THE HOUSE OF TRUTH

THE HOUSE OF TRUTH

A WASHINGTON POLITICAL SALON AND THE FOUNDATIONS OF AMERICAN LIBERALISM

BRAD SNYDER

OXFORD
UNIVERSITY PRESS

OXFORD
UNIVERSITY PRESS

Oxford University Press is a department of the University of Oxford. It furthers the University's objective of excellence in research, scholarship, and education by publishing worldwide. Oxford is a registered trade mark of Oxford University Press in the UK and certain other countries.

Published in the United States of America by Oxford University Press
198 Madison Avenue, New York, NY 10016, United States of America.

Library of Congress Cataloging-in-Publication Data
Names: Snyder, Brad, author.
Title: The House of Truth : a Washington political salon and the foundations of American liberalism / Brad Snyder.
Description: New York, NY : Oxford University Press, [2017] | Includes bibliographical references and index.
Identifiers: LCCN 2016014092 | ISBN 9780190261986 (alk. paper)
Subjects: LCSH: Washington (D.C.)—Politics and government—20th century. | Washington (D.C.)—Intellectual life—20th century. | Washington (D.C.)—Social life and customs—20th century. | Salons—Washington (D.C.)—History—20th century. | Political culture—Washington (D.C.)—History—20th century. | Politicians—United States—Biography. | Intellectuals—United States—Biography. | Liberalism—United States—History—20th century. | United States—Politics and government—1913–1921. | United States—Politics and government—1919–1933.
Classification: LCC F199 .S67 2017 | DDC 975.3/04—dc23
LC record available at https://lccn.loc.gov/2016014092

1 3 5 7 9 8 6 4 2

Printed by Sheridan Books, Inc., United States of America

To Shelby, Lily, and Max

Contents

Introduction   I

1. Expanding Horizons   6

2. 1727 Nineteenth Street   13

3. The Call of the Moose   38

4. The Center of the Universe   61

5. Buddha   84

6. The Soldier's Faith   98

7. Temperamentally Unfit   122

8. Our Founder   147

9. Fighting Valentine's Fight   158

10. The House at War   167

11. One-Man War   188

12. Uniting the Labor Army   209

13. The Inquiry   226

14. The Wonderful One   237

15. "The H/T Cannot Be Re-constituted"   270

16. Harvard's Dangerous Men   274

17. Touched with Fire   305

18. Protestant of Nordic Stock   322

19. We Live by Symbols   341

20. The 1924 Election and the Basic Issues of Liberalism   365

21. Eloquence May Set Fire to Reason   384

22. A Fly on an Elephant   396

23. No Ordinary Case   409

24. This World Cares More for Red Than for Black   442

25. A Damn Poor Psychologist   477

26. The Happy Warrior   488

27. Freedom for the Thought That We Hate   498

28. America's Shrine for Political Democracy   508

29. The Best Men   516

30. A Very Great Beginning   541

31. The Hard Case Has Melted   556

    Epilogue   565

Appendix   581
Notes   583
Selected Bibliography   741
Acknowledgments   773
Index   777

Introduction

In 1918, a small group of friends gathered for dinner at a row house near Washington's Dupont Circle: a young lawyer named Felix Frankfurter; a seventy-seven-year-old Supreme Court justice, Oliver Wendell Holmes Jr., and his wife, Fanny; and perhaps the most unlikely guest, the sculptor Gutzon Borglum. As they sat around the dining room table, Borglum described his latest idea for a sculpture. He wanted, he explained to the other guests, to carve monumentally large images of Confederate war heroes into the side of Stone Mountain, Georgia. Justice Holmes, a Union army veteran who had always admired his Confederate foes, expressed interest in Borglum's idea. Yet he could not fully grasp the sculptor's vision.[1]

Borglum, a Westerner whose cowboy hat, bushy mustache, and stocky frame reflected his frontier beginnings, pushed the plates to the center of the table and began drawing on the white tablecloth.[2] He depicted three men in the foreground, all of them on horseback: Robert E. Lee on his legendary horse, *Traveller*; Stonewall Jackson, slightly in front of Lee; and Jefferson Davis closely behind them. There were clusters of cavalrymen in the background. The desired effect, Borglum explained, was to march the Confederate army across the 800-by-1,500-foot face of the mountain. Holmes was delighted and astonished. Frankfurter never forgot the encounter.

As it turned out, Borglum never finished his Confederate memorial (mainly because of a dispute with the Ku Klux Klan, an organization he had embraced). Nonetheless, his first attempt at mountain carving led to what became the major work of his lifetime: memorializing four American presidents in the Black Hills of South Dakota at Mount Rushmore.

By the time Frankfurter, Holmes, and Borglum dined there that night, they had eaten many meals together at this narrow, three-story, red-brick row house that its residents self-mockingly but fondly referred to as the "House of Truth." The name was inspired by debates between Holmes and its residents about the search for truth. During these discussions, Frankfurter

Gutzon Borglum's vision of Robert E. Lee (center), Stonewall Jackson (left), and Jefferson Davis (right) marching across the face of Stone Mountain

and other Taft and Wilson administration officials who lived there from 1912 to 1919 turned the House into one of the city's foremost political salons. They threw dinner parties, discussed political events of the day, and wooed young women and high government officials with equal fervor. Ambassadors, generals, journalists, artists, lawyers, Supreme Court justices, cabinet members, and even a future US president dined there. "How or why I can't recapture," Frankfurter recalled, "but almost everybody who was interesting in Washington sooner or later passed through that house."[3]

For Frankfurter and his friends, the House was a place to gather information, to influence policy, and to try out new ideas. In 1912, many of them wanted Theodore Roosevelt once again in the White House and supported his third-party presidential run. Two years later, they founded the *New Republic* as an outlet for their political point of view. Above all, the House of Truth helped them created an influential network of American liberals who would influence American law and politics from Theodore Roosevelt's defeat in 1912 to Franklin Roosevelt's victory in 1932.

This book tells the story of how the House built a professional network that shaped the foundations of American liberalism. The network revolved around and changed the personal and professional lives of four individuals in particular: Frankfurter, journalist Walter Lippmann, Borglum, and Holmes. Frankfurter met his wife there, gained a national reputation as a labor expert in the Taft and Wilson administrations, and landed a job as a Harvard Law School professor. Lippmann lived there with his new wife while on leave from the *New Republic* and became a foreign policy expert while working in the Wilson administration. Borglum was attracted to the House's support of Theodore Roosevelt in 1912 and often returned there in 1918 while investigating a subject he became as passionate about as mountain carving: wartime aircraft production. And largely because of his friendship with this younger crowd, Holmes saw his reputation evolve from a relatively obscure member of the Supreme Court into a judicial icon.

Though I refer to people associated with the House as "liberals," they were liberals not in the nineteenth-century sense of classical liberalism, with its emphasis on individual liberty, but in the twentieth-century sense of liberalism, with its emphasis on government. Like progressivism, "liberalism" has many definitions.[4] Progressives believed in government regulation; liberals also believed in government regulation, but they recognized government's limits. During the early twentieth century, the terms were sometimes used interchangeably. After World War I, however, the House of Truth crowd stopped referring to themselves as "progressives" and began calling themselves "liberals." This may have been clever rebranding, but it also reflected growing and genuine concern over the abuse of government power and the potential of courts, especially the Supreme Court, to protect civil liberties.

The network created by these men and women defined and then redefined American liberalism.[5] "The word, liberalism, was introduced into the jargon of American politics by that group who were Progressives in 1912 and Wilson Democrats from 1916 to 1918," Lippmann wrote in 1919. "They wished to distinguish their own general aspirations in politics from those of the chronic partisans and the social revolutionists. They had no other bond of unity. They were not a political movement. There was no established body of doctrine. American liberalism is a phase of the transition away from the old party system."[6]

This new liberalism began to take shape in 1912 during Theodore Roosevelt's third-party presidential bid—with the House of Truth serving as the Bull Moose campaign's de facto DC headquarters.[7] Frankfurter, Borglum, and their friends viewed Roosevelt as representing the best hope of achieving their political goals—a government run by experts rather than political party hacks, more aggressive prosecution of illegal monopolies, and new state and federal laws to protect workers and organized labor. They believed that government could make people's lives better through the passage and enforcement of antitrust laws, minimum wage laws, maximum hour laws, and workers' compensation laws. In their eyes, Roosevelt was the only politician willing to push for those laws; to stand up to big business; and to fight for working men, women, and children in an age of industrial accidents and violent labor disputes.

Before the First World War, one institution had stood in the way of their political goals—the Supreme Court. The Court struck down state minimum wage and maximum hour laws, limited the enforcement of antitrust laws and the rights of organized labor, and curbed congressional power. Part of the attraction of Theodore Roosevelt for the House of Truth crowd was his willingness to put "the fear of God into judges."[8]

After the 1919 Red Scare prosecution and deportation of radical immigrants and the Red Summer of racial violence, Frankfurter and his allies began to change their view of the Court. They looked to the Court, and especially to Holmes and Louis D. Brandeis, to protect free speech and fair criminal trials.[9] During the Harding, Coolidge, and Hoover administrations of the 1920s and early 1930s, Frankfurter, Lippmann, and their liberal friends found themselves out of political power. They never lost faith in the democratic political process, but they turned to the judiciary when the political process failed them.

The story of the House begins with the friendship and professional aspirations of its three original residents: Frankfurter, Winfred T. Denison, and Robert G. Valentine. Together with Frankfurter, they stood out in the Taft administration as three of the most fervent supporters of Theodore Roosevelt. Though Denison and Valentine have been forgotten by history, all three men played central roles in the formation of the House of Truth.

The House broke up as a political salon in 1919 after its residents fell out of political power. Yet their faith in government and their old friendships never waned. In the years to come, they argued about which presidential candidates to support in the *New Republic*. They lobbied for and against

Supreme Court nominees. They took sides in 1927 on the efforts to save Italian anarchists Sacco and Vanzetti from the electric chair. They repeatedly celebrated the career milestones and opinions of Justice Holmes. And in 1932, they helped to elect a president and another Roosevelt.

In its own way, nothing captured the House of Truth's belief in government better than Borglum and his monument at Mount Rushmore, a mountain carving inspired by the Confederate memorial he had started to draw on the tablecloth that night in 1918. His desire to create a "shrine to democracy" began after Theodore Roosevelt's defeat in 1912. That election galvanized Borglum, just as it did the group of young men, beginning with an Austrian-Jewish immigrant who ascended through the ranks of the federal government of his adopted country.

I

Expanding Horizons

At 7:15 p.m. on October 31, 1910, five cars left the Lexington Avenue home of New York Republican gubernatorial candidate Henry Stimson. New York City police escorted them with shrill whistles blaring until they arrived at the Grand Music Hall, a Yiddish variety theater located at the corner of Grand and Orchard Streets on the Lower East Side. Men, women, and children clogged the streets and made it impossible for Stimson and his campaign aide Felix Frankfurter to get to the front door. Police finally cleared a path for them. More than 2,500 people were waiting inside.[1]

The audience cheered as Stimson entered the room. After the crowd quieted, the master of ceremonies told a story about how as Manhattan's US attorney Stimson had hired Frankfurter as an assistant US attorney though most Wall Street law firms had refused to hire Frankfurter because he was Jewish. "And if Tammany Hall tries this year to work off the oldtime tale of Republican race prejudice," the master of ceremonies continued, "you answer with the tale of the appointment of Felix Frankfurter, Jew." The audience, which knew the story of the Lower East Side boy who had made good, "shouted and cheered and cheered again."[2] Then Stimson spoke and appealed to the crowd of Jewish voters. "If there was one of my assistants in the District Attorney's office to whom I owe personal gratitude for the work done by my assistants," Stimson said, "Felix Frankfurter is that man. And I take great pleasure in expressing that obligation to him publicly."[3]

★★★

When he arrived at Ellis Island on August 9, 1894, on the steamship *Marsala* from Hamburg, Germany, eleven-year-old passenger Felix Frankfurter could not speak a word of English and had never heard one spoken. The young Austrian quickly learned the language because his teacher at New York City's P.S. 25, Miss Hogan, had threatened his German American classmates with physical punishment if they spoke to him in German.[4] He filled

Henry L. Stimson (sitting third from left), Denison (sitting far left), and
Frankfurter (standing third from left)

the gaps of his American education at Cooper Union, where he devoured
the nation's daily newspapers in the top-floor reading room and attended
Friday night political discussions. He became so interested in politics that
he skipped school when he was thirteen to witness the arrival of 1896
Democratic presidential candidate William Jennings Bryan in Hoboken,
New Jersey. At his grammar school graduation the following summer,
Frankfurter recited a speech by John Adams.[5]

Frankfurter declined a partial scholarship to the private school Horace
Mann because his family could not afford to pay the rest of the tuition.
Instead, like many other Jewish immigrants, he enrolled in the five-year
combined high school and college program at City College of New York.
He joined the City College debate team and finished third in his class. He
was nineteen. After working for a year in the city's new Tenement House
Department, he decided to go to law school and enrolled at Harvard.[6]

Harvard Law School intimidated Frankfurter. His roommate Sam
Rosensohn thought he was a "Mama's boy" because Frankfurter's mother

had packed his clothes. Frankfurter's classmates had attended elite colleges and universities, were taller and more self-assured, and spoke eloquently in class.[7] Dimple-chinned, five-foot-six, and with a slight foreign accent, the baby-faced Frankfurter did not think he would survive. The annual tuition was only $150; more than 20 percent of his class flunked out after a single set of exams at the end of the year.[8] Frankfurter's grades on the exams were so good that they qualified him for membership on the *Harvard Law Review*. By graduation, he was first in his class.[9]

Yet the top student in Harvard Law School's class of 1906 struggled to find a job. Most Wall Street law firms in the early twentieth century did not hire Jews.[10] Not yet knowing he was first in his class, Frankfurter recalled feeling like a beggar as he took sealed letters of recommendation from the dean of the law school from firm to firm. Finally, Hornblower, Byrne, Miller & Potter, a respected firm with a number of Harvard law alumni, offered him a job. One of the partners asked him to change his last name to something less "odd, fun-making" (and presumably less Jewish-sounding).[11] Frankfurter accepted the job but kept his surname. He was the firm's first Jewish associate.

Soon after he began his professional life as a Wall Street lawyer, Frankfurter received a phone call from Stimson, who had just been named US attorney. Stimson had a long, thin face, an aquiline nose, short black hair parted down the middle, and a dark mustache. He also had degrees from Phillips Academy, Yale College (where he belonged to the secret society Skull and Bones), and Harvard Law School. At age thirty-eight, he had left his $20,000 salary at his Wall Street law firm to go into government. He landed the US attorney post on the recommendation of his former law partner Elihu Root, Theodore Roosevelt's secretary of state, and because Stimson shared Roosevelt's love for the outdoors and his progressive spirit.[12]

Like Roosevelt, Stimson and other progressives believed in using the federal government to protect workers from the effects of industrialization and to prosecute illegal monopolies for destroying competition. Big government could be imperialistic—the United States was emerging as a world power after the Spanish-American War with territorial acquisitions in Puerto Rico, Cuba, and the Philippines. But big government could also be used to stand up for the little guy—prosecuting the robber barons for anticompetitive contracts and breaking up illegal monopolies. Roosevelt appointed Stimson to reorganize the office and to prosecute the sugar trust.

Stimson transformed the Southern District of New York into one of the nation's premier federal prosecutor's offices. He reorganized it into criminal, civil, and customs divisions and divided the criminal division into miscellaneous and antitrust sections. He ended the practices of farming out high-profile cases to private lawyers at great public expense and of keeping a percentage of the customs fees collected. He hired assistant US attorneys based on merit rather than political affiliation. With a budget of less than $30,000, he replaced holdover patronage appointments by asking law school deans about their best recent graduates.[13] Frankfurter's name was at the top of Stimson's list. Harvard Law School dean James Barr Ames informed Stimson that Frankfurter was "the most able man of the graduates of that school within the past three or four years."[14] Stimson offered Frankfurter a job. Frankfurter, torn more about leaving his Wall Street firm so soon than about taking a $250 pay cut, consulted Dean Ames, who replied: "I suggest you follow the dominant impulses of your nature."[15]

On August 7, 1906, Frankfurter joined Stimson in the US attorney's office as a junior assistant. Under Stimson's direction and with President Roosevelt's support, Frankfurter and his fellow assistants prosecuted railroads for illegal shipping rebates to the American Sugar Refining Company, bank executive Charles W. Morse for defrauding the National Bank of North America, and the American Sugar Refining Company again for manipulating scales and defrauding the federal government of customs fees.[16] The sugar trust prosecutions continued in 1909 and 1910 after Stimson had left office to return to private practice.[17] Frankfurter and others stayed on as special prosecutors, and they pursued criminal fraud charges and appeals against the secretary of the American Sugar Refining Company, Charles R. Heike.[18] Heike's conviction and eight-month prison sentence for conspiring to defraud the federal government of sugar import fees kept Stimson in the headlines. After the Heike case, Frankfurter joined Stimson's law firm for eight months in 1909 before returning to the Manhattan federal prosecutor's office. During the fall of 1910, he took a month off to work on Stimson's gubernatorial campaign.[19]

In Frankfurter's mind, Stimson's prosecution of the sugar trust had made him the natural candidate to replace Republican reformer Charles Evans Hughes as governor of New York. "He has never stood for peanut politics nor peanut politicians," Frankfurter told the *New York Times* in late September. "Mr. Stimson has no love for the grafter, never had and never will."[20]

★★★

Fifteen minutes after Stimson had finished his October 31 speech on the Lower East Side and had left for his next campaign stop, five more cars pulled up at the Grand Music Hall. This time, a swelling crowd of 3,000 people surrounded the lead car. The star attraction had arrived. The police tried but failed to create a path for him to the front door, so Theodore Roosevelt hopped onto a fire escape on the side of the building, bounded up a flight of stairs two at a time, and approached a window leading into the hall. Before he entered, he turned back and waved his hat at the cheering crowd below.[21]

Roosevelt was deeply invested—some thought too invested—in Stimson's campaign. As president, he had made Stimson one of the nation's foremost prosecutors. As an ambitious ex-president, he had orchestrated Stimson's Republican Party nomination for governor, turning the campaign into a full-scale war against the Tammany Hall political machine and a litmus test for another presidential bid. Introduced as "the greatest citizen in the world," Roosevelt received three cheers from the crowd and "three cheers more before he could be heard." New Nationalism with Stimson as governor, Roosevelt told the crowd of garment workers and merchants, offered them "the chance to work for a reasonable wage under healthy conditions, and not for an excessive number of hours." It also offered "the chance for the small business man to conduct his business without oppression, without having to be blackmailed" and the chance to "stand against the worst alliance of crooked politics and crooked business that this State has seen, or this city has seen, since the days of Tweed."[22]

That night, Stimson and Roosevelt spoke to nine different audiences throughout New York City and only crossed paths at the last stop. "Isn't it bully?" an energized Roosevelt repeated as he encountered Stimson in a narrow stairwell.[23] With the election nine days away, Stimson trailed Tammany Hall candidate John Alden Dix in the polls.

As successful as he had been as a prosecutor, Stimson was not much of a political candidate. "Darn it, Harry," Roosevelt told Stimson in Frankfurter's presence, "a campaign speech is a poster, not an etching!"[24] Roosevelt overshadowed Stimson on the stump and dominated the political conversation. Indeed, Frankfurter informed Roosevelt that the New York *World* was keeping a running tally of how often Roosevelt used "I" in his speeches on Stimson's behalf.[25] Tammany Hall fought to keep Roosevelt's handpicked candidate out of Albany and to tarnish Roosevelt's reputation as rumors swirled that he would run for president again in 1912.

Unable to escape Roosevelt's shadow or to overcome his own inadequacies as a candidate, Stimson never stood a chance. At the Stimson campaign headquarters on election night, Frankfurter and other current and former assistant US attorneys celebrated their defeated chief. Winfred T. Denison, who had joined the Justice Department as an assistant attorney general after trying and appealing the *Heike* case with Frankfurter, came up from Washington.[26] Denison brought one of his Harvard College classmates, President Taft's commissioner of Indian affairs, Robert G. Valentine. That night, Denison almost certainly introduced Frankfurter to Valentine.[27]

Clifford Berryman cartoon about 1910 New York governor's race

For the twenty-seven-year-old Frankfurter, the Stimson campaign had
educated him about electoral politics, had whetted his appetite for a career in
public service, and had brought him into the orbit of Theodore Roosevelt.[28]
"I feel exactly as you do, that there never was a more genuine fight for the
people than we made; and I am mighty glad to have had my hand in it,"
Roosevelt wrote Frankfurter in December 1910. "Let me also say that it
was a genuine pleasure to have gotten to know you. I value you and believe
in you."[29] Stimson believed in Frankfurter, too. In June 1911, President Taft
needed a progressive in his cabinet and named Stimson secretary of war. At
first, Stimson tried to arrange a job for Frankfurter with Attorney General
George W. Wickersham. The position did not materialize.[30] Instead, Stimson
offered, and Frankfurter accepted, a $4,500-a-year job as a law officer in the
Bureau of Insular Affairs overseeing US territories and as Stimson's "junior
partner."[31]

Before leaving for Washington, Frankfurter accompanied his boss on a
tour of territories acquired during the Spanish-American War.[32] Frankfurter
boarded the USS *North Carolina* in Puerto Rico and saw Santo Domingo
and Cuba. "His eyes are sticking out of his head with [the] novelty of the
experience," Stimson wrote of the "Faithful Frankfurter," adding, "and we
all feel a little expanded in horizon."[33] Frankfurter's horizons expanded
even further upon his arrival in Washington.

2

1727 Nineteenth Street

In September 1911, Frankfurter arrived in Washington, DC, knowing only a handful of people.[1] Walking the streets of the nation's capital, the new War Department aide fell in love with the "charming, large, peaceful, equable big town."[2] The sidewalks along tree-lined Connecticut Avenue were twice their current width because streetlights had not yet been installed and automobiles were scarce. Most people walked to and from their offices and worked at a leisurely pace. A month into his job, Frankfurter encountered Solicitor General Frederick W. Lehmann on the street and discussed the latest Supreme Court vacancy and Lehmann's disagreement with President Taft on the enforcement of the Sherman Antitrust Act.[3] Two mornings later, Attorney General Wickersham saw Frankfurter walking to work and offered the young man a carriage ride. During the ride, Wickersham opined on law, history, and politics, including Frankfurter's role in the sugar fraud prosecutions.[4] Frankfurter liked Washington because it was not driven by money like New York City but by political power and ideas.[5] He did not care about money and did not "collect books or pictures," one of his friends explained, "he collects people."[6]

Frankfurter's mission was to turn the most important person in his professional life so far, Secretary of War Stimson, into the Taft administration's leading progressive voice on trust busting. Like many Roosevelt supporters, Frankfurter doubted Taft's willingness to prosecute monopolies and deemed the president too deferential to the Supreme Court. Since its 1895 decision preventing the prosecution of the sugar trust, most progressives viewed the Court as the biggest obstacle to enforcement of the antitrust laws.[7] In 1910 and 1911, the Court had permitted the Roosevelt-initiated antitrust actions against John D. Rockefeller's Standard Oil Company and the American Tobacco Company.[8] Despite these apparent victories, the Court's decisions limited the broad language of the Sherman Antitrust Act's ban on any

Felix Frankfurter

contracts or combinations in restraint of trade to a "rule of reason"—meaning only *unreasonable* restraints of trade violated the law. Progressives worried that the rule of reason gave the Court too much power to decide what mergers were unreasonable. Instead, they wanted tougher enforcement of the Sherman Act, amendments to the law, and new legislation creating an administrative agency to regulate unfair competition. They saw antitrust enforcement as one way to strike the right balance between management and labor, producers and consumers, robber barons and small businesses.

During his first few months as Stimson's aide in the War Department, Frankfurter drafted a trust-busting speech for his boss to deliver on November 14 before the Kansas City Commercial Club. He wanted Stimson to invigorate the Taft administration's antitrust policy and to bring liberals into the Republican Party. "I assume that your larger purpose is to identify the Republican Party in the public mind as the liberal party and thereby more immediately further the interests of the administration [as the exponent of] liberalism," he wrote Stimson on September 9. Frankfurter argued that it started with the belief that government could improve the lives of working people by protecting the rights of organized labor; by passing minimum wage, maximum hour, child labor, and workmen's compensation laws; and by prosecuting monopolies. Frankfurter invoked themes from his boss's past speeches about "the changed industrial condition," "interdependence of people," and "a discarding of the old *laissez-faire* philosophy." Frankfurter proposed "a social program" that addressed the two most pressing areas of regulation: industrial relations and antitrust prosecutions.[9]

The dilemma for Stimson in his Kansas City speech was to reframe the debate about trust busting without undermining President Taft. Stimson had urged Taft to write out his speeches to convey a clear and constructive message on the trust issue during a month-long trip west.[10] Instead, Taft crisscrossed the country delivering a series of extemporaneous remarks that muddled the debate: he defended the Court's two recent antimonopoly decisions, opposed amendments to the Sherman Act, described literal enforcement of the Sherman Act as the road to socialism, and promised more prosecutions under the statute.[11] Stimson believed that Taft's speeches managed to alienate both conservatives and progressives.[12] Frankfurter encouraged Stimson to use the Kansas City speech to clarify the confusion over Taft's speeches and to chart a more progressive course. Attorney General Wickersham agreed that Stimson should address the trust issue. Frankfurter conferred with Stimson and other members of the administration.[13]

By the end of October, Frankfurter and Stimson had drafted a speech declaring the Sherman Act unclear and insufficient. They proposed to amend it and to pass new legislation, including specific criminal offenses and penalties and an administrative body like the Interstate Commerce Commission to provide guidance to businesses and to declare monopolistic practices anticompetitive. "I think we realize now better than ever before," the draft concluded, "how the interests of the manufacturer, the laborer and the consumer—the corporation, its employees, and the public—are alike bound up in common in its solution."[14] They showed the draft to several people. Former sugar trust prosecutor and Justice Department lawyer Winfred Denison read the speech and remarked that "this is exactly the sort of stuff that I think the administration ought to issue." But he cautioned Stimson that the proposal to amend the Sherman Act clashed with some of Taft's recent speeches and used Taft's prepresidential statements "against himself."[15] Instead, Denison argued, the best tactic was to propose new legislation preventing unfair competition.[16] Denison also wrote Stimson a follow-up note: "F.F. had the notion that I did not like your speech because I didn't say more in the letter the other day. He's very much mistaken. I'm very much for it."[17] Charles Nagel, Taft's secretary of commerce and labor, endorsed the speech and believed that it did not show up the president: "I am satisfied you will find him fully committed to it." Nagel echoed Denison's concerns about the proposal to amend the Sherman Act and preferred new legislation. Overall, Nagel encouraged Stimson: "I am very glad that you are going to speak along these lines. It is just what Kansas City will want to hear."[18]

When the Kansas City Commercial Club asked for a title for advertising purposes, Stimson met with Taft to ask permission to give the Sherman Act speech. The president immediately said yes. Stimson relayed the title, "The Sherman Law and Our Industrial Problem,"[19] but insisted that Taft read the speech. After he read it, Taft suggested a different topic—the soon-to-be-completed Panama Canal.[20] Taft planned to include remarks about the Sherman Act in his message to Congress, preferred different points of emphasis and tone, and wanted the entire cabinet's input about antitrust policy. The president did not know that influential members of his cabinet had been encouraging Stimson, but that did not matter.[21] Stimson was a team player; his Sherman Act speech was off.[22]

On November 3, Stimson broke the news to Frankfurter.[23] The two men had less than two weeks to prepare a Panama Canal speech. As Frankfurter worked on it, he realized that Stimson "hasn't got his heart in it as he had in [the] trust speech."[24] The Kansas City Commercial Club wired Stimson begging him to return to the original topic; Stimson refused.[25] After receiving the telegram, he remarked to Frankfurter: "I'd give $1,000 to make that trust speech."[26] The *New York Times* buried Stimson's Panama Canal speech on page eight.[27]

Instead of burying his ideas about antitrust policy, Stimson included them in a memorandum to the president for the message to Congress.[28] As predicted, Taft's December 5 message opposed amending the Sherman Act but endorsed supplemental legislation including a Federal Corporation Commission. In reality, however, Taft's support for new legislation was tepid. In Taft's mind, the Sherman Act was sufficient. After all, his administration had initiated more Sherman Act prosecutions than Roosevelt's.[29]

Taft's critics believed that he was too content to allow the Supreme Court to define the contours of prosecuting illegal monopolies. In less than two years, he had remade the Court by nominating five justices: Horace

Stimson

H. Lurton in December 1909; Charles Evans Hughes in April 1910; and Willis Van Devanter, Joseph R. Lamar, and the elevation to Chief Justice of Associate Justice Edward Douglass White in December 1910. And with Justice John M. Harlan's death in October 1911, Taft had another vacancy to fill and nominated Mahlon Pitney. Indeed, Taft, a former federal appeals court judge, had made it no secret that he longed to be chief justice. "It does seem strange," Taft said of the chief justiceship, "that the one place in the government which I would have liked to fill myself I am forced to give to another."[30]

Ten days after the president's message to Congress, Stimson delivered a revised version of his Sherman Act speech to the New York City Republican Club.[31] With Taft's permission, Stimson proposed new legislation calling for criminal antitrust penalties and a federal administrative body.[32] But it was not the progressive rallying cry that Frankfurter had hoped it would be. For Frankfurter, the episode "left a painful impression and a striking demonstration of Taft's lack of leadership and constructive thinking. Here he floats around the country talking on the industrial situation without having the thing at all thought out, without having formulated a definite policy after Cabinet consultation."Taft, according to Frankfurter, was "amiable and well-intentioned" but lacked "vision and decision. He is indeed the tragedy of opportunities of greatness unrealized."[33]

★★★

Disillusioned with Taft and unable to persuade Stimson to become the administration's progressive voice, Frankfurter formed a social circle of like-minded friends. His most important ally was Assistant Attorney General Winfred T. Denison.

Denison had made a national name for himself prosecuting the sugar fraud cases with Stimson and Frankfurter. Hired to be an assistant US attorney at about the same time as Frankfurter, Denison had left the Wall Street firm of Stetson, Jennings & Russell to be a senior assistant at $4,000 a year (Frankfurter initially made $750).[34] Denison took a lead role in prosecuting the sugar fraud cases as the head of the office's interstate commerce bureau and later as a special prosecutor.[35] After joining the Justice Department in early 1910, he continued to prosecute customs fraud in Philadelphia and other cities.[36] And in public speeches, he credited Stimson for ridding the federal prosecutor's office of political hacks and argued that the New York sugar fraud prosecutions never would have happened without Stimson's merit-based hiring practices.[37]

Denison hailed from a prominent Portland, Maine, family, graduated from Phillips Exeter and Harvard College, traveled in Europe for a year, then graduated in 1900 from Harvard Law School.[38] His six years of private practice made him one of the US attorney's office's more senior and accomplished trial lawyers. He also was a skilled appellate advocate. As assistant attorney general, he regularly argued before the Supreme Court, priding himself on never using the entire hour allotted to him.[39] In October 1911, he agonized with Frankfurter about whether to become a judge.[40]

Denison was closer in age to Stimson but closer in personality to Frankfurter. Both Frankfurter and Denison were social animals. A lifelong bachelor, Denison was 5-7½ and wore wireless oval pince-nez. He had prominent eyebrows, a wide nose, full lips, gray eyes, and thinning dark brown hair streaked with gray at the roots and temples.[41] Winnie, as his friends called him, entertained at the Metropolitan Club and Chevy Chase Country Club and earned a place in the *Social Register* and in the Washington society pages.[42]

Clifford Berryman cartoon of William Howard Taft

Frankfurter recalled that Denison "once said of himself about going out often, perhaps too often, with a childlike innocence, 'It's that damn charm of mine!'"[43] Denison's charms came with high highs, low lows, and bouts of nervous exhaustion because of a history of depression.[44] In February 1911, he contracted typhoid fever.[45] He convalesced that summer in Britain with his sister and social companion, Katherine.[46] By October, he still had not recovered, and Katherine moved from New York City to Washington to live with him for the winter.[47] A twenty-four-year-old Wellesley graduate, Katherine hit it off with the Washington society crowd and was "fresh and lovely," according to Frankfurter, "revelling in the richness of Washington life and absorbed in Winnie's future and greatness."[48]

On October 20, 1911, Frankfurter brought Denison to lunch with the People's Lawyer, Louis D. Brandeis.[49] Frankfurter and Brandeis had been corresponding about antitrust matters for at least a year. As a law student, Frankfurter had heard Brandeis speak at the Harvard Ethical Society on "The Opportunity in the Law" about the roles that lawyers could play

Winfred T. Denison

in public service.[50] A Boston lawyer, Brandeis frequently found himself in Washington on business. He had become wealthy representing smaller manufacturers and corporations. Yet he became the People's Lawyer by representing the public's interests in political and legal controversies and by spearheading reform efforts against unscrupulous banks, railroads, and other monopolies. At lunch, Brandeis discussed the Sherman Act, the dangers of monopolies to capitalism, and the need for new antitrust legislation and more administrative oversight.[51] Representing smaller manufacturers, Brandeis opposed the American Tobacco Company's proposed reorganization plan and urged Frankfurter and Denison to lobby

Attorney General Wickersham.[52] Unfortunately for Brandeis, Wickersham approved the company's plan. Brandeis, in looks and bearing, was often compared to Lincoln. Journalist Ray Stannard Baker, whom Frankfurter met at Denison's home in November 1911, first saw Brandeis a year earlier and recalled his "tall, spare, rugged, slightly stooping figure" and "high, rather harsh voice, but with perfect command." Baker wrote that Brandeis's "face, indeed, at a certain angle, and especially in repose, recalls almost star-tlingly one of the portraits of Abraham Lincoln."[53]

Born and raised in Louisville by middle-class Jewish parents from Prague, Brandeis graduated from high school at fourteen, traveled with his family in Europe and studied in Germany for two years, and entered Harvard Law School at age eighteen. He graduated with the "highest known average" in the history of the law school.[54] As a lawyer, he possessed the mind of a skilled advocate and able politician. In 1908 in *Muller v. Oregon*, he had de-fended the constitutionality of the state's maximum hour law for women. Three years earlier in *Lochner v. New York*, the Supreme Court had struck down a similar law for bakers as violating the Due Process Clause's "liberty of contract."[55] In *Muller*, Brandeis found a way around *Lochner*. Submitting a 100-page brief based on sociological research by his sister-in-law Josephine Goldmark and other members of the National Consumers' League, he argued that the Court should uphold the Oregon law because of physical differences between men and women. The Court agreed.[56] Because the "Brandeis Brief" provided a new method of defending labor laws based on social scientific evidence, Frankfurter believed that the *Muller* decision was "epoch making."[57]

In addition to *Muller*, Brandeis challenged J. P. Morgan's monopolistic control of the New York, New Haven & Hartford Railroad's rail and trol-ley lines. Brandeis aroused public suspicion about the company's finances and succeeded in forcing the New Haven Railroad to relinquish control of the Boston & Maine Railroad.[58] In 1910, he represented *Collier's* maga-zine and advised US Forest Service chief Gifford Pinchot and field agent Louis Glavis in their allegations against Taft's Secretary of the Interior Richard Ballinger. Pinchot and Glavis charged that Ballinger had enabled Morgan- and Guggenheim-backed interests to exploit coal-rich public land in Alaska. Pinchot, an ally of Roosevelt, was fired from his Forest Service post after backing Glavis against Ballinger. The Ballinger-Pinchot Affair, as it came to be known, divided pro-business and conservationist wings of the Republican Party and pitted Taft's loyalists against Roosevelt's. Brandeis revealed that Taft had exonerated Ballinger based on an undisclosed memorandum that had been backdated.[59] Brandeis's investigation and cross-examination of Ballinger made him a hero in the eyes of Frankfurter and his anti-Taft friends.

As great a lawyer as Brandeis was, his reserve did not endear him to Frankfurter and Denison. In time, Brandeis considered Frankfurter "half brother, half son,"[60] financed Frankfurter's pro bono activities, and supplied Frankfurter and his friends with ideas. Yet as much as they admired him, they did not love him—at least not at first. "Brandeis has depth and an intellectual sweep that are tonical," Frankfurter wrote after the October 20 lunch. "He has great force; he has Lincoln's fundamental sympathies. I wish he had his patience, his magnanimity, his humor."[61]

The person in Washington who made the greatest first impression on Frankfurter and Denison was Justice Oliver Wendell Holmes Jr. Frankfurter possessed the ultimate entrée to the justice—a letter of introduction from one of Holmes's oldest and dearest friends and Frankfurter's property law professor at Harvard, John Chipman Gray.[62] Like Holmes, Gray hailed from a prominent Boston family, attended Harvard College, and served in the Union army during the Civil War. After the war, Gray started one of Boston's leading law firms, Ropes & Gray. He also joined the Harvard law faculty and became the nation's preeminent property law scholar. One of his lasting contributions to history was introducing Frankfurter, his former research assistant, to Holmes.

On November 27, 1911, Justice and Mrs. Holmes invited Frankfurter to lunch for the first time. "I came away with the keen relief of having been on Olympus and finding that one's God did not have clay feet," Frankfurter wrote Gray. "There is a brilliance and range in the justice's conversation. ... But over and above his keen penetration, his contempt for mere words and formula, and his freshness of outlook, give lasting zest and momentum to one's groping and toiling."[63]

Frankfurter, who initially lived in an apartment only a block away, became a regular visitor to Holmes's large three-story residence at 1720 Eye Street. The nerve center of 1720 Eye Street was the second floor. In those days, the Supreme Court did not have its own building and heard oral argument in the old Senate chamber in the Capitol. The justices worked out of their homes, and Holmes turned his second floor into an office and social gathering place. His beloved books filled floor-to-ceiling built-in bookshelves that covered the walls and even above the doorway to his study. His secretaries, as his law clerks were known then, sat in the front study at a small desk under

For Felix Frankfurter
with great appreciation and high hopes.

Most Cordially
Louis D Brandeis

May 31/1914

Louis D. Brandeis circa 1914

a large lamp suspended from the ceiling. The double doors between the secretary's study and the justice's were always open.

Holmes worked and entertained in his rear study. He sat in a simple mahogany chair at a seven-drawer cherry wood desk that had belonged to his maternal grandfather, former Massachusetts Supreme Judicial Court Judge Charles Jackson. Several volumes of Supreme Court decisions and a small lamp sat on Holmes's desk. He wrote his judicial opinions at his grandfather's mahogany stand-up desk by the window and read for pleasure in a comfortable leather chair near the sitting desk. His great-grandfather's swords from the French and Indian War hung above the fireplace.[64] Even at age seventy, Holmes still possessed the erect posture and tall, lean frame from his Union army days. He wore three-piece suits and ties but was anything but formal in his manner. His full head of hair was gray on top and white on the sides; his flowing white handlebar mustache gave him a regal appearance. His aristocratic Boston accent made him sound oddly British. His piercing blue eyes twinkled with mischief.

What made Frankfurter's visits to Holmes special was the conversation. Of all the great talkers in Washington, none compared to Holmes. Frankfurter recalled sitting in front of the fire or in the study and listening as the justice "did practically all of the talking." Frankfurter did not dare interrupt him because "it was such a wonderful stream of exciting flow of ideas in words."[65] Holmes could discuss philosophy, law, history, literature, and culture, high and low. He cared little about politics and did not read newspapers, but he liked to gossip. He loved his wife, Fanny, yet flirted with other women well into old age. He told tall tales, especially about his Union army days. He delighted in young people and their idealism, even though he was skeptical about their ideas.

In 1911, Holmes's skepticism nonetheless endeared him to many young progressives. Thirty years earlier, in *The Common Law*, he had written one of the most famous sentences in the history of American jurisprudence: "The life of the law has not been logic; it has been experience."[66] As a member of the Massachusetts Supreme Judicial Court for twenty years and the Supreme Court of the United States since 1902, he had dissented from decisions that struck down pro-labor legislation—though not because he believed that the laws would accomplish anything. For example, he thought the Sherman Act's ban on all contracts and combinations in restraint of trade was "a foolish law."[67] But he was no more willing to declare the Sherman Act unconstitutional than he was labor laws. "I have little doubt that the country likes it and I always say, as you know, that if my fellow citizens want to go to Hell I will help them," he wrote. "It's my job."[68] What drew Frankfurter and Denison to Holmes was his personality and open-mindedness. Holmes did not subscribe to their ideas, but he was willing to listen to them. They admired his intellectual curiosity, conversational skills, and sense of fun. Mephistopheles, as Holmes often referred to himself, admired their ambition, intelligence, and optimism about the future.[69]

Frankfurter and Denison were beginning to form a new social circle. Brandeis inspired them with ideas and served as a role model for his fellow social and economic reformers. Holmes was their intellectual idol, who embraced them but not their ideas. Frankfurter was the *kochleffel*, the Yiddish word for cooking spoon or busybody, the avid collector of people who stirred the pot and introduced new ingredients into the mix.[70] Denison was Frankfurter's social companion and just as adept at flattery, charm, and friendship. All Frankfurter and Denison needed now was a house and a man named Valentine.

★★★

Soon after Frankfurter arrived in Washington, Denison reintroduced him to Taft's commissioner of Indian affairs, Robert G. Valentine. On the night of November 2, Denison brought Frankfurter to Valentine's home at 1727 Nineteenth Street for the first time. Valentine's fifteen-month-old daughter, Sophia, was in a long flannel nightgown and almost ready for bed. The guests, however, delayed the baby's bedtime. Denison, Sophia's godfather, and Frankfurter went up to the baby's room. "They each held her for a few moments," Valentine's wife, Sophie, wrote in her diary, "and the baby was rosy and sweet. She did not quite enjoy their call, or wish being held, but bore it without crying."[71] After a few months, Frankfurter and Valentine had become the best of friends. At Christmas, Frankfurter dined with Stimson and his wife out of professional obligation but spent half the day with Valentine out of personal pleasure. "We had a wonderful half day with Valentine," Frankfurter wrote his friend Emory Buckner. "He is the very *realest* of men I know here; next to you, Emory, he gets beneath my skin and touches my vitals more than any man I know."[72]

By early 1912, Valentine, Denison, and Frankfurter formed an inseparable trio, and the salon was beginning to take shape. "The days have been good to me down here," Frankfurter wrote to Buckner on April 20. "I should like to talk of Holmes and Bryce and Judge Mack (the real stuff) and Borglum and an Indian night at Val's etc. etc. with all that and so much more."[73] Julian W. Mack was a federal judge on the short-lived Commerce Court and later

Justice Oliver Wendell Holmes circa 1915

on the court of appeals, a prominent Harvard law graduate, and principal ally of Frankfurter and Brandeis in progressive and Zionist causes.[74] James Bryce was British ambassador to the United States. Holmes and Borglum, like Brandeis, were becoming regulars at Valentine's dinners.

Valentine, the Taft administration's leading outcast, turned his home into a political salon and into the center of a new liberal network. He clashed with Taft not simply as a holdover from the Roosevelt administration but as a direct result of Valentine's own policy decisions. As the commissioner of Indian affairs, Valentine put the economic self-sufficiency and assimilation of Native Americans first and governmental, business, and religious interests a distant second, third, and fourth. He alienated conservatives with his liberal policies. Lumber industry interests, for example, pegged Valentine as an ally of Gifford Pinchot, the conservationist Forestry Service chief who had been fired by Taft. Indeed, Valentine succeeded Pinchot in challenging the administration.

On January 27, 1912, Valentine issued a one-page order banning teachers at government-sponsored Indian schools from wearing religious "insignia and garb." The order appealed to the "essential principle of our national life—separation of church and state" and gave anyone with objections to the order until the next school year to comply.[75] Primarily aimed at sixty Catholic priests and nuns still teaching at Indian schools after the government had taken them over, Valentine's order caused a firestorm. Protestant and anti-Catholic organizations cheered. The Catholic Church and some members of Congress complained. Representative Bird S. McGuire of Oklahoma phoned Taft to say that Valentine possessed "not one particle of loyalty" and "has declared himself as a rank, violent Pinchot follower; that he has absolutely no loyalty whatever."[76]

Taft, with his re-election bid looming in November, was furious with Valentine for putting him in a no-win situation. Neither Taft nor Secretary of the Interior Walter L. Fisher had been consulted about Valentine's order, and Valentine had issued it while the president was out of town. Taft wanted to revoke the order immediately and then to investigate the issue. Fisher and other members of the cabinet urged the president to investigate first and then revoke Valentine's order before it took effect in the fall. One of the few progressives in the administration, Fisher presented the president with two proposed revocation orders: the first designed not to alienate Protestants, the second designed to humiliate Valentine. Taft chose the second option. "I fully believe in the principle of separation of the Church and State on which our government is based," Taft wrote Fisher, "but the questions presented by this order are of great importance and delicacy."[77] In revoking the order on February 3, Taft explained that the government had taken over the schools from the Catholic Church and that for these Catholic teachers Valentine's order "almost necessarily amounts almost to a discharge from the Federal service of those who have thus entered it."[78]

The Valentine who had united his friends against Taft was a divided soul. With his neatly combed, auburn-tinged hair, starched white spread-collar shirts, perfectly knotted ties, and dark suits, he looked as if he still belonged on Wall Street. Yet he possessed the spirit of an aspiring poet and had spent much of his early professional life chasing both banking and poetry

Robert G. Valentine

before he turned to government service. Born in 1872 in West Newton, Massachusetts, to an invalid mother and abandoned by his adventurer father, Valentine was raised by his aunts on a farm in nearby Holliston and attended a country school until he was fourteen. His beloved Aunt Beth made sure that he received an elite secondary education at Boston's Hopkinson School, which sent Valentine and many of its all-male graduates to Harvard College.

Valentine distinguished himself in Harvard's class of 1896.[79] In addition to Denison, his close friends included future New Hampshire governor Robert P. Bass; future lawyers and public servants Joseph P. Cotton and John Lord O'Brian; and future Boston lawyer John G. Palfrey. At Harvard, Valentine rowed freshmen crew, debated, played on the chess team, and was one of several graduation speakers.[80] His first love was poetry and literature. He published a student essay on Keats, made an aborted attempt at Harvard's graduate school in government, and then from 1896 to 1899 pursued his literary interests while teaching composition writing to MIT undergraduates.[81] He published articles about how to teach students to write in clear and effective ways in their chosen fields and prepared them for careers in government, business, and engineering.[82] He wrote poetry but viewed "writing *as an avocation*, not taking it seriously except in trying to write *accurate* verses." He burned many poems that he found unsatisfactory, bound the rest into a book, and looked for something else that inspired him.[83]

Wall Street lured Valentine to New York City. In June 1899, he subleased an apartment overlooking Washington Square and went to work as private secretary to James Stillman, the father of one of his Harvard classmates and the owner of the National City Bank (later Citibank).[84] Valentine learned how Wall Street worked from Stillman, who had allied his business interests with those of John D. Rockefeller and Edward H. Harriman.[85] After an apprenticeship lasting a year and a half, Valentine jumped at the chance to move to Omaha, Nebraska, to look after Stillman's interests as a member of the accounting department at the Union Pacific Railway.[86]

Poetry and literature brought Valentine back to MIT. In September 1901, he resumed his job as an assistant writing instructor and corresponded with another aspiring poet, Amy Lowell.[87] He spent the summer of 1902 working for Stillman and left MIT again for New York in November 1903 to work full-time for the Stillman-owned Farmers' Loan and Trust Company. Neither arts and letters nor making money satisfied him.[88] "In literature he felt the lack of actual human experience," his college roommate John Palfrey explained. "He turned to industry, the actual; but there at first the poet missed, or rather was baffled in his eagerness to reach, the human touch."[89]

Searching for the human touch in New York City, Valentine became active in political and social movements. In 1901, he campaigned for the successful anti–Tammany Hall mayoral candidate Seth Low, who introduced the merit-based civil service system in city government.[90] Valentine and four friends lived in a house in old Greenwich Village, then a crowded, poor, Italian immigrant neighborhood. In 1902, they co-founded Greenwich House, a settlement house for young immigrant women who lived and worked in the cooperative in exchange for food, shelter, and help in assimilating to American life. Valentine and his friends were known in their social circle as the "benefactors of Greenwich House."[91] The strain of trying to do too much—poetry and business and New York politics and settlement house work—proved too great. In February 1904, Valentine suffered a nervous breakdown as well as heart trouble and was ordered to rest for six months.[92] His cousin Sophie French inspired him to get well. After a prolonged courtship, her own nervous breakdown, and multiple marriage proposals, the thirty-one-year-old Valentine and thirty-six-year-old French announced in March 1904 that they were engaged.[93]

Valentine looked for a fresh start and left for Washington in December 1904, ostensibly to attend the National Civil Service Reform League annual meeting but in reality to find a government job so that he could marry Sophie.[94] He was so confident of his job prospects that on December 10 he proposed that they get married in two weeks.[95] "My situation comes very near to life and death with me," he wrote Sophie.[96] *Outlook* magazine's editor-in-chief Lyman Abbott, the father of one of Valentine's Harvard classmates, introduced him to one of the progressive magazine's longtime Washington reporters, Elbert F. Baldwin. Baldwin took a personal interest in Valentine, accompanied him to Washington for the Civil Service Reform meeting, and introduced him to many leading politicians, including President Roosevelt.[97] "Wonderful Wonderful Wonderful!" Valentine wrote Sophie on New Willard Hotel stationery. "That's been running in my mind ever since. It is not because he is President. You absolutely forget that when you are talking with him. He is a man; and your friend, in so far as there is good in you. Absolute quiet, a gentle voice, and strength, strength behind." After three minutes with Roosevelt, Valentine was sure that he belonged not in banking with Stillman but in public service in the Roosevelt administration. "I shall never mind Mr. Stillman again," Valentine wrote, referring to Roosevelt. "This is a great man."[98]

The day after he saw the president, Valentine met Roosevelt's newly appointed commissioner of Indian affairs, Francis E. Leupp.[99] The author of an early Roosevelt biography and a former newspaperman with a lifelong interest in Native Americans, Leupp wanted to pursue a progressive approach to Indian affairs. He respected Native American culture and believed that secular education, financial and land reforms, and skills training could make Native Americans more self-sufficient.

Leupp and Valentine hit it off. Having submitted an application to the Foreign Service, Valentine began a tryout of sorts with the new Indian affairs commissioner.[100] On December 21, he went to work for the first time in more than ten months.[101] The next day, after Valentine handed in his first report, Leupp asked if he was "open to negotiations." With a permanent job in sight, Valentine knew he could get married. On December 31, 1904, at 1:30 p.m., he and Sophie were married at the French family homestead in South Braintree in a small ceremony witnessed by a few Harvard friends, including Denison.[102] Sophie joined her husband in Washington. On February 12, 1905, Leupp offered Valentine a full-time job as the commissioner's private secretary.[103]

Valentine embarked on a new life in Washington and new adventures in Indian affairs. For four months of every year, he lived on reservations, rode with Native Americans on horseback, and learned about their problems.[104] The other eight months, he assisted Leupp, learned the ins and outs of the bureau, and rapidly ascended through its ranks. Leupp named him superintendent of Indian schools. In December 1908, outgoing President Roosevelt promoted Valentine to assistant commissioner of Indian affairs. Six months later, when Leupp resigned citing physical and mental exhaustion, Taft nominated the thirty-six-year-old Valentine as commissioner.

As commissioner of Indian affairs, Valentine sought to continue Leupp's policy goals of economic self-sufficiency and "treating the Indian as a man."[105] Valentine brought economic efficiency and scientific management skills to improving the lives of 300,000 Native Americans. He focused on Native American health, education, and industry. His oft-stated goal was simple—the elimination of the Indian Affairs Bureau.[106] He launched programs designed to make self-sufficiency and citizenship the only course.[107] He established local competency commissions to determine which Native Americans could control their finances and property. He endeavored to pay his field agents and superintendents more money and to hire them based on civil service standards rather than political patronage. He tried to stem the spread of tuberculosis and trachoma, to create Indian schools that emphasized English and vocational skills, to integrate Indians into white schools, and to encourage Native Americans to farm their land and to sell excess acreage. The results of these programs and others were mixed; failures were frequent.[108] Administrative problems, public corruption, private greed, and cultural barriers turned health, education, and industry into elusive goals and the elimination of the Indian affairs bureau into a pipe dream.

Valentine's home life was equally stressful. In May 1910, he accompanied forty-two-year-old Sophie back to Boston so that she could give birth to their first and only child.[109] On July 23, their daughter, Sophia, was born. His wife suffered life-threatening postpregnancy complications. His daughter had trouble gaining weight. While they recovered in South Braintree outside Boston, Valentine rented and furnished a three-story Dupont Circle row house at 1727 Nineteenth Street.[110] In preparation for his family's return, he had the walls scraped and painted cream white, hardwood floors and stairs waxed, and the baby's room decorated.[111] Every day he visited to check on the progress. He promised Sophie to make the House "healthy," "bright and happy," and "basically furnished" and hired two servants to cook and clean.[112] A month later, Valentine's wife and daughter joined him there. "And such a fascinating house as this I am sure you have never seen!" Sophie wrote.[113] She liked the big room on the main floor and the roses on the upstairs wallpaper, and she described her sitting room—with two bureaus, three chairs, a cheval glass, a photograph of an Indian painting, and an etching of her family homestead in Braintree—as a "bower of loveliness."[114]

For Valentine, the house was the perfect place to entertain friends. The main floor opened up to a thirty-two-foot living and dining room with "burnt orange walls," a large fireplace "of reddish brownish black speckled bricks," and a "double mantel of black wood." "Sophie's French Coat of Arms" hung above the fireplace; Indian baskets decorated several shelves.[115] One side of the room included a small desk, a piano, and several comfortable chairs on an Indian rug near the fireplace, china displayed over the double mantel, a lawyer's bookshelf on the adjacent wall, and a skylight overhead. The other side included a china cabinet and a small round dining room table.[116]

The joys of his house and family could not prevent his job from getting to Valentine. He confessed that "no man can stand up to the remorseless

Sophie French Valentine with her infant daughter, Sophia

inconsequence of things below and of things above him and take all the attacks from right, left, behind and before and not have it reduce his efficiency."[117] He prided himself on eighteen-hour days yet was so fatigued that he could manage only three hours in the morning and three in the afternoon on Indian affairs matters.[118] He looked gaunt and tired, and in May 1911 he suffered another nervous breakdown and headed to Atlantic City to recuperate with Denison.[119] After nearly two months, Valentine returned to work in Washington.

The poor health of Valentine's family added to his stress. Baby Sophia still could not gain weight because of an undiagnosed milk allergy. Doctors insisted that she needed specialized medical care, and in March 1912 Sophie and Sophia returned to the French family's home in South Braintree for good.[120] For the next three years in Massachusetts, a team of doctors and servants helped nurse baby Sophia back to health. Valentine was living all alone in the three-story, Nineteenth Street row house that he had decorated for his family. He opened his home to his friends Denison and Frankfurter.

In early May 1912, Frankfurter agreed to pay half the rent and expenses and moved into Valentine's house.[121] A month later, Denison followed suit.[122] Frankfurter exulted over the "great time we are having."[123] Valentine wrote

The living room of the House of Truth

his wife about their dinner parties and five-hour Sunday lunch: "Sunday at
our regular general invitation we had besides FF & myself, [Louis G.] Bissell
and [Thurlow M.] Gordon, Winnie's assistants at the Dept. of Justice, Lord
Eustace Percy, & [Loring] Christy [sic]. We talked & talked after 1:30 feast
and the first thing we knew it was 6:45!"[124]

A year later, two regular guests at the House, Loring Christie and Lord
Eustace Percy, became its fourth and fifth original residents. Denison's assistant at the Justice Department, Christie had worked on the New York
customs fraud prosecutions with Denison and Frankfurter and had come to
Washington in October 1910 to assist Denison with briefs and arguments
before the US Supreme Court and Commerce Court.[125] On one of his first
nights in Washington, Christie had dined with Denison at Valentine's new
home.[126] Three years behind Frankfurter in law school, Christie had been
the *Harvard Law Review* president in 1908–9 and had finished in the top
three in his class.[127] Christie and two other top classmates joined Stimson's
law firm, Winthrop & Stimson. At Stimson's firm, Christie met and began
a lifelong friendship with Frankfurter. Frankfurter probably urged Christie
to leave the firm, where he was reputedly earning $10 a week, to work for
Denison at a $2,500 annual salary.[128] Unlike other top Harvard law gradu-
ates, Christie and Frankfurter chose public service over a Wall Street law
firm and knew that "our friends think us damn fools."[129] In Washington,
Christie initially lived a few buildings down from Frankfurter at Eighteenth
and I Streets and less than one block from Holmes.[130] Frankfurter and
Christie often visited the justice at his home and admired Holmes's judicial
philosophy.[131]

With his high cheekbones, cleft chin, prim expression, and commanding
eyebrows, Christie looked like his Scottish ancestors. A product of a middle-
class Baptist family from Amherst, Nova Scotia, and a graduate of a small
Baptist college, Acadia University, he viewed Washington, just as he had
Harvard Law School, as an escape from a provincial life in Nova Scotia.[132]
He was practicing law at the highest levels of the federal government yet
never forgot his Canadian roots or his interest in diplomatic and international affairs. "Christie is an attractive fellow with a fine mind; still rather
restless," Frankfurter wrote in his diary. "He seems to have a deep emotional
side which is not always administered."[133]

The fifth and final original resident at 1727 Nineteenth Street, Percy, arrived in Washington in early May 1910 to serve as an attaché to the British
Embassy under Ambassador Bryce.[134] Soon after his arrival, Percy began

Loring Christie circa 1910

visiting Valentine's house.[135] Valentine described Percy as "a younger son of the head of the famous Percy family that owns a large part of England."[136] The seventh son of the seventh duke of Northumberland, Percy possessed the bloodlines of landed British nobility but none of the land or wealth. Educated at Eton College and Christ Church, Oxford, he believed in public service and belonged to the Catholic Apostolic Church that awaited the early Second Coming of Jesus Christ. According to Frankfurter, Percy was "much more of a dreamer and a mystic than the son of a great land-owner."[137] He was not always sympathetic to his housemates' politics, but he shared their love of conversation, interest in social reform, and Christie's ties to Great Britain. Percy and his British friends brought a transatlantic perspective to the discussions.[137]

By the summer of 1912, the House was beginning to take shape. Frankfurter, Denison, and Valentine lived there, and Christie and Percy were soon to follow. They threw dinner parties that drew Justice Holmes, Brandeis, Borglum, Judge Mack, Ambassador Bryce, and many others.

To Felix, always Transoceanically constant
Eustace Percy

Eustace Percy

Valentine's dispute over his religious garb order in government-run Indian schools symbolized growing frustration with Taft. It also reflected differences between Taft and Roosevelt supporters, between big business and organized labor, between old ideas about laissez-faire capitalism and new ones about government regulation of both trusts and labor-management relations.

That summer the residents and guests at 1727 Nineteenth Street began referring to it as the House of Truth. The name has been misattributed to Holmes.[138] In fact, Holmes credited the name to Denison.[139] And Frankfurter could not remember who named it.[140] Regardless of its origin, the name

self-mockingly referred to the ideological debates between the justice and his young friends about the search for truth. They believed in an objective truth based on empirical data and analysis by social scientists and nonpartisan government experts. Holmes, on the other hand, believed that truth was "the system of my (intellectual) limitations"[141] or "the majority vote of that nation that could lick all others."[142] Philosophical debates about truth soon morphed into political debates about whether Theodore Roosevelt should challenge his handpicked successor for the presidency. 1727 Nineteenth Street was not just a home for ambitious and disaffected Taft administration officials. It became the unofficial headquarters for Roosevelt supporters. More than anything else, the prospect of a Roosevelt presidential bid made the House of Truth the place to be in Washington.

3

The Call of the Moose

At 1:00 p.m. on January 12, 1912, Frankfurter ate lunch with Theodore Roosevelt at the former president's office at *Outlook* magazine near Union Square in New York City.[1] A few days later, he sent Roosevelt a copy of Holmes's 1911 Harvard commencement speech on the fiftieth anniversary of the justice's graduation and employed the type of flattery Frankfurter usually reserved for his judicial idol.[2] "[W]hat I really want to send you is some indication of what *you* mean to me," Frankfurter wrote Roosevelt, "in dealing with the raw stuff of life, even if the common obscurity of the vast majority were my lot for the rest of my life."[3]

Long before his lunch with the former president, Frankfurter, like many others, had sensed Roosevelt's desire to run for a third term. Roosevelt had already served nearly two terms in the White House, from 1901 to 1905 after William McKinley's assassination and a second, elected term from 1905 to 1909. In 1908, Roosevelt had declined to run again, though he would have been only fifty years old on Election Day. Instead, he had groomed his friend William Howard Taft, a former state and federal judge, as his successor by naming Taft secretary of war. Roosevelt's anger and frustration with President Taft had been building for months. The Ballinger-Pinchot controversy about Alaska coal field claims in early 1910 turned into a proxy war between Taft and Roosevelt loyalists and had begun the formal split between the two men. By the time Roosevelt returned from Africa (where he was on safari) and Europe (where he accepted the Nobel Peace Prize for ending the Russo-Japanese War) in June 1910, his war with Taft was in the open. The final break between the two former friends came in October 1911 when Taft's Justice Department charged U.S. Steel with antitrust violations based on a merger that Roosevelt had approved as president after discussing it with his cabinet, including then Secretary of War Taft. In reality, Roosevelt was looking for excuses to run again.[4] A week before their

lunch, Frankfurter had predicted that Roosevelt would be drafted into the Republican presidential race: "The thing is in the air; people of intelligence and observation here 'feel' he will be nominated," he wrote to Emory Buckner. "Right now, however, if I had to stake my life on it I should stake it on Taft's re-nomination—but I'm damn glad I don't have to stake it!"[5]

On February 10, a week after Taft revoked Valentine's religious garb order, seven Republican governors petitioned Roosevelt to accept his party's presidential nomination.[6] Roosevelt's lone progressive rival for the presidency, Wisconsin Senator Robert La Follette, had lashed out at a group of newspaper publishers during a rambling two-hour speech on February 2 in Philadelphia. The press reported that La Follette was "ill" and had suffered a "mental collapse."[7] The next day, La Follette took a break from campaigning, opening the door for Roosevelt to challenge Taft. The petition from the state governors, which Roosevelt had orchestrated, precipitated an intraparty showdown between the former president and his handpicked successor.

Roosevelt's much-anticipated February 21 speech before the Ohio Constitutional Convention in Columbus raised expectations. "We Progressives," Roosevelt began, "believe that the people have the right, the power, and the duty to protect themselves and their own welfare; that human rights are

Theodore Roosevelt speaking at Grant's Tomb in 1911

supreme over all other rights; that wealth should be the servant, not the master, of the people. We believe that unless representative government does not absolutely represent the people it is not representative government at all." Roosevelt described a war against privilege and on behalf of the common man; he vowed "to free our government from the control of money in politics" and to put government back "in the hands of the people" and to make their representatives "responsible to the people's will."[8]

Roosevelt's "Charter of Democracy" addressed the issues most important to Frankfurter, Denison, Valentine, and other regulars at the House of Truth.

First, Roosevelt took on the issue of trusts. He did not attack big business simply because it was big but because the government should pursue illegal monopolies. He believed that, with the aid of new legislation, he could distinguish between good and bad trusts.[9]

Second, Roosevelt asserted that both the federal government and the states had the power to protect working people, particularly women and children, from long hours, low wages, and unsafe conditions.[10] Finally and most controversially—in the eyes of even his supporters—he attacked the courts by endorsing the popular recall of judges and their decisions.[11] State court judges, he argued, claimed to be interpreting the Constitution when they struck down legislation that protected small businesses and consumers from illegal monopolies and working men and women from unfair labor practices. He singled out a New York Court of Appeals decision that had invalidated the state's worker's compensation law and left a crippled railroad worker with no legal remedy.[12]

Although his recall proposal was aimed at state judges and not the Supreme Court of the United States, Roosevelt's speech put the Court's nine justices on notice.[13] Throughout his speech, he invoked Lincoln's reaction to Chief Justice Roger B. Taney's *Dred Scott* decision that invalidated the Missouri Compromise and exacerbated divisions over slavery.[14] In Roosevelt's telling, the people trumped the Court by electing Lincoln, overruling *Dred Scott*, and passing the Fourteenth Amendment. Roosevelt implicitly cast himself as the Lincolnesque hero, the Court as a historically reactionary institution, and Taft as the reactionary institution's enabler and biggest defender.

Attacking the Court was nothing new for Roosevelt. Two years earlier in a speech in Denver, he had criticized the Court's decisions in *E. C. Knight*, which excluded manufacturing from the reach of the antitrust laws, and *Lochner*, which invalidated a New York maximum hour law for bakers.[15] The Court's *E. C. Knight* and *Lochner* decisions, Roosevelt had argued, created a no man's land where neither the federal government nor the states could regulate unfair competition and unfair labor practices. He also had attacked the courts and unpopular judicial decisions in a series of 1911 *Outlook* magazine articles, private correspondence, and stump speeches in the spring of 1912, as well as in an introduction to a book attacking the judiciary.[16] Roosevelt's latest broadside against state supreme court decisions was an extension of his earlier remarks and another effort to pit the judiciary against the will of the people. "I may not know much about law," Roosevelt told Frankfurter, "but I do know one can put the fear of God into judges."[17]

Roosevelt's Columbus speech did not officially announce his candidacy; newspapers, however, picked up his off-the-record response to a question about whether he would run: "My hat is in the ring."[18] Three days later, on February 24, he replied to the seven Republican governors that, if it were offered to him, he would accept the Republican nomination.[19]

★★★

After Roosevelt's announcement, Frankfurter could not contain his inner turmoil about how a progressive Roosevelt loyalist could remain in the Taft administration. In an eight-page letter circulated to his friends, Frankfurter confessed his "prepossessions against Taft" upon arriving in Washington, prejudices that were reinforced by the Kansas City speech debacle with Stimson. Taft, Frankfurter believed, was a former judge miscast as president. He had no clear beliefs other than "textual worship of the Constitution," no passion for the presidency, and no ideas for the country. As a result, conservatives ended up controlling Taft's political agenda, even though he was neither liberal nor conservative. Taft, Frankfurter argued, had done nothing to further the progressive goal of social reform.[20]

Roosevelt, by contrast, understood that the president possessed the constitutional power to change the direction of the country—to enforce the antitrust laws and to lobby for the passage of supplemental legislation, to protect the rights of workers, and to exhort the courts not to obstruct these endeavors. Frankfurter recognized Colonel Roosevelt's limitations as a thinker, as someone far more "keen to scent a wrong, far less resourceful to suggest a remedy." Roosevelt's idea about popular recall of judges and their decisions was antithetical to Frankfurter's legal training, yet the Colonel's criticism of judges for thwarting legislation based on narrow interpretations of vague constitutional commands, in Frankfurter's view, was absolutely correct. Though Frankfurter was well aware of Roosevelt's imperfections, his heart and mind were unreservedly with the Colonel. Their bond had been forged two years earlier during Stimson's New York gubernatorial campaign. And Frankfurter could not support Woodrow Wilson, despite the New Jersey Democrat's "moral endowment" and "more disciplined intellect," because of "his party's traditions on States' Rights," because "the Republican Party is the party of liberal construction of the Constitution," and because Roosevelt possessed the ability to transform the Republican Party into "the distinctly liberal party."[21]

Frankfurter's dilemma about staying in the Taft administration was heightened by his boss Henry Stimson's decision to support Taft. On March 5, Stimson publicly endorsed the president and asserted that he had "carried out this Progressive faith of the Republican party."[22] Though he owed his career in public life to Roosevelt, Stimson believed that Roosevelt's campaign was a "great mistake" that would divide the party and prevent a Republican victory in November.[23] Stimson also believed that Roosevelt had shown poor leadership and judgment by leaving the door open to running and allowing others to draft him into the race.[24] During a series of honest conversations with his boss, Frankfurter openly disagreed with Stimson's endorsement of Taft.[25] He also advised Stimson to refrain from making any further comments about the presidential race.[26] For most of the campaign, Stimson heeded Frankfurter's advice. Stimson valued Frankfurter's loyalty and counsel, and the two men agreed to disagree about Roosevelt.

As early as March 1912, Frankfurter seriously considered resigning from the Taft administration. But after discussions with Stimson, Valentine, and others, he decided to stay for the time being. An unsolicited message from Roosevelt instructed him to keep his day job; Brandeis offered the same advice.[27] Frankfurter could barely stand it as the Roosevelt campaign began without him. He knew in his heart that Roosevelt would not win the Republican nomination, that it was a mistake to challenge an incumbent president in the same party, and that Roosevelt should have waited until 1916 to try for a third term.[28] Nonetheless, Frankfurter hoped that Roosevelt would take the fight to the convention and, if that failed, run as a third-party candidate. After Frankfurter wrote his eight-page confession, he vowed to read it to his friends and housemates, Valentine and Denison, who were struggling with their own conflicts between their political beliefs and staying in the administration.[29]

A week before the Columbus speech, Valentine met with Roosevelt and "came back with at least a hundred spiritual years added to my life."[30]

Valentine believed Roosevelt was a changed man since leaving the White House; the former president had gained more physical strength, a gentler personality, and "a real grip on the social movement."[31] Valentine knew after the "Charter of Democracy" speech that he, too, needed to leave the Taft administration and to join the man who had stirred his soul during his Washington job search in 1904 and who had appointed him assistant commissioner of Indian affairs. Roosevelt's Columbus speech changed everything for Valentine.[32] It articulated the differences between Taft Republicans and Roosevelt Republicans and laid out the blueprint for the government's role in creating a more just, progressive nation.

Valentine did not immediately resign because he did not want people to think that he was leaving because of the controversy about his religious garb order. A few days before a hearing on the issue, he had spoken at the graduation ceremonies for the Carlisle Indian Industrial School in Pennsylvania about the need for Native American self-governance. He was at peace physically and mentally on April 8 when he testified about his religious garb order before Secretary of the Interior Walter Fisher.[33] Fisher's pretense of impartiality, the testimony of various religious organizations, and the accompanying briefs were something of a joke.[34] Everyone knew that Taft would not reinstate the order. Valentine, however, was pleased to get his side of the story on the record and felt "'without care'" and as if "he had 'won a spiritual victory.'"[35] Not even trumped-up charges in Congress that he had brought alcohol onto an Indian reservation and had committed other improprieties could dampen his spirits.[36] He was "amused" by letters from friends in Massachusetts suggesting that he was in "in danger!" "Not much!" Valentine replied. "The President's statement about his not favoring Catholics was a great mistake. That's the common statement here."[37] After the April hearing, people began treating Valentine "with the tenderest consideration" and allowed him to "accomplish more things."[38]

By mid-May, Valentine was handicapping the November presidential election. His career in the Bureau of Indian Affairs depended on it. It also affected his desire to buy the House at 1727 Nineteenth Street. He told Sophie that buying it would save them $20 on their $240 monthly rent and would be a good investment regardless of who won the election.[39] "The chances of Mr. Taft's return are very small, I should say not more than one out of twenty," he wrote Sophie. "If TR came in I should want to stay in some capacity. With TR, Hughes or Wilson I might well stay. If the

Democrats win with other than Wilson, we should probably leave & I think we should have no difficulty in renting."[40]

★★★

Roosevelt's campaign was also welcome news for Denison, who felt as weary as Valentine felt rejuvenated. Denison had left Washington in April 1912 for a vacation and much-needed rest.[41] He was always in danger of spreading himself too thin, overworking, and sliding into deep depression. Slowing down did not come naturally to him. Earlier that year, he had argued before the Supreme Court that the Commerce Court could not interfere with the Interstate Commerce Commission's factual findings on railroad rate-fixing.[42] He also had made a series of headline-grabbing speeches: he argued that sugar fraud resulted from political patronage and demonstrated the need for civil service reform, and he advocated for supplemental legislation to prevent unfair competition.[43]

Denison believed that Roosevelt was the only man willing to make these proposed new laws a reality. But he could not bring himself to quit his job as assistant attorney general in charge of customs affairs and to join the campaign—at least not yet. He owed too much to Attorney General Wickersham. Wickersham had kept his job open for nearly a year in 1911 while Denison battled typhoid fever.[44] In February 1912, Wickersham had defended Denison after Senator Boies Penrose of Pennsylvania questioned the propriety of Denison's customs fraud speeches and their effects on Pennsylvania business interests.[45] And Wickersham tolerated Denison's progressive political views and had accepted Denison's refusal to campaign for Taft in New Hampshire.[46]

Christie, Denison's assistant counsel at the Justice Department, felt less hamstrung by his position in the Taft administration. Christie was not a high-level official, nor did he have aspirations for higher office. The official search for his replacement had begun in November 1911.[47] Christie felt free to support Roosevelt's campaign and planned to attend the Republican National Convention in June.

Roosevelt's presidential campaign stumbled out of the gate. La Follette, a Wisconsin progressive popular with western farmers, captured the first primary on March 19 in North Dakota, as well his home state on April 2. After Taft was awarded most of the delegates at the state convention in New York on March 27, Roosevelt threatened to run as a third-party candidate and won a string of Republican primary victories: Illinois on April 9, Pennsylvania on April 13, and Nebraska and Oregon on April 19.

Things turned ugly in Massachusetts. Roosevelt looked as if he would sweep the remaining primaries against Taft, run away with the Republican nomination, and embarrass a sitting president. It was make or break for Taft, and Taft knew it. In an April 25 speech in Boston, the president broke his promise to Stimson not to attack Roosevelt personally, used Roosevelt's private letters as ammunition, and charged the former president with preaching "class hatred."[48] Roosevelt replied that pro-labor legislation to protect working women and children was not class hatred.[49] On the night of the Massachusetts primary, Frankfurter was "making the rounds at the newspaper offices" and told Valentine that "early returns look as if TR were carrying Massachusetts." By 10:30 p.m., the Associated Press and Hearst Papers indicated that Roosevelt had won. "I'm *so glad*," Valentine wrote.[50] The next morning, however, Valentine and Frankfurter learned that Taft had eked out his first and only primary victory in Massachusetts, 50 percent to 48, though Roosevelt was awarded more delegates.

After his narrow defeat in Massachusetts, Roosevelt captured the last five primaries in May, including Taft's home state of Ohio and nine of twelve primaries in all. In 1912, however, most states did not hold primaries.[51] Everyone knew that party leaders, not state conventions or primaries, would choose the Republican nominee at the convention in Chicago in June. But defeating a sitting president in his home state meant something. "Isn't Ohio grand!" Valentine wrote Sophie. "But I appreciate how you are filled and properly so with pity for the President's humiliation. It's a national humiliation that he could be the kind of man that should get such a rebuke. ... Whether Roosevelt is nominated at Chicago or not is a matter of minor importance *compared* with the importance of not having a man like Mr. Taft President another term."[52]

As Roosevelt's campaign surged, more people wanted to dine at the House. "Sunday we had a good truth teller," Valentine wrote of a May 19 lunch. From New York City, Frankfurter brought two friends from law school, Sam Rosensohn and Buckner. Other guests included Christie, Percy, Indian affairs official Arthur Ludington, New York lawyer Sanford Freund, and of course Justice Holmes. Valentine had known Holmes since their mutual friend John G. Palfrey, Valentine's college roommate and Holmes's lawyer, had introduced them soon after Valentine had arrived in Washington.[53] "It was good talk," Valentine wrote of Sunday dinner, "and the Justice I think enjoyed himself."[54]

All the talk, of course, was about Roosevelt. "T.R. is creating new, needed and healthy political organisms," Valentine wrote after a May 27 dinner party. "[W]hatever the immediate results may be politically, there is a real social democracy ahead, and with an increase instead of a lessening of individual achievement and a lifting of all standards including the highest." The May 27 dinner included Roosevelt loyalists Herbert Knox Smith, Ludington, Frankfurter, Denison, and Percy; Captain Frank R. McCoy, an aide to General Leonard Wood; and the sculptor Borglum.[55] Borglum often traveled to Washington and in April 1912 had testified before the Senate Foreign Relations Committee about the need for a memorial to recognize the centennial of the 1814 Treaty of Ghent between the United States and Great Britain. Monuments, he argued, "are built to celebrate great events, great ideas, or great ideals, and artists are employed to celebrate those ideals."[56] He proposed a monument to be erected on the US–Canadian border, consisting of a series of giant boulders and bronze tablets, but Congress never funded it.[57]

It is unclear how Borglum ended up at the House, but it was probably through Frankfurter. The previous year, Borglum had sent Frankfurter a signed photograph of the sculptor's statue of a seated Lincoln in Newark, New Jersey, a memento that Frankfurter considered "a permanent treasure."[58] Frankfurter's and Borglum's interests converged over the opening of the Panama Canal; Borglum had lobbied for an amendment to the bill to specify its artistic design.[59] Valentine and Borglum also hit it off. Having grown up in the West, Borglum engaged Valentine about Indian affairs. He had been raised with Indians as a boy in Nebraska and elsewhere in the West and had been interested in them his entire life. Valentine sent Borglum a report about the Indian Affairs bureau and requested Borglum's comments and criticism.[60]

Borglum also shared his new friends' enthusiasm for Roosevelt. In 1896, Borglum had received a letter of introduction to Roosevelt, who was then a New York City police commissioner and Borglum was new to the New York art world. Roosevelt championed the sculptor's work.[61] In 1908, then-President Roosevelt unveiled Borglum's Embassy Row statue of Civil War General Philip Sheridan.[62] A great admirer of Borglum's marble bust of Lincoln, Roosevelt successfully lobbied for its permanent display in the rotunda of the US Capitol.[63] Finally, on May 30, 1911, Roosevelt unveiled Borglum's statue of a seated and melancholy Lincoln, his hat resting on a bench, in Newark, New Jersey, after Roosevelt had admired the unfinished work in Borglum's studio.[64]

Borglum, who claimed that he could judge a man by his facial structure and expressions, did not think much of Taft.[65] "Taft is a good man naturally but weak and so much flesh without purpose, will, nor moral courage or even constancy to his own convictions," Borglum wrote. "His indecision serves crime, and he has not the will to see that the criminal only threatens and he yields to fears of one sort or another."[66] Taft did not respond to Borglum's letter about a proposed Lincoln statue in Taft's hometown of Cincinnati. Borglum also attempted to engage Taft in a discussion of the sixteenth president at a Lincoln birthday celebration in Newark on the first anniversary of the dedication of Borglum's Lincoln statue.[67] It could not have helped matters when, after laying a wreath at Borglum's statue, Taft described progressives as "political emotionalists and neurotics."[68] "I got interested in politics when Roosevelt broke loose in 1912," Borglum wrote.[69] The sculptor admired the Roosevelt campaign's regard for the rights of working people and western farmers, its contempt for the financiers who controlled the Republican Party, and its insurgent, antiestablishment themes.

Borglum (sitting second from back) at the 1912 Progressive Party convention in Chicago

"In God's name I wish I could serve you these days," he wrote Roosevelt in April. "I do at every chance."[70] Borglum passed along wild rumors he heard in Washington, chaired the Progressive Party in Stamford, and organized political rallies in Connecticut.[71]

By going all in for Roosevelt, Borglum and his new friends Valentine, Frankfurter, and Denison found themselves drawn to each other. On June 19, Valentine finished a three-page poem, "A Nation's Prayer," which began by trying to inspire a new political generation:

> A Nation, young, deliberate and keen
> Bulks huge against the sunset,
> Her eyes
> Fixed on the outstanding stars.
> Millions of men, arise!
> This night in prayer are met
> We who have seen
> How fateful is the dawn tomorrow brings.
> Millions on millions we, as one voice sings,
> Now lift our hymn to light
> Our plea for Truth, our Country's might.
> Lord God of all the worlds that be
> Guide us to Thee,
> Help us to serve thy earth aright.

He sent the poem to Borglum. "Here's my latest use of the knife," Valentine wrote Borglum next to the first paragraph, "in the eternal attempt to cut through to Truth. You are one of my Gratitudees."[72] "Your prayer is so much mine it is hard for me to prove it," Borglum wrote Valentine. "Still if it is too my prayer it's wonderful. God bless you for it." The sculptor promised to read Valentine's poem to 200 people in Stamford, explained how he had challenged the Republican political establishment in Connecticut, and confessed to Valentine: "I'm still a Bull Moose whatever that may mean." At the end of his letter, Borglum invited his friends from the House to his Stamford, Connecticut, estate known as Borgland. "What chance is there of having you and Frankfurter & Denison honor my inn by a visit here. I'll write them."[73]

The House of Truth attracted not only true believers like Borglum but also its share of converts like Francis Biddle. A recent Harvard law graduate tapped to work as Justice Holmes's secretary from 1911 to 1912, Biddle was invited to a few Sunday lunches at the House and never forgot the big personalities of the men who lived there—Valentine ("the center of a group of young men who were stirred by a sense of needed change in American life"); Frankfurter ("wonderfully stimulating and exciting"); Denison ("gifted and forthcoming, whose friendly ease covered desperate periods of depression"); Percy ("appealingly attractive and companionable, yet with something hidden and inviolate deep in his personality that suggested a diffident mysticism"); and Christie two years ahead of him in law school.[74] A blue-blooded Philadelphian and graduate of Groton, Harvard College, and Harvard Law School, Biddle was conservative to his core and had believed since college that Roosevelt was "demagogic, bumptious, untruthful."[75]

A few lunches and dinners at Valentine's home transformed Biddle's political outlook. "It was Bob Valentine who turned me into a Roosevelt man," Biddle recalled. "Yes, he said, to these hackneyed expressions of distrust on my part, he may be all these, but you must judge a man by his direction and by his positive virtues, not by his faults, not by what he lacks: and Roosevelt has done a good deal for the country, he has a forthright outlook, and a real, not a spurious, moral sense."[76] After leaving Holmes's employ, Biddle shocked his family by becoming the Philadelphia chairman of the Bull Moose Party's speakers' bureau.

Biddle's boss, Justice Holmes, could not understand the younger generation's fascination with Roosevelt. "My wife tells me that you have become a Rooseveltian and think that a great moral issue is involved," Holmes wrote Biddle. "I wish you had said what one, for I don't discover it. I fear, if a lot of you young men are on that side and take that view, that there is something that I don't see and that I am showing myself to be an old fogy, but it has seemed to me that the most striking difference between Taft and R. is that the latter thinks that everything is about right when it is under his hat."[77] Had he not stopped voting since taking the bench, Holmes insisted that he would have voted for Taft even though the justice disagreed with the president's Sherman Act prosecutions. Holmes admired the success of the robber barons. He once told Taft that "if they could make a case for putting Rockefeller in prison I should do my part; but if they left it to me I should put up a bronze statue of him."[78]

Holmes knew Roosevelt's faults better than any of his young friends and probably owed the Colonel the largest professional debt. In 1902, Roosevelt nominated Holmes to the Supreme Court at the urging of Senator Henry Cabot Lodge and after an interview at Roosevelt's Long Island home, Sagamore Hill.[79] Roosevelt admired Holmes's famous "Soldier's Faith" speech, thought Holmes's speech about Chief Justice John Marshall was not respectful enough, but considered Holmes's Massachusetts Supreme Judicial Court "labor decisions criticized by some of the big railroad men and other members of large corporations ... a strong point in [his] favor."[80] Roosevelt had assumed that Holmes would enforce the Sherman Act and support the administration's antitrust prosecutions. Holmes quickly disappointed him. During his second term on the Court, he dissented from the *Northern Securities* decision that dissolved a massive railroad trust owned by J. P. Morgan and John D. Rockefeller.[81] In an apocryphal remark, Roosevelt is quoted as saying that "he could carve out of a banana a Justice with more backbone than that."[82]

The quotation may have been made up, but the tension between Holmes and Roosevelt was real. Although they privately aired their differences about *Northern Securities* and Holmes later dined with Roosevelt at the White House, the justice never forgave the president who had put him on the Court.[83] "We like each other by temperament though I cannot again take his friendship seriously," Holmes wrote.[84] The justice never failed to mention *Northern Securities*.[85] Nor did he consider Roosevelt one of the nation's great presidents. "He was very likeable, a big figure, a rather ordinary intellect, with extraordinary gifts, a shrewd and I think pretty unscrupulous politician," Holmes wrote after Roosevelt's death. "He played all his cards—if not more."[86]

In 1912, however, Roosevelt reigned as the hero of the House. Frankfurter conceded to Mrs. Holmes that the Roosevelt fixation was a passing fad, "the undisciplined exuberance of youth," an excitement about "the aspirations of the man rather than the man himself." Frankfurter reassured Mrs. Holmes that her husband's legacy would endure "long after the turmoil and noise of present-day politics."[87] For the time being, however, Holmes was perplexed by and a bit lost amid the Bull Moose fervor.

Another regular at the house, Brandeis, was not a Roosevelt supporter either. Personally and politically, he was extremely close to Wisconsin senator Robert La Follette and initially supported him for the Republican nomination.[88] Until Roosevelt entered the race, La Follette had been the leading progressive candidate. Like Roosevelt, he attacked the reactionary judiciary for invalidating socioeconomic legislation, thwarting the prosecution of illegal monopolies, and interfering with "the movement toward democracy."[89] But La Follette's rambling Philadelphia speech had cost him any realistic shot at winning the presidency in 1912. Even so, Brandeis believed that Roosevelt's

fight with Taft was counterproductive, for it had divided progressives among
La Follette, Roosevelt, and Taft. During the close primary in Massachusetts,
Brandeis remarked: "If we could only have had such an impasse between
conservatism & progress—instead of the issue of T.R.!"[90]

The three-way battle between Roosevelt, Taft, and La Follette came to
a head in June at the Republican National Convention in Chicago. A few
days before the convention, party leaders had awarded 235 of 254 disputed
delegates to Taft. "I don't see anything but a bolt unless we are willing to
compromise pretty far," Christie reported to Frankfurter from Chicago.[91]
Unsure how Roosevelt would react to defeat, Christie wrote: "He is strong
enough to stand by & we ought to be able to count on keeping him up to
the mark—& we could say, God help him if he doesn't."[92] With his defeat all
but assured, Roosevelt delivered one of the best speeches of his career. On
the eve of the convention, he charged "big bosses" and the "great crooked
financiers" who back them with stealing his nomination and giving it to
Taft.[93] Arguing that the "good of mankind" was at stake and vowing to continue his campaign, Roosevelt concluded with one of the most memorable
perorations in American political history: "We fight in honorable fashion
for the good of mankind; fearless of the future; unheeding of our individual
fates; with unflinching hearts and undimmed eyes; we stand at Armageddon,
and we battle for the Lord."[94]

Valentine was so inspired by Roosevelt's "Armageddon Speech" that he
fired off a fifteen-page letter to a longtime family friend about the merits
of Roosevelt's campaign.[95] Valentine had been receiving updates from
a trio of Roosevelt insiders and friends of the House: lawyer Joseph P.
Cotton, Valentine's Harvard classmate; George Rublee, Cotton's law partner and Roosevelt's speechwriter during the early stages of the campaign;
and Judge Learned Hand, a federal district judge in Manhattan and one of
the nation's most promising jurists.[96] Valentine believed them when they
said that Roosevelt did not want to be president again, that he had been
dragged into the campaign, and that it was up to him to challenge Taft as a
matter of "principle" and to bring about a "true social democracy in this
country."[97] Even if Roosevelt lost the nomination, Valentine believed, the
campaign would unite progressive Democrats and Republicans into a third
political party. Like Frankfurter, Valentine did not believe that Roosevelt
was "doing any real thinking himself"; Roosevelt, however, had returned
from Africa with an understanding of "the real spirit of social movement

in this country" and dedicated to the belief that "the real function of government in these days is social reform."[98]

During the next several days at the Republican convention, party stalwart Elihu Root, Roosevelt's former secretary of war and secretary of state, was elected chair and engineered Taft's renomination. Prior to the final vote, Roosevelt instructed his delegates to walk out and announced his third-party campaign for the presidency. A month earlier, newspapermen had asked Roosevelt how he was feeling after several months of vigorous campaigning. "Fine! fine!" he replied at his *Outlook* magazine office, "just like a bull moose."[99] With his defeat at the Chicago convention, Roosevelt's Bull Moose campaign had begun.

★★★

As Bull Moosers stuck in the Taft administration, Valentine, Frankfurter, and Denison continued to explore the possibility of leaving their jobs to join the campaign. Frankfurter met with Roosevelt in early July and was eager to discuss the meeting with Stimson.[100] Brandeis counseled Frankfurter to stay in the administration and discussed possible future public service jobs for Valentine.[101]

Brandeis's influence was limited, particularly after July 10, when he informed his friends that he would support the Democratic nominee, Woodrow Wilson.[102] At the Democratic National Convention in Baltimore, Speaker of the House James Beauchamp "Champ" Clark of Missouri led after the first few ballots. But with Tammany Hall backing Clark, William Jennings Bryan threw his support to Wilson, and on the forty-sixth ballot Wilson captured the two-thirds votes needed for the nomination.[103] Brandeis believed that progressives should realign the nation's political parties and unite behind Wilson and the Democrats.[104]

As much as Frankfurter and Valentine wanted to join the campaign, Roosevelt kept dissuading them. He only encouraged "men of the crusading temperament" and with "little or nothing to lose" to join him. In July, he instructed an intermediary to inform Frankfurter and Valentine that, as much as Roosevelt would like them on board, "you would not do enough good to the cause to counterbalance the damage you would do by leaving your present position."[105] To friends and acquaintances, Valentine and Frankfurter insisted that they had no intention of resigning. Valentine dispelled swirling rumors about his imminent resignation, believed that he would serve until after Inauguration Day, and contended that Taft would

Clifford Berryman cartoon of 1912 presidential election

have to fire him.[106] Valentine refused to leave until he could find a successor who would put the interests of Native Americans above the interests of businessmen and party politicians.[107] Frankfurter wrote on July 17 that "here I am quite happy in good fun work, unhappy that I can't be out where my political heart is (tho I'm exposing it to every passerby) and serenely lucky to have the pal-ship of Valentine and Denison. We're having great times."[108]

That summer, in addition to Christie, Percy, Borglum, Biddle, and Holmes, the rotating crew of guests at the House included new Children's Bureau Commissioner Julia Lathrop, her private secretary Fanny Howe Fiske, Judge

Mack, and British attaché Alfred Mitchell-Innes.[109] One night, Valentine, Frankfurter, and Lathrop dined at the New Willard Hotel, then Denison, Biddle, and Justice Department lawyer Thurlow M. Gordon joined them to see *Carmen*.[110] "All the world were their friends," Gordon's wife, Pauline, wrote in a poem about the House of Truth, "and the merry parties they had became famous."[111] Secretary of War Stimson and his wife dined there; another night the group went to the British embassy for dinner.[112] Valentine and Denison's Harvard classmate Elliot Goodwin stayed at the House in August while working as the general secretary of the National Chamber of Commerce; like Stimson, Goodwin was a Taft supporter.[113] They not only convened over dinners but also took day trips to Great Falls and weekend trips to Carlisle, Pennsylvania, and Hampton, Virginia.[114] Valentine, Frankfurter, and Denison led the House's activities. "You would have been joyous to see the Three Musketeers leaving the House this morning," Valentine wrote his wife one Saturday, "kicking up their heels and each with a rose in his button-hole—a little rose."[115]

Another of the House's regulars, Taft's Commissioner of Corporations Herbert Knox Smith, returned from a meeting at Sagamore Hill in mid-July and informed them that he was leaving the administration to join the Bull Moose campaign. "He's going to help T.R. in the construction work," Valentine wrote Sophie. "This is *confidential* till you see it in the papers. ... We are greatly excited, waiting for Smith's resignation to appear." Even though it had been rumored in the papers for several days, the announcement of the first Taft administration official to jump ship for Roosevelt was front-page news.[116]

The calls for Frankfurter, Valentine, and Denison to get personally involved in Roosevelt's campaign came in late July from New Hampshire governor Robert P. Bass. One of the seven Republican governors who had petitioned Roosevelt to accept the party's nomination, Bass was a Harvard College classmate of Valentine and Denison and well known to Frankfurter. Bass's decision to bolt the Republican Party would cost him a second term as governor and future elected offices.[117] But once he put his political career in jeopardy by joining the Progressive Party, Bass was looking for others to join him. "Now is the time," he wrote Valentine on July 31, "for you to quit your job and join the 3rd party movement. In it lies the promise of the future, provided it remains in control of the right men. It need[s] such men now."[118] Three days later, Valentine replied that he had been thinking about leaving the administration since Roosevelt's "Charter of Democracy" speech but also wanted to find a successor who would not undo in a few months what he had accomplished in seven years at the Indian Affairs bureau.[119]

Bass refused to take no for an answer—especially after the Progressive Party Convention on August 5 through 7 in Chicago. On August 6, Roosevelt delivered his "Confession of Faith" speech at a convention that Herbert Knox Smith described to Valentine as "more like a religious meeting than a political gathering."[120] The next day, Progressive Party delegates including Borglum nominated Roosevelt as their presidential candidate and California governor Hiram Johnson as their vice-presidential candidate. A few days after the convention, Bass insisted that Valentine could make more of an impact on the future of Indian affairs by joining the campaign and electing Roosevelt.[121] Smith emphasized to Valentine the "moral effect created by men of prominence, like yourself, when they voluntarily give up office to join the party of their convictions. ... There are vast numbers of people just waiting [for] a slight impetus from the outside to turn them our way."[122] Valentine confided to his wife, Sophie, back in Massachusetts that he planned on staying until Taft left office on March 4.[123] Whatever happened with the election, Valentine still wanted to buy the House because they could always rent it after the inauguration and because "it is a headquarters for us."[124]

At the end of August, Bass continued to pressure Valentine to join the campaign. Valentine once again pleaded that there was no one he trusted to run the Indian Affairs bureau.[125] After Bass's letters, Valentine discussed the issue with his boss, Secretary of the Interior Fisher. Fisher asked if Valentine were "actively supporting the Third Party movement."[126] Valentine replied that he was "heart and soul for the Third Party Movement" and was "losing the chance of my life" in not joining it, but the only active part he was taking in the campaign was in discussing it privately with his friends.[127] Valentine's primary concern remained finding a nonpolitical successor who would put the interests of the Indians first; Fisher agreed yet also conceded that he had given up trying to find someone. Then he added: "'As you doubtless feel, the President would be undoubtedly most delighted to lose you.'"[128]

Something changed after Valentine's August conversation with Fisher. It may have had to do with the religious garb order. On August 22, Valentine wrote Fisher about the still-pending decision and laid out his differences with his boss.[129] Two days later, Fisher informed Valentine and Taft that the order would not be reinstated.[130] Taft affirmed Fisher's decision a month later.[131] With his religious garb order permanently revoked, few allies left in the administration, and a president who wanted him gone, Valentine knew he was a man with nothing left to lose. As he told Frankfurter, "The difference [between Taft as president and Roosevelt] was that when you left TR's presence 'you were ready to eat bricks for lunch,' and when you left Taft, you thought, 'What's the use.'"[132]

In June, Valentine had declined to be considered for a job as the general manager of the Rockefeller Institute for Medical Research. He did not want to take money from the Rockefeller fortune, he sought to "re-enter public life," and he considered himself a "social democrat."[133] Valentine's commitment to government service trumped his financial concerns—even with his wife and daughter still living with her family in South Braintree, Massachusetts, and his daughter, Sophia's, costly medical bills. And yet he bought the House, both for what it represented and because it would save the family twenty dollars a month. The safe thing to do, especially because he had just bought the House, was to stay in the administration until Inauguration Day. The Roosevelt campaign forced him to stand up for his ideals and to see the bigger picture. "We must not forget that WE HAVE HAD A REAL LIFE—more than all people or any people deserve and more than most people get," he wrote Sophie in mid-August. "We have two things left to do: See that Sophia gets her chance, and help a few others to get theirs by the kind of work we do in the world."[134]

Valentine became the second member of the Taft administration to leave to join Roosevelt, news that on September 11 made the *New York Times* front page.[135] "Last winter I felt that the Progressive movement in the Republican Party was the beginning of a new day in the betterment of living conditions throughout the country," Valentine wrote President Taft. "Now, however, the case is different. The program of the Progressives has been pushed aside by the national leaders of the Republican Party."[136] A weight had been lifted off Valentine's shoulders. "*Everything* that's happened since my resignation," he wrote Sophie, "only confirms the wisdom of the decision."[137]

Valentine sent Bass a copy of the resignation statement, planned on joining him in New Hampshire to work on the campaign, and vowed to bring another Bull Mooser along with him—Felix Frankfurter.[138] In a late August letter to a skeptical Sophie Valentine, Frankfurter defended Roosevelt and the Bull Moose campaign against charges (in the *Boston Evening Transcript* from the La Follette camp) that Roosevelt was a fly-by-night progressive. Frankfurter knew that progressivism was an elusive trend, but he also knew Roosevelt's record. As governor of New York, Roosevelt had played ball with party bosses, yet he also had fought for a more progressive tax system.[139] As president, Roosevelt had come into office at "the high tide of national smugness," not to mention his imperialistic control of territories gained during the Spanish-American War and acquisition of the Panama Canal Zone. Yet Roosevelt's administration also had championed conservation efforts, civil service reform, and protective labor legislation. Frankfurter recognized Roosevelt's "deep blemishes, the crudities, at times even the brutalities, of a fighter," but he believed above all in Roosevelt's "open-mindedness, his responsiveness to new insights, to new convictions—this is one of the great gifts of his usefulness—his capacity for growth." Frankfurter concluded by apologizing, for he had been "very derelict in my duty as a reporter of the truth, but that is because Bob and I have been having such a riotously sober good time of it."[140]

In his September 10 letter to Bass, Valentine predicted that Frankfurter would resign along with him.[141] Valentine believed that the best place for Frankfurter would be on the campaign trail with Roosevelt. During Stimson's New York gubernatorial campaign, Frankfurter had always seemed to have the right speech or document at his fingertips for Stimson to use on the stump, and along the way Frankfurter had developed a good rapport with Roosevelt. Valentine urged Bass to write to Roosevelt but to keep the whole thing quiet until Frankfurter could inform Stimson.

The day that Valentine resigned, Frankfurter wrote a tortured resignation letter to his boss. The timing certainly was not convenient. Frankfurter was vacationing in Sharon, Massachusetts; Stimson was out west. But Frankfurter's letter could not wait. "I find now the call for active work in the Progressive Party is too insistent, too dominant, not to be heeded if I have fairly considered all the controlling considerations," he wrote.[142] Frankfurter felt great loyalty to Stimson, loyalty that had kept him from joining the Bull Moose campaign sooner. He planned to return to Washington in a few days but vowed not to leave his post until he heard from Stimson.

Frankfurter's resignation letter was forwarded to Stimson at Yosemite, and Stimson answered it on September 19 in San Francisco. He wrote that he was extremely grateful for Frankfurter's loyalty over the years and blessed his decision to join the Roosevelt campaign, though he also believed that Frankfurter was making a big mistake.[143] There was not enough time left in the campaign for Frankfurter to make much difference. He would be better off waiting until after the campaign when the "real work to be done" would be uniting the progressive factions.[144] Frankfurter promised to think it over, returned to work in Washington, and awaited Stimson's return the first week of October before making any final plans.[145]

With Frankfurter's resignation in limbo, Valentine attempted to sway his friend's decision. "If you haven't heard from T.R. by the time you get this, please wire me, letting me know also when you feel you can cut loose," Valentine wrote on September 22.[146] Valentine attacked the two people advising Frankfurter to stay: Brandeis and Stimson. "I return Brandeis's note to you," Valentine wrote Frankfurter. "He is making such remarkable statements in this campaign that I do not like to keep such incriminating documents in my possession."[147] After a three-hour meeting with Wilson on August 28 at the New Jersey governor's summer home in Sea Girt, Brandeis came away "favorably impressed" and believed Wilson "has the qualities of an ideal President"—"strong, simple, serious, openminded, eager to learn and deliberate."[148] Brandeis helped Wilson articulate a "New Freedom" business platform so as not to attack big business per se but to attack monopoly. Brandeis also wrote pro-Wilson articles and editorials for *Collier's Weekly* and attacked the Progressive Party's approach to trust busting.[149] In September and October, he traveled the country speaking about trusts and advised the Wilson campaign.[150]

As for Stimson's suggestion that Valentine had regretted resigning, Valentine told Frankfurter that he had never been happier than he was in working with Bass in New Hampshire on Roosevelt's behalf.[151] Valentine insisted that Frankfurter's "real job at the present time is with the Colonel himself" and instructed Frankfurter to wait for a call from the candidate.[152] Roosevelt needed Frankfurter more than Stimson. The stakes, according to Valentine, were high: "With the Colonel you might well be a turning factor in the whole campaign."[153]

Just why Frankfurter decided not to resign in order to work for Roosevelt is unclear. Perhaps the call from Roosevelt never came. Perhaps the advice of his mentors Stimson and Brandeis gave him pause. Perhaps he knew that resigning in September was futile, and that Roosevelt's campaign was doomed. Perhaps he was worried about his future career prospects. In later years, Frankfurter recalled that Taft had offered him a federal judgeship in Manhattan, but that at age twenty-nine Frankfurter thought he was too young to lead the monastic life of a federal judge.[154] The only federal judicial opening in Manhattan had been filled in February 1912; Frankfurter may also have wanted to remain in good standing with the Taft administration.[155] "[A]fter much and dubious searching of heart I have decided it's my bigger job to stay and I can only hope that it won't come up to plague me in the years to come," Frankfurter wrote fellow Bull Mooser Learned Hand. "I'm clearer than ever in the *raison d'etre* of the movement and equally clear that it should be fought on the assumption of not being successful this year."[156]

The same mix of pragmatic and career concerns may have motivated Denison to stay in the Taft administration. One of Denison's college classmates, Governor Bass, also tried to pull him into the campaign. Like Valentine and Frankfurter, Denison had made no secret of the fact that he wanted to join the fight for Roosevelt. Earlier that summer, he had offered his resignation to Attorney General Wickersham, but Wickersham refused it because he believed that Denison had kept his progressive politics from affecting his first-rate work.[157] Denison was reluctant to leave Wickersham after the loyalty his boss had shown him during his typhoid fever recovery and after his controversial sugar fraud speeches. Denison also knew that the physical rigors of a political campaign might not be the best place for someone prone to overwork and depression. In July, he told Bass that he was too tired to hit the campaign trail and decided to wait and see how the election developed. A month later, after many discussions with Valentine and Frankfurter, Denison insisted to Bass that "I do intend to get into the fight just as soon as I honorably can."[158] In addition to lingering loyalty to Wickersham, Denison wanted to continue litigating a case that he had been working on for six months and that would not be resolved until September 1. Denison added in a postscript: "I hear the call of the Moose so loud and clear I can hardly sit still."[159]

September came and went without any word from Denison; career ambitions may have stood in his way. Denison harbored dreams of a judgeship or some other higher office. On August 21, Taft appointed him to a three-member commission to investigate allegations of neglect and customs fraud against the Board of the United States General Appraisers.[160] Nearly two months later, when one of the three members dropped out, Taft designated Denison the commission's chairman and added a new third member— Denison's housemate Frankfurter. Denison and Frankfurter accepted these posts less than a month before the election.[161] As the two men who principally prosecuted the sugar fraud cases, they were uniquely qualified to investigate additional customs fraud allegations. They were also young and ambitious lawyers who may have been reluctant to risk everything by joining the final months of a quixotic campaign.

★★★

With Denison and Frankfurter sitting on the sidelines and Valentine aiding Bass in New Hampshire, there was no shortage of drama on the campaign trail. Roosevelt was shot as he prepared to get into a car on his way to an October 14 speech in Milwaukee. The bullet was slowed by his eyeglasses case and a copy of the speech in his right breast pocket and lodged in his ribcage. Before he went to the hospital, he insisted on delivering the speech. After asking the crowd to be as quiet as possible and revealing that he had been shot, he remarked: "It takes more than that to kill a Bull Moose."[162] He spoke in a low voice for fifty minutes even though he was noticeably fatigued and his shirt was soiled with blood. Finally, after finishing his speech, he went to a nearby hospital, where doctors elected not to operate on what they described as a superficial wound.

The assassination attempt did not determine the outcome of the election. As Brandeis and Stimson had predicted, Republicans voted for Taft and Roosevelt, and Progressives voted for Taft, Roosevelt, Wilson, and Socialist Party candidate Eugene V. Debs (who received 900,000 votes).[163] The result was a victory for Wilson (435 electoral votes) over Roosevelt (88 votes), a pitiable third-place showing for Taft (8 votes), and a cloud of uncertainty at 1727 Nineteenth Street.

Roosevelt never again held such a firm grip on the ideals and aspirations of the House of Truth. Valentine moved out and returned to Boston. Frankfurter and Denison took charge of the House and waited for Wilson to take over in March. All three men needed to decide what to do next, and how best to achieve their political and legal goals with a new administration.

4

The Center of the Universe

During his seven weeks on the Bull Moose campaign, Valentine felt more alive than he had ever been in his life. He no longer regretted not having lived during the Revolutionary War or Civil War eras, and believed that he was participating in one of the most important moments in American history.[1] After Roosevelt lost, Valentine and his housemates took different career paths.

Fortunately for Valentine, he had a plan. The previous July, he and Frankfurter had lain on the floor of the House of Truth and had "worked out our general scheme of the Universe."[2] Four days later, they had finished it with some assistance from Denison and were "very proud of it."[3] In an eight-page outline titled "A Tentative Social Program," Valentine and Frankfurter took aim at one of the most important issues of their time—the effects of industrialization on workers.[4] Industrial accidents, strikes, and union busting plagued the nation's economic life. Women and children worked long hours and in inhumane and unsafe conditions. On March 25, 1911, 146 female garment workers, most of them recent Jewish and Italian immigrants, had died in New York City's Triangle Shirtwaist fire. Management had increased the loss of life because of its practice of locking the doors to stairwells and exits to keep the women at work on cutting and sewing blouses. With no way out of the top three floors of the burning ten-story building, more than sixty women had leaped to their deaths. Labor and management were at each other's throats during this period; strikes over low wages, long hours, and inhumane conditions were common.

One of the largest strikes, which lasted from January to March 1912, was at the Lawrence, Massachusetts, textile mill. Organized by the radical Industrial Workers of the World (IWW), 23,000 workers, most of them immigrants, left their jobs and destroyed machinery after management cut their wages 3.5 percent in response to a state law that reduced the

The four original residents of the House of Truth (clockwise from left): Winfred T. Denison, Robert G. Valentine, Felix Frankfurter, and Loring C. Christie. The fifth resident, Eustace Percy, not pictured here, did not move into the House until late 1913.

maximum hours for women and children from fifty-six to fifty-four per week. Before the strike, men earned an average of $8.76 per week, women and children $6.[5] After a labor victory in Lawrence, the IWW led strikes among waiters in New York City in 1912 and 1913, and among silk mill workers in Paterson, New Jersey, from February to July 1913.

In their "Social Program," Valentine and Frankfurter believed that they had discovered the solution to the nation's labor problems—a stronger, more powerful government. "Government," they wrote in the manifesto, "is the readiest and best fitted administrative means through which the conception of the people as to their welfare may find realization in action and, rightly understood, becomes the most potent affirmative social agency on behalf of all the people."[6] They believed that they could tap into the unused power of the federal government, the states, and the US Constitution to level the playing field between management and labor. Their examples included empowering administrative agencies, changing election laws, and making the tax laws more progressive. Above all, they envisioned experts in and out of government as facilitators of an "industrial democracy" in which workers were represented by organized labor; management recognized the rights of workers to unionize and agreed to negotiate with them collectively; unions embraced efficiencies associated with industrialization; and labor and management worked together to solve their problems. "Let us build up the personal manhood of our poets, scientists and politicians," they concluded, "as we seek to take the child out of the factory and men and women out of all kinds of poverty."[7]

Valentine and Frankfurter had thought that the key to implementing this social program was to oust Taft and to return Roosevelt to the White House. Roosevelt would maximize the use of federal laws and administrative agencies to protect working men, women, and children and to put the "fear of God into judges" who tried to stop them. The failure of the Bull Moose campaign left the "Social Program" in Valentine's and Frankfurter's hands.

To turn his ideas into a means to support his wife and daughter in Massachusetts, Valentine set up shop on Boston's State Street as the nation's "first industrial counselor."[8] He wanted to bring to industry the same principles that he had relied on as Indian affairs commissioner—disinterested expertise, efficiency, and the public good. He envisioned himself, depending on the project, as working for labor, management, municipalities, or consumers. He could report on working conditions, employment schedules, manufacturing difficulties, and consumer prices. He believed that management had nothing to fear from workers represented by organized labor. And he believed that labor had nothing to fear from efficiency studies championed by industrial engineer Frederick W. Taylor and other Taylorists who believed in scientific management.[9] Valentine described his efficiency studies as "industrial audits"—evaluating a company's books, employment, and wage schedules; working conditions; and the location and types of machinery on the factory floor. Valentine saw himself as the disinterested expert who could bridge the gap between labor and management. He removed himself from politics, declining Governor Bass's invitation to a Progressive Party convention in December 1912. He knew that he needed to establish himself as neutral and nonpartisan, and after seven years of government service, he needed to earn enough money to support his family.[10]

What Valentine wanted most was for his fellow visionary Frankfurter to join him as a business partner. During the summer of 1912, they had formed a close bond. Frankfurter encouraged Valentine's poetry and his Bull Moose sympathies and joined him in a twelve-hour session from 3:00 p.m. to 3:00 a.m. one Sunday in June that resulted in Valentine's poem "A Nation's Prayer."[11] "I don't know how long you have known him," Valentine wrote his friend Julia Lathrop about Frankfurter, "but certainly long enough to have discovered that he is an inspired child."[12] For Frankfurter, the feeling was mutual. "I found a soul-mate down here in Valentine, the Indian Commissioner."[13]

With their "Social Program," Valentine believed that he and Frankfurter had seen the future. "We have discovered—you and I—the center of the universe," he wrote his "co-trustee" Frankfurter. "Don't make any plans for the future—either for yourself or the Universe—until we have stood at the center of it together and discussed things. This is a far cry from lying on the floor of the front room at 1727."[14]

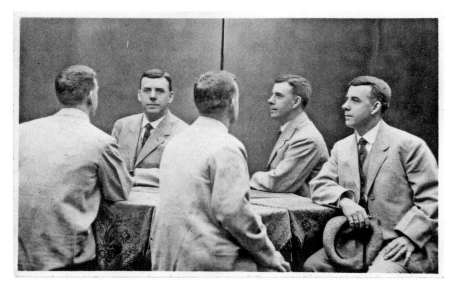

Valentine in Atlantic City

Though he continued to work for Stimson in the final months of the Taft administration, Frankfurter seemed eager to explore the universe with Valentine. "Dear Pardner ...," Frankfurter wrote, "I don't know what else you've done but you've sent coursing through my veins the rapturous champagne of your courage and imagination and humor and sanity that cannot be in vain, were it not sufficient unto itself."[15] In mid-January 1913, Frankfurter, Denison, Christie, and Frankfurter's friends Emory Buckner and Sam Rosensohn dined with Valentine in New York City and spent the entire evening critiquing and refining Valentine's prospectus.[16] The debate continued the next day during the car ride to and from a visit with Borglum at his Connecticut home.[17] They admired Valentine's fearlessness and determination in "going it alone."[18] Frankfurter passed along additional comments about the statement of services and praise for the venture from Holmes ("delighted, no almost awed"), Hand ("enthusiastic hopefulness"),[19] and Brandeis ("joyous surprise that you should do as well as you do")[20] and drummed up potential business in the private sector and federal government.[21] "The *practical* appeal of the idea," Valentine wrote his wife, "is cumulatively tremendous."[22] Frankfurter, however, remained noncommittal about joining his friend. "The silence is the silence of much thinking and more longing for a union of the universe," he wired Valentine in February. For the time being, Frankfurter was tied up with War Department work and awaited Valentine's draft prospectus for their new venture.[23]

With Valentine starting his industrial counseling business in Boston, Frankfurter and Denison took charge of running the House. "We enjoy living in this nice house very much and Felix keeps us alive most of the time," Denison wrote Frankfurter's mother. "The only trouble with him is that he wants to sit up all night and sleep all day. And he's terribly slow about getting dressed and washed and down to breakfast. Why in the world did you fail to teach him that black air means night and time to sleep and that white air means day and time to be awake? Otherwise than that you've brought him up tip top and I am very grateful to you."[24] Valentine instructed Denison and Frankfurter to send him the bills, to hang the curtains and drapes, to select wallpaper for the newly renovated bathroom and guest room, and to move the bed out of the upstairs parlor.[25] In late January 1913, Valentine asked that his reference books, including William James's *Principles of Psychology*, be sent to Boston.[26] Two months later, Sophie Valentine made sure that one of Washington's foremost political salons would survive her husband's return to Massachusetts. On March 12, 1913, she paid $10, borrowed $2,000, and assumed $4,500 remaining on the mortgage on the House.[27] Frankfurter and Denison ran it the way that their friend would have wanted. Valentine's picture above the mantel reminded them of their spiritual leader.[28] "I'd rather canvas the universe here," Frankfurter wrote Valentine, "in the living room of the House of Truth than even spend a day together Boston way."[29]

In late March, Valentine made a triumphant return to the House that he and his wife now owned. Frankfurter and Christie met him at Union Station; Denison joined them at the House for lunch.[30] Valentine ran into Justice Holmes, who reiterated his admiration for the industrial counseling idea.[31] Valentine discussed Indian affairs during a long dinner with Wilson's Secretary of the Interior Franklin K. Lane, who was "very much interested" in Valentine's business venture.[32] Valentine, Frankfurter, and "all the House of Truth" attended a dinner for British ambassador Bryce. Bryce was so impressed with Valentine's plans that the ambassador sent for him the following day and told Valentine to "use his name" as a reference.[33] "This is being a most helpful trip for the Adventure ...," Valentine wrote his wife. "Even [his conservative Harvard classmate] Elliot Goodwin thinks it is a *great* idea."[34]

Valentine and Frankfurter visited one afternoon with Justice Holmes. On Saturday night, Valentine, Frankfurter, Christie, Percy, Alfred Mitchell-Innes of the British embassy, Roosevelt speechwriter George Rublee, and Learned Hand dined at the home of writer Herbert Croly.[35] Croly's book *The Promise of American Life* served as the bible of progressives.[36] Finally, they held a Sunday night dinner in Valentine's honor at the House. The guests included Frankfurter; Denison; Christie, Percy; Croly; Denison's new boss, Attorney General James C. McReynolds; Learned Hand; Mitchell-Innes; former Indian affairs official Arthur Ludington; Sam Rosensohn; and Rublee.[37] Frankfurter boasted: "We dished up three cabinet members and one ambassador and one Justice for Val in three days."[38]

Upon his return to Boston, Valentine wrote a report on the working conditions at the Charlestown Naval Yard; his client, thanks to Frankfurter's War Department contacts, was Assistant Secretary of the Navy Franklin D. Roosevelt.[39] Although he lived only a few blocks across Connecticut Avenue from 1727 Nineteenth Street, Roosevelt was not part of the Bull Moose crowd; he was a Democrat and an ardent Wilson supporter. He probably never set foot in the House of Truth. Even so, Frankfurter knew Roosevelt well enough to prepare him for Valentine's recommendations.[40]

The House of Truth living room

"Cousin Roosevelt seems to have borne my report to him with equanimity," Valentine reported.[41] The assistant navy secretary was one of Valentine's first satisfied customers. But in 1913, he was far from the center of Frankfurter's and the House's universe.

Frankfurter and Denison stayed at the House until the final days of the Taft administration and beyond. They used their positions to pursue their political aims of bringing expertise to government, prosecuting fraud, busting trusts, and fighting for the rights of working men, women, and children. Since August 1912, Denison had chaired a three-person committee, including Frankfurter, to investigate the Board of General Appraisers in charge of hearing customs cases. The committee held a series of private hearings and interviews in Washington and New York and investigated how similar customs courts operated in other countries. On February 15, 1913, they issued an eighteen-page report with recommendations that included reducing the number of people on the board, dividing the functions of classifications for tariff purposes and reappraisals, and making appointments nonpartisan to prevent political agendas from dominating the process.[42] Taft took the report seriously. On the last day of his administration, the president fired two life-tenured members of the Board of Appraisers for cause.[43]

Frankfurter's War Department work at the end of Taft's administration was equally hectic. Stimson was constantly trying to prevent "blunders" caused, according to Frankfurter, by Taft's "impotence and incompetence."[44] Frankfurter accompanied Stimson to the opening of the Panama Canal and remained loyal to the secretary of war until the bitter end.[45] He coauthored a memorandum (abridged in the *Boston Evening Transcript* as "The 'War Record' of Henry Stimson") that read like a history of the War Department since the Spanish-American War and praised Stimson's management of the Panama Canal Zone, the insular territories, and peacetime reorganization of the military.[46]

Stimson urged Frankfurter to stay in the Wilson administration to see through two projects: hydroelectric power and governance of the Philippines. Frankfurter's knowledge of public utility regulation and the War Department made him one of the nation's experts on how federal agencies worked and how to effect social change. He agreed to stay on with the new administration. Stimson's successor, Lindley M. Garrison, was not the intellect or the administrator that Stimson was, but Frankfurter liked and admired his new boss.[47] He continued to learn about how federal agencies operated and made new contacts within those agencies. Something about the Wilson administration, however, rubbed him the wrong way. He observed a "regenerative righteousness" and "assumption, for instance, that the McKinley-Roosevelt-Taft policy in the Philippines was one of exploitation, and that we are the instrument of liberation."[48] Yet, as of May 1913, Frankfurter conceded that "Wilson has done mighty well thus far."[49]

Denison, who had submitted his resignation to President Wilson and had planned on returning to New York to practice law, was coaxed into staying by Attorney General McReynolds. From Denison's perspective, McReynolds had been a good choice because he was "not a politician," was a former assistant attorney general who "knows the department," and was "able and pleasant."[50] A prominent Tennessee lawyer who had prosecuted trusts in the Roosevelt Justice Department and as a special prosecutor, McReynolds had asked two men to resign—Solicitor General William Marshall Bullitt and William Henry Lewis. The Lewis resignation confirmed McReynolds's notorious racism. A Harvard law graduate, Lewis was the Justice Department's only black lawyer.[51] McReynolds met with Denison and asked him to stay and to argue some of Bullitt's cases pending before the Supreme Court. Denison agreed to stay "indefinitely, until fall anyway."[52] As early as February, rumors swirled that Wilson would nominate him for

THE CENTER OF THE UNIVERSE

higher office.[53] A few months later, Frankfurter reported to Valentine that "Winnie is really turkey-trotting with the Administration."[54]

Though Frankfurter viewed his Wilson administration post as temporary and Denison saw his as a means for career advancement, they shared the same social instincts and sense of fun. "The House is flourishing," Frankfurter reported to Valentine. "We have moved some of its furniture around, yet, I think, as Bryan would say, 'we have kept the faith.' I rather love to think we have done so uninfluenced by your stern countenance that frowns down on us from the heights of the mantel-piece. Winnie, I think has never been better, more steadily on the job, or more wholesomely buoyant. He says I am improving in general conversation, which, curiously enough, means that he talks more. We had a kids' luncheon here yesterday, which would have warmed the hearts of both of you."[55]

Some people with sterner dispositions, such as frequent visitor Brandeis, were not as enamored with the House's social activities.[56] He attended a lunch with Christie, Stanley King and his wife, Gertrude, Justice Department lawyer Louis G. Bissell, and Borglum. The brash, outspoken Borglum and the cold, reserved Brandeis exchanging ideas over lunch must have been a sight to behold. The People's Lawyer thought that Frankfurter and Denison needed to socialize less and to work more. "You are right about Frankfurter's excessive sociability," Brandeis wrote his wife. "[Attorney General] McReynolds criticised Denison also on that score."[57] Brandeis's humorlessness was one of the reasons why, despite his ideological affinity with Frankfurter, Denison, and Christie, the People Lawyer's was not the hero of the House. That honor belonged to Holmes. With Theodore Roosevelt out of the political picture and Valentine in Boston in 1913, Holmes took center stage at the House of Truth.

And with good reason. The Court remained the biggest obstacle to laws regulating unfair competition, maximum hours, minimum wages, workers' compensation, and child labor. With the Wilson administration poised to introduce a federal child labor law, Frankfurter stepped up his attacks on the Court's defenders. In a January 1913 *Survey* magazine article, "The Zeitgeist and the Judiciary," he criticized an American Bar Association report that condemned, without offering any alternatives, Roosevelt's idea of popular recall of state judges. Frankfurter knew that judges were by their very natures conservative because they tended to be old men who relied on past decisions to resolve contemporary issues. He also knew that labor and unfair competition laws developed from detailed factual investigations rather than old legal principles. New types of "social legislation," which he defined as addressing "economic and social conditions" and "the stuff of life," faced resistance from the Constitution's judicial guardians.[58]

Instead of simply attacking the Court and its defenders in "The Zeitgeist and the Judiciary," Frankfurter celebrated Holmes as the Court's true intellectual leader. Holmes did not believe that unfair competition and labor laws would make people's lives better. Yet, as he wrote in his 1905 *Lochner* dissent about the maximum hour law for bakers, he also believed that the justices had no business reading laissez-faire economic philosophy into the Constitution by making up concepts such as "liberty of contract." In his article, Frankfurter quoted Holmes's introduction to *The Common Law* and argued that Holmes had been "a powerful influence in the changed attitude of the Supreme Court."[59]

By championing Holmes, Frankfurter revealed that he had not lost all faith in the Court as an institution. He believed that the best way to help working people was not through litigation but through state and federal regulation and through a government run by experts like the Board of Appraisers investigation that he and Denison led. Nonetheless, Frankfurter's job still brought him before the Court. On April 24, he defended the decision by the governor of the Philippines to deport a Chinese immigrant. Holmes, speaking for a unanimous Court, affirmed the governor's deportation power and refused to interfere with the decision.[60] Frankfurter's argument won praise from other justices besides Holmes.[61] One evening, Frankfurter mixed cocktails in a shaker for his housemates and their guest, Justice Horace Lurton. A Taft appointee, Lurton was a Kentucky Democrat who during his four years on the Court often sided with Holmes. "I hope you mix drinks as well as you argue cases," Lurton said to Frankfurter. After trying one of Frankfurter's cocktails, Lurton added: "You mix drinks even better than you argue cases."[62]

Frankfurter and his friends at the House of Truth embraced Holmes because they knew he would vote to uphold pro-labor legislation. They also liked him on a personal level and because they admired his dedication to his craft. Holmes was skeptical about all ideas except his "Jobbist" philosophy— his desire to do his job as well as he could (and better than anyone else) every single day.[63] And he could turn a phrase better than any other justice on the Court and perhaps any in the Court's history. The House's residents repeated Holmes's zingers as if he were writing for them. And maybe he was. Holmes loved flattery, and Frankfurter and Denison were expert flatterers.

In March, Holmes sent a copy of his Harvard class speech to Denison. "The House of Truth is happier," Denison replied, "every time Mephistopheles crosses its threshold."[64] Two months later, Holmes sent Denison a new edition of the justice's collected essays and speeches.[65] "You know what I think of the philosophy which pervades this book and every contact one has with you," Denison wrote. "It has gusto and inspiration, and has given me a good pull over some hard places."[66]

An equally important part of the House was Holmes's wife, Fanny, whom even her husband portrayed as a recluse.[67] But her visits to 1727 Nineteenth Street and friendships with the men who live there offer a fuller picture. They loved her as much as they loved her husband. She liked to play practical jokes and to surprise the justice. And, though childless, she loved children. No one ever forgot her surprise at the House of Truth's children's party, and little wonder. "Mrs. Holmes sent a big pie for dessert, which had ribbons running out of it, one ribbon for each child, and when they pulled the ribbon, there came out of the pie a present instead of food," Denison recalled. "Then when they had just finished that a live monkey jumped right onto the table thru the dining room window, and a hand-organ began to play."[68] Mrs. Holmes also bought the men a housewarming gift, a small wren house, that they put on the sleeping porch out back. "I wait for wrens—," Frankfurter wrote his friend Marion Denman, "but only sparrows come."[69] Before the Holmeses left Washington for the summer, Frankfurter made sure to say good-bye to Mrs. Holmes and let her know that she was an integral part of the House. "Truth may still be at the bottom of the well," he wrote her, "but you have brought up for us—joy. A bountiful summer to you! In grateful humility. *Your* House of Truth."[70]

On June 15, 1913, Holmes was leaving for an overseas voyage to Britain, a solo trip to visit Lady Clare Castletown, his flirtatious correspondent in Ireland, as well as other friends.[71] It was his last journey across the Atlantic. Mrs. Holmes accompanied her husband as far as New York City to see him off and must have known the reason for his trip. The House's residents let Holmes know that he would be missed. Christie greeted Justice and Mrs. Holmes in New York City.[72] Frankfurter sent the justice a note along with a copy of Mary Antin's autobiography, *The Promised Land*, about a Russian-Jewish woman's migration to Boston.[73] Holmes read the book on board the *Mauritania* and said it "stirred my vitals." "It seems as if the gift of passionate enthusiasm were racial," he wrote of her Jewishness. "It is a great one."[74] Denison sent Holmes a telegram on board the *Mauritania*:

"A happy and trifling summer to you and the eager friends across the sea; in the gay[e]ties and frivolities do not entirely forget Truth and its abode and the squatters therein laboring here in its vineyard but repine as of today tunc pro nunc with the same old inspiration."[75]

The House's young men faced impending career decisions and needed Holmes's wise counsel more than ever.

★★★

Christie was the first to leave. Alfred Mitchell-Innes, a regular visitor from the British embassy, wrote to the new Canadian prime minister Robert Borden and described Christie as "one of the two cleverest young men in Washington and is a particular friend of mine and Percy's."[76] Mitchell-Innes informed Borden that Christie "does not at all want to become a Yankee and would, so Percy tells me, much like to return to Canada."[77] Borden asked for more information about Christie.[78] Innes replied, reporting Christie's age (twenty-seven), experience, and status as a British subject and added: "Both the Attorney General and the Solicitor General have a high opinion of him."[79] After a short interview in New York City, the Conservative prime minister offered Christie a job in the Department of External Affairs.[80]

In March 1913, Christie announced that he was leaving the House, but his last month in Washington was unforgettable.[81] On March 9, President Wilson accepted Solicitor General William Marshall Bullitt's resignation effective two days later. Several newspapers reported that James Fowler, assistant to Attorney General McReynolds, was the acting solicitor general.[82] Others reported that the acting solicitor general was Christie.[83] Although Fowler may have held that title, it was well known among Christie's friends that a twenty-eight-year-old Canadian citizen was running the solicitor general's office representing the US government before the Supreme Court.[84] Before Christie left town, Frankfurter and Denison threw a dinner party on March 28 at 1727 Nineteenth Street. Christie was "the guest of honor." Justice and Mrs. Holmes, Holmes's secretary Stanley Clarke, Mr. and Mrs. Arthur Willert of *The Times* of London, Percy, Mitchell-Innes, and eight others attended one of the House's rare gatherings that made the Washington *Evening Star* society page.[85]

★★★

With Christie departing, Frankfurter faced his biggest career decision so far—whether to accept a Harvard law professorship. Without telling

Frankfurter, Denison had written to Professor Edward "Bull" Warren.[86] A year ahead of Denison in law school, Warren had started teaching at Harvard in 1904 during Frankfurter's time as a student. He terrified first-year students in his property class by employing the Socratic method with unrelenting harshness and earned the nickname "Bull."[87] Warren had taught Frankfurter Equity as a second-year student and Corporations as a third-year student and almost certainly knew that Frankfurter had graduated first in the class of 1906. "You know what I think of him and what everybody thinks of him down here, and you know him yourself," Denison wrote Warren. "He has made a tremendous impression with the Supreme Court. The Chief Justice and two of the other Justices have spoken to me with great enthusiasm of his work and I understand their views are shared by the other members of the court."[88]

Warren needed no convincing. "To a man, we want Frankfurter," he reported after reading Denison's letter at a faculty meeting.[89] The faculty member pushing hardest for Frankfurter's appointment was Roscoe Pound, who wanted to collaborate on new approaches to criminology.[90] Frankfurter greatly admired Pound's pioneering sociological approach to legal scholarship and his criticism of *Lochner v. New York*. Before they started raising money to endow a new professorship, Warren wanted to know if Frankfurter was interested and instructed Denison to show him both letters.[91] "If I had received a letter from an Indian princess asking me to marry her," Frankfurter recalled, "I wouldn't have been more surprised."[92] He did not think he was worthy of a position on a faculty that had included Christopher Columbus Langdell, the founder of the casebook method; James Barr Ames, the dean who had brought the school to national prominence and had recommended Frankfurter to Stimson; John Chipman Gray, the property scholar who had introduced Frankfurter to Holmes; and James Bradley Thayer, whose view that judges should overturn federal statutes only in extreme circumstances profoundly influenced Frankfurter. Nor did Frankfurter regard himself as a traditional legal scholar who could spend his career churning out law review articles. Of Frankfurter's unworthiness, Brandeis replied: "I would let those who have the responsibilities for selecting you decide your qualifications and not have you decide that."[93]

The thirty-year-old Frankfurter knew that he was at a career crossroads and that the country was at a political crossroads. He was trying to find himself professionally just as America was trying to grow into its status as a world power and to take care of its citizens in the age of industrialization.

He yearned to be at the center of the universe and grapple with the so-cioeconomic issues of his time, and he believed that law would play a central role. Teaching at Harvard Law School, he wrote in a four-page memorandum, would allow him to mold the nation's future leaders who would shape "jurisprudence to meet the social and industrial needs of the time" and wrestle with "the great procedural problems of administration and legislation." Together with Roscoe Pound, Frankfurter believed that he could apply the social sciences to law in a way that would revolutionize Harvard Law School and transform its future graduates. Valentine identi-fied Frankfurter's "gift of tapping people of all kinds," his "coordinating facilities," gifts that he could use to identify future leaders who could move public opinion and change the future of America. "'To enlighten public selfishness and harmonize the public will,'" Frankfurter wrote, "—that may be my job."[94]

Frankfurter wrote a memorandum outlining several competing options. First, there was what he called "the Valentine thing."[95] That path would force him to give up the law and waste his legal training and experience. As his financially strapped friend Emory Buckner remarked of Valentine's work, "You are about as unfit for that as I should be to become President of the National Provident Savings Bank."[96] Second, he could choose to stay in the Wilson administration. He never warmed to Wilson, whose "inscrutable secretiveness," "Southern-Democrat atmosphere," and "'party solidarity'" bothered him. Frankfurter's boss, Lindley Garrison, was nice enough but a "first-class mediocrity." Nor did Wilson use his cabinet as extensively as his predecessors Roosevelt and Taft.[97] Finally, he could practice law in New York City. Both Stimson and Roosevelt had been urging Frankfurter to take this route, to become the city's "citizen-lawyer," and to emulate Brandeis's "people's lawyer" status. Private practice, however, never appealed to Frankfurter. He did not like kowtowing to clients or advocating positions in which he did not believe. Harvard Law School, he concluded, was the "best five years' investment ahead." If he didn't like it, he would be young enough to change course.[98]

Before he confirmed his interest in the job, Frankfurter showed his men-tors and friends his memorandum and asked for their blessings. The child-less Stimson and his wife, who looked after Frankfurter like a surrogate son, were against the idea. Stimson worried that Frankfurter's "greatest faculty of acquaintance, for keeping in touch with the center of things,—for know-ing sympathetically men who are doing and thinking," would be wasted at the law school. Frankfurter, Stimson argued, belonged "at the center of the great liberal movement which [is] now going on in national and industrial life." Studying criminology with Pound would be "'a side track.'"[99] Stimson did not think that Frankfurter and Pound were compatible personalities. Stimson believed that Frankfurter should return to New York City not out of some selfish desire to practice law with him again but because it was best for Frankfurter.[100]

Though appreciative of Stimson's opinion, Frankfurter believed that the offer was not limited to criminology and that the divide between universities and the world of politics was not so vast. He admired University of Wisconsin professors who had shown that they could influence the political sphere—at least at the state level. He did not believe that New York City law practice would put him at the center of a liberal movement in government.[101]

Learned Hand was also against the move, but for reasons different from Stimson's. Hand thought that Frankfurter should stay in the Wilson administration and continue to work for Secretary of War Garrison. Harvard Law School and Roscoe Pound were not going anywhere. And Frankfurter's experience gained in government would aid his future endeavors. "What does Holmesy say?" Hand asked. "I suppose that you have writ[ten] him before now."[102]

Of all the people Frankfurter asked for advice, Holmes's carried the most weight. The justice, however, was out of the country. Frankfurter had asked to delay his decision for a few weeks so that he could hear back from the justice.[103] In a lengthy July 4 letter to Holmes, Frankfurter pitched it as a five-year tryout.[104] Holmes's experience with academia had been short and unfulfilling—he had abruptly resigned from the Harvard law faculty after only a few months in the fall of 1882 to accept an appointment to the Massachusetts Supreme Judicial Court. He believed that Frankfurter needed to leave Washington but preferred legal practice or business to law teaching; he also ventured that Frankfurter would get "more nourishment from economics than from criminal law." The only positive Holmes offered was that by accepting Harvard's offer to teach, Frankfurter might slow down a little bit and protect his health. The justice echoed Stimson's skepticism based on "the objection that ... academic life is but half-life—it is a withdrawal from the fight in order to utter smart things that cost you nothing except the thinking them from a cloister."[105]

Perhaps unsurprisingly, Valentine was no more receptive to the idea. He reacted to Frankfurter's inclination to teach at Harvard Law School with silence. It is understandable why Valentine might be lukewarm—Frankfurter had failed to join him on the Roosevelt campaign and had declined to explore the "center of the universe" with him as an industrial counselor. Frankfurter insisted that one of the side benefits of teaching at Harvard would be opportunities to collaborate with Valentine.[106] But as the summer months passed without any advice and with hardly any correspondence, Frankfurter was "saddened by" his friend's "loss of warmth."[107] He hoped that the possibility of living near Valentine in Boston might rekindle their friendship.

The last person Frankfurter asked for advice was Marion Denman, the twenty-two-year-old woman he had met at the House during the summer of 1913.[108] The daughter of a Congregationalist minister and president of the class of 1911 at Smith College, Marion was everything that Felix was not: a tall, beautiful WASP.[109] Her lanky frame, high cheekbones, and especially her wide eyes were so striking that Holmes believed she looked like the subject of one of Bernardino Luini's Italian Renaissance portraits; Holmes referred to her as Luina.[110] Frankfurter asked her whether he should accept the Harvard offer. She declined to answer the question, she angrily told him, because she felt unqualified to do so.[111]

After canvassing his closest friend and advisers, Frankfurter accepted Harvard's offer of a full professorship.[112] One obstacle stood in the way—money—until his friends rescued the situation. Brandeis pledged $1,000 a year for five years to pay Frankfurter's salary.[113] With help from Judge Mack and Eugene Meyer's brother Walter, Brandeis secured $1,000 pledges from Sears, Roebuck part owner and philanthropist, Julius Rosenwald; financiers Felix and Paul Warburg; and a wealthy law school alumnus.[114] Holmes and Hand each pledged $500.[115]

The funding for Frankfurter's professorship was no longer an issue, and the prospect of teaching a public utilities course opened because of the forced resignation of Professor Bruce Wyman.[116] Wyman had failed to disclose that he had been receiving a $10,000 annual retainer from the New Haven Railroad monopoly owned by J. P. Morgan; Wyman had testified on the railroad's behalf before the Interstate Commerce Commission and had employed several family members to testify before trade boards and other organizations.[117] Wyman's loss of a professorship was Frankfurter's gain. Because he would not start until the 1914–15 academic year, Frankfurter agreed to stay in the administration and live at the House until the following summer.

★★★

As Frankfurter planned his future during the fall of 1913, Denison explored a different opportunity—secretary of the interior for the Philippines. On October 6, Denison informed Valentine that the White House would be nominating him. He planned to leave for San Francisco three weeks later, had "no doubt of [the] wisdom of the move," and promised to "carry [the] matter of our house into the orient."[118] As Denison waited to be nominated, doubt crept in. He had gathered facts and wrestled with the decision. Frankfurter, who knew a lot about the Philippines because of his work in Insular affairs, tried to be as supportive as possible without influencing the final decision. Frankfurter predicted that his friend would take the job.[119] Valentine, for his part, was against it. He had known Denison since their college days and appreciated better than anyone his friend's fragile physical and mental constitution. Valentine also had learned from his experience in Indian affairs how difficult it was to fight the existing power structure and to change conditions among a subjugated or colonized people. The Philippines was a backwater where Denison would be marginalized forever.

Denison nonetheless decided to go if the president nominated him. He knew it would be difficult to effect real change in the Philippines and distrusted the government officials there. But what Valentine saw as a "permanent and serious" move Denison saw as a three-year sojourn. Denison's other option would be to return to a New York law firm. In the Philippines post, he saw three distinct advantages: (1) a $25,000 to $30,000 salary with all living expenses paid for, both of which allowed him to save money for the future; (2) an adventure—he had always yearned to travel around the world; and (3) an opportunity—he wanted to test his mettle, to challenge himself.[120]

On November 6, 1913, three days after Denison explained his final decision to Valentine, President Wilson nominated the forty-year-old Justice Department lawyer to be secretary of the interior of the Philippines and a few weeks later as a member of its governing body, the Philippine Commission.[121] Denison had only a few weeks left at the House. "What can I say to you?" he wrote to Frankfurter from the rear bedroom. "I suppose you have no real conception of what you have done for me these years and how your unwavering patience has filled me with astonishment and your wonderful wisdom and ideals with inspiration and a glimmering hope, which your final magic touch these last few weeks has changed to a final confidence. You were there at the Crossing of my Rubicon, and built in a good many of the timbers of my bridge."[122] Before he left, Denison

Denison and Valentine

also sent an inscribed photograph of himself to his favorite two people in Washington: "Dear Justice and Mrs. Holmes: Will you take this from a heart of yours in the Far East? Lest you forget me when I again search your inspired doorstep."[123]

Denison headed for San Francisco so that he could sail for the Philippines as soon as the Senate confirmed him. It took a lot longer than he had anticipated. Senate Republicans blocked his nomination amid charges that he had been involved in politics while working for the Justice Department. His status as a known Bull Mooser in the Taft administration had come back to haunt him. He also had alienated the business community with his customs fraud prosecutions and public speeches about those prosecutions. And he had created still more enemies while investigating the Board of Appraisers.

With Denison's nomination bottled up in committee for more than a month, his former boss, ex–Attorney General Wickersham, rushed to his defense. On January 12, 1914, Wickersham wrote directly to one of Denison's most vocal and influential opponents—Senator Reed Smoot of Utah. Wickersham explained that Denison was an "idealist," had got "carried away" by Roosevelt's campaign, and had immediately offered his resignation (which Wickersham had rejected). Denison had refrained from campaign work, excelled at his job in the Justice Department, and served on committees devoted to civil service reform. Finally, Wickersham said, Denison did not seek his position on the committee that investigated the Board of Appraisers, and that an ex-member of the board was simply seeking "mean revenge."[124] Wickersham urged Senator Smoot to reconsider and opined that "failure to confirm [Denison] would be a greater injury to the public service than to him."[125] Wickersham sent a copy of his letter to Frankfurter, urged him to show it to Secretary of War Garrison, and wrote: "I have been boiling with indignation over the grounds of opposition to Denison's confirmation."[126]

Denison's limbo situation in San Francisco captured front-page headlines and the imaginations of political cartoonists. The *New York Times* reported on page one that seven times Denison had booked a stateroom on steam liners bound for Hong Kong, sent his trunk down to the dock, and waited for a telegram announcing his confirmation. The seventh time, on January 22, 1914, Denison waited on the dock until the last minute, "but no word came."[127] Five days later, he again waited on the dock and missed his eighth steam liner because the official news of his confirmation had arrived a half hour late.[128] The next ship was not leaving for another five days. A Chicago newspaper depicted him sitting on his trunk on the dock watching a ship sail away under the headline: "'WIN' DENISON IS GREATEST LITTLE WAITER."[129]

Denison did not just sit around and wait. He visited friends in Seattle and over Christmas sailed to Alaska. In San Francisco, he stayed at the Fairmont Hotel, discussed the Philippines over tea with General John J. Pershing, and amassed a circle of Bay Area friends from country club types to professors of mathematics and Sanskrit.[130] He threw a luncheon party for twenty-five friends on board the SS *China*; the guests disembarked five minutes before the ship sailed at 1:00 p.m. on February 3 with Denison finally bound for Manila.[131]

★★★

The second-to-last person to leave the House of Truth was its last original resident, Percy. At first glance, the third secretary at the British embassy did not seem to have a lot in common with his housemates. He was not a Bull Mooser, not a lawyer, and not all that progressive. The politics of his friends, however, rubbed off on him—he had attended the 1912 Republican Party convention in Chicago, revered Justice Holmes, and in late 1913 found himself living at 1727 Nineteenth Street.[132] "Percy is now living at the House," Frankfurter wrote, "and he is a good sceptic on a good deal of this 'modern reform'—but largely he is ready to concern himself with much more ultimate problems, to which he is in deep search for peace-bringing solution. For sheer beauty of character—he is exquisitely rare."[133]

Percy shared Frankfurter's gift of befriending people of all professions, personalities, and political persuasions. He was especially close to Christie. And he brought interesting people to the House, including *The Times* of London correspondent Arthur Willert and counselor to the British embassy Alfred Mitchell-Innes.[134] "That household had a touch of du Maurier's Quartier Latin, with law and the erratic politics of the then infant *New Republic* taking

Denison in Atlantic City

the place of art as the focus of its endless talk and even more endless casual guests," Percy recalled. "The range of our talk and our entertainment was 'extensive and peculiar'; but we hardly took ourselves or our symposia seriously enough to deserve the nickname of the 'House of Truth' which some humorist conferred upon us."[135]

Percy had a strong idealistic streak. He was fascinated by Valentine's "Social Program" and authored an anonymous pamphlet known as the "blue memorandum," a blue-bound volume of seventeen printed pages about how disinterested men in government can write laws and regulations to achieve social advancement. The cover indicates that it was "the outcome of discussions recently held by a small group of men"; everyone associated with the House knew that the author of the anonymous document was Percy.[136] "Felix tells me you have a matter of much importance to impart to me regarding the 'blue memorandum,'" Percy wrote Valentine. "I wish I could come and sit at your feet to hear it."[137] Percy wished Valentine luck on his new industrial counseling business and admired the prospectus, for "it seems to proceed on the realisation that the only possible cure for oppression is *not* rebellion of the oppressed but the enlightenment of the oppressor—a realization which I take to be the essence of all peacemaking."[138]

In January 1913, Frankfurter sent the "blue memorandum" to a number of people, including Brandeis, whose response sparked a debate about its application in America. Brandeis rejected the idea of a small group of men running the government, as in the British civil service, because social legislation is a scientific study that requires "discovery and invention," trial and error, success and failure.[139] "Of course," Frankfurter replied, "we can't hand the government over to a little group of experts, because the kind of government we want must have a base as broad as all the people." Yet they agreed with Brandeis that they wanted people in government interested in "social invention" and "to combine ... the efforts of such laboratory men with the work of our public leaders."[140]

Six months later, Percy announced that his time at the embassy was at an end, but that his efforts to implement the "blue memorandum" back home in the British government were just beginning. "We have seen a great deal of one another," Frankfurter wrote of Percy, "and while our angles of approach considerably differ, he has such a sense of the challenge of life's deep earnestness, that far and away he is one of the most worth-while men we have seen here."[141]

The night before Percy sailed for Britain from New York City, Frankfurter organized a send-off. New York City was the perfect location because it allowed Christie to come from Canada and was convenient for those living in New England and New York. He invited a long list of regular guests "and the House."[142] At 7:00 p.m. on May 25, 1914, they met at The Players, an exclusive club for men of arts and letters on Gramercy Park. The dinner menu in Percy's honor consisted of littleneck clams, clear green turtle soup, roast Long Island chicken, green peas, rice croquettes, sweet potatoes, asparagus, Hawaiian salad, ice cream, cheese, and coffee.[143] Each guest contributed $7.45.[144]

Frankfurter served as toastmaster over a group that included a who's who of the House of Truth and its friends: Justice Department lawyer Louis G. Bissell, New York prosecutor Emory R. Buckner, New York lawyer Charles C. Burlingham, Christie, writer Herbert Croly (in absentia), Winfred Denison (in absentia), Customs Department agent Guy Emerson, writer Francis Hackett, Learned Hand, counsel to the New York federal reserve Edward H. Hart, British businessman Maurice Hely-Hutchinson, War Department official Stanley King, writer Walter Lippmann, Judge Julian W. Mack (in absentia), Canadian lawyer C. S. MacInnes, Frank McCoy of the Army General Staff, Canadian lawyer Vincent Massey, New York political activist Henry Moskowitz, former Senator Root staffer Phillips Robinson, lawyer Samuel J. Rosensohn, lawyer George Rublee, Valentine (in absentia), *The Times* of London correspondent Arthur Willert, and a late addition— sculptor Gutzon Borglum.[145]

Valentine was disappointed that he could not make it from Boston for the May 25 dinner.[146] His industrial counseling business was booming. Starting at the end of the previous year, companies had begun hiring him to do the internal analyses that he called industrial audits. He was appointed the first chairman of the Massachusetts Minimum Wage Commission—despite opposition from Catholics who had not forgotten his religious garb order as Indian affairs commissioner.[147] In many ways, Percy's dinner was a product of the House that Valentine had created. "I should say you were missed at the dinner to Percy—to a much greater extent were you represented," Frankfurter wrote Valentine. "In fact, it was so much a House of Truth dinner that the cosmic modesty of the founder of the House would have been somewhat disturbed."[148]

In early June 1914, Frankfurter resigned his Wilson administration post, departed the House of Truth, and prepared for his first year of teaching at

Harvard Law School.[149] "Three happy years are within a few minutes of being at end," he wrote to Robert and Sophie on 1727 Nineteenth Street stationery. "And yet what is it ends? Surely nothing of that which was permanent and significant in the vitality of life."[150]

Neither the House of Truth nor Frankfurter's time there was at an end. The people at Percy's farewell dinner moved into the House and started a new magazine that served as an outlet for the group's ideas.

5

Buddha

Six weeks before Percy's farewell dinner in New York, a group including Valentine, Frankfurter, and Learned Hand had dined at The Players to introduce the idea of a new political magazine initially called the *Republic*. The gathering of the magazine's "counsellors, contributors, and friends" had included its founder, Herbert Croly; its patron Willard Straight; and its founding editors Francis Hackett, Robert Hallowell, Walter Lippmann, and Philip Littell.[1]

The one who probably spoke the least at these two dinners was twenty-four-year-old Lippmann. His large wide eyes, portly frame, and predilection for silence earned him the nickname Buddha.[2] Many interpreted his demeanor as signaling arrogance and condescension. His political leanings, until the last year or so, had leaned toward Fabian Socialism. A college classmate and radical former friend, John Reed, satirized the "calm, inscrutable" Lippmann in verse:

> Who builds a world, and leaves out all the fun,—
> Who dreams a pageant, gorgeous, infinite,
> And leaves all the color out of it,—
> Who wants to make the human race, and me,
> March to a geometric, Q.E.D.—
> Who but must laugh, if such a man there be?
> Who would not weep, if WALTER L. were he?[3]

Lippmann responded with a vicious editorial, "Legendary John Reed."[4] And yet no one, not even Reed, denied Lippmann's genius. The youngest of the magazine's founding editors had already published one critically acclaimed book on American politics and had another book on the way.

With Valentine in Boston, Frankfurter headed for Cambridge, Denison in the Philippines, Christie in Canada, and Percy returning to Britain, the

Walter Lippmann

House of Truth's founding residents were in exile. In their absence, however, the magazine soon to be called the *New Republic* invigorated it. The *New Republic* kept the House together, expanded its network of liberal allies, and provided the perfect outlet for its ideas.[5] No one was more important to the magazine's success—or to the House of Truth's future—than Lippmann.

The only child of wealthy, assimilated third-generation German Jews, Lippmann grew up on New York's Upper East Side (where he lived with his parents until he married in his late twenties), summered in Europe, attended the private Sachs School for Boys, and headed to Harvard College to study art history before switching to philosophy. He was not close to his father and adeptly collected male mentors who contributed to his intellectual development and furthered his career. In Harvard's philosophy department, he had impressed and befriended William James, George Santayana, and visiting professor and Fabian Socialist Graham Wallas. Lippmann distinguished himself not only as a fine writer but also as a campus rabble-rouser and founder of the Harvard Socialist Club. As a budding Socialist, he disavowed religion and his reform Jewish upbringing at Temple Emanu-El.[6] He was even more assimilationist than Frankfurter; it was easier for Lippmann, two generations removed from Europe, to forget his Jewish past.[7]

Another mentor, muckraking journalist Lincoln Steffens, encouraged Lippmann to pursue journalism. After graduating from Harvard in three years, Lippmann accepted a job with a weekly newspaper, the *Boston Common*, yet soon became disenchanted with its editor and with "work so mechanical that I am learning nothing. I might as well be attached to a clipping bureau."[8] He begged Steffens for a job and became Steffens's secretary and "leg man" for a story about the banking industry for *Everybody's Magazine*.[9] Steffens bet an editor at *Everybody's* that in a year he could turn a recent college graduate into a magazine writer, a bet that Steffens won when the magazine accepted Lippmann's anonymously submitted article about pragmatist philosopher William James.[10] Lippmann landed an editorial position at *Everybody's*, wrote for Socialist and mainstream publications, and became an integral member of Mabel Dodge's radical Greenwich Village salon.[11]

On Steffens's recommendation, Lippmann joined the staff of George Lunn, the Socialist mayor of Schenectady, New York. The arrangement began in January 1912 and lasted less than six months, mainly because Lunn abandoned his Socialist principles in favor of policies designed to gain reelection.[12] Lippmann resigned and attacked Lunn's administration as proof "that Socialists in power follow their prejudices like most other administrations."[13] Lippmann's ties with many of his radical friends began to fray. Mabel Dodge later remarked that unlike radical labor leader William "Big Bill" Haywood, "Walter was never, never going to lose an eye in a fight. 'He might,' I thought, 'lose his glow, but he will never lose an eye.'"[14]

At loose ends, Lippmann wrote freelance articles and reviews and resumed work on his first book, *A Preface to Politics*. Writing during the 1912 election, he was searching for a new theory of politics based on the philosophy that he had learned from James, Santayana, and Wallas; his experiences in Socialist politics and in journalism with Steffens; and his interest in Freudian psychology.[15] But Lippmann also was deeply affected by the Lawrence textile strike and the need for government to play a strong role in dealing with "moral and social problems" as "fine opportunities."[16] "The party platform will grow ever more and more into a program of services …," he predicted. "A political revolution is in progress: the state as policeman is giving place to the state as producer."[17]

The country needed a "statesman" to help government solve people's moral and social problems. Lippmann greatly admired the past leadership of Theodore Roosevelt yet also saw the promise of a future leader in Woodrow Wilson. "I am attempting to suggest some of the essentials of a statesman's equipment for the work of a humanly centered politics," Lippmann wrote. "Roosevelt has seemed to me the most effective, the most nearly complete …; Wilson, less complete than Roosevelt, is worthy of our deepest interest because his judgment is subtle where Roosevelt's is crude. He is a foretaste of a more advanced statesmanship."[18]

After he published *A Preface to Politics* in May 1913, Lippmann sent a copy to Herbert Croly. Croly admired the book's "sound thinking," "suggestive ideas," and "intellectual honesty."[19] In his note to Lippmann, Croly wished that there were a political journal that applied "such an intellectual attitude to current affairs."[20] Croly was amused by how similar the ideas in *A Preface to Politics* were to the ones in his forthcoming book, a few chapters of which he had just delivered as the Godkin Lectures at Harvard.[21] Croly concluded by wishing that their like-minded friends could convene and agree "on a statement of philosophy of progressive democracy."[22]

Lippmann described Croly as "the first important political philosopher who appeared in America in the twentieth century"; Frankfurter dubbed Croly the "philosopher" of the progressive movement and *The Promise of American Life* as its mission statement.[23] The son of New York City journalists, Croly was ignored by his hard-driven mother and showered with attention by a father obsessed with Auguste Comte's reconciliation of science and religion known as positivism. The younger Croly pursued a philosophy degree at Harvard College for nearly twelve years without success and edited *Architectural Record* magazine through family connections. He accomplished almost nothing until 1909 when at age forty he published his first book.[24] *The Promise of American Life* sold only about 7,500 copies in Croly's lifetime yet earned him great fame among the intellectual and political elite.[25] The dense book grappled with the problems afflicting industrialized America and was debated at the House of Truth's dinner parties. Croly's *Promise* advocated Alexander Hamilton's belief in a strong central government to achieve Jeffersonian democratic ends, coined the phrase New Nationalism that Roosevelt adopted in 1910 as a political slogan, and championed Roosevelt as a big government reformer.[26] "The nationalization of reform endowed the movement with new vitality and meaning," Croly wrote. "What Mr. Roosevelt really did was to revive the

Hamiltonian ideal of constructive legislation. ... Mr. Roosevelt and his hammer must be accepted gratefully, as the best available type of national reformer; but the day may and should come when a national reformer will appear who can be figured more in the guise of St. Michael, armed with a flaming sword and winged for flight."[27]

Like Valentine, Croly believed that federal legislation must recognize the rights of big corporations as well as those of labor unions.[28] In December 1912, Valentine's prospectus for his industrial counseling business found its way into Croly's hands. "I admire particularly the courage and intellectual sureness of foot ... of a man who proposes to create a new profession," Croly wrote Valentine. "I can see that there may be a scientific basis for such a professional practice and I envy the experience of one who undertakes to convert this science into a practical art. It will be the noblest of professions if you can pull it off."[29]

In January 1913, Croly rented a small Connecticut Avenue apartment and fell in with Valentine's friends Frankfurter, Denison, Percy, and the rest of the House of Truth. After a single dinner, Croly was a Frankfurter fan. "It was my first chance to get anywhere near him and I liked him thoroughly," Croly wrote Learned Hand. "He is one of the most completely alive men whom I have ever met, and I feel now as if I could not see enough of him." Croly also liked Denison, who supplied "the latest gossip about Wilson" and the administration.[30] By March, Croly had reconsidered his "wholly erroneous" first impression of Percy: "His face is a little weak, but it is rather spiritual in expression ... he is an interesting man—different from anything we produce."[31] When Valentine visited Washington later that month, Croly invited them all over for dinner and then dined at the House of Truth.[32] Like Valentine, Croly was planning a venture of his own.

"There is a matter of some importance which I should like to discuss with you," Croly wrote Lippmann on November 1, 1913. Croly invited Lippmann to lunch at 1:00 p.m. six days later at the Players Club.[33] Though he had sent him a copy of *A Preface to Politics*, Lippmann knew Croly only through reading and admiring *The Promise of American Life*, which Lippmann later described as "the political classic which announced the end of the Age of Innocence with its romantic faith in American destiny and inaugurated the process of self-examination."[34] Croly shared Lippmann's penchant for silence. In large groups, the bespectacled, dour-looking Croly was often introverted and shy (perhaps a reason he did not attend Percy's farewell dinner). One-on-one, however, Croly could be charismatic and persuasive;

he knew that he had to be, given that he badly wanted Lippmann for his new project—a political magazine.

Their initial meeting went well; Croly invited Lippmann to Washington, DC, in late December for an extended "series of conversations."[35] "I want you to feel that the Republic," as Croly referred to the magazine at the time, "is yours quite as much as it is mine."[36] Croly also wanted to make sure that they were ideologically compatible. That winter, Croly was living in "a little dinky two by four apartment" in the Dupont, a building on Twentieth Street two blocks from the House of Truth, and working out of an extra room in George Rublee's spacious Constitution Avenue home where Croly

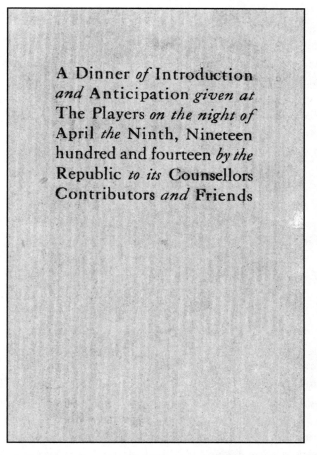

A Dinner *of* Introduction *and* Anticipation *given at* The Players *on the night of* April *the* Ninth, Nineteen hundred and fourteen *by the* Republic *to its* Counsellors Contributors *and* Friends

Valentine's invitation to a dinner at The Players in New York City on April 9, 1913

likely met with Lippmann.[37] "I have just been keeping some long sessions with Lippmann," Croly wrote Learned Hand. "I have tested him all along the line—that is I have tried to discuss how he will react on every phase of current public policy, and he seems always to ring true and sound."[38]

After their Washington conversations, Croly grasped Lippmann's potential and limitations. "Lippmann is as you say an interesting mixture of maturity and innocence," Croly wrote Hand in early January 1914. "The *Preface to Politics* is an astonishing book for a fellow three years out of college to write, but no matter how he turns out as a political philosopher, he certainly has great possibilities as a political journalist. I consider him a gift from heaven for the enrichment of the Republic."[39] Croly described the proposed publication as "radically progressive" but "not socialistic," a "weekly review of current political and social events and a discussion of the theories they involve," intended "to represent progressive principles but ... independent of any party or individual in politics."[40] Croly was outraged that Norman Hapgood had turned *Harper's Weekly* into a shill for Wilson and the Democratic Party; he envisioned the new magazine as a counterweight.[41] Croly wanted to call it "The Nation," but that name was already taken. So was Croly's second choice, "The Republic," by a failing Boston newspaper purchased by former congressman John "Honey-Fitz" Fitzgerald as a Democratic mouthpiece that helped elect him the city's mayor. Croly eventually settled on the *New Republic*.[42]

Besides the progressive point of view and name, Croly secured four years of guaranteed funding from J. P. Morgan banker Willard Straight and his wife, Dorothy, an heiress to the Whitney family banking fortune. The Straights, who had become Croly's patrons after reading *The Promise of American Life*, endorsed the idea of a magazine based on the book's "political and social ideas."[43] Croly was mired in financial difficulties, and the Straights vowed to help.[44] In addition to financing the *New Republic*, they purchased Croly's New York brownstone (which he had been unable to sell) and remodeled it into the magazine's book-lined, wood-paneled headquarters and intellectual playground staffed with French chefs. "I really have a vision of the New Republic in my head," Croly wrote Hand. "The vision will, I fear, set angel Dorothy back some hundreds of thousands of dollars, and may never be realized at that; but she will get a little education for her money, and so will I and so, I hope, will you and others."[45]

Lippmann's radical friends blanched at the idea that he would join a publication financed by the very banking interests that he had investigated with Steffens.[46] The funding for the magazine, slated for fall 1914, comforted Lippmann as did the editorial arrangement. The Straights would have only one vote on the editorial board; all editorials would be approved by major-ity vote, assigned, then published anonymously.[47] Croly offered Lippmann the prestige and respectability of a founding editorship, a sixty-dollar-a-week salary, and the freedom to freelance for other publications and to write books. Lippmann accepted immediately. "The age of miracles, sir, has just begun," he wrote author Van Wyck Brooks in February 1914. "Our general form will be that of the [British] *Saturday Review*. The substance will be American, but sophisticated and critical."[48] In an effort to entice Brooks to be a contributor, Lippmann contradicted Croly by adding: "We shall be socialistic in direction, but not in method, or phrase, or allegiance. If there is any word to cover our ideal, I suppose it is humanist."[49] Croly knew what he was getting in Lippmann: "He'll throw a few firecrackers under the skirts of the old women on the bench and in other high places."[50]

Joining Croly and Lippmann as the third founding editor and principal political writer was Walter Weyl, a trained economist, freelance journalist, and author of another important work of progressive political philosophy, *The New Democracy*. Other original members of the editorial board included book review editor Francis Hackett, an Irishman who had overseen the *Chicago Evening Post* literary supplement; Phillip Littell, a longtime friend of Croly's and author of the magazine's "Books and Things" column; and Charlotte Rudyard, a Vassar graduate and former associate editor at *Harper's Weekly* whom Lippmann described as "a kind of assistant magazine editor."[51]

In January 1914, Croly invited Lippmann to a Saturday lunch at the Harvard Club to meet another influential founder of the magazine, Felix Frankfurter.[52] Croly, recalling his frustrated academic odyssey in Cambridge, urged Frankfurter to turn down the Harvard law professorship and (along with Hand) to join the magazine's editorial board full-time.[53] Croly knew that Frankfurter's personality, peripatetic travels, and zest for politics better suited him for journalism than for law.[54] "If I only had Felix too," Croly wrote Hand, "I should look forward to the approaching campaign with confidence."[55] Because Frankfurter's professorship did not start until the fall of 1914, Croly and Hand pulled him into the planning stages of the publica-tion. Croly practically begged Frankfurter to maintain editorial ties to the magazine.[56] Frankfurter was listed as a trustee on the magazine's first state-ment of ownership, attended staff meetings, and later wrote many signed and unsigned editorials on political and legal issues.[57] He soon recognized that juggling the magazine's strong personalities would be a challenge. "I wish Walter & Francis [Hackett] would feel more zestful about [the *New Republic*]," Frankfurter wrote Hand. "Francis I'm afraid doesn't temperamentally get with Herbert. I've talked frankly to him and time may help some. Discounting all my enthusiasm I still think [the magazine] is a startling achievement."[58]

The impact of the *New Republic* crowd on Walter Lippmann was profound. In the initial pages of his diary, he described the winter of 1914 as "an important change for me. Perhaps I have grown conservative. At any rate I find less and less sympathy with revolutionists ... and an increasing interest in administrative problems & constructive solutions."[59]

Besides their belief in a strong central government, their support for Roosevelt in 1912, and their wait-and-see attitude about Wilson, the main issue that united the *New Republic* and House of Truth crowds was their support for organized labor. The nation's labor unrest initially dominated their agenda. On April 20, 1914, the Colorado National Guard attacked

Herbert Croly, Founding Editor

Herbert Croly

1,200 striking coal miners in Ludlow, Colorado, and killed between nineteen and twenty-five people (including two women and eleven children). The "Ludlow Massacre" set off violent counterattacks against Rockefeller's Fuel and Iron Corporation. The death tolls climbed, and the United Mine Workers–initiated strike lasted all year.[60]

Those associated with the *New Republic* and the House of Truth shared a belief in the power and potential of an expert-run federal government and that the government should support organized labor—not the radical labor movement of the IWW, Emma Goldman and Big Bill Haywood, wildcat strikes, threats of violence, and ties to Socialism, but the institutional organizations and leadership of the American Federation of Labor (AFL) and Samuel Gompers. Though they recognized organized labor's corruption and flaws, they believed that it held out the best chance of ending labor unrest; for providing living wages and humane working conditions for men, women, and children; and for representing them in the workplace.

They also clung to the idea, despite the progressive aims of the Wilson administration, that only one politician could implement their pro-labor ideas—Theodore Roosevelt. Like Valentine, Denison, and Frankfurter, Croly and Weyl were ardent Bull Moosers and friends of the former president. Roosevelt had praised *The Promise of American Life* after reading it in Europe in April 1910.[61] Weyl had been active in the labor movement before turning to journalism and, like Croly, held Roosevelt's ear. During the Bull Moose campaign, Croly had defended Roosevelt's antitrust policy against Brandeis's pro-Wilson attacks. Even after Roosevelt lost, Croly and his friends had not given up on the Colonel.

Lippmann had never met Roosevelt, but *A Preface to Politics* had "used him as a working model for statesmanship."[62] Roosevelt took the book with him on his trip to Brazil in the winter of 1913 and wrote Lippmann a "long enthusiastic letter."[63] Lippmann yearned for a meeting with the Colonel upon his return.[64] "You can readily see from it that it owes a great deal to you," Lippmann wrote him, "and for that reason I was very eager to have your opinion of it."[65] Lippmann met twelve presidents in his lifetime, but only Roosevelt captivated him. Lippmann described himself as an "unqualified hero-worshipper."[66] Roosevelt later dubbed Lippmann "the most brilliant young man of his age in all the United States."[67]

Lippmann met Roosevelt for the first time with Frankfurter in May 1914 at a group breakfast at the Harvard Club.[68] Later that afternoon, Lippmann and Frankfurter met privately with Roosevelt at the Hotel Belmont to discuss the labor situation in the wake of the Ludlow Massacre. Lippmann volunteered to draft a position paper on labor issues, and the Colonel enthusiastically accepted.[69] Lippmann enlisted Weyl's help and formulated the rough outline that he sent to Roosevelt, Croly, and Frankfurter. The platform consisted of two main points—maintaining a decent standard of living and obtaining worker representation through the organized labor movement.[70] Lippmann knew that unions, like democracies, were often corrupt, but he also believed that unions provided the best chance of breaking the cycle of labor violence exemplified by the Ludlow Massacre and its aftermath.[71] "With all its crudities," Lippmann wrote Roosevelt, "the union is the first instrument by which the people in a factory can obtain some representation in the management of business."[72]

On July 1, 1914, Lippmann sent Roosevelt a revised labor platform after further consultation with Weyl and Frankfurter.[73] The *New Republic* editors went their separate ways for the summer. Croly and Weyl left New York City for their summer homes in Cornish and Woodstock; Frankfurter headed to Harvard Law School. Lippmann left for Europe and did not plan on returning until mid-September. Roosevelt continued to rely on Frankfurter, Weyl, and others for advice.[74] In August, he invited Frankfurter and Valentine to lunch in New York to discuss "'labor matters.'"[75] Lippmann vowed to resume work on the platform upon his return and urged Roosevelt to guard his health. "The campaign on which you are engaged," Lippmann wrote, "is larger than any issue that could possibly arise this Fall."[76]

★★★

On June 28, a few days before Lippmann sailed for Britain on July 2, the Archduke Franz Ferdinand and his wife were assassinated in Sarajevo. Most Americans barely noticed the significance of a Serbian nationalist murdering the heir to the Austro-Hungarian Empire. The Austrian-born Frankfurter heard the news in Boston's South Station and predicted to his friends Valentine and Henry Kendall: "Well, the fat is in the fire, and the European war is just a matter of weeks, if not days."[77] A few months later, Frankfurter wrote: "There weren't two dozen people who had the faintest suspicion how fraught with danger the incident was to the peace of the rest of the world."[78]

Lippmann, for his part, thought little of the news. Not even the declaration of war between Austria and Serbia on July 26 altered his travel plans. The next day, he left Britain after several weeks for a short trip to

Belgium.[79] One day, he was sunning himself on a beach in Ostend, the next day he was touring fifteenth-century Bruges, and the day after that people in Brussels "were weeping in the streets" and a bank panic caused the credit market to collapse with the threat of a German invasion.[80] He had bought a train ticket to meet his parents in Zurich but turned around and traveled all night to Britain.[81] He arrived at the home of Graham Wallas and immediately collapsed into bed.[82] For the next few weeks, he watched and waited at Wallas's as events unfolded.[83] Lippmann felt "a sort of blank stupidity with [the] inability to realize the situation."[84] On August 2, he wrote Frankfurter that Germany had declared war against Russia, the fate of France was unknown, and all of Britain was on edge.[85] Three days later, Britain declared war on Germany. The events changed Lippmann's life goals. "My own part in this," he wrote in his diary, "is to understand world-politics, to be interested in national & military affairs, and to get away from the old liberalism which concentrates entirely on liberal problems. We cannot lose all that, but I see now that all our really civilized effort is set in a structure of hard necessities."[86]

Lippmann returned home for the fall publication of his second book, *Drift and Mastery*; Croly's new book, *Progressive Democracy*, also came out that fall. Both Lippmann and Croly advocated Valentine's view of unions as giving workers a seat at the table and the linchpin to creating an "industrial democracy."[87] "The unions are struggling to give the wage-earners representation, and that is why the hopes of democracy are bound up with the labor movement ...," Lippmann wrote. "Labor needs criticism, needs inventive thought, needs advice and help. But no one can give any of these things who has not grasped with full sympathy that impulse for industrial democracy which is the key to the movement."[88]

Both books received polite reviews, but the war had shifted everyone's focus overseas.[89] For the same reasons, the first issue of the *New Republic*, which hit newsstands on November 7, 1914, fell flat. With only 875 initial subscribers, the magazine's lead editorial focused on the domestic issues that had preoccupied the House of Truth before the war—the future of progressivism. "Progressivism of all kinds has fared badly," the editorial page lamented after the defeat of progressive candidates in the November 1914 elections. "The Progressive Party has been reduced to an insignificant remnant."[90] Despite the magazine's vow to revive "non-partisan progressivism,"[91] the war had changed everything. Roosevelt could no longer lead them. The federal government could not be all-powerful. The nationalism that Lippmann and Croly espoused for the domestic sphere seemed suspect in light of what was happening abroad—especially in the hands of the militaristic, imperialist former President Roosevelt.

At first, the *New Republic* praised Roosevelt's supposed stance that American neutrality should not prevent the US government from expressing outrage about the German invasion of Belgium. In an editorial "Timid Neutrality," the magazine championed Roosevelt's leadership: "We believe that of all Americans commenting on the war his judgment is the ripest. We reject as the idlest superstition the idea that he enjoys war and despises peace."[92] Roosevelt toasted the magazine's founding editors by inviting them to spend the night at Sagamore Hill and keeping them up half the night talking.[93] By 2:00 a.m., Croly fell asleep.[94] "'Don't wake him. Don't wake him,'" Roosevelt said, according to Lippmann, "and went on talking."[95] That same month, Roosevelt reviewed Croly's and Lippmann's new books in *The Outlook* and believed "[b]oth of these writers stand foremost among those of our thinkers who recognize the grave abuses of our present system."[96]

The warm feelings between Roosevelt and the *New Republic* were short-lived. The magazine criticized Wilson's Mexico policy as inconsistent with his policy of neutrality and nonaggression in Europe.[97] Wilson had sent troops to capture the port of Vera Cruz in an unsuccessful effort to block a German weapons shipment from reaching Mexican General Victoriano Huerta, but the military maneuvers helped to topple Huerta's regime. In a December 6 *New York Times Magazine* article, Roosevelt blasted Wilson for starting an unauthorized war in Mexico, compared it to the German invasion of Belgium, and accused Wilson of enabling Venustiano Carranza and Pancho Villa to commit atrocities against Mexican Catholics.[98] Roosevelt, Lippmann recalled, was "practically charging" the Wilson administration "with personal responsibility for the rape of nuns in Mexico."[99] In an attempt to demonstrate its fairness, the *New Republic* charged that Roosevelt had "struck blindly and unfairly" at the president, and that Roosevelt's article on Mexico was "driven by his prejudice" against Wilson and "was an example of the kind of fighting which has turned so many of [Roosevelt's] natural admirers into bitter enemies."[100] Roosevelt reacted by accusing Croly and the magazine of disloyalty and slamming its editors as "three anemic Gentiles and three international Jews."[101] The former president never again held the magazine in high regard and referred to the editors as "nice well-meaning geese—early Victorian Geese" and "talking like nice, kindly old ladies over their knitting."[102] "He broke with us," Lippmann recalled, "and we never saw him again."[103]

The war and the break with Roosevelt forced the *New Republic* and the House of Truth crowds to rethink their political agenda and to expand their network into the Wilson administration. The federal government still held the key to their vision of an industrial democracy that recognized organized labor and protected the rights of workers. But with the war increasing the use of government power, the people at the House of Truth began to look to the judiciary to strike the proper balance between their belief in democracy and their growing concern for civil liberties and fair criminal trials.

6

The Soldier's Faith

After their break with Roosevelt, the *New Republic*'s editors and their friends from the House of Truth turned to Justice Holmes. He might have seemed like an odd choice. Holmes did not read newspapers and was not interested in politics, but he was so enamored with the new magazine that it was his primary source of news. "[Y]ou young fellows in the *New Republic* show that we can write as well in this country as anywhere," Holmes wrote Frankfurter, "and fill me with courage even though you humble me personally."[1]

Holmes was an unlikely hero for this group of intellectuals because he did not share their desire for pro-labor legislation or their belief that government recognition of organized labor would create an industrial democracy. Yet his willingness to allow the government to experiment with different types of socioeconomic legislation made him their best hope on the Supreme Court. His Union army experiences made him their leading authority on war. And his interest in new ideas and talented young people drew him to the *New Republic* crowd just as he had gravitated to Frankfurter, Denison, and others at the House of Truth.

Holmes, in turn, took to the magazine's two biggest stars, Croly and Lippmann. Both editors sent the justice copies of their new books.[2] Neither book persuaded Holmes of anything except the greatness of the writers. "Alas, my doubts attach to many of the shibboleths of the young—(your gifted lot of chaps)," he wrote Frankfurter. "I don't believe some of the things deeply implied in the writings of Croly and Lippmann, much as I delight in them and I almost need your encouragement not to think that I am an old hulk on the sands."[3] The justice nonetheless began recommending their books and the new magazine to his friends. "Do you know Walter Lippmann's books—A Preface to Politics and (just out) Drift & Mastery?" he wrote John Chipman Gray. "He is young—and one thinks at times proceeding on an inadequately founded faith—but Lord, how good a writer—what discernment of impalpables and enumeration of infinitesimals—What delightful cheek and what sound criticism for the meditation of the elders." Holmes urged Gray to subscribe to the magazine and to read Lippmann: "He is one of the lads that give me courage for the future."[4]

To Croly, Holmes sent a four-page handwritten letter praising *Progressive Democracy* but emphasizing their points of disagreement.[5] To Lippmann, Holmes drafted a letter about *Drift and Mastery* "with some criticism and much praise, but it was unsatisfactory and so burned."[6] Instead, the justice quoted from his letter to Gray.[7] Three days later, after he had finished reading Lippmann's book, Holmes wrote him that "while I have found no further ground for disagreement I have found much more to admire."[8] To thank him for the book and sealing the bond of their new friendship, Holmes made sure that Lippmann received a copy of Holmes's *Speeches* "which may disclose in an accidental way here and there the readiness of my mind to accept most of your views."[9]

Holmes with the *New Republic* at right

Soon both Lippmann and Croly were making pilgrimages to 1720 Eye Street. No one captured the experience better than Lippmann. In contrast to the hot, cigar-reeking halls of Congress, he wrote in the *New Republic*, "there is at least one place in Washington where things have an altogether different quality, and no one I think comes away from it unmoved. It is the house of Mr. Justice Holmes. When you enter, it is as if you had come into the living stream of high romance. You meet the gay soldier who can talk of Falstaff and eternity in one breath, and tease the universe with a quip."[10] The laconic Lippmann engaged Holmes in completely different types of conversations from those engaged in by the frenetic Frankfurter; Holmes, of course, did most of the talking.[11] "If you found Croly solemn Lippmann has great gifts of silence," Holmes wrote to Clara Stevens. "I like to talk with both of them, however. Their wisdom in the paper sometimes depresses me—perhaps it is also points of management in which they may be right."[12]

★★★

In addition to recommending Lippmann, Croly, and the *New Republic* to his friends, Holmes provided another connection between the magazine and the House of Truth and supplied 1727 Nineteenth Street with a much-needed commodity—new residents.

Each year, a Harvard law professor selected a top graduate to be Holmes's secretary sight unseen. There was not much legal work for them to do because he wrote all his own opinions. Besides drafting one- or two-page summaries of the incoming petitions to hear new cases, the secretaries mostly kept Holmes company. The justice used his secretaries, today referred to as law clerks, as sounding boards and companions. The childless Holmes and his wife treated them like surrogate sons. Robert Taft, the top student in the law school class of 1913 and president of the *Harvard Law Review*, had declined the offer to be Holmes's secretary.[13] Taft's father, the lame-duck president in mid-November 1912, had advised his son that a year with Holmes was not as valuable as a year of practicing law in their hometown of Cincinnati.[14]

When the House of Truth first started in 1912, Holmes's secretary Francis Biddle had sat at the feet of Valentine, Frankfurter, and other Bull Moosers, and had become enamored with Roosevelt and his campaign. Despite his dismay over his secretary's political conversion, Holmes introduced Biddle's successor, Stanley Clarke, to Frankfurter and Loring Christie "to give him a start as he knows no one. If you chaps like him you probably will pass

Holmes's study at 1720 Eye Street

him around."[15] Clarke socialized at the House.[16] In the fall of 1913, Clarke's
successor, George Harrison, moved into the House when Frankfurter and
the other original residents started moving out. Harrison's successor, Harvey
Bundy, another Yale College graduate and member of the *Harvard Law
Review*, also lived in the House.[17]

By the fall of 1914, when Bundy moved in, the composition of the House
had changed completely. Two of Frankfurter's friends, Justice Department
and Interstate Commerce Commission lawyer Louis G. Bissell and former
State Department lawyer Edward H. Hart, lived there. Bissell had been
the editor-in-chief of the *Columbia Law Review*, and Hart had been one of

Bissell's fellow editors. Both Bissell and Hart had attended Percy's farewell party in New York City. So had the House's fourth new resident, Franklin Ellis, a 1906 Harvard graduate and businessman described by Bundy as a "rather queer addition" to the House and "jolly man about town."[18] Ellis's main interests consisted of playing bridge and golf, not law and politics.[19]

Bundy, too, spent much of his year with Holmes socializing. He usually arrived at 1720 Eye Street at 9:00 a.m. and stayed there until Holmes left for the Court at noon. From noon to 4:00 p.m., Bundy was on his own. He had so much free time that he won Chevy Chase Country Club's tennis championship.[20] Bundy usually returned at 4:00 p.m. to discuss the justice's day at the Court.[21] His social life at the House, not his legal work for the justice, dominated the year. "The House of Truth was still going strong," Bundy recalled, "and we had the most wonderful times. Life was by no means monastic. One was out for dinner, or had people in for dinner, at the House of Truth, almost every night."[22]

In the fall of 1915, Bundy's successor as Holmes's secretary moved into the House. His name was Chauncey Belknap, but his friends called him Chick. Orphaned as a boy and raised by aunts and uncles, he graduated from New York City's High School of Commerce and was a prize-winning debater at Princeton.[23] After his graduation in 1912, he enjoyed his summer travels in Europe a little too much; he arrived that fall at Harvard Law School ten days late.[24] Initially horrified by his casual lateness, his classmates soon forgot about it. Based on his first-year grades, Belknap qualified for membership on the *Harvard Law Review*.[25]

Belknap was the first Holmes secretary who had known Frankfurter as a law professor.[26] Belknap's last year at the law school coincided with Frankfurter's first year of teaching. The youngest professor at the school, Frankfurter looked like a student and made it his business to get to know the students on the *Law Review*. Still a bachelor, he spent "a very substantial amount of time" with Belknap and his friends.[27] They must have heard Frankfurter's tales of 1727 Nineteenth Street. Frankfurter arranged for Belknap and another classmate to live there after graduation. "I never can repay the debt of gratitude I owe to Felix for this introduction," Belknap recalled. "It meant that I was immediately introduced to the liveliest and most interesting group of people of my own age and a little older in the city."[28]

Belknap's unpublished diary of his year as Holmes's secretary provides a window into work with the justice, life at the House of Truth, and how the war and pro-labor causes captured the attention of the House's friends and former residents. On October 7, 1915, Belknap arrived in Washington, DC, on the overnight train from New York City. As he was eating eggs for breakfast, he learned the "strange news" that President Wilson, whose wife, Ellen, had died the previous year, was marrying the widow of a jewelry store owner, Edith Galt. Despite a heavy rain, Belknap proceeded "by trolley to 1727 Nineteenth St., between R and S Streets, Frankfurter's famous House of Truth. It's a narrow, red brick three story affair, a bit dingy outside and in. I soon discovered the passage into our dining-living room, a converted studio of generous proportions, with skylight and broad windows."[29]

The day after Belknap arrived in Washington, he reported to 1720 Eye Street at 11:00 a.m. as instructed and "was ushered up to [Holmes's] study on the second floor back, by the negro messenger." There Belknap found Holmes writing at his desk. "He is a good specimen for 74,—deep, sparkling eyes under bushy brows, hair thick & not yet white, flowing white mustache. He stands a trifle over 6 ft. I should say, erect & a clean cut figure, in his purple velvet jacket, with a long cigar, he looks more like a

Chauncey Belknap circa 1912

cavalry captain than the popular conception of a jurist." The justice showed Belknap the adjoining library. "It reveals versatile tastes, from the Year Books to Walter Lippman [*sic*], William James to Rabelais. Over [his] mantel is what the Justice describes as 'the family mausoleum, where I keep all my fathers' books in their various editions and my grandfathers'—both of them wrote books.'" Finally, Belknap met Mrs. Holmes, whom he described as "a peculiar looking woman of the Justice's age with a reputation for extraordinary brilliancy."[30] Holmes gave his new secretary free rein over his bookshelves and presented him with a copy of the justice's *Speeches*, which Belknap believed "is not so widely known as it should be."[31]

It did not take Belknap long to join the House of Truth social scene that included intelligent and attractive single women, led by the daughter of the president of the Washington *Evening Star*, Frances Noyes. She was not like many women of that era, who often were forced to sacrifice their ambition and sublimate their personalities to find a husband. In 1913, she had published a novel, *Mark*, and later wrote short stories, a Pulitzer Prize–winning play, and nonfiction.[32] Educated at the Sorbonne and Columbia, the twenty-five-year-old Noyes was not afraid to speak her mind, liked to have fun, and was comfortable in the company of men. Noyes, Belknap wrote in his diary, was "keen, vivacious, cultivated—attractive without beauty—a tiny bundle of nerves."[33] Belknap and his housemates were in love with her.[34] One of them, Edward Hart, later married her.[35] Soon after Belknap had arrived in town, Noyes began inviting him and his housemates to her family's home in Silver Spring, Maryland. She also began teaching him French.[36] He, in turn, introduced her to one of the most cultivated and flirtatious men in Washington, Justice Holmes. "He jokingly said to me when I started to work," Belknap recalled, "to bear in mind that part of my duty was to make sure that the liveliest girls in Washington attended his and Mrs. Holmes' parties."[37] Noyes, a regular at the teas, was the liveliest; Holmes described her as "the heroine of our Monday afternoons."[38]

Justice and Mrs. Holmes loved young people and loathed the stuffy, self-importance of official Washington. On the justice's seventy-fifth birthday, Belknap helped Mrs. Holmes pull off one of her beloved surprises. During the early evening, she threw a dinner party consisting of cabinet secretaries, congressmen, and their wives whom Mrs. Holmes referred to as "pouter pigeons." It was Belknap's job to make sure that all those guests left by 10:00 p.m. and to arrange for "the best of the young people—you young fellows from the 'House of Truth' and your girls" to hide downstairs by 10:15. At the appointed time, they blew bird whistles provided by Mrs. Holmes. The justice came downstairs, and the real party began. The champagne flowed, and the conversation continued past midnight.[39]

Holmes often talked to his secretaries about his Civil War experiences. "The Judge was a solider," Belknap's predecessor Bundy recalled, "and he always talked in terms of a soldier."[40] With the war in Europe on everyone's mind, the justice's friends from the House of Truth and the *New Republic* turned to him and his writings for advice and inspiration. Philip Littell wrote an entire "Books and Things" column about Holmes's 1884 Memorial Day address that recounted the deaths of friends on the battlefield.[41] Others found inspiration from "The Soldier's Faith," Holmes's 1895 address about his Civil War experiences. "The Soldier's Faith," as much as any of Holmes's judicial opinions, resonated with his young friends.

Loring Christie sought the justice's counsel about staying at home in Canada instead of joining the British on the front lines in France and Belgium.[42] In September 1914, Christie had gotten engaged to a twenty-one-year-old Ottawa woman named Marie Armstrong and was eager to introduce her to the justice. Marie had relieved Christie of a "sense of loneliness" that he had felt for many years.[43] Yet his engagement could not relieve Christie of the feelings of guilt and worthlessness as he worked day and night behind a desk in Ottawa while Canadian men, including his brother, enlisted. He vowed to do the same if he ever felt that he were not adding value to Prime Minister Borden's administration and told the prime minister so.[44] Christie unburdened himself, first to Frankfurter and then to Holmes: "I have faith somehow that a world brought to its knees may learn some of the things that you learned in your dark days of half a century ago. For myself it seems I am not to be allowed to find the Soldier's Faith; I must content myself with hoping I may count a little here."[45] Holmes was "deeply moved" by Christie's letter and reminded him "that it takes romantic faith to do unromantic things."[46]

Christie tried to take Holmes's words to heart in February 1915, as the first Canadian division left for France and "our next word of it will be that some have gone to stay."[47] A few months later, Christie reported how Canadian forces "fought like very devils" holding the line in France and half an infantry was killed or wounded during three days of fighting. "I have several friends gone," Christie wrote Frankfurter. "We are beginning to get what Englishmen have had to put up with since August—what Eustace has been seeing when he wrote a while ago 'we shall emerge from this war with all our private life a desert around us.' It's got to go on & on a very long while."[48] Christie disagreed with the *New Republic*'s call for "an inconclusive fight" as "intellectualizing a situation" rather than understanding the costs and consequences to the Allies in not achieving victory.[49]

On a Sunday in mid-January 1916, Christie visited the House of Truth and its new residents. Belknap, who described Christie as the "private secretary" to Prime Minister Borden, enjoyed the visit: "As Felix F put it in his matchless phrase, he reverted much to reticences & [on] some things to talk. He spent some time in England with the chief last year & had unmitigated disgust for most liberal leaders [including British Prime Minister H. H.] Asquith & [Asquith's successor David] Lloyd George."[50]

On board the *Mauritania* in May 1914 on his trip home to Britain, Percy wrote Holmes thanking him for his influence and for inspiring future trips to America. "You know, too, I am sure," Percy wrote, "all that you represent today to the young men of my own age with whom I have lived in Washington during the last two years, but especially the last winter."[51] Since the war broke out, he had been working fourteen- to fifteen-hour days in the Foreign Office in London for Edward Grey and in the newly created War Department.[52] By his bedside, he kept a copy of Holmes's *Speeches*.[53] Like Christie, Percy yearned to put on a uniform and join the front lines yet contributed to the war effort sitting behind a desk. The experience changed him. "In the House of Truth we youngsters used to be so gay in our estimates of social ills and remedies, and this blithe survey of causes and effects drew, I fear, half its charm from the knowledge that no one could ever *prove* us wrong!" he wrote Holmes. "In such an atmosphere future stress comes to be laid on clear and convincing *statement*. War ends that. It provides an infallible touchstone. ... The rightness or wrongness of that estimate is written the next month in blood."[54]

As the months passed, Percy worked with Christie on matters related to the British Empire, updated Frankfurter on the war effort, and wondered when America would join forces with the Allies. Percy let Frankfurter know just how life-changing the war would be: "Well, we have schemed together and filled our little heads full of gaudy plans of statesmanship—but now every Englishman who stands near to politics should be able to give you *one* piece of news. From this nightmare of a month I bring you at least this message—Never believe again, as we have believed in the past, that this world is ours to shape."[55]

With the war raging in Europe, the *New Republic* tried to maintain its own neutrality between Roosevelt's militarism and Wilson's caution and between Germany and the Allies. After an early pro-Ally editorial, a British publisher tried to bribe the nascent magazine by offering to purchase 50,000 copies each week if the magazine agreed to publish weekly pro-British editorials; the editors declined.[56] The magazine favored the Allies but assessed blame on both sides. On February 13, 1915, the *New Republic* equated the German declaration of British and French waters as war zones with the British use of an American flag on the *Lusitania* to avoid a German submarine attack.[57] Others accused Croly of being "pro-German" and Lippmann of "becoming a pro-British maniac."[58]

Everything changed—for the magazine and the nation—on May 7, 1915, the day that a German submarine sunk the *Lusitania*, a British-bound ocean liner, killing 1,198 people on board, including 123 Americans. Wilson exchanged several strongly worded notes with Germany, notes that led to the resignation of his isolationist secretary of state, William Jennings Bryan.[59] Though Germany had warned Americans not to travel on munitions-carrying British vessels, the sinking of the *Lusitania* caused the *New Republic* and its editors to change their tune. The magazine blamed Germany for the loss of lives yet resisted Roosevelt's demands that the nation enter the war. The editors considered Roosevelt "too much of an agitator." "We sympathize," the editorial continued, "with the man who recently said that he has had to spend too much of his energy recently in wishing that Mr. Roosevelt would be more discreet and Mr. Wilson less so."[60] In an editorial, "Not Our War," the *New Republic* advocated a disinterested neutrality that sided with the Allies, considered Germany the aggressor, and urged America to prepare for a war that it hoped to avoid.[61] "It will be well for the world to keep one great Power disinterested," the editorial concluded. "The United States ought to be that Power."[62] The war was great for the magazine's readership. By September 1915, it was selling 9,000 copies per week.[63]

Lippmann was furious with Germany for sinking the *Lusitania*, but he endorsed the magazine's restrained position.[64] "We have been going through a bad month here ever since the *Lusitania* went down," he wrote to his British friend Alfred E. Zimmern. "Our press has been very misrepresentative. The feeling against war in this country is a great deal deeper than you would imagine by reading the editorials."[65] That same day, Lippmann echoed Wilson's caution to another friend: "We have got to stay out if there is any way of doing so."[66]

During the summer of 1915 on Long Island, Lippmann tried to make sense of it all by writing his first book on foreign policy, *The Stakes of Diplomacy*. He was troubled by the thought that the democratic political process would not have stood in Wilson's way if, after the sinking of the *Lusitania*, the president had wanted to go to war.[67] *The Stakes of Diplomacy* sought an alternative to war that recognized the dangers of patriotism and the necessity of internationalism. Lippmann advocated government participation in creating a more peaceful world, just as he supported government intervention in creating an industrial democracy at home. "The strategy of peace is to use the democratic governments as organs of leadership in world politics …," he wrote. "These, as I see them, are the conditions under which an internationalist remains a patriot, not in order to support his country right or wrong, not in order to aggrandize it, but in order to use it as a lever to influence world politics."[68] *The Stakes of Diplomacy*, published in November 1915, was dedicated to the editors of the *New Republic*, which made Frankfurter proud.[69] As his reputation as a foreign policy expert grew, Lippmann began to make more frequent trips to Washington, and in December he visited the House. "He is quiet but not unassuming," Belknap wrote in his diary. "His talk is not nearly as brilliant as his books and ideas … but he supports thoughtful argument."[70]

After the sinking of the *Lusitania*, the annoyances that Percy and Christie had felt about Wilson's neutrality began to dissipate. "I just want to say a word—to speak my prayer for those who must speak America's voice today, for the man on whose shoulder the thing rests," Christie wrote Frankfurter four days after the incident. "I am sorry for some personal irritations I may have felt at his way of saying things. In the ultimate voice & doings of America herself, whatever is done, I have an abiding faith."[71] Percy's and Christie's ties to America were too deep not to be sympathetic. Both men looked back with fondness on their days at the House of Truth and often asked about its founder, Valentine.

★★★

Valentine, Denison, and Frankfurter all watched the war unfold from outside Washington. Less than two years after he had left the Taft administration to join Roosevelt's Bull Moose campaign, Valentine returned to the city an industrial relations expert and a visionary. On April 14, 1914, in the assembly room of the Shoreham Hotel, he testified before the US Commission on Industrial Relations about how unions must be represented in the process of scientific management. At the outset, he described his profession of industrial counselor as that of "a man who is devoting all of his time to studying the relations between employers, employees, and the public."[72] He explained how industrial relations benefited from a combination of efficiency and democracy. The reason that labor and management must be represented in scientific management decisions, Valentine said, was that "in my experience, I have found that neither side possessed a monopoly of the brains."[73] He recounted, without mentioning the company by name, how the Plimpton Press in Massachusetts had implemented scientific management studies but only after bargaining with unions over wages and hours. Collective bargaining, Valentine argued, gave labor input into the process.[74]

During the summer of 1914, Valentine, Frankfurter, and textile mill and Plimpton Press owner Henry P. Kendall met with the father of scientific management—Frederick W. Taylor—at Taylor's summer home in Kennebunkport, Maine. Valentine and Frankfurter argued that scientific management and unions could be compatible; Taylor saw no need for negotiating with employees.[75] Though he could not persuade Taylor to change his mind about organized labor, Valentine won the argument by testing his scientific management theories in the real world at Kendall's mills and elsewhere. Before the commission, Valentine had suggested that the only way to understand how scientific management shops worked in practice was to study them. The commission took him up on his offer. Valentine was management's expert on a three-person committee that studied thirty-five scientific management shops and produced a report, written by University of Chicago economist Robert F. Hoxie, concluding that "scientific management presents certain possible benefits to labor and to society."[76]

Like Brandeis, Valentine believed in the importance of a fair minimum wage, though not at the expense of regular employment. Scientific management again held the key. The minimum wage depended on the cost of production and the cost of living and varied city by city and industry by industry and factory by factory. Scientific management and a fair minimum wage drew support from Lippmann, Croly, and others associated with the *New Republic*. In a March 1915 article, Lippmann blasted critics of minimum wage laws and cited the Massachusetts Minimum Wage Commission, chaired by his friend Valentine, as an example of how to make such laws work.[77] A few months later, Lippmann mocked the National Association of Manufacturers for insisting that a fair minimum wage would result in widespread layoffs.[78] In November 1915, Judge Learned Hand wrote an article about the eight-year impact of Australia's minimum wage laws and a *Harvard Law Review* article about how that country's courts set minimum wages. "Minimum wage laws," Hand wrote, "are to all practical intents as yet untried in the United States."[79]

As the first chairman of the Massachusetts Minimum Wage Commission, Valentine presided over six employee representatives, six employer representatives, and three public representatives.[80] With the commission's support and input, he negotiated a minimum wage with the brush industry. Brush workers were mostly female Irish, Italian, and Jewish immigrants who earned $5 to $6 per week. The workforce was unsteady because the wages were so low. The board established a minimum wage of 15½ cents an hour ($8 to $9 per week), not quite the cost of living but designed to provide stability to both workers and manufacturers. The fears of scientific management opponents—rising prices or calls for increased efficiency by replacing workers with machinery—had not materialized. Enforcement of the minimum wage, however, was difficult. Though the *New Republic* did not mention Valentine by name, it described the effort as "one well calculated to afford a practical test of the theory."[81]

Valentine had succeeded in creating a new business of industrial counseling and in establishing himself as one of the nation's foremost labor relations experts.[82] In addition to serving on the Massachusetts Minimum Wage Commission, he had accepted a position on the Corset Makers' Wage Board to help them receive weekly rather than hourly minimum wages. He also enjoyed living with his family near Boston. The health of his daughter, Sophia, had finally improved.[83] "It is doing me great good to have Felix in my vicinity again," he wrote Denison, "and he ... and I are laying our plans to rattle a whole lot of dead bones here in New England."[84] Otherwise, Valentine vowed to stay out of national domestic or international politics.

Valentine's belief in "the need of every concern in the United States to analyze its labor relations" assumed added importance as the war loomed.[85] "You'll think for a minute—but not longer—that I've gone crazy over my idea of what there is to be done in industrial relations," he wrote Loring Christie, "when I say that it is building right relationships in industry out of which is to come a vigorous affirmative, manly, and womanly peace of the world."[86] Three months after the sinking of the *Lusitania*, Valentine argued in the *New Republic* that the war made it even more imperative for Americans to strive for an industrial democracy. He saw the war as affording an opportunity for the United States to lead with its labor policy. He argued that representation was the key to national unity and labor peace, and he challenged businessmen like Elbert Gary of the steel industry and Senator Henry Cabot Lodge to learn from Britain's mistakes and to make sure that workers were represented. "In every place men meet," Valentine wrote, "we should try to carry to our dangerously complacent business men this tremendous story of the need of industrial organization along lines of representation."[87]

No former House of Truth resident was further removed from talk of the war than Valentine's former housemate Denison. It took Denison only six months as the secretary of the interior in the Philippines to stir up controversy. During a June 30, 1914, speech at the City Club in Manila, derisively known as his "White Hope Speech," Denison parried questions about Philippine independence but insisted that money should be spent for Filipino, not American, interests and should be spent only on things that the Filipino people wanted. He contended that $500 for photographs of mollusks should have been spent on a schoolteacher's salary; that $14,000 to print an ethnological study should have been spent on teachers for the teacher-less Mountain Province; a single doctor for the doctor-less 40,000 people in Palawan; or medical assistance for six nuns taking care of 250 patients at a leper colony. Denison believed that "the money is theirs" and "we shall spend it for what they want."[88]

Denison's ideas did not go over well with his fellow commissioners running the island as an American colony and spoil of the Spanish-American War. They believed that democracy was incompatible with a colonial government and US foreign policy interests.[89] The Portland *Oregonian* accused Denison of slandering fellow Americans who had preceded him in office.[90] A Filipino newspaper accused Denison of "blowing off for the benefit of his friends back in the States."[91]

Denison's friends back home, however, were not impressed. Of his White Hope Speech, he wrote Valentine:

> Now I lay me down to sleep
> Expectations blown away;
> When they get it in the States
> What in the hell will Teddy say?[92]

Denison still admired Roosevelt, asked him for an autographed picture, and described himself as "the only living Bull Moose in the Government service, now that Frankfurter has been corralled by Harvard."[93] Denison sent

Roosevelt the White Hope Speech. Roosevelt agreed that money should be spent for Filipinos, but not on whatever they want if that included weapons and ammunition.[94] Ex-president Taft, a former governor general of the Philippines, informed Stimson that Denison had "made such an infernal ass of himself out there."[95] Denison's friends who knew something about Insular affairs—Stimson, Frankfurter, and Alfred Mitchell-Innes—all thought that the speech was unwise from a foreign policy standpoint.[96] Stimson, Denison's former boss, read the White Hope Speech and informed Denison that it made "the same unfortunate impression."[97]

As the negative reactions to his speech poured in, Denison chafed at the silence and lack of support from his closest friends at home, the Valentines and Frankfurter.[98] For several months at the beginning of 1915, Denison cut off contact with them.[99] His period of "selfish unhappiness" soon gave way to loneliness, frustration, and regret. Any hope for reform in the Philippines depended on action from Washington, action that was not forthcoming given the country's growing preoccupation with the war. As Valentine and Frankfurter thrived in their new occupations, Denison began second-guessing his own career choice. "For the first time in my life I am HUMBLE," he wrote Frankfurter and Valentine. "I'm ashamed of the easy overconfidence I had of my fitness for this job, and of much that I have done here or rather said. I'll try to keep my incapacity as SECRET as possible, and so I hope you won't tell anybody who doesn't know it, but I want to go on record to you two and Sophie. Never expect me to touch another political or administrative office!"[100]

As unhappy as Denison was, Frankfurter was happy and in his element in the job that Denison had nudged him into—a Harvard law professorship. Frankfurter found a kindred spirit in Roscoe Pound, adopted Pound's sociological approach to legal scholarship, and loved molding smart young men and teaching public utilities through detailed factual investigations of cases. Frankfurter's first major publication, a casebook about the Interstate Commerce Act, included an epigraph from Holmes about the difficulty of arriving at an "absolutely final and quantitative determination" in the law because of "competing social ends," and therefore "a judgment for the plaintiff or the defendant cannot be reduced to number and accurately fixed."[101] The first opinion in the book was a 1913 Supreme Court case argued by Denison.[102] After reviewing the casebook, Christie remarked: "Will you forgive an immodest first impression, viz. that the House of Truth and environs comes off very well."[103]

One weekend in November 1915, Frankfurter visited Belknap and the other residents living at the House of Truth. Frankfurter had so many places to go and people to see that they barely saw him—except for an extravagant dinner that reminded them what the House used to look and sound like. He invited *Harper's Weekly* editor Norman Hapgood, Justice Department lawyer Thurlow Gordon, lawyer Robert Szold, new Federal Trade Commission (FTC) commissioner George Rublee, and "half a dozen others." After dinner, the conversation grew even livelier during a debate about US entry into the war. "Hapgood and Felix debated the President's preparedness program with warmth and brilliance, and it seemed to most of us that Hapgood made out a strong case for the administration," Belknap wrote in his diary.[104]

★★★

At Harvard Law School and in the pages of the *New Republic* and the *Harvard Law Review*, Frankfurter made it his mission for the rest of the country to recognize the greatness of Belknap's boss, Justice Holmes. Indeed, Frankfurter and other contributors to the magazine portrayed Holmes as their only hope on an otherwise reactionary Court. There was only one problem—Holmes was not that liberal. He merely believed that the justices should not read their personal views into vague clauses of the Constitution to trump majority rule. He was neither liberal nor conservative but simply believed that the government should be allowed to experiment with socio-economic legislation. Holmes's philosophy, therefore, led to outcomes that pleased his friends—especially in cases involving organized labor.

In January 1915, Holmes dissented from the Court's decision in *Coppage v. Kansas* invalidating the state's ban on yellow-dog contracts that forbade union membership as a condition of employment. The Court's majority struck down the law as a violation of the Fourteenth Amendment Due Process Clause's "liberty of contract."[105] The decision invalidated not only the Kansas law but also similar laws in thirteen states and Puerto Rico.[106] A few years earlier, in *Adair v. United States*, the Court had struck down a similar federal law.[107] Holmes rejected "liberty of contract" theory as the justices reading their laissez-faire economic views into the Constitution. "The Fourteenth Amendment," he wrote in his 1905 *Lochner* dissent, "does not enact Mr. Herbert Spencer's Social Statics."[108] The Due Process Clause's prohibition against the deprivation of "life, liberty, and property without due process of law" said nothing about "liberty of contract." Holmes did not believe that

the "upward and onward" pro-labor legislation would accomplish anything
or that unions would create industrial democracy.[109] Legislative majorities,
however, rendered his personal views irrelevant. "Whether in the long run
it is wise for the workingmen to enact legislation of this sort is not my concern," he wrote in a one-paragraph dissent in *Coppage*, "but I am strongly of
the opinion that there is nothing in the Constitution of the United States to
prevent it, and that *Adair v. United States* ... and *Lochner v. New York* ... should
be overruled."[110]

The *New Republic* quoted Holmes's *Coppage* dissent and lauded him as
"a judge who deals with things, not words, and who realizes that a document which is to rule a great people must in its very nature allow for a
wide and growing field for experimentation."[111] A week later in another
unsigned *New Republic* editorial, Learned Hand attacked the Court's majority opinion in *Coppage* as undemocratic and anti-union. "He puts his wine
in a tiny cup," Hand wrote of Holmes's dissent, "but for that we taste it the
better."[112] Frankfurter thanked Holmes, one of three dissenters along with
moderates Charles Evans Hughes and William R. Day, even before reading
the opinion: "I'm stirred up about the case but not at all as an onward-
and-upwarder. ... But I *am* stirred up about the decision as a student of
constitutional law and how she is made. ... I thoroughly dislike the majority
decision, so perhaps it won't be *lese* judiciary to say it on paper."[113]

Frankfurter and his friends were not simply praising Holmes for Holmes's
sake. They were trying to remove the Court as an obstacle to socioeconomic legislation. They were laying one of the foundations of American
liberalism, a belief in government's role in regulating the nation's economic
life, in managing labor-management relations, and in recognizing the rights
of unions. The *Coppage* case was bigger than a ban on yellow-dog contracts.
The Court was the only thing standing in the way of industrial democracy.

The People's Lawyer, Brandeis continued to lead the defense of state
minimum wage and maximum hour laws.[114] Six years after his "Brandeis
Brief" had persuaded the Court in *Muller v. Oregon* to uphold a maximum
hour law for women, he returned to the Court to defend an Oregon law
establishing an industrial commission to set minimum wages for women
and children. He employed the same "Brandeis Brief" technique, citing 369
examples of why the minimum wage law was a reasonable exercise of state
power. Brandeis's advocacy skills were every bit as good as his brief writing.
Few in attendance on December 17, 1914, forgot his Supreme Court argument in defense of the minimum wage law. "I have just heard Mr. Brandeis

make one of the greatest arguments I have ever listened to, and I have heard a many great arguments ...," William Hitz, a special attorney in the Justice Department, wrote Frankfurter. "He not only *reached* the Court, but he *dwarfed the Court*, because it was clear that here stood a man who knew infinitely more, and who cared infinitely more, for the vital daily rights of the other people than the men who sat there sworn to protect them."[115]

Hitz, who in 1916 became a justice on the Supreme Court of the District of Columbia, was not the only one impressed with Brandeis's performance. Charles Warren, a lawyer and constitutional historian, was in attendance that day and recalled how the Court had deferred to Brandeis. Chief Justice White gave each side an extra half hour, then gave Brandeis another half hour, and then said: "'Mr. Brandeis, your time is up but we will consider that the clock has stopped and you may continue.' The Clerk of the Court told me later that he never recalled such a thing ever before being done by a Chief Justice."[116]

As masterly as the performance was, Brandeis's argument was not carrying the day with the justices. A few weeks after he had started work, Belknap learned from Holmes's files that the Court had voted 5–4 to strike down the Oregon minimum wage law. "Holmes seemed to have noted with pleasure Pitney's comment in conference [about a] 'Communist proposition'; this over [his own] vigorous 'I take the more pleasure in voting to affirm that I regard the law as the imbecile product of incompetence,'" Belknap wrote in his diary. "Imagine Pitney's expression!"[117] As early as February 1916, Brandeis knew that the Court was "having some trouble" with the case because the justices had already affirmed California's maximum hour law, and that case had been argued after his.[118]

The Oregon minimum wage law remained on the Court's docket when Belknap started the following fall. Holmes, who was reading a *Harvard Law Review* article about Australia's minimum wage laws, began discussing the Oregon case with his new secretary.[119] Chief Justice White was presumably writing an opinion for a five-member majority including Pitney, Willis Van Devanter, Joseph Rucker Lamar, and James C. McReynolds. Holmes, along with Day, Joseph McKenna, and Hughes, had voted the other way. "The Justice said he is afraid it will be knocked out and he read me a dissent he had prepared if such proves to be the case," Belknap wrote. "If this has to come forth as a dissent, it will rank beside his opinion dissenting from Lochner vs. N.Y. as a classic utterance for those who believe that the Court does not stand in the way of all social reform."[120]

A month later, the chief justice's proposed majority opinion arrived at the Holmes residence. Holmes read it and remarked: "'Oh, I hope I'm not prejudiced. I think it awful stuff.'" Holmes then read most of it aloud while making comments along the way. "I think it will hurt the court more than anything it has done in my time," he told Belknap. Holmes vowed to write something "solemn and nasty about the Chief's opinion. . . . I take delight in upholding the law because I simply abominate its policy, but the Chief is so solemn about it I mustn't let levity detract from my words."[121] Fate, however, intervened. On January 2, 1916, Justice Lamar died after a prolonged illness, and his absence left the Court divided 4–4.

Before the United States entered the war, Frankfurter and his liberal friends believed that the political process was the best way of protecting less fortunate members of society. In the spring of 1915, however, Holmes began to show liberals that the Supreme Court could be another way to protect the politically powerless. Although many associate him with his free speech dissents, he also protected people from the government when it came to fair criminal trials. At the time, the Court had never overturned a state criminal conviction on due process grounds no matter how unfair the trial had been. Holmes believed that some state criminal trials could be so unfair as to violate due process, especially in the case of politically unpopular minorities.

In April, for example, Holmes dissented from the Court's decision to uphold the capital murder conviction of Leo Frank.[122] The Brooklyn-born Jewish manager of an Atlanta, Georgia, pencil factory, Frank was convicted of murdering Mary Phagan, a thirteen-year-old factory worker, based on the false testimony of a black janitor with a criminal past. A lynch mob outside the courthouse delayed the case's submission to the jury for several days and prevented Frank's presence in the courtroom to hear the jury's verdict.[123]

Holmes believed that the mob had compromised Frank's right to a fair trial. "Whatever disagreement there may be as to the scope of the phrase 'due process of law,' there can be no doubt that it embraces the fundamental conception of a fair trial, with opportunity to be heard," Holmes wrote. "Mob law does not become due process of law by securing the assent of a terrorized jury. . . . [W]e think the presumption overwhelming that the jury responded to the passions of the mob."[124] Seven of his brethren, despite their willingness to invalidate the Kansas law banning yellow-dog contracts, refused to invoke due process to interfere with the Georgia criminal justice system. Only Hughes joined Holmes's dissent.

Holmes felt "a good deal" in coming to Frank's defense.[125] So did his friends from the House of Truth. Brandeis and Frankfurter may have been privy to an early draft of Holmes's dissent and encouraged others, including Pound, to speak out about the case because "it is important that this protest should be made by a non-Jew."[126] An unsigned editorial in the *New Republic*, probably written by Frankfurter, urged the state of Georgia to heed "the delivered opinion of the most distinguished intellectual and moral membership of the United States Supreme Court, the judgment of men least likely to be swerved by the interest of a particular case, and most zealous to maintain the authority of the separate states." The editorial demanded action from the governor: "There is now left to Georgia only the pardoning power to wipe away the stain of legalized lynch law which Justice Holmes and Justice Hughes were compelled to disclose. That power must be exercised for Georgia's sake, as well as Frank's."[127]

As he languished in prison, the Cornell-educated Frank wrote Holmes, thanking him for the dissent and informing him that the governor of Georgia had stirred up the same mob violence that had marred Frank's trial by commuting his sentence to life imprisonment. "My life is preserved and I live on in the confident trust in God and man, that the day is not far

Leo Frank

distant when Truth and Reason will hold sway, and Right and Innocence come into their own. On that day, the vindication and liberty, justly mine even now, will be meted out to me. I hope, and verily believe, that you, too, will live to see that day," Frank wrote on July 15. "With liberty and honor restored, it would be a pleasure for me to greet you in person."[128] Holmes was deeply moved by Frank's note. "A man who could write to him so sensitively as Frank," Holmes told Frankfurter, "couldn't have raped and murdered a girl."[129]

A month after Frank's letter to Holmes, the most prominent citizens of Mary Phagan's hometown, Marietta, Georgia, organized a lynch mob of twenty-five men and broke Frank out of the prison hospital where he was recovering from having had his throat slashed.[130] The so-called Knights of Mary Phagan drove Frank 150 miles to Marietta and hanged him from a tree. A photograph of Frank's body, beaten and blindfolded, was sold on postcards throughout the South.

Holmes's dissent in the Leo Frank case and belief in the right to a fair criminal trial had implications for racial justice but were not motivated by racial sympathies—at least not yet. During his initial years on the Court, he had been reluctant to interfere with majority rule in almost any context except criminal law and often allowed state legislatures to trample on the rights of southern blacks. In 1903, he had upheld an Alabama constitutional provision disenfranchising black voters because the Court lacked the power to compel registration and was unwilling "to supervise the voting in that state by officers of the court."[131] A few years later, he voted to uphold a Kentucky law designed to forbid interracial colleges and dissented from a decision that overturned an Alabama peonage statute that had forced a man into indefinite hard labor for stealing fifteen dollars.[132] Even Frankfurter acknowledged that Justice Hughes had "much better a nose ... for the actual operation of peonage laws in the South than Holmes."[133] During his early years on the Court, Holmes's record on race was bad but not all bad. In the spring of 1915, he joined a unanimous opinion (except for McReynolds, who recused himself) holding that Oklahoma's and Maryland's grandfather clauses exempting white voters from literacy tests violated the Fifteenth Amendment.[134]

Holmes's contact with blacks in segregated Washington was essentially limited to his Supreme Court messenger. Each justice was assigned a black messenger who often played the roles of valet, cook, and chauffeur. The jobs were so coveted that messengers worked for the Court for years.

Holmes's first messenger, John Craig, had begun working at the Court in 1872 for Justice Joseph P. Bradley, then for Holmes's predecessor Horace Gray, and then for Holmes for five years. When Craig died in late 1907, Holmes and Chief Justice Melville Fuller attended the funeral at a private home in a black section of town.[135] For a brief period before and after Craig's death, Joseph Wilson "looked after" Holmes.[136] Craig's permanent replacement was George Marston, who had been working at 1720 Eye Street for Mrs. Holmes and was offered the job based on her recommendation.[137] Marston's death in June 1915 delayed Holmes's summer return to Massachusetts.[138] The funeral was held at Marston's home at 1616 Corcoran Street, four blocks from the House of Truth.[139]

The House of Truth and the *New Republic* crowds were not passionate in 1915 about eliminating racial injustice. They were not ardent segregationists like some progressives (or many southern populists).[140] It was not noteworthy that a black cook and black maid attended the House's residents. Such was the norm in segregated Washington, DC, of that era. Certainly, however, there was nothing radically egalitarian about their racial views. In late November 1915, the *New Republic* published an article written by Brandeis's nephew and namesake, Louis Brandeis Wehle, defending racial segregation in his hometown of Louisville and other southern cities.[141] Any reaction to the article from the Louisville-born Brandeis is unknown.

Croly solicited a response to Wehle's article not from W. E. B. Du Bois or another member of the nascent National Association for the Advancement of Colored People (NAACP) but from a more palatable black leader, Booker T. Washington.[142] Washington's article denounced segregation but not with the tone or flair that Du Bois or another eloquent radical black voice would have brought to the task.[143] Croly should be credited with soliciting a response to Wehle's article that the editor described to Washington as "dispassionate" but with a "tendency to favoring segregation"; Croly's choice, however, revealed his upper-crust establishment view of race and his limited knowledge of American black leaders. In 1915, race was not a salient issue for Valentine, Frankfurter, Lippmann, Croly, and their colleagues. Nothing could distract them from their single-minded focus on supporting unions, establishing minimum wage laws, and banning child labor. As long as Justice Holmes continued to uphold labor laws, he was as liberal as they needed him to be. But Holmes's support for fair criminal trials had long-term implications for racial justice and for the role of the Court in the House of Truth's liberal activism.

Holmes's change of heart about race could not come soon enough for
Washington's vibrant black middle class. The presence of Howard University
and the prospect of federal employment had turned Washington into a
mecca for the nation's educated, upwardly mobile blacks. Yet the election
of Woodrow Wilson three years earlier had dealt their hopes a cruel blow.
Washington was a Jim Crow town, and Wilson's administration made it
even more segregated. As president of Princeton University, Wilson had prevented the enrollment of black students.[144] As the first southern-born president since Andrew Johnson and the first Democrat since Grover Cleveland,
Wilson took his cue from southern Democrats. He named McReynolds,
a racist southerner, his first attorney general and in August 1914 his first
Supreme Court nominee.[145] Wilson's Treasury secretary William Gibbs
McAdoo and his postmaster general Albert S. Burleson, both southerners,
introduced racial segregation into the workplaces and lunchrooms of their
agencies as well as at the Bureau of Engraving and Printing. Wilson also
allowed southern Democrats to thin the ranks of black clerical and lower-
level government employees by requiring photographs on all civil service
applications and to bar black appointments to high-ranking positions. Aside
from the reappointment of Robert H. Terrell as a DC municipal judge in
1914 over the opposition of southern Democrats, Wilson made life worse
for the city's black middle class.[146]

The behavior of the Wilson administration outraged blacks who had supported him based on his campaign promise, "Should I become President of
the United States, they may count upon me for absolute fair dealing and
for everything by which I could assist in advancing the interest of their race
in the United States."[147] One of Wilson's most prominent black supporters,
William Monroe Trotter, a Phi Beta Kappa graduate of Harvard and editor
of the *Boston Guardian*, brought a group of black leaders to the White House
on November 12, 1914, and confronted Wilson for forty-five minutes about
segregation in federal agencies. Wilson was offended by Trotter's tone, accused him of blackmail, and threw Trotter and his group out of the Oval
Office.[148] A few days later, a crowd of 500 black Washingtonians heard Trotter
mention Wilson's name and "hooted and hissed."[149] A *New Republic* editorial
condemned Wilson: "The President used fair words in 1912 in his appeal to
the negroes for votes. We know now that those words meant nothing."[150]

Wilson soon added insult to injury. On March 21, 1915, he invited his
cabinet members and their children to a White House screening of *The Birth
of a Nation*, D. W. Griffith's silent propaganda film based on Thomas Dixon's

novel *The Clansman.* The film, which lampooned blacks and Reconstruction and lionized the Ku Klux Klan, sparked protests in New York, Philadelphia, and Boston (where William Monroe Trotter was arrested after he was denied admission) and was banned in Chicago and other cities to prevent racial violence.

In the *New Republic*, Francis Hackett wrote a scathing review in which he described the film as "aggressively vicious and defamatory" and a "spiritual assassination. It degrades the censors that passed it and the white race that endures it."[151] Walter Lippmann was outraged that New York City's censorship board had allowed the film to be shown there with only minor changes and suggested a town hall meeting at Cooper Union to discuss the issue.[152] "We think here that it is the most serious case in regard to the use of the 'movies' that has come to public notice," Lippmann wrote.[153] Instead, the editors published an explanation from the National Censorship Board that historical accuracy was not a factor in its decision to permit the showing of a film.[154]

And yet, like most white publications, the *New Republic*'s editors were silent about the White House screening of the film.[155] It took a letter to the editor from a woman from Washington, DC, to raise the issue and to ask the White House whether Wilson had endorsed the film.[156] As the film's producers fought censorship efforts by disingenuously claiming that Wilson as well as Chief Justice White had endorsed the film after the private screening, Wilson was forced to issue a statement that indicated he "was entirely unaware of the character of the play before it was presented and has at no time expressed his approbation of it" and that described the screening as "a courtesy extended to an old acquaintance."[157] The nation's leading black newspaper, the *Chicago Defender*, accepted Wilson's statement at face value: "We take great pleasure in erasing one demerit mark from our high chief and suggest that if it isn't too painful, he might keep the good work up."[158]

Despite Wilson's entrenchment of segregation in the federal government, his confrontation with Trotter, and his screening of *The Birth of a Nation* at the White House, the *New Republic* and the House of Truth were not as persistent critics of the president's racial politics as NAACP founder Oswald Garrison Villard was in *The Nation* and the *New York Evening Post*. Nor did Wilson's racial politics deter growing support for his administration among the *New Republic* and House of Truth crowds, support that began with Wilson's nomination of Louis Dembitz Brandeis to the Supreme Court.

7

Temperamentally Unfit

On January 27, 1916, Loring Christie wrote a memorandum to his boss, Canadian prime minister Robert Borden, about Woodrow Wilson's re-election prospects in November. Four years earlier, Wilson had captured the presidency with less than 42 percent of the popular vote because Taft and Roosevelt had divided the Republican Party and progressives had split their votes among Wilson, Roosevelt, and Eugene Debs. Christie reported that his friends from the *New Republic* and the House of Truth had never warmed to Wilson and were seeking a Republican or Progressive Party challenger. They could not agree on a candidate. Lippmann proposed Fisher, Taft's former interior secretary.[1] Frankfurter preferred giving Roosevelt another chance even though the former president had lost some of his allure.[2] After the magazine's interest in Fisher waned, Frankfurter tried and failed to generate support for his former boss Stimson.[3] "I attended a dinner of the staff of the *New Republic*," Christie wrote Borden. "They were attempting to fix on a man whom they could support for the presidency against Wilson. They failed utterly to reach anything like a decision. … There seemed to be no man and no cause that could command the nation. Unity seems in abeyance. There is something like political anarchy."[4]

The next day at noon, however, things began to change—Wilson shocked the US Senate by submitting Brandeis's name to replace Justice Lamar, a Taft nominee who had died. "If Mr. Wilson has a sense of humor left, it must be working overtime today," Taft confidant Gus Karger wrote to the former president. "When Brandeis's nomination came in yesterday, the Senate simply gasped. Today some of the Senators are coming up for air and trying to take stock. There wasn't any more excitement at the Capitol when Congress passed the Spanish War Resolution."[5]

Brandeis and his wife, Alice, were already in Washington for a dinner party that night at the home of Treasury Secretary McAdoo and his wife

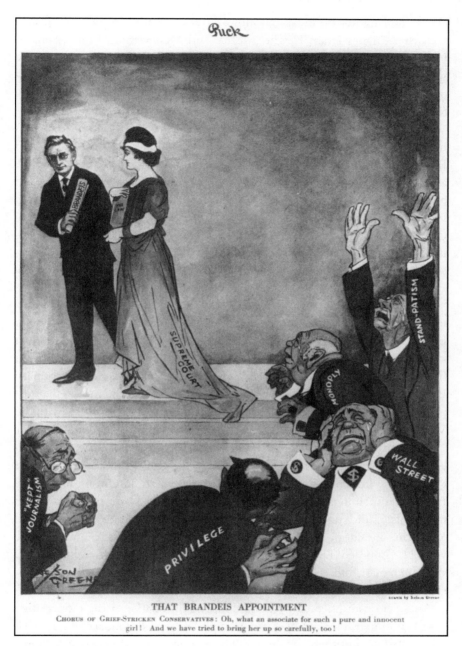

THAT BRANDEIS APPOINTMENT

CHORUS OF GRIEF-STRICKEN CONSERVATIVES: Oh, what an associate for such a pure and innocent
girl! And we have tried to bring her up so carefully, too!

Puck's cartoon about Brandeis's Supreme Court nomination

(Wilson's daughter Eleanor) in honor of President and Mrs. Wilson.[6] Justice and Mrs. Charles Evans Hughes, Justice and Mrs. Mahlon Pitney, Senator James D. Phelan of California, and lawyer Samuel Untermyer and his wife were among the twenty guests at the McAdoos' R Street home.[7] The president and Mrs. Wilson left the dinner to catch a train for a ten-day speaking tour in the Midwest to rally support for his military preparedness program.[8] Wilson, therefore, was not around to hear the opposition to Brandeis's nomination, opposition that the president had anticipated. He had wanted Brandeis in his cabinet, as attorney general, solicitor general, or commerce and labor secretary, but presidential adviser Colonel Edward M. House and business leaders had scuttled that plan.[9] In February 1915, Wilson had intervened to prevent opponents from blocking Brandeis's membership in the Cosmos Club.[10] Brandeis had been one of Wilson's most trusted advisers during the 1912 campaign and continued to advise the president on antitrust matters, as well as the creation of the Federal Reserve System and the Federal Trade Commission.[11]

Although several members of his cabinet proposed the idea of nominating Brandeis to the Supreme Court, Wilson was quite familiar with Brandeis and his views and did not need any prompting.[12] The president knew that he needed to win over former progressives, especially after his first nominee, McReynolds, had emerged as the Court's leading reactionary. Putting Brandeis on the Court was the first in a series of moves that appealed to the *New Republic* and House of Truth crowds, allied them with the Wilson administration, and improved the president's chances of re-election.

The hard part was getting Brandeis confirmed. He did not earn the sobriquet the "People's Lawyer," oppose the J. P. Morgan–orchestrated merger of the New Haven Railroad, and embarrass the Taft administration in the Ballinger-Pinchot Affair without making rich and powerful enemies. In fact, Wilson did not even consult Brandeis's home-state senators from Massachusetts about the nomination because the president knew that they would be opposed. That his enemies accused Brandeis of self-righteousness, sharp practices, and conflicts of interest by acting as "counsel to the situation" made the lines of opposition to his nomination clear.

Anti-Semitism hovered over the confirmation battle of the Court's first Jewish nominee, cloaked by his opponents' professed concern about what they called his unfitness for the job. Those who branded Brandeis as "temperamentally unfit" or lacking "judicial temperament" included Republican Senators Henry Cabot Lodge and John W. Weeks of Massachusetts, Harvard

University president A. Lawrence Lowell and fifty-one of Boston's most prominent citizens, and six of the seven former American Bar Association presidents, including former president William Howard Taft.[13]

Brandeis's nomination, Taft wrote, "is one of the deepest wounds that I have had as an American and a lover of the Constitution and a believer in progressive conservatism. ... He is a muckraker, an emotionalist for his own purposes, a socialist, prompted by jealousy, a hypocrite, a man who has certain high ideals in his imagination, but who is utterly unscrupulous, in method in reaching them, a man of infinite cunning, of marked ability in that direction that hardly rises above the dignity of cunning, of great tenacity of purpose, and, in my judgment, of much power for evil."[14] Brandeis had humiliated Taft and his administration during the Ballinger-Pinchot Affair by showing that the administration had withheld and backdated a key memorandum. Taft was often mentioned for the Supreme Court vacancy, a position he coveted.[15] More, however, was at stake than Taft's personal pride and ambition.

Brandeis's nomination galvanized liberals as they began to warm to Wilson. During the 1912 presidential campaign, Croly and Brandeis had served as opposing advisers and speechwriters on trust busting—Croly for Roosevelt, Brandeis for Wilson. Unlike Brandeis, Croly and Lippmann had little faith in the antitrust laws as the mechanism to stamp out monopolistic practices. Their philosophical differences persisted after the campaign even as their friendship grew.[16] Croly disagreed with Brandeis's ideas published in *Harper's Weekly* and in Brandeis's book *Other People's Money and How the Bankers Use It.*[17] Brandeis initially took a dim view of Croly's qualifications and leadership abilities to run a magazine and adjudged the new publication's success as "improbable."[18] After the nomination, however, Croly and his editors rallied around Brandeis. "I have not been so pleased in a great many years over anything connected with the public welfare of the whole country as I have with your appointment to the Supreme Court," Croly wrote Brandeis.[19] "It was good to get your and the other greetings from the New Republic," Brandeis replied. "I feel almost as if you and your associates must carry the responsibility."[20]

The *New Republic* and House of Truth fought for Brandeis's confirmation for several reasons. First, it was like having one of their own nominated to the Court, an authentic liberal voice on a historically reactionary institution. Second, the business establishment opposed to Brandeis's nomination also opposed minimum wage and maximum hour laws and the rights of

organized labor. Finally, Croly, Lippmann, Frankfurter, Hand, and others understood the nomination fight as a contest over the future of the Supreme
Court's role in defining the scope of government power and regulation.

The Supreme Court had been the biggest obstacle to government's ability to regulate the economy, to recognize the rights of organized labor, and
to create a social welfare state. The bedrock principle of twentieth-century
American liberalism—government's ability to make people's lives better—
was at stake. Liberals had already adopted Holmes as an unlikely standard-
bearer because of his willingness to uphold labor laws. If they could get him
confirmed, Brandeis would be a much-needed ally. The fight for Brandeis's
confirmation was a fight for control of the Court and for American liberalism's democratic faith in government. "One public benefit has already
accrued from the nomination of Mr. Brandeis," the *New Republic*'s February 5
unsigned editorial began. "It has started discussion of what the Supreme
Court means in American life."[21] The editorial explained that "the Court
deals primarily with problems of government, and that is why its personnel is of such nation-wide importance." It reviewed the Court's history of
defining federal and state power and its invocation of liberty of contract to
strike down social welfare legislation, yet optimistically predicted that "[t]he
period of individualism and fear is over. Occasionally there is a relapse, but
on the whole we have entered definitely upon an epoch in which Justice
Holmes has been the most consistent and dominating force, and to which
Justices Day and Hughes have been great contributing factors."[22]

The editorial further challenged the notion that Brandeis was unfit for
the Court. It reviewed his fact-intensive argument in favor of Oregon's
maximum hour law and how that case inaugurated a supposedly new era in
constitutional law and epitomized his approach to legal problems. The editorial argued that "Mr. Brandeis is no doctrinaire," "[t]he very processes of
his mind are deliberate and judicial," and he possesses "that balance of head
and heart and will which constitutes real judicial-mindedness."[23] Finally, the
editorial urged Brandeis's opponents to specify the charges against him so
that they may be answered and "so that the nation may begin to employ this
man who has at once the passion of public service and the genius for it."[24]

The author of the editorial, with its prolix style and references to Holmes
and James Bradley Thayer as dead giveaways, was Frankfurter.[25] Frankfurter
was overjoyed by the nomination and determined to do all he could to
get Brandeis confirmed.[26] "Brandeis is sure to go through," he wrote
Lippmann shortly after the nomination. "I don't know when I've had a

joyous emotion that was as intense & so long sustained as Brandeis' appointment has aroused."[27] To Learned Hand, Frankfurter wrote: "Isn't the Brandeis thing fine—if only to hear them howl & to drag into the aerated open all this bunk of sterilized removal of the Court from the issues of life on which they pass."[28]

Brandeis let his guard down during his confirmation fight and shed the cold reserve that Frankfurter and the House's other residents had found so off-putting. "The other night I had the most intimate personal talk I have ever had with Brandeis," Frankfurter wrote Lippmann. "He talked with the complete depth of impersonalness, and, as he himself said, 'I have never talked this way before to a soul.' He is anxious to tell in complete detail the forces and the purposes that have made and moved his life. He wants to tell it so that his own career may be of use 'to the young fellows' who come along."[29] Frankfurter's passion and hard work on Brandeis's behalf cemented a lifelong "half brother, half son" relationship between the two men, a relationship that led Brandeis to act as Frankfurter's financial patron for the time and effort the Harvard law professor put into future social welfare campaigns and other pro bono work.[30]

Frankfurter, however, did not lead the fight for Brandeis's confirmation. Brandeis's law partner Edward F. McClennen coordinated the confirmation process and appeared repeatedly before the Senate Judiciary subcommittee on the nominee's behalf.[31] In those days, Supreme Court nominees did not testify. Although he stayed away from Washington and heeded the attorney general's advice not to try to defend himself in person, Brandeis worked behind the scenes.[32] Neither he nor Frankfurter wanted the confirmation battle to be viewed as a Jewish fight or to characterize the opposition as anti-Semitic; they wanted to win on the merits.[33] And the Wilson administration did not want the confirmation fight to be viewed as an ideological struggle but as one that relied on Democratic Party loyalty.

The other person writing pro-Brandeis *New Republic* editorials besides Frankfurter was Walter Lippmann. For several weeks, Frankfurter had been encouraging Lippmann "to get [the magazine] in to the fight."[34] After attending the February 17 Senate hearings on the nomination, Lippmann left "with the feeling that *The New Republic* must get into the Brandeis fight with its heaviest guns."[35] He told Frankfurter about "a war council the other day— Norman Hapgood, George Rublee and I, and we decided that *The New Republic* was the paper that ought to do the aggressive fighting for Brandeis. There is no daily paper doing it and *Harper's Weekly* goes to press so late that they are almost out of it."[36] Frankfurter, who had investigated each of the issues, agreed and wanted to meet to discuss a plan of attack. He believed that "the fight is not Brandeis's fight, but our fight. ... [T]he situation is peculiarly one that belongs to the *New Republic*, for it presents in its concreteness loyalty to the ideas and forces in our national life that we care about."[37]

The night before he attended the hearings, Lippmann dined at 1720 Eye Street with Justice and Mrs. Holmes and discussed Brandeis's nomination.[38] Brandeis had admired Holmes since Holmes's lectures on *The Common Law* in 1881, lectures that revolutionized American jurisprudence and that helped transform Brandeis's vision of the law as based on facts and social scientific data. Holmes and Brandeis had been friends since Brandeis arrived in Boston in 1882 to practice law with Samuel Warren, a former associate in Holmes's law firm.[39] Their friendship continued after Holmes joined the Court. Brandeis often dined with the Holmeses when he came to Washington and on March 8, 1916, sent Holmes a telegram congratulating him on his seventy-fifth birthday.[40] Responding to charges that he did not believe in a written constitution, Brandeis replied to Attorney General Thomas Watt Gregory: "My views in regard to the constitution are as you know very much those of Mr. Justice Holmes."[41]

In truth, their philosophies differed though they often arrived at similar results. Brandeis believed in the efficacy of reform legislation; Holmes did not, but his personal doubts about such legislation did not render it unconstitutional.[42] Brandeis believed in a factual and scientific approach; Holmes was more of a philosopher-king. Their admiration for each other's intellectual gifts was deep and enduring. Holmes, like the other justices, remained publicly silent about Brandeis's nomination. Privately, Holmes expressed some unease about the unseemliness of the confirmation battle.[43] To Lippmann, he was more encouraging. Lippmann informed Brandeis that Holmes "spoke of you with such affection and admiration that I have come home feeling extremely happy."[44]

Lippmann pledged the *New Republic*'s support in the confirmation fight. He had known Brandeis for several years, and Brandeis had consulted him about past labor matters.[45] They agreed about the importance of organized labor in an industrial democracy. A vote for Brandeis was a vote for a more labor-friendly Supreme Court. "You know of course that all of us here look upon the fight as the most important one now taking place in this country ...," Lippmann wrote Brandeis. "The thing at stake is much greater than our personal affection for you."[46]

Two days after his letter, Lippmann met with Brandeis for three hours about the opposition's allegations about conflicts of interests in the United Shoe Machinery Company case and several family estate matters. During their discussion, Brandeis maintained his cold reserve. "I had to rub my eyes every once in a while and remind myself that the whole row was about him," Lippmann later wrote to FTC counsel Raymond Stevens. "We went over all the cases, especially the Shoe Case in a great deal of detail, and I am convinced that when we talked of it the other day we did not begin to realize how favorable to Brandeis all the facts were."[47]

Lippmann and Frankfurter were energized about the nomination fight and tackled each controversial issue that arose during the Senate hearings. In an unsigned March 4 editorial, Frankfurter answered charges that Brandeis had acted unethically as a counsel and director of the United Shoe Machinery Company.[48] Brandeis had resigned in 1907 after the company's president refused to alter contracts that compelled purchases of all the company's machines to buy a single product. In the ensuing years, the company acquired a competitor before that competitor could bring a rival machine to market. Several years after his resignation, Brandeis advised a potential competitor to United Shoe Machinery about how to draft legislation that would forbid such monopolistic practices.[49] His advice relied on no prior knowledge gained as counsel or director (as even the company's president conceded); he provided the advice pro bono; and he paid $25,000 to his law firm to compensate his partners for the time he had spent on the matter. The Shoe Machinery Company attacks on him began, the editorial asserted, only after the company faced federal antitrust charges and his subsequent testimony in favor of new legislation. "In good truth the Shoe Machinery case is proof," Frankfurter's unsigned editorial concluded, "perhaps more than any other event in his life, that Louis D. Brandeis is at once judicial, rarely courageous, possessed of an ardent and calm sense of justice which to him is truth in action."[50]

The theme of the *New Republic*'s campaign against Brandeis's Boston Brahmin opponents who had signed President Lowell's petition emerged from a chart that Lippmann had obtained from Brandeis.[51] The chart, prepared by one of the young lawyers in Brandeis's firm, revealed the social and economic connections among the signers by classifying them in overlapping categories of "Member Somerset Club," "Trustee or Banker," "State Street Office," "Back Bay Resident," and "Large Corporation Connections and Corporate Activities."[52] The chart, Lippmann informed Frankfurter, "is expected to raise more trouble than any other outrage ... which we have ever perpetrated here. It seems that I commit all the outrages and Herbert suffers all the trouble."[53] Croly sent the chart and accompanying editorial to publisher Willard Straight. The purpose of the editorial and chart, Croly's five-page letter explained, was to show that Boston was "an in growing community" that objected because Brandeis had taken on two of its biggest businesses, the New Haven Railroad and the United Shoe Machinery Company.[54] Straight, outraged by Brandeis's past criticisms of J. P. Morgan interests in the New Haven Railroad merger, killed the chart and watered down the editorial.[55] For nearly a century, the chart and Croly's letter to Straight hung in the office of the *New Republic*'s editor.[56]

Even without the chart, Lippmann's revised editorial exposed the insularity and small-mindedness of President Lowell's petition: "Mr. Brandeis has been a rebellious and troublesome member of the most homogeneous, self-centered and self-complacent community in the United States. ... It was a special community that had found Mr. Brandeis untrustworthy—the powerful but limited community which dominated the business and social life of Boston." The editorial declared that the petition signed by fifty-one Bostonians was a product of "group psychology" and not "fifty-one individual investigations" but "one investigation and one verdict which had been repeated so often that it ceased to require the confirmation of facts." After revealing the insular bonds among the petitioners, the editorial concluded: "They undertook to destroy the reputation of a man, to prevent a public servant from using his great abilities to the best public advantage. They have exhibited only their own disqualification to draw an indictment."[57]

Incensed that the president of Harvard had organized a campaign against the nomination of one of its most distinguished law school graduates and knowing that "Brandeis is simply paying the price for the rest of us," Frankfurter launched a counterattack from members of the Harvard community.[58] In February, the *Boston Post* published endorsements from nine of the eleven members of the Harvard law faculty.[59] Of the remaining two, one had been out of the country and unwilling to opine on the issue; the other, Edward "Bull" Warren, had clashed with Brandeis over a dispute about Boston's street railway consolidation bill.[60] A few months later, Harvard law dean Roscoe Pound and the revered former Harvard president Charles W. Eliot wrote letters to the Senate Judiciary Committee in support of the nomination. Pound argued that Brandeis was a "great lawyer" based on the "Brandeis Brief" in defense of the Oregon maximum hour law and

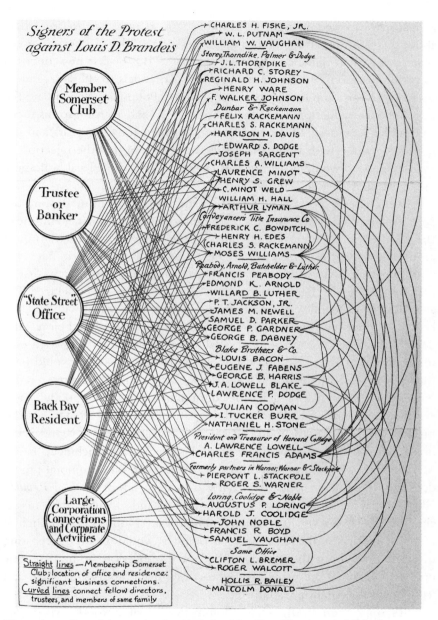

Chart about Brandeis nomination that the *New Republic* never published

a great scholar based on a groundbreaking 1890 *Harvard Law Review* article about the right to privacy. Pound also observed that the Harvard Board of Overseers, which included many leaders of the Boston bar now opposed to his nomination, had repeatedly appointed Brandeis to the law school's board of visitors. The Boston bar's "objections," Pound concluded, "are the unconscious product of fear of his political views and aversion to his social and public activities."[61] Eliot had known Brandeis for forty years and did not always agree with Brandeis's causes, but believed that the rejection of his nomination "would be a grave misfortune for the whole legal profession, the court, all American business, and the country."[62]

A week after exposing the nature of the opposition from Boston, the *New Republic* confronted the dissenting opinions of seven former American Bar Association presidents by singling out the motives of that letter's most prominent signer, William Howard Taft. Brandeis believed that Taft's opposition was a political blessing. Frankfurter and Lippmann knew that as counsel during the Ballinger-Pinchot Affair, Brandeis had disgraced Taft and Attorney General Wickersham by exposing that they had withheld and backdated their seventy-five-page investigatory memorandum before Taft's decision backing Interior Secretary Ballinger.[63] Lippmann's unsigned editorial dismissed Taft's opposition in a single paragraph. "One would have supposed that ex-President Taft was the last man qualified to express a judgment on Mr. Louis D. Brandeis," the editorial began. It then reminded readers how President Taft had "deceived the public" and then "tried to conceal his deception with a falsehood." "If Mr. Taft does not like Mr. Brandeis the human explanation is exceedingly simple," the editorial concluded. "It was Mr. Brandeis who demonstrated to the country Mr. Taft's immoral procedure in a disreputable incident."[64] Taft was so angry about the *New Republic* editorial that he considered suing the "socialistic and so-called uplift magazine" for libel.[65] Wickersham talked him out of it: "Nobody but a bunch of Hebrew uplifters of the same stripe as Brandeis would dream of repeating the criticism" about the Ballinger-Pinchot investigation.[66] The "Hebrew uplifters" included the magazine's editors Lippmann and Walter Weyl and its frequent contributor Frankfurter.

Taft's opposition to Brandeis's nomination went beyond revenge for Ballinger-Pinchot. His letters to confidant Gus Karger, a Washington correspondent for the *Cincinnati Times-Star* (a newspaper owned by Taft's half-brother), reveal the former president's deep-seated animus toward Brandeis. Based on a conversation with his New Haven friend Isaac Ullman, whom he described as sitting "on all the great Jewish committees," Taft asserted that Brandeis's devoted work on Zionist causes was a calculated reaction to his failed bid to be attorney general and enabled him to portray himself as a "representative Jew" and to show that he "has metaphorically been re-circumcised. ... If it were necessary, I am sure he would have grown a beard to convince them that he was a Jew of Jews."[67] This made it impossible, Taft argued, for Jews to oppose him and also made it impossible for Senators Lodge and Weeks to lead the opposition to Brandeis's nomination and thus risk alienating Boston's Jewish community. Lodge and Boston's most prominent citizens, Taft reminded Karger, "regard Brandeis as the most exalted type of the dishonest trickster."[68] Finally, Taft disclaimed that he was not motivated by a jealous desire to be on the Supreme Court.[69] Scholars have not portrayed Taft as anti-Semitic and have pointed out that the former president was dismayed at anti-Semitic remarks made about Brandeis.[70] Taft's friend, Gus Karger, was Jewish; Taft had included Brandeis's former brother-in-law, Charles Nagel, in his cabinet.[71] If not anti-Semitic, however, Taft's opposition to Brandeis was personal and ideological and strayed into using anti-Semitic stereotypes.

After the nineteenth and final day of Senate hearings, the *New Republic*'s March 25 editorial, "The Case against Brandeis," concluded that "those who followed the testimony knew that the case against Mr. Brandeis had collapsed by its own weight." The opposition had contradicted itself in charging Brandeis with resorting to any tactic to help his clients win and not being loyal enough to them: "Those who attacked him seemed unable to agree on whether he is a ruthless partisan, or a man who is not partisan enough." It then reviewed each of the charges against Brandeis, highlighted that he had alienated the "twin pillars" of the Boston business establishment in the United Shoe Machinery Company and the New Haven Railroad, and concluded: "The sense of betrayal is not based on evidence of particular betrayals. ... He has outraged a group loyalty."[72]

With all the evidence in, the Senate did what it often does—delay. Not just any delay, but the second-longest delay in the entire history of Supreme Court nominations. No Supreme Court nominee until Merrick Garland one hundred years later waited longer (117 days) for a committee vote than did Brandeis.[73] On April 3, 1916, the Senate Judiciary subcommittee voted, 3–2, along party lines to send Brandeis's nomination to the full committee. Then nothing happened. "The Senate of the United States is about 85 percent dignity, 14 percent bunkum and 1 percent horse sense," Lippmann wrote Frankfurter. "If the dignity is left to itself the horse sense will carry through. ... The real fact is probably that the Senate has got to confirm and it wants to seem to do it of its own free will. That also is dignity."[74]

Beginning in mid-March, Frankfurter was preoccupied with personal tragedy and professional responsibilities. He returned to New York City because his father, Leopold, had died on March 6 at age sixty.[75] "Yes, the world called him a failure—but it makes me have more respect for 'failures,' it makes me less interested in external standards ...," Frankfurter wrote Emory Buckner. "If you had known him my 'queerness' would be explicable to you and you would know the source of much that you like in me."[76]

Holmes and Brandeis had largely supplanted Leopold as Frankfurter's father figures. With Brandeis's nomination leaving the National Consumers' League in need of new counsel, Frankfurter assumed the lead role in defending labor laws before the Supreme Court. On April 11, Frankfurter arrived in Washington to defend Oregon's maximum hour law limiting all mill, factory, and manufacturing workers to ten hours per day (with up to three hours paid overtime). Frankfurter's brief, Belknap wrote in his diary, was "practically asking for an explicit overruling of Lochner v. N.Y."[77] Frankfurter stayed at the House of Truth and charmed its new residents. "He is ebullient as ever," Belknap wrote, "full of words & phrases with a joy for living."[78] Justice and Mrs. Holmes threw a dinner party for Frankfurter. Washington agreed with him. He enjoyed living in "the House here—Oh! It has ravaging absences for me—has the peace of the preciously familiar."[79]

While in Washington waiting for the Court to call his case, Frankfurter missed a House of Truth reunion in New York City. Percy was in town and ate lunch in the *New Republic* offices, then dined with Brandeis, Emory Buckner, Christie, Croly, Winfred Denison, Francis Hackett, Learned Hand, Stanley King, and Valentine. Only Frankfurter, among the House's original residents, was absent.[80] The Sunday before the dinner, he took the train to New York to see Percy but missed the midweek dinner because of his involvement in something "as vital as this case."[81] In addition to arguing the case, Frankfurter wrote a letter to the *Boston Evening Transcript* chiding the paper for crediting him with defending the Oregon law but failing to mention the lawyer who had written the brief and popularized the use of social scientific facts to defend such laws—Brandeis.[82]

After Frankfurter's oral argument, he and Lippmann continued to work behind the scenes on Brandeis's nomination. They had lined up people to speak on Brandeis's behalf but put their plans on hold. "Otherwise active endeavors have been stopped on alleged authoritative desire of Washington to lie low," Frankfurter wired Lippmann from Washington. "Cannot help feeling that policy of lying low giving clear field for misrepresentation by other side is all wrong."[83] By early May and with no further action in the Senate, Lippmann began to panic. He identified key recalcitrant senators in a meeting with Attorney General Gregory, who insisted that Brandeis would be confirmed based on Democratic Party loyalty. That night Lippmann, Norman Hapgood, and George Rublee met with Attorney General Gregory, Secretary of the Interior Lane, and Secretary of Labor William B. Wilson to discuss the best way to achieve Brandeis's confirmation. Lippmann wrote Frankfurter that we "talked over the thing and we shouted so hard at the Attorney General that this ought to be an administration matter that when he left he said with a confidential voice: 'I think something will happen within the next forty-eight hours that will please you boys.'"[84]

President Wilson ended the delay, orchestrating an inquiry about Brandeis's nomination from Senate Judiciary Committee chairman Charles Culberson and replying with a letter that the president released to the press.[85] The charges, Wilson wrote based on a memorandum from his attorney general, "threw a great deal more light upon the character and motives of those with whom they originated than upon the qualifications of Mr. Brandeis." Wilson had investigated those charges when considering Brandeis for the cabinet, had gotten to know him over the years, and respected his talents as a lawyer and his record of public service. "I nominated Mr. Brandeis for the Supreme Court," Wilson concluded, "because it was, and is, my delib-erate judgment that, of all the men now at the bar whom it has been my privilege to observe, test, and know, he is exceptionally qualified."[86] Wilson had stirred the Senate into action, but the final vote was still in doubt. "The President's letter helps," Hapgood wrote Lippmann, "but by no means settles it."[87]

Wilson and members of the cabinet must have agreed with Hapgood be-cause they corralled the votes of opposed Democrats on the Senate Judiciary Committee. Hapgood arranged for two senators, Hoke Smith of Georgia and James Reed of Missouri, to meet Brandeis at an informal party in New York City, and after the meeting they agreed to vote yes.[88] Wilson won the vote of Senator James O'Gorman of New York by urging the British to commute the death sentence of a New York resident to ten years' imprison-ment.[89] Wilson charmed Senator Lee Overman of North Carolina during a May 20 train trip to Charlotte, North Carolina. Wilson stopped the train in

Overman's hometown of Salisbury and praised the senator; Overman voted for Brandeis.[90] And Wilson's son-in-law and Treasury Secretary McAdoo lobbied a fellow Tennessean, Senator John Shields.[91] Wilson confided to his future biographer Ray Stannard Baker that he had lobbied senators to confirm Brandeis and George Rublee as FTC commissioner because "the only way for a party to live was to be going somewhere—moving—in short, being *progressive*."[92]

On May 24, 117 days after Wilson nominated Brandeis, the Senate Judiciary Committee voted 10–8, along strict party lines, to send the nomination to the Senate floor. A week later, the Senate voted to confirm him, 47–22. Only three Republicans—Robert La Follette of Wisconsin, George W. Norris of Nebraska, and Miles Poindexter of Washington—voted for Brandeis; the other forty-four votes came from Democrats. The remaining twenty-seven senators present abstained.[93] Wilson's party-based strategy carried the day.

The big winner was Wilson, who had endeared himself to those who had worked so hard to confirm Brandeis—Frankfurter, Lippmann, and the *New Republic*. Some of their friends hoped that they would move on, as Valentine quipped, "now that Mr. Brandeis is safely on the Supreme Court and Felix's judgments are at last swinging back toward normal."[94] Frankfurter and his *New Republic* allies knew, however, that the Supreme Court battle was not over. In many ways, it had just begun. "The Brandeis case is closed," the magazine's editorial concluded. "The country has been spared humiliation, and the authority of the Court has been immeasurably strengthened." But the editorial warned that future nominees, some of them conservative, might be afforded the same treatment that Brandeis had received: "Mr. Brandeis's enemies have done more to drag the Supreme Court into politics than the most extreme radical."[95]

★★★

The House of Truth's shift from Roosevelt to Wilson began with the Brandeis nomination and continued with Wilson's war policies. During his ten-day tour of the Midwest after nominating Brandeis, the president touted the benefits of military preparedness. The *New Republic* praised Wilson's preparedness campaign for "converting it into a political asset rather than a liability."[96] Wilson, the magazine argued, had improved his negotiating position with Germany, had silenced Roosevelt, and had "made it increasingly difficult for ordinary pacifist Democrats and militarist Republicans to oppose him."[97] The editorial cited the preparedness campaign and the Brandeis nomination as signs that Wilson was asserting his leadership over the country: "If the President holds to his present militant course he may become what he has hitherto failed to be—a forerunner, a leavening intellectual and moral ferment, a leader and moulder of progressive opinion."[98]

Though it recognized some of Wilson's past foreign policy failures in Mexico, the *New Republic* assailed critics of his approach to the war in Europe as second-guessers with no plan of their own.[99] Indeed, the magazine praised Wilson's response to the *Sussex* crisis. On March 24, a German U-boat had torpedoed the *Sussex*, a French ferry, which the Germans mistook for a minelaying vessel. Of the eighty casualties, twenty-five were Americans. On April 19, Wilson addressed Congress and vowed to sever diplomatic relations with Germany unless it stopped sinking passenger and merchant ships. Realizing that it was on the brink of war with the United States, Germany acceded to Wilson's demands. The magazine declared that the president's "decision to settle accounts with Germany may be one of the most momentous acts in American history," one that would "transform" American foreign policy.[100]

In a May 27 speech to the League to Enforce Peace, Wilson signaled an end to American isolationism. Only an international organization and co-operation could end the war, avert armed US involvement, and create a lasting peace. Wilson's speech, Lippmann's editorial declared, "may well mark a decisive point in the history of the modern world";[101] Lippmann believed that it was "one of the greatest utterances since the Monroe Doctrine."[102] To Percy, who was still working for the British government and hopeful for more US involvement, Lippmann wrote: "We all think it was a highly significant one in that it is practically the first official statement ever made in America that we were ready to do our part and take our responsibilities in the world at large."[103]

As he became more confident in Wilson's leadership on international affairs, Lippmann became more disenchanted with the militarism of Roosevelt. "I am pretty well convinced that T.R. will not do ...," Lippmann wrote Frankfurter in January 1916 after Roosevelt's criticism of Wilson's nonintervention in Mexico. "After all, you and I have been banking on a theoretical Roosevelt, a potential Roosevelt, but not the Roosevelt who at this moment is actually at work."[104] During the next several months, Roosevelt's second-guessing of Wilson's foreign policy seemed to confirm Lippmann's assessment. In March, the magazine's editors objected to

Roosevelt's criticisms of Wilson's failure to protest Germany's invasion of Belgium because Roosevelt's own 1914 *Outlook* articles about Belgium had been isolationist.[105] This inconsistency "shocked" Lippmann about "how [Roosevelt's] mind works."[106]

Lippmann feared Roosevelt's entry into the 1916 presidential race. In March, Roosevelt declared that he had no interest in the Republican nomination or in running in any presidential primaries. He blasted the "unmanly failure" of the Wilson administration and looked forward to the party conventions in Chicago in June.[107] His statement, however, left open the possibility of accepting the Republican nomination if a divided convention led to a draft Roosevelt movement. Lippmann explained his objections to his pro-Roosevelt publisher, Willard Straight. "Roosevelt is the best man in sight for the job, but Roosevelt himself is not one man but many men ...," Lippmann wrote. "If Roosevelt is nominated this campaign is going to be the most crucial test of our independence that has ever been presented to us."[108] Lippmann expected that the magazine would have "to lean towards Roosevelt," but it would not refrain from criticizing him.[109] As the Republican Party and Progressive Party conventions approached in Chicago, Lippmann considered other candidates. "My preference is for [Justice Charles Evans] Hughes although I am not at all certain that I shall not line up for Wilson in the end," Lippmann wrote Percy. "T.R. gets on my nerve so much these days that I shall become a typical anti-Roosevelt maniac if I do not look out."[110]

The Republican Convention disgusted Lippmann. He described it in the *New Republic* as "a nightmare, a witches' dance of idiocy and adult hypocrisy" and deplored how the name of Abraham Lincoln was "mauled and dragged about" and "taken in vain and his spirit degraded, prostituted to every insincerity and used as window dressing for every cheap politician."[111] The Republicans were angry that Roosevelt had betrayed them four years earlier and refused to nominate him. Instead, they tapped Hughes, a sitting Supreme Court justice and former governor of New York. The *New Republic* described him as "a man of unimpeachable moral independence and austere personal integrity" and urged him to woo the 1.5 million people who had voted for Roosevelt in 1912, not by running an anti-Wilson campaign but by laying out his ideas for the future.[112]

As bad as the Republican Convention was, Lippmann thought that the Progressive Party convention was worse. The Progressives had tried and failed to bluff the Republican Party into nominating Roosevelt. Instead, they nominated Roosevelt only to see him decline the nomination and insult them by suggesting that the party nominate his archconservative friend Henry Cabot Lodge.[113] Roosevelt then urged the Progressives to join forces with Republicans, and he endorsed Hughes against Wilson.[114] The *New Republic* eulogized the Progressive Party and blamed its death on Roosevelt: "Its epitaph should read: 'Here lie the remains of a party which lived to make Theodore Roosevelt President of the United States and died as the penalty of its failure.'"[115] The magazine's lead editorial described Roosevelt as "a militant moralistic nationalist" and suggested that in order to remain politically relevant he should run for the US Senate.[116]

Not everyone associated with the House of Truth had given up on Roosevelt, especially Borglum. The sculptor had attended the Progressive Party convention with the hopes of uniting the Progressive and Republican parties behind his own preferred candidate—General Leonard Wood. A former army chief of staff, Wood was Roosevelt's friend and had been commander of their Rough Rider volunteer army unit during the Spanish–American War. Borglum believed that he needed only one thing to make Wood's nomination a reality—Roosevelt's endorsement. He claimed that Roosevelt privately supported Wood but held out long enough for the Republican nomination and then endorsed Lodge, effectively killing Wood's chances. "[Roosevelt] seems with all his magnificent power and opportunity determined to be completely ruined," Borglum wrote Wood.[117] Borglum's disappointment soon gave way to anger: "Mr. Roosevelt double-crossed his best friend—about the only big friend of the old group he has left. I shall never forget it, nor forgive him."[118] Borglum nonetheless knew that the Republican Party was "pretty well satisfied with Hughes" and predicted that Hughes would defeat Wilson.[119]

Lippmann, on the other hand, returned from both conventions even more convinced that Wilson would prevail.[120] Though Hughes was "able and respectable," his election meant "a return of the most evil-smelling plutocracy that the country has." In Lippmann's mind, Hughes was "a pretty conservative man and his party was unspeakable."[121] By contrast, Wilson was gaining in stature because of his improved foreign policy and his support for the Allies.[122] Lippmann, therefore, attempted to promote the president's re-election bid to his friends from the House of Truth. He told Frankfurter to forget about Roosevelt: "He does not understand industrial preparedness; he does not know what he means by social justice. He has no vision of the class struggle and you cannot jolly him into an understanding."[123] Hughes,

Lippmann wrote Frankfurter, "has not said one word that is interesting."[124] To Percy, Lippmann predicted that Wilson's foreign policy would be better than the alternative and described Hughes as "protectionist" regarding tariffs, industry, and military affairs.[125]

All this revealed that Lippmann was becoming increasingly close with the Wilson administration. He and Croly began meeting with Wilson's influential adviser Colonel Edward M. House.[126] Lippmann's letters to Senator Henry F. Hollis of New Hampshire were often passed on to the president. After Lippmann complimented Wilson's May 27 speech at the League to Enforce Peace, the president replied: "I value his high opinion very much indeed."[127] Lippmann also began corresponding with Wilson's secretary of war, Newton D. Baker, who passed along Lippmann's comments to Wilson. Through Baker, Lippmann urged Wilson to use an upcoming speech to address "the economic war after the war," including international economic alliances and tariffs.[128]

Despite Lippmann's hard turn toward Wilson, the *New Republic* remained "perched on the fence." After the Democrats renominated Wilson in St. Louis, the magazine argued that though "valid reasons exist for preferring Mr. Wilson to Mr. Hughes or Mr. Hughes to Mr. Wilson they cannot from the point of view of *The New Republic* be called decisive."[129] Some of it was a personal dislike of Wilson, his sanctimonious attitude, and his professorial tone. Some of it was a wait-and-see approach to Hughes, whether he would embrace progressive ideas during the campaign or just attack Wilson. Some of it was skepticism about both parties, the pro-business and antilabor platform of the Republicans and the southern and antilabor stance of the Democrats. The magazine viewed both parties as obstacles to change. Finally, some of it involved a dance with Willard Straight, the magazine's pro-Roosevelt publisher and a rock-ribbed Republican. "I am enclosing a note from one of the writers for the *New Republic*," *Harper's* editor and Wilson confidant Norman Hapgood wrote the president. "They are having a hard time with themselves."[130]

One *New Republic* writer requesting an interview with President Wilson was a twenty-three-year-old British Socialist and Oxford graduate named Harold Laski. Though he had been one of Laski's earliest champions, Hapgood was reluctant to recommend that the president see him for even fifteen minutes.[131] British Socialists were not often granted White House interviews. Then again, Hapgood knew that Laski was no ordinary Socialist. He had discovered Laski, an instructor in history at McGill University, in

1914 in Montreal and told Frankfurter to go to Canada to meet "an extraordinary young man."[132] During an early spring 1915 visit to Ottawa to see Loring Christie, Frankfurter stopped in Montreal to meet Laski. "Everything that Hapgood said about his extraordinary qualities," Frankfurter recalled, "was verified within an hour."[133]

Laski was Hapgood's discovery, but he was Frankfurter's creation. Frankfurter introduced Laski—bespectacled, "undersized, sparse looking, Oxford all over and under" in his three-piece suits—to the House of Truth and to the editors at the *New Republic*.[134] Laski quickly ingratiated himself with his tall tales about beating the American tennis champion, his precocious intelligence, his belief in organized labor, and his powerful pen.[135] By June 1915, Laski was writing book reviews for the *New Republic*. That summer, Frankfurter began trumpeting Laski's reviews and forthcoming *Harvard Law Review* article as part of a larger plan—to bring Laski to Harvard.[136] Beginning in the fall of 1916, he arranged an instructorship for Laski teaching government and political theory. Frankfurter asked his closest friends to finance Laski's $2,000 salary so that the instructor could support his wife, Frida, and young daughter on the way.[137] Five years earlier, Laski had been disowned by his family of wealthy British Jews for marrying a non-Jew.[138] Finally, Frankfurter helped Laski enroll in the law school so that he could one day join him and Pound on the faculty as a legal historian and public law scholar.[139] "Poor President Lowell," Frankfurter wrote, "doesn't know what a rebel we concealed in the Trojan horse when we rolled Laski in."[140]

In July 1916, Frankfurter bestowed his most enduring gift upon Laski—a trip to Beverly Farms to meet Justice Holmes.[141] Thus began a lifelong friendship between Holmes and Laski and one of the most remarkable exchanges of correspondence in the history of American and British letters. With his ties to Holmes and Frankfurter and his fast friendship with Valentine, Laski became an integral member of the House of Truth crowd and an important voice in the *New Republic*.[142] Randolph Bourne, a *New Republic* staff member, declared that Laski, Frankfurter, and Lippmann "make up a Jewish trinity which is the wonder of the world or, at least, of my world."[143]

Though he did not grant Laski an interview, Wilson was intrigued by the young man's letter. Hapgood explained that Laski wanted to hear what the president had been telling others in private about a more liberal direction for the country, but Hapgood believed that Wilson's "big legislative program, your foreign policy and your two last appointments to the supreme court are more than enough to prove to any observant mind that you are

Harold Laski with wife, Frida, and daughter, Diana

the real liberal leader." Hapgood, however, also advised Wilson that many former Bull Moosers were undecided about the election and would be more inclined to vote for a Democrat but wanted "an expression of general liberal doctrine, especially in the form of a program for the future."[144] One of those undecided Bull Moosers, Learned Hand, was still on the fence and wanted to hear more about plans for Wilson's second term. Hand, Hapgood informed Wilson, was a "Federal Judge and a man of much intelligence and some influence. His view is interesting to me, because I have never known an election in which the number of persons on the fence was nearly as large as it is today."[145]

With Hughes's presidential run leaving a vacancy on the Supreme Court, Wilson had another opportunity to appeal to Hand, Frankfurter, and other former progressives. What they feared was another McReynolds. Frankfurter counted only three justices with "a consistently open-minded and forward-looking point of view"—Brandeis, Day, and Holmes—and the latter two were getting up in years. Other members of the Court, Frankfurter argued, had "very little experience in or imagination about the forces and the needs of a modern industrial democracy."[146] Frankfurter advised House that Wilson should nominate former solicitor general Frederick W. Lehmann or Attorney General Gregory.[147] After Gregory declined the appointment, Wilson chose a liberal federal district judge from Cleveland, John Hessin Clarke.[148]

Clarke was important in light of Wilson's significant legislative achievements, socioeconomic legislation that endeared him to liberals by using the federal government to regulate the economy and to stand up for small businesses and the rights of labor. The president had signed the Federal Reserve Act creating the Federal Reserve System, the Federal Trade Commission Act to prevent unfair competition, the Clayton Antitrust Act to aid in the prosecution of monopolies and to protect labor unions, and the Keating-Owen Child Labor Act banning the transportation of goods across state lines made by children. On September 1, Wilson signed the federal child labor law "with real emotion."[149]

Wilson's stature with liberals continued to grow with his handling of the nationwide railroad strike. He met with representatives from labor and management and addressed a joint session of Congress on August 29 to urge the passage of legislation limiting interstate railroad workers to eight-hour days plus overtime pay.[150] Congress quickly complied, and Wilson signed the Adamson Act into law. He earned bonus points by naming George Rublee, who had served on the FTC as a recess appointee but whose nomination had been blocked by the Senate, to a three-person commission entrusted with enforcing the railroad law.[151] That October, the AFL's Samuel Gompers endorsed Wilson and encouraged the union's members to vote to re-elect the president.[152]

Yet as hard as he worked to court liberals and organized labor, Wilson brushed aside pleas from prominent black leaders, including W. E. B. Du Bois. Writing on behalf of the NAACP, Du Bois informed Wilson that his false promises of justice had "grievously disappointed us." Du Bois referred to the dismissal of black public officials, the segregation of the federal civil

service, and the administration's silence about lynching, black disenfranchisement, and southern segregation. He offered Wilson an opportunity to
make a statement on these issues.[153] As he did with an earlier letter from
Georgia Nugent of the National Association of Colored Women about
the president's position on lynching, Wilson delegated a response to his
personal secretary, Joseph Tumulty.[154] Leading black newspapers reacted to
Wilson's record on race and his unwillingness to court black voters by
urging their readers to vote for Hughes.[155] In a June 1916 article, "The
Superfluous Negro," the *New Republic* opined that immigration and racial
prejudice often limited the job prospects and economic mobility of northern blacks. "We often wonder," the article said, "what the reflective Negro
thinks as he listens to our orators, who welcome the Immigrant to this land
of liberty, to this free world of opportunity for all men." The article held
out hope that limited immigration during wartime might provide economic opportunities for northern blacks.[156] Yet the *New Republic* remained
silent about Wilson's stance toward people of color. Race was simply not
a compelling issue as the magazine and its editors decided on their presidential candidate.

That summer, Wilson invited Lippmann to the summer White House
in Shadow Lawn, New Jersey. The two men sat on the upstairs veranda.
Lippmann, who was satisfied with Wilson's foreign policy and support for
the League to Enforce Peace, asked about the president's domestic views.
Wilson, however, wanted to talk about how, after the election, the Germans
intended to declare unilateral submarine warfare.[157] "I came back and told
that to Croly and the other editors," Lippmann recalled, "and said, 'Now
we'll face it. What we're electing is a war President—not the man who kept
us out of war—and we've got to make up our minds whether we want
to go through the war with Hughes or with Wilson.'"[158] By late August,
Lippmann had moved closer to endorsing Wilson.[159] He applauded the
president's response to the potential railroad strike and rejected Hughes's
criticism of the Adamson Act as putting legislation ahead of investigation as
"pure buncum."[160] In "The Puzzle of Hughes," Lippmann described "the
evolution of a distinguished man into an undistinguished candidate."[161] Two
weeks later, in "The Case for Wilson," Lippmann touted the president's
legislative achievements and his League to Enforce Peace speech as proof
of his "extraordinary growth" and lauded Wilson's ability to transform the
Democratic Party into "the only party which at this moment is national is
scope, liberal in purpose, and effective in action."[162]

In September, Lippmann pushed Croly and the *New Republic* to endorse Wilson.[163] A week after Lippmann's endorsement, Croly announced his support for Wilson but "reluctantly and only after prolonged hesitation."[164] A lifelong Republican and Roosevelt supporter, Croly had started the magazine partly as a counterweight to Hapgood's pro-Wilson *Harper's Weekly* and to the Jeffersonian Democratic principles of Wilson's New Freedom. It was remarkable, then, that a few years later Croly would praise the Democratic Party as the party of nationalism. Indeed, Croly now supported Wilson for many of the same reasons that moved Lippmann—for transforming the Democratic Party into "the more promising of the two party organizations," for incorporating "progressive principles,"[165] and for learning from past foreign policy mistakes.[166]

The endorsement of Croly's magazine soon followed. On October 28, the lead *New Republic* editorial wondered what had happened to Hughes's progressivism as governor of New York and viewed Wilson and the Democratic Party as their best hope for the future of liberalism. "The defeat of Mr. Wilson and the triumph of Mr. Hughes would be interpreted as a liberal setback and would increase the formidable obstacles to the success of the liberal cause," the editorial stated. The magazine vowed, just as it had in the past, not to be pro- or anti-Wilson in the future. But for now, the magazine supported the president for re-election.

The *New Republic*'s endorsement of Wilson was not without controversy. In the same issue, the magazine's publisher Willard Straight wrote about why he supported Hughes. Straight credited Wilson with "certain admirable pieces of legislation" but believed that Wilson had "lowered the prestige of the United States" and "aggravated the problems which the American people will be called upon to face in connection with the world readjustment after the European war." Straight, who had vetoed the publication of the chart about the Boston interests arrayed against Brandeis's nomination, praised the magazine as an experiment and expressed his continued support for the venture.[167] At least Straight did not prevent the magazine from endorsing Wilson. The agreement to disagree about the election, the *New York Times* observed, was "[e]vidence of editorial independence."[168]

Frankfurter's endorsement of Wilson was nearly as tortured as the *New Republic*'s. As much as he admired Hughes as a justice and a person and preferred his personality to Wilson's, Frankfurter backed the president. Wilson's nomination of Brandeis, his support for the federal child labor law and the eight-hour day for railroad workers, and his improvement in the international sphere all swayed Frankfurter. Frankfurter was neither a committed Democrat nor an ardent Republican; he was, however, committed to liberal ideas about government regulation and socioeconomic legislation. It was a close call, but in 1916 he voted for Wilson. In late October, he circulated a twenty-three-page memorandum about the candidates to close friends and mentors such as Hand, Holmes, Christie, Stimson, and Valentine.[169]

Like Frankfurter, Valentine was not keen on either man, but saw Wilson as the lesser of two evils. After reading Frankfurter's memorandum, Valentine expressed frustration with Hughes's comments about organized labor. "Apparently his whole conception of the labor movement is included within the pale of protection," Valentine wrote. Valentine worried about Hughes's vow to intervene in the volatile political situation in Mexico, vague remarks about big business, and parting comment that his supporters "'believe in the honesty of the working man.'"[170]

Frankfurter's mentors Holmes and Stimson, on the other hand, were loyal Republicans who backed Hughes. Holmes had admired Hughes on the Court, and Stimson had served as an aide to Hughes's campaign. "Your paper is forceful and candid," Holmes wrote Frankfurter. "I will not attempt to state what I consider fundamental facts in the controversy, but will unite with you in the prayer, May the Best Man Win."[171]

The 1916 election was one of the closest in American history. On election night, Wilson refused to concede defeat to Hughes until the returns from western states came in. He went to bed at midnight not knowing the outcome but assumed that Hughes had won. Two days later, thanks to a narrow victory in California (4,000 votes), Wilson was declared the winner with 277 electoral votes to Hughes's 254 and 9.1 million popular votes to Hughes's 8.6. Many factors, large and small, contributed to Wilson's victory and Hughes's defeat. In hindsight, Hughes's unintentional snub of California Governor Hiram Johnson at a Long Beach hotel in August may have cost him the election. After the snub, Johnson refused to help Hughes's candidacy.[172]

Wilson's victory was aided by the support of liberals who had backed Roosevelt, including Frankfurter and Lippmann. Brandeis's nomination started it all. Wilson's pro-labor legislation and internationalist stance on the war also helped. After Wilson's re-election, Frankfurter and his friends returned to power in his administration, put their liberal ideas about government and labor in action, and reunited at the House of Truth.

8

Our Founder

Four days before the 1916 presidential election, Valentine convened a meeting of the Bureau of Industrial Audit at the offices of the *New Republic*. Croly, Lippmann, Frankfurter, former New Hampshire governor Robert Bass, journalist and labor researcher Robert W. Bruère, and Valentine's partner Ordway Tead discussed two industries plagued by labor disputes during the summer of 1916—New York City's transit system and garment industry.[1]

Valentine wanted the group's advice on how to navigate New York City politics so that he could conduct an industrial audit of the New York Railways and Rapid Transit Company. In August, he helped Mayor John Purroy Mitchel negotiate an end to the transit strike.[2] "Congratulations on your brilliant tramway settlement," Stanley King wired him. "You have become a national figure."[3] From his friends at the *New Republic*, Valentine wanted advice on when he should release his proposed report on the garment industry. All summer long he had served on an arbitration board along with its chairman, Judge Mack, and had attempted to bring peace to the industry and to implement a new protocol that included a minimum wage and other fair labor practices.

In the previous year or so, Valentine's industrial counseling business had begun to receive national recognition. In July 1915, Richard Washburn Child wrote an article for *Harper's Weekly*, "The Human Audit," explaining that "until three years ago, when Robert G. Valentine, formerly Indian Commissioner of the United States, became the pioneer, the profession of labor auditing was unknown."[4] In January 1916, *American Magazine* published a photograph of Valentine, wearing glasses and a suit and tie, sitting outside at a table underneath a tree, work in hand and a pot of daises beside him. Describing him as the country's "First Expert in Industrial Relations" and "the only man in America who is a whole profession all by himself," the magazine recounted some of his successes—how he had advised Boston's female telephone operators in their labor negotiations and had persuaded an industrial client to permit union representation—both of which averted strikes. Valentine boldly stated one of the primary goals of industrial counseling: "I will settle strikes before they ever become strikes."[5]

Valentine's business thrived because he had the courage to implement part of the "Social Program" that he and Frankfurter had outlined on the living room floor of the House of Truth when they had discovered "the center of the universe." Through his work in industrial relations, Valentine strengthened the bonds between the House of Truth and the *New Republic*. He made the groups realize that they did not need the Progressive Party or Roosevelt to further their pro-labor agenda. He pushed them to clarify their ideas about organized labor and showed how those ideas could be implemented. He was the group's leading idealist but also its true reformer who was experimenting with his ideas. Even though he no longer lived there, Valentine was the House of Truth's spiritual leader.

Valentine, "the nation's first industrial counselor"

Valentine forced his friends to explain what they meant by industrial democracy. On March 7, 1916, he sent a letter to a dozen people, including Frankfurter and *New Republic* editors Lippmann, Croly, Weyl, Hackett, and Alvin Johnson. "I find among my clients an increasing desire, becoming in many cases pathetically insistent, to have a definition of 'Industrial Democracy,' and should be deeply grateful if you could give me your definition of Industrial Democracy," Valentine wrote. "As a sort of take-off, I enclose a document containing a definition which I recently gave to a man. How wrong is it?" To most of his friends, industrial democracy meant that workers received representation in business through organized labor. But to Valentine, industrial democracy meant that all parties—owners, managers, workers, state governments, and the federal government—played a role in "the government of industry."[6]

Valentine's letter "stumped" Lippmann. During the last two years, Lippmann had considered him an intimate friend and had consulted him about their interests in the labor movement while "working for some time on some articles about his experiments."[7] Though Lippmann could not provide a better definition of industrial democracy, he believed that it meant that "every adult has enough education not only to do a job but to know why he is doing a job," and "every adult is sufficiently insured for the primary needs of life so that he is capable of making some kind of free contract with other men." "Sufficient education and a sufficient stake in the community," Lippmann concluded, "are necessary to what in the modern sense we may call a free man."[8]

For much of the spring and summer of 1916, Valentine was in New York City helping to avert a garment industry strike. He had taken Brandeis's place on the arbitration board and in maintaining the agreement between management and labor known as the protocol. He spent a lot of time conferring with both sides, with arbitration chairman Julian Mack, and with Brandeis.[9]

Like Valentine, Brandeis believed that scientific management could benefit organized labor. In January 1911, Brandeis had employed scientific management techniques to cross-examine railroad executives, and based on this testimony he had submitted a brief to the Interstate Commerce Commission opposing railroad rate increases.[10] He had helped negotiate an end to the 1910 New York City garment workers' strike by establishing a protocol that consisted of a board of grievances with appeals to a board of arbitration.[11] Indeed, it was Brandeis who had recommended Valentine as chairman of the Massachusetts Minimum Wage Commission and presumably as the new head of the protocol.

The protocol, which had been in place for five years, may have been Brandeis's brainchild, but it was Valentine's job to keep it going. Valentine found himself avoiding grievances and arbitration by mediating disputes between the unions and manufacturers. The agreement with the dress and waist industry was imperiled by a strike of 60,000 cloak, suit, and skirt workers. "Things …," Valentine wrote in May, "are very brittle, & the best hope through them is mediation, & I think I am strengthening my powers as a mediator."[12]

Valentine's presence in New York enabled him to build his business with help from his friends. Thanks to a letter of introduction from Frankfurter, Valentine met in Chicago with Sears, Roebuck's Julius Rosenwald.[13] Governor Bass and his wife joined in the garment mediation and planned on entering the industrial counseling business.[14] Denison, back from the Philippines, was helping with legal research about some of Brandeis's prior arbitration decisions.[15] Valentine was doing his part. "Yesterday, partly at my instance," he wrote on May 17, "the Board of Arbitration *mediated* a case which would have probably split the Protocol if it had been *decided*."[16]

Valentine was making ends meet with the income from his industrial counseling business and the rent from the House of Truth.[17] He had taken in two partners, Ordway Tead and Richard Gregg.[18] He helped the mayor of New York City avert a transit strike. And that fall, he was finishing a report about a new protocol for the dress and waist industry.[19] "After conference with dress executive protocol looks hopeful," Bruère wired him in mid-September. "Free your mind of worry. God bless you and bring you back refreshed."[20]

Valentine was spending so much time in New York that he wanted to move his wife and daughter there after the election.[21] All the talk about the future made him think about his mortality. "When I die I don't want you to build any romantic sorrow around me," he wrote his wife, Sophie, on September 24. "Whatever you feel about me now it will be your duty to feel about me then. The slightest word or thought that I was any good to you more than I was will not be honest."[22]

Less than two weeks later, the garment industry needed Valentine back in New York City. On Saturday, November 11, he kissed Sophie and headed for the train station. The next day, he attended a conference in Scarsdale, and on Monday he worked all day in his New York City office. He sent a telegram to Brandeis and left to meet Frankfurter.[23]

At 11:00 p.m., Valentine checked into the Hotel Manhattan at Forty-Second and Madison Avenue, near his office. He dropped off his things and joined Frankfurter and friends three blocks away for a late-night dinner at Delmonico's. Frankfurter had invited Emory Buckner, Sam Rosensohn, and the Harvard psychiatrist and criminologist Herman Adler to join them.

Around midnight at the restaurant, Valentine fell ill. His friends helped him back to the hotel and called the hotel doctor.[24] Dr. McIntyre arrived quickly, but there was nothing he could do—Valentine had suffered a massive heart attack.[25]

Valentine was calm and in good spirits despite obvious pain. He was the "master of the situation" and seemed more concerned that Frankfurter was going to miss his train back to Boston than about himself. With his friends at his bedside, Valentine gently fell asleep in the early morning hours and never woke up. He was forty-four.[26] "Poor Valentine died of heart failure after a gallant and cheering struggle," Frankfurter wired Brandeis at 3:44 a.m. "His last act before the attack was to telegram to you which he showed me with deep feeling."[27] Upon arriving home in Boston, Frankfurter sent Sophie red roses along with a note: "With love from House of Truth to our founder."[28]

Newspaper coverage of Valentine's death was sparse, in part because he had died after the morning papers had gone to press and because, unlike Frankfurter and Brandeis, the press did not understand his contributions to labor relations. Most obituaries focused on Valentine's dispute with Taft over the religious garb order. A few mentioned his prior career as an investment banker. Most failed to grasp his growing profile as an industrial relations expert, his work on the Massachusetts Minimum Wage Commission, and his behind-the-scenes role in averting strikes in Boston and New York. None conveyed what Valentine meant to the *New Republic* and the House of Truth.

Valentine's friends made sure that he and his ideas would not be forgotten. "His larger plans were about to mature," Lippmann wrote in an unsigned *New Republic* editorial, "the opportunity for a full test of his ideas had been won, his own novitiate was over, when senselessly, capriciously so it seems now, he was stricken."[29] Lippmann's editorial revealed how much the magazine's editors had absorbed Valentine's ideas about the benefits of a fair minimum wage but only with regular employment, scientific management for labor, and industrial audits for management. For Valentine combined the balance of idealism and scientific expertise that they admired most. "Valentine had hold of the largest truth which inspires the experiment under which he lived," Lippmann wrote. "He testified splendidly to the fact that opinion based on class feeling, drawn from motives unanalyzed, breeds tyranny and disorder, that science is the only method of thought through which democracy can be workable."[30]

Other progressive publications lauded Valentine and his pioneering work. "Such a man," an *Outlook* editorial said, "should be counted among the real makers of America."[31] His client Henry P. Kendall attested to Valentine's vision and impact on industry. "To know Mr. Valentine," Kendall wrote in *The Survey*, "was to respect and admire him, and one could not commune with him long without getting a wider vision of our industrial and social life."[32] The *Independent* ran a long article, written before Valentine's death, about his new profession of industrial counseling. "In the weeks since this article was written, Robert Valentine has suddenly died," the magazine added. "But the profession which he invented, the new method of reconciliation and readjustment of the human relations in industry which he created, will not die."[33]

Frankfurter lived up to the nicknames that Robert, Sophie, and their daughter, Sophia, had been calling him for years—Mr. Fix It, Mr. Fix, or simply Fix. Frankfurter took control of the funeral arrangements. He wired Valentine's friends and admirers, including Theodore Roosevelt. "Your husband," Roosevelt wrote Sophie the day before the funeral, "was one of the most upright and efficient public servants, and one of the most disinterested and fearlessly independent citizens, whom it has ever been my good fortune to know. There were in all the United States few more valuable men. He was one of the staunchest and most loyal of friends. I mourn his loss."[34]

Frankfurter consulted with Sophie and chose the other pallbearers—Governor Bass, Judge Mack, and Kendall; Valentine's business partners Tead and Gregg; his college classmates John Palfrey, Eliot Jones, and Joseph Cotton; and House of Truth visitor Stanley King—and included Laski among the ushers.[35] Frankfurter rode with Sophie, who wore Robert's favorite purple dress, to Boston's Trinity Church. The day before the November 17 funeral, Frankfurter read to her from Holmes's 1884 Memorial Day address and "The Soldier's Faith." "'The man who wrote that,'" she remarked, "'knew Robert before their hands met.'"[36]

Sophie and Robert had gone through so much to get married, overcoming familial opposition, their bouts of depression, and his lack of employment. He would never see their six-year-old daughter, Sophia (whose name was later changed to Charlotte in honor of Robert's mother), grow up. Two days after his death, Sophie wrote a letter that she enclosed in a small envelope labeled "My Robert—November 16, 1916." She kept the letter in Robert's wallet along with a lock of his hair, a small photo of Sophia, a few business cards, and a few fragments and poems in Robert's handwriting.[37]

Frankfurter's friends from the House of Truth knew that he, too, had suffered a great loss.[38] "You will know when I say that the closest friend of my own years is gone," Frankfurter wrote Holmes the day of the funeral.[39] Holmes sent Frankfurter a telegram that comforted him. "I grieve at Valentine's death as a public loss," Holmes wrote Laski. "I saw him but two or three times. What I did see impressed me much."[40]

Laski, like Frankfurter, considered Valentine "the closest of friends."[41] The feeling between Laski and Valentine was mutual. "Laski in his way is a first Felix," Valentine had written his wife that summer. "I'm not sure he has not considerably more depth and creative power. I believe you will like him."[42] In a remarkable four-page essay, Laski recalled his friendship with Valentine of less than a year and how they spent time together during a long summer in New York City. Laski remembered a walk from Washington Square to 180th Street when they discussed "industrial theory, religious theory, Plato, Kipling, Henry James, Lloyd George, the history of the papacy, the character of the Indians—all of them with a vigor that was to make most of what he said easily and naturally memorable."[43] Like Lippmann and Frankfurter, Laski was extremely sympathetic to Valentine's views on labor and drawn to his personality. "He lived greatly and he died greatly—," Laski wrote, "died in the full vigor of his powers and at the threshold of his achievement."

Christie and Percy sent notes to Frankfurter and Mrs. Valentine; Christie regretted not being able to come down from Canada to serve as a pall-bearer.[44] Frankfurter made sure that everyone who ever set foot in the House of Truth knew that Valentine was the House's leader. "[I] want to tell you about Valentine," he wrote Learned Hand. "Altogether it seems about as cruelly a wasteful a thing as life has revealed to me. He died with the same kind of gay intrepidity that he lived all his life. The job now is to keep what he was trying to do together."[45]

On a Sunday afternoon in mid-January 1917, Frankfurter presided over a celebration of Valentine's life and work before 250 to 300 people at Boston's Faneuil Hall.[46] Frankfurter set the meeting's celebratory tone: "We have come to gather wisdom and strength and joy of life by sharing our devotion to Robert Valentine."[47] Frankfurter described Valentine as someone who "asked questions and relentlessly put them to the test. He was Socrates, Socrates in action."[48] As an MIT writing instructor, in the banking business, in Indian affairs, and as an industrial counselor, Valentine "not only sought, he not only found, he followed truth." "Surely if any man did," Frankfurter said, Valentine "thought under fire."[49]

Frankfurter did not want the event to be a second funeral but akin to one of the evenings at the House of Truth. Speakers included Valentine's college roommate John Palfrey, labor and manufacturing clients, and Bull Moose allies. Frankfurter read notes of appreciation from clothing store magnate Edward Filene, Judge Mack, and Justice Brandeis.

Brandeis's letter praised Valentine for carrying on the work of trying to solve industrial problems by combining scientific management with representation from organized labor. "He did not delude himself by a belief that he had discovered a cure-all ...," Brandeis wrote. "He worked like the scientist with patience and without assumptions. He worked like the pioneer with vision and with courage. He gave to humanity a religious devotion. Such are the heroes of peace."[50] Brandeis had learned from his wife, Alice, that Sophie and Sophia had been "financially unprovided for" and sent Frankfurter a $1,000 check.[51]

For Frankfurter, the most "profoundly eloquent" tribute came from Sol Polakoff of the International Ladies' Garment Workers' Union.[52] With some assistance from Frankfurter, Polakoff told the story of how a self-educated "Russian Jewish outcast of the Ghetto" learned to trust a Harvard-educated "Puritan aristocrat."[53] Polakoff recounted his initial suspicion in February 1916 when Valentine had been introduced as the new director of the protocol for the dress and waist industry. It was the same suspicion that Polakoff harbored toward social workers, one founded on the belief that Valentine could not possibly understand the depth and complexities of the problems facing garment workers. A few days later, Valentine invited Polakoff for a walk to discuss the industry and won over Polakoff by sincerely referring to him as "Brother." In less than a year, Polakoff had discovered in Valentine "not only a friend of the laboring class, but a true friend of justice and a brother to me."[54]

The meeting's final speaker was closer to Valentine than anyone who had spoken that day—Denison. Health problems had forced Denison to return from the Philippines in September 1915 after less than a year and a half there.[55] The Filipino newspapers regretted Denison's departure because he possessed the same sort of disinterested civil service mentality that Valentine had brought to Indian affairs and industrial counseling.[56]

Denison had returned to America a broken man. Malaria had left him severely jaundiced, stress had made his hair much grayer, and his body was wracked by possible gallstones.[57] He spent the early part of 1916 at a Marblehead, Massachusetts, sanitarium.[58] "Win is getting on—I think decidedly," Frankfurter reported to a mutual friend. "He's gained 13 pounds!"[59] By the end of March, Denison was well enough to venture to Washington to persuade President Wilson that the country's policies toward the Philippines were "not only mistaken but absurd."[60] While in Washington, Denison dined with Holmes and his secretary Chauncey Belknap. A week later, Belknap attended another dinner at the justice's where a dismayed Denison revealed that his briefing with President Wilson had lasted only four minutes.[61] Undeterred, Denison followed up his disappointing meeting with the president with a twenty-five-page memorandum.[62]

That fall, Denison had recovered enough to rejoin his old New York law firm of Stetson, Jennings & Russell. Immediately after Robert's death, Denison wired Sophie: "I will come up as soon as possible. Just leaving Washington. Tell Sophia to count on me."[63] Two days later, Denison wired Sophie from Dayton, Ohio: "I am with you all. Never fear about his friends. They have always been yours on your own account as well as Sophia's. We have all much to do and will do it pulling together."[64] He was conspicuously absent from the list of pallbearers and ushers at Valentine's funeral. Perhaps he feared that the pain of his friend's death and the strain of the funeral would have been too much for his weak constitution. At the memorial meeting, however, Denison revealed the depth of his admiration for Valentine. "Of all the men in and about my time," Denison told the audience, "Valentine seemed to me the one most likely to make an epochal change in human life in this country."[65]

Denison recalled a discussion with Valentine about the impact of the war in Europe on their careers. Denison believed that they should get involved in the biggest historical event of their lifetimes. Valentine vehemently disagreed: "Why, the European war is a drop in the bucket to the tragedy of the industrial life of this country. The millions who suffer and die in that drama are not a tithe of those who suffer and die and live-without-living in our factories and mines. I would not interrupt my work for anything I could do in that war."[66]

Denison also recounted his final conversation with Valentine, ten days before the dinner at Delmonico's. Valentine was at peace with his professional life, his contribution to society, and his creation of the profession of industrial counseling. "At last I believe this thing can go without me," he told Denison. "For the first time I feel easy about it." "I believe he was right," Denison added. "He had lived his full life and done his job."[67]

To Denison, Valentine had confided his one regret about his industrial counseling business—the impact of financial sacrifices and physical separation on Sophie and Sophia.[68] Valentine could have gone back into banking or worked for management and provided for his family. Instead, he chose to follow his passion, to strike out on his own without any financial backing, an act that Denison described as "the bravest thing I ever saw a man do."[69]

Denison tried to fill the void left by Valentine's death. He worked with Frankfurter and Brandeis to keep Valentine's industrial counseling business afloat by encouraging Governor Bass to join Tead and Gregg in the firm.[70] He managed Valentine's DC real estate interests and owned a half stake with Sophie in the R Street house. He looked after his goddaughter Sophia and even offered to marry Sophie.[71] Sophie, however, turned him down. Denison remained a lifelong bachelor and close Valentine family friend.

For the most part, Frankfurter lived up to his Mr. Fix reputation when it came to looking after Valentine's family and legacy. He peppered Sophie with letters and notes of encouragement in the weeks and months after Valentine's death. He never made good on his pledge to publish the speeches and letters from Valentine's memorial service in book form, yet he carried on Valentine's legacy in other ways. He used his government contacts to steer work to Valentine's industrial counseling firm. And he created a historical record by writing lengthy articles about Valentine for the *Harvard Alumni Bulletin* and *Dictionary of American Biography*.[72] "Valentine was a pioneer ... ," Frankfurter wrote. "The permanence he achieved, and the triumphant marvel is that he should have been able to achieve it in so short a time. His work will go on."[73]

After Valentine's death, Frankfurter emerged as the nation's leading expert on labor-management relations. He embraced Valentine's ideas about minimum wages and eight-hour days, cooperation between labor and management, and scientific expertise and showed how they could be applied by industrial counselors as well as government civil servants. He encouraged

American liberals not to rely on the Supreme Court to solve all their problems. He began to build an industrial democracy by using the power of the
federal government, especially with the proliferation of agencies, boards,
and commissions in wartime Washington. He made sure that the House of
Truth would not die with Robert Valentine.

9

Fighting Valentine's Fight

Eight days after Valentine's memorial service in Boston, Frankfurter was back in Washington, pursuing Valentine's vision of an industrial democracy, and in residence once again for a few days at the House of Truth. "Here again—in the familiar room, with its silence and life," Frankfurter wrote Sophie Valentine on 1727 Nineteenth Street stationery. "It *is* our House of Truth—and our life, Robert's and the first of us, pervades."[1]

In Washington, Frankfurter tackled the biggest obstacle to labor laws—the Supreme Court. The constitutionality of every state's minimum wage and maximum hour laws was at stake. Valentine had devoted much of the remarkable third and final act of his life to leading the Massachusetts Minimum Wage Commission. Frankfurter fought Valentine's fight by defending an Oregon minimum wage law for women and children and an Oregon ten-hour law for mill, factory, and manufacturing workers.

For several days, Frankfurter bided his time as the Court heard other cases. He caught up with Brandeis, Denison, and other old friends. "It's good to be here," he wrote Sophie Valentine. "The House has its flavor, its traditions to an extraordinary degree."[2]

On Thursday, January 18, 1917, the Court called the cases that Frankfurter had taken over from Brandeis for the National Consumers' League. Brandeis recused himself because in 1914 he had defended the Oregon minimum wage law. Justice Lamar's death had prevented Chief Justice White from releasing an opinion striking down the law and deadlocked the Court, 4–4. The following year, Justice Hughes had left the Court to run for president, and Hughes's replacement, John Hessin Clarke, had been not sworn in until October 1916.

This was Frankfurter's second time before the Court in the last two years. In April 1916, he had defended the Oregon ten-hour law. That law's fate also remained in limbo because of the Court's changing personnel. That

Frankfurter (left) and Percy (far right) in front of the House of Truth

fall, Oregon attorney general George M. Brown requested that the case be submitted on the briefs without further argument—and without consulting the National Consumers' League or Frankfurter.[3]

Years later, Frankfurter recalled learning about the submission in the *New York Times*, but such an item cannot be found.[4] More likely, he learned the news from Josephine Goldmark at the National Consumers' League. Goldmark, who had been closely monitoring the case with the Clerk of the Court, learned that the ten-hour-law case would be decided the week of October 23, 1916, without oral argument.[5] On October 17, she wrote to the state attorney general about the issue's "national importance" and warned him that the lack of another oral argument could be "fatal to [the] case."[6] The state attorney general, however, disagreed.[7]

With less than a week before the Court decided the case, Frankfurter wired Chief Justice White that he would "take the liberty of calling" at the chief justice's home the next morning at 10:00 a.m.[8] A few years earlier, he and Denison had made an annual tour of Washington homes on New Year's Day and always saved White's house at 1717 Rhode Island Avenue for last because the chief justice served the best egg nog in town.[9] Frankfurter still felt some unease about taking the train from Boston and showing up at the chief justice's front door to discuss Supreme Court business. White welcomed him. After some small talk about the number of southern students at Harvard Law School and the effects of the Civil War on the South, the chief justice asked why Frankfurter had come to see him.

After Frankfurter explained the situation, White asked if it would resolve the problem if the Court issued an order denying the submission on the briefs without oral argument and returning the case to the Court's calendar for argument. Frankfurter said it would.[10] On October 24, the Court therefore denied the request to submit the case without argument, ordered the ten-hour-law case restored to the calendar, and paired it with the argument about the Oregon minimum wage law in late January.[11]

Frankfurter had not expected to argue these cases so soon after Valentine's memorial service.[12] Fortunately, he had defended the ten-hour law the previous year. He also had published a *Harvard Law Review* article that defended the constitutionality of wage and hour laws and that criticized a Massachusetts Supreme Court decision declaring the state's minimum wage law unconstitutional as "inadequately presented."[13] Frankfurter argued that the Supreme Court had changed its position about these cases. *Lochner*'s invocation of "a 'common understanding'" about a particular industry—in that case bakeries—was based on misassumptions and prejudices and was "no longer 'controlling.'" Three years after *Lochner*, the Court in *Muller* had declared Oregon's maximum hour law for women constitutional and, Frankfurter argued, had changed the debate to one about the reasonableness of legislation based on a scientific investigation of "economic and social facts."[14] He had requested another oral argument because he did not want the justices to dismiss the brief of nearly 1,000 pages as merely an unmanageable mountain of statistics; he wanted to confront the justices with the reasonableness of the Oregon laws.

In the small old senate chamber in January 1917, Frankfurter stood before the Court to warn the justices not to act like superlegislators. *Lochner* and its "common understanding" about maximum hours legislation, Frankfurter argued, was no longer good law, and a *Muller*-like scientific factual investigation had revealed the Oregon laws to be justified and reasonable. More than the constitutionality of the Oregon laws was at stake. "It would, in truth, be a strange and monstrous thing, if those who framed the Constitution had rendered it impermeable to the experience of a changing time," the *New Republic* concluded about Frankfurter's brief.[15] "The decision in this case," the *Independent* wrote, "will be awaited with the greatest eagerness by all those who realize the importance to the welfare of the whole community of legislative protection of the workers against unhealthful and oppressive conditions of labor."[16]

Frankfurter's friends had helped him prepare for the argument. Denison and Laski had worked on the briefs.[17] "I have nothing but dislike for the Supreme Court," Laski wrote Justice Holmes and regretted that he could not see Frankfurter's argument in person. "But you will please tell me how he behaved and if we may be proud of him."[18]

Those who witnessed Frankfurter's two days of argument were impressed. The justices, *The Nation* wrote, listened "intently" to the "small, dark, smooth-faced lawyer, mostly head, eyes, and glasses, who looked as if he might have stepped out of the sophomore classroom of a neighboring college."[19]

The facts of Frankfurter's cases were straightforward. Frank Stettler, the owner of a Portland box factory, and one of his employees, twenty-two-year-old Elmira Simpson, challenged the constitutionality of the Oregon minimum wage law in which an industrial commission set a minimum wage for women factory workers at $8.64 per week and limited their hours to nine per day and fifty-four per week. Simpson made $8 per week; Stettler paid some of his female employees as little as $6 per week.[20]

Franklin Bunting operated the Lake View Flouring Mills and had been convicted and fined $50 because his employees had worked thirteen hours in a day without overtime pay.[21] Oregon's ten-hour law (plus three hours overtime) was not an easy sell. A maximum hour law for women working in sweatshops, which the Court had upheld in 1908 based on alleged physiological differences between the sexes, was one thing. A maximum hour law for able-bodied men working in mills, factories, or manufacturing was quite another. The Oregon Supreme Court believed that the laws were different only by degree—an important point according to Frankfurter. "Once [we] admit it is a question of degree," he wrote in the *Harvard Law Review*, "there follows the recognition—and the conscious recognition is important—that we are balancing interests, that we are exercising judgment, and that the exercise of this judgment, unless so clear as to be undebatable, is solely for the legislature."[22]

Not all the justices were willing to defer to the wisdom of state legislatures, especially not Justice McReynolds. A notorious racist and anti-Semite, McReynolds was the Court's most stubborn reactionary.[23] Born in Kentucky and educated at Vanderbilt and the University of Virginia Law School, he had practiced law in Nashville and taught at Vanderbilt Law School. He had made a national name for himself in the Roosevelt Justice Department as a trustbuster. Upon returning to private practice, he vigorously prosecuted the American Tobacco Company and other trust cases for the Taft administration, "which made him appear as liberal."[24] House, who had dissuaded Wilson from naming Brandeis attorney general, succeeded in installing McReynolds instead.[25] Attorney General McReynolds continued his aggressive prosecution of trusts, including the American Telephone & Telegraph Company and the J. P. Morgan–backed New Haven Railroad, and proposed tax legislation to weaken the tobacco trust.[26] Though the attorney general had been an unpopular member of the cabinet, his record as a trustbuster, his ambition, and most of all his connection to House landed him on the Court.[27]

Frankfurter and McReynolds had some history. In 1913, McReynolds had dined with Valentine, Frankfurter, and others at the House of Truth.[28] They had encouraged Wilson's new attorney general to maintain the Justice Department's civil service system—hiring the best men regardless of political affiliation—practiced by McReynolds's predecessor, Attorney General Wickersham. "What you young gentlemen say is all very fine," McReynolds responded, "but I am afraid you don't see as I do the 96 members of the US Senate all standing hungrily in your outer office."[29] Frankfurter, whose belief in civil service had been instilled in him by Henry Stimson at the US attorney's office and in the War Department, refused to give any ground. "May I suggest, Mr. Attorney General," he told McReynolds, "that you let the 96 Senators block your vision of the 96 million citizens of the United States." After Frankfurter's retort, the dinner "broke up."[30]

McReynolds interrupted Frankfurter's argument about the ten-hour law. Frankfurter respected McReynolds's intelligence and knew what to expect from him. The first time that Frankfurter had argued the Oregon minimum wage case, McReynolds had interrupted him at every turn. The second time Frankfurter argued the minimum wage case, McReynolds had leaned back in his chair, read the other side's brief while holding it at arm's length, and ignored Frankfurter's argument.[31] Frankfurter preferred the silent treatment to McReynolds's questions about the maximum hour law.

"Ten hours! Ten hours! Ten!" McReynolds asked, "Why not four?"

Frankfurter paused and approached McReynolds, who was sitting on the extreme right of the bench: "Your honor, if by chance I may make such a hypothesis, if your physician should find that you're eating too much meat, it isn't necessary for him to urge you to become a vegetarian."[32]

Frankfurter could hear Holmes say from the other side of the bench and loudly enough for everyone to hear: "Good for you!"[33] Others were equally impressed with Frankfurter's argument that Oregon should be allowed to experiment with ways to protect its workers as long as the laws were reasonable. He proved their reasonableness by comparing them to laws in other states and countries; the wages and conditions for women and child labor; and scientific studies of fatigue in mills, factories, and manufacturing. "Mr. Frankfurter's argument before the Supreme Court last week was brilliant," *The Independent* wrote. "What is better, it was convincing."[34]

Frankfurter felt good about it, too. "IN THAT FAVORITE BLUE TIE I FACED THE FIRE AND CAME OUT HAVING FOUGHT THE FIGHT," he wired Sophie Valentine. "THE JUSTICE WAS SATISFIED AND I DID MY BEST."[35] "The justice" was undoubtedly Holmes.[36] Holmes was "mighty skeptical" of minimum wage and maximum hour laws, knew that this put him at odds with Brandeis and other liberals, but believed that life was more like survival of the fittest, and a little wealth redistribution would not help.[37] That said, Holmes had no intention of substituting his personal views for those of the Oregon legislature.

On April 9, the Court upheld Oregon's ten-hour law by a 5–3 vote. The Court's opinion quoted the Oregon Supreme Court decision that the law was not unreasonable based on the industrial practices in other states and countries.[38] The Court divided 4–4 on the minimum wage law and, without a formal opinion, permitted the Oregon Supreme Court decision upholding the law to stand.[39] Brandeis's recusal had prevented two victories, but a victory and a tie were better than two defeats. Frankfurter had struck a partial blow against *Lochner* and "liberty of contract," added another precedent for *Muller's* scientific investigation of the reasonableness of labor laws, and allowed the Oregon legislature to protect its industrial workers.

A few weeks earlier, the Court had handed another major victory to organized labor when it upheld the Adamson Act, which established an eight-hour day (plus overtime) for all railroad workers on cargo trains. Frankfurter had defended the Adamson Act in the *Boston Herald* in October 1916 when

Congress had passed it and President Wilson had signed it into law and averted a massive railroad strike.[40] A lower court had declared that the act exceeded Congress's power to regulate interstate commerce and enjoined the law's enforcement. In a 5–4 opinion by Chief Justice White, the Court upheld the legislation as within the scope of Congress's power.[41] McKenna, the fifth vote, wrote a separate opinion. Brandeis, Clarke, and Holmes joined White's opinion. Holmes, who believed that White's conception of congressional power was too narrow, signed onto the opinion without writing one of his own. "As I put it after the argument," he told Laski, "I think if Congress can weave the cloth it can spin the thread."[42] Holmes also expressed doubts to Frankfurter about White's opinion: "If absolute certainty is the condition of Constitutional power, God help us. I hear rumors that we came near universal anarchy if the strike had gone on. I don't know, but it is getting to be time to find out what is/who are the governing powers in this country."[43] A decision striking down the Adamson Act would have been disastrous to the railroad industry as it helped prepare the country for war. The Court had announced its decision days before Wilson asked Congress for a declaration of war.

★★★

By 1917, the House of Truth was in favor of war. Lippmann and others believed that America should break free of its isolationism and assert itself as a world power. They placed their faith in scientific management and expertise to solve the twin problems of nationalism and imperialism plaguing Europe. They believed that America was the only country that could end the war and broker the peace. And they had not yet discovered the limits of government power.

After the 1916 election, the *New Republic* had become a cheerleader for the Wilson administration. Lippmann and Croly met regularly in New York with Colonel House.[44] Lippmann attended a White House state dinner on December 12, the night that Germany sent a "peace note" that attempted to thwart American efforts to set the terms of a peace accord.[45] Lippmann returned to the *New Republic* intent on supporting the president and exposing the peace note as a German ploy to remain Europe's preeminent power.[46] The title of Lippmann's follow-up editorial, "Peace without Victory," soon became the administration's mantra.[47]

Behind the scenes, Lippmann and Croly conveyed their support for the administration. "Both Mr. Lippmann and I are more interested in doing what little we can to back the President up in his work than in anything else we have ever tried to do through the *New Republic*," Croly wrote to House, describing Wilson's interventionism as "one of the greatest enterprises ever undertaken by an American president."[48] Wilson read the magazine and appreciated its support. On January 8, he told the magazine's Washington correspondent: "I wish you would write Mr. Croly and Mr. Lippmann and tell them that I appreciate the work they are doing and THAT I AM IN ENTIRE AGREEMENT WITH THEIR ARTICLES ON PEACE."[49] Two weeks later, in an address to the US Senate, Wilson tried to sell the nation on his vision of peace: a League for Peace and a settlement based on "peace without victory," freedom of the seas, and respect for the sovereignty of other nations. Wilson's speech pleased Lippmann and Croly because Wilson had exhorted America to end its neutrality and isolationism.[50] "An American revival will be under way when the President has integrated in one purpose our membership in a league of nations, industrial and social preparedness, and free and material service to the sufferers of Europe," one editorial declared.[51] In another unsigned editorial, "America Speaks," Lippmann urged Americans to support the president: "His address to the Senate Monday is primarily a summons to the American nation to share the responsibilities of the peace. Mr. Wilson is asking his people to prepare themselves for the work which the world has begun to expect of them."[52]

At the end of January, Lippmann sent Wilson an updated version of *The Stakes of Diplomacy*. He also included an excerpt of a letter from H. G. Wells about Wells's forthcoming book, *War and the Future*, suggesting that the solution to war would come "not from the point of view of victory but of the point of view of Right." "The good effects of your move grow more evident as time goes on," Lippmann wrote Wilson. "Everywhere I hear even among political opponents an extraordinary enthusiasm and affection for what you have done."[53] Frankfurter defended the president's speech to a table of ten people, described it as "great fun," and added in a handwritten note to Lippmann: "Not a little of my zest these days comes from 'defending,' no, expounding you. From Wilson & peace to NR & you is an easy transition."[54] After Germany resumed its submarine warfare in February, as Wilson had predicted before the election, the *New Republic* demanded an end to American neutrality. "The immediate duty of this country is clear," the magazine declared in a postscript to its February 3 issue.[55]

On February 3, Wilson addressed both houses of Congress and announced that the United States had broken off diplomatic relations with Germany.

"It is a deep consolation to feel we should have no regrets—come what may," Frankfurter wrote a friend. "That much Wilson has done for us—and a great thing it is." Two days after Wilson's announcement, Frankfurter took the train from Cambridge to New York City to attend what he described as the magazine's "'War' meeting."[56]

Then, much to the chagrin of Wilson and his supporters at the *New Republic*, nothing happened. After visiting Washington to survey the scene, Lippmann reported to Frankfurter that the White House had "miscalculated the facts" and underestimated the country's "pacifist and isolationist sentiment."[57] And without any further action, the United States, not Germany, would look like the aggressor. Frankfurter was not worried. "Germany is forcing action on us," he wrote Lippmann and added in a postscript: "I'm still putting my faith in W. W."[58]

On March 1, the Wilson administration revealed the existence of the Zimmermann telegram—a British-intercepted cable from Germany to Mexico that proposed an alliance among Germany, Mexico, and Japan and promised Mexico its former territory in the southwestern United States if it agreed to join Germany in the war.[59] The Russian Revolution began that month and left the outcome of the European war even more in doubt. Isolationists in the Senate nonetheless blocked the passage of the Armed Neutrality Bill that would have armed American merchant ships. After a March 9 visit from Lippmann and Croly, House wrote, "I am finding it difficult to keep them in line because of the President's slowness of action."[60]

Finally, on April 2, President Wilson asked Congress to declare war against Germany based on the theme of "making the world safe for democracy." In a letter to the president, Lippmann included part of his editorial that "'our debt and the world's debt to Woodrow Wilson is immeasurable.'"[61] With some hesitation and sadness, Frankfurter agreed that the decision to go to war "could not have been otherwise."[62]

The US entry into the war brought Frankfurter and Lippmann to Washington and back to the House of Truth.

10

The House at War

On a "golden Sunday morning," Frankfurter was riding on a train from Boston to Washington. As the train approached the nation's capital, he thought about his impending visit to the White House, his stay at the House of Truth, and his dinner at Justice Holmes's.[1]

The day that Wilson asked for a declaration of war, Frankfurter was in Washington for a meeting of the Advisory Committee on Labor of the National Council of Defense. Frankfurter's aim was to prevent the United States from making the same mistakes that Britain had made in 1914 in removing all labor standards and restrictions. He knew that such issues as the influx of women and unskilled workers and their threat to skilled workers would be raised. "I don't know how much we shall be able to avoid mistakes that England has paid for," he wrote, "without paying them ourselves."[2]

The call for Frankfurter's help came from Secretary of War Newton D. Baker. A progressive former mayor of Cleveland, a pacifist, and with no previous experience in the federal government, Baker had been an unlikely choice in March 1916 to run Wilson's War Department.[3] Much of Baker's job had focused on preparedness and avoiding labor unrest that might impede the war effort. On the eve of the United States' entry into the war, he supported a draft of 1 million men and vowed to have them trained by June 1918.[4]

As president of the National Consumers' League, Baker had learned about Frankfurter's knowledge of labor issues and experience under Secretary of War Stimson. "When the war broke out for us in 1917, I had a wire from Secretary Newton D. Baker asking me to come down for the weekend, if I could," Frankfurter recalled. "I packed my suitcase, and the weekend didn't terminate until the fall of 1919."[5] This was almost true. Two weeks after his initial visit, he was back in Washington at Baker's behest—this time, for the duration of the war. "I'm here on the Labor job, indefinitely," Frankfurter

Frankfurter circa 1917

wrote. "We are in for long, long days. I seriously doubt our entrance will shorten the war. I fear the contrary."[6]

Baker, who had received permission from President Lowell to borrow the Harvard law professor, did not have to twist Frankfurter's arm.[7] Frankfurter valued his American citizenship more than any other possession. After arriving at Harvard in 1914, he had agreed to serve as a major in the reserves of the Judge Advocate General's office.[8] Because US intervention had become more likely in early March 1917, he had begun to think about ways to serve his beloved adopted country. Though he had been at the law school for only two years, he had arrived as a full professor, would not be jeopardizing his career, and wanted to serve. He explained his reasons to Justice Holmes. "Your discourse as to your own attitude in case of war seems to me to put it rightly and brings peace to my heart," Holmes replied. "And I only rejoice that if you have to serve, it is not likely to be in the field."[9]

Frankfurter intended to serve. To him, the war represented not only an end of isolationist US foreign policy but also a domestic opportunity—to remake labor-management relations; to recognize the rights of organized labor; and to improve hours, wages, and working conditions. He wanted to realize Valentine's vision of an industrial democracy in ways that his late friend had never dreamed of—by using the power of the War Department.

Frankfurter loved everything about Washington—walking its wide boulevards and avenues, working in the corridors of political power, writing as many as thirty-four letters in a single evening on 1727 Nineteenth Street stationery (many of them responding to congratulatory letters about his victory in the Oregon cases), and living in his beloved House of Truth. Not even having his tonsils out could dampen his mood.[10] After his recovery, he began seeing old friends and reviving the dinners at the House. Justice and Mrs. Holmes were "more Holmesy than ever—their sauciness, their youth, above all their imaginative tenderness."[11]

In April 1917, Percy returned to Washington with British foreign secretary Arthur Balfour and worked out of the British embassy for another year. Upon his arrival with the British delegation at the Shoreham Hotel, Percy caught up with friends for more than an hour in the lobby. "Probably he is older, but he doesn't look more than thirty," the *Washington Times* wrote. "Fair-haired, blue-eyed, and broad-shouldered, he lounged about in a loose-fitting grayish suit, and smoked innumerable cigarettes."[12] That winter, he moved back into the House.[13] The war had changed Percy. His twenty-four-year-old cousin and fellow former attaché, the "piercingly beautiful" Ivar Campbell, had died on January 8, 1916, fighting the Turks at the Battle of Sheikh Sa'ad.[14] Percy, Frankfurter wrote, was "a bit older, a bit more a man of affairs, not a whit less St. Francis."[15]

Stanley King, a frequent visitor, also worked for Secretary of War Baker and began living in the House. Other former visitors such as *The Times* of London correspondent Arthur Willert and his wife, Flo, returned. Flo Willert liked to chastise Frankfurter for the "loose" way he ran the House, the lack of control over the staff, and the expensive dinner parties.[16] "The H of T looks as of old," Frankfurter reported to Marion Denman. "Stanley King is now here & Eustace is coming and—well Mrs. Willert says we ought to have the old fashioned parties."[17] To another correspondent, he wrote: "The H of T is a blast again. I'm very well & happily at work."[18]

The House's cook complained that preparing food was impossible because she never knew "how many people thay [sic] are going to bring in to dinner" and that one meal had been ready for an hour "when Mr. Frankfurter came in" at eight p.m. "I can't surve [sic] good meals."[19] Frankfurter enjoyed the informality. "If something happened to the soup, so what?" he re-called. "If the ice cream that was to have turned up for dessert didn't turn up, then so what. Nobody worried about it. One ate sufficiently well, nothing to write home about, but plenty of good food in an easy, devil-may-care sort of way." The atmosphere led to conversation characterized by "great informality, great ease, free flow of talk. There were no sacred cows."[20]

A dinner invitation to the House became so coveted that newspapers began to write about the place. "Did you ever hear of the 'House of Truth'?" a Washington newspaper columnist asked. "It is a brand new one on me, but it seems that several smart young bachelors have a house together, somewhere in Nineteenth street, to which they give that name and where they have the most wonderful parties."[21]

No new visitor made a bigger impression at the House than Herbert Hoover. A mining engineer who had made millions before turning to public life, Hoover became a national hero by organizing Belgian relief efforts. When the United States formally entered the war, he headed the US Food Administration. "The last two days I have seen much of a truly great man," Frankfurter wrote. "Belgium has smelted clean any alloy of self-concern that Hoover ever had. Now, he is an extraordinarily competent man completely devoted to keep life going in half the world—literally to keep life going."[22] Hoover revealed that he "had designs" on hiring Frankfurter. Already committed to Baker, Frankfurter regretted having to turn Hoover down. "I'd rather work with him than anyone I have seen in Government," Frankfurter wrote. "He is the biggest thing here."[23]

Agreeing with Frankfurter's assessment, Lippmann thought Hoover "had the greatest gift for exposition of a public question of anybody I'd met."[24] In mid-May, Lippmann took the night train from New York to Washington just to see Hoover. "He was beaming," Lippmann wrote. "He'd seen the President late last night and had been told he could have what power he needed [for food relief]—that's by far the best news since the war began."[25] To Lippmann and Frankfurter, Hoover represented what a competent expert could accomplish in government. He was doing for food relief in Europe what Frankfurter and Lippmann wanted to accomplish for American labor.

★★★

By early May, Frankfurter was trying to facilitate Lippmann's installation as a resident at the House and as a pro-labor ally in the War Department.

Lippmann and Frankfurter were closer at this point than at any other in their lives. Their friendship had begun with the founding of the *New Republic*, had grown while they were writing unsigned editorials and working behind the scenes on Brandeis's confirmation, and peaked in wartime Washington.

Only twenty-seven and eligible for the draft, Lippmann asked Frankfurter to put in a good word for him with Secretary of War Baker. It was not a tough sell. Lippmann was already a Wilson administration insider who met and corresponded with presidential adviser Colonel House and was already assisting the Colonel in organizing a wartime propaganda bureau.[26] Indeed, House talked Lippmann out of enlisting or trying to join the American mission to Russia, but he kept Wilson apprised of Lippmann's desire to join the administration.[27] In the past, Lippmann had conveyed ideas to Wilson and Secretary of War Baker in private meetings and correspondence. He had written three books, including one on foreign policy, and in April had addressed the American Academy of Political and Social Science.[28] To Frankfurter, Lippmann confided his lofty wartime ambitions: "What I want to do is to devote all my time to studying and speculating on the approaches to peace and the reactions from the peace. Do you think you can get me an exemption on such high falutin' ground? Somehow or other I have to ask Baker for it and yet I feel that that plus the N.R., plus special publicity work is my job. May I put the matter in your hands?"[29]

Not content to rely on Frankfurter, Lippmann wrote Baker a long, personal letter reiterating a desire to serve in the War Department rather than get drafted. "I have made it my business to understand the administration of foreign policy," he wrote, "and to realize the problems it was up against." Lippmann wanted no special favors even though he claimed that his father was dying (his father would not die for another ten years) and that his mother would be "absolutely alone in the world." He planned on coming to Washington and hoped to speak to Baker personally.[30]

Baker had already hired a small team of special assistants: Frankfurter on labor issues, Stanley King on industrial relations, and former Columbia University dean Frederick Keppel on personnel. Yet Baker was eager to add Lippmann to the mix. Three days after his first letter to Baker, Lippmann wrote him again: "Felix has told me of his talk with you this morning and I just want to put in another word of enthusiasm and confidence in the plan. It's a job at which I could work with all my heart, because I'd be under a man whose whole view of life there is just the quality which alone can justify this high enterprise."[31]

With his naked ambition and naive belief that he could plan world peace, Lippmann was on his way to living at the House of Truth. There was only one catch. The House would have to accept its first female resident since it had become a bachelor pad—Lippmann's fiancée and soon-to-be wife, Faye Albertson.

Lippmann confided to Frankfurter and Baker about his impending marriage. Faye was the daughter of Lippmann's surrogate father, Ralph Albertson. A former Congregationalist minister who had once started a Georgia commune, Albertson had given young Lippmann his first job after college as a reporter at the *Boston Common*, a Socialist weekly newspaper. Hazel Albertson, Ralph's second wife and eighteen years younger than him, had been like a wise older sister to Walter (and had given him the nickname "Buddha"). Walter and Faye had known each other since she was a fifteen-year-old with a crush on the young Harvard Socialist.[32] They had been dating for the last year.

Mabel Dodge, whose Greenwich Village salon had been a haven for Lippmann during his Socialist phase, thought that the pair were woefully mismatched. Faye was a dance instructor who liked to frequent the theater. She cared little for politics and did not fit in with Lippmann's old intellectual crowd. After entertaining the couple for a weekend in November 1916, Dodge wrote Hazel Albertson that Walter was "preoccupied" with Faye but that Faye was "indifferent" to Walter. "Frankly, he bores her when he comes to her level, where he is not at his best. People are only really amusing and at their best when in their highest levels—but Faye probably would never 'get' Walter on his."[33] Though she confessed her own "fantasies" about Lippmann, Dodge perceived what Walter and Faye could not.[34]

Lippmann, who was attracted to "Nordic blonds," was smitten with Faye.[35] He wrote Frankfurter on April 27 that he was getting married to her in June: "It's an old love and a very happy one, and it's been the only one. Faye knows all about you. What friends we are, and we'll make it a threesome."[36] Frankfurter's enthusiastic reply triggered the type of emotion that Lippmann rarely displayed.[37] "Your letter moves me profoundly," Lippmann wrote. "It nourishes the thing—that communion which sustains us."[38]

As he usually did with his closest friends, Frankfurter solidified the bond with Lippmann by corresponding with the bride-to-be. "It's not Walter, the wunderkind, that I ferociously care about," he wrote Faye on May 23. "It's

Walter the friend, the happy companion in purpose and in play. Him I love very dearly. And I want you to become dear to me as Walter's wife."[39]

On May 24, Walter and Faye were married by a New York magistrate in a small ceremony at his parents' home.[40] At twenty-seven, Walter finally moved out of his parents' East Eightieth Street apartment and prepared to move in with Faye at the House of Truth. Frankfurter looked forward to their arrival. "Somehow I'm glad that it should be from the House of Truth that I send you my affectionate good wishes, dear Walter. You see the place is hallowed with gayety and purpose and grief and hope for me."[41] Frankfurter informed Lippmann that Sophie Valentine was an admirer of Faye's and "'tremendously happy'" about their marriage, that "the Holmeses ... are awaiting the two of you," and that Percy "has a more than mystic fondness for you."[42]

With Frankfurter's assistance, Walter and Faye's transition into the House was a smooth one. "A little bedroom on the second floor was set aside for the newlyweds," wrote Lippmann biographer Ronald Steel, who had interviewed both Lippmann and his wife. "The situation was an odd one for Faye but she handled it well, bringing some order into the household accounts and providing a welcome adornment at dinner. The men teased and doted on her, and it was a tribute to her easygoing nature that she could get on so well with such ambitious and independent-minded intellectuals."[43]

Like her new husband and her new friend Frankfurter, Faye was drawn to Justice Holmes, or more likely the justice, who enjoyed the company of attractive young women, was drawn to her. Holmes "used to come from the Court chambers in the late afternoons to play double solitaire with her. Once during a game she gently pointed out to him that he was cheating. 'But it's such a small thing, my dear,' he sighed through his great drooping mustache, 'and no one will suffer from it but me.'"[44]

With Faye leaving the Washington heat in mid-July, Lippmann played the role of bachelor at the House of Truth. He met Winfred Denison, who stayed there one weekend. "Last night Denison slept in your bed and snored so hard I had to get up and sleep on the couch in the living room," he wrote Faye. "To-night the house is deserted."[45]

Professionally, Lippmann was happier than ever with his decision to work for Secretary of War Baker. He admired Baker as a "great combination of mind and heart" and, with the war going on, vowed to take a break from journalism "until the end of the war, though I shall have to do some to make up for what the Government doesn't pay me."[46]

Croly, for one, was blindsided by Lippmann's decision to refrain from writing for the magazine.[47] Lippmann was much younger than Croly, a far better writer, and with deeper contacts inside the Wilson administration. Croly also relied on him to get out the magazine during the summer months that Croly spent in Cornish, New Hampshire. The magazine was finally beginning to thrive during the United States' run-up to the war. By July 1916, paid subscribers topped 17,000 and included Holmes, Brandeis, former justice Charles Evans Hughes, and Secretary of War Baker.[48] People subscribed because it was an insiders' publication with real insight and knowledge about the Wilson administration's war plans. Now the magazine was losing its best writer and chief insider.

Croly conveyed his despondence and dependence on Lippmann to Frankfurter, who had visited the Crolys in Cornish over Memorial Day weekend.[49] Frankfurter encouraged Lippmann to placate Croly by writing some non–war themed unsigned editorials. "Do be nice to Herbert," Frankfurter wrote Lippmann. "I mean—Coddle his dependence on you. It is that. If in doubt ask Faye."[50]

★★★

Almost as soon as he helped the Lippmanns get settled at the House of Truth, Frankfurter embarked on a secret mission orchestrated by former Turkish ambassador Henry Morgenthau. The public purpose of the Morgenthau Mission was to go to Egypt to monitor the treatment of Jews in Palestine. The secret purpose, as conceived by Morgenthau, was to negotiate a separate peace with Turkey.[51] Secretary of War Baker asked Frankfurter to go. Frankfurter was not keen on the assignment. He did not know anything about Turkey, nor did he like what he had seen and heard from Morgenthau.[52] After consulting with Brandeis, Morgenthau personally appealed to President Wilson to send Frankfurter.[53] At that point, Frankfurter could not say no. "May I convey to you the depth of my thanks for the confidence implied in your selection," he wrote Wilson. "These days we are all soldiers. As such I go obedient to the duty with which you have generously charged me."[54] Yet Frankfurter preferred to focus on the labor issues at home and to serve as de facto social director of the House of Truth.[55]

He was also keen on pursuing his romantic interest with Marion Denman. After meeting Frankfurter at the House of Truth in the spring of 1913, Denman had worked as a secretary at Miss Spence's School and enrolled in the New York School of Social Work. The rigors of social work, however, had triggered a nervous breakdown. She recovered at a sanitarium in Saranac Lake, New York; Frankfurter continued to court her through relentless correspondence and periodic visits. The Congregationalist minister's daughter struggled to reconcile their religious and temperamental differences. Yet he needed her, and she needed him. Before leaving on the mission, he visited her at her family's home in Springfield, Massachusetts. She gave him a letter to read on board the ship, a letter that he "read & reread" and carried "as a talisman."[56] He sent her his photograph and recalled that "very first Ontario glimpse of you, that night at the House of Truth."[57]

Frankfurter's worst fears about Morgenthau and the mission were realized. A New York City real estate magnate, a German Jew, a former Democratic National Committee finance chairman, and a Wilson campaign contributor, Ambassador Morgenthau knew less about Turkey than Frankfurter did after a few briefings from friends. Frankfurter quickly tired of Morgenthau and began avoiding him on the voyage to neutral Spain.[58] Frankfurter sent Lippmann a jolly July 4 postcard from Spain before the mission began to go sour.[59]

Within ten days, the Wilson administration learned that the mission was a "fiasco."[60] Morgenthau had been telling everyone about the real purpose of the mission and overestimated Allied support for negotiating with Turkey.[61] Based on his personal relationship with one of the Turkish rulers, Morgenthau believed that he could go to Switzerland and negotiate peace with Turkey. Neither the British government nor the Zionist movement had any interest in negotiating a separate peace. The British wanted to capture Palestine from Turkey, and the Zionists believed that a British takeover was the surest way to a Jewish homeland.[62] At a meeting in Gibraltar on July 4 and 5, two Zionists, British representative Chaim Weizmann and French representative Colonel Ernest Weyl, persuaded Morgenthau of the somewhat dubious proposition that Turkey lacked any incentive to sign a peace accord because the Central Powers looked stronger than ever. Weizmann was as dismissive of Morgenthau and his lack of concrete knowledge and planning as Frankfurter was.[63] Frankfurter had never met Weizmann before but came away incredibly impressed.[64] Their Gibraltar meeting was the first of Weizmann's many future contacts with Frankfurter and Brandeis based on their mutual interest in Zionism.

The Wilson administration panicked when it heard from Frankfurter and others that Morgenthau had exceeded his marching orders—purporting to represent President Wilson's views and trying to negotiate a separate peace with Turkey on his own.[65] Things fell apart in Paris. Morgenthau arranged a meeting with General John J. Pershing, the commander in chief of the American Expeditionary Forces in Europe, and proposed attacking Turkey. When Pershing asked if the former ambassador had any military maps, Morgenthau went out and bought a pocket map from Brentano's bookstore. Frankfurter understood that he was there to babysit Morgenthau and to make sure that the ambassador did not embarrass the administration.[66] They were supposed to go to Cairo to talk to the Turks (and supposedly assess the Palestine situation), but they never made it there because of Morgenthau's freelancing.[67] In an attempt to salvage the mission and at Weizmann's urging, Frankfurter asked to go to Russia to influence Jewish opinion there. The request, however, was denied.[68]

The trip was not a total loss for Frankfurter. Instead of going to Russia or Cairo, the State Department asked him to write a report about the situation in France. Fortunately for Frankfurter, he had invited one of his protégés, Max Lowenthal, on the trip.[69] A 1912 Harvard law graduate and former law clerk to Judge Julian W. Mack, Lowenthal left his budding New York law practice to accompany Frankfurter on the first of several investigations. With Lowenthal's assistance, Frankfurter spent days gathering information in Paris and the French countryside and cabled a detailed report home while on board the SS *Espagne*. The report explained that 2 million French casualties had destroyed the country's morale. The US entrance in the war had provided a boost, but the French saw a League to Enforce Peace as a utopian solution. Secretary of State Robert Lansing was impressed with the level of detail in Frankfurter's report and with Frankfurter. "This morning I had an hour's talk with Frankfurter, which was most enlightening," Lansing wrote Wilson on August 13. "I believe that you should see him and hear the story."[70]

Though he had not wanted to go on the Morgenthau Mission and it had turned out to be a colossal failure, Frankfurter showed his ability to go into the field, assess a situation, and write a comprehensive report. "I'm keen to tell you the effect my intelligence—my report—made on those in authority," he wrote Brandeis. "The trip was deeply worthwhile."[71] Frankfurter had enhanced his reputation within the administration. He had gained first-hand knowledge about the war from the perspectives of Britain and France and had made important Zionist contacts. He returned home with "the sense of what the war is and the peace that ought to be is in my marrow," "full of energy," and "of course at 1727 again."[72]

Frankfurter enjoyed living with the Lippmanns. "At the House of Truth we are much as of old. The Lippmanns fit in—very well," he wrote to Katharine Ludington. "Yes—[Learned] Hand is right, she is a 'roadside rose' and proves that Walter is—no denizen of fine reason! From which remark you must only gather that I love him more than ever & we are truly happy together." Stanley King also was living in the house and working in the War Department. Judge Mack lived there too while drafting the Military and Naval Insurance Bill. And, according to Frankfurter, "Brandeis is the sage adviser of all."[73]

Frankfurter, however, was not at 1727 for long. On September 1, Baker suggested to President Wilson and Secretary of Labor William B. Wilson that Frankfurter join a proposed commission to investigate the labor unrest that had begun to plague the western United States.[74] Frankfurter, however, opposed a public commission as attracting unnecessary attention.[75] Three days later, he wrote Baker a lengthy memorandum proposing a low-key investigation and explaining the subtleties of the labor movement. Frankfurter, who had consulted with Brandeis about the issues, distinguished between the establishment union leaders such as Samuel Gompers at the AFL, the Socialist labor leaders in the IWW, and non-IWW radicals who could be trusted and practical.[76] Frankfurter incorrectly believed that his memorandum had headed off the idea of a public commission—at least that's what he wrote House.[77] Baker, however, sent Frankfurter's memorandum to President Wilson, praised Frankfurter as a "very thorough going and thoughtful fellow," and recommended that Frankfurter serve as the secretary to the President's Mediation Commission.[78] Secretary of Labor Wilson, the chair of the commission, agreed.[79]

With his labor expertise in high demand, Frankfurter headed west for three months with the commission to resolve strikes that could impair the US war effort—copper-mining strikes in Arizona, a telephone operator strike in California and the Pacific Northwest, and a railroad strike in Minnesota. Though he had opposed the idea of a commission, he enjoyed seeing the West as well as getting to know Secretary of Labor Wilson and the labor and management representatives on the commission. Most of all, the commission offered the chance to test Valentine's ideas about the role of mediation in labor-management relations.[80] "The trip is going very nicely …," Frankfurter wrote Lippmann in October. "However, do not jump to a hasty conclusion—my patience has plenty new fields for conquest. 'The Education of Mr. Felix' is certainly what my historian will call this year."[81]

Frankfurter relied on the House's residents for assistance in resolving the Arizona copper-mining strikes. Lippmann and Stanley King supplied him with contact information for several New York men connected to the mine owners.[82] Percy helped him break the last holdout among Arizona copper-mining companies, a British-owned operation with a stubborn Scottish manager who refused to settle with the union.[83] "At last the mess here is settled," he wrote Lippmann. "It was a very nasty tangle."[84]

The commission's investigation of the copper-mining strikes in the wilds of Arizona led to a Frankfurter-authored report about the Bisbee deportation. A year earlier, in July 1916, an Arizona sheriff and his deputies had rounded up 1,186 striking miners like cattle and had dumped them in New Mexico without food, water, or a way to contact their families. Federal troops were forced to rescue the miners—some US citizens and mostly European immigrants—and to provide food and shelter for them until the strikes were settled in mid-September. Frankfurter's report to the president concluded that the deportations violated Arizona law and interfered with the Selective Service draft, and recommended that Congress make future deportations illegal.[85]

After the commission settled the mining strikes and reported on the Bisbee deportation, Frankfurter spent ten days in San Francisco settling the strike of female telephone operators and investigating the case of jailed labor leader Tom Mooney. "Out of the wilderness of Arizona we came into this most fascinating of cities, but during the ten days we have been here I have worked longer hours than for many a moon," Frankfurter wrote Lippmann on November 22.[86]

When President Wilson instructed the commission to look into the Mooney case, Frankfurter was so unfamiliar with it that he was not even sure how to spell Mooney's last name.[87] Frankfurter had been in Europe during the summertime hue and cry about the case. Mooney had been tried and sentenced to death for the Preparedness Day Parade bombing in San Francisco. In the middle of the parade on July 22, 1916, a suitcase containing a pipe bomb had exploded just south of Market Street, killing ten bystanders, wounding forty-one, and blowing a little girl's legs off. It was the worst terrorist attack in San Francisco history. Although the police originally suspected anarchists, Mooney and several of his radical labor associates had been arrested and tried for murder. Mooney was the only one sentenced to death.[88]

Frankfurter's report found that Mooney's conviction had been based on perjured testimony. The chief eyewitness was so discredited after Mooney's trial that the witness was not called in the subsequent trials of Mooney's alleged co-conspirators, both of whom were acquitted. The California Supreme Court lacked the jurisdiction to declare a new trial. Frankfurter's report recommended that the president encourage the governor of California and state prosecutors to retry Mooney. "[T]he feeling of disquietude aroused by the case must be heeded, for if unchecked, it impairs the faith that our democracy protects the lowliest and even the unworthy against false accusation," the report said. "War is fought with moral as well as material resources."[89]

The Bisbee and Mooney reports subjected Frankfurter to harsh criticism and contributed to his growing reputation as a dangerous radical. Theodore Roosevelt accused him of "taking, on behalf of the Administration an attitude which seems to me to be fundamentally that of Trotski [sic] and the other Bolsheviki leaders in Russia; an attitude which may be fraught with mischief to this country."[90] Roosevelt believed that the Mooney report sided with IWW radicals and anarchists sympathetic to the German cause and that the Bisbee report impugned the reputation of Roosevelt's old friend and fellow Rough Rider John C. Greenway.[91] Frankfurter knew that Roosevelt's criticism was coming because TR had wired the district attorney in Mooney's case a telegram of support; Frankfurter's earlier efforts to reach Roosevelt through intermediaries had failed.[92] Now Frankfurter responded to Roosevelt's letter point by point, and their disagreement showed how far TR had fallen in the eyes of many of his former supporters.[93] For Roosevelt, militarism and nationalism trumped the labor issues that Frankfurter and other former Bull Moosers held dear. In late 1917 and early 1918, Frankfurter still believed that government could be used to advance his pro-labor agenda, but the war revealed some of government's limits—especially when it came to the right to fair trials for politically unpopular defendants.

A few years later, conservative attorney James Beck debated Frankfurter about the Mooney case in the pages of the *New Republic*.[94] By all accounts, Frankfurter bested Beck because of superior knowledge of the procedure and the facts of the case; Frankfurter pointed out that the trial judge and the California Supreme Court had been procedurally powerless to declare a new trial and that the governor had commuted Mooney's sentence from death to life in prison. In 1939, after the US Supreme Court found that the prosecution had knowingly used perjured testimony, Mooney was pardoned and the next day marched at the head of a victory parade down Market

Street.[95] It was not the last time that Frankfurter tried to change public opinion about a highly charged criminal case.

After three months of settling strikes and investigating the Bisbee deportation and the Mooney case, Frankfurter had emerged as the nation's foremost expert on wartime labor relations. He did not regret the experience, even if it briefly took him away from Washington and may have cost him other diplomatic opportunities. He had made contacts at the highest levels of the War and Labor Departments. He was poised to manage the country's domestic labor situation for the rest of the war.[96]

★★★

Like Frankfurter, Lippmann made a name for himself as one of Secretary of War Baker's top assistants. Through a combination of flattery, political skill, and intelligence, Lippmann quickly became an administration insider. He wrote the president and praised his June 14, 1917, speech about "the German plot" as "the most adequate and searching expression of the meaning of this war that has yet been uttered."[97] He wrote many memoranda, including one that Baker passed along to Wilson about Pope Benedict XV's August 1 call for a negotiated peace. "Walter Lippmann is attached to my office," Baker wrote Wilson. "He makes me memoranda on many things. This one, I venture to submit to your thought only because you know how thoughtful he is."[98]

Like Frankfurter, Lippmann worked on labor issues—both domestic and military.[99] One of those issues included introducing black soldiers into the armed forces.[100] Since the United States had declared war, black leaders pushed the Wilson administration to include African American officers.[101] The presence of black officers led to lynchings and race riots in Houston, Memphis, and East St. Louis.

As a showing of good faith, Emmett J. Scott of the Tuskegee Institute was made a special assistant to Baker in charge of black troops. Scott, however, faced a lack of support from Baker and racist attitudes. "Baker asked me whether Scott had any perspective because that day he had sent in an order for a private room & a private stenographer & a private messenger," Lippmann wrote in his diary on October 10, 1916. "I told Baker that so far as Scott was concerned the more alone the better and he said: 'I'm happy if 11,000,000 darkies want to think that Scott is Asst. Sect. of War.'"[102]

Lippmann's biggest booster was Colonel House. The transplanted Texan with the purely honorific title was thought to be running the White House out of his New York and Massachusetts homes.[103] Before he arrived in Washington, Lippmann had worked for House on special projects such as creating a war publicity bureau and had earned House's trust and confidence.[104]

House helped Lippmann achieve his "high falutin'" dreams of planning the country's diplomatic responses to the war by tapping him for a special assignment—the Inquiry. The idea behind the Inquiry was to plan for America's central role in the inevitable peace negotiations by assembling a small team of experts to gather data about all the countries involved in the war, to assess their political situations and interests, and to figure out what it would take to have them agree to a negotiated peace. The Inquiry embodied the belief in scientific investigation and expert-run government. Lippmann jumped at House's offer to remap the postwar world. "Nothing has ever pleased me more or come as a greater surprise," he wrote House on September 24. "I'd literally rather be connected with you in this work in no matter what capacity than do anything else there is to do in the world."[105]

After four months, Walter and Faye Lippmann moved out of the House of Truth for good and returned to New York so that he could work on the Inquiry. "I am in a great rush at this time as I am leaving Washington tomorrow afternoon," Lippmann wrote Frankfurter on October 3. "I saw the Colonel on Sunday in New York and he told me to get free immediately and come with him so I am leaving many things unfinished."[106]

House intended the Inquiry to be operated with as much secrecy as possible and outside the channels of Washington gossip. The Inquiry, therefore, would be run out of New York—with a guard at the door of offices in the New York Public Library.[107] Two of Lippmann's friends from the *New Republic*, Croly and Judge Learned Hand, were privy to the organization's beginnings.[108] Hand was so interested in joining the organization that he asked whether he should resign from the bench, but Lippmann "was somewhat discouraging & noncommittal because I do not see how he is to be fitted into [the] organization."[109]

Much to House's and Wilson's consternation, the press revealed the unnamed organization's existence after an October 10 meeting between the two, its purpose of collecting data for the peace conference, and its leadership in House and his assistant Lippmann. Lippmann, the *New York Times* reported, was already on the job "devoting his time especially to mapping out a preliminary plan for collecting data under well defined heads."[110] While House was meeting with Wilson, Lippmann was in Washington conferring with members of the War Department. Lippmann dined at the House of Truth with Frankfurter protégé Gerry Henderson, Walter Meyer, and Sam Rosensohn and after dinner discussed the progress of the war with Secretary Baker.[111]

Lippmann had been keeping Frankfurter, who was out west, apprised of the plans for the Inquiry. "[W]e are to go ahead but ... the bigger plans for organization in Europe must be held up," Lippmann wrote. "We have to work on a modest basis and chiefly through agencies already in existence. This means that we have to draw very heavily upon the sources that are in Washington which have connections abroad. And I have been wondering whether the most immediate useful thing you could do would not be to organize the Washington end of this thing? This would enable you to keep your hand on the labor situation as well, and then after a few months if the point of view changes we can go on with a bigger idea."[112]

No one wanted to work on the Inquiry more than Frankfurter.[113] Unable to plead his case from Arizona, he asked Lippmann to plead his case just as he had done so for Lippmann with Secretary Baker. Before he left for New York City, Lippmann had spoken with House about Frankfurter "at length and in the most satisfactory way. He has you very actively in mind as soon as you return."[114]

As he was about to leave Arizona for San Francisco to investigate the Mooney case, Frankfurter continued to express his interest in joining the Inquiry. He was fluent in German and had learned a lot about the peace preferences among the Allies during the Morgenthau Mission. "I feel I can be of most use for this peace preparedness business ...," he wrote Lippmann. "If that appeals to you and the Colonel for me, why of course that's the thing I want to do most eagerly. ... I make you trustee of my usefulness."[115]

Lippmann, however, was unable to deliver. "Strictly between ourselves the job goes well but it has not reached a point where you can be drafted into it with any fairness to the work you are now doing," he wrote Frankfurter a week later.[116] Lippmann explained the research he was doing on other failed attempts at internationalization, then listed House's small staff and their respective projects.[117] Frankfurter was not impressed with the list and suggested that Laski could aid the project.[118] Lippmann promised to send for Frankfurter as soon as an opening became available.

The truth was that no opening was likely for Frankfurter as long as the final decision maker was Colonel House. When President Wilson had initially raised the idea of the Inquiry in early September, Frankfurter immediately came to the president's mind. "Have you had a talk with

Frankfurter?" Wilson wrote House. "If you have not, I wish you would have. He knows what some of the other governments are doing to get their cases ready and their pipes laid, and he might be able to give you a lead as to doing what I am here suggesting."[119] House, however, had already de-briefed Frankfurter after the Morgenthau Mission and did not seem nearly as impressed as Wilson.[120]

Neither Frankfurter nor Lippmann understood the depths of House's anti-Semitism. In 1912, House had kept Brandeis out of Wilson's cabinet either as attorney general or as secretary of commerce and labor and even opposed Brandeis for solicitor general.[121] It was no coincidence that Wilson had nominated Brandeis to the Court when House had been out of the country.[122] Why, then, did House hire Lippmann on the Inquiry? Lippmann, as House had explained to Wilson, was the right type of Jew—a fully as-similated, moneyed, German Jew, and most of all quiet. "The objection to Lippmann is that he is a Jew," House wrote Wilson, "but unlike other Jews he is a silent one. The small group around me must be in thorough sympa-thy with your purposes."[123]

Not content to exclude Frankfurter based on pure anti-Semitism, House sullied his reputation with the president by blaming Frankfurter for press leaks about the Inquiry and related matters.[124] Both David Lawrence of the *New York Evening Post* and Lincoln Colcord of the *Philadelphia Public Ledger* had broken the news about House's new organization and its preparation for the eventual peace negotiations.[125] Colcord was in "constant contact" with House. House had sponsored Colcord's appointment to the *Public Ledger* and had cultivated Colcord and the *Public Ledger*'s Washington bureau chief, William C. Bullitt.[126]

A month after Colcord's article, Bullitt broke a story that House would represent the United States at the upcoming Inter-Allied Conference and that Lippmann would be accompanying House there.[127] House once again blamed Frankfurter, who was friends with Bullitt. "I am sorry about all this public-ity in regard to the work you have asked me to do but it was inevitable after Frankfurter told Bullitt of the Ledger ...," House wrote Wilson. "The Jews from every tribe have descended in force, and they seem determined to break in with a jimmy if they are not let in."[128] Wilson was extremely annoyed by "the very inconsiderate talk of some people who ought to have known better" and wanted Bullitt removed as the *Public Ledger*'s Washington bureau chief.[129]

It is true that Frankfurter's ties to "Billy" Bullitt ran deep—Bullitt frequented the House of Truth, as did his wife, Ernesta Drinker Bullitt. Frankfurter teased Lippmann about being "a rival inside tracker" for the

affections of Ernesta, who "needs no description."[130] Ernesta's aunt, portrait painter Cecilia Beaux, obsessively captured her development from a
girl to young woman.[131] Both Frankfurter and Lippmann may have been
courting Ernesta.[132] Everyone else was. Frankfurter, however, saw Ernesta
as more than an object of desire. Homeschooled in Pennsylvania and privately tutored in Paris, Ernesta spoke with an affected aristocratic accent of
long *a*'s and dropped *r*'s but lacked a proper education.[133] " Bob [Grosvenor]
contributed to my scientific & medical education, Arthur Ludington to my
economic & sociological, Billy to my literary, Felix Frankfurter to my political," Ernesta wrote in an unpublished memoir.[134]

Ernesta Drinker Bullitt, painted by her aunt, Cecilia Beaux

In the fall of 1915, twenty-two-year-old Ernesta had enrolled at Radcliffe without taking any examination or any formal high school education. She claimed that she had sweet-talked the dean into admitting her; others attributed her admission to Frankfurter. "I don't know how the powers were persuaded to enroll a girl without degrees or academic credits, except that Felix Frankfurter, then teaching at the Harvard Law School, had something to do with it," Ernesta's homely but talented younger sister, author Catherine Drinker Bowen, wrote. "He admired Ernesta, and, like various of her men friends, desired to 'educate' her. Actually, Ernesta was the only one of the family with a social conscience."[135]

At Radcliffe, Ernesta lived in the top-floor bedroom of a house occupied by "two old maids" who took an active interest in her comings and goings and questioned her choice of friends. "My association with Felix Frankfurter and Walter Lippmann worried them greatly," Ernesta wrote in her unpublished memoir. "Did my parents know that I was associating with Jews? ... I have always liked Jews. Their quickness, their swift appreciation of any lovely thing, their ardor, the intensely personal quality of their friendship, their gift of swift intimacy. As I look back on it, I see how much the Jew there was in Billy."[136]

Bullitt, whose mother's family was Jewish, hailed, like the Drinkers, from a prominent Philadelphia family of lawyers and was voted "most brilliant senior" in Yale's class of 1912.[137] He dropped out of Harvard Law School after less than a year because of his disenchantment with the law and his father's death.[138] Bullitt embarked on a career in journalism and landed a job at the *Public Ledger*, where he quickly rose from cub reporter to editorial writer to war correspondent. Before his overseas assignment, he asked Ernesta to marry him and to accompany him to Europe.[139] She agreed and left Radcliffe. In May 1916, Billy and Ernesta were married.[140] The following year, she gave birth to a son, who died two days later.[141] They returned to the United States because of her health and his designs on government service. For the time being, he served as the paper's Washington bureau chief and started all the trouble with his story about House, Lippmann, and the Inter-Allied Conference.

Despite his friendship with the Bullitts, Frankfurter denied that he had been the leaker. Since returning from the Morgenthau Mission in August 1917, he had spoken to the Washington correspondent, but Bullitt had already learned about the Inquiry from his colleague Colcord, who had learned about it from House directly. Bullitt also knew that Frankfurter had met with House. "I told Bullitt nothing," Frankfurter wrote in a private memorandum, "except the vaguest generalities of my talks with the Colonel, such as his liberal outlook, etc., and Bullitt said, that I suppose he told you himself now the things that I told you."[142] Frankfurter also pointed out that many people, including Laski, had been discussing the need to prepare for the eventual peace conference and that Frankfurter had shown Bullitt some of Laski's outlines of an idea of what should be done about Germany.[143]

Frankfurter first heard about definitive plans for the Inquiry from the most likely source of the leak besides House himself—Lippmann. It was Lippmann who had alerted Bullitt to House's plans for the Inquiry.[144] Lippmann had been friends with Bullitt for several years, believed that Bullitt was "by all odds sharpest of the American [war] correspondents," and recommended him for a position in the State Department as a "man of very rare ability and character."[145] In Frankfurter's absence, Bullitt had been a frequent guest at the House of Truth. In June, Lippmann also entertained Bullitt's colleague Colcord for breakfast at the House and solicited Colcord to write for the *New Republic*.[146] It was Lippmann who had alerted Frankfurter to House's and the president's suspicions. Out west at the time, Frankfurter entrusted Lippmann to set House straight and expected House to clear things up with the president.

Yet by late December Frankfurter realized that the president's mind had not been changed. "Now on the matter that bothers me, for once," he wrote Lippmann. "I've heard the President said, 'Frankfurter is fine, etc. but—he can't keep a confidence.' Clearly the Colonel passed on to him what he told you before its correction by you. I asked to see the Colonel with a view of having him correct the President."[147] In Frankfurter's absence, Lippmann had tried to smooth things over with House. "I am very much disturbed at what you said on Saturday about possible 'leaks' through indiscretions of Frankfurter," Lippmann wrote. "I have inquired about it and I am satisfied that what came out came through other sources, and not through him."[148] Finally, in January 1918, Frankfurter discussed the rumors with House in person. "I told the Colonel that I did not want an impression as to a breach left in his or the President's mind," Frankfurter wrote, "and he tended to dismiss the subject, saying that it was all over and everybody involved had long since forgotten about it."[149]

House certainly held no grudge against Bullitt. In July 1917, Bullitt, then working for the Committee on Public Information, enlisted House's assistance to avoid military service by landing a job as personal secretary to the president.[150] " I have thought that he might need the services of a young man who is used to keeping his mouth shut and to dealing confidentially with all sorts of men from Foreign Ministers and Ambassadors to day laborers," Bullitt wrote. After apologizing to House in October for the leak in the *Public Ledger*, Bullitt landed a job as assistant secretary of state and began a checkered diplomatic career and lifelong friendship with House.[151] As fond as he was of Bullitt, House never changed his mind about Frankfurter, who continued to correspond with House but never worked on the Inquiry.

In December 1917, Lippmann and his Inquiry colleagues drafted a memorandum about the interests of all the "great powers" in any future peace conference.[152] On January 4, House and Wilson discussed the memorandum, "The Present Situation: War Aims and Peace Terms It Suggests," and the president wrote the first draft of the Fourteen Points in the margin.[153] Four days later, Wilson delivered his address to Congress containing the Fourteen Points.[154] After hearing Wilson's message, Lippmann believed that he had "put words into the mouth of the President."[155] Through his work on the Inquiry, Lippmann was helping Wilson to remap the world.

Frankfurter's exclusion from the Inquiry and his undeserved reputation as a leaker did not dampen his friendship with Lippmann. He visited the Lippmanns in New York several times in 1918 and was philosophical about their departure from the House of Truth. " I had a bright thought this morning as I reflected on the many changes in the House of Truth these last few years," Frankfurter wrote Lippmann on a postcard while out west. "To wit: If Truth is like the H. of T., her shell may be absolute and permanent, but her content is temporary and pragmatic."[156]

The House's last original resident, Frankfurter enjoyed his life and work in wartime Washington and expanded his network of liberal allies. He was still in the good graces of Secretary of War Baker. He was still in close contact with his mentors Brandeis and Holmes. He had mastered the ins and outs of the War and Labor Departments. He had assumed Valentine's role as the nation's foremost expert on mediating labor disputes. On Christmas Day 1917, Frankfurter was in Chicago settling a meatpacking strike.[157] He also presided over the residents and gatherings at the House of Truth. Indeed, Frankfurter ended his final letter of 1917 to Lippmann with a postscript: "The H of T still lives!"[158]

II

One-Man War

In the summer of 1915, Gutzon Borglum received a letter from one of Atlanta's oldest living Confederate widows, eighty-six-year-old C. Helen Plane. Plane's husband, Captain William F. Plane, was a surgeon who had been shot in the chest on September 17, 1862, at Antietam. He was left by the Confederate army on the battlefield, was taken by the enemy to a farmhouse, and died as night fell. After the war, Plane had her husband's body removed and reburied in his hometown of Macon, Georgia.[1] She never remarried and dedicated her life to carrying on the memory of the Confederacy.

The founder of the Atlanta chapter of the United Daughters of the Confederacy, Plane spearheaded the drive for a Confederate memorial at Stone Mountain, Georgia.[2] She was inspired by two 1914 newspaper columns. In May, the brother of Georgia's former governor had proposed the idea of a Greek temple at the base of the mountain.[3] Later that summer, journalist John Temple Graves suggested carving a bust of Robert E. Lee.[4] Plane persuaded Sam Venable, whose family owned Stone Mountain, to donate twenty feet at the base of the mountain for a memorial.[5] She pitched the idea to the Atlanta chapter of the United Daughters of the Confederacy and was named president of the Stone Mountain Confederate Memorial Association.[6] All she needed was a sculptor.[7]

In July 1915, Plane invited Borglum to Atlanta to discuss the memorial and to see Stone Mountain. Enthralled with "the idea of having a whole mountain to chisel," the sculptor began asking southern friends if they had contacts with members of the memorial committee.[8] "It would be a great work—could be," he wrote, "or it could be a great failure."[9] On August 9, Borglum informed Plane that he would be in Atlanta within ten days.[10] When he arrived at the train station, she refused to shake his hand out of

Borglum with his son, Lincoln

fear that the sculptor's northern relatives improbably might have killed her husband.[11] Plane and other members of the commission drove Borglum to Stone Mountain. They pointed out the twenty feet of rock donated for the memorial and asked him what he thought about carving Lee's head there. "Ladies," he said, "I don't know what to think. But it seems to me that a twenty-foot head of Lee on the side of that mountain would look like a stamp on a barn door."[12]

Instead of returning to Atlanta for a luncheon with his hosts, Borglum stayed at Stone Mountain for three days. He befriended its owner, Sam Venable, and bunked in the Venable family summer home at the base of the mountain. Borglum hiked all over the mountain and scaled its northeastern face. He watched the sun rise and fall on the mountain and marveled at its purple hues. As the sun set on the third day, he had a vision. He saw the Confederate army—led by Lee, Stonewall Jackson, and Jefferson Davis—marching across the mountain's face.[13]

Venable asked how much of the mountain Borglum would need to execute his vision. With the Venable family's blessing, Borglum initially requested 200 feet and eventually took over the entire 800-by-1,500-foot face. Borglum could not wait to get home and to begin drawings of the Confederate army with its most famous figures leading the way. Before he left Atlanta, he wrote Plane that his vision of the memorial was "practical," "possible," and "need not be overly expensive—and yet can be so executed as to be the most significant monument in the western world. ... I can see Lee's Jackson's Johnson's Army finding their way across the Mountain."[14]

Borglum vowed that his Confederate memorial would be "an American monument."[15] For years, he had advocated a type of cultural nationalism associated with leftist writer Randolph Bourne and other *New Republic* contributors.[16] "[A]rt in America," Borglum wrote in June 1914, "should be American, drawn from American sources, memorializing American achievement."[17] He blasted Daniel Chester French's design for the Lincoln Memorial as "a Greek temple without a mark or relief or any record on it anywhere of thirty years of the most heart-rending story that a people ever went through; a cold, classical, meaningless temple of two or three thousand years ago."[18] Borglum's own tributes to Lincoln, his marble bust in the US Capitol and seated Lincoln in Newark, brought him praise from Lincoln's son Robert and enough national acclaim to attract the attention of an eighty-six-year-old Confederate widow.[19] As he explained to Plane and others, Stone Mountain would allow Borglum to create a uniquely American monument that would put the Sphinx and the Pyramids to shame. "Had the Egyptians possessed Stone Mountain," he told the Daughters of the Confederacy, "there can be little doubt they would have shaped it into the first wonder of the world."[20]

Money was the only obstacle. The United Daughters of the Confederacy had refused to fund the project. Later that year, Plane informed Borglum that filmmaker D. W. Griffith had pledged proceeds from a local Monday matinee of his racist propaganda film, *The Birth of a Nation.* "Since seeing this wonderful picture of Reconstruction in the South I feel that it is due the Ku-Klux Klan which saved us from negro domination and carpet-bag rule, that it be immortalized on Stone Mountain," Plane wrote. "Why not represent a small group of them in their *nightly* uniform approaching in the distance?"[21] There is no record of Borglum's response. On Thanksgiving night in 1915, fifteen men burned a cross atop Stone Mountain and, for the first time since Reconstruction, revived the Ku Klux Klan.[22]

In January 1916, Borglum revealed his idea for the Confederate memorial in a national publicity campaign.[23] The nation's largest newspapers published his early sketches, a first-person account, and lengthy articles promoting the project.[24] The estimated size of the three Confederate heroes—fifty feet high. The estimated cost of the memorial—$2 million. The estimated time to complete it—eight years.[25]

Five months later, about 20,000 people gathered at the foot of the mountain for the May 16 dedication. Borglum, Plane, and a few remaining Confederate veterans watched local Masons lay the cornerstone. The band played "Dixie" and "Yankee Doodle." A fifty-foot Confederate flag was unfurled on the face of the mountain and looked tiny by comparison. Borglum knew that his carvings would have to be at least fifty feet high, if not bigger. He also knew that this would be a massive undertaking. He told the crowd that he hoped to live to see it finished.[26]

For two years, Borglum prepared the mountain for carving. The first step was surveying its granite face, which was so steep that local workers were afraid to scale it below a red line that had been drawn into the mountainside. A man named Jesse George Tucker showed them it could be done and became the project's superintendent.[27] Tucker and his men established a hoist system with 2,000 feet of steel cable to carry small trucks of materials. They built horizontal cables across the mountain and cleared the surface of loose stone. They purchased 11,000 pine planks and built 500 feet of steps with four platforms at various intervals. They planned a road to the top of the mountain.[28]

While his men overcame technological hurdles, Borglum worked on plaster models of the main groups of soldiers on horseback and traveled the country making speeches and seeking donations. "If I can create this memorial in America," he wrote his wife, Mary, "I will do the greatest possible service to the Heart and Soul of this great part of America and will do the most important service to the honest belief in greatness and our place in great annals of this world that has been undertaken or done and that will be something."[29]

The US entry into the war in Europe brought the building of Borglum's Confederate Memorial to a standstill. The war dried up his funding and manpower. It took his trusted superintendent, Tucker, into the army. It also brought Borglum back to Washington, DC, on a regular basis. During this period, he astonished Frankfurter and Justice and Fanny Holmes by drawing Lee, Jackson, Davis, and the rest of the Confederate army on the dining room tablecloth at the House of Truth.

Borglum's faith in the federal government was sorely tested by what he saw and heard about war-related industries. In November 1917, he traveled to Cleveland to discuss some technological problems related to Stone Mountain's hoisting system. While in Ohio, he stopped in Dayton and toured the Dayton-Wright Company's aircraft factory. What he saw appalled him—it had been seven months since the United States entered the war, and the company had not produced a single fighter plane.

Borglum believed that state-of-the-art fighter planes could save American lives and end the war. He made it his mission to expose what he viewed as corruption and profiteering in an aircraft industry captured by the automobile industry and in need of a major overhaul. He became a fixture in wartime Washington and the center of public controversy. He put his reputation and financial solvency on the line and began fighting what the title of his unfinished autobiography described as a "one-man war."[30] "Gutzon was for war, for all sorts of war, six wars at a time," Frankfurter recalled. "People weren't wrong; they were crooked. People didn't disagree with him; they cheated him."[31]

★★★

Borglum—his full name was John Gutzon de la Mothe Borglum—developed his fighting spirit on the western frontier. His father, Jens (later James), had converted to Mormonism in Denmark, learned English while working as a Mormon missionary, and in April 1864 left Denmark for the United States. Just before his ship arrived in New York, James married another Mormon émigré, twenty-two-year-old Ida Michelson.[32] The newlyweds headed for Salt Lake City. With the church's blessing, James also married Ida's younger, more beautiful sister Christiane (later Christine or Christina).[33]

The Borglums soon moved to Bear Lake Valley, Idaho, near the town of Ovid. James built a two-room cabin, but the family spent much of the winter of 1866 living in a log fort with other Mormon families to protect themselves from Indians.[34] On March 17, 1867, Gutzon was born to Christine, the first of her two sons. James moved his growing family to Ogden, Utah, to build the transcontinental railroad. Christine's second son, Solon, was born there. After the railroad was finished, the Borglums left the Mormon Church and moved to Omaha, Nebraska.

Gutzon grew up with feelings of abandonment. His mother, Christine, listed in the 1870 census as a "domestic servant," left the nontraditional family two years later by "mutual consent" when he was five.[35] He remembered the day that she said good-bye. " Gutzon," she said, "take care of little Solon." Gutzon's account made it seem as if she had been on her deathbed.[36]

In reality, Christine started a new life and a new family with a thirty-six-year-old blacksmith and Union army veteran, Joseph Wilson. They had three children and a long-buried Borglum family secret: Joseph Wilson was a light-skinned black man.[37]

During the Civil War, Wilson had worked as a blacksmith in the Fifty-Fourth Massachusetts Regiment. On May 12, 1863, he had been mustered into the Union army's most famous black regiment as a private in Company K by Oliver Wendell Holmes Jr.'s best friend, Norwood "Pen" Hallowell.[38] Wilson was with the regiment during its famous assault on South Carolina's Fort Wagner. A year into his service, he contracted a lung ailment that his wife claimed bothered him for the rest of his life. In 1871, Wilson was working in Omaha as a blacksmith and met Borglum's mother, Christine.[39] In October 1872, they moved to Muncie, Indiana, got married, and started a family there.[40]

In 1871, the same year that Joseph Wilson and Christine Michelson had met, James Borglum moved his family from Omaha to St. Louis to study homeopathic medicine. Three years later, Dr. Borglum moved his family back to Omaha to start his medical practice and later took over a practice in Fremont, a Nebraska frontier town about thirty-five miles west of Omaha.

From ages seven to twelve, Gutzon repeatedly ran away from home. He thrived on adventure. He bought a wild horse for sixty-five cents from an Indian and tamed the horse himself.[41] He served as his father's trusted assistant on medical calls for births and gunshot wounds.[42] He yearned to attend West Point or to return to Denmark to build ships. Instead, the fourteen-year-old was sent to a Catholic boarding school, St. Mary's College in Kansas. At St. Mary's, he developed a love for drawing and painting. It was his only formal schooling.

Three years later, Gutzon and his family moved to Los Angeles. His father may have tried to reunite with Christine.[43] After a few months in Los Angeles, James Borglum moved the family back to Nebraska and later ordered his son Solon never to reveal the "sickening details" of the family's past.[44]

Christine's second husband, Joseph Wilson, had died at forty-four in 1880 in Muncie, Indiana, and was considered one of the town's "best colored citizens."[45] After Joseph's death, Christine and her three children moved to Chicago. During the 1880s, she worked as a laundress and petitioned the federal government to collect her husband's Union army pension of twelve dollars per month plus two dollars for each child under sixteen. "I have never in any manner," she swore in her petition, "aided or abetted the rebellion."[46] After she succeeded in collecting the pension, Christine moved to Los Angeles with her children. Two children died in their twenties nearly a year apart; their death certificates listed them as white.[47] Christine worked as a dressmaker and lived in Los Angeles with her youngest child, a daughter.[48] On February 3, 1901, Gutzon's mother died of bronchitis at fifty-four in the same city where he began his career as an artist.[49]

Though it is unknown whether he ever reunited with his mother, eighteen-year-old Gutzon stayed in Los Angeles after the rest of his family had left town. He learned engraving as an apprentice to a lithographer and worked on a crew of fresco painters.[50] He soon moved into the studio of a thirty-six-year-old portrait painter and divorcee, Elizabeth "Lisa" Jaynes Putnam. Together they studied painting in San Francisco. At twenty-two, he married Lisa and became a fixture in the Los Angeles art scene.[51] He painted the portrait of General John C. Fremont and won an important patron in Fremont's wife, Jessie Benton Fremont.[52]

With Jessie Fremont's support, he and Lisa left Los Angeles in 1890 and headed east. Along the way, Gutzon visited his family in Omaha, reunited with his younger brother, Solon, and encouraged Solon to become an artist.[53] In New York City, Gutzon sold forty of his paintings thanks to Jessie Fremont's contacts, including Borglum's new friend, police commissioner Theodore Roosevelt.[54] Gutzon and Lisa earned enough money from the successful New York exhibition to go to Paris.

During two years in Paris, a year in Spain, a brief return to California, and a move to London, Gutzon made a living as a painter and dabbled in sculpture. His early sculptures consisted of Indian sentinels, a warrior fallen from his horse, and the face of a young girl. In Paris, Borglum studied art at the Académie Julian and École des Beaux-Arts and met the person who inspired him to become a sculptor—Auguste Rodin. Though he never formally studied with him, Gutzon frequented Rodin's studio and regarded Rodin as a mentor, friend, and "one of the greatest individuals of history."[55]

Besides Rodin, the other factor that turned Borglum into a sculptor was the success of his brother, Solon. In 1893, Solon had abandoned his life as an Omaha rancher and had moved to California intent on becoming an artist like his brother. For a time, Solon lived with Gutzon in California but clashed with Lisa.[56] Solon eked out a living for several years as a California artist; he then studied drawing, painting, and sculpture for two years at the Cincinnati Academy of Art and earned enough money to go to Paris. In Paris, other American artists, including Augustus Saint-Gaudens, encouraged him to capture the Old West in sculpture. Solon's *Stampede of Wild Horses* was chosen for the entrance to the US pavilion at the 1900 Paris Exhibition, and two other works won silver and bronze medals there.[57] He married a Frenchwoman and returned to New York City. By the fall of 1901, Solon had become the best-known sculptor named Borglum.

Gutzon's decision to focus on the same medium as Solon created a lifetime of sibling rivalry and public confusion.[58] They competed for the same projects, including a $250,000 prize to memorialize General Ulysses S. Grant.[59] After that experience, they pulled out of several competitions rather than vie with each other for business. Yet Gutzon irritated Solon's family by referring to his younger brother as his pupil. Solon, according to his family, was supposed to be the sculptor named Borglum who was hired to carve Stone Mountain.[60] Solon had endeared himself to the people of Atlanta with his 1907 monument to General John G. Gordon and had memorialized other Confederate generals at Vicksburg. Sam Venable's sisters told Solon's family in 1924 that they thought Stone Mountain was going to be "a joint enterprise" by the Borglum brothers.[61] But Plane, the driving force behind the project, told a different story.[62] More likely, Gutzon invited Solon to assist him on the Confederate Memorial project. Days before the initial dedication in May 1916, Solon joined Gutzon for a weekend visit to Venable's house at Stone Mountain.[63] The visit, however, never resulted in a collaboration or a thawing of relations between the two families.

Whether it was his brother's rapid rise or his own failure to achieve widespread fame by age thirty, Gutzon left Lisa and Paris in November 1901 and moved to New York City to reinvent himself as a sculptor. His sculpting career did not get off to an auspicious start. In September 1902, he suffered from a mysterious fever and a nervous breakdown. He recovered after a brief reunion with his family in Omaha and returned to New York to begin his sculpting career and to be with his new love, twenty-seven-year-old Mary Montgomery.[64]

Borglum had met Montgomery on the ship home from Paris. Born in Turkey to American missionaries, a graduate of Wellesley College, and fluent in Sanskrit, Hebrew, Turkish, Arabic, Greek, and Egyptian, Montgomery had earned a PhD in linguistics from the University of Berlin.[65] A Berlin correspondent described her as "a delicate-looking little Yankee girl with bright blue eyes and rosy cheeks, who looks frail and tiny, as if a strong gust of wind might pick her up and carry her away. It seems incredible that so much learning can be compressed into such a small compass."[66]

With Mary at his side, Gutzon returned to health and devoted himself to becoming a great sculptor. His *Return of the Boer* won a gold medal at the 1904 St. Louis Exposition, and two years later banker James Stillman purchased one of Gutzon's most famous works, *The Mares of Diomedes*, for the Metropolitan Museum of Art. The bust of Lincoln in the US Capitol, statue of General Philip Sheridan on horseback at Sheridan Circle, and chummy relationship with Theodore Roosevelt established Gutzon's reputation in Washington, DC.

After finalizing his divorce from Lisa in 1909, Gutzon and Mary were married and settled on 300 acres of Stamford, Connecticut, property that they called Borgland.[67] Mary bore him two children, a son, Lincoln, in 1912 and a daughter, Mary Ellis, in 1916, and held together the family's finances. Gutzon's business instincts were his Achilles' heel. He was perpetually indebted to New York financiers, including Eugene Meyer, who had bought Borglum's bust of Lincoln and donated it to the US Capitol and had lent the sculptor $40,000 plus 6 percent interest to purchase Borgland.[68] Meyer's loan dogged Borglum for years and became a source of contention during the sculptor's wartime inquiries into the aircraft industry.

★★★

Borglum's faith in the federal government led him to take his information about corruption in the aircraft industry straight to the White House. He had known Woodrow Wilson since his days as the president of Princeton. In 1904, Princeton had commissioned Borglum to create gargoyles atop Class of 1879 Hall. Five years later, the sculptor had returned to Princeton to create more gargoyles for Guyot Hall and to receive an honorary degree.[69] He frequently wired the president political suggestions and in May 1915 called on Wilson at the White House.[70]

In November 1917, Borglum arrived in Washington and requested a meeting with the president to discuss the aircraft situation.[71] Wilson admitted that he was in no position to discuss the issue and asked his personal secretary, Joseph Tumulty, to inquire about the matter.[72] Borglum refused to be put off. A week later, he pressed for a meeting with Wilson about the aircraft situation "because of a desire deeper than any I have outside my immediate family's happiness, that of helping the country at this hour." He then explained that the automobile industry had captured the aircraft board and has led to "cheap, grandiose projects, incapable of fulfillment, which cannot but bring scandal or disaster, and which in turn can harm none but the Administration."[73] Wilson took Borglum's concerns seriously. " Gutzon Borglum is a sincere fellow and this letter disturbs me," he wrote Tumulty. " Is there not somebody you can consult about how to reply to it? Perhaps you might have a few words with Baker about it."[74]

Secretary of War Baker informed Tumulty that the aircraft board had consulted with some of the nation's top experts, as well as its European allies, in designing and producing aircraft. The country's inexperience in manufacturing warplanes made technological delays and setbacks inevitable. Baker, who knew Borglum "personally" but thought that the sculptor's patriotism may have clouded his judgment, reassured Tumulty that "our aircraft program and the progress made in it are wholly worthy of the confidence of the people."[75]

But where Secretary Baker saw excusable inefficiency, Borglum saw corruption. The sculptor had been fascinated with airplane technology since Samuel P. Langley's early flight experiments at the Smithsonian Institution. Three years after the Wright brothers' first flights in 1903 at Kitty Hawk, Borglum had joined the Aero Club of New York. In September 1908, he had represented the club at one of Orville Wright's military demonstrations at Fort Myer, Virginia. Wright had stayed airborne for more than an hour thanks in part to Borglum's suggestion to station a man on the roof of a shed and to alert Wright when he had reached the sixty-minute mark.[76] During a similar test flight a week later, Wright had crashed his plane, killing his passenger and nearly himself.[77] " I am but one of millions who shall ever be grateful to you and your brother for what you have done," Borglum wrote to Wright after the accident, "and kindly count me ever ready to do anything within my power to aid you both."[78] Once Orville had recovered, Borglum had chaired an Aero Club committee that presented gold medals to the Wright brothers at the White House.[79]

Borglum fashioned himself something of an airplane expert who believed that airplanes should be less like gliders and more aerodynamic. He had been tinkering with designs for an airplane that looked like a fish, a new air brake, and an improved propeller. He compared his fascination with airplane technology with that of Leonardo da Vinci and believed that he was qualified to judge the shocking state of aircraft production in Dayton.[80]

With Secretary Baker skeptical about the vagueness of Borglum's allegations, Wilson pressed the sculptor for specifics.[81] In December 1917, Borglum visited other airplane factories and found additional evidence of "irregularities, graft, self-interest, and collateral profiting."[82] He asked the president to establish a three-person commission of aviation experts, including Borglum; Wilson refused. "I had a very full report about it not long ago and things seemed going very satisfactorily," he wrote Tumulty. "If Mr. Borglum has a grievance or has any personal element in it, it is rather important that we should know."[83]

At Secretary Baker's suggestion, however, Wilson invited Borglum to come to Washington to substantiate the allegations.[84] "I urge you to come at once to Washington, lay the whole matter frankly and fully before the Secretary, and by your own investigation discover the facts in this business," Wilson wrote Borglum in a January 2 letter drafted by Baker. "The Secretary of War assures me that he will be delighted to clothe you with full authority to get to the bottom of every situation."[85]

Borglum mistakenly believed that the letter granted him a commission as the administration's official investigator. At 10:00 a.m. on January 7, 1918, he arrived in Washington and started a three-week preliminary investigation. At 6:00 p.m. that first day, he consulted a "personal friend" from the House of Truth and a veteran of many investigations on the public's behalf—Justice Brandeis.[86]

Sitting in the justice's library, Brandeis encouraged Borglum's efforts and supplied the name of a crackerjack investigator. Borglum showed him Wilson's letter.

"Well—That will get you as far as they want you to, and no harm done," Brandeis predicted. "And then—they will stop you."

"But," Borglum replied, "I won't be stopped."

"Supposing the plan to stop you comes from the White House," Brandeis asked. "What will you do?"

"I will follow it to the White House."

Brandeis, who had investigated Taft's firing of his forestry chief, Gifford Pinchot, during the Ballinger-Pinchot Affair, laughed.[87]

As Brandeis had predicted, Borglum encountered resistance from Secretary Baker and members of his staff, beginning with House of Truth resident Stanley King.[88] A classmate of Frankfurter's at Harvard Law School, King looked like a Massachusetts Yankee with his tall frame, long face, and narrow, slightly downward-sloping eyes. A second-generation Amherst College graduate, King had read law for a year with his father, a prominent Springfield lawyer, city solicitor, and future judge. The younger King had entered Harvard Law School as a second-year student and against his father's wishes, but his grades had earned him a spot on the *Law Review*.[89] After graduation, King had gone to work for the W. H. McElwain Company, a Boston shoe manufacturer that had tried to hire Frankfurter in 1914 and had been represented by Brandeis.

Stanley King and his wife, Gertrude, had been frequenting the House of Truth since its inception and had participated in some of its early intellectual debates. They befriended Valentine, Percy, and Holmes. Lippmann wrote that Gertrude King, a Vassar-educated poet and essayist, had "a cavalry temperament which made her wish to go fast and take a chance, to swim too far out in bad weather and drive too quickly on slippery roads, which made her in controversy a distressingly incisive and ironical adversary."[90]

Gertrude King debated Justice Holmes about the meaning of truth. She offered four different definitions. Holmes liked some of them, disliked others, and countered with one of his own: "Objective truth is a pure ideal that if everyone was as clever and educated as you they would agree with you and then the universe would be conquered. But even if we all agreed in everything, I don't see the guaranty that this universe would agree with us."[91] Gertrude added her fifth and final definition. "Truth," she wrote, "is the realization of the manageableness of facts."[92]

The elusive manageability of facts about aircraft production was a major source of friction between Borglum and Stanley King. Shortly before the United States entered the war, Frankfurter had assisted King in finding a job with Julius Rosenwald on the Council of National Defense's Committee on Supplies.[93] On October 4, 1917, King joined Frankfurter and Lippmann as one of Secretary Baker's confidential advisers on business matters at $1,200 per year.[94] With Gertrude staying in Boston to care for their two young children, Stanley lived at the House of Truth with Frankfurter, Lippmann, and Percy.[95]

King's connections to the House of Truth did not help Borglum, however. According to Borglum, King obstructed requests for documents, spied on him for Baker, and discouraged several key Dayton witnesses from talking to the sculptor.[96] King worked in Room 237 of the War Department, just down the hall from Borglum, who was in Room 225. Borglum became so suspicious that his investigation was being sabotaged that he set up shop at the Albany Hotel and the Metropolitan Club. He avoided official channels, invoked the president's letter, and gathered information on his own time and money.

After a three-week investigation in Washington and several trips to aircraft manufacturing plants, Borglum requested a meeting with the president. Instead, Wilson asked him to put all his findings and evidence in writing and urged the sculptor to be discreet.[97] Baker had informed Wilson about Borglum's frequent invocation of presidential authority based on the January 2 letter and urged Wilson to "examine just what he has and form some judgment as to how dangerous he is."[98]

Borglum waited around Washington for several days to meet with the president and to hand deliver the report.[99] Wilson, citing a cold, asked the sculptor to send it to him.[100] Borglum detailed a pattern of War Department obstruction that forced him to invoke Wilson's January 2 letter and to investigate "without aid."[101] In his nine-page "Preliminary Report on Aeronautic Conditions," he repeated that the automobile industry had captured the aircraft industry and frittered away $640 million in federal funds. "Our aeronautic board of production has been frankly and flatly a promoter's exercise ...," he wrote, and has "not produced a single service or battle plane that could be ordered across the lines." In seven months, these aircraft companies had produced only 1,444 training planes unfit for overseas use, and 40 percent of those planes were "worn out or useless."[102] The United States had been forced to buy Italian and French warplanes. Borglum believed that he had discovered "a chain of dishonesty and disorder that runs throughout our production department" and recommended that the president "might seize the whole bankrupt program."[103]

The villain of Borglum's story was Colonel Edward A. Deeds. Deeds had founded the Dayton-Wright Company when the United States had entered the war and volunteered for government service on the Aircraft Board. It was Deeds who had shown Borglum around the Dayton-Wright factory in the fall of 1917 and who had disclosed the automobile industry's capture of wartime aircraft production while on the same train bound for New York. After his conversation with Deeds, Borglum had left the train in Harrisburg and headed straight to the White House.[104]

According to Borglum's report, Deeds was the "dominant figure" in the scheme to funnel airplane contracts to Dayton-Wright as well as other

Deeds-owned companies.[105] A former executive at the National Cash Register Company, Deeds had been sentenced to a year in jail for criminal antitrust violations, later overturned on appeal. In 1915, he had founded Dayton Engineering Laboratories Company (Delco), which built ignition systems. Delco's ignition system was the only one compatible with the "Liberty Motor" that the automobile companies were manufacturing for the airplanes.

Some of Borglum's allegations about Deeds were way off-base—that Deeds's last name was originally Dietz and that he was of German descent. "My sympathies are with Germany," Borglum quoted Deeds, "but we must win the war."[106] Borglum's report also failed to disclose his own checkered history with Deeds. In 1913, Borglum had agreed to build a memorial to Wilbur Wright based on a model of a naked man with wings about to take flight. But after a flood that year had devastated Dayton, Deeds's committee had canceled the project after paying Borglum only a fraction of his $10,000 contract.[107] Four years later, Deeds hired Borglum to create a bronze bust for the mausoleum of his son, E. A. Deeds Jr.[108]

Despite the exaggerations and omissions in the report, Borglum's three-week investigation confirmed his initial fears—the US government had spent $640 million and did not have a single fighter plane to show for it. He begged Wilson to act: "Mr. President, the aeronautic program is as serious a piece of business as confronts the world. It might win the war. It, if it can do what its advocates boast, can save us from a hundred to two or three hundred thousand of our boys. Must it continue [to be] the butt of graft or inefficiency?"[109]

Borglum's preliminary report and persistent follow-up letters convinced the president of only one thing. "I think he is crazy," Wilson confided to House, "—and therefore, perhaps, all the more dangerous."[110] Instead, Wilson asked Secretary of War Baker to find someone impartial to read it.[111] Baker chose another of his volunteer assistants who frequented the House of Truth—financier Eugene Meyer Jr.[112]

Meyer's brother Walter lived in the House of Truth. A member of the Council of National Defense, Walter had graduated two years ahead of Frankfurter in law school and had befriended Frankfurter when the two men had worked in New York City.[113] Walter Meyer was one of several prominent Jews, along with Brandeis and Jacob Schiff, who had pledged money for Frankfurter's professorship.[114] Part of a wealthy California Jewish family, Walter and Eugene had grown closer after their youngest brother, Edgar, had died on April 15, 1912, aboard the *Titanic*.[115]

In Washington, Frankfurter introduced Eugene Meyer and his wife, Agnes, to Holmes, Brandeis, and the rest of the crowd.[116] The eventual owner of the *Washington Post*, Eugene Meyer recalled his evenings at the House of Truth with a mixture of awe and disdain: "They had a good many highbrow conversations, discussions and debates at the House of Truth and I was occasionally condescendingly invited by this highbrow as a sort of Philistine observer and recipient of their superior thinking."[117] Of all the men whom Meyer met there, including Frankfurter, Lippmann, and Percy, the resident who impressed him the most was a young lawyer on the US Shipping Board, Gerard C. "Gerry" Henderson. Meyer recalled that "they all did a lot of talking, and that sometimes after listening a while this little fellow, who had tousled hair, a very negligee shirt, unpressed trousers and unblackened shoes, would come into the discussion and finish it by a complete, comprehensive and convincing statement about what the right and wrong of it all was, after which debate ceased."[118] The president of the *Harvard Law Review*, Henderson, according to Frankfurter, was "by long odds the ablest man in the School."[119] A few years after meeting him at the House of Truth, Meyer hired Henderson to be general counsel of the War Finance Corporation.[120]

Meyer could afford to work in the Wilson administration as a "dollar a year" man. He had worked for Lazard Frères after graduating from Yale and had made millions by starting his own investment banking firm, Eugene Meyer Jr. & Company. When the United States entered the war, Meyer had dissolved his firm and had asked Brandeis to find him a job in the administration.[121] At first, Meyer had worked for Julius Rosenwald on the Committee on Finished Goods and later had distinguished himself with his knowledge of the copper industry while working for Bernard Baruch on the War Industries Board. In the War Department, Meyer was Secretary Baker's liaison to the Aircraft Board.[122] Thus, Baker chose Meyer to investigate Borglum's report. "It happens that Mr. Meyer has known Mr. Borglum for a long time," Baker wrote Wilson, "and believes that his presence at the interview will have considerable weight with Mr. Borglum in bringing him to a reasonable and proper attitude toward your confidence with regard to the whole subject."[123]

Though he was Baker's liaison to the aircraft board and a friend of the House of Truth, Meyer was in fact the wrong person to review Borglum's report. First, Meyer owned more than $5 million in stock in Fisher Body, an automobile company that was manufacturing the fuselages for the government's warplanes.[124] Second, he had helped Baker avert a political scandal by divesting Baker's brother of stock ownership in one of the Ohio aircraft companies.[125] Third, he had purchased Borglum's bust of Lincoln for the US Capitol and held a $40,000 mortgage plus 6 percent interest on Borgland. Both Baker and Meyer rejected the idea of seizing the aircraft production facilities. Instead, Baker charged Meyer with investigating Borglum's allegations against Colonel Deeds that the secretary of war described as recycled rumors in the press and "villainy … too monumental to be believed."[126]

Once he learned who would be reviewing the report, Borglum refused to turn over his data and charged the War Department with sabotaging his investigation. He told Meyer that he was "an improper person to be given a report by me, because you were my friend."[127] For years, he had resented Meyer's insistence that Borglum immediately repay the $40,000 mortgage plus interest.[128] The outstanding debts and bad feelings between Borglum and Meyer lingered for years.[129] Three months and an additional $300 million later, Borglum insisted that nearly a billion dollars had not produced a single warplane and that he had "done great national service in bringing on this investigation."[130]

With or without Meyer's review, the administration still faced trouble over Borglum's allegations. On March 12, 1918, Wilson appointed H. Snowden Marshall, former US attorney for Manhattan, to chair a three-person committee to investigate Borglum's accusations and to report within a month. Wilson asked Borglum to turn over his materials to the committee and insisted that "the whole aircraft matter is undergoing a very thorough review."[131] A few days after Wilson had formed the Marshall Committee, word of Borglum's secret report began to leak.[132] Herbert Bayard Swope, eager to defend the administration in the New York *World*, asked Wilson for a copy of Borglum's full report and informed the president that "in the abstracts that Borglum prepared he takes shots at [Bernard] Baruch and Meyer and others."[133]

At first, Borglum publicly praised Wilson for authorizing the investigation and urged the country to get its aircraft production in order.[134] But in the coming weeks, Wilson repeatedly refused the sculptor's offers of further assistance. Borglum continued to visit aircraft production facilities and met with federal officials, including Assistant Secretary of the Navy

Franklin Roosevelt, General Leonard Wood, and Senator Gilbert Hitchcock of Nebraska.[135] Upon hearing rumors that Deeds's friends would be put in charge of the aircraft program, Borglum was beside himself. "Is it possible no man of the Assistant Secretary of Navy's standing, ability and loyalty can be found?" he asked Wilson because of the sculptor's admiration for Roosevelt. "Mr. President, I've gone too deeply into this miserable business to be a silent partner in a patched up arrangement to further deceive this nation and the world and I cannot do it."[136]

Borglum soon found himself under attack. The pro-Wilson New York *World* reported that the Marshall Committee had found "no suspicion of graft or profiteering" and that the sculptor had "submitted no proof to back up his sensational conclusions."[137] After reading the *World* article, Borglum complained to Wilson: "It's been very unfair to me that I have been obliged to establish my own organization and with my own resources made my investigation. What your reason has been to leave me in this unpleasant position unsupported I do not know."[138] Wilson responded by disavowing that the administration had ever agreed to aid Borglum's investigation with expert assistance: "I never at any time constituted you an official investigator. I merely gave you the right to look into the matter of your own motion. ... [W]e have at no time regarded you as the official representative of the administration in making the investigation."[139]

Refusing to back down from Wilson and finding an ally in the *New York Times*, Borglum called for a criminal investigation. He disagreed with the Marshall report' and the Senate Committee on Military Affairs' conclusions that the solution lay in government reorganization—specifically in consolidating power in a new head of the aircraft board. On April 28, 1918, he issued his first detailed public statement in the *Times* arguing for a "judicial inquiry" into the "ring of aircraft manufacturers" who engaged in "corralling contracts" and "colossal profiteering" by spending "nearly a billion without the delivery of a serviceable plane."[140] The *New York Times* agreed: "We do not know whether Mr. Borglum's investigation discloses anything like knavery, with intent to aid the enemy, but even if there was no intentional obstruction, the result is the same, the enemy has been distinctly aided. It is enough that public funds have been squandered, and to a very large amount. For that somebody is responsible, and whoever it is should be exposed and fitly punished."[141]

After Senator Hitchcock conceded that the aircraft program had failed but that a Senate investigation was unnecessary because "the material

Mr. Borglum had would not be of any great value," a May 1 *New York Times* editorial defended Borglum's investigation: "He has brought to light the astonishing conditions that exist in the field of aircraft production, he has exposed the failure of the Aircraft Board and of the Signal Corps to construct airplanes. Is that 'material' of no value to the Senate?"[142]

The day after the *New York Times* editorial, Borglum testified for three hours before the Committee on Military Affairs behind closed doors. The Senate delayed in launching a full-blown investigation because some senators preferred that it be led by the Justice Department.[143] Borglum's secret Senate testimony and calls for a criminal investigation landed him on the front pages of the nation's newspapers but also exposed him to withering criticism.

Eight days after his Senate testimony, Borglum found himself at the center of a public controversy. The press and members of the Senate, wielding White House and army intelligence documents, accused Borglum of using his investigation for personal gain. They charged him with establishing an aircraft company with a British official and trying to steer government contracts their way.[144] Borglum denied the charges as a "scurrilous frameup" and declared his chief accuser, Kenyon W. Mix of the Dodge Manufacturing Company, "a confessed tool of Deeds."[145] He did not deny that he had experimented with designs for airplanes, air brakes, and propellers and had encouraged others to develop new technology in an effort to accelerate American airplane production—but only to end the war, not for personal gain. To President Wilson, Borglum vowed to testify publicly to rebut "certain false charges as to motive or monetary interest in my investigation" and to explain that "my *interest* was *to get planes*, of some kind, *built* and *delivered* to our army."[146]

The Wilson administration, undoubtedly aiding Borglum's accusers in the press and Senate, was privately gleeful. Wilson's personal secretary, Joseph Tumulty, believed that Borglum had "destroyed himself."[147] Wilson agreed: "I think Borglum is sure to make an ass of himself when he tries to make good."[148]

Despite these personal attacks on Borglum, his charges against the Wilson administration—what happened to the nearly $1 billion in federal money intended to produce military aircraft—refused to die.[149] Others agreed that automobile manufacturers, which were supposed to be producing the Liberty Motor for the airplanes, knew nothing about aircraft design, ignored foreign models, and had not produced any fighter planes.[150]

As a way to fend off a congressional investigation, Wilson initiated a Justice Department inquiry led by his Republican opponent in the last election—former Supreme Court Justice Charles Evans Hughes. Hughes had achieved fame in 1905 and 1906 for investigating the New York Gas and Electric monopoly and the state's insurance industry, investigations that had propelled Hughes to the governor's mansion.[151] By having liberal journalist Lincoln Colcord plant the idea with Colonel House, Borglum took credit for suggesting that Hughes lead the investigation.[152] On May 16, Hughes agreed to Wilson's request.[153] Borglum vowed to help even if it elected Hughes president and despite Hughes's lack of knowledge about the aircraft industry. "Justice Hughes knew as much about the aironautics [sic]," the sculptor wrote, "as I do about the underwear of a Japanese Prince."[154]

Borglum's frustration stemmed from Hughes's failure to connect all the dots even though Borglum had supplied him with more than 100 of the investigation's 280 witnesses. During his investigation, Hughes took more than 17,000 pages of testimony, and on October 25, 1918, he issued a 182-page report that saved the Wilson administration from embarrassment.[155] "Mr. Hughes's report," Borglum concluded nearly four years later, "was a failure."[156]

Yet Hughes vindicated Borglum's charges in fundamentally important ways—particularly as they related to Colonel Deeds.[157] President Wilson had relieved Deeds and the two other members of the Aircraft Board and instructed them to aid Hughes's investigation. Hughes's report recommended that Deeds be court-martialed for acting as a confidential adviser to one of his former business associates at Dayton-Wright and for issuing false and misleading public statements about aircraft production.[158] Hughes's report also detailed how Deeds had funneled government contracts to several of his former companies and that Deeds had held onto stock in these companies for much longer than he publicly had represented. Attorney General Gregory agreed that Deeds was "guilty of censurable conduct" and recommended "disciplinary measures."[159] Deeds, however, was never punished. A War Department review panel exonerated him and recommended against a trial by court-martial.[160] A *New York Times* editorial blamed Secretary Baker for letting Deeds off the hook.[161] Wilson had already pardoned two others whom Hughes had recommended for prosecution.[162] Though Deeds and his associates escaped punishment, Hughes's report, a subsequent congressional investigation, and media accounts revealed profiteering and waste in the aircraft industry that Borglum insisted had been there all along.[163]

The conventional historical wisdom about Borglum's aircraft investigation often echoes the Wilson administration's view—that the corruption charges were overblown and that Borglum had been humiliated.[164] The aircraft investigation was a complicated affair, and it is difficult a century later to determine where the truth lies.[165] Though at times Borglum made overheated and unsubstantiated allegations, he brought national attention to the problem that Deeds and other profiteers had wasted hundreds of millions of federal dollars and had not produced any airplanes suitable for combat. Yet the sculptor's faith in the federal government was unshaken. Writing years later, he recommended that the federal government take over all patents and inventions related to airplane technology and invest in new ideas in propellers, wings, fuselages, easier controls, more powerful engines, and "a noiseless plane."[166]

Borglum was deeply committed to winning the war and considered his aircraft investigation to be his wartime service to the nation. In a June 1918 civil service application, he listed the following men as his references: Theodore Roosevelt, Taft, Wilson, Rodin (deceased), and Frankfurter. He listed as his full-time job the aircraft investigation: "The greatest service I could at this time perform for the immediate good of the Nation, and aid to our Allies would be to completely rebuild our Aeronautic Department on *sane, informal* lines that would make it possible to function within a reasonable time and produce this war instrument of such character and standard as would answer the needs abroad and protect the lives of our students at home."[167]

Borglum's aircraft investigation came at great personal cost. He had neglected his commissions and had spent his own money on his investigation. His efforts to get the Wilson administration to reimburse his expenses repeatedly failed. He fell further in debt, took out additional mortgages on Borgland, and owed more interest to financiers, including Eugene Meyer. Borglum was briefly kicked out of the Metropolitan Club, allegedly for unpaid bills but in reality "because he had brought the name of the Club disrepute or least unpleasant notoriety in regard to the aviation matter."[168] He had clashed with President Wilson, Secretary of War Baker, and other members of the administration. He had made enemies of some men at the House of Truth, including Eugene Meyer and Stanley King, but had maintained friendships with others, including Frankfurter and Brandeis. He had been publicly humiliated. And yet, after all the hue and cry about the aircraft investigation had died down, Borglum continued his one-man war against the establishment and continued to stand up for the common man. He continued to believe in the federal government's ability to invest in new projects and new technology. And he continued to believe in art as a way not just of preserving but of understanding American history.

12

Uniting the Labor Army

Frankfurter was conspicuously silent about Borglum's aircraft investigation—not because his House of Truth friends King and Eugene Meyer were intimately involved but because his outlook was so different from Borglum's. Borglum was an outsider who saw corruption and self-dealing by a handful of individuals involved with the aeronautics industry; Frankfurter was an insider who saw inefficiency on a much grander scale.

During the last few months of 1917, Frankfurter had been mediating labor disputes in the Pacific Northwest's lumber industry, an industry that produced lightweight spruce essential to building aircraft wings. Yet every time that he and his fellow mediators appeared close to a deal, Secretary of War Baker undermined his negotiations by conferring with the AFL's Samuel Gompers. With Frankfurter unable to broker an agreement, the military assumed control of spruce production. Out of his frustration, he discovered what he believed ailed not just aircraft production but the entire war effort. "But I'm glad—for it's now going to go straight up to the President," he wrote to Brandeis. "The confusion of authority, its haphazardness, the multiplicity of agencies without a central direction cannot go on much longer." He added: "Dear good Baker is swamped. ... This isn't a jeremiad at all, but the time has come when we cannot afford to continue the mistakes England taught us to avoid two years ago."[1,2]

Decades before the New Deal, Frankfurter began to use the power of federal agencies to change domestic labor policy to help the Wilson administration to fight the war. Based on his three years in the War Department from 1911 to 1914, Frankfurter knew that Secretary Baker was trying to do too much. His department was overburdened by too many agencies, boards, and committees and lacked the ability to control them. And based on his experiences in the field as a Valentine-inspired industrial relations expert, Frankfurter knew that the biggest issue facing the American war

effort was labor. With a more efficient administrative state and more efficient labor practices, critics like Borglum would fall by the wayside, aircraft
production would increase, and the United States would be able to end
the war.

After mediating a few more labor disputes in December, Frankfurter
returned to Washington to tell his boss the straight truth. On January 7,
1918, the same day that Borglum arrived in Washington to begin his aircraft
investigation, Frankfurter wrote Baker a confidential nine-page memorandum titled "Necessary Reorganization of the Functions Exercised by
the Secretary of War." After dismissing much of the criticism as partisan or
ill-informed and describing "shortcomings" in war mobilization as "inevitable," Frankfurter laid the problem bare: "The system under which we are
operating is inadequate and the heart of the trouble is the system and not
the persons who are operating it."[3] Baker, Frankfurter wrote, was trying
to do three jobs instead of one—running the army, managing war-related
industries and munitions, and setting labor policy.[4] "It is a responsibility," he
concluded, "which no mortal can discharge."[5]

Frankfurter

Frankfurter proposed consolidating numerous wartime agencies, committees, and departments under three executives in charge of the military,
industry, and labor. The secretary of war would maintain control over the
military but would name executives to oversee war-related industries/
munitions and labor relations.[6] With Baker due to testify before Congress
at the end of the month and at least one senator proposing a head of
munitions, Frankfurter advised his boss to take the lead in any potential
reorganization.[7] And Frankfurter intimated that others agreed with him.[8]
He shared a copy of his memorandum with Colonel House, who claimed
that "Baker was rather dumbfounded at the audacity of it."[9]

Frankfurter, however, had an important ally in Justice Brandeis. House
agreed to raise the issue with the president if, as Frankfurter had promised, Brandeis agreed to write a similar memorandum.[10] On January 9,
Brandeis wrote House that "the situation" was "very serious" and that
"betterment can come only through radical changes in systems."[11]
Brandeis advocated abolishing the War Industries Board and all of its
committees and putting a single executive in charge of munitions and
a single director with an advisory committee in charge of labor.[12] He
envisioned a war department "dealing then only with purely military
matters" by placing each branch of the military under a single department head. And he proposed a single Central Intelligence Office, a single
Shipping Board for the transportation needs of the War and Munitions
Departments, and a small war council "freed from the detail of administration and of executive responsibility."[13] Echoing Frankfurter, Brandeis
concluded: "It is only by freeing Secretary Baker from many of the burdens now improperly resting upon him that the country can get the full
benefit of his great ability and fine qualities."[14]

Despite his barely disguised anti-Semitism, House took their concerns
seriously because other people were saying the same thing. "Men of every
shade of political opinion condemn the organization as it now exists," House
wrote in his diary. "The President and Secretary Baker seem to be the only
ones that think the organization is as it should be."[15] House, however, had
already raised his organizational concerns with Wilson and was reluctant to
do so again.[16] He also had tried to oust Baker from the War Department
by shifting him to Interior.[17] It is unclear whether House kept his promise
to Frankfurter and Brandeis, but his resentment of the justice ran deep:
"I cannot quite understand why a Justice of the Supreme Court should
bother about other people's business as Brandeis does."[18]

Frankfurter's stock in the Wilson administration was rising. His reports the previous summer from Paris had revealed his skill in gathering facts and discerning the different European perspectives on the war. He had survived the allegations at the end of 1917 that he had leaked the existence of the Inquiry, and his letter of denial to House seemed to have rehabilitated his reputation. And on January 8, 1918, the President's Mediation Commission published Frankfurter's report on the Bisbee deportation and the Mooney case, a report criticized by Theodore Roosevelt and others but praised by liberals.[19]

On January 27, at House's suggestion, Secretary Baker authorized Frankfurter to travel to Britain and France to study "the machinery organized for the adjustment of labor disputes and the results attained, and also some other questions about which we have spoken confidentially."[20] Baker was particularly interested in "the solution of industrial questions affecting the production of war materials." Three days later, Frankfurter took the train to Boston to confer with Colonel House.[21] Not everyone was thrilled with Frankfurter's assignment, least of all British ambassador Walter Hines Page, who wrote: "But what the 'hot dog of war' (Frankfurter) has come over for ... I can't imagine. ... This little Jew comes for the War Dep't, after every General we have has been here and made a report. What he can find out that escapes them, the Law of Israel only knows."[22]

On January 31, Frankfurter sailed from New York harbor for London.[23] After what he described as "long days on the water," including several in life vests, he arrived in London on the night of February 8 to air raid sirens.[24] During his eighteen days there, he met with so many people that he did not have five minutes to sightsee. His British friends, Percy and Laski, provided him access to all the right people—members of the Labour, Liberal, and Conservative Parties; the radical left and radical right; and Prime Minister David Lloyd George and his government. "I've seen pretty much all the people I want to see," Frankfurter wrote, "from Lloyd George down—or up—and gauged the trend of events here."[25]

In early March, Frankfurter continued his hectic schedule in Paris. "I find the American pace is a bit swifter than the English and French are accustomed to," he wrote.[26] His second visit to Paris in two years reinforced why the United States had entered the war. "One feels here a little bit more vividly that it is liberty we are fighting for, the right to our own adventure of life, even tho there be much of 'inefficiency' of carelessness about us," he wrote. "And there is. But we prefer salvation by our own errors."[27]

Frankfurter hoped that America could learn from its mistakes and from the European labor situation. On March 24, while heading home aboard the USS

America, he transmitted a sixteen-page report to House on British and French labor attitudes. In both countries, the dissatisfaction of labor was political and unrelated to industrial conditions. They distrusted their own governments and looked to Wilson for leadership and for his democratic vision of a postwar future. "The ascendency of President Wilson among the great masses of both England and France is all pervading," Frankfurter wrote House. "Their dependence upon his leadership, the child-like trust in his authority is the most touching and awing fact in the present life of England and France. Intellectuals and proletariat are united in their devotion."[28] Frankfurter was concerned that Wilson was not using his goodwill to his advantage and needed to send better diplomats to these countries. "Some one should be on the spot, filled with understanding and belief in the President's policies," he wrote, "and with wisdom to enforce them both upon the English and French Governments."[29] On March 27, back in the States, Frankfurter reported to House in person.[30] It is unknown whether the confidential aspects of Frankfurter's mission, the ones that Baker had alluded to in his letter, stayed confidential. House's diary does not mention them. And Frankfurter definitely did not include anything about them in his written report.

★★★

Perhaps Frankfurter's biggest secret was his deepening relationship with Marion Denman, the Smith College graduate whom he had first laid eyes on five years earlier at the House of Truth. Before his trip to Europe, he had facilitated her return to Washington by helping her sister Helen land a job as a confidential clerk to Frederick Keppel in the War Department.[31] Soon after Frankfurter returned to Washington, Marion also found a War Department job as a special assistant to Raymond Fosdick, the chair of the Commission on Training Camp Activities (CTCA) overseeing the health and recreation of American troops at home and abroad.[32] The Denman sisters lived together at 2506 K Street, NW, near the Georgetown waterfront and a little more than a mile walk from 1727 Nineteenth Street.

From London, Paris, and Washington, Frankfurter overwhelmed Denman with increasingly passionate letters. Six weeks after he returned home, it became her turn to travel. She agreed to join Fosdick in Paris and London in early May to study women workers in military camps. The twenty-seven-year-old Denman's passport listed her as a social worker.[33] Before she left for Europe, Felix and Marion spent their last night together in New York City by taking a horse-drawn carriage ride around Central

Park. He proposed; she accepted. Though neither of them was religious, the pair knew that a mixed marriage between a Congregationalist minister's daughter and an Austrian-Jewish immigrant would face stiff resistance from both families. They decided to keep their engagement secret.[34]

On the morning of May 7, Denman boarded the SS *Espagne* on the French Line for Paris. "And now I'm off. I wish you were here to talk to—I *wish* I would tell you some things," she wrote during her first day aboard the ship. "I want you to know while I'm gone that I love you with all of me, know it every day afresh, be happy in it & sure of it, and work & play hard until I arrive back—to you." She signed it "L," for Luina—Holmes and Frankfurter's nickname for her.[35]

As Frankfurter knew from his own recent voyages, the Atlantic Ocean was rife with German submarines. The US Navy requested that daily newspapers stop reporting ship movements for fear of aiding the enemy and putting American ships in danger.[36] He learned that Denman had made it safely to France. From there, she accompanied Fosdick for a weeklong tour of the Western Front to survey the recreation and comfort provided by

Marion Denman

nonmilitary organizations, including the Red Cross. They returned to Paris and then went to Great Britain to study naval training camp activities.[37] Frankfurter worried that he would never see her again. "This is a hello and a wonder if you're not ever coming back," he wrote to her on June 9. "Not ever. It's good I have a 48 hours [a] day job."[38]

On July 12, Denman left Brest, France, on the USS *Von Steuben* and arrived in New York City nine days later.[39] She was greeted by her sister Helen at the gangplank. The first words out of Marion's mouth were: "You know that I am going to marry Felix."[40] For more than a year, they did not tell another soul. After eight weeks abroad, Denman returned to Washington. Frankfurter was of course delighted to have her back despite the fragile state of her health. "France seemingly gripped her—," he wrote one of their friends, "she is grave, of course, as every sensitive nature in immediate contact with the issue of life & death is bound to be. She's doing a real job and *that* I [believe] is therapeutic."[41]

Denman did not last long in Washington. In 1918, a flu pandemic spread across the globe, and soldiers returning from France brought it back to the United States. Having just returned from visiting French soldiers on the Western Front, Denman felt her own precarious health begin to fail. In an abundance of caution, she was sent to Saranac, New York, where they had treated her for her breakdown in the past but this time as a possible tuberculosis patient. A chest X-ray revealed an old lung infection but no signs that she was suffering from the flu or tuberculosis.[42] "That's very, very, very happy news you gave me tonight, dearest Marion," Frankfurter wrote after speaking to her on the phone. "Of course you whistled—and there was spring and color and body in your voice."[43]

After leaving Saranac for her parents' home near Springfield, Massachusetts, Denman was gaining weight by drinking a quart of milk a day and relaxing by napping and taking long walks. She returned to Washington after recovering her health and finished a report on women workers at military camps.[44] For the next two years, even after she had resigned from the commission and had left the city for good, she remained on the War Department payroll and wrote a history of the Commission on Training Camp Activities.[45] More than an administrative assistant to Chairman Fosdick, she was an investigator and writer greatly admired and respected by her boss. Her wartime service was nonetheless overshadowed by the increasingly high-profile work of her secret fiancé.

★★★

Soon after Denman accepted his marriage proposal, Frankfurter saw the recommendations in his January 7 report come to fruition. Nothing could stop the reorganization of the War Department, not with Borglum investigating aircraft production and mounting criticism of the war administration from Democrats and Republicans. On January 28, 1918, Secretary of War Baker testified for five hours before the Senate Committee on Military Affairs and fended off congressional attempts to reorganize his department long enough to pass legislation that empowered the president to do so.[46] Wilson appointed financier Bernard Baruch chair of the reorganized War Industries Board to supervise production. He also agreed to convene a war cabinet and established the National War Labor Board to resolve labor disputes—it would be co-chaired by former president Taft representing management and Kansas City lawyer Frank P. Walsh representing labor.[47]

Despite these changes, Frankfurter and others believed that the administration needed a director general of labor to coordinate the government's labor policies and procurement among the many wartime agencies. They lobbied for the person they thought was perfect for the job: Justice Brandeis.[48] Frankfurter offered to ask Holmes to speak to Chief Justice White about the necessity of Brandeis's temporary appointment to win the war—if Wilson so desired.[49] Wilson, however, was reluctant to take Brandeis away from the Court, even for a short time, and promised "to give the matter a little further thought."[50] Frankfurter and King urged Baker to influence the president's decision. They wrote him that they thought "the handling of the labor problem is the only crucial unresolved task of the war administration," and no one was better suited than Brandeis to take it on.[51]

Instead of a single labor czar, Wilson created the War Labor Policies Board and named as chairman the thirty-five-year-old Frankfurter. Frankfurter's appointment thrust him into the national spotlight. "In Washington," the New York Tribune wrote, "Professor Frankfurter is known as a 'liberal.' ... It generally is believed, however, that the appointment will be acceptable to both labor and capital."[52] A New York Times magazine headline a few weeks later described Frankfurter as "Uniting the Labor Army on a Single War Front."[53]

Though nominally reporting to Secretary of Labor William B. Wilson as one of his assistant secretaries, Frankfurter was charged with preventing wartime labor shortages by coordinating the labor needs of the War Department, the navy, the Department of Agriculture, the Shipping Board, the Railroad Administration, the War Industries Board, the Aircraft Board, and the Council of National Defense. Each of these departments would be represented on the War Labor Policies Board chaired by Frankfurter. "Since the outbreak of the war the United States government has come to be the greatest single employer of labor in the country," he said in his first public statement. "But it has had no operating policy with regard to the plants as a whole. Each one has been operated individually as a separate enterprise, quite apart from the others and, so far as the labor supply has been concerned, in actual competition with the others."[54]

Frankfurter's friends cheered his appointment. "I was pleased last night to have Walter Lippman[n] tell us that you knew more about labor than any man in Washington with the possible exception of Brandeis," Emory Buckner wrote.[55] The *New Republic* described Frankfurter's experience—mediating labor disputes, prosecuting fraud, and teaching administrative law—and added that "his chief qualification is that he has been able to win his way into the esteem and confidence of the men with whom he is now associated, men preeminently representative of business, the professions and labor."[56]

In accepting the chairmanship of the War Labor Policies Board, Frankfurter rejected the entreaties of *New Republic* editor Herbert Croly to become the chairman of the faculty of the newly formed New School for Social Research in New York City. Two days before he accepted, Frankfurter had informed Croly about the new labor post: "It is a man's—several men's jobs and high time that it is done. Incidentally, while I don't breathe a word about it, it ought to furnish a medium for dealing with the problems that loom beyond."[57] Frankfurter was fulfilling Valentine's vision by bringing efficiency to labor policy and the industrial workforce. His first goal was to centralize the government's labor procurement so that the United States could win the war. His second but equally important goal was to implement new policies that organized labor had been clamoring for and Valentine had fought for before his death—eight-hour workdays, workers' compensation, and child labor regulations.

During the course of 1918, Frankfurter revealed the power of federal agencies to make economic and social policy, to operate under the nation's radar, and to counteract reactionary decisions of the Supreme Court of the United States. On June 3, the Court struck down the Keating-Owen Child Labor Act that prohibited the interstate shipment of goods made by children under fourteen and by children between fourteen and sixteen who had worked more than eight hours a day, overnight, or more than six days a week. Roland Dagenhart worked with his two sons, Reuben, fourteen, and John, twelve, in a Charlotte, North Carolina, cotton mill and had challenged the law as exceeding the power of the federal government and infringing on the power of the states.[58] Reuben, who had quit school after the third grade to work in the mill with his father, believed that the heavy lifting and dusty conditions had stunted his and his brother's growth. The only thing they had received from the lawsuit was a bottle of Coca-Cola when they had visited the company's lawyers. When asked about the case, he referred to the owner of the mill: "You mean that suit the Fidelity Manufacturing Company won?"[59] In *Hammer v. Dagenhart*, five justices found that the child labor law exceeded Congress's power under the Commerce Clause and infringed on the power of the states because manufacturing was a purely local activity.[60] And, unlike similar federal bans on interstate transportation, the goods themselves were not inherently harmful.[61]

At the urging of Brandeis, Holmes wrote a dissent on behalf of four justices.[62] Holmes found it impossible to distinguish a child labor law from federal laws banning the sale of alcohol, the production of oleomargarine, or the interstate transportation of lottery tickets—laws that the Court had found to be constitutional.[63] He also recognized that the states were unable to deal with the problem of child labor on their own: "The national welfare as understood by Congress may require a different attitude within its sphere from that of some self-seeking State. It seems to me entirely constitutional for Congress to enforce its understanding by all the means at its command."[64]

Holmes knew that his liberal friends were interested in the child labor case.[65] As dismayed as they were by the Court's decision, they praised his dissent. The *New Republic* wrote: "No one, and particularly no lawyer familiar with the prior rulings of the Court, can read the dissenting opinion of Mr. Justice Holmes and retain a reasonable doubt that the majority wholly misconceived the issue. ... In an opinion of calm and luminous eloquence for which generations to come will be grateful, Mr. Justice Holmes makes short shrift of the wholly artificial issue of the majority opinion."[66]

As chairman of the War Labor Policies Board, Frankfurter was able to circumvent the Court's decision in *Hammer v. Dagenhart* and other antilabor rulings. Within six weeks of the decision, the board adopted a July 12 resolution that inserted the same prohibition of child labor into all future government contracts.[67] It was one of many contractual provisions that the board drafted to create fair labor standards for all war industry employees. Frankfurter accomplished his goals without congressional authorization or an executive order but merely the agreement of all the agencies that something had to be done to coordinate the government's wartime labor policy. And with the help of the War Industries Board he attempted to enforce these policies against private war-related industries.

Frankfurter pursued his goals with help from friends of his and Valentine's who were sympathetic to their ideas about labor-management relations. The professor-turned-bureaucrat recruited assistants, counsel, and support staff from his connections to Brandeis, Harvard Law School, and elsewhere. His trusted investigator Max Lowenthal was his assistant; his law school roommate Sam Rosensohn served as counsel and drafted pro-labor contractual language; another classmate, King, represented the War Department on the board. Valentine's college friends, former New Hampshire governor Robert Bass and Boston lawyer John Palfrey, represented the Shipping Board and were assisted by Frankfurter's former research assistant Herbert Ehrmann. "It is an extraordinary lark that I find myself in," Frankfurter wrote Laski. "Val would enjoy it with all his enthusiasm."[68]

Chairman Frankfurter grew close to another of the board's representatives—Assistant Secretary of the Navy Franklin D. Roosevelt. They had met in 1906 in New York City through one of Frankfurter's law school classmates and had seen each other from time to time at the Harvard Club.[69] Seven years later, Frankfurter and Roosevelt renewed their friendship in the early days of the Wilson administration. Frankfurter decided to remain in the War Department; Roosevelt became Wilson's assistant naval secretary. They worked on the same floor of the State-Army-Navy Building (the Old Executive Office Building). Frankfurter and Valentine had introduced Roosevelt to scientific management to resolve labor and supply issues at the Charlestown Naval Yard.[70]

But it was not until Frankfurter became chairman of the War Labor Policies Board and Roosevelt represented the navy on the board that their friendship blossomed. They respected each other's abilities and believed in using the power of federal agencies. Although Roosevelt attended only three of the board's weekly meetings, he impressed Frankfurter and others.[71] "I reported to my wife that on the whole Board I could discern only two first-rate minds," recalled Ehrmann, the Shipping Board's representative at the meetings. "One was the Chairman's and the other belonged to a

handsome Assistant Secretary of the Navy, named Roosevelt."[72] Frankfurter
and Roosevelt were in complete harmony because, according to Frankfurter
biographer Max Freedman, "scarcely a day passed when he did not have a
conference with Roosevelt or talk with him on the phone."[73] In October
1918, after Franklin had brought him home for lunch, Eleanor described
Frankfurter to her mother-in-law: "An interesting little man but very Jew."[74]

   In the fall of 1917, the Roosevelts rented a mansion at 2131 R Street,
NW—only a few blocks from 1727 Nineteenth Street. It is unlikely, however, that Franklin or Eleanor socialized at the House of Truth. Franklin was
in the midst of an affair with Eleanor's social secretary, Lucy Mercer, a relationship that Eleanor learned about in September 1918 when she unpacked
her husband's suitcase upon his return from Britain with double pneumonia
and discovered Mercer's love letters. Eleanor threatened to divorce Franklin
unless he immediately ended the affair. He stopped seeing Lucy Mercer for
a while but not for good.[75]

★★★

Even without the presence of the Roosevelts, the House of Truth in 1918
was a revolving door of wartime residents and guests. Frankfurter invited
Lowenthal and Rosensohn, who worked with him on the War Labor Policies
Board, to live there along with Judge Mack. At Secretary of War Baker's re-
quest and based on Frankfurter's proposal, Mack served on a three-person
Board of Inquiry that heard appeals for conscientious objector status.[76] In
April, Percy left the House again to return to the British Foreign Mission's
London office. Captain Harold Armstrong, the secretary to the Canadian
mission, replaced Percy.[77]

   Holmes continued to visit the House and to meet new residents. On
March 14, while Frankfurter was on his fact-finding mission about the labor
situation in Europe, Holmes dined there as Percy's guest. "You may gather
from this that I dined out last night," Holmes wrote Laski. "It was at the
House of Truth with Lord Eustace Percy as host—2 dames and a lot of men
all much younger than I. They made me laugh consumedly."[78]

   The war dominated the dinner party conversation. On May 8, Holmes
again dined at the House, but the guest of honor was Major Édouard
Réquin of the French High Commission to the United States.[79] Réquin
had arrived in America a month after it had entered the war and was helping the country mobilize its military forces. That night, just as Borglum
had done in demonstrating his idea for memorializing the Confederacy,

Réquin drew on the white tablecloth the position of the French army on the Western Front.[80] Réquin also regaled them with tales of serving at the side of Marshal Ferdinand Foch—chief of the General Staff of the French Army and eventual supreme commander of the Allied armies.[81] A month later, Réquin wrote an article, "Our Faith in Foch," for the *New Republic*.[82] "I wish you would tell Major Réquin how admirable I thought his article about General Foch," Holmes wrote Frankfurter.[83]

The House continued to be a source of social activity but also an un-official center for discussion about wartime administration. Holmes's former secretary Shelton Hale spent the last night before his marriage at 1727 Nineteenth Street. "And the house was gay tonite," Frankfurter wrote Denman. "Max and Mack talking honeymoon places, Mack volun-teering that Felix has a place tucked away in the Pyrenees—a year ago!"[84] A few weeks later, Bernard Baruch of the War Industries Board dined with Frankfurter and his housemates.[85] Like Réquin and the American military and Baruch and the War Industries Board, Frankfurter was reorganizing the American labor force. "It is not what I thought should have been done— I thought [Brandeis] the man—but I am not wasting much thought or energy in idle questioning," Frankfurter wrote Percy.[86]

With the support of steel magnate Charles M. Schwab of the US Shipping Board, Baruch, King, and Roosevelt, Frankfurter coordinated the federal government's labor standards and procurement and pursued his most controversial goal—the eight-hour workday. The eight-hour day became a liberal rallying cry, one that Wilson had supported and that Hughes had opposed during the 1916 presidential campaign.[87] At the start of the war, however, Wilson had issued an executive order that prior legislation limiting government and government-contracted workers to an eight-hour day be suspended because of the "extraordinary emergency" of wartime.[88] Instead, the president had ordered a "basic eight hour-day"—eight hours plus time and a half for overtime.[89] But because of exceptions in prior laws, different factories and different agencies had adopted different policies.[90]

On June 28, the War Labor Policies Board adopted a resolution that in-serted a basic eight-hour-day provision into all government contracts, that vowed to enforce the basic eight-hour day where the law permitted, and that attempted to extend enforcement of the basic eight-hour day to pri-vate industry through conference and mutual agreement.[91] Frankfurter's compromise position alienated the co-chairmen of the National War Labor Board, Taft and Walsh. From the outset, they had opposed the formation of the War Labor Policies Board as usurping their authority as the last word on labor disputes. They rejected the secretary of labor's invitation to sit as representatives on Frankfurter's board.

Taft's frustration with Frankfurter boiled over at one of the War Labor Board's early executive sessions. "Mr. Frankfurter is like a good Chancellor," Taft said, "he wants to amplify his jurisdiction and he is very anxious to be able to say that this Board is under him."[92] Walsh and the other board members joined Taft in blasting Frankfurter and rejecting any notion that they were bound by the War Labor Policies Board's decisions.[93] Taft, no doubt recalling Frankfurter's tortured service in his administration yet open support for Roosevelt, concluded: " My only experience with the gentleman whom we have been discussing from what I have heard is that if we just keep away he will tie himself up. There is no trouble about that."[94]

On the surface, Frankfurter was diplomatic in his correspondence and in meetings with Taft and Walsh. During a September 12 conference at the secretary of labor's office, Frankfurter attempted to mollify their objections to inserting a basic eight-hour provision into Governmental Readjustment Boards.[95] " I did a nifty job with Walsh today," he wrote Denman, "by getting the big fat Taft boy (who is dull & honest so that Walsh usually 'plays' him but today I was around &—it was fun.) on my side."[96] Frankfurter was well aware that the War Labor Board was undermining his gradual implementation of the basic eight-hour day. Based on allegations in one of their labor disputes, Walsh and other pro-labor representatives accused him of opposing the eight-hour principle.[97] They challenged Frankfurter to name a single private industry that had voluntarily adopted the basic eight-hour day.[98]

Unbeknownst to his opponents on the War Labor Policies Board, Frankfurter had been wrangling for months with a leading private-sector opponent of the basic eight-hour day, the chairman of U.S. Steel, Judge Elbert Gary. U.S. Steel had earned record profits in 1917 and had enjoyed its best quarter in the beginning of 1918. Yet Gary opposed the basic eight-hour day and feared that the board was trying to make it standard practice after the war. On July 9, at the suggestion of Charles Schwab, Frankfurter invited Gary to assemble a committee of industry representatives to come to Washington to discuss the basic eight-hour day.[99] Ten days later, Gary suggested that he would put a committee together only after Frankfurter agreed to come to Gary's office in New York City.[100] Frankfurter refused and suggested dates that Gary could come to Washington to discuss "our common problem."[101]

A week later, Frankfurter followed up with Gary about pinning down a specific date.[102] Months passed without any response. Finally, on September 17, Frankfurter wired Gary: "In view of the definite government policy with regard to the eight hour day, it is important for me to learn from your Committee its views with regard to this policy and the steel industry."[103] Two days later, having heard no response, Frankfurter wrote Gary again and then threatened to make their correspondence public.[104]

The next day at 9:15 a.m., Gary and one of his colleagues arrived at Frankfurter's office at the Slidell House across Lafayette Park from the White House. Frankfurter decided not to prepare any remarks but to engage Gary, who was twice his age, in a conversation.[105] Gary believed that the basic eight-hour day was "a sham"—the time and a half for overtime was "a method of obtaining a wage increase under false pretences," and therefore "he was strongly opposed to it."[106] Frankfurter believed that the overtime provision would encourage industry to adopt a true eight-hour day. A true eight-hour day, Gary replied, was impossible given the wartime labor shortages. Frankfurter interrupted when Gary accused him of having already made up his mind on the issue. He told Gary that he could not simply do nothing because some government and government-contracted employees worked eight-hour days while others did not, some received time and a half for overtime while others did not—a situation he described as "impracticable."[107] He pressed Gary for input on a solution to this problem, but the U.S. Steel chairman offered nothing but resistance. At Gary's mills, blue-collar workers toiled for more than ten hours a day at forty-two cents an hour.[108] Frankfurter pointed out that Henry Ford had moved his plants to a basic eight-hour day and predicted that the War Labor Policies Board's decisions would continue the trend in that direction.[109] As Gary stood up to leave, he said: "Professor Frankfurter, you work more than eight hours every day." Gary indicated that he worked more than eight hours in a day and that men and women laboring in the factories should, too. "Ah, Judge Gary," Frankfurter replied, "but think what interesting jobs you and I have."[110]

Immediately after the meeting, Frankfurter wrote a short memorandum to Secretary of Labor Wilson and Bernard Baruch summarizing the conversation, as well as a conciliatory letter to Gary.[111] Five days later, Gary announced that U.S. Steel would adopt the basic eight-hour day on October 1.[112] Frankfurter wired the news to Secretary Wilson and remarked: "This records a really big achievement—in its immediate significance as well as in its implications for the days beyond."[113] In the end, it was Frankfurter's pragmatism—learned from Brandeis and Valentine—that won out. He advocated for a basic eight-hour day, not an actual eight-hour-day.[114] Nor did he attempt to enforce the basic eight-hour day across the board, as pro-labor groups had insisted, but only where it was feasible. He kept his eye on the larger goals of leading the country to make an actual eight-hour workday standard practice. "This standard, during the war, has perhaps been honored more in breach than in observance, but the principle has been firmly established," he wrote.[115]

Frankfurter knew Valentine would have been proud of the eight-hour-day mediation efforts. Their old friends from the House of Truth saw the parallels. In August 1918, Winfred Denison wrote Sophie Valentine: " I had a letter from Felix—he feels, correctly, that he's working as a disciple of Robert! How the leader himself would grapple it. I should gather F. is doing well with it, and in the spirit."[116]

Not everything about Frankfurter's War Labor Policies Board was a success. As the basic eight-hour-day controversy indicated, it took months to formulate new labor policies based on input from both labor and management, and it was even harder to enforce them. Since early June, he had been secretly working on plans for "reconstruction"—planning for the reintroduction of returning soldiers into the workforce and adjusting wartime labor standards and production schedules after the war.[117] Indeed, the board did not consider regulations governing night work for women until mid-September, regulations that were not adopted for another two months.[118] By that time, the war had come to an end.[119]

★★★

On November 11, Germany and the Central Powers surrendered. Three months later, Frankfurter resigned as assistant secretary of labor and the chairman of the War Labor Policies Board. He felt he had done his job. "What American business needs is a substitution of law and order for the present status between anarchy and violence, by which it is governed," he wrote a month after the war had ended. He had helped bridge the gap between management and labor and had found alternatives to violent strikes and lockouts by getting both sides to see the other's point of view. "Not until American industry realizes that the problems are too vast and too intricate to be dealt with only by looking at one side," he wrote, "not until the management realizes that the labor movement is essentially not a belly movement, but a movement for the assertion of personality, and the workman recognizes that industry is a complicated organism, shall we see the light."[120] The war had shown him the way to achieve Valentine's vision of America as an industrial democracy through the power of federal agencies. If Valentine's legacy was as the nation's first industrial relations counselor, Frankfurter was beginning to establish his legacy as an expert on administrative law.

13

The Inquiry

Six days before Germany surrendered, Lippmann had written Frankfurter from the American embassy in Paris: "The propaganda business got shipwrecked very early, so I was turned loose for the Inquiry." Lippmann had elided over his difficulties in House's secret peace planning organization and described this period as "most 'fruitful' months," but he recognized that the key to achieving their war aims lay with "demobilization and reconstruction" on the home front.[1]

No one knew more about the preparation for the Paris Peace Conference than Lippmann. He had been planning for the end of the war for more than a year. In June 1917, he had stopped writing books and taken a leave of absence as one of the founding editors of the *New Republic* to join Frankfurter in the War Department. By early October, he and Faye had left Washington and their life at the House of Truth to return to New York City so that he could work for Colonel House on the secret peace planning organization, the Inquiry. The Inquiry epitomized the old progressive belief in government by experts. The group, which eventually included some 150 academics, was directed by philosopher Sidney Mezes, and its original members included historian James T. Shotwell of Columbia University and geographer Isaiah Bowman of the American Geographical Society. Lippmann was head of research.

In December, Lippmann, Mezes, and lawyer David Hunter Miller drafted a memorandum based on the Inquiry's statistics and research that became the broad outlines of the conditions of Germany's surrender, the new boundaries of a reconstituted Europe, and many of Wilson's Fourteen Points.[2] Wilson's famous Fourteen Points speech to Congress on January 8, 1918, delighted Lippmann. "This is the second time," he told Bowman, "that I have put words into the mouth of the President."[3] But Lippmann's doubts about the Inquiry's ability to reshape the world from the confines of a secret office in the New York Public Library were growing. Infighting also had begun; Bowman was jealous of Lippmann's relationship with House. The conflict-averse Lippmann was looking for an excuse to leave the Inquiry and to go overseas where the action was.

On June 15, 1918, Captain Heber Blankenhorn approached him with a proposition. A former labor journalist for the *New York Sun*, Blankenhorn was working for the army's military intelligence branch and wanted Lippmann's help in sending American propaganda—about Wilson's Fourteen Points and other democratic ideals—behind enemy lines. "Can't we catch up with the British and French? They're distributing leaflets," Blankenhorn argued to Lippmann. "We have the most important message of them all. We have Wilson's words." Lippmann told an astonished Blankenhorn this was something he would like to try.[4]

Public opinion, Lippmann believed, held the key to winning the war. And he feared that the Wilson administration was beginning to lose the support of liberals by resorting to unnecessary censorship. In October 1917, Lippmann had met with House about Postmaster General Albert Burleson's decision to rescind the mailing privileges of the *Jewish Daily Forward* as well as several Socialist publications.[5] In a follow-up letter, Lippmann informed

Lippmann (left) with Assistant Naval Secretary Franklin D. Roosevelt (center)

House that "radical and liberal groups are in a sullen mood over the government's attitude towards the socialist press." Liberal philosopher John Dewey, Lippmann's friend and a *New Republic* contributor, had lost faith in the administration. "Liberals cannot understand," Lippmann wrote House, "why the government is apparently more apprehensive about what an obscure and discredited little sheet says about Wall Street and munition makers than about Mr. Roosevelt's malicious depreciation of the American army." Lippmann believed that only actual threats to military secrets should be suppressed and that the administration should stop censoring harmless radical publications.[6] House conveyed Lippmann's concerns to Wilson.[7]

Blankenhorn later claimed that Lippmann wanted to go overseas because of a "quarrel" with House.[8] The evidence does not support Blankenhorn's recollection. On June 16, 1918, the day after he had spoken with Blankenhorn, Lippmann asked for House's permission to work for the military intelligence branch while continuing to work for the Inquiry.[9] For another month, Lippmann continued to advise House.[10] And once overseas, Lippmann kept in frequent contact with him. More likely, tension with Bowman and other members of the Inquiry and Lippmann's desire to be at the center of things in Europe motivated his departure.[11] Blankenhorn used Lippmann to get Secretary of War Baker who, unbeknownst to President Wilson, greenlighted the project and made Lippmann a captain.

In mid-July, Lippmann left the Inquiry's New York headquarters and his wife of thirteen months and headed overseas.[12] Blankenhorn described the newly made captain and his lieutenant, *New Republic* colleague Charles Merz, "as unsoldierly soldiers as you could see" and recalled Lippmann's disregard for military life and protocol.[13] "Lippmann had a reporter's flair for interrogation, but God how he hated the army!" Blankenhorn recalled. "At the inconvenience of the camps he said, 'This place is a prison!'"[14]

Lippmann and his fellow propagandists also butted heads with Wilson's wartime censorship agency, the Committee on Public Information led by George E. Creel, and with British military officials who refused to drop American leaflets behind enemy lines. Lippmann's negotiations with British officials got him into hot water with Blankenhorn for ignoring protocol about not entering into binding agreements.[15] Lippmann also annoyed House by using State Department cables to criticize Creel and the Committee on Public Information.[16] Lippmann voiced his frustration with bureaucratic hurdles and with propaganda accompanied by a lack of political intelligence. "Unless the men who are writing and directing propaganda are in close touch with political developments they cannot of course do anything effective," he wrote House on August 9.[17]

Lippmann also passed along British ideas and intelligence.[18] One of his sources was Percy, his old friend from the House of Truth now in the British Foreign Office. Lippmann wrote that Percy "always speaks to me quite candidly as we are old friends, and who often gives a good hint of what is being thought in official circles in the Foreign Office."[19] Percy charmed several Americans, including Blankenhorn, who wrote that Percy was "a Tory of Tories in the most Tory of offices who nevertheless has an intellectual grasp of Liberalism, almost of Radicalism."[20] Journalist Ray Stannard Baker dined with Percy and described him as a "charming and likeable young man" and a Tory who had supported the Bull Moose Party. "It is amusing to find Englishmen so strong about democratic movements in America and so doubtful about them at home."[21] Percy belonged to a pro-Wilson group of British Tories known as the Round Table, a group that favored the League of Nations and that "should be in closer touch" with American liberals led by Lippmann.[22]

One person not enthralled with Lippmann's propaganda work, his criticisms of the Committee on Public Information, or his connection to Percy was President Wilson. "I am very much puzzled as to who sent Lippmann over to inquire into matters of propaganda," Wilson wrote House after reading two of Lippmann's letters. "I have found his judgment most unsound, and therefore entirely unserviceable, in matters of that sort because he, in common with the men of The New Republic, has ideas about the war and its purposes which are highly unorthodox from my own points of view."[23] Wilson also blasted Lippmann's reliance on Percy, whom the president found to be "one of the most slippery and untrustworthy of the men we have had to deal with here."[24] Seemingly aware of Croly's souring *New Republic* editorials and Washington correspondent William Hard's criticism of the War Department, Wilson wanted complete control over American propaganda and was determined to find out more about Lippmann's doings. "Who is 'Captain' Lippmann and who commissioned him to assess our propaganda?" the president asked Secretary of State Robert Lansing.[25]

Explaining that the War Department had sent Lippmann over to deal with propaganda in enemy countries and that he was a former aide to Baker, House rose to Lippmann's defense. "I do not know how recently you have been in touch with Lippmann, but my impression is that he is not now in sympathy with the men who govern the policy of the New

Republic," House wrote Wilson. "He went with Baker immediately after we declared war. He was always the ablest of that group and he is young enough to wean away from them and [be] broadened."[26] House's response mollified the president. Though he claimed to have "a high opinion" of Lippmann, Wilson wanted complete control over American propaganda: "I would not think of interfering with the activities of the War Department's intelligence agents, but I want to keep the matter of publicity entirely in my own hands."[27] After Wilson's inquiries, the War Department shut down Blankenhorn's propaganda efforts.[28]

With his propaganda assignment "shipwrecked," as he put it, Lippmann turned his attention to gathering political intelligence for House and the Inquiry.[29] On October 25, 1918, House arrived in Paris and transferred Lippmann to his staff. Lippmann lobbied House to bring the entire Inquiry to Europe so that they could learn what is happening on the ground and establish contacts with British and French officials. "The greatest weakness of the Inquiry is its divorce from responsibility and from intimate knowledge of current affairs," Lippmann wrote House on October 26.[30]

Lippmann's enemies on the Inquiry lay in wait. On November 1, American newspapers carried stories revealing that news of the impending armistice was being dropped across enemy lines and that Lippmann was involved.[31] At the time, Lippmann did not know that his cover had been blown and he had been exposed as a propagandist. The person who leaked the story was Bowman, the Inquiry's de facto leader, who remained jealous of Lippmann's relationship with House.

In Paris, Lippmann became indispensable to House for two reasons: first, Lippmann had been in Europe since mid-June and had made numerous contacts among British, French, and Italian officials; second, the problem with most of Wilson's Fourteen Points was that they were so vague that no one knew what they meant—except perhaps Lippmann and New York *World* editor Frank I. Cobb. On October 28, Lippmann and Cobb wrote a memorandum for House interpreting what the Fourteen Points meant, how they could be used to override secret treaties among the Allies and to prevent them from consolidating their empires, and how to draw geographic boundaries in postwar Europe to make a lasting peace.[32] House had instructed them to write the memorandum, which was approved by President Wilson and which helped House negotiate an armistice between Germany and the Allies.[33] "I must write you this morning because I couldn't possibly tell you to your face how great a thing you have achieved ...," Lippmann wrote House on November 7. "The President and you have more than justified the faith of those who insisted that your leadership was a turning point in modern history. No one can ever thank you adequately."[34] The day after Germany surrendered, Lippmann also congratulated his former boss, Secretary of War Baker, and updated him about the impending Paris Peace Conference. He explained that he had been working for House and admired "his kindly skill in the midst of formidable difficulties. But the most difficult period of war lies ahead."[35]

For Lippmann and other liberals, the war reinforced their faith in government, yet it also showed them how government officials could abuse their power. Lippmann's crisis of conscience had begun in the fall of 1917 with the postal service's censorship of Jewish and Socialist publications. It had continued with the Inquiry's infighting and lack of knowledge about what was happening on the ground in Europe. If Wilson's vision of a League of Nations was to become a reality after the peace conference, Lippmann knew the American people needed to be educated, not censored. Without public opinion on their side, American officials in Paris faced a severe handicap.

In November 1918, Lippmann encouraged House to devise a plan of disseminating information among the massive American press corps in Paris and to establish that "no political or diplomatic censorship will be exercised."[36] Lippmann knew that the press was the lifeline to influencing public opinion: " So far as possible they should be made to feel that they are actually taking part in one of the most important phases of the conference, that they are regarded as insiders and that their curiosity is legitimate."[37] Both Wilson and Creel ignored Lippmann's advice, commandeered the transatlantic cables from Paris, and censored the American press rather than using it to influence public opinion through the power of Wilson's ideas.[38] It was a sign of House's waning influence on Wilson, who had not yet arrived in Paris. Lippmann was happy to be working at House's side again and to be preparing for the peace conference.[39] For a time, Lippmann contemplated accompanying Herbert Hoover to Austria and Germany "for the purpose of getting a first hand view of the situation" in advance of the conference.[40] He awaited Hoover's arrival in Paris and continued to work closely with House.

Lippmann's private life began to intervene. He was homesick and missed his wife, Faye. They had been married for only thirteen months before he had left her with his parents in New York City and had joined the army.

In November, he tried to bring Faye to Europe, but army regulations prohibited it.[41] He was hoping to be transferred to the State Department for
the peace talks in order to facilitate her arrival.[42] To make matters worse,
Faye's letters reached him in Paris three to four weeks later. He wrote to her
almost daily in what amounted to a virtual diary of his army service.

    He also became anxious over the ill health of the publisher and financial
backer of the *New Republic*, Willard Straight. Major Straight had worked for
the American Expeditionary Forces and then joined House's staff after the
armistice. Straight, along with House, Lippmann, and many others, suffered
from the influenza epidemic sweeping across Europe and the United States.[43]
Straight's influenza turned into pneumonia. On November 25, Lippmann
moved into the Hôtel de Crillon to be closer to his boss and ailing friend.
"Yesterday the thing looked hopeless, but last night there was a turn for
the better, though he is by no means out of danger," he wrote Faye.[44] On
a dreary Thanksgiving Day, little had changed. "Willard is desperately ill,"
Lippmann wrote, "and everybody else is immeasurably homesick."[45]

Colonel Edward M. House

For the next week, Lippmann spent his days by Straight's bedside. Finally, at 12:45 a.m. on December 1, Straight died.[46] He was only thirty-eight. "I was with Willard Straight last night when he died, and I am lonely to the point of heartbreak for the love which you alone can give me," Lippmann wrote Faye. He arranged for his friend's funeral. Two days later, after a small military parade to an American church about a mile away, Major Willard D. Straight was laid to rest at an American cemetery in Suresnes, about seven miles from Paris. Lippmann inventoried Straight's things and collected his letters, a diary, a cable to Croly, and other keepsakes to send in a diplomatic pouch to his widow, Dorothy.[47] She was the real driving force behind the Straights' investment in the *New Republic*, not only because she came from the Whitney family but also because she was a true believer in Croly's and Lippmann's political ideas. "In the last eight weeks I was closer to Willard than ever before," Lippmann wrote her the day that her husband had died. "He was as quick and fine and true as a man could be, and in his young maturity."[48] Lippmann watched as the life of an up-and-coming internationalist like himself was cut much too short. Straight's death probably did not precipitate Lippmann's departure from Paris, but it made him miss his wife and likely increased his desire to return home to his true calling as a journalist.

If it wasn't Straight's death that sent Lippmann home, then it was the arrival of Lippmann's former adversaries on the Inquiry. On December 14, President Wilson arrived in Paris to a carnival-like atmosphere on the city's streets. Lippmann's colleagues on the Inquiry accompanied Wilson aboard the USS *George Washington* and received a briefing from the president. "Naturally we are pleased that he is going to use us," Yale historian Charles Seymour wrote his family after the talk with Wilson, "for we have been worried by the feeling that Lippmann's connection with the Inquiry had discredited the whole organization."[49]

Lippmann tried to patch things up with his former colleagues but soon realized that his usefulness was nearing an end. He walked the streets of Paris for two hours with Inquiry executive director Sidney Mezes discussing the challenges that lay ahead. "The next part of my own work is completed here," Lippmann wrote Faye, "and now everything is in the pot. The big decisions will be made this next month, and then our biggest job is in the United States."[50]

He also cleared the air with Isaiah Bowman, his biggest enemy on the Inquiry. He did not care to revisit the fact that Bowman had neglected to mention, much less apologize for, leaking Lippmann's name in connection with American propaganda, "but Bowman is probably aware that a gentleman does not attack another man while he's away, and then continue to write him cordial letters in the manner of a colleague."[51] Infighting at the Inquiry was beneath Lippmann, who sensed that the organization would play a minimal role at the peace conference. Lippmann was ready to come home and return to his life as a political journalist and to his wife, who yearned to start having children. "Lonely as I've been, there is a satisfaction in having been a tiny part of the A.E.F. which is for both of us and for our children," he wrote Faye.[52]

Lippmann knew what his task would be at home—to write books and *New Republic* articles enlightening American public opinion. Even from Europe, he knew that the isolationist impulses of the American political establishment, led by Wilson's Republican enemies Theodore Roosevelt and Henry Cabot Lodge, were opposed to the idea of a League of Nations. "I'm sure that the people who are gathering against the President have no conception of what is boiling and bubbling everywhere under the surface in Europe, and that Wilson is the hope of European conservatism," Lippmann wrote Faye. Wilson's success would "depend in large measure upon the feeling back home," and that is what Lippmann was determined to write about.[53]

Wilson's earlier displeasure over the control of propaganda was not the reason for Lippmann's departure. Lippmann had redeemed himself in late October by interpreting Wilson's Fourteen Points for House and the president. Years later, however, an article attacking Lippmann asserted that Wilson had refused to see him and sent him home.[54] Lippmann denied those allegations, and the contemporaneous evidence supports him and not his detractors.[55]

Instead, Lippmann had realized two things: first, that he had fallen out of favor with the Inquiry, and, second, that the Inquiry was unlikely to play a large role at the peace conference. A good friend of Lippmann's, Ralph Hayes, assessed the situation for their former boss, Secretary of War Baker. Hayes reported that the members of the Inquiry were told that "this is a State Dept. show" and that Lippmann was prepared to leave Paris and was "greatly discouraged."[56] On December 22, Hayes wrote Baker: "Lippmann has been much troubled for many weeks. Walter's liberalism is the source of much whispering about him whenever he gets measurably close to a throne."[57] Though Hayes reported to Baker four days later that the Inquiry had regained some of its responsibilities, that gain did not affect Lippmann.[58]

On December 28, Lippmann informed Faye about his decision to come home. He had made up his mind before Wilson and the others had arrived on the *George Washington*, a decision complicated by an opportunity to join Hoover on a mission to Austria and Germany. Lippmann turned down the new assignment and reported that House was "splendid about it." He alluded to the ill will on the Inquiry but did not bother House with the details. "I shall have my say," Lippmann wrote his wife. He possessed "an inner satisfaction that in the meanest experience of my life I have not stooped to wrangle and dispute and argue, and to clutter up the place with my ego while the world is on fire." He suggested that Faye show the letter to Croly, Dorothy Straight, and Frankfurter.[59]

Like Frankfurter and his report on the Bisbee deportation and the Mooney case, Lippmann had seen how government officials misuse their power and fail the American people. He had objected to the postal service's censorship of Socialist newspapers in October 1917; he had disagreed with the administration's decision a year later to censor rather than inform the American press corps in Paris; and he had witnessed firsthand the infighting and lack of knowledge on the ground among the members of the Inquiry. Without knowledge of the facts on the ground, respect for civil liberties, and an educated public opinion, government, he believed, ran into trouble.

The politician who placed too much faith in government and too little concern for civil liberties in wartime, Theodore Roosevelt, died in his sleep on January 6, 1919. The *New Republic*'s January 11 lead editorial about Roosevelt's death quoted him as saying, "I'm a warrior and not a prophet," and opined: "He was a warrior on behalf of what he believed to be and usually were morally decisive causes. The most poignant tragedy of his life was that he was unable to fight sword in hand in the war which raised one of the clearest and greatest moral issues in history."[60] The war had cost Roosevelt dearly. On July 14, 1918, his youngest son, Quentin, had been killed when his plane was shot down behind enemy lines by two German flyers. Roosevelt lived only another six months after his son's death.[61] His final days had been spent not advocating the causes that drew Croly, Frankfurter, and Lippmann to him but promoting a reactionary imperialism and intolerance that they abhorred. The ties that bound Frankfurter, Lippmann, and their network of liberal allies were stronger than those to Roosevelt.

On January 13, 1919, a week after Roosevelt's death, Frankfurter attempted to boost Lippmann's spirits and get him up to speed on the domestic difficulties facing the Wilson administration. "I think I know a little of the atmosphere and circumstances under which you are laboring, and I want to send you this word of anxious good wishes and eager affection," Frankfurter wrote. He was "pessimistic" about the peace conference, feared "reactionary forces" on the scene, and predicted that what they had begun would "have to be done all over again and I think mostly from the outside."[62] Frankfurter and Lippmann were trading places, with Frankfurter heading to Paris soon after Lippmann's return. "I would give a lot for a talk with you," Frankfurter concluded. "The months will grow apace and one of these days we shall have it."[63]

On February 7, Lippmann arrived home to Faye and to the well wishes of many of his friends from the House of Truth.[64] Frankfurter was busy extricating himself from the Labor Department and unable to see Lippmann in person, but Laski caught up with him. Laski had been urging Lippmann to return to the *New Republic* because the magazine needed him.[65] "I had some good talk with Walter Lippmann last week before he left for a holiday," Laski reported to Holmes. "I am eager for you to see him again—he is more critical, less facile, and, to say something differently, with a deeper sense that you don't find truth by skimming milk."[66]

Lippmann never had any intention of leaving the *New Republic*.[67] He came home from Paris to enlighten the American people, to criticize the American delegation, and to define the country's role in the future of the world. Though he was no longer in Paris, he pledged to help people understand the peace conference and become one of the chief arbiters of the nation's public opinion. He would have his say.

14

The Wonderful One

The row house on Nineteenth Street was cold, dark, and almost empty. The only lighted window was likely Felix Frankfurter's. After seven years of living in the House of Truth, he was in a reflective mood. His time there was nearing an end. It was where he had met his fiancée, Marion Denman; where he had befriended his judicial idols, Holmes and Brandeis; and where he had met Robert Valentine, "the likes of him as friend there never was or will be for me."[1] "What a procession of memories passes through the House …," he wrote Denman in the early morning hours of January 19, 1919. "I'm so happy about it for the House has been the shell of so much for me these years and now we have shared it not merely as narrative but by the mere warmth of its fire, and its glow and generosity."[2]

On February 8, Frankfurter resigned as assistant secretary of labor and chairman of the War Labor Policies Board.[3] Before he left, he mediated the New York City garment workers strike and established forty-four-hour weeks as the industry standard.[4] A week after his resignation, he embarked for Europe to attend the Paris Peace Conference and to secure a Jewish homeland in Palestine. Frankfurter, who had been dithering about whether to return to the Harvard law faculty, decided not to ask university officials for permission before he left. He was concerned about the reaction of Harvard's anti-Semitic president, A. Lawrence Lowell, who believed that the professor's wartime service was devoted to furthering the Zionist cause.[5] Indeed, some of it was. During the summer of 1917, Frankfurter had accompanied Henry Morgenthau on the former ambassador's ill-fated mission to woo Turkey away from the Central Powers. In Gibraltar, Frankfurter had met Zionist leader Chaim Weizmann, and together they had scotched Morgenthau's plan because it would have jeopardized Zionist hopes for a British takeover of Turkish-controlled Palestine.

Aaron Aaronsohn

The Balfour Declaration had changed everything. In November 1917, after months of lobbying and internal negotiations, British foreign secretary Arthur Balfour wrote: "His Majesty's Government view with favour the establishment in Palestine of a national home for the Jewish people and will use their best endeavours to facilitate the achievement of this object, it being clearly understood that nothing shall be done which may prejudice the civil and religious rights of existing non-Jewish communities in Palestine, or the rights and political status enjoyed by Jews in any other country."[6]

In February 1918, Frankfurter returned to Europe at Colonel House's behest to investigate the labor and political situation in Britain and France, but he pursued an unpublicized secondary agenda. With the permission of Secretary of War Baker, Frankfurter conferred with Weizmann and other Zionist leaders about British plans to send a commission to Palestine. In the process, Frankfurter had earned Weizmann's trust and confidence.[7] With the peace negotiations about to start, Weizmann begged Frankfurter to join the American Zionist delegation in Paris.[8]

The plan was for Frankfurter to stay in Paris until June 1919 to influence negotiations over the League of Nations, to make sure that the British received a mandate over Palestine, and then to visit the Holy Land that summer with the man who had inspired his interest in Zionism—Brandeis. It was Brandeis who had arranged for Frankfurter to go on the Morgenthau Mission in 1917 and to confer with Weizmann a year later. Despite long-standing rumors that he would temporarily leave the Supreme Court to aid President Wilson at the Paris Peace Conference, Brandeis stayed in Washington to tend to his judicial duties. For Weizmann and other Zionists, Frankfurter's presence in Paris was the next best thing.

On the surface, Brandeis and Frankfurter's interest in Zionism was odd because neither man had a religious bone in his body. They were secular Jews who were fluent in German but were otherwise fully assimilated into American society. For years, Brandeis had donated sparingly to Jewish and Zionist causes, and his interest in the movement had been modest.[9] Brandeis's Zionist conversion is often attributed to a 1910 interview with the editor of Boston's *Jewish Advocate*, Jacob de Haas. The former secretary to Zionist leader Theodore Herzl, de Haas had been sent to Boston by Herzl ten years earlier to organize American Zionists. After their interview, Brandeis had accompanied de Haas to the train station. As the two men were about to part, de Haas had referred to Brandeis's revered uncle Lewis Dembitz, a Louisville lawyer and religious scholar, as "a noble Jew."[10] Brandeis, who had changed his middle name to Dembitz in honor of his uncle, wondered what de Haas had meant by the comment. De Haas launched into an explanation of Zionism, and the two men returned to Brandeis's home and talked for hours.[11] A divisive personality within the Zionist movement, de Haas believed that in Brandeis he had discovered the next Herzl.[12]

By 1914, Brandeis was leading the American Zionist movement and had recruited Mack and Frankfurter as his chief lieutenants.[13] Brandeis gained his two most steadfast Zionist allies by tapping into their Americanism. The same nationalism that had caused Croly to start the *New Republic*, galvanized liberal support for US entry into the war, and inspired Mack and Frankfurter to leave their jobs and to aid the government's war effort resulted in their conversion to Zionism. "My approach to Zionism was through Americanism," Brandeis explained to a crowd at Boston's Symphony Hall in September 1914. "Gradually it became clear to me that to be good Americans, we must be better Jews, and to be better Jews, we must become Zionists."[14]

Brandeis's vision of a Jewish homeland in Palestine was a liberal one. He did not believe that all 12 million Jews should repatriate, only the ones who wanted to live there. Nor did he believe in an exclusively Jewish state; everyone in Palestine—Arabs and Jews, Christians and Muslims—should enjoy full rights of citizenship.[15] For Brandeis, a Jewish state represented a Jeffersonian ideal of an agrarian society, a place where labor and management could create an exemplar for democracy by working together and embracing scientific management rather than violent strikes, substandard wages, and inhumane conditions. In one of his later Supreme Court opinions, Brandeis described America's states as laboratories of experimentation.[16] For Brandeis, Frankfurter, and Mack, Palestine was their liberal laboratory.

A few days before Frankfurter left for Paris, he visited Brandeis and was inspired yet again by the justice's vision for Palestine and for America. "I wish you might have heard L.D.B. on the aims of my trip—you would have felt the reach of a profound mind and a truly 'deep' person," Felix wrote Marion. "[Y]ou would have also felt the world scope of the Zionist conception, as he & I perceive it."[17] Brandeis urged Frankfurter to survey the situation and promised to meet him in Palestine as soon as the Court adjourned. Of socialized medicine, the land problem, and labor cooperatives, he told Frankfurter: "For we must make of Palestine a laboratory for our problems here."[18]

The only downside of Frankfurter's trip to Paris was prolonged separation from his fiancée. Before he set sail for London, he sent Marion flowers and wrote her notes about how much he loved and missed her.[19] Though not an overly emotional person, she saw his little notes and flowers, and "they made me cry as I haven't cried before."[20]

One of the last people Frankfurter visited before he left Washington was Justice Holmes, who mockingly remarked: "You're going off to see great men but I bet it'll be hell to find a better nucleus than us."[21] What Holmes probably did not know was how integral the House of Truth's residents and visitors had been and would be to Frankfurter's mission to Paris to secure a Jewish homeland.

★★★

Frankfurter arrived at the Piccadilly Hotel in London early on April 26 after ten days aboard the SS *Baltic*. During the last leg of the journey from Liverpool to London, he and the other passengers had been "without food, in shivering cold" because of the "incompetence" of the White Star Line.[22] During the Atlantic crossing, he wrote Roscoe Pound and declared his intention to delay his return to the faculty until September: "There was no way out—Either Brandeis or I had to go on this Zionist business, and of course he couldn't." Frankfurter made his summer trip to Palestine sound like a sociolegal experiment: "We shall make, we hope, an intensive study of the social-economic problems on the spot—to know the elements of the experiment that will be established." He promised to return in September.[23]

After a day of debriefing in London by de Haas and prominent American Zionist Bernard Flexner, Frankfurter left the next morning for Paris.[24] He arrived to a city jammed with people and discovered that Weizmann had already presented the Zionist proposal to the Council of Five (Britain, France, Italy, United States, Japan). Secretary of State Lansing offered Frankfurter another opportunity to speak, but Frankfurter declined. Weizmann had done a fabulous job, and Frankfurter was "not interested in fireworks." Instead, Weizmann updated him about the last year of Zionist activity.[25]

Born in Pinsk, Belarus, Weizmann was trained in chemistry in Germany and Switzerland and became a British citizen while teaching at the University of Manchester. He was bald with a dark complexion and Vandyke beard, and he spoke in a "rich and resonant" voice.[26] After the outbreak of the war, he rose through the ranks of the Zionist movement, charmed influential British officials, and found several of them supportive of a Jewish state in Palestine. Frankfurter, who respected Weizmann but considered him a "most worrisome fellow," hoped to serve as a peacemaker among various Zionist factions and to make the proposed British mandate a reality based on his contacts with American, British, and French officials.[27]

Everywhere he went near the Hôtel Meurice in Paris, Frankfurter ran into old friends from the House of Truth. Christie joined the Canadian delegation as aide to Prime Minister Robert Borden; Percy was assisting the British delegation and was an important Zionist ally; Walter Meyer and Mack were representing the American Zionists; another former housemate, Captain Harold Armstrong of the Canadian military, was there as well; and Bullitt aided the State Department. "You find Washington all over Rue de Rivoli," Frankfurter wrote.[28]

★★★

No former House of Truth resident was more important to Frankfurter's Zionist mission than a botanist and British spy from Palestine named Aaron

Aaronsohn. Aaronsohn's claim to fame was his discovery of how to grow wild wheat in Palestine's arid soil. A self-taught botanist, he directed the Jewish Agricultural Experiment Station south of Haifa and conducted hybridizing experiments on wheat, oats, and barley. His discovery and experiments impressed US Agriculture Department officials enough to publish them in an official departmental publication.[29]

A large, ruddy-faced man who was fluent in multiple languages but still learning English, Aaronsohn possessed Svengali powers over seemingly everyone he had spoken to, whether about wild wheat or Palestine. Originally from Romania, the Aaronsohn family had emigrated to Palestine when Aaron was five. Led by their father, Ephraim, they had taken up farming and settled in Zichron Ya'akov about twenty miles south of Haifa on the Mediterranean Coast. Aaron and his brother, Alex, became the Palestinian-Jewish community's best ambassadors among American intellectuals. From 1910 to 1913, Alex had lived in the United States, had worked in the Agriculture Department, and had taken initial steps toward American citizenship. In 1909 and 1910, Aaron had traveled to the United States to raise money for an Agricultural Experiment Station from wealthy German American Jews, including Louis Marshall, Julius Rosenwald, and Jacob Schiff.[30]

The story of Aaronsohn's wild wheat discovery, which Rosenwald recounted in July 1912 at a Washington banquet, had astonished Brandeis and—perhaps as much as his 1910 conversation with Jacob de Haas—had inspired Brandeis's Zionist conversion. For Brandeis, Aaronsohn was transforming Palestine into Jefferson's vision of an agrarian society and into a laboratory of experimentation. "The talk was the most thrillingly interesting I have ever heard," Brandeis wrote his brother Alfred, "showing the possibilities of scientific agriculture and utilization of arid or supposedly exhausted land."[31] In May 1913, Brandeis recounted the story of the Aaronsohn family to encourage American Jews to "support the Zionist movement, whether you or I are interested or never think of going to Palestine. ... If we aid that effort the Jew will be brought to the full development of this manhood and thus be enable to do his full duty to his race and his country."[32]

It did not take long for Aaronsohn to ingratiate himself with the House of Truth crowd, which made influential contacts for him. Brandeis urged Norman Hapgood to commission Aaron to write a Zionism article for *Harper's*.[33] In New York City, Mack and Frankfurter took Aaronsohn to an exhibition of Cubist painters and then to the offices of *Outlook* magazine to meet Theodore Roosevelt.[34] It was March 15, 1913—Roosevelt was still the idol of 1727 Nineteenth Street. During a lunch at the Art Club attended by social reformer Jacob Riis, Frankfurter, Mack, and several others, Aaronsohn sat to Roosevelt's immediate right and told the story of the wild wheat discovery and the Aaronsohn family's colonization of Palestine. "My talk lasted for one hour and forty minutes," Aaronsohn wrote. "All who know the Colonel are surprised; from now on my reputation will be the man who made the Colonel shut up for 101 minutes."[35]

With the outbreak of the war in Europe, Aaronsohn needed the House of Truth more than ever. The war had shifted the balance of power in the Zionist movement from Europe to the United States and from Weizmann to Brandeis, and the war changed the lives of the Aaronsohn family forever. Turkey's decision to join Germany and the Central Powers had coincided with a shift in policy toward the Jews of Palestine from toleration to a reign of terror and starvation. The Turkish government had shut off all aid from Britain and the United States. In 1915, Brandeis had organized relief efforts among wealthy American Jews, including Rosenwald, Schiff, and Nathan Straus. With Morgenthau's diplomatic assistance, Brandeis had persuaded Secretary of the Navy Josephus Daniels and Secretary of State William Jennings Bryan to transport the supplies to Egypt and Palestine on the USS *Vulcan*.[36] After the supplies had arrived in Palestine in March 1915, Brandeis wrote President Wilson: "I desire to express the high appreciation by the Jews of America of the important services rendered by the Department of State and the Navy Department in protecting and relieving the distress of their bretheren [*sic*] in Palestine."[37] The person who had distributed the supplies to Palestine's Jews was Aaron Aaronsohn.[38]

The Aaronsohn family had kept a low profile in 1914 and 1915 but did not suffer in silence. In the July and August 1916 issues of the *Atlantic Monthly* and in book form, Alex Aaronsohn had detailed Turkish atrocities and Jewish suffering.[39] He told his family's story of emigrating to Palestine thirty-five years earlier, of creating an egalitarian farming community in Zichron Ya'akov, of establishing a Jewish court system, and of the absence of Jewish crime.[40] The Turks, having joined forces with Germany, had pressed Alex and other Jewish settlers into military service, where they performed back-breaking manual labor.[41] Alex bribed his way out the Turkish army upon hearing stories of soldiers raping Jewish women and children and pillaging Jewish villages.[42] He returned to Zichron Ya'akov; sent his sister Sarah to Beirut, where she would be safe from Turkish troops; and buried a cache of weapons in a wheat field.[43] The Turkish military responded by imprisoning Alex and his father and beating them into unconsciousness. They were released when their fellow villagers revealed the location of the weapons after the army had threatened to rape all the village's young girls.[44] Alex headed to German-infiltrated Jerusalem in January 1915 as the Turks prepared for their failed attempt to cross the Suez Canal, to invade Egypt, and to defeat the British (who were waiting for them and repelled the attack).[45] Finally, after a failed attempt to board the USS *Tennessee* without a passport, he escaped in a Turkish officer's uniform to Beirut, conferred with British officials in Alexandria, and in October returned to the United States.[46]

The House of Truth crowd embraced Alex Aaronsohn with the same fervor that it had his brother. With encouragement from Brandeis and Frankfurter, he embarked on a speaking tour to Jewish groups to raise money for the Zionist cause.[47] Brandeis encouraged Alex, who was much more fluent in English than his brother, to write the story of Zichron Ya'akov, a suggestion that may have led to his *Atlantic Monthly* articles and book. Frankfurter, for his part, encouraged him to contact the most literary man among them, Justice Holmes. "I had a letter from Alex Aaronson [*sic*] forwarded to me here," Holmes wrote Frankfurter in October 1915. "He, I think, was the brother of the wonderful one and didn't see that I had anything to say."[48] "The wonderful one"—in case Frankfurter or anyone at the House of Truth needed clarification—was Alex's brother, Aaron.

Aaron Aaronsohn remained in good stead with Turkish officials because in February 1915 locusts had descended upon Palestine for the first time in forty years and threatened a massive famine.[49] Not even he could prevent the insects, followed by a heat wave, from destroying all the crops. Despite this failure, he remained a valuable asset to Turkish officials because of his agricultural knowledge and international standing.[50]

In an October 1916 "confession" to Judge Mack, however, Aaronsohn had described Turkish atrocities even worse than what Alex had revealed in the *Atlantic Monthly*.[51] Then he unmasked the instigator of the Turkish attacks on the Jews—the German government. For several years, he had warned Mack and his American Jewish allies of the danger that Germany posed to the Jews and the need for a British protectorate in Palestine.[52] Finally, Aaronsohn revealed why he had stayed in Palestine when his brother had escaped: "I stood where I was, I organized a whole movement, I became connected with the [British] Intelligence Office, as people who are afraid of words call it. I do not like mincing words. Put it clearly,

I became a Spy."[53] Aaronsohn and his family had started a spy network known as NILI. The purpose of NILI—a Hebrew acronym that means "The Eternity of Israel will not lie"—was to gather intelligence about the Turkish army's movements for British troops in Egypt and to help the British seize Palestine.[54]

Aaronsohn wanted his confession shown to select American Zionists beginning with Frankfurter. "First of all I think of Felix," he wrote Mack. "He is open-minded, free and prudent and has such a wonderfully subtle mind. I have been too well treated at the 'House of Truth'; I owe him the truth. I would like you to show him the letter."[55] Though he considered Mack and Frankfurter friends and full-fledged Zionist converts, Aaronsohn was not yet sold on Brandeis: "I gather that Brandeis publicly declared me somewhat responsible for his conversion. But I do not believe it is going very deeply with him."[56] He left it up to Mack and Frankfurter whether to show the letter to Brandeis and other American friends, including Henrietta Szold, Mr. and Mrs. Julius Rosenwald, Jacob Schiff, and Louis Marshall. Aaronsohn knew that many of them would not understand his decision to become a British spy.[57]

Aaronsohn wrote his confession to Mack from Copenhagen. He had left Palestine during the summer of 1916 via Damascus, Constantinople, and Berlin to get to Denmark and Sweden. In Denmark, he was supposed to help Djemal Pasha, the Turkish ruler of Palestine, discover how to turn sesame seeds into fuel.[58] In reality, he had betrayed the Turkish government and accomplished what his brother, Alex, and another member of the NILI network could not—earning the trust and confidence of the British government.

From Denmark, Aaronsohn had boarded a ship bound for the United States, but he disembarked on October 24, 1916, at his secret final destination—London. There he impressed Scotland Yard officials with his knowledge of the Turkish military and spent much of 1917 in Cairo providing intelligence to the British military through the NILI network.[59] At the end of 1917, he returned to London and conferred with British officials and fellow Zionists. He was not an "official" Zionist who believed that the best way to obtain a Jewish state was through negotiation; he believed in military might and action.[60] That said, the Balfour Declaration of November 2, 1917, was a triumph for Aaronsohn and Weizmann and a real opportunity for a Jewish homeland. Weizmann and the British government wanted support for the declaration from the Wilson administration and prominent

American Zionists. They chose Aaronsohn to go to the United States to do their bidding.[61]

Despite considerable tension between him and Weizmann, Aaronsohn left for the United States. He arrived in New York on December 2 with Judge Mack as his guide. At Mack's New York chambers, he received a horrifying telegram dated November 27 informing him of a family tragedy at home. The Turks had arrested and tortured members of his family. His sister Sarah had killed herself. His father, at least according to the initial report, had died from shock.[62] How the Turks discovered NILI, the Aaronsohn family's spy network, remains a mystery. Alex Aaronsohn claimed it started with an intercepted carrier pigeon; others have attributed it to villagers in Zichron Ya'akov or a possible leak within the British government or Zionist movement.[63] Whatever the cause, the leader of the family's spy network was dead.

Sarah Aaronsohn had returned to Palestine to run NILI in her brothers' absence. Headstrong and quite beautiful, she had probably been in love with another NILI member who had been killed in 1916. She was also deeply committed to the cause. During five days of brutal torture by her Turkish interrogators, she refused to break. Her transfer to a Damascus prison, where several of her collaborators were later executed, was imminent. To inspire her fellow NILI members, she took a gun she had hidden in the bathroom of her family's house and shot herself in the mouth. She survived for four days in "intense agony, but not a minute ceasing to exalt her comrades," her brother Alex wrote. "Her last words were a prophecy of British triumph."[64] Aaron was despondent but not shocked that NILI had been discovered. "The sacrifice is accomplished," he wrote in his diary. "I knew that we still had to face the great misfortune. But it is one thing to fear and another to know that all hope is lost. Poor father. Poor poor Sarati. It is her loss that certainly is the most cruel."[65]

Shortly after hearing about his family tragedy, Aaronsohn took the train to Washington to meet with Brandeis. He later discovered that the news was not as bad as initially reported. "Aaron is beyond wonder," Frankfurter wrote Marion Denman. "Thrice of the happiness that three words from Alex from Jerusalem brought them—Rivka and Aaron—'Father is alive.'"[66]

During his stays in Washington at the end of 1917 and beginning of 1918, Aaron Aaronsohn lived at 1727 Nineteenth Street. Frankfurter introduced him to the House's friends and former residents. In early February 1918, Aaronsohn, Frankfurter, and housemate Walter Meyer traveled to Halifax,

Nova Scotia, where they reunited with Loring Christie. Aaronsohn reported to his sister Rivka about Frankfurter's nocturnal habits: "Felix is taking it easy; he stays in bed to noon. I grant him that for a few days, but not for any longer. I am very severe with him. I started a French school for him and made him work hard. What a shame that he, of all men, should not know French! Walter reads fluently, but the most awful accent you ever heard."[67]

Aaronsohn also befriended another House of Truth resident, British Foreign Service officer Percy. Both in Washington and in London, Percy had been using British diplomatic pouches to send uncensored letters among Aaronsohn, Brandeis, and Weizmann. Percy was an important contact for the Zionists; he had arranged a meeting between Brandeis and Lord Balfour before the issuance of the Balfour Declaration. But, like many in the British government, Percy's support for Zionism masked a deep ambivalence about a Jewish homeland. "I had long had a number of contacts with American Jewry and I now felt overwhelmed by the enthusiasm with which it greeted the Balfour Declaration," he wrote. Despite his ambivalence, he confessed, "I could not help sunning myself in the jubilation of my friends, and perhaps I cannot be much blamed for letting the sun get a little in my eyes."[68]

Aaronsohn had managed to touch Percy's mystical side. The news of Sarah's death must have triggered painful memories. Percy's cousin and fellow attaché at the British embassy had been killed by Turkish forces in January 1916. Now the Turks had killed Sarah. "Perhaps I may *write* what I had no words to *say*, how deeply I share with you, not merely your grief, but the hope and faith which, thank God, already swallows it up and will, ere long, turn it into joy," Percy wrote Aaronsohn.[69]

Even people with little or no interest in Zionism wanted to meet Aaronsohn. Lippmann, who like many assimilated German Jews never embraced Zionist causes, was desperate to meet him.[70] It would not take long for both Aaronsohn brothers to charm Lippmann, just as they had charmed everyone else at the House of Truth. In August 1918, Aaron Aaronsohn discovered that Lippmann was in Europe "camouflaged as a Captain," caught up with him in London, and urged him to go to Egypt and Palestine. "He would do it if I were with him, but would gladly accept you as a substitute," he wrote Alex.[71] Lippmann never went to Palestine while stationed in Europe, but his friendship with Aaronsohn grew. A few months later, they reunited in Paris with Lippmann's time at the peace conference nearly finished and his spirits low. "He is displeased with his work, with

Col. House and the whole Wilson administration," Aaronsohn wrote in his diary. "He is under the impression—justified or not—that they are trying to rid the administration of all Liberals—and he is surprised that Felix manages to stay there."[72]

Of all the House's residents and friends, Aaronsohn's admiration ran deepest for Frankfurter. When he heard about the ill-fated Morgenthau Mission in July 1917, he described the ambassador to Turkey as "a soap bubble" and the other American representative as a "vulgar demagogue … Felix is the only man with a level head. Even if they should oppose the arrival of the whole Commission, Felix's coming can only be beneficial."[73]

Indeed, Frankfurter's secret travel companion during his second European reconnaissance trip in March 1918 was none other than Aaronsohn. "Our times were too full to write down impressions," Aaronsohn wrote, explaining the five-month gap in his diary.[74] In addition to assessing the labor situation in Britain and France for House, Frankfurter—with Aaronsohn's assistance—explained to Chaim Weizmann why the United States could not send delegates to join a commission to Turkey-controlled Palestine.[75] America had not declared war against Turkey, and House had discouraged Brandeis and other American Zionists from participating.[76] Indeed, with Frankfurter preoccupied with Labor Department work and Brandeis with Supreme Court business, Aaronsohn served as Brandeis's eyes and ears on the trip and accompanied Weizmann's group to Palestine.[77] He returned home deeply saddened by the death of his sister, the destruction of his family, and his lukewarm reception as a spy. He yearned to hear from Frankfurter: "I have been waiting for a line from you in vain. What is the matter with you? Is it really possible that since I left Paris you have not written or did your letters go astray?"[78]

In late November 1918, Aaronsohn briefly returned to the United States to smooth over relations between Brandeis and Weizmann and finally warmed to the justice. "He is great. He is a statesman," Aaronsohn reported to his brother. "The first day we had a session of 14 hours, I doing the talking all the time. The next day, a six-hour session, and I was dead. But, L.D.B. thought it was Chaim's happiest inspiration to have sent me over, and he discovered that I had 'character, judgment, and wisdom,' the three things he appreciates most. You easily imagine how happy little Felix—who *is* a dear—felt when L.D.B. told him that."[79] Aaronsohn left what was to be his last trip to America convinced that it had been a success. "The organization in the States is growing," he wrote. "With L.D.B., Felix, Judge M. at the head, we stand a fair chance."[80] After his meeting with Brandeis, he returned to Paris for the peace conference and awaited the men he considered key figures in the American Zionist delegation: Judge Julian Mack, Rabbi Stephen S. Wise, and Frankfurter.[81] Only Brandeis was not coming, at least not yet.

★★★

After only a few days in Paris, Frankfurter realized that the peace conference was all about meeting and understanding leaders from all over the world. He reported that "so much of it is personalia," which kept him occupied day and night.[82] In this regard, he possessed the perfect skills to achieve the Zionist movement's goals. He understood the movement's vulnerabilities based on the potential clash of egos and nationalities and was adept at mediating interpersonal conflicts. He could navigate bureaucratic hurdles based on his experiences in the War and Labor Departments. Thanks to his government service and network of liberal allies from the House of Truth and *New Republic*, he knew everyone worth knowing in Paris, particularly the key British and American players. And he could befriend anyone he did not know. No one was better at collecting friends and allies than Frankfurter. According to his secretary Ella Winter, he "had a foothold, or at least a toehold, it seemed, in every delegation."[83]

Just days after arriving in Paris, Frankfurter met his most important new ally, an Arab delegate at the peace conference, Prince Feisal. Prior to the peace conference, the British government had persuaded Feisal that forging an Arab-Jewish alliance and acceding to Jewish settlement in Palestine was the surest way for Feisal and his family to maintain control of the rest of the Arab Kingdom of Syria and Iraq. During much of 1918, Chaim Weizmann had laid considerable groundwork in securing an alliance with Feisal.[84] On January 3, 1919, Feisal and Weizmann had signed a peace accord that bore both their names.[85] But it was Feisal's meeting with Frankfurter three months later in Paris that gained national headlines and produced lasting historical documents.

No matter how much support the Zionist movement received from the British and American governments and how much it overcame French opposition and territorial aims, Frankfurter knew that the fate of a Jewish homeland depended on Arabs in Palestine. "THE ARAB Question has ceased to exist as a difficulty to the realisation of our programme before the Peace Conference," he wrote Brandeis. "The locus of trouble from the Arabs is Palestine and not Paris. The Arab question is and will continue [to be] a source of friction in the actual life in Palestine and as such it is a challenge, to the wishes, to the sympathetic understanding and the generosity of Jewish statesmanship."[86]

American Zionists were eager to sit down with Arab leaders and sent Frankfurter as their representative at a March 3 interview with Prince Feisal. Frankfurter, accompanied by Weizmann, called on the Arab leader at a small private hotel that the prince had rented on the fashionable Avenue du Bois. There they met Feisal accompanied by members of his staff, as well as his British adviser and translator, Colonel T. E. Lawrence—known today as Lawrence of Arabia.[87] "Lawrence is a quiet dare-devil" and a "fascinating Englishman," Frankfurter noted in the handwritten margin of a long typewritten report. Frankfurter was equally taken with Prince Feisal: "The Arab prince & I had a grand time—he makes you think of the face of Jesus, except black-bearded, fine silken hair with a sparkling but remote smile—remote to me. The Ends of the Earth met in him & me & yet I'm simple enough to think that he & I dealt & can deal as human beings who understand one another."[88] Through Lawrence, Feisal spoke first and "said all the right things" about the Jews and the Zionist movement. Frankfurter then replied "what I felt our attitude should be towards the Arabs, drawing upon our own sad experience dealing with the Southern Negroes." It was Frankfurter who suggested that the two men exchange letters of mutual understanding, letters that could be the basis of a formal public announcement; Feisal agreed.[89]

Immediately after the March 1 interview, Frankfurter and Lawrence returned to the Hôtel Meurice, where Frankfurter and his fellow Zionists were staying. Lawrence drafted a letter embodying Feisal's comments during the interview and "prepared under the most responsible conditions."[90] Later that day, Frankfurter received a copy of the letter signed by Feisal and published two days later in the *New York Times*.[91] "We feel that the Arabs and Jews are cousins in race, having suffered similar oppressions at the hands of powers stronger than themselves, and by a happy coincidence have been able to take the first step towards the attainment of their national ideals together," Feisal wrote Frankfurter. "We Arabs, especially the educated among us, look with the deepest sympathy on the Zionist movement." Feisal welcomed the Jews and pledged to support the proposal for a British-mandated Jewish homeland in Palestine. After mentioning Weizmann's helpfulness and support, Feisal wrote: "We are working together for a reformed and revised NEAR EAST, and our two movements complete one another. The

Jewish movement is national and not imperialist. Our movement is national and not imperialist, and there is room in Syria for us both. Indeed, I think that neither can be a real success without the other."[92]

Frankfurter wrote his response on the same day that Lawrence had drafted Feisal's letter. A flu bug, however, forced Frankfurter to rest and, as he explained to Lawrence, delayed the delivery of his response to Feisal for more than twenty days.[93] Frankfurter's March 23 response began by expressing gratitude about the burgeoning relationship between Feisal and the Weizmann-led Zionist movement: "We knew it could not be otherwise; we knew that the aspirations of the Arab and the Jewish peoples were parallel, that each aspired to re-establish its nationality in its own homeland, each making its own distinctive contribution to civilization, each seeking its own peaceful mode of life." Frankfurter concluded on a prophetic note: "For both the Arab and the Jewish peoples there are difficulties ahead—difficulties that challenge the united statesmanship of Arab and Jewish leaders." Overcoming those difficulties, Frankfurter wrote, would take cooperation: "We each have our difficulties; but there are no substantial differences between us. These difficulties we shall work out as friends, friends who are animated by similar purposes, seeking a free and full development for the two neighboring peoples. The Arabs and Jews are neighbors in territory, we cannot but live side by side as friends."[94]

At the end of March, Frankfurter participated in a farewell lunch before Feisal's departure. Feisal was wearing a black, floor-length cashmere coat with "Oriental embroidery" and a gold and silver turban. Frankfurter described Feisal as "wise" but couldn't "help detecting a contempt ... for all our Western civilization." And yet Frankfurter liked Feisal. "After Feisal appeared before the Council of Ten to state the Arab claims someone asked him what he thought of them & he replied 'a caravan of camels led by an ass,'" Frankfurter wrote. "That's the kind of customer he is."[95]

Frankfurter knew that his relationship with Prince Feisal was only the first of many necessary steps to a Jewish homeland and a successful resolution to the peace conference. Given his myriad personal contacts and experience with bureaucracy, Frankfurter took charge of the details in preparation for a presentation before the Commission on Mandates. One of the most important details, the boundaries of the proposed British mandate over Palestine, he delegated to the person most familiar with the territory—Aaron Aaronsohn.

Aaronsohn was a forgotten man at the peace conference. His repeated clashes with Weizmann and disregard for "official" Zionism had marginalized him within the movement.[96] And his reputation as a former spy made it hard for him to win people's trust and confidence.[97] His intelligence and maps of the region had been a crucial component of the British victory over the Turks in the Middle East, as many British military officers attested.[98] When Alex Aaronsohn received the Distinguished Order of Merit, one British officer said, "Aaron should have had two."[99]

Frankfurter was one of the few people who recognized Aaronsohn's status as the only Zionist in Paris with on-the-ground knowledge and expertise about Palestine. He urged Brandeis to overlook Aaronsohn's personal flaws and clashes with Weizmann and other Zionists: "He is *persona gratissima* to everybody who matters for us in the English and American delegations and instead of utilizing him as a scientist all these weeks he has been allowed to fritter away his spirit and energy in futile bickering and disorganizations. I think I have put an end to it at least during our stay in Paris."[100]

Another controversial figure who aided the Zionist mission was William C. Bullitt. Bullitt took an interest in the movement because his mother was Jewish and because of his friends at the House of Truth. A State Department official at the peace conference, he had been a regular visitor to 1727 Nineteenth Street at the end of 1917.[101] His *Philadelphia Public Ledger* articles leaking details about the Inquiry had gotten Frankfurter in hot water with House and Wilson. Yet Bullitt and his wife, Ernesta, remained close to Frankfurter and Lippmann and struck up a friendship with Aaronsohn.

In Paris, Bullitt arranged a meeting between Weizmann and House and at Aaronsohn's request read an early draft of the Zionist movement's proposed mandate.[102] Aaronsohn was privy to Bullitt's misgivings about the drafting of the League of Nations and his thoughts about resigning.[103] Indeed, Aaronsohn was there the day that House dissuaded Bullitt from resigning and instead suggested that Bullitt go to Russia to report on the nascent Bolshevist regime.[104] After several days of indecision, Bullitt agreed to go. He had left on his secret mission to Russia with journalist Lincoln Steffens shortly before Frankfurter arrived in Paris. Frankfurter knew all about Bullitt's threats to resign over the League of Nations and described him as "the enfant terrible" at the Hôtel de Crillon, the American delegation headquarters.[105] Yet Frankfurter conceded that, when it came to the Zionist movement, Bullitt "has aided us greatly, opening all the doors that needed to be opened."[106]

Unlike Bullitt, Frankfurter had not yet soured on the potential of the League of Nations. He could see the bigger picture about the importance of the United States in the fate of the British mandate over Palestine and in not imposing too harsh sanctions on Germany. Britain, France, and Italy wanted Germany to pay even though the German economy was already in shambles. A lot depended on the leadership of President Wilson, whose brief departure from the Paris Peace Conference left everything suspended in uncertainty and doubt. Dismayed at the news from home about isolationist opposition to the League of Nations, Frankfurter wished that those senators could spend a day or two in Paris so that they could "realise that unless we create a very effective world structure very quickly things will have become so disintegrated in Europe and in the world that no underpinning of a League of Nations will hold it up."[107]

In mid-March, House sent for Frankfurter, asked for his expertise on labor matters, and urged him to stay until the end of the peace conference. Frankfurter knew he was being flattered, describing House as a "most genial queen," but had no idea about the depths of House's anti-Semitism or the anti-Semitism of many of Zionism's supposed friends in the British government.[108] Shortly after his arrival in Paris in December 1918, House had spoken with Balfour about the reason for the Balfour Declaration's support for a Jewish homeland in Palestine. "He presented a very curious theory regarding Jews," House wrote in his diary. "Some told him, and he is inclined to believe it, that nearly all Bolshevism and disturbances of a like nature, are directly traceable to the Jews of the world. They seemed determined either to have what they want or to upset present civilization." House, for his part, "suggested that we put them in Palestine, at least the best of them, and hold them responsible for the orderly behavior of the rest of the Jews throughout the world." It is unclear how much of that diary entry reflected House's anti-Semitism or Balfour's.[109]

Frankfurter and his Zionist colleagues were putting the finishing touches on a draft of their proposed British mandate for Palestine and needed all the support from the British and American governments that they could get.[110] His faith still lay with President Wilson for "fighting hard against a retributive peace."[111] Events, however, upset the Zionists' best-laid plans. Some prominent American Jews, including Adolph Ochs of the *New York Times*, opposed a Jewish homeland in Palestine.[112] Arab uprisings in Palestine tested the faith of British loyalists, including Alex Aaronsohn, who believed that the British were encouraging the uprisings to prevent the establishment of a

Jewish state.[113] And the Inter-Allied Syrian Commission alarmed Frankfurter enough to write Colonel House to make sure that Palestine would not be on the itinerary and, if it were, that Zionist leaders would be consulted.[114]

Frankfurter realized that the British were not as committed to a Jewish state as they were to expanding the British Empire into Palestine. His former housemate Percy had introduced Frankfurter to many members of the British delegation, including Percy's initial boss in Paris, Lord Robert Cecil, and Prime Minister David Lloyd George's right-hand man, Philip Kerr. Kerr had visited the House of Truth during a 1912 trip to Washington and edited the influential foreign policy journal the *Round Table*.[115] The "acetic intellectual who largely guides" Lloyd George in Paris, Kerr made Frankfurter privy to "mischievous gossip" about the peace conference "because in a way I belong to the club via Eustace."[116]

Percy and Kerr also introduced Frankfurter to Nancy Astor, an American living in Britain whose country estate was home to the politically influential Cliveden Set during the late 1930s and who converted Kerr to Christian Science. A notorious anti-Semite, Astor asked a bemused Frankfurter and Weizmann, "Why don't you Jews give up Palestine?" She then tugged on Lloyd George's sleeve and said: "Tell these Jews why they can't have Palestine." Lloyd George smiled and responded: "I can't because I promised they shall have it, & I must keep my promise." Astor, Frankfurter reported, acted as if "Palestine was a little play thing" and Lloyd George "an accommodating playmate."[117]

Frankfurter was more alarmed that his close friend Percy seemed to be backpedaling from the Zionist cause. Percy assisted Cecil in Paris from January to March 1919 in drafting the League of Nations and then returned home to run for election to Parliament in the Central Hull district. During his failed bid for public office, he had misrepresented himself to the district's large Jewish constituency as a committed Zionist who had been one of the insiders responsible for the Balfour Declaration.[118] Returning to Paris as Balfour's secretary after his political defeat, Percy revealed his more ambivalent true colors. Frankfurter departed a luncheon with Percy and his wife disappointed that his close friend would not level with him about the issue.[119]

Sensing a weakening of British resolve about the Balfour Declaration, Frankfurter took desperate measures—a direct appeal to President Wilson. "As a passionate American I am, of course, most eager that the Jew should be a reconstructive and not a disruptive force in the new world order," Frankfurter wrote Wilson. "I have reassured their leaders, with the conviction born of knowledge of your purposes."[120] Frankfurter's May 8 letter sought to get the president on record as supporting the Balfour Declaration as well as permission for Frankfurter and Weizmann to go to Palestine to reassure Jewish leaders there. Five days later, Wilson responded with a single sentence acknowledging Frankfurter's letter and assuring him "how deeply I appreciate the importance and significance of the whole matter."[121] Frankfurter could not hide his disappointment. "You know how profoundly words, even familiar words, move people to-day—how their hopes and their faith are sustained or saddened, by what you say, or fail to say," he replied the next day. He told the president that his response "has occasioned almost despair to the Jewish representatives now assembled in Paris, who speak not only for the Jews of Europe but also for the American Jewish Congress, the democratic voice of three million American Jews." Frankfurter begged the president for some words of hope.[122] Taken aback by Frankfurter's response, Wilson failed to allay Zionist concerns: "I never dreamed that it was necessary to give you any renewed assurance of my adhesion to the Balfour Declaration, and so far I have found no one who is seriously opposing the purpose which it embodies. ... I see no ground for discouragement and every reason to hope that satisfactory guarantees can be secured."[123]

The importance of the Balfour Declaration was not just academic or political posturing. On May 12, Frankfurter received an urgent letter from Henry Alsberg in Warsaw about the persecution and starvation of more than 1 million Polish Jews. Alsberg reported that another 600,000 Jews in Eastern Galicia, a battleground between Poles and Ukrainians, "are slowly also rotting to death." His letter described in detail how Polish Jews were being starved to death and slaughtered, and "if something is not done of a radical nature to relieve the situation, there will be no Jews left to go to Palestine."[124]

Alsberg recommended that the Polish government be "bullied and brow-beaten" into protecting and feeding its Jews, that American Jews be allowed to enter the country as observers, that the peace conference explicitly protect minority rights, and that relief organizations work to move Polish Jews closer to Palestine. "I tell you quite plainly that Zionism will have to show the Jews of the world that it has saved the Jews in the Diaspora and made their life possible," Alsberg wrote, "as well as that it has gotten us back Palestine."[125] Alsberg's letter, Frankfurter wrote House, represented facts from "a most dependable observer, a disciplined mind, not one of 'the dispossessed,' and neither by temperament nor training a radical."[126] It explained why Frankfurter had urged President Wilson to express support for the Balfour Declaration. Unlike House and Wilson, Frankfurter understood the stakes for the Jewish people.

As the peace conference wore on, Frankfurter's concerns about Wilson were growing, and not just about the Palestine question. Frankfurter and his friends in Paris believed that Wilson was being outnegotiated and outmaneuvered—resulting in a peace treaty that severely punished Germany and made no explicit provision to protect minority rights in Eastern Europe. Wilson kept his two closest advisers, Secretary of State Lansing and Colonel House, at bay and was negotiating directly with the rest of the Big Four—Georges Clemenceau of France, David Lloyd George of Great Britain, and Vittorio Orlando of Italy.[127] Frankfurter lamented that Wilson had not asked a skilled negotiator such as Brandeis, Herbert Hoover, or Elihu Root to come to Paris.[128] Wilson, however, seemed to want only yes-men. Norman Hapgood, a longtime friend of Brandeis and Wilson's ambassador to Denmark, told Frankfurter that Wilson did not ask Brandeis to come to Paris because of the latter's work on the Court and because "'[Wilson] can't have about him any man who fights for his ideas.'" By the time the president realized that he needed help, it was too late—Wilson had already been bested at the negotiation table. "No wonder," Frankfurter wrote of Wilson, "he is one of the saddest looking men I've ever seen."[129]

Disappointment bordering on heartbreak for Frankfurter seemed to come in pairs. He was planning his trip to Palestine in June along with Brandeis and other Americans on the Zionist Commission. Aaron Aaronsohn was to be their guide. At Frankfurter's insistence, Aaronsohn had finished several maps proposing boundaries for British-controlled Palestine, maps that were to play a key role in the peace treaty negotiations as Britain, France, and Italy laid claims to different parts of the Middle East. Perhaps because he had finished his maps, perhaps because the end of the peace conference was near and he would be returning home to Palestine, Aaronsohn was rejuvenated. He was a lot of things—agricultural wizard, spy, military strategist, and larger-than-life personality—but he was not a diplomat, and the backslapping and socializing needed at the peace conference and navigating the internecine disputes in the Zionist movement had been getting him down. Indeed, Frankfurter had spent much of his time in Paris keeping Aaronsohn in line and making sure that his expertise about Palestine would not go untapped. Hence, the maps. At one point, Frankfurter lit into Aaronsohn so hard that the big man broke down in tears. At others,

Frankfurter defended him in letters home to Brandeis.[130] Through it all, Frankfurter and Aaronsohn remained the closest of friends, and as they prepared for their trip, Aaronsohn kept saying, "I must show you Palestine."[131]

Aaronsohn arrived in Frankfurter's hotel room on the morning of May 11 happier than he had been in weeks. With the final drafts of his maps in hand, he was set to fly to London that day to meet with Weizmann and British officials. Three days earlier, his brother, Alex, had sent a panicked cable that the British were letting the Arabs run roughshod over the Jews in Palestine and were insufficiently committed to the idea of a Jewish state.[132] During four days in London, Aaronsohn wanted to make sure that his family's sacrifices had not been in vain and that the British government was still committed to the Balfour Declaration.

Four days later, Frankfurter was waiting in Paris for his friend's return flight.[133] A dense fog had settled over the English Channel; the wind howled. Aaronsohn, who had flown between Paris and London a month earlier and had been taking risks his entire life, was unconcerned.[134] He boarded a Royal Air Force plane loaded with mail and confidential documents for the British mission. The plane was so overloaded that there was not even enough room for his luggage and supplies (khakis and boots) that he had bought for his return to Palestine. A man as large as Aaronsohn must have been crammed into his seat on the small postal plane. Weizmann, who was supposed to go with them and left a box of cigarettes on board, promised to take Aaronsohn's luggage with him by boat and train.[135] The plane took off once but returned to the base because of a problem with the propeller. Despite the poor weather conditions, the decorated Royal Air Force pilot decided to try again. The plane was last seen over the harbor of the French port city of Boulogne. It got lost in the fog and landed in the sea. A French fishing captain and his son saw the plane fall from the sky, its engine roaring as it landed in the water.[136]

The plane and the mail were recovered in the English Channel, but the bodies of Aaronsohn and the pilot were never found.[137] A French newspaper reported that a second British plane had been seen falling from the sky in the exact same spot—prompting conspiracy theories that Aaronsohn's plane had been shot down by enemies in the British government and that he had been assassinated.[138] The inept British investigation of the crash—as well as delayed reports in the British press—fueled rumors of foul play.[139] In 1919, however, air travel was risky; planes were frequently lost at sea—especially in foggy, windy weather.

Frankfurter wired the news to Brandeis and Aaronsohn's other friends in America.[140] For Frankfurter, Aaronsohn's death rekindled memories of seeing Valentine stricken at Delmonico's and sitting at Valentine's bedside as his closest friend breathed his last breath. Once again, Frankfurter took charge after a friend's death—gathering Aaronsohn's papers and effects; comforting his love interest, a married aspiring opera singer; and relaying respects from Brandeis and other American dignitaries to the Aaronsohn family.[141] While performing these unpleasant duties, Frankfurter implored President Wilson to express his support for the Balfour Declaration and worked with Weizmann to maintain their alliance with Prince Feisal as the best hope for an Arab-Jewish rapprochement.[142]

"And now Aaron is gone," Frankfurter wrote in his first letter about the tragedy to Marion Denman.[143] Yet he did not fully mourn Aaronsohn's death for nearly a month. For her part, Denman was relieved that Frankfurter was alive and had not been on Aaronsohn's airplane—something not entirely clear when she had received a phone call about the initial May 19 *New York Times* story and not clarified until she received Frankfurter's first letter.[144] Frankfurter regretted not sending her an official cable. He had gotten so used to discussing Aaronsohn's death in a "cold cable way" that it took a while for him to process it and to share his feelings with Marion. "I hear his warm, shrill voice, his pervasive frame fills in the room," he wrote her, "—in ceaseless ways." The writer of the liberal *Manchester Guardian*'s obituary described Aaronsohn as "the great Romantic figure in the history of the Jews." In Frankfurter's mind, Aaronsohn and Valentine were dreamers; he shared the same dreams and treasured their friendship.[145]

Others connected with the House of Truth mourned Aaronsohn's death. Judge Mack had known Aaron since 1909 and had been his "closest friend in America."[146] Brandeis, who credited his Zionist conversion in part to Aaronsohn, knew that his chief lieutenants in Paris, Mack and Frankfurter, were crestfallen. "I SORROW WITH YOU AND MAC[K] OVER THE LOSS OF AARON," Brandeis wired Frankfurter.[147]

No one took Aaronsohn's death harder than William and Ernesta Bullitt. Billy had confided in him before deciding to go to Russia and shared his iconoclasm. "Billie Bullitt and Ernesta, over whom [Aaron] cast the spell of a god walking the earth, kept on saying 'he isn't lost; he just isn't,'" Frankfurter wrote. "'Aaron will find some way, somehow.'"[148] A year later, Bullitt wrote Alex Aaronsohn that his brother was unequaled in terms of intellectual and emotional intelligence and recalled how Aaron had "astonished" diplomats in Washington. "Aaron, to me, was not merely the flaming embodiment of the determination of the Jewish race to have a home and to be again a nation," Bullitt wrote, "but rather a captain in the foremost company of that small army of humanity which marches ever against ignorance, superstition and hatred."[149] Indeed, Bullitt never forgot Aaron Aaronsohn and considered him "the greatest man I have known."[150]

After returning from his secret mission to Russia, Bullitt was furious about the Allies' refusal to remove their blockade, as well as President Wilson's refusal to recognize Lenin's Bolshevik regime. "You ought to hear Billie Bullitt rant—he is just wild, shrieking Bolshevistics at the top of his lungs, while Ernesta exhibits goodness that no real civilization should do without," Frankfurter wrote. "There is a dark incongruity about it all."[151] Bullitt was one of the few American delegates willing to criticize his country's efforts at the Paris Peace Conference.[152] No one was more upset with Wilson's handling of the negotiations than Bullitt. It was no surprise on May 19 when Bullitt resigned from the American delegation. "Poor Billie," Frankfurter wrote, "he needs steadying lots, for he wants of life a steady stream of exciting adventures and emotionally he, like Walter L. is, as I told him, a short distance sprinter. He won't do the drudgery of fighting. He is fine, tho & full of real, generous manhood."[153] Ernesta, for her part, was "fine and steady about it" but "lots grayer."[154] Frankfurter encouraged Bullitt to join forces with Croly, Lippmann, and other critics of Wilson's handling of the peace conference. "I wish you were here for this last beautiful fight on Russia," Bullitt wrote Lippmann soon after returning from Moscow.[155] Bullitt and Lippmann grew closer over their disappointment with Wilson and became two of the administration's most outspoken critics.

★★★

The *New Republic* announced Lippmann's return on a printed postcard that looked handwritten: "Walter Lippmann is back—back from France—back once more on the staff of 'The New Republic.' As Captain of Military Intelligence, he has until recently been attached to the personal staff of Colonel House."[156] Lippmann had returned to the pages of the *New Republic* with a bang. Before, during, and after his vacation with Faye to Camden, South Carolina, he had been writing everything he had been thinking about the war and the peace conference but could not say as a commissioned military officer. He sent the massive manuscript to Croly, who set it in type before even reading a word of it. No one was happier about Lippmann's return than Croly.[157] The magazine had missed Lippmann's strong opinions, unmatched prose style, and inside scoop on the peace conference. Croly had missed Lippmann's ideas and presence in the magazine's New York offices. Croly informed Lippmann of an intention to publish Lippmann's manuscript, which consisted of ten parts, "in the first issue after you return in one whole lump."[158] Lippmann's essay, *The Political Scene*, comprised a bound supplement to the March 22, 1919, issue, a magazine unto itself. Lippmann dedicated the essay to the magazine's late publisher, Willard Straight. *The Political Scene* was part polemic, part history lesson, and part prophecy.

The polemic critiqued President Wilson for his inability to translate his idealistic reasons for entering the war into a workable peace treaty. Once the war was over, Lippmann argued, Wilson had lost all his leverage over European leaders, as well as the overwhelming support of the Europeans. He was trapped between the reaction of European imperialism and the revolution of Bolshevism. "Many who have supported Mr. Wilson and still support him in all loyalty," Lippmann wrote, "know that his ideas have never had the precision and downrightness which characterizes both the Reaction and the Revolution."[159]

The history lesson reviewed the reasons why the United States had been drawn into the war (and implicitly why Lippmann and others associated with the *New Republic* had supported it), why Wilson's Fourteen Points (which Lippmann had helped interpret) had not resulted in an earlier attempt at peace, and why European allies (Britain, France, Italy) had insisted on absolute victory over Germany.

The prophecy outlined why the League of Nations was doomed to fail not only with American isolationists at home but also in preserving the peace abroad. Lippmann argued that Article X about league signatories preserving and protecting territorial integrity should be rewritten and that congressional representation on the league should be included. He criticized the creation of new barrier nations between Germany and Russia, including Poland, Czechoslovakia, Greater Romania, and Jugo-slavia as "a very dangerous bit of fooling" that attempted to paralyze Germany, to exile German-speaking people to foreign countries, and to isolate Bolshevist Russia. The treaty, he argued, should have checked Bolshevism economically by using the League of Nations to maintain control over Russian ports. He concluded by urging America to agree to enforce "a peace that Europe will endure" but to retreat into isolationism if it is "a peace that can be maintained only by the bayonet."[160]

The Political Scene signaled the beginning of the end of the *New Republic*'s pro-Wilson, pro–League of Nations editorial stance. Lippmann's left-wing friends cheered him on. "I thought your supplement was extraordinarily effective and I would underwrite every word of it," Laski wrote.[161] Laski recommended *The Political Scene* to Justice Holmes because it was "an exceptionally profound piece of analysis and I think as true as a generalisation can hope to be."[162] Holmes, who had seen the Lippmanns on their way home from Camden, South Carolina, agreed.[163] Judge Learned Hand lauded Lippmann's essay, encouraged him to write a history of the war, and recognized changes in Lippmann's style and outlook: "You have a breadth and certainty of treatment, a kind of depth in foundation, which makes what you say massive and correspondingly impressive." As one of the founders of the *New Republic*, Hand described Lippmann's return to the magazine as "a thing of genuine public interest. If you can sustain such power and scope you will make yourself a noticeable force in American political ideas. The war was a bad enough thing, but it certainly has been a blessing for you."[164]

Frankfurter, for his part, knew that Lippmann's more critical view of the Wilson administration was changing the direction of the *New Republic*—and for the better.[165] The book had arrived from the publisher days before Aaron Aaronsohn's death. Aaronsohn and Frankfurter had read it together "with admiration and pride," Frankfurter wrote Lippmann.[166]

Given the chaos after Aaronsohn's death and his frantic letters to President Wilson about the Balfour Declaration, Frankfurter did not correspond with Lippmann for nearly two months after the publication of *The Political Scene* and after Wilson's failure in Paris had been assured. They had in many ways changed places, with Frankfurter now the diplomatic insider and Lippmann the outsider. Yet their views on the peace conference and the people they blamed—perhaps rightly, perhaps wrongly—were remarkably similar. "At least at bottom, if not *the* bottom fact is that neither the President nor the Colonel had an adequate conception of what the problem of peace-making was …," Frankfurter wrote. "Without exception, the saddest day of the war for me was Labour Day of last year when the Colonel outlined to me the plan for the Peace Conference. I knew then (and I told L.D.B. at the time) that they were the naïvest children in the world and the President's efforts to achieve his principles were doomed to failure." Despite these perceived mistakes, Frankfurter believed that the peace conference could have been salvaged: "I have not a particle of doubt that just one personality like L.D.B. would have made a world wide difference—and of course it is of the essence of any consideration of [Wilson's] personality that he did not bring L.D.B. with him or ever realize the need of having him."[167]

A few weeks later, Lippmann responded to Frankfurter that he had written the essay "at a stage in the proceedings when I was still determined to hope against hope." He agreed with Frankfurter that Wilson's failure had been "a failure of technique. What Paris has demonstrated is, that you cannot in ignorance improvise a structure of good will." Wilson, Lippmann wrote, had failed in early 1917 to get an agreement among the Allies about war aims before America committed its troops. Then Wilson had "compounded" his mistake by not having an effective diplomatic service in place. And the diplomatic service he had "was insulated from the President, who worked by intimation from Colonel House, who had his own irresponsible diplomatic service." Finally, Lippmann criticized the president for creating an "atmosphere of unreality" about American diplomacy, as well as most "so-called liberals" who have "entered a monastery where they contemplate ecstatically the beatitudes of the League of Nations."[168]

Lippmann did not just write this way in private. In the July 1919 issue of the *Yale Review*, he laid much of the blame for the Paris Peace Conference at Wilson's feet—for ignoring the State Department, for eschewing diplomacy for George Creel's propaganda bureau, and for "failing to realize that his position would be radically altered by the conclusion of the war." In the process, Lippmann argued, Wilson had lost his chance to negotiate a just peace in the summer of 1918 with "the whole working and middle classes in every Allied country" behind him and "had lost his grip on America." Above all, Lippmann argued, Wilson failed by negotiating with the Big Four on his own. The secret treaties between the Allies (which Wilson knew all about) and secret negotiations were no excuse. "What happened in the so-called secret conferences of the Big Four is not so secret after all," Lippmann concluded. "It is written in the Treaty of Versailles."[169]

★★★

Before he left Paris, Frankfurter made a last-ditch effort to save the prospect of a Jewish homeland and to make sure that his close friend Aaron Aaronsohn had not died in vain. Even with Wilson's tepid support for the Balfour Declaration and diplomatic failure at the peace conference, a British mandate over Palestine still had a chance. To lock in British support, Frankfurter played his final trump card—he demanded that the leader of the American Zionist movement travel to Palestine.

Brandeis was planning to leave Washington on June 9 and to join Frankfurter and the rest of the Zionist Commission in Palestine.[170] That was until Mack and others persuaded him to postpone his trip because of Arab uprisings in the region, because of questions whether the British mandate over Palestine would be written into the peace treaty, and because the Middle East situation would not be resolved until the fall.[171] Frankfurter, however, would not be denied. Brandeis needed to gather facts on the ground in Palestine, to persuade the British to accede to a mandate over the land, and to emerge as the movement's public face. "I made up my mind that Brandeis can't continue to lead this movement from the securities of the eighth floor of Stoneleigh Court, overlooking the Potomac and the imperturbable Washington Monument," Frankfurter wrote. "He's got to *feel* the facts, get their subtle weight on the spot and in the perverse and misfiring and blended details."[172] Rather than resign himself to Brandeis's decision, on June 6 Frankfurter dashed off a wire begging the justice to reconsider. Brandeis tried to put him off, but Frankfurter pressed the issue. "Your failure to come may have consequences that I contemplate with the utmost anxiety," Frankfurter replied in a second cable that day. "Have consulted Mr. Balfour who fully agrees with need of your coming. Weizmann has read this cable and concurs."[173]

Frankfurter's telegrams worked; Brandeis changed his mind and agreed to take what the newspapers called a "vacation" to Palestine.[174] On June 14, five days after the Supreme Court adjourned for the summer, Brandeis, his eldest daughter, Susan, and Jacob de Haas joined 658 other passengers aboard the *Mauretania* bound for Southampton, England. Six days later in Southampton, Frankfurter and fellow Zionist Bernard Flexner were waiting for the *Mauretania* to make its way through the fog.[175]

After a night of debriefing, Brandeis described Frankfurter and Flexner "as blue as men can be over the Peace Treaty, and the League to Enforce Peace."[176] Frankfurter described Brandeis as "at the very best of his powers," "bursting quiet eagerness," and dwarfing the supposedly great yet timid men already in Paris.[177] During the two nights in London, Brandeis and Frankfurter dined with Weizmann and met with Socialist political scholar Graham Wallas. "London is civilization," Brandeis wrote, "& it would be worth millions of men's lives to preserve it."[178]

Brandeis made a briefer stopover in Paris. Balfour, Percy's boss, was waiting for him and insisted on meeting Brandeis before the justice left for Palestine. For nearly two hours at Balfour's apartment at the British headquarters on the Rue Nitot, the two men found common ground about Zionism. They realized that Palestine could be an outlet for Jews desperate to leave Eastern Europe. Brandeis outlined three conditions for a successful Jewish state: (1) "that Palestine should be the Jewish homeland and not merely that there be a Jewish homeland in Palestine"; (2) that Palestine's

boundaries extend far north enough to control its water supply as well as
far enough south and east; and (3) "that the future Jewish Palestine must
have control of the land and the natural resources which are at the heart
of a sound economic life."[179] Balfour agreed with Brandeis's conditions yet
explained that President Wilson's insistence on self-determination conflicted
with preexisting agreements with France about Syria, as well as with the concept of a Jewish homeland in Palestine given the Arab majority there. Brandeis
responded that a Jewish homeland was not simply about Palestine but about
a "world problem." He reiterated the importance of his three conditions and
asked that no final decision be made about Palestine until he returned. In the
end, Balfour promised to wait for Brandeis's report on the conditions there.
Frankfurter, who along with Percy was present at the meeting, concluded
in a memorandum: "No statesman could have been more sympathetic than
Mr. Balfour was with the underlying philosophy and aims of Zionism as they
were stated by Mr. Justice Brandeis."[180] Indeed, as they were leaving Balfour's
apartment, Brandeis remarked that "it is a great joy to deal with a gentleman,"
and Frankfurter described it as a "deeply important meeting."[181]

Thanks to Brandeis, the Balfour Declaration was alive and well. In addition to seeing Balfour in Paris, Brandeis crammed in meetings with Herbert
Hoover, Colonel House, Lincoln Steffens, Baron de Rothschild, and European
and Russian Zionist leaders in what Frankfurter described as "their first
glimpse of the real Joshua." "I wish you could have seen LDB & Hoover &
LDB & Balfour together," Frankfurter wrote Marion Denman. He was
amazed at how Brandeis was "simple and profoundly impressive" with everyone from Balfour to the run-of-the-mill Russian Jew.[182] For Frankfurter and
Brandeis, Hoover and Lewis Strauss—the two-man Commission for Relief
in Belgium—embodied everything that liberals in Paris yearned for—experts
who ran the administrative state by gathering facts on the ground and helping
people who needed it the most.[183] They were the only ones looking out for
Europe's starving and dispossessed minorities; the peace treaty did not provide
for them; and the United States would be compelled to feed and protect them.
Hoover, according to Frankfurter, knew "more deeply about the Economics of
Europe than any man in Paris" and exhibited complete disdain for Wilson and
the peace treaty. "Hoover has guts," Frankfurter wrote, "—the *only* man here
who has tried to make the poor Wilson man see what's what."[184]

Frankfurter hoped that Brandeis could have a similar impact on the
Zionist movement. He believed that Brandeis would have to choose between life in America and his position on the Supreme Court and life in the

future Jewish homeland of Palestine and political leadership of the Zionist movement.[185] And in the end, he wanted Brandeis to resign from the Court and to choose Palestine.[186]

After a few days in Paris, Frankfurter put Brandeis on a train to Marseilles to board a ship bound for Egypt. Frankfurter could barely hide his disappointment that he was also not going to the Promised Land, to feel and to see Palestine for himself. Brandeis's friend from the British government, Alfred Zimmern, was his companion along with Jacob de Haas.[187] Someone had to stay in Paris and make sure that the Palestine question would not be decided in the Zionist Commission's absence. So Frankfurter stayed. He saw the peace treaty signed and President Wilson leave a beaten man and waited for Brandeis to return.

Instead of simply waiting for Brandeis, Frankfurter threw himself into investigating and stopping the slaughter of Polish Jews. Henry Alsberg had followed up his May 12 letter to Frankfurter about the atrocities with a phone call a month later about the poverty and starvation in Hungary, Poland, Austria, and Czechoslovakia.[188] In a meeting arranged by House and with Brandeis present, Frankfurter urged American diplomat Hugh Gibson to leave his posh hotel in Warsaw and to investigate the starvation and extermination of Polish Jews.[189] Frankfurter was also trying to prevent the anti-Zionist Morgenthau from getting involved. Sure enough, Wilson appointed Morgenthau to make a fact-finding mission to Poland. Lippmann's low opinion of Morgenthau's "character" was one of several reasons why he had turned down House's offer to go on the Polish mission.[190] Despite his own disdain for Morgenthau given their disastrous 1917 mission to Gibraltar and Paris, Frankfurter went along.[191] Amazed that Frankfurter had gone not to Palestine but to Poland, Lippmann wrote: "I really think that the kind of problem raised there requires your abilities even more than those in Palestine."[192]

Frankfurter thought he knew what poverty and squalor were until he visited Poland. Though he was ready to leave after a few days, he knew that six months of mediating disputes between the Jews and the Poles could make things better there. He debriefed the American Commission to Negotiate Peace and only wished Wilson would send someone to Poland to do the job.[193] More than 3 million Jews, Frankfurter wrote Lippmann, face "systematic, pervasive anti-Semitism," "live in a state of terror," and are isolated from other German-speaking people. "And to study, to understand that most complicated problem Wilson sends that unsurpassed vapid Megalomaniac Morgenthau." The only thing that cheered Frankfurter upon returning to

Paris was reading the *New Republic*. "I read the leader 'Mr. Wilson Forgets' and spotted you and want to say FINE!" he wrote Lippmann. "*That's* the way to go after that gent—stick the Knife of concreteness into him and don't let him wiggle. It was well done—and the paper is in fine form."[194]

Frankfurter's best hope for the Jews of Poland awaited Brandeis's return from Palestine. Brandeis and his party cooled their heels for a week in Egypt to wait for the return from Syria of General Edmund Allenby. After dinner with the general, his wife, and other British officials, Brandeis and Allenby talked privately from 10:15 p.m. to midnight about the problems of Palestine. As with other British officials, Brandeis made a good first impression on Allenby. Palestine awed Brandeis. "It is a wonderful country, a wonderful city," he wrote upon arriving in Jerusalem. "Aaronsohn was right. It is a miniature California, but a California endowed with all the interest which the history of man can contribute and the deepest emotions which can stir a people. The ages-long longing, the love is all explicable now. . . . The way is long, the path difficult and uncertain; but the struggle is worthwhile. It is indeed a Holy Land."[195]

Brandeis toured the country for more than two weeks, visited all the cities and twenty-three of the forty-three Jewish settlements, heard about all the problems, and learned to love the Mediterranean cuisine.[196] He was glad to have learned the facts on the ground and radiated optimism about the future. "What I have seen and heard strengthen greatly my conviction that Palestine can and must become the Jewish Homeland as promised in the Balfour Declaration," he wrote General Allenby. "The problems and difficulties are serious and numerous, even more so than I had anticipated; but there is none which will not be solved & overcome by the indomitable spirit of the Jews here and elsewhere."[197] Above all, Brandeis was grateful to Frankfurter for shaming him into going to Palestine: "Felix was very wise in insisting upon our coming. There was, in fact, no basis whatsoever for a different view."[198]

Brandeis's visit to Palestine, as Frankfurter learned upon the justice's return to Paris and London, was not a panacea. The Commission on Mandates was no closer to resolving Middle Eastern territorial and sovereignty questions. Opposition to the League of Nations was growing in the United States. "The President has his hands pretty full," Brandeis wrote, "and even my revered associates on the Bench (of whom I rarely think) must begin to realize that we are not living in the Nineteenth Century."[199] The justice, however, had no intention of leaving the bench to run the Zionist movement. "On the whole," he wrote, "I think Zionist affairs about the most hopeful of all the world's problems."[200]

The post-Palestine, European version of Brandeis, according to Frankfurter, was "a different man."[201] Others noticed it, too. Lincoln Steffens, after seeing him in Paris, wrote that Brandeis "even looks different. It's as if he had seen a vision."[202] In Europe, the austerity that marked so much of Brandeis's cloistered life on the bench and sheltered Washington existence under the watchful eye of his wife was gone. He liked good food, good wine, and fine hotels such as Claridge's in London.[203] Over lunch, Brandeis debriefed Balfour and other British officials. Balfour "was thrilled" by Brandeis and urged Frankfurter to "talk Poland."[204] For several weeks, Brandeis and Frankfurter made the rounds in London. The leader of the American Zionist movement brought gravitas and factual knowledge about the Palestine problem.[205] He put the British on notice that he would not let the Balfour Declaration die, and he and Frankfurter put Weizmann and other European Zionists on notice that democracy and inclusion would be hallmarks of the movement going forward.[206]

Brandeis in Palestine in 1919

An embittered Weizmann believed that Brandeis and Frankfurter were abandoning the Jewish people by returning home. "Brandeis could have been a prophet in Israel," Weizmann wrote in an unsent August 27 letter to Frankfurter. "You have in you the making of a Lassalle. Instead, you are choosing to be only a professor in Harvard and Brandeis only a judge in the Supreme Court."[207] Weizmann wrote the letter days before Frankfurter and Brandeis returned home. After several weeks of fun and frolic in Britain, Frankfurter said good-bye to Percy and Harold Armstrong and joined Brandeis's party on the SS *Rotterdam* for the voyage back to America.[208]

During nine months in Paris, Frankfurter failed to achieve a Jewish homeland in Palestine, but he learned how difficult government intervention was at home and abroad. As he confided to Brandeis, he believed that the stars were aligned to send him to Paris with the Zionist movement rather than with the disastrous American delegation at the peace conference. In response, Brandeis "buried his chin in his neck" and replied, "You

Frankfurter

know—I've thought the same thing about myself."[209] They were deter-mined to keep alive the cause of a Jewish homeland. Frankfurter, however, could not wait to return home. He missed his fiancée, Marion Denman, whom he had written almost every day from Europe; he missed fighting the reactionary forces against him and Roscoe Pound at Harvard Law School; and he missed the last days of the Dupont Circle row house he loved so dearly.

15

"The H/T Cannot Be
Re-constituted"

The most poignant aspect of Felix Frankfurter's nine-month absence from America was the end of the House of Truth as a political salon. Robert Valentine's widow, Sophie, and their daughter, Charlotte (née Sophia), returned to Washington in early February 1919 and stayed for the remainder of the school year. The first place that Sophie wanted to go when she arrived on the train from Boston was 1727 Nineteenth Street. Instead, she waited until she got settled in their apartment half a mile away at 2326 California Street.[1]

For the next two days, Sophie visited the houses that she and Robert had lived in and walked the sidewalks that they had walked. She put off returning phone calls from Alice Goldmark Brandeis and Gertrude King and instead spent two days re-living her former life in Washington with her husband. "Never since his going has he seemed so near—never since his going has the anguish of the separation been so great," she wrote Frankfurter of her husband. "I walked as in a dream: the tears running down my face—but I have not been so happy for two years."[2]

Sophie Valentine wanted to talk with Frankfurter about the memory book about her husband that had not been finished (and never would be) and about the future of the House.[3] Frankfurter showed the letter to Denman. The letter was so grief-filled that Denman could not bear to throw it away. "[Robert Valentine] was a tragic man to lose because in going he tore away so much of her own life that had become his," she wrote Frankfurter."[4]

After the end of the influenza epidemic that had forced her to convalesce at her parents' home near Springfield, Massachusetts, Denman returned to Washington to work again for the War Department's Commission on Training Camp Activities and to live with her sister and

Frankfurter (left) and Percy in 1918 in front of the House

fellow War Department employee, Helen. Denman maintained a long friendship with Sophie Valentine, renewed acquaintances with her in the spring of 1919 in Washington, and took an instant liking to Robert and Sophie's eight-year-old daughter, Charlotte.[5] Denman pitied Charlotte. Her mother had been forty-two when Charlotte was born, and Sophie was still living in the past. "She always was elusive and a bit vague, but she's vapory now …," Denman reported. "There's very little real sympathy between them, for Mrs. V is an *old* person. I think Charlotte will be an interesting person with plenty of force."[6]

Denman also updated Frankfurter about the fate of the House of Truth. He knew that the end was near in March when she had informed him that the House was being "papered and painted." "I did not know news of a cleansing process could so reopen?—and yet, for me, it's like white-washing the Palais Royal or the facades of the Place Vendome," he wrote with tongue in cheek and a reference to his dictionaries. "I wonder what the vandals will do to my centuries!"[7] The news brought Frankfurter a tinge of sadness. The House for so long had been a bachelor pad in which its residents reveled in its disorderly messiness and borderline disrepair. He would not recognize it repainted, wallpapered, and pristine.

Denman's warnings grew louder a month later after she had dined with Sophie and Charlotte. She reported that an army officer and his family were living in the House, but the temporary military assignment left open the possibility that Frankfurter and his friends could reclaim it.[8] Sophie Valentine wanted it that way. "She said that Walter L. has refused to give up his key to the house," Denman wrote, "which seemed to please her immensely."[9]

But Lippmann was living in New York City with his wife, Faye, and working out of the *New Republic*'s office there. Frankfurter was engaged to Denman and promised to return to Cambridge after the Paris Peace Conference and to rejoin the Harvard law faculty. Christie was with Frankfurter in Paris as counsel to Canadian prime minister Borden, married, and permanently living in Ottawa. Percy was married and living in Britain. There was no one who could run the House as a political salon/ bachelor pad the way that Valentine, Lippmann, Frankfurter, Christie, or Percy once did.

One person knew this above all the others—Winfred Denison. He had been instrumental in starting the House with Valentine and Frankfurter and the least capable of keeping it going. He had never recovered from his disastrous two-year stint as secretary of the interior to the Philippines. He had returned home a broken man in 1916 and knew that his career in government was finished. He had attempted to resurrect his legal career in New York City, first with his old firm of Stetson, Jennings & Russell and then by starting his own firm.[10] He was so far removed from public life that he had never entertained the thought of joining his old housemates Frankfurter, Christie, and Percy in Paris. Denison lived on Quogue, Long Island, and only recently had begun leaving the house. He vowed to try to put his life back together again.[11]

As Charlotte's godfather, Denison continued to try to look after Sophie and her daughter. He also managed the Valentines' Washington real estate interests, including the investment property he co-owned with them on R Street. Denison's interest in the House of Truth was proprietary, but not in the legal sense. He had introduced Frankfurter to Valentine and had invited Christie, his assistant at the Justice Department, to live there. There would have been no group house without Denison. He was the one who self-mockingly had named it the House of Truth because of their debates with Holmes. Denison had helped Frankfurter turn the House into a liberal network. And it was Denison who, along with Frankfurter and Christie, had begun championing Holmes as a judicial hero. Yet he informed Sophie Valentine in February 1919 that the House had entered a new phase: "I think the H/T cannot be re-constituted as a *physical* institution, and ought to be regularly rented or sold. Its soul goes marching on—."[12]

Denison's friends were no longer at the center of American politics the way they had been in 1912 or even in 1919. After the Paris Peace Conference, Frankfurter, Lippmann, and other liberals had given up on Wilson. For the next decade, they tried and failed to return to political power. They turned to the Supreme Court to protect free speech and fair criminal trials, and they transformed Holmes into a liberal icon. They may not have needed to live at 1727 Nineteenth Street anymore, but they needed the liberal network they had created there more than ever.

16

Harvard's Dangerous Men

Before he left for Paris in 1919, Frankfurter tapped into his liberal network from the House of Truth, *New Republic*, and Harvard Law School for the "one tie all of us have in common—affection for Mr. Justice Holmes."[1] He wanted to raise $350 for a bronze bas-relief by sculptor Bashka Paeff of Holmes in his judicial robes.[2] For the past six years, Holmes had delighted his friends by dissenting from the Court's antilabor decisions. Though no liberal, Holmes also helped show his friends that the Court could protect them from abuses of government power and safeguard their free speech.

Holmes's free speech dissents are generally considered his most important contribution to American liberalism. During a span of six months in 1919, he went from authoring majority opinions upholding the criminal convictions of wartime radicals to dissenting on their behalf. Most scholars attribute Holmes's shift on free speech to key encounters with friends and the influence of their work—a chance meeting on a train with Judge Learned Hand, a summertime visit from Harold Laski and Harvard law professor Zechariah Chafee, Laski's new book on sovereignty, and Chafee's law review article on free speech.[3] "[T]he shift in Holmes' consciousness," Holmes biographer G. Edward White wrote, "is best explained by Holmes' personal experiences and relationships."[4]

One of the most important but often overlooked episodes during Holmes's summertime shift on free speech was his behind-the-scenes defense of his friends from postwar fears of Communism in the United States, which led to arrests, deportations, and accusations known as the Red Scare. The attacks on Frankfurter and Roscoe Pound imperiled their jobs and even threatened the future of Harvard Law School. With prodding from Brandeis, Holmes sprang into action with Harvard president A. Lawrence Lowell. Holmes cared little about the fate of wartime radicals, but he cared greatly about the academic freedom of Frankfurter, Pound, and other left-leaning Harvard intellectuals, including Laski and Chafee. Holmes's response to the red-baiting of Frankfurter and Pound is an underexplored reason for the transformation of his views on free speech. Even less well known is that Holmes rose to their defense.[5]

For much of the war, civil liberties had not been high on the agenda of the House of Truth's liberals. Yet in September 1917, Frankfurter and others in the War Department had attempted to protect conscientious objectors.[6] A month later, Lippmann had advised against the Wilson administration's press censorship.[7] And in January 1918, Frankfurter's report for the President's

January 16, 1920, cover of the *Harvard Lampoon*

Mediation Commission on the Bisbee deportation and the Tom Mooney case had triggered backlash from Theodore Roosevelt and others. But it took longer for Frankfurter and his liberal allies to object to the administration's biggest assault on civil liberties.

After declaring war on Germany in 1917, Wilson had signed into law the Espionage Act, which made it a federal crime to interfere with military operations, to promote the success of the country's enemies, or to obstruct military recruitment. The Espionage Act was aimed chiefly at German and Russian immigrants sympathetic to their home countries, as well as to Communists, Socialists, and anarchist radicals opposed to the war. It was the Espionage Act that empowered the postmaster general to suspend the mail privileges of publications in violation of the act. A year later, the Sedition Act amended the Espionage Act to criminalize disloyal and profane speech about the US government. The Wilson administration used these laws to prosecute wartime radicals, several of whom appealed their convictions to the Supreme Court.

On March 3, 1919, Holmes wrote the first of three unanimous opinions affirming the Espionage Act convictions. Charles Schenck, the secretary of the Socialist Party, had printed 15,000 leaflets urging prospective draft-ees not to serve.[8] He was tried, convicted, and sentenced to six months in federal prison. The Court upheld Schenck's conviction for conspiring to obstruct the draft and rejected a free speech defense.

Holmes's opinion introduced two of the most quoted phrases into the American constitutional lexicon. He analogized wartime obstruction of the draft as akin to "falsely shouting fire in a crowded theatre" and rejected Schenck's free speech defense because his leaflets had created a "clear and present danger." "The question in every case is whether the words used are used in such circumstances and are of such a nature as to create a clear and present danger that they will bring about the substantive evils that Congress has a right to prevent," Holmes wrote. "It is a question of proximity and degree. When a nation is at war many things that might be said in time of peace are such a hindrance to its effort that their utterance will not be endured so long as men fight and that no Court could regard them as pro-tected by any constitutional right."[9]

A week after upholding Schenck's conviction, Holmes upheld the Espionage Act convictions of both an unknown German newspaper editor and a national political figure. Jacob Frohwerk, editor of the *Missouri Staats Zeitung*, had written editorials denouncing America's decision to send troops to France and to participate in the war as "outright murder."[10] Eugene V. Debs, the leader of the Socialist Party, had received 900,000 votes in the 1912 presidential election. At a 1918 antiwar rally in Canton, Ohio, Debs had praised fellow Socialists convicted under the Espionage Act for encouraging others to refuse induction into military service.[11] Both Frohwerk and Debs were sentenced to ten years in federal prison.[12]

Holmes's opinions in *Schenck, Frohwerk*, and *Debs* masked his evolving views on free speech. In 1907, he had believed that the First Amendment protected nothing more than freedom from prepublication censorship.[13] Eight years later, he rejected a free speech challenge to a Washington State law for criminalizing a pamphlet encouraging nudism.[14] Holmes began to reconsider his views in June 1918 thanks to a chance meeting on a train from New York City to Boston with Learned Hand. A federal district judge and founder of the *New Republic*, Hand wrote a 1917 opinion rejecting Postmaster General Burleson's decision to revoke the second-class mailing privileges of *The Masses*, a Socialist magazine edited by Max Eastman. Hand's opinion ventured that in order to censor a political publication there must be a "direct incitement" by another person to break the law. Hand's test, however, was reversed on appeal.[15] On the train to Boston in June 1918, Hand and Holmes had debated their different conceptions of free speech and continued their discussion by mail.[16] "Rarely does a letter hit me so exactly where I live as yours, and unless you are spoiling for a fight I agree with it throughout," Holmes wrote. "My only qualification, if any, would be that free speech stands no differently than freedom from vaccination."[17] In late 1918, Holmes wrote a dissent in a draft obstruction case arguing that "the emergency would have to be very great" for the government to suppress political speech. He had distributed the opinion to his colleagues on December 3 but had withdrawn it when the government confessed error and dropped the case.[18]

Holmes "greatly regretted having to write" the three Espionage Act opinions and believed that he had been assigned them precisely because of his evolving views on free speech.[19] "As it happens I should go farther probably than the majority in favor of it," Holmes wrote to Frederick Pollock, "and I daresay it was partly on that account that the C[hief] J[ustice] assigned the case to me."[20] He blamed federal trial judges for growing "hysterical about the war" and hoped that "the President when he gets through his present amusements [in Paris] might do some pardoning."[21] He sent the opinions to Laski in the hopes that his young admirer would agree with him. Laski

conceded "with deep regret they are very convincing" and agreed that the
Court should not substitute its judgment for the president's. "Your analogy of a cry of fire in a crowded theatre is, I think excellent, though in the
remarks you make in the *Schenck* case I am not sure that I should have
liked the line to be drawn a little tighter about executive discretion." Laski
believed that the Espionage Act had given Wilson too much power to
punish his political foes.[22]

The *Debs* case troubled Holmes the most and cast the justice into the
national spotlight. The *New Republic* initially sided with Holmes, yet
it argued that Debs's ten-year prison term was too harsh: "His Canton
speech clearly violated the Espionage Act. But since that act ceases to have
force when peace is declared, and since the emergency which might have
justified it has passed, to let Debs serve his sentence would be both cruel
and blind."[23] Holmes believed that the *New Republic* had gotten it "exactly
right." He was no fan of Debs and thought the Socialist leader's ideas were
"rather silly," yet he was coming around to the view that Debs was "not
dishonest."[24]

Criticism of Holmes's first three Espionage Act opinions soon followed.
A year after their discussion on the train, Hand criticized Holmes's "clear
and present danger" test. Hand did not deny that Debs had been guilty
under the law, but questioned the applicability of a test that depended on
the intent of the speaker. Juries would not apply it properly, Hand wrote,
and "it will serve to intimidate,—throw a scare into,—many a man who
might moderate the storms of popular feeling. I know it did in 1918."[25]
Holmes replied, "I am afraid that I don't quite get your point." Nor did he
understand how the "incitement" test would have led to a different outcome
in *Debs* or *Schenck*.[26] In addition to Hand's criticism, Ernst Freund, a longtime free speech advocate, wrote in the *New Republic* that Holmes "takes
the very essentials of the entire problem for granted, and intimates that
they are conceded even by the defendant."[27] Freund also found Holmes's
analogy about falsely shouting fire in a crowded theater unhelpful in the
political sphere.[28] Holmes thought Freund's article was "poor stuff," drafted a
response to Croly, but never sent the letter.[29]

The *Debs* opinion triggered hostile letters and even an attempt on
Holmes's life.[30] In late April, followers of Italian anarchist Luigi Galleani
mailed bombs to the homes of thirty-six elected officials with the hope that
the packages would explode on May Day. One of the packages, marked as a
sample from the Gimbel Brothers department store, arrived at the doorstep

of Senator Thomas Hardwick of Georgia. Before leaving the Senate, Hardwick had co-sponsored the Immigration Act of 1918 that enabled the government to deport radical anarchists. The package blew off both hands of Hardwick's maid and burned the face and upper body of the senator's wife.[31] The Post Office and Secret Service intercepted similar packages intended for other public officials associated with prosecutions of radicals, including a package at a New York post office intended for Holmes. " I suppose it was the Debs incident that secured me the honor of being among those destined to receive an explosive machine, stopped in the Post Office as you may [have] seen," Holmes wrote Laski. " It shows a want of intelligence in the senders."[32]

Some have attributed Holmes's free speech switch to Laski's influence.[33] A Harvard instructor in history and government, Laski had dropped out of the law school during his second year yet somehow remained the war-depleted *Harvard Law Review*'s book review editor and intellectual compass.[34] Pound, who along with Frankfurter had been grooming him to join the law faculty, wrote: "Laski is a joy forever. I don't know how I could get on without him."[35] Pound encouraged Laski's scholarship; Laski, in turn, em-boldened Pound. In March 1919, they joined several Harvard professors on the staff of the new Boston Trade Union College run by the Boston Central Labor Union.[36] No one flattered and admired Holmes more than Laski. In March 1919, Laski sent an advance copy of his new book, *Authority in the Modern State*, to Holmes as a seventy-eighth birthday present, a book dedi-cated to " Mr. Justice Holmes and Felix Frankfurter: The Two Youngest of My Friends." The dedication "moved" Holmes, who read the book "with en-thusiasm."[37] Yet even as he praised the book, Holmes did not endorse Laski's ideas—whether they were about sovereignty, socialism, or free speech. " The combination of learning and ability is very impressive to me—and to a very great extent I follow you with agreement," he wrote Laski. "We both are ideasts rather than thingsters and your attitude is what I should expect from that. There is no doubt a slight tint of rose to you in what I should see blue."[38]

Others writing about Holmes's free speech switch have pointed to a late July 1919 meeting that Laski arranged between Holmes and Zechariah Chafee Jr.[39] Chafee was one of Pound's liberal law faculty hires to whom Laski had grown close during Frankfurter's wartime absence. The scion of a prominent family of Rhode Island industrialists, Chafee had graduated second in his law school class in 1913, practiced law for three years before joining the faculty as an assistant professor, and was promoted to professor of law three years later.[40] He made his scholarly reputation by producing groundbreaking scholarship about free speech.[41] During the summer of 1919, he criticized Holmes's Espionage Act decisions in a *Harvard Law Review* article, "Free Speech in War Time." Holmes, Chafee argued, had missed a "magnificent opportunity" to distinguish between political speech protected by the First Amendment and unprotected speech, including incitement, libel, slander, and indecency. "He, we hoped, would concentrate his great abilities on fixing this line," Chafee wrote.[42] He took issue with Holmes's *Schenck* opinion because it "seems to mean that the Supreme Court will sanction any restriction of speech that has military force behind it, and reminds us that the Justice used to say when he was young, 'that the truth was the majority vote of that nation that could lick all others.'" Holmes's error, Chafee argued, was his overwhelming deference to majority rule without doing anything "to emphasize the social interest behind free speech, and show the need of balancing even in war time."[43]

Laski devoured Chafee's article, invited him to spend the weekend at Laski's small summer home in Rockport, and arranged for Holmes to visit on July 28 from nearby Beverly Farms. For most of the year, Holmes and Laski were no more than frequent correspondents. During the summertime, however, they saw each other socially. "Holmes is coming to tea, & I want you to arrive in good time," Laski wrote Chafee. "For I have given him your article and we must fight on it. I've read it twice, & I'll go to the stake for every word. Bless you for it."[44]

After his meeting with Holmes, Chafee did not think he had made any headway. "I have talked with Justice Holmes about the article but find that he is inclined to allow a very wide latitude to Congressional discretion in the carrying on of the war ... ," Chafee wrote Judge Charles Amidon. "He further thinks that he could not have gone behind the jury verdict in the Debs case." Still, Chafee sensed that the justice was sympathetic to the plight of Debs and other radicals: "It is clear from the way Justice Holmes talks that if he had been on the jury in the Debs case he would have voted for acquittal."[45] Holmes, for his part, did not indicate that the meeting or article had transformed his thinking. Holmes liked Chafee but did not mention their meeting in his extensive correspondence until nearly a year later and even then only in passing.[46]

In the end, Holmes's thinking on free speech changed when the Red Scare came to Harvard Law School and jeopardized the careers of Frankfurter and Pound. As early as February 1919, Holmes learned that

Frankfurter's trouble at Harvard was instigated by some of the justice's friends from Boston.[47] Richard W. Hale, founder of the Boston law firm of Hale and Dorr and leader of the Harvard was Law School Association, was a longtime admirer of Holmes.[48] Yet Hale and other prominent Harvard law alumni in Boston made their hostility to Frankfurter well known. Thomas Nelson Perkins, a member of the Harvard Corporation and leader of the Harvard Endowment Fund drive in Boston, acted as the public face of the opposition.[49] A wartime assistant to Secretary of War Baker, Perkins had known Frankfurter's from their War Department work and in 1918, had dined at the House of Truth.[50] Back in Boston, however, the Perkins-Frankfurter relationship was more contentious. "Why do you rock the boat?" Perkins asked Frankfurter over lunch. Perkins also informed Frankfurter that he was a "very unreasonable man."[51]

Word filtered back to Holmes. "Every once in a while, faintly and vaguely as to you, a little more distinctly as to Frankfurter, I hear that you are dangerous men," Holmes wrote Laski soon after the *Debs* decision. "What does it mean? They used to say in Boston that I was dangerous."[52] Laski, who was serving as Frankfurter's eyes and ears during his absence from the law school, informed Holmes that Hale and Perkins were behind it: " Hale is abominable. He actually sent for the editor of the *Law Review* early in the year and warned him against Felix. Why he adopts this attitude I do not know though [law school librarian] Ned Adams suggests that it is anti-semitism." Laski suggested that if Holmes were "to drop a hint to Hale or Perkins you would do us all a great service."[53] Initially, Holmes was reluctant to intervene. " I thought and think that Perkins was converted to Frankfurter by meeting him in Washington," Holmes replied to Laski. " I have hesitated about writing to Hale—and still hesitate."[54]

The purported reason for Frankfurter's troubles was his report for the President's Mediation Commission alleging that Tom Mooney had been convicted of the 1916 Preparedness Day bombing based on perjured testimony. For his enemies at Harvard, Frankfurter's Mooney report was the gift that kept on giving. With each subsequent anarchist-inspired bombing, critics pointed to his report as exhibit A for why he should not be on the law faculty. It did not matter that he had drafted the report for a government commission that President Wilson had charged with investigating Western labor unrest as well as the Mooney case. It was enough that the late Theodore Roosevelt had accused Frankfurter of adopting a position consistent with "that of Trotski and other Bolsheviki leaders in Russia" and dangerous to the American people.[55]

Beneath it all was the fear that Frankfurter and Pound were radicalizing the students. Pound was one of the first scholars to celebrate Holmes's dissent in *Lochner*, which invalidated a New York maximum hour law for bakers, as a classic statement of judicial deference. And Pound's sociological jurisprudence based on scientific investigation captured the techniques of Brandeis and other progressive lawyers. Frankfurter and Emory Buckner had been instrumental in Pound's move in 1910 from the University of Chicago to Harvard and his elevation five years later to the Harvard deanship.[56] In 1916, Pound had joined Frankfurter's fight for Brandeis's Supreme Court nomination. And both Frankfurter and Pound had assumed Brandeis's role in defending pro-labor legislation on behalf of the National Consumers' League. To the old guard, it seemed that Frankfurter and Pound had hijacked the law school. "The real truth is," Laski explained to Holmes, "that there's a great fight on as to the future of the School and the older Tories are eager to make the place unbearable by Pound."[57]

The whole controversy reached Frankfurter soon after he had arrived in Paris. On March 1, 1919, Pound sent word through Mack that Frankfurter would be receiving a summons and to get in touch with the dean before responding. "Very likely it will be informal, but it will be a summons," Pound warned Mack. "All this between you and me and Frankfurter."[58] Frankfurter knew that the reason for the uproar was not the Mooney report, which he described as "a tame legal document that no self-respecting lawyer could have failed to write."[59] Yet since the summer of 1918, Frankfurter had been corresponding with Perkins about rumors of displeasure among the Boston establishment.[60] When the rumors resurfaced a year later, he wrote Perkins a point-by-point procedural history of the Mooney case, presidential commission, and subsequent report.[61] A "very much worried" Pound described the attacks on Frankfurter as part of "a general crusade here against all things liberal—which is a reality in spite of the liberal pronouncements in the President's report—and that Mooney report of yours." Pound also revealed the rejections of several new proposed faculty members, including former House of Truth resident Gerry Henderson, because "we were told that we were recommending three Bolshevists."[62]

At first, Frankfurter was amused by the controversy. He read bits and pieces of Pound's letter to the professors working for the American delegation at the Hôtel de Crillon. "It's a real fight—and a fight that matters," Frankfurter wrote Denman.[63] A few weeks later, Pound wrote Frankfurter even more "discouraged" about the future. The son of a member of the Harvard Corporation

Harvard Law School dean Roscoe Pound

remarked that "if he had his way [Frankfurter] would be deported." Pound also revealed that they were making him take a one-year leave of absence as dean in the midst of new faculty hires and curricular reform and were replacing him with an interim dean, Edward "Bull" Warren, who had been the only faculty member to oppose Brandeis's Supreme Court nomination. If asked to take a leave of absence, Pound did not think he was going to return. And Frankfurter should not expect a pleasant return, either. "All in all the prospects are so utterly and hopelessly reactionary that I should not expect you to be very comfortable," Pound wrote Frankfurter. "The whole country is going the same way."[64]

On May 24, 1919, Pound wrote Brandeis about the troubles at the law school and the corporation's rejection of faculty hires as "'too radical.'" The dean also explained to Brandeis that "there is a great deal of hostility to Frankfurter," who was being denied a chair as the Byrne Professor of Administrative Law. It was clear that they were trying to make it so uncomfortable that Frankfurter would leave. Finally, Pound mentioned his forced leave of absence, vowed not to return if it happened, and revealed that his "first inclination was to threaten to resign at once."[65]

Pound's threat to resign made Frankfurter want to board the first ship back to Cambridge, for he was ready to fight.[66] Instead, he wired Brandeis to meet with Pound before leaving for the European part of the Palestine trip.[67] After a meeting with Pound at the City Club in New York, Brandeis reported to Frankfurter: " Pound is very depressed. They're after him but he says they are really gunning for you. In short you are a 'dangerous man.'"[68]

The charges against Frankfurter—made by prominent Harvard Law School alumni who had opposed Brandeis's nomination, including President Lowell, lawyer and NAACP founder Moorfield Storey, former Boston mayor Nathan Matthews Jr., and others—was that Frankfurter was corrupting young minds with dangerous ideas.[69] After Brandeis heard these allegations, he made Pound promise not to resign and to abide by one rule: " Do nothing till Felix returns."[70] Frankfurter asked how much of it was anti-Semitism, and Brandeis replied: " It's a make-weight, that's all."[71] A few days later, they talked more about the law school controversy and were almost giddy about it. As Brandeis told Pound: "'Don't worry about Felix. He'll be entirely happy. This will be something he'll like.'"[72]

For several years, Brandeis had been telling his wife, Alice, that his enemies would come after Frankfurter just as they had come after him during the confirmation fight.[73] " Old Boston is unregenerate and I am not sorry to have escaped a struggle there that would have been as nasty as it is unending," Brandeis wrote Alice. " F.F. is evidently considered by the elect as 'dangerous' as I was; and it looks as if some whom F. considered his friends are as unrelenting as were some who were called mine."[74]

Brandeis enlisted the most powerful ally he could find in the fight to keep Frankfurter and Pound at Harvard Law School—Justice Holmes. Since joining the Court in 1916, Brandeis had been encouraging him to write dissents—including the dissent on behalf of four justices about the federal child labor law—when Holmes otherwise would have simply noted his dissent or joined someone else's.[75] He also challenged Holmes to expand his mind. Brandeis loved facts; Holmes loathed them. In May 1919, Brandeis urged Holmes to quit reading books on philosophy for the summer and to learn something about one of the pressing issues of the day. He suggested that Holmes read a government report on the Lawrence, Massachusetts, textile strike of 1912 and then go visit the mill to understand why the workers struck again in 1919. "Talking with Brandeis yesterday (a big chap) he drove a harpoon into my midriff by saying that it would be for the good of my soul to devote my next leisure to the study of some domain of fact …,"

Holmes wrote. "Well—I hate facts—and partly because of that am impressed by Brandeis's suggestion."[76] Nowhere was Brandeis's influence on Holmes greater than in the law school fight about Pound and Frankfurter. "I've had great fun in awakening Holmes to the facts," Brandeis told Frankfurter in London. "He is as innocent as a sixteen year old girl as to the facts of human conduct. He is so tender & so sensitive [a] being that he can't conceive of conduct like Lowell's & those men. I showed him Pound's letter & he was stunned. But he's learned a lot."[77]

After consulting with Brandeis, in May 1919 Holmes wrote Frank W. Grinnell, the secretary of the Harvard Law School Association, the secretary of the Massachusetts Bar Association, and Richard W. Hale's longtime law partner.[78] He wrote not as a Supreme Court justice but in his capacity as the newly elected president of the Harvard Law School Association. In his letter to Grinnell, Holmes introduced a resolution in appreciation of Pound and suggested that Pound receive an honorary L.L.D. degree from Harvard, just as he had at several other universities. Holmes knew that the only way to prevent Pound from resigning was a public showing of support. Grinnell showed the letter to Pound, who thanked Holmes for the proposed resolution but was more concerned about Frankfurter. "Unhappily most people hereabout seem to be chiefly concerned to push Frankfurter out of the school," Pound wrote. "If such a thing were to happen it would be nothing short of a calamity. What I fear is that he will be made uncomfortable and will go."[79] Holmes knew that he had to do more. "If the school should lose Pound and Frankfurter it would lose its soul, it seems to me ...," he wrote Laski. "By Jove, I think I'll say that to Lowell."[80] The presidency of the Harvard Law School Association was supposed to be an honorary position, but by now Holmes had determined that the future of the school was at stake.

In a June 2 letter to President Lowell, Holmes alluded to one of Aesop's fables by joking that upon learning of his election as alumni president, "I found I was King Log," and apologized for not consulting Lowell about the Pound resolution. "I should have consulted you had I not been taken rather suddenly," Holmes wrote. "But I have a very strong feeling that Pound and in his place Frankfurter have and impart the ferment which is more valuable than an endowment, and makes of a Law School a focus of life."[81]

Eight days later, Lowell replied that he was "very glad" that Holmes had suggested "a resolution recognizing" Pound. Lowell knew that Pound "had been somewhat discouraged" about the law school, but the Harvard president attributed it to wartime conditions and overwork. Lowell said he had been encouraging Pound to take an overseas sabbatical so that the law dean could rest. He also agreed that Pound deserved an honorary degree, though it was too late to vote him one for the 1919 commencement. "What you say about his value to the school," Lowell wrote to Holmes, " I agree with entirely."[82] Lowell's letter said nothing about Frankfurter; Holmes's message, however, had been received. The fight for academic freedom had only just begun, but Frankfurter was humbled by support from his judicial idol. "Think of Holmesy going into that fight—," Frankfurter wrote Marion Denman, "and to put it in he wrote Lowell that he must show Pound how grateful the University is for what he together with Frankfurter have done for the Law School. Ain't that grand!"[83]

On June 3, 1919, Holmes looked outside his home at 1720 Eye Street and saw a police officer stationed near the front door. The justice knew something had happened but was not sure what.[84] Officers had been ordered to watch the homes of all cabinet officials and Supreme Court justices.[85] At 11:15 p.m. the previous night, Attorney General A. Mitchell Palmer had just turned off the lights in the first-floor library of his home at 2132 R Street and headed upstairs to bed when he heard an explosion. Palmer rushed outside to find that a bomb had destroyed the first floor of his home and blown out the windows on the first three floors, as well as the windows of nearby homes.[86]

The bomb also blew out the windows of the home of Assistant Secretary of the Navy Franklin Roosevelt, who lived across the street at 2131 R Street. Three minutes before the bomb exploded, he and Eleanor had driven onto R Street, parked their car in the garage, and walked into the house. Some of the remains of the Italian anarchist bomber landed on their doorstep; the bomber's spinal cord landed in the bedroom of the son of the Norwegian minister at 2137 R Street.[87] Roosevelt drove Palmer's wife and daughter to a safe house. Neither was hurt in the explosion.[88] Though the bomber had failed in his mission to harm Palmer and his family, newspapers published the message found in the bomber's suitcase: "There will have to be bloodshed; we will not dodge; there will have to be murder; we will kill, because it is necessary; there will have to be destruction; we will destroy to rid the world of your tyrannical institutions."[89]

The nation's leading crusader against Communist, Socialist, and anarchist radicals, Attorney General Palmer vowed to redouble his efforts. He described the bombings that had destroyed buildings in seven cities as "nothing but the lawless attempt of an anarchistic element in the population to terrorize the country and thus stay the hand of the government. This they have utterly failed to do. ... These attacks by bomb throwers will only increase and extend the activities of our crime detecting forces."[90] On June 12, he requested another $500,000 (and $2 million total) from the House Appropriations Committee to establish a special division within the Bureau of Investigation of the Justice Department to hunt down dangerous anarchists and radicals.[91] On August 1, Palmer designated a twenty-four-year-old agent, J. Edgar Hoover, to run it.[92]

The country was on fire during that Red Summer of 1919, not only because of anarchist bombings but also because of postwar racial violence. The migration of blacks to northern cities and returning soldiers of both races created massive housing shortages and a scarcity of employment. Tensions boiled over at the epicenter of the Great Migration—Chicago. A black man drowned in Lake Michigan after being hit with a rock when he had swum into the white section of the lake. The lack of an arrest despite several eyewitnesses triggered three days of violence and bloodshed—mostly ethnic whites attacking blacks on the city's South Side. Thirty-eight people died, including twenty-three blacks and fifteen whites. Hundreds were injured.[93]

Economic tension fueled racial violence during the fall of 1919, tension that was not confined to northern cities. In Phillips County, Arkansas, a meeting between the Progressive Farmer and Household Union of America and about 100 black sharecroppers led to gunfire and four days of violence and murder. On September 30, several whites fired shots into the meeting at a black church; the black farmers returned fire. A white railroad agent was killed, and a deputy sheriff was wounded. Local whites, outnumbered by blacks in Phillips County four to one, called in federal troops and hunted down black suspects in what was initially portrayed as a black insurrection and massacre of whites. During the next four days, five whites and at least twenty-five blacks were killed. Dozens of black farmers were arrested and tortured into testifying against each other about the murder of the railroad agent. No witnesses were called for the defendants at trial. Twelve blacks were sentenced to death by an all-white jury after deliberations that lasted less than ten minutes. Sixty-seven others received lengthy prison sentences.[94] NAACP assistant secretary Walter White, passing as a white reporter for the *Chicago Daily News*, investigated the case, interviewed Arkansas governor Charles H. Brough, and recast the story as one of whites trying to maintain the peonage system that had replaced slavery. White's stories ran in the *Chicago Daily News*, the black press, and *The Nation.*[95]

The few liberal whites who spoke out about the sham trials after the Elaine Riots suffered professional consequences. An English professor at Virginia Military Institute wrote an "open letter" to the next Arkansas governor about the unfairness of the trials and urged the governor to grant the prisoners clemency.[96] Less than three months later, the school's board of visitors asked the professor to resign.[97] When it came to pleas for fair criminal trials, the right to unionize, or free speech, academic freedom often fell by the wayside. Even liberal members of the Harvard faculty were under siege.

During the fall of 1919, Holmes's liberal friends tested the limits of academic freedom and gave reactionary forces at Harvard new fodder to attack. Laski weighed in on the biggest issue facing the city of Boston—the police strike. On September 9, more than 1,200 members of the police force went on strike, and the lack of police presence in the city led to two days of looting and mob violence. On the first night of rioting, President Lowell encouraged Harvard students to volunteer for police duty yet denied that they would be serving as strikebreakers.[98] Fifty students immediately volunteered.[99] The Boston Police Union tried and failed to affiliate with the American Federation of Labor. Massachusetts governor Calvin Coolidge and Boston Police Commissioner Edwin U. Curtis refused to negotiate with the striking officers and chose to replace them instead.

Laski supported the strikers in the *Harvard Crimson* and at a public rally. He blamed Commissioner Curtis for refusing to consider the union's grievances prior to the strike, urged the mayor to negotiate with the strikers, and proclaimed that "[a]ffiliation with the American Federation of Labor is the right of any red-blooded American."[100] At an October 15 meeting of 2,000 women who supported the striking officers, Laski continued to criticize the police commissioner: "We are told the police are deserters. The deserter is Commissioner Curtis, who was guilty at every point of misunderstanding his duties and failure to perform his functions."[101]

Laski's comments did not sit well with some Harvard faculty. Dr. Edwin Hall, a longtime physics professor who had been the first faculty member to volunteer for the police force and had encouraged students to do the same, responded to one paragraph in the *Boston Herald* under the headline: "HARVARD PROFESSOR QUOTED FOR UNION."[102] Though conceding that Laski "is a very brilliant young man, whose teachings have attracted much attention in Cambridge during the last year or two," Hall claimed that in a lecture the previous spring Laski had defended and glorified Bolshevism. "The fact is that I felt toward him a certain measure of gratitude," Hall wrote, "the same that I should feel for a rattlesnake that had given me timely warning."[103] When pressed for specifics, Hall later conceded to Lowell and to angry alumni that Laski never advocated overthrow of the government or uttered the word "Bolshevism."[104] Other faculty and students dismissed Laski's comments as those of a "Parlor Bolshevist" and "Boudoir Bolshevist."[105] To which Laski replied: "No one—not even my own colleagues—has the right to condemn the police without enquiry."[106]

In an October 28 letter to Justice Holmes, Laski tried to downplay the episode: "I have had a fight here, but am, I think, out of danger. Lowell was magnificent and I felt that I had a president in him I would fight for. ... But the atmosphere is clear again and I don't think there will be any difficulties over academic freedom in the future." He thought Frankfurter was also safe, for when people meet him "the adjective 'dangerous' melts as the snow before the sun."[107]

Despite Laski's assurances, the Red Scare in America had reached a fever pitch. At 9:00 p.m. on November 8, federal and state officials raided Communist Party and other radical offices across the country, rounded up suspected anarchists and revolutionists, and sent many of them to Ellis Island to be deported. In New York City alone, 700 officers raided seventy-three offices, arrested 500 suspects, and intended to charge 100 of them.[108] The first of these Palmer Raids, named after Attorney General Palmer and directed by J. Edgar Hoover, led to the deportations of more than 200 people, including anarchists Alexander Berkman and Emma Goldman.[109]

A week before he received Laski's letter, Holmes had heard the first of two days of oral argument about the convictions of five Russian-born Socialists and anarchists convicted under the Espionage Act. Their crime: printing and distributing two leaflets, one in Yiddish and one in English, criticizing American intervention in the Russian Revolution and calling for a general strike. Jacob Abrams, who owned and operated the printing press and printed 5,000 copies of the leaflets, received a twenty-year prison sentence.[110]

Two days after the initial Palmer Raids, seven members of the Supreme Court affirmed the convictions of Abrams and his co-conspirators.[111] Holmes, joined by Brandeis, authored one of the most famous defenses of free speech in constitutional history, a dissent that transformed both justices into civil libertarians in the eyes of their liberal admirers. Holmes insisted that his prior Espionage Act cases had been "rightly decided" and that the power to abridge free speech was greater in wartime.[112] Unlike Schenck's case, however, Holmes found no clear and present danger in Abrams's; the leaflets were not intended to impede the government's war effort. Nor could any criticism of the war be a crime. As an example, Holmes alluded to his friend Borglum's aircraft investigation: "A patriot might think that we were wasting money on aeroplanes. … No one would hold such conduct a crime."[113] Even if intent to impede the war effort could be found in this case, Holmes described Abrams and his co-defendants as "poor and puny anonymities" who deserved only "the most nominal punishment," not twenty years in jail.[114]

With the Red Scare jeopardizing the careers of his "dangerous" friends at Harvard Law School, Holmes warned about government limits on political speech by introducing the metaphor of a marketplace of ideas: "that the best test of truth is the power of the thought to get itself accepted in the competition of the market, and that truth is the only ground upon which their wishes safely can be carried out." The US Constitution, he argued, "is an experiment, as all life is an experiment." He refined his clear and present danger test to protect unpopular political speech because we needed to "be eternally vigilant against attempts to check the expression of opinions that we loathe and believe to be fraught with death, unless they so imminently threaten immediate interference with the lawful and pressing purposes of the law that an immediate check is required to save the country."[115]

Holmes knew that his *Abrams* dissent was important and mailed copies to Lippmann, Laski, Pound, and Frankfurter because he wanted their approval and because the Red Scare had affected all their lives.[116] Lippmann was so moved by the *Abrams* dissent that he asked Holmes "if you would send me a copy of the dissent with something of your own written on it I shall treasure it and teach my children to treasure it."[117] The *New Republic*, he informed Holmes, was reprinting the opinion.[118] In an unsigned editorial by Croly, the magazine hailed "the remarkable dissenting opinion of Mr. Justice Holmes" and predicted it would be as famous as his *Lochner* dissent that argued that states have the power to protect the health and safety of workers.[119] With the Red Scare raging, Croly's editorial, "A Call to Toleration," highlighted what was at stake for America: "At the present time American public opinion in its relation to freedom of speech, as expressed by the Supreme Court itself, is in danger of sacrificing the benefits of liberty to a headstrong impulse to cure its abuses."[120]

Lippmann was emerging as the nation's pre-eminent authority on the formation of public opinion. In the same letter to Holmes praising the *Abrams* dissent, he enclosed the first of two articles on liberty, free speech, and public opinion in the November issue of the *Atlantic Monthly*. He published a second article in the December issue, then packaged them into a book, *Liberty and the News*. "Public opinion," Lippmann wrote in the book's introduction, "is blockaded."[121] Before he left Paris, Lippmann had confided to Aaronsohn that the Wilson administration was ridding itself of liberals and wondered how Frankfurter had managed to survive.[122] Even after Lippmann returned home, hostility toward him remained high. During a February 22 meeting with Secretary of State Lansing and Colonel House, the AFL's Samuel Gompers charged that "faddist parlor socialists were more agreeable to the Commission than the representatives of American labor." Those Socialists, according to Gompers, included Bullitt and Lippmann. It did not matter that Lippmann's Socialist phase had long since passed. Neither House nor Lansing rose to Lippmann's defense. Lansing managed to reply that "he had not seen Captain Lippmann for ten months, and he had never had a private conversation with him; that he heard of him as an editor of the 'New Republic.'"[123]

His unhappy experiences with the American propaganda machine in Paris inspired Lippmann to embark on a new project after *The Political Scene*. He began writing an article about the effect of "freedom of thought and speech" on the manufacturing and manipulation of public opinion. Lippmann expected to write another long article, something better suited to the *Atlantic Monthly* than the *New Republic*, about the formation of public opinion.[124] Given the reactionary postwar political scene, Lippmann wisely stayed out of politics in favor of journalism. That fall, he declined an invitation to testify against the League of Nations before the US Senate and instead suggested his friend Bullitt. During sensational testimony before the Senate Foreign Relations Committee on September 12, Bullitt recounted his secret mission to Russia and how the Wilson administration had suppressed his report and ignored his recommendations.[125] In private, he blamed both Wilson and House but remained close to Lippmann. "We had never been flim-flammed before & I suppose one has to be sold out at least once in politics before one acquires the appropriate distrust of statesmen," Bullitt wrote Lippmann. "And besides you fooled me & I fooled you & Colonel House bamboozled us both."[126]

Lippmann's frustration with censorship during the war and at the Paris Peace Conference inspired *Liberty and the News*; Holmes's *Abrams* dissent gave him hope for the future. "The theory of our constitution, says Mr. Justice Holmes, is that truth is the only ground upon which men's wishes safely can be carried out," Lippmann wrote in the book's introduction. He referred to *Abrams* and proclaimed that "[t]here can be no higher law in journalism than to tell the truth and shame the devil."[127] Lippmann admired Holmes as much as anyone in America. In February 1920, he and Faye dined with Justice and Mrs. Holmes at 1720 Eye Street.[128] "Walter L. wrote me a very enthusiastic letter about his dinner," Laski reported to Holmes. "You put heart and truth into him as, indeed, you do into us all."[129]

The signs were everywhere that Lippmann was outgrowing the *New Republic*. He had published his two long articles about liberty and the news in the *Atlantic Monthly* and aspired to write a big book on public opinion. He still agreed with the magazine's anti-Wilson editorial stance. He and Frankfurter had facilitated the publication of British economist John Maynard Keynes's article blaming the failure of the peace conference on Wilson.[130] Yet Lippmann was growing apart from the magazine's editors. Croly had found religion; Francis Hackett was obsessed with his native Ireland's independence movement from Britain.[131] Lippmann was thinking bigger thoughts.

In June 1921, he informed Frankfurter of his decision to leave the *New Republic*. Ever since he had returned from Europe, he thought he was going through the motions with Croly. "Herbert and I no longer learn from each other, and for two years our intellectual relationship has been a good natured accommodation rather than an inspiring adventure," Lippmann wrote Frankfurter. Although he was one of the magazine's founding editors, Lippmann believed that he was "not essential to the present N.R. because the N.R., a good 70% of it, is in tone, selection, and emphasis not the paper I would want to make it."[132] Lippmann's only influence on the magazine was through his own articles. To make matters worse for Croly, Lippmann took the magazine's managing editor, Charles Merz, with him.[133] Croly, who had struggled to maintain the magazine's influence and subscription base after the war, was bitter about Lippmann's parting and reminded Frankfurter that Lippmann had been a Socialist before joining the magazine as a twenty-four-year-old editor. Croly also predicted that Lippmann would make "a further movement toward conservatism."[134] To his credit, Croly ran excerpts of Lippmann's next book in the *New Republic*, commissioned a lengthy positive review from pragmatist philosopher John Dewey, and allowed Lippmann to contribute occasional articles to the magazine.[135]

In leaving the *New Republic*, Lippmann accepted a job as an editorial writer for the New York *World*. The Pulitzer-owned *World* was famous for its award-winning exposure of the Ku Klux Klan, as well as its Democratic Party loyalties. Lippmann joined the newspaper because he admired its editor, Frank I. Cobb. During the war, Cobb and Lippmann had co-authored a detailed interpretation of Wilson's Fourteen Points for House and the president. Lippmann's new job with the *World* did not start until January 1, 1922. The six-month break allowed him to finish his biggest and most important book yet about the formation of public opinion and its impact on American democracy. The book was inspired, in part, by wartime censorship and post-war suppression of civil liberties of people like Jacob Abrams.

★★★

Holmes's *Abrams* dissent also inspired Laski, who wrote Justice Holmes that "amongst the many opinions of yours I have read, none seems to me superior either in nobility or outlook, in dignity or phrasing, and in that quality the French call *justesse*, as this dissent in the Espionage case."[136] Laski's predictions that he was "out of danger" because of his comments during the Boston police strike had been premature. "Just now the tide of battle rages about Laski," Pound reported to Brandeis on October 31, 1919.[137] Faculty and alumni protest over Laski's comments escalated from letters in the *Boston Herald* to an inquiry by the Board of Overseers into whether he harbored radical tendencies. The Overseers interrogated Laski at the Harvard Club. He did not seem to mind and later described it as "a dinner at which we exchanged opinions in a friendly fashion" and only wondered whether "the Committee realized how very conservative my opinions really were in this changing social world."[138] On January 12, 1920, the Overseers announced that they "were satisfied that Mr. Laski's opinions had been misunderstood and misinterpreted" and recommended "that no further action should be taken."[139]

Laski avoided injury but not insult. Three days after the Board of Overseers had cleared him, the *Harvard Lampoon* skewered him. With encouragement and editorial contributions from alumni, faculty, and members of the Board of Overseers, the magazine devoted an entire January 16 special issue to Laski.[140] The issue, "Laski: Lampy's Expose," included a naked image of him on the cover; comments about his appearance, Jewishness, and Socialist politics; and this stanza from the poem "Alone at Laski":

> 'Twould be greatly to his liking
> If the whole world started striking,
> With himself established at the strikers' head;

> In the parlance of the ghetto
> He would "shake a mean stiletto"
> From the firstski to the laski he's a Red![141]

The public humiliation was too much for Laski and his wife, Frida, to bear. They took the *Lampoon* spoof hard, some thought too hard.[142] Holmes rushed to Laski's defense. "It is disgusting that so serious a scholar and thinker as he should be subject to the trampling of swine," he wrote Frankfurter.[143] Frankfurter passed along Holmes's comments to President Lowell.[144] But even with the sympathetic Holmes, Laski retreated into "silence." Holmes tried to cheer him up, insisting that the *Lampoon*'s portrayal was "a childish and rotten little show" that had swung public opinion Laski's way.[145]

Even before the *Lampoon* came out, Laski knew that the damage to his academic reputation had been done.[146] He would never join Frankfurter and Pound on the law faculty or get promoted to a professorship in any department. And he could not get his articles published in the Boston-based *Atlantic Monthly* because Ellery Sedgwick did not want "to reawaken the very foolish discussion which is gradually dying down."[147] Though he continued to travel, teach, and publish in America for years, Laski accepted a full professorship in political science at the London School of Economics.

Holmes, hearing rumors of Laski's departure for several months, was disappointed that his young friend was leaving Boston. "When next you write," Holmes asked Frankfurter, "tell me if Laski did not leave Harvard College of his own choice. I came across the belief that he was compelled or requested to leave and that Lowell no longer stood by him."[148] President Lowell, according to Laski and others, said if the Board of Overseers had asked for Laski's resignation, Lowell would have offered his own.[149] But Lowell also made it known that Laski would never be promoted beyond instructor.[150] Some of Laski's friends, according to journalist Upton Sinclair, questioned the "genuineness" of Lowell's support and sincerity.[151] In his book about higher education, Sinclair observed that Lowell had studied at Oxford and enjoyed a considerable academic and professional reputation in Britain; Laski came from a prominent Manchester Jewish family. One of Sinclair's Harvard friends wondered what Lowell would have done amid the postwar hysteria about Eastern European radicals "'if Laski had been a German Jew, or a Russian Jew.'"[152]

★★★

Under fire much like his protégé Laski, Frankfurter responded enthusiastically to Holmes's *Abrams* dissent. "And now I may tell you the gratitude
and, may I say it, the pride I have in your dissent," he wrote Holmes. "You
speak there as you have always spoken of course. But 'this time we need education in the obvious' and you lift the voice of the noble human spirit."[153]
A week before the publication of the *Abrams* dissent, Frankfurter visited
1720 Eye Street and revealed the secret that he had been keeping for nearly
six months: he was going to marry Marion Denman. As soon as he heard
the news, Holmes "jumped up and shouted" for his wife. "Dickie," he said.
"Dickie bird!" Fanny Holmes, who had been battling an illness for several
months, shuffled into the room. She had known Holmes since her youth
and was regarded as a beautiful young woman until two bouts with rheu-
matic fever had caused her to lose some of her hair and may have disfigured
her face. A classic New Englander, she was quiet and reserved, yet quick and
witty.[154] "Tell her! Tell her!" Holmes said. As soon as she heard the news,
Mrs. Holmes left the room without saying a word. She quietly returned
and extended her fists. She opened one fist containing a piece of jade and
another containing a piece of amber and asked which one Denman would
like. Frankfurter pointed to the amber.[155] Mrs. Holmes gave it to him and
expressed her regard for Denman and for the happy couple before she left
the room.[156] Both Holmes and his wife reacted like "loving parents."[157] The
Holmeses were not the only ones excited for Frankfurter and Denman.
Frankfurter was reluctant to tell Brandeis after keeping the secret from him
for so long. Brandeis, however, displayed a rare show of emotion. "[H]e is
very devoted to me," Frankfurter wrote.[158]

Frankfurter's happy news was tempered by tragedy. On the afternoon of
November 5, a well-dressed man nervously paced up and down a crowded
New York City subway platform. As a train approached the station at
Thirty-Fourth Street and Seventh Avenue, the man pulled an overcoat over
his head and jumped in front of it. Women on the platform fainted. It took
police twenty minutes to remove the body from between the wheels of the
front car. Inside the man's pocket was a monogrammed gold watch: "With
kindest regards and best wishes from directors and assistants of the Bureau
of the Department of Interior, Philippine Islands, Manila. September 15,
1914."[159] It was Winfred Denison.

Chauncey Belknap, Holmes's former secretary, identified the body.[160]
Belknap had met Denison in the spring of 1916 while dining with the
justice at 1720 Eye Street and living at the House of Truth.[161] Meeting

Denison changed Belknap's life. During the fall of 1916, Denison had persuaded Belknap to leave C. C. Burlingham's Wall Street law firm and to work with Denison at Stetson, Jennings & Russell. After serving overseas during the war, Belknap had returned to Stetson, Jennings to work with Denison. He had just joined Denison's new firm, Denison & Curtis.[162] Then Denison killed himself. After he identified the body, Belknap no doubt informed Justice Holmes, who was "saddened" and shocked by Denison's death. "I had thought that things were going well with him," he wrote Nina Gray of Denison. "He used to live in the House of Truth when Frankfurter was there—and I rather think gave it its name. He was a fine fellow and an able man."[163]

Denison's suicide was no surprise to friends who knew his family history of mental illness, and to some it was seen as a relief to his "endless misery."[164] He was never the same after the Philippines. He had recovered well enough to rejoin his old law firm Stetson, Jennings & Russell. But in late July or August 1917, his mental illness had returned; in March 1918 it had landed him in a sanitarium similar to the one he had stayed in after his return to the United States.[165] By the end of the year, he was living in Roslyn, Long Island, under the constant care of a doctor and nurse.

One of the few people Denison stayed in touch with, because of their joint real estate holdings, his lifelong bond with her husband, and her own history of depression was Sophie Valentine. "I don't see any daylight ..., but Dr. P and the nurse say the depression is breaking up," Denison wrote her on December 10, 1918. "I did have one 'light' day (but rather feverish) last week—the only one this year. They say it's a good sign."[166] Denison tried to arrange for Robert Bass to take over the renting and possible sale of the R Street house that Denison and Sophie Valentine co-owned.[167] As absentee landlords, they continued to have difficulties with the real estate agent and tenants there.[168] The House of Truth was never far from Denison's mind. In his last letter to Sophie in May 1919, Denison asked about the family living there and delighted in seeing and receiving letters from Charlotte Valentine. He wanted Sophie to tell Charlotte the story about the children's party with the pie from Mrs. Holmes and the monkey that had played the hand organ.[169]

Frankfurter had tried to keep tabs on Denison after the Philippines and had monitored Denison's mental health with his friend's doctor.[170] He thought Denison had recovered upon returning to New York law practice.[171] Denison had provided some research assistance in 1916 and 1917 for Frankfurter's defense of the Oregon maximum hour law before the Supreme Court and had watched Frankfurter argue the case. In January 1917, they had spoken at Valentine's memorial service. And in July 1917, Denison had snored in Faye Lippmann's empty bed at the House of Truth.[172]

The last time Denison and Frankfurter saw each other had been in late September 1917 in Washington. "Had a talk with Felix, who was very lively. His usual self," Denison wrote Sophie. "I feel jealous of his intensity of vital interest!"[173] Denison had longed to visit Washington during the summer of 1919, but his mental health never recovered enough to allow it.[174] By 1919, the man who had prosecuted the sugar fraud cases and had named the House of Truth had been gone for years.

A month earlier, Frankfurter had included Denison on his wedding announcement list and had written notes to all forty people.[175] After hearing about Denison's death, Frankfurter phoned Sophie Valentine and then Denison's sister Katherine Gignoux in Portland, Maine, "to give her the feeling that [her brother's] life was not all poisoned and while we're bowed by his death we're proud of him."[176] Frankfurter planned to accompany Sophie Valentine to the Episcopalian service in Portland. He could not stop thinking "idle irrational thoughts" about his wedding note to Denison. "I wish Winnie had had my note," he thought. From the US attorney's office in the Southern District of New York, to Denison's role in introducing him to Valentine and living with him at the House of Truth, to their work in the Taft administration, including serving as customs fraud commissioners, to their Bull Moose presidential enthusiasm tempered by their day jobs, Frankfurter recognized that "my first six years out of Law School are bound up with him—and much that matters all these years."[177]

Denison's death, the Palmer Raids, *Abrams*, and the Red Scare at Harvard made Frankfurter reluctant to revel in his joy about his impending marriage. "The times also make me especially shy about my personal happiness," he confided to Holmes.[178] The justice was giddy about the union that had begun at the House of Truth. "Nothing to tell except the delightful visit of Frankfurter and his joyful news—I think it will be a good thing for him as well as for her," Holmes wrote Laski.[179] Of all people, Laski understood why it had taken so long for Frankfurter, a Jew, and Denman, a Gentile, to marry. In order to marry his non-Jewish wife, Frida, Laski had severed ties with his family. He was glad that Frankfurter and Denman had looked past their different religious backgrounds. "It couldn't have been better if I had deliberately arranged it," he wrote Holmes.[180]

Judge Learned Hand was supposed to marry the couple but lacked the legal authority in the state of New York. Holmes later agreed to marry them but was not empowered to do it either.[181] The third judge was the charm: Benjamin Cardozo of the New York Court of Appeals married Frankfurter and Denman in Hand's chambers on December 20, 1919.[182] Felix's mother did not attend the ceremony but came to accept the union. The newlyweds returned from their Southern Pines, North Carolina, honeymoon and started their new life together in Cambridge happy as "two cooing doves," Laski reported to Holmes.[183]

Though happy at the law school and with Marion, Frankfurter seemed intent on testing the limits of what a member of the faculty could do or say. He did not care whether or not Harvard made him the Byrne Professor of Administrative Law. He believed that he could not be fired because he had always been a full professor, which was considered a lifetime appointment, and because he had an inside man—his friend Judge Mack had been elected to Harvard's Board of Overseers and would never allow anything to happen to him. "He and Mack are too guileless," Pound wrote Brandeis on October 31. "They don't appreciate the Puritan conscience that enabled these people to stick a knife into those with whom they maintain cordial relations with a serene consciousness that they are doing god's will." Pound let Brandeis know that people in Boston were still bent on destroying Frankfurter: "I rejoice that Frankfurter appraises the situation so cheerfully. But he ought not to talk freely to everyone who greets him cordially and expresses delight at his return."[184]

Much to Pound's dismay, criticism and controversy emboldened Frankfurter. On November 11, 1919, the first anniversary of Germany's surrender on Armistice Day, he chaired a meeting at Boston's Faneuil Hall urging the Wilson administration to recognize Russia's Bolshevik regime.[185] Frankfurter was no Bolshevist; indeed, most of his remarks consisted of quoting Prime Minister David Lloyd George's and President Wilson's rejection of military intervention against Russia during the Paris Peace Conference.[186] In any case, Frankfurter refused to be cowed by his enemies in Boston, including the city's leading Harvard fundraiser, Thomas Nelson Perkins. "You know as well as I do that at present there is a raging form of lynch law in the North, much more ominous, because less crude, than the well-known brand of the South," he wrote Perkins. "It is led by some of the so-called most respectable, by some of the educated and the rich. I should feel like a poltroon if I suppressed my convictions." Frankfurter was unwilling to sacrifice academic freedom because people like Perkins surmised that the endowment might suffer.[187] Their correspondence continued through November and December, in part because both men wanted to get the last word. Frankfurter showed the correspondence to Holmes, who cautioned that academic freedom was not absolute when it jeopardized student enrollment and endowments.[188] The law school's endowment suffered, but not because of Frankfurter's activities.[189] Nonetheless, Holmes urged him to be careful.

Frankfurter refused to back down. He was angry that Pound was "being harassed to the point where they have been near to firing him"; that Gerry Henderson, "*the* best brains from the Law School in my time," was denied a faculty appointment as a falsely alleged Bolshevik; that Laski was "inquisitioned" for his support of the Boston police strike; and that "instructors are cowed and scared out of [their] lives." He explained the situation at the law school to former classmate Emory Buckner: "You see I'm free & don't give a damn. If I have to leave here I can make a living elsewhere. But 90% of teachers can't, so I wanted them to know what's what."[190]

The payback for Frankfurter's political activities and outspokenness with Perkins was the withholding of the Byrne professorship. Pound and Mack spent months fighting for Frankfurter's chair.[191] Perkins led the opposition alleging that Frankfurter "has no character" and is a "poor teacher"; Perkins, however, "didn't give a damn about scholarship."[192] Pound wrote Brandeis and asked him to show the letter to Holmes. The letter, Holmes replied, "causes me the greatest concern—I only write to ask you to let me know if there is anything that I can do."[193] Frankfurter was sorry that Pound had bothered Holmes about it and told the justice not to worry about Perkins or the chair.[194] In May 1920, Pound reported to Brandeis that all the named professorships had been filled except the Byrne and that "everyone is talking about it." After much wrangling by Pound, in October Frankfurter received his chair.[195]

Even before he had received his chair, Frankfurter continued to stand up for civil liberties and to speak his mind as if nothing had happened. In February 1920, he agreed to serve on the national committee of a new organization, the American Civil Liberties Union (ACLU). His expertise on labor matters, report on the Bisbee deportation and Mooney case, and litigation for the National Consumers' League made him a natural fit. "What I have to give in 'judgment from time to time on tactics and policies' you are, of course, free to lean on," he wrote founder Roger Nash Baldwin, "for the Civil Liberties Union."[196]

In April 1920, Frankfurter and Chafee appeared at the request of Judge George W. Anderson on behalf of twenty immigrants who had been rounded up during the Palmer Raids, detained in horrible conditions, and scheduled for deportation because of alleged membership in the Communist Party or Communist Labor Party.[197] After 1,600 pages of factual investigation and fifteen days of testimony, Frankfurter and Chafee revealed numerous flaws in the Justice Department's pre-arrest investigation of the suspected radicals.[198] In his opinion, Judge Anderson detailed the warrantless searches and arrests throughout New England, the horrifying conditions of confinement, and hearings before Department of Justice officials without any meaningful legal representation.[199] He refused to deport the immigrants and released all but four of them from custody because of a "lack of due process."[200] The Justice Department appealed only four of the twenty cases and succeeded in reversing only the part of Anderson's ruling that immigrants could not be deported because of Communist Party membership.[201] Judge Anderson's opinion saved sixteen immigrants from deportation and laid bare the Justice Department's unconstitutional conduct of the Palmer Raids in New England.

To bring the Justice Department's "continual illegal acts" to the attention of the American people, Frankfurter and Chafee signed a report by the National Popular Government League.[202] Twelve prominent lawyers, including Pound, alleged that the attorney general had made warrantless arrests, had imprisoned suspects without access to counsel, had searched homes and seized property without warrants, had infiltrated radical organizations with Justice Department spies, and had flooded newspapers and magazines with propaganda.[203] The Department of Justice's "illegal acts," the report argued, "have caused widespread suffering and unrest, have struck at the foundation of American free institutions, and have brought the name of our country into disrepute."[204]

During testimony before the House Rules Committee on June 2, 1920, Attorney General Palmer could not reconcile Frankfurter's decision to represent Communist Party members with the duty to uphold the Constitution. In response, Frankfurter and Chafee wired Palmer and explained that they had appeared at the request of Judge Anderson and that the Constitution explicitly protected the rights of defendants by providing for the writ of habeas corpus and due process.[205] Palmer replied that Frankfurter and Chafee's allegations of misconduct were false and demanded that they issue a retraction.[206] Frankfurter and Chafee refused and informed Palmer and the chairman of the House Rules Committee of their willingness to substantiate these allegations in person.[207] Frankfurter also humiliated the attorney general in the press. In the *Baltimore Sun*, he took Palmer to task for insinuating that the central issue in Judge Anderson's opinion—the Justice Department's flagrant violations of due process during the Palmer Raids—had been appealed when it had not.[208]

The whole controversy brought Frankfurter to the attention of the Bureau of Investigation and J. Edgar Hoover. On May 20, 1920, the bureau ordered an investigation of Frankfurter, Chafee, and other defense lawyers in Anderson's courtroom at the "earliest practicable date."[209] After receiving a memorandum six days later, Hoover started several secret files on Frankfurter's activities and kept tabs on his foreign travel.[210] A June 20 memorandum to Hoover described Frankfurter as a "parlor bolshevist" and "confirmed radical" who "has been one of the most active elements in the stirring up and inciting to disturbances … particularly among the foreigners."[211] Hoover reputedly declared that Frankfurter was "the most dangerous man in the United States."[212]

Unlike Frankfurter, Pound was an "essentially timid creature" who believed that the sky at the law school was always falling.[213] Yet the dean was more privy than Frankfurter, Laski, or any other liberal to Harvard's reactionary forces, including President Lowell, the Board of Overseers, alumni, law faculty, and other members of the ruling class. Beneath Pound's institutional timidity lay a devoted liberal and one of the signers of the National Popular Government League report about the Palmer Raids. Pound sympathized wholeheartedly with Holmes's *Abrams* dissent, was a bit ashamed that he had not read it right away, and predicted that it would become canonical. "It is worthy to stand with your opinion in the Lochner case as one of the classics—yes one of the landmarks—of our law," Pound wrote Holmes.[214] Pound's letter gave Holmes "the greatest pleasure."[215]

Despite his timidity in the eyes of his colleagues, Pound had triumphed over most of the reactionary forces at Harvard. He had fought hard for Laski (unsuccessfully) and Frankfurter (successfully) and had hired three new members of the faculty, including Manley Hudson. In June 1920, Pound received his honorary degree from Harvard, and President Lowell reiterated that the push had begun with the resolution from Holmes. "To have been thought worthy of the highest degree Harvard has to give by the first of our legal scholars as well as the first of living judges," Pound wrote Holmes, "is a decoration beyond any that the corporation may bestow."[216]

When Pound took his sabbatical in Britain during the 1920–21 academic year, however, the reactionary forces at Harvard pounced. They could not force Pound or Frankfurter to resign, yet they had humiliated Laski into leaving for the London School of Economics. They focused their energies on a new target at the law school who, unlike Laski, was a full professor of law—Zechariah Chafee. Chafee's ostensible crime stemmed from his published account of the arrest, forced confessions, and trial of Jacob Abrams and his co-conspirators. "The whole proceeding, from start to finish, has been a disgrace to our law," Chafee concluded, "and none the less a disgrace because our highest court felt powerless to wipe it out."[217] Of Holmes's dissent, Chafee wrote:"While the decision of the majority has done a lasting injustice to the defendants, its effect on the legal conception of freedom of speech should be temporary in view of its meager discussion of the subject and the enduring qualities of the reasoning of Justice Holmes."[218]

Chafee's real crimes were that he and Frankfurter had written the friend of the court brief on behalf of Russian immigrants scheduled for deportation; that he, Frankfurter, and Pound had signed the National Popular Government League report exposing the Justice Department's unconstitutional conduct during the Palmer Raids; and that he, Frankfurter, and Pound had signed a clemency petition on Jacob Abrams's behalf. With his groundbreaking 1920 book on free speech, Chafee symbolized everything that reactionary alumni feared—a radical takeover of the law school. Aided and abetted by the Justice Department, twenty Harvard law alumni led by Wall Street lawyer Austen G. Fox filed formal charges with the university against Frankfurter, Pound, Chafee, and other liberal members of the faculty for errors in their clemency petition for Abrams and for errors in Chafee's account of Abrams's trial. Only the charges against Chafee stuck.[219] The Board of Overseers allowed the case to go to a May 22, 1921, inquiry known as the "Trial at the Harvard Club."[220] "I wish you could have been at the meeting on Sunday—," Frankfurter wrote Lippmann. "Chafee the very epitome of naïve & complete honesty, Fox the fit instrument of ignorant intolerance." And, despite his antipathy for Lowell, Frankfurter described Harvard's president as "an avowed champion" of Chafee and the school.[221]

President Lowell had indeed defended Chafee in the name of academic freedom. At the trial, Lowell cross-examined Fox and gave the closing argument on Chafee's behalf.[222] But a panel of state and federal judges nearly voted to dismiss Chafee from the faculty. Chafee won by a single vote, that of Judge Cardozo.[223] *The Nation*, though praising the final decision, insisted

Zechariah Chafee Jr.

that Chafee was "only the first target" and that the "reaction's real scheme" was to drive Frankfurter and Pound from the school.[224] An embarrassed Lowell kept the entire proceedings secret and pressured Chafee to publish five pages of corrections and qualifications about his *Harvard Law Review* article on the *Abrams* case.[225] Yet twenty years later Chafee dedicated his book *Free Speech in the United States* to Lowell because of the president's unwavering support.[226] "Lowell," Chafee wrote Holmes, "was splendid."[227] Holmes had lifted Chafee's spirits with a letter of support. "[I]t was as good as a hand upon my shoulder to have you write as you did," Chafee wrote Holmes and noted the importance of Holmes's *Abrams* dissent in the outcome of the "Trial at the Harvard Club." "The fact that the President of the Harvard Law School Association had denounced the conviction and the sentences was a crushing argument."[228]

But no son of Harvard was safe, not even Oliver Wendell Holmes Jr. Holmes's *Abrams* dissent had subjected him to similar attacks from conservatives. He should have known they were coming. Three of his colleagues,

Justices William R. Day, Willis Van Devanter, and Mahlon Pitney, had called on Mrs. Holmes at 1720 Eye Street, and together they had urged her husband not to dissent. They believed that Holmes had adopted "a somewhat quixotic view" of the case and had been "influenced toward it by Justice Brandeis's arguments."[229] Holmes's friend John Henry Wigmore, a Northwestern law professor who had served in the Judge Advocate General's Corps during the war, described the dissent as "poor law and poor policy" with "dangerous implications." "In a period when the fate of the civilized world hung in the balance," Wigmore wrote, "how could the Minority Opinion interpret law and conduct in such a way as to let loose men who were doing their hardest to paralyze the supreme war efforts of our country?"[230] Holmes insisted that Wigmore's article "wasn't reasoning but emotion." Frankfurter replied that "[t]he poor man has not yet come out of his uniform and thinks the War is still on."[231] But it was not just Wigmore. The conservative magazine *The Review* argued that Holmes was "clearly and palpably wrong."[232] Thomas Nelson Perkins and other members of Boston's ruling class also expressed their misgivings.[233] Holmes seemed to take pride in the fact that "some of our friends in Boston again have been discovering me to be dangerous and have been cursing me. ... But some of those whose judgment I most respect have said things that warmed my heart."[234]

Holmes was one of them now. His switch on free speech from April to October 1919 can be explained by many factors. In truth, the justice played an active role in his own transformation when the Red Scare came to Harvard Law School. During the summer of 1919, Holmes had invoked his honorary title as president of the law school's alumni association and, with prodding from Brandeis, had intervened with Lowell to protect Pound and Frankfurter. He had made his first stand for free speech several months before his *Abrams* dissent by vouching for his liberal friends.

As a champion of free speech, Holmes emerged as an even greater hero to the liberals at the law school, the *New Republic*, and the House of Truth. His *Abrams* dissent began the process of identifying the limits of government power and the role of the Supreme Court in protecting free speech and fair criminal trials. His *Abrams* dissent also accelerated his transformation from a relatively obscure justice into a liberal icon. That transformation began the moment he had set foot in the House of the Truth in 1912. Of the House's three original residents—Valentine, Denison, and Frankfurter—only Frankfurter lived to see the remarkable third and final act of Holmes's life.

17

Touched with Fire

Before he left Harvard for the London School of Economics in June 1920, Laski lamented that he could not make one more visit to 1720 Eye Street.[1] Instead, he spent his final days in America finalizing the publication of a collection of Holmes's essays, law review articles, and speeches about law—an oddly titled book known as Holmes's *Collected Legal Papers*. In a preface written days before his friend's departure, Holmes thanked Laski "for gathering these little fragments of my fleece … A later generation has carried on the work that I began nearly half a century ago, and it is a great pleasure to an old warrior who cannot expect to bear arms much longer, that the brilliant young soldiers still give him a place in their councils of war."[2]

Ten years earlier, Holmes had almost laid down his arms and surrendered. He was frustrated on the Court and considering retirement.[3] Despite having written *The Common Law* and "The Path of Law," he had failed to achieve his ambition of becoming "the greatest jurist in the world."[4] In 1910, he was an obscure justice. He had even circled his planned departure date—December 8, 1912—the tenth anniversary of his joining the Supreme Court of the United States and the guarantee of a lifetime pension. Two years passed, and his planned retirement date came and went. Frankfurter, Denison, and other men at the House of Truth lured him to their dinners, engaged him in debates about the search for truth, and praised his judicial opinions old and new. Starting with his initial visits to the House of Truth in 1912 and continuing with his *Abrams* dissent in 1919 and the publication of *Collected Legal Papers* at the end of 1920, his young friends played an integral role in Holmes's transformation into a liberal hero.

Part of the reason for Holmes's insecurity about his contribution to American life stemmed from the long shadow cast by his famous physician-poet father. Dr. Oliver Wendell Holmes Sr. practically owned Boston. He had nicknamed the city the Hub, coined the phrase "Boston Brahmin,"

Lieutenant Oliver Wendell Holmes Jr. in August or September 1861

and ruled the city's intellectual roost. A Paris-trained and Harvard-educated physician, he had written an article in 1843 about the cause of puerperal fever, a bacterial infection afflicting pregnant women, and had saved the lives of thousands of women by discovering that doctors were transmitting it by not washing their hands. He lectured at Harvard on anatomy. But Dr. Holmes was best known for his poetry, his novels, and his essays in the Boston-based *Atlantic Monthly*. In 1858, he collected many of his poems, essays, and table talk into his best-known book, *Autocrat at the Breakfast-Table*. He was not only one of Boston's leading public figures and intellectuals but also a full-blown national celebrity.

As a boy, Holmes Jr. was not even known by his first name. Family and friends in Beacon Hill called him by his middle name, Wendell. He thrived at school and during nightly dinner table discussions. He attended Harvard College, contributed essays to and edited the *Harvard Magazine*, and, in an obvious reference to his father, was named class poet.[5] Like his father, he began his adult life as an ardent abolitionist who "shuddered" at a minstrel show. In January 1861, Holmes and his friend Norwood Penrose "Pen" Hallowell served as bodyguards for Anti-Slavery Society speaker Wendell Phillips.[6] After Fort Sumter fell in April, Holmes, Hallowell, and many of their Harvard classmates left school prior to graduation and volunteered for the Union army. "The tendencies of the family and of myself have a strong bent for literature, etc., at present I am trying for a commission in one of the Massachusetts Regiments, however, and hope to go south before very long," Holmes wrote in his Harvard College yearbook. "If I survive the war I expect to study law as my profession at least for a starting point."[7]

Enlisted as a first lieutenant in the Twentieth Massachusetts Volunteer Regiment, Holmes began the war as an idealistic abolitionist like his father and ended it as a skeptic who admired men of action who did their jobs well. The Twentieth Massachusetts was composed of young Harvard gentlemen like Holmes, experienced German soldiers, and older Nantucket whalers. The regiment quickly "divided into factions" not only over class lines but also between abolitionists and Unionists.[8] Holmes and his fellow Harvard men were made officers even though many had not even graduated from college, much less had experienced combat.

Holmes's first battle was almost his last. On October 21, 1861, Union forces crossed the Potomac River and climbed the 150-foot cliff known as Ball's Bluff. At the top and with no means of escape, they soon discovered that they were surrounded by Confederate troops waiting in the forest.[9] Some regiments ran, but not Holmes's.[10] An hour into the battle, Lieutenant Holmes was encouraging his men forward when a spent musket ball hit him in the stomach and knocked the wind out of him. He got up and with a sword in his hand again rushed ahead when another shot entered his left breast, passed through his lungs, and was extracted from his right breast. He was spitting blood. His men carried him down the bluff's steep, densely wooded terrain, onto a pontoon boat, and over to a makeshift hospital at Harrison's Island in the middle of the river.[11]

Even amid the scores of wounded men at Harrison's Island, Holmes was quickly identified as the son of a celebrity.[12] Dr. Holmes received detailed letters from several officers about his son's condition. *Harper's Weekly* boasted that "New England Never Runs" and emphasized that Holmes was "'wounded in the breast': not in back; no not in the back. In the breast is Massachusetts wounded, if she is struck. Forward she falls, if she falls dead."[13] After Holmes had recovered sufficiently from his wounds at a hospital in Poolesville, Maryland, and at the Philadelphia home of his friend Hallowell, Dr. Holmes arrived from Boston and brought his twenty-year-old son home.

Five months later, Holmes returned to the Twentieth Massachusetts Regiment, was promoted to captain, and once again saw his bravery overshadowed by his father's celebrity. He was wounded a second time on September 17, 1862, at the bloodiest battle of the Civil War—Antietam. Holmes and his men stood in the middle of the West Woods and were ordered "up so close to the front line that we could have touched them with our bayonets."[14] They could not shoot back for fearing of killing their own troops. The Confederates broke through the line and ambushed them from the rear.[15] Given orders to retreat, Holmes and the Twentieth Massachusetts ran. With bullets flying all around him and running as fast as he could, he was shot in the back of the neck near the middle seam of his collar, with the bullet passing through the left side of his neck. His bearded friend Hallowell was shot in the left arm above the elbow. As Holmes was leaving the battlefield with a wound in the back and not the front, he "remember[ed] chuckling to myself," recalling the *Harper's Weekly* story after Ball's Bluff, and thought: "It's all right—but not so good for the newspapers."[16]

Holmes and Hallowell managed to make it to a farmhouse known as the Nicodemus House. With wounded men scatted all over the front lawn, Holmes and Hallowell lay down in the front parlor. The farmhouse soon fell behind enemy lines.[17] A Confederate soldier poked his head through the window.

"Yankee?"

"Yes."

"Wounded?"

"Yes."

"Would you like some water?"

The Confederate soldier threw his canteen inside, fought for another fifteen minutes, and then returned.

"Hurry up there! Hand me my canteen! I am on the double-quick now!" They threw it back to him.[18]

Holmes was not sure if he would make it out of the Nicodemus House alive or if he would remain conscious, so while he was lying in the house he found a pencil and wrote a note on a small piece of paper:

I am
Capt 20th Mass
OW Holmes
Son of Oliver Wendell Holmes MD
Boston[19]

He stayed conscious long enough to help save Hallowell's arm. A doctor, believing he could save it, needed a long, thin board to make a splint. Holmes told the doctor to check behind the looking glass of the clock; the doctor found what he needed.[20] A day or so later, a surgeon salvaged Hallowell's arm by removing a three-quarter-inch piece of bone.[21]

Holmes's neck wound was more serious. The first doctor who saw him refused to treat him because there was no "chance of recovery." The second doctor, General William G. LeDuc, decided to try—washing and plugging Holmes's wound with lint, giving him opium, and transporting him by ambulance to nearby Keedysville, Maryland. At the first house not occupied by soldiers, LeDuc forced the owner to move a featherbed to the first floor for the

Norwood Penrose Hallowell

wounded captain. LeDuc was amazed at Holmes's "escape from instant death," and that the wounded soldier was joking and in good spirits. Well aware of who the young man's father was, LeDuc wired Dr. Holmes: "Captain Holmes wounded shot through the neck thought not mortal at Keedysville."[22]

Holmes left Keedysville in a milk wagon for Hagerstown and was seen walking slowly around town with a bandage around his throat.[23] Mrs. Kennedy, a Union sympathizer and owner of a big white brick house on a hill, sent her son to ask if the wounded officer needed anything. Holmes explained that he was waiting for a train to Philadelphia. She offered him a place to stay. "He accepted the invitation and introduced himself as Oliver Wendell Holmes Jr.," Mrs. Kennedy's daughter recalled. "Of course we

Holmes's letter to his parents on September 22, 1862

recognized him as the son of Dr. Oliver Wendell Holmes." She thought the doctor's son, with his tiny black mustache, was "very tall and very good looking."[24] Holmes saw the house's grand piano and one of his father's books there and was relieved.[25]

With the help of another young woman in the house, Holmes dictated a letter to his parents because his wound had caused some numbness in his left arm. He could write well enough to sketch a picture of himself at the bottom of the letter and described himself as "disgracefully well" for someone "who has been hit again within an inch of his life." He planned on leaving for home in a few days and warned his father: "I neither wish to meet any affectionate parent half way nor any shiny demonstrations when I reach the desired haven."[26]

The warning had arrived too late. After he had received LeDuc's telegram, Holmes Sr. left Boston by train to find his son. And rather than simply find his son and bring him home, he turned the search-and-rescue mission into a magazine story for the *Atlantic Monthly*, "My Hunt after 'The Captain.'"[27]

Dr. Holmes stopped first in Philadelphia at the Hallowells' home, where their sons were recovering from their wounds, but there was no sign of the younger Holmes. Holmes Sr. boarded a train to Baltimore, stayed overnight there, then continued to Frederick, Middletown, and finally to Keedysville. In Keedysville, he learned that his son had left for Hagerstown and from there probably for Philadelphia. Dr. Holmes retraced his steps back to Philadelphia.[28] Finally, at the train station in Harrisburg, he boarded the 7:00 a.m. train from Hagerstown, and "[i]n the first car, on the fourth seat to the right, I saw my Captain. ..."

"How are you, Boy?" Dr. Holmes asked.

"How are you, Dad?" Captain Holmes replied.[29]

In his article, Dr. Holmes recalled the matter-of-fact manner in which father and son greeted each other and chalked it up to "the proprieties of life, as they are observed among us Anglo-Saxons of the nineteenth century."[30] He neglected to mention a prior episode with his son—the "young soldier's show of contempt for his [father's] lack of restraint" upon greeting his wounded son in Philadelphia after Ball's Bluff. Holmes was incensed by his father's portrayal of the Antietam greeting on the train. "This was play acting," Holmes recalled, "and we both knew it."[31] "My Hunt after 'the Captain'" annoyed Holmes on multiple levels—that his "Governor" (as he referred to his father) had tried to find him against his wishes and had hijacked the most harrowing episode of his life and turned it into a literary set piece.

After two months of recovery in Boston, Holmes returned to his regiment, but a bad case of dysentery prevented him from fighting and forced him to recover again at the Hallowell home in Philadelphia.[32] Finally, after he had rejoined his regiment in Falmouth, Virginia, he was wounded a third time during the Battle of Chancellorsville. Confederate sharpshooters near Fredericksburg sent Holmes and his fellow soldiers sprawling to the ground. The first shot barely missed him; the second blew off his knapsack; the third shattered his left heel.[33] "I've been chloroformed & hard bone extracted—probably shant lose foot," he wrote his mother. The next day he added to his father: "Foot didn't have to come off as was feared."[34] Losing his foot would have ended two hard years of military service that his fellow soldier Henry Abbott recognized had been "particularly trying to Holmes, who is a student rather than a man of action."[35]

Perhaps the most admired man in the Twentieth Massachusetts, "Little" Abbott wrote that Holmes was "a remarkably brave & well instructed officer, who has stuck to his work, though wounded often enough to discourage any but an honorable gentleman."[36] A Harvard-educated son of a prominent Lowell, Massachusetts, lawyer and former judge, Abbott and his family were Democrats, anti-Lincoln, and almost anti-war Copperheads. Abbott loathed Holmes Sr., whom he described as a "miserable little mannekin [sic]" for his "little fool make orations" about abolitionism. But his son was a different sort—"a good fellow & remember 6 feet high."[37]

Abbott was "delighted" that Holmes had decided to return to the army.[38] After six months, Holmes indeed returned, though not to the Twentieth Massachusetts. His abolitionist idealism was gone. He also had declined his friend Pen Hallowell's invitation to join the Fifty-Fourth Massachusetts Regiment, the legendary all-black regiment that made the bloody assault on Fort Wagner. It turned out to be a wise choice. Hallowell returned home for good in November 1863 because of prior wounds.[39]

Instead Holmes returned to service on horseback as an aide-de-camp to General Horatio Wright. With General Wright, Holmes saw Jubal Early's Confederate troops approach the outskirts of Washington, DC, at Fort Stevens. President Lincoln, wearing his stovepipe hat, was trying to get a better look by standing on the parapet as Confederate snipers took aim at the men up there. Holmes is often quoted as yelling at Lincoln: "Get down you, you fool!" or "Get down, you damn fool, before you get shot."[40]

Holmes told many people the story of having seen Lincoln at Fort Stevens, but not of yelling at or even speaking to the president.[41] The quotations are almost certainly apocryphal.[42]

As an aide to General Wright in the Sixth Corps, Holmes acted as an advance scout and carried dispatches on horseback by riding day and night. He experienced at least one more brush with death on a wild nighttime ride. He encountered by his own estimate twenty Confederate cavalry while carrying a dispatch. His gun misfired, and he dodged a hail of bullets by "lying along the side of [my] horse Comanche fashion."[43] After his three years of required service, the thrice-wounded twenty-three-year-old veteran elected to return home to Boston for good in July 1864.[44] He could not bear the physical or mental strain of returning to line duty with his old regiment.[45] His wrote his parents that everyone from the Twentieth Massachusetts whom he "knew or cared for is dead or wounded."[46] Two months earlier, his good friend Henry Abbott had died at age twenty-two leading the regiment during the Wilderness Campaign. "He was little more than a boy, but the grizzled corps commanders knew and admired him," Holmes wrote of Abbott in his 1884 Memorial Day address, "and for us, who not only admired, but loved [him], his death seemed to end a portion of our life also."[47]

His war experiences imbued in Holmes an intense skepticism about abolitionism and other moral causes. They also reinforced the challenges of escaping a lifetime in his father's shadow and taught him to admire the quiet professionalism of fallen soldiers such as Henry Abbott. In his 1895 Memorial Day speech, "The Soldier's Faith," Holmes wrote that the war had taught him, among other things, "to keep the soldier's faith against the doubts of civil life, more besetting and harder to overcome than all the misgivings of the battle-field, and to remember that duty is not to be proved in the evil day, but then to be obeyed unquestioning; to love glory more than the temptations of wallowing ease, but to know that one's final judge and only rival is oneself."[48] He described his Southern enemies in Virginia, Georgia, and Mississippi as "noble" and learned something from his near-death combat experiences. "Through our great good fortune," Holmes wrote of the war, "in our youth our hearts were touched with fire."[49]

His wartime experiences with the Twentieth Massachusetts Regiment instilled in him a lifelong belief in what his biographer G. Edward White described as "unadvertised professional craftsmanship."[50] Holmes was determined to be the best lawyer, the best legal scholar, and the best judge by doing his job well every single day—what he later referred to as his "job-bist" philosophy. "The lessons he learned then he carried with him always," Marion Frankfurter recalled near the end of his life. "They were the simple principles on which his way was made. Mrs. Holmes once said that if it hadn't been for the Civil War, 'Wendell would have been a coxcomb.'"[51]

At his father's urging and consistent with his Harvard College yearbook, Holmes enrolled at Harvard Law School and hoped to combine his interest in philosophy with law. He tried to make a life of his own in Boston. He be-friended William and Henry James, and together with John Chipman Gray they formed a loose-knit dinner group of young philosophers known as the Metaphysical Club.[52] Holmes was courting the beautiful and witty Fanny Dixwell, his schoolmaster's daughter whom William James described upon meeting her as "decidedly A-1, and (so far) the best girl I have known." James flirted with Fanny, yet knew he had no chance; he wrote his brother Henry "that villain Wendell Holmes has been keeping [Fanny] all to himself out at Cambridge for the last eight years."[53]

"Little" Henry Abbott

As an apprentice at a Boston law firm, he lived in his father's house on Beacon Street. He knew that his future lay not in legal practice but in scholarship. He worked punishingly hard first as a contributor to and then as editor of the *American Law Review* and the twelfth edition of Kent's Commentaries.[54] In 1872, he finally married Dixwell, whom he described as "for many years my most intimate friend."[55] It was not a happy time for the couple. They were living with Holmes Sr. on Beacon Street, and Holmes often neglected his young wife in those early years in Boston for his work.[56] William James wrote that he had seen his closest friend at the time only twice that winter: "I fear he is at last feeling the effects of his overwork."[57] Holmes Sr. satirized his son's ambition by publishing a series of *Atlantic Monthly* stories, *The Poet at the Breakfast Table*, about a young astronomer who harbored dreams of being a poet.[58] In reality, his son was working on a series of lectures about the common law for the Lowell Institute and wrote with a "sense of urgency" because he believed "that if a man was to do anything he must do it before 40."[59]

Before his fortieth birthday, Holmes succeeded in turning his law review articles and lectures into a major book. Published in February 1881, *The Common Law* remains one of the most influential works in American legal history. It reflected Holmes's belief in the development of judge-made law as one of ongoing scientific discovery rather than dogmatic absolutes. "The life of the law has not been logic: it has been experience," he wrote in the introduction to the first lecture. "The felt necessities of the time, the prevalent moral and political theories, intuitions of public policy, avowed or unconscious, even the prejudices which judges share with their fellow-men, have had a good deal more to do than the syllogism in determining the rules by which men should be governed."[60]

Neither the publication of *The Common Law* nor joining the Supreme Judicial Court of Massachusetts after a semester teaching at Harvard Law School brought Holmes the type of public recognition he craved. He dedicated himself to the craft of judging during twenty years as a state supreme court justice (like his maternal grandfather, Charles Jackson), the last few as chief justice. His 1884 Memorial Day address and his 1895 "The Soldier's Faith" recalled friends and fellow soldiers in the Twentieth Massachusetts Regiment.[61] His 1897 address "The Path of Law" rejected "the fallacy of logical form" and inspired future generations of progressive scholars to take a social scientific approach to law.[62]

Yet as long as he and Fanny lived in Boston, even after Dr. Holmes's death in 1894, he remained the physician-poet's son. His relationship with his father was complicated.[63] No one could criticize his "Governor" except Holmes.[64] He believed that his father had frittered away considerable scientific and literary gifts on light verse and fluffy short stories and novels rather than devoting himself to one thing—becoming the world's greatest doctor or greatest novelist, poet, or essayist.[65] Holmes, by contrast, dedicated himself to becoming the world's greatest judge but found public recognition slow in coming and his father's fame difficult to overcome.[66]

Even after Theodore Roosevelt appointed him to the Supreme Court of the United States in 1902, Holmes contended with his father's reputation. During his second year on the Court, Holmes attended a Washington cocktail party and was introduced to a senator's wife. She went on and on about how much she enjoyed Holmes's novel *Elsie Venner*. Holmes tried to explain that his father had written the book, but the senator's wife said the justice was being "entirely too modest, and should not hide his literary light under a bushel. Justice Holmes sighed and resumed the supping of his punch."[67]

During his first ten years on the Court, Holmes labored in relative obscurity. To be sure, he had infuriated Roosevelt in 1904 by dissenting in the *Northern Securities* case about the enforcement of the Sherman Antitrust Act (which Holmes believed was a "foolish law").[68] And a year later, Holmes cryptically dissented in *Lochner v. New York* that "[t]he 14th Amendment does not enact Mr. Herbert Spencer's Social Statics." With his allusion to the work of an English philosopher and sociologist who coined the phrase "survival of the fittest," Holmes argued in his *Lochner* dissent that the Fourteenth Amendment did not embody any particular economic or social theory and should not be used to invalidate state labor laws.[69] But newspapers did not quote Holmes's dissent in that case; they quoted Justice John Harlan's dissent instead.[70] It was not until 1909 that Roscoe Pound argued that Holmes's *Lochner* dissent contained "a few sentences that deserve to become classical."[71] The public, however, still ignored it and largely ignored Holmes.

In March 1911, a small story on page two of the *Washington Post* acknowledged Holmes's seventieth birthday with a photograph and five terse paragraphs. The story mentioned that Justice Harlan had placed a "bouquet of violets" on Holmes's seat on the bench, that Holmes had served nine years on the Court, that he had fought and been wounded in the Civil War, and that he had "rendered the famous decision in the beef trust case."[72]

The article said nothing about *The Common Law* or his *Lochner* dissent. Several other newspapers mentioned Holmes's birthday in a single small paragraph.[73] Boston was the only place where Holmes had achieved anything approaching celebrity status, a fame largely derived from that of his father. In a 1911 series, "Gems and Wit" and alluding to his father's poetry, the *Boston Globe* published some of the younger Holmes's speeches.[74]

As his seventieth birthday approached, Holmes was not only trapped in his father's shadow but also so frustrated on the Court that he considered retirement. "I have not as much recognition as I should like," he wrote.[75] One source of frustration was the attitudes of his colleagues. "I sit in my library and scribble away when I am not in Court, and as of old my brethren pitch into me for being obscure and when I go nasty I say that I write for educated men—of course, as if referring to some others than my interlocutor," he wrote in 1908.[76] After his Supreme Court nomination, newspapers described him as "more of a 'literary feller' than one often finds on the bench, and he has a strong tendency to be 'brilliant' rather than sound."[77] Holmes's new colleagues did not appreciate his literary and philosophical qualities. In 1911, he complained that his "brethren pulled all the plums out of my pudding and left it rather a sodden mess. Tis ever thus. I get in a biting phrase and of course someone doesn't like it and out it goes."[78] Nor was he as close with his colleagues as he was with his friends in Boston. "The brethren are kind, friendly, able men, but for the most part the emphasis of their interests and their ideals are not the same as mine and I happen at this moment to be realizing that our conceptions of the best way to do things is not the same," he wrote John Chipman Gray in 1914. "I daresay it is all the better that it should be so and I try to profit by it, but at times I have to fall back on Luther's Ich Kann nicht anders." [Here I stand. I cannot help it.][79] But even Gray, one of Holmes's oldest and dearest friends, conceded to then president Taft that Holmes's opinions "seem to lack lucidity."[80]

In many ways, Gray's letter of introduction to Frankfurter came at the right moment. Holmes's old friends from the Civil War were on their last legs. Gray had been suffering from heart disease that forced him to retire from Harvard Law School in 1913 and that killed him two years later.[81] Holmes had not been as close of late with Pen Hallowell, who died in 1914, yet considered Hallowell "the greatest soul I ever knew" and wrote that "his death leaves a great space bare."[82] Holmes needed new friends. His association with the House of Truth in 1912 was perfect timing and not just because his friends were dying and he was contemplating retirement. During the 1912 presidential race, two potential progressive candidates, Theodore Roosevelt and Robert La Follette, attacked the Supreme Court for its reactionary, anti-labor decisions and advocated the recall of judges and their decisions.

The House of Truth attacked the Supreme Court by reviving Holmes. They pointed to his *Lochner* dissent as a classic statement about judges reading their economic views into the Constitution. They cheered his pro-labor dissents in yellow-dog contract and child labor cases. And they influenced his shifting views on free speech because of their own professional difficulties during the Red Scare. Holmes, in turn, showed his liberal friends how the Court could aid their political and legal activism—particularly when it came to free speech and fair criminal trials.

★★★

The public recognition that he had long sought finally began to come Holmes's way beginning in November 1919, with his *Abrams* dissent, and continued a year later with the publication of his *Collected Legal Papers*. Holmes sent advance copies of the book to his friends, including Frankfurter, Croly, and Lippmann.[83] Croly and Lippmann, in consultation with Frankfurter, determined that Lord Haldane should review *Collected Legal Papers* for the *New Republic*.[84] Haldane admired Holmes, and the magazine's editors knew that the approval of the British would bring Holmes pleasure.[85] They knew that it would be some time before Haldane's review came out, but that it would generate a lot of publicity. Croly offered the possibility that other people would review Holmes's book. "[I]t is very likely that Walter Lippmann and I may want to do so, too," Croly wrote Holmes.[86]

Several people beat them to it. The philosopher Morris R. Cohen, Frankfurter's former law school roommate, praised *Collected Legal Papers* in the *New Republic* as "an extraordinary book of thoroughly matured human wisdom."[87] Cohen described Holmes's "urbane or civilized skepticism" and "complete freedom from all the current cant phrases about liberty and equality, democracy and progress."[88] Holmes wrote Cohen about his "happiness" with the review that "makes life easier." He acknowledged that was "an odd phrase" for someone about to turn eighty, but "as a corner is turned the road stretches away again and ambition to go farther returns."[89] Philip Littell, in the magazine's "Books and Things" column, quoted four sentences from *Collected Legal Papers* as proof that they represented "'the finest modern English prose.'"[90] Holmes appreciated Littell's "little side puff."[91]

Positive reviews poured in throughout 1921 and generated scholarly and professional reappraisals of Holmes's career in law reviews, political science journals, and several magazines.[92] The reviewers recognized that Holmes's speeches and writings placed him a cut above his brethren and made him an important judicial figure. They saw greatness in Holmes just as the House of Truth did. "*Collected Legal Papers*," Judge Learned Hand concluded in yet another review, "is a good vertical section of the mind of that judge who beyond any other of his generation has impressed his ideas on the structure and course of the law."[93] Frankfurter maintained his steady stream of flattery by discussing reviews with Holmes and sending him copies. The justice was a little concerned about "the outpouring. Pride goeth before a fall and whenever anything sets me up, I expect very shortly to get taken down."[94] Frankfurter replied that his wife heard about Holmes's fears and remarked: "'Why doesn't he realize what he is and what he means to men.' Whereupon, I tried to explain to her how thoroughgoing your scepticism and how deep your humility."[95] Holmes was a skeptic; humility was another matter. The reception of his *Collected Legal Papers* fed his ego and his vanity. Hand commented on Holmes's "childlike simplicity. The last made it very easy to exploit him, and, as I look back on it, we all did exploit him by playing upon his vanity which we could not have done if he had not been as guileless as he was."[96]

Holmes was well aware of what Old Boston thought about his new friends, many of them Jewish—Brandeis, Frankfurter, Laski, and Lippmann. "I am tickled at your 'If only you stay thoroughly Anglo-Saxon,'" Holmes wrote Nina Gray. "I take the innuendo to be that I am under the influence of the Hebs. I am comfortably confident that I am under no influence except that of thoughts and insights." He acknowledged that Brandeis—"my brother B. seems to me to see deeper than some of the others"—had swayed his thinking and had often encouraged him to write dissents.[97]

The *Milwaukee Leader* case may have been on Holmes's mind. The day before his eightieth birthday, the Court affirmed the constitutionality of Postmaster General Burleson's suspension of the second-class mailing privileges of the Socialist and antiwar newspaper. Both Holmes and Brandeis wrote dissents. After praising Brandeis's opinion and admitting that it had changed his mind about the case, Holmes accused the postmaster general of interfering with "very sacred rights" and concluded that the revocation of the paper's mailing privileges "was unjustified by statute and was a serious attack upon liberties that not even the war induced Congress to infringe."[98]

Just as they did with *Abrams*, his liberal friends lavished praise on his dissent. "What a 'Magisterial' opinion you wrote in the *Milwaukee Leader* case. You said it all in the few, pungent sentences," Frankfurter wrote.[99] The *New Republic* added: " Mr. Justice Holmes with a few strokes of his pen brought down the house of cards of the majority opinion."[100] The flattery was genuine and had a purpose. With civil liberties under attack at Harvard and elsewhere in 1921, Frankfurter and friends needed Holmes to fulfill their liberal aspirations on the Court.

A little before eight o'clock on March 6, 1921, Holmes was sitting in the library of 1720 Eye Street with his wife; she had convinced him to "dress, tails and all," to go out for Sunday dinner.[101] It was two days before his eightieth birthday. They headed downstairs to find more than a dozen of his former secretaries, including Chauncey Belknap, Francis Biddle, and Harvey Bundy, as well as former House of Truth residents Edward H. Hart (and his wife, Frances Noyes Hart) and Louis G. Bissell standing around the dining room table. Fanny had arranged for them to enter the house through the kitchen on the lower level. Holmes, by his own admission, was "flabbergasted."[102] His secretaries were the closest things he had to sons. Biddle recalled that "he shaded his eyes, as he looked at them," and Holmes exclaimed: "'Ghosts! ... Well, I'll be damned.'"[103] Holmes "yelled with joy" as they began to pour glasses of champagne from a "case or two" that he had received before prohibition.[104] "The Eighteenth Amendment," he told his secretaries, "forbids manufacture, transportation and importation. It does not forbid possession or use."[105]

The celebration of Holmes's eightieth birthday continued in print. Pound praised *Collected Legal Papers* in another *Harvard Law Review* volume dedicated to Holmes and declared that "the author of 'The Path of the Law,' and of the dissenting opinion in *Lochner v. New York* may await the assured verdict of time."[106] Haldane wrote in his long-awaited *New Republic* review that "[e]very nation forms an intellectual type which is peculiarly its own" and considered Holmes "a striking example of it."[107] Both reviews, Holmes wrote a friend, "show that I have achieved what I longed to do."[108] His father's fame, however, still loomed in the lay public's mind. The *New York Times* review, "A 'Legal' Autocrat," claimed that Holmes's modest preface about the "fragments of my fleece" "might have been written by his universally beloved father. One can pay his distinguished son no greater compliment than that."[109]

With all the praise for *Collected Legal Papers*, the tributes in the *Harvard Law Review*, and his companionship with Brandeis on the Court, Holmes no longer harbored thoughts of retirement. Opinion writing came as easily for him at eighty as it had been at seventy.[110] He set a new goal—to stay on the Court another ten years and to live to see ninety years old.[111] The House of Truth shared his goal. There was important work ahead, and his young friends were counting on their beloved justice.

18

Protestant of Nordic Stock

After failing to get President Wilson to pay the expenses he had incurred during the aircraft investigation, Borglum was in such dire financial straits that he appealed to President Harding for reimbursement.[1] During the 1920 presidential election, Borglum had been active in the Nonpartisan League, a progressive group of North Dakota and other northwestern farmers. After his friend General Wood had failed to get the Republican nomination, he had persuaded the organization to endorse Harding.[2] Before and after the election, he and Harding dined and corresponded.[3] Thanks to Borglum, Harding knew all about the aircraft investigation.[4] Upon receiving Borglum's request for reimbursement, Harding had his secretary of war look into it.[5] Harding's administration determined that, because of Wilson's disavowal that Borglum had been working on behalf of the executive branch, any reimbursement would have to come from an act of Congress.[6]

Though he desperately needed money, Borglum decided not to press the issue, possibly because he needed Harding and Congress to help with his Confederate Memorial at Stone Mountain. As his drawing on the House of Truth's tablecloth attested, the Confederate Memorial was never far from his mind during the war. He stuck to his vision of carving Lee, Jackson, and Davis and the Confederate army marching across the 800-foot high mountain, to immortalize these men as well as himself, and to keep his promise to a Confederate widow. "I hope you are keeping well and not discouraged," he wrote C. Helen Plane during the war. "I want to assure you that I am going to finish the Memorial—whether Georgia raises her finger or not in the work!"[7] On April 23, 1919, the ninety-year-old Plane resigned as president of the Stone Mountain Memorial Association. She was "worn out and unable to stand up any longer under the strain of responsibility." The people of Atlanta had let her down by promising to raise $100,000 for the memorial but doing nothing. She praised Borglum for working for nearly three years at his own expense and without pay. During the war, however, all the infrastructure that he had added to the mountain had fallen into disrepair from "neglect and exposure." The memorial association's coffers stood at $1,055.72.[8]

Borglum's financial situation was even worse. His commissions had dried up during the war. Eugene Meyer, his nemesis during the aircraft investigation, had called in his $40,000 loan plus compound interest on Borglum's New York studio and Stamford, Connecticut, home, a loan that Borglum could not repay.[9] Dorothy Straight, the widow of the founder of the *New Republic*, sued Borglum on her late husband's behalf for failing to repay $3,151 on a $5,000 loan.[10] Borglum was mired in debt, had mortgaged his property in Stamford and New York City multiple times, and had borrowed another $12,000 to finance his aircraft investigation.[11] He was so desperate that he broke his rule of not entering competitions; his entry for a $175,000 prize from the Cuban government for a monument to General Maximo Gomez finished a disappointing third.[12]

The postwar desire for memorials once again put Borglum's services in demand. He was hired to create another monument to General Philip

Borglum carving Lee's nose

Sheridan, this one in Chicago's Lincoln Park. He landed a $100,000 commission from the estate of a Civil War veteran to create a war memorial in Military Park in downtown Newark. The city was already home to Borglum's seated Lincoln and would feature another work, *Wars of America*. The monument started with four figures from the Revolutionary War, the Union army, the world war, and the navy, followed by a tangled mass of thirty-eight soldiers and two horses. "We do things in the mass, not as individuals," Borglum said when he unveiled his plaster model in April 1921. "Mass action is the keynote of our monuments."[13]

Borglum's biggest monument to date, *Wars of America* borrowed conceptually from his proposed Confederate Memorial, with four soldiers in the foreground followed by men and horses in the background. The *Atlanta Constitution* noticed the similarities.[14] Like Stone Mountain, *Wars of America* would take years to complete. The biggest difference, however, was that *Wars of America* was to be cast from a forty-ton plaster model into "the largest bronze group in the United States, if not in the world."[15] The Confederate Memorial had to be carved into the granite face of an 800-foot-high mountain, a technical challenge on a different order of magnitude.

Though he was not working on the project during those first two years after the war, Borglum kept the Confederate Memorial on track. He resisted efforts to reserve part of the mountain for a memorial to the 1,405 Georgians who had died during the world war.[16] He sustained interest in the project in 1919 and 1920 through speaking engagements.[17] In January 1919, an *Atlanta Journal* reporter spoke with superintendent Tucker and declared: "Borglum Says He Will Finish Stone Mountain Memorial as Planned."[18] Later that year, an *Atlanta Constitution* reporter wrote Borglum about starting "an intensive media campaign patterned somewhat after the Red Cross" for fundraising.[19] He agreed to cooperate and encouraged the reporter's efforts: "I know the sources where large sums could be obtained if a group of men thoroughly in earnest will take charge."[20]

Borglum was both in earnest and willing to take charge. When no Georgia fundraising effort was forthcoming, he approached one of the richest men he knew, financier Bernard Baruch. Born in Camden, South Carolina, Baruch was the son of a Confederate surgeon and of an active member of the United Daughters of the Confederacy.[21] Baruch, moreover, was interested in the history of the Confederacy.[22] The sculptor asked Baruch for $200,000, with $100,000 of this to restart the memorial and to make a film about Confederate war heroes and another $100,000 to remove all the mortgages on his homes and to get him out of debt. He offered Baruch the $100,000 contract on *War of America* and the $50,000 contract on the Sheridan Memorial as collateral and, if Baruch did not wish to donate any money to the memorial, a $100,000 possible return on the movie. "Your aid in the great memorial would result in its completion," Borglum wrote.[23] Baruch declined to contribute but remained on good terms with the sculptor. Indeed, Baruch was one of the few Wilson administration officials who had encouraged Borglum's aircraft investigation, who sympathized with Borglum's progressive politics on behalf of northwestern farmers, and who somehow managed to escape Borglum's negative stereotypes about Jews.[24]

Nothing was more complex about Borglum than his relationship with Jews. He counted Baruch, Brandeis, Frankfurter, and especially Jewish scholar Isidore Singer among his friends. Singer edited the *Jewish Encyclopedia*, to which Borglum's wife, Mary, contributed and which the sculptor lauded in print and in fundraising efforts. He considered Singer a fellow "artist" and "creative genius" and created a bust of Singer in the scholar's honor.[25] Yet Borglum had come to loathe Eugene Meyer, Jacob Schiff, Felix Warburg, and other New York Jewish financiers who had purchased some of his best work for pittances and had refused to forgive his loans or compound interest. As a result of these negative experiences, Borglum bought into growing conspiracy theories about Jewish financiers running the world and lapsed into anti-Semitic rants about Jews as middlemen and moneylenders. "So you think the Jews control the unions as they also control capital!" Borglum wrote a friend in 1920. "I know the latter is true, but don't believe the former. I don't think there are enough Jews that *work* in this world to control any union!"[26]

Borglum needed money—whether Baruch's or someone else's—because the work he had already done on the mountain was in a sorry state. On July 10, 1920, Tucker reported after inspecting the mountain that some of the stairs needed "small repairs," a few stairs were gone, and sections of handrails and cables had "rusted entirely off."[27] With no memorial to work on, Tucker had taken on a Georgia highway project. But by January 1921, he was ready to rejoin Borglum to work on the mountain.[28] The biggest obstacle to bringing Tucker back and repairing the decaying infrastructure was a lack of funding. For the past six years, Borglum had worked on Stone Mountain without a contract and without collecting any salary. The memorial association covered some of the expenses, but he paid others out of his own pocket.

It was, he believed, time for the people of Atlanta to step up. He sought to shake Atlanta from its apathy beginning in January 1921 with his week-long stay there accompanied by the half-brother to the king of Spain, thirty-six-year-old Prince Alfonso Louis de Bourbon. Together Borglum and his friend stayed at the Atlanta home of Stone Mountain owner Sam Venable and toured the mountain.[29] The prince accompanied Borglum everywhere and generated interest in the project. They proposed a propaganda film, undoubtedly inspired by D. W. Griffith's *The Birth of a Nation*, about the "lost cause" by telling a fictionalized version of Plane's story and her dream of making the Confederate Memorial at Stone Mountain.[30] The prince made headlines by wearing the bronze cross of the Confederacy.[31] And Borglum announced to the Atlanta Chapter of the United Daughters of the Confederacy that he planned to carve the head of General Lee by July or August.[32] But the people of Atlanta raised no funds, the movie never happened, and Borglum's timeline proved to be too ambitious. He was finishing the Sheridan memorial in Chicago. And he still had to finish the plaster cast of *Wars of America* so that it could be sent to Italy and cast in bronze, a project that was worth $100,000 and that took him most of 1922.

The one man who could have helped him finish Lee's head at Stone Mountain was no longer alive. Borglum's younger brother, Solon, died on January 30, 1922, after an emergency appendectomy. The two brothers shared the same mother, the same artistic talent, and the same medium, but they had wildly different artistic temperaments. Gutzon battled members of the art establishment; Solon befriended them. While Gutzon had made headlines with his aircraft investigation, Solon had volunteered for the French army during the world war and had received the Croix de Guerre. The two brothers both lived in Connecticut yet rarely collaborated on projects. A renowned sculptor in his own right, Solon struggled to escape his publicity-hungry brother's considerable shadow. Though his appendix had ruptured, Solon was expected to survive the operation, and his family was not called to Stamford Hospital until the last minute. By the time Gutzon arrived, his brother was in a "very deep sleep." Solon's family could hear the cries from down the hall.

"*We shall do great works together!*" Gutzon screamed, according to family members. "Wake up, Solon. Wake up!"[33]

Solon's daughter rushed into the room and ordered Gutzon to leave. "It's too late," she said. "You should have told father that when he could hear you."[34]

Solon died at 7:00 p.m. at age fifty-two.

Solon's family prevented Gutzon from speaking at the funeral or the subsequent New York City memorial service.[35] Gutzon contented himself with eulogizing his brother in a long letter to the *New York Times*, and he grieved for several months.[36] He regretted that they would never work together on the Confederate Memorial. He had asked Solon to sculpt three big horses in the cavalry and, in the event of his own death, had authorized only his younger brother to finish the project.[37] "If Solon were only here to help me!" he wrote.[38]

Borglum tried to lose himself in his work. He was making progress on *Wars of America* and the Sheridan Memorial in Chicago, and the Confederate Memorial was "calling loudly." In mid-March, he brought his family to Stone Mountain because in Atlanta "they have money."[39]

What he did not reveal was the source of the new funds—the Ku Klux Klan. The Klan's influence on the project had always been present. Sam Venable, Borglum's close friend and a proud member of the organization, had permitted the Klan to inaugurate its revival by burning crosses atop his mountain on Thanksgiving night 1915. A month later, C. Helen Plane had asked Borglum to incorporate the Klan somewhere in his memorial.[40] In recent years, Borglum had mentioned General Nathan Bedford Forrest, a founding member of the original Klan, as one of the first cavalrymen to be carved on the mountainside trailing Lee, Jackson, and Davis.[41]

By 1922, Borglum needed assistance, and the Klan was the only organization offering it. "Mr. Sam showed me a letter from Mr. Forrest saying they were ready for action as soon as the association approved their proposition but he did [not] think they would get any action until you come," Tucker wrote Borglum.[42] "Mr. Sam" was Sam Venable. "Mr. Forrest" was Nathan Bedford Forrest II, the grandson of the Confederate general and a leader of the revived Klan. In September 1921, Forrest had been named secretary and business manager of Lanier University, an Atlanta college purchased by the Klan and designed to "teach pure, 100 per cent. Americanism."[43] Forrest was nominated to the revived Stone Mountain Memorial Association's board of directors in May 1922 and was planning to enlarge Borglum's studio at the base of the mountain.[44] A month later, Borglum wrote another Klan leader, E. Y. Clarke, about "Gen. Forrest's proposal for the studio, [and] your own later offer to piece out the present needed funds to put the big design on the mountain."[45]

Borglum's relationship with the Klan was more than just financial opportunism; he was interested in the Klan as a growing political force. "Have you paid any attention to what the Klan are doing?" Borglum wrote a friend in May 1922. "It seems to me there is a group of men that are worth something."[46] A month later, Borglum proposed another friend, Lynn Haines, the Washington, DC–based editor of the *Searchlight*, for Klan membership. Borglum described Haines as "a blue lodge Mason. … He is head and heart our kind."[47] The Klan's anti-Semitism, cultural nationalism, and concern for the common man appealed to Borglum.

And of course the money did not hurt. The Klan's financial support made it possible to begin repairs to the mountain's stairs, railings, and other infrastructure destroyed due to neglect and what the *Atlanta Constitution* described as "wanton vandalism" and "shameful mischief."[48] Tucker also had returned to the project. By July 1922, he had repaired the stairs, replaced the railings, and created a new platform at the bottom of the stairs 550 feet above the studio.[49] He also outlined a $5,400 budget needed for wood flooring for the new platform, steel cable, a steel cage on vertical and horizontal wheels, and other labor and materials so that the sculptor could begin carving. A month later, the *Atlanta Constitution* announced that Borglum had returned to Stone Mountain to begin "actual work" there.[50] "Gutzon Borglum is with us," the newspaper declared, "and one fancies something like the light of a congratulatory smile on Stone Mountain's rugged face."[51]

Newspapers began to publish photos of Borglum standing on the mountain's platform with a giant drawing of General Robert E. Lee, in profile, wearing a hat.[52] The sculptor was wrestling with his biggest technological hurdle yet—how to transfer his design for the memorial to a mountainside. He decided to project the image of his design onto it. Experts, however, dismissed the idea because projectors at that time could only display images from 270 to 300 feet and the face of the mountain was 1,500 feet wide and 800 feet high.[53] "I could throw my pictures on the moon," he boasted, "if I could get a slide between the sun and the moon."[54] He wanted a projector with a triple lens and high-powered light that would "throw" an image 600 feet or more. For $2,200, he commissioned a projector that weighed 901 pounds, was powered by a 150-ampere arc, and contained a water-cooling system to prevent the lenses from burning up.[55] To test his giant projector, he took it to his Stamford, Connecticut, farm and hung giant white sheets several hundred feet away. At first, the image on the slide did not show up on the sheets. As he was trying to focus the slide, his six-year-old daughter, Mary, cried, "Oh, Daddy, look! Horses riding through the field."[56]

The Klan's financial backing was indispensable to progress on the memorial. Borglum had paid for the $2,200 projector and had been covering the $120 to $160 weekly payroll out of his own pocket. And he needed another $15,000 to bring the remaining machinery to the mountain.[57] He did not want to return to the same situation as before the war, when he had been responsible for the memorial association's debts.[58] The Klan could help him raise funds, and he could help the Klan with his contacts in the federal government. Indeed, his belief in the Klan and his belief in government were, in his mind, one and the same.

In 1922, the Klan was a formidable political force in Texas, Louisiana, and elsewhere, a force that he attempted to legitimize despite growing state and federal opposition to its anti-Catholicism, anti-Semitism, and racial violence. On December 14, he wired President Harding: "I have two friends possibly three from west who will be in Washington Monday are very anxious to have half hour conference with you. I believe this very important. Can I bring them?"[59] The president agreed to see them four days later at 5:30 p.m.[60] Harding, who had sponsored antilynching legislation in the Senate and whose attorney general had investigated the Klan, repeatedly denied accusations that he was a Klansman or that he supported the organization.[61] On December 18, Borglum and his guests had met at the Willard Hotel with one of the Klan's most outspoken critics, Kansas governor Henry J. Allen.[62] At 5:30, Borglum arrived at the White House with his "friends ... from the west," including Dr. H. W. Evans of Texas, the Imperial Wizard of the Ku Klux Klan.[63] To the *Atlanta Constitution*, Borglum cryptically "explained that he wanted to present friends to the president to pay respects."[64] It was not the last time that he interceded with Harding on the Klan's behalf.

The same day that Borglum took his friends to the White House, he learned that Klan leaders Nathan Bedford Forrest II and E. Y. Clarke had offered to raise funds for the Confederate Memorial.[65] They wanted Borglum to present their proposal to the board. During a January 17 meeting with the memorial association's executive committee, Borglum explained the project's "imperative" financial situation. What he really wanted was a long-term financial commitment, and he argued that Clarke and Forrest had made "the only proposition we are in [a] position to accept."[66] The Klan pledged to raise $250,000 in thirty to sixty days from Atlanta and Georgia and then shift its fundraising operations into other states, taking a 5 percent commission for its efforts. "The proposition in itself," Borglum declared, "is probably the easiest thing [for] Mr. Forrest to finance today in America."[67]

Though he embraced the Klan's financial possibilities, Borglum also wanted plausible deniability. "Neither you nor I can afford to be involved in any question relating to the Klan," he wrote memorial association chairman Forrest Adair. Borglum attempted to rewrite history, insisting that the previous summer he had declined $10,000 from the Klan on Adair's advice. Borglum claimed to Adair, who had not attended the meeting when they had voted on the proposal, that neither the Klan nor any of its subsidiaries

Borglum in front of the White House

was in charge. "The Stone Mountain Confederate Memorial Association surrenders nothing," he wrote Adair. It was merely accepting funds from the Klan-run Southern Advertising Association.[68] Three days later, Adair resigned from the memorial association, citing business and personal commitments and without mentioning the Klan.[69]

The Klan's fundraising proved to be a disappointment. After a month, Borglum was still covering the weekly payroll and had personally guaranteed the $1,900 needed to run power lines from the streetcar to the mountain.[70] He needed the power lines in order to set up his new projector. He complained to Klan fundraiser E. Y. Clarke, but Clarke had his own problems: he was indicted under the Mann Act for transporting a woman across state lines, and the Klan canceled his fundraising contract and banned him from the organization.[71] Borglum bemoaned the whole situation after reading about it in the *New York Times* and continued to count on Clarke's assistance.[72] The sculptor later credited Clarke for what progress had been made in 1923.[73]

The Klan nonetheless continued to rely on Borglum's connections in the White House. On March 5, he attempted to make another personal appeal to President Harding. Unable to see the president because it was the end of the congressional session, Borglum met with Harding's private secretary, George Christian. He informed Christian that public officials were being dismissed because they were Klansmen and that "there was an organized movement on foot, directed by subordinates in the Department of Justice— possibly Mr. Burns against your Klan." Christian replied: "They, the Klan, are fighting catholics and other people not in their organization in different parts of the country." To which Borglum, who claimed to be acting as an intermediary and could not speak for the organization, replied that "'they are fighting no sect; they are refusing to permit membership to their organization to any one not white, not native-born not protestant;' and I considered it a very serious matter if the administration is permitting any sect, whether it be protestant, catholic, or jew, to drive from office any man because he is a protestant, a catholic, a jew, or a klansman, if he is honest, honorable, and an efficient public servant."[74] Borglum reported his conversation to one of his Klan contacts and sent a copy of the letter to President Harding.[75]

With or without the Klan's financial assistance, Borglum moved forward with the Confederate Memorial. After the power lines were extended to the mountain in late February 1923, he began experimenting with his new projector.[76] One problem was immediately apparent: tracing the image at an elevation of 350 feet distorted it. He and Stamford photographer Charles D'Emery solved the program by creating a photograph of the image at an angle equal to the distortion.[77] They continued to experiment with different slides until they perfected their discovery. Bolted to a concrete floor, the projector moved from side to side or up and down and produced such a clear image of Borglum's design at night that men could trace it in white onto the mountainside.[78] The projector aroused interest from the editors of *Scientific American* and *Popular Mechanics* and saved Borglum an estimated one to three years of work.[79]

During a March 1 national radio address, Borglum boasted of the physical scope of his memorial and his technological breakthroughs. He described a ninety-foot-high image of Lee on horseback, plans for a memorial hall at the base of the mountain, and the new projector as resolving "the greatest difficulty experienced in working out plans for the memorial."[80] He explained how the projector enlarged his drawings with such precision. "We have tested it, and it works perfectly," he told the audience. " It will carry a needle-scratch on a black surface 700 feet, enlarging it in this distance to a width of 9 inches."[81] Tucker experimented with different slides and awaited machinery needed to carve the mountain. After a month, he received a check for the compressor that would send compressed air through the pneumatic drills, and the motor generator arrived. Borglum wired congratulations, planned to return to Atlanta to make further experiments, and instructed Tucker: "Want everything in readiness."[82]

The Klan's connection to Borglum and Stone Mountain overshadowed his progress. On April 22, the *Baltimore Sun* claimed that the Klan "came out in the open today and virtually took charge of the movement to raise the $2,000,000 to cover the expenses of carving a great memorial to the Southern Confederacy."[83] The *New York Tribune*'s front-page headline declared: "Confederate Memorial Seized Upon by Klan as Huge 'Ad.'"[84] Dr. H. W. Evans announced plans to raise the $2 million for the memorial and that Borglum "has been a frequent visitor at the Imperial Palace since he came to Atlanta and that the klan had a satisfactory understanding with him."[85] The *Tribune* quoted Evans as saying that he would raise the $2 million "if he has to place an arbitrary assessment on every Klan in the country."[86] Nathan Bedford Forrest II was described as holding a "whip hand" over the memorial association.[87]

The Pulitzer-owned New York *World*, which had published a twenty-part series on the revival of the Klan in September 1921, wired questions to

Borglum and the United Daughters of the Confederacy demanding to know which organization was in charge of the memorial and whether Borglum was a member of the Klan.[88] Borglum responded to "that impudent paper" with half-truths and lies. In a letter to the president of the United Daughters of the Confederacy, he denied that the Klan had anything to do with the memorial, claimed that the Daughters of the Confederacy owned title to the property, and asserted that the Stone Mountain Memorial Association "was in complete control of the work." In the same letter he maintained that "a Klan outrider would not be placed on the mountain with General Lee, nor would a Klansman appear anywhere with the confederate forces, nor on the mountain, nor had there been any proposal of that kind." He insisted the work was financed by the city of Atlanta at $25,000 a year for five years and that Fulton County and the state of Georgia would also contribute. And he rejected the paper's questions and sources of information as coming from "people who were enemies to the true history of this country." Finally, he added that while he had "nothing against the Klan what so ever" and hoped they would contribute funds, he refused to allow "any influence of any kind … that will affect the historical accuracy and the art product, in so far as is in my power."[89]

In the meantime, internecine Klan disputes jeopardized the memorial. After ousted Imperial Wizard William J. Simmons sued his successor, Evans, memorial association president Hollins Randolph wrote Borglum that the whole thing was likely "to upset your entire plans."[90]

Borglum's plans included an April 20 banquet at Atlanta's Capital City Club, featuring southern governors and US senators and their representatives and highlighted by the appearance of a very special guest—President Harding. Ever since his early March intercession on the Klan's behalf, Borglum had been lobbying Harding to come to Stone Mountain. The sculptor promised to turn on the projector and put up slides on the mountain for a special nighttime showing. Harding's visit seemed possible. Eight days earlier, Harding's father had told the United Confederate Veterans that Robert E. Lee was "the greatest of American generals" and Jefferson Davis was "one of the country's greatest statesmen" and had assured them that "[t]he South never had a better friend than Warren G. Harding."[91] Despite a White House meeting with Stone Mountain Memorial Association officials and numerous telegrams and last-minute pleas from Borglum, Harding opted not to make a personal appearance.[92] Instead, he sent a letter of endorsement: "It will be one of the world's finest testimonies, one of history's complete avowals, that unity and understanding may be brought even into the scene where faction, hatred and hostility have once reigned supreme."[93]

Harding may not have wanted to go to Stone Mountain along with the 400 other southern dignitaries because of the project's ties to the Klan. During the weekend of the Capital City Club dinner, the most important order of business was how to select Confederate heroes from each state to carve into the mountain as members of the cavalry. Instead of leaving the selection to the governors, special committees from each state would handle the task. And thanks to an amendment by Nathan Bedford Forrest II, those committees included not only governors and their representatives but also state representatives from the United Daughters of the Confederacy and the Stone Mountain Memorial Association.[94] In other words, the Klan's fingerprints remained on the mountain, and the organization dogged Borglum as a source of controversy. In early June, Klan members filed a lawsuit alleging mismanagement of funds, succeeded in temporarily freezing the organization's assets, and named members of the Klan's Imperial Kloncilium as defendants, including Borglum. To Atlanta newspapers, the sculptor wired from his Stamford, Connecticut, home: "Kindly publish that they have no right to involve my name, as I am not a member of Kloncilium. Am not a Knight of the Ku Klux Klan, and I say this as a matter of fact, without any prejudice to the Klan whatsoever."[95]

Two months later, several newspapers reported that a member of the Klan had read Borglum's biography in *Who's Who in America* listing the sculptor as a member of the Catholic Church and that Klan officials were "mortified to learn that a Catholic had been a member of their inner circles."[96] This is not surprising given that Borglum's only schooling had been at Saint Mary's, a Jesuit school for boys in Kansas that he had attended after his family had renounced its Mormon roots. The article revealed that "Borglum did not stand for re-election to the Kloncilium at the last election," though he continued to be an active member. Finally, the article said that Stone Mountain officials were worried that Borglum's Catholicism would jeopardize the Klan's interest in the project. Borglum's wife, Mary, alerted him to the article and said Forrest and other Klan officials dismissed it because of the newspaper editor's Catholicism.[97] Borglum's *Who's Who* biography listed him as a Catholic until 1924, when he changed it to "Protestant of Nordic stock."[98]

Borglum's religious background was the least of his family secrets. Had the Klan known that his biological mother had married a former slave and ex–Union soldier and that the sculptor's half-sister Charlotte Pierce was a person of color, passing in Los Angeles as a white person, the organization would have severed ties with him altogether.[99] Borglum may have come from Nordic stock, but his family could not escape Du Bois's prediction that "the problem of the Twentieth Century is the problem of the color-line."[100] With his secret safe and despite the negative media attention, Borglum remained privy to the Klan's inner workings. During the summer of 1923, he served as an intermediary between warring factions of the organization.[101] One faction was led by Borglum's good friend and leader of the Indiana Klan, David C. Stephenson. To Stephenson, Borglum wrote racist and nativist screeds against blacks, Jews, and immigrants.[102] The sculptor also discovered that someone within the organization was reporting his visits to the Klan's Imperial Palace to federal officials in Washington.[103] Above all, he learned that the Klan was in turmoil and not nearly the political force he had hoped it would be.

★★★

By the summer of 1923 and unable to wait any longer for fundraising from the Klan, Borglum began carving Lee's head on Stone Mountain. He inaugurated the carving process, as he usually did, in grand style. Beginning at 10:00 a.m., people lined the streets of Atlanta for a parade. Police rode on horseback. A band sponsored by the rail and power company played. The motorcade was led by a convertible carrying Georgia governor Thomas Hardwick, Virginia governor Lee Trinkle, Borglum, Sam Venable, and of course Mrs. Plane.

Governor Trinkle, representing Lee's home state, spoke on the steps of the Atlanta capitol and then laid wreaths at Solon's sculpture of General John B. Gordon on the grounds and at the memorial of General Henry W. Grady in the heart of Atlanta.[104] The motorcade continued another eighteen miles until it almost reached the summit of Stone Mountain.[105] The main event took place 800 feet above thousands of cheering people. Borglum and the two governors ascended to the summit and then climbed down the newly repaired steps onto a wooden platform covered with American flags. Governor Trinkle, a portly man dressed in a dark suit and holding a cane, spoke to the crowd below through a megaphone and dedicated the pneumatic drill. Governor Hardwick flipped an electric switch that turned on compressed air.[106] After Trinkle handed him the drill, Borglum strapped himself into the leather harness secured by a steel cable, scaled the mountain's

Borglum carrying C. Helen Plane on January 19, 1924, General Lee's birthday, before the unveiling of Lee's head

face, and drilled the first hole in the space designated for General Lee's nose and mustache. Dressed in a white suit and a white panama hat, he looked small and insignificant on the mountain's massive face.[107]

He was so eager to begin carving General Lee that the sculptor did not wait for the arrival of a giant steel hoisting system. The drawing of the hoisting system depicted a complicated contraption—a 100-foot steel truss with a track underneath connected to an inverted steel tower, which connected to a 133-foot pantograph and a 16-by-16-foot self-leveling platform. The purpose of this swinging steel platform was to allow fifteen to twenty men to carve at one time and to allow them to scale up to 200 feet of the mountainside.[108] Borglum told an Atlanta audience that the hoisting system would allow him to complete the project in "six or seven years."[109] After having spent $2,000 to retain his friend Lester Barlow's firm to design the system, Borglum discovered that it was too costly and too complicated. Tucker continued preparation for carving. He was putting scaffolding down to the area near Lee's head, and his men began slowly removing the top layer of stone.[110] The men discovered that they preferred to drill sitting in a leather swing designed by Tucker rather than a steel cage.[111]

Atlantans were captivated by the spectacle of mountain carving. Margaret Mitchell, then a young *Atlanta Journal* reporter, strapped herself into the chair while hanging six stories down the side of a "very high" building. Mitchell survived the dizzying experience and wrote a Sunday magazine article about it titled, "Hanging Over Atlanta in Borglum's Swing." The future author of *Gone with the Wind* refused to do it again for the newspaper's photographer: "'If the fate of the whole Confederacy rested on my being hung six stories from the ground again,' I declared firmly, 'Sherman would have to make another march to the sea!'"[112]

Two or three times, Tucker was asked by members of the memorial association to slow down work on the mountain "because of funds"—meaning the lack thereof.[113] Borglum instructed them to keep going but not to remove any stone near Lee's head until he arrived. Tucker kept his men drilling elsewhere "as it seems to interest the public."[114] During the month of August, 12,534 people signed the Stone Mountain visitors' book, and an estimated 35,000 to 100,000 people visited that summer.[115]

Some tourists must have been disappointed to arrive at the mountain and to see no one working on it. In mid-August 1923, Borglum left Atlanta and ordered Tucker to stop all drilling and work on the mountain.[116] The sculptor was tired of middling fundraising efforts, of assuming all the financial and legal risks, and most of all of working without a contract. "I cannot continue alone with merely promises ...," he wrote a member of the executive committee. "We might as well be honest about these things."[117] His biggest fear was that one of his men was going to get hurt drilling on the mountain and that he would be responsible, given that he was the person who paid the wages. The memorial association's executive committee claimed that it had been trying to get Borglum to sign a contract for months.[118] Yet one of its members acknowledged to Tucker that total funds, including the Klan's fundraising efforts, amounted to $40,000.[119] The two sides agreed on a contract by early September, but the dispute revealed lingering tensions and mistrust.

Once the contract was signed, Borglum made a stunning announcement— he planned to finish the Lee head by January 19, 1924, the general's birthday. The sculptor was pleased with the progress that had been made of removing the initial layer of granite around the central group of figures.[120] He instructed Tucker not to let anything "interfere with the carving which is the big thing" and to "double up" work on the mountain.[121] In mid-October, Tucker installed lights at Stone Mountain so that ten men could carve day and night.[122] To remove the granite, they sat in leather harnesses and wielded pneumatic drills. A compressor, 6,500-pound electric motor, and 15,000-pound engine atop the mountain powered the drills. All this equipment had to be hauled up the mountain on a track with wheels. Five men worked with jackhammers to remove massive chunks of granite.[123] Though the mountain had started to get very cold at night, morale had improved among the men.[124] They installed canvas over the scaffolding near Lee's head to protect them from the wind and cold. They slept in shifts atop the mountain in two camp shacks and reached the platform by climbing down 720 feet of steps.[125] Tucker had plotted a rough image of Lee's head on the mountain in ten-foot squares. He and his men continued to stay away from Lee's head, but the superintendent believed that the mountain was almost ready for Borglum to begin carving.[126]

While Tucker and his men worked around the clock removing large granite blocks from the mountain, Borglum was holed up in his Stamford, Connecticut, studio building a life-size model of Lee's head and the rest of the central group.[127] Borglum intended this to be his master model, the one from which his assistants could make plaster models, scaling up the central figures to one-quarter the size of the mountain sculpture. The top of Lee's head to the knee of his horse, *Traveller*, was 120 feet. The plaster models, therefore, would be 30 feet high.[128] The sculptor shipped his models to his newly enlarged studio at the base of the mountain, and in December he and several of his assistants began carving out the details of Lee's head.[129]

Strapped into a leather harness, Borglum stood next to Lee's nose, his foot wedged into a ledge on Lee's mustache, and instructed his assistants on the details of the carving. They quickly carved Lee's eye and nose; the general's profile was beginning to take shape.[130] Borglum worked alongside his men day and night. They stood most of the time on a small wooden ledge and used their pneumatic drills with impressive precision. The head was so big that while Borglum worked on carving Lee's lower eyelid he could not even reach the upper lid. They worked for three weeks straight in order to have it ready for the January 19 unveiling on Lee's 117th birthday. "Don't worry—," Borglum told the press, "the head will be finished."[131] He was at peace while on the mountainside with his men. "There is something else at work in that granite besides myself and the drillers and stone cutters," he said. "I don't know what it is, but I know it is there. I feel it. My men feel it. The face of Lee up there on the mountain is going to represent something more than I have put into it."[132]

No one could unveil a monument better than Borglum. Southern governors past and present and representatives from the US military had arrived.[133] The day before the unveiling, Borglum and his wife hosted a select group for lunch high up on the mountain on Lee's shoulder.[134] On the morning of Lee's birthday, cars jammed the wet roads from Atlanta to Stone Mountain and created a backup a mile long. Memorial association officials borrowed 200 cars for the dignitaries alone. The streetcar company ran special trains from Atlanta. Some people walked there from surrounding areas. Many of those stuck in traffic never made it in time for the 2:30 p.m. unveiling.[135] Rabbi David Marx gave the invocation to an estimated 10,000 to 20,000 people who stood 1,500 feet away from the base of the mountain in the drizzling rain. Some waved Confederate flags, others wore the Confederacy's old gray uniforms, and all of them waited for the sight of their beloved general.[136]

The honor of unveiling Lee's head was reserved for the driving force behind the memorial, ninety-four-year-old Confederate widow C. Helen Plane. When she had met Borglum in 1914, she had refused to shake his hand because his northern relatives might have killed her surgeon husband at Antietam. Nearly ten years later on Lee's birthday, she allowed Borglum to carry her from a limousine up the stairs to a chair on the platform.[137] Someone held an umbrella over her head. The petite southern lady, dressed in a black fur hat and a black fur coat and carrying a bouquet of flowers, managed to maintain her dignity on the day that her dreams came true. With Plane sitting on the platform, Borglum waved a white handkerchief, and his men on the mountainside dislodged some large boulders that came rumbling down. Now it was Plane's turn. She waved a small Confederate flag over her head, and Borglum's men pulled up the folds of two huge American flags and revealed Lee's hatband and profile in white granite on the dark gray surface of the mountain.[138] A hush fell over the crowd. A wave of applause began and soon exploded into a roar. Borglum was speechless. He finally managed to say: "The head of Lee is on Stone Mountain!"[139] It took a few days for Borglum to put the whole experience into words. He realized that he had been too close to the work in those final frenetic weeks. He was, he said, "amazed as I looked at it" because the head was "perfect in scale on the great wall of granite. ... It is twenty-one feet from his chin to the top of his head and yet it looks like a normal head. We stood fifteen hundred feet away from it and although the day was mild and gray and therefore without the aid of light and shade of the sun, each part of the face took its place and I was very very happy."[140]

Borglum did what people said could not be done. He had employed the latest technology to overcome the challenges of carving a mountain. He had drilled for the ages a hero of the Confederacy into the side of Stone Mountain and in the process had kept his promise to an old Confederate widow. He still needed more money and another two to three years to finish the central group and perhaps another ten years for the entire project. With the Klan proving to be more a curse than a blessing, Borglum began to call on his friends in the federal government to help him finish the job.

19

We Live by Symbols

For much of the spring and early summer of 1921, Lippmann canceled his social engagements and kept correspondence to a minimum, holing himself up at his home on Wading River, Long Island, in order to finish his biggest and most important book yet, *Public Opinion*. He had been thinking about writing a book on public opinion for nearly five years. His unhappy experiences with the Inquiry and overseas propaganda, his disillusionment with the peace conference, and his outrage over wartime censorship and postwar abridgment of civil liberties drove his efforts, as did his desire to finish it before he started as an editorial writer at the New York *World*. Published in March 1922, *Public Opinion* argued that people lack access to facts on the ground because of censorship, propaganda, and "stereotypes" (a word he coined) and therefore form their opinions based on "fictions" and "symbols"—what he referred to as the "pictures in our heads." Like many former progressives, Lippmann believed in the importance of experts. He called on the political science community to investigate the facts and to inform public opinion. The biggest problem facing American democracy, both in politics and in industry, was that "the pictures inside people's heads do not automatically correspond with the world outside."[1] Two decades before Lippmann wrote about "pictures in our heads," Holmes had spoken from the bench of the Supreme Judicial Court of Massachusetts on the 100th anniversary of Chief Justice John Marshall's first day on the Supreme Court of the United States. Addressing Marshall's place atop the pantheon of American jurists, Holmes had seized on a similar idea. "We live by symbols," he said, "and what shall be symbolized by any image of the sight depends upon the mind of him who sees it."[2] After seeing excerpts in the *New Republic*, Holmes could not wait to read *Public Opinion*. When he did, he praised it not because of the originality of Lippmann's ideas or the novelty of his solutions but because of what he called Lippmann's "intimate perception of the subtleties of the human mind and of human relations."[3] Holmes told a friend that the book was "really extraordinary" and that Lippmann was one of the "few living I think who so discern and articulate the nuances of the human mind."[4]

Frankfurter was also one of *Public Opinion*'s great admirers. Lippmann had read portions of it to the Frankfurters during a weekend at their summer residence in Hadlyme, Connecticut. After its publication, they read the entire book together. Frankfurter agreed with Holmes's emphasis on the centrality of symbols and on one in particular.

Together—Frankfurter in the pages of the *New Republic* and *Harvard Law Review* and Lippmann in the New York *World* editorial page and elsewhere—they used their respective platforms to create a symbol or picture in people's heads of Justice Holmes as the judicial face of American liberalism. In their view, after the world war Holmes exemplified liberalism's ideal role for the Court in modern America: upholding laws that protected

Lippmann (seated center) with the New York *World* editorial page staff

workers and addressed the problems of industrialization while protecting people's rights to free speech and fair criminal trials.

Though he increasingly came to see the importance of the courts in protecting individual rights, Frankfurter would have preferred that the Constitution did not contain a due process clause. Like Holmes, he believed that some of the other justices used it to trump the democratic political process in the name of economic liberty. In 1921, Holmes wrote a 5–4 decision upholding the Washington, DC, postwar rent control law.[5] The four justices who voted to strike down the law, based on their reading "liberty of contract" into due process, troubled Frankfurter. "It was a close shave, wasn't it?" he wrote Holmes after reading about the decision in the *Boston Evening Transcript.* "All of which makes me wonder more and more and about the 'due process' clause." A hypothetical Court consisting of Holmes, Brandeis, Learned Hand, and Benjamin Cardozo would invoke the clause more sparingly, but Frankfurter refused to entrust the current or future justices with this much power. Relying on the Court to solve all the nation's problems, he argued, resulted in "the weakening of the responsibility of our legislators and of our public opinion, or rather, the failure to build up a responsible public opinion. We expect our Courts to do it all."[6]

By 1922, Frankfurter was using Holmes to attack an increasingly conservative Court. In July 1921, President Harding had replaced Chief Justice White with ex-president William Howard Taft. Taft was no reactionary and, according to both Holmes and Brandeis, a much better chief justice than president.[7] Yet Frankfurter and his friends could not erase their image of Taft circa 1911 to 1913 as a lazy and incompetent chief executive. Their relations did not improve after Taft had left office. In 1916, Taft had opposed Brandeis's Supreme Court nomination. Two years later, Taft and Frankfurter had clashed over wartime labor policy.[8] "I never liked Frankfurter," Taft wrote Elihu Root in 1922, "and have continued to dislike him more the more I have known him. Indeed the only thing I know against Stimson is his good opinion of Frankfurter."[9]

Already one of the Court's chief critics, Frankfurter became more vigilant after Taft joined the Court. When Taft's nomination as chief justice received nearly "universal acclaim," Frankfurter reminded the *New Republic's* readers how much Taft resented criticism of the Court. Frankfurter, on the other hand, believed the Court's "social control allowed the states under the fourteenth amendment" was fair game because "the only safeguard

against the terrible powers vested in the Supreme Court" lay in "continu-
ous, informed, and responsible criticism."[10]

Taft's first major opinion about organized labor confirmed Frankfurter's
fears. Cooks and waiters from the English Kitchen restaurant in the copper-
mining town of Bisbee, Arizona, went on strike and picketed the restaurant
because its owner, William Truax Sr., one of the town's most powerful men,
had cut their pay and increased their hours. Truax sought a court order
to stop the strikers from picketing because it interfered with his property
rights—his restaurant business. An Arizona law, however, prohibited "labor
injunctions." After the Arizona Supreme Court upheld the statute, Truax
appealed to the US Supreme Court. Taft's opinion in *Truax v. Corrigan* declared the Arizona law unconstitutional because it violated Truax's right
to property under the Fourteenth Amendment's Due Process Clause.[11] Taft
also concluded that the Arizona law violated the Fourteenth Amendment's
Equal Protection Clause because the law favored former employees over
employers.[12]

In an unsigned *New Republic* editorial, "The Same Mr. Taft," Frankfurter
criticized the chief justice's opinion because it "deals with abstractions and

President Harding (left) and Taft (right)

not with the work-a-day world, its men and its struggles." The decision "justified the worst fears" about Taft, making clear that he would read his personal views "in the most sensitive field of social policy and legal control."[13] As proof, Frankfurter quoted the first few lines of Holmes's dissent about "[t]he dangers of a delusive exactness in the application of the Fourteenth Amendment" and "a source of fallacy throughout the law." The fallacy, according to Holmes, was equating the loss of business revenue with property and "the use of the Fourteenth Amendment beyond the absolute compulsion of its words to prevent the making of social experiments that an important part of the community desires."[14]

Two other Taft opinions from 1922 prompted additional comments, if slightly less criticism. First, a unanimous Court held that the United Mine Workers could be sued under the antitrust laws but could not be held liable based on the evidence in that particular case.[15] Frankfurter wrote a bylined *New Republic* article explaining the ramification of decisions on organized labor but without his usually harsh rhetoric.[16] Second, eight justices struck down a second attempt at a federal child labor law. In 1918, the Court had invalidated the first child labor law, over Holmes's dissent, as an unconstitutional exercise of Congress's power to regulate interstate commerce because manufacturing was a purely local activity. Congress repassed the law as a tax because it generally had broad discretion over taxing power. The Court, however, struck it down because the law's purpose was the same—to interfere with the states' rights whether or not to regulate child labor.[17] In the second case, neither Holmes nor Brandeis dissented. Frankfurter did not disagree, either. In another bylined *New Republic* article, he wrote: "We must pay a price for Federalism."[18] In Frankfurter's mind, Taft, in his opinion about the Arizona law in *Truax v. Corrigan*, was not willing to pay that price. The case raised larger concerns for Frankfurter about whether the Court would use the Fourteenth Amendment to turn American democracy into a government by judiciary and, if so, how that power could be checked. The justices, he argued, should be held accountable to the people during the Senate confirmation process: "Surely the men who wield this power of life and death over legislation should be subjected to the most vigorous scrutiny before being given that power."[19]

Though he would have preferred to write the Due Process Clause out of the Constitution as a way of curbing judicial power, Frankfurter refused to support proposed constitutional amendments to the Fourteenth Amendment, to protect child labor, or to recognize equal rights for women.

He believed that the slim chances of ratification and the lengthy amendment process stifled the push for new laws. Repealing the Due Process Clause was neither feasible nor effective. As Brandeis told Frankfurter during their private conversations about the Court, the other justices would find another clause in the Constitution to strike down laws in the name of contractual freedom.[20] Instead, Frankfurter preferred Holmes's democratic solution that the Fourteenth Amendment should not be invoked "'beyond the absolute compulsion of its words to prevent the making of social experiments.'"[21]

The Supreme Court's antilabor decisions provoked radical proposals to curb judicial power. Senator La Follette of Wisconsin attacked Chief Justice Taft and the Supreme Court as "the actual ruler of the American people" in a June 14, 1922, speech at the AFL convention in Taft's hometown of Cincinnati.[22] La Follette proposed a constitutional amendment that prevented lower federal courts from voiding a federal law and that granted Congress the power to nullify a Supreme Court decision by re-enacting the statute.[23] His comments prompted a national debate about the role of the judiciary. Frankfurter sympathized with La Follette's ends of curbing judicial power but not the means. Instead of endorsing the proposed amendments, Frankfurter continued to attack the Court by building up Holmes's liberal reputation.

There was one problem with the strategy—Holmes was eighty-one, the fourth-oldest justice ever to sit on the Court at that point. A health scare made his days on the Court seem numbered. In early June, he took a hot, jolting train back to Boston.[24] He was spotted on Boston's State Street looking "remarkably well for a man of his years," yet he did not feel like himself.[25] He was preparing to accept an honorary degree at Amherst, to celebrate his fiftieth wedding anniversary, and to spend the summer at his home in Beverly Farms. The press knew that something was amiss when he did not attend Amherst's graduation ceremonies to receive his honorary degree. His doctors determined that he needed prostate surgery. Though they gave him a nine out of ten chance of survival, Holmes at least deemed the operation "serious."[26] His doctors performed two operations, a minor one to insert a catheter on June 27 and a major one on July 12 at Brookline's Corey Hill Hospital.[27] Frankfurter received updates from Brandeis, learning that the second operation had been successful. " I continue to hear good reports about Holmes—thus far all is going well," Frankfurter wrote Lippmann. " It looks as tho he again cheated the surgeons—LDB says as he did sixty years ago."[28] September 17, as Holmes liked to remind people, marked the sixtieth anniversary of his being wounded at Antietam. After nearly a month in the hospital reading detective stories and writing short letters in pencil, he returned to Beverly Farms, yet was still so weak and unsteady that his doctor sent him straight to bed. Though he hoped to live to see ninety, he said he felt like a "feeble old man."[29] Nonetheless, when people mentioned that he might think about retiring, he would have none of it.[30] " I do hope to turn up in Washington as if nothing had happened," he wrote.[31] Yet the whole episode shook him, making him feel "so little confidence in the future."[32]

Holmes returned to a much different Court.[33] On September 1, Justice John Hessin Clarke resigned. Wilson's third and final nominee to the Court, Clarke was supposed to lead the liberal wing along with Brandeis but never warmed to the job. He clashed with Wilson's racist and reactionary first nominee, McReynolds, and found himself "agreeing less & less frequently" with Brandeis about "liberal principles."[34] Clarke stood out as the staunchest defender of the Wilson administration—writing the majority opinion that affirmed Jacob Abrams's Espionage Act conviction and the lone dissent when the Court invalidated the second attempt at a federal child labor law. His replacement was former senator George Sutherland of Utah, a staunch conservative. With Taft lobbying for colleagues like Sutherland, Harding was able to transform the Court into a far more conservative institution in a short period of time.[35] The retirements of several other aging justices were imminent.

Liberals therefore needed more than ever for Holmes to stay on the Court. He left Beverly Farms on September 26 for Boston and then proceeded to Washington.[36] His first few months were not restful. He and Mrs. Holmes stayed in a ninth-floor suite at the Powhatan Hotel for a month while an elevator was installed from the first to second floor at 1720 Eye Street. The construction scattered the books in Holmes's library, forcing him to work out of a hotel at a time when the justices worked out of their homes.[37] Holmes felt "weak in the joints" and walked slowly and somewhat unsteadily.[38]

Not all of Holmes's decisions, moreover, pleased Frankfurter and his liberal friends. On December 11, 1922, the Court invalidated a Pennsylvania law banning mining beneath people's homes. Holmes authored the Court's 5–4 majority opinion declaring the law violated the Fourteenth Amendment right to property. He argued that the law deprived the mining company of subterranean rights to the land, rights that it legitimately owned.[39] Brandeis dissented and sided with the homeowners, even though they owned only surface rights to the land.[40] Privately, he blamed Holmes's opinion on his postsurgery fatigue and on his secretary Robert Benjamin for "accentuating the tendency of age to conservatism."[41] After a month of silence from Frankfurter, Holmes knew that his liberal cheering section was not pleased.[42] A *New Republic* editorial ghostwritten by former Brandeis secretary and Frankfurter protégé Dean Acheson pitted Holmes's "tolerant skepticism" and belief that the homeowners were trying to "get something for nothing" against Brandeis's belief in "the power of the community to protect itself" and concluded that "Brandeis's view seems the superior statesmanship."[43]

His decision on the Pennsylvania law notwithstanding, Holmes's liberal coronation continued in the *New Republic*. The magazine noted that December 8, 1922, marked his twentieth anniversary on the Supreme Court and that December 15, 1922, was his fortieth anniversary on the bench. An unsigned editorial, "Mr. Justice Holmes," quoted "We live by symbols" and proclaimed that Holmes's opinions were "the symbol at once of the promise and the fulfillment of the American judiciary."[44] The editorial argued that his dissents were among "some of his greatest utterances." It mentioned in particular his 1918 dissent in the first child labor case about the scope of federal power and his 1922 dissent in the Arizona anti-injunction case as a warning against the misuse of the Fourteenth Amendment to eviscerate state power. "Behind the sceptic is invincible faith …," the editorial concluded. "And ours still the glory of his labor, still ours the music of his dream."[45] As Holmes suspected, the prose belonged to Frankfurter. A "deeply moved" Holmes confessed his fears of getting old to Frankfurter: "The terror is not only that one may fall down but that when people go to the top of the hill, the next stop seems to come down again."[46] Holmes was improving physically and by 1923 was mentally sharper. Taft, for one, described him as a "delight," observing that his mind seemed sharp and that he remained "the life of the Court."[47]

Whether or not he was the life of the Court, Holmes was one of its few constants. At the end of 1922, two of his septuagenarian colleagues, Mahlon Pitney and William R. Day, retired within a matter of weeks. Pitney and Day both had occasionally voted with the more liberal bloc; both justices had joined Holmes's 5–4 DC rent control decision. With Taft's endorsement, Harding nominated federal appeals court judge Pierce Butler to replace Day and federal trial judge Edward Terry Sanford of Tennessee to replace Pitney. Butler, a Minnesota Catholic and

noted railroad lawyer, was a lightning rod for opposition. The Ku Klux
Klan opposed him because he was Catholic. Liberals opposed Butler as
antilabor and because of his role as a member of the Board of Regents in
ousting "radical" or "disloyal" University of Minnesota professors.[48] The
New Republic described Butler as "a reactionary of the most pronounced
type"; *The Nation* labeled him a "friend of intolerance."[49] Rumors flew
that Frankfurter and his friend Max Lowenthal would testify against
Butler before the Senate Judiciary Committee. Frankfurter, however,
refused to testify; he had taught Butler's son at Harvard and remained
close to him.[50] Both Butler and Sanford were easily confirmed, giving
Harding a total of four Supreme Court nominees in three years. Though
his short presidency is associated with scandal and corruption, Harding's
most enduring legacy may be his impact on the future of the Supreme
Court.

Frankfurter walked straight into the teeth of this more conservative
Court. He continued to believe that state laws, not pie-in-the-sky constitutional amendments, were the best ways to protect the rights of women
and children workers. He continued to work for the National Consumers'
League, drafting model minimum wage legislation and defending the laws
in court. In 1921, he defended the Washington, DC, minimum wage law for
women and children before the D.C. Court of Appeals. Children's Hospital
as well as a hotel operator earning thirty-five dollars a month challenged
the minimum wage law for women.[51] Jesse Adkins, the chairman of the DC
Minimum Wage Board, had worked with Frankfurter and the late Winfred
Denison when they had been federal prosecutors in lower Manhattan
and Adkins had been in the Justice Department.[52] A few years later in
Washington, they continued to work together, and Adkins had frequented
the House of Truth (where his rugs were part of the house's furnishings).[53]
Frankfurter did not defend the case out of friendship and fond memories.
If the DC law were declared unconstitutional, he knew, all state minimum
wages would be imperiled.

The first time he defended the law before a three-judge panel in February
1921, Frankfurter won the case on appeal. Adkins congratulated Frankfurter
on the victory but spoke too soon.[54] One of the two judges who had voted
in Frankfurter's favor was a trial judge sitting in place of an appellate judge
who had been ill. The D.C. Court of Appeals granted reargument and replaced the trial judge with the absent appellate judge.[55] Frankfurter considered the court's decision to change judges in rehearing the case "nothing

short of scandal."[56] The second time, thanks to the new judge, he lost and was forced to appeal to the Supreme Court.

Frankfurter thought that there was no question about the constitutionality of minimum wage laws for women and children. *Lochner*, the 1905 case that had struck down the New York maximum hour law for bakers based on "liberty of contract" in the Due Process Clause, was presumed dead.[57] Three years later, Brandeis had defended the Oregon maximum hour law for women.[58] And in 1916 and 1917, Frankfurter had successfully defended Oregon's minimum wage law for women and children and maximum hour laws for industrial workers.[59] In December 1921, the Court, in a 5–4 Holmes decision, had rejected a due process challenge to a Washington, DC, rent control statute.[60] Nonetheless, with all state minimum wage laws at stake, Frankfurter was not taking any chances. He submitted a brief from the National Consumers' League, similar to one that he and Brandeis had used in the Oregon cases, which was more than a thousand pages long. He solicited help with the new facts and unusual procedure from the League's staff as well as from his protégé Dean Acheson, who after two years as Brandeis's secretary was an associate at Covington & Burling.[61]

The Court that Frankfurter argued before on March 15, 1923, was much different than the one he had appeared before six years earlier. Clarke was gone. Day and Pitney, two possible votes at least based on their positions in the DC rent control case, were gone, too. And Brandeis recused himself not because of the work he had done for the National Consumers' League from 1908 to 1916 or because he was once again funding Frankfurter's pro bono activities but because his daughter Elizabeth worked as Adkins's personal secretary at the DC Minimum Wage Board.[62] Without Brandeis, Holmes looked like Frankfurter's only sure vote.

The day before the argument, Frankfurter visited the justice at 1720 Eye Street and "had one of the very best talks we ever had—he took me with both his hands, his eyes all afire" when they said good-bye.[63] The argument weighed on Frankfurter's mind—and with good reason. The justices, he knew, would not be a receptive audience. And they were not. "Saw the Court today—and wish I had a cocktail before I spoke to them," he reported. "With exception of Holmes & L.D.B., what a sight!! But—I'm still confident for I'll land Taft & he is key to Court."[64]

Though Frankfurter impressed neutral observers with his "very able argument," he could not overcome the Court's more conservative personnel.[65] Less than a month later, he learned that he had lost the case, *Adkins v. Children's Hospital*, 5–3, and that *Lochner's* liberty of contract was alive and stronger than ever. Usually a state or federal law is entitled to a presumption of constitutionality. Writing for the five-justice majority, Justice Sutherland turned "freedom of contract" into "the general rule and restraint the exception."[66]

Harding's nominees had made a difference on both sides. Frankfurter did in fact win the key vote of Taft, who wrote a dissent that fellow Harding nominee Sanford joined. Taft believed, as Frankfurter did, that the Oregon cases in 1908 and 1917 had implicitly overruled *Lochner's* liberty of contract. Though the chief justice did not like to dissent, he was even more loath to depart from the Court's prior decisions.[67] He also was worried about the rising tide of criticism against him and the Court and the calls for judicial reform.[68]

The last dissent announced on April 9 was from Holmes. He pointed out that every law interferes with economic liberty, including those that the Court had upheld such as Sunday laws and usury laws. He could not understand how maximum hour laws could be constitutional when minimum wage laws were not. He charged the majority with reading the word "contract," as well as their personal preferences, into the liberty provision of the Due Process Clause. "The criterion of constitutionality is not whether we believe the law to be for the public good," Holmes wrote and confessed his own doubts about the efficacy of the law. Yet he insisted that the law's costs and benefits were "not for me to decide."[69]

Holmes seemed not to care that Taft and Sanford both refused to join his dissent and instead challenged the liberty of contract crowd to pay the same attention to liberty of free speech. "The C.J. [Taft] and Sanford seemed to think I said something dangerous or too broad so they dissented separately …," Holmes wrote Laski. "It was intended *inter alia* to dethrone Liberty of Contract from its ascendancy in the Liberty business. I am curious to see what the enthusiasts for liberty of contract will say with regard to liberty of speech under a State law punishing advocating the overthrow of government—by violence."[70] Brandeis read a draft of Holmes's dissent and declared: "It ought to make converts."[71] After reading it in published form, Laski replied: "If I were Frankfurter I should rest content that I had secured that dissent from you. … Please go on dissenting."[72] Holmes tried to console Frankfurter that "no one could have brought about a different decision."[73]

Frankfurter, however, never argued another case before the Supreme Court. Everything that he, Pound, Brandeis, and other liberal lawyers had been doing to chip away at the *Lochner* decision and liberty of contract and to pass labor laws state by state seemed to have been lost. Sutherland's opinion, Frankfurter recalled, "struck the death knell not only of this legislation, but of kindred social legislation because it laid down as a constitutional principle that any kind of change by statute has to justify itself, not the other way around."[74] Most of all, Frankfurter questioned his faith in the Court as an institution: "[T]he possible gain isn't worth the cost of having five men without any reasonable probability that they are qualified for the task, determine the course of social policy for the states and the nation."[75]

Even when he believed that the state law was illiberal or detestable, Frankfurter believed that the Court should not invoke the Due Process Clause's liberty provision to invalidate it. For example, the Court nullified a Nebraska law that had banned the teaching of foreign languages to public and private school students who had not reached the eighth grade.[76] Holmes noted his dissent in that case and wrote a short dissent in a companion case about a similar Iowa law because it was "reasonable" to force students to speak English at school.[77] Based on his belief that the Court was undermining the democratic political process, Frankfurter would have joined Holmes's dissent. "Of course, I regard such know-nothing legislation as uncivilized, but for the life of me," Frankfurter wrote Learned Hand, "I can't see how it meets the condemnation of want of 'due process' unless we frankly recognize that the Supreme Court of the United States is the revisory legislative body." Frankfurter's concern was that legislatures would have no incentive to legislate, and that people would have no incentive to elect better legislators. The result would be a government by judiciary. "The more I think about this whole 'due process' business," he wrote, "the less I think of lodging that power in those nine gents at Washington."[78]

Though deeply skeptical of judicial power because the justices were using the Due Process Clause to read their social and economic views into the Constitution, Frankfurter and other liberals soon adopted Holmes's belief that the clause should be invoked in two categories of cases: those involving the protection of free speech and fair criminal trials. During the Red Scare and the Red Summer of racial violence, the government had run roughshod over the right to free speech of radicals like Jacob Abrams and the right to a fair trial of southern blacks and other unpopular minorities. In both instances, Holmes showed his liberal friends when to limit governmental power and the role that the judiciary could play in protecting minority rights.

A month before the Court decided *Adkins*, Holmes had given hope to Frank Moore and four black farmers sentenced to death for the 1919 murder of a white railroad agent during the sharecroppers' union meeting that sparked the Elaine Riots in Phillips County, Arkansas. The NAACP took the cases on appeal. The state supreme court reversed six of the death sentences. NAACP president Moorfield Storey and another lawyer argued Moore's case before the Supreme Court of the United States.

Writing on behalf of six justices in *Moore v. Dempsey*, Holmes laid out the allegations that Moore's trial had been a mob-dominated sham. The defendants' preferred trial lawyer had been run out of town. A lynch mob had been quelled based on assurances that the defendants would be found guilty and electrocuted. Defendants had been whipped, beaten, and tortured into testifying against each other. Court-appointed counsel had not been permitted to speak with the defendants before the trial, had not called any witnesses on their behalf, and had not asked for a delay or change of venue. The trial had lasted about forty-five minutes; the all-white jury had deliberated for five. "[N]o juryman," Holmes wrote, "could have voted for an acquittal and continued to live [in] Phillips County and if any prisoner by any chance had been acquitted by a jury he could not have escaped the mob."[79]

Holmes distinguished *Moore v. Dempsey* from his dissent eight years earlier in *Frank v. Mangum* when his colleagues upheld the murder conviction of Atlanta pencil factory manager Leo Frank. Holmes conceded that the Supreme Court does not correct "mere mistakes of law" made during a criminal trial; it was a different story when "the whole proceeding is a mask—that counsel, jury and judge were swept to the fatal end by an irresistible wave of public passion, and that the State Courts failed to correct the wrong." If Moore's criminal trial had been so mob-dominated as to be a sham, Holmes argued, nothing could "prevent this Court from securing to the petitioners their constitutional rights."[80]

In a lengthy dissent, McReynolds decried Holmes's departure from the Court's *Leo Frank* decision and declared that the use of the federal courts to delay criminal punishment was "a national scandal."[81] McReynolds, joined by Sutherland, objected to second-guessing the "solemn adjudications by courts of a great state" based on sworn declarations "of interested convicts joined by two white men—confessedly atrocious criminals. The fact that petitioners are poor and ignorant and black naturally arouses sympathy; but that does not release us from enforcing principles which are essential to the orderly operation of our federal system."[82]

Though Holmes remanded the case to the federal district court for a hearing on the allegations about the sham trials, the governor of Arkansas intervened, commuting all the death sentences to twelve years in prison. By January 1925, the last of the men had been released.[83] Holmes's majority opinion in *Moore v. Dempsey* had saved the men's lives, established that mob-dominated trials violated the Due Process Clause, and marked the first time a majority of the Supreme Court had interfered with a state criminal trial on due process grounds.

What Holmes had shown Frankfurter and his friends was that they could use the Court to pursue their agenda. Liberal publications cheered Holmes's decision to protect blacks from unfair criminal trials. "It is a fine thing to have one's faith in the courts restored," *The Nation* wrote of *Moore v. Dempsey* and two state supreme court decisions reversing the criminal convictions of members of the IWW.[84] *Outlook* declared that *Moore v. Dempsey* was "one of the greatest cases in American legal procedure that has received little notice in the press of the country."[85] The *New Republic* noticed. The magazine re-printed large sections of Holmes's opinion and then noted that, if the facts were true, "[i]t would be hard to imagine a situation which was more clearly within the scope of the Fourteenth Amendment, born in the reconstruction period, than this judicial murder of five Negroes by an enraged white population." With no federal antilynching law on the books, the magazine saw Holmes's decision in *Moore v. Dempsey* as the best hope of protecting black defendants: "By stating what the Fourteenth Amendment requires, he has written an opinion which will rank with those in which he has stated what it does not require."[86]

The timing of Holmes's opinion could not have been better, particularly in light of proposals to curb the Court's power, proposals that Frankfurter dismissed as either hopeless or pointless. He told the National Consumers' League that constitutional amendments about child labor, equal rights of women, or minimum wage laws had no chance of ratification.[87] He wrote that the bills proposed by Senator La Follette and Senator William Borah of Idaho to require a 7–2 or 6–3 vote to overturn a federal law had little chance of passage and "at the rate which the Sutherlands and Butlers are being appointed to the Court, it wouldn't do any good if it did."[88]

Ever practical, Frankfurter called a minimum wage conference on April 20, 1923, with an eye toward salvaging existing laws in other states. He wanted to continue to enforce the DC law and state laws about children because *Adkins* did not address that portion of the law. He also wanted to amend the DC and state minimum wage laws to change from mandatory enforcement to enforcement by publicity, as in the Massachusetts law.[89] His goal was to establish a livable minimum wage without incurring the Court's wrath: "We have got to be practical and fight inch by inch, while we do the larger thing."[90]

Finally, Frankfurter had decided that he would change the Court's mind by commissioning economic studies about the assumptions that Sutherland had made in his *Adkins* opinion. "The heart of the difficulty was that the Supreme Court assumed certain things to be facts which are not facts," he said. He blamed the justices for having outdated pictures in their heads: " I am sure if you could get an intellectual X-ray of Sutherland and Pierce Butler's minds and [Mc]Reynolds, you would find an [antiquated] notion of American society."[91] Like Pound and other liberal lawyers, he believed in educating the bench and bar, informing public opinion, limiting the Due Process Clause to procedural matters, and electing a president who, in Pound's words, would appoint "a type of man upon the Supreme Court who will administer constitutional provisions in a more enlightened fashion."[92]

Until liberals were appointed to the Court, Frankfurter's main strategy was to promote Holmes as the model of what a justice should be. Frankfurter had been waiting to publish a law review article, "Twenty Years of Mr. Justice Holmes' Constitutional Opinions," until after the Court decided the minimum wage case in *Adkins*.[93] In June 1923, he published it in the *Harvard Law Review* along with an appendix listing more than 500 of Holmes's constitutional opinions organized into thirteen categories.[94] The first half of the article read like a rebuttal to the Court's decision in *Adkins*. Frankfurter outlined the proper theory of judicial review based on Cardozo's book of lectures, *The Nature of the Judicial Process*, Charles Warren's three-volume history of the Supreme Court, and private conversations with Brandeis.[95] The Court, Frankfurter argued, had been most destructive in interpreting due process and equal protection because the vagueness of those clauses forced each justice to rely on the picture inside his head, a picture, according to Frankfurter, "bound to be determined by his experience, environment, imagination, his hopes and fears,—his 'idealized political picture of the existing social order.'"[96] For Frankfurter, this raised a larger concern: " Should such power, affecting the intimate life of Nation and States, be entrusted, ultimately, to five men?"[97] Short of repealing the Due Process

Clause, Frankfurter urged a more vigilant process of selecting justices. Based on his review of history, they would be neither liberal nor conservative but rich in life experiences.[98] Holmes, Frankfurter argued, was "the great exception."[99] He had transcended the idea of judge as philosopher-king and viewed the Constitution not as a revered document but as a practical guide for governing the country. "He has found the Constitution equal to the needs of a great Nation at war," Frankfurter wrote. "But according to the same Constitution the individual must not be sacrificed to the Moloch of fear. To be sure, some of his weightiest utterances applying these views are merely dissenting opinions—but they are dissents that shape history and record prophecy."[100] Frankfurter then quoted from some of the justice's opinions from the past twenty years to show why the rest of the Court had a lot to learn from his opinions: "The Supreme Court, like all human institutions, must earn reverence through the test of truth. He has built himself into the structure of our national life. He has written himself into the slender volume of the literature of all times."[101]

This portrait of Holmes was beginning to reach a national audience. His House of Truth friends played a role. In 1923, one of Frankfurter's former students, the aspiring poet Archibald MacLeish, began writing the education column at a new national magazine known as *Time*.[102] MacLeish most likely turned his new employer on to Frankfurter's article about Holmes. Beneath the headline "Honor to Justice Holmes," a one-paragraph notice in *Time*'s July 16 issue mentioned Frankfurter's article (though not his name) and marked the beginning of a national trend.[103] The *New Republic* echoed that Frankfurter's tribute to Holmes should be "read not only by lawyers, who would presumably be technically interested in its contents, but by laymen to whom the traditional American system of law and government is a cherished inheritance."[104]

Though not mentioned in this coverage, Frankfurter emerged in 1922 as one of the Court's chief critics. He was one of Harvard Law School's brightest stars, had served in three presidential administrations, had argued several big cases before the Supreme Court, and wrote for multiple magazines and newspapers. Most of all, he used his unparalleled access to the secret world of the Court. This was partly because each year he sent top Harvard law students to work as secretaries for Holmes and Brandeis, and these young men served as Frankfurter's eyes and ears. But Frankfurter's real access was due to his friendship with Brandeis. They had become even closer after their European sojourn on behalf of Zionism. The Frankfurters spent the

summers of 1922 and 1923 with the Brandeises at their Chatham home.[105]
Through Brandeis, Frankfurter gained access to the latest US Supreme
Court Reports and the freshest gossip.[106] Through Brandeis, Frankfurter
kept tabs on Holmes and the dynamics among the other seven justices.

No one knew more about how the Taft Court operated than Frankfurter,
and no one, including Lippmann, would dare challenge that. Politics, however, was another story. Their differing reactions to two events in particular
revealed their diverging conceptions of liberalism, as well as their fraying
friendship. Part of the problem was one of temperament. Lippmann preferred praise to conflict and argument. Frankfurter was an expert flatterer,
but he also loved debate—so much so that he never seemed to want to end a
discussion. After Lippmann moved from the weekly *New Republic* to the daily
New York *World*, this proved problematic, for Frankfurter offered a constant
stream of comments, favorable and unfavorable, about the paper's editorials.

Their first major disagreement was over Harvard College's proposed
quota for Jewish students. During the mid-1920s, anti-Semitism in America
was rampant, as evidenced by the political ascendancy of the Ku Klux Klan,
as well as by Henry Ford's anti-Semitic newspaper the *Dearborn Independent*
and its republication of the *Protocols of the Elders of Zion* alleging international
Jewish banking conspiracies. It had also reached the gates of Harvard Yard.
Frankfurter had pegged Lowell as an anti-Semite ever since the Harvard
president had led Old Boston's opposition to Brandeis's Supreme Court
nomination. Six years later, Lowell proposed capping the number of Jewish
students at Harvard College at 15 percent. A committee was established to
examine "principles and methods for more effective sifting of candidates for
admission."[107] Lowell appointed thirteen faculty members to the committee, including three Jews, but not Frankfurter.[108]

There was no love lost between Frankfurter and Lowell. In 1916,
Frankfurter and Lippmann had humiliated the Harvard president in the
New Republic by exposing his anti-Brandeis alliance with Old Boston, as
well as by receiving a Brandeis endorsement from Lowell's beloved predecessor, Charles W. Eliot. Frankfurter, moreover, had known of Lowell's
suspicion that his wartime public service was a cover for Zionist activities.
He did not stand up for Frankfurter during delays in his promotion to the
Byrne Professor of Administrative Law. It must be said that Lowell had been
a staunch defender of academic freedom, serving as Chafee's advocate during
his trial at the Harvard Club. Yet Frankfurter's outside work irritated Lowell
because of what he deemed its "unfortunate effect upon the School."[109] In

1920, Frankfurter and Chafee had represented immigrants facing deportation in Boston federal court and, along with Pound and others, had challenged the legality of the Palmer Raids. In December 1921 and January 1922, Frankfurter had debated Solicitor General James Beck in the *New Republic* in response to Beck's attack on Frankfurter's Mooney report (which even Lowell conceded showed that Beck "was in a hopeless situation").[110] Around the same time, Frankfurter declined a $2,000 honorarium for more than six months of work as co-chairman (with Pound) of the Cleveland Crime Survey and asked that it be given to Harvard Law School. Lowell's response was that "now that the pressing calls for public service caused by the war are over, I think that Professor Frankfurter would be wise in paying practically his whole attention for a time to his work in the Law School."[111] Thus it came as no surprise that Lowell refused to appoint the law school's first Jewish professor to the sifting committee to study the Jewish quota issue. The Harvard president's reasoning was that Frankfurter lacked "the quality of solid judgment."[112]

Harvard president A. Lawrence Lowell

Frankfurter was livid about the prospect of a Jewish quota. Judge Mack, the first Jewish member of Harvard's Board of Overseers, fought Lowell over the Jewish quota and defended Frankfurter at every turn.[113] For his part, Frankfurter confronted Lowell with rumors that the Harvard president considered his views on the subject "'violent'" and "'extreme.'"[114] Lowell continued to defend his decision not to put him on the committee and to deny Frankfurter's argument that he stacked the committee with "'safe Jews.'"[115]

What the debate over a Jewish quota at Harvard College needed was a prominent Jewish alumnus to stand up and be counted. Frankfurter called on the author of *Public Opinion* to prevent people from relying on Jewish stereotypes and the "pictures in their heads" about a Jewish-dominated Harvard. Though he had been urging the New York *World* to investigate, Frankfurter decided to "ask more" of Lippmann.[116] "You are one of the most influential of Harvard's alumni," Frankfurter wrote. "The thing is bound, very soon, to have rather sensational publicity. In the language of one of the most respected of the Faculty (not a Jew), 'it will become necessary to try to make clear that this action was not taken by Harvard's better self, but by fear & snobbery led by a man, the President, who all his life has hated Jews.' I ask you to inform yourself of the facts." As far as Frankfurter was concerned, the issue of a Jewish quota went "to the very core of honor & honesty in the guidance of the University with the most liberal traditions." "Don't dismiss this as my hysteria," he added. "I am not wont to ask you to go on crusades."[117]

Though both assimilated Jews who had married Gentiles, Frankfurter and Lippmann came from very different backgrounds and took very different approaches to their Jewishness. Frankfurter had arrived in America as an eleven-year-old immigrant who later made a conscious break from religion. Lippmann had grown up in the thoroughly assimilated world of Upper East Side German Jewish privilege, with summer trips to Europe and education at the Sachs School and Harvard. Frankfurter was an idealist who believed, like Brandeis, that Zionism offered an alternative to European persecution of Jews and a potential liberal beacon for the rest of the world. Lippmann never embraced Zionism. He had met Chaim Weizmann when the European Zionist leader came to America, and he offered to broker a truce between European and American leaders.[118] Ultimately, he believed that "Zionism in America" was "a romantic lost cause."[119] Frankfurter was proud to be the first Jewish professor at Harvard Law School but did not go looking for anti-Semitism. Lippmann wanted people to forget that he was Jewish.

Lippmann's attitudes toward anti-Semitism reflected his upbringing and snobbery. In a solicited article about the country's growing anti-Semitism for the *American Hebrew and Jewish Messenger*, Lippmann blamed "the rich and vulgar and pretentious Jews of our big American cities" as the true sources of anti-Semitism. "I waste no time myself worrying about the injustices of anti-Semitism. There is too much injustice in the world for any particular concern about summer hotels and college fraternities. But the anti-Semitism which has its root in our own weaknesses and failings I do worry about."[120]

Rather than accept Frankfurter's challenge, Lippmann may have aided the other side. When asked about his views by government professor Arthur Holcombe, Lippmann wrote: "Naturally I resented the way in which the proposal was made and many of the reasons that were given; and of course I felt that for Harvard to give its sanction to a policy of discrimination was an abandonment of its best tradition." Still, Lippmann not only shared Frankfurter's outrage but also thought the quotas might be beneficial because "it would be bad for the immigrant Jews as well as for Harvard if there were too great a concentration." Lippmann suggested that Massachusetts establish a state school "under Jewish leadership to persuade Jewish boys to scatter."[121] He did not stop there. In response to another faculty member's request in October 1922 to state his views on the issue, Lippmann wrote but probably did not send a letter contending that "a concentration of Jews in excess of fifteen percent will produce a segregation of culture rather than a fusion." He also did "not regard Jews as innocent victims. They hand on unconsciously and uncritically from one generation to another many distressing personal and social habits."[122]

In the spring of 1923, the Committee of Thirteen ostensibly rebuked Lowell by unanimously rejecting a proposal for proportional representation and reaffirming "the policy of equal opportunity for all regardless of race and religion."[123] The school's intent, however, was to institute a de facto quota against Jews. During the fall of 1922, Harvard's application included questions about race or color, where the father was born, and whether the family had changed its last name.[124] And the committee's report recommended the need for geographical diversity by focusing on the South and West, thereby reducing the number of Jews largely concentrated in northeastern cities. Indeed, a memorandum to Lowell projected the number of

Jewish undergraduates under this "new plan."[125] Lippmann and Frankfurter agreed to disagree about the situation and about Lowell, whom Lippmann defended but whose leadership, as Frankfurter put it, "sickens my soul."[126] Others agreed with Frankfurter, and with good reason. In January 1923, Lowell excluded black undergraduates, including Roscoe Conkling Bruce Jr., from the school's freshman dormitories. Bruce was the son of a Harvard graduate and grandson of Mississippi Senator Blanche K. Bruce. The Board of Overseers reversed Lowell's Jim Crow policy after four months of outrage from public officials with ties to Harvard, the New York *World*, and its columnist Heywood Broun, but not from Lippmann.[127]

Lippmann and Frankfurter's disagreement over Harvard's plan for a quota system for Jews was mild compared with the controversy in June 1923 over the decision of Amherst College to oust its president, Alexander Meiklejohn. Meiklejohn alienated the faculty with his new hires and a revamped curriculum. And he alienated alumni with liberal faculty hires, even more liberal guest speakers, and comments such as that he would hire a Bolshevik if the person "were a good teacher."[128] Prodded by the alumni and based on his alleged mismanagement of university resources and messy personal finances, the trustees forced Meiklejohn to resign. Unpopular as he might have been with alumni, Meiklejohn was adored by students. At graduation, thirteen students protested by refusing to accept their diplomas. George W. Plimpton, the nephew of the president of the Board of Trustees, accepted his diploma "under protest."[129] Meiklejohn gave a valedictory address that made national headlines. The *Boston Herald* reprinted the address in full under the headline "AMHERST HEAD TELLS FOES THEY WILL RUE BLOW AT LIBERALISM."[130] " I am a minority man," he told the crowd. " I'm always wanting change. I am almost invariably in an issue against the large number. That being the case, I am perfectly willing to take my medicine." Meiklejohn laid out his vision for the future of higher education: "America can't think in democratic terms. America still thinks in terms of privilege and possession and position and social clubs. America must learn to think in other terms than those, and it has a long task."[131]

Frankfurter, who recalled the attempt of Wall Street lawyer Austen G. Fox and other powerful Harvard alumni to run him and Pound and Chafee out of the law school, was outraged at Meiklejohn's ouster.[132] He admired how Meiklejohn had transformed the curriculum and faculty and had enjoyed teaching Amherst graduates at the law school. And he was incensed that a group of rich trustees saw fit to terminate "the most significant educational achievement in our times."[133]

Not surprisingly, Lippmann reached the opposite conclusion. He spent two days on the Amherst campus and wrote a bylined article for the *World* four days after Meiklejohn's ouster blaming the former president for privileging his new faculty hires over his old ones, refusing to play the political games that most college presidents play, and losing a majority of the faculty's support. "Amherst has lost a fine educator and a great spiritual leader of youth because he was an unsuccessful leader of men," Lippmann wrote. "He did magnificently with students. He failed lamentably with the grown-ups. He could inspire but he could not manage. He was lots of Woodrow Wilson but none of Lloyd George."[134] Frankfurter admitted to Lippmann he was "much dissatisfied" by the piece: "You are not a reporter—and you did a reporter's job. From you we want not 'the facts' but a critique of the facts. And that couldn't be done, even by you, under the limitations, particularly of time, under which that piece was produced."[135]

Frankfurter was equally upset with the tepid response of Lippmann's former employer, the *New Republic.* He was disappointed with Robert Morss Lovett's article and irritated that the magazine had refused to take an editorial stance.[136] For Frankfurter, "to a journal committed to the espousal of the liberal faith, a courageous and luminous exposition of the factors that brought about such a tragedy in American liberalism would seem to be nothing less than a primary duty."[137] At a meeting in New York with *New Republic* editors as well as with Lippmann, Frankfurter implored the magazine to demand a public explanation from the ringleader among the trustees, New York banker Dwight Morrow. Lippmann, a friend of Morrow's, conceded that he had played a central role. The *New Republic* editors were unmoved. "I'm not easily disappointed, as you know, but that was a very disheartening experience for me," Frankfurter wrote Lippmann. "Here was the end of probably the most significant effort in contemporary American education, and the attitude of the table was 'yes, it's too bad—but let's get on with business as usual.'" He was particularly upset that the comment came from "men whose self-assumed job is reforming the world by transforming opinion."[138]

Nearly two weeks later, *New Republic* editor Alvin Johnson relented and drafted an "Open Letter to Dwight Morrow" based on Frankfurter's suggestions. Johnson conceded to Frankfurter that "it isn't the letter you want.

One can't live up to your ideal specifications."[139] Morrow was deemed to have the power to fire Meiklejohn because of "the prestige that goes with membership in the House of Morgan." The letter argued that since Morrow had exercised that power, "the responsibility for an accounting rests squarely on you."[140] When Morrow did not respond for several months, Frankfurter wrote a signed letter to the *New Republic* taking Morrow to task. Based on his continued silence, Frankfurter argued, Morrow either believed that he had no "responsibility to the public" or "that if he and his fellow-trustees will only lie low for a little while, the storm raised by the Meiklejohn affair will blow over."[141]

Frankfurter was not satisfied with Lippmann's silence, either. He peppered Lippmann with letters all summer.[142] Finally, Lippmann blew his top and terminated the discussion.[143] "You hate discomfort, and our correspondence has been uncomfortable to you …," Frankfurter wrote. "And so you allowed yourself to get hot and to find comfort in the approval of your article by others, instead of trying to get what it is that so aroused me."[144] Frankfurter tried to conclude on a conciliatory note about their friendship: "Even if I temporarily irritate you, surely you must realize that what I have written you in our recent correspondence, I have written not only because I care greatly about the issues in the Meiklejohn case, but also because I deeply care about you."[145] Lippmann responded with more silence. Three months later, he wrote Frankfurter and came the closest he could to a fence-mending gesture about "the Meikeljohn [*sic*] business. No doubt I was as impertinent with you as you seemed intolerant of me." Lippmann looked forward to seeing Frankfurter "soon, and then often." Yet he still refused to discuss the issue with Frankfurter.[146]

The Meiklejohn affair took on much greater significance than the future of Frankfurter's friendship with Lippmann or even Meiklejohn's impact on American education (he landed on his feet at the University of Wisconsin, where he established an experimental curriculum and flourished as a First Amendment scholar). It revealed that American liberalism was at a crossroads. Liberals, the *New Republic* declared the same month as Meiklejohn's ouster, were "adrift." Though liberalism "was regaining some of the ground lost during the period of the war," the magazine lamented the "increasing assault" on free speech and press. An even bigger issue, the editorial contended, was "the failure of American liberals up to the present time to agree upon a program or even upon a body of views which may be regarded as their common articles of faith."[147]

During the Meiklejohn affair, Frankfurter championed the liberal faith in academic freedom and in challenging the status quo. He believed that the biggest threat to higher education was not aggressive liberals but "the corrosive influence of business aims and processes in the world of the spirit." He charged one of his anti-Meiklejohn friends with leaving "wholly out of account the true function of a 'liberal.'" In Frankfurter's mind, a liberal served as "a ferment and a fighter" who was "apt to be a bit of a nuisance simply because he is tilting against entrenched complacency, he is seeking to dislodge injustice and to arouse indifference. The amenities are naturally on the side of things as they are; the 'liberal' aims to change things and almost invariably he disturbs the amenities. But the proprieties and amenities are among the most powerful preservatives of ignorance and injustice."[148]

As liberals took different paths during the 1924 presidential election, one thing bound them together—faith in Justice Holmes to strike the right balance between belief in government and freedom from injustice, between security and liberty. Far removed from the corridors of government, liberals lived by the symbol of Justice Holmes.

20

The 1924 Election and
the Basic Issues of Liberalism

During the 1924 presidential election, the fissures in the Frankfurter–Lippmann friendship and in American liberalism continued to grow. After nearly a year of physical decline due to coronary artery disease, President Harding died on August 2, 1923, in San Francisco's Palace Hotel while on a tour of the western United States. Harding's successor was Vice President Calvin Coolidge, the former Massachusetts governor who had risen to prominence in 1919 for crushing the Boston police strike. At the time, Frankfurter did not see much difference between the two presidents. "As for Harding and Coolidge, you once remarked that it is a tough old world," he wrote Lippmann. "Having survived Harding, I don't fear anything in particular will happen through Coolidge."[1] The 1924 election, however, was a different story. It was a battle for public opinion, for control of the country's domestic and foreign policy agenda, and, perhaps most of all, for the future of the Supreme Court. Frankfurter and Lippmann started out in agreement about who should be the next president, but their different conclusions revived the clash of temperaments and diverging political visions. Wilson's death on February 3, 1924, underscored the search for someone who could emerge as a liberal leader.

Lippmann and Frankfurter agreed at least that the Court was heading in the wrong direction and that Holmes and Brandeis were its only beacons. Yet in 1924, Holmes was still considering whether he should retire. "I can't help wondering whether I am finished and ought to say so—but I can't see that my work has fallen off," he wrote Laski.[2] Laski begged his friend not to resign and appealed to the justice's sense of duty, arguing that he was "laying the foundations of the next age in jurisprudence. ... Don't desert your post until you have convinced yourself that it is essential. Every liberal

mind in America would despair if you resigned."[3] At the beginning of the
term the previous October, Brandeis had walked with Holmes from the
John Paul Jones statue near the Tidal Basin to 1720 Eye Street—a distance
of about a mile—and reported that Holmes was in "fine shape physically &
mentally. ... His mind is in much better condition than at any time during
the 1922 term & quite as good as at any time during the 1921 term."[4]

Holmes's national recognition, which had begun to reach a mass audience
with the brief notice in *Time* magazine, continued during what President
Coolidge described as a "simple little ceremony" in the East Room of the
White House.[5] On June 2, 1924, Coolidge awarded Holmes the Roosevelt
Memorial Association's gold medal "for distinguished service in the
development of public law."[6] Two of Theodore Roosevelt's children, half of
Coolidge's cabinet members and their wives, the French ambassador and
his wife, Senator Henry Cabot Lodge, and most of Holmes's fellow justices
and their wives were on hand.[7] Holmes was "in fine form again," Brandeis
reported, and "had the joy of a child" at the ceremony.[8] "One cannot but

Senator Robert M. La Follette Sr.

well feel very confident that President Roosevelt would have been peculiarly gratified to know that this distinction was to be conferred upon you,"
Coolidge said to Holmes of the late president. "During your long service
there you have, I think, almost unerringly interpreted the institutions and
aspirations of your country with the liberality, the understanding and vision
that would have unfailingly earned his approval."[9] Holmes replied: "For
five minutes, Mr. President, you make the dream of a life seem true."[10]
Lippmann recognized the Roosevelt Medal winners in a New York *World*
editorial and described Holmes as a "scholar whose integrity is written in a
hundred bold decisions."[11] Frankfurter watched the East Room ceremony
on the newsreels. "The present occupant of the White House is not one of
my heroes ...," he wrote Holmes, "but last Monday he was the instrument
of a very gracious event, and to a good many of us, a very happy one."[12]

For several months, Frankfurter believed that Coolidge's first run for pres-
ident would be his last. Few people considered that Coolidge could win
the 1924 election given his ties to the corrupt Harding administration. The
Teapot Dome scandal revealed that oil companies had bribed Secretary of
the Interior Albert Bacon Fall for access to government-owned oil reserves.
Congress also investigated corruption in the Justice Department, including
Harding's attorney general. In an unsigned editorial in the *New Republic*,
Frankfurter chastised Coolidge for lecturing the Senate for trying to investi-
gate a scandal in the Internal Revenue Bureau of the Treasury Department.[13]

Everyone expected that the next president would be a Democrat.
Frankfurter feared that the Democrats would nominate John W. Davis.
A former West Virginia congressman, Davis was Wilson's solicitor general
from 1913 to 1918 and ambassador to Great Britain from 1918 to 1921.
Davis's legal and political credentials were impeccable. As solicitor general,
he had earned the reputation as one of the best Supreme Court advo-
cates in American history. In 1922, he had declined a seat on the Supreme
Court that went to Pierce Butler because Davis wanted to make money.[14]
Taft and Van Devanter had lobbied Davis to take Justice Day's seat. Davis,
however, had returned from Britain "dead broke."[15] Instead of the Supreme
Court, he joined the Wall Street law firm of Stetson, Jennings & Russell.
The last part of his biography was the problem for Frankfurter. For nearly
three years with Chafee and Pound, Frankfurter had signed the clemency
petition for Jacob Abrams, challenged mass deportations of immigrants in
Boston, questioned the constitutionality of the Palmer Raids, and suffered
the consequences of Harvard's Red Scare. Prominent members of the bar,

including former Justice Hughes, had spoken out against the Red Scare and the deportation of suspected radicals. Davis, the president of the American Bar Association (ABA) from 1922 to 1923, was neither seen nor heard from on any of these topics. Instead, he was lining his pockets by working for J. P. Morgan & Co.[16]

Two months before the Democratic Convention, Frankfurter tried to stave off Davis's candidacy with an April 16 *New Republic* article, "Why Mr. Davis Shouldn't Run." "Mr. Davis is under retainer by the house of Morgan," Frankfurter charged. A friend had suggested that Davis sever his ties with J. P. Morgan before running for president, but Davis had dismissed the suggestion as "'a gust of popular opinion.'" Leaders of the bar, Frankfurter wrote, should live up to ideals espoused by Brandeis and Pound and engage in public service by standing up for the rights of the less fortunate. New York, however, changed Davis. "He has become the close associate of the most powerful banking house in the world," Frankfurter wrote. "He has ceased to be merely a distinguished advocate."[17] Brandeis approved of Frankfurter's efforts: "The N.R. has painted J.W.D. so well that he who reads will have no excuse for letting him run."[18] The source of Frankfurter's information about Davis was the New York *World*'s editorial page edited as of mid-March by Lippmann.[19] The *World*'s April 2 editorial revealed that Davis had rejected advice to quit his New York law firm and to run for the US Senate from his home state of West Virginia if he were serious about running for president. Davis lectured his adviser about the duties of a corporate lawyer to his clients. The *World* questioned Davis's fitness for the presidency based on his response: Not "a mere 'gust of popular opinion,'" Davis "is confronted with an ancient doubt, based on long democratic experience, as to whether a man in public office can with a perfectly free mind approach questions affecting the interests of his old business associates." The *World* concluded that his failure to acknowledge the conflict of interest "is therefore in effect a withdrawal of Mr. Davis's name from the list of active candidates."[20]

Thus, as of April 1924, Lippmann and Frankfurter appeared to be on the same page. Still, Frankfurter was "puzzled" as to why, on the same day as the Davis editorial, the *World* praised the "honesty" and "disinterested-ness" of Coolidge's Treasury secretary Andrew Mellon. When it came to the Treasury Department's Internal Revenue Bureau, Frankfurter wrote Lippmann, Mellon was the fox guarding the henhouse and no freer of conflicts of interest than Davis.[21] In a letter to Frankfurter, Brandeis went

John W. Davis

even further about the new editorial page editor's judgment: "Walter L. will need a lot of education before he will be competent to guide opinion on American affairs."[22]

Frankfurter and Lippmann attended the Democratic National Convention in Madison Square Garden, the longest convention in history. It lasted for thirteen trying days, included fifteen candidates, and took a record 103 ballots to produce a nominee. The convention became known as the "Klanbake," for the Klan backed the Georgia-born and Tennessee-raised William Gibbs McAdoo, Wilson's former Treasury secretary and son-in-law, and a "dry" candidate in favor of Prohibition. Northern Democrats backed New York

Governor Al Smith, a Catholic and "wet" candidate against Prohibition, anathema to the anti-Catholic Klan and most southern Democrats. With the party split between McAdoo and Smith, Davis emerged as the compromise candidate.

Even before the convention, Frankfurter and Lippmann concurred in their low opinion of McAdoo and not just because he had refused to renounce the Klan. It had come to light that Edward Doheny, who had been implicated in the Teapot Dome oil scandal, had given McAdoo $20,000. McAdoo's decision to return the money did not improve their opinion of him. "Let me thank you for your fight on McAdoo," Frankfurter wrote Lippmann. "To nominate him is to adopt William Allen White's slogan for McAdoo, 'To make the world safe for plutocracy.'" Frankfurter quoted another newspaper editor that "'the nomination of McAdoo would be a direct invitation to the youth of the country to make money their god.'"[23]

The next day, however, Frankfurter informed Lippmann that just because they agreed about McAdoo did not mean that Frankfurter would vote for Davis. For some reason, Lippmann suddenly seemed to consider Davis a liberal. Frankfurter questioned Davis's "disqualifying silences" as ABA president about "cardinal issues of liberalism concerning freedom of speech and constitutional observances of law and order—what makes you regard him as a liberal? Do you know his views on economic and social issues, or do you know people who know his views intimately?"[24]

In the same letter, Frankfurter announced that he planned to vote for Senator Robert M. La Follette, the third-party candidate.[25] Many believed that La Follette, not Roosevelt, would have been the Progressive Party's candidate for president in 1912. But his intemperate speech to newspaper publishers in Philadelphia and physical exhaustion had doomed his candidacy that election cycle. His progressive bona fides were unmatched. As a Wisconsin governor and US senator, he helped make his state a leader in pro-labor legislation.

La Follette also had been a longtime critic of the judiciary. "The judiciary has grown to be the most powerful institution in our government," he wrote in 1912 in the introduction to the book *Our Judicial Oligarchy* by his former law partner, Gilbert Roe. "Evidence abounds that, as constituted to-day, the courts pervert justice almost as often as they administer it. Precedent and procedure have combined to make one law for the rich and another for the poor."[26] A dozen years later, La Follette was back on the stump chastising the courts, proposing constitutional amendments for a congressional override of the Court's power to overrule federal laws, and abandoning the Republican Party for a presidential bid reminiscent of Roosevelt's Bull Moose campaign.

Holmes had seen the newspaper stories that indicated Brandeis might leave the bench to be La Follette's running mate. "Do you suppose it possible that he has political *velléités* underneath?" Holmes wrote Laski. "I shouldn't be surprised if judging didn't satisfy him—taking all the conditions."[27] Brandeis was indeed La Follette's first choice for a running mate. The two families had been close for years. La Follette did not approach Brandeis directly but sent an emissary to the justice's summer home on Cape Cod.[28] Brandeis declined to be considered and did not want to leave the Court, but his heart was in politics. "The Senator will have (if he keeps his health) a grand fight," Brandeis wrote his brother Alfred. "If I had several watertight compartment lives, I should have liked to be in it. The enemies are vulnerable & the times ripe."[29]

Lippmann, for his part, could not understand why Frankfurter was supporting La Follette given the law professor's opposition to reform-based constitutional amendments. "I am honestly interested to know just what your attitude toward La Follette is, and what you're aiming at in giving him support," Lippmann wrote Frankfurter on July 17. "That isn't a question for debate. It's a genuine inquiry."[30] The next day Frankfurter replied earnestly and in language that the author of *Public Opinion* would understand: "You see, I'm incorrigibly academic, and, therefore, the immediate results of the 1924 election do not appear very important. The directions which we further or retard for 1944 are tremendously important. Coolidge and Davis have nothing to offer for 1944; they have no dreams, no 'pictures in their heads' (which *Public Opinion* has taught me is the all-important thing) except things substantially as is. The forces that are struggling and groping behind La Follette are, at least, struggling and groping for a dream, for a different look of things in 1944."[31] During their July correspondence, Frankfurter realized that he and Lippmann would be taking, as Frankfurter put it, "very different roads in this campaign."[32] But, as during the Meiklejohn affair, they could not simply agree to disagree and projected very different visions of American liberalism.

After Frankfurter's letter about the pictures inside the heads of Coolidge, Davis, and La Follette for 1944, a July 22 New York *World* editorial, "The Superpurists," took dead aim at Frankfurter and his ilk for dismissing Davis "before he has had a chance to open his mouth." The editorial also attacked the *New Republic*—founded, after all, by the late J. P. Morgan banker Willard

Straight with Frankfurter's full support—for assuming "that any man who has ever touched money made in the vicinity of Wall Street is forever after a lost soul." Davis's critics, the editorial concluded, ought to hold their fire: "The violent prejudging of Mr. Davis will injure him far less than it will injure the credit of liberalism."[33]

That same day, Frankfurter dashed off a four-page letter to the editor of the *World* reminding the newspaper of its April 2 editorial about Davis's refusal to consider severing his connections to J. P. Morgan & Co. before running for president. "Of course the World may now think that it was wrong in characterizing Mr. Davis as 'a conservative' in April, or it may believe that the fact that he was a conservative in April becomes irrelevant in July," Frankfurter wrote, and challenged the *World* to explain its change in editorial stance.[34] After three days without a response, Frankfurter wired Lippmann and asked if the *World* was going to print the letter.[35] After six days without a response, Frankfurter wrote Lippmann again: "Surely I am entitled to an answer, not out of any consideration of friendship, but simply because, presumably, the World deals with public issues in a public spirit."[36]

Borglum with his 1924 LaFollette-Wheeler campaign medallion

On July 28, Lippmann replied that he would print Frankfurter's letter only if it were cut to 300 words.[37] Frankfurter cut the letter, but pointed out that more than half of his 1,100 words reprinted the *World's* April 2 editorial and that several of the newspaper's recently published letters were between 400 and 600 words.[38] Rather than simply print the truncated version of Frankfurter's letter, Lippmann added an "Editor's Note" denying that Davis had "at any time been attorney" for J. P. Morgan or that his firm was on retainer to the bank. Davis's refusal to sever his ties with Wall Street, the *World's* note concluded, demonstrated his "rare courage and distinguished fineness."[39]

"Astounded" by Lippmann's "Editor's Note," Frankfurter asked him to print a 250-word reply referring to newspaper articles in which Davis admitted that J. P. Morgan was his client.[40] Lippmann refused, citing his "editorial right to close a correspondence in which the correspondent has no further claim upon our space."[41] Frankfurter wrote Lippmann asking him to reconsider, reciting the history of the *World's* coverage and its "flank movement" on Frankfurter's letter and appealing based on "the claim for a generous and free-spirited discussion of the issues vital in this Campaign."[42] Lippmann conceded that the *World* had "changed its views," but he refused to "engage in a public controversy" with Frankfurter and considered "the matter definitely closed."[43] Frankfurter wanted the last word in their private correspondence: "Really, Walter, I had no desire for a debate. I simply wanted The World to say publicly what you now write me in your letter—instead of red-herringing an absurd bit of misinformation about Mr. Davis's law practice."[44]

Frankfurter fired back at Lippmann and Davis in the *New Republic*. The day after Lippmann's "Superpurists" editorial, Frankfurter attacked Davis's personality as a "handsome façade—but only a façade" and explained why the *New Republic* opposed him and why all former progressives should be opposed to him. "By 'progressivism' we mean active dissatisfaction with the present social and economic government of the nation, and the necessity and hope for a drastically more humane, more just, and more beautiful ordering of the lives of men, women and children …," he wrote. "Social-industrial problems, therefore, are the very heart of politics." Frankfurter ticked off the reasons why Davis was a conservative, not a liberal. Unlike Hughes, Davis had represented only big business since becoming a Wall Street lawyer and indeed embraced the role of corporate defender. And in his address as president of the ABA, Davis had criticized some of the

Supreme Court's decisions as "too liberal for him." Frankfurter exposed "Mr. Davis's support of things as they are" and predicted that he "will use his influence to keep alive and respectable a concentration of economic power which is dangerous and intolerable."[45]

After he realized that Lippmann would not print his reply to the *World*'s "Editor's Note," Frankfurter countered Lippmann's assertions in an unsigned August 6 *New Republic* editorial, "Abstemious Liberalism." It cited as examples Davis's decision not to leave his Wall Street law firm before his presidential run; his conspicuous silence as ABA president during the Red Scare, the Palmer Raids, and mass deportations; and his defense of "the constitutional sanctity of property rights" and criticism of the Supreme Court because "'[c]onstitutional limitations have yielded to the police power under the pressure of real or supposed emergencies.'" Frankfurter pressed Davis to specify which Supreme Court decisions the former ABA president was referring to and reminded the *New Republic*'s readers of the stakes—future Supreme Court appointments and "his own attitude on the comprehensive issue of redistribution of social and economic power." After reviewing Davis's entire record from West Virginia congressman to Wall Street lawyer, Frankfurter concluded: "If, after such a record on such basic issues of liberalism, Mr. Davis can be claimed as a 'liberal,' 'liberalism' has lost all meaning."[46]

★★★

The intensity of the Frankfurter-Lippmann debate about the best candidate for American liberals paled in comparison to the political machinations of Borglum. After the unveiling of Lee's head in January, the sculptor received an unexpected boost as he and his men were carving the head and shoulders of Jackson. A vacationing Belgian engineer named Jean Vanophem stopped by the mountainside and watched the engineers and workers using the same pneumatic drills that they had used day and night to bore through layers of granite and to carve Lee's head. The Belgian engineer was puzzled why Borglum's men were not using dynamite. The problem with dynamite, Borglum replied, was that it would split the brittle granite into pieces. Vanophem explained how to overcome this problem by using small amounts of dynamite. Borglum called his friend Coleman du Pont, who sent some of DuPont's dynamite along with one of the company's experts.[47] The expert was soon sent home because he was using too much dynamite. Tucker discovered that half an ounce of dynamite would suffice. One of Tucker's men, Cliff Davis, became so adept and precise at using dynamite that he was nicknamed "Dynamite Davis."[48]

Even more than the giant projector, the use of dynamite in mountain carving became the biggest technological achievement of the memorial and accelerated Borglum's timetable. On March 9, the Stone Mountain Memorial Association announced that it had authorized him to hire enough workers to finish the heads of Jackson and Davis by June 1 "if his progress is not halted by the lack of funds." Hollins Randolph, the president of the association, vowed that his organization would raise the money but did not say how.[49]

During the daytime, visitors watched Borglum and his men work on the heads of Jackson and Davis. From 7:00 to 9:00 p.m., they visited the sculptor's studio at the base of the mountain as he worked on his master model. He had finished a sketch model that was nine feet high and three and a half feet wide at his Stamford studio and had it shipped to Stone Mountain. The Georgia studio contained an "armature," or base wall, that mirrored the contours of the mountain. On this wall, Borglum worked in the evenings on his master model, which was fourteen feet high and thirty-two feet wide, featured the central group of Lee, Jackson, and Davis on horseback followed by another group of cavalrymen, and was illuminated every evening. "The master model will stand in the studio until the central group is finished on the precipice," the *Atlanta Constitution* reported. "Then it will be available for preservation in the great memorial hall to be cut out of the breast of the mountain below the central group, or in any other institution to which the memorial association might present it as a gift."[50]

Instead, progress came to a halt. Randolph, the great-great-grandson of Thomas Jefferson and an alleged member of the Imperial Kloncilium, chaired the Georgia delegation at the 1924 Democratic National Convention and led the efforts to nominate the Klan's candidate, McAdoo.[51] Randolph was instrumental in persuading a member of the Georgia delegation to change her vote to secure the passage of the party platform that did not condemn the Klan.[52] Either despite or because of his silence on the Klan issue, McAdoo lost the nomination to Davis after having led the balloting for much of the convention.[53] His defeat marked the end of the Klan as a national political force.

Borglum undoubtedly annoyed Randolph and the Klan for failing to support McAdoo. A self-described "Independent Republican," Borglum never considered any of the Democratic candidates. Smith was out of the question as a New York governor and Catholic. Davis was too closely tied to the New York banking interests that Borglum despised. And McAdoo was a nonstarter because of his connection to the Wilson administration that Borglum considered corrupt and dishonest during the sculptor's aircraft investigation. Active in the Nonpartisan League and its fight to protect northwestern farmers, Borglum endorsed La Follette, whom he met with twice, in late June and early July.[54] He liked La Follette's Midwestern roots and concern for farmers, his independence, and his freedom from the northeastern business interests that had captured the Republican and Democratic Parties.[55] And he believed that La Follette could carry fifteen to twenty states and throw the election into the liberal House of Representatives and produce a liberal president.[56] "I was a La Follette man before I became a Roosevelt man," Borglum wrote Senator James E. Watson, an Indiana Republican. Borglum was so committed to improving the lot of northwestern farmers that "today I find myself actually aiding in a movement which I have prayed and labored to prevent."[57] He even asked for a copy of La Follette's platform to try to entice Randolph and the Klan to endorse the third-party candidate.[58]

The Klan was unmoved. It may also have soured on Borglum for a second reason: the sculptor's continued friendship with the former Grand Dragon of the Indiana Klan, D. C. Stephenson. The charismatic thirty-three-year-old coal dealer had raised the Klan's membership in Ohio from 4,000 to 265,000 and in Indiana from 7,000 to 380,000.[59] His power increasing, he split with the Atlanta-based Klan in May 1924, formed his own organization, and sued the Klan's leadership for libel, slander, and $200,000 in damages.[60] He amassed even greater political power in Indiana by switching his political affiliation from Democrat to Republican and by backing Edwin L. Jackson for governor. Jackson won the primary and went on to win the general election. Borglum continued to confide in Stephenson after the Indiana leader's split from the Klan—perhaps because the sculptor owed him money. Either way, they remained friends and political allies throughout the 1924 presidential campaign.

For a time, Borglum harbored delusions of grandeur about his role in the La Follette campaign. He believed that he would introduce labor leader Warren Stone as La Follette's running mate at the Progressive Party convention and that the senator might even ask Borglum to join the ticket.[61] Borglum was pleased with La Follette's eventual choice, Senator Burton Wheeler of Montana, because Wheeler was a westerner and progressive who would fight for northwestern farmers. In mid-July, Borglum boosted the La Follette–Wheeler campaign by designing a campaign button made of bronze and reminiscent of the profiles of the central figures on the Confederate Memorial. The buttons were distributed to anyone donating one dollar or more to the campaign. They also landed the sculptor back in the headlines.[62]

Soon after Borglum finished the campaign button, he became disillusioned with La Follette's presidential bid. In September, he declined a position on the New York State Campaign Committee. "I have been a progressive all my life—an Independent Republican, very active in progressive politics, and I don't approve at all of the way this campaign has been bungled from the beginning," he wrote La Follette campaign chairman Arthur Garfield Hays.[63] To his friend Stephenson, Borglum blasted La Follette's proposals about the Supreme Court and the July endorsement of Socialist Party leader Morris Hillquit.[64] "I am supporting Mr. Coolidge and supporting him openly, first because I don't believe in La Follette's plan to destroy the Supreme Court— as he proposes to make Congress supreme, it would mean the destruction of the Court," Borglum wrote. He believed that Hillquit, "Jews, Socialists, and alien forces in this country" were trying to get their claws into La Follette, and if they succeeded in destroying the Court, "our present government which is the most stable form of republic, would melt away in a single administration."[65] In declining Oswald Garrison Villard's mid-September request to include his name on a list of artists and writers who endorsed La Follette, Borglum wired: "NO I AM OUT OF THIS FIGHT I DON'T THINK A SANE CLEAN ANGLO SAXON PROGRESSIVISM IS BEFORE THE VOTERS THIS YEAR IN THE SO CALLED LAFOLLETTE GESTURE."[66] Borglum requested one of the campaign buttons, though the sculptor's name had been left off the design.[67]

The same day that he declined an invitation to join La Follette's New York Campaign Committee, Borglum received President Coolidge's permission to design a campaign button and requested some profile pictures.[68] By October, Borglum considered himself one of Coolidge's intimate advisers.[69] The sculptor turned political operative was determined to swing the northwestern states populated by the Nonpartisan League's farmers the president's way: "I want Mr. Coolidge to defeat the Socialistic group in the East and win over the Farmers in the West."[70]

Borglum's switch from La Follette to Coolidge may have been a product of the anti-Semitic, anti-immigrant, anti-Socialist fervor sweeping the country and coloring the sculptor's worldview. But it was also a product of political opportunism. Coolidge was likely to remain in the White House the next four years and had already approved a Stone Mountain half dollar that was the key to financing and finishing the memorial. The Stone Mountain half dollar turned out to be Borglum's ultimate undoing with the Klan. During the summer of 1923, he had been working his Republican political contacts in Congress and with Harding to obtain federal legislation authorizing the minting of 5 million Stone Mountain half dollars, with the proceeds to go to the memorial.[71] The coin honored the leaders of the Confederacy as well as Harding. The bill passed the House on March 6 and the Senate five days later. On March 17, Coolidge signed it into law.

Borglum had not been able to spend as much time as he wanted at Stone Mountain during the spring and summer of 1924 because he was busy designing the coin. By May, he had completed a medal of Lee, Jackson, and Davis on horseback to raise funds. He incorporated part of that design into the half dollar, with Lee and Jackson on horseback on the front and an American eagle on the back. The sculptors and artists advising the US Mint, however, rejected several of his designs; Coolidge objected to Harding's inclusion. Borglum was forced to redesign the coin nine times.[72] "There were very serious attacks made upon the Memorial itself that I had to face, and am still facing in Washington," Borglum wrote Stephenson. "This has in the past two weeks blocked the coinage of the Memorial half dollar. Where this comes from I don't know."[73]

By the summer, the sculptor realized that he had fallen out of the Klan's good graces. He informed Stephenson that "your ancient Texas friend," Klan leader H. W. Evans, "organized an attack upon us for efforts misunderstood by him in my desire to help everything in an upward trend."[74] Borglum's failure to endorse McAdoo and his continued friendship with Stephenson, however, made Evans's attacks unsurprising. Regardless of the identity of the next president, Borglum's problems with the Klan, the half dollar, and the Stone Mountain Memorial were far from over.

★★★

That fall, Frankfurter campaigned to make La Follette the next president. He worked with the senator's campaign, tried to persuade Republican friends, and took to the pages of the nation's newspapers as well as the *New Republic*. The future of the country, American liberalism, and the Supreme Court, he believed, hung in the balance.

The Harvard law professor was most effective in critiquing the three candidates' attitudes toward the Supreme Court. In an unsigned October 1 *New Republic* editorial, "The Red Terror of Judicial Reform," he began with side-by-side quotations from Coolidge and Davis in defense of the Court. The purpose of the Constitution, Coolidge asserted in a September 5 speech in Baltimore, was "that the minority, even down to the most insignificant individual, might have their rights protected." The next day in Dubuque, Iowa, Davis defended the Court against charges of despotism: "There must be in this country some power to which the American citizen can appeal when these sacred rights of his are invaded."[75] Frankfurter's editorial savaged Coolidge and Davis not for what they said but for what they did not say. He dismissed the comments by Coolidge, the author of *The Reds in Our Colleges*, because the president "knows no better." Davis, a former ABA president, solicitor general, and leader of the New York bar, knew better yet "conveyed a mutilated, and, therefore, untrue picture." Despite the need for "an independent Supreme Court," Frankfurter argued that it should not decide all state and federal political controversies. He criticized the Court's crabbed interpretation of the commerce power to strike down the first child labor law as a product of "the unconscious rationalizations of the economic and social biases of individual justices." He quoted Holmes that the country would not cease to exist if the Court lost the power to strike down federal laws, but it needed the power to nullify state laws.[76]

Instead of addressing the commerce power, Coolidge and Davis focused on the Constitution's Bill of Rights. Yet the Court had not done well in this area, either. Channeling Holmes and Brandeis in *Abrams*, Frankfurter remarked that "the record of the Supreme Court in interpreting the guarantee of 'freedom of speech' shows how, with rare exceptions, passions lay prey even the courts."[77] Frankfurter then challenged Coolidge and Davis over the Court's misuse of the Due Process Clause and Equal Protection Clause. The Fourteenth Amendment, instead of protecting the rights of blacks as was intended, has been used to strike down pro-labor legislation. What Coolidge extolled as "'protecting the freedom of the individual, of guarding his earnings, his home, his life,'" was a defense of the Court's invocation of freedom or liberty of contract to strike down "workmen's compensation laws, the ten-hour law for bakers, laws prohibiting discrimination against trade union workers, [and] the minimum wage law for women." Or, as Frankfurter described liberty of contract: "[T]his doctrine which the Supreme Court has used as a sword with which to slay most important social legislation and to deny the means of freedom to those least free." He went after Davis again for disparaging the dissenters on the Court as merely a cheap shot against opponents of liberty of contract—Justices Hughes, Holmes, Brandeis, and "occasionally" Chief Justice Taft. This coming from a candidate who on the stump defended "'the right of free contract'" yet said nothing about the Court's antilabor decisions from *Lochner* to *Adkins*. "Mr. Davis is silent about such decisions," Frankfurter wrote, "but he cannot be ignorant of them."[78]

On the other hand, Frankfurter defended La Follette's attacks on the Court not because he agreed with the precise solutions but because of their impact on public opinion. The Bull Moose campaign of 1912, Frankfurter argued, "was mainly responsible for a temporary period of liberalism" about the Due Process Clause because Roosevelt had threatened to impose a recall of judges. "The public opinion which the Progressive campaign aroused subtly penetrated the judicial atmosphere," Frankfurter wrote. Roosevelt had taught Frankfurter about the impact of public opinion on the Court. "'I may not know much about law,'" Roosevelt told Frankfurter, "but I do know one can put the fear of God into judges.'" Like Roosevelt in 1912, La Follette's proposals would once again shake up federal and state court judges and the justices who struck down the Washington, DC, minimum wage law for women in *Adkins*. "The 'fear of God,'" Frankfurter wrote, "very much needs to make itself felt in 1924."[79] The fear of God, however, was not enough. Any "informed study" of the Supreme Court would conclude that "no nine men are wise enough and good enough" to be entrusted with this power, therefore, "[t]he due process clauses ought to go." Without them, he argued, the Court could play its proper role and "exercise the most delicate and powerful function in our dual system of government."[80]

Frankfurter threw himself into the La Follette campaign. Both he and Marion took to the stump, and he wrote impassioned editorials and letters to the editors endorsing and defending La Follette in the *Boston American*, the *Boston Herald*, the *Boston Traveller*, the *Harvard Crimson*, and the *Independent*.[81] For the Frankfurters and Brandeises, a vote for La Follette was a litmus test of liberalism. As successful as he was in defending the candidate's stance on the Supreme Court, however, Frankfurter was unsuccessful in persuading his friends to vote for La Follette. Much to Frankfurter's dismay, New York lawyers C. C. Burlingham and Raymond Fosdick, Judge Learned Hand, and Rabbi Stephen Wise all decided to vote for Davis; Boston lawyer George Roberts decided to vote for Coolidge; Judge Mack may have been Frankfurter's only La Follette convert.[82]

During the final days of the campaign, Frankfurter went toe to toe in the *New Republic* with Lippmann. The two had not spoken or corresponded about the election for months. Frankfurter and Croly wrote *New Republic* endorsements for La Follette; Lippmann wrote one for Davis. In "Why I Shall Vote for La Follette," Frankfurter observed that the "'great inequality of property' is the most significant characteristic of our social-economic life" and that solutions to the problems of accumulating wealth in the power of a few lay with neither the "stand-pat" Republican Party nor the Democratic Party controlled by the "'solid South' ... the greatest immoral factor of American politics." He compared La Follette's campaign to John Fremont's 1856 third-party run that helped Lincoln win four years later. The 1924 presidential campaign was a transitional election freighted with political significance. Industrialization, the great black migration, and immigration promised a realignment of the nation's political parties. And in the face of this realignment, the only person "educating public opinion" about "the claims and needs of labor and agriculture" was La Follette. Unlike Roosevelt's Bull Moose campaign based on his cult of personality, La Follette's third-party run was premised on standing up for labor and agriculture. "I am not voting for him for his sake," Frankfurter wrote of La Follette. "I do not regard him as a Messiah." But during his forty years of serving Wisconsin and of making the University of Wisconsin a centerpiece of the state's political and intellectual life, La Follette had espoused many of the same ideas as the men who had lived at the House of Truth. "Probably no other man in public life today compares with La Follette in the extent of his reliance on disinterested expertness in the solution of economic and social questions," Frankfurter wrote. Focused on the future, he urged people to abandon their party affiliation and to vote for La Follette, if only to prove that "all the talk of 'throwing one's vote away' is the cowardly philosophy of the bandwagon."[83]

Lippmann's contribution to his old magazine, "Why I Shall Vote for Davis," consisted solely of hard-boiled realism. "I shall vote for Mr. Davis because he is the only man who can be elected in place of Mr. Coolidge," Lippmann wrote, "and I do not wish directly or indirectly to give the present administration another term of power." In supporting Davis, Lippmann denied that he was abandoning liberalism. He believed that Davis's "strong Jeffersonian bias against the concentration and exaggeration of government is more genuinely liberal than much that goes by the name of liberalism."[84] Most of Lippmann's essay knocked La Follette, who, he argued, was liberalism's pipe dream and would not lead to the predicted demise of the Democratic Party or the solid South. Nor was Lippmann impressed with La Follette's political platform, which was "almost violently nationalistic and centralizing; that seems to me reactionary and illiberal." Charging that La Follette's views on monopoly veered toward prewar Socialism and his foreign policy ignored everything in Europe since the Treaty of Versailles, Lippmann added that he refused to cast his vote for a candidate who could not win. He argued that "at least I ought to be able to vote for a man who is bravely and lucidly expounding what seems to me a liberal program. Mr. La Follette does not offer me that compensation." Almost as an afterthought, he concluded that he was voting for Davis based on the Democratic nominee's foreign policy experience and "personal character."[85]

Lippmann was right about the outcome of the 1924 election. Aided by La Follette's third-party candidacy, Coolidge won by a landslide, with 15.7 million popular votes and 382 electoral votes. La Follette captured only his home state of Wisconsin, but he beat Davis in twelve states, and his 4.8 million votes made Fighting Bob one of the twentieth century's most successful third-party candidates. Yet, as Lippmann had predicted, the main byproduct of La Follette's campaign was that it kept Coolidge in the White House. After the election, Lippmann tried to mend fences with Frankfurter and wrote: "Some time soon I hope we shall get together for a post-mortem, to confess our mistakes, admit our prejudices and match minds for the future."[86]

The 1924 election marked the beginning of the end of Frankfurter's friendship with Lippmann. They were not nearly as close as they had been when they had lived together in the House of Truth. They hardly ever saw each other in person and maintained their relationship through steady correspondence about the *World*'s editorials and current affairs. When Frankfurter agreed with the paper's stance on an issue (such as the Scopes trial), things were fine because Lippmann loved praise. But when they disagreed (such as about the 1924 election), Lippmann resented Frankfurter's deluge of lengthy letters and cut off the correspondence. Their cooling friendship suffered from this pattern of praise and discord, correspondence and silence.

The truth was that Lippmann and Frankfurter had begun to take different approaches to American liberalism. The best evidence that Lippmann was abandoning many of his principles was his November 1925 sequel to *Public Opinion, The Phantom Public. Public Opinion* was premised on faith in the democratic political process and a belief that public opinion could be educated based on an expert-led factual discovery. *The Phantom Public,* however, indicated that Lippmann had lost faith in democracy because the American people were too diffuse and uninterested in public affairs to be worth educating. His Upper East Side elitism was difficult for Frankfurter, Brandeis, and other liberals to swallow. Lippmann had sent Frankfurter an inscribed advance copy of the book. Frankfurter emphasized their areas of agreement such as the need for better legislation, but he added that the Supreme Court had erected unnecessary roadblocks.[87] Brandeis also described it as a "remarkable book" yet recognized the author's limitations. "The defects are the inevitable ones due to his qualities and lacks which we have often discussed," he wrote Frankfurter. "Denn der Sonne Busen ist libeleer" [For the sun's bosom is without love].[88] In the *New Republic*, philosopher John Dewey challenged *The Phantom Public*'s premises about democracy as "aimed in some degree at a man of straw" and motivated by Lippmann's distaste for contemporary political events such as Prohibition and the Tennessee creationism legislation at issue during the Scopes trial. Dewey was optimistic that the American people could again become politically re-engaged.[89] Like others, liberals looked to the dissenters on the Supreme Court for guidance and inspiration.

21

Eloquence May Set Fire to Reason

Both Frankfurter and Lippmann believed that one of liberalism's best hopes was the not-so-liberal Justice Holmes. Holmes loved them like sons. In August 1924, Frankfurter had visited 1720 Eye Street; much to Holmes's delight, they talked for nine straight hours. Holmes greatly admired Lippmann's *New Republic* editorial "Why I Will Vote for Davis" and thought it far superior to Croly's editorial about La Follette. (Holmes had missed Frankfurter's the week before.)

During the 1924 election, Holmes sympathized with Coolidge—and not simply because the president had awarded him the Roosevelt Medal. A Republican since before the Civil War, Holmes never would have voted for a Democrat, let alone voted for La Follette; the justice admired the robber barons and big business far more than his young friends cared to admit. Plus, a Republican president made it easier for Holmes to retire. "If I had had a vote I should have voted for Coolidge—quite apart from the fact that his election relieves my conscience from the doubt whether I ought to resign so as to give the appointment to him," Holmes wrote a dismayed Laski, who described Coolidge to the justice as "a fool and a mean fool."[1] "I think your judgment of Coolidge is prejudiced," Holmes replied, "and while I don't expect anything very astonishing from him I don't want anything very astonishing."[2] Laski, whose hatred for Coolidge stemmed from the 1919 Boston police strike, was more concerned with Holmes's talk of retirement: "You seem in great form; and so long as I hear that you don't intend to resign, I am happy. For (a) you have no moral right to resign until you have been on the Court as long as Marshall, (b) it would be a crime to give Coolidge another nomination and (c) it would leave Brandeis lonely and miserable."[3]

Holmes (right) and Elihu Root (left) receiving the Roosevelt Medal from
President Coolidge (center)

Coolidge's judicial appointments after the election were not as bad as Laski
and others feared. After Justice Mahlon Pitney died on December 4, 1924,
Coolidge nominated his attorney general and former Columbia law dean
Harlan Fiske Stone. Stone ended up joining Holmes and Brandeis in the
Court's liberal bloc. Coolidge also promoted Judge Learned Hand from the
federal trial court to the court of appeals. Some thought that the president
would soon have the opportunity to replace Holmes.

Holmes reassured his friends, young and old, that the January 7, 1925, *Boston
Evening Transcript* "scoop" that he was retiring was false.[4] He suspected that
Chief Justice Arthur P. Rugg of the Supreme Judicial Court of Massachusetts
had circulated the rumor because Rugg, a friend and former Amherst classmate of Coolidge's, coveted Holmes's job. "As old [Melville] Fuller said to me
when he was [chief justice]," Holmes wrote, "'I am not to be paragraphed out
of my place.'"[5] Aside from occasional bouts of lower back pain, Holmes was in
fine shape physically and had never been better mentally.[6] Newspaper rumors
may not have "paragraphed" him into retirement, but they prompted reassur-
ances from Frankfurter that he was up to the task. "I say without hesitation that

your opinions this term show the same eye for the jugular, the same powerful deftness in striking it as of old," Frankfurter wrote Holmes.[7]

Holmes justified Frankfurter's faith in him with a dissent in the free speech case of radical Socialist Benjamin Gitlow. Arrested on November 8, 1919, during the second day of the Palmer Raids, Gitlow was charged with publishing a thirty-four-page manifesto criticizing the legislative efforts of moderate Socialism and predicting that the nation's increasingly violent strikes would lead to "a 'revolutionary dictatorship of the proletariat.'"[8] Published in 1,600 copies of the Left Wing Socialist Party organ, *The Revolutionary Age*, the manifesto led to no violence. Nonetheless, Gitlow was tried and convicted under a New York criminal anarchy statute passed in 1902 after President William McKinley's assassination. Sentenced to five to ten years of hard labor, Gitlow had served nearly three by the time the Court decided his case.[9]

At the time, states could use their "police powers" to abridge free speech or press. During the Red Scare, many states echoed federal legislation and passed criminal laws designed to punish objectionable speech or publications. The First Amendment's prohibition that "Congress shall make no law …" says nothing about the states. In a 1920 dissent about a similar Minnesota criminal law, Brandeis suggested that if the Fourteenth Amendment's Due Process Clause protects the liberty of contract or right to property, it also should protect fundamental liberties, including freedom of speech.[10] Holmes had alluded to the same idea after the Court had invoked the liberty of contract doctrine to invalidate the Washington, DC, minimum wage law in *Adkins*.

The Court first heard oral argument on Gitlow's case in April 1923, three days after it had announced *Adkins*. *Gitlow* was reargued in November 1923, but the Court failed to issue a decision before the end of the term. Finally, after two arguments and three years of Gitlow's hard labor, the Court held that free speech and press were "among the fundamental personal rights and 'liberties' protected by the due process clause of the Fourteenth Amendment from impairment by the States." The Court, however, affirmed Gitlow's conviction because states have the power to ban speech advocating overthrow of the government. It was of no moment that Gitlow's publication did not lead to any violence; it was enough that it might have. "A single revolutionary spark," Justice Edward T. Sanford wrote for the Court, "may kindle a fire that, smouldering for a time, may burst into a sweeping and destructive conflagration."[11]

BENJAMIN GITLOW

Business Manager of " The Revolutionary Age," official organ — Left Wing Section of Socialist Party.

Arrested on charge of Criminal Anarchy by direction of the Committee, December 1, 1919, tried, convicted and sentenced to State Prison for not less than five years nor more than ten years.

Benjamin Gitlow

Holmes, joined by Brandeis, dissented from the Court's decision for its failure to apply the "clear and present danger" test as Holmes had defined it in *Schenck* and redefined it six months later in his *Abrams* dissent. "There was no present danger of an attempt to overthrow the government by force on the part of the admittedly small minority who shared the defendant's views," he wrote. He did not elaborate on a clear and present danger test that continued to vex courts and lawmakers about how to draw the line between lawful and unlawful speech. But as in *Abrams*, he attacked the majority opinion with his rhetoric and his metaphor about the marketplace of ideas. Gitlow's manifesto, Holmes argued, was not an "incitement" because "[e]very idea is an incitement. ... The only difference between the expression of an opinion and an incitement in the narrower sense is the speaker's enthusiasm for the result. Eloquence may set fire to reason. But whatever may be thought of the redundant discourse before us it had no chance of starting a present conflagration." When it came to the threat of Communism in America, Holmes continued to put his faith in the marketplace of ideas: "If in the long run the beliefs expressed in proletarian dictatorship are destined to be accepted by the dominant forces of the community, the only meaning of free speech is that they should be given their chance and have their way."[12]

Even in defeat in *Gitlow*, Holmes and Brandeis could claim a major victory—the Court's decision to protect some of the most cherished First Amendment freedoms from the states. The *Gitlow* majority conceded that freedom of speech and press were "fundamental personal rights and liberties" that applied to the states. The Due Process Clause, as Holmes had demonstrated in his 1923 opinion in *Moore v. Dempsey*, could be used to protect both the powerful and the powerless. Just as *Moore v. Dempsey* protected blacks from mob-dominated state criminal trials, Holmes's dissent in *Gitlow* sought to protect political radicals from criminal prosecution for free speech. In both cases, Holmes sided with the least popular and least powerful members of society against state prosecutors. No one was a more devout believer in majority rule than Holmes, yet in *Moore v. Dempsey* and *Gitlow* no one articulated more fundamental limits on government power.

At eighty-four, Holmes proved that he was still at the top of his game. He sent copies of his *Gitlow* dissent to those who would appreciate it most— Frankfurter and Laski. "I gave an expiring kick on the last day (Brandeis was with me) in favor of the right to drool on the part of believers in the proletarian dictatorship—only a page—please read it," Holmes wrote Frankfurter.[13] As he had repeatedly stated, Frankfurter abhorred the Due Process Clause because judges had used it to invalidate labor laws and other socioeconomic legislation; Holmes's *Gitlow* dissent and the invocation of due process to protect free speech provoked a different reaction. Judge Benjamin Cardozo, who had dissented from the New York Court of Appeals decision upholding the state anarchy law in *Gitlow*, relayed kind words to Frankfurter, which "deeply gratified" Holmes.[14] "I find that I gain more from Holmes than from any one else, alive or dead," Cardozo wrote. "Pick up his opinions haphazard, even the early ones in Massachusetts, one finds them studded with sentences that illumine the dark places. I find no equal inspiration anywhere."[15] Others also praised the dissent. In an unsigned New York *World* editorial commissioned by Lippmann, Columbia law professor Thomas Reed Powell described the differences between the majority and the dissent as "the fruit of divergent social outlooks." The two dissenters had "adhered to the older, and it seems to us, the sounder doctrine that the speech of a wind-bag like Gitlow ... should, however much we may dislike it, nevertheless be tolerated."[16] In an unsigned *New*

Republic editorial, Chafee tried to find the silver lining in *Gitlow's* application of the First Amendment's speech and press clauses to the states. He
imagined a future in which the Court thwarted states from abridging free
speech: "A more liberal Court may prevent a checker-board nation, with
ultra-conservative states into which moderately radical Americans come at
peril of imprisonment for sedition."[17] Chafee preferred to look to politics
before turning to the courts. He recognized that "freedom must be secured through state legislatures and state governors" like New York governor Alfred E. Smith, who had pardoned Gitlow's associates and, six months
later, pardoned Gitlow.[18] For Chafee and others, the value of Holmes's
and Brandeis's dissents was in their impact on everyday Americans: "The
victories of liberty of speech must be won in the mind before they are won
in the courts," Chafee wrote. "The majority opinions determined the cases,
but these dissenting opinions will determine the minds of the future."[19]

Not content merely to applaud Holmes's *Gitlow* dissent, Frankfurter used
it to educate public opinion and to keep the Supreme Court on its toes.
With the help of his protégé James M. Landis, Frankfurter reacted to several
of the Court's antilabor decisions with scholarly broadsides. In response
to decisions thwarting two federal attempts to regulate child labor, he and
Landis published a May 1925 *Yale Law Journal* article exploring the history
of the Compact Clause that enables states to enter into agreements to solve
interstate problems.[20] A month later, they wrote about the Court's pre–
Civil War history in the first of seventeen *Harvard Law Review* articles that
Frankfurter coauthored on "The Business of the Supreme Court," which
evolved into his annual evaluation of the Court's output.[21] And he continued
to critique the Court, its procedures, and its decisions in the pages of the
New Republic, The Nation, and other publications—all aided and abetted by
summertime talks with Brandeis, who supplied him with gossip about the
Court's inner workings.

Though he praised the *Gitlow* dissent and believed that the judiciary
should protect free speech and fair criminal trials, Frankfurter cautioned
liberals about waiting for the Court to solve all their problems. In an unsigned
New Republic editorial, "Can the Supreme Court Guarantee Toleration?," he
highlighted the dangers of using the liberty and property provisions of the
Due Process Clause to protect individual rights.[22] Such decisions put state
social welfare experiments at risk.

Exhibit A for Frankfurter was another June 1925 decision—McReynolds's
majority opinion in *Pierce v. Society of Sisters*, which invalidated an Oregon

The Taft Court in 1925: McReynolds (sitting left), Holmes, Taft, Van Devanter, Brandeis, Sanford (standing left), Sutherland, Butler, and Stone

law that compelled all children between ages eight and sixteen who had not finished the eighth grade to attend public schools. Oregon's 1922 compulsory public education law, sponsored by the Ku Klux Klan and due to go into effect in September 1926, would have put the state's Catholic (and other private) schools out of business. These schools sued to protect their property interests. The decision built on the trio of 1923 decisions invalidating state laws that banned the teaching of German and other foreign languages in public schools. The Oregon public education law, the Court held, violated "the liberty of parents and guardians to direct the upbringing and education of children under their control."[23] *Pierce*, Frankfurter admitted, "gives just cause for rejoicing. The Supreme Court did immediate service on behalf of the essential spirit of liberalism." But he warned that it might turn out to be a double-edged sword for liberals because it strengthened the power of the Due Process Clause. McReynolds argued that the states violated the fundamental liberty of parents to choose where to educate their children, but the Court had invoked the same right to liberty and property to invalidate state labor laws about maximum hours, minimum wages, and the rights of unions. In *Adkins*, as Frankfurter knew all too well, the Court had revived liberty of contract to invalidate the DC minimum wage laws for women and children. "These words mean what the shifting personnel of the United States Supreme Court from time to time makes them mean," he wrote. "The inclination of a single Justice, the tip of his mind—or his fears—determines the opportunity of a much-needed social experiment to survive, or frustrates, at least for a long time, intelligent attempts to deal with a social evil."[24]

Frankfurter's message was not to elect a better president who would appoint more liberal justices. Coolidge had just been elected for another four years; the Progressive Party's standard-bearer, Robert La Follette, died on June 18, shortly after his seventieth birthday. If anything, the electoral emphasis should shift to producing better state governors and state legislators. Frankfurter refused to worship at the god of the judiciary or "to make constitutionality synonymous with propriety. ... Such an attitude is a great enemy of liberalism. Particularly in legislation affecting freedom of thought and freedom of speech much that is highly illiberal would be clearly constitutional."[25] He praised Holmes's dissent in the Nebraska foreign language case and predicted that McReynolds's decision in *Pierce* would encourage states to pass laws requiring teachers and students to exhibit "'good moral character'" and "'patriotic disposition.'" He warned that "the real battles of liberalism are not won in the Supreme Court."[26] The future of American liberalism, he argued, depended on winning in the court of public opinion because the Court, as presidential candidates Roosevelt and La Follette had shown in attacking its antilabor decisions, reflected "the general drift of public opinion." "Only a persistent, positive translation of the liberal faith into the thoughts and acts of the community," Frankfurter wrote, "is the real reliance against the unabated temptation to straitjacket the human mind."[27]

Frankfurter's faith in the democratic political process and the educability of public opinion made Holmes—the Court's most consistent defender of majority rule—the ideal liberal judge. Holmes did not believe that legislation would accomplish social change. Nor was he sympathetic to the Socialism espoused by Laski in his latest book, *A Grammar of Politics.*[28] "I don't agree with the premises as to human rights etc.," Holmes wrote Frankfurter. "I think the passion for equality is more likely to be a noxious humbug than an inspiration."[29] Holmes said as much to Laski, who replied: "I have convictions built on faith while you (forgive me!) have doubts built on fears."[30] Holmes pleaded guilty to Laski's charges and admitted that he had heard similar ones in the past. For Holmes, it always came back to the Civil War: "The only thing that I am competent to say from the experience of my youth is that I fear your getting into the frame of mind that I saw in the Abolitionists (and shared)—the martyr spirit."[31] Despite his fears and doubts about noble causes, Holmes consistently voted to uphold pro-labor social and economic legislation and, since November 1919, to protect the right to free speech and fair criminal trials. As his *Gitlow* dissent and summertime letters to Frankfurter and Laski indicated, he showed no signs of slowing down, and talk of retirement ceased.

A number of young admirers made the pilgrimage to 1720 Eye Street. Frankfurter wrote a letter of introduction to Holmes for *New Republic* contributor Elizabeth Shepley Sergeant.[32] Born in Massachusetts and educated at Bryn Mawr, the forty-five-year-old Sergeant had worked for then editor Willa Cather at *McClure's Magazine*, served as the *New Republic's* Paris-based war correspondent, and lived in the Southwest writing about Pueblo Indians. In December 1925, she arrived at Holmes's doorstep. He was eager to impress a well-bred, well-educated younger woman with his gift of conversation. For an hour and a half, he regaled her with stories. He only stopped so that he would not get too tired.[33] Near the end of her visit, Sergeant revealed her desire to a write a profile of him.[34] And, with Frankfurter's assistance and encouragement, she did. Frankfurter wrote her: "You certainly have bagged the Justice."[35]

In January 1926, Frankfurter inquired about sending another sparkplug Holmes's way to be his secretary for the following term—Thomas Gardiner Corcoran. Along with Landis, Corcoran stood out among Frankfurter's many protégés who made teaching at Harvard so fulfilling. Both Landis and Corcoran stayed at the law school an extra year to earn their doctorates, to serve as Frankfurter's de facto research assistants and coauthors, and to be groomed for public service. Frankfurter selected Landis to work for Brandeis, and Corcoran for Holmes. Whereas Brandeis expected his secretaries to work in monastic silence in a separate apartment, bury themselves in the Library of Congress in search of sociological and economic studies, and contribute to his fact- and footnote-laden opinions, Holmes wanted his secretaries to balance his checkbook, listen to his tall tales, and serve as his surrogate sons. Frankfurter described Corcoran to Holmes: bright-eyed, ebullient, and Irish-Catholic (a first for Holmes). Corcoran could match Holmes's penchant for tall tales and liked to burst into Irish songs.[36] Holmes accepted Corcoran sight unseen. But in January 1926, he issued a disclaimer before Corcoran started that fall— one that the justice repeated every year thereafter. "Of course Mr. Corcoran will appreciate the increasing chance that death or resignation may cut his career here short," Holmes wrote Frankfurter.[37]

With no end in sight to his career, however, Holmes appreciated that his friends celebrated his eighty-fifth birthday. "Wherever law is known, he is known," Frankfurter wrote in an unsigned *New Republic* editorial.[38] Lippmann dedicated much of the New York *World's* March 8, 1926, editorial page to the justice: "The fame of Holmes is of an altogether different quality from that of the celebrities about whom we read and write. It is the kind of fame that only a few men in any age acquire; it is the fame of those minds of the first order who affect the character of thought itself." Recalling Holmes's interactions with him and other young men at the House of Truth, Lippmann zeroed in on the source of Holmes's power and influence: "The true disciples of Holmes are the first-rate men now in law school or just recently graduated. Between him and them there is a sympathy of spirit and a community of method which the pedants and legalists do not understand and look upon with some apprehension." The legal establishment, Lippmann argued, has nothing to fear from Holmes and his "revolutionary influence" on these young men because that influence has been "profoundly civilizing," for he taught them to doubt their own "first principles." "He is a thinker who has made thinking, even about law, beautiful." To Holmes, Lippmann identified himself as the author of the editorial.[39]

Lippmann also alerted Holmes that the author of a second essay published in the *World* that day was by another longtime admirer, Judge Learned Hand. Hand annoyed Lippmann by refusing to sign the essay, which came out a week after Hand had visited Holmes at 1720 Eye Street and Holmes had reversed one of Hand's judicial opinions in a patent case.[40] But Hand had come to admire Holmes's skepticism years earlier. In a story that he revealed in Sergeant's *New Republic* profile later that year, Hand recounted a carriage ride with Holmes through Washington, DC. As they parted ways, Hand called out: "Do justice, sir!" Holmes turned around: "Come here, young feller!" "I am not here to do justice," he told Hand. "I am here to play the game according to the rules."[41]

In his essay, Hand defined Holmes's skepticism as the belief that "truth is a dangerous experiment and man is a bungling investigator." Holmes's skepticism made him more comfortable with legislative experiments and resulted in a more limited role for judges. Holmes believed "that the Constitution did not create a tri-cameral system," that judges should not act like legislators by imposing their political beliefs as constitutional commands. Though Holmes's influence on the Court had been "indirect" because he often found himself in dissent when the Court invalidated controversial pieces of legislation, Hand, like Lippmann, understood that Holmes's view of the Constitution had "gained a currency among the younger profession due very largely to his consistent presentation of it." Holmes's skepticism made him different from his fellow judges who imposed their political will in the name of protecting the liberty of the individual. He was an outlier. As a result of his different approach, he was unlikely to win a popularity contest or become famous. And yet, in a "curious phenomenon," Holmes had managed to achieve "a general recognition which puts him among the highest figures in American law."[42]

Holmes's unexpected fame had reached new heights. His eighty-fifth birthday made the national newsreels. The *New York Times* profiled him in its Sunday magazine.[43] An accompanying *Times* editorial, "The Captain," began by quoting his father's *Atlantic Monthly* article, "The Hunt after the Captain" (which must have made Holmes groan). The editorial then recognized the impact of Holmes's book *The Common Law* on legal history and jurisprudence and quoted from Frankfurter's 1923 *Harvard Law Review* article assessing Holmes's judicial career.[44]

A week later, *Time* put Holmes's portrait on a white cover above words that must have been gratifying: "—as venerable as his father."[45] Started in March 1923 by two aspiring journalists from Yale, Henry Luce and Briton Hadden, *Time* had seen its circulation grow from 18,500 at the end of its first year to more than 100,000 in 1926 and rising.[46] Its brief articles and punchy writing style attracted a mass audience. And its covers, featuring portraits of politicians and businessmen, turned them into national celebrities. *Time*'s article about Holmes rehashed some of the same biographical comparisons to his father, noting that the elder Holmes had lived eighty-five years and thirty-nine days. "But Justice Holmes is as venerable as his father, and equals his sire in other respects."[47] The *Time* story began by noting that on his birthday, Holmes dissented from a decision striking down a Pennsylvania law that prohibited the use of "shoddy" in bedding. The Court held that the law was "purely arbitrary" and therefore violated the Due Process Clause. Holmes, joined by Brandeis and Stone, believed that if unsterilized shoddy could spread disease, then Pennsylvania could ban its use in bedding: "I think that we are pressing the Fourteenth Amendment too far."[48]

Time advanced the House of Truth's image of Holmes as a liberal icon. After comparing him to his father, the magazine argued that Holmes "is now and always has been regarded as one of the liberals of the Court. He has never been known as an old fogy. He is no stickler over small technicalities, not one to place the tradition of the law above the majesty of justice." The article quoted Chief Justice Taft that Holmes is the Court's "'most brilliant and learned member'" and a newspaper correspondent's prediction that he and Chief Justice Marshall would be viewed as "'the greatest two men that ever sat in the Supreme Court.'"[49]

In beginning with his dissent about stretching the Fourteenth Amendment beyond its limits, *Time*'s story ended with a mental image of Holmes on the bench: "Last week, white haired, white mustached, 85, and carrying himself like the veteran which he is, Mr. Holmes could well afford to laugh at the suggestion that the greater part of a man's active years are behind him at 60."[50] Holmes not only was a liberal icon but also had achieved national celebrity that would soon eclipse his father's. His reputation, thanks to Frankfurter and friends and now the national news media, was secure. And his goal of living to see ninety was in sight. His friends continued to pursue goals of their own.

22

A Fly on an Elephant

On a February night in 1925, a police car chased Tucker and Borglum's car through Georgia's dark and treacherous back roads. At times, the officers were so close that Tucker ordered Borglum to lie down to avoid being seen or, even worse, getting shot.[1] A few hours earlier, the sculptor had learned from reporters that the executive committee of the Stone Mountain Memorial Association not only had fired him but also had obtained a court order barring him from the premises. He had to leave the mountain right away. With tears in his eyes, he took a final glance at his master model of Lee, Jackson, and Davis on horseback followed by a small cavalry of their lieutenants. And without consulting Tucker or anyone else, he handed a crowbar to Homer, one of his most loyal and trusted men, and ordered him to destroy it.[2] Homer and several other men smashed the master model to pieces. Nothing remained of it besides two or three lower legs of horses.[3] Borglum then gathered all his drawings in his studio and burned them. He went up the mountain and ordered that the models of Jackson's head and Lee's shoulders be dropped off the platform and onto the rocks below.[4]

By nightfall, word had reached Atlanta that the models had been destroyed. One of the association's vice presidents swore out warrants for Tucker's and Borglum's arrest, charging them with malicious mischief, larceny, and larceny from the house. The association also filed a lawsuit charging Borglum with destruction of property worth $50,000. Before the police arrived, someone had tipped off Tucker, who put Borglum in the car and sped east toward Lawrenceville and Athens.[5] The police pursued them for several hours, but Tucker and Borglum lost them. They were later spotted stopping for gasoline in Grayson, Georgia, crossed the border into South Carolina, and dropped out of sight. Police were on the lookout for them in Greenville, South Carolina; Greensboro, North Carolina; and Richmond, Virginia.[6] The two men were rumored to be headed to Washington, DC, or to Cincinnati, Ohio.[7] No one, not even Borglum's wife and children, who had remained back in Atlanta, knew where they were headed.

Anyone reading the nation's newspapers in February 1925 knew that Borglum's days with Hollins Randolph and the Stone Mountain Memorial Association were numbered. In mid-February, the sculptor had nonetheless proceeded to Washington, DC, with his friend Lester Barlow to lobby for legislation that would award Barlow money for patents that had been used for bombing during the war. Barlow agreed to donate $100,000 from the patents to the Confederate Memorial and another $100,000 for a different project that Borglum was planning out west. While Borglum was in Washington, Randolph had offered the job of finishing the Confederate Memorial to Tucker. Tucker declined and immediately called Borglum back to Stone Mountain. Borglum had arrived the next morning at Atlanta's Peachtree Station and was greeted by his wife, Mary, two children, Lincoln and Mary Ellis, and Tucker. Mary and Tucker told him about the committee's plans to seize his work and to remove him. They picked up Stone Mountain owner

Borglum and his model for the Confederate Memorial

Sam Venable from the executive committee meeting, learned more about the committee's imminent plans to fire Borglum, and arrived around 12:30 p.m. at the mountain. Four hours later, the models had been destroyed, and Borglum was on the run.[8]

Both sides had been airing their grievances for some time. Borglum charged that the memorial association lacked the funds for him to finish the central group before the mountain reverted to its owner, Sam Venable. The association had not raised the money it had promised in the spring of 1924. He could not spend as much time as he would have liked working on the mountain because he was so busy making speeches to citizen groups, lobbying congressmen in Washington, and designing the association's two fundraising vehicles—the children's medal and the Stone Mountain half dollar. The association, Borglum told the *Atlantic Constitution*, "has shrunk into a local habitation with no funds and with scarcely a name."[9]

What Borglum did not tell the press was that he desperately needed money. His creditors were still hounding him. Eugene Meyer wanted the $40,000 plus interest that Borglum still owed him.[10] D. C. Stephenson, the rogue Indiana Klansman, wanted his money, too. He tried to attach 100 acres at Borgland, but there was nothing left to attach because the sculptor had mortgaged the property "piece by piece, year after year" to cover his debts.[11] Stephenson had his own problems: he was charged with the rape and murder of a young woman and would soon be convicted and imprisoned. As his legal bills mounted, he sued Borglum for $30,000.[12]

For years, of course, Borglum had poured money into the Confederate Memorial but had been reimbursed only for his expenses and received almost no salary in return. He had declined numerous, more lucrative projects to work on the mountain. In December 1924, he had demanded that the Stone Mountain Memorial Association advance him $40,000 of the remaining portion of the $250,000 that it owed him for the project.[13]

The problem, at least according to Randolph and the association, was not money; it was Borglum. The sculptor had not finished the heads of Jackson and Davis by June 1924 as he had promised. The association also alleged that "it has been extremely difficult to get him to do any work at all at the mountain," that "his main desire seems to be to get his name in the newspapers as often as possible."[14] Nor should it have taken him seven months to design the half dollar. Randolph charged that Borglum had "loafed on the job" from March to October 1924 in designing the coin, a job that should have taken him a matter of weeks. After eight years, the association was not about to pay him for services not rendered, having already paid him $50,000.[15] Borglum's friend Lester Barlow countered with the claim that Borglum had lent the association $20,000 of that money for expenses and had been paid only $30,000 for nearly nine years of work. Randolph disputed Barlow's figures.[16]

Neither Borglum nor Randolph was willing to state publicly that the sculptor had fallen out of favor with the Ku Klux Klan. Borglum's failure to support McAdoo during the 1924 presidential election and his friendship with Stephenson had hurt the sculptor's standing with the Klan leadership.[17] "The Klan were the real issue between them," sculptor William James Robinson said, "although the committeemen were not game enough to admit it." Robinson cited Borglum's supposedly "outspoken opposition" to the Klan and concluded the whole thing was "largely a Ku Klux Klan matter."[18] Borglum denied that the dispute was about the Klan.[19] The New York *Amsterdam News* reminded its primarily black readership about Borglum's comments a few years earlier in the New York *World* that "praised the Klan highly, saying that many of his best friends were Klansmen—perfect gentlemen incapable of wrong doing!"[20] But the *World* and others defended Borglum's artistic rights to his creation.[21]

What it was really about was money—$5 million worth of coins to be precise. Borglum lost his job carving the mountain because he had tried to stop the Klan from controlling the proceeds for the sale of the 5 million Stone Mountain half dollars at a dollar apiece. The sculptor suspected that the Klan was prepared to line its own coffers rather than use the proceeds to fund the memorial.[22]

On January 21, 1925, he wrote President Coolidge, imploring him to establish a national advisory committee to work with the memorial association in selling the Stone Mountain half dollar. Borglum even supplied Coolidge with the names of prominent Democrats and Republicans who could serve on the committee.[23] Coolidge, however, believed that taking ownership of the project was "unwise."[24] Borglum begged the president to reconsider because of the sculptor's "deep anxiety for the welfare and happy conclusion of a work, in which I have given so much, involved our country, and explain my hope that you would help me a little more in insuring its happy conclusion."[25] Upon discovering the date of Borglum's initial letter to Coolidge, Randolph was furious; it was clear that the sculptor had tried to double-cross the association. After Randolph fired him, Borglum tried to intercede with Treasury Secretary Andrew Mellon to have the US Mint directly issue the coins.[26] That, too, proved unsuccessful: the legislation gave the Treasury Department no authority to issue the coin; that power rested solely with the Stone Mountain Memorial Association.[27]

Two days after he and Tucker had vanished into the Georgia night, they resurfaced in Raleigh, North Carolina. The sculptor told the press he had destroyed the models because they were rough, "imperfect," and "useless" and would lead astray any future work. He also openly defied the association's executive committee: "I'll rot in jail forever before I give the key to my design ... to that committee."[28] However, the association was so determined to prosecute Borglum that on February 28 it had him arrested as he was leaving a train in Greensboro and sought to extradite him to Georgia. He was released two hours later on $5,000 bond.[29] He immediately left by train for New York City, where he again defended the destruction of his models based on "the inalienable right of an artist to his own creation."[30] On March 7, the extradition proceedings were dropped after North Carolina governor Angus W. McLean urged his Georgia counterpart to back down.[31] Though he was no longer under arrest, Borglum was still a wanted man in Georgia and did not dare go back. If he did, he believed, he would be killed. "Had it not been for Tucker," he wrote to a friend, "I would have been mobbed and lying in the Dekalb [County] jail or worse."[32]

Unable to prosecute Borglum, the Stone Mountain Memorial Association vowed to remove Lee's head from the mountainside and to replace Borglum with another sculptor, Augustus Lukeman.[33] Privately, Borglum was furious that he was being replaced by Lukeman, "an unprincipled Jew" and a sculptor whom he considered no better than a carpenter.[34] The association's decision to hire another sculptor to complete Borglum's work, however, backfired by swinging the art establishment in his favor. Several prominent artists urged Borglum's reinstatement.[35]

Finally, Hollins Randolph consolidated his power at the association's annual meeting on April 22. He removed Borglum's allies, Stone Mountain owner Sam Venable and the head of the Georgia chapter of the United Daughters of the Confederacy, from the board. Re-elected as president of the association, Randolph announced the official hiring of Lukeman. With Randolph secure in his power and Lukeman the new sculptor, there was no hope of Borglum's return.

All this drama was too much for C. Helen Plane at age ninety-six. The Confederate widow's family allowed the *Atlanta Constitution* to publish parts of her scrapbook detailing how she had spearheaded the building of the memorial and hiring of Borglum. Since the March 10 death of her sixty-five-year-old son, she had become too ill and anguished to talk to the press.[36] She remained the association's president emerita, but her dream of building a Confederate memorial was falling apart. Randolph's April 22 re-election confirmed it.[37] Plane died two days later in a private hospital sixty-three years after her husband's death at Antietam.[38] An *Atlanta Constitution* editorial declared her "the south's noblest woman" and concluded: "She worked incessantly on the fruition of the plan and lived to see the work begun, as she had prayed that she might."[39]

Borglum took the news of Plane's death hard: "Heaven has taken from them every soul and every hand that has aided in lifting Lee to his place on the Mountain."[40] Despite his pugnacious public front, the sculptor was overcome by a profound sadness. He had lost a project to which he had dedicated nearly nine years. He planned to rebuild his working model of the Confederate Memorial's central group at his Raleigh studio.[41] He found it hard to let go and planned to build the monument in North Carolina by carving the granite cliffs of Chimney Rock twenty-five miles from Asheville.[42] But that was just talk. For the rest of his life, he held out hope of finishing what he had started at Stone Mountain. He turned to other projects. On June 3, 1925, he signed a $100,000 contract to build a monument for the Trail Drivers' Association in San Antonio and soon relocated his studio and his family there.[43] The monument was similar in concept to his *Wars of America* memorial (which he was then packing up to be bronzed in Italy). He was busier than ever with work yet could not get mountain carving out of his system.

In January 1924, the state historian of South Dakota, Doane Robinson, had made some offhand remarks in a speech about the value of monuments to tourism and how a monument might be constructed in the granite of the Black Hills. "I can think of nothing in America that would outrival such a spectacle, with the possible exception of Stone Mountain, near Atlanta, Georgia," he said.[44] His idea was ridiculed as an attempt to destroy the natural beauty of the peaks or "needles" along the highway in the Black Hills. He believed that the highest point, Harney Peak, was the perfect place for a monument and that no tourist would pass through the West without seeing it.[45]

Robinson began to reach out to artists, beginning with Chicago-based sculptor Lorado Taft. Robinson inquired about Taft's interest, asked him to survey the location, and suggested carving a Sioux Indian or Red Cloud there.[46] "Near the summit is a little park through which the highway passes," Robinson wrote Taft. "It is no larger than a large hall, but it is studded about with column after column of these great pinnacles and in my imagination I can see all the old heroes of the west peering out from them." To Robinson, these western heroes included the explorers William Lewis and Meriwether Clark, their Native American guide Sacagawea, General John C. Fremont, explorer Jedediah Smith, and showman Buffalo Bill Cody.[47] After Taft declined citing ill health, Robinson contacted the only sculptor who had attempted to carve a mountain. "In the vicinity of Harney Peak, in the Black Hills of South Dakota are opportunities for heroic sculpture of unusual character," he wrote Borglum on August 29, 1924, and asked if he would be interested in creating "a massive sculpture there."[48] The letter arrived at Stone Mountain while Borglum was home in Connecticut. Tucker opened it and wrote across the top: "Here it is Borglum; let's go."[49]

A few days later, Borglum revealed to the press his desire to build a centrally located national memorial not to the Confederacy but to the Union. The location was in the Black Hills of South Dakota. "I wanted a mountain of granite to carve," he said, "and this state reports that it has a mountain, just a little larger than Stone Mountain, with all the conditions to make it a splendid national park." He also announced that he planned to inspect the site and hinted at the grand scope of his ambitions: "The United States is without a real memorial to our Union—a memorial to Washington who forged it, to Lincoln who welded it together, and to our other great national heroes."[50]

In late September 1924, he pulled his twelve-year-old son, Lincoln, out of school for several days. He was grooming the boy to be his protégé and wanted him along for the first visit to the Black Hills. Borglum arrived in Rapid City on September 25 with Lincoln and Tucker in tow. They were met at the train station by Robinson as well as prominent local citizens. There was supposed to be no publicity, but Lester Barlow's brother happened to live in Rapid City and had alerted people to Borglum's arrival. They insisted on fêting the sculptor at an organized lunch, where he spoke to the audience about the importance of national memorials.[51]

Robinson drove Borglum's party that afternoon though the Needles Highway to Sylvan Lake among the granite peaks. The next morning, they climbed Harney Peak, at 7,242 feet above sea level the highest mountain between the East Coast and the Rockies. He continued south of Harney Peak until he saw a "vast line of rock that hides the Peak from view" and that overlooks a "deep canyon" and proclaimed: "Here is the place, American History shall march along the skyline."[52]

After a brief examination of the granite and a survey of the surrounding area, Borglum was steadfast in choosing the peak that soon became known as Mount Rushmore. They returned after two days to Rapid City, where he spoke to the local Rotary Club and "created the utmost enthusiasm" about the monument. "The entire outlook of the people of the Hills is changed," Robinson wrote.[53]

Before he left by train for the East Coast, Borglum had issued a short statement to the Associated Press: "My visit here has been at the earnest request of men interested in the history of our country and its founders. I knew slightly the Hills and I had a day to spare. We walked through the veritable garden of the gods, up Mount Harney. I know the west, much of my life has been spent in the Rockies, yet I know of no grouping of rock formation that equals those found about this mountain in the Black Hills of South Dakota, nor do I know of any so near the center of our country that is so available to the nation or so suitable for colossal sculpture." He disclaimed any intent to carve the needles along the highway and suggested that the granite south of Harney Peak "should be examined for definite historical portrait characters, preferably national in the largest sense. One group alone of this character would single out your great national park and give it a place entirely its own."[54]

The sculptor charmed everyone he met in South Dakota, including Robinson, whom he left with a small sketch of George Washington composed on the morning train and based on a mountain of inspiration.[55] "Borglum has come and gone," Robinson wrote. "I count it one of the great experiences of my lifetime to have spent two days with a man of his genius and high character."[56] Borglum and Robinson agreed that the best way to sell the monument was to limit the initial proposal to the two heads, those of Washington and Lincoln. Each would be 200 feet high. The sculptor believed that the project would require an annual state appropriation of $200,000 for the next three years.[57] By November 24, he had sent Robinson a preliminary sketch of Washington cloaked and Lincoln hatless.[58]

The project started with a built-in advantage over the Confederate Memorial, with its problematic politics and ties to the Ku Klux Klan: political clout in Washington. Before agreeing to carve another mountain, Borglum conferred, in December 1924, with Peter Norbeck, the progressive US senator from South Dakota. It was a meeting of kindred spirits. Borglum and Norbeck were both independent Republicans who had fought for western farmers. Moreover, in Norbeck, Borglum had found someone who could navigate the political waters more adeptly than the sculptor with his bull-in-a-china-shop approach. At first, Norbeck was skeptical, especially with the Confederate Memorial floundering and in need of federal funds. He insisted that the federal government did not like to fund monuments and that some money for the Black Hills monument would have to come from the state of South Dakota. But after a three-hour meeting with Borglum on January 20, 1925, the senator "got a better line on the man than I had had before" and was infected with the sculptor's optimism. "He is a peculiar combination of a promoter, publicist, politician and, last but more important, he is one of the great artists of the world," Norbeck wrote Robinson. "The remarkable trait that I discovered today is probably the fact that he refuses to be discouraged. He looks upon it as a weakness, and almost a disease."[59] During their second meeting, Norbeck was persuaded that Borglum's "mind is on South Dakota now." Borglum told Norbeck that he had but one "big mission in life … to get the American people to look at art in a big way and to get away from this petty stuff."[60]

When the Confederate Memorial fell apart, the competition from a second mountain-carving project was not lost on Hollins Randolph and the memorial association. In their postfiring bill of particulars against Borglum, they cited the exploration of a Union memorial in the Black Hills as one of the reasons he had neglected the Confederate Memorial during the summer and fall of 1924. They predicted that Borglum would take his know-how about mountain carving, his superintendent Tucker, and his loyal crew and relocate them from the southern to the western monument.[61] Borglum's enemies in Georgia tried to derail the Black Hills memorial by flooding South Dakota with nasty letters about the sculptor.[62] The campaign was successful in its way, given that it came while state and federal legislation was pending about the project. The state funding fell through. And the federal reimbursement from Lester Barlow's proceeds from his wartime patents never materialized.[63] The only legislation that passed merely authorized Borglum to carve the mountain because of its proximity to Custer State Park and the Harney National Forest. Therefore, Robinson, Borglum, and Norbeck formed the Harney Memorial Association and pledged to raise the money and to see the project to completion.

Borglum threw the Black Hills monument in the Confederate Memorial Association's face. On March 7, 1925, the same day that the state of Georgia dropped its extradition proceedings and the charges against him in Greensboro were dismissed, he announced that he had been authorized to carve the heads of Washington and Lincoln into a mountain in the Black Hills. He estimated that the project would cost $1 million.[64] About to turn fifty-eight, he felt as if this project would make or break him. "I am determined to put a couple of great figures in your Hills," he wrote Robinson from Raleigh. "I want the vindication it would give me, and I want to give it to my Old West. We will let those people in the South fry in their fat for a year or two."[65] Refusing to repeat the mistake of paying his own expenses as he had at Stone Mountain, Borglum requested $10,000 (which he later reduced to $5,000) in initial funding to survey the mountain and to drill deep into the granite to make sure that it was suitable for carving.[66] The next step was to raise the seed money.

In August 1925, Borglum and his son spent nearly two weeks in South Dakota. The sculptor fished with Senator Norbeck on August 12. The next morning, Borglum and his son left the game lodge and camped for two days at the foot of Rushmore Peak.[67] The sculptor sketched pictures of the mountain in his diary and found the stone to be not only sound enough for carving but also larger than expected. He emerged with a much grander vision—an entablature about America's history and westward expansion, as well as three or four or even five presidents down to their chest and shoulders. Each president would be 200 feet high. In his diary, Borglum described "a group of the Empire Makers" and listed Jefferson, Lincoln, and Roosevelt.[68] "The portraits should be of Washington and Lincoln, the founder and the saviour, should be the portraits of Jefferson, who is the first expansionist and Roosevelt, who completed commercial control by securing Panama," Borglum wrote Norbeck after returning home.[69]

Borglum also began referring to the site of the memorial in his diary and letters by a much catchier name—Mount Rushmore. It was named for Charles Rushmore, a New York lawyer and businessman who had journeyed to the Black Hills in 1884 following the discovery of tin there. Rushmore had spent several weeks with prospectors in the Black Hills to purchase options on the tin mines and had made several return trips. One afternoon, he had stood before the massive granite rock with two tall peaks and had asked the prospectors its name. They told him it didn't have a name. "We will name it now," one of them apparently said, "and name it Rushmore Peak."[70]

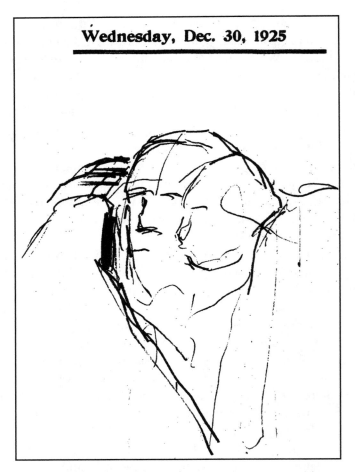

Wednesday, Dec. 30, 1925

Borglum's sketch for Mount Rushmore during an August 1925 visit

Forty years later, Borglum wrote in his diary that the "shoulder of Rushmore is far and away the best that I have seen."[71] After twenty-five Rapid City businessmen raised $5,000, Borglum made his third visit to Rushmore in mid-September 1925 accompanied by ever-loyal Tucker and former Stone Mountain engineers Hugo Villa and Dynamite Cliff Davis.[72] They surveyed and tested the stone in great detail and found it suitable for carving.

Borglum insisted that they dedicate the national memorial that fall. He wanted to raise money over the winter and not lose a year of work on the mountain.[73] He lobbied President Coolidge to dedicate the memorial and scheduled the dedication for October 1, when he knew that Coolidge would be in Omaha for the American Legion national convention. Two weeks before the dedication, the sculptor leaked the invitation to the press and urged friends and politicians to wire the president.[74] Coolidge, however, said it would be "impossible" for him to attend. Borglum returned to Washington to try to change the president's mind—to no avail. Still, he would not concede defeat. More than anyone else, he recognized that Rushmore's ultimate success or failure would depend on the support of Coolidge and the federal government.

Without Coolidge, the October 1 dedication was low-key, particularly by Borglum's standards. Only about 3,000 people showed up. A detachment of soldiers from Fort Meade, South Dakota, led the procession; the Rapid City band played; and a high school glee club sang "America the Beautiful." Senator Norbeck, Governor Carl Gunderson, and state supreme court Judge Dwight Campbell all spoke. Atop the mountain, Borglum, his son, and Norbeck planted flags from France, Spain, and the United States to symbolize how all three countries at various points had claimed sovereignty over the territory. Joining them at the flag ceremony was a Sioux chief, as well as men dressed in American colonial garb and as French and Spanish trappers.[75] Borglum assured those gathered that Washington's head would be completed in a year. "Meet me here a year from today," he told the crowd. "The statue of Washington will exceed in dimensions the Sphinx of Egypt. The entire memorial will be a great thing for your state and for the nation. It will help America to know better the great Northwest and will be an inspiration to patriotic citizens of all generations."[76] Borglum estimated that Rushmore would cost $1 million. He had no signed contract, no funding, yet lots of optimism. Not long after the dedication ceremony he began sketching a detailed rendition of the four American presidents he planned to carve.

Mount Rushmore would be different from the Confederate Memorial, with its Klan funding and racist underpinnings. This new monument celebrated the heroes not of a rebellion but of the founding and the preservation of America's democratic experiment. Of course, it had its own cultural overtones and moral complexities. After all, Borglum was proposing to carve a peak in the Black Hills that the Sioux named *Paha Sapa* (*paha* means hills, and *sapa* means black) and considered sacred land.[77] And he was building a monument ultimately to Manifest Destiny—celebrating "empire builders" who had subjugated indigenous peoples everywhere.

Yet in its way Mount Rushmore reflected a belief in government. By turning heads of Washington, Lincoln, Jefferson, and Roosevelt into towering
embodiments of democratic power, the project tapped into one of liberalism's central tenets that government was a force for good and that its leaders
could be great. In Borglum's mind, the federal government was critical to
his latest masterpiece as a source of funding and approval.

Mount Rushmore was in some ways the monumental apotheosis of
the House of Truth. Though the Stone Mountain memorial had gone
badly wrong, it had driven Borglum's obsession with mountain carving,
and in the process made him unforgettable to Justice Holmes. Recalling
their evening at 1727 Nineteenth Street when the sculptor impressed him
with his tablecloth drawing of the Confederate Memorial, Holmes wrote
Frederick Pollock: "He said to me that when he began he felt like a fly on
an elephant—at the end he felt as if the mountain were a handful of clay
in his hand."[78]

The Confederate Memorial had become for Borglum what the Civil
War had been for the South—a lost cause. Yet it had inspired the sculptor's belief in the country's growing industrial and technological power—
projecting images from hundreds of yards away, blasting dynamite to remove
granite, and devising a hoisting system that allowed men to hang off a
mountainside.[79] It also represented his faith in the power of the federal
government. He had courted Presidents Harding and Coolidge and had
secured funding from the Stone Mountain half dollar. He recognized that
Rushmore would present its own unique set of challenges and struggles,
though ultimately it also would rise or fall based on federal support. And,
like the challenges and struggles facing the country as it debated government's powers and limits, it could result in something timeless.

23

No Ordinary Case

The Frankfurters, the Brandeises, and everyone in their social circle called her Auntie Bee. Brandeis's daughters, Susan and Elizabeth, had called her Auntie Bee as children, and the nickname stuck. Auntie Bee was practically a member of the Brandeis household and considered Brandeis her older brother.[1] Her full name was Elizabeth Glendower Evans, and she and Frankfurter played an integral role in turning the case of two Italian immigrants into one of the trials of the century.

In 1886, Elizabeth's husband, Glendower "Glen" Evans, had died after a brief illness just three years into their marriage. Glen Evans had attended Harvard Law School a few years after Brandeis, read law with Oliver Wendell Holmes Jr., and given Holmes valuable feedback on the proofs of his book *The Common Law*.[2] The young Boston lawyer Glen Evans and his wife had befriended Brandeis, and the trio had become inseparable. After Glen Evans's death, his widow had no idea what to do with the rest of her life. Brandeis helped her find her way. On a Sunday morning walk through the streets of Boston, he encouraged her to expand her mind and to throw herself into political and social causes.[3]

Auntie Bee—known professionally as Elizabeth Evans—dedicated the rest of her life to helping the less fortunate. From 1886 to 1914, she served on the state board of industrial schools for troubled boys. Through Brandeis, she became interested in the problems of industrialization and organized labor. At his urging, she traveled to Britain to study Socialism and to Wisconsin to meet Robert La Follette and to learn about the state's social programs. In 1914, she was the president of Massachusetts's new minimum wage board and worked with the House of Truth's founder Robert Valentine.[4] In 1919, horrified by the treatment of the striking workers at the second textile strike in Lawrence, Massachusetts, she marched with them and encouraged others, including then Harvard instructor Laski, to join her.

She also embraced the cause of woman's suffrage and joined La Follette's wife, Belle, to promote the issue on the Chautauqua lecture circuit. In 1914, Evans headed a White House delegation and confronted President Wilson about the issue.[5] Wearing plain dark dresses that went up to her neck and a fluffy black hat with a large plume, she looked and dressed the part of a suffragette.[6] Evans's familial relationship with the Brandeises never waned. She often spent her summers at their summer cottage on Cape Cod, and the Frankfurters often joined her there. She grew close to Alice Brandeis and Marion Frankfurter, both of whom battled depression yet strived to emulate their friend's social activism.

In 1920, Evans was inspired by Frankfurter and Chafee's success in preventing the deportation of Boston immigrants after the Palmer Raids. She became particularly invested in the case of two Italian anarchists charged with robbery and murder. At 3:00 p.m. on April 15, 1920, the scene on Pearl Street in South Braintree, Massachusetts, was pure chaos. Two men shot and killed a paymaster and his security guard carrying two boxes that contained the Slater and Morrill Shoe Company's payroll of $15,778.51. An

Nicola Sacco (right) and Bartolomeo Vanzetti (left)

open touring car carrying three other men drove up, the two men jumped in after grabbing the boxes of money, and the car fled the scene.

The two anarchists—a shoe factory worker named Nicola Sacco and a fish peddler named Bartolomeo Vanzetti—were arrested twenty days later. Both men were armed—Sacco with a fully loaded Colt automatic .32 caliber pistol and twenty-two extra cartridges, and Vanzetti with a fully loaded .38 caliber pistol.[7] During their interrogation, they lied about their whereabouts on the day of the murders.[8]

Sacco had been planning to return with his family to Italy. On May 2, Vanzetti had been to New York City to try to secure the release of their friend and fellow anarchist, Andrea Salsedo, who had been rounded up during the Palmer Raids and was in the custody of the Justice Department's Bureau of Investigation. On May 4, they learned that Salsedo had been found dead on the sidewalk after being held incommunicado on the fourteenth floor of a Park Row building—the victim of suicide or murder.[9] The next day, Massachusetts police arrested Sacco and Vanzetti.

Because of shotgun shells found on him at the time of his arrest, Vanzetti was first charged and tried in the December 24, 1919, attempted holdup of another shoe company paymaster in Bridgewater, Massachusetts. During an eight-day trial in late June 1920, Vanzetti's lawyers had refused to put him on the stand because, according to Vanzetti, they feared that his anarchist beliefs would be used against him.[10] He was convicted of assault with intent to rob and murder in the Bridgewater case and sentenced to twelve to fifteen years in prison. This was before he and Sacco went on trial for the South Braintree murders.

Evans befriended Sacco and Vanzetti during regular jailhouse visits. She joined the Sacco-Vanzetti Defense Committee and helped finance their legal team. And at the behest of Fred H. Moore, a Socialist lawyer from California, she attended their murder trial in Dedham from May 31 to July 14, 1921. As she sat in the courtroom during those seven weeks taking notes, she was convinced that the two men were innocent and would be acquitted. She began to notice that the jurors would not look the accused men in the eye and would barely glance at the exhibits. After the jury returned a guilty verdict, she wrote Sacco and Vanzetti that she believed that they were innocent, and she vowed not to rest until they were freed.[11]

Evans pestered Marion Frankfurter for her husband's views about the case. As a former assistant US attorney for Henry Stimson in Manhattan, Frankfurter had tried numerous defendants and knew how criminal prosecutions should be conducted. As a Harvard law professor, he had stood up for the rights of Boston immigrant radicals rounded up during the Palmer Raids. Now two more radicals were charged at the height of those raids and faced a fate much worse than deportation. And as co-chair of the Cleveland Crime Survey, Frankfurter understood that big-city criminal justice systems needed reform and that sensationalistic newspaper coverage often jeopardized the fairness of criminal trials. Yet he had no interest in opining about a case that he knew nothing about except for inflammatory newspaper headlines. He told his wife that without having read the record he could not comment about either the trial or the conviction.[12]

Evans would not let it go. Neither would Marion Frankfurter. After two years and with new trial motions pending, they continued to hound him.[13] Two things changed Frankfurter's mind. First, William G. Thompson agreed to represent the two men on appeal. One of the most respected members of the Boston bar and one of the city's most accomplished trial lawyers, Thompson was a good friend of Frankfurter's mentor Stimson, as well as with the late Harvard Law School dean Ezra Thayer, who had hired Frankfurter. Unlike the California lawyer who had represented Sacco and Vanzetti at trial, Thompson was a Boston Brahmin who would not treat the appeal like a social cause and who would have the instant respect of local judges.[14]

Second, Frankfurter read a newspaper account of one of Thompson's new trial motions, which was based on an affidavit from the state's ballistics expert, Captain William Proctor. The head of the Massachusetts State Police for thirty years, Proctor claimed that the prosecution had knowingly misused his testimony. Prior to trial, he had repeatedly informed the prosecution that he was unwilling to testify that the .32 caliber Colt automatic pistol found on Sacco at the time of his arrest was the same one that had fired one of the fatal bullets. Instead, based on a pretrial agreement with the prosecution, Proctor testified: "My opinion is that it is consistent with being fired by that pistol."[15] Proctor meant that the fatal bullet could have been fired from any .32 caliber Colt automatic pistol, not necessarily Sacco's. The jury, however, missed this distinction during Proctor's lengthy and highly technical testimony. The prosecution did not deny Proctor's story except to say that Proctor had not "repeatedly" told them that he would refuse to testify that the fatal bullet came from Sacco's gun. "When I read about that motion something happened to my insides," Frankfurter recalled. All the lessons that Stimson had taught him about how

Elizabeth Glendower Evans

to prosecute a case came flooding back. It was not all about winning but winning the right way. The disclosure of potentially exculpatory evidence was not required by the law at the time, but it was required by the ethical standards of any self-respecting prosecutor. "If what Proctor said was true, it was reprehensible beyond words," Frankfurter said, "and it undermined any confidence in the conduct of the case, that a district attorney should try to get an expert to swear to something that he repeatedly said that he couldn't swear to." After the district attorney did not deny Proctor's story except the detail that Proctor had not told them "repeatedly," Frankfurter knew what he had to do: read the record.[16]

Frankfurter helped transform a case that for six years had outraged people all over the world into an American obsession. But he accomplished something much more important: he turned the case into nothing less than a litmus test for American liberalism. Liberals lined up for or against a new trial for Sacco and Vanzetti. The Red Scare and the Palmer Raids were admittedly deplorable. But it was one thing to object to the deportation of European immigrants, to rush to the defense of Harvard law professors from rich reactionary alumni, or to protest the ouster of an Amherst College president by a repressive board of trustees. It was another to stand up for the rights of two men who held abhorrent political views, who had fled to Mexico rather than serve in the US military during the world war, and who had been convicted by a jury of cold-blooded murder. Frankfurter forced his old friends from the House of Truth—Lippmann, Holmes, and Borglum, among them—to choose sides. Like Holmes, he helped put fair criminal trials on the liberal agenda and redefined what American liberalism stood for.

★★★

In January 1926, Frankfurter watched as Thompson tried to persuade the five justices on the Supreme Judicial Court of Massachusetts to grant the two men a new trial. The justices were not as impressed as Frankfurter had been. Five months later, they ruled that the trial judge had not abused his discretion in refusing to grant a new trial.[17] "I wish you had been present and heard the whole argument …," Frankfurter wrote Laski. "The poor Judge is himself the victim of forces and of emotional and intellectual limitations he has not a glimmer of. I am very pessimistic of the outcome. I cannot believe that the Governor will ever allow them to be hung, but I fear they will not get a new trial, confident as I am that a new trial would acquit them."[18]

Frankfurter left nothing to chance. With the assistance of Sylvester Gates, an Oxford-educated graduate student spending two years at Harvard Law School, he began working on a *New Republic* article about the case.[19] He thought highly of Gates and wanted him to succeed Tom Corcoran as Justice Holmes's next secretary; Gates, however, turned the offer down because he did not think it would advance his legal career in Britain.[20] Frankfurter allowed Gates to write the first draft of the *New Republic* article; Frankfurter rewrote, edited, and supervised its final publication.[21] In preparation, Frankfurter read the 2,000-page trial record, the trial judge's denial of a new trial, and the prosecution's and defense's objections and appellate briefs; attended the three days of oral argument before the Massachusetts Supreme Judicial Court in January 1926; and dissected the court's May 1926 decision denying a new trial.[22]

Yet no one knew that Frankfurter had co-authored the unsigned June 9 *New Republic* article, "The Sacco and Vanzetti Case." The article was consistent with Frankfurter's work on the Cleveland Crime Survey—a fact-intensive inquiry into what had happened at the trial. To the magazine's liberal readers, Frankfurter and Gates explained in three pages of detail how the two Italian anarchists had been railroaded. The article questioned the reliability of the prosecution's eyewitnesses—two women had seen the getaway car crossing the railroad tracks from a second-floor window sixty feet away but did not come forward for a year; a man had been working in a nearby shoe factory and had seen them through an open window; another woman had seen nothing at the time, then changed her story because the police were "'bothering the life out of me'"; another man, who unbeknownst to the jury was facing a larceny charge, identified them from a pool hall thirty feet away yet had told others at the time that "'he was so scared he never saw the men's faces.'" Some of the eyewitnesses never saw a lineup, only the two defendants. "Under such conditions," Frankfurter and Gates wrote, "identification of foreigners is a farce."[23]

As "foreign radicals" arrested at the height of the Red Scare and the Palmer Raids, the article argued, Sacco and Vanzetti never stood a chance of receiving a fair trial. Not with armed guards marching them handcuffed together through the streets of Dedham to the courthouse each day and the two defendants sitting in the courtroom in a cage. Not with District Attorney Frederick G. Katzmann questioning them about their draft dodging and anarchist views and ending his closing statement to the jury with "'[S]tand together, you men of Norfolk County!'" Or with Judge Webster Thayer charging the jury that "'you, like the true soldier, responded to that call in the spirit of supreme American loyalty.'" Not with the prosecution papering over the shakiness of the eyewitness testimony with a theory of "consciousness of guilt" based on the nervous lies the defendants had told after their arrest. "The prosecution harped on 'consciousness of guilt,'" Frankfurter and Gates wrote. "But was this consciousness of being a murderer or consciousness of being a Red at a time when, beneath the generous impulse of patriotism and the distorting energy of fear, the government was hunting Reds like wild beasts?" They invoked Holmes's comment in the Leo Frank case that "'any Judge who has sat with juries knows that in spite of forms they are extremely likely to be impregnated by the environing atmosphere.'"[24]

The article laid out the motions for a new trial. Jury foreman Walter Ripley, a former Quincy, Massachusetts, police chief, had brought in his own bullets for the jury to examine and in response to a comment before trial that the defendants were innocent had replied: "Damn them, they ought to hang them, anyway." Eyewitness Roy Gould, who believed that a man who had fired at him from the getaway car did not look like Sacco or Vanzetti, was not called by the prosecution or revealed to the defense. Captain Proctor swore that he had refused to testify that the fatal bullet had come from Sacco's gun, yet the prosecution had given the jury that mistaken impression. Based on the record and Thompson's argument before the Massachusetts Supreme Judicial Court, the article concluded: "The 2,000 pages of the record reveal the presence of other passions than that for justice, other tempers than the 'calmness of a cool mind.'"[25]

Frankfurter made sure that at least one person knew that he and Gates had written the unsigned *New Republic* article. Relations between Frankfurter and Lippmann had improved since their differences over the 1924 presidential election, Lowell's Jewish quota at Harvard, and the Meiklejohn affair at Amherst. They had agreed to collaborate on the Harvard Crime Survey's analysis of newspaper coverage of Boston's criminal trials. Frankfurter had been contributing ideas to the New York *World*'s editorial page and had written and declined payment for an unsigned editorial about the prosecutions of corrupt Harding administration officials. And Frankfurter's presence in New York City during the summer of 1926 undoubtedly helped the relationship given that Lippmann loathed responding to Frankfurter's letters. Frankfurter revealed his co-authorship with a sense of purpose—he wanted the *World* to take a lead role in making the public case for a new trial. He wrote Lippmann that Harvard historian Samuel Eliot Morison said of the Sacco-Vanzetti case that "'the honor of the Commonwealth is at stake' & hardly anybody cares."[26] Lippmann cared. "As to Sacco Vanzetti, I'll wait to hear from you further," he wrote Frankfurter in June. "I'm thinking about it, bear in mind the great difficulty of discussing the details of the evidence for a newspaper audience that has no background of the case."[27] Whether Lippmann cared as a newsman or because of his politics remained to seen. And whether he cared as much as Frankfurter was extremely doubtful. Yet Frankfurter was doing exactly what Lippmann's books had suggested that experts do—educate public opinion.

In the meantime, new evidence cast doubt on the verdict. On November 18, 1925, twenty-three-year-old Celestino F. Medeiros, who was in the same Dedham jail awaiting his execution for murdering a bank cashier, had passed a note to Sacco: "I hear by confess to being in the South Braintree shoe company crime and Sacco and Vanzetti was not in said crime."[28] Medeiros's "confession" was not immediately made public or pursued by the defense because his appeal was pending before the Massachusetts Supreme Judicial Court (he was granted a new trial and convicted again). In a jailhouse deposition on June 28, 1926, however, Medeiros testified that he had been one of the men riding in the back of the getaway car from the South Braintree murders with the Providence-based Morelli gang.[29] He again insisted that Sacco and Vanzetti had not been involved.[30]

The Medeiros confession and Morelli gang story gained credence thanks to a lawyer whom Frankfurter had solicited to join the defense team, Herbert "Brute" Ehrmann. In 1914, Ehrmann had been a third-year Harvard law student looking for a job when he had met the newly arrived Frankfurter; they became fast friends and longtime collaborators. During the war, Ehrmann had replaced former New Hampshire governor Robert Bass as the US Shipping Board's representative to Frankfurter's War Labor Policies Board. Ehrmann had been the one who had recognized Frankfurter and Franklin Roosevelt as the board's "only two first-rate minds."[31] Ehrmann also had dined at the House of Truth. "The talk was fast and sprightly," he recalled, "although a number of Harvard College professors seemed more interested in scuttle butt about their colleagues back home than in the 'Truth.'"[32] After the war, Ehrmann had worked at the Boston firm of Hale & Dorr and with Frankfurter and Pound on the Cleveland Crime Survey. In May 1926, Frankfurter asked him to assist Thompson on the Sacco and Vanzetti case.

Ehrmann was as skeptical as anyone about the truthfulness of Medeiros's confession and thought that the story about the Morelli gang was simply the lies of a condemned man. The more Ehrmann investigated the facts of the Bridgewater and South Braintree shoe factory robberies, however, the more the evidence suggested that the Morelli gang had committed them. He used the skills he had learned on the Cleveland survey to investigate the gang, which had been prosecuted in Rhode Island for a string of train robberies of shoes and textiles. Some of the shoes were from the South Braintree factory.[33] Eventually, Ehrmann became so convinced of the gang's guilt in the South Braintree robbery that he wrote a book laying out all the connections.[34] As a result of Ehrmann's investigative work in 1926, Thompson made the Medeiros confession another basis for a motion for a new trial.

With the Medeiros motion pending, Frankfurter spurred the *World* into action, and the newspaper sent its Pulitzer Prize–winning labor and economics reporter, John J. Leary, to cover the new trial hearings. Leary wrote a story, based on two former agents' testimony in Thompson's new trial motion, in which he argued that the Department of Justice had secretly collaborated with District Attorney Katzmann in prosecuting Sacco and Vanzetti.[35] Frankfurter thanked Lippmann for help and putting "your finger on the vitals of the case. ... In simple truth, you are again rendering a notable public service."[36]

During a four-day hearing from September 13 to 17, Judge Thayer rejected the defense's request to allow Medeiros to testify in open court and instead relied on the prisoner's prior statements.[37] After witnessing the hearings, Frankfurter prepared Lippmann for the worst: "I am so pessimistic about the outcome of the Sacco case from what I know and saw of the judge's attitude. It is quite incredible! I don't seem to be able to free my mind from preoccupation from what is a truly terrible thing."[38] Lippmann promised to do more. "I'm prepared to go to pretty broad lengths in the Sacco matter, if I saw my way clearly how to do it," he wrote Frankfurter on September 23. He expressed willingness to come to Boston for a day to learn more about the facts of the case.[39] A few days later, Frankfurter replied: "We surely will want you to come if Thayer fails."

On October 22, Thayer denied the Medeiros motion for a new trial. Thompson once again appealed to the Massachusetts Supreme Judicial Court. Three days after Thayer's decision, Frankfurter wired Lippmann: "STRONGLY URGE YOU TO COME UP FOR SESSION WITH THOMPSON AND ME."[40] Lippmann replied that it was "impossible" for at least three weeks.[41]

Instead of waiting for Lippmann, Frankfurter made inroads closer to home with the *Boston Herald*'s editorial page editor, F. Lauriston Bullard. Three days after Judge Thayer denied the Medeiros motion, Bullard wrote and published an editorial, "We Submit." "We do not know whether these men are guilty or not," he wrote. "We have no sympathy with the half-baked views which they profess. But as the months have merged into years and the great debate over this case has continued, our doubts have solidified slowly into convictions, and reluctantly we have found ourselves compelled to reverse our original judgment." A number of things troubled the paper: Judge Thayer's decision denying a new trial "carries the tone of the advocate rather than the arbitrator"; the Justice Department's files should be produced because federal officials admitted working on the case with the state police; Medeiros's confession to the crime should be heard "in open court"; and Captain Proctor's ballistics testimony misled the jury. "And if on second trial Sacco and Vanzetti should be declared guiltless everybody would rejoice that no monstrous injustice shall have been done," the editorial concluded. "We submit these views with no reference whatever to the personality of the defendants and without allusion now to that atmosphere of radicalism of which we heard so much in 1921."[42] Few expected the *Herald* to come out in favor of a new trial. The editorial won Bullard the Pulitzer Prize. Brandeis congratulated Frankfurter: "You have done an extraordinary thing in educating the Herald to its stand on S. V.; the World also."[43]

Frankfurter continued to take matters into his own hands. In November 1926, he and Gates began expanding upon their *New Republic* article. Their goal was to distill the 2,000-page trial transcript into prose that the average person could read and draw a conclusion as to the fairness of the proceedings. The transcripts were proving "very difficult" to summarize, and the "pamphlet," as Frankfurter described it, was "long."[44] After reviewing the evidence again and working on the expanded article, he became more convinced that an injustice had been done. "As I read that record, the more I read it the more flimsy the case against the men appears, the more obviously biased Thayer's conduct is revealed," he wrote his wife, Marion. "But—Moore was an incredibly poor lawyer! The Proctor motion ('consistent with') is absolutely conclusive. And so it goes."[45]

In his longer article, Frankfurter laid out the case that the Massachusetts judicial system had failed. Initially, he planned on publishing it in the *New Republic.*[46] The magazine had seen better days, having declared bankruptcy in October 1924.[47] Its circulation had plummeted from a postwar high of 27,500 on Armistice Day in November 1919 to 14,500 in mid-1925.[48] As a result of Croly's decision to oppose the ratification of the Treaty of Versailles, the magazine had lost many of its subscribers as well as its political influence.[49] It also had lost many of its founding editors. In November 1919, Walter Weyl had died of cancer. Lippmann's departure in 1920 with Charles Merz did not help. By the fall of 1926, editors Francis Hackett, Alvin Johnson, and Philip Littell also had left the magazine. Croly was not the intellectual force he had been when he had started the magazine in 1914 or when he had written *The Promise of American Life* in 1909. He had become so disillusioned with the Harding and Coolidge administrations that he threw himself into a religious mysticism that one of the magazine's editors described as a "quasi-Oriental cult."[50] Though he had resigned as one of the magazine's trustees in December 1924, Frankfurter remained loyal to Croly and to the magazine and planned on publishing the pamphlet there.[51]

Until, that is, Ellery Sedgwick caught wind of it.[52] The owner and editor of the Boston-based *Atlantic Monthly*, Sedgwick went way back with Frankfurter. A friend of Winfred Denison's since their Harvard College days, he had been a regular visitor and overnight guest at the House of Truth.[53] Through Denison, he had met Holmes and the House's other regulars and had begun a lifelong friendship and correspondence with Frankfurter. A native of Stockbridge, Massachusetts, Sedgwick had worked at several magazines after college before buying the *Atlantic Monthly*—which had been founded in 1857 by proper Bostonians including Ralph Waldo Emerson, Henry Wadsworth Longfellow, and Oliver Wendell Holmes Sr.— for $50,000. Sedgwick married into a Boston Brahmin family, knew and liked all the proper Bostonians, yet wanted to prove his bona fides to his young intellectual friends. "He was also one of these compounded creatures like the rest of us," Frankfurter recalled. "He wanted to be on the side of the angels. He wanted to be for decency. He wanted to be for 'liberalism'— provided it didn't cost him too much, particularly if it didn't cost him too much with what he regarded as the 'right people.'"[54]

After suffering a nervous breakdown five years earlier, Sedgwick had traveled to South America and in Montevideo, Uruguay, was shocked to a find "a throng of people" in the town square stirred up over newspaper headlines about Sacco and Vanzetti. A few years later, every newspaper editor in London wanted to discuss the case with him. A slightly embarrassed Sedgwick returned home determined to publish something in the *Atlantic Monthly*.[55] He phoned Frankfurter, inquired about the existence of the article, and asked to publish it. Frankfurter, however, insisted that he was committed to Croly and the *New Republic*.[56] Sedgwick refused to take no for an answer. The *Atlantic Monthly* reached a much larger audience (132,000 circulation) than the *New Republic* (25,000), and the Boston-based magazine would make a much bigger impact on the people and politicians of Massachusetts.[57] Besides, the *New Republic* already had two editors, Bruce Bliven and Robert Morss Lovett, writing about the case.[58] To his fellow editors, Croly did not seem particularly interested in Sacco-Vanzetti.[59] Finally, Frankfurter had already published a shorter article in the magazine. His conversation with Croly, in which he asked to be released from his commitment and to publish the article in the *Atlantic*, was an easy one. Croly agreed and released Frankfurter without any bitterness.[60]

In the *Atlantic Monthly*'s March 1927 issue, Sedgwick published "The Portentous Case of Sacco and Vanzetti: A Comprehensive Analysis of a Trial of Grave Importance." The article was twenty-three pages long. A month later, the Boston-based Little, Brown and Company published the piece, including additional facts and footnotes left out of the magazine, as a short book, *The Case of Sacco and Vanzetti: A Critical Analysis for Lawyers and Laymen.*[61] Frankfurter directed all the proceeds from the article and the book to the Sacco-Vanzetti Defense Committee.[62] He also paid his British graduate student Sylvester Gates $125, half of what the magazine paid for the article.[63]

The article—and the ensuing controversy it produced—tested Sedgwick's resolve. Shortly after its initial publication, he received a letter of protest from Justice McReynolds, who remained just as anti-Semitic and reactionary as ever. On the bench, McReynolds was cold to Brandeis and had been hostile to former colleagues Pitney and Clarke.[64] "McR is a very extraordinary personality—what matters most to him are personal relations, the affections," Brandeis confided to Frankfurter. "He is a *Naturemensch*—he has very tender affections and correspondingly hates. … He is a lonely person, has few real friends, is dilatory in his work."[65]

McReynolds was no friend of Frankfurter's. As Wilson's new attorney general, McReynolds had clashed with Frankfurter in 1913 around the House of Truth's dinner table about maintaining the Justice Department's civil service system. Four years later, McReynolds had been hostile to Frankfurter during the oral argument about Oregon's maximum hour law.[66]

McReynolds questioned why Sedgwick had published Frankfurter's article: "The purpose of the writer seems plain enough and harmonizes with what he has done in other times."[67] Sedgwick's defense of Frankfurter was tepid at best: "With many of Professor Frankfurter's activities, I have no personal sympathy. He is hot-headed, not always temperate, radical in his instincts, but upright, courageous, and able. I personally went through his article with great care."[68] McReynolds was not mollified: "I must think your estimate of the writer of the article is very much too high & that this misleads you. Other performances by him indicate what lies in the back of his head." McReynolds was furious about "unsympathetic assaults upon the courts by men with crooked minds" and reasserted his faith in the Massachusetts courts and lack of faith in Frankfurter. "My faith in them cannot be shaken by the ill-natured flings from an exotic mind." McReynolds wanted to send a message to a member of Old Boston society: "Perhaps I may venture to add that to me it is a really annoying thing to find such a man teaching American boys at Harvard. Do the responsible managers of the institution realize what the results will be, surely they cannot."[69]

Frankfurter was writing in real time to influence public opinion and to move people of Massachusetts to right a wrong. He wanted the public to make up its mind before it was too late. "The Sacco-Vanzetti case has been before the courts and the public for more than six years. It has divided opinion at home and been the cause of demonstration abroad, and the end is not yet," he wrote in the prefatory note to the book dated February 15, 1927. "This is no ordinary case of robbery and murder. More issues are involved in it than the lives of two men. Had that been all, its history could never have been so prolonged. Other factors, little known and less understood, explain its extraordinary vitality. What they are, these pages seek to make clear, for the first time so far as the general public is concerned."[70]

Lippmann echoed Frankfurter's call for public concern. A New York World editorial recommended Frankfurter's article to the newspaper's readers "who wish to understand this case." The editorial summarized the article's main points—the Red Scare prejudices of Judge Thayer and the prosecutor, the misleading ballistics testimony of Captain Proctor, and the Medeiros confession that the robbery and murder were the work of the Morelli gang. "A new trial can do no harm if Sacco and Vanzetti are guilty; it may prevent a great wrong if they are innocent," Lippmann's editorial concluded. "Mr. Frankfurter and the other men who have taken the side of these friendless agitators, in the face of intense popular prejudice against them, have done a generous and valuable service to the cause of justice."[71] Frankfurter thanked Lippmann for the editorial; Lippmann replied that he kept two copies of Frankfurter's Atlantic Monthly article—one at home and one at the office. "You've done a fine, disinterested job," Lippmann wrote, "which ought to give you great satisfaction."[72] Others agreed. Later that summer, Time magazine wrote: "Felix Frankfurter's study of the Sacco-Vanzetti case has become a sort of Sacco-Vanzetti Bible, excerpts from which have been read from many a soap-box on many a public square."[73]

One of the most controversial aspects of Frankfurter's article was the matter of when it was published—with the appeal of Medeiros's new trial motion pending before the Massachusetts Supreme Judicial Court. On January 27 and 28, 1927, Thompson argued the motion before the state supreme court and was awaiting the outcome of his latest appeal. On February 10, Thompson wrote Frankfurter questioning the wisdom of publishing before the court ruled.[74] The next day by telephone, Frankfurter indicated his willingness to defer to Thompson's judgment because it was Thompson's case. Frankfurter, however, pointed out that Judge Thayer was not above reproach and that the public had a right to know about his judicial conduct. Frankfurter also observed that Thayer's hometown Worcester County Bar had passed a formal resolution approving the trial judge's conduct; Frankfurter's "scientific discussion" would prevent the debate from being one-sided. After he talked with Frankfurter, Thompson's doubts disappeared.[75]

On April 5, after the publication of the article and the book, the Massachusetts Supreme Judicial Court denied the appeal based on the Medeiros motion. The Court refused to address the new evidence or to order a new trial. It merely said that in denying the new trial motion, Judge Thayer had not abused his discretion.[76] In other states but not in Massachusetts, appellate judges inquired into the evidentiary basis for a criminal conviction. Judge Thayer, however, was the only judge who had reviewed the facts of the case.

At 10:00 a.m. on April 9, sheriff's deputies and court officers armed with shotguns stood guard inside and outside the crowded Dedham courtroom to hear Sacco's and Vanzetti's sentencing. Evans, her hair now completely white, sat in the front row flanked by two women supporting her. Frankfurter watched the proceedings from the jury box with the press. Sacco and Vanzetti were brought into the courtroom handcuffed together and sat in an enclosed cage in the center of the courtroom.[77]

The clerk asked Sacco if he wanted to say anything about why he should not be sentenced to death. Sacco, who had been resigned to his execution for many months and had been protesting his conviction with periodic hunger strikes, spoke in halting English: "I am not an orator. It is not very familiar with me the English language." Yet he lashed out at Judge Thayer and the cruelty of the court: "As I said before, Judge Thayer know all my life, and he know that I am never been guilty, never—not yesterday nor today nor forever."[78]

The clerk then asked the same question of Vanzetti. The mustachioed and more intellectual Vanzetti was similarly unbowed. He launched into a forty-minute soliloquy that astonished Frankfurter and others in attendance. Vanzetti declared his innocence in the Bridgewater and South Braintree robberies. He discussed the Medeiros confession and accused Judge Thayer and District Attorney Katzmann of highlighting their radical views to prejudice the jury.[79] "I would not wish to a dog or to a snake, to the most low and misfortunate creature of the earth—I would not wish to any of them what I have had to suffer for things that I am not guilty of," Vanzetti concluded. "But my conviction is that I have suffered for things that I am guilty of. I am suffering because I am a radical and indeed I am radical; I have suffered because I was an Italian, and indeed I am an Italian; I have suffered more for my family and for my beloved than for myself; but I am so convinced to be right that if you could execute me two times, and if I could be reborn two other times, I would live again to do what I have done already."[80]

Emotionless, Judge Thayer began to speak and insisted that he was bound by Massachusetts law. First, he sentenced Sacco to death. As the judge started to pronounce the second death sentence, Vanzetti asked to speak to his lawyer. Judge Thayer kept going. Then Sacco cried out: "You know I am innocent. That is the same word I pronounced seven years ago. You condemn two innocent men."[81]

Ignoring the interruption, Judge Thayer explained that Sacco and Vanzetti would be killed "by the passage of a current of electricity through your body" during the week of July 10. "This is the sentence of the law."[82]

After the court adjourned, the pair's loyal supporters, including Evans, rushed to Sacco and Vanzetti's cage and whispered "words of encouragement."[83] The press and other onlookers could not stop talking about the eloquence of Vanzetti as he faced the prospect of death. Frankfurter told the New York *World* that "he never had been more moved than by Vanzetti's speech."[84]

"The S.V. decision came quick & of course was not unexpected by you," Brandeis wrote Frankfurter after the state supreme court's decision. "It will perhaps heighten the already great impression your book has made."[85] Frankfurter was assisting the New York *World* editorial page and advising the Sacco-Vanzetti Defense Committee.[86] Indeed, the legal efforts to save Sacco and Vanzetti and the backlash against Frankfurter's recently published book had only just begun.

Old Boston lashed out at Frankfurter for publishing during a pending appeal and other ethical violations. Moorfield Storey, one of the founders of the NAACP and a leading opponent of Brandeis's Supreme Court nomination, accused Frankfurter of serving as pro bono defense counsel and writing the book. Both Frankfurter and Thompson denied that Frankfurter was part of the defense team.[87] Others charged that prominent graduates refused to contribute to the law school's endowment fund because of

Frankfurter's activities.[88] Finally, Storey vowed to "have nothing to do with the Law School as long as Frankfurter is on the Faculty" because of a false rumor that Frankfurter had written an initial report concluding that Tom Mooney was guilty but had withdrawn it because of "political pressure."[89] It was no coincidence that the *Boston Evening Transcript* reprinted Theodore Roosevelt's 1919 letter attacking Frankfurter's Mooney report.[90] Two days later, the paper was shamed into republishing Frankfurter's response to the late president.[91]

With alumni attacking him from all sides, Frankfurter was deeply disappointed with the "timidity," "fear," and lies of his dean, Roscoe Pound. "For once I'm stumped in deciding what is the wise thing to do with R.P.," Frankfurter confided to Brandeis. An apologetic Pound told Massachusetts Supreme Judicial Court justices that he had urged Frankfurter not to publish until after their decision. In private conversations with Frankfurter, Pound had initially disagreed with Frankfurter's decision to publish. Two days later, however, Pound had changed his mind. "I have thought a good deal about our last talk re: S.V.," he told Frankfurter. "I'm glad you published your book—it was in the interest of justice that you should have done so."[92] Frankfurter wisely chose to wait to confront Pound until after the case was over.[93] Their deteriorating relationship never recovered from this episode.[94] Pound privately agreed that Sacco and Vanzetti had been railroaded and privately defended Frankfurter's book against charges that it was "'one-sided,'" but the dean declined to voice opinions about the case or to support Frankfurter—not even from his highest-profile attacker.[95]

John Henry Wigmore, the dean of Northwestern University Law School and the nation's leading expert on the rules of evidence, was one of the most respected members of the legal academy. He was also a longtime friend and correspondent of Justice Holmes. The war, however, tested their friendship. Wigmore had worked on the staff of General Enoch Crowder in the judge advocate general's office; he had attained the rank of major and received a Distinguished Service Medal. The war had turned him into a superpatriot who supported Attorney General Palmer's roundups of radicals and immigrants. Indeed, Wigmore attacked anyone who tried to defend their civil liberties. He had criticized Holmes's dissent in the *Abrams* case as "poor law and poor policy" and with "dangerous implications."[96] Now he took aim at Frankfurter's Sacco-Vanzetti book. Frankfurter was just as anti-Communist and pro-America as Wigmore was, but Wigmore had disagreed with Frankfurter's recommendation to Newton D. Baker that the

War Department take a more flexible approach in handling conscientious objectors.[97] He had undoubtedly blanched at Frankfurter's Mooney report, as well as the Harvard professor's support for amnesty for Jacob Abrams and legal challenge to the Palmer Raids. To people in Chicago, Wigmore began referring to Frankfurter as "the most dangerous man in the U.S."[98]

As soon as Frankfurter's *Atlantic Monthly* article was published, Wigmore began telling his colleagues that he planned on writing a reply. "Sacco and Vanzetti are dangerous enemies to society," Wigmore announced. He intended to reveal "the character of the men, the influences behind them" in an effort to help the public understand how dangerous they were. When a colleague responded that he would "be playing directly into Frankfurter's hands" based on the argument that Sacco and Vanzetti were convicted because of their radical beliefs, Wigmore insisted that "the facts are not as Frankfurter says they are" and vowed to contact Judge Thayer to "find out what the facts really are."[99]

Judge Thayer seemed emboldened by Wigmore's support. "I have nothing and nobody to fear …," Thayer told the *New York Times* on the day that he sentenced Sacco and Vanzetti to death. "In reference to the articles published by Professor Frankenstein [*sic*] of Harvard in the *Atlantic Monthly*, I would say that these will be answered by one of the best authorities in the United States at the proper time."[100] In addition to Thayer, Wigmore sought information about the case from Hoover's Bureau of Investigation.[101] The evidence professor tried to publish his response in the *Massachusetts Law Quarterly*, the journal of the Massachusetts Bar Association. State bar secretary Frank Grinnell suggested that the article would get more publicity in the *Boston Evening Transcript*.[102] Four days later, the *Transcript* accepted it for publication.[103]

Wigmore's article never mentioned Frankfurter by name; instead, it repeatedly referred to him as "the plausible pundit." It accused him of making "errors and misstatements" and committing "libel on Massachusetts justice." Wigmore further charged that the defense had never objected to the composition of the jury pool; that Judge Thayer had not said that the Massachusetts Supreme Judicial Court had "approved" (as opposed to "affirmed") the verdict; and that the Massachusetts Supreme Judicial Court could (and did) review the facts of the case.[104]

At 3:00 p.m. on April 25, Frankfurter received a phone call alerting him to Wigmore's front-page *Boston Evening Transcript* article: "J. H. Wigmore Answers Frankfurter Attack on Sacco-Vanzetti Verdict." Frankfurter and his secretary rushed to Harvard Square, bought a copy of the newspaper, and brought a typewriter with them to Frankfurter's home at 192 Brattle Street. Marion Frankfurter saw the article while riding on a streetcar and rushed home by taxi to tell her husband. By the time she arrived, he was already writing his response. He also had called a friend at the *Boston Herald* and persuaded the paper to hold the presses so that the next morning's paper could contain his response.[105] Later that afternoon, Sedgwick phoned him in a panic. He urged Frankfurter to "be temperate, be cool" in response. Wigmore's article, combined with the criticism of some of Old Boston's most esteemed lawyers, was too much for the *Atlantic Monthly* publisher to bear. Frankfurter later learned that "Sedgwick took to bed when he saw this attack by Wigmore."[106]

Frankfurter knew how to defend himself. He had responded in print to both Theodore Roosevelt and Solicitor General James Beck about his memorandum in the Mooney case and bested both men on the facts. Wigmore's article suffered from a fatal flaw: he had not read the record. Instead, he relied on conversations with Judge Thayer and on Thayer's written opinion. Frankfurter, on the other hand, had based his article and book on the record and more specifically on the bill of exceptions— the prosecution's and defense's objections at each stage of the trial and appeals process.[107] In a response long on facts and short on invective, he quoted from the trial record and the bills of exceptions about the defense's objections to the composition of the jury pool and Thayer's claim that the state supreme court had "approved" of the verdict. "I say without fear of contradiction that Dean Wigmore could not have read the record, could not have read with care the opinion of Judge Thayer, on which his article is largely based, could not even have examined my little book," Frankfurter wrote. He then proceeded to rebut Wigmore's allegations of inaccuracy "one by one."[108]

Two weeks later, Wigmore returned to the pages of the *Boston Evening Transcript* with more vitriol. He continued to refer to Frankfurter only as "the plausible pundit" and "the contra-canonical critic." He accused the *Atlantic Monthly* and Frankfurter of violating the American Bar Association's canon of ethics by commenting on a pending case—though the case had been on appeal rather than before a jury. And Wigmore continued to defend Judge Thayer's honor.[109] "I shall continue to leave vituperation to Dean Wigmore, while I stick to facts," Frankfurter replied, then reviewed, point by point, the "serious charges" in Wigmore's April 26 article and how each of "his original charges have evaporated."[110] Frankfurter denied new allegations that he was serving as Sacco and Vanzetti's co-counsel; Thompson wrote a letter to the *Boston Evening Transcript* confirming that Frankfurter has never been part of the defense team.[111] Emory Buckner, for one, believed that Wigmore's attacks were "very fortunate" and that Frankfurter's article and book "brought for the first time portions of the 'conservative' element into the controversy on the side of the defendants, or at least on the side of urging a board of review."[112]

The verdict against Wigmore was overwhelming. H. L. Mencken wrote Frankfurter to offer his "congratulations upon your slaughter of Wigmore. It was done neatly, and it was complete! Wigmore is wasted in a law-school. He should have been a federal judge."[113] Heywood Broun, the left-leaning New York *World* columnist who outflanked Lippmann's editorial page throughout the case, described Wigmore's first attack as "a disgraceful performance" and the second one as "subversive of all logical and honest argumentation."[114] Norman Hapgood wrote that Wigmore had "destroyed his own reputation."[115] Robert Maynard Hutchins, the dean of Yale Law School, wrote that Wigmore was becoming a "public menace."[116] Corcoran, Holmes's secretary, wrote Frankfurter: "I think that you gave Grand Duke Wigmore a beautiful sock in the guts and that (although you mustn't quote him) the Boss says so too!"[117] *The Nation* declared that Wigmore "has gone to war again" and that his attack "was consistently and almost incredibly wrong."[118]

Frankfurter was more sanguine about the Wigmore affair. To their mutual friend General Crowder, whom Frankfurter also had worked with in the War Department, Frankfurter declared that Wigmore's treatise on evidence was "the greatest law-book not only of our generation, but of modern times." He added that the Wigmore who had written that book was not the Wigmore who had written those articles: "I think the wisest and the acutest judgment that has been passed on the Wigmore of today is the remark by one of his colleagues that 'Wigmore is one of the casualties of the War.'"[119] Justice Holmes put it slightly more colorfully to his secretary Corcoran: "Wigmore—a casualty of war—wearing spurs to keep his feet from slipping off the table. Flying off astride his own testicles."[120] Even Frankfurter's nemesis, Harvard President Lowell, declared him the winner. "Wigmore is a fool! Wigmore is a fool!" Lowell told Hapgood. "He should have known that Frankfurter would be shrewd enough to be accurate."[121] Lowell's description of Frankfurter as "shrewd" revealed the depth of Old

Boston's enmity toward Harvard's first Jewish law professor. Frankfurter's enemies, Lowell included, were not going away.

After his second response to Wigmore, Frankfurter wrote nothing about the Sacco-Vanzetti case until after it was over. Instead, Frankfurter devoted the summer of 1927 to trying to save the two men from the electric chair. The battle to save Sacco and Vanzetti shifted from an appeal to the Massachusetts Supreme Judicial Court to petition Governor Alvan T. Fuller. On April 7, Thompson met with concerned citizens, including the Frankfurters, about the next steps in the case. Thompson still believed in Sacco and Vanzetti's innocence and that they had not received a fair trial. He contended that an appeal to the Supreme Court of the United States would not be successful: all legal remedies had been exhausted, and the governor's clemency power was the pair's only hope.

Only Vanzetti signed the petition to Governor Fuller. Sacco had given up hope.[122] The petition reviewed Captain Proctor's misleading ballistics testimony and the prosecution's "conscientiousness of guilt" arguments and offered new evidence that they had been victimized by the prejudices of Judge Thayer.[123] Thayer had commented about the case at the University Club, where he had resided during the trial, to members of the press, and to his friends at a Worcester country club. The defense submitted five sworn affidavits from some of Boston's most upstanding citizens who had reported that Thayer had referred to the defendants as "those bastards down there" and their lawyers as "those damn fools." He boasted, "Just wait until you hear my charge" and referred to the defense's trial counsel, Fred H. Moore, as "that long-haired anarchist."[124] A few days later, more of Thayer's extrajudicial comments came to light. After denying Sacco and Vanzetti a new trial a few years earlier, the judge had told a Dartmouth College professor at a football game: "Did you see what I did to those anarchistic bastards the other day? I guess that will hold them for a while. Let them go to the Supreme Court now and see what they can get out of them."[125]

★★★

Before the revelations about Judge Thayer's extrajudicial comments, Lippmann was wavering in the New York *World*'s editorial commitment to the Sacco and Vanzetti case. Lippmann seemed to be falling into his old pattern of halfhearted support for a liberal cause. The *World*'s April 18 editorial, "Calmness and Fairness Needed," responded to radical demonstrations by viewing "two sets of shrill extremists with equal repugnance"—those writing Governor Fuller to pardon Sacco and Vanzetti and those calling for the pair's immediate execution. "What we want is justice, not a victory for either violent radicalism or hidebound conservatism," the editorial said. "Who knows whether Sacco and Vanzetti are guilty or innocent. ... What we need is a careful determination of guilt or innocence, and since the Massachusetts Legislature declines to act, we must hope that Gov. Fuller takes steps to insure it."[126] The *World's* caution may have reflected the moderate editorial stance of its publisher, Ralph Pulitzer, rather than Lippmann, who had been out sick.[127] Lippmann, however, seemed deeply concerned about the effect of the radical demonstrations at home and abroad.[128]

The day after the *World's* call for calmness, Heywood Broun protested his own editorial page's position: "The World has advised calmness to all contenders. ... I must dissent." Broun urged the paper's subscribers to read Frankfurter's book.[129] Unlike Broun, Lippmann did not defend Frankfurter's book against Wigmore's attacks; Lippmann believed that the attacks were not worthy of publicity. To Frankfurter, Lippmann expressed confidence that Governor Fuller "will interfere."[130]

The affidavits exposing Judge Thayer's biases and prejudices brought Lippmann back into the fold. Frankfurter let Lippmann know they were coming, and Lippmann responded in kind.[131] The *World's* May 6 editorial, "The Prejudices of Judge Thayer," was the paper's most outraged thus far: "What comes out of all of these statements is a picture not of a judge but of an agitated little man looking for publicity and utterly impervious to the ethical standards one has the right to expect of a man presiding in a capital case." It was, the editorial argued, "absolutely essential" that Governor Fuller reopen the case.[132]

On May 12, Lippmann wrote another editorial about a petition written by Columbia law professor Karl Llewellyn and signed by sixty-one law professors asking Governor Fuller to form a commission of inquiry to investigate the case.[133] Thirteen Columbia law professors, nine Yale law professors (including Dean Hutchins), six Kansas law professors, six Missouri law professors, and the entire Minnesota law faculty signed Llewellyn's petition.[134] Two days later, the *World* listed all the petitioners to date, a list that included Harvard's Dean Pound.[135]

Sacco and Vanzetti's defenders needed the *World's* courage and support. Frankfurter lamented to Lippmann that Boston newspapers, including the Pulitzer Prize-winning *Herald*, "have editorially abdicated their function on this case."[136] Lippmann suggested that Bullard should either return his Pulitzer Prize for his editorial about the case or resign from the *Herald*.[137] The *Springfield Republican* was the only Massachusetts newspaper consistently calling for a new trial. The New York papers were not much better. The conservative *Herald-Tribune* decried Frankfurter's book for its "partisan distortions" and criticized the Harvard law professor for "fanning anarchistic flames of prejudice against the courts of Massachusetts."[138] The *Times* refused to run H. G. Wells's article about the case even after requesting that Frankfurter review it for factual accuracy. The paper claimed that its counsel feared a libel lawsuit. Frankfurter was shocked. "I wonder whom they think the article libeled," he wrote the *Times*'s Sunday editor.[139]

Only the *World* stepped up—beginning with Lippmann's "Prejudices of Judge Thayer" editorial and Rollin Kirby's accompanying cartoon, "The Breaking Wave," depicting a wave of protest about to break over the outstretched arm of Judge Thayer.[140] Yet Lippmann's editorial page reflected both his and publisher Ralph Pulitzer's goal of moderation. A May 16 editorial, "Zealots and Extremists," criticized Boston's business community for boycotting Thompson's law firm and Sacco and Vanzetti defenders for threatening Governor Fuller if he did not do the right thing.[141] Lippmann's support for the cause was tenuous at best.

On June 1, Governor Fuller appointed a three-member advisory committee and stayed the July 10 execution pending the outcome of the committee's investigation. Each of the governor's appointees was cause for concern for Frankfurter and other supporters. Samuel Wesley Stratton—president of MIT, a mathematician, and the committee's only nonlawyer—was "unquestionably conservative" and "not very bright."[142] At least Stratton had not opined about the case. Judge Robert Grant, a retired Suffolk County probate judge and novelist, had expressed "hostility" to Sacco and Vanzetti before Fuller's appointment. Yet to the governor Grant claimed not to have an opinion about the case and merely objected to Frankfurter's article because of its potential effect on Harvard Law School's endowment campaign.[143] But the committee chairman really worried the pair's supporters—the self-appointed leader of Old Boston, Harvard President Lowell. Lowell's appointment should not have come as a shock. He had met with Governor Fuller three times during the last few weeks.[144] Lowell and Frankfurter were archenemies after the Harvard president's efforts to impose a quota on Jewish undergraduates.

Nonetheless, the day that the governor announced the committee members, Frankfurter wired Lippmann that Lowell was Sacco and Vanzetti's "only hope." He maintained his optimism despite some unsettling developments. The Lowell Committee conducted its investigation and took testimony from witnesses in secret. To Thompson, Lowell displayed alarming "instances of impatiences, lack of understanding and indifference" about the facts of the case. Lowell also refused to allow Thompson to watch the committee's two-hour interview with Judge Thayer and other witnesses. Governor Fuller's independent investigation was similarly secretive. Still Frankfurter believed that Lowell would not overlook Judge Thayer's bias during the trial. "I still

THE BREAKING WAVE

Rollin Kirby's New York *World* cartoon, "The Breaking Wave" have hope in him because it is simply inconceivable to me how, upon the facts, they can dare send Sacco and Vanzetti to the electric chair," he wrote Lippmann.[145]

Given the cowardice of the Boston press corps, to save Sacco and Vanzetti Frankfurter needed Lippmann's and the *World's* support. "'One courageous paper,'" according to Frankfurter's friends in the Boston press, could have settled the matter. At least he had Lippmann and the *World*. On July 12, Frankfurter begged Lippmann (or in Lippmann's absence, Leary) to come to Boston and praised the paper's coverage: "[T]he World has made this case its own and journalistically it is more alive than ever."[146]

As the Lowell Committee finished its investigation, however, Lippmann's editorials began to give Frankfurter cause for concern. In discussing the four-day-old hunger strike by Sacco and Vanzetti, the *World* described the prisoners as "behaving irrationally" if they believed that the strike would influence Governor Fuller and praised the governor for acting "promptly, energetically and conscientiously in their case."[147] Two days later, the *World* criticized the Sacco-Vanzetti Defense Committee for asking the governor to put an end to the secrecy surrounding his and the committee's inquiry into the case: "Gov. Fuller is entitled to credit for going into the merits of the case so carefully and thoroughly. He is entitled to the presumption that he desires only to see justice done." The *World* opined that an open inquiry was "impracticable" and that Fuller was not conducting a retrial.[148] Lippmann was also troubled about the protest bombings in Massachusetts and at US embassies and consulates abroad. He urged Frankfurter to advise Sacco and Vanzetti to "make a statement urging their sympathizers throughout the world to refrain from all acts of violence which might injure innocent people."[149]

Frankfurter passed along the suggestion, yet he found that Lippmann's criticism of the defense committee, of which Frankfurter was not a member, was "very puzzling." "It could have been written only by one who knew very much less or very much more than we do here," he wrote Lippmann.[150] Governor Fuller was retrying the case; the evidence, according to Frankfurter, pointed to only one conclusion. Frankfurter imparted that his "own belief in the innocence of the men has been strengthened *by everything* that has turned up since I wrote my book," and he described the testimony before the Lowell Committee about Judge Thayer's "prejudice" as "simply crushing."[151]

Lippmann and Frankfurter viewed the Sacco-Vanzetti case differently. Lippmann placed too much faith in people in positions of power and was not as concerned with their biases and prejudices. Frankfurter wanted to use the press to educate public opinion and to persuade government officials to protect Sacco and Vanzetti's right to a fair criminal trial. Frankfurter regretted that the *World* lacked a Boston correspondent gathering the facts on the ground and reminded Lippmann that Fuller was not legally trained to conduct a retrial on his own: "I am greatly worried that [the] *World* should be praising Fuller instead of investigating the S.V. and thereby miseducating the public."[152] Lippmann was not nearly as worried: "I have been hopeful ever since Fuller started—I can't say why—except that he's given me the impression that he does not intend to have the sentence carried out and that he's fortifying himself against the attacks of his friends and supporters. That may be wish thinking."[153]

Frankfurter's fears proved justified. At 9:10 p.m. on August 3, Sacco and Vanzetti were secretly transferred to the death house.[154] That night, Governor Fuller announced that he would not intervene in the case and that the two men had received a fair trial. He based his written decision on his own independent investigation, as well as the report of the Lowell Committee. The committee, which presented its findings to the governor on July 27, was unanimous. The Boston papers praised the governor's decision and considered the case closed.[155]

The next morning, Frankfurter wired Lippmann: "[THE GOVERNOR'S] DECISION IS MONSTROUS WONT YOU PLEASE NOW COME ON AND CHARGE YOURSELF PERSONALLY WITH A CAUSE THAT COMES IF EVER ANY DID WITHIN THE TERMS OF JOSEPH PULITZER PLATFORM FOR THE WORLD I BESEECH YOU TO DO THIS IN TWO DAYS YOU CAN BECOME MASTER OF THE ESSENTIALS ON THE ABSOLUTELY DOCUMENTED AUTHORITY."[156]

"The outcome fills me with sorrow," Lippmann replied in a handwritten telegram. After a day of considering Frankfurter's suggestion and conferring with the *World* staff, Lippmann once again declined to come to Boston: "We agree that no conceivable practical results can be achieved by my attempting to master a case in a few days for which a great deal more time and far better equipment are required."[157]

The telegrams reflected the very different paths that Frankfurter and Lippmann took during the case's final days and weeks. The *World*'s initial editorial respected the legal authority of the governor's decision and believed that "Massachusetts law has run its course." It politely suggested that the governor's inquiry, "assisted by three prominent citizens," did not "quiet the doubt that an injustice may have been done."[158] The next day, the *World* appealed to Governor Fuller to commute the sentences to life imprisonment "as an act of wise mercy."[159]

The *World's* muted and respectful editorials contrasted with the initial reactions of its most popular columnist. Heywood Broun excoriated Governor Fuller and Judge Thayer and questioned their fairness and impartiality: "Men like Holmes and Brandeis do not grow on bushes. Popular government, as far as the eye can see, is always going to be administered by the Thayers and Fullers." Broun also explained how the district attorney had fooled the jury with Captain Proctor's testimony about the fatal bullets and referred his readers to Frankfurter's book. "It is ridiculous to say that Sacco and Vanzetti are being railroaded to the chair," Broun wrote. "The situation is much worse than that. This is a thing done cold-bloodedly and with deliberation. But care and deliberation do not guarantee justice."[160] The next day, Broun exposed the biases in Governor Fuller's decision, questioned those who were praising the governor, and expressed befuddlement "that a vast majority of the voters in the Bay State want to see the condemned men die." Ultimately, Broun blamed the committee report's authors, President Lowell and Judge Grant, and other sons of Harvard. "From now on," Broun concluded, "I want to know, will the institution of learning in Cambridge which once we called Harvard be known as Hangman's House?"[161]

Lippmann's editorial page took the opposite approach. A few days after the governor's decision, the Lowell Committee released its report. Lippmann's deference to President Lowell and Old Boston came through in a two-paragraph editorial that continued to call for commuting the sentences to life imprisonment: "Gov. Fuller made a very serious mistake in not publishing the report of the Lowell committee along with his own statement. For the report of the committee is an incomparably abler and more convincing document. It has the earmarks of fairness, consideration, shrewdness and coolness." Lippmann concluded that for the first time since the trial "the case against Sacco and Vanzetti has been plausibly and comprehensibly stated."[162]

The *World's* praise for the Lowell report and Broun's inflammatory columns were on a collision course. Calling Harvard a "Hangman's House" was the last straw. Publisher Ralph Pulitzer instructed Broun to stop writing about the case; Broun refused. In an open letter on the August 12 editorial page, Pulitzer announced: "The *World*, therefore exercising its right of final decision as to what it will publish in its columns, has omitted all articles submitted by Mr. Broun."[163] Pulitzer, whose name stood for journalistic excellence based on the prize endowed by his late father, Joseph, censored Broun's two subsequent Sacco and Vanzetti columns. The difference of opinion between Lippmann's editorial page and Broun's columns came down to tactics. "There is no use in my pretending that I do not believe myself right and The World wrong in the present controversy …," Broun responded five days later in the paper. "The editorial strategy of The World seemingly rested upon the theory that in a desperate cause it is well to ask a little less than you hope to get. I think you should ask more." At the end of the column, Broun announced that he was quitting the paper: "In farewell to the paper I can only say that in its relations to me it was fair, generous, and gallant. But that doesn't go for the Sacco-Vanzetti case."[164] Pulitzer replied on the same page. He cited his editorial right not to run Broun's columns because the "unmeasured invective against Gov. Fuller and his committee seemed to The World to be inflammatory, and to encourage those revolutionists who care nothing for the fate of Sacco and Vanzetti, nor for the vindication of justice, but are using this case as a vehicle of their propaganda." As a result, Pulitzer argued, Broun was undermining any chance of saving Sacco and Vanzetti from the electric chair.[165]

Lippmann defended his publisher's decision. The editorial page had praised the governor's review and the committee's report and pleaded for mercy and commutation because "what counted was the impression we might be able to make upon the moderate conservative opinion in newspaper offices in Massachusetts."[166] Broun's columns impugning the governor's and the committee's motives had contradicted the paper's message and confused the public. Lippmann blamed the whole affair on Broun's absence from the office, and the failure of the paper's news editors to ask him to take out two or three of the most inflammatory sentences prior to publication. "Having failed to edit Heywood when he needed to be edited, we suppressed two columns—one of which at least I read—which were harmless and dull," Lippmann wrote. The censorship and Broun's decision to quit had turned the columnist into a martyr and hero. The editorial page editor was not altogether sorry to see Broun go. "Sorry as I am that Heywood is out of the paper," Lippmann wrote a few days later, "his disappearance, so far as our influence in the Sacco-Vanzetti case is concerned, has been an enormous relief."[167]

Broun's resignation had left the World's editorial page in turmoil. Lippmann's brief editorial praising the fairness of the Lowell Committee's report exacerbated the unrest and displayed a lack of knowledge of the factual details of the case. Fortunately for Lippmann, Frankfurter came to the rescue.

Frankfurter worked behind the scenes because he was a marked man. Old Boston considered him a "hard-headed lawyer" and an "officious damned radical jew who has meddled with this case."[168] Governor Fuller believed the lies that Frankfurter's enemies were spreading that the law professor had made $100,000 from the sale of his book and *Atlantic Monthly* article. Neither the governor nor Old Boston would have believed that by the end of the case Frankfurter had made $413.73 in royalties and had donated them all to the Sacco-Vanzetti Defense Committee.[169] On August 1, the Massachusetts attorney general authorized the state police to wiretap Frankfurter's telephone "to procure official information" about the case. For the next several months, the police transcribed all of the Frankfurters' phone conversations.[170]

To escape the political turmoil in Boston during the summer of 1927, the Frankfurters had rented a house thirty-five miles south of the city in Duxbury, Massachusetts. The small white house with light green blinds and blue plant pots out front was next to the Bay Farm, where they bought fresh milk, eggs, and chickens, and the house was a short walk to an inlet on Kingston Bay.[171] Duxbury was the Frankfurters' sanctuary. It was close enough for Frankfurter to take the train from Kingston back to Boston or Cambridge, but far enough away to keep the press and members of the Sacco-Vanzetti Defense Committee at bay. He was trying to keep a low profile. He knew that any public comments that he made about the Sacco-Vanzetti case would only hurt the cause. He did not want to turn the last-ditch effort to save the men into a debate between him and Lowell because that was a debate, at least in Boston, that Frankfurter could not win and that would cost Sacco and Vanzetti their lives.[172] Frankfurter therefore stayed silent, but he did not sit still.

Frankfurter turned his summer home into the shadow headquarters to save Sacco and Vanzetti. He worked with Gardner "Pat" Jackson, a former *Boston Globe* reporter who had left his Harvard graduate studies at the end of 1926 to join the Sacco-Vanzetti Defense Committee.[173] Frankfurter did not believe that Jackson was up to the task of getting the truth out about the case.[174] Jackson was not a lawyer and lacked a strategy for stopping the executions. Frankfurter used all of his legal, political, and media contacts to influence public opinion and to persuade Massachusetts officials or federal judges to intervene. "This really has been the most difficult thing I have gone through in my life," he confided to a friend, "but I am still hanging on."[175]

Frankfurter played a major role in orchestrating the final efforts to save Sacco and Vanzetti in the courts. For three long years, Thompson and his co-counsel Ehrmann had been appealing Sacco and Vanzetti's convictions and pursuing a new trial. The ordeal had been particularly hard on Thompson. He continued to represent both men long after his payment of $37,500 for three years of work had run out and his reputation in Old Boston had sunk to new lows. He did so because of his firm belief in his clients' innocence, his friendship with the more intellectual Vanzetti, and his sympathy for Rosina Sacco and her fourteen-year-old son, Dante.[176] Since July, the attorneys had been hearing rumors out of the state house that both Governor Fuller and the Lowell Committee had their minds set on Sacco and Vanzetti's guilt and that the hearings and investigation were just a show. Continuing to believe in the good faith of Lowell, Thompson worked himself to the point of exhaustion. By the end, he was mumbling to himself in his office.[177]

Frankfurter's chief source of information was Elizabeth Evans. She wrote him that the "situation is pretty grim," Thompson and Ehrmann do not "have hope of the men's freedom," and only Ehrmann believes there is a "chance" of a commutation to life imprisonment. She tried to buoy Thompson's depleted spirit by telling him "that his children and children's children would live to be proud" of his work on the case.[178] After receiving Evans's letter, Frankfurter tried to buck up the defense team. "Thompson is fearfully frayed out," he wrote Ehrmann and exhorted the younger co-counsel to pick up the slack: "After all, no fight is lost until it is lost. And you cannot possibly know either what is in Lowell's mind or what the Governor may finally decide upon. I know the outlook is very gloomy indeed."[179]

After Governor Fuller refused to intervene and the Lowell Committee released its report, Thompson and Ehrmann withdrew from the case. They criticized Fuller for conducting his investigation in secret, disputed the Lowell Committee's conclusions, and insisted that their clients were innocent. That night at 6:55 p.m., Thompson made a surprise visit at the death house. Sacco, in the midst of a twenty-three-day hunger strike, refused to see him, so Thompson spent nearly an hour with Vanzetti, who had eaten only twice during that same period.[180] The exhausted Thompson headed for a rest in New Hampshire, continued to advise the defense, but explained that it was time for some other lawyer to try to save them.

That someone would not be the publicly silent Frankfurter, though he knew just the man to be the pair's new chief counsel during those final days—Arthur Dehon Hill. The Paris-born son of a Harvard English professor, Hill had founded one of the city's most respected law firms, Hill, Barlow & Homans, and in 1909 had served as the Suffolk County district attorney.[181] The boyish-looking, quick-witted Hill had alienated Old Boston in 1912 by supporting Roosevelt's Bull Moose presidential campaign and four years later Brandeis's Supreme Court nomination. Old Boston, led by Moorfield Storey, retaliated by opposing Hill's permanent appointment to the Harvard law faculty. Frankfurter countered by soliciting an endorsement letter from Hill's longtime mentor and family friend, Justice Holmes.[182] In 1890, Hill had met with Holmes when Holmes was a justice on the Supreme Judicial Court of Massachusetts and Hill a Harvard undergraduate seeking career advice. After the meeting, Hill left the college without a degree and enrolled in the law school.[183] "My whole life would have been a different & a poorer business if I had not known you and I can't thank you enough for all you have done for me since I went to see you in the old court house in 1890," he later wrote Holmes.[184] Holmes's 1916 letter of endorsement to Pound described Hill as "enthusiastic" and "noble in his way of thinking" and with "an epigrammatic wit."[185] From 1915 to 1919, Holmes entrusted Hill and Frankfurter with selecting a Harvard law graduate to be his secretary.

Holmes's letter to Pound did the trick. Hill joined the Harvard faculty full-time in the fall of 1916, teaching evidence and criminal law. His stay, however, was brief. During the war, he worked for the Red Cross in France, joined the judge advocate general's office as a major in December 1917, and from January 1918 to June 1919 again served in France. Frankfurter and Hill often saw each other in Paris but took different paths after the war. Frankfurter returned to the Harvard faculty; Hill resigned, returned to private practice, and served as the city of Boston's corporation counsel.[186] Hill and Frankfurter remained close friends, bonded by their Bull Moose political pasts and their love of Holmes, left-wing politics, and public service. Ehrmann described the Boston Brahmin Hill and immigrant Jewish Frankfurter as "brothers under the skin."[187]

After Thompson's resignation, Frankfurter phoned Hill and wanted to discuss something serious. Hill suggested lunch first. After lunch at the Somerset Club, they walked across the Boston Common and sat on a bench near the Frog Pond.[188] Frankfurter asked Hill about the possibility of becoming Sacco and Vanzetti's new chief counsel. This was not Hill's

first involvement with the case. In 1923, he had assisted Thompson in arguing one of the new trial motions before Judge Thayer.[189] To Frankfurter's
immense relief, Hill accepted the job of exhausting their appeals.[190] Despite
agreeing to take on the appeals for a minimum of $5,000 or "whatever was
reasonable," Hill refused to collect his fee.[191] He asked only that the Sacco-
Vanzetti Defense Committee pay his expenses and the fees of his two associates. Hill agreed to become Sacco and Vanzetti's new chief counsel not
for the money or because he believed that the men were innocent but because of a sense of duty.[192] He reasoned that every lawyer in Boston would
appeal the murder conviction of the wife of a rich banker for a $50,000
fee. "I do not see how I can decline a similar effort on behalf of Sacco and
Vanzetti simply because they are poor devils against whom the feeling of
the community is strong and they have no money with which to hire me,"
he told Frankfurter.[193]

Hill started with the Massachusetts courts. On August 6, he filed a motion
for a new trial and another motion to revoke the death sentences.[194] There
was only one problem: the state's chief justice had designated Judge Thayer
to hear the motions. During a two-and-a-half-hour hearing on Monday,
August 8, Hill argued that Judge Thayer was too prejudiced to hear the
motions and that they should be heard by another judge. Thayer, unsurprisingly, disagreed.[195] He denied the new trial motion and refused to revoke
the death sentences. Hill appealed Thayer's rulings to the Massachusetts
Supreme Judicial Court. Hill also appealed to Justice George Sanderson of
the same court for a writ of error; the justice denied the motion.[196]

Sacco and Vanzetti were supposed to die at midnight on Wednesday,
August 10. That day, Hill refused to rest until he had exhausted every option
to try to save them. At 10:00 a.m., he and one of his associates went to the
courthouse to persuade Justice Sanderson to allow the defense to appeal the
decision on the writ of error before the entire court. From 11:45 a.m. to
12:15 p.m., Hill conferred with Justice Sanderson and the attorney general
in the supreme court's lobby. Both Hill and Justice Sanderson assumed that
Sacco and Vanzetti would receive a stay of execution because the justice
was not prepared to make a decision until the next morning. "We expect
to see Judge Sanderson tomorrow morning and obtain his final decision,"
Hill said.[197]

All Hill needed was a stay of execution. At 12:23 p.m., he arrived at the
state house to make his case to Governor Fuller and his executive council
to stay the executions so that Hill could exhaust Sacco and Vanzetti's appeals

in the state and federal courts. Around the same time, the governor sought advice from seven former attorneys general while the governor's executive council met in special session. At 1:00 p.m., the executive council broke for lunch and was not scheduled to return until 3:30. Hill realized that neither the governor nor his executive council was going to see him, and therefore that the stay of execution was in doubt.[198] With no assurances from the governor and the executions scheduled to take place in less than twelve hours, Hill knew what he had to do next—appeal for a writ of habeas corpus with his friend and mentor, Justice Holmes.

24

This World Cares More for Red Than for Black

Shortly before 3:00 p.m. on August 10, 1927, two cars pulled into a gravel driveway off Hale Street in Beverly Farms, Massachusetts. Five men emerged, looking solemn and with a sense of purpose, armed only with a writ of habeas corpus.

At the end of every Supreme Court term, Justice and Fanny Holmes retreated to his family's large Victorian house with its ivy-covered front porch, three chimneys, and a majestic view of Manchester Bay.[1] From June to September, he read philosophy and literature, watched the sailboats go by, and wrote letters to friends. Occasionally, he was interrupted by work—reading petitions for certiorari asking the Court to hear a case and entertaining stays of execution.

Though only twenty-nine miles north of the city, Holmes's North Shore enclave was a world away from the turmoil surrounding the Sacco–Vanzetti case back in Boston. The men in the car were interrupting Holmes's serenity. Hill had brought four lawyers with him, including former chief defense counsel Thompson. Together, Hill and Thompson intended to press Holmes for a writ of habeas corpus—an extraordinary remedy to challenge the fairness of Sacco and Vanzetti's convictions. Short of granting the writ, Holmes could grant them a stay of execution. A single justice could grant a stay so that, come October, the entire Court could consider hearing the case.

Holmes knew this day was coming. As early as May, he had suspected that the case would land on his doorstep.[2] The papers had been rife with rumors since early August that defense counsel would appeal to him.[3] His familiarity with the case came from a single source—Frankfurter's book. In March, Holmes had written Frankfurter that the book "leaves me with a suspicion that the evidence against the defendants could be stated more strongly but with painful impressions that seem hard to remove." He applauded "the self-sacrifice and devotion to justice that led you to write the book."[4] Frankfurter was so proud of Holmes's letter that he pasted a copy next to the prefatory note in his annotated edition of the book.[5] But Holmes had chosen his words carefully. Old Boston, including Judge Robert Grant before he had joined the Lowell Committee, had been providing a different perspective. And from Brandeis, Holmes knew that Frankfurter's book "has kicked up a commotion" and that "Beacon Street is divided."[6]

With good justification, Holmes suspected that Frankfurter was behind Hill's plea.[7] The day that Hill had agreed to become chief counsel, Frankfurter wrote him a memorandum laying out the case against Judge Thayer. "The point is this, as I see it: An accused is not entitled to a wise judge, or a learned judge, or a wholly calm judge," Frankfurter wrote on August 6. "But, surely the essence of an Anglo-American trial, particularly in a capital case, implied a *judge*." Frankfurter believed that due process required "observance of the elementary decencies of Anglo-American criminal procedure." He proposed a strategy on appeal: to prove that Thayer had prejudged the case, "manifested a rooted prejudice, and continued to hold it throughout all the proceedings that came before him." This argument was

Holmes's summer cottage at Beverly Farms

particularly important in Massachusetts because a trial judge's rulings were virtually unreviewable, given the limited scope of the state's appeals process compared with other states at the time. Yet Frankfurter acknowledged the lack of evidence in the trial record of Thayer's overt prejudice. The only place that it could be found was in the affidavits attesting to the judge's extrajudicial comments about "those anarchistic bastards" and their lawyers. Nonetheless, he was convinced that Thayer's prejudice and bias amounted to a denial of due process.[8] On the morning of August 10, Frankfurter boarded a train from Duxbury to Boston. By 10:00 a.m., he was in Hill's office discussing how to save Sacco and Vanzetti on the final day before their executions.[9] Later that afternoon, Frankfurter returned to Duxbury. He did not dare go with Hill to Beverly Farms.

Both Hill and Frankfurter, longtime friends of the justice and students of his opinions, knew that Holmes was the ideal judge to hear these due process claims. In those days, the Supreme Court of the United States was extremely reluctant to interfere with state criminal trials. Yet Holmes had made his position known that a state criminal trial could be so prejudicial and so unfair as to violate a defendant's right to due process of law. His 1915 dissent had argued that the Jewish Atlanta pencil factory manager Leo Frank had not received a fair trial because the lynch mob outside the courthouse had made it impossible for the jury to acquit him.[10] Eight years later, Holmes vindicated his dissent in the *Frank* case with his majority opinion in *Moore v. Dempsey* about the mob-dominated sham trials of Arkansas sharecroppers and which led to their release from prison.[11] *Moore v. Dempsey* was Sacco and Vanzetti's best hope.

Hill and Thompson planned to persuade Holmes that Judge Thayer's extrajudicial comments about the defendants and their lawyers and Thayer's conduct of the trial had been just as prejudicial as *Moore v. Dempsey*'s mob-dominated sham trials; that the trial before Judge Thayer was like having no judge at all; and that Sacco and Vanzetti, like the black sharecroppers on trial for their lives in Arkansas, had not been afforded due process of law. When they arrived at Beverly Farms at 2:50 p.m., Holmes greeted them at the front door. The justice, who had been alerted that they were coming, ushered the lawyers into the first-floor parlor. Thompson's son, who served as one of the drivers that day, waited with the press corps outside the house.[12]

For two and a half hours, Hill and Thompson pressed their case. At age eighty-six, Holmes was as mentally sharp as ever, but he tired more easily. He let them have their say until he began to fade. At the end of the argument, he wrote his one-paragraph decision in longhand. After finishing, he was so exhausted that he declined to give any interviews and went straight to bed. At 6:30 p.m., a grim-faced Hill rushed out of Holmes's residence. Before racing back to Boston, he told a *Boston Post* reporter: "I know of no human power at this time that can save them."[13]

Hill and Thompson went immediately to see Judge George W. Anderson, the liberal federal trial judge who had invited Frankfurter and Chafee to participate in Boston's Palmer Raids deportation cases in 1920. Anderson knew that Holmes had denied the writ and that the defense's argument was based on Holmes's opinion in *Moore v. Dempsey*. Like Holmes, Anderson refused to issue a writ of habeas corpus.[14]

Back in Duxbury, Frankfurter waited by the phone. That night he and his wife were supposed to join another couple to see the Jitney Players, a theatrical troupe that toured New England during the summer. He told Marion to go, but she stayed by his side.[15] Just before 8:00 p.m., he learned that Holmes had denied the petition. Frankfurter refused defense counsel's request to come to Boston that night to help them.[16] After learning that the state house still had not granted a stay, he offered one final suggestion about whom to approach for a writ of habeas corpus.

"You know where the other Justice is?" Frankfurter asked.

"No."

"In Chatham. Phone 330."

"330?"

"Yes. You will be kind enough not to talk about this talk between us. Layman cannot sometimes appreciate."[17]

Back in Boston, the Sacco-Vanzetti Defense Committee was panicking. At 9:00 p.m., Sacco's wife, Rosina, collapsed at the committee's headquarters. Her husband was supposed to die in three hours. At the state prison in Charlestown, Warden William Hendry was preparing for the executions; 800 police officers stood guard with high-pressure fire hoses and machine guns.[18] Sacco, Vanzetti, and Medeiros waited in their death cells. Police arrested thirty-nine protesters, including writers John Dos Passos and Dorothy Parker, for illegal picketing in front of the state house.[19]

Hill arrived at the state house and still could not find anyone to grant a stay of execution. Governor Fuller and his executive council were furious that Hill had circumvented their authority by appealing to the federal courts. At 7:30 p.m., upon hearing about Hill's comments to the press, the executive council adjourned for an hour. Later that night, Hill pleaded with the governor and his executive council to grant the stay so that the entire state supreme court could review Justice Sanderson's decision refusing to grant a writ of error. Governor Fuller and his attorney general favored granting the stay; his parole board–like executive council did not. Finally, at 11:27 p.m., thirty-three minutes before they were set to begin, Governor Fuller stayed the executions for twelve days until August 22.

Soon after Governor Fuller's announcement, Holmes's handwritten opinion was released to the press and shared the next day's headlines. Most newspapers printed it in full. Holmes refused to grant the writ not because he agreed or disagreed with Judge Thayer's conduct but because the justice felt that he lacked the power to grant it. "I have no authority to issue it unless it appears that the Court had not jurisdiction of the case in a real sense so that no more than the form of a court was there," Holmes wrote. "But I cannot think that prejudice on the part of the presiding judge however strong would deprive the Court of jurisdiction, that is of legal power to decide the case, and in my opinion nothing short of want of legal power to decide the case authorizes me to interfere in this summary way with the proceedings of the State Court."[20] Holmes's opinion did not mention *Moore v. Dempsey* and revealed little of his feelings about the merits of the case. But during his discussion with Hill and Thompson, Holmes had distinguished between the lynch mob outside the courthouse in *Moore v. Dempsey* and a trial dominated by Judge Thayer's prejudices. Hill and Thompson argued "what was the difference whether the motive was fear or the prejudices alleged in this case." Holmes disagreed: "I said most differences are differences of degree, and I thought that the line must be drawn between external force, and prejudice—which could be alleged in every case."[21]

The night after his decision, Holmes declined police protection. A few days earlier, a postcard, "Free Sacco and Vanzetti," had arrived at the US Supreme Court. "If there is any more trouble in our ranks," it said, "they are going to blow up some of you big boys."[22] In Washington, plainclothes officers guarded the homes of justices and cabinet members.[23] A neighbor volunteered to guard the justice's residence at Beverly Farms; Holmes declined.[24] Letters poured in, one of them calling him a "monster of injustice."[25] Newspapers carried rumors that Hill once again would appeal to Holmes to grant a stay of execution so that the entire Court would hear the case. "So I have no perfect peace," Holmes wrote.[26] He questioned why his friends Frankfurter and Laski were so "stirred up" about the case and criticized his friends who had turned him into a national icon. "If justice was what the world is after, this case is not half so bad as those that are more or less familiar in the South," Holmes wrote to another overseas correspondent, Lewis Einstein. "But this world cares more for red than for black."[27] He was not just talking about the black sharecroppers in *Moore v. Dempsey*. For Holmes, the Sacco-Vanzetti case revealed the limits of his younger friends' liberalism and his own complex postwar views on race.

★★★

With twelve days to save Sacco and Vanzetti from the electric chair, Frankfurter was not content to wait for the case to return to Holmes or for the consciences of Governor Fuller and President Lowell to kick in. He called on his network of lawyers and journalists to try to sway public opinion and to create a groundswell of support for a new trial.[28] If Hill could not get a new trial in the courts, then Frankfurter would find a way to get one from the people themselves.

The collapse of the New York *World's* editorial coverage—Broun's resignation and Lippmann's editorial praising the Lowell Committee's report— spurred Frankfurter into action. He was convinced that the two events were related and that Broun's resignation was accompanied by instructions to Lippmann to "tone down" his editorials.[29] More than any other newspaper, the *World* was the best hope for getting out the truth about the case. At first, Frankfurter requested Judge Mack to persuade Lippmann to come to Boston for a day, to review the trial record, and to learn the facts on the ground: "All I want him to do is to inform his mind now when there is time—to come and get the setting and do something about it."[30] On August 14, the *World* sent one of its reporters to see Frankfurter. The reporter spent "many hours" in Duxbury, and Frankfurter made him privy to evidence that the *World* had not seen. The reporter promised to relay the evidence to Lippmann, who "will have knowledge that he never had before," Frankfurter said. "I think he will be very receptive to printing [the] entire question in the World."[31]

Unwilling to leave anything to chance, Frankfurter went to New York to make the case to Lippmann himself.[32] He brought along a key reinforcement and eminent New York lawyer in Charles Culp ("C. C.") Burlingham. A lifelong Republican, Burlingham was one of the city's leading admiralty lawyers, had represented the White Star Line after the 1912 sinking of the *Titanic*, and soon became president of the City Bar Association. He was also an outspoken believer that Sacco and Vanzetti had not received a fair trial. Of all Frankfurter's friends in the legal establishment, Burlingham may have been the most important convert. "That the Epicurean C. C. Burlingham should have become a S.V. protagonist," Brandeis had written Frankfurter, "is a remarkable manifestation of the power in your story & the deep down possibilities for Americans."[33]

Frankfurter and Burlingham "did a job" with Lippmann. After an August 18 session lasting "many hours," the *World* devoted its entire August 19 editorial page to reviewing the evidence in the case.[34] "Doubt That Will Not Down" refuted the Lowell Committee's report point by point, rebutting each piece of evidence based on citations to the trial record. Of the three men—Burlingham, Frankfurter, and Lippmann—only Frankfurter had read the record. The editorial was a Felix Frankfurter production. "The Sacco-Vanzetti case is clouded and obscure," the editorial concluded. "It is full of doubt. The fairness of the trial raises doubt. The evidence raises doubt. The inadequate review of the evidence raises doubt. The Governor's inquiry has not appeased these doubts. The report of his Advisory Committee has not settled these doubts. Everywhere there is doubt so deep, so pervasive, so unsettling, that it cannot be denied and it cannot be ignored. No man, we submit, should be put to death where so much doubt exists." The only "real solution," the editorial asserted, was a new trial in front of a new judge.[35] Thanks to Frankfurter and Burlingham, Lippmann and the *World* had returned to the fold.

The other major publicity effort involved making the case for a new trial with President Lowell. Gardner Jackson believed that once Lowell was named the chairman of the advisory committee, Sacco and Vanzetti were doomed because Lowell would view the evidence through the lens of his dislike of Frankfurter. The Harvard president, Jackson recalled, simply would not be able to "surmount the depth of his feeling of hostility to Felix Frankfurter."[36] Frankfurter knew this, of course.[37] He conferred with Judge Mack and others about enlisting conservative Harvard alumni to appeal to Lowell to reconsider his advisory report.[38] He also found another way to persuade Lowell—by having the *New Republic* take out a full-page ad in the August 19 *New York Times*. Reprinting "A Letter to President Lowell" from the magazine's editors, the ad reviewed the now-familiar reasons for a new trial: Judge Thayer's prejudicial behavior, District Attorney Katzmann's prejudicial cross-examination, Captain Proctor's misleading ballistics testimony, the unreliability of other supposedly key pieces of evidence, and the withholding of a key eyewitness. "We believe that the questions we ask demand answer," the letter challenged Lowell, "even if such answer involves the reconsideration of the report of the Advisory Committee appointed by Governor Fuller. We await your reply."[39]

Meanwhile, Frankfurter holed himself up in Burlingham's Connecticut country house, where the two men worked on a letter to the editor at the request of the *New York Times*.[40] The *Times* published Burlingham's August 20 letter over the headline: "The Advisory Report: A Review of Some of the Findings of the Lowell Committee; With Indication of Errors." Burlingham then proceeded to review the report "with the advantage of having at hand a copy of the record and of the affidavits submitted on motions." The tone of Burlingham's letter was respectful but firm: "The personnel of the committee is so distinguished that one is naturally disposed to accept their report as conclusive, but a careful study of the report has led me to a different view." Instead of relying on the credibility of liberal *New Republic* editors to attack Lowell's report, this attack came from one of the most eminent members of the New York bar. Burlingham's letter once again picked apart the evidence in the report. The letter was signed: "CHARLES C. BURLINGHAM, New York, Aug. 19, 1927."[41]

The same day as Burlingham's letter, Frankfurter assisted the Sacco-Vanzetti Defense Committee in organizing a final public appeal to Governor Fuller either to commute the sentences to life imprisonment or to stay the executions. The appeal was signed by many of Frankfurter's friends and a who's who of American liberals: Jane Addams of Hull House, historian Charles Beard, *New Republic* editor Bruce Bliven, Burlingham, *Springfield Republican* editor Waldo Cook, Columbia philosopher John Dewey, University of Chicago law professor Ernst Freund, Harvard Medical School professor Alice Hamilton, journalist Norman Hapgood, *The Survey* editor Paul Kellogg, and Columbia economics professor Henry Seager.[42] Frankfurter, however, did not sign it.

Frankfurter left the public appeals to others and the last-minute legal appeals to Hill. The cost to Hill's social reputation in Boston for taking on the case was enormous. "He is an outcast—," Frankfurter told Jackson, "he is worse than Thompson because he took up the fight when Thompson said nothing could be done—there was an end to the matter."[43] On August 19, the Massachusetts Supreme Judicial Court rejected Hill's appeal on the writ of error. This was the court's final ruling in the case.[44] That same day, defense counsel petitioned Judge James M. Morton Jr. of the US District Court for a writ of habeas corpus based on the same evidence presented to Justice Holmes and Judge Anderson.[45] Judge Morton agreed with Holmes and Anderson, denied the writ, and refused to grant the defense a certificate of probable cause for an appeal.[46] With one day left before the executions, Hill had Frankfurter's complete confidence and support. "[I]t is very important to keep Hill on the situation until the last minute," Frankfurter told Jackson. "There is nothing of a quitter about him—he doesn't quit."[47]

Hill knew that his only chance of saving Sacco and Vanzetti from the electric chair was to persuade one of the Supreme Court's liberal justices to stay the execution until October so that the full Court could decide whether to hear the case. In 1925, the Supreme Court had received the power to control most of its docket, and it established a rule of four—four justices had to vote to hear a case. That would put the case on the Court's fall calendar for full briefing and oral argument before all nine justices. For now, Hill needed only a single justice to stay the executions until the fall. On August 20, he returned to Beverly Farms to get it.

Hill went back to Holmes because the justice had heard the earlier appeal, because of Holmes's decision in *Moore v. Dempsey*, and because of the practical reason that Beverly Farms was close to Boston. In the past, Frankfurter and his network of friends from the House of Truth had always rallied around Holmes for different reasons—initially because Holmes's belief in majority rule would have prevented the Court from invalidating state and federal pro-labor legislation and later because he protected free speech and fair criminal trials. Yet, in some ways, Holmes outflanked his liberal friends on the issue of race. He did not understand their obsession with the Sacco-Vanzetti case given all the injustices he saw involving black criminal defendants in the Jim Crow South. His critique that "this world cares more for red than for black" revealed that Frankfurter and his allies had a long way to go in 1927 in protecting minority rights.

Holmes did, too. During the previous term, he had written the majority opinion in *Buck v. Bell* upholding Virginia's compulsory sterilization law of the "feebleminded." The state was determined to make a test case out of the sterilization of seventeen-year-old Carrie Buck. Like her supposedly "feebleminded" and "sexually promiscuous" mother, Buck was institutionalized at the Virginia Colony of Epileptics and Feebleminded.[48] She had given birth to a daughter, Vivian, who at seven months old was deemed "not quite normal."[49] The doctor who ran the mental institution had rammed the sterilization law through the state legislature and had orchestrated Buck's lawsuit as a test case. Her lawyer had failed to bring out pertinent facts at trial and on appeal, probably because he had been handpicked by the opposition. He was one of the doctor's oldest friends, a former member of the institution's board of directors, and a proponent of sterilization.[50]

In his opinion for the nearly unanimous Court, Holmes had rejected Buck's due process challenges by emphasizing the law's procedural protections and "the proven absence of danger to the patient."[51] And, as with his defense of pro-labor legislation, he was loath to strike down state laws as violating the liberty provision of the Due Process Clause. He also rejected the argument that the statute denied Buck equal protection of the laws, which he dismissed as "the usual last resort of constitutional arguments to point out shortcomings of this sort." Finally, he could not resist a Holmesian rhetorical flourish: "It is better for all the world, if instead of waiting to execute degenerate offspring for crime, or to let them starve for their imbecility, society can prevent those who are manifestly unfit from continuing their kind. The principle that sustains compulsory vaccination is broad enough to cover cutting the Fallopian tubes. ... Three generations of imbeciles are enough."[52] That six-word sentence—"three generations of imbeciles are enough"—encapsulated the dangers of leaving the protection of civil rights and civil liberties to majority rule. Only Justice Pierce Butler, the Court's lone Catholic, dissented, without writing an opinion.

Holmes was proud of his decision, which not only allowed Virginia to make Buck its first sterilization victim but also implicitly upheld thirty similar state laws.[53] During the 1920s, eugenics in America was championed by many of the country's leading doctors and scientists and liberal thinkers. Eugenics also was consistent with Holmes's worldview. Ever since his three Civil War wounds, he had believed in survival of the fittest—hence, his faith in majority rule and his definition of "the truth as the majority vote of that nation that can lick all others."[54]

In his defense, Holmes did not know the real story of *Buck v. Bell*. Carrie Buck was not one of three generations of imbeciles. Her mother could read and write. Buck had received good marks in school; she had been institutionalized because she had been raped by the nephew of her foster family, and the family wanted to hide the pregnancy.[55] Her daughter, Vivian, was a B and C student who received As in deportment and made the school's honor roll.[56]

Neither Frankfurter nor Laski challenged Holmes's assertion that "my cases this term have been of rather a high average of interest," singling out his opinion about "the Virginia Sterilization Act."[57] At the end of the term, Frankfurter remarked that Holmes's opinions had never been "more vigorous, nor sprightlier, and no batch will live longer than what you gave us this Term."[58] He went on to compliment several of Holmes's opinions, except *Buck v. Bell*. In the *Harvard Law Review*, Frankfurter tried to put the best spin on *Buck* as one of several examples of a judge who "enforces statutes based upon economic and political theories which he does not share and of whose efficacy in action he is sceptical."[59] Privately, Holmes confided that writing the opinion had given him "pleasure."[60] He alerted Laski that *Buck* was coming and revealed clashes with other justices about his harsh rhetoric.[61] The justice may have known Laski's history with eugenics. Laski had met his future wife, Frida Kerry, in late 1909 when she was giving a eugenics lecture.[62] Laski had become so interested in the topic that he worked at the Eugenics Institute at University College in London, and upon entering Oxford in fall 1910, he had initially pursued science before switching to history and politics.[63] Indeed, many liberals embraced eugenics, as they did the birth control movement, and many heralded Holmes's opinion as legalizing population control and the evolution of the human race.

A few people, notably African Americans, attacked Holmes for legitimating the use of sterilization against them. The *Chicago Defender* observed that Holmes had "started something when he suggested sterilization as a cure for mental defectives and inferior peoples. Immediately the idea has been pounced upon and broadcast as a possible cure for all race ills. 'Sterilize all colored people, they are our inferiors,' some white Americans are now suggesting."[64]

Yet most of black America embraced Holmes because of another decision that term. The NAACP financed a lawsuit challenging a 1923 Texas law banning blacks from participating in Democratic Party primary elections. Dr. Lawrence Aaron ("L. A.") Nixon, an African American physician from El Paso and a registered Democrat, had been denied the right to vote in the 1924 primary elections for the US Senate and House of Representatives and had sued county election supervisors for $5,000 in damages. The Texas trial judge had dismissed the case, which was appealed directly to the Supreme Court. The NAACP's national counsel—Arthur Spingarn, Moorfield Storey, Judge James Cobb, and Louis Marshall—took control of the briefing from local counsel. Marshall agreed to write a reply brief that the NAACP hoped would make up for local counsel's mediocre oral argument.[65]

Holmes announced the decision, *Nixon v. Herndon*, for a unanimous Court.[66] He wrote that the law did not violate the Fifteenth Amendment's prohibition against denying a citizen the right to vote on the basis of race but was "a more direct and obvious infringement" of the Fourteenth Amendment. "That Amendment," he wrote, "while it applies to all, was passed, as we know, with a special intent to protect the blacks from discrimination against them."[67] He invoked the amendment's guarantees of the privileges or immunities of citizenship and of equal protection of the laws (which two months later in *Buck v. Bell* he claimed was "one of the last resorts of constitutional argument").

To support his Fourteenth Amendment argument in *Nixon v. Herndon*, Holmes quoted the Court's 1917 decision in *Buchanan v. Warley*, which invalidated a Louisville law that prohibited blacks from living on a majority-white block. He neglected to mention that he had nearly dissented because he believed that the case brought by a white real estate agent was "manufactured" and did not concern "the constitutional rights of the blacks."[68] Nor did he mention that in 1903 he had written one of the more egregious decisions about race in the Court's history in *Giles v. Harris*, which upheld an Alabama constitutional amendment that used poll taxes, grandfather clauses, literacy tests, and good character tests to disenfranchise the state's black voters.[69] Or that in 1908 he had concurred in the Court's upholding of a Kentucky law that prevented a private college from enrolling black and white students.[70] Or that in 1911 he had dissented from a decision that overturned Alabama's peonage laws and that he had reluctantly joined the majority in a case about a revised Alabama law three years later.[71] Or that in 1914 he had refused to endorse the Court's Fourteenth Amendment reasoning in a decision that invalidated an Oklahoma separate railroad car law that refused to provide sleeping and dining cars for blacks.[72] Indeed, he wrote a harsh memorandum in the Oklahoma railroad case, which Justice Hughes replied did not interpret the Fourteenth Amendment as prohibiting racial discrimination.[73]

Something happened to Holmes's views on race after the summer of 1919. The Red Scare and the Red Summer of racial violence had made him more sensitive to the limits of government power. Beginning in October 1919, he had defended the free speech rights of Jacob Abrams and other "poor and puny anonymities."[74] Less than four years later, he had safeguarded the due process rights of Frank Moore and other black Arkansas sharecroppers sentenced to death after the 1919 Elaine Riots. With his decision in the 1927 Texas White Primary case, Holmes provided more evidence that his views on race had changed in recent years. "States may do a good deal of classifying that it is difficult to believe rational, but there are limits," he concluded, "and it is too clear for extended argument that color cannot be made the basis of a statutory classification affecting the right set up in this case."[75] Holmes's newfound willingness to enforce the Fourteenth Amendment to protect the rights of black voters showed that, skeptical as he was, he had not completely abandoned his abolitionist roots.[76]

Brandeis reported to Frankfurter that Holmes had "delivered with much joy the Negro primary opinion."[77] Kelly Miller, a Howard University dean and law graduate, was in the courtroom that day to hear another case and was "doubly repaid by the privilege of listening" to Holmes deliver the unanimous opinion—which Miller pointed out garnered the vote of even the notoriously racist Justice McReynolds. "The decision was clear-cut and decisive from beginning to end ...," Miller wrote. "The most significant feature of this decision consists in the fact that it is not based on race or color, but fundamentally upon citizenship rights."[78] NAACP assistant secretary Walter White, who was also in the courtroom that day, thanked him for *Nixon v. Herndon*: "This decision will be of tremendous encouragement to the eleven million Negroes of America and a further affirmation of the fact that whatever injustices may be done to Negroes because of their color[] in lower courts they have always refuge in the United States Supreme Court."[79] A black Philadelphia bank president read about the decision in the newspaper and wrote the justice to congratulate him on the Texas primary opinion. When Holmes's secretary Tom Corcoran replied with a form letter on the justice's behalf, the bank president demanded "a bona fide letter from the Boss!"[80]

More than his 1923 decision in *Moore v. Dempsey* and the Texas primary case from the previous March were on Holmes's mind when he critiqued his friends about their obsession with Sacco and Vanzetti and lack of interest in issues of race. "Your last letter shows you stirred up like the rest of the world on the Sacco Vanzetti case," he wrote Laski. "I cannot but ask myself why this so much greater interest in red than black. A thousand-fold worse cases of negroes come up from time to time, but the world does not worry over them. It is not a mere simple abstract love of justice that has moved people so much."[81]

Holmes's experience with the criminal justice system's unfairness toward African Americans was more immediate. Every summer at Beverly Farms, he received pleas from black men to stay their executions so that the Court could consider their certiorari petitions. The summer of 1927 was no different. On July 15, 1927, Nathan Bard and Bunyan Fleming were scheduled to hang for the rape of a sixteen-year-old white girl, Nellie Catherine Breithaupt, during a robbery outside a country club in Madisonville, Kentucky. The small town, because of about a half dozen similar crimes in the past ten days, was on edge.[82] The police arrested a white prostitute because of a photograph of her with a black man and letters that revealed she and another prostitute had been with black men.[83] The letters led police to three black suspects. One of the suspects confessed to being an accomplice and (after being given two dollars to buy tobacco) implicated two other men in the rape—Bard, a coal miner, and Fleming, a chauffeur.[84]

Before the trial, the three men were imprisoned in Louisville for their safety and were scrambling to find counsel. Three days after their arrest, Bard and Fleming found themselves on trial for their lives. A black Louisville attorney from the city's NAACP branch had come to Madisonville to represent both men, but was "advised" to leave town along with the editor of a black Louisville newspaper for their own safety.[85] The threat of a lynching hovered over the proceedings. Soldiers armed with machine guns stood guard in front of the jail and the courthouse, as well as in the hallway outside the courtroom.[86] Fleming's lawyer, a white Louisville attorney, was not allowed to speak to his client until fifteen to twenty minutes before trial and only in the presence of two court officers. Bard's lawyer, a black attorney from nearby Hopkinsville, was not allowed to speak to his client at all. The wife of one of the defendants was arrested and jailed until the end of the trial; the other defendant's wife was not allowed to attend the trial either.[87] The defense attorneys did not file a motion for a change of venue because Kentucky law required them to get someone else to sign the motion, and no one, white or black, dared sign it. An all-white jury convicted Fleming after deliberating for ten minutes; the next day, the jury convicted Bard in eight minutes.[88]

US District Court Judge Charles I. Dawson held a two-day habeas corpus hearing, expressed deep concerns about the fairness of the trials because they were not postponed or moved to another county, yet denied Bard and Fleming's petition.[89] The Sixth Circuit Court of Appeals in Cincinnati affirmed the trial judge's decision. On July 9, Brandeis granted a temporary stay of execution. At Beverly Farms, Bard's and Fleming's attorneys sought a permanent stay.[90] When presented with the facts of the case, Holmes immediately recognized another potentially mob-dominated trial when he saw one. On July 14, the day before Bard and Fleming were supposed to die, Holmes scrawled at the bottom of the stay petition:

> Motion allowed. Mandate stayed until the petitioners shall have presented a petition for certiorari to the Supreme Court at its next term provided such petition is presented at the earliest date when it is possible by law & any bond given to question law requires it be approved by this Court.

> Oliver Wendell Holmes
> Justice Supreme Court of United States[91]

The black press, which had been covering the Bard and Fleming case for months, hailed Holmes's stay; most white newspapers barely noticed it.[92]

On August 20, two days before Sacco and Vanzetti's execution date, Hill and two attorneys set out for Beverly Farms, trailed by a carload of newspapermen. The attorneys knew all about Holmes's stay. They cited the Bard and Fleming case in their briefs submitted to the justice before their second trip to Beverly Farms.[93] Holmes had given Bard and Fleming exactly what Sacco and Vanzetti wanted—a stay of execution until October so that the entire Supreme Court could vote to hear the case. The lawyers stopped for lunch in Salem and arrived at Holmes's doorstep at 2:30 p.m. The newspapermen sat on the stone wall on the edge of the property while Hill made

Holmes's order granting a stay of execution for Bard and Fleming his case inside the house. At 4:30 p.m., Hill came outside and announced to them that the application had been denied.[94]

This time, instead of a single paragraph, Holmes laid out his reasoning in a three-page, handwritten opinion that was reprinted in newspapers everywhere.[95] He remained persuaded that the prejudices and biases of Judge Thayer had not voided the trial because, as he wrote in his opinion, it had not been "invaded by an infuriated mob ready to lynch prisoner, counsel, and jury if there is not a prompt conviction." This was not a mob-dominated trial such as in *Moore v. Dempsey* and as Bard's and Fleming's seemed to be. At best, Holmes argued in his opinion, Sacco and Vanzetti's trial may have been "voidable" by the Massachusetts Supreme Judicial Court, but not by him: "I have no power to set the proceeding aside—that, subject to the exception that I shall mention, rests wholly with the State." Holmes argued that Supreme Court intervention in state criminal cases on due process grounds "is a power rarely exercised and I should not be doing my duty if I exercised it unless I thought there was a reasonable chance that the Court would entertain the application and ultimately reverse the judgment. This I can not bring myself to believe."[96]

Judge Thayer's prejudicial comments, discovered after the verdict and reviewed only by Thayer, did not sway Holmes. He argued to Hill that it would have been constitutional if the state of Massachusetts had refused to allow any appeals from the rulings of a single trial judge. He also rejected Hill's hypothetical of a "corruptly interested or insane" judge because that was not the case here. "I will not attempt to decide at what point a judgment might be held to be absolutely void on these grounds."[97]

Finally, Holmes refused to be influenced by the intense media scrutiny surrounding the Sacco-Vanzetti case. His opinion mentioned that, after his first opinion, he had received "many letters from people who seem to suppose that I have a general discretion to see that justice is done." He tried to explain that the role the Supreme Court plays in a federal system "is a very delicate matter that has occupied the thoughts of statesmen and judges for a hundred years and can not be disposed of by a summary statement that justice requires me to cut red tape and to intervene." Almost as an aside, he added: "Far stronger cases than this have arisen with regard to the blacks when the Supreme Court has denied its power."[98]

Aside or not, Holmes's comment caught the eye of the *Chicago Defender*, the nation's leading black newspaper, as did his racial terminology. "We cannot rejoice wholeheartedly at what Justice Holmes said in this case because of the manner in which he said it," the *Defender* wrote. The editors rejected as "patronizing" the word "blacks" to describe a race of people: "We want to be known only as Americans—just Americans."[99] Holmes was almost certainly alluding to the case of Bard and Fleming. He also may have been thinking about another case that summer in which he denied certiorari for two men facing execution.[100] And he was speaking to Frankfurter, Laski, and their liberal friends who care "more for red than for black."

If there was a silver lining in Holmes's second Sacco-Vanzetti opinion, it was that he had explicitly permitted Hill and his colleagues to approach other justices about a stay. The race to save Sacco and Vanzetti was on. Hill did not divulge to the waiting newspapermen where he was going next.

Frankfurter knew exactly where. At 7:40 p.m. that night, he learned from Gardner Jackson that Holmes had turned them down and that Hill was heading to Cape Cod to see Brandeis. "Don't dissuade him," Jackson told Frankfurter by phone from Hill's office. "Don't try to put any obstacles in his way. This is the only thing left to do. ... You go ahead and encourage him to try to do every damn thing."[101] Jackson did not know that twelve days earlier Frankfurter had provided one of the lawyers with Brandeis's phone number in Chatham. Frankfurter did not discourage Hill, who recognized that Brandeis "may feel himself disqualified from sitting for reasons you can divine."[102]

Lawyers and nonlawyers associated with the Sacco-Vanzetti Defense Committee bothered Frankfurter day and night about how to save the two men. At 1:00 a.m., Jackson called again and asked Frankfurter to review with Hill the evidence in the record of the judge's and district attorney's prejudice. He also begged Frankfurter to go to Chatham to talk with Brandeis.[103] Frankfurter refused and intimated that he knew things that Jackson did not. "You do not know what transpired in Mr. Holmes' parlor when this was put before him," he told him. He added that he could not tell Jackson over the phone or even in person, and suggested that if he had read Holmes's August 10 memorandum that "a statement of prejudice, no matter however strong." Jackson replied: "I read it and I don't agree with it." Frankfurter, whose phones were being tapped by the state police, reminded Jackson that the argument about prejudice had been made to Holmes and would be made to Brandeis. "I haven't the slightest idea what will happen tomorrow—what Brandeis will do with it," Frankfurter told the nonlawyer Jackson. "I would not be a bit surprised if he disqualified [himself] from sitting and nothing more could cinch it than for me to go down to Chatham. I can't say any-thing more."[104]

At 2:00 a.m., Hill and his fellow attorneys checked in at the Chatham Bars Inn.[105] At 8:35 a.m., Frankfurter phoned while they were having breakfast, apologized for calling on "a fool's errand," and reiterated Jackson's points about District Attorney Katzmann's prejudicial cross-examination in the record.[106] After breakfast, the lawyers left to see Brandeis. Disqualified or not, Brandeis was Hill's best hope. He was the most liberal justice on the Court, more liberal than Holmes, and the most intellectually influential elder statesman at the House of Truth. Though they loved and admired Holmes, they followed Brandeis's lead.

By 1927, Brandeis had emerged as an intellectual force on the Court every bit Holmes's equal and then some. "Justice Holmes is not a liberal, in the sense that Justice Brandeis is," Brandeis's longtime friend Norman Hapgood wrote that year. "[Holmes] is not excited about what may be done by legislation to make better the lot of man. Rather is he impressed with the futility of most such dreams."Yet, as Hapgood observed, Brandeis and Holmes often ended up in the same place "from partly opposite di-rections"—especially as it related to free speech.[107] A year after joining Holmes's dissent in *Abrams*, Brandeis established himself as a protector of free speech by writing dissenting opinions about the Espionage Act convic-tions of Philadelphia publishers of German-language newspapers and from Joseph Gilbert's conviction for a Nonpartisan League speech that violated a Minnesota law about interfering with the draft.[108] Five months before Holmes, Brandeis had graced the cover of *Time* magazine on October 19, 1925, under the tagline "The rights of man—." "He is an admitted liberal," the magazine wrote of Brandeis, "a Justice in whose decisions the rights of property are likely to be subordinated to the rights of man."[109]

On November 13, 1926, editorials in the *New Republic* and New York *World* celebrated Brandeis's seventieth birthday and tenth year on the bench.[110] "Justice Brandeis and Justice Holmes for years have stood apart as the two most progressive-minded members of the Supreme Court ...," Learned Hand wrote in the unsigned *World* editorial. Hand noted Brandeis's "wisely liberal stand" with his dissents in several Espionage Act cases, as well as his dissent about the president's removal power.[111] Chief Justice Taft attributed Holmes's proliferating dissents to Brandeis and charged that Holmes was "so completely under the control of brother Brandeis that it gives to Brandeis two votes instead of one."[112] The profoundest insight about Brandeis's heavily footnoted, fact-laden opinions came from Hand: "Mr. Brandeis's thoroughness is such that his opinions have sometimes been criticized as too 'exhaustive;' and it springs from his feeling that a search for the truth, if carried far enough, will always dispel any conflict in opinions. This passion for truth and his deep acquaintance with modern social and industrial developments are Justice Brandeis's two chief contributions to our highest court."[113]

Brandeis had been itching to publish his views on free speech and finally did so in a May 1927 concurring opinion in the case of Charlotte "Anita" Whitney.[114] The Wellesley-educated daughter of a prominent San Francisco family (she was the niece of the late Justice Stephen J. Field), Whitney had begun her career as a settlement house worker.[115] She had joined the Oakland branch of the Communist Labor Party and had been arrested after delivering a November 28, 1919, speech, "The Negro Problem in the United States." Because of her membership in the Communist Labor Party, she had been tried and convicted under a California criminal syndicalism law and faced up to fourteen years in prison. Brandeis doubted whether the syndicalism law could be squared with the First Amendment. He believed the Fourteenth Amendment protected fundamental rights, protections that included not only property rights but also freedom of speech and assembly.[116] "Fear of serious injury cannot alone justify suppression of free speech and assembly," he wrote. "Men feared witches and burnt women. It is the function of speech to free men from the bondage of irrational fears."[117]

Invoking the Founding Fathers' lack of fear of political change and belief in reason in popular government, Brandeis used his dissent to redefine the "clear and present danger" test: "[N]o danger flowing from speech can be deemed clear and present, unless the incidence of the evil apprehended is so imminent that it may befall before there is opportunity for full discussion. If there be time to expose through discussion the falsehood and fallacies, to avert the evil by the processes of education, the remedy to be applied is more speech, not enforced silence. Only an emergency can justify repression. Such must be the rule if authority is to be reconciled with freedom. Such, in my opinion, is the command of the Constitution." Brandeis concurred in the case because Whitney had failed to argue that "there was no clear and present danger of serious evil."[118] Though he had voted to uphold her conviction, Whitney was not bitter. "I have nothing to complain of," she said, "in comparison to Sacco and Vanzetti."[119] A month later, the governor of California pardoned her based in part on Brandeis's opinion.[120]

Brandeis's record on race was not any better than Holmes's was initially. A Louisville native, he was a southern Democrat who was nominated to the Court by a southern Democrat (Wilson) and only confirmed because of the Senate votes of southern Democrats.[121] Nearly two years before he joined the Court, Brandeis had discouraged the NAACP from seeking his advice and had refused to serve as counsel in a potential lawsuit attacking racial segregation on interstate train travel—though no one had litigated more effectively before the Interstate Commerce Commission. When it came to "the Jim Crow car situation," he had abandoned his role as the "People's Lawyer."[122] The following year, his nephew and namesake, Louis Brandeis Wehle, had written a *New Republic* article extolling the benefits of racial segregation in Louisville and other southern cities.[123]

On the Court, Brandeis had been conspicuously silent about race.[124] He had voted with the majority in many decisions that permitted racial segregation or discrimination—including a 1926 decision that upheld racially restrictive covenants in Washington, DC, just a few blocks from 1727 Nineteenth Street.[125] "I can tell most of the time when I'm reading a brief by a Negro attorney," he said in advising Howard University president Mordecai W. Johnson to hire a full-time faculty and to turn the law school into a day program.[126] (Holmes, by contrast, remarked in 1927 on "a very thorough and really well expressed argument by two colored men—one bery [sic] black—that even in intonations was better than, I should say, the majority of white discourses that we hear.")[127] Unlike Holmes, Brandeis had not written a single opinion vindicating the rights of African Americans. He had, moreover, joined Holmes's opinion in *Buck v. Bell* and later cited it with approval.[128] Yet Brandeis had issued a temporary stay of execution that summer in the Bard and Fleming case before Holmes issued a permanent stay.

Brandeis remained Hill's best hope to save Sacco and Vanzetti. At 9:30 a.m. on August 21, Hill and three lawyers arrived at Brandeis's summer home in Chatham. Only the gable roof was visible from the dirt road entrance. In 1922, the Brandeises had summered in Chatham on Cape Cod and had liked it so much that the following year they purchased a nineteenth-century wooden home there tucked far enough away from the town's main street to give them privacy, and only a short walk to a creek off the Oyster River where the justice liked to go canoeing. The main house was modest and covered with gray wooden shingles. Behind it were a two-story kitchen and a single-story guest house where the Frankfurters, Elizabeth Glendower Evans ("Auntie Bee"), and Brandeis's children and grandchildren stayed.[129] Beginning early in his legal career, the justice always took the month of August off. "I soon learned that I could do twelve months' work in eleven months," he said, "but not in twelve."[130]

Dressed in knickers and a cap and having finished his breakfast, Brandeis was sitting on the front porch waiting for Hill and his colleagues to arrive.[131] They did not get past the front door. "I know what you are here for," Brandeis said, "and I can't take any action at all." Hill replied: "Let me tell you what we have to say." Brandeis refused. Hill insisted on having his say. Brandeis repeated that he was disqualifying himself. The entire conversation lasted three minutes.[132] He did not even write an opinion—justices do not typically explain why they disqualify themselves from cases. To a *Boston Herald* reporter on hand, Hill cited Brandeis's "personal relations with some of the people interested in the case."[133] Brandeis's personal connections to the case were indeed many. Evans, one of the largest contributors to the Sacco-Vanzetti Defense Fund, was practically a member of his family. During the Sacco-Vanzetti trial in 1921, she had put up Sacco's wife, Rosina, and their two children, Dante and Inez, in Brandeis's home in Dedham and not far from the jail where Sacco was being held.[134] Evans and Frankfurter had been staying at Brandeis's summer home in Chatham as late as mid-June 1927, and they likely discussed the case with the justice at length.[135] Second, Alice Brandeis had donated money to the Sacco-Vanzetti Defense Fund in 1921; both she and her eldest daughter, Susan, were personally invested in the case because of their relationship with "Auntie Bee."[136] Finally, there was Brandeis's "half brother, half son" relationship with Frankfurter, with whom Brandeis had been engaged in a running dialogue about the case at least since the October 1926 publication of Frankfurter's unsigned *New Republic* article.[137] In June 1927, the justice had offered to supplement Frankfurter's income for work on the Sacco-Vanzetti case in addition to funding his other pro bono activities.[138] In early August, Brandeis wrote Frankfurter, lamenting the postponement of a summer visit to Chatham because of Sacco-Vanzetti and observing: "You & Auntie B. have played noble parts."[139] After turning them down, Brandeis walked Hill and the lawyers to their car and spoke with them for a few minutes in a friendly way through the driver's side window. The engine was running, and before long they headed north, to the coast of Maine.[140]

If Brandeis turned them down, Hill and Frankfurter had already agreed that they would seek out the remaining liberal justice on the Court, Harlan Fiske Stone. A New Hampshire Republican, Stone had served in the War Department during the world war, reviewing conscientious objector cases, and had been critical of Attorney General Palmer's postwar deportation of aliens. The longtime dean of Columbia Law School, Stone had announced his resignation in October 1923 after clashing with the university's conservative president, Nicholas Murray Butler. In April 1924, six months after Stone's return to Sullivan & Cromwell as its head of litigation, his Amherst College classmate President Coolidge had named him attorney general.[141] As attorney general, Stone had cleaned up a Justice Department plagued by scandal under Harding's attorney general, Harry M. Daugherty. Stone had received help rebuilding the Justice Department from an unexpected source—Frankfurter. "The key to Stone's problems is, of course, men," Frankfurter wrote Lippmann in April 1924. "Everything is subordinate to personnel, for personnel determines the governing atmosphere and understanding from which all questions of administrative organization take shape."[142] In the same letter, Frankfurter had indicated which people Stone should keep, which people he should fire, and who would be good replacements. Lippmann had sent the letter to Stone, who replied directly to Frankfurter: "I have followed almost exactly the suggestions contained in your letter."[143] The "almost" was notable. Frankfurter disagreed with Stone's decision to allow the prosecution of Senator Burton K. Wheeler to go forward; he viewed it as payback for Wheeler's Senate hearings on the Harding administration.[144] Yet Frankfurter agreed with Stone's decision to fire the director of the Bureau of Investigation, William J. Burns, who had been "shadowing" congressmen who were investigating Harding administration scandals.[145] Stone replaced Burns with J. Edgar Hoover, who, the attorney general predicted to Frankfurter, would "make good in a way which would be gratifying to all those with liberal ideas" about the Justice Department.[146] Though publicly silent about Hoover's promotion, Frankfurter and Chafee were unhappy with Hoover's appointment because of his ties to the Palmer deportations. Frankfurter warned Stone that Hoover might be a less "effective and zealous instrument for the realization of the 'liberal ideas' which you had in mind" under a different attorney general.[147]

Before Stone joined the Court, Frankfurter had harbored doubts about the sincerity of his liberalism. Stone's pro-Coolidge speeches during the 1924 presidential election attacking La Follette for criticizing the Supreme

Frankfurter with Brandeis in Chatham

Court had given Frankfurter pause "not about Stone's honesty but his quality." Stone had conflated the Court's child labor decisions, and he had seemed untroubled by "some aspects of the power which the Court enjoys," Frankfurter had written Learned Hand in November 1924. "If Stone is a liberal, so is Sutherland, so is Pierce Butler. If you call Stone a liberal, I wonder what degree of wildness attaches to Brandeis and Holmes."[148] After Coolidge nominated Stone on January 5, 1925, to replace Joseph McKenna on the Supreme Court, Stone made it his life's goal to be thought of in the same breath as Holmes, Brandeis, and Cardozo (then a judge on the New York Court of Appeals). Stone, like Brandeis, fawned over Holmes. "When I read any opinion like this," Stone wrote in joining Holmes's opinion in a trade-mark case, "I feel like taking up ditch digging or carpentry as a more suitable occupation."[149] Stone had made a less than favorable impression on his colleagues. Van Devanter had "unmeasured contempt for him"; Brandeis was not sold on him, either.[150] Perhaps based on his summertime conversations with Brandeis, Frankfurter believed that Stone wanted to be viewed as lib-eral more out of ambition than conviction. Frankfurter was sure that he was "in a different class from Butler and McReynolds," he wrote Learned Hand. "The latter haven't the slightest desire to be thought well of, let us say, by the New Republic. Stone has—but he also wants to be thought well of by those who regard the general direction of the New Republic as subversive. And so, occasionally, we will find him with Holmes and Brandeis." Frankfurter expected of Stone "little as a clear-cut propulsion of insight like Holmes' and Brandeis'."[151] Putting his reservations aside, Frankfurter persuaded Hill that Stone was the third-best option to obtain a stay for Sacco and Vanzetti.

The problem for Hill was that Stone was at his summer home on Isle au Haut, an island off the Maine coast and unreachable by telephone or wire. As soon as Brandeis had turned him down, Hill instructed his co-counsel to find out the boat and ferry schedules. The last boat had left at 5:00 a.m.[152] Undeterred, Hill began driving to Rockland, the closest mainland town. At noon, Hill's co-counsel called Frankfurter from Plymouth. He advised them to "skillfully weave in" New York and British cases from Frankfurter's book and to remind Stone that the evidence of Judge Thayer's prejudice had not been available for seven years. Flattery was also important because Stone was "a vain man."[153]

Hill drove through Boston without stopping at his office. At 3:00 p.m., he telephoned his office, got stuck in bad traffic on the Newburyport Turnpike, and at 5:55 p.m. phoned again from Portsmouth, New Hampshire.[154] They finally arrived in Rockland "shortly before" 2:00 a.m. Hill decided to get a few hours' sleep and to charter a fishing boat early the next morning.[155] Sacco and Vanzetti's executions were less than twenty-four hours away. Hill barely slept. He took the ferry from Rockland to Stonington on Deer Isle, thirty-five nautical miles, and then chartered a fishing boat another eight miles to the even more remote Isle au Haut, a four-hour trip. He arrived at Stone's summer home at 9:00 a.m. and spoke with the justice for an hour and fifteen minutes. The answer, however, was the same. Stone issued a two-line order: "Application considered and denied without prejudice to application to any other justice. I concur in the view expressed by Justice Holmes as to the

Holmes (center), Harlan Fiske Stone (left), and Brandeis (right)

merits of the application and action of the counsel in presenting it."[156] After returning to Searsport, Maine, Hill called his office: "Nothing else could be done."[157] An exhausted Hill spent the night in Portland, Maine.

With the clock ticking, new lawyers injected themselves into the case with the encouragement of the Sacco-Vanzetti Defense Committee.[158] Hill had filed a petition for certiorari with the clerk's office at the US Supreme Court in Washington. He mailed the clerk a copy of the record after another lawyer had taken the train to Washington to file the petition—but neglected to bring the record.[159] The new lawyers were intent on finding a judge who would grant a stay so that the entire Court could consider hearing the case. They began trying things that Hill and Frankfurter had rejected as bad strategy. Michael Musmanno, a publicity-seeking Pittsburgh lawyer, repeatedly wired Chief Justice Taft at his summer home in Pointe-au-Pic in Quebec, Canada. At 9:00 p.m., Musmanno phoned the chief justice and offered to meet him at the US-Canadian border; Taft refused because he agreed with Holmes.[160] Musmanno also wired President Coolidge in Rapid City, South

Dakota, unsuccessfully tried to get the president on the phone, and offered to charter a plane there to argue that Coolidge should pardon Sacco and Vanzetti. Coolidge's aide refused: no federal crime had been committed, and the former Massachusetts governor was unlikely to interfere with the state's legal establishment. Besides, the president was leaving early the next morning for Yellowstone National Park.[161]

Three hours before the scheduled executions, four lawyers led by civil libertarian John Finerty returned to Beverly Farms at 9:00 p.m. Justice Holmes again refused to grant a stay.[162] The lawyers also unsuccessfully sought stays from several lower court judges. Frankfurter and Jackson clashed about Holmes's memorandum concluding that the Court lacked the power to interfere in state criminal proceedings absent a trial by mob. Jackson, echoing other nonlawyers on the Sacco-Vanzetti Defense Committee, complained that "it is a most awful situation where your legal system will not insure moral demands; that is what leads to revolution." Frankfurter, after months of working behind the scenes to save the two condemned men, was having none of it: "Now don't talk to me about that because I have had to listen to my wife all day. I can shut you up but not her."[163]

On the morning of the executions, the Frankfurters returned from Duxbury to Boston. With a sympathetic friend, they walked the streets of Beacon Hill past midnight and at 12:19 a.m. heard the news on the radio: "Sacco gone, Vanzetti going!" Marion "collapsed and would have fallen to the pavement if the two men had not caught her."[164] She sank into a depression that lasted many months. Frankfurter arranged for her to co-edit Sacco and Vanzetti's jailhouse letters for publication as a way of helping her recover and bringing her back to life.[165] Indeed, Frankfurter had worked himself to the point of exhaustion. "To the end, you have done all that was possible for you," Brandeis wrote him. "And that all was more than would have [been] possible for any other person I know. But the end of S.V. is only the beginning. 'They know not what they do.'"[166]

★★★

Following the executions of Sacco and Vanzetti, American liberalism was at a crossroads. A *New Republic* editorial probably written by Herbert Croly characterized the case "as a revelation of liberal impotence. The agitation did not carry any conviction with those socially important mediating minds which occupy the grand-stand of American public opinion."[167] Liberals had never been more united behind a cause, yet never more incapable of influencing its outcome. They had placed their faith in the ability of facts and reason to change public opinion and to persuade elected officials to do the right thing. Despite Holmes's and Brandeis's refusal to stay the executions, they began to view the Court, more than ever, as an ally in their efforts to emphasize fair procedures to obtain just results. Yet public opinion, elected officials, and the legal system had failed them. "It is this bloc state of mind on the part of the responsible people which accounts for the impotence of liberals even when they are united," the *New Republic* concluded. "They would do well to recognize the fact, and to consider its causes and consequences. How far is it their own fault that they count so little in the eyes of their official and responsible fellow countrymen? Can they do anything about it?"[168]

The fight was not over. The man who had united so many people behind the cause of Sacco and Vanzetti was once again fighting to keep his job. Old Boston was spreading false rumors to try to force Frankfurter's resignation from Harvard Law School. They charged that his book had stalled the law school's $5 million endowment drive. In truth, only a few people had reneged on small pledges totaling no more than $2,000 to $3,000, and philanthropist Julius Rosenwald made his support for Frankfurter and the law school known by pledging $10,000 for a Frankfurter-directed publication fund.[169] Old Boston also claimed that Frankfurter had been secretly on the Sacco-Vanzetti Defense Committee's payroll. To Judge Mack and others, Frankfurter wrote a detailed recitation of his involvement in the case since 1923 which refuted the financial allegations.[170] During a September 27 meeting, Mack defended Frankfurter before Harvard's Board of Overseers.[171]

Given Pound's timidity, Frankfurter needed Mack's support more than ever. After the executions, Pound wrote that he was "fearful of trouble."[172] Frankfurter reminded him of their agreement about Frankfurter's decision to publish while the case was pending before the Massachusetts Supreme Judicial Court. Frankfurter was unrepentant about anything he had written or done in trying to save the two men.[173] For many months, Pound had been defending Frankfurter before the American Bar Association and at Harvard law alumni meetings, but the dean was tired of it all: "The persistently hostile attitude of the University authorities generally toward the Law School makes one wonder whether it is worthwhile to continue trying to do anything here."[174]

The Sacco-Vanzetti case had exacerbated Frankfurter's already toxic relationship with President Lowell. Even before the case was over, Frankfurter had written Lowell an eleven-page letter attacking the Lowell Committee's factual conclusions about Sacco and Vanzetti's guilt and Judge Thayer's prejudices.[175] As John Moors, Frankfurter's friend, Lowell's Harvard College classmate, and a member of the Harvard Corporation, said, "Lawrence Lowell was incapable of seeing that two wops could be right and the Yankee judiciary could be wrong."[176] To Pound, Frankfurter made it clear that he would not succumb to pressure from Lowell or anyone else: "When people ask me, 'Do you plan to resign?' I say to them, 'Why should I? Let Mr. Lowell resign.'"[177]

The Harvard alumni who wanted Frankfurter's resignation would not get it—Lowell himself defended Frankfurter's academic freedom.[178] However, he also made Frankfurter's professional life difficult. Frankfurter threatened to resign from the Harvard Crime Survey upon hearing that Lowell was holding up its funding, presumably because of Sacco-Vanzetti.[179] Lowell tried to block Frankfurter's protégé Landis from joining the faculty in 1928 and vetoed a five-year appointment for a second Jewish professor, Nathan Margold, despite faculty and judicial support.[180] Pound declined to confront Lowell about Margold or about what Frankfurter saw as "the ugly atmosphere of anti-Semitism."[181] The Harvard president reputedly told Pound: "[O]ne Frankfurter to the Pound should be enough."[182]

The day after the executions, one publication praised both Lowell's service on the committee and Frankfurter's calls for a new trial—and somehow managed to straddle both—Lippmann's New York *World*. Of Lowell and fellow committee member Samuel Stratton, the *World* wrote: "Whether they were right or whether they were wrong, well-advised or ill-advised, is a matter which will long be in dispute. But that as individuals they faced a disagreeable duty bravely is something that cannot be disputed." The *World*'s editorial, "Patriotic Service," singled out Thompson, Hill, and Frankfurter as "those who gave freely, and at great cost to themselves." Though the lawyers failed to obtain a new trial, they "placed indelibly on the record the fact there are men in Massachusetts now, as in the past, who are ready to uphold the right of the humblest and the most despised. Those who are prepared to generalize glibly about the conservative classes in Boston and about Harvard might remember these three names. For they stand very high and very honorably in the roster of patriots."[183]

The penultimate line was a reference to the paper's erstwhile columnist, Heywood Broun. Writing in *The Nation*, Broun took the *World* and *Boston Herald* to task for their attempts at postexecution even-handedness: "Here in America the word 'liberal' has lost its savor. Many have come to think of a liberal as a good-humored fellow with some sense of sportsmanship. He strides into a dispute and sagely ventures: 'There is much to be said on both sides. The truth lies somewhere between the two.' And that's a silly thing to say because it does not indicate just where truth sits in the charted field lying between the left and right. Liberalism deserves decay if it has nothing more to offer than the worship of Mrs. Winslow['s soothing syrup]."[184]

On October 4, 1927, the *New Republic* hosted a dinner to honor liberal lawyers, literati, and other volunteers who had devoted their time to the cause of Sacco and Vanzetti and "to discuss what ought to be done in order to keep the flag flying."[185] Thompson and Hill spoke about the case. Thompson moved the crowd with his speech about the two men and his belief in their innocence. Hill insisted he was just doing his legal duty and was "revolted" at criticisms of Lowell and the committee's report. Frankfurter, in turn, rebuked Hill for defending Lowell, attacked the report's facts and conclusions as "an obstruction to a free inquiry into this case," and urged that the obstruction be "removed" by continuing to critique the report.[186] Frankfurter's rebuttal buoyed the spirits of the literary crowd on hand, including "the forlornly cynical" Dorothy Parker, "the flint-like crusading" John Haynes Holmes, the *New Republic*'s Socialist book review editor Edmund Wilson, and of course Broun.[187] The *New Republic* dinner gave Broun the perfect opportunity to confront Lippmann for flip-flopping about the case and to call him out as a faint-hearted liberal. "Broun gave Walter Lippmann unshirted hell in front of him about his open mind, that was so open the wind whistled through and nothing stuck," Jackson recalled. "It was a devastating attack to which Walter had no answer at all."[188]

Lippmann had revealed his ambivalence about the Sacco-Vanzetti case in response to a letter from Judge Learned Hand. Hand thought that Frankfurter was unhinged about the case. He described listening to Frankfurter discuss Sacco-Vanzetti at a conference in Hanover, New Hampshire, in late summer as "exquisitely painful." He agreed that Frankfurter had mastered every detail about the case, but that "his conclusions ... were without weight, because it was so apparent that no more light could then come into his mind, and that passion had seized all." Hand wrote Lippmann: "What I needed was someone who could give me conclusions that I could accept. Plainly he was in no condition to do that." Hand praised Lippmann's initial editorial about the Lowell report. "Everybody up here was with you on that except Felix to whom it was monstrous," Hand wrote of his friends who summered in Cornish, New Hampshire. The judge confessed his doubts about whether

Sacco and Vanzetti had a fair trial or whether "there was evidence to convict them." But not until after they had been executed.[189]

To Hand, Lippmann revealed that all summer long he had been distracted by others things—working on his next book during the morning, supervising the *World*'s editorial page during the afternoons and evenings, and dealing with his father's death. Lippmann never had taken the time to come to Boston and to investigate the facts, and he did not trust Frankfurter's version of events. Through the entirety of the Sacco-Vanzetti "horror," Lippmann wrote Hand, he had not been so troubled about anything since 1919 "when against what I really believe was my own deepest and best feeling I let irritation against Wilson's stupidity push me into intransigent opposition to the Treaty." Lippmann conceded that he had placed too much faith in people in positions of power, starting with President Lowell. He had "confidently" assumed that the Lowell report would not result in the executions of Sacco and Vanzetti. "The briefness of the time allowed for reaching an opi[ni]on, the atmosphere of horror and the very real danger of red violence followed by white violence," he wrote Hand, "made me feel as if we were being rushed into the gravest kind of decision without freedom of mind to consider it."

Unlike Frankfurter, Lippmann chose to sit on the sidelines and let others educate public opinion. Broun and others were right to question Lippmann's liberalism. "You know that I was never convinced that they were innocent," Lippmann wrote Hand. "At the end, my feeling was (a) that Sacco might be guilty and Vanzetti less probably, (b) that the evidence against both was insufficient, (c) that the trial was almost certainly conducted in a prejudiced atmosphere, (d) that the governor, though probably sincere within his lights, was infected with the psychology of the class conflict which the case had provoked, (e) that a commutation was the wiser course even though one could sympathize with the governor's difficulty in yielding after the threats had been made." Rather than question Old Boston's reaction to the case, Lippmann tried to rationalize it. He wished that the "conservative classes" could "abandon their panicky state of mind and rule the country with some flexibility and ease. They sit upon the rock of Gibraltar and behave as if they were upon a raft at sea."[190] Lippmann biographer Ronald Steel suggested that Lippmann's reaction to the case "revealed a deep vein of conservatism running through his brand of liberalism."[191]

Frankfurter's work on Sacco-Vanzetti made him a liberal hero, and his commitment to liberalism was stronger than ever.[192] Indeed, his most enduring act in the Sacco-Vanzetti case occurred after their executions when he spearheaded the publication of all six volumes of the record in the case, though, as he discovered, much of the Lowell Committee's investigation was conveniently not recorded for posterity. The publication was made possible because leading members of the bench and bar—Newton D. Baker, Emory R. Buckner, C. C. Burlingham, John W. Davis, Bernard Flexner, Raymond B. Fosdick, Charles P. Howland, Victor Morawetz, Charles Nagel, Walter H. Pollak, and Elihu Root—contributed to the $30,000 cost covered mostly by John D. Rockefeller Jr. and Julius Rosenwald.[193] The project was Frankfurter's idea, though his name was nowhere to be found. Except for responding to a reviewer in the *Illinois Law Review* questioning his motives for writing the book, Frankfurter stayed publicly silent about the case.[194] He believed that the publication of the six-volume record would persuade people, as he had been persuaded, that Sacco and Vanzetti were innocent and that at the very least they could not have been convicted on the evidence presented at trial.[195] He would not rest until copies of the record were "in every library in the world."[196] He had not lost his faith in factual investigation and reason to move public opinion and elected officials, and he was unwavering in his belief that the Court could be an ally it if consisted of more justices like Holmes and Brandeis.

For several days after the executions, police guarded Holmes's summer residence at Beverly Farms. Frankfurter was disturbed by the news that the serenity of the justice's summer vacation was interrupted by night-time guards.[197] Three times, Sacco and Vanzetti lawyers had sought stays of execution from Holmes, and three times he had turned them down. "Judge Holmes has steadily been the advocate on the bench of tolerance of liberal and even 'advanced' views," a *New York Times* editorial said. "He, if any Federal Judge, was indicated as the most hopeful recourse for the lawyers making their last gallant but desperate plea for the men condemned to death in Boston."[198]

Holmes's views of the case were anything but liberal. He thought the *New Republic*'s August 31 editorial was "hysterical," welcomed news from his new secretary Arthur Sutherland Jr. that Frankfurter's "general frame of mind is to drop the matter as finished," and considered "the row that has been made [over the case] idiotical. ... If justice is the interest why do they not talk about the infinitely worse cases of the blacks?" he wrote Laski. Though he agreed with Frankfurter's book, he believed all it showed was that "the case was tried in a hostile atmosphere. I doubt if anyone would say that there was no evidence warranting a conviction."[199] Holmes complained to Frankfurter about the *New Republic*'s fixation on reasonable doubt: "[I]t seems quite clear that this one is not due to abstract love of justice but to the undue prominence given to red opinions which interest more than black skins."[200]

The radical left angered Holmes with its criticism of his closest colleague on the Court. Brandeis was bombarded with "abusive letters."[201] The day after the executions, the Communist *Daily Worker* compared him to Pontius Pilate. Rejecting Brandeis's recusal because of his family's interest in the case as a "flimsy excuse," the *Daily Worker* accused him of being "part of the capitalist machine that intends to make an example of Sacco and Vanzetti ... the dominant section of the American ruling class is intent on their death. And the 'liberal' Brandeis is going along. A Pilate has come to judgment."[202] Holmes's secretary Sutherland had seen the article in the New York newspaper's front window and reported the contents to his boss. "How can one respect that sort of thing?" Holmes asked his Socialist friend Laski. "It isn't a matter of reason, but simply shrieking because the world is not the kind of a world they want—a trouble that most of us feel in some way."[203]

Frankfurter and his friends still believed in representative government, still believed that the legal system worked, and still believed in Holmes and Brandeis. In a December 1927 *Harvard Law Review* article about Holmes's twenty-five years on the Supreme Court, Frankfurter wrote: "Where others are guided through experience of life, he is led by the divination of the philosopher and the imagination of the poet. He is, indeed, philosopher become king."[204] The following year, Frankfurter dedicated his new book, *The Business of the Supreme Court*, to "Mr. Justice Holmes, who, after twenty-five terms, continues to contribute his genius to the work of a great Court."[205] Frankfurter enlisted the *New Republic*'s assistance in responding to Brandeis's critics. The magazine took Frankfurter's suggestion and published a one-paragraph editorial comparing Brandeis's ethics to Judge Thayer's.[206] Lippmann wrote Brandeis praising the justice's decision to disqualify himself from hearing the Sacco-Vanzetti case as "the conception of what real disinterestedness in a judge ought to be."[207] On October 22, the Court dismissed Sacco and Vanzetti's petition for certiorari as moot. They were already dead.

The Court, however, still held the lives of two black Kentucky men in its hands. Nathan Bard and Bunyan Fleming were alive thanks to stays of execution from Brandeis and Holmes. Yet the NAACP's National Legal Committee refused to take the lead in appealing the case to the Court.

Louis Marshall read the record and did not find any issues to appeal because trial counsel had not moved to change the venue and had agreed
to a one-day extension of time.[208] A due process claim based on *Moore
v. Dempsey*, according to Marshall, was not enough.[209] Marshall did not
want the NAACP's National Legal Committee to sponsor cases "in which
there is not a fair fighting chance and which do not involve an important
principle or some outstanding act of prejudice and injustice."[210] Though the
NAACP donated $250 to the local Louisville branch's defense fund, the or-
ganization's experienced Supreme Court advocates—Marshall, Moorfield
Storey, and James Cobb—stayed on the sidelines.[211]

On November 21, the Court declined to hear the case. It did not matter
that Bard and Fleming had been given two days to find lawyers; that Bard
had not conferred with his counsel and Fleming did so for only fifteen to
twenty minutes before trial; that the NAACP's Louisville counsel had been
run out of town; that Bard's wife had been arrested and jailed so she could
not testify on her husband's behalf; that armed state troopers had guarded the
courthouse to prevent a lynching; or that the two men had been convicted by
an all-white jury in ten minutes or less. The Court, as in most cases, did not
say why it declined to hear the case. Not a single justice voted to hear it.[212]

On November 25, 8,000 white people stood in the Hopkins County,
Kentucky, jail yard, on fences, on nearby rooftops, on sheds, on telephone
poles, and anywhere else they could find to watch Bard and Fleming hang.[213]
Both men died professing their innocence. White newspapers buried the
Bard and Fleming story.[214] Black newspapers made it front-page news.[215]
The black *Louisville Leader* attacked the white *Louisville Times*'s editorial
analogizing the case to Sacco-Vanzetti because "there was as much difference between the Bard and Fleming case and that of Sacco and Vanzetti as
between noon and midnight." The *Leader* observed that Bard and Fleming
was an interracial rape case lasting several days without pretrial access to
counsel and with the threat of a lynching hanging in the air, and that Sacco-
Vanzetti was a double-murder case that lasted months and an appeals process
that lasted seven years. "In the next place Bard and Fleming were Negroes
and Sacco and Vanzetti were white," the *Leader* continued. "This makes a big
difference in Kentucky." The paper pointed to a case in Lexington where
a white man accused of raping a black girl had been sent to an insane
asylum. Nor did the NAACP play as big a role as the white newspaper
alleged.[216] The NAACP's National Legal Committee had abandoned Bard

EXECUTION PASS

—The Bearer—

O. A. Link

Is entitled to admittance as a witness to the hanging of Bunyan Fleming and Nathan Bard at Madisonville, Ky., on Nov. 25, 1927.

This Pass is not transferable.

C. E. Barnett

Sheriff, Hopkins County, Ky.

Sheriff's pass to the public hangings of Bard and Fleming

and Fleming, who, unlike Sacco and Vanzetti, did not have first-rate counsel on appeal.

Though it began to protect the rights of southern blacks to fair criminal trials in *Moore v. Dempsey* and black voting rights in *Nixon v. Herndon*, the Supreme Court circa 1927 was far from a panacea for people of color. That fall, Gong Lum, a Chinese grocer in Rosedale, Mississippi, challenged a school principal's decision to send his nine-year-old daughter, Martha, home from school after recess. Martha and other Chinese students in Mississippi attended Rosedale's white schools, though the state constitution mandated separate "white or colored" schools. State officials ended the practice because Martha Lum "was of Chinese descent, and not a member of the white or Caucasian race."[217] Lum argued that the school board had failed to set up a separate school for Chinese students and therefore must admit his daughter to the white school. The trial court agreed and ordered the school board to readmit her. The state supreme court, however, reversed because the state constitutional provisions were designed "to preserve the integrity and purity of the white race," and Martha Lum was not white or Caucasian.[218] The only options for her were to pay for private school or to attend the nearest public school for colored children.

The Court unanimously affirmed the state supreme court's decision based on the 1896 decision in *Plessy v. Ferguson* establishing the racially "separate but equal doctrine," as well as prior decisions about racially segregated schools. "[W]e cannot think that the question is any different, or that any different result can be reached, assuming the cases above cited to be rightly decided, where the issue is as between white pupils and the pupils of the yellow races," Chief Justice Taft wrote. "The decision is within the discretion of the state in regulating its public schools, and does not conflict with the Fourteenth Amendment."[219] Holmes and Brandeis both joined *Gong Lum v. Rice*'s unanimous reaffirmation of the separate but equal doctrine. Holmes's secretary Arthur Sutherland asked the justice about the fairness of the decision to Martha Lum. "I expressed some sympathy for the appellant," Sutherland recalled. "Holmes grumbled and swore but concurred."[220] Frankfurter was well aware of the problems of racial segregation—his black former graduate student Charles Hamilton Houston had written him in 1925 about the DC Bar's refusal to allow black lawyers to use the bar's law library.[221] Yet neither Frankfurter, Lippmann, nor any other white liberal associated with the House of Truth mentioned the outcome of Martha Lum's case.

Holmes was right about Sacco and Vanzetti—the world did care more for red than for black. Though no racial egalitarian, he made overlooked contributions to the Court's role in protecting the Bill of Rights, voting rights, and the rights of minorities. In defending the right to fair criminal trials, he articulated a limit on government power as important and enduring as his free speech dissents. *Moore v. Dempsey* provided an opening, in extreme cases, to protect the due process rights of southern blacks. He continued to champion those rights with his second opinion denying a stay in the Sacco-Vanzetti case and his stay of execution for Bard and Fleming. In doing so, he helped show his liberal friends the role that the Supreme Court could play with regard to race and the criminal justice system. It would not be long before Frankfurter and other liberals began to accept Holmes's challenge.

25

A Damn Poor Psychologist

The unlikeliest of individuals memorialized Sacco and Vanzetti after their executions—the nativist former Klansman, self-proclaimed "protestant of Nordic stock," and creator of the South Dakota monument to America's presidential heroes. Borglum's connection to the two martyred Italian anarchists stemmed from his House of Truth friendship with Frankfurter and specifically from a bet Frankfurter and Gardner Jackson made in May 1928. Jackson had purchased a small house on Beacon Hill to serve as a Sacco and Vanzetti memorial, proposed a bas-relief for the front entrance, and believed that Borglum was the perfect person to do it. "Felix just hooted at the idea," Jackson recalled. "He said I was, in effect, nuts to think that I could persuade Gutzon Borglum to do this. I bet him he was wrong."[1] Immediately after speaking with Frankfurter, Jackson headed to the Western Union office in Harvard Square and wired Borglum at the sculptor's San Antonio, Texas, studio. In his telegram, Jackson wrote what Frankfurter had said about the chances that Borglum would create a bas-relief in honor of Sacco and Vanzetti and about their bet. It was a clever strategy because no one could tell Borglum that he could not or would not do something. "YOU TELL FELIX FRANKFURTER HE IS A DAMN POOR PSYCHOLOGIST," Borglum replied five hours later. "AT SAME TIME GIVE HIM MY LOVE AND TO YOU. OF COURSE I WILL MAKE A BAR [sic] RELIEF OF SACCO AND VANZETTI."[2]

After Borglum agreed, Jackson articulated a vision of the memorial and proposed unveiling the bas-relief in three months' time on the first anniversary of Sacco's and Vanzetti's executions. In a follow-up letter to Borglum, Jackson explained why Frankfurter had not gotten in touch with the sculptor instead. Their mutual friend was keeping his distance from the case because he had been "charged with being the master mind of our dangerous defense organization with its tentacles throughout the world. If only people really knew." Despite Frankfurter's lack of involvement with

Borglum's bas-relief of Sacco and Vanzetti

the defense committee or the memorial, Jackson assured Borglum that "when your wire of acceptance came back, boy, O boy, he was joyful and excited." It was Frankfurter who suggested that Borglum leave San Antonio and immediately come to Boston to inform himself about the case. "Both Felix and Marion," Jackson reported to Borglum, "are keen to have you."[3] Borglum was delighted to join forces with his old friend. "Felix knows perfectly well what side to find me on when a decision must be taken as to whether I will be with Tom Paine, Jefferson, and their kind, or with their opponents," the sculptor replied to Jackson. "Fear not, I will take up the cause of these two men if they have been wronged. ... I will do anything I can to make the martyrdom of these men a burning, living protest against the injustice practiced in the name of modern jurisprudence!"[4]

Still, Borglum's lingering questions about Sacco's and Vanzetti's guilt or innocence and practical questions about the bas-relief brought him to Boston. That summer, he and Mary drove from San Antonio and were seen riding in a Packard convertible down Hanover Street in Boston's North End. Borglum visited Jackson's proposed museum, measured the entranceway, and obtained photographs of Sacco and Vanzetti.[5] But the main purpose of the trip was to learn the facts of the case and reunite Borglum with Frankfurter. They had not seen each other in many years, probably since the war, when Frankfurter was living at the House of Truth and Borglum was fighting the Wilson administration about the aircraft

Gardner Jackson (right) and Frankfurter

scandal. They were no longer united as they had been by Roosevelt's Bull Moose campaign and indeed had traveled very different political paths after 1912, yet they still had a lot in common. Both were politically independent and believed that government could make people's lives better. Both had a knack for ingratiating themselves with people in positions of power yet were unafraid to take on the establishment. And both liked to talk—a lot. "Felix must be mellowing," Borglum told Jackson and Jackson's wife, Dodi, as the sculptor was saying good-bye to them on Cape Cod. "This was the first time I've been able to get a word in when he was around." As Frankfurter walked the Jacksons back to their cottage, he said, "Gutzon must be mellowing. This was the first. ..."[6]

Political differences aside, Frankfurter and Jackson changed Borglum's mind about the Sacco-Vanzetti case. As Frankfurter had suspected, the sculptor initially believed that the two men were guilty.[7] After hearing the facts, Borglum offered to construct the bas-relief merely for the cost of materials.[8] He joined Frankfurter's fight, albeit after it was over.

★★★

Borglum had a lot of time on his hands during the summer of 1928 because the money for Mount Rushmore had run out. He did not make good on his promise that he would complete the head of Washington in a year. In fact, he had barely started carving. The state of South Dakota had appropriated no money for the memorial; fundraising had stalled. The only way he could begin was with the help of the federal government. Even after President Coolidge had declined to appear at the October 1925 unveiling, Borglum refused to give up on him. The sculptor sent the president a copy of the program from the unveiling, the 1926 annual report, and a sketch of the proposed head of Washington.[9]

Good fortune intervened. During the spring of 1927, the president decided to replace the White House's leaky roof and to expand the attic into a third-floor residence. In April, President and Mrs. Coolidge moved into a house at 15 Dupont Circle and were looking for a summer vacation spot out west. Senator Peter Norbeck and others urged Coolidge to consider the Black Hills. Borglum also weighed in, telling the president how important Mount Rushmore was as "the first purely national monument of this character." The sculptor explained how he was beginning to work on Washington's sixty-foot-high head and wanted the president to preside over a dedication ceremony.[10] His entreaties seemed to have worked.

The president announced on May 24 that he would be leaving the following month for the Black Hills. At 9:00 p.m. on June 13, a special nine-car presidential train left Union Station, carrying seventy-five people, including President and Mrs. Coolidge, the president's staff, Secret Service, and newspapermen. Grace Coolidge brought her five pet canaries, two collies—Rob Roy and Prudence Prim—and Rebecca, the family's pet raccoon. After brief train stops in Hammond, Indiana, and Pierre, South Dakota, the presidential train arrived in Rapid City at 5:30 p.m. on June 15 to a cheering throng of nearly 10,000 people and a twenty-one-gun salute. Rob Roy and Prudence Prim bounded off the train in front of the Coolidges. A car was waiting for them. At the small village of Hermosa, a hundred or so cowboys joined the presidential party and escorted the motorcade the last twelve miles to the president's summer residence at the thirty-room State Game Lodge in the Black Hills.

The people of South Dakota made sure President Coolidge had a good time. State officials and Colonel Edmund Starling, Coolidge's trusted Secret Service man, had stocked the creek next to the president's lodge with large trout. The fish had been raised on liver and horsemeat and would bite at anything; they were also hemmed in by wire mesh hidden by rocks. His first time out fishing, the president caught five rainbow trout, including one weighing one pound, fourteen ounces. Coolidge caused a national controversy by admitting that he had baited his hook with worms rather than flies. No self-respecting trout fisherman used worms; the president switched to flies.

President Coolidge received gifts everywhere he went and proved willing to show them off for photographers, much to the chagrin of his friends and family. At a July 4 celebration, he wore a ten-gallon hat and white chaps with the letters "C-A-L" on each side. A month later, when the Sioux tribe of South Dakota made him a chief named Wamblee-Tokaha (Leading Eagle), he wore a war bonnet with elaborate feathers.[11] The state legislature renamed the creek near the game lodge Grace Coolidge Creek and a nearby mountain Mount Coolidge. Still, it was not all play and no work. The president had an office on the first floor of the high school building in Rapid City, the site of biweekly talks with the press corps. Numerous government officials, including Secretary of Commerce Herbert Hoover and General John J. Pershing, came to Rapid City to meet with the president. It was there that lawyer Michael Musmanno had tried to get Coolidge on the phone about pardoning Sacco and Vanzetti.

Though Coolidge's presence had diverted the attention of the people of South Dakota and stalled fundraising efforts, Borglum knew that both the president and the national media were captive audiences for the rededication of Mount Rushmore. For a time, it was touch-and-go as to whether Coolidge would even visit the site of the memorial, much less speak at a rededication ceremony.[12] The sculptor left nothing to chance. On July 22, he invited Coolidge to draft the monument's inscription. Borglum envisioned a 160-foot tablet containing a frontier history of America—250 words each about the Declaration of Independence in 1776, the drafting of the Constitution in 1787, Jefferson's Louisiana Purchase in 1803, the cession of Florida from Spain in 1819, Texas's statehood in 1845, the acquisition of the Oregon Territory and California, and the purchase and opening of the Isthmus of Panama. "My own thought on this is expressed in my earnest wish that you be the one author of that tablet," he wrote Coolidge. "It should be simple, brief, biblical in its simplicity. It becomes part of the art work we are building."[13]

The entablature, as Borglum referred to it, later embroiled him in yet another public controversy, but it was the worm that he needed to bait the hook. The ploy worked. Coolidge agreed to participate in an August 10 ceremonial carving of Washington's head. The only problem was getting him there. The dirt road from the old mining town of Keystone to Rushmore was steep, narrow, and winding; heavy rains had made it impassable.[14] People abandoned their cars and hiked the rest of the way as temperatures topped eighty degrees. "Soft white clouds with silvery edges crept over the mountain as the crowd assembled," the *Rapid City Daily Journal* reported. "They cast a welcome shade upon those who had walked to the peak, and made it an ideal day."[15] After arriving at Keystone by car, the president rode his favorite horse, *Mistletoe*, three miles up a steep trail to Mount Rushmore. He wore his ten-gallon hat, riding boots, stirrups, and buckskin gloves, in addition to his suit and tie. Senator Simeon D. Fess of Ohio, presidential adviser Colonel Blanton Winship, presidential physician Major James F. Coupal, presidential riding instructor "Dakota Clyde" Jones, and four Secret Service men accompanied the president on horseback.[16]

A cheering throng of 1,000 to 2,000 people and a presidential salute of twenty-one blasts of dynamite greeted Coolidge's party at the base of Mount Rushmore.[17] As the president dismounted, the crowd sang the first verse of "America the Beautiful," and a fighter plane flew over and dropped a wreath bearing Washington's name.[18] After he removed his hat, stirrups, and gloves, the president put on his glasses and delivered his first formal speech of the summer. It was an ode to the four featured presidents, to the monument, and to the nation. "The union of these four Presidents, carved on the face of the everlasting hills of South Dakota, will constitute a distinctly national monument," President Coolidge said. "It will be decidedly American in its conception, in its magnitude, in its meaning and altogether worthy of our country. No one can look upon it understandingly without realizing it is a picture of hope fulfilled." Lauded for his fiscal conservatism, Coolidge endorsed the project as worthy of the federal treasury: "Money spent for such a purpose is certain of adequate returns in the nature of increased public welfare." He called on "private beneficence and the national government" to aid the people of South Dakota in raising the funds for the project, which was expected to cost $437,000 and to take five years to complete. After the president finished his speech, he handed six drills to Borglum and expressed "my hope that he begin the work at once and push it to a speedy conclusion."[19]

Taking center stage, Borglum publicly invited Coolidge to write the monument's inscription: "We want your name on that mountain as well as

President Coolidge (center) at the dedication of Washington's head at Mount Rushmore

those of your illustrious predecessors. I want the name Calvin Coolidge on that monument. There's plenty of stone up here; I'm not very old, and I may still have a chance to do more."[20] After his speech, Borglum began to climb the 1,400 wooden steps to the top of the mountain. As he climbed, South Dakota politicians spoke about each of the four presidents. The French, Spanish, and early colonial American flags were raised and lowered, signifying earlier conquests of South Dakota. When he reached the top of the mountain, Borglum and Tucker were lowered over a wall and drilled six holes that supposedly formed the outlines of Washington's head. The crowd sang the last verse of "America the Beautiful." At the close of the program, people cheered when Senator Norbeck predicted that the memorial would be finished in four years "and the inscription will be in the words of Calvin Coolidge."[21] Every major newspaper in America covered Coolidge's speech and rededication of Mount Rushmore. "I made the address very brief and explicit," Coolidge told Rushmore's director of publicity, Doane Robinson, "for I thought you might want to print it in a little booklet to help you get the money."[22] Immediately after the ceremony, Borglum instructed his San Antonio studio to ship his huge plaster model of Washington's head to South Dakota so that the men could begin blocking it in the rock.[23] The seven-foot tall, 800-pound model was one-twelfth the actual size of what Washington's head would look like on the mountain.

Yet Borglum harbored serious doubts that Washington's head would ever be carved there. Since he had arrived in South Dakota in early August, the sculptor had enlisted Coolidge's aid in writing the inscription; he also had persuaded some of his friends in Chicago to donate equipment for the memorial's power plant, placed some models in a small miner's cabin, and made some measurements. Mostly, however, he sat on his hands, stewing about not having a proper place to work and about ignored orders.[24] He found the workmanship on the wooden stairs, the buildings, and the power plant constructed by Tucker to be shoddy. He blamed this on Tucker's contract, which provided for a bonus for cost savings. He also blamed Robinson for releasing cheap public relations materials and for not capitalizing on Coolidge's speech. And he was so dismayed about working out of a small miner's cabin that he returned to his San Antonio studio to work on the models.[25] "I have been annoyed and pained to find my plans questioned, delayed and set aside and of course this can not continue without great expense to the work, loss of character to the work itself, to the natural injury that comes from a recession of interests," he wrote Tucker.[26] Most of all, Borglum could not believe the lack of support from the people of South Dakota. By December 1927, the money had run out, and the weather had turned cold. Washington's head had been blocked out to his ears.[27] The idea that Borglum would carve Washington's head and unveil it on July 4, 1928, seemed like a pipe dream. He feared that it might take seven or eight years to complete, and without federal funding there might be no memorial at Mount Rushmore.[28] In January and February 1927, a few months before the Rushmore dedication ceremony, he had been in Washington lobbying for a coast-to-coast national highway system.[29] He also had approached Treasury Secretary Mellon's office about minting a special coin to fund the Rushmore project. After the disastrous experience with the Stone Mountain half dollar, the Treasury Department was not keen on minting special coins. Mellon, however, suggested the possibility of as much as $500,000 in federal funding.[30] Borglum, overestimating his ability to raise private matching funds, countered with $250,000.[31] Coolidge supported the idea and was even more enthusiastic after spending the summer in the Black Hills.[32] In May 1928, Senator Norbeck, the bill's driving force on Capitol Hill, gave it "an even chance" of getting at least $75,000 before the end of the session.[33]

They needed to work fast because Coolidge's White House days were numbered. A week before he rededicated Mount Rushmore, he had ordered twenty-five copies made of a slip of paper and called journalists into his Rapid City office. He had handed each of them a slip that contained a single sentence: "I do not choose to run for President in 1928." The press had asked Coolidge, who had assumed the presidency upon Harding's death in August 1923 and won re-election the following year, to elaborate about his decision not to run for another term. "There will be nothing more from this office today!" was all Coolidge would say.[34] He was tired of being president and had never recovered after his sixteen-year-old son, Calvin Jr., died of blood poisoning in July 1924 after getting a blister on his toe while playing tennis on the White House's south lawn. "When he went," Coolidge wrote of his son, "the power and glory of the Presidency went with him."[35] After Coolidge's speech at Mount Rushmore, the time to get federal funding through Congress was short.

In May 1928, Senator Norbeck pushed a bill through the Senate that provided for a Mount Rushmore National Memorial Commission and $250,000 in federal matching funds. The House, however, attached a series of amendments to the bill. Norbeck, who was so exhausted from overwork that he had to be hospitalized, did not have time to get the amended bill through the Senate before the summer recess. The amendments would have to be taken up in a conference committee in December.[36] With no federal funding in 1928, the precious summer and fall months in South Dakota came and went without any progress on Washington's head.

It may have been a lost year for Mount Rushmore, but not for Borglum. In 1928, he was flush with commissions in Texas and elsewhere, and not even the destruction of his carving of Lee and the partial carving of Jackson off the side of Stone Mountain could dampen his mood. Borglum's successor, Lukeman, had made almost no progress on the Confederate Memorial and indeed had gotten no further than creating a tiny head of Lee. In March 1928, Borglum broke his silence about the court-ordered destruction of his work at Stone Mountain by pointing out that he had recently finished a marble statue of the vice president of the Confederacy, Alexander H. Stephens, for the US Capitol and the previous month had donated the original marble statue to the state of Georgia. Because of his fear of being arrested again, he declined to go to the statue's dedication ceremonies. "I have given much to Georgia," he wrote. "The entire Confederate Memorial is my invention, my creation; its art, its engineering, its acceptance by the nation stands forever as my service to the South—to America. It has been my pleasure and honor to further the life record of the South's and of Georgia's noblest men, to high places in the realm of memorial art."[37]

One of the projects that Borglum turned to during the summer of 1928 was the Sacco-Vanzetti memorial. Indeed, Jackson's telegram in May 1928 had arrived just as federal funding for Mount Rushmore had been delayed. Borglum's anti-immigrant leanings came out in one of his early reactions to constructing a bas-relief for two Italian anarchists. "I am not blind to the frightful character of much of our alien population," he wrote to Jackson, "and equally ignorant, witch-burning masses, descendants of the Puritan group, that still affect our public opinion and public life."[38]

Freed from his responsibilities at Mount Rushmore, Borglum finished a plaster cast of the bas-relief and shipped it to Boston before the anniversary of the executions. Now all the Sacco-Vanzetti Defense Committee needed was a place to unveil it. The committee's first choice was the Old South Meeting House, but Richard W. Hale of Old Boston's Hale & Dorr law firm prevented it. The city of Boston denied permission to use Faneuil Hall. The Tremont Temple and other meeting halls also refused to host the event. One hall manager cited pressure from state and city officials. Finally, the Jewish immigrant owner of Scenic Auditorium in Boston's South End granted the group permission but only after the American Civil Liberties Union had received assurances of no police retaliation against the owner.[39] At the least the liberals had found a place indoors. The Communists were forced to hold their meetings outdoors—500 people in Boston's South End and 2,500 in New York City's Union Square.[40]

On the night of August 23, 1928, more than 2,000 people crowded into the Scenic Auditorium to honor Sacco and Vanzetti a year after their deaths. The auditorium was packed to the doors; several hundred people were turned away.[41] The master of ceremonies was Robert Morss Lovett of the *New Republic* and University of Chicago. Alexander Meiklejohn, ousted Amherst College president and University of Wisconsin professor, urged the audience to seek justice: "They have not died in vain if we and other men, because of them, are stirred to keep the faith, are made to see again that justice is more precious than life itself, injustice far more terrible than death."[42] Another speaker, Harvard philosophy professor Horace M. Kallen, was arrested and charged with blasphemy after contending that "if Sacco and Vanzetti were anarchists, so were Christ and Socrates."[43] The charges were later dropped, but they drew more attention to Boston's intolerance for

Sacco-Vanzetti dissenters. Other speakers that night included the Reverend Harold Stratton of Worcester, the British writer John Cowper Powys, and Jackson.[44] Telegrams and cables were read from defense lawyer Clarence Darrow, writer Edna St. Vincent Millay, philosopher Morris R. Cohen, writer Upton Sinclair, *Nation* publisher Oswald Garrison Villard, journalist William Allen White, and French novelist Romain Rolland.[45] Frankfurter, still keeping a low profile about the case, was nowhere to be found.

The most emotional moment of the night belonged to Elizabeth Evans.[46] Years after alerting Frankfurter and other liberals about the importance of the case, she unveiled Borglum's four-by-seven-foot bas-relief. The white plaster sculpture on the black velvet dais created a "stark" contrast.[47] The left side of the work featured Sacco and Vanzetti in profile, looking at the arm of justice balancing the scales of life and death. Superimposed over the arm of justice was a quotation by Vanzetti from shortly before his execution: "What I wish more than all in this last hour of agony is that our case and our fate may be understood in their real being and serve as a tremendous lesson to the forces of freedom so that our suffering and death will not have been in vain." The bas-relief was greeted with "universal enthusiasm."[48] "We are profoundly moved by the work you have done …," Jackson wired Borglum. "The symbolism is perfect."[49]

At the meeting, the defense committee announced that Borglum's bas-relief would grace the front of a Sacco-Vanzetti museum on Beacon Hill.[50] It turned out to be a struggle to keep the flame alive. Jackson could not afford to pay the property taxes on the house and lost it to foreclosure. After Jackson and others pleaded for decades with state and city officials to display the memorial on Boston Common, the plaster draft of Borglum's bas-relief finally found a home in 1979 in the Boston Public Library. In 1997, on the seventieth anniversary of the anarchists' executions, the city officially accepted the memorial at a dedication ceremony.[51]

The initial unveiling of Borglum's bas-relief was overshadowed the next day by coverage of Governor Al Smith's acceptance speech as the 1928 Democratic presidential nominee. Many liberals, Frankfurter included, had not forgotten about Sacco and Vanzetti, but they had moved on. They invested their energies on trying to elect the Catholic son of German-Italian and Irish immigrants the next president of the United States.

26

The Happy Warrior

No one had more impressed the inhabitants of the House of Truth during his wartime visits than Herbert Hoover. A former mining engineer and multimillionaire by age forty, he had worked as a dollar-a-year man in the Wilson administration and had epitomized how government experts with a grasp of the facts on the ground could make a difference in people's lives. During the war, he had led the organization that helped feed the starving people of Belgium. After the war, he had expanded his efforts to all of Europe. He was viewed as a problem solver, someone who could get things done. Both Frankfurter and Lippmann had wanted to work for him. As Wilson's reputation unraveled in their eyes during the Paris Peace Conference, Frankfurter and Lippmann looked to Hoover as the country's next great leader.

Something happened to Hoover's liberal reputation on the way to the White House. Denied the Republican Party's nomination for president in 1920, he had served for the next seven years in the Harding and Coolidge administrations as the secretary of commerce. After the Great Mississippi River Flood of 1927, he had supervised relief efforts, displaying the same talents that he had exhibited during the war. In the eyes of American liberals, however, Hoover was no longer the same candidate. The *World*, which had proclaimed Hoover the "best qualified man to succeed Woodrow Wilson" in 1920, withdrew its endorsement eight years later: "In 1920, Mr. Hoover was a free man, with a superb record of achievement in the war. In 1928 he is a partisan Republican, with a record of eight years in the Harding and Coolidge Cabinets. Those eight years are what matter to-day."[1]

Frankfurter, Lippmann, and others deserted Hoover because of what the *World* described as the "spiritual sloth" of Harding's administration and the "inertia" of Coolidge's administration.[2] They believed that Hoover had sat on his hands during the Teapot Dome oil scandal and the corruption of

Frankfurter (left) and Al Smith (right)

Harding's Justice Department. And Hoover's calls for increased industrial efficiency reflected a lack of concern for the effects of industrialization on American workers. "It is highly revealing that in the field of his greatest competence he has seen merely the technological and not the social significances," Frankfurter wrote Lippmann in June 1928.[3]

Exhibit A for Frankfurter was Hoover's 1922 book, *American Individualism*. "I am an American individualist," Hoover declared in response to the rise of Communism and Socialism in postwar Europe. "For America has been steadily developing the ideals that constitute progressive individualism." Hoover distinguished America's individualism from Europe's by emphasizing "equality of opportunity"—the American belief in social and economic mobility.[4] Though just as much a believer in equal opportunity as Hoover, Frankfurter saw the nation's future as more complicated than reliance on terms like "capitalism" or "individualism" and believed that *American Individualism* ignored the role that government played in regulating the economy and creating an industrial democracy. "I think the vapidity and ineptitude and errors (demonstrable errors of fact) in that book are a good index to his social philosophy because I think they really point the direction of his mind," Frankfurter wrote Lippmann.[5] Lippmann did not need convincing that Hoover was not their candidate. After the stock market dropped in mid-June 1928, Lippmann and others predicted that an economic catastrophe was on the horizon. "I am coming to believe that by early Autumn we shall have had a big smash on the stock market and a much more evident industrial depression," he wrote Frankfurter in July 1928. "I don't know just what the political effects of that will be, but they may be very great."[6]

During the 1928 presidential campaign, Frankfurter and Lippmann joined forces for the last time. Four years earlier, they had clashed. Frankfurter supported the third-party candidate, La Follette, and Lippmann backed the Democratic nominee, Davis. But after eight years of the pro-business Republican Party's "spiritual sloth" and "inertia," Frankfurter and Lippmann were united in their belief that the future of American liberalism lay with the pro-worker and pro-farmer Democratic Party. Scholars dispute whether the 1928 presidential election was the politically realigning contest that it seemed with hindsight.[7] Indeed, former progressives divided their support between the Republican and Democratic presidential candidates. But the choice for Frankfurter and Lippmann was clear. They urged liberals to vote for Al Smith.

With Smith as their leader, Frankfurter and Lippmann envisioned the Democratic Party as the liberal party. "In the nomination of Gov. Smith the Democratic Party is making its third serious attempt since the Civil War to transform itself from an asylum for lost and discredited causes into a responsible and liberal instrumentality of government," Lippmann's *World* declared. The *World* reviewed the "lost causes" of slavery, populism, and Prohibition that had "wrecked" the Democratic Party and the attempts of Grover Cleveland in 1884 and Woodrow Wilson in 1912 to resuscitate it. "The task which now confronts Gov. Smith is no easy one," Lippmann wrote, reciting how the Republican opposition encountered difficulties that helped Cleveland and Wilson. "The Republican Party under Herbert Hoover is a formidable thing ... only the most sure-footed leadership can break its ranks."[8]

This was Smith's third presidential run. He had run in 1920 and had nearly captured the Democratic nomination in 1924, but a deadlock between him and McAdoo had thrown the nomination to Davis. It was not the first time that Franklin D. Roosevelt nominated Smith for the presidency. At the 1924 convention in New York City, Roosevelt had returned to public life three years after polio had paralyzed him from the waist down.[9] Roosevelt had been Wilson's assistant secretary of the navy, Frankfurter's ally on the War Labor Policies Board, and the Democratic vice-presidential nominee in 1920. On June 26, 1924, Roosevelt had walked to the podium on crutches, had nominated Smith for the presidency, and had famously called him "the 'Happy Warrior' of the political battlefield."[10] Four years later, Roosevelt again nominated Smith for the presidency at the Democratic convention in Houston. This time, Roosevelt walked to the podium aided only by his son Elliott and a pair of canes.[11] After the convention, Roosevelt confided to Lippmann that the speech had been written "wholly for the benefit of the radio audience and press rather than for any forensic effect it might have on the delegates and audience in the convention hall."[12] Roosevelt praised Smith's record as governor and his understanding of "the popular need, because he himself has lived through the hardship, the labor and the sacrifice which must be endured by every man of heroic mold who struggles up to eminence from obscurity and low estate."[13] Smith's humble background had its downsides. The four-time governor had grown up on the Lower East Side and had risen through the ranks of the Tammany Hall political machine. He was a "wet candidate" who opposed Prohibition. And as the son of an Irish mother and German-Italian father, he was trying to become the nation's first Catholic president.

If Prohibition was Smith's initial Achilles heel, then Lippmann was partly to blame. Northern and southern Democratic Party leaders were so divided on the issue that they took no stance on it in the party platform. In those days, the nominee did not attend the convention or accept the nomination in person. At Lippmann's urging, Smith had sent a telegram to the convention advocating that the enforcement of Prohibition be left up to the states.[14] Roosevelt was happy that Lippmann and the *World* had dropped the issue. "I still fail to see how Smith can by any possibility lose the wet votes which are now his," Roosevelt wrote Lippmann in August and urged him to focus on other issues.[15] Two years after the election, Roosevelt still ridiculed Lippmann and the *World* for "that fool telegram ... telling how wet he was. Al had every wet vote in the country but he needed a good many millions of the middle of the road votes to elect him President." Roosevelt believed that Lippmann and the *World* had done "more harm to Al Smith's candidacy than all the Republican newspapers in the United States put together."[16]

The Tammany Hall issue was equally polarizing but in many ways the easiest one to address. There was no question that Smith had received his start as a machine politician. But there was no evidence that as governor he had allowed New York City political bosses to dictate state policy. Frankfurter believed that the Tammany charges could be rebutted and instead used to attack Hoover's blind eye to corruption during the previous seven years in the Harding and Coolidge administrations. "If Tammany left no trace or trail in Albany during Al's governorships," Frankfurter wrote Lippmann, "the argument becomes a false bogey & even worse when the alternative is continuance in power of the G.O.P. after its Harding saturnalia and Coolidge-Hoover indifference."[17] Lippmann agreed and revealed that the *World* was investigating Smith's eight years as governor along the lines that Frankfurter suggested.

That did not stop others, including former progressives, from tarring Smith as a corrupt political hack. Journalist William Allen White, the editor of the *Emporia Gazette* in Kansas, charged that as a state legislator Smith had voted for bills in favor of saloons, gambling, and prostitution and that if elected Smith would be a "Tammany President" and a threat to "Puritan Civilization." After conferring with his friend Lippmann, White publicly retracted the allegations about prostitution, yet continued to attack Smith's voting record twenty years earlier in the New York Assembly on saloons and liquor traffic.[18] On the *World's* editorial page, Lippmann questioned the relevance of Smith's twenty-year-old voting record to the presidential race and challenged White to find any evidence that Smith was "a friend of the unregenerate saloon and subservient to Tammany" during his four terms as governor.[19] The same day as Lippmann's editorial, Frankfurter reminded White that Albert J. Beveridge's biography of Lincoln revealed that the sixteenth president had been just as much of a party man in the Illinois legislature as Smith had been in the New York legislature. Yet Lincoln "rose above this early record, and achieved moral distinction." Rather than acknowledge Smith's similar moral arc, White chose to traffic in stereotypes about corrupt big-city politicians. "Instead of helping the American people to understand the exhilarating and heartening meaning of Al Smith's achievements as a personality and as a public figure," Frankfurter wrote White, "you have, I am sorry to say, joined the blind forces of Pharisaism so rampant in America today."[20] Lippmann chalked up

White's accusations to "carelessness, an amateur investigation and muddle-headedness." He added that White was "a sweet fellow and I think was very contrite."[21] Frankfurter agreed that White was a "sweet fellow," recalling his "kindly humanity in those horrid Paris 'Peace' days" and support during the Sacco-Vanzetti controversy. Yet given White's past support for liberal causes, Frankfurter could not explain his opposition to Smith aside from stemming from "some deep unconscious motivation."[22]

As Frankfurter, Lippmann, and many other people knew, Tammany was code for anti-Catholic bias, a rallying cry for the Ku Klux Klan in the South and Midwest, and religious intolerance. Having lived through a year of anti-immigrant rhetoric about Sacco and Vanzetti, Frankfurter saw the same sort of prejudices re-emerge in Boston during the Massachusetts Democratic primary as Republicans appealed to the city's "'snobs and bigots'" while trying not to offend its "fair-minded" residents. "The job to be done—and I wish there were more time to do it in—," Frankfurter wrote Lippmann in September, "is to replace the grotesque 'pictures in the heads' of people of abstract vices labeled Al Smith with the concrete, flesh and blood Al & his achievements & qualities."[23] Lippmann's *World* spearheaded the opposition to the Tammany Hall charges as religious bigotry. Next to Lippmann's editorial, Rollin Kirby drew a Pulitzer Prize–winning cartoon depicting the Republican Party as a fat man with his hands up and back turned to the seventeen Republican politicians jailed or charged with corruption in recent years.[24]

Smith's opponents seized on both Prohibition and Tammany Hall to pit Protestants against the Catholic candidate. Mabel Walker Willebrandt, a Harding and Coolidge Justice Department lawyer charged with enforcing Prohibition, traveled the country appealing to Methodist and Presbyterian ministers to work for Hoover and to preach to their parishioners to vote against Smith en masse. "While Mr. Hoover permits her to go from one sectarian meeting to another asking ministers to work for Hoover," the *World* charged, "all of Mr. Hoover's fine protestations about avoiding the religious issue are utterly meaningless."[25] The *World* spoke for many leading intellectuals who were disgusted with Hoover for using Willebrandt as an attack dog. For Frankfurter, who had overcome anti-Semitism despite finishing first in his Harvard Law School class, the issue was personal. "The people of New York have learned to realize that Smith the human being is more significant than Smith the Catholic," he wrote his Harvard colleague Samuel Williston. "It would be a great thing for the people of this country to gain such an experience in humanity and reason."[26]

The Prohibitionists and the religious bigots did not disturb Frankfurter and Lippmann as much as White and other former progressives who continued to support Hoover and who could not see the potential of the Democratic Party as the liberal party. The Bull Moose Party was as dead as TR was. The Republican Party had become the party of big business and would not stand up for the issues former progressives cared about most—such as the welfare of industrial workers and farmers. Frankfurter also blamed the Smith campaign for not courting former progressives hard enough. "On his record, the Governor deserves the progressive vote—the great bulk of liberal independents who supported T.R. in '12 and La Follette in '24," Frankfurter wrote Smith campaign adviser Belle Moskowitz in August. "As yet, the vote is torpid—certainly it has not yet moved towards Al. Don't be sore at the progressives. Win them."[27]

Lippmann and Frankfurter took very different approaches to selling Smith to liberals. Despite months advising Smith on Prohibition and other issues and writing pro-Smith editorials in the *World*, Lippmann took the

Rollin Kirby's Pulitzer Prize–winning cartoon about Tammany Hall allegations and Al Smith

same on-the-one-hand and on-the-other-hand approach with the election as he had taken with the Sacco-Vanzetti case. An exasperated Frankfurter admired Lippmann's editorial writing skills but criticized his "excessive appreciation or, rather, attribution of Hoover's talents."[28] In a September *Vanity Fair* article, "Hoover and Smith: An Impartial Consideration of the Candidates for the American Presidential Office," Lippmann emphasized the candidates' similarities rather than their differences. Both candidates, Lippmann argued, would take the country out of the "private selfishness" of the Harding and Coolidge eras and would "represent a very real change."[29] Lippmann argued that Hoover's strengths lay with "government of business" and Smith's with the "business of government." Like many liberals, Lippmann sided with Smith because "he would enormously broaden the popular base upon which the government rests."[30] By endorsing Smith for president, Lippmann revealed the liberal belief in democracy and capitalism and in government's ability to help workers and farmers, not just to facilitate big business. "You better than Smith himself," Frankfurter wrote Lippmann, "can bring home Smith's consistent respect for liberty and his human sympathy which transcends intolerance."[31]

To attack Hoover on the issues, Frankfurter enlisted the same liberal Harvard law professors who had helped him with Sacco-Vanzetti. He and Landis wrote a memorandum for the Smith campaign on electric power because Hoover was opposed to building a dam on the Tennessee River to create a government-owned hydroelectric power facility in Muscle Shoals, Alabama. Many believed that the government-owned facility would help farmers.[32] Frankfurter's memorandum, follow-up letters, and *New Republic* article inspired Lippmann to write editorials about the issue.[33] Frankfurter's Harvard law colleague Calvert Magruder wrote a memorandum advising Smith on how to navigate tricky immigration issues in an increasingly isolationist country and in nativist cities such as Boston.[34] After Frankfurter's work on Smith's behalf during the 1928 election, Brandeis declared his protégé "clearly the most useful lawyer in the United States."[35]

As he had in prior elections, Frankfurter made his case in the *New Republic*. For Croly, Frankfurter's article was a godsend. Earlier that fall, the author of *The Promise of American Life* had suffered a massive stroke that would take his life two years later. He was in no condition to write lead editorials. As soon as Frankfurter's article had arrived, the *New Republic* editor scrapped short election articles by John Dewey and another writer in favor of Frankfurter's. "It is the most comprehensive and at the same time succinct

statement of the salient reasons for voting for Smith that I have seen anywhere," Croly wrote Frankfurter.[36] In "Why I Am for Smith," Frankfurter
offered many reasons to vote for Smith: the rejection of religious bigotry
and the social class system as creating latent requirements for the presidency; the recognition that Prohibition was a failed experiment that needed
modification; and the confirmation that politics was "a process of popular
education" and that Smith was "the master of politics." Smith's combination
of the common touch and ability to surround himself with experts who
might navigate the path to real reforms was "indispensable for the adjustment through government of the conflicting economic interests among different sections and different classes in the country." The American people,
Frankfurter argued, should vote for Smith because his "election will give
decided momentum to the liberalizing American social economy," and as
governor of New York he "has achieved great things for liberal causes." And
Frankfurter rejected the Tammany label affixed to Smith by arguing that
it was Hoover who had been in the cabinet of the corrupt Harding administration and the do-nothing Coolidge administration. Smith's election
would send the Republican Party and its corruption of the last eight years
"into the wilderness."[37]

During the final week of the campaign, Frankfurter and Lippmann gave
Smith's election everything they had. "Your editorial today is, I believe, a
prophetic interpretation of next Monday's significance," Frankfurter wrote
Lippmann. "And what a thrilling thing it would be if Smith actually won!"[38]
The Friday before the election, in opening remarks at Boston's Symphony
Hall, Frankfurter declared a political victory for Smith for making "the
people of the United States think" about the issues after more than seven
years of Republican rule in which people were encouraged not to think
or to think only about themselves. "Governor Smith," Frankfurter told the
crowd, "has vitalized politics and lifted them to their rightful plane of discussion, debate, controversy, exchange of opinion, full and frank, about the
pressing problems of society."[39]

On election night, however, they saw their hopes dashed. And it was not
close—at least not in the electoral college. A candidate who was Catholic,
wet, and associated with Tammany Hall never stood a chance in the West
and nearly lost the solid South. And perhaps no one stood a chance against
Hoover. Hoover captured 444 electoral votes and forty states; Smith won
87 electoral votes and only eight states. Even New York went for Hoover.

Lippmann was angry—angry with Smith for running such a poor campaign and angry with the Democratic Party for not disavowing tariffs and Prohibition. To *Atlantic Monthly* editor Ellery Sedgwick, Lippmann proposed to write an analysis of everything that had gone wrong with Smith's campaign: "I am convinced that for over a year his whole approach was wrong, due to bad advice, inexperience and a failure to grasp the significance of his own candidacy." Others, including Roosevelt, blamed Lippmann and the *World* for bad advice regarding the convention telegram about Prohibition. Lippmann was pessimistic about the prospects for the Democratic Party and posited that "a union of the South and the Northeast is demonstrably impossible."[40] Though he abandoned the article because it would not write, his pessimism about the future of the Democratic Party and doubts about American liberalism continued to grow.[41]

The day after the election, Frankfurter walked the streets of Boston in a daze. It reminded him of the January day when his mother had died. "There was something unreal about my surroundings, something precious had gone out of life," he wrote to Smith aide Belle Moskowitz, "but the people about me seemed to be unaware of it."[42] Despite his profound sadness about Smith's defeat, Frankfurter was as optimistic about the future as Lippmann was pessimistic. He believed that the Democratic Party could remake itself into the liberal party.[43] And he saw Franklin Roosevelt, who had been drafted as a candidate and swept into office as the governor of New York, as the future of the Democratic Party. For the time being, Frankfurter envisioned Smith as an effective leader of the Democratic opposition. "Certainly there is no one in sight who can begin to assume such a function," Frankfurter wrote Lippmann, "and there will be no one unless and until Roosevelt emerges to such leadership in four years."[44] Lippmann was not nearly as high on Roosevelt as Frankfurter. But Frankfurter saw the future where Lippmann could not—and in it saw the role the Supreme Court would play.

27

Freedom for the Thought That We Hate

Following Hoover's election in 1928, Frankfurter and others worried about the impact on the future of the Court. Liberals had already been out of political power for eight years. Harding's and Coolidge's appointments, with one or two exceptions, had created a Court as "reactionary" as it had been during Frankfurter's early House of Truth days when Theodore Roosevelt had "put the fear of God" into the justices. Yet with Roosevelt long gone from the political scene, no one in politics or journalism was engaged in the "awakening of public interest" about the Court's invocation of the Due Process Clause and the Equal Protection Clause to invalidate state socioeconomic legislation. "The simple truth is that the Supreme Court is at present in an even more reactionary period than it was before Roosevelt let loose liberalizing influences," Frankfurter had written Lippmann in late May 1928. "Some of their decisions are at least as bad as the famous *Lochner* case."[1]

Frankfurter and his allies continued to celebrate the dissents of Justice Holmes. Holmes often dissented after prodding from Brandeis, who asked him to write the lead dissent or at least to write a short dissent in addition to joining one of Brandeis's. This may have been what prompted Chief Justice Taft to charge Brandeis with wielding "two votes instead of one."[2] Three days before Frankfurter's letter to Lippmann, Holmes had dissented from the Court's decision that invalidated a Pennsylvania law that taxed taxicab corporations, but not taxicabs owned by individuals or partnerships, on equal protection grounds.[3] Nothing in the Fourteenth Amendment, Holmes wrote, prevented the taxation of larger corporations to protect smaller business.[4] In addition to his one-paragraph dissent, Holmes joined Brandeis's lengthy and heavily footnoted denunciation of the Court's decision. Brandeis, who believed in the power of states to experiment with economic regulation, discussed the Court's long history of upholding state taxes and regulations on corporations and decried the decision's usurpation of state power.[5]

A few weeks before his dissent in the Pennsylvania taxicab decision, Holmes had dissented in another case known as *Black and White Taxicab*.[6] At Brandeis's urging, Holmes dissented that the Court should not make up its own commercial law in cases between citizens or corporations of two different states. Instead, Holmes argued, the Court should follow the applicable state law, in this case Kentucky's. Brandeis believed that the dissent,

Holmes (right) and Brandeis leaving the Court

which he and Justice Stone joined, would carry more weight coming from Holmes—the author of *The Common Law*, a history of judge-made law. "The common law," Holmes had written in 1917, "is not a brooding omnipresence in the sky, but the articulate voice of some sovereign or quasi sovereign that can be identified."[7] Holmes's dissent contended that one of the Court's long-standing decisions on this issue should be overruled (and was later overruled by Brandeis a decade later) and that Supreme Court justices should relinquish to state judges some of their control over making commercial law. Holmes's dissent in *Black and White Taxicab* signaled a way to curb the Court's power and to respect state power, and it demonstrated that Holmes was still at the top of his game. "You have written, if I may say so, a landmark opinion," Frankfurter wrote Holmes. "To think that it has taken a century to expose the fallacy of one of the most obstinate doctrines of your Court!"[8] Holmes, as always, basked in Frankfurter praise.[9]

Frankfurter encouraged Holmes's and Brandeis's efforts to use the Court's power to protect the right to fair criminal trials as well as the right to privacy. In 1928, the two justices dissented from the Court's decision upholding the federal government's illegal wiretaps to gather evidence and to convict the head of a bootlegging operation, Roy Olmstead. Once again, Brandeis influenced Holmes's thinking on the issue. The co-author of an 1890 article on the "right to privacy," Brandeis wrote a landmark dissent in *Olmstead* that federal wiretapping violated the Fourth Amendment's prohibition against unreasonable searches and seizures and the Fifth Amendment's prohibition against self-incrimination. By relying on the broad purposes of these amendments, he articulated a constitutional right to privacy and argued that the drafters of the Constitution "conferred, as against the Government, the right to be let alone—the most comprehensive of rights and the right most valued by civilized men."[10] Although he did not agree that the Fourth and Fifth Amendments applied to the defendant's case and therefore did not join Brandeis's dissent, Holmes was troubled that the evidence had been obtained "by a criminal act."[11] At Brandeis's urging, he published a short dissent and read it from the bench with "words and voice and manner [that] were disdainful."[12] "If the existing code does not permit district attorneys to have a hand in such dirty business," Holmes wrote, "it does not permit the judge to allow such iniquities to succeed."[13] Holmes's *Olmstead* dissent infuriated Chief Justice Taft, who described it as the "nastiest" opinion in the case and contrasted it with Brandeis's "eloquence and idealism." Taft, per usual, blamed Holmes's dissent on Brandeis: "The truth is that Holmes wrote it the other way till Brandeis got after him," describing Holmes as "a law unto himself if Brandeis says yes."[14]

Despite his willingness to protect the right to fair criminal trials, Holmes held a less expansive view of the right of privacy than Brandeis. In another wiretapping and entrapment case that term, Holmes wrote the majority opinion upholding the conviction of a lawyer who had sold morphine-soaked towels to a prisoner.[15] Brandeis dissented not only because federal agents had bugged the jailhouse meeting room but also because they had induced the prisoner to ask the lawyer to commit the crime.[16] Holmes was relieved by Brandeis's dissent because it showed that "there is no pre-established harmony between us."[17] Nonetheless, Brandeis influenced Holmes's thinking, as well as the frequency of Holmes's dissents. There was no denying their close relationship.[18]

The wiretapping cases aroused Frankfurter and other liberals who had challenged the constitutionality of the Palmer Raids against immigrants and suspected radicals and who had argued that Sacco and Vanzetti deserved a new trial. Immediately after the Court's decision in *Olmstead* on June 4, 1928, Frankfurter phoned Lippmann's deputy editorial page editor, Charles Merz, and urged him to publish an editorial about the evils of wiretapping. "Mitchell Palmer's worst deeds were breaches of the tradition against unlawful search and seizure," Frankfurter wrote Lippmann. "I think you ought to pounce hard on the terrible doctrine that Taft announced for the majority."[19] The *World* responded with two wiretapping editorials on consecutive days. The first quoted Brandeis's dissent and used it to try to rally American liberals, quoting his line that "'the greatest dangers to liberty lurk in insidious encroachment by men of zeal, well-meaning, but without understanding.'"[20] The second editorial attacked Chief Justice Taft's opinion as enabling use of wiretapping in a wide variety of cases including Prohibition, radical politics, or business methods in which "the Government's agents find themselves pressed for evidence." The liberal distrust of the Court's conservative majority was palpable. "Since the Supreme Court does not choose to stand as a bulwark between this tyranny and the rights of the private citizen," the *World* concluded, "the public has no relief except Congressional action."[21]

Brandeis and to a lesser extent Holmes helped put privacy on the liberal agenda. Instead of simply attacking the Court's position on privacy issues, Frankfurter and his friends brought Holmes into the liberal fold. "You said what needed to be said about prosecutorial indecencies," Frankfurter wrote Holmes.[22] He also sent Holmes a copy of a letter from Cardozo. One of the nation's great judicial stylists, Cardozo insisted that Holmes had "written some of the great dissents of the last few months—as fine as anything ever written by him or by any one else." Cardozo referred to him as "the Master."[23] Even Taft conceded that Holmes was "as bright as ever."[24] All the praise may have put to rest the rumors swirling in the nation's major newspapers that the eighty-seven-year-old justice was contemplating retirement. Several conservative newspapers, including the *New York Herald-Tribune* and the *Chicago Tribune*, published editorials praising the "freshness" of his opinions and his "penetrating" mind and urging him to stay "as long as his powers permit."[25] Holmes had no intention of retiring. But the rumors "pleased" him because they prompted a series of "flattering articles" that "encouraged me to believe that in remaining I am not yielding to the illusions of old age."[26]

What made Holmes "fresh" was his willingness to consider new ideas—whether it was new legal ideas such as Brandeis's about state commercial law and the right of privacy or new ideas in American literature, such as Ernest Hemingway's first novel, *The Sun Also Rises*. The book was a gift from Holmes's friend and correspondent Owen Wister. A Harvard-educated lawyer, longtime friend of Theodore Roosevelt, and eastern aristocrat, Wister had given up the law to write western novels, including *The Virginian*.[27] While relaxing at Beverly Farms in mid-July, Holmes read *The Sun Also Rises*. Or, rather, Mrs. Holmes read it aloud to him until she got to the parts about the bullfights, "which she didn't want to read out, and she had enough."[28] He acknowledged to Wister that Hemingway was "quite remarkable" and his book was "singular." Though he disapproved of the foul language and "hints of fornication" and thought the book had "no ideas," it did not bore "with the details of an ordinary day."[29] To his friends, Holmes described *The Sun Also Rises* as a "queer book." He was interested in it because "the narrative had a masterly simplicity and fact followed fact as of course," and he suspected it to be a "work of art."[30]

Holmes's hunger for fame had not abated. He did not achieve milestones; he stalked them. In his sights ever since his eighty-seventh birthday seven months earlier was Chief Justice Roger B. Taney's record as the oldest sitting justice.[31] On October 4, 1928, the day arrived—Holmes passed Taney by reaching eighty-seven years, six months, and twenty-six days. "Today I am older than Taney when he died—," Holmes wrote, "and of greater age than any judge of the court has been while still sitting."[32] His liberal friends took notice of the milestone. In a one-paragraph New York *World* editorial, "The Oldest Justice," Lippmann expressed "some diffidence" about congratulating Holmes: "[W]e feel as though something historical had happened and we cannot let the event pass without saying something about it."[33] After reading the editorial, Frankfurter wrote Lippmann: "You did the thing for Holmes just right."[34]

Holmes had every intention of sitting on the bench until age ninety—a milestone he had been talking and writing about for several years.[35] But he was not immortal, and the odds were that the next president would select his replacement. A dyed-in-the-wool Republican, Holmes never would have voted for Al Smith and was not troubled by Hoover. Before the election, Holmes had described Hoover as "on faith to be a considerable person."[36] After reading a paper written about Hoover by Lewis Einstein, the US ambassador to Czechoslovakia, Holmes concluded that "the next president is a great man or very near it."[37] In March 1929, the justice attended Hoover's inauguration, sat "within two yards" of the president-elect, and thought that "Hoover's looks did not make it impossible for me to stick to my impression that he may be a great man."[38]

On April 30, almost two months after the inauguration, Fanny Holmes died in her sleep at age eighty-eight.[39] Two weeks earlier, Holmes had been absent from the Court. Word had reached his colleagues that Fanny was "seriously ill." She had fallen in the house and had broken her hip. There had been signs of trouble—a chronic cough and three prior falls. Death relieved her of suffering. After Fanny had broken her hip but before her death, Brandeis remarked that Holmes had shown up at the justices' private conference and "seemed crushed, and fully twenty years older than he has been for months—actually the old man."[40] Chief Justice Taft was the first person to see Holmes after Fanny's death and arranged for her burial at Arlington National Cemetery. Frankfurter, Hill, John G. Palfrey, and "much of Boston" came down for the funeral.[41] "It is a beautiful little spot," Holmes wrote Nina Gray. "I have ordered a granite stone on the form in use there—it seems queer to put up one's own tombstone—but I suppose in a military place a woman has to be accounted for—This will be on it":

Oliver Wendell Holmes
Brevet Colonel & Captain; 20th Mass. Voluntary Infantry
Justice Supreme Court of the United States
March 1841   _____
His Wife
Fanny B. Holmes
Dec. 1840   April 30, 1929[42]

Holmes squelched any talk about retirement. "You understand, of course, this will make no difference," he told Taft the morning after Fanny's death. "I shall carry on."[43]

Despite his vow to keep working, Holmes was not the same without Fanny. She had read to him, needled him, tolerated his flirtatious behavior with attractive women, and shared his Boston Brahmin roots. She had also delighted Holmes, his secretaries, and his liberal friends Frankfurter and Lippmann with her quick wit and charm. She threw a children's party at the House of Truth that people talked about for years. She could be enigmatic and very sensitive about perceived slights toward her husband. "Things hurt her that I didn't mind," Holmes wrote, describing her as "almost a recluse" with few "very intimate" friends.[44] Except for her husband. "For sixty years she made life poetry for me and at 88 one must be ready for the end," he wrote. "I shall keep at work and interested while it lasts—though not caring very much for how long."[45]

Without Fanny, Holmes was, according to Taft, "very lonely."[46] He retreated to his house at 1720 Eye Street. The house was staffed with a cook, two maids, and a driver on call. His secretary, John Lockwood, was his closest companion and agreed to stay with him at Beverly Farms for most of the summer. Lockwood, who was "needed as no Secretary ever has been & is evidently much beloved" by his boss, kept both Frankfurter and Brandeis informed of Holmes's condition.[47] "I can only say that he stands square with eyes forward …," Lockwood wrote Frankfurter. "He goes about his work as before and faces the world with unabated interest."[48] From time to time, Brandeis dropped by 1720 Eye Street to check on his colleague.[49] After learning from Brandeis that Holmes had written all his assigned opinions, Taft assigned Holmes three more cases and instructed him to write one each week.[50] Both Brandeis and Taft knew that the only thing that could keep Holmes going was work.

Just a few months after Fanny's death, Holmes wrote what was to be his last great dissent about free speech in the case of Rosika Schwimmer. A Hungarian-born Jewish writer and linguist, Schwimmer had been active in the international feminist and suffragist movements. She was also a pacifist. During the war, she had persuaded Henry Ford to sponsor an international meeting in an unsuccessful effort to broker an early peace. After the war, she returned to her native Hungary and participated in the new democratic regime until the Communists took power and persecuted her. To escape the Communists, she fled to Vienna, took up residence in the

United States, and in 1924 applied for US citizenship.[51] The fifty-year-old Schwimmer met all the qualifications except one: she refused to take up arms for the United States because of her pacifist beliefs. After a lengthy interrogation, the trial judge denied her citizenship. The court of appeals disagreed and reversed. The Department of Labor appealed to the Supreme Court. Six justices reversed the court of appeals and made her denial of citizenship permanent. "The fact that she is an uncompromising pacifist, with no sense of nationalism, but only a cosmic sense of belonging to the human family, justifies belief that she may be opposed to the use of military force as contemplated by our Constitution and laws," Justice Butler wrote for the Court. "And her testimony clearly suggests that she is disposed to exert her power to influence others to such opposition."[52]

In a dissent joined only by Brandeis, Holmes described Schwimmer as "a woman of superior character and intelligence, obviously more than ordinarily desirable as a citizen of the United States." At trial, Schwimmer had agreed to take the oath of allegiance to her adopted country. She simply did not believe in bearing arms. Nor was there any chance that a fifty-year-old woman would be asked to take up arms for her country. For Holmes, her pacifist beliefs were beside the point: "Some of her answers might excite popular prejudice, but if there is any principle of the Constitution that more imperatively calls for attachment than any other it is the principle of free thought—not free thought for those who agree with us but freedom for the thought that we hate."[53]

The *New Republic* reprinted his dissent in full: "We feel that it sets out, far more ably than any words of ours can do, the attitude which any person who calls himself a liberal ought to take toward this decision."[54] Lockwood rejoiced over the dissent for what it said about free speech and about the health of his boss. "The Schwimmer dissent is truly a magnificent document," Lockwood wrote Frankfurter. "I rejoice at such tangible evidence that the divine fire burns as brightly as ever."[55] Frankfurter, who had urged the *New Republic* to publish the dissent, wrote Holmes: "I had assumed that you exhausted my capacity for being thrilled by magisterial utterance on behalf of sanity in your Abrams opinion. But you have done it again and anew."[56] Frankfurter also enclosed a *New York Times* editorial praising Holmes and Brandeis as "the defenders of minorities, of not only theoretic but applied freedom."[57] Discussing the case in the *New Yorker*'s "Talk of the Town" section, E. B. White wrote: "One profession that is more noble today than that of soldier is Dissenting Justice of the Supreme Court."[58] In

addition to national recognition, Holmes received a thank-you note from
Schwimmer.[59] She was allowed to stay in the United States for the rest of
her life—as a resident alien. Her note initiated a warm correspondence between the pacifist and the Civil War hero.

For all that the *Schwimmer* case delighted most liberals, it frayed the
friendship between Frankfurter and Lippmann. For years, Lippmann had
been slow to defend civil liberties—whether Meiklejohn's at Amherst,
those of Jewish students at Harvard, or Sacco and Vanzetti's right to a fair
trial. Frankfurter found the New York *World's* editorial about the *Schwimmer*
case "disappointing." He did not believe that his friend could have written
it, and asked him to read the opinions.[60] Lippmann replied that he had "read
both opinions several times and couldn't make much out of either of them.
I may be quite foolish about this, but for the first time I felt that Holmes
had not come to grips with the question, though naturally I liked his general remarks." He conceded that Schwimmer's denial of citizenship was
"persecution" but confessed that about the "theoretical issue raised" about

Rosika Schwimmer

conscientious objectors "I haven't been able to form an opinion."[61] There was little that Lippmann hated more than conflict and especially conflict that precipitated a steady stream of letters from Frankfurter. "Your letter flabbergasts me," Frankfurter replied. He could not believe that Lippmann could disagree with "the two greatest judges in the land (barring Holmes)," referring to Brandeis and Cardozo and including excerpts from Cardozo's letter about Holmes's dissent. "That six Justices should have gone the other way does not bother me in the slightest, knowing as I do the characteristics of those Justices," Frankfurter wrote. He thought that Lippmann was "creating difficulties" to dismiss the decision and that his doubt about the case was "one of the w[ei]rdest intellectual experiences of my life."[62] An angry and annoyed Lippmann waited six days to respond and consulted with an equally outraged Learned Hand. He was "irritated at the tone" of Frankfurter's letter "and its assumption that a failure to agree immediately and whole-heartedly with Holmes, Brandeis and Cardozo was a weird and strange procedure."[63] Frankfurter, however, refused to let the exchange go. After apologizing for having irritated and offended Lippmann, he wondered why their friendship could not include disagreement as well as agreement.[64] Lippmann claimed that he did not mind disagreement and criticism: "Once in a while, as in your Schwimmer letter, there is an unconscious dogmatism which gives me a sense of being rushed and pushed, not unlike that of being physically jostled."[65]

It had become clear that Frankfurter and Lippmann adopted different approaches toward the future of American liberalism. Frankfurter was hopeful and expansive about politics; Lippmann retreated into pessimism and detachment. Frankfurter stood up for free speech and fair criminal trials of radicals, immigrants, and minorities; Lippmann shied away from any unpopular political causes. Frankfurter believed in the Democratic Party as the liberal party and saw Franklin Roosevelt as its future leader; Lippmann thought that the Democratic Party could not unite the country and that Roosevelt was a lightweight. Indeed, their next major political disagreement over Roosevelt would be one of their last.

One of the only things Frankfurter and Lippmann continued to agree upon was the greatness of Holmes.

28

America's Shrine for Political Democracy

The man building a public monument to America's heroes needed Hoover's election more than anyone. For more than a year after Coolidge's visit to the Black Hills, work on Mount Rushmore had been at a standstill. Without financial support from Republicans in Congress and the White House, Borglum knew perfectly well that the project would never be finished.

Less than ten days before Hoover's March 4 inauguration, the federal government rescued Rushmore. On February 22, Washington's birthday, Senator Norbeck asked to bring legislation to the floor for a vote. The Senate had just finished reading Washington's Farewell Address, which Norbeck said "gives new inspiration to meet every national problem and combat every difficulty."[1] After Norbeck described the project in the Black Hills and Borglum's progress on Washington's head, the Senate passed a bill creating a new twelve-member Mount Rushmore National Memorial Commission and authorized $250,000 for the monument. Though the money was contingent on raising matching private funds, the bill made $100,000 available immediately. Three days later, Coolidge signed it into law. "Wish I could have flown to Washington and been present at that signing," Borglum wrote Norbeck.[2] At Borglum's request, the president's secretary sent him the pen used to sign the legislation.[3]

Before work on the project could proceed, Hoover needed to appoint another member to the commission because Coolidge had named only eleven of the twelve members before leaving office. Borglum suggested that the new president meet with the commission personally at the White House. Though the idea was endorsed by Norbeck and Robinson because it would generate publicity for the project, Mount Rushmore was not

Gutzon Borglum and Supt. inspecting work on face of Washington - Mt. Rushmore # 40

Borglum scaling the nose of George Washington at Mount Rushmore

Hoover's first priority upon taking office.[4] The May meeting was pushed back to June and jeopardized another summer of work. "The apparent thing is that the Rushmore deal is dragging along in '29 just like it did in 1928," Norbeck wrote Borglum. "I am not saying that in criticism—I am stating it as an apparent fact. ... Last year put us in jeopardy and left a feeling both in South Dakota and Washington that 'Borglum starts a lot of things and doesn't finish them.'"[5] As he made his way from North Carolina to Washington, DC, to encourage Hoover to meet with the commission, Mary Borglum rushed to her husband's defense. She challenged Norbeck to name one project besides the Confederate Memorial that Borglum had not finished, and she blamed that "miserable Atlanta crowd have spread their calumny" about what had happened at Stone Mountain.[6] In fact, he had not given up on finishing the Confederate Memorial. He had made three visits there during the summer of 1928 at the request of people who wanted him to salvage the project.[7] In February 1929, he had boasted that he was going back and would "dominate the project without interference."[8] The sculptor also assured Norbeck that there would be no return to Stone Mountain for at least two years and vowed: "Now let us finish the Black Hills first."[9]

Borglum's presence in Washington did not help matters. Hoover was too busy to meet with the commission. Norbeck could not make it happen, either. A progressive Republican who had refused to endorse Hoover for president in 1928, he was not even on speaking terms with the administration and was forced to rely on others. The sculptor failed to exert the same influence on Hoover as with past presidents. Despite numerous letters, he could not get the president to meet with him; Hoover would meet only with members of Congress. Borglum's meddling in Washington political affairs tested his alliance with Norbeck. "Mr. Borglum is an artist and not a business man, but he is not satisfied with being the artist," Norbeck wrote a South Dakotan on the commission. "He wants to be the whole show and sit in the front seat, etc., etc. He has made me no end of trouble here."[10]

On June 6, Hoover finally met with the commission in the Cabinet Room and named philanthropist Julius Rosenwald as the last member. Work on Mount Rushmore resumed. On July 17, Borglum gave Rosenwald and other members of the commission a grand tour of the mountain. Then Borglum got back to doing what he did best—sculpting. He hoped to finish carving Washington's head by the end of the year and to complete the entire project in five years. "We shall place the Father of the Republic in the center, somewhere above the others, silent as the Sphinx, because his selfless, far-seeing character suggests that," he wrote the *New York Herald-Tribune* in June 1929. "But we mean to give him feeling that will indicate his broad world purpose, a purpose broader than anything Europe ever conceived."[11]

During the summer and early fall, work on Washington was in full swing. Borglum had created several large-scale clay models by studying Jean-Antoine Houdon's 1785 life mask and portraits by Charles Wilson Peale and Gilbert Stuart.[12] The sculptor hired scores of unemployed miners, retrained them to be mountain carvers, and taught them techniques that he had refined at Stone Mountain. By mid-August, he and his men had blocked out the sixty-foot-high head from the top of the forehead to the chin. The carvers were removing rough stone before Borglum began to use a new master pointer to locate Washington's eyes, nose, and mouth on the mountainside.[13] Not even the departure of Tucker, who sued for his pay under his old contract and settled for $7,500, could slow the work's progress.[14] The drillers also began removing stone to the left of Washington for Jefferson's head.[15] "I'm working on the Jefferson head," Borglum wrote Norbeck in September. "So I shall be able to block that head into recognizable shape besides finishing the face of Washington by November 1st."[16] No one was allowed to publish photographs of Washington's head until its unveiling.[17] By November, Borglum had finished Washington's eyebrows and half of his nineteen-foot-long nose. Meeting with the commission in Chicago at the Standard Club, Borglum promised to have the entire head completed for a July 4 unveiling.[18] The commission's first annual report to Congress was even more ambitious—indicating that Jefferson's head had been "roughed out," models of Lincoln and Roosevelt will be ready by the spring, and "the heads of Washington and Jefferson will be finished for unveiling on Independence Day, 1930. The completion of the memorial will take at least four years."[19]

Mount Rushmore's prospects gave America something to feel good about. In late October 1929, the stock market had collapsed—as Lippmann and others had predicted. With $100,000 in federal funding in hand and another $150,000 so long as he raised matching funds, Borglum proceeded with a project that reminded America about its glorious past and that relied on federal money to put people to work when jobs were scarce. Rushmore exemplified the good things that government could do.

The only thing standing in the way of Rushmore's success was Borglum's self-sabotaging desire to be "the whole show"—even if it meant overshadowing the ex-president most responsible for the project's survival. No one had done more for the Black Hills and Mount Rushmore than Coolidge. Coolidge's decision to turn the area into his Summer White House in 1927 had started another "Black Hills boom." Instead of a second gold rush,

Borglum's model for Mount Rushmore

railroads and commercial clubs started a boom in tourism. Since the president's stay, 400,000 people had visited the area.[20] His only speech that summer, his inspired rededication of Mount Rushmore, had landed the project on the front pages of the nation's newspapers for all the right reasons. He also had lent the project the federal government's imprimatur and financial support. Just before leaving office, he had signed the legislation that guaranteed funding; had the government waited another few months, the stock market crash likely would have killed the project.

In short, Borglum owed Coolidge. Instead of repaying the former president with gratitude, he returned the project to the nation's front pages. The sculptor started a controversy over Coolidge's drafting of the monument's inscription. The president was supposed to draft a 500-word history of America based on eight major historical events starting with the Declaration of Independence and the Constitution. To the right of the four presidents, Borglum wanted to carve the dates of the events and Coolidge's words to be large enough (three feet high) for all to see and deep enough (five inches deep) so that they would remain for thousands of years. And he wanted to carve the inscription about the first two historical events for the unveiling of Washington's head.[21] In January and February 1930, Borglum conferred with Coolidge about the inscription by mail and in person as Coolidge passed through the sculptor's home in San Antonio.[22] Two problems emerged. First, Coolidge took his time to write the first two passages about the Declaration of Independence and the Constitution. The short paragraphs did not arrive until April 1.[23] Second, Borglum did not like what Coolidge had written. Instead of consulting the former president about proposed changes, the sculptor simply edited the text himself and released it to the press. In mid-April, Coolidge privately rejected Borglum's changes and found the publicity "exceedingly distasteful." My object in trying to do this," he wrote to Borglum, "was to help the project a little and not from any desire to advertise myself."[24] In an attempt to mend fences, Borglum apologized for the publicity and the distress it had caused the former president.[25] Coolidge was not mollified: "You can see where your improvements published without consulting me landed me."[26]

The worst was yet to come. In early May, the *New York Times* discovered that Borglum had changed Coolidge's passages about the Declaration of Independence and the Constitution and wired Borglum. After a series of telegrams between the sculptor and the newspaper, the *Times* broke the story on May 13. Every major newspaper in America ran a version of it, some on the front page and some mocking Borglum on their editorial pages.[27] In truth, he had changed only a few words here and there. And privately, he was not so contrite and rather amused by the whole controversy. "First, he seeks me to write the inscription, or tell him what to say; then, he seeks me to improve on what he finally says …," Borglum wrote to Coleman du Pont. After that, "Coolidge gets peevish and tells the world I have meddled with his text."[28]

At a July 3 meeting at Mount Rushmore, the commission agreed to suspend all carving of the inscription and gave Coolidge until its November meeting to finish the entire text. The text would be subject to review by the commission, not by Borglum.[29] Coolidge refused to write another word.[30] At its November meeting at Chicago's Union League Club, the commission decided to table the issue of a new author for another year. Borglum was unbowed about editing the former president: "Posterity will hold me responsible for it, whether I wrote it or not, and I want it right."[31]

The hue and cry over Coolidge's inscription undermined the July 4 unveiling of Washington's head. Borglum's boasts that Hoover and Coolidge would attend did not materialize.[32] After Hoover had declined because Congress might be in session, Borglum asked him to send Coolidge as the federal government's official representative.[33] The commission also wired the former president directly.[34] Not surprisingly, Coolidge was in no mood to participate. A year later, Paul Bellamy, a friend from Rapid City, asked if the former president had been in touch with Borglum. Coolidge asked how far it was from his home in Northampton, Massachusetts, to the Black Hills. Bellamy said 1,500 miles. "Well ... Y' know, Mr. Bellamy," Coolidge replied, "that's about as close t' Mr. Borglum as I care t' be."[35]

The July 4 ceremony went forward without a real-live president. At noon, buglers from Fort Meade, South Dakota, started the proceedings. A crowd of 2,500 people gathered near Borglum's studio at the base of Mount Rushmore and sang "America the Beautiful." Speeches celebrated not only Washington but also the American form of government. Commission chairman Joseph Cullinan echoed Borglum's theme that the monument was "America's shrine for political democracy."[36] People watched and waited for the giant American flag draped over the top of the mountain to reveal the head of Washington. With the press of a button, the flag was released. Riflemen from Fort Meade delivered a twenty-one-gun salute. Airplanes from Rapid City Port flew overhead. An American Legion drum and bugle corps played.[37]

As the crowd gazed up at the sixty-foot head on Mount Rushmore, which was 6,200 feet above sea level, Borglum described his artistic vision. Washington's forehead alone was "twenty feet from wig to nose, as animate and carefully constructed as the Houdon mask which I have followed, together with the portraits by Peale and Stuart." He boasted about the "mass, vigor, and beauty" of Washington's brow and declared that the nose was "better" than the Stuart. He also explained that the depth of the eye sockets made the eyes "unnecessary." Washington's "great face seemed to belong to the mountain; it took on the elemental courage of the mountains around."[38] The press reported that Borglum planned to unveil one president per year, with the entire project completed by 1933 with Theodore Roosevelt and the inscription.[39] That turned out to be wishful thinking. But by completing Washington's head, he had quieted the skeptics and critics and boosted his reputation.

Back in Georgia, people noticed the publicity and tourism that Borglum's monument had attracted to South Dakota. A movement started for the sculptor to finish the Confederate Memorial at Stone Mountain.[40] "Bring Borglum Back," the Atlanta Constitution pleaded.[41] Even with the issuing of yet another warrant for his arrest for destroying his plaster models in 1924, Borglum accepted a late August invitation from Atlanta's mayor-elect to consider resuming the project.[42] The sculptor kept a low profile but told the *Atlanta Constitution* that the Confederate Memorial was "uppermost in his thoughts."[43]

South Dakotans, who for some years had viewed the sculptor as another huckster trying to swindle them out of their money and natural resources, changed their tune. The day after the July 4 unveiling, the *Rapid City Journal* repeated Borglum's boast that the memorial "would outlast this government." He had said the same thing three years earlier, when Coolidge had rededicated the project. "The first time it was received in silence," the newspaper reported. "Yesterday the crowd applauded vigorously."[44] In 1927, South Dakotans had been skeptical about a national memorial in their state and did not know what to make of Borglum. He was, according to the *Rapid City Journal*, "regarded as a dreamer, a bit impractical, a little disrespectful of the government whose chief, Mr. Coolidge, was in his presence." Three years later, he had created a shrine to Washington and captured what he meant to "American life and the civilization of the world." They knew that Washington's head was not finished, that Jefferson's head and the entablature had just been started, and that the project would take years to complete. But after the unveiling of Washington's head, they believed Borglum's matter-of-fact statement that Mount Rushmore "would outlast this government."[45]

Something else had changed as well—people's trust in their government. The Great Depression was less than a year old, and many blamed the policies of the Harding, Coolidge, and Hoover administrations. "America's shrine for political democracy" reminded them of what our government had achieved in the past and what it was capable of in the future. It instilled a sense of faith in democracy—federal funds could be used for great works of art and for public works projects that put people back to work. And it reminded people that, with the right leadership, government could make their lives better again. In one of their darkest economic hours, the American people needed Mount Rushmore. They put their faith in one of the oddest yet most compelling figures in American history, an artist with something to prove to himself and an important message for the nation, its government, and its leaders.

29

The Best Men

In a series of lectures he gave at Yale Law School during the spring of 1930, Frankfurter argued that the nation's best men should go into government service. He believed that career politicians like Lincoln and Theodore Roosevelt should be cultivated and not scorned, that in a democracy the key to "politics is a process of popular education," and that "*expertise* is indispensable." "The difficulties of our social-economic problems will not abate with time …," he said. "They will make increasing demands upon trained intelligence. If government is to be equal to its responsibilities, it must draw more and more on men of skill and wisdom for public administration."[1] One institution that Frankfurter had in mind was the Supreme Court. In his Yale lectures and subsequent articles, he continued to celebrate the public servant he admired most and used Holmes's opinions to criticize the Court.[2]

For several years now, Frankfurter and his allies had recognized that the Court could play a positive role in achieving their political and legal goals. The key was to keep it from becoming too conservative. They pursued three strategies. First, they attacked Hoover's Supreme Court nominees and pressured him to nominate more liberal justices. Second, they criticized the Court's rulings that usurped the authority of state governments to pass socioeconomic legislation. Third, they continued to promote Holmes as a judicial icon and great jurist of his time.

The most important concern was Hoover's choice of a new chief justice. On January 6, 1930, Chief Justice Taft announced that he was taking a month-long leave of absence for health reasons. He was suffering from a recurring bladder problem; he was emotionally exhausted from the death of his half-brother Charles; and he was so physically exhausted that he checked himself into the hospital for the second time in six months. In Taft's absence, the eighty-nine-year-old Holmes assumed the role of acting chief justice. The burden of presiding at oral argument and the justices' private conferences terrified him.[3] Despite his fears, his first day of leading the Court was a success. "O.W.H. is indeed 'to the manner born,'" Brandeis wrote Frankfurter. "He is presiding with great fondness, alertness and joy. A marked rejuvenescence has been effected; and he is definitely without worry in those unaccustomed duties incident to his new office. It is several years since we have had so good a C.J."[4] The glowing reviews continued after the justices' private conference two days later. "O.W.H. presided beautifully & calmly at today's conference," Brandeis wrote Frankfurter. "Stone says it was the best conference he has attended since coming onto the Court."[5] In revealing some of Brandeis's confidential comments to Lippmann, Frankfurter wrote: "Isn't it thrilling to have man at the threshold of 90 as the spiritual leader of the Court?"[6]

Nearly a month later, Taft announced his retirement.[7] Frankfurter's first choice for the new leader of the Court was Cardozo, chief judge of the

Chief Justice Charles Evans Hughes (left) and Holmes on Holmes's ninetieth birthday

New York Court of Appeals.[8] But Frankfurter and others were content
with Stone, a Republican and Hoover adviser, in the center chair. That
would have enabled Hoover to appoint Cardozo or Learned Hand to
replace Stone as associate justice. Frankfurter even had an inside man in
the administration—Undersecretary of State Joseph P. Cotton also urged
Hoover to elevate Stone in the hopes of getting Hand on the Court.[9]
However, two of the Court's conservative justices, Van Devanter and Butler,
had gone to New York to meet with their own preferred candidate, and
they had the support of Attorney General William D. Mitchell. During
dinner at Hand's apartment with Lippmann, Frankfurter predicted that
Stone's nomination as chief justice would be scuttled by "'the boys' …
because he has shown himself to be unreliable, from their point of view, on
social-economic questions."[10]

As Frankfurter feared, Hoover passed over Stone and replaced Taft with
former associate justice and 1916 Republican presidential nominee, Charles
Evans Hughes. Frankfurter was furious with the *World*'s initial editorial
claiming that Hughes's nomination as chief justice had received "'universal approval.'"[11] Frankfurter was also angry with Hoover for caving to the
conservative wing of his party. After all, Hoover had thought so highly of
Stone as to want to make him secretary of state, attorney general, or chairman of the crime commission. Frankfurter asserted that the president had
nominated the sixty-eight-year-old Hughes, "if I am right, because of the
hostility which Stone has aroused for having decently liberal views on constitutional issues."[12] Frankfurter did not believe that Hughes was a staunch
conservative, but, as the second justice from New York, he all but eliminated
Cardozo and Hand, also New Yorkers.[13] What really worried Frankfurter
was that Hoover had "yielded to influences that are reactionary" in not
nominating someone more liberal and moreover that the president would
do so again to tilt the Court in an even more conservative direction.[14]

After several letters from Frankfurter, Lippmann wrote a New York *World*
editorial, arguing that the protest over Hughes's nomination was "directed
only incidentally at Mr. Hughes; its real animus has been against the pre-
vailing majority of the court." The Court, Lippmann's editorial argued,
was "out of harmony" with the American people's desire to regulate utilities and other monopolies at the state level. And Hoover and eight years
of Republican rule were to blame. "When American insurgency is intense enough to challenge fundamental decisions of the Supreme Court,"
Lippmann wrote, "then we may be certain that it is no petty revolt."[15]

Thanks to Frankfurter, Lippmann's editorial reached Hoover's desk, and "Hoover read it." "But, alas, the President's attitude, on the whole, is still that of the New York Herald Tribune," he wrote Lippmann, referring to the conservative newspaper. "He thinks the criticism against Hughes was all captious and mere sniping, and he does not take in the forces that you so acutely analyzed."[16] Several senators attacked Hughes's nomination on the Senate floor. They objected to Hughes's decision to leave the Court to run for president in 1916, his political activity on behalf of the Republican Party since then, and his Supreme Court arguments on behalf of the railroad industry and other big businesses.[17] After three days of intense debate, the Senate voted to confirm Hughes, 52–26.[18] "Not since Jackson nominated Taney," Hughes's biographer Merlo J. Pusey noted, "had the Senate raised such a furor over the confirmation of a Chief Justice."[19]

Frankfurter and Lippmann joined forces for one more judicial nomination battle. March 8 was Holmes's eighty-ninth birthday; the US Senate honored him.[20] Just as his colleagues gathered in their private conference room to celebrate the occasion, they learned some grim news. Their colleague, sixty-four-year-old Justice Edward T. Sanford, had collapsed in a dentist's chair after a tooth extraction and died at home a short time later. Sanford's six years on the Court were quiet and undistinguished (his only notable opinion rejected Benjamin Gitlow's free speech claims). Even in death, Sanford received second or even third billing. Five hours after his death, Taft died at age seventy-two.

Rumors swirled about Sanford's successor. Coolidge's name was floated.[21] Frankfurter wrote the Hoover administration a memorandum, making the case for Cardozo.[22] But the search soon focused on four federal court of appeals judges, three of them southerners. Replacing the Tennessee-born Sanford with another southerner would help the Republican Party make inroads into the solidly Democratic South. On March 21, Hoover nominated John J. Parker, a forty-four-year-old federal appeals court judge from North Carolina. The New York Times declared: "Senate Approval Likely."[23]

Liberals had tried to fend off Parker's nomination.[24] Now they mobilized for a nomination battle that presaged an alliance between labor and civil rights groups. In 1916, Frankfurter and Lippmann had cemented their friendship by using the New Republic to fight for Brandeis's confirmation. Fourteen years later, they reunited to oppose Parker's. Still, what he viewed as the even-handedness of Zechariah Chafee's unsigned New Republic editorial about Parker's nomination annoyed Frankfurter. Chafee's editorial raised concerns about Parker's experience with major constitutional questions and characterized his judicial opinions as pedestrian. "Even a layman cannot read decisions by Cardozo or Learned Hand without realizing that he is in contact with a great judge," Chafee wrote. "In contrast, Judge Parker's scores of opinions yield hardly a single passage which would be quoted as a distinctive statement of a legal principle."[25] Frankfurter wired Lippmann that "my own views are even less favorable than Chafee's."[26]

The *World*'s April 1 editorial, "The Opposition to Justice Parker," warned about the impact of Hughes's and Parker's nominations on the future of the Supreme Court. "President Hoover either missed or chose to ignore the chief point in the Senate's recent attack on the nomination of Chief Justice Hughes," the *World* wrote. "The motive behind this attack was a belief in the Senate that the Supreme Court is already top-heavy with extremely conservative sentiment and that the times call for nomination of a liberal."[27] After reading the editorial, Frankfurter reminded Lippmann that Brandeis's confirmation battle had lasted four months and that other great judges, including the recess appointees Taney, Harlan, and Holmes, took months to be confirmed. "*A propos* the Parker nomination," he wrote Lippmann, "there is one thing that ought to be insisted upon, namely, thorough deliberation."[28] Frankfurter started by reading all of Parker's judicial opinions during his five years on the federal bench. His biggest problem with Parker's opinions was not that they were antilabor or antiblack but that they were mediocre. Holmes ranked lawyers based on their sharpness: stings, razors, and kitchen knives ("the average able lawyer"); Parker, according to Frankfurter, was "just a kitchen knife."[29] "I think he is one of these extreme 'conservatives' because of the limited nature of his mind," he wrote Lippmann. "Why is that not the best of all reasons for not having him on the Supreme Court— particularly for not having him for the next forty years!"[30] Lippmann incorporated Frankfurter's information in a follow-up editorial, but he needed more ammunition. "If you can send me some more material I'll go on with this," Lippmann wrote. "But I feel quite helpless to do it alone."[31]

Lippmann and Frankfurter were not alone, however. Organized labor and the NAACP led the way. On April 5, William Green, the president of the AFL, testified before a Senate judiciary subcommittee against Parker's nomination. Parker had written a 1927 opinion rejecting the United Mine Workers' (UMW) challenge to yellow-dog contracts, which forced West Virginia coal miners to agree not to join a union as a condition of employment.[32] His opinion had enjoined the UMW from urging its members

not to honor the contracts and had followed a long line of antilabor decisions enforcing them. Labor injunctions and these yellow-dog contracts
were the two biggest obstacles for unions. For Green and the AFL, the issue
was clear: Parker's confirmation would hurt unions and "strengthen the
reactionary side of the Supreme Court, by adding another to that powerful
influence." The AFL's wish, like that of Frankfurter and Lippmann, was "to
see the greatest legal tribunal in all the world humanized and liberalized."[33]

The NAACP also joined the fight. For the first time in its history, the organization opposed a Supreme Court nominee. On the same day as Green's
testimony, Walter White, acting secretary of the NAACP, offered new revelations against Parker. During his 1920 campaign for governor, Parker had
praised a state constitutional amendment passed in 1900 that used poll taxes,
literacy tests, and grandfather clauses to disenfranchise black voters. He told
the *Greensboro Daily News* that "the participation of the negro in politics
is a source of evil and danger to both races and is not desired by the wise
men in either race or by the Republican Party of North Carolina."[34] After

Judge John J. Parker

discovering the article, the NAACP wired Parker to ask him whether he still held those views ten years later, but it received no response. White described Parker's comments as "open, shameless flouting of the fourteenth and fifteenth amendments," and argued that anyone who held those views was not fit to sit on the Supreme Court.[35]

Yet the AFL, according to White, "was exceedingly anxious to prevent the identification of its opposition against Parker with that of Negroes."[36] The AFL's Green went so far as to avoid White at the Senate subcommittee hearings. The NAACP, however, could not be ignored. White orchestrated a grassroots mobilization effort among its local branches, black churches, and black newspapers and in the white press. The organization intensely lobbied members of the US Senate, urged President Hoover to withdraw the nomination, and asked Vice President Charles Curtis not to cast the tie-breaking vote in Parker's favor.[37]

One person interested in the NAACP's campaign was, of course, Frankfurter. In 1929, after the deaths of Louis Marshall and Moorfield Storey, he had joined the NAACP's national legal committee.[38] After testifying against Parker, White sent Frankfurter a copy of the testimony and asked him for legal assistance.[39] Frankfurter, in turn, asked White for copies of the *Greensboro Daily News* article and the organization's latest letter to President Hoover and complimented the tone of the NAACP's campaign. "I know how distressing the whole controversy raised by Parker's nomination is to you," Frankfurter wrote White, "but I think you ought to have the satisfaction of feeling that you have conducted your fight with serenity, dignity and impersonal relevance."[40] White was "most pleased" by Frankfurter's comments. He told Frankfurter that the campaign was bigger than Judge Parker and the Supreme Court, that it would "serve as a warning to others who may share Parker's views and who have national ambitions not to indulge in anti-Negro statements for political advantage."[41]

Frankfurter, meanwhile, continued to work behind the scenes. Many of his ideas found their way onto the New York *World* editorial page that, for much of April, deputy editorial editor Charles Merz ran while Lippmann was in Europe.[42] "Judge Parker's views, so far as they are known, appear to be much more conservative than those of the present Chief Justice," the *World* wrote on April 17. "Instead of moving to make the court more liberal, Mr. Hoover has leaned in the opposite direction."[43] The issue for the *World* was not Parker's opinion in the yellow-dog contract case but "that the Supreme Court is unhealthily conservative and that the times call for the nomination of a liberal."[44]

Frankfurter wanted Lippmann and the *World* to stress Parker's mediocrity. Before the Senate floor vote, Frankfurter asked Lippmann to write one
more editorial "summing up" the case that Parker "is not good enough" and
that his confirmation "threatens us for the next thirty years with mediocrity and blindness in the most sensitive phase of government for no other
reason in the world than temporary exigencies of Southern and Republican
politics."[45] To Frankfurter's delight, Lippmann's editorial incorporated those
ideas almost word-for-word and argued that "an appointment like Judge
Parker's threatens us for the next thirty years with mediocrity and blindness
in the most sensitive phase of government, for no other reason in the world
than the temporary exigencies of Republican politics in the South."[46]

With opposition from organized labor, the NAACP, and American liberals, the Senate rejected Parker's nomination, 41–39. Lippmann's newspaper
led the way (with a little help). "The World has again proved how influential a newspaper can be," Frankfurter wrote Lippmann. "Unquestionably its
series of articles on the Parker nomination added considerably to the forces
that prevailed in his rejection."[47] Brandeis credited Frankfurter with the
World's editorial stance. "In the defeat of Parker—or rather of H.H.—you
have played an important part, through The World and otherwise," he wrote
Frankfurter and predicted gains for organized labor, African Americans, and
liberals from both parties.[48]

In Parker's place, Hoover nominated Owen J. Roberts. A prominent
Philadelphia lawyer and a prosecutor of Harding officials implicated in
the Teapot Dome scandal, Roberts was easily confirmed. "In every way,"
Frankfurter predicted to Brandeis, "Roberts is superior to Parker."[49] Brandeis
agreed that Roberts's confirmation "closes happily a worthy struggle."[50]
Roberts, however, was not the reliable vote on economic issues that liberals
thought he would be.[51]

Throughout the Parker fight, Frankfurter continued his critiques of the
Court itself. During the spring and early summer of 1930, he used his Yale
lectures and wrote several magazine articles to focus on the Court as the
biggest threat to American liberalism because it was "putting constitutional
authority behind the personal opinion of its members in disputed and difficult questions of social policy." The Court, he argued, invoked due process
and equal protection to exercise a judicial veto against state regulation.[52]
Like Brandeis, Frankfurter believed that the states served as laboratories
of experimentation and that the justices had squelched those experiments
by reading their political and social views into the Constitution.[53] Against

them, Frankfurter argued, stood Holmes, who like all great judges considered the Constitution "not primarily a text for interpretation but the means of ordering the life for a progressive people." Holmes, Frankfurter contended, perpetuated John Marshall's belief that the Constitution was a "broad outline" for a workable, adaptable government. "Great constitutional provisions must be administered with caution," Holmes wrote in one of his early Supreme Court opinions quoted by Frankfurter. "Some play must be allowed for the joints of the machine, and it must be remembered that legislatures are ultimate guardians of the liberties and welfare of the people in quite as great a degree as the courts."[54] Frankfurter revered Holmes because the justice allowed the "flexible scope" of the Constitution to adapt to modern problems and encouraged people to look to legislatures and not the courts for policy solutions. The Holmesian Constitution was not a roadblock to but a facilitator of government action. "He has found the Constitution equal to the needs of a great nation at war," Frankfurter wrote, "and adequate to the desires of a generous and daring people at peace."[55]

That spring, Holmes—thanks to liberal admirers—achieved more national recognition. In the March 1930 issue of *Harper's* magazine, Laski honored the justice on his eighty-ninth birthday with a seven-page essay that Senator Robert La Follette Jr. reprinted in the *Congressional Record*.[56] "Since John Marshall revealed to the American people what their new constitution might imply," Laski wrote, "none has so clearly molded its texture as Mr. Justice Holmes." Laski used his *Harper's* essay not only to praise Holmes but also to attack the Supreme Court for failing to recognize that "the American constitution does not forbid experiment" and, like Marshall, "he has ceaselessly remembered that the constitution is not a gate but a road." Laski praised Holmes for being a "judge and not the legislator," for allowing states to experiment, and for enabling the administrative state to grow along with the nation's problems and population. But Holmes's most "enduring" contribution, Laski argued, was "the attitude he has revealed to the individual rights the Constitution has sought to safeguard." He was, of course, referring to Holmes's opinions about freedom of speech.[57]

A month after Laski's *Harper's* essay, Hand unveiled a portrait of Holmes at Harvard Law School. Faculty and students crowded in the courtroom at Langdell Hall for the unveiling of Charles Hopkinson's full-length portrait of Holmes standing in judicial robes. To Holmes's great delight, law school officials decided to hang the portrait across from one of Chief Justice Marshall.[58] Though Holmes was unable to attend because of his judicial duties, Hand represented the justice's friends and delivered a stirring address. "He has been called a liberal, a champion of freedom, and surely it is true, if those words are to have any meaning," Hand said. But words like "liberal" and "freedom" did not capture what made the eighty-nine-year-old justice so special. It was his openness to new ideas. "If we measure youth by the power to assimilate what is new, by freshness of outlook, by sympathy, by understanding, by quickness of response, by affection, by kindness, by gentleness, by magnanimity," Hand said in remarks reprinted in the New York World, "he is not old."[59]

Privately, however, Hand told Frankfurter that Holmes's opinions were "not quite adequate any longer."[60] Frankfurter was concerned that Holmes was "overworked" and that the duties as acting chief justice had taxed the justice's health. In addition to presiding at oral argument and private conferences, Holmes assigned extra cases to himself. He was also responsible for drafting a congratulatory letter to Taft upon his retirement. Taft's mental collapse and disoriented picture in the newspaper "haunted" Holmes. "For about a week he was tired, worried & quite miserable," his secretary reported.[61] Without his wife, Fanny, by his side, Holmes relied on his secretaries for companionship seven days a week. His new secretary, a twenty-five-year-old Harvard law graduate from Baltimore, was Alger Hiss. Holmes took Hiss to his favorite spots around Washington, including Fort Stevens.[62] Hiss, in turn, initiated the practice of reading books aloud to the justice in the afternoons and evenings as Fanny had done.[63] One of the novels they read was Hemingway's A Farewell to Arms, which the justice said "moved me moderately, not to a superlative degree."[64] Hiss even got away with breaking one of Holmes's cardinal rules by getting married during his year with the justice.[65]

The deaths of Taft and Sanford had added to the justice's burdens. As acting chief justice, Holmes was tasked with writing to the House and Senate as well as the Court's memorial notices.[66] Hiss tried to take some of the burden off the justice by replying to more than 200 birthday wishes save for those from a few close friends.[67] Holmes showed other small signs of getting older. He complained to Hiss about not "seeing the spring colors so clearly as last year—particularly the faint fire of the red maples." An outing at the theater "depressed" Holmes, and for several days he was "unhappy" and "very tired." Hiss, who had suggested going to see The Journey's End after the justice had read the play in French and English, was "tearfully anxious" about his boss. Hiss feared that the justice's depression stemmed from memories that the play triggered but also that Holmes felt that he had missed some of its "quips and subtleties." Hand had visited 1720 Eye Street when Holmes was "most depressed" and "couldn't but notice that time was bound to vanquish even the great one."[68]

At the end of the term in May 1930, however, Holmes proved that he could still write stinging dissents. Joined by Brandeis and occasionally Stone, Holmes continued to rail against the Court's invocation of the Due Process Clause to invalidate state laws simply because the justices disagreed with them. Three times that term, the Court struck down state taxes. Three times, Holmes dissented. The last of his three dissents, about a Missouri estate tax, was quintessential Holmes. He chided his fellow justices for reading their economic views into the Constitution just as he had warned them against doing in *Lochner*, the 1905 New York bakeshop case: "As the decisions now stand I see hardly any limit but the sky to the invalidating of those rights if they happen to strike a majority of this Court as for any reason undesirable." The Fourteenth Amendment, he argued, was not "intended to give us carte blanche to embody our economic or moral beliefs in its prohibitions."[69] McReynolds was incensed by Holmes's dissents and

Holmes and his secretary Alger Hiss at Beverly Farms during the summer of 1930

his refusal to follow the Court's decisions earlier that year. During the courtroom announcement of his majority opinion in the Missouri estate tax case, McReynolds opined that the rule "laid down" in those prior cases "ought to be clear to an unclouded mind." McReynolds's comment, which was not included in his published opinion, seemed like a reference to Holmes and his advanced age.[70] An "amused" Holmes told Brandeis as they were riding home from the Court that day: "I feel a great relief at having spoken my mind."[71]

Holmes's dissent in *Baldwin v. Missouri* justified everything Frankfurter had been writing and saying over the years. Frankfurter wrote Lippmann that Holmes had written one of the finest opinions of his career: "For he spoke with a candor and explicitness hardly ever equaled, and certainly never exceeded, in the history of the Supreme Court, as far as my reading of the cases of that Court go." After urging Lippmann to read the opinion, Frankfurter believed that Holmes's opinion had justified "everything that was said and done in the Hughes and Parker debates."[72] In a *World* editorial praising Holmes's dissent, Lippmann agreed: "Nothing said in the course of the Senate debate on the Hughes and Parker nominations was more outspoken than this warning to the conservative majority of the Supreme Court spoken by a member of the court itself."[73]

Not everyone bought into the liberal embrace of Holmes. H. L. Mencken, for one, wrote that liberals were "frantically eager" to find someone on the Court "who was not violently and implacably against them, seized upon certain of Mr. Justice Holmes's opinions without examining the rest, and read into them an attitude which is actually as foreign to his ways of thinking as it is to those of Mr. Chief Justice Hughes." In a May 1930 review of a collected volume of Holmes's dissents, Mencken argued that the Fourteenth Amendment was meant to protect "minorities," and thus he was concerned about Holmes's reluctance to invoke it against "novel and oppressive laws. ... If what he says in some of those opinions were accepted literally, there would be scarcely any brake at all upon lawmaking, and the Bill of Rights would have no more significance than the Code of Manu." What Mencken failed to mention was that in 1930 only a few provisions of the Bill of Rights applied to state laws. He also did not specify which minorities he deemed worthy of protection. His critique of Holmes as a liberal, however, hit closer to home: "He is a jurist of great industry, immense learning and the highest integrity, but ... to call him Liberal is to make the word meaningless."[74]

Despite Mencken's reservations, liberals remained convinced that Holmes would help lead the Court in a new, more liberal direction. Hughes, according to Brandeis, was a big upgrade over Taft, who in his later years "had really lost his grip" so that Van Devanter, Butler, and McReynolds "were running him." Brandeis admired Hughes's "real energy and intelligence," yet he conceded that Hughes's opinions were "like his old opinions on the Court—he has no imagination but he is a good artisan." The hope for liberals, according to Brandeis, lay with its newest member: "[I]f Roberts is what we expect him to be, I think we may gradually see a decidedly different temper on the Court."[75]

Holmes returned to Beverly Farms after the Court adjourned for the summer with his secretary Hiss in tow. During a stopover in Boston, Marion Frankfurter took Holmes to see his portrait at Harvard Law School.[76] "I have that face every day but of course can't tell what he really looked like," he remarked as he looked at the portrait. "But that does seem to me to look like a smart fellow!!"[77] The Frankfurters lunched with Holmes at Beverly Farms and were amazed at how energetic he was. "He seemed more like the earlier Holmes than at any time in recent years," Frankfurter reported to Lippmann.[78] After Harvard's commencement, Frankfurter, Hand, and Lippmann drove up from Cambridge to see the justice. Holmes, who often tired after an hour and a half, was buoyed by the visit. He told them that "the best thing I could do was to die. Everything has been so smiling to me this last year that I tremble, and fear that I shall do some damned thing that will put a fly into the ointment." Holmes reported that Hand replied, "'All life is taking a risk. Go ahead and take it'—and I thought he was right. But still I tremble."[79]

In early August, Frankfurter brought another special guest to Beverly Farms, Benjamin Cardozo—his first choice for the Court and a longtime Holmes admirer. Holmes was delighted by the visit and by Cardozo. "He is one of the few who have said in print and private the things that make my life seem worth having been lived," Holmes wrote Laski.[80] Several times that summer, Holmes's mind wandered back to the day that he was shot in the neck at Antietam. In particular, he recalled General Sumner's unfortunate decision to send Holmes and other members of the Twentieth Massachusetts Regiment "so close to the front line that we could have touched them with our bayonets."[81] Holmes's regiment was too close—they could not fire back for fear of shooting their fellow Union soldiers on the front line in the back. He was more focused on the past than the future.[82]

As the justice approached his ninetieth birthday, he soldiered on, returning to Washington that October for another term. He remained receptive
to new ideas. His new secretary read him books by Jerome Frank of Yale
and Karl Llewellyn of Columbia about a cutting-edge theory called "legal
realism"—emphasizing facts, outcomes, and the human element and de-
emphasizing formal rules in legal decision-making.[83] Frank's book, *Law and
the Modern Mind*, Holmes wrote, "has ideas but too many words, I think, and
seems to show some confusion about the emotional reaction of judges as if
it were all to be set against the rules."[84] Even as he authorized Frankfurter
to hire another secretary for the following year, Holmes worried that he
was losing his mental acuity and was not keeping up with his work. His
colleagues were kind to him, but he was concerned that he was no longer
"pulling my weight."[85] Frankfurter tried to reassure Holmes that his work
was of the same high quality. "I speak as a zealous student of your Court's
work when I say that I could not, at pistol's point, find warrant in the
remotest degree, for any concern of yours as to your share of the Court's
work ...," Frankfurter wrote. "So—write on!"[86]

Holmes's admirers turned his ninetieth birthday into a national celebration. Frankfurter organized a book of essays, mostly consisting of former *New
Republic* and *Harvard Law Review* articles, by Lippmann, Cardozo, Dewey,
Phillip Littell, Sergeant, Wigmore, and of course Frankfurter himself.[87] In
a review in the *American Bar Association Journal*, former attorney general
Wickersham contended that "without exception the writers of all the essays
in this volume represent a school of thought to which, in general, the majority of the Supreme Court has been consistently opposed."[88] Frankfurter
replied that if he and his Sacco and Vanzetti antagonist Wigmore belonged
"to the same 'school of thought,' then I should think the 'school' is sufficiently comprehensive for Mr. Wickersham also to find himself at home in
it."[89]

One place where Holmes was not universally celebrated was in Boston,
his hometown, where, according to Frankfurter, "a Holmes is an exotic
and a Coolidge its natural symbol and glory." After hearing a remark about
the justice's "vanity" by a noted Boston physician, Richard C. Cabot,
Frankfurter exploded at his friend historian Arthur Schlesinger Sr.: "That
Cabot should have put Holmes' vanity in the foreground of his characterization of Holmes/the person, is for me—who has observed rather closely
Cabotese culture for now these seventeen years—a perfect symbol of its
limitation and meagreness." Frankfurter apologized to Schlesinger for the

outburst and wished he had taken "the opportunity of telling you with great particularity what manner of man this Holmes is."[90] For Frankfurter, Holmes's ninetieth birthday reminded him of meeting his wife, Marion, and introducing her to Holmes at the House of Truth. "Holmes is a bond between us, as he is with no other pair," he wrote Marion the day before the justice's birthday.[91] Laski accepted a visiting professorship at Yale Law School during the spring of 1931 primarily so he could celebrate Holmes's ninetieth birthday with the justice in Washington.[92] Laski paid tribute to Holmes in the *Yale Law Journal*; Frederick Pollock and Morris R. Cohen did the same in the *Columbia Law Review*; the *Harvard Law Review* dedicated its entire volume to Holmes, with short contributions from Chief Justice Hughes, Frankfurter, and others.[93] In Britain, Holmes was elected honorary bencher of the Honorable Society of Lincoln's Inn in London. President Hoover released a letter congratulating Holmes and "our country upon the continuance of your splendid services."[94]

Everyone connected to the House of Truth recognized the milestone. For so long, Holmes had represented their hopes and decided cases how they would have decided them: to keep the Court's hands off federal and state socioeconomic legislation, to protect free speech, and to guard against unfair criminal trials. They wanted a civil libertarian Court, one that instead of protecting property rights protected human rights. With the rise of fascism in Europe, Holmes's free speech dissents and fair trial opinions took on even greater significance. "Never was there a time," *The Nation* argued, "when we Americans and the peoples of the world at large needed more than today the profound faith in freedom that lies at the heart of the work of Justice Holmes."[95]

A *New Republic* editorial declared Holmes's ninetieth birthday "an event which belongs not to him but to the nation."[96] The magazine's founder, Herbert Croly, had died in May 1930. Croly's book *The Promise of American Life* had made him the intellectual leader of the late progressive movement. Yet Croly had failed to live up to the "promise" of *The Promise* in his subsequent books and had been so disillusioned by the terms of the Treaty of Versailles that he soured on politics and turned to religion.[97] The Harding and Coolidge administrations made him even less engaged by the liberal political causes of 1920s. His lack of interest in the Sacco-Vanzetti case reflected his failure to grasp liberalism's enduring power, a belief in government coupled with an interest in protecting civil liberties and promoting fair criminal trials.[98] Croly's magazine, however, continued to promote liberal ideas and to celebrate Holmes as a national figure. The magazine remained Holmes's only source of news. The *New Republic*'s other famous founding editor, Lippmann, wrote: "As for the greatest man I have personally ever known apart from Einstein himself, who I have met only once for a short time, I should perhaps say Mr. Justice Holmes."[99]

Lippmann, however, lacked a public outlet to praise Holmes. On February 27, 1931, the New York *World* ceased publication. The Pulitzer-owned paper was sold to the Scripps-Howard chain and merged into the *New York World-Telegram*. With the emergence of the *New York Times* and the *New York Herald-Tribune* as the city's two leading newspapers, the *World* could no longer compete for readership and was suffering "heavy financial losses."[100] Lippmann was the newspaper's last editor. At a 200-person dinner in his honor a month after the paper's final issue, he discussed the future of American liberalism as demanding "the capacity to act resolutely while maintaining a skeptical mind, the willingness to take all the risk of action knowing what those risks are."[101]

Not everyone still viewed Lippmann as a friend to liberalism. Though many attended the dinner in his honor, including Newton D. Baker, Hand, Emory R. Buckner, C. C. Burlingham, and even Heywood Broun, Frankfurter was not among them.[102] On March 28, Lippmann announced upon returning from a European vacation that he was joining the *New York Herald-Tribune*. For Frankfurter, it was not a shock that Lippmann had agreed to be a columnist at a conservative newspaper, for, as he wrote their mutual friend Ralph Hayes, "he has steadily moved to the right, and the logic of psychological forces will continue that process. ... Of course I know that you believe that Walter will tincture the Tribune and its readers with liberalism rather than strengthen the conservative forces. I think I know the argument and understand it, but am wholly unpersuaded by it."[103]

Laski, like Frankfurter, had soured on Lippmann. In March, Laski had spent an hour with Lippmann and "not very profitably." "I think wealth has done two things to him," he wrote Holmes. "A good deal of his sensitiveness has gone." The first problem was that he was "interested in external things, queer little worthless comforts," like yelling at a waiter for not bringing him coffee. The second was that "he has arrived at the stage where he is no longer eager to take intellectual risks."[104]

Everyone from the old House of Truth days, even Borglum, took notice of Holmes's ninetieth birthday. From McAllister, Oklahoma, while driving through the West, Borglum wired Holmes. They had been out of touch for so long that the sculptor even passed along his well wishes to the late Mrs. Holmes.[105] Ever since his showdown in May 1930 with Coolidge over the inscription and the unveiling of Washington's head a month later, Borglum had been struggling to raise the funds to complete Jefferson's head. The sculptor had spent much of 1931 crisscrossing the country soliciting "'Big Democrats in America," including financier Bernard Baruch, in the hopes that they would embrace a project memorializing the nation's most famous Democrat.[106] "I have not been able to interest a single one of them," Borglum glumly informed President Hoover. All the sculptor needed was $25,000 in private donations (and $25,000 in federal matching funds) to complete Jefferson's head. But with the country mired in the Great Depression, people believed that there were more worthy causes than carving the images of presidents into rock. Worried that the work would be shut down because of lack of funds in a matter of weeks, Borglum appealed to the president to commemorate Mount Rushmore through a US stamp.[107]

Borglum remained a rock-ribbed Republican and Hoover supporter. Yet he warned the president that northwestern Republicans, many of them progressive, held the key to the White House in 1932 and that Hoover should do nothing to alienate them. If Norbeck found his Senate seat imperiled, Borglum vowed to take to the stump to campaign for him. There would be no Mount Rushmore without federal funding, and no federal funding for Mount Rushmore without Norbeck. Borglum admired not only the senator's political skill but also his progressive politics. "Draw men like Norbeck close to your administration," Borglum advised Hoover. "Men of selfish interest and small political ambition stick with the machine for selfish reasons, but men like Norbeck ... must be disarmed by reason, into effective alliance."[108]

Technology helped Holmes's friends and admirers around the nation celebrate his ninetieth birthday. That night the Columbia Broadcasting System (CBS) aired a thirty-minute live nationwide radio program, organized by law review editors at Harvard, Yale, and Columbia. Six hundred Harvard law students and faculty gathered at Langdell Hall to listen to the address from two large loudspeakers. Before the broadcast, Professor Eugene Wambaugh extolled Holmes's decisions on "due process of law, the most important doctrine in this country," and Pound remarked that Holmes "thinks as the legal world is thinking and changing."[109] Preferring a more intimate gathering, Frankfurter invited ten to twelve people to listen to the broadcast at his Cambridge home at 192 Brattle Street. The guests included Holmes's former secretary Alger Hiss and historian Samuel Eliot Morison. To the other guests,

Morison remarked that Holmes "never made any sense economically" and that his economic theory "wasn't mature." Hiss grew so incensed that he "wanted to get Frankfurter's permission to kick Morison out of the house."[110]

At 10:30 that evening, American Bar Association president Charles Boston and Yale Law School dean Charles Clark spoke from a New York studio followed by Chief Justice Hughes from Washington. "We honor him, but, what is more, we love him," Hughes concluded. "We give him tonight the homage of our hearts."[111] Holmes, however, stole the show. At 10:55, he recited brief concluding remarks that he had written out in longhand. The previous day, a live microphone and receiver had been installed in his second-floor study at 1720 Eye Street. A CBS representative was on hand to make sure that the broadcast went off without a hitch.[112] "There is time to hear the kind voice of friends and to say to one's self, 'The work is done,'" Holmes said in an aristocratic, British-sounding voice. "But just as one says that, the answer comes: 'The race is over, but the work never is done while the power to work remains.'" Holmes concluded by quoting a Latin poem: "'Death plucks my ear and says, "Live—I am coming."'"[113]

The next day, the national media embraced Holmes as an American hero. The front-page New York Times story described him as a "soldier, lawyer, leader of public opinion, and associate justice" and noted the "series of tributes such as have rarely been paid to any man in his own lifetime."[114] The humorist and sportswriter Ring Lardner, not knowing that the justice cared nothing and knew nothing about sports, wrote: "In the opinion of the undersigned, who has had some slight experience in talking into a microphone, Justice Oliver Wendell Holmes did pretty well in his radio debut last night, at least well enough to be entitled to another trial. You must remember he is just a kid breaking in and it is no wonder his voice was a little shaky. With the right kind of teaching he ought to be ready to step in next fall and take charge of one of the minor games like Harvard and Bates or Army v. Ursinus."[115] Holmes thanked Dean Clark of Yale: "Everything went off delightfully and even the dread plunge into the unknown of the radio became a pleasure."[116] A man who lived in "a metal lath house" near Los Angeles complained that he could not hear the broadcast. A Boston company recorded the celebration and sold copies of it on records.[117]

A week after the radio broadcast, fifteen of Holmes's former secretaries, including Francis Biddle, Harvey Bundy, Chauncey Belknap, Tom Corcoran, and Alger Hiss, came from all over the country to see the justice at 1720 Eye Street for about fifteen minutes. They presented him a parchment scroll signed by all of them, and informed him that they had commissioned another portrait by the artist Charles Hopkinson, a sitting portrait for the unfinished Supreme Court building.[118] Before they arrived at the house in which each one had spent a memorable year, the secretaries had gathered at the Mayflower Hotel and shared stories about the justice.[119]

They knew what everyone suspected: that Holmes would not be sitting on the Court much longer. During the summer at Beverly Farms, the justice was "recovering from fatigue."[120] Visitors, including Judges Learned and Augustus Hand and portrait artist Hopkinson, tired him. His young friends were not around to invigorate him. Laski had returned to Britain. The Frankfurters were in Los Angeles, where he was working on a survey of the criminal justice system. By early fall, the justice had his bed moved downstairs. He was stooped and had trouble navigating steps.[121] His devoted Irish housekeeper, Mary Donnellan, kept a close watch over him. He was so tired that he declined to accept the American Bar Association Medal by making another radio address. Instead, he accepted the award with a note in handwriting that was smaller, crabbed, and unsteady.[122] It had become physically hard for him to write.

A month later, Holmes's return to the Court did not go well. "The enervating heat of Washington has left me very languid," he wrote to Frankfurter. "I infer that I must be careful about my heart." He was struggling to keep up with the demands of his work on the Court. He reported feeling "stupid and muddle-headed at the oral arguments" and relied heavily on Brandeis to keep up.[123] Brandeis tried to implement rules to prevent Holmes from getting too fatigued—that Holmes only write opinions during the Court's recess, that he rest for an hour from five to six when the Court was in session, and that visitors stay no longer than an hour and a half.[124] "Matters are not going too well," Brandeis reported to Frankfurter on October 5. The doctor recommended that Holmes resign, but Brandeis talked his friend out of it.[125] Holmes regularly rode out to Arlington Cemetery and silently rubbed his fingers over Fanny's headstone.[126] By the end of October, his condition remained much the same. "OWH is bearing up pretty well," Brandeis wrote Frankfurter again, "but is undoubtedly older; doesn't catch on as he did at arguments and is not having a good time."[127] Holmes's attention span was briefer and briefer. The fatigue brought on by his work cast "a pall" over his face.[128] On Christmas Day, his secretary Chapman Rose phoned Brandeis. Holmes's health had deteriorated, and his doctor advised the justice to refrain from doing any work.[129]

On January 10, 1932, Chief Justice Hughes made a late Sunday morning appointment to see Holmes at 1720 Eye Street. They talked for about half an hour in Holmes's second-floor study. A majority of the justices had asked the chief justice to encourage Holmes to resign because "he could no longer do his full share" of the Court's work. After conferring with Brandeis, Hughes agreed to "take up the matter."[130] Hughes recalled that he told Holmes "a man who had been forty-nine years on the benches of his state and nation should not strain himself by continuing to carry the load when his strength was no longer equal to it."[131] Chapman Rose was called in to retrieve the statute book about tenure and retirement, then waited downstairs. Holmes wrote a letter of resignation to President Hoover dated January 12, 1932, so that the justice could deliver his final opinion. Rose recalled the white-bearded and imposing chief justice walking down the stairs "with tears just streaming down his face."[132] Rose and Mary Donnellan went upstairs to find the justice stoically sitting in his study. Within fifteen minutes, Brandeis arrived and found his friend "as calm and gallant as ever in his life."[133] The day it became official, Rose wired Frankfurter: "THE JUSTICE RESIGNED THIS MORNING. NO SUDDEN REASON. HE IS WELL AND LOOKS FORWARD TO SEEING YOU ON SUNDAY. SENDS LOVE TO BOTH."[134]

When Holmes's letter of resignation was made public, the nation learned what Brandeis and Frankfurter already knew. The letter, Lippmann wrote in his *Herald-Tribune* column, was evidence of "a life done in a great style"; Lippmann predicted that Holmes would live on with Ralph Waldo Emerson and William James as proof of "the American spirit ... He has the gift of delivery. I have no doubt that his prose is the purest American writing in our time."[135] A week later, Lippmann wrote that Holmes's retirement left a void on the Court and left President Hoover with an important decision; Lippmann urged the president to nominate someone who believed that law was not an "iron frame" but "a garment which can be cut and altered. ... That has been the work of the judges from Marshall to Holmes and those who see ahead ought to hope ardently for a true successor in that great line."[136] What Lippmann failed to grasp was that Holmes's retirement also represented a threat to the future of liberalism.[137]

Holmes's retirement triggered an intense behind-the-scenes political battle for control of the future of the Supreme Court. Frankfurter and other liberals immediately began pressuring Hoover to nominate the one judge who could match Holmes's judicial approach and stylistic abilities—Cardozo. A gentle, kind, and soft-spoken man, Benjamin Nathan Cardozo was a lifelong bachelor

who had lived much of his adult life with his two sisters. He was reeling from
the death of his older sister, Nellie, who had raised him as a boy. His father,
Albert, had been a New York Supreme Court judge who had resigned in
disgrace for doling out favors to the Tammany Hall kingpin Boss Tweed. The
son charted a different judicial path than his father. Tutored by Horatio Alger
as a child, he finished first in his class at Columbia at age nineteen, attended
Columbia Law School, and then forged a judicial reputation that was above
reproach. He wrote groundbreaking books on jurisprudence, including *The
Nature of the Judicial Process*, and as a judge and later chief judge on New York's
highest court had written landmark and beautifully crafted opinions, including one of the first on product liability. In experience, writing ability, and
intellect, Cardozo was every bit Holmes's equal.

Clifford Berryman's cartoon about Hoover's nomination of Hughes and Parker

Frankfurter had known Cardozo since the heyday of the House of Truth in 1914 and had been promoting him for the Supreme Court for several years. Cardozo's path to the Court, however, posed multiple political obstacles. The Court already had two New Yorkers, Hughes and Stone, and four easterners in Hughes, Stone, Brandeis, and Roberts. And it already had one Jew in Brandeis. A third New Yorker, a fifth easterner, and a second Jew were not easy sells.

Working with Judge Mack and Rabbi Stephen S. Wise, two of his Zionist allies at the 1919 Paris Peace Conference, Frankfurter pressed Cardozo's case. Hoover's decision to nominate Cardozo involved a number of complicated political calculations in an election year.[138] But Frankfurter and his allies were determined to make it happen. The battle for a more liberal Court, one that began with the displeasure over the nomination of Hughes as chief justice and continued with the fight to reject Parker's nomination, ended with the bid for Cardozo's.

In a January 19 letter to Frankfurter, Rabbi Wise discussed his three days of lobbying in Washington, DC, on Cardozo's behalf. Senator William E. Borah, a progressive Idaho Republican who had supported Hoover during the 1928 election but also had led the charge against Hughes and Parker, joined Wise's cause. Borah met with the president and assured him that Cardozo would be swiftly confirmed.[139] Mark Sullivan, the syndicated *New York Herald-Tribune* columnist and Hoover confidant, also vouched for Cardozo. Stone, a member of Hoover's medicine-ball cabinet that spent mornings playing a medicine-ball game on the south lawn of the White House, went so far as to offer his resignation so that Cardozo could be nominated.[140] Stone feared a nomination that would "emphasize the Court's conservative tendencies."[141]

The Mastiffs, the epithet for the Court's conservative justices McReynolds, Butler, Sutherland, and Van Devanter, also wanted another ally.[142] Even before Holmes's resignation had been made public, they made their first choice known—Hoover's attorney general William D. Mitchell. They figured that Mitchell was the only conservative whom the Senate would confirm.[143] Even Stone predicted to Van Devanter that Mitchell would get the nomination.[144]

Reluctant to part with his attorney general, however, Hoover was swayed more by sectional considerations. Nominating a southerner or westerner would help his 1932 re-election campaign. Stone knew the president's mind and was worried that Hoover would appoint Judge Orie L. Phillips, a federal court of appeals judge from New Mexico.[145] Stone passed along two critiques of Judge Phillips to the president: a *St. Louis Post-Dispatch* editorial and a memorandum about Phillips's opinions from Frankfurter via Brandeis.[146] The memorandum, according to Frankfurter, "proves to the hilt what was to be expected from a young man of our generation who got his law in a correspondence school, and whose strong allegiances are with the Elks."[147] Hoover's other sectional candidate, Senator Joseph T. Robinson of Arkansas, also lacked creativity. A progressive southern Democrat, Robinson had attacked anti-Catholic bigotry and the Ku Klux Klan in a 1928 Senate speech and had been Al Smith's vice-presidential running mate that year. Though he admired Robinson's "large-mindedness" at the 1929 London Naval Disarmament Conference, Frankfurter believed that Robinson's appointment to the Court would be "nothing short of a calamity." Robinson, Frankfurter argued, was "an old-fashioned Democrat in his constitutional outlook," and the Court needed "strengthening not on its stand-pat side but on its imaginative side."[148]

Frankfurter conveyed these thoughts to his first mentor and the highest-ranking member of the Hoover administration he knew well, Secretary of State Stimson. During a meeting in Washington four days after the announcement of Holmes's resignation, Stimson had asked for Frankfurter's views about the vacancy.[149] The day after he wrote Stimson a letter about Joe Robinson, Frankfurter wrote another letter to Stimson championing Cardozo as "*the* only appointment which would be received with national enthusiasm." Frankfurter made the political case that Cardozo's appointment would help Hoover with more voters than Robinson's or anyone else's because of Cardozo's stature not only with the legal community but with the country as a whole. Frankfurter insisted that "the geographic argument"— Cardozo was another New Yorker—"would evaporate like snowflakes in the face of the national acclaim." Finally, Frankfurter rejected the argument that there was a Jewish seat on the Court and therefore that Cardozo, a Sephardic Jew, could only be nominated if Brandeis retired. Cardozo's replacement of Holmes, Frankfurter argued, would send the message that "what counts is not geography, race or religion or party, but unqualified fitness for the functions exercised by the Supreme Court."[150]

Stimson had indeed been discussing the Supreme Court vacancy with the president.[151] At first, he recommended Cardozo and Learned Hand as "good candidates." A few days later, he told the president that Cardozo was the "safest bet," but that Hand also would be "a good candidate."[152] By mid-February, Stimson assured Frankfurter that, based on Stimson's last conversation with the president, Cardozo was "Hoover's first choice." Stimson, who of course had hired Frankfurter in 1906 when most New York law firms had refused to hire Jews, vowed to relay Frankfurter's "objections to making such an appointment in place of Brandeis."[153] Stone maintained that he had no idea what the president would do; Stimson, however, thought it was a done deal.[154] The secretary of state believed that rather than Senator Borah influencing Hoover, it was the other way around. In his February 14 diary entry, Stimson noted that Hoover had talked with Borah about the Supreme Court vacancy and "had very skillfully maneuvered Borah into just the position that we want him on Cardozo, where he has to support Cardozo."[155]

On the morning of February 15, 1932, Hoover phoned the sixty-two-year-old Cardozo, but the judge was on a train to Albany. As soon as he arrived, Cardozo returned Hoover's call and accepted the president's nomination to the Supreme Court.[156] There are many reasons why Hoover ultimately decided to nominate Cardozo. The president had been scarred by the criticism over Hughes's nomination and the rejection of Parker's and could not afford more controversy in an election year. He needed to replace Holmes with someone of equal stature, someone the Senate could not possibly reject. And even he was concerned that the Court was dominated by too many conservatives. Indeed, Hoover's nominees—Hughes, Parker, Roberts, and Cardozo—were neither as liberal as Brandeis nor as conservative as the Mastiffs.[157] The only ones who objected to Cardozo's nomination were the conservative justices. Justice Van Devanter deemed Cardozo "an unfortunate selection" and the national media's reaction as "largely propaganda."[158]

Not surprisingly, Frankfurter was ecstatic. He thanked Secretary of State Stimson for his "not inconsiderable share in the process which led to the result."[159] He also thanked Justice Stone for his "decisive help in achieving a great national good."[160] And he knew that Rabbi Wise and Senator Borah also deserved credit.[161] Ultimately, however, Cardozo was Hoover's call.[162] In a letter to the president, Frankfurter wrote that "never in the history of the Court has an appointment been made to it more fitting to the needs of the Court at the particular period than is true of your appointment of Chief Judge Cardozo."[163] And in an unsigned *New Republic* editorial, Frankfurter explained that Hoover "appointed Cardozo not because he came from the East or the West, not because he was Catholic, Jew or Protestant; he appointed him because he was Cardozo."[164]

To Felix Frankfurter
with the friendship and admiration of
Benjamin N. Cardozo
October, 1929.

Benjamin N. Cardozo

The message of Frankfurter's 1930 book, *The Public and Its Government*, was about getting the best men in government. For Frankfurter, that was what Parker's rejection and Cardozo's nomination were about. That is also why Frankfurter admired Holmes and turned him into a liberal icon. The Supreme Court was only part of the equation. The other part was getting the best man into the White House.

30

A Very Great Beginning

At the same time that he was lobbying Hoover to nominate Cardozo to the Supreme Court, Frankfurter was ramping up the campaign to replace the thirty-first president. Soon after Hoover's victory over Smith in 1928, Frankfurter had started informally advising New York governor Franklin D. Roosevelt, re-establishing a friendship that had begun ten years earlier when Frankfurter had chaired the War Labor Policies Board and Roosevelt had served on the board as assistant naval secretary. Roosevelt had reluctantly entered the New York gubernatorial race in 1928 and had won despite Smith's having lost the state to Hoover. With Frankfurter as his adviser on hydroelectric power, public utilities, and other issues, Roosevelt won re-election two years later (the governorship was a two-year term then). During that time, the political climate had completely changed. The 1929 stock market crash and widespread bank failures had caused financial ruin and left many New Yorkers unemployed and in bread lines. For Frankfurter, Roosevelt was the ideal career politician who could rescue the country from the Hoover administration's failed economic policies and return liberals to political power.

Not everyone shared Frankfurter's faith in Roosevelt. The rap on the governor, according to Frankfurter, was that he "smiles too much" and he was "a little too boyscoutish."[1] Basically, people thought he was an intellectual lightweight. Reformers also thought that Roosevelt had managed to get re-elected in 1930 by taking it easy on the Tammany Hall political machine. These stereotypes took on new life thanks to the man who had first used that term "stereotype" in his book *Public Opinion*. The lack of respect that Lippmann had for Roosevelt was mutual.[2] Roosevelt had repeatedly questioned Lippmann's political acumen ever since the journalist had advised Smith to come out strongly against Prohibition during the 1928 presidential campaign. Since 1930, Frankfurter had been acting as a one-way intermediary between Roosevelt and Lippmann, conveying Roosevelt's ideas to Lippmann as subtly as he could but with little effect.[3]

In his January 8, 1932, *Herald-Tribune* column, "The Candidacy of Franklin D. Roosevelt," Lippmann tried to squelch Roosevelt's political viability by portraying the governor as soulless, two-faced, and unqualified for the presidency. "In the case of Mr. Roosevelt it is not easy to say with certainty whether his left-wing or his right-wing supporters are the more deceived," Lippmann wrote. He described Roosevelt as "a highly impressionable person, without a firm grasp of public affairs and without very strong convictions." Above all, Lippmann reinforced the image of Roosevelt as a lightweight and a "cautious politician" who had accomplished little as governor. "I doubt whether anyone can point to a single act of his which involved any political risk," he wrote. He described Roosevelt's water power policy as having "cost him nothing" and argued that Roosevelt was "forced into assisting the exposure of corruption in New York City." Lippmann also raised the bugaboo that had doomed Smith's 1928 campaign—"that,

Lippmann with photo of Holmes at far right

through his patronage," Roosevelt had "supported the present powers at Tammany Hall." Lippmann predicted that Roosevelt would "fight Tammany only if and when he decides it is safe and profitable to do so." Roosevelt, in Lippmann's view, "is no crusader. He is no tribune of the people. He is no enemy of entrenched privilege. He is a pleasant man who, without any important qualifications for the office, would very much like to be President."[4]

Lippmann's column did not surprise Frankfurter. As he wrote Stanley King, another House of Truth roommate who had worked in the War Department with Lippmann, some of their friends failed to realize how far Lippmann had moved to the right.[5] Yet, as much as he understood Lippmann's growing conservatism, Frankfurter could not fathom the *Herald-Tribune* columnist's ignorance about policy matters, especially about state control of water power. Just to be sure, Frankfurter checked Lippmann's facts with Columbia economics professor James Bonbright, who thought that the column was "grossly unfair" on the issue and wrote: "One trouble with Lippmann is that he knows nothing about the power question himself."[6] Roosevelt, who encouraged one of his power experts to write Lippmann, added: "In spite of his brilliance it is very clear that he has never let his mind travel west of the Hudson or north of the Harlem!"[7]

Lippmann harbored a not-so-secret agenda—promoting the candidacy of Newton D. Baker. Baker had been Wilson's secretary of war and Lippmann and Frankfurter's former boss. Frankfurter professed "a deep personal attachment" to Baker and described their relations as "sweet and candid."[8] Though he supported Baker for a Supreme Court vacancy "because his tolerant nature would satisfy the narrow requirements of liberalism that make a man liberal on the Court," the Democratic presidential nomination was a different matter.[9]

On January 9, Frankfurter wrote a memorandum that he privately began circulating to his closest friends who wanted Baker for president. Baker continued to believe that the United States should join the League of Nations nearly twelve years after the Senate had declined to ratify the Treaty of Versailles. Frankfurter, however, opined that Baker's support for the League of Nations was "not a test of liberalism," for fellow "League of Nationists" included Taft's conservative attorney general Wickersham and Harvard president Lowell.[10] Frankfurter objected to Baker as president for reasons similar to those that had kept him from supporting Davis in 1924. In Frankfurter's view, Baker had been captured by big business while in private practice. Frankfurter ticked off his bill of particulars against Baker as a corporate mouthpiece. As president of the Cleveland Chamber of Commerce, he had supported the open shop, an anti-union position that had prompted Florence Kelley to request his resignation as the president of the National Consumers' League. As founding partner of a powerhouse Cleveland law firm that became Baker Hostetler, he had established himself as one of "the most-sought-after lawyers in big corporate litigation"—much like Davis and Hughes. Baker had represented monopolists who wanted to merge Bethlehem and Youngstown Steel and to consolidate eastern railroads. On behalf of other corporate interests, he had attacked the constitutionality of the Federal Power Act, which established a commission to coordinate hydroelectric power projects.[11]

Though Baker had protected conscientious objectors as secretary of war, he had not stood out as a civil libertarian while in private practice. He had defended free speech in several cases, but only on behalf of the Scripps-Howard newspaper chain. And on the Wickersham Commission on law enforcement, he had signed a report calling for no jury trials in Prohibition cases and had endorsed the "non-publication" of a report about the eyewitnesses who had committed perjury at the trial of jailed labor leader Tom Mooney. "Baker, I am afraid, is fast getting to be a myth," Frankfurter wrote. "I am afraid Baker's liberalism has largely evaporated."[12]

Frankfurter had known about Lippmann's support for Baker since the previous November when they had talked in Cambridge the morning of the Yale-Harvard football game. What troubled Frankfurter were the differences between their private conversations about Baker and Roosevelt and Lippmann's public pronouncements. He felt that Lippmann failed "to realize his responsibility now that he is writing over his own signature and is not anybody else's mouthpiece." In private, he says one thing and in print he continues to "pontificate like Sir Oracle ...," Frankfurter wrote Ellery Sedgwick. "To me, however, he said quite candidly when I said that Baker had a kind of soft quality, 'I know what you mean. He lacks blood and iron.'" Lippmann also conceded that Roosevelt had worked with the legislature "with real understanding and grip" on the issues of unemployment and taxation. Yet in Lippmann's columns about Roosevelt, "so possessed was he to paint a black picture that no chiaroscuro was allowed to enter. Not a word about unemployment and taxation."[13]

Roosevelt had a bigger problem than the biases of Lippmann—opposition from aides to failed 1928 Democratic nominee Smith. Publicly, Smith insisted that he was not a candidate, yet his handlers put his name on the ballot in the Massachusetts primary. Frankfurter was furious. "OUT OF A GREAT PUBLIC FIGURE YOU FELLOWS ARE MAKING A SMALL OFFICE SEEKER," he wired Smith aide Joseph Proskauer.[14] Proskauer insisted that Frankfurter wait until the play's "last act."[15] Frankfurter was dismayed that Smith's aides were tarnishing his brand: "Smith's special contribution to American political life is an infusion of truth-speaking into the fetid atmosphere of dissembling and evasion."[16] A strong Smith supporter in 1928, Frankfurter claimed that Smith was his "first choice" but believed that Smith could not be nominated because "racial and religious intensities are still more virulent than I should have supposed."[17] The opposition by the Smith forces to Roosevelt's candidacy created the perfect opening for Lippmann and other Baker supporters.

In the last of a four-part series on the Democratic Party, Lippmann capitalized on the "increasing tension" between Roosevelt and Smith supporters—how Governor Roosevelt tried "to dissociate himself" from Smith, how Smith "ought to be eternally grateful" that Roosevelt had nominated him for the presidency, and how Roosevelt owed the governor's mansion to Smith—all as a vehicle to promote Baker's candidacy. Lippmann argued that all the infighting between them would hurt the Democrats on a national level, and therefore the best thing they could do was to nominate someone else. That someone was, of course, Baker. Lippmann argued that Baker was "the logical candidate," and that once Americans realized that he was their best hope "in adjusting their policies to their new world position," Baker would be "the inevitable candidate."[18]

Refusing to bow to Lippmann's inevitabilities yet agreeing that Smith's only goal was to prevent Roosevelt's nomination, Frankfurter implored Smith's advisers not to hand the nomination to Baker. To Belle Moskowitz, Frankfurter argued that the Democrats were "jeopardizing what I regard as the predominant national interest, namely, to terminate Hoover's administration, even if a Democratic one were no better." Frankfurter conceded Roosevelt's "limitations" yet insisted that his "general socio-economic directions" were far better than those of Baker or Owen Young, the president of General Electric and another Democratic candidate.[19]

With Smith pledging that he would "fight to the end against any candidate who persists in any demagogic appeal," Lippmann was growing increasingly confident of Baker's chances.[20] Smith's candidacy weakened Roosevelt in the East. In March, Roosevelt defeated Smith in New Hampshire. A month later, however, Smith routed Roosevelt in Massachusetts by a three-to-one margin.[21] "Mr. Roosevelt does not ring true," Lippmann wrote after the Massachusetts defeat.[22] Despite his strong support in the South and West, Roosevelt did not fare well in California, where Speaker of the House John Nance Garner of Texas won a three-way race. "What has been happening in the last few weeks is that the inflated strength of Roosevelt is being deflated as the voters learn more of the record in New York and take their own measure of the candidate," Lippmann wrote after the California primary.[23] Though Roosevelt had captured a majority of the Democratic primaries, Lippmann was so confident of Baker's chances of emerging from a brokered convention that the journalist drafted a foreign policy platform for Baker's campaign.[24] The day in late June 1932 that he arrived at the Democratic National Convention in Chicago, Lippmann announced his endorsement, "Baker for President": "The strength of Baker derives from an almost universal confidence in his ability and in his character. He is profoundly trusted." After a deadlock on the first few ballots, Lippmann predicted that the convention would turn Baker's way.[25]

Roosevelt did not capture the Democratic nomination on the first, second, or even third ballot. He was about a hundred votes shy of the two-thirds needed for the nomination. Lippmann's predictions about Baker's emergence as a compromise candidate appeared to be coming true. Baker's right-hand man, Ralph Hayes, worked behind the scenes, and several states indicated that they would jump to Baker on the fourth or fifth ballot. But on the fourth and final ballot, Speaker Garner pledged his California delegates to Roosevelt in exchange for the vice-presidential spot on the ticket. Publisher William Randolph Hearst and former Treasury secretary McAdoo urged Garner to make the move because they preferred Roosevelt to the internationalist Baker.[26] Thanks to the back-room deal, Roosevelt was the Democratic nominee. Bucking the long-observed tradition of not accepting the Democratic nomination in person, Roosevelt flew to Chicago, addressed the convention on July 2, and promised the American people a radical departure from the Republican policies of the previous twelve years. "I pledge you—I pledge myself—to a new deal for the American people," Roosevelt said. "Let us all here assembled constitute ourselves prophets of a new order of competence and of courage. This is more than a political campaign; it is a call to arms."[27]

The "new deal" line, a nod to Theodore Roosevelt's Square Deal, ushered in a new era in American politics. Just what Roosevelt meant by it no one knew, but some were not impressed, including Lippmann. He was so disgusted by the convention that he took a vacation in mid-July and did not plan on returning until after Labor Day. Before he left, Lippmann asked Baker's advice about whom to support in the upcoming campaign. He could not stand the idea of voting for Hoover because it "would signify forgiveness of the Republican record," and yet he had "no confidence in Roosevelt."[28] Baker advised him to wait as long as possible before making an endorsement.

During his trip to Chicago, Roosevelt called Frankfurter to congratulate him on news from Massachusetts.[29] On June 22, Governor Joseph B. Ely had nominated Frankfurter to the Massachusetts Supreme Judicial Court. The idea, the product of an intense lobbying campaign by Frankfurter's friends, including Sacco-Vanzetti lawyers Thompson and Ehrmann, was to restore the prestige of the state's highest court. Instead, the appointment, which was subject to approval by the governor's executive council, revived the whole controversy. Ex-governor Fuller, who had refused to pardon the Italian anarchists or to commute their death sentences, predicted that with Frankfurter on the bench, "I see no reason why murder should not flourish here in Massachusetts."[30] Governor Ely countered that Holmes, Brandeis, and Cardozo all endorsed Frankfurter. Yet no one seemed to have inquired whether Frankfurter would accept the nomination. Brandeis believed that Frankfurter could do more good at Harvard and advised him not to take the job.[31] And Holmes refused to take sides.[32] On June 29, Frankfurter declined the nomination but was sworn to secrecy until July 12, when Governor Ely, unable to persuade him to change his mind, made the letter public.[33]

Frankfurter believed that he would be "more useful both to the law and to the country" by staying where he was. In the short run, he wrote Roosevelt, he wanted to work "to turn out Hoover and help elect you."[34] In mid-July, Frankfurter pumped Roosevelt aide Sam Rosenman and two old friends from the National Consumers' League for information about Roosevelt's record as governor.[35] "You see one of the gains from not having gone on the Massachusetts Court," Frankfurter wrote Molly Dewson, "is that I can be alive during the campaign."[36] At Roosevelt's invitation, the Frankfurters stayed overnight at the governor's mansion.[37]

As a legal adviser, Frankfurter helped Roosevelt achieve a major political victory, one that changed some people's minds about the candidate's presidential timber. The biggest knock against Roosevelt was that he had ignored evidence of corruption against Tammany Hall. For nearly two years, Samuel Seabury had been investigating Tammany's influence on all phases of New York government. In February, New York County sheriff Thomas Farley resigned. Seabury's chief target, however, was New York City mayor Jimmy Walker. In late July, Seabury presented Roosevelt with a report charging Mayor Walker with corruption. Walker responded in writing, and Seabury replied to Walker's response. After reading all the reports, Frankfurter advised Roosevelt that, if true, "the facts ineluctably compel removal of the Mayor."[38] Backed by Frankfurter, Roosevelt decided to hold his own trial instead of turning the case over to the courts. After Roosevelt heard witnesses for several weeks and cross-examined Walker for several days, the mayor resigned on September 1 without mounting a defense. "WARM CONGRATULATIONS," Frankfurter wired Roosevelt. "RESIGNATION IS CONCESSION AND COMPLETE VINDICATION OF YOUR FIRMNESS, SKILL, AND FAIRNESS AS CHIEF EXECUTIVE."[39] After Roosevelt's ousting of Mayor Walker, Frankfurter promoted the idea that the trial had answered Roosevelt's critics. In a September 7 letter to the *New York Times*, Frankfurter blasted a New York trial judge's support for Walker and criticism of Roosevelt: "No one who has disinterestedly followed in detail the Walker hearings in Albany can have failed to be impressed with the Governor's mastery of a series of complicated transactions and with his skill and patience in exploring them."[40]

That summer, Hoover contributed to his declining popularity. In late July, he ordered General Douglas MacArthur to evict 45,000 unemployed war veterans who were camped out in Washington, DC, while seeking early payment of their bonuses. The Bonus Army petitioned Congress for the immediate payment of wartime bonuses due in 1945. The legislation died in the Senate. The veterans occupied Anacostia, a neighborhood in southeast Washington, as a sign of peaceful protest. With tanks, bayonets, and tear gas, General MacArthur beat the bonus marchers, burned their camp, and forcibly removed them.[41] A month later, hundreds of banks collapsed and plunged the country deeper into economic despair. The Bonus Army fiasco, bank collapse, and nearly 25 percent unemployment further eroded whatever public confidence was left in the Hoover administration.

Between Roosevelt's conduct of the Walker hearings and Hoover's ineptitude on domestic issues, Lippmann had no choice but to announce his support for Roosevelt. Even a muted endorsement from Lippmann, whose "Today and Tomorrow" column was syndicated in newspapers with more than 6 million readers, meant something. "It seems probable," Allen Nevins wrote in a *Herald-Tribune* Sunday magazine profile, "that Mr. Lippmann is gaining a greater influence than any other editor in the country."[42] In his

Herbert Hoover

October 7 *Herald-Tribune* column, Lippmann wrote that "after much hesitation and serious misgiving, the election of Governor Roosevelt now seems to me preferable to the re-election of President Hoover." After revealing his distaste for the back-room dealings that handed Roosevelt the nomination and the belief that the governor was "distinguished more for his amiability than for his grasp of public affairs," Lippmann conceded that events of the previous two months had forced him to revise his thinking. The Walker hearings loomed largest for Lippmann, a long-standing critic of Roosevelt's coziness with Tammany Hall and a purveyor of the image of Roosevelt as a lightweight. For Lippmann, the Walker hearings were "a very severe test" and demonstrated Roosevelt's "capacity to master an exceedingly intricate mass of evidence." Complimenting Roosevelt's "wisely conceived campaign" and pledging to vote "cheerfully" for him, Lippmann looked ahead to the next two years and predicted that Roosevelt would work better with the Democratic Congress and would make "many readjustments that it is imperative to make." For Lippmann, Roosevelt's election would produce national unity whereas Hoover's re-election would open up "a long vista of frustrated discontent and recrimination."[43]

Despite his endorsement, Lippmann never warmed to Roosevelt. He criticized Roosevelt's refusal to take a firm stand on whether the members of the Bonus Army should receive their bonuses early despite bulging budget deficits.[44] Frankfurter agreed with Lippmann's criticisms, assuring him that Roosevelt was privately opposed to the Bonus Bill and defending the candidate against charges of "indecisiveness."[45] At times, however, even Lippmann defended Roosevelt. When the pro-Hoover *Herald-Tribune* editorial page questioned Roosevelt's "2 a.m. courage" in times of crisis and revisited Roosevelt's preconvention compromises with Tammany Hall, Lippmann reminded his readers that the election was a choice between Roosevelt and Hoover: "I do not know that Mr. Roosevelt has such courage. It can hardly be argued that Mr. Hoover has displayed much of it."[46]

Another person who had changed his mind about the presidential election was Borglum. In a June article "Why I Am a Republican," he explained how Americans had accumulated great wealth based on technological innovations, including the telegraph, telephone, automobile, airplane, highways, motion pictures, radio, and submarine. In addition to these innovations, Americans have "forced a new standard of economics" and a "new philosophy of government." His article radiated his cultural nationalism and explained his longtime political activism. Since he was "a good Republican" yet had resisted partisanship and supported Theodore Roosevelt in 1912, he had fought "when the issues permitted me to help the farmer against known political enemies, and *kept the non-partisana still within the old party*." At first, Borglum endorsed Hoover out of a reluctance "to turn the national government over to strange hands." After predicting Hoover's re-election, he explained his sectional interests: "I want the west, the north-west, to win, because I want the farmer to get his share of America's *freedom* and *smiles*."[47] Just as he had warned Hoover in October 1931 about the "delicate condition of the entire northwestern part of the Republican Party" and had urged Hoover to court western progressives, including Senator Norbeck, "Why I Am a Republican" attempted to "interest the independent voter, the class I belong to anyway."[48]

A few weeks after the publication of his article endorsing Hoover, Borglum proposed a Hoover campaign pin and button for sale by the women's division of the Republican National Committee. The button that he had made for La Follette in 1928, Borglum wrote, had raised $150,000.[49] The Republican National Committee agreed to a Hoover button.[50] But just as he had switched from La Follette to Coolidge during the 1928 campaign, Borglum jumped ship in the middle of the 1932 presidential race and in early August began making a campaign medallion for Roosevelt and Garner. It looked very much like the La Follette medallion, with the two Democratic candidates in profile as if they were minted on a US coin. The bronze medallions would be on sale for one, five, and ten dollars to benefit the campaign. On September 4 at Hyde Park, Roosevelt bought the first bronze medallion from Borglum for one dollar.[51] "I am an independent Republican," Borglum announced, "and I am voting for Governor Roosevelt for the same reasons I was for T.R."[52]

In a September 6 speech in Stamford, Connecticut, to 200 Roosevelt supporters in the Nonpartisan League, Borglum framed his decision to vote for Roosevelt as one of principle. He praised Roosevelt's trial of Mayor Walker and his support for the "small home owner, for the farmer, for the forgotten man." Borglum believed that it was time to end "12 years of Republic misrule." Hoover, Borglum argued, had never shown much interest in farm relief and bungled his handling of the Bonus Army. Above all, the sculptor explained that he was a Republican voting for Roosevelt because Roosevelt shared the political philosophy of Abraham Lincoln. He saw Roosevelt as the candidate "who thinks the whole nation and not simply the Wall Street interests need his unprejudiced care."[53]

Borglum's change of heart was also personal and instrumental—he blamed Hoover for the lack of work during the summer of 1932 at Mount Rushmore. The project was entirely dependent on the support of the federal government. From the moment he had taken office, however, Hoover had been slow to appoint members of the project's governing body, the Mount Rushmore National Memorial Commission. And when the first wave of commissioners including Coleman du Pont and Julius Rosenwald died or retired, Hoover dragged his heels about replacing them. "I have deep and bitter grounds for resentment that I can neither rub out nor overlook," Borglum wrote a Republican newspaper editor. "For three years, I have waited, hoped and waited."[54]

Because of his frustration with the lack of progress at Mount Rushmore during the summer of 1932, Borglum began making noises again about returning to Stone Mountain. The indictments against him were finally dropped in early June, and he met with Georgia officials, including Governor Richard B. Russell Jr., about resuming work on the Confederate Memorial.[55] The talks, however, went nowhere because of a lack of funds. The sculptor knew that his legacy lay at Mount Rushmore and that he needed the federal government's interest and financial support to finish it: "This is a Government work."[56]

Impassable roads from Keystone, South Dakota, to the top of the mountain made it difficult for Borglum to get his car to Mount Rushmore without ending up in a ditch. The state government refused to contribute anything for the monument, only for new roads that had not yet been built.[57] The sculptor knew that he needed the federal government's help now more than ever if work resumed in 1933 or beyond. In the fall of 1932, Mount Rushmore received a $100,000 federal appropriation—enough money to allow him to continue work on Washington's shoulders and coat and on Jefferson's head.[58] But to complete the project, the sculptor needed more funding and a new administration behind him.

By September 1932, Borglum was writing everyone he knew in politics about why he was supporting Roosevelt. He had known Roosevelt since the sculptor's House of Truth days. Indeed, Borglum had wanted Roosevelt to oversee the aircraft investigation because the sculptor considered the then assistant naval secretary an honest man.[59] Fourteen years later, Borglum backed Roosevelt for the presidency. "I am for Roosevelt," he wrote un-convinced journalist William Allen White. "I am for a new day and a new deal."[60] Borglum joined the National Progressive League led by Republican senator George W. Norris and composed largely of former Bull Moosers who had supported Theodore Roosevelt and now backed Franklin.[61] "[T]he big thing I see is that in Franklin Delano Roosevelt America has a new instrument, keen, well-tempered, seasoned and unafraid," Borglum wrote Senator Norris.[62] He saw a direct connection between the 1912 and 1932 elections. "America's republic has been saved by the independents, by the mature revolters of the 1912 split ...," Borglum wrote Gardner Jackson the day before the election. He wondered if Franklin Roosevelt would "take the great mandate given him and be, in addition to the routine admin-istration president, another Jefferson, Jackson, Lincoln or T.R.?" Borglum made many suggestions to Jackson about agriculture, flood control, and Roosevelt's cabinet. And he "would put Frankfurter in as Attorney General even if hell froze over."[63]

Newspaper rumors and Borglum's wishes to the contrary, Frankfurter was not angling to be attorney general or solicitor general. But he joined his old friend in the National Progressive League and since late summer had been appealing to his friends, many of them independents and undecided voters, to vote for Roosevelt. Shortly before the election, Frankfurter hosted a reception for Roosevelt with the Progressive League of Massachusetts at Parents House in Groton. Frankfurter introduced Roosevelt to Elizabeth Evans, who was voting for Socialist Party candidate Norman Thomas. "Gov. Roosevelt," Evans said, "I would rather see you in the White House than anyone since Abraham Lincoln and Norman Thomas, Oh, Oh, I beg your pardon, I mean Woodrow Wilson."[64] Everyone laughed. Frankfurter, however, was determined to persuade his friends who supported Thomas or Hoover or who chose to sit out the race entirely.[65]

Rabbi Wise, Frankfurter's ally in promoting Cardozo's Supreme Court nomination, was one of the New York reformers on the sidelines. In 1930, Wise and others had presented Roosevelt with evidence of Mayor Walker's corruption, yet Roosevelt had done nothing. Recalling Frankfurter had refused to support Davis and instead campaigned for La Follette in 1924, Wise predicted that Frankfurter would regret supporting Roosevelt. "I say to you as a liberal and a progressive and a Democrat,—you will rue your decision to give your support to him," Wise wrote, arguing that Roosevelt was only progressive because his handlers had told them that it would get him elected. Wise bought into the stereotypes about Roosevelt, that "there is no basic stuff in the man." He believed that there would be no real difference between a Roosevelt administration and that of Harding, Coolidge, or Hoover.[66]

Insisting that he had voted for a Democratic presidential candidate only twice in his life, Frankfurter downplayed his close working relationship with Roosevelt in favor of arguments based on pragmatism and personal experience. "I can with an easy conscience vote for Roosevelt," Frankfurter wrote Wise. "I know his limitations and inadequacies, but I also know his qualities, and I know you do them very much less than justice." Frankfurter ticked off Roosevelt's accomplishments with water power, public utilities, and the recent Walker hearings. He told Wise to stop being so idealistic and to vote for the best candidate on the ballot. "Politics, perhaps you sometimes forget, is a choice of the second best," he reminded Wise.[67]

On the campaign trail, Frankfurter made it his mission to help Roosevelt win Massachusetts, where he had been trounced in the state's primary. Frankfurter looked to the only candidate who could win the state for Roosevelt, Al Smith. Irish Catholics committed to Smith were threatening to stay home on Election Day. After Smith had endorsed Roosevelt in Albany in mid-October, Frankfurter lobbied Smith confidants Belle Moskowitz and Herbert Bayard Swope to persuade the former nominee to come to Massachusetts on Roosevelt's behalf.[68] Over lunch, Frankfurter made his pitch directly to Smith and then followed up with a note of encouragement: "Your speech here will bring wisdom and guidance not only for our own day but for generations of Americans to come."[69] Smith agreed to speak in Providence and Boston, to put aside his differences with Roosevelt, and to support the Democratic ticket. Frankfurter joined Smith's party in Providence and for the train ride to Boston.[70] Thanks to a national radio broadcast, Smith's October 27 Boston speech projected a Democratic Party unity not seen at the convention. "Al's visit had the effect of a mass movement," Frankfurter wrote Swope.[71] He also reported on Smith's Boston speech to Lippmann and predicted that even though Hoover would probably win Massachusetts, "Al was at his very best. And the outpouring of affection and devotion to him both at Providence and here had a quality about it such as I have never seen given to any American political figure."[72]

Frankfurter also made his pitch directly to Massachusetts voters. In an October 15 *Harvard Crimson* article, "Why I Am Voting for Roosevelt," he

Franklin D. Roosevelt (waving at center)

reached out to disenchanted Massachusetts Democrats who would otherwise vote for Hoover. He blamed Hoover for the Great Depression and
contrasted Hoover's handling of the Depression with Roosevelt's response
in New York. Finally, Frankfurter urged Massachusetts voters to vote for a
Democratic president: "To reward Mr. Hoover with re-election would be to
deny party responsibility. The best hope of the country as well as the effective
working of our party system requires the rejection of President Hoover and
his party.[73] Beneath the headline "FRANKFURTER FOR CHANGE," the *New York
Times* reprinted part of his *Crimson* essay.[74] A week later, he elaborated on his
support for Roosevelt at Boston's Mount Vernon Church.[75] At Roosevelt's
request, he also attacked Hoover's economic policy during a November 5
campaign speech on Boston's WBJ radio station.[76] "Neither before the depression nor since has Mr. Hoover shown any awareness that we are living
in a new economic world," Frankfurter said. After reviewing Roosevelt's
record as governor on taxation, power regulation, and unemployment relief,
Frankfurter concluded: "Governor Roosevelt's outlook and achievements
and the courage and hope of which his life is a triumph, justify us in following his lead. Supported by the liberal and progressive sentiment of the
country, he can help us out of our present moral and material morass and
start new ways of thought into new deeds of action." Roosevelt's election,
he predicted, could "well be the augur of happier days."[77]

Roosevelt carried Massachusetts and forty-one other states, winning 472
electoral votes to Hoover's 59. Even Lippmann declared that Roosevelt's
victory was an "electoral revolution."[78] Frankfurter agreed with Lippmann
that Roosevelt's victory was epochal. "YOUR CAMPAIGN HAS EDUCATED THE
HOPES OF THE NATION AND INVIGORATED ITS FAITH," he had wired Roosevelt
a few days before Election Day. "AS A RESULT, NOT SINCE WILSON'S CAMPAIGN
IN 1912 HAS THE PUBLIC TEMPER BEEN MORE RIPE TO SUPPORT THE PROGRES-
SIVE LEADERSHIP WHICH YOU HAVE ESPOUSED."[79] For Frankfurter, Roosevelt's
victory was "a very great beginning."[80]

Roosevelt's election ended an era. With their preferred candidate in the
White House, liberals struggled with what role the Supreme Court, sans
Justice Holmes, would play in the realization of their political agenda.

31

The Hard Case Has Melted

Roosevelt's election had little or no impact on Justice Holmes. Three days before Election Day, he had confessed his preference for Hoover. Never much of a political animal, not having voted in years, though a lifelong Republican, Holmes recognized that Hoover "had little political judgment."[1] As Wilson's assistant secretary of the navy, Roosevelt had attended Holmes's Sunday afternoon teas but did not make a great first impression on the justice.[2] "Roosevelt when I knew him," Holmes recalled, "struck me as a good fellow with rather a soft edge years ago."[3] A quotation often attributed to Holmes about Roosevelt—"A second-class intellect. But a first-class temperament"—probably referred to Theodore, not Franklin.[4]

Holmes continued to serve as an important symbol for the role that the Supreme Court could play in his friends' political activism. They still admired him for his refusal to interfere with most state and federal economic regulation and his pioneering opinions protecting free speech, voting rights, and fair criminal trials. He had allowed the political process to play out in most instances, yet after the world war he had begun to protect the rights of the politically powerless. He had shown how to strike a balance between democracy and liberty.

After retiring in January 1932, Holmes recovered his physical health, but his memory and attention span continued to fade.[5] His reading interests consisted of mostly detective stories, "with an emphasis on the need for action on every page."[6] His secretary reread to him the complete run of Sherlock Holmes.[7] The retired justice found it increasingly hard to write letters to friends. The only thing that he published after leaving the bench was a short introduction to a Frankfurter-edited volume commemorating Brandeis's seventy-fifth birthday. "Whenever he left my house I was likely to say to my wife, 'There goes a really good man …,'" Holmes wrote of

Eleanor (left), Franklin (center), and James (right) Roosevelt outside 1720 Eye Street on the justice's ninety-second birthday

Brandeis. "In the moments of discouragement that we all pass through, he always has had the happy word that lifts up one's heart."[8]

In retirement, Holmes revealed his softer side. "The hard case of O.W.H. has melted; he now would like petting, the kind of tender affection that Mary [Donnellan, his housekeeper] gives him," Frankfurter wrote. During the summer of 1932, the Frankfurters often visited Holmes at Beverly Farms, where he had an elevator installed like the one at 1720 Eye Street so that he could greet his frequent visitors on the first floor without having to sleep there. The presidential campaign that summer did not interest him. "It's all very remote to me," Holmes said. "I'm dead. I'm like a ghost on a battlefield with bullets flying through me." Marion gently reminded him that he had never been interested in politics. Yet sometimes she visited him alone and saw how sad and lonely he was. "Hasn't a man a right to be dead at 91?" he asked her.[9]

After one lunch with the Frankfurters, Holmes asked if they had ever read the Civil War poem "The Old Sergeant." They had not, so he pulled a copy from his bookshelf. "I don't know whether I can read this," he said, "the last few times I made a mess of it." They encouraged him to try. The poem told the story of a Confederate soldier wounded at Shiloh and dying in an army hospital. "He was terribly moved by it," Marion recalled, "and before the end the tears were streaming down his face and his voice broke and trembled. I couldn't control myself either." Holmes asked them in a lighthearted way: "Doesn't that *get* you?" He then read them another Civil War poem, and "we wept all over again."[10]

The Civil War had taught Holmes about duty, honor, and the virtues of doing one's job well every single day. Yet it also taught him to care less about ideology and political or social causes and more about his craft as a lawyer, a scholar, and a judge. "The capacity to care like the devil about something and to care all the time is a gift like any other," he told Marion, "and it makes the difference between people."[11] The problem with Holmes in retirement was that he had nothing left to care about. He returned to live in Washington every fall, still hired a new secretary every Term, but took little interest in the daily work of the Supreme Court. Shortly after his retirement, someone asked him if he ever read the Court's opinions, and he replied: "Not a damned one."[12]

If he had, Holmes would have seen how his opinions continued to influence the role of the Court. His defense of fair criminal trials started to gain traction, especially for southern blacks. In November 1932, the Court reversed the death sentences of the Scottsboro Boys, young black men convicted of raping two white women on an Alabama freight train. The allegations began in 1931 after a fight between nine black teenagers and several whites who had been thrown off the train. The police stopped the train, the two white women cried rape, and the nine black youths were taken to the nearest county seat in Scottsboro for trial. The military kept the suspects under constant guard. The trial judge generally charged the entire local bar to represent them; a Tennessee lawyer volunteered his assistance but had not prepared the case or spoken with any of the defendants. Twelve days later, an all-white jury convicted and sentenced eight of the nine to death. As with the Bard and Fleming case in Kentucky, the NAACP's National Lawyers Committee had been reluctant to get involved. Instead, the International Labor Defense, the legal arm of the Communist Party, appealed the convictions. The Alabama Supreme Court denied the appeals of all but one defendant, though the state's chief justice dissented because of the unfairness of the trials.[13] The appeal relied on Holmes's decision in *Moore v. Dempsey*

Holmes in spring 1928 at the Old Soldiers' Home

about mob-dominated criminal trials, the only Supreme Court case that had ever interfered with a state criminal conviction on due process grounds.

In a 7–2 decision known as *Powell v. Alabama*, the Supreme Court found that the trial of the Scottsboro Boys had violated their constitutional rights to due process but for entirely new reasons—the "failure of the trial court to give them reasonable time and opportunity to secure counsel" and "the failure of the trial court to make an effective appointment of counsel." Justice Sutherland's majority opinion cited "the ignorance and illiteracy of the defendants, their youth, the circumstances of public hostility," their imprisonment by "military forces," their inability to communicate with their friends and families in other states, and "above all that they stood in deadly peril of their lives."[14]

Though a member of the National Lawyers Committee of the NAACP, which had been slow to take on the case, Frankfurter celebrated the Court's decision in the *New York Times* and noted that "even lay comment upon the Scottsboro decision was alive to a significance that went beyond a respite from death for seven illiterate Negro boys." He argued that the Court had written "a notable chapter in the history of liberty." It was one thing, according to Frankfurter, to use the Due Process Clause to strike down state socioeconomic legislation in order to protect liberty or property rights. It was another to invoke basic notions of due process to protect fair criminal trials, especially those of southern blacks. The immediate purpose of the Fourteenth Amendment, he argued, was to protect "black men from oppressive and unequal treatment by whites." In the criminal justice system, the unpopular and less fortunate deserved basic procedural protections that prevented a rigged game. That was Frankfurter's problem with the Sacco-Vanzetti trial, Holmes's problem with the trials of Bard and Fleming, and the Court's problem with the Scottsboro trials. Frankfurter believed that *Powell v. Alabama*, like *Moore v. Dempsey*'s prohibition of mob-dominated criminal trials, made the system more fair: "Not only must there be a court free from coercion, but the accused must be furnished with means of presenting his defense. For this the assistance of counsel is essential."[15]

With Roosevelt in office and filling future vacancies, Frankfurter expected the Supreme Court to be composed of more justices like Holmes, Cardozo, Stone, and Brandeis; that it would be able to resist the temptation of using the Due Process Clause to strike down socioeconomic legislation based on political and economic predilections; and that it would invoke due process to guard against blatantly unfair criminal trials as in *Powell v. Alabama*.

Roosevelt's presidency, as well as his future Supreme Court nominations, almost never happened. On the evening of February 15, 1933, three weeks before his inauguration, the president-elect returned from a two-week fishing vacation to a cheering throng at Miami's Bayfront Park. Immediately after Roosevelt delivered some brief remarks while sitting on top of an open car, Giuseppe Zangara, an unemployed bricklayer and anarchist, stood on a small chair and began firing his .32 caliber pistol from less than twenty-five feet away. Zangara wounded the mayor of Chicago, Anton Cermak, and four others before someone grabbed his arm.[16] Roosevelt was unharmed because he had just slid into his seat, because Zangara stood only just over five feet tall, and because of sheer luck.[17] Cermak, who died a few weeks later from his injuries, told Roosevelt in the hospital: "I'm glad it was me instead of you."[18]

In the days and weeks before the inauguration, Frankfurter had been advising Roosevelt on the composition of his cabinet and other matters. "You have got the essentials under way," he wrote Roosevelt in late February. "Now I look forward to having your Inaugural modify greatly the defeatist attitude so sedulously cultivated recently."[19] On Saturday, March 4, Roosevelt took the oath of office from Chief Justice Charles Evans Hughes. In one of his most famous speeches, the nation's thirty-second president gave hope to the starving and unemployed American people, that in times of suffering "the only thing we have to fear ... is fear itself."[20]

Four days after the inauguration, Frankfurter arranged a surprise for Holmes's ninety-second birthday.[21] That afternoon, Frankfurter joined former secretary Tom Corcoran and current secretary Donald Hiss for lunch with the justice at 1720 Eye Street. Donald, who like his older brother Alger worked for Holmes after graduating from Harvard Law School, had purchased some champagne from a bootlegger and informed the justice that it had been a gift from an ambassador.[22] Holmes knew better. "Young fellow," he told Frankfurter, "I don't want you to misunderstand things: I do not deal with bootleggers but I am open to corruption."[23] After drinking three or four glasses, Holmes announced: "It feels good to your face."[24] Frankfurter, who had instructed Hiss to hold all telephone calls, was interrupted by a call from the White House and was informed that Roosevelt was expecting him. "I am at a better place," Frankfurter told the White House aide. "I am at Justice Holmes'."[25]

At 3:30 p.m., Frankfurter left for the White House. Only he, Hiss, and housekeeper Mary Donnellan knew about the birthday surprise. Hiss read to the justice. Instead of an afternoon drive, Holmes decided to take a nap in his alpaca coat that he often wore around the house. Hiss kept checking the front window.

Shortly after 5:30 p.m., a black convertible Packard pulled up in front of 1720 Eye Street.[26]

"Mr. Justice," Hiss said.

"Yes."

"I think the President—President Roosevelt is calling."

"Don't be an idiot, boy," Holmes replied, as he often referred to his secretaries. "The President wouldn't call on me."[27]

Hiss checked again. A crowd had gathered around the convertible outside. He quickly helped the justice change from his alpaca to his swallowtail coat. The doorbell rang.[28] The president wore a double-breasted suit and a light gray fedora. Mrs. Roosevelt wore a short brown beaver fur coat, matching hat, and brown walking shoes.[29] Their strapping twenty-five-year-old son, James, wore an overcoat and a dark bowler hat. It is unclear whether FDR used his son and a cane or a ramp and a wheelchair to navigate the brownstone's nine front stairs. With or without his braces, the president could not navigate stairs; the Secret Service usually installed ramps for his wheelchair.[30]

Roosevelt had broken presidential protocol by calling on a private residence. He did not seem to care much about tradition. Two days after taking office, he had suspended gold payments from the Treasury and had declared a national bank holiday to prevent any more banks from collapsing. At 10:00 a.m., he had conducted the first press conference in the White House in nearly twelve years as approximately 130 reporters crowded around his desk in the Oval Office and peppered him with questions for forty-five minutes.[31] If he could suspend gold payments, close the banks, and banter with reporters, he could visit 1720 Eye Street. Frankfurter joined the presidential party for the surprise.

Roosevelt, his son James, and the Secret Service men rode in the elevator; Frankfurter and Mrs. Roosevelt took the stairs. They all greeted the justice in his second-floor study. The conversation was "very animated" and "very easy."[32] The president admired the two swords over Holmes's fireplace. Holmes said his paternal great-grandfather had carried them with him when he fought in the French and Indian War.[33] James Roosevelt recalled his father's "monumental glee when we found that wonderful old Yankee browsing through his noted collection of French novels which he kept hidden behind his law books."[34] Frankfurter recalled that they talked about "prize fights—John L. Sullivan and Jim Corbett."[35] Eleanor presented Holmes with a bouquet of roses and enjoyed her time with him. "He is a fine old man," she wrote her friend Lorena Hickok, "with flashes of his old wit and incisiveness."[36]

Holmes thought that polio had changed the president. The "soft edge" that Holmes had detected in 1918 was gone. "He has a much stronger face than when I knew him before," Holmes told Hiss. "He had a very handsome

The last known photo of Holmes, in December 1934

face then, but there was a weakness in it. Now, there is strength in it."[37] Four days into his presidency, Roosevelt asked if Holmes had any advice. The justice is often apocryphally quoted as saying "Form your battalions and fight, sir."[38] The truth is more complicated and more revealing of Holmes and of the dilemmas facing a country mired in an economic disaster. "No, Mr. President," Holmes said, according to Donald Hiss. "The time I was in retreat, the Army was in retreat in disaster, the thing to do was to stop the retreat, blow your trumpet, have them give the order to charge. And that's what you are doing. This is the admirable thing to do and the only thing you could have done."[39] Roosevelt also asked if there was anything he could do for him. Holmes joked about lifting the bank holiday or making an exception for retired justices because he had not been able to pay his household staff.[40]

By the end of the president's forty-minute visit with Holmes, a large crowd had gathered in the dark outside the justice's red-brick townhouse near

Seventeenth and Eye Streets. Harvard law professor Thomas Reed Powell was there and shouted: "Hey Felix!"[41] Frankfurter waved and jumped into the back of the Packard convertible with Roosevelt and his son James.[42] Members of the press also waited outside.[43] Eleanor saw Associated Press reporter Bess Furman, who accompanied the First Lady and her little black dog, Meggie, on the short walk to the White House.[44] Furman's wire story described the Frankfurter-arranged visit as when "a President called 'liberal' was talking with the venerable Ex-Justice famed for liberal opinions."[45]

Epilogue

Sometime between his lunch with Holmes on his ninety-second birthday and the president's visit to 1720 Eye Street later that afternoon, Frankfurter had declined Roosevelt's offer to be solicitor general.[1] Roosevelt said he needed Frankfurter in Washington for advice on a wide range of issues. Frankfurter had already prepared his answer, since rumors about his being named attorney general or solicitor general in the new administration had been swirling since early November. In the meantime, he had been conferring with Brandeis, who had been advising him to decline either post.[2]

At the start of their conversation, Frankfurter assured Roosevelt that he was more invested in the success of this administration than in any that had come before, including TR's or Wilson's. Serving as the government's representative before the Supreme Court, Frankfurter explained to Roosevelt, was a sixteen-hour-a-day job and would leave him no time to advise the president on other issues. Frankfurter argued that he could do the administration more good from the outside. Soon after the election, he had accepted the Eastman Fellowship to spend the 1933–34 academic year at Oxford. "I think I can be of use to you even while I am abroad," he told the president, "and of more use to you than as Solicitor General."[3]

"I am going to talk Dutch to you," Roosevelt replied. He explained that he eventually wanted to nominate Frankfurter to the Supreme Court, and it would be much easier to nominate the solicitor general who had defended the US government rather than a Harvard law professor who had declined a position on the Massachusetts Supreme Judicial Court and had defended Sacco and Vanzetti. "[T]hen there is ... your race," Roosevelt said, referring to Frankfurter's Jewish heritage. "But once you are Solicitor General, these various objections will be forgotten or disappear." Roosevelt said all this while smiling. Frankfurter was flattered but unmoved. He refused to take one job that he did not want in the hopes of landing another. "All that must be left to the future," he told the president. "I really don't think I ought to

Roosevelt (center) with Borglum (right) at Mount Rushmore dedication on
August 30, 1936

take a post at which I know I cannot be of the use that I can be in remaining where I am, simply because it may promote my going elsewhere."[4]
Frankfurter never regretted his decision. "Everyone has been after me—as
tho I could move mountains ...," he wrote Marion from Washington in
April 1933. "I'm so glad we're not in office—it would be awful & distract-
ing beyond measure & truly not satisfying."[5] The Frankfurters were never
happier than they were at Oxford.[6]

Before, during, and after the year in Oxford, Frankfurter's influence
on the Roosevelt administration, the New Deal, and the future of federal regulation was incalculable. For example, when the first draft of the
Securities Act of 1933 met resistance in Congress, Frankfurter enlisted two
former students and another protégé—Tom Corcoran, James Landis, and
Benjamin Cohen—and for two weeks straight all three redrafted the bill.[7]
When the Securities Act of 1933 proved insufficient, Corcoran and Cohen
wrote the Securities Exchange Act of 1934, as well as the Public Utility
Holding Company Act of 1935—all the while backed by Frankfurter.[8] In
the press, Frankfurter defended the constitutionality of early New Deal
legislation, just as he had defended the constitutionality of Wilson-era

socioeconomic legislation that expanded the number and power of federal agencies. "If the court, aided by an alert and public-spirited bar, has access to the facts and follows them," Frankfurter said in a May 1933 radio interview, "the Constitution is flexible enough to meet all the new needs of our society."[9]

More than an outside adviser as House had been during the Wilson administration, Frankfurter was a legal and political tactician, fixer, occasional speechwriter, and above all a talent scout. During the depths of the Great Depression in 1932, the low demand for lawyers in Wall Street law firms was compensated for by the high demand by the federal government. No one was better connected to the nation's best and brightest young lawyers than Frankfurter. He sent dozens of his former students and protégés into the administration led by Dean Acheson in the Treasury Department, Corcoran in the Reconstruction Finance Corporation (where he had begun under Hoover's RFC chair Eugene Meyer), Cohen as counsel in the Public Works Administration, and Landis as a commissioner at the Federal Trade Commission and Securities and Exchange Commission (SEC) and later as SEC chairman. Former House of Truth visitor (and Holmes secretary) Francis Biddle was the chairman of the National Labor Relations Board and later became attorney general. In every department, every new administrative agency, Frankfurter knew a former student or disciple. Critics referred to them as Frankfurter's "Happy Hot Dogs."[10] Many Frankfurter protégés happened to be talented Jewish Harvard law graduates shut out of Wall Street law firms.[11] The virulently anti-Semitic Joseph Kennedy charged that Frankfurter was running the Roosevelt administration. "Why I don't see Frankfurter twice a year," Roosevelt said. "You see him twenty times a day," Kennedy replied, "but you don't know it because he works through all these other groups of people without your knowing it."[12] Another Frankfurter adversary, General Hugh S. Johnson, labeled him "the most single influential individual in the United States." Johnson claimed Frankfurter had "his 'boys' ... insinuated into obscure but key positions in every vital department."[13]

Of all Frankfurter's "hot dogs" in the Roosevelt administration, Corcoran wanted to re-create his mentor's old political salon. He had heard stories from Frankfurter about the row house on Nineteenth Street and had sat at the feet of Holmes as one of his most devoted secretaries. From 1933 to 1936, Corcoran, Cohen, and a rotating cast of friends and Washington lawyers lived in what Roosevelt's critics derisively named "The Little Red House." "The famous Little Red House in Georgetown was neither little nor red," one of its residents recalled of the rented five-story old Italianate mansion at 3238 R Street. Thanks to Corcoran, many young Harvard law graduates working in Washington lived there and turned it into a political playhouse.[14] The house got its name from right-wing conspiracy theorists who charged that Roosevelt was the New Deal's Kerensky about to be overthrown by the Frankfurter-inspired Communists led by "the ten to 18 men of radical minds" who met nightly in "The Little Red House."[15]

In 1937, Frankfurter had not been consulted before Roosevelt announced his "court-packing plan" to add six additional justices to the Supreme Court—one for every justice over seventy years old.[16] Roosevelt was incensed that the Court had struck down several key pieces of New Deal legislation.[17] Though privately opposed to many aspects of the court-packing plan, Frankfurter maintained a conspicuous public silence and counseled Roosevelt throughout the ordeal.[18] Two years later, Roosevelt nominated Frankfurter to the Supreme Court to replace Cardozo, who had retired because of ill health. After a brutal confirmation process, one that forced him to testify before the Senate to rebut questions about his loyalty to the country, Frankfurter joined the Court on January 17, 1939, and overlapped for a few months with Brandeis before the latter retired. As a sitting justice, Frankfurter continued to advise Roosevelt on political matters. In 1942, Frankfurter successfully lobbied Roosevelt to make Stimson secretary of war—the same job that Stimson had held under Taft and that had brought Frankfurter to Washington in the first place.

To many, Frankfurter was not a liberal justice. Like his judicial idols Holmes and Brandeis, Frankfurter believed in a more limited role for the Supreme Court in our democracy. Frankfurter's liberal critics charged that he sided too often with democracy and not enough with liberty—particularly in the wartime flag salute cases. But he often sided with criminal suspects in Fourth Amendment cases and believed in the Court's power of habeas corpus to review unfair state criminal trials. He also played an important role in dismantling the Court-sanctioned system of racial segregation. In 1954, he helped the Court achieve a unanimous opinion in *Brown v. Board of Education* outlawing racially segregated schools. Despite his contributions to the moral triumph in *Brown*, he urged his Warren Court colleagues to exercise caution about expanding the judicial branch's power to all aspects of American life. He wanted people to rely on the democratic political process to pursue economic and social change. Yet, like Holmes, he saw a role for the Court when the political process broke down.[19]

Over the years, Frankfurter corresponded with the other two surviving original House of Truth residents, Loring Christie and Eustace Percy, until the end of their lives. Christie was visiting Frankfurter in Cambridge the day after Roosevelt had announced his Supreme Court nomination.[20] Two years later, in April 1941, Christie died at age fifty-six as Canadian minister to the United States. Percy, who had served as a conservative member of the House of Commons from 1921 to 1937 and had enjoyed brief stints in the British cabinet, died at age seventy-three in 1958. "The United States," Frankfurter wrote after Percy's death, "seemed to tap a deep democratic strain in him."[21] The same could be said of Frankfurter. Just before his own death in 1965 at age eighty-two, he told his biographer: "Tell the whole story. Let people see how much I loved Roosevelt, how much I loved my country, and let them see how great a man Roosevelt really was."[22]

★★★

Frankfurter had arranged Roosevelt's birthday visit to Holmes not only to celebrate the justice but also to mute one of the president's most influential critics—Walter Lippmann. "Roosevelt had called to pay his respects to Justice Oliver Wendell Holmes, the *pater familias* of all liberals and intellectuals," Corcoran recalled. "Lippmann might belittle the new President, but every thoughtful reader of the next morning's papers would know Roosevelt had his head on straight."[23]

During the early days of Roosevelt's administration, Frankfurter stayed in close contact with the *New York Herald-Tribune* columnist. "The 'New Deal' may be a phrase but it may also be translated into realities," Frankfurter wrote Lippmann. "And I have very high hopes that circumstances are cooperating with Roosevelt's temperament and desires for a less greedy, a less jug-handled society."[24] Indeed, Lippmann praised Roosevelt's response to the banking crisis and predicted he would be a president "whose power to act in the emergency will not be questioned."[25] Yet both Frankfurter and Roosevelt knew that Lippmann's support for the administration would not last. After reading Frankfurter's correspondence with Lippmann, Roosevelt predicted that "Lippmann's philosophy of government and of social organization would make him a determined opponent of the New Deal, and all his talk about the necessity of strong Presidential leadership would not prevent his ultimate divergence and opposition."[26] As Roosevelt had predicted, Lippmann became one of the New Deal's most prominent detractors.[27]

The Frankfurter-Lippmann friendship did not survive the first half of 1933. The last straw for Frankfurter was an appeasing *Herald-Tribune* column about Adolf Hitler. With German Jews no longer safe from Nazi violence and Jewish scholars losing their positions at German universities, Frankfurter and other American Jewish leaders understood the grave threat that Hitler posed to the Jewish people.[28] A week after writing about how the Nazis had burned books and terrorized Jews, Lippmann described Hitler as "the authentic voice of a civilized people."[29] Frankfurter decided that he could no longer be friends with Lippmann. Three years later, in 1936, the columnist was shocked to learn the source of the rift and claimed that Frankfurter had taken "authentic voice of a civilized people" out of context.[30]

Frankfurter was not the only former Bull Mooser fed up with Lippmann. With his "Today and Tomorrow" column syndicated in 126 newspapers, Lippmann was an inviting target for liberal critics. In a four-part series in *The Nation*, Amos Pinchot excommunicated Lippmann from American liberalism. Based on Lippmann's early books, Pinchot described Lippmann as a "publicist" and "a salesman for plutocracy" who argued that the "criticisms and exposures of big business are exaggerated and on the whole unwarranted."[31] Pinchot exposed Lippmann's hypocrisy in decrying the Tammany charges against Smith in 1928, then hurling those same charges against Roosevelt in 1931 and 1932.[32] In the next installment, Pinchot attacked Lippmann's "desire to maintain an attitude of unoffending independence" in the Sacco-Vanzetti case. "The important thing is that the contending factions should be united by a common appreciation of Walter Lippmann's fairness," Pinchot wrote. "And so Mr. Lippmann takes his way back to his pent-house tower, leaving his public with the comforting assurance that, whatever may have happened to Sacco and Vanzetti, the honor of Massachusetts is safe."[33] Pinchot's final article concluded that it was unhelpful to criticize Lippmann for "his swing to the right" because, other than a youthful dalliance with Socialism, Pinchot argued, Lippmann's books and articles revealed that he had always been a conservative.[34]

After reading the first installment, Frankfurter congratulated Pinchot for "a notable public service in your Lippmann series." Pinchot's article, Frankfurter wrote, had exposed what years of reading Lippmann's work had revealed—"he is not a scholar in his reporting of the social-economic scene and is quite lacking in that disinterestedness which is his moral panacea."[35] Laski was so impressed with "Pinchot's remarkable articles" that he began circulating them "though W.L. just at present is a 'sacred cow' in London."[36] But what goes around comes around. In 1941, Pinchot attacked the Roosevelt administration as "delivering the United States to socialism" because of Roosevelt's ties, via Frankfurter, to Laski.[37]

Lippmann launched his own attacks on the Roosevelt administration and on Frankfurter. For the 300th anniversary of Harvard College in 1936, Frankfurter helped Roosevelt navigate ex-president Lowell's inquiries about the length and content of Roosevelt's remarks.[38] In June 1936, Lippmann, by then a member of the Harvard Board of Overseers, wrote: "Members of university faculties have a particular obligation not to tie themselves to, nor to involve themselves in, the ambitions and purposes of the politicians."[39] Hand, who was still on good terms with both men, believed that Lippmann had taken a cheap shot at Frankfurter.[40] By the fall of 1937, Hand's relationship with Lippmann soured after the columnist had left his wife, Faye, for the wife of his best friend, Hamilton Fish Armstrong.[41]

During the Roosevelt years and after, Lippmann and Frankfurter could not stand each other. "I might as well put it in the record that I found it impossible to be an independent journalist and be a good friend of Frankfurter's at the same time," Lippmann recalled. "If you gave him a chance, you'd get such a *deluge* of letters, and the passion would be so heavy, and the intimation was always that if you didn't agree with him there was some moral turpitude about it. I found it boring and I just cut it off." Lippmann rarely saw Frankfurter in Washington and avoided corresponding with him at all costs.[42]

Frankfurter, too, could not tolerate Lippmann, who basked in adulation yet chafed at the slightest disagreement or criticism. "For my taste," Frankfurter wrote, "he [became] more and more worldly-wise, and there set in an imperceptible alteration of our relationship." Whatever "fire" was left in their relationship had "gone out."[43] Frankfurter could not get past Lippmann's appeasing 1933 columns toward Hitler. He also considered Lippmann's oracular status as something of a joke given the columnist's poor track record on major domestic and foreign policy issues including pre–World War I interventionism, opposition to the Treaty of Versailles, opposition to Franklin Roosevelt and the New Deal, Nazi appeasement, and pre–World War II isolationism. As late as 1950, Frankfurter wrote that Lippmann "has, on balance, long exerted mischievous influence, both here and abroad" and that "someone ought to demonstrate that he whose lucid writing gives the delusion of wisdom is really one of the unsafest of guides."[44] British philosopher Isaiah Berlin noted that at his December 1955 lecture in Washington, Lippmann and Frankfurter sat "at opposite ends."[45]

Despite his rift with Frankfurter and his abandonment by American liberals, Lippmann wrote groundbreaking books about democracy and public opinion. He never overcame his initial objections to Roosevelt. In addition to his opposition to the New Deal, Lippmann had encouraged people to vote against Roosevelt in 1936 and had advised Roosevelt's opponent Wendell L. Willkie in 1940.[46] After Roosevelt's death, Lippmann's stature and influence as a nationally syndicated columnist continued to grow—he popularized the phrase the "Cold War," advised presidents and their administrations, and broke with Lyndon B. Johnson in 1966 over the Vietnam War.[47] Liberals may have abandoned Lippmann with good reason, but they continued to read his columns, his books on public opinion, and the magazine that he, Croly, and Frankfurter had founded more than a century ago—the *New Republic*.

★★★

Borglum resumed work on Mount Rushmore thanks to federal funding that Norbeck and others maneuvered through Congress. Roosevelt signed a bill granting $100,000, which was enough funding for 1933 and part of 1934. Rushmore was a proto–Works Progress Administration project. In June 1934, the memorial received another federal appropriation, and Borglum was "quite enthusiastic" about getting Roosevelt to the Black Hills to unveil one of the three remaining presidents.[48]

With regular federal appropriations, Borglum found a new friend and inside man in the administration—Herman Oliphant. A former Columbia Law School and Johns Hopkins professor, Oliphant was general counsel in the Treasury Department. Though he had helped Frankfurter and others draft the Norris–LaGuardia Act of 1932 outlawing labor injunctions, Oliphant was an ally of Treasury Secretary Henry Morgenthau Jr. and was "'meanly jealous'" of Frankfurter's influence on the Roosevelt administration.[49] During the summer of 1934, the Borglums visited Oliphant in Annapolis, and the sculptor explained his vision of the project, his timetable, and his funding needs. Oliphant, in turn, spent two weeks at Mount Rushmore and "informed himself about every phase of it."[50] After several days there, Oliphant said: "I never would have believed so seemingly useless a creation was necessary to humanity. Silently they come in thousands, silently they sit for hours, silently, reluctantly they go away."[51] In Oliphant, Borglum found someone able to pry money out of appropriation bills. The bond between Borglum and Oliphant was not just business; it was personal. "I see you in the 'News Behind the News,'" Borglum wrote Oliphant in August 1935. "Hell, I've known that for a long time! Swat Felix for me if you get a chance. He belongs to the ant family."[52]

Frankfurter and Borglum rarely crossed paths in later years. Then Justice Frankfurter spied Borglum across the room at the 1939 Gridiron Club dinner, but the sculptor was too shy to stop by the head table. Instead, they exchanged warm letters that reminisced about the Sacco-Vanzetti memorial and that revealed Borglum's interest in finishing the Confederate Memorial at Stone Mountain.[53] "I have been down here to answer a restlessness in the hearts of some old Confederates," Borglum wrote Frankfurter, "still dreaming of a proper record to their forebears who fought and died between '60 and '65."[54]

What helped Borglum most was Roosevelt's decision to come to Mount Rushmore during the summer of 1936 to dedicate Jefferson's head. The project had not been without its difficulties. Lincoln's head had to be moved to where the entablature was supposed to be (the controversy over Coolidge's inscription ended after the former president had died in 1933 and a contest was held for a new inscription). Theodore Roosevelt's head was moved between Washington's and Jefferson's. In November 1935, the sculptor wrote the president that Jefferson's head was finished. A flag lay over Jefferson's head; the public had not seen it. After accepting the Democratic nomination for a second term in late June 1936, Roosevelt wrote that he might be in Pierre, South Dakota, at the end of August, would try to dedicate Jefferson's head then, but asked the sculptor to keep the visit a secret in case it did not materialize.[55]

On August 30, 1936, Roosevelt arrived at the mountain in the passenger seat of his Packard convertible wearing sunglasses and waving his hat to the crowd.[56] The sculptor gave the signal, and the American flag was removed from Jefferson's head. Roosevelt was awestruck. "I had seen photographs, I had seen the drawings and I had talked with those who are responsible for this great work," he told the crowd, "and yet I had had no conception until about ten minutes ago, not only of its magnitude, but of its permanent beauty and of its permanent importance."[57]

Building on the momentum of Roosevelt's visit, Borglum and his son Lincoln finished Abraham Lincoln's head in the summer of 1937 and began work on Theodore Roosevelt's. They had difficulties finding suitable stone to carve a fourth president and were forced to set Roosevelt's head back from the others. They also began work on the hall of records at the bottom of the mountain. The hall was never finished because in order to obtain more federal funding they had to agree to finish the heads of the four presidents first. Borglum did not live to see his memorial completed. In 1941, he died in Chicago after a bladder operation at age seventy-three. His son Lincoln supervised the remaining work on the mountain.

★★★

If Rushmore was Borglum's best-known work, then one of his least-known works was of the man who connected everyone to the House of Truth—Justice Holmes. On March 8, 1934, Holmes celebrated his ninety-third birthday at 1720 Eye Street. Three days earlier, the Court had upheld a New York law fixing milk prices, a decision that confirmed the views in Holmes's 1905 dissent in *Lochner* invalidating a New York maximum hour law for bakers.[58] As his secretary read him excerpts of the majority and dissenting opinions from the *New York Times*, Holmes listened "with real and unusual interest."[59] For a time, the Court looked as if it were moving in a more democratic, Holmesian direction. Roosevelt was unable to visit Holmes in person but sent him a handwritten birthday note "wishing all good things for the most splendid and the wisest of all American Liberals."[60]

In the fall of 1934, Holmes left Beverly Farms and returned to Washington, DC, for the last time. In late February, he caught a cold while taking one of his regular automobile rides and contracted pneumonia. Frankfurter, who had been kept apprised of the justice's condition, was told to come to Washington immediately.[61] Even while hooked up to an oxygen tank, the justice maintained his sense of humor. "Every soldier to his tent, Captain Holmes," his secretary James Rowe joked. Holmes thumbed his nose at him.[62] Two days shy of his ninety-fourth birthday, Holmes lapsed into a coma and died at 2:30 a.m. with Rowe, former secretaries Corcoran and Mark DeWolfe Howe, Frankfurter, and members of the household staff at his bedside.[63] The last book that Rowe had read to the justice was Thornton Wilder's *Heaven Is My Destination*. In his closet, Holmes had left his two Civil War uniforms, one of them caked with blood and with a note attached indicating that the blood was his. He had donated half of his $550,000 estate to the US Treasury. Roosevelt's public statement declared: "The Nation has lost one of its first citizens."[64]

On the morning before the funeral at All Souls' Unitarian Church, Holmes's body lay in state at 1720 Eye Street. Marion Frankfurter never forgot the sight of Holmes dressed in robes in his bed. She had never come so close to death before. "'That is not real; for me he is living here,'" Marion said as she "touched her heart."[65]

Borglum, who had visited Holmes in retirement and had entertained him just as the sculptor had years earlier at the House of Truth, was one of the few mourners allowed to pay his respects at 1720 Eye Street.[66] As he often did with people he admired, Borglum made a plaster death mask of the justice's mustachioed face. That morning, he described Holmes's face as "one that ranked with 'the best in Anglo-Saxon, Greek or Roman history.'"[67] The mask was stashed in the sculptor's Stamford studio for years until Holmes's biographer and former secretary Mark DeWolfe Howe inquired about its whereabouts. In 1953, Harvard Law School purchased it from Mary Borglum for $1,000 as well as permission to make reproductions.[68]

With rain and sleet falling at Arlington National Cemetery on March 6, 1935, Eleanor Roosevelt stood next to Marion Frankfurter at a grave marked "Holmes" on the lovely spot on the hill where the justice had regularly visited his wife, Fanny. President Roosevelt, his head uncovered and only partially shielded by the canopy covering the casket, stood in the sleet and rain clutching the arm of a military aide.[69] Frankfurter, his head bowed, stood next to the bugler who played "Taps."[70] During the justice's final days, the Frankfurters had stayed with the president at the White House. "And I shall always associate his meaning for me *with you*," Frankfurter wrote Roosevelt, "at the most poignant and triumphant hours of life."[71] The Frankfurters also spent time with Brandeis, who was "too stricken with grief" to attend his friend's funeral.[72]

During his final days and in obituaries, newspapers referred to Holmes as the Court's "great liberal."[73] Holmes was not a liberal like his friend Brandeis or a conservative like his friend McReynolds. Neither label fits. Yet the liberals associated with the House of Truth loved Holmes and adopted him as one of their own because he upheld pro-labor legislation, defended the right to free speech and fair criminal trials, and articulated their preferred vision of a flexible Constitution. His pedigree, his ebullient personality, and his uncanny ability to turn a phrase made him the perfect symbol for American liberals as they struggled with the role that the Court should play in their political and legal activism.

Frankfurter (left), his wife, Marion (center), and Eleanor Roosevelt (right) at
Holmes's funeral at All Souls' Unitarian Church

Holmes's national recognition and identification as a liberal can be traced
directly to his association with the people at the House of Truth. The political salon began in 1912 as the place to be for supporters of Theodore
Roosevelt's Bull Moose presidential campaign. The House survived
Roosevelt's defeat and thrived under the leadership of Frankfurter, Winfred
T. Denison, and Robert G. Valentine. In many ways, Valentine was the beating heart of the house. Holmes may have inspired its name, but Valentine's
galvanizing energy and vaulting sense of possibility filled it. Frankfurter
and Denison carried it on. They befriended Herbert Croly and Walter
Lippmann and helped start the *New Republic* as an outlet for their ideas.
During the war, some of them worked in the Wilson administration and
mastered wartime administrative agencies to achieve their goals. They embraced Holmes and transformed the unhappy seventy-year-old jurist on the
verge of retirement into a ninety-year-old liberal icon. Over time, Holmes
replaced Theodore Roosevelt as their lodestar.

Frankfurter (right, head bowed) at Arlington National Cemetery

The people associated with the House made two major contributions to American liberalism. First, Holmes and Brandeis showed liberals how the Court could come to the aid of political and racial minorities by protecting free speech, voting rights, and fair criminal trials. Liberals spent the 1920s and early 1930s out of political power, but they fought for and against judicial nominees and used the courts to advance their political and legal agenda. As the Sacco-Vanzetti case illustrated, they did not always succeed. The courts, like electoral politics, produced victories as well as defeats. But the legal system offered another path to success.

Second, Frankfurter and his friends created an influential liberal network, one that long survived the breakup of the House in 1919. From 1912 to 1932, American liberalism was an evolving concept. During the Taft and Wilson administrations, the people associated with the House of Truth used the federal government and the political process to shape liberalism's content. The wartime suppression of civil liberties and the failure of the Treaty of Versailles forced them to confront government's limits. Once they fell out of political power during the Harding, Coolidge,

and Hoover administrations, they increasingly relied on the courts to protect civil liberties and fair criminal trials. They did not, however, abandon
electoral politics. Instead, they amassed a collection of the best men
ready for government service. It should be no surprise that Frankfurter
supplied the New Deal with brains and manpower. For twenty years, he
had been collecting people—a collection he brought together at a red-
brick Dupont Circle row house.

The House of Truth's network is a monument to the power of American
democracy every bit as enduring as Mount Rushmore. Both were products

Borglum's death mask of Holmes in 1935

of decades of work, and both went through periods of activity and despair, periods of belief in government's potential and cynicism about whether that potential could ever be brought to bear.

Both the House of Truth and Mount Rushmore were premised on high ideals. The House's liberals believed that government was good and could make people's lives better. They believed that government could force big business to recognize the rights of organized labor and could protect industrial workers from long hours, inhumane conditions, and unconscionably low pay. Borglum also believed in the power of the federal government and built Mount Rushmore as a "shrine to democracy." Without federal financial assistance and support from Presidents Coolidge, Hoover, and Franklin Roosevelt, the sculptor never would have been able to realize his vision.

Yet both the House of Truth and Mount Rushmore had dark sides. The House's liberals were so focused on labor issues that they often neglected issues of race. Mount Rushmore desecrated sacred Native American land and was a shrine to Manifest Destiny and the subjugation of indigenous peoples as much as it was a shrine to democracy. Still, both the House of Truth and Mount Rushmore created legacies that are worth celebrating. Since the House's heyday, the liberal political and legal network in this country has expanded almost as exponentially as the power of the government to create a social safety net. Indeed, during the 1980s conservatives began to create an influential political and legal network of their own. Both liberals and conservatives have used these networks to influence the political process and the judiciary to try to achieve their goals. The House's celebration of the life and work of Justice Holmes transformed him into a liberal judicial icon and a national hero. Without his friends' influence, Holmes would not be second to Chief Justice John Marshall in the pantheon of American jurists.

Whatever the ideology of those associated with it, the people at the House of Truth were dreamers—of bigger, better government; protection of civil liberties and fair criminal trials; and gigantic monuments in stone. They were bold, ambitious, and driven to succeed. They believed that if they worked hard and dreamed big, they could make lasting contributions to our nation's history.

Appendix

Warum

(With apologies to A. T. Slosson.)

By Pauline Gordon[*]

Why was it called the House of Truth you ask! Listen, and I will tell you.

Once there was a man. He was a very nice man, and he owned a very nice house. This house had belonged to others before him, who had lived in it and found it a good one. A house has to be lived in, you know, to be really good, and all good things have souls—even houses! All the people who had lived there had contributed to its growth without losing anything from their own. For soul, you know, is something you can give away and give away, and then, like the miraculous pitcher, have all the more left for yourself.

All this happened a long time ago, before the days that you and I remember. History does not record more than what I have told you.

One day the man said he must go away. Some duty he felt, to himself and to his country, was beckoning him to another land, to begin a new work among different people. He was sad at heart to leave his house with things in it, and memories and atmosphere which he could not take with him, and sorely grieved to think that his gardens and fields might be left to grow waste and barren. Oh, I almost forgot to tell you of those fields. They were all round the house—beautiful fertile lands where the man had spent many happy hours working, and where others had worked and played with him. People had always loved to work there in the sunshine—many did not call it work, but play. It would be hard to decide which it really was—work or play. It was life.

Trees grew there, harboring gay, sweet-throated birds and giving down restful shade. When the wind blew they made soft noises overhead. Every pretty flower was there in its season, fragrant herbs and nourishing fruits. Everything lovely was here surrounding the house, and in the care, there was always much to be done.

"Someone must come and live in my house for me," said the man. "My lands must be kept growing, and the weeds rooted up. I want the fire always burning on the hearth, and the latch-string forever out, for some day I may come back again."

[*] Wife of Thurlow Gordon, a Justice Department attorney from 1912 to 1916, friend of Frankfurter and Denison, and House of Truth regular along with Pauline.
"Warum" is German for "why." Annie Trumbull Slosson was an American author and entomologist.

And this is where history of which we have accurate knowledge begins. He told it to one man, who told it to another, who told still another—and so the rumor went out.

One day three friends came and said, "We will live in your house, and keep your fields."

The men liked them, and so they came, and they continued the hospitable traditions of the house—played in the gardens, and worked in the fields. Everyone was welcome there, and people from far and near came to visit the place. They always went away smiling, and with a warm and happy feeling in their hearts. In the house and out there was always peace, plenty and happiness. The soul of the house still grew, and the souls of all who came there absorbed of its grace.

Once, one man of them left to go far away, as the owner man had done. And then another left them, and all the friends lamented deeply. All persons who had ever been there, came to bid him adieu, and they tried hard to be glad, because he was going away to fill a place of great honor.

Soon other men came to take the vacant places, and presently a fourth joined them. All the world were their friends, and the merry parties they had became famous. One day they brought there some little children and did things to give them a good time. But old people and young had a good time at the house always—they could not help it. Good will was in the air.

"Yes, but why was it called the 'House of Truth'! You haven't told us that yet."

Why, isn't that the *true* way to live?

Notes

INTRODUCTION

1. FFR, 110–11.
2. *Id.* Frankfurter recalled Borglum's "plan of doing the three great figures in American history on the Black Mountains." *Id.* at 111. That could refer to Borglum's most famous work–the four American presidents in the Black Hills known today as Mount Rushmore. But Borglum did not make his first trip to Rushmore until September 1924, five years after the House's existence as a political salon. Frankfurter was recalling Borglum's efforts to carve the three Confederate war heroes at Stone Mountain. Indeed, Holmes's correspondence refers to Borglum and Stone Mountain. *See* OWH to FP, 4/30/1926, 2 H-P Letters at 181.
3. FFR, 106. For more on the House, *see id.* at 105–12.
4. On recent scholarship about liberalism, *see* Edward Fawcett, *Liberalism: The Life of an Idea* (2014); Alan Ryan, *The Making of Modern Liberalism* (2012); James T. Kloppenberg, *The Virtues of Liberalism* (1998); James T. Kloppenberg, *Uncertain Victory* (1986). For some of the vast scholarship about the reform movements during the Progressive Era spanning roughly from 1877 to 1920, *see* Michael McGerr, *A Fierce Discontent* (2003); Daniel T. Rodgers, *Atlantic Crossings* (1998); Steven J. Diner, *A Very Different Age* (1998); Nell Irvin Painter, *Standing at Armageddon* (1987); Otis L. Graham, *The Old Progressives and the New Deal* (1967); Robert H. Wiebe, *The Search for Order, 1877–1920* (1967); Gabriel Kolko, *The Triumph of Conservatism* (1963); Richard Hofstadter, *The Age of Reform* (1955); Daniel T. Rodgers, "In Search of Progressivism," *Reviews in American History* 10, no. 4 (December 1982): 113–32; David M. Kennedy, "Overview: The Progressive Era," *Historian* 37, no. 3 (May 1975): 453–68; David M. Kennedy, "Introduction," in *Progressivism: The Critical Issues* (David M. Kennedy, ed., 1971); Peter Filene, "An Obituary for 'The Progressive Movement,'" *American Quarterly* 22, no. 1 (April 1970): 20–34.
5. On the creation of political and legal networks outside of the traditional political party framework, *see* Sidney M. Milkis, *Theodore Roosevelt, the Progressive Party, and the Transformation of American Democracy* (2009); N. E. H. Hull, *Roscoe Pound and Karl Llewellyn* (1997); Sidney M. Milkis, *The President and the Parties* (1993).
6. Walter Lippmann, "Liberalism in America," TNR, 12/31/1919, at 150.

7. James T. Kloppenberg, "Liberalism," in *The Princeton Encyclopedia of American Political History*, Vol. 1, at 479–80 (2010) (defining "new liberalism" as an abandonment of laissez faire economics and that was associated with Holmes, Brandeis, Herbert Croly, and Lippmann); Charles Forcey, *The Crossroads of Liberalism* xiii–xiv, xxvii–xxviii (1961) (referring to a "new liberalism" that arose out of Theodore Roosevelt's 1912 presidential campaign and the ideas of *New Republic* founding editors Lippmann, Croly, and Walter Weyl).

8. TNR, 10/1/1924, at 113 & *in* Felix Frankfurter, *Felix Frankfurter on the Supreme Court* 142 (Philip B. Kurland ed., 1970).

9. Laura Kalman, *The Strange Career of Legal Liberalism* 2 (1996) (using "the term *legal liberalism* to refer to trust in the potential of courts, particularly the Supreme Court, to bring about 'those specific social reforms that affect large groups of people such as blacks, or workers, or women, or partisans of a particular persuasion; in other words, *policy change with nationwide impact*'") (emphasis in original).

CHAPTER 1

1. NYTrib, 11/1/1910, at 1.

2. *Id.*

3. *Id.* The article does not specifically mention that Frankfurter was in attendance, but he handled Stimson's correspondence and accompanied Stimson on the campaign trail. *See* HLSP, Reels 20–22; FFR, 50–53; Henry L. Stimson and McGeorge Bundy, *On Active Service in Peace and War* 26 (1948).

4. New York Passenger Lists, 1894, Roll M237_60, line 34; NYTrib, 8/10/1894, at 19; NYT, 8/10/1894, at 3; FFR at 4–5.

5. Program, Grammar School No. 25, 6/29/1897, FFLC, Box 234, Folder "Personal Material." *Cf.* FFR 3–4, 6–8 (recalling it was speech by William Pitt in the House of Lords). On Bryan speech, NYT, 9/24/1896, at 2.

6. FFR at 9–10, 13–16; NYT, 6/24/1897, at 3. On City College, *see* FFR at 11–12, 14; Matthew Josephson, "Jurist-II," New Yorker, 12/7/40, at 37; NYT, 6/20/1902, at 5. On Frankfurter's early years, *see* Michael E. Parrish, *Felix Frankfurter and His Times* 10–16 (1982); H. N. Hirsch, *The Enigma of Felix Frankfurter* 11–24 (1981); Joseph P. Lash, "A Brahmin of the Law," in DFF, 3–5; Josephson, "Jurist II," at 36–38.

7. FFR, 17–18.

8. Daniel R. Coquillette and Bruce A. Kimball, *On the Battlefield of Merit* 580 & tbl. 15.2 (2015); Bruce A. Kimball, "Before the Paper Chase," *Journal of Legal Education* 61, no. 1 (August 2011): 47 (estimating that 21 percent of the class of 1906 flunked out).

9. Austin Wakeman Scott to Monte Lemann, 5/28/1946, Scott Papers, Box 11, Folder 11-8; Arthur E. Sutherland, *The Law at Harvard* 241 (1967). On Frankfurter's time at Harvard, *see* Parrish, *Felix Frankfurter and His Times*, 16–22.

10. *See* Jerold S. Auerbach, *Rabbis and Lawyers* 150 (1990) ("The entry of Jews into the legal profession was prolonged and painful, strewn with obstacles of exclusion and discrimination set by law schools and law firms."); Auerbach, *Unequal Justice*, 106–8, 121–23 (1976) (discussing the New York bar's attempts to exclude Jewish lawyers after World War I).

11. FFR, 34–38. *See* FF to LH, 10/19/1931, at 1, LHP, Box 104-B, Folder 104-21 (recounting law firm interviews over his spring vacation, including one with Dwight Morrow at Reed, Simpson, Thacher, and Varbum).

12. Memorandum, 1/17/1909, HLSD, Reel 1, Vol. 1, at 1–10.

13. Stimson and Bundy, *On Active Service*, 5–7; FFR, 38–40; Memorandum, 1/17/1909 & 8/15/1909, HLSD, Reel 1, Vol. 1, at 6–14; Diary Entry, 11/8/1930, at 2, HLSD, Reel 2, at 135 (recalling he had hired Frankfurter and Winfred T. Denison even though they "were at no time and in no possible way party men, but who had become most valuable assistants").

14. HLS to AG Moody, 8/10/1906, at 6, HLSP, Reel 11, Vol. I, 155 & NARA Department of Justice, RG 60, Box 596. On soliciting Ames, *see* HLS to Ames, 6/30/1906, at 1–3, HLSP, Reel 11, Vol. 1, at 126–28.

15. FFR, 39. Frankfurter could not have been at the firm more than two months, since he spent the first month of that summer as a research assistant to Harvard property professor John Chipman Gray. *Id.* at 23.

16. Stimson and Bundy, *On Active Service*, 8–17; FFR, 41–49.

17. Stimson and Bundy, *On Active Service*, 12–14; FFR, 50.

18. FF to HLS, 6/7/1911, at 1, HLSP, Reel 25 at 114; ERB to FF, 6/22/1911, at 1–2, FFLC, Box 30, Folder "Buckner Emory R. 1911 #2."

19. FFR, 50. The firm was Winthrop & Stimson. Before and after the campaign, Frankfurter worked in the Southern District of New York. AG Wickersham to Henry Wise, 12/21/1909, Department of Justice Records, NARA, RG 60, Applications & Endorsements, 1901–1933, S.D.N.Y., Box 600, Folder "Felix Frankfurter" (confirming Frankfurter's appointment); FF to Wickersham, 7/14/1911, *id.* (thanking him for raise from $3,000 to $4,000 in US attorney's office).

20. NYT, 9/28/1910, at 5.

21. NYSun, 11/1/1910, at 4; NYH, 11/1/1910, at 6; NYW, 11/1/1910, at 4.

22. NYT, 11/1/1910, at 3.

23. *Id.*

24. Stimson and Bundy, *On Active Service*, 26. *See* FFR, 50.

25. FFR, 51–52.

26. *See* Wickersham to WTD, 1/4/1910, Department of Justice Records, DOJ NARA, RG 60, Appointment Letters Books, 1884–1934, Vol. 62, at 88 & Appointment Clerk to WTD, 2/1/1910, *id.*, Vol. 63, at 148.

27. RGV to SFV, 11/9/1910, trans. at vi99, RGVP, Carton 21, Folder 29.

28. "Personal Recollections of the Convention and Campaign of 1910," at 1–8, HLSD, Reel 1, Vol. 2; Stimson and Bundy, *On Active Service*, 21–28; FFR, 50–53, HLS to FF, 12/2/1910, FFLC, Box 103, Folder "Stimson, Henry L. 1908–12."

29. TR to FF, 12/2/1910, FFLC, Box 98, Folder "Roosevelt, Theodore 1910–16."
30. HLS to FF, 6/30/1911, FFLC, Box 103, Folder "Stimson, Henry L. 1908–12." *See* HLS to FF, 7/1/1911, at 2, *id.* (claiming he had turned down on Frankfurter's behalf a high-paying post as assistant attorney general in charge of customs affairs); Wickersham to FF, 7/13/1911, at 1–2, Department of Justice Records, NARA, RG 60, Applications & Endorsements, 1901–1933, S.D.N.Y., Box 600, Folder "Felix Frankfurter" (indicating that Wickersham had no vacancies, that he thought highly of Frankfurter's work, but that Stimson needed Frankfurter more in the War Department).
31. FFR, 56. *See* HLS to FF, 5/30/1911 & 7/1/1911 & 7/3/1911, FFLC, Box 103, Folder "Stimson, Henry L. 1908–12."
32. FFR, 56–57; HLS to FF, 7/3/1911, FFLC, Box 103, Folder "Stimson, Henry L. 1908–12"; "Trip to the West Indies and Panama," HLSD, Reel 1, Vol. 1, at 43–46.
33. HLS to Lewis Stimson, 8/3/1911, at 6, HLSP, Reel 25, at 611.

CHAPTER 2

1. FF to ERB, 9/26/1911, at 3, FFLC, Box 30, Folder "Buckner, Emory R. 1911#2."
2. FFR, 57–58.
3. DFF, 10/22/1911, at 104.
4. *Id.*, 10/24/1911, at 107–8.
5. FF to ERB, 9/26/1911 at 5 ("the road to relish here is from contract to status").
6. HL to OWH, 7/20/1925, 1 HLL, 766.
7. United States v. E. C. Knight Co., 156 U.S. 1 (1895).
8. Standard Oil Co. v. United States, 221 U.S. 1 (1910); United States v. American Tobacco Co., 221 U.S. 106 (1911).
9. *Id.* at 5–6.
10. HLSD, Reel 1, Pages 54–56; HLS to WHT, 9/13/1911, at 1–3, HLSP, Reel 26, Pages 292–94.
11. HLSD, Reel 1, Pages 57–58; NYT, 9/19/1911, at 5, NYT, 9/23/1911, at 1–2; NYT, 9/29/1911, at 3; NYT, 10/7/1911, at 6; NYT, 10/8/1911, at 6, NYT, 10/24/1911, at 6; NYT, 10/28/1911, at 1, NYT, 11/1/1911, at 1.
12. HLS to wife, 9/21/1911, at 3, HLSP, Reel 26, Page 473 (referring to Taft's September 18 speech in Detroit).
13. DFF, 10/23/1911, at 106; *id.*, 10/24/1911, at 108; *id.*, 10/26/1911, at 111–12.
14. Speech at 24, WHTP, Reel 361, Series 6, CF42, at 10657. *See* DFF, 10/27/1911, at 112; *id.*, 10/28/1911, at 114; *id.*, 10/29/1911, at 114; FF to Philip Miller, 10/31/1911, at 1–3, FFLC, Box 84, Folder "Miller, Philip L. 1911–12."
15. WTD to HLS, 10/31/1911, at 1–2, HLSP, Reel 26, Page 785.
16. *Id.* at 2–3.
17. WTD to HLS, 11/2/1911, at 2, HLSP, Reel 26, Page 825.
18. Nagel to HLS, 10/31/1911, at 1–2, HLSP, Reel 26, Page 791. Nagel was Brandeis's former brother-in-law; he was married to Brandeis's sister, Fannie, who died in 1889.

19. On Taft's permission, *see* HLS to Lewis Stimson, 11/7/1911, at 1–3, HLSP, Reel 26, Pages 891–93; DFF, 11/3/1911, at 115–16; HLSD, Reel 1, Pages 57–58. On the title, *see* KC Commercial Club to HLS, 11/6/1911 tel., HLSP, Reel 26, Page 860.

20. WHT to HLS, 11/2/1911, HLSP, Reel 26, Page 824; HLSD, Reel 1, Pages 57–58.

21. DFF, 11/3/1911, at 116.

22. HLS to Lewis Stimson, 11/7/1911, at 1–3; DFF, 11/3/1911, at 115–16.

23. DFF, 11/3/1911, at 115.

24. DFF, 11/6/1911, at 118. *See* HLS to Lewis Stimson, 11/7/1911, at 1–3.

25. KC Commercial Club to HLS, 11/6/1911 tel., HLSP, Reel 26, Page 860; HLS to KC Commercial Club, 11/6/1911 tel., *id.*, Page 871.

26. DFF, 11/6/1911, at 118.

27. NYT, 11/15/1911, at 8.

28. Memorandum to WHT, 11/3/1911, HLSP, Reel 26, Page 841.

29. NYT, 12/6/1911, at 8. *See* James C. German Jr., "The Taft Administration and the Sherman Antitrust Act," in *The Monopoly Issue and Antitrust, 1900–1917*, at 172–86 (Robert F. Himmelberg, ed., 1994).

30. Archie Butt, Diary Entry, 7/8/1910, 2 *Taft and Roosevelt* 439 (1930).

31. Address to New York City Republican Club, 12/15/1911, HLSP Reel 130, at 57–70.

32. HLSD, Reel 1, Pages 60–61.

33. DFF, 11/4/1911, at 116.

34. HLS to AG Moody, 8/10/1906, at 2, HLSP, Reel 11, Page 152 & Department of Justice Records, NARA, RG 60, Applications & Endorsements, 1901–1933, S.D.N.Y., Box 596. Stetson, Jennings was the predecessor to Davis, Polk & Wardwell.

35. WP, 1/16/1910, at 4.

36. NYT, 12/9/1911, at 2; NYT, 1/7/1912, at 6; WP, 1/28/1912, at 6; NYT, 2/4/1912, at 14; WP, 2/4/1912, at 1.

37. NYT, 12/17/1910, at 9; WP, 2/4/1912, at 1.

38. Harvard College Class of 1896, Secretary's Fourth Report, at 80–81 (June 1911).

39. FFR, 108.

40. DFF, 10/24/1911, at 109.

41. Winfred Denison, 10/7/1896, Passport Application, No. 17390, U.S. Passport Applications, 1795–1905, NARA Series m1372, Roll 3477.

42. WES, 12/19/1911, at 7 (hosting Valentine, Frankfurter, Christie, Solicitor General Lehman, Brigadier General Enoch Crowder, Captain McCoy, Mr. Clarence B. Wilson, U.S. Attorney James C. Crawford). *See Social Register*, Washington, D.C., 1911 & 1913, at 35; WP, 2/3/1911, at 7; WP, 2/7/1911, at 7.

43. FFR, 108.

44. *Id.*

45. LCC to FF, 2/25/1911, at 1–2, FFLC, Box 43, Folder "Christie, Loring C. 1911–1914"; Harvard College Class of 1896 Secretary's Fourth Report at 81; WP, 4/6/1911, at 7.

46. WP, 4/6/1911, at 7; WP, 6/24/1911, at 7.

588 NOTES TO PAGES 19–22

47. LDB to AGB, 10/21/1911, FLLDB, at 172; WP, 10/28/1911, at 7; WP, 10/12/1911, at 5.
48. DFF, 10/24/1911, at 109.
49. DFF, 10/20/1911, at 103–4; LDB to AGB, 10/21/1911.
50. A. L. Todd, *Justice on Trial* 256 (1964) (based on interview with Frankfurter).
51. DFF, 10/20/1911, at 103–4.
52. LDB to AGB, 10/21/1911; NYT, 10/6/1911, at 1.
53. Baker, "Short Article on Brandeis," at 2, RSBP, Reel 55, Container 56 & Melvin I. Urofsky, *Louis D. Brandeis* 392 (2009). On Brandeis, *see* Urofsky, *Louis D. Brandeis*; Lewis J. Paper, *Brandeis* (1984); Philippa Strum, *Louis D. Brandeis* (1984); Alpheus Thomas Mason, *Brandeis* (1946).
54. Brandeis graduated with a score of 97 out of 100 based on the grading scale at the time. James M. Landis, "Mr. Justice Brandeis and the Harvard Law School," 55 Harv. L. Rev. 184, 184 (1941). *But see* Garfield Horn, Landis Research Assistant, Original Draft of "Mr. Justice Brandeis and the Harvard Law School," at 1 n. 2, 10/28/1941, James McCauley Landis Papers, Box 169, Folder "Justice Brandeis and the Harvard Law School, *Harvard Law Review* 1941") (explaining that "his average for the two-year course of those days was 97 (*but it should be remembered that the marking system at that time differed to some extent from what it now is, so that grades of 90 or better, while exceptional, were not extraordinary*)" and noting that "subsumed in this [mark of] 97 were three marks of 100 and two of 99") (emphasis added) (based on "Law School records, Secretary's Office, Gannett House").
55. Lochner v. New York, 198 U.S. 45 (1905).
56. Muller v. Oregon, 208 U.S. 412 (1908).
57. Felix Frankfurter, "Hours of Labor and Realism in Constitutional Law," 29 Harv. L. Rev. 353, 365 (1916).
58. *See* Harry Lee Staples and Alpheus Thomas Mason, *The Fall of a Railroad Empire* (1947); Mason, *Brandeis*, 172–214; Strum, *Louis D. Brandeis*, 159–60; Urofsky, *Louis D. Brandeis*, 181–200.
59. On the Ballinger-Pinchot controversy, *see* Lewis L. Gould, *Chief Executive to Chief Justice* 62–63 (2014); Lewis L. Gould, *The William Howard Taft Presidency* 76–78 (2009); Mason, *Brandeis*, 254–82; 1 Henry F. Pringle, *The Life and Times of William Howard Taft* 470–514 (1939); Strum, *Louis D. Brandeis*, 132–45; Urofsky, *Louis D. Brandeis*, 254–76.
60. LDB to FF, 9/24/1925, HBHS, at 212. *See* LDB to MD, 11/3/1919, FFLC, Box 26, Folder "Brandeis, Louis D. 1919–" (describing them as "half son, half brother").
61. DFF, 10/21/1911, at 104.
62. JCG to OWH, 11/17/1911, Bureau of Insular Affairs Records, NARA, RG 350, Series 5A, Box 666, Page 12607. On the Holmes-Gray relationship, *see* Holmes, Address to Massachusetts Historical Society, 3/12/1915, in *John Chipman Gray* 48–50 (Roland Gray, ed., 1917).
63. FF to JCG, 11/27/1911, at 1, Bureau of Insular Affairs Records, NARA, RG 350, Series 5A, Box 666, Page 12607.

64. "Residence of Justice Oliver Wendell Homes, 1720 I Street," 14 photographs circa 1935, Lot 10304 (G), Library of Congress, Prints and Photographs; "Library of Justice and Mrs. Oliver Wendell Holmes' Washington, D.C. residence," 4/9/1905, Holmes Digital Suite, Harvard Law School, http://via.lib.harvard .edu:80/via/deliver/deepLinkItem?recordId=olvwork392139&component Id=HLS.Libr:1476778; G. Edward White, *Justice Oliver Wendell Holmes: Law and the Inner Self* 310, 313 (1993) (about Holmes's books and relationship to secretaries); John S. Monagan, *The Grand Panjandrum* 36–38, 121 (1988) (describing house); Augustin Derby, "Recollections of Mr. Justice Holmes," 12 N.Y.U. L.Q. Rev. 345, 346 (1935); Donald Hiss Interview in Katie Louchheim, ed., *The Making of the New Deal* 38 (1983) (recalling swords used in "the Indian Wars" but mistakenly attributing them to his maternal grandfather, not his paternal great-grandfather, David Holmes, a colonel in the French and Indian War).

65. FFR, 58.

66. Oliver Wendell Holmes, *The Common Law* 1 (1881). On Holmes, *see* White, *Law and the Inner Self*; Liva Baker, *The Justice from Beacon Hill* (1991); Sheldon M. Novick, *Honorable Justice* (1989); Monagan, *The Grand Panjandrum*; Mark DeWolfe Howe, *Justice Oliver Wendell Holmes: The Proving Years 1870–1882* (1963); Mark DeWolfe Howe, *Justice Oliver Wendell Holmes: The Shaping Years, 1841–1870* (1957).

67. OWH to HL, 3/4/1920, 1 HLL, at 248.

68. *Id. See* OWH to FF, H-FF Corr., 3/24/1914, at 19 ("a law should be called good if it reflects the will of the dominant forces of the community even if it will take us to hell").

69. Holmes, "Law and the Court," in *Collected Legal Papers* 295 (1921) ("Judges are apt to be naif, simple-minded men, and they need something of Mephistopheles."); Francis Biddle, *Mr. Justice Holmes* 124 (1942) ("[Holmes] knew he himself had something of Mephistopheles."); OWH to NG, 10/23/1910, at 1, OWHP, Reel 23, Page 506, Box 32, Folder 5 ("I am much pleased with my secretary, Olds. ... I don't quite know how far to introduce him to Mephistopheles. ....").

70. According one of his former law clerks, *kochleffel* was one of Frankfurter's favorite words. Philip Elman, interviewed by Norman Silber, "The Solicitor General's Office, Justice Frankfurter, and Civil Rights Litigation, 1946–1960: An Oral History," 100 Harv. L. Rev. 817, 832 (1987).

71. SFV Diary 1910 (misdated), 11/2/1911, RGVP, Carton 16, Folder 3. *See* SFV to RGV, 11/3/1911, at 2, *id.*, Carton 7, Folder 54 (describing a similar scene).

72. FF to Maggie and John, 12/26/1911, at 2, FFLC, Box 30, Folder "Buckner, Emory R. 1911 #2."

73. FF to ERB, 4/20/1912 at 7, *id.*, Folder "Buckner, Emory R. 1912 #4."

74. On Mack, *see* Harry Barnard, *The Forging of an American Jew* (1974).

75. RGV to Superintendents in Charge of Indian Schools, 1/27/1912, WHTP, Series 6, No. 515C, Reel 397, Page 56765.

76. Memorandum, 2/3/1912, *id.*, at Page 56777.

77. WHT to Fisher, 2/3/1912, at 1, *id.* at Page 56775.

78. *Id.* at 2.

79. John Lord O'Brian COH, Vol. I, at 26–27. On O'Brian, *see* Daniel R. Ernst, *Tocqueville's Nightmare* 91–93 (2014).

80. On crew, see HCrim, 10/6/1892; HCrim, 11/29/1893. On debate, *see* HCrim, 1/19/1894; HCrim, 3/2/1895; HCrim, 4/26/1895; HCrim, 1/22/1896. On chess, *see* HCrim, 10/18/1892; HCrim, 11/4/1892. On graduation speaker, *see* HCrim, 5/22/1896.

81. On Keats, *see* HCrim, 2/19/1896. On Harvard graduate school, *see* Harvard College, Class of 1896, Secretary's Fourth Report, at 307–8.

82. Robert G. Valentine, "On Criticism of Themes by Students," Technology Review 4, no. 4 (1902): 459–78; Robert G. Valentine, "Introduction in English at the Institute," Technology Review 1, no. 4 (1899): 441–56; David R. Russell, *Writing in the Academic Disciplines, 1870–1990*, at 109–17 (2d ed., 2002).

83. RGV to SFV, 3/29/1899, at 4, RGVP, Carton 2, Folder 51 (emphasis in original).

84. RGV to Elizabeth Caldwell Stevens ("Aunt Beth"), 6/6/1899, RGVP, Carton 1, Folder 57; RGV to SFV, 6/10/1899, *id.*, Carton 2, Folder 52.

85. On working for Stillman, RGV to SFV, 8/1–4/1899, Carton 2, Folder 54. On Stillman's alliance with Rockefeller and Harriman, *see* Felix Frankfurter, "Valentine, Robert Grosvenor," Dictionary of American Biography Vol. 19 (1936): 142; John Moody, *The Truth about the Trusts* 4–5 (1904).

86. RGV to ECS, 10/6/1900, RGVP, Carton 1, Folder 69; Harvard College, Class of 1896, Secretary's Second Report, at 117 (June 1901).

87. On returning to MIT, RGV to SGV, 9/30/1901, RGVP, Carton 2, Folder 76; Diane T. Putney, "Robert Grosvenor Valentine, 1909–12," in *The Commissioners of Indian Affairs* 233 (1979). On his correspondence from 1900 to 1907 with Amy Lowell, *see* RGVP, Carton 9, Folders 30–35.

88. On summer with Stillman, *see* RGV to SFV, 5/26/1902, at 1–2, RGVP, Carton 3, Folder 48. On leaving MIT again, *see* SFV Diary Entry, 11/17/1903, trans., RGVP, Carton 21, Folder 48.

89. Seventh Report of Harvard College, Class of 1896, at 2, FFLC, Box 188, Folder "Valentine, Robert G. 1916–17."

90. RGV to SFV, 10/12/1901, at 3–4, RGVP, Carton 2, Folder 81 ("The city is boiling with politics. ... The chances for the election of the Reform Ticket seem fair.").

91. NYT, 8/14/1903, at 10.

92. RGV to E. S. Marston, circa 1904, at 3, RGVP, Box 1, Folder 20 (indicating that his doctor must watch his heart for a few months before he can go back to work); RGV to ECS, circa 6/20 or 21/1904, *id.*, Carton 2, Folder 8; RGV to SFV, 12/20/1904, *id.*, Carton 5, Folder 79; Seventh Report of Harvard College, Class of 1896, at 2 (citing "ill health from overwork").

93. Aunt Caroline to RGV, 3/20/1904, RGVP, Carton 5, Folder 5 (acknowledging announcement of engagement); ECS Diary Extract, 4/19/1904, at 2, *id.*, Carton

21, Folder 49 ("Robert and Sophie announced their engagement shortly before Easter").

94. RGV to SFV, 12/7/1904, at 3, Carton 5, Folder 74.

95. RGV to SFV, 12/10/1904, at 1, *id.*, Folder 75.

96. RGV to SFV, 12/12/1904, *id.*, Folder 76.

97. RGV to SGV, 12/8/1904, at 1–2, *id.*, Folder 74; RGV to ECS, 12/11/1904, at 1, *id.*, Carton 2, Folder 9 ("I was personally introduced to the President and it was a wonderful three minutes. This week takes its place next to the two or three greatest experiences through which I have passed.").

98. RGV to SFV, 12/8/1904, at 1–2.

99. RGV to SFV, 12/10/1904, at 2, RGVP, Carton 5, Folder 75.

100. RGV to SFV, 12/17/1904, at 3, *id.*, Folder 78 ("I am very anxious to write to you about my call on Mr. Leupp, yesterday. ..."); RGV to ECS, 12/22/1904, at 3, *id.*, Carton 2, Folder 9 (submitting an assignment to Leupp); Report of the 1908 Lake Mohonk Conference at 30 (Leupp's remarks).

101. RGV to SFV, 12/20/1904, RGVP, Carton 5, Folder 79. *See* RGV to SFV, 12/22/1904 tel., RGVP, Carton 5, Folder 80; RGV to ECS, 12/23/1904, at 3.

102. ECS Diary Extract, 12/31/1904, at 6–7, *id.*, Carton 21, Folder 49.

103. Green Leaved Book, 2/12/1905, *id.*, Carton 11, Folder 41.

104. WP, 11/28/1909, at SM4; "Mr. Leupp and Mr. Valentine," Outlook, 6/26/1909, at 421.

105. "Mr. Leupp and Mr. Valentine," at 421.

106. WP, 7/18/1909, at ES4; WP, 1/11/1910, at 6.

107. Report of 1909 Lake Mohonk Conference at 18–19.

108. Janet A. McDonnell, "Land Policy on the Omaha Reservation: Competency Commissions and Forced Fee Patents," *Nebraska History* 63 (Fall 1982): 399; Diane T. Putney, "Fighting the Scourge" (PhD diss., 1980), 110–24, 162–66 (detailing Valentine's efforts to stop the spread of tuberculosis and trachoma).

109. Extracts from ECS Date Book for 1910, 5/2/1910, RGVP, Carton 21, Folders 50.

110. SFV to ECS, 9/16/1910, trans. at q106, *id.*, Carton 21, Folder 44.

111. RGV to SFV, 9/8/1910, RGVP, Carton 7, Folder 27.

112. RGV to SFV, circa 10/1/1910, "On Train," RGVP, Carton 7, Folder 52.

113. SFV to ECS, circa 11/1910, trans. at q108, *id.*, Carton 21, Folder 44.

114. *Id.* at q109.

115. Extracts from ECS Date Book, 2/17/1911, *id.*, Carton 21, Folder 52.

116. Photos of 1727 Nineteenth Street interior, Dorothy Koval Collection (on file with author).

117. Report of 1912 Lake Mohonk Conference at 81.

118. *Id.* at 81–82.

119. Francis Fisher Kane to RGV, 6/17/1911, trans. at d110, RGVP, Carton 21, Folder 31 (telling Bass he saw Valentine "looking very ill and thought he ought to go on a holiday"); Extracts from ECS Date Book for 1911, 5/19/1911, at 6, *id.*, Folder 52; Mrs. Abbott to SFV, 7/5/1911, RGVP, Carton 15, Folder 12.

120. Extracts from ECS Date Book for 1912, 4/1/1912, at 3–4, RGVP, Carton 21, Folder 52.

121. FF to ERB, 5/4/1912 at 2, FFLC, Box 30, Folder "Buckner, Emory R. 1912 #4"; RGV to SFV, 5/6/1912, at 1–2, RGVP, Carton 7, Folder 60 (proposing to send check for Frankfurter's half of the May expenses on June 1 "and Winnie's share when he comes in").

122. RGV to Dr. Mumford, 6/18/1912, at 15, RGVP, Box 8, Folder 82 (noting Denison and "another man" lived in the House).

123. FF to ERB, 5/4/1912, at 2.

124. RGV to SFV, 5/6/1912, Carton 7, Folder 60. See RGV to SFV, 5/10/1912, at 1–2, id. (discussing Thursday night dinner with Frankfurter, the Ludingtons, and the Smiths and that "everyone had a wonderfully particularly good time").

125. Memorandum from WTD, 11/28/1911, at 1, LCCP, Vol. 19, Reel 3888, at 18014; Wickersham to LCC, 10/5/1910, NARA, Department of Justice, RG 60, Appointment Letter Books 1884–1934, Vol. 69, at 486.

126. RGV to SFV, circa 9/30/1910, at 2, RGVP, Carton 7, Folder 32 (Christie and WTD among guests).

127. Robert Bothwell, *Loring Christie* 10 & 21 n. 14 (1988) (based on July 1970 interview with Austin Wakeman Scott).

128. On making ten dollars a week at Winthrop & Stimson, see Bothwell, *Loring Christie*, 15 (based on interview with Scott). On his Justice Department salary, see id.; Memorandum from WTD, 11/28/1911, at 1; Wickersham to LCC, 10/5/1910.

129. DFF, 10/29/1914, at 114.

130. 1911 D.C. City Directory at 411 (listing Christie at 1808 I Street); 1912 D.C. City Directory at 416 (same); but listing FF at 1801 I Street at 618.

131. LCC to FF, 2/25/1911, at 2–3, FFLC, Box 43, Folder "Christie, Loring C. 1911–14."

132. Bothwell, *Loring Christie*, 7–14; A. R. M. Lower, "Loring Christie and the Genesis of the Washington Conference of 1921–22," *Canadian Historical Review* 47, no. 1 (March 1966): 40 (recalling Christie denigrated Halifax as "The Garrison").

133. DFF, 10/29/1911, at 114.

134. Eustace Percy, *Some Memories* 22 (1958) (arriving May 6, 1910).

135. *Id.* at 40; RGV to SFV, 5/6/1912, at 1.

136. RGV to SFV, 5/10/1912, at 1.

137. FFR, 105. See "Eustace Percy," Oxford Dictionary of National Biography, Vol. 43, at 687 (2004); Percy, *Some Memories*, 9–21.

138. On the transatlantic influence on the American progressive movement, see Rodgers, *Atlantic Crossings*.

139. "Felix Frankfurter," *Fortune*, 1/1936, at 88; Joseph P. Lash, "A Brahmin of the Law," in DFF, 8. *But see* Jeffrey O'Connell & Nancy Dart, "The House of Truth," 35 Cath. U.L. Rev. 79, 79 (1985) (doubting attribution to Holmes).

140. OWH to NG, 11/6/1919, at 2–3, OWHP, Reel 23, Page 684, Box 32, Folder 12.

141. FFR, 107 (describing the House as "a place where truth was sought, and everybody knew that it couldn't be found, but even trying to seek the truth conscientiously is a rare occupation in the world.").

142. Oliver Wendell Holmes, "Natural Law," 32 Harv. L. Rev. 40, 40 (1918). *See* Oliver Wendell Holmes, "Ideals and Doubts," 10 Ill. L. Rev. 1, 2 (1915) ("I therefore define the truth as the system of my limitations, and leave absolute truth for those who are better equipped."); OWH to LH, 6/24/1918, OWHP, Reel 26, Page 486, Box 36, Folder 3 ("I don't bother about absolute truths or even inquire whether there is such a thing, but define the Truth as the system of my limitations. I may add that as other men are subject to a certain number, not all, of my Cant Helps, intercourse is possible. When I was young I used to define the truth as the majority of that nation that can lick all others. So we may define the present war as an inquiry concerning truth.").

143. Holmes, "Natural Law," 40.

CHAPTER 3

1. TR to FF, 1/6/1912, TRP, Series 3A, Vol. 39, Reel 371.
2. OWH speech 2/28/1911, TRP, Series 1, Reel 109.
3. FF to TR 1/15/1912, TRP, Series 1, Reel 123.
4. On Roosevelt's break with Taft, *Taft and Roosevelt*; John Milton Cooper Jr., *The Warrior and the Priest* (1983); Lewis L. Gould, *The William Howard Taft Presidency* (2009); Doris Kearns Goodwin, *The Bully Pulpit* (2013).
5. FF to ERB at 1/6/1912, at 5, FFLC, Box 30, Folder "Buckner, Emory R. 1912 #3."
6. Republican Governors to TR, 2/10/1912, 17 *The Works of Theodore Roosevelt*, at 149–50 n. 1 (Hermann Hagedorn, ed., 1926).
7. NYT, 2/4/1912, at 1. Others have suggested that La Follette was not ill but criticized the corporate-controlled newspaper industry. Gabriel Snyder, "Something's Wrong with La Follette," 2/6/2012, at http://www.thewire.com/politics/2012/02/introducing-our-1912-project-somethings-wrong-la-follette/48316/.
8. TR, "A Charter of Democracy," 2/21/1912, Columbus, Ohio, 17 *The Works of Theodore Roosevelt*, at 120.
9. *Id.* at 126–30.
10. *Id.* at 131.
11. *Id.* at 135–39.
12. *Id.* at 143–45 (discussing Ives v. South Buffalo Ry. Co., 201 N.Y. 271 (1911)).
13. *Id.* at 146–47; TR to HLS, 2/5/1912, at 3, HLSP, Reel 28, Page 190.
14. "A Charter of Democracy," at 120–21, 139.
15. TR, "The Nation and the States," 8/29/1910, Denver, CO, http://www.theodore-roosevelt.com/images/research.txtspeeches/691.pdf. *See* United States v. E. C. Knight, 156 U.S. 1 (1895); Lochner v. New York, 198 U.S. 45 (1905). On

Roosevelt's attacks on *Lochner, see* Victoria F. Nourse, "A Tale of Two Lochners," 97 Cal. L. Rev. 751, 778–85 (2009); William E. Forbath, "Popular Constitutionalism in the Twentieth Century," 81 Chi.-Kent L. Rev. 967, 977–84 (2006).

16. Theodore Roosevelt, "Nationalism and the Judiciary," Outlook, 2/25/1911, at 383–85; Theodore Roosevelt, "Nationalism and the Judiciary," Outlook, 3/4/1911, at 488–92; Theodore Roosevelt, "Nationalism and the Judiciary," Outlook, 3/11/1911, at 532–36; TR to HLS, 2/5/1912, at 1–4, HLSP, Reel 28, Pages 188–92; Theodore Roosevelt, "The Right of the People to Rule," 3/20/1912, Carnegie Hall, New York City; Theodore Roosevelt, "Recalls of Judges and Referendum of Decisions," 4/10/1912, Philadelphia, Pa., in http://www.theodore-roosevelt.com/images/research/treditorials/078.pdf; Theodore Roosevelt, Introduction, 7/1/1912, in William L. Ransom, *Majority Rule and the Judiciary* 3–24 (1912).

17. Felix Frankfurter, "The Red Terror of Judicial Reform," TNR, 10/1/1924, at 113, in *Felix Frankfurter on the Supreme Court* 166; Felix Frankfurter, "The Supreme Court and the Public," *Forum*, June 1930, at 334, in *id.* at 226.

18. NYT, 2/22/1912, at 1.

19. NY Trib, 2/26/1912, at 1.

20. FF to ERB, 3/4/1912, at 2–4, FFLC, Box 30, Folder "Buckner, Emory R. #3."

21. *Id.* at 4–6.

22. HLS, "The Progressive Character of President Taft's Administration," 3/5/1912, at 3, HLSP, Reel 130, Page 76.

23. HLS to Lewis Stimson, 2/28/1912, at 2–3, HLSP, Reel 28, Pages 490–91.

24. "Personal Reminiscences, 1911–1912," HLSD, Reel 1, Vol. 2, Pages 32–35.

25. FF to ERB, 3/4/1912, at 7.

26. FF to HLS 4/30/1912, at 1–3, HLSP, Reel 29, Pages 279–81.

27. FF to ERB, 3/4/1912, at 8.

28. *Id.*

29. FF to ERB, 3/4/1912 P.S., FFLC, Box 30, Folder "Buckner, Emory R. #3."

30. RGV to Dr. Mumford, 6/18/1912, at 2, RGVP, Carton 8, Folder 82.

31. *Id.*

32. *Id.*; RGV to RPB, 8/2/1912, at 1, RGVP, Carton 9, Folder 27.

33. FF to SFV, 4/3/1912, at 2, RGVP, Carton 15, Folder 67.

34. FF to SFV, 4/9/1912, *id.*; FF to RGV, 4/17/1912, *id.*

35. FF to SFV, 4/9/1912, at 1.

36. LCC to RGV, Apr. 1912, RGVP, Carton 8, Folder 80 (enclosing 4/24/1912 clipping and adding: "I take off my hat & bare & bow my head to this performance. . . .").

37. RGV to SFV, 5/15/1912, at 2, RGVP, Carton 7, Folder 60.

38. RGV to SFV, 4/21/1912, at 3–4, *id.*, Folder 59.

39. RGV to SFV, 5/10/1912, at 2–3.

40. RGV to SFV, 5/17/1912, at 1–2, *id.*, Folder 61.

41. FF to SFV, 4/9/1912, at 3.

42. NYT, 1/14/1912, at C10; CT, 1/12/1912, at 11. *See* Hooker v. Knapp, 225 U.S. 302 (1912).

43. NYTrib, 1/7/1912, at 3; NYT, 1/7/1912, at 3; WP, 1/28/1912, at 6; NYTrib, 1/28/1912, at 7; NYT, 1/9/1912, at 12; NYT, 2/4/1912, at 14; WP, 2/4/1912, at 1; NYTrib, 2/14/1912, at 4; WP, 3/2/1912, at 6.

44. WTD to RPB, 7/12/1912, at 1, RGVP, Carton 9, Folder 50.

45. Penrose to Wickersham, 2/2/1912, WTD to Wickersham, 2/7/1912, Wickersham to Penrose, 2/7/1912, *id.*, Folder 49.

46. WTD to RPB, 7/12/1912, at 1–2.

47. Memorandum from WTD, 11/28/1911, at 1, LCCP, Vol. 19, Reel 3888, at 18014.

48. FF to ERB, 4/20/1912, at 3–4, FFLC, Box 30, Folder "Buckner, Emory R. 1912 #4."

49. NYT, 4/30/1912, at 5; *see* RGV to Mumford, 6/18/1912, at 3.

50. RGV to SFV, n.d. 1912, RGVP, Carton 7, Folder 56.

51. Geoffrey Cowan, *Let the People Rule* (2016).

52. RGV to SFV, 5/22/1912, at 4, 6–7, RGVP, Carton 7, Folder 61 (emphasis in original).

53. John G. Palfrey to OWH, 12/9/1904, RGVP, Carton 8, Folder 61.

54. RGV to SFV, 5/22/1912, at 2.

55. RGV to SFV, 5/28/1912, RGVP, Carton 7, Folder 62.

56. Statement of GB, 4/24/1912, at 7, Committee on Foreign Relations, U.S. Senate, 62nd Cong., 2d Sess., S. 4256 (Washington, DC: GPO, 1912).

57. NYT, 12/6/1913, at 13.

58. FF to GB, 10/4/1911, at 2, GBP, Box 16, Folder "F." *See* Felix Frankfurter Visual Materials, Harvard Law School Historical & Special Collections.

59. GB to General Wood, 2/1/1912, GBP, Box 81, Folder "Politics 1912"; FF to GB, 8/12/1912, *id.*

60. RGV to GB, 5/23/1912, *id.*

61. Howard Shaff and Audrey Karl Shaff, *Six Wars at a Time* 51, 87 (1985).

62. WP, 11/26/1908, at 1; NYT, 11/26/1908, at 6.

63. TR to GB, 2/17/1908, TRP, Series 2, Reel 348, Vol. 78, Page 364; TR to GB, 3/28/1908, TRP, Series 2, Reel 348, Vol. 79, Page 404; TR to GB, 4/1/1908, TRP, Series 2, Reel 348, Vol. 79, Page 439; TR to GB, 5/11/1908, TRP, Series 2, Reel 349, Vol. 81, Page 61.

64. GB to TR, 11/12/1910, TRP, Series 1, Reel 94; GB to TR, 5/31/1911, TRP, Series 1, Reel 107; TR to GB, 6/2/1911, TRP, Series 3A, Reel 367, Vol. 20.

65. WashHerald, 7/7/1912, §2, at 7.

66. GB to H. R. Probasco, circa 1912, at 2, GBP, Box 81, Folder "Politics 1912."

67. *Id.*

68. CPD, 2/12/1912, at 4.

69. Note, GBP, Box 12, Folder "D."

70. GB to TR, 4/3/1912, TRP, Series 1, Reel 135.

71. *See* GB to TR, circa 1912, TRP, Series 1, Reel 163; Herbert Knox Smith to GB, n.d., GBP, Box 81, Folder "Politics 1912."

72. RGV, "A Nation's Prayer," 6/16/1912, at 1 & RGV to GB (handwritten), GBP, Box 45, Folder "V."

73. GB to RGV, 7/12/1912, at 1–2, RGVP, Carton 8, Folder 83. *See* RGV to SFV, 8/3/1912, at 2, *id.*, Carton 7, Folder 69 ("I have a good letter from Gutzon Borglum which I shall send along when I have answered it.").

74. Francis Biddle, *A Casual Past*, 265–67 (1961). *See* FB to SFV, 12/12/1916, at 1–3, RGVP, Box 15, Folder 32.

75. Biddle, *A Casual Past*, 268.

76. *Id. See* RGV to SFV, 6/6/1912, at 2, Carton 7, Folder 63 (placing Biddle at one of the House's dinners); RGV to SFV, 3/26/1913, at 4, *id.*, Folder 76 (same).

77. OWH to FB, 7/17/1912, at 2, FBP, Box 2, Folder 31; Biddle, *A Casual Past*, 270.

78. OWH to LE, 10/28/1912, H-E Letters at 74. *See* OWH to LE, 9/28/1912, *id.* at 72–73; OWH to LE, 11/24/1912, *id.* at 75–76; OWH to Canon Sheehan, 11/23/1912, H-S Corr., at 52.

79. TR to HCL, 7/10/1902, *The Letters of Theodore Roosevelt*, Vol. III, 1901–1903, at 288–89 (Elting E. Morison, et al., eds., 1951). On the Holmes-Roosevelt relationship, *see* White, *Law and the Inner Self*, 298–307; Richard H. Wagner, "A Falling Out: The Relationship between Oliver Wendell Holmes and Theodore Roosevelt," *Journal of Supreme Court History* 27, no. 2 (December 2002): 114–37; John A. Garraty, "Holmes's Appointment to the U.S. Supreme Court," *New England Quarterly* 22, no. 3 (September 1949): 291–303.

80. TR to HCL, 6/5/1895, 1 Correspondence of Theodore Roosevelt and Henry Cabot Lodge, 1:146; TR to HCL, 7/10/1902, *id.* at 2:517–18.

81. Northern Securities v. United States, 193 U.S. 197, 364 (1902) (Holmes, J., dissenting).

82. Newspapers did not include the quotation at the time of the dispute; the quotation surfaced the year that Holmes retired, in one of the first biographies. Silas Bent, *Justice Oliver Wendell Holmes* 251 (1932); Owen M. Fiss, 8 *History of the Supreme Court of the United States: Troubled Beginnings of the Modern State, 1888–1910*, at 138 n. 94 (1993). Bent may have pulled this quotation from two different parts of Owen Wister's Roosevelt biography published two years earlier. *Cf.* Bent, *Justice Oliver Wendell Holmes*, 260 (quoting Wister's book on *Northern Securities*) with Owen Wister, *Roosevelt* 50 (1930) (containing Roosevelt's description of McKinley as having a "chocolate éclair backbone").

83. OWH to NG, 5/30/1908, at 2, OWHP, Reel 23, Page 454, Box 32, Folder 3.

84. OWH to NG, 1/4/1909, *id.* at Page 470.

85. Fiss, *Troubled Beginnings*, 138 nn. 94–95.

86. OWH to FP, 2/9/1921, 2 H-P Letters, at 64.

87. FF to FH, 5/24/1912, H-FF Corr., at 7

88. LDB to Walter Pollock, 4/9/1912, at 2 LLDB, at 577.

89. Robert M. La Follette, Introduction (March 1912), in Gilbert E. Roe, *Our Judiciary Oligarchy* v (1912).

90. LDB to Alfred Brandeis, 4/30/1912, FLLDB, at 190 & 2 LLDB, at 611. On divisive, LDB to George Rublee, 3/16/1912, 2 LLDB, at 568–69.

91. LCC to FF, 6/20/1912, at 1, FFLC, Box 43, Folder "Christie, Loring C. 1911–14."

92. *Id.* at 5.

93. TR, "The Case against the Reactionaries," 6/17/1912, Chicago, 17 *The Works of Theodore Roosevelt,* 209.

94. *Id.* at 231.

95. RGV to Dr. Mumford, 6/18/1912, at 3.

96. *Id.* at 3–4.

97. *Id.* at 4.

98. *Id.* at 8–11. *See* George Rublee COH, at 79–98.

99. NYT, 5/29/1912, at 4.

100. HLS to mother, 7/10/1912, at 3, HLSP, Reel 29, Page 945 ("Frankfurter is back fresh from an interview with T.R. but I have not yet heard the details which he is anxious to communicate.").

101. LDB to FF, 7/12/1912, HBHS, at 20.

102. LDB to Alfred Brandeis, 7/10/1912, FLLDB, at 192.

103. John Milton Cooper Jr., *Woodrow Wilson* 140–58 (2009).

104. LDB to FF, 7/12/1912, HBHS, at 19–20 & 2 LLDB, at 648; LDB to Hapgood, 7/3/1912, 2 LLDB, at 633–34.

105. TR to Ewert, 7/5/1912, *The Letters of Theodore Roosevelt, Vol. VII, 1909–1914* at 572 (Elting E. Morison, ed. 1954).

106. WP, 7/11/1912, at 6; RGV to SFV, 7/12/1912, RGVP, Carton 7, Folder 65 ("While nothing that might happen would surprise me, I supposed that conservative view of the chances indicates that I shall remain at this job until the fourth of next March. ..."); RGV to Dr. H. B. Frissell, 7/12/1912, at 1, *id.*, Carton 21, Folder 32.

107. RGV to Dr. H. B. Frissell, 7/12/1912, at 2–3.

108. FF to Sofy Buckner, 7/17/1912, at 2, FFLC, Box 30, Folder "Buckner, Emory R 1912 #4." *See* FF to Philip Miller, 6/20/1912 & 7/15/1912, *id.*, Box 84, Folder "Miller, Philip 1911–12."

109. RGV to SFV, 6/6/1912, at 1–2, RGVP, Carton 7, Folder 63 (mentioning dinner with Lathrop, Judge Mack, and Frankfurter); RGV to SFV, 7/19/1912, at 2–3, *id.*, Folder 66 (Percy and Innes at dinner to discuss trip to Panama Canal); RGV to SFV, circa August 1912, at 1, *id.*, Folder 68 (Great Falls with Denison, Frankfurter, Innes, Percy, Christie, and Elliot Goodwin).

110. RGV to SFV, 6/6/1912, at 2.

111. *See* appendix; "Warum," at 3, RGVP, Carton 9, Folder 55 (identifying Mrs. Gordon as the author on typewritten version); LHP, Box 104B, Folder 104–12 (containing handwritten version).

112. RGV to SFV, circa 8/1912, at 2.

113. RGV to SFV, 8/6/1912, RGVP, Carton 7, Folder 70 ("Elliot is now with us."); RGV to SFV, 8/11/1912, at 1, *id.*; RGV to SFV, 8/18/1912, at 1, *id.*, Folder 71 (describing Goodwin as "strongly anti Roosevelt").

114. RGV to SFV, 6/8/1912, at 2, RGVP, Carton 7, Folder 63 (mentioning trips to Carlisle and Hampton); RGV to SFV, 6/19/1912, at 1–2, *id.*, Folder 64.

115. RGV to SFV, 6/8/1912, at 1.

116. NYT, 7/17/1912, at 1; WP, 7/17/1912, at 1; BG, 7/17/1912, at 1.
117. George Rublee COH at 96–97 (remarking how the Republican Party never forgave Bass for joining the Progressive Party).
118. RPB to RGV, 7/31/1912, RGVP, Carton 9, Folder 27.
119. RGV to RPB, 8/2/1912, at 1–2, *id.*
120. Herbert Knox Smith to RGV, 8/10/1912, RGVP, Carton 8, Folder 84.
121. RPB to RGV, 8/10/1912, RGVP, Carton 9, Folder 27.
122. Herbert Knox Smith to RGV, 8/10/1912.
123. RGV to SFV, n.d., RGVP, Carton 7, Folder 55 (intending to be in office until March 4); RGV to SFV, n.d., at 1, *id.*, Folder 56.
124. RGV to SFV, 8/17/1912, RGVP, Carton 7, Folder 71. *See* RGV to SFV, 8/24/1912, at 2–3, *id.*, Folder 72; RGV to SFV, n.d., *id.*, Folder 55 (asking his wife to negotiate the sale of the House).
125. RGV to RPB, 8/28/1912, RGVP, Carton 9, Folder 27.
126. RGV to SFV, n.d., at 2, RGVP, Carton 7, Folder 56.
127. *Id.*
128. *Id.* at 4.
129. RGV to Walter Fisher, 8/22/1912, RGVP, Carton 12, Folder 40 & Walter L. Fisher Papers, Box 12, Folder "Indians."
130. Fisher to WHT, 8/24/1912, WHTP, Series 6, 515C, Reel 398 & Walter L. Fisher Papers, Box 12, Folder "Indians."
131. NYT, 9/23/1912, at 5; WP, 9/23/1912, at 1.
132. FFR, 85.
133. Memorandum, 6/14/1912, at 1, RGVP, Carton 8, Folder 81. *See* Jerome Greene to RGV, 6/11/1912, *id.* (proposing job).
134. RGV to SFV, 8/11/1912, at 2, RGVP, Carton 7, Folder 70.
135. NYT, 9/11/1912, at 1.
136. RGV to WHT, 9/10/1912 & Resignation Statement at 1, WHTP, Series 625, Reel 358, at 6688–89; BG, 9/11/1912, at 18.
137. RGV to SFV, 9/12/1912, RGVP, Carton 7, Folder 73. *See* TR to RGV, 9/27/1912, *id.*, Box 8, Folder 84 ("extremely pleased" and "a thing that only a man with its crusading spirit would have done & I appreciate it very greatly.").
138. RGV to RPB, 9/10/1912, at 1, RGVP, Carton 9, Folder 29.
139. FF to SFV, 8/28/1912, at 1–3, FFLC, Box 108, Folder "Valentine, Sophie 1912–1931."
140. *Id.* at 4–5. *See* FFR, 3/17/1953, at 1–5, FFLC, Box 205, Folder "Felix Frankfurter Reminisces Transcript."
141. RGV to RPB, 9/10/1912, at 1.
142. FF to HLS, 9/10/1912, at 1, FFLC, Box 103, Folder "Stimson, Henry L. 1908–12."
143. HLS to FF, 9/19/1912, at 1–2, *id.*
144. *Id.* at 2.
145. FF to HLS, 9/26/1912, *id.*
146. RGV to FF, 9/22/1912, RGVP, Carton 9, Folder 68.
147. *Id.*

148. LDB to Alfred Brandeis, 8/29/1912, 2 LLDB at 661; LDB to Josephus Daniels, 9/4/1912, *id.* at 663.

149. LDB to Norman Hapgood, 9/4/1912, 2 LLDB at 663–64; LDB to Norman Hapgood, 9/13/1912, *id.* at 671–72; LDB to Alfred Brandeis, 9/15/1912, *id.* at 673.

150. LDB to WW, 9/30/1912, 2 LLDB, at 686–94; LDB to William McAdoo, 10/2/1912, *id.* at 697–98. *See* Melvin I. Urofsky, "Wilson, Brandeis and the Trust Issue, 1912–1914," *Mid-America* 49, no. 1 (1967): 3–28.

151. RGV to FF, 9/28/1912, at 1, RGVP, Carton 9, Folder 68; Entry from ECS Daybook 1912, 9/16/1912, at 9, RGVP, Carton 21, Folder 52.

152. RGV to FF, 9/28/1912, at 1.

153. *Id.*

154. FF to Herbert Brownell, 3/19/1957, at 2, FFLC, Box 30, Folder "Brownell, Herbert, Jr. 1953–1957"; FF to ERB, 2/6/1932, at 2, FFLC, Box 206, Folder "Felix Frankfurter Reminisces Miscellany #28"; FFR, 279.

155. On February 19, 1912, Taft, over the objections of prominent New York lawyers and judges Learned Hand, Augustus Hand, and C. C. Burlingham, as well as Florence Kelley of the National Consumers' League, nominated Julius M. Mayer as a judge on the Southern District of New York. Mayer, the former state attorney general, was Jewish. For the objections of the Hands and Burlingham, *see* HLSP, Reel 27. For Kelley's objection, *see* NYT, 1/23/1912, at 3. Many believed that Mayer, as state attorney general, had not adequately defended the New York maximum hour law for bakers in the *Lochner* case.

156. FF to LH, 8/26/1912, at 2, LHP, Box 104A, Folder 104-1.

157. Wickersham to Senator Reed Smoot, 1/12/1914, RGVP, Carton 9, Folder 51.

158. WTD to RPB, 8/21/1912, at 1, *id.*, Folder 50.

159. *Id.* at 2.

160. WHT to WTD, 8/21/1912, WHTP, Reel 361, Series 41J at 9930; WP, 8/23/1912, at 4.

161. WHT to WTD, 10/12/1912, WHTP, Reel 361, Series 41J at 9965; FF to WHT, 10/19/1912, WHTP, Reel 361, Series 41J at 9966 & env. 9967.

162. BaltSun, 10/15/1912, at 1.

163. On the 1912 election, *see* Lewis L. Gould, *Four Hats in the Ring* (2008); James Chace, *1912* (2004).

CHAPTER 4

1. Extracts from ECS Date Book for 1912, 11/3/1912 & 11/6/1912, at 7–8, RGVP, Carton 21, Folders 52.

2. RGV to SFV, 7/16/1912, at 2, RGVP, Carton 7, Folder 66.

3. RGV to SFV, 7/21/1912, at 1, *id.* ("We have just finished our Social Program, and are very proud of it. We is chiefly Felix and I as W.T.D. has gone with Ellery Sedgwick to the mountains of West Virginia. ... Winnie helped, however, on all except the first page and the loose sheet.").

4. Frankfurter and Valentine, "A Tentative Social Program," at 1, RGVP, Carton 9, Folder 67 & FFLC, Box 216, Folder "Valentine, Robert G. Speeches & Articles."

5. Chas. P. Neill, *Report on the Strike of Textile Workers in Lawrence, Massachusetts, in 1912*, at 31, 72, 74 (Washington, DC: GPO, 1912). On labor problems of that period, *see* David Montgomery, *The Fall of the House of Labor* (1987); William E. Forbath, *Law and the Shaping of the American Labor Movement* (1991); Daniel R. Ernst, *Lawyers against Labor* (1995); David Von Drehle, *Triangle* (2003).

6. FF and RGV, "A Tentative Social Program," at 1.

7. *Id.* at 8.

8. Henry P. Kendall, "The First Industrial Counselor–Robert G. Valentine, 1871–1916," The Survey, 11/25/1916, at 189.

9. RGV, "The Progressive Relation between Efficiency and Consent," Bulletin of the Society to Promote the Science of Management, Vol. 1, No. 6, 11/1915, at 26–30, RGVP, Carton 22, Folder 35.

10. RGV to RPB, 12/5/1912, RGVP, Carton 9, Folder 29.

11. RGV to Gertrude King, 6/19/1912, RGVP, Carton 8, Folder 82.

12. RGV to Julia Lathrop, 6/19/1912, *id.*

13. FF to LH, 8/26/1912, at 2, LHP, Box 104A, Folder 104-1.

14. RGV to FF, circa 12/1912, at 1–2, RGVP, Carton 9, Folder 69.

15. FF to RGV, circa 12/1912, at 1–2, *id.*

16. Office of Robert G. Valentine Counsellor of Industrial Relations, 1/3/1913, *id.*, Carton 13, Folder 26.

17. RGV to SFV, 1/14/1913, at 1, RGVP, Carton 7, Folder 75.

18. FF to RGV, 1/7/1913, at 1, RGVP, Carton 9, Folder 70.

19. FF to RGV, circa 12/1912, at 2–3. Hand, however, initially remarked that the "program is rather app[e]alling. I have only read it once and could find no detail to dissent from, tho some of it remained a little uncertain in my mind." LH to FF, 8/26/1912, at 1–2, LHP, Box 104A, Folder 104-1.

20. FF to RGV, 5/18/1913, at 2, RGVP, Carton 9, Folder 71.

21. FF to RGV, 12/30/1912, *id.*, Folder 69.

22. RGV to SFV, 1/14/1913, at 2.

23. FF to RGV, 2/10/1913 tel., RGVP, Carton 9, Folder 70.

24. WTD to Emma Frankfurter, 10/26/1912, at 2, FFLC Box 51, Folder "Denison, Winfred T. 1910–13."

25. RGV to WTD, 10/14/1912, RGVP, Carton 9, Folder 38.

26. RGV to FF, 1/30/1913, at 2, *id.*, Folder 70.

27. Deed from Elizabeth Fealy to SFV, 3/13/1913, Lot 92, Subdivision 133, Liber 12, Folio 63, Washington DC Land Records, 3612, at 223–27; WP, 3/14/1913, at 9.

28. FF to RGV, 5/18/1913, at 4.

29. FF to RGV, 3/10/1913, at 1, RGVP, Carton 9, Folder 70.

30. RGV to SFV, 3/22/1913, at 1, RGVP, Carton 7, Folder 76.

31. *Id.* at 2–3.

32. *Id.* at 2; RGV to SFV, 3/26/1913, at 5, *id.* ("very much interested").

33. RGV to SFV, 3/26/1913, at 1, 2.

34. *Id.* at 5.

35. *Id.* at 2–3.

36. Herbert Croly, *The Promise of American Life* (1909). For more on Croly, *see* chapter 5 nn. 23–27.

37. RGV to SFV, 3/26/1913, at 3–4.

38. FF to ERB, 3/26/1913, at 1, FFLC, Box 30, Folder "Buckner, Emory R. 1913 #6."

39. RGV, "Report of Investigation of Labor Conditions at Charlestown Navy Yard, Boston Massachusetts," 7/17/1913, U.S. Commissions on Industrial Relations, 1912–1915, Reel 8, Page 490.

40. FF to RGV, 7/14/1913, RGVP, Carton 9, Folder 71.

41. RGV to FF, 7/25/1913, *id.*

42. Report, 2/15/1913, FFLC, Box 51, Folder "Denison, Winfred T. 1910–13."

43. NYT, 3/4/1913, at 4.

44. FF to RGV, 3/10/1913, at 3.

45. On the Panama Canal trip, *see* WP, 11/13/1912, at 7; FF to HLS, 3/3/1913, FFLC, Box 103, Folder "Stimson, Henry L. 1913–14"; HLS to FF, 3/18/1913, *id.*

46. BET, 3/12/1913, § 2, at 20; Felix Frankfurter and Capt. George H. Shelton, "Secretary Stimson's Administration of the War Department: A Review," HLSP, Reel 140, Page 59.

47. FF to RGV, 3/5/1913; FF to RGV, 3/10/1913, at 3–4; FF to ERB, 3/11/1913, FFLC, Box 30, Folder "Buckner, Emory R. 1913 #6"; FF to ERB, 3/26/1913, at 2, *id.*

48. FF to RGV, 5/18/1913, at 3.

49. *Id.* at 4.

50. WTD to SFV and RGV, circa 3/1913, at 2–3, RGVP, Box 9, Folder 46.

51. *Id.* at 1; Coquillette and Kimball, *On the Battlefield of Merit*, 539–42.

52. WTD to SFV and RGV, circa 3/1913, at 1. *See* FF to RGV, 3/10/1913, at 1 (handwritten at top) (indicating that Denison would be arguing several important cases).

53. FF to RGV, 2/13/1913 tel., RGVP, Carton 9, Folder 70.

54. FF to RGV, 5/18/1913, at 4.

55. *Id.*

56. FF to RGV, 3/10/1913, at 4.

57. LDB to AGB, 11/24/1913, FLLDB, at 224.

58. Felix Frankfurter, "The Zeitgeist and the Judiciary," The Survey, 1/25/1913, at 543.

59. *Id.*

60. Tiaco v. Forbes, 228 U.S. 549 (1913).

61. See WTD to SFV, 6/13/1913, at 2–3, RGVP, Box 15, Folder 58 (recalling Justice Joseph Rucker Lamar's praise for Frankfurter's argument in the Philippines case).

62. FFR, 109.

63. OWH to Charlotte Moncheur, 7/23/1917, OWHP, Reel 26, Page 436, Box 36, Folder 2. *See* OWH to Wu, 3/26/1925, in H-Wu Corr., 27–28; OWH to HL, 3/26/1925, 1 HLL, at 723; OWH to HL, 12/9/1921, *id.* at 385; Holmes to Ford, 12/29/1917, *Progressive Masks*, at 130–31 (David Burton, ed., 1982).

64. WTD to OWH, 3/3/1913, at 2, OWHP, Reel 31, Page 232, Box 41, Folder 19.
65. Oliver Wendell Holmes, *Speeches* (rev. ed. 1913).
66. WTD to OWH, 5/10/1913, at 2, OWHP, Reel 31, Page 235, Box 41, Folder 19.
67. OWH to Ethel Scott, 1/6/1912, at 1, OWHP, Howe Research Material, Group II, Box 17, Folder 28 & in Howe, *The Proving Years*, 103 ("She is a very solitary bird, and if her notion did not compel her to do otherwise, she would be an absolute recluse, I think."). *See* Albert W. Alschuler, *Law without Values* 35 (2000); Baker, *The Justice from Beacon Hill*, 221, 224; Monagan, *The Grand Panjandrum*, 47–64.
68. WTD to SFV, 5/20/1919, at 6–7, RGVP, Carton 15, Folder 64.
69. FF to Marion Denman, 7/15/1913, at 7, FFLC, Box 5, Folder "Denman, Marion 1913–14."
70. FF to Fanny Holmes, circa 1913, OWHP, Reel 61, Page 440, Box 79, Folder 11.
71. The consensus on the Holmes-Castletown relationship is that it was not sexual. *See* White, *Law and the Inner Self*, 225–52; Monagan, *The Grand Panjandrum*, 71–94; John S. Monagan, "The Love Letters of Justice Holmes," *Boston Globe Magazine*, 3/24/1985, at 15. Holmes destroyed her letters, but she did not destroy his.
72. OWH to FF, 6/15/1913, H-FF Corr., at 9.
73. FF to OWH, 6/9/1913, *id.*
74. OWH to FF, 6/15/1913, *id.* On Holmes and his relationship with Jews, *see* David Hollinger, "The 'Tough-Minded' Justice Holmes, Jewish Intellectuals, and the Making of an American Icon," in *The Legacy of Oliver Wendell Holmes* (Robert W. Gordon, ed., 1992).
75. WTD to OWH, 6/10/1913 tel., OWHP, Reel 31, Page 238, Box 41, Folder 19.
76. Alfred Mitchell-Innes to Robert Borden, 5/22/1912, at 2, RBP, Reel 15, Page 8278; Bothwell, *Loring Christie*, 18–19.
77. Mitchell-Innes to Borden, 5/22/1912, at 2.
78. Borden to Mitchell-Innes, 5/28/1912, RBP, Reel 15, Page 8281; Bothwell, *Loring Christie*, 18–19.
79. Mitchell-Innes to Borden, 6/9/1912, at 1–2, RBP, Reel 15, Pages 8288–89.
80. Borden to Mitchell-Innes, 1/3/1913, RBP, Reel 15, Page 8343.
81. FF to RGV, 3/10/1913, at 1 (handwritten at top).
82. WP, 3/15/1913, at 6; BaltSun 6/27/13, at 2.
83. BET, 3/11/1912, at 2, RGVP, Carton 22, Folder 7.
84. FFR, 106; WP, 4/9/1941, at 10.
85. WES, 3/28/1913, at 7.
86. Frankfurter's account does not credit Denison. FFR, 77–87.
87. Felix Frankfurter, "Edward Henry Warren," 58 Harv. L. Rev. 1128, 1128–29 (1945); ERB to FF, 2/5/194?, FFLC, Box 32, Folder "Buckner, Emory R. undated." *See* Edward H. Warren, *Spartan Education* (1942); Paul D. Carrington, "The Pedagogy of the Old Case Method: A Tribute to 'Bull' Warren," 59 J. L. Educ. 457, 462–63 (2010).

88. WTD to Edward Warren," 6/12/1913, FFLC Box 51, Folder "Denison, Winfred T. 1910–13."

89. Edward Warren to WTD, 6/16/1913, *id.*

90. Pound to Ezra Thayer, 6/19/1913, Harvard Law School Dean's Office, Box 1, "Correspondence about Positions in the Law School and Elsewhere, 1912–1920," Folder "Frankfurter, Felix." On Pound, *see* Ernst, *Tocqueville's Nightmare*, 108–15; Hull, *Roscoe Pound and Karl Llewellyn*; Laura Kalman, *Legal Realism at Yale, 1927–1960* (1986); David Wigdor, *Roscoe Pound* (1974).

91. Warren to WTD, 6/16/1913; Warren to Thayer, 6/26/1913, Harvard Law School Dean's Office, Box 1, Folder "Frankfurter, Felix."

92. FFR, 78.

93. *Id.* See FF to Warren, 6/25/1913, Harvard Law School Dean's Office, Box 1, Folder "Frankfurter, Felix."

94. FFR, 81–82 (quoting memorandum, 7/5/1913).

95. *Id.* at 83.

96. ERB to FF, 7/7/1913, at 2, FFLC, Box 30, Folder "Buckner, Emory R. 1913 #7."

97. FFR at 83 (quoting memorandum, 7/5/1913).

98. *Id.* at 83–84.

99. HLS to FF, 6/28/1913, at 2–3, FFLC, Box 103, Folder "Stimson, Henry L. 1913–14."

100. *Id.* at 4.

101. FF to HLS, 7/7/1913, at 3–5, *id*; FF to LH, 6/28/1913, LHP, Box 104A, Folder 104-2.

102. LH to FF, 7/3/1913, at 2, LHP, Box 104A, Folder 104-2. *See* LH to FF, 7/18/1913, *id.*; FF to LH, 7/8/1913, *id.*

103. FF to Warren, 6/25/1913; FF to RGV, 7/7/1913, at 2, RGVP, Carton 9, Folder 71.

104. FF to OWH, 7/4/1913, H–FF Corr., at 10–11.

105. OWH to FF, 7/15/1913, *id.*, at 12–13.

106. FF to RGV, 7/7/1913, at 3.

107. FF to RGV, 8/26/1913, at 1, RGVP, Carton 9, Folder 71.

108. FF to MD, 6/11/1913, FFLC, Box 5, Folder "Denman, Marion 1913–14"; FF to MD, 7/15/1913, *id.*

109. CSM, 10/1/1910, at 13.

110. OWH to LH, 4/19/1918, OWHP, Reel 26, Page 477, Box 36, Folder 3; OWH to HL, 1/15/1920, 1 HLL, at 234.

111. FFR, 79.

112. FF to Thayer, 7/30/1913, Harvard Law School Dean's Office, Box 1, Folder "Frankfurter, Felix."

113. LDB to Ezra Thayer, 11/4/1913, *id.*

114. Felix Warburg to Thayer, 11/17/1913, *id.*; Walter Meyer to Thayer, 11/7/1913, *id.*; Mack to Thayer, 11/29/1913, *id.* (Rosenwald); Thayer to Meyer, 12/3/1913, *id.*

115. Thayer to OWH, 11/25/1913, *id.*; Thayer to Hand, 11/13/1913, *id.*

116. FFR, 80; Thayer to Felix Warburg, 1/31/1914, Harvard Law School Dean's Office, Box 1, Folder "Frankfurter, Felix."

117. NYT, 5/12/1914, at 6; Cornell Daily Sun, 1/6/1914, at 3.

118. WTD to RGV, 10/6/1913 tel., RGVP, Carton 9, Folder 39.

119. FF to RGV, 10/30/1913, at 4, *id.*, Folder 72.

120. WTD to SFV & RGV, 11/3/1913, *id.*, Folder 47.

121. NYT, 11/25/1913, at 7.

122. WTD to FF, 11/27/1913, at 1–2, FFLC, Box 51, Folder "Denison, Winfred T. 1910–13."

123. WTD to OWH and Mrs. Holmes, 11/19/1913, OWHP, Visual Materials Collection, http://ids.lib.harvard.edu/ids/view/9281631.

124. Wickersham to Smoot, 1/12/1914, at 2, RGVP, Carton 9, Folder 51.

125. *Id.* at 3.

126. *Id.*

127. NYT, 1/23/1914, at 1.

128. NYT, 1/28/1914, at 1.

129. Day Book Chicago, 2/12/1914, at 30.

130. WTD Diary, 1/31/1914, at 1, RGVP, Carton 9, Folder 51.

131. WTD Diary, 2/3/1914, at 1–2, *id.*

132. Percy, *Some Memories*, 24–25, 35.

133. FF to LH, 12/9/1913, at 2, LHP, Box 104A, Folder 104-2. In 1912, Percy had lived in the house of Taft military aide Archie Butt. *See* Archie Butt to Clara Butt, 2/23/1912, 2 *Taft and Roosevelt*, 848.

134. On Willert's connection to Percy and memories of the House of Truth, *see* Sir Arthur Willert, *Washington and Other Memories* 47, 64–65 (1972).

135. Percy, *Some Memories*, 40.

136. RGVP, Carton 22, Folder 4.

137. Percy to RGV, 2/18/1913, RGVP, Carton 8, Folder 86.

138. *Id.* at 2.

139. LDB to FF, 1/28/1913, 3 LLDB, at 19–20 & HBHS, at 22.

140. FF to LDB, 1/30/1913, FFLC, Box 26, Folder "Brandeis, Louis D. 1911–13" & RGVP, Carton 8, Folder 86. Brandeis had "very warm regard" for Percy. LDB to Maurice Hely-Hutchinson, 10/30/1914, 3 LLDB, at 344.

141. FF to LDB, 1/30/1913.

142. FF to LH, 5/2/1914, LHP, Box 104A, Folder 104-2; FF to LH, 5/9/1914, *id.*; FF to WL, 5/2/1914, WLP, Reel 164, Box 1, Folder 29; FF to WL, 5/9/1914, *id.*

143. "Farewell Dinner to Lord Eustace Percy," 3/25/1914, at 3, RGVP, Carton 22, Folder 5.

144. FF to LH, "Percy Dinner," circa 5/16/1914, LHP, Box 104A, Folder 104-2.

145. "Farewell Dinner to Lord Eustace Percy," 3/25/1914, at 2; FF to LH, 5/2/1914; FF to ERB, 5/20/1914, FFLC, Box 30, Folder "Buckner, Emory R. 1914 #8."

146. RGV, 6/5/1914, RGVP, Carton 9, Folder 73.

NOTES TO PAGES 82–87

147. LDB to FF, 10/24/1913, 3 LLDB, at 203 & HBHS, at 23; FF to RGV, 10/30/1913, at 2–3, RGVP, Carton 9, Folder 72.

148. FF to RGV, 5/28/1914, RGVP, Carton 9, Folder 73.

149. WP, 6/7/1914, at E12; FFR, 86.

150. FF to RGV & SFV, n.d., at 1–2, RGVP, Carton 9, Folder 75.

CHAPTER 5

1. "A Dinner *of* Introduction *and* Anticipation *given* at The Players *on the night of* April *the* Ninth, Nineteen hundred and fourteen *by the* Republic *to its* Counsellors, Contributors *and* Friends," Invitation to Robert Valentine (on file with author). The magazine's other founding editor, Walter Weyl, was not part of the April 9 dinner.

2. Mabel Dodge Luhan, *Movers and Shakers* 89, 119 (1936); Ronald Steel, *Walter Lippmann and the American Century* 31 (1980).

3. John Reed, *Day in Bohemia* 42 (1913) & Luhan, *Movers and Shakers*, 180–81.

4. TNR, 12/26/1914, at 15–16.

5. FF to Alfred Mitchell-Innes, 11/7/1914, FFLC, Box 30, Folder "Buckner, Emory R. 1914 #9."

6. WL to Lucile Elsas, 5/10/1908, PPWL, 4; WL to Lucile Elsas, circa 1908, *id.* at 5.

7. See Steel, *Walter Lippmann and the American Century*, 3–11 (early years), 12–32 (Harvard), 23–32 (socialism).

8. WL to LS, 5/18/1910, PPWL, at 6.

9. WL to LS, 4/17/1911, *id.* at 6–7.

10. Lincoln Steffens, *The Autobiography of Lincoln Steffens* 592–94 (1931).

11. Luhan, *Movers and Shakers*, 23, 89, 92, 118–19; Steel, *Walter Lippmann and the American Century*, 50–55; Christine Stansell, *American Moderns* 100–111 (2000).

12. WL to Hazel Albertson, 1/8/1912, PPWL, at 8; WL to Hazel Albertson, 3/4/1912, *id.* at 9; WL to Hazel Albertson, 3/11/1912, *id.* at 10; WL to Graham Wallas, 7/31/1912, *id.* at 11–12; Walter Lippmann, *A Preface to Politics*, 182–83 (1913).

13. NY Call, 6/9/1912, at 16.

14. Luhan, *Movers and Shakers*, 119.

15. *See* Lippmann COH at 35 (describing it as "an amateurish attempt to translate the Wallas form of interpretation into a Freudian interpretation").

16. Lippmann, *A Preface to Politics*, 270, 277–78.

17. *Id.* at 270–71.

18. *Id.* at 103. On Roosevelt and Wilson, *see id.* at 97–105.

19. HC to WL, 5/16/1913, at 1, WLP, Reel 164, Box 1, Folder 20.

20. *Id.* at 2.

21. *Id.* at 2–3.

22. *Id.* at 3.

23. Walter Lippmann, "Notes for a Biography," TNR, 7/16/1930, at 250; Felix Frankfurter, "Herbert Croly and American Political Opinion," TNR, 7/16/1930, at 247.

24. On Croly's early life, *see* Levy, *Herbert Croly of* The New Republic, 3–95.

25. Frankfurter, "Herbert Croly and American Political Opinion," at 247. On the reception of *The Promise of American Life, see* Levy, *Herbert Croly of* The New Republic, 132–61.

26. Forcey, *The Crossroads of Liberalism*, 29 ("The pursuit of Jeffersonian ends by Hamiltonian means, therefore, became Croly's prescription for a new liberalism."); Sean Wilentz, preface, *The Promise of American Life* ix–xi (Princeton University Press ed., 2014); Croly, *The Promise of American Life*, 169 (using the phrase "New Nationalism"); George E. Mowry, *Theodore Roosevelt and the Progressive Movement* 145–46 (1946) (describing New Nationalism as "combining Hamiltonian means with Jeffersonian ends" and attributing New Nationalism to Croly).

27. Croly, *The Promise of American Life*, 168, 175.

28. *Id.* at 386 ("The labor unions, consequently, like the big corporations, need legal recognition; and this legal recognition means in their case, also, substantial discrimination by the state in their favor."). *See id.* at 357–68 (on the recognition of corporations); *id.* at 385–98 (on organized labor).

29. HC to RGV, 12/26/1912, at 1–2, RGVP, Carton 8, Folder 85.

30. HC to LH, circa late 1/1913, at 3, LHP, Box 102, Folder 102-20. *See* LH to HC, 1/30/1913, at 1, *id.* ("I am very glad you like Frankfurter; he is all that you think … he is a wonderfully keen and wholly disinterested man. I think he may go anywhere provided he keeps his health. He is a little bit too much alive, and at times gets looking badly. Dennison [*sic*] is himself just as fine a fellow, but I don't think he has the intellectual outfit of Frankfurter. However, he makes up for it by having a little bit broader base to sit on. There is danger that Frankfurter may lose his balance, but unless I am all wrong he is just as pure as a diamond, or as Phil [Littell] recently said, as a newly fallen woman.").

31. HC to LH, circa early 3/1913, *id.*, Folder 102-21.

32. RGV to SFV, 3/26/1913, at 2–4, RGVP, Carton 7, Folder 76.

33. HC to WL, 11/1/1913, WLP, Reel 164, Box 1, Folder 20.

34. Lippmann, "Notes for a Biography," at 250. For influences on Croly and *The Promise of American Life, see* Levy, *Herbert Croly of* The New Republic, 96–131 (his father's religious positivism); Forcey, *The Crossroads of Liberalism*, 20–21 (James's pragmatism).

35. HC to WL, 12/5/1913, at 1, WLP, Reel 164, Box 1, Folder 20.

36. *Id.*

37. HC to LH, 12/13/1913, at 1, LHP, Box 102, Folder 102-21.

38. HC to LH, 12/21/1913, at 2–3, *id.*

39. HC to LH, 1/5/1914, at 2–3, *id.*

40. NYT, 4/24/1914, at 11.

41. HC to LH, 1/5/1914, at 3–4 (bemoaning *Harper's* editorial); HC to LH, 1/8/ 1914, at 1–2, *id.* (discussing *Harper's* falling circulation).

42. Lippmann, "Notes for a Biography," at 251. On the history of the magazine, *see* Forcey, *The Crossroads of Liberalism*; Levy, *Herbert Croly of The New Republic*; David Seideman, The New Republic (1986).

43. Herbert Croly, *Willard Straight* 472 (1924).

44. HC to LH, n.d. 1913, LHP, Box 102, Folder 102-21 (asking for loan, paying debts at Harvard Club); HC to LH, 6/21/1913, *id.* (receiving $2,000 loan).

45. HC to LH, 3/7/1914, *id.*

46. Luhan, *Movers and Shakers*, 298 (reporting that Lippmann's joining the magazine upset Reed and caused a split in their relationship).

47. Croly, *Willard Straight*, 473–74.

48. WL to Van Wyck Brooks, 2/5/1914, PPWL, 16.

49. *Id.* at 17.

50. HC to LH, 1/5/1914, at 4.

51. Lippmann, "Notes for a Biography," at 250.

52. HC to WL, n.d., WLP, Reel 164, Box 1, Folder 20.

53. HC to LH, 12/21/1913, at 3; HC to LH, 6/29/1914, at 1–2, LHP, Box 102, Folder 102-21 (enticing Hand); FF to HC, n.d., LHP, Box 104A, Folder 104-2 (explaining his decision to go to Harvard).

54. HC to FF, 6/29/1913, FFLC, Box 50, Folder "Croly, Herbert 1913"; FF to HC, 7/4/1913, *id.*; FFR, 92.

55. HC to LH, 12/21/1913, at 3.

56. HC to FF, 9/4/1913, FFLC, Box 50, Folder "Croly, Herbert 1913."

57. On Frankfurter as trustee, *see* Forcey, *The Crossroads of Liberalism*, at 181–82.

58. FF to LH, circa 12/26/1914, at 2, LHP, Box 104A, Folder 104-3.

59. WL Diary, 7/4/1914, at 1–2, Reel 160, Box 236, Folder 1.

60. Howard M. Gitelman, *The Legacy of the Ludlow Massacre* (1988).

61. TR to HCL, 4/27/1910, *The Letters of Theodore Roosevelt*, Vol. VII, at 76.

62. WL Diary, 7/4/1914, at 2. *See* Lippmann, *A Preface to Politics*, 24 ("The Roosevelt regime gave a new prestige to the Presidency by effecting through it the greatest release of political invention in a generation.").

63. WL Diary, 7/4/1914, at 2.

64. WL to TR, 5/6/1914, TRP, Series 1, Reel 182. *See* TR to WL, 5/22/1913, PPWL, at 14 n. 1 (TR letter is lost).

65. WL to TR, 5/30/1913, PPWL, at 14.

66. Walter Lippmann, *Public Persons* 126 (1976).

67. TR to Romulo Sebastian Naon, 1/6/1915, *The Letters of Theodore Roosevelt*, Vol. VIII, 1914–19 (Elting Morison, ed., 1954), at 872.

68. WL Diary, 7/4/1914, at 2–3; Steel, *Walter Lippmann and the American Century*, 65.

69. WL Diary, 7/4/1914, at 3.

70. WL Diary, 7/4–5/1914, at 3–4.

71. *Id.*

72. WL to TR, 6/1/1914, at 2, TRP, Series 1, Reel 185.

73. WL Diary, 7/4–5/1914, at 4.
74. TR to Weyl, 8/6/1914, *The Letters of Theodore Roosevelt*, Vol. VII, at 793.
75. FF to ERB, circa August 1914, FFLC, Box 30, Folder "Buckner Emory R. 1914 #9."
76. WL to TR, 7/1/1914, at 2, TRP, Series 1, Reel 187.
77. FFR Transcript, 6/27/1957, at 6, FFLC, Box 205, Folder "Felix Frankfurter Reminisces Transcript 27 June 1957 #12" (recalling returning to Boston from Kennebunkport, Maine, with Kendall and Valentine from meeting with Frederick W. Taylor).
78. FF to Alfred Mitchell-Innes, 11/7/1914, at 1, FFLC, Box 30, Folder "Buckner, Emory R. 1914 #9."
79. WL Diary, 7/27/1914, at 17.
80. WL to Hazel Albertson, 9/25/1914, PPWL, at 19–20; WL Diary, 7/30/1914, at 17.
81. WL to Graham Wallas, 7/30/1914, at 1–2, WLP, Reel 32, Box 33, Folder 1244; WL Diary, 7/30/1914, at 17.
82. WL Diary, 8/1/1914, at 17; Steel, *Walter Lippmann and the American Century*, 71.
83. On the causes of the war, *see* Christopher Clark, *The Sleepwalkers* (2012); Max Hastings, *Catastrophe 1914* (2013); Margaret MacMillan, *The War That Ended Peace* (2013); Sean McMeekin, *July 1914* (2013).
84. WL Diary, 8/2/1914, at 17.
85. WL to FF, 8/2/1914, PPWL, at 18–19.
86. WL Diary, 8/5/1914, at 20.
87. Herbert Croly, *Progressive Democracy* 378–405 (1914) (discussing "industrial democracy"); Walter Lippmann, *Drift and Mastery* 77–100 (1914) (discussing the "key to the labor movement" as an "industrial democracy").
88. Lippmann, *Drift and Mastery*, 99.
89. HC to Straight, 12/17/1914, at 2, WSP, Reel 5, Section 3, at 85 ("The difficulty is, I think, that the people are not seriously concerned with domestic social and political problems now. They are still so much preoccupied by the war and by the attempt to think out its cause and effects, that they cannot concentrate upon a book which is confined entirely to the discussion of domestic policy.").
90. TNR, 11/7/1914, at 3.
91. *Id.* The progressive movement is not easily defined, and "progressive" is not a synonym for "liberal." This book distinguishes progressivism from liberalism based on progressivism's faith in the state. Of course, there were many types of progressives. David Kennedy identifies the "semantic" problem that "hundreds, no doubt thousands, of public men in the first two decades of this century referred to themselves as 'progressive.'" Kennedy, "Introduction," xii. The House of Truth generally consisted of "regulationists" who believed that experts could implement economic reform, particularly in the field of labor-management relations. Kennedy also describes Richard Hofstadter's failure to recognize "regulationists like Theodore Roosevelt and Herbert Croly and Walter Lippmann as authentic progressives." Kennedy, "Overview: The Progressive Era," at 462.

92. TNR, 11/14/1914, at 7.

93. WL to TR, 11/12/1914, TRP, Series 1, Reel 193; WL to Mabel Dodge, 11/20/1914, in Luhan, *Movers and Shakers*, 164; Lippmann, *Public Persons*, 100; Steel, *Walter Lippmann and the American Century*, 76.

94. Lippmann COH at 54; Lippmann, *Public Persons*, 100.

95. Lippmann COH at 54.

96. Theodore Roosevelt, "Two Noteworthy Books on Democracy," Outlook, 11/18/1914, at 648.

97. TNR, 11/21/1914, at 3–4.

98. NYTM, 12/6/1916, at SM1.

99. Lippmann, *Public Persons*, 100–101.

100. TNR, 12/12/1914, at 4–5. *See* HC to Willard Straight, 12/13/1914 or 12/17/1914, DWSEP, Reel 14.

101. Alvin Johnson, *Pioneer's Progress* 245 (1952). *Cf.* Steel, *Walter Lippmann and the American Century*, 76 ("three circumcised Jews and three anemic Christians") (with no citation). Some of Roosevelt's correspondence with Lippmann was stolen in the 1940s. *Id.* at 606 n. 7. Lippmann described it as a "savage letter." Lippmann, *Public Persons*, 101. The three Jews were Frankfurter, Lippmann, and Walter Weyl.

102. TR to Willard Straight, 2/8/1916 at 8. *The Letters of Theodore Roosevelt* Vol. VIII, 1914–1919, at 1020. *See* TR to Owen Wister, 9/28/1916, TRP, Reel 386, Series 3A, Vol. 96; TR to Owen Wister, 11/3/1916, *id.*

103. Lippmann COH at 55. For similar comments, *see* Lippmann, "Notes for a Biography," at 251.

CHAPTER 6

1. OWH to FF, 5/29/1915, H-FF Corr., at 30.

2. HC to OWH, 11/15/1914, at 1, OWHP, Reel 30, Page 358, Box 40, Folder 21; OWH to FF, 11/27/1914, H-FF Corr., at 23.

3. OWH to FF, 1/21/1915, H-FF Corr., at 25.

4. OWH to JCG, 10/27/1914, at 3–4, OWHP, Reel 35, Pages 532–33, Box 33, Folder 25. *See* OWH to FP, 11/7/1914, 1 H-P Letters at 224; OWH to LE, 12/10/1914, H-E Letters at 102.

5. OWH to HC, 11/22/1914, Autograph File "H," Harvard University.

6. OWH to WL, 10/27/1914, at 1, WLP, Reel 165, Box 2, Folder 39, "Holmes, Oliver Wendell 1914–1916."

7. *Id.* at 2–3.

8. OWH to WL, 10/30/1914, *id.*

9. *Id.*

10. TNR, 3/11/1916, at 156. Lippmann wrote Holmes: "I have tried to write for this week's New Republic what I felt to say. But of course I couldn't succeed ... a lady to whom I showed the article said that the most serious

fault was the omission of Mrs. Holmes. I told her it couldn't be done by mortal pen." WL to OWH, 3/8/1915 [*sic*], OWHP, Reel 35, Page 338, Box 46, Folder 27 (ellipses in original).

11. OWH to HL, 11/25/1916, 1 HLL at 38.

12. OWH to Clara Stevens, 2/9/1916, OWHP, Reel 26, Page 354, Box 35, Folder 32.

13. Robert Taft's good friend from Yale and Harvard Law School, George Harrison, accepted instead. Harrison was the best man at Taft's wedding. WES, 10/14/1914, at 7.

14. WHT to RT, 11/19/1912, WHTP, Reel 452, Image 177; WHT to JCG, 11/19/1912, *id.*, Image 176.

15. OWH to FF, 10/12/1912, H-FF Corr., at 7.

16. WES, 1/8/1913, at 7; WES, 3/28/1913, at 7.

17. He is the father of McGeorge Bundy, who later befriended Frankfurter, assisted Henry Stimson during World War II and on his memoir, and was Kennedy's and Johnson's national security adviser. *See* Kai Bird, *The Color of Truth*, 23–41 (1998).

18. Harvey Bundy COH at 66 ("rather queer addition"); Belknap Diary, 10/7/1915 ("jolly man about town") (on file with author); Harvard College Class of 1906, Third Report at 124 (1914) (listing him as member of Chevy Chase Country Club and Metropolitan Club and as secretary and treasurer of Harper & Voigt Company general contractors); FF to TR Powell, 12/13/1915, FFLC, Box 91, Folder "Powell, Thomas Reed" (describing Bissell's background).

19. Bundy COH at 66.

20. *Id.* at 67; WES, 5/1/1915, pt. 1, at 10.

21. Bundy COH at 67.

22. *Id.* at 65–66.

23. Chauncey Belknap, Undergraduate Alumni Records, Princeton University, Box 381.

24. Recollection of Robert Patterson by Chauncey Belknap COH at 1, 4/27/1960 (1961).

25. *Id.* at 4–5.

26. *Id.* at 12. Harvard law dean Ezra Thayer had selected Belknap to be Holmes's secretary. Belknap to FF, 3/29/1935, at 1–2, FFLC, Box 145, Folder "Rowe, James Mar.–June 1935 #6"; FF to Belknap, 3/27/1935, *id.* After Thayer committed suicide in 1915, Holmes designated Frankfurter and Arthur Hill to select the new secretaries. Frankfurter selected all the remaining secretaries until Holmes's death.

27. Recollections of Patterson by Belknap COH at 12; Belknap COH, 4/29/1975, at 7.

28. Belknap COH, 5/6/1975, at 14–15. The classmate was Montgomery Burns Armstrong. *Id.*; Belknap Diary, 10/7/1915.

29. Belknap Diary, 10/7/1915. *See* I. Scott Messinger, "The Judge as Mentor: Oliver Wendell Holmes, Jr. and His Law Clerks," 11 Yale Journal of Law & the Humanities 119 (1999). I thank Scott for his assistance in obtaining a copy of the diary, which is written in part in Pittman shorthand.

30. Belknap Diary, 10/8/1915.

31. Belknap Diary, 10/29/1915.

32. WP, 10/26/1943, at 6; NYT, 10/26/1943, at 23.

33. Belknap Diary, 10/11/1915.

34. Phone interview with Robert Belknap, Chauncey's son, with author, 7/13/2012.

35. NYT, 1/7/1921, at 13; WES, 1/6/1921, at 8.

36. Belknap Diary, 10/11/1915 & 12/16–18/1915 (French lesson).

37. Belknap COH, 5/6/1975, at 15.

38. OWH to HL, 12/13/1916, 1 HLL at 42. See OWH to HL, 11/22/1917, id. at 111 (moving the teas to Thursday and inviting Noyes); OWH to HL, 2/7/1918, id. at 133 (recommending her for an overseas post he described as "some job I don't approve of but, as in duty bound, [I] gave her a character in writing to help her get the place"); OWH to HL, 2/12/1918, id. at 135 ("She is a nice gal–and I like her very much."); Belknap Diary, 11/1/1915 & 11/8/1915.

39. Belknap COH, 5/6/1975, at 16–17. See Belknap Diary, 3/8/1916 (describing a party in "two installments").

40. Bundy COH at 68.

41. TNR, 5/29/1915, at 100.

42. OWH to Charlotte Moncheur, 12/30/1915, at 1, OWHP, Reel 26, Page 345, Box 35, Folder 31.

43. LCC to FF, 9/10/1914, at 2, FFLC, Box 43, "Folder Christie, Loring C. 1911–1914."

44. LCC to FF, 11/11/1914, at 4, id.; Marie Armstrong to FF, 11/15/1914, at 4, id.; FF to Frederick Lehmann, 1/8/1915, at 2, WLP, Reel 164, Box 1, Folder 29.

45. LCC to OWH, 3/6/1915, at 1, OWHP, Reel 31, Page 73, Box 41, Folder 12.

46. OWH to Charlotte Moncheur, 12/30/1915, at 1. See OWH to FF, 4/16/1915, H-FF Corr., at 29; LCC to FF, 11/21/1915, at 2, FFLC, Box 43, Folder "Christie, Loring C. 1915."

47. LCC to FF, 2/22/1915, at 3, FFLC, Box 43, Folder "Christie, Loring C. 1915."

48. LCC to FF, 5/3/1915, at 2–3, id.

49. LCC to FF, 12/21/1915, at 1–2, id.

50. Belknap Diary, 1/15–29/1916.

51. EP to OWH, 5/17/1914, at 2–3, OWHP, Box 48, Folder 27, Reel 36, Page 914.

52. Percy, Some Memories, 41–42; FF to Frederick Lehmann, 1/8/1915, at 2.

53. EP to OWH, 12/24/1914, at 1–2, OWHP, Box 48, Folder 27, Reel 36, Pages 918–19.

54. EP to OWH, 6/13/1915, at 2–3, id., Pages 922–23.

55. EP to FF, 8/29/1914, at 3–4, FFLC, Box 89, Folder "Percy, Eustace 1913–15."

56. WL, "Notes for a Biography," at 251.

57. TNR, 2/13/1915, at 35.

58. WL to FF, 2/29/1916, WLP, Reel 9, Box 10, Folder 419.

59. See Arthur S. Link, 3 Wilson: The Struggle for Neutrality, 1914–1915, at 368–455 (1960); Cooper, Woodrow Wilson, 285–98.

60. TNR, 9/4/1915, at 111.
61. TNR, 6/5/1915, at 109.
62. *Id.* at 110. TNR, 8/7/1915, at 11 ("The fact that one great democratic nation has remained disinterested and detached will be of peculiar value when the war is over.").
63. "A Review of the Growth and Prospects of the New Republic," 8/19/1916, WSP, Reel 5, Segment 4, April 1916–August 1917.
64. Hutchins Hapgood, *A Victorian in the Modern World* 402–3 (1939).
65. WL to Alfred Zimmern, 6/7/1915, PPWL, at 27.
66. WL to Robert Dell, 6/7/1915, *id.* at 28.
67. Walter Lippmann, *The Stakes of Diplomacy* 15–25 (1915).
68. *Id.* at 228–29.
69. FF to WL, 11/16/1915, at 2, WLP, Reel 164, Box 1, Folder 29.
70. Belknap Diary, 12/6/1915.
71. LCC to FF, 5/11/1915, at 1, FFLC, Box 43, Folder "Christie, Loring C. 1915." *See* EP to FF, 5/23/1915, FFLC, Box 89, Folder "Percy, Eustace 1915–16."
72. Industrial Relations, Final Report and Testimony 852 (1916).
73. *Id.* at 854.
74. *Id.* at 855.
75. *See* Frank Barkley Copley, 2 *Frederick W. Taylor* 417–32 (1923); FFR Transcript, 6/27/1957, at 1–6, FFLC, Box 205, Folder "Felix Frankfurter Reminisces Transcript 27 June 1957 #12"; Taylor to Valentine, 9/23/1914, RGVP, Carton 13, Folder 3.
76. Industrial Relations, Final Report and Testimony, 128.
77. TNR, 3/27/1915, pt. 2 at 2, 8. *See* FF to WL, 3/23/1915, WLP, Reel 164, Box 1, Folder 29 (arranging a meeting with Valentine).
78. TNR, 7/3/1915, at 221–23.
79. TNR, 11/20/1915, at 66.
80. Industrial Relations, Final Report and Testimony, at 856.
81. TNR, 1/16/1915, at 16.
82. FF to Alfred Mitchell-Innes, 11/7/1914, at 3; RGV to WTD, 7/27/1914, at 1–2, RGVP, Carton 9, Folder 41.
83. RGV to WTD, 10/23/1914, RGVP, Carton 9, Folder 44.
84. RGV to WTD, 7/27/1914, at 2.
85. RGV to WTD, 10/23/1914.
86. RGV to LCC, 12/1/1914, at 2, RGVP, Carton 9, Folder 2.
87. TNR, 7/7/1915, at 286.
88. Winfred T. Denison, "What the Filipinos Want," The Independent, 11/16/1914, at 237–39.
89. WTD to RGV, 5/12/1914, at 4–5, RGVP, Carton 15, Folder 59.
90. Oregonian, 8/23/1914, at 6.
91. Colman's Weekly, 7/4/1914, at 4, RGVP, Carton 9, Folder 53.
92. "Re White Hope Speech," n.d., RGVP, Carton 9, Folder 51.
93. WTD to TR, 3/24/1915, TRP, Series 1, Reel 182 & RGVP (on file with author).

94. TR to WTD, 8/3/1914, at 1–2, TRP, Series 3A, Reel 384 & RGVP, Carton 9, Folder 53; WTD to TR, 11/27/1914, at 1, *id.*, Folder 54 & TRP, Series 1, Reel 194; TR to WTD, 1/7/1915, TRP, Reel 357, Vol. 100, Page 247.

95. WHT to HLS, 2/2/1915, HLSP, Reel 38, Page 506. See WHT to WTD, 2/2/1915, at 1–2, *id.*, Pages 514–15. Taft was initially "severe," then softened his tone in a follow-up letter because of Denison's "efforts at good things in the Philippines." WHT to WTD, 1/25/1916, WHTP, Vol. 43, Page 261. Taft sent his January 25 letter to Denison, who was in a sanitarium at the time, care of Frankfurter at Harvard Law School.

96. FF to Alfred Mitchell-Innes, 11/7/1914, at 3.

97. HLS to WTD, 2/27/1915, at 1, HLSP, Reel 38, Page 698. *See* HLS to WTD, 1/9/1915, HLSP, Reel 38, Page 150; FF to HLS, 3/3/1915, at 1–2, *id.* at Pages 774–75; HLS to FF, 3/6/1915, FFLC, Box 103, Folder "Stimson, Henry L. 1915–16."

98. WTD to SFV, 7/14/1914, RGVP, Carton 15, Folder 59; WTD to SFV, 7/18/1914, *id.*; WTD to RGV & SFV, 11/30/1914, *id.*, Carton 9, Folder 44.

99. WTD to SFV, 4/18/1915, RGVP, Carton 15, Folder 60.

100. WTD to RGV & FF, 5/28/1915, at 1–2, RGVP, Carton 9, Folder 45.

101. Felix Frankfurter ed., *A Selection of Cases under the Interstate Commerce Act* (1915) (quoting Holmes, "Law in Science and Science in Law," 12 Harv. L. Rev. 443, 456 (1899)).

102. *Id.* at 1 (including Omaha Street Rwy. v. ICC, 230 U.S. 324 (1913)).

103. LCC to FF, 5/3/1915, at 1, FFLC, Box 43, Folder "Christie, Loring C. 1915."

104. Belknap Diary, 11/14/1915. Belknap misspelled his name as Irving. Dr. Erving, an orthopedic surgeon, was a friend of Brandeis's. *See* LDB to FF, 11/19/1916, HBHS, at 26 & 27 n. 5. For more on the Hapgood-Frankfurter debate, *see* FF to WL, 11/16/1915, at 1, WLP, Reel 164, Box 1, Folder 29 ("I had a set to with Hapgood in which he was brilliant, but found me as lacking in sense as he had found you.").

105. Coppage v. Kansas, 236 U.S. 1, 11 (1915).

106. *Id.* at 47 n. 2 (Day, J., dissenting).

107. Adair v. United States, 208 U.S. 161 (1908).

108. Lochner v. New York, 198 U.S. 45, 75 (1905) (Holmes, J., dissenting).

109. OWH to HL, 12/13/1916, 1 HLL at 42. *See* OWH to HL, 1/8/1917, *id.* at 51–52.

110. Coppage, 236 U.S. at 27 (Holmes, J., dissenting).

111. TNR, 1/30/1915, at 4. *See* Oliver Wendell Holmes, "Law in Science and Science in Law," 12 Harv. L. Rev. 443, 460 (1899) ("We must think things not words, or at least we must constantly translate our words into the facts for which they stand, if we are to keep to the real and the true.").

112. TNR, 2/6/1915, at 6–7, LHP, Box 104A, Folder 104-4.

113. FF to OWH, 1/27/1915, H-FF Corr., at 25–26.

114. Muller v. Oregon, 208 U.S. 412 (1908). *See* chapter 2 nn. 56–58.

115. Hitz to FF, 12/17/1914, LDB-Louisville, Reel 119 & Mason, *Brandeis*, 253 (emphasis in original).

116. Charles Warren to FF, 4/6/1939, FFLC, Box 127, Folder "Brandeis, Louis D. 1939–59."
117. Belknap Diary, 10/29/1915.
118. LDB to Alfred Brandeis, 2/27/1915, 3 LLDB at 444.
119. Henry Bournes Higgins, "A New Province for Law and Order," 29 Harv. L. Rev. 13 (1915).
120. Belknap Diary, 11/22/1915.
121. Belknap Diary, 12/23/1915.
122. Frank v. Mangum, 237 U.S. 309 (1915).
123. *See* Steve Oney, *And The Dead Shall Rise: The Murder of Mary Phagan and the Lynching of Leo Frank* 339–42 (2003); Leonard Dinnerstein, *The Leo Frank Case* 54–56, 60 (1968).
124. Frank, 237 U.S. at 347, 349 (Holmes, J., dissenting).
125. OWH to LE, 4/10/1915, H-E Letters at 112.
126. LDB to RP, 11/27/1914, 3 LLDB at 373.
127. TNR, 4/24/1915, at 290.
128. Leo Frank to OWH, 7/10/1915, at 2, OWHP, Reel 31, Page 364, Box 43, Folder 2.
129. Memorandum of talk with FF, 8/10/1964, at 1, MDHP, Box 22, Folder 26.
130. Oney, *And the Dead Shall Rise*, 513–28, 560–71 (on the role of prominent Marietta citizens in planning the lynching).
131. Giles v. Harris, 189 U.S. 475, 488 (1903). Legal scholars regard Holmes's opinion as one of the worst decisions about race in the Court's history. Jamal Greene, "The Anticanon," 125 Harv. L. Rev. 379, 429 (2011) (asserting that *Giles* "should be–the most prominent stain on the name of Oliver Wendell Holmes"); Richard H. Pildes, "Democracy, Anti-Democracy, and the Canon," 17 *Constitutional Commentary* 295, 306 (2000) (describing it as "the most legally disingenuous analysis in the pages of the U.S. Reports"); Gerard Magliocca, "The Worst Supreme Court Opinion Ever?," *Concurring Opinions* blog, posted May 20, 2011.
132. Berea College v. Kentucky, 211 U.S. 45 (1908) (Holmes, J., concurring in the judgment); Bailey v. Alabama, 219 U.S. 219, 245 (1911) (Holmes, J., dissenting).
133. FF to Morris Cohen, 10/3/1916, in *Portrait of a Philosopher: Morris R. Cohen in Life and Letters* 248 (Leonora Cohen Rosenfield, ed., 1962). *See* United States v. Reynolds, 235 U.S. 133, 150 (1914) (Holmes, J., concurring) ("There seems to me nothing in the 13th Amendment or the Revised Statutes that prevents a state from making a breach of contract, as well a reasonable contract for labor as for other matters, a crime and punishing it as such.").
134. Guinn v. United States, 238 U.S. 347 (1915); Myles v. Anderson, 238 U.S. 368 (1915).
135. BAA, 1/11/1908, at 1; BAA, 1/18/1908, at 1; WashBee, 1/11/1908, at 5.
136. Thomas E. Waggaman to Catherine Drinker Bowen, 4/7/1943, CDBP, Box 60, Folder "Yankee from Olympus."
137. *Id.*

138. OWH to FF, 7/5/1915, H-FF Corr., 32.

139. WP, 6/25/1915, at 14; WES, 6/25/1915, at 8.

140. Diner, *A Very Different Age*, 125–54 (discussing the black loss of "political and civil rights" and "tightening segregation" during this period); McGerr, *A Fierce Discontent*, 182–218 (discussing the "shield of segregation"); Painter, *Standing at Armageddon*, 216–30 (discussing race and disenfranchisement); David W. Southern, *The Progressive Era and Race* 111–36 (2005) (discussing national politics and race from 1900 to 1917); Wiebe, *The Search for Order, 1877–1920*, at 107–10, 156–57 (discussing populism and Jim Crow and scientific racism).

141. TNR, 11/27/1915, at 88–89.

142. HC to Washington, 6/18/1915, 13; *The Booker T. Washington Papers: 1914–15*, Vol. 13, at 320 (Louis R. Harlan and Raymond W. Smock, eds., 1984).

143. TNR, 12/4/1915, at 113–14.

144. Cooper, *Woodrow Wilson*, 88; Arthur Link, 1 *Wilson: The Road to the White House* 502 (1947).

145. On McReynolds, *see* chapter 9 nn. 23–27.

146. Cooper, *Woodrow Wilson*, 204–6; Arthur Link, 2 *Wilson: The New Freedom* 243–54 (1956); Nicholas Patler, *Jim Crow and the Wilson Administration* (2007); Eric S. Yellin, *Racism in the Nation's Service* (2013); Constance McLaughlin Green, *The Secret City* (1969).

147. TNR, 11/21/1914, at 5. On Wilson's campaign and the race question, *see* Link, 1 *Wilson: The Road to the White House*, 501–5.

148. On Trotter, *see* Cooper, *Woodrow Wilson*, 270–73; Link, 2 *Wilson: The New Freedom*, 252.

149. CT, 11/16/1914, at 1.

150. TNR, 11/21/1914, at 5.

151. TNR, 3/20/1915, at 185.

152. WL to John Collier, 3/22/1915, PPWL, at 26 & n. 1.

153. *Id.*

154. TNR, 4/10/1915, at 262–63.

155. The exception was a blind *Washington Post* item. WP, 2/19/1915, at 4.

156. TNR, 5/8/1915, at 17.

157. WW to Tumulty, 4/28/1915, 33; WWP at 86. *See* Link, 2 *Wilson: The New Freedom*, 253 (suggesting that Wilson "fell into Dixon's trap"); *id.* at 252–54. For the best review of the controversy, *see* John Hope Franklin, "*Birth of a Nation*—Propaganda as History," in *Race and History* 10–24 (1989) & *Massachusetts Review* 20, no. 3 (October 1979): 417–34.

158. CDEF, 5/8/1915, at 8.

CHAPTER 7

1. WL to FF, 1/17/1916, at 1–2, WLP, Reel 9, Box 10, Folder 419; FF to LH, 1/22/1916, LHP, Box 104A, Folder 104-5.

2. FF to ERB, 1/26/1916, FFLC, Box 30, Folder "Buckner, Emory R. 1916. #12."
3. FF to LH, 1/30/1916, at 2–3, LHP, Box 104A, Folder 104-5.
4. LCC to Borden handwritten memorandum, 1/27/1916, at 4, LCCP, Reel 3887, Vol. 2, at 1744. See Arthur S. Link, 4 *Wilson: Confusions and Crises, 1915–16*, at 44 & n. 95 (1964) (mentioning the memorandum).
5. Karger to Taft, 1/29/1916, WHTP, Reel 162, Series 3. On the Taft-Karger relationship, *see* Gould, *Chief Executive to Chief Justice*, 24–25.
6. LDB to Alfred Brandeis, 1/28/1916, 4 LLDB at 25.
7. WP, 1/29/1916, at 7.
8. NYT, 1/29/1916, at 1; WP, 1/29/1916, at 1.
9. House Diary, 1/8/1913, 27 WWP at 23 (opposing LDB for commerce and labor secretary); EMH to WW, 1/19/1913, *id.* at 27; House Diary, 1/17/1913, *id.* at 62 (saying LDB had been "practically eliminated" from any cabinet position); House Diary, 1/25/1913, *id.* at 71 (persuading president not to appoint him solicitor general or "anything of a legal nature"); House Diary, 2/13/1913, *id.* at 110 (recollecting that WW rejected criticism of Brandeis).
10. WW to Cosmos Club, 2/1/1915, 32 WWP at 167; Hitz to WW, 1/30/1915, *id.* at 163–64.
11. Link, 4 *Wilson: Confusions and Crises*, at 324; 29 WWP at 30 n. 1 (noting Wilson read Brandeis's article on the money trust); LDB to WW, 6/14/1913, 27 WWP at 520–21 & 3 LLDB at 113–16 (advising on federal reserve legislation). On Brandeis and the FTC, *see* Marc Winerman, "The Origins of the FTC," 71 Antitrust L.J. 1, 32–38 (2003).
12. *See* 4 LLDB at 25–26 n. 2; Link, 4 *Wilson: Confusions and Crises*, 323–25. On the story of Brandeis's nomination, *see* Urofsky, *Louis D. Brandeis*, 430–59; Strum, *Louis D. Brandeis*, 291–308; Lewis J. Paper, *Brandeis* 209–40 (1983); A. L. Todd, *Justice on Trial* (1964); Mason, *Brandeis*, 465–508; Melvin I. Urofsky, "Wilson, Brandeis, and the Supreme Court Nomination," *Journal of Supreme Court History* 28 (July 2003): 145–56; Melvin I. Urofsky, "Attorney for the People: The 'Outrageous' Brandeis Nomination," *Yearbook: 1979 Supreme Court Historical Society* 8–19 (1979).
13. NYT, 1/31/1916, at 18; NYT, 2/13/1916, at 16; NYT, 3/15/1916, at 4.
14. WHT to Karger, 1/31/1916, at 1, WHTP, Reel 162, Series 3. For the best account of Taft's opposition to Brandeis, *see* Gould, *Chief Executive to Chief Justice*, 62–69.
15. *See* chapter 2 n. 30 (citing Archie Butt, Diary Entry, 7/8/1910, in 2 *Taft and Roosevelt*, 439); Alpheus Thomas Mason, *William Howard Taft: Chief Justice* 66–71 (1965).
16. HC to LH, 12/13/1913, at 4–5, LHP, Box 102, Folder 102-21. *See* Levy, *Herbert Croly of* The New Republic, 155–59.
17. HC to LH, 1/8/1914, at 1–2, LHP, Box 102, Folder 102-21 (discussing how Brandeis's articles "have not helped" *Harper's* circulation). Even though he disagreed with Brandeis ideologically, Croly came to respect him. *See* HC to LH, 12/13/1913, at 4–5. On Croly's disagreement with *Other People's Money, see* Levy, *Herbert Croly of* The New Republic, 188.

18. LDB to AGB, 12/5/1913, FLLDB at 227.
19. HC to LDB, 2/9/1916, 4 LLDB at 45 n. 1.
20. LDB to HC, 2/11/1916, *id.* at 45. *See* LDB to LH, 2/9/1916, *id.* at 37.
21. TNR, 2/5/1916, at 4.
22. *Id.* at 5.
23. *Id.* at 5–6.
24. *Id.* at 6.
25. FFLC, Box 194, Folder "Addenda 1916–24"; ERB to FF, 2/7/1916, *id.*, Box 30, Folder "Buckner, Emory R. 1916 #2."
26. FF to KL, 1/27/1916, at 1, FFLC, Box 79, Folder "Ludington, Katharine 1916 #2."
27. FF to WL, 2/2/1916, at 2, WLP, Reel 9, Box 10, Folder 419.
28. FF to LH, 1/30/1916, at 1–2.
29. FF to WL, 3/20/1916, at 1, WLP, Reel 164, Box 1, Folder 29. See FF to KL, 2/16/1916, at 3, FFLC, Box 79, Folder "Ludington, Katharine 1916 #2" ("I … dined with Brandeis–on business. He made me feel as never before, the priest in him–the austere nobility of his dedication. He'll go through all right–and a wonderful thing it is!").
30. LDB to FF, 9/24/1925, HBHS, at 212. *See* LDB to FF, 11/19/1916 & 11/25/1916, *id.* at 26–27. Some scholars have made much of this financial relationship. *See* Bruce Allen Murphy, *The Brandeis/Frankfurter Connection* (1982). Others claim the ethical charges have been grossly exaggerated. *See* Robert Cover, "The Framing of Justice Brandeis," TNR, 5/5/1982, at 17–18.
31. Nomination of Louis D. Brandeis, Hearings before the Senate Judiciary Subcommittee, 64th Cong., 1st Sess., Vol. 1, at 682–705, 713–47, 773–807, 815–45, 847–93, 986–1021 (Washington, DC: GPO, 1916).
32. LDB to McClennen, 3/9/1916, 4 LLDB at 114.
33. FF to Julian Mack, 1/31/1916, FFLC, Box 81, Folder "Mack, Julian W. 1924–26" ("It is terribly important that no Jews should make the slightest peep about a race issue. You know as I do that the Jew in Brandeis has nothing to do (I except negligible isolated individuals) with the grounds of opposition.").
34. FF to WL, n.d. 1916, WLP, Reel 9, Box 10, Folder 419.
35. WL to FF, 2/18/1916, at 1, PPWL at 37 & WLP, Reel 9, Box 10, Folder 419.
36. *Id.* WL Diary, 2/16/1916, at 66, WLP, Reel 160, Box 236, Folder 1 (recording tea with Hapgood and Rublee about Brandeis).
37. FF to WL, n.d. 1916, at 3, WLP, Reel 9, Box 10, Folder 419. *See* FF to KL, 2/16/1916, at 5, FFLC, Box 79, Folder "Ludington, Katharine 1916" ("Of course you'd like Walter L. He is human and simple and deep. Don't worry, he was grateful for what I told him through you.").
38. WL Diary, 2/16/1916, at 66; WL to OWH, 2/14/1916, WLP, Reel 13, Box 14, Folder 556.
39. Oliver Wendell Holmes, Introduction, *Mr. Justice Brandeis* ix (Felix Frankfurter, ed., 1932); OWH to Clara Stevens, 5/13/1916, at 2, OWHP, Reel 26, Page 376, Box 35, Folder 32.

40. LDB to OWH, 3/8/1916, 4 LLDB at 109.

41. LDB to Gregory, 4/14/1916, *id.* at 165.

42. OWH to Wigmore 2/12/1916, OWHP, Reel 26, Page 356, Box 35, Folder 32.

43. OWH to Clara Stevens, 5/13/1916, at 2; OWH to LE, 5/14/1916, at 1–2, *id.* at Pages 377–78 & H-E Letters at 128.

44. WL to LDB, 2/18/1916, PPWL, 38.

45. LDB to WW, 5/26/1913, 3 LLDB at 97–99.

46. WL to LDB, 2/18/1916.

47. WL to Raymond Stevens, 2/21/1916, PPWL, 41.

48. TNR, 3/4/1916, at 117–19.

49. *Id.* at 118–19.

50. *Id.* at 119. *See* NH to WL, 3/7/1916, at 2, WLP, Reel 164, Box 2, Folder 35 (writing that the editorial was "very helpful").

51. LDB to WL, 2/21/1916, 4 LLDB at 80–81 & n. 1.

52. Chart, 3/2/1916, WSP, Reel 5, Segment 3 & FFLC, Box 128, Folder "Brandeis, Louis D. Nomination to Supreme Court 1916 #1"; 4 LLDB 80–81 n. 1 & Mason, *Brandeis*, 484–85.

53. WL to FF, 2/29/1916, WLP, Reel 9, Box 10, Folder 419.

54. HC to WS, 3/2/1916, WSP, Reel 5, Segment 3.

55. For the original version, *see* n.d., WLP, Series II, Box 19, Folder 109; Seideman, The New Republic, 24–25.

56. Jeffrey Rosen, "Why Brandeis Matters," TNR, 7/22/2010, at 19.

57. TNR, 3/11/1916, at 139.

58. FF to KL, 5/12/1916, at 1–2, FFLC, Box 79, Folder "Ludington, Katharine 1916 #2."

59. WP, 2/3/1916, at 5 (containing each professor's comments). The reporter was a third-year Harvard law student, Shelton Hale, who interviewed each member of the Harvard law faculty. FF to NH, 2/5/1916, FFLC, Box 128, Folder "Brandeis, Louis D. Nomination to Supreme Court 1916 #1." A month earlier, Frankfurter had selected Hale to be Holmes's secretary for the 1916 term. OWH to FF, 1/29/1916, H-FF Corr., at 45; OWH to FF, 3/27/1917, *id.* at 70. ("The lad here calls himself a pacifist as well as a socialist and exhibits a thin and stubborn rationality. I find myself very fond of him. ..."); OWH to HL, 12/31/1916, 1 HLL at 49 ("I have a secretary who has socialistic velleities, though with a very rational nature, and I see in him the tendency common to the time to believe in regulating everything. ...").

60. LDB to Edward McClennen, 3/14/1916, FFLC, Box 128, Folder "Brandeis, Louis D. Nomination to Supreme Court 1916 #1."

61. RP to Sen. Chilton, n.d., Brandeis Nomination Hearings, Vol. 2, at 251–52 (1916).

62. Charles Eliot to Sen. Culbertson, 5/17/1916, *id.* at 241–42.

63. LDB to FF, 3/18/1916, at 1–2, FFLC, Box 128, Folder "Brandeis, Louis D. Nomination to Supreme Court 1916 #1" (attaching newspaper articles about

the controversy). *See* LDB to NH, 3/14/1916, 4 LLDB at 118–19; chapter 2 n. 59 (citing Gould, *Chief Executive to Chief Justice*, 62–63).

64. TNR, 3/18/1916, at 165.

65. WHT to Wickersham, 3/27/1916, WHTP, Reel 538, Vol. 46, Page 255.

66. Wickersham to WHT, 3/26/1916, at 2–3, WHTP, Reel 164, Series 3. *See* GW to WHT, 3/29/1916, at 1, *id.*

67. WHT to Karger, 1/31/1916, at 2. Ullman was treasurer of the American Jewish Committee and a corset manufacturer. He had arranged for Taft's housing in New Haven. *See* Frederick C. Hicks, *William Howard Taft* 5 (1945). That same day, Taft made similar but even worse comments to his brothers, Henry and Horace. *See* WHT to Henry Taft, 1/31/1916, WHTP, Reel 437, Vol. 43, at 315 (claiming Brandeis "became a Jew of the Jews after that, a Zionist, a new Jerusalemist, was metaphorically circumcised again, spent his time addressing in every city and country, wearing his hat, and out Jewing the Rabbis of all but the most bearded orthodox of the Sanhedrin. It has worked to a charm."); WHT to Horace Taft, 1/31/1916, at 1, *id.* at 339 ("while Brandeis was a very poor Jew down to the time that he was defeated for Attorney General, he has been a hat-wearing Jew since that time, and has been preaching a return to Zion and Jerusalem. ... Now he is a Jew all over, and I presume it will arouse jealousy throughout the country if any attempt is made to best him, and indeed the racial question has already been introduced by publishing fake telegrams as to the opposition to him because he is a Jew.").

68. WHT to Karger 1/31/1916, at 2. *See* WHT to Karger, 3/27/1916, at 3, WHTP, Reel 538, Series 8, Vol. 46, Page 258A ("I see that the Jews have selected Brandeis to preside over them in Philadelphia at their world convention. I am really sorry for this. I should not be at all surprised if our worthy President had something to do with it in calling on other prominent Jews to help him to use this to secure confirmation.").

69. WHT to Karger, 1/31/1916, at 3.

70. *See* Gould, *Chief Executive to Chief Justice*, 64 ("An undercurrent of anti-Semitism accounted for much of the opposition to the Brandeis nomination. That noxious sentiment did not animate William Howard Taft in his reaction to the president's selection."); Jonathan Lurie, *William Howard Taft* 180–83 (2012); Urofsky, *Louis D. Brandeis*, 438–49; Todd, *Justice on Trial*, 256–57; Mason, *William Howard Taft*, 72–74; Pringle, 2 *The Life and Times of William Howard Taft* 898–99, 952–53.

71. On Nagel's role in the Taft administration, *see* Michael J. Churgin, "Immigration Internal Decisionmaking," 78 Texas L. Rev. 1633 (2000).

72. TNR, 3/25/1916, at 202–4.

73. Denis Steven Rutkus and Maureen Bearden, "Supreme Court Nominations, 1789–2009: Actions by the Senate, the Judiciary Committee, and the President," at 13 (Congressional Research Service, 5/13/2009).

74. WL to FF, 3/16/1916, at 1–2, WLP, Reel 9, Box 10, Folder 419.

75. FF to FH, 3/5/1916 & FF to OWH, 3/6/1916, H-FF Corr., at 46.

76. FF to ERB, 3/1916, FFLC, Box 30, Folder "Buckner, Emory R. 1916. #12."

77. Belknap Diary, 4/11/1916.

78. *Id.*

79. FF to KL, 4/15/1916, at 3, FFLC, Box 79, Folder "Ludington, Katharine 1916."

80. WL Diary, 4/18/1916, at 79–80, WLP, Reel 164.

81. FF to KL, 4/15/1916, at 1–2. *See* FF to KL, 4/16/1916, FFLC, Box 79, Folder "Ludington, Katharine 1916."

82. BET, 5/10/1916, pt. 2, at 2.

83. FF to WL, 5/4/1916, FFLC, Box 128, Folder "Brandeis, Louis D. 1916–24 #3."

84. WL to FF, 5/6/1916, at 2, PPWL, 47–48 & WLP, Reel 9, Box 10, Folder 419.

85. Brandeis Hearings, Vol. 2, at 5–7.

86. WW to Culberson, 5/5/1916, 36 WWP at 609–11.

87. NH to WL, n.d., at 2, WLP, Reel 164, Box 2, Folder 35.

88. Mason, *Brandeis*, 503–4; Urofsky, *Louis D. Brandeis*, 458.

89. Todd, *Justice on Trial*, 230–31.

90. 37 WWP at 78–79; Josephus Daniels, *The Wilson Era*, at 545–47 (1944).

91. Todd, *Justice on Trial*, 238–41.

92. Ray Stannard Baker, Memorandum, 5/12/1916, 37 WWP at 34.

93. 53 Cong. Rec. 9032 (1916).

94. RGV to Marie Christie, 6/12/1916, RGVP, Carton 9, Folder 5.

95. TNR, 6/10/1916, at 134.

96. TNR, 2/5/1916, at 1.

97. *Id.*

98. *Id.* at 2.

99. TNR, 5/4/1916, at 4.

100. TNR, 4/22/1916, at 301.

101. TNR, 6/3/1916, at 102. *See* Walter Lippmann, *Early Writings* 37 (Arthur Schlesinger Jr., ed., 1970) (revealing Lippmann's authorship and correctly pointing out the speech was given on May 27, not May 22 as the editorial says).

102. WL to Sen. Henry F. Hollis, 5/29/1916, 37 WWP at 166.

103. WL to EP, 5/29/1916, PPWL, 49.

104. WL to FF, 1/17/1916, at 1, WLP, Reel 9, Box 10, Folder 419 & PPWL, 33–34. *See* TNR, 1/22/1916, at 287–88 (on Mexico).

105. TNR, 3/25/1916, at 204.

106. WL to WS, 4/6/1916, PPWL, 45 & WSP, Reel 5, Segment 4.

107. TR statement to press, 3/9/1916, 17 *The Works of Theodore Roosevelt*, at 410–13.

108. WL to WS, 4/6/1916.

109. *Id.*

110. WL to EP, 5/29/1916, PPWL, 50.

111. TNR, 6/17/1916, at 164.

112. TNR, 6/17/1916, at 158–59.

113. TNR, 6/17/1916, at 164–65.

114. The Nomination for the Presidency, 6/22/1916, 17 *The Works of Theodore Roosevelt*, at 414–24.
115. TNR, 6/17/1916, at 160.
116. *Id.* at 155.
117. GB to Wood, n.d. tel., GBP, Box 81, Folder "Politics 1916."
118. GB to Probasco, 8/26/1916, GBP, Box 35, Folder "P." Borglum's story of the 1916 Progressive Party convention (that Roosevelt preferred Wood) did not check out with Roosevelt biographer Hermann Hagedorn. *See* John Taliaferro, *Great White Fathers* 142–45 (2002).
119. GB to Probasco, 8/22/1916, GBP, Box 35, Folder "P."
120. WL to Sen. Henry Hollis, 6/12/1916, 37 WWP at 212.
121. WL to S. K. Ratcliffe, 6/15/1916, PPWL, at 51.
122. *Id.*
123. WL to FF, 6/30/1916, at 1, WLP, Reel 9, Box 10, Folder 419.
124. *Id.*
125. WL to EP, 7/5/1916, PPWL, 53.
126. *See* chapter 9 n. 44.
127. WW to Hollis, 6/7/1916, 37 WWP at 166. Lippmann saw the letter. WL to Hollis, 6/12/1916, *id.* at 212.
128. WL to NDB, 8/2/1916, 37 WWP at 525.
129. TNR, 6/24/1916, at 181.
130. NH to WW, 8/7/1916, 38 WWP at 3.
131. *Id. See* NH to WW, 8/10/1916, 38 WWP at 23.
132. "Justice Frankfurter's Contribution to the Harold Laski Programme," British Broadcasting Corporation, 11/15/1961, at 1, FFLC, Box 200, Folder "Writings of Felix Frankfurter 1956–1963," & *id.*, Box 207 & Felix Frankfurter, *Of Law and Life & Other Things That Matter* 217 (Philip B. Kurland, ed., 1965).
133. *Id.* at 218. On Laski, *see* Isaac Kramnick and Barry Sheerman, *Harold Laski: A Life on the Left* (1993). Kramnick and Sheerman place the first Frankfurter-Laski meeting in "early spring" 1915, which must be correct given Laski's trips to Harvard in July. *Id.* at 86.
134. FF to MD, 6/26/1916, at 7, FFLC, Box 5, Folder "Denman, Marion 1916 #3."
135. OWH to FP, 2/18/1917, 1 H-P Letters at 243 (repeating the American tennis champion anecdote); Felix Frankfurter, Foreword, 1 HLL, at xv ("Good talkers are apt to embellish their tales and Laski's stories often gained in the telling.").
136. HL to Benjamin Huebsch, 6/5/1915, BHP, Box 16, Folder "Laski, Harold J. 1914–15"; HL to FF, 7/18/1915, FFLC, Box 74, Folder "Laski, Harold J. 1915–19."
137. FF to KL, 1/27/1916, at 1–2, FFLC, Box 79, Folder "Ludington, Katharine 1916."
138. FF to LH, 1/22/1916, at 2, LHP, Box 104C, Folder 104-5; FF to KL, 1/27/1916, at 2.
139. FF to LH, 1/22/1916, at 1–2.
140. FF to MD, 6/26/1916, at 8.

141. Frankfurter, Foreword, 1 HLL, at xiv; HL to OWH, 7/11/1916, *id.* at 3; OWH to LE, 7/11/1916, H-E Letters at 132 ("We had a visit from two young Jews who hit me where I live. ..."); OWH to FP, 7/12/1916, 1 H-P Letters at 237 (describing Laski as "an astonishing Jew, whom Frankfurter brought over here the other day").

142. Johnson, *Pioneer's Progress*, 243 (describing Laski as "a visitor so frequent as to be almost a member of the staff").

143. Randolph Bourne to Alyse Gregory, 11/10/1916, Bourne Papers & *The Letters of Randolph Bourne* 382 (Eric J. Sandeen, ed., 1981).

144. NH to WW, 8/10/1916, 38 WWP at 23.

145. NH to WW, 8/9/1916, *id.* at 14–15. *See* LH COH at 118–19 (recalling he voted for Wilson but later regretted it).

146. FF to EMH, 6/14/1916, at 1–2, LCCP, Vol. 3, Reel 3877, Page 1914 & EMHP, Box 45, Folder 1443.

147. *Id.* at 3–4.

148. WW to NDB, 7/10/1916, 37 WWP at 397; WW to EMH, 7/23/1916, *id.* at 467; EMH to WW, 7/25/1916, *id.* at 475.

149. Remarks upon Signing the Child Labor Bill, 9/1/1916, 38 WWP at 123–24.

150. A Statement, 8/14/1916, 38 WWP at 32; An Address to a Joint Session of Congress, 8/29/1916, *id.* at 96–101.

151. On Rublee's role in crafting the FTC legislation, *see* William Kolasky, "George Rublee and the Origins of the Federal Trade Commission," *Antitrust* 26, no. 1 (Fall 2011): 106–12.

152. Gompers to WW, 10/17/1916, 38 WWP at 468–72 (enclosing endorsement of 10/14/1916).

153. Du Bois to WW, 10/10/1916, 38 WWP at 459–60.

154. Du Bois to JT, 10/24/1916, 38 WWP at 522; Georgia Nugent to WW, 8/9/1916, *id.* at 15; WW to JT, 8/11/1916, *id.* at 24. On Tumulty, *see* John M. Blum, *Joe Tumulty and the Wilson Era* (1951).

155. CDEF, 11/4/1916, at 12; BAA, 11/4/1916, at 4; Philadelphia Tribune, 11/4/1916, at 1.

156. TNR, 6/24/1916, at 187–88.

157. Lippmann COH at 91.

158. *Id.* at 92.

159. WL to NDB, 8/21/1916, 38 WWL at 62–63; WL to NH, 8/23/1916, *id.* at 87; NDB to WW, 9/23/1916, *id.* at 238.

160. WL to NH, 9/25/1916, *id.* at 274.

161. TNR, 9/30/1916, at 210.

162. TNR, 10/14/1916, at 263.

163. Lippmann COH at 89 ("It was a great struggle. Croly didn't want to do it. Straight didn't want to do it. I did. Finally, by September I persuaded them that Hughes was taking a pro-German line with a feeling toward the pro-German vote, and that Wilson was the man for us.").

164. TNR, 10/21/1916, at 286.

165. *Id.*

166. *Id.* at 289–90.

167. TNR, 10/28/1916, at 313. For negotiations between Croly and Straight, *see* HC to WS, 10/17/1916, WSP, Reel 5, Series 4; WS to TNR editors, 10/23/1916, *id.*

168. NYT, 10/29/1916, at 9.

169. "The Election of 1916," FFLC, Box 204, Folder "The Election of 1916," & RGVP, Carton 9, Folder 78.

170. RGV to FF, 10/30/1916, RGVP, Carton 9, Folder 74.

171. OWH to FF, 11/5/1916, H-FF Corr., at 59.

172. Merlo J. Pusey, 1 *Charles Evans Hughes* 335–49 (1951).

CHAPTER 8

1. Meeting of the Bureau of Industrial Audit at New Republic, 11/3/1916, RGVP (on file with author).

2. Mitchel to RGV, 8/7/1916, RGVP, Carton 13, Folder 21.

3. Stanley King to RGV, 8/9/1916 tel., *id.*

4. Richard Washburn Child, "The Human Audit," *Harper's Weekly*, 7/17/1915, at 50–51 in RGVP, Carton 13, Folder 38.

5. Bruce Barton, "Moses Could Have Used This Man," *American Magazine*, 1/1916, at 52 in *id.*

6. RGV to FF, 2/14/1916 & "Industrial Democracy," at 1, RGVP, Carton 9, Folder 74. He sent it to the *New Republic* editors on March 7. *See id.*, Carton 13, Folder 17.

7. WL to Dorothy Alden, WLP, 2/14/1916, WLP, Reel 21, Box 22, Folder 877. *See* FF to WL, n.d., WLP, Reel 164, Box 1, Folder 29.

8. WL to RGV, 3/17/1916, RGVP, Carton 9, Folder 90 & PPWL, 43–44.

9. *See* RGV to SFV, 3/11/1916, at 1, RGVP, Carton 7, Folder 83; RGV to SFV, 4/19/1916, at 2, *id.*, Folder 84; RGV to SFV, 5/7/1916, at 1, *id.*, Folder 85.

10. Louis D. Brandeis, *Scientific Management and Railroads* (1911).

11. Louis D. Brandeis, Foreword, *Wages and Regularity of Employment in the Cloak, Suit, and Skirt Industry* 5–7 (1915).

12. RGV to SFV, 5/9/1916, at 1–2, RGVP, Carton 7, Folder 85.

13. RGV to SFV, 3/8/1916, at 2, *id.*, Folder 83.

14. RGV to SFV, 5/10/1916, at 1, *id.*, Folder 85.

15. RGV to SFV, 5/13/1916, at 3, *id.*, Folder 86.

16. *Id.* at 1.

17. RGV to SFV, 5/17/1916, at 1, *id.*

18. Partnership Contract, 5/26/1916, *id.*, Carton 13, Folder 33.

19. "Work Analysis of the Board for Control Enforcement of Protocol Standards in the Waist and Dress Industry," 9/25/1916, RGVP, Carton 13, Folder 99; RGV to SFV, 9/5/1916, at 1 & RGV to SFV, 9/6/1916, at 1, *id.*, Carton 7, Folder 88.

20. Robert Bruère to RGV, 9/15–16/1916 tel., RGVP, Carton 13, Folder 22.
21. "N.Y. v. Boston," RGVP, Carton 7, Folder 84; RGV to SFV, 11/1/1916, *id.*, Folder 89.
22. RGV to SFV, 9/24/1916, at 1-2, RGVP, Carton 7, Folder 88.
23. SFV, 11/16/1916, at 3–5, RGVP, Box 2, Folder 8.
24. NYH, 11/15/1916, at 5.
25. Dr. Herman Adler to SFV, 11/16/1916, at 2, RGVP, Carton 15, Folder 20.
26. FF to OWH, 11/16/1916, H-FF Corr., at 60.
27. FF to LDB, 11/15/1916, LDB-Louisville, Reel 47.
28. FF, 11/14/16, RGVP, Carton 15, Folder 23.
29. TNR, 11/25/1916, at 84.
30. *Id.* at 85.
31. Outlook, 11/22/1916, at 629.
32. H. P. Kendall, "First Industrial Counselor–Robert G. Valentine," The Survey, 11/25/1916, at 190.
33. Ordway Tead, "Industrial Counselor, a New Profession," The Independent, 12/4/1916, at 393.
34. TR to SFV, 11/16/1916, RGVP, Carton 15, Folder 20.
35. BET, 11/17/1916, at 1.
36. FF to OWH, 11/16/1916.
37. RGVP, Box 2, Folder 8. *See* SFV, 11/16/1916, *id.*
38. HL to LDB, 11/20/1916, LDB-Louisville, Reel 47.
39. FF to OWH, 11/16/1916. Valentine's influence on the first half of Frankfurter's life is not well documented. *But see* Parrish, *Felix Frankfurter and His Times*, 76. This may be because part of Frankfurter's oral history about Valentine was omitted from the published volume. *See* FFR Transcript, 6/27/1957, at 1–6, FFLC, Box 205, Folder "Felix Frankfurter Reminisces Transcript 27 June 1957 #12."
40. OWH to HL, 11/19/1916, 1 HLL at 35–36.
41. HL to OWH, 11/20/1916, *id.* at 36.
42. RGV to SFV, circa 7/3/1916, at 1, RGVP, Carton 7, Folder 88.
43. HL Remarks, at 4, RGVP, Box 2, Folder 17.
44. LCC to FF, 11/15/1916, FFLC, Box 43, Folder "Christie, Loring C. 1916"; EP to FF, 12/31/1916, at 1–2, FFLC, Box 65, Folder "Percy, Eustace 1916."
45. FF to LH, 11/22/1916, LHP, Box 104A, Folder 104-6. *See* RGV secretary to LCC, 12/11/1916, RGVP, Carton 13, Folder 23 ("As Mr. Frankfurter says, 'we have lost a leader and the deepest of friends.'").
46. BG, 1/8/1917, at 9.
47. Remarks of Felix Frankfurter in Presiding at the Memorial Meeting for Robert G. Valentine at Faneuil Hall, 1/7/1917, at 1, FFLC, Box 188, Folder "Valentine, Robert G. memorials 1916–17" & RGVP, Box 2, Folder 15.
48. *Id.*
49. *Id.* at 2. Frankfurter was alluding to Holmes's 1884 Memorial Day Address ("Through our great good fortune, in our youth our hearts were touched with fire.").

50. LDB, "For FF," 1/3/1917, RGVP, Box 2, Folder 17.

51. LDB to FF, 12/1/1916, 4 LLDB at 268. *See* AGB to FF, 11/15/16, RGVP, Carton 9, Folder 79; FF to LDB, 12/5/1916, at 1–2, LDB-Louisville, Reel 47; LDB to FF, 5/3/1917, HBHS, at 28.

52. FF to OWH, 1/12/1917, H-FF Corr., at 65.

53. FF to MD, 1/10/1917, FFLC, Box 5, Folder "Denman, Marion A. Jan.–Mar. 1917 #4."

54. Sol Polakoff Remarks (possibly edited by Frankfurter), at 1, RGVP, Box 2, Folder 16.

55. War Department to FF, 10/7/1915, at 1, RGVP, Carton 9, Folder 73.

56. Editorial, 9/17/1915 and other Filipino editorials, FFLC, Box 51, Folder "Denison, Winfred T. 1914–16."

57. FF to ERB, 11/11/1915, FFLC, Box 30, Folder "Buckner, Emory R. 1915 #11"; FF to KL, 11/18/1915, at 6, FFLC, Box 79, Folder "Ludington, Katharine 1914–15."

58. The sanitarium was at the Devereux Mansion. WTD to FF, 3/8/1916, FFLC, Box 51, Folder "Denison, Winfred T. 1914–16." *See* Dr. Isaac Adler to FF, 3/18/1916, at 2, *id.*, Box 19, Folder "'A' Misc. Ad."

59. FF to ES, 12/8/1915, ESP, Carton 4, Folder "Frankfurter, Felix N.D.–1927."

60. Chauncey Belknap to Mark DeWolfe Howe, 4/12/1963 (containing 3/30/1916 diary transcription), MDHP, Box 22, Folder 26 "Anecdotes 1895–1964"; Belknap Diary, 3/30/1916.

61. Belknap Diary, 4/6/1916.

62. WTD to WW, 5/15/1916, WWP, Series II, Reel 79, at 83644.

63. WTD to SFV, 11/15/1916 tel., RGVP, Carton 15, Folder 60.

64. WTD to SFV, 11/17/1916 tel., *id.*

65. Denison Revised Remarks, at 1, RGVP, Box 2, Folder 13.

66. *Id.* at 1–2.

67. *Id.* at 3.

68. WTD to SFV, 2/23/1917, at 7–8, Carton 15, Folder 62.

69. Denison Revised Remarks, at 1.

70. WTD to SFV, 5/13/1917, RGVP, Carton 15, Folder 62; WTD to LDB, 11/20/1916, LDB-Louisville, Reel 47; FF to LDB, 11/19/1916, *id.*; RPB to FF, 1/16/1917, RGVP, Carton 13, Folder 24.

71. Notation, n.d., RGVP, Box 15, Folder 57; Telephone Interview with Dorothy Koval, 2/12/2012, Lake Elmore, Vermont. Koval was friends with Charlotte (Sophia) Valentine Taylor and spent years organizing Valentine's papers with her.

72. FF, "Robert Grosvenor Valentine '96," Harvard Alumni Bulletin, Vol. 19, No. 12, 12/14/1916, at 228–30; Frankfurter, "Valentine, Robert Grosvenor," 142.

73. FF, "Robert Grosvenor Valentine '96," at 228, 230.

CHAPTER 9

1. FF to SFV, 1/15/1917, RGVP, Carton 15, Folder 72.

2. FF to SFV, 1/17/1917, at 2, *id.*

3. Bunting v. Oregon, No. 38, 1916 Term Supreme Court Docket Book, at 7, NARA, M216, Roll #15, Dockets of the Supreme Court of the United States, 1915–18, Original and Appellate; George M. Brown to James D. Maher, 10/3/1916, and accompanying stipulation, Bunting v. Oregon Clerk's Office File, NARA, RG 267, Appellate Case File 24346.

4. FFR, 98.

5. Josephine Goldmark to James Maher, 9/1/1916, Maher to Goldmark, 9/6/1916, Goldmark to Maher, 10/13/1916, Maher to Goldmark, 10/14/1916, Bunting v. Oregon Clerk's Office File, NARA, RG 267, Appellate Case File 24346.

6. Goldmark to Brown, Goldmark to Teal, 10/17/1916, FFLC, Box 128, Folder "Bunting v. Oregon 1916."

7. Brown to FF, 10/18/1916 tel., id.

8. FF to CJ White, 10/20/1916, FFLC, Box 183, Folder "Supreme Court 1870–1935 #1." Cf. FFR, 99.

9. FF to AMB, 12/11/1964, at 1–2, FFHLS, Box 206, Reel 33, Pages 135–36.

10. FFR, 99–101.

11. NYT, 10/25/1916, at 18; Bunting v. Oregon, No. 38, 1916 Term Supreme Court Docket Book, at 7.

12. FF to KL, 1/14/1917, at 3–4, FFLC, Box 80, Folder "Ludington, Katharine 1917."

13. Frankfurter, "Hours of Labor and Realism in Constitutional Law," 369 (citing Commonwealth v. Boston & M.R.R., 110 N.E. (Mass.) 264 (1915)).

14. Id. at 369–70.

15. TNR, 2/3/1917, at 8.

16. "Labor, Law and Life," The Independent, 4/24/1916, at 123.

17. WTD to James Mather, 9/8/1916, Stettler v. O'Hara Clerk's Office File, NARA, RG 267, Appellate Case 24,248; LDB to HL, 4/3/1916, at 4 LLDB at 142.

18. HL to OWH, 1/15/1917, 1 HLL at 55.

19. "Notes from the Capital: Felix Frankfurter," The Nation, 3/15/1917, at 320.

20. Complaint in Simpson case, at 2–3, 10–11, Stettler v. O'Hara Clerk's Office File, NARA, RG 267, Appellate Case 24,248.

21. Bunting v. Oregon, 243 U.S. 426, 434 (1917).

22. Frankfurter, "Hours of Labor and Realism in Constitutional Law," 367 (citing State v. Bunting, 71 Ore. 259, 271, 139 Pac. 731, 735 (1914)).

23. On allegations that McReynolds turned his back on Charles Hamilton Houston during a 1938 school desegregation argument, see Robert L. Carter, "The Long Road to Equality," The Nation, 5/3/2004, http://www.thenation.com/article/long-road-equality#; CDEF, 11/19/1938, at 2 (reporting McReynolds left the bench halfway through the state's argument); PC, 3/21/1937, at 2 (protesting McReynolds's public comment that "he had tried to protect 'the poorest darky in the Georgia backwoods as well as the man in the mansion on Wall Street'"). McReynolds was not on speaking terms with Jewish justices Brandeis and Cardozo. John Knox, The Forgotten Memoir of John Knox: A Year in the Life of a Supreme Court Clerk in FDR's Washington 36–37 (Dennis J. Hutchinson and

David J. Garrow, eds., 2002). But the story that there was no official Supreme Court portrait in 1924 because McReynolds would not sit next to Brandeis for an official portrait is apocryphal. There was only a new portrait in those days when there was a new justice (and there was no new justice in 1924). In any case, the justices did not sit in order of seniority in older portraits. McReynolds's objections were to sitting for a third photographer's studio in 1923, not to sitting with Brandeis. *See* Franz Jantzen, "From the Urban Legend Department: McReynolds, Brandeis, and the Myth of the 1924 Group Photograph," *Journal of Supreme Court History* 40, no. 3 (2015): 326–38. For more on McReynolds, *see* chapter 23 nn. 64–69.

24. EMH to Frank Buxton, 4/8/1936, FFLC, Box 127, Folder "Brandeis, Louis D. 1890–1938."

25. *Id.*; House Diary, 12/18/1912, Series II, Vol. 1, at 35; *id.*, 2/15/1913, at 100; *id.*, 2/16/1913, at 101–2; Link, 2 *Wilson: The New Freedom*, 13; Charles E. Neu, *Colonel House* 78–79, 82 (2015).

26. Link, 2 *Wilson: The New Freedom*, 417–23. For more on his time as attorney general, *see id.* at 117–19.

27. House Diary, 1/1/1914, Series II, Vol. 2, at 2; *id.*, 7/12/1914, Series II, Vol. 2, at 128; *id.*, 1/11/1917, Series II, Vol. 5, at 17; EMH to Frank Buxton, 4/8/1936; EMH to WW, 7/16/1914, 30 WWP at 285; Neu, *Colonel House*, 143–44; Daniels, *The Wilson Era*, 540–41.

28. *See* nn. 28–29; chapter 4 n. 37 (citing RGV to SFV, 3/26/1913, at 3–4, RGVP, Carton 7, Folder 76).

29. Joseph Alsop and Robert Kintner, *Men around the President* 49 (1939) & Frankfurter Interview with Joseph Alsop, at 3–4, n.d., circa 1938, Joseph and Stewart Alsop Papers, Box 93, Folder 3.

30. *Id.* & Frankfurter Interview with Alsop, at 4. *See* FF to HLS, 4/16/13, FFLC, Box 103, Folder "Stimson, Henry L. 1913" ("What a horde of office seekers is wearing away the strength and time of men like McReynolds–who let them!").

31. FFR, 102–3.

32. *Id.* at 102.

33. *Id. See* "Notes from the Capital: Felix Frankfurter," at 320 ("He lectured the court quietly, but with a due sense of its indebtedness to him for setting it right where it had been wrong, and giving it positive opinions where uncertainty had been clouding its mental vision. He was becomingly tolerant when the gray-haired learners asked questions which seemed to him unnecessary, and gentle when he had to correct a mistaken assumption.").

34. "Oregon May Be Right," The Independent, 2/5/1917, at 203.

35. FF to SFV, 1/20/1917 tel., RGVP, Carton 15, Folder 72.

36. FF to MD, 4/17/1917, FFLC, Box 5, Folder "Denman, Marion A. Apr.–June 1917 #5."

37. OWH to HL, 1/8/1917, 1 HLL at 51–52.

38. Bunting v. Oregon, 243 U.S. 426, 438–39 (1917).

39. Stettler v. O'Hara, 243 U.S. 629 (49/1917) (per curiam).

40. FF, "The Adamson Law," BH, 10/9/1916, in FFLC, Box 194, Folder "Writings 1913–24."

41. Wilson v. New, 243 U.S. 332 (1917).

42. OWH to HL, 3/23 or 29/1917, 1 HLL at 69.

43. OWH to FF, 3/27/1917, H-FF Corr., at 69–70.

44. House Diary, 12/28/1916, Series II, Vol. 4, at 326; *id.*, 1/14/1917, Series II, Vol. 5, at 25; *id.*, 1/22/1917, at 30; *id.*, 1/25/1917, at 33, *id.*, 2/5/1917, at 44; *id.*, 3/9/1917, at 67; *id.*, 4/17/1917, at 110. *Cf.* Lippmann, "Notes for a Biography," at 251.

45. Steel, *Walter Lippmann and the American Century*, 108–9.

46. *Id.*; TNR, 12/16/1916, at 168–70.

47. TNR, 12/23/1916, at 201–2.

48. EMH to WW, 12/29/1916, 40 WWP at 360.

49. Charles Merz, "Memorandum of Meeting with Woodrow Wilson," 1/8/1917, 40 WWP at 423.

50. TNR, 2/3/1917, at 3–4; TNR, 2/3/1917, at 5; House Diary, 1/22/1917, Series II, Vol. 5, at 30; *id.*, 1/25/1917, at 33.

51. TNR, 2/3/1917, at 5.

52. TNR, 1/27/1917, at 341.

53. WL to WW, 1/31/1917, 41 WWP at 83.

54. FF to WL, 1/31/1917 (#9), WLP, Reel 9, Box 10, Folder 420.

55. "Postscript," TNR, 2/3/1917 Supp., in FFLC, Box 80, "Ludington, Katharine 1917."

56. FF to KL, 2/5/1917, at 1, *id.*

57. WL to FF, 2/19/1917, WLP, Reel 9, Box 10, Folder 420 & PPWL, 61–62.

58. FF to WL, 2/1917, WLP, Reel 9, Box 10, Folder 420.

59. WW to EMH, 2/26/1917, 41 WWP at 288; EMH to WW, 2/27/1917, *id.* at 296–97; Robert Lansing, "Memorandum on the Message of Zimmermann to the German Minister to Mexico," 3/4/1917, *id.* at 321–27. On the Zimmermann telegram, *see* Arthur S. Link, 5 *Wilson: Campaigns for Progressivism and Peace 1916–1917*, at 342–61 (1965); Barbara W. Tuchman, *The Zimmerman Telegram* (1958).

60. House Diary, 3/9/1917, Series II, Vol. 5, at 67.

61. WL to WW, 4/3/1917, 41 WWP at 537 (quoting TNR, 4/7/1917, at 280).

62. FF to MD, 4/6/1917, at 3, FFLC, Box 5, Folder "Denman, Marion A. Apr.–June 1917 #5." *See* FF to MD, 4/1/1917, at 2–6, *id.*

CHAPTER 10

1. FF to MD, 4/1/1917, at 1, 7.

2. *Id.* at 1–2.

3. On Baker's selection as head of the War Department, *see* Douglas B. Craig, *Progressives at War* 65–67 (2013); Daniel R. Beaver, *Newton Baker and the American*

War Effort 1–8 (1966); Frederick Palmer, 1 *Newton Baker: America at War* 6–10 (1931).

4. NYT, 4/6/1918, at 1. *See* Beaver, *Newton Baker and the American War Effort*, 37 (noting that more than 600,000 men were drafted between September 1917 and March 1918).

5. FFR, 114.

6. FF to KL, 4/27/1917, at 1, FFLC, Box 80, "Ludington, Katharine 1917." *See* FF to MD, 4/22/1917, at 2–3, FFLC, Box 5, Folder "Denman, Marion A. June 1917 #5."

7. NDB to ALL, 4/22/1917 tel. & 4/23/1917, A. Lawrence Lowell Official Papers, Box 85, Folder 1163.

8. FFR, 114–15.

9. OWH to FF, 3/5/1917, H-FF Corr., at 68. Frankfurter's letter is missing.

10. FF to MD, 4/22/1917 at 1.

11. *Id.* at 4.

12. WashTimes, 4/23/1917, at 2.

13. Percy, *Some Memories*, 53, 59; FF to MD, 4/22/1917, at 1–2; WES, 12/18/1917, at 8.

14. FF to KL, 2/16/1916, at 4, FFLC, Box 80, "Ludington, Katharine 1916"; *Letters of Ivar Campbell* (privately printed, 1917).

15. FF to MD, 4/30/1917, at 4, FFLC, Box 5, Folder "Denman, Marion A. Apr.–June 1917 #5."

16. FFR, 109–10.

17. FF to MD, 4/30/1917, at 4.

18. FF to KL, 4/27/1917, at 2.

19. Note to "Mr. Henderson and the Gentlemen of the House," circa 10/1918, at 1–2, FFLC, Box 5, Folder "Denman, Marion A. October 1918 #12."

20. FFR, 111.

21. Clipping, n.d., RGVP, Carton 22, Folder 7. Frankfurter sent the clipping to Sophie Valentine and wrote: "To have escaped this till the end. Yours in H of T. Think–of the opportunity of living *that* down." *Id.*

22. FF to MD, 5/15/1917, FFLC, Box 5, Folder "Denman, Marion A. Apr.–June 1917 #5."

23. FF to MD, 6/8/1917, *id.*

24. WL COH at 98. *See* WL to HH, 5/15/1917, PPWL at 66–68; WL to FA, 5/15/1917, at 4, WLP, Reel 165, Box 2, Folder 54.

25. WL to FA, 5/15/1917, at 4.

26. WL to EMH, 4/12/1917, WLP, Reel 14, Box 14, Folder 564.

27. EMH to WL, 5/7/1917, *id.*; House Diaries, 5/7/1917, Series II, Vol. 5, at 142.

28. Walter Lippmann, "The World Conflict in Its Relations to American Democracy," *Annals of the American Academy of Political and Social Science*, July 1917, at 1–10.

29. WL to FF, 4/1917, at 2–3, Box 77, FFLC, Folder "Lippmann, Walter 1914–19."

30. WL to NDB, 5/7/1917, at 2–3, NDBP, Reel 2. *See* House Diary, 5/7/1917.

31. WL to NDB, 5/10/1917, at 1–2, NDBP, Reel 2.

32. Steel, *Walter Lippmann and the American Century*, 118.
33. MDL to Hazel Albertson, 11/14/1916, in Steel, *Walter Lippmann and the American Century*, 118–19.
34. Luhan, *Movers and Shakers*, 310.
35. *Id.*
36. WL to FF, 4/23 or 4/27/1917, FFLC, Box 77, Folder "Lippmann, Walter 1914–19."
37. *See* FF to WL, n.d. 1917 #16, at 1–2, WLP, Reel 9, Box 10, Folder 420.
38. WL to FF, 4/1917, at 1.
39. FF to FL, 5/23/1917 #15, at 1–2, WLP, Reel 9, Box 10, Folder 420.
40. Steel, *Walter Lippmann and the American Century*, 120; NY Trib, 5/27/1917, at 25.
41. FF to WL, n.d. 1917 #16, at 1.
42. FF to WL, n.d. 1917 #17, at 2.
43. Steel, *Walter Lippmann and the American Century*, 120. The bedroom Steel referred to was likely the House's top-floor crow's nest.
44. *Id.* For Lippmann's recollections of the House, *see* WL COH at 97–98.
45. WL to FL, circa late May/early June 1917, WL, Reel 165, Box 2, Folder 54.
46. WL to NH, 7/20/1917, PPWL at 68.
47. FF to WL, n.d. 1917 #13, WLP, Reel 9, Box 10, Folder 420; FF to WL, n.d. 1917 #17, at 1, *id.*
48. "A Review of Growth and Prospects of The New Republic," at 1, Aug. 1916, WSP, Reel 5, Segment 4.
49. FF to MD, 5/30/1917, at 1, FFLC, Box 5, Folder "Denman, Marion A. Apr.–June 1917 #5."
50. FF to WL, n.d. 1917 #13, at 3.
51. Lansing to WW, 5/17/1917, *Papers Relating to the Foreign Relations of the United States: Lansing Papers, 1914–20*, Vol. 2, at 17–19 (J. S. Beddie, ed., 1940); Memorandum re: Morgenthau Secret Mission, 6/10/1917, at 101–5, in Unpublished Lansing Diary Blue Boxes, Box 2, 4/4/1916 to 12/30/1919, Reel 1; William Yale, "Henry Morgenthau's Special Mission of 1917," *World Politics* 1, no. 3 (April 1949): 308–20.
52. FF to WL, 3/20/1916, at 2–3, WLP, Reel 164, Box 1, Folder 29.
53. Morgenthau to WW, 6/7/1917, 42 WWP at 462–63. The president wrote Frankfurter thanking him as if it were a fait accompli. WW to FF, 6/11/1917, *id.* at 475.
54. FF to WW, 6/12/1917, *id.* at 486.
55. FFR, 146.
56. FF to MDF, 2/21/1933, at 2, FFLC, Box 14, Folder "Denman, Marion A. (Frankfurter) 1933 #123." *See* FF to MD, 6/20/1917, at 3, FFLC, Box 5, Folder "Denman, Marion A. Apr.–June 1917 #5".
57. FF to MD, 6/20/1917, at 1; FF to MD, 6/21/1917, at 3, FFLC, Box 5, Folder "Denman, Marion A. Apr.–June 1917 #5."
58. FFR, 146–48.
59. FF to WL, 7/4/1917, WLP, Reel 9, Box 10, Folder 420.
60. House Diary, 7/14/1917, Series II, Vol. 5, at 213.

61. *Id.; id.*, 6/11/1917, Series II, Vol. 5, at 179.

62. Yale, "Henry Morgenthau's Special Mission of 1917," 316–18.

63. CW to Sir Ronald Graham, 7/5/1917 & CW to RG, 7/6/1917, *The Letters and Papers of Chaim Weizmann*, Series A, Vol. 7, at 460–65 (Leonard Stein, ed., 1975).

64. FFR, 149.

65. *Id.*, 151; Frank Polk to WW, 7/12/1917, 43 WWP at 159–60 & n. 1 (containing telegram from FF and Henry Morgenthau, 7/8/1917); House Diary, 7/14/1917, Series II, Vol. 5, at 213.

66. FFR, 151–52; Henry Morgenthau Sr. Diary, 7/13/1917, Henry Morgenthau Papers, Box 2, Reel 2.

67. William Graves Sharp to Lansing, 7/17/1917, 43 WWP, at 201; Polk to WW, 7/18/1917, *id.* at 206–7.

68. Polk to WW, 7/12/1917, *id.* at 159–60.

69. FFR, 149.

70. Robert Lansing to WW, 8/13/1917, 43 WWP, at 442. *See id.* at 442–48 (containing FF to Lansing, 8/7/1917); WW to Lansing, 8/14/1917, *id.* at 460.

71. FF to LDB, 8/14/1917, FFLC, Box 29, Folder "Brandeis, Louis D. from Frankfurter 1915–19" & LDB-Louisville, Reel 59A at 36.

72. FF to KL, 8/14/1917, at 2, FFLC, Box 80, "Folder Ludington, Katharine 1917."

73. FF to KL, 9/6/1917, at 6–8, *id. See* Barnard, *The Forging of an American Jew*, 209.

74. NDB to WW, 9/1/1917, 44 WWP at 120.

75. FF to MD, 10/1/1917, at 1, FFLC, Box 6, Folder "Denman, Marion A. 1917 #6."

76. FF, Memorandum for the Secretary of War, 9/4/1917, 44 WWP at 161–64. *See* David M. Kennedy, *Over Here* (1980).

77. FF to EMH, 9/4/1917, at 2, EMHP, Box 45, Folder 1443.

78. NDB to WW, 9/7/1917, 44 WWP at 161 (enclosing FF, Memorandum for the Secretary of War, 9/4/1917).

79. WBW to WW, 9/18/1917, *id.* at 213–15 (enclosing Memorandum for the Secretary of Labor, 9/18/1917).

80. FF to MD, 10/1/1917 & 10/9/1917 & 10/17/1917, FFLC, Box 5, Folder "Denman, Marion A. 1917 #6"; FF to KL, 10/4/1917, at 1–3, FFLC, Box 80, Folder "Ludington, Katharine 1917"; FF to LDB, 10/20/1917, at 1–8, LDB-Louisville, Reel 59E & FFLC, Box 29, Folder "Brandeis, Louis D. from Frankfurter 1915–19."

81. FF to WL, 10/3/1917, FFLC, Box 77, Folder "Lippmann, Walter 1914–19."

82. FF to WL, 10/2/1917 tel., *id.*; Stanley King to FF, 10/4/1917, *id.*

83. FFR, 120–21.

84. FF to WL, 10/22/1917, at 1, WLP, Reel 9, Box 10, Folder 420.

85. WBW to WW, 11/6/1917, 44 WWP at 520. *See* FF to LDB, 11/7/1917, at 1, LDB-Louisville, Reel 59F & FFLC, Box 29, Folder "Brandeis, Louis D. from Frankfurter 1915–19."

86. FF to WL, 11/22/1917, at 1, WLP, Reel 9, Box 10, Folder 420 & FFLC, Box 77, Folder "Lippmann, Walter 1914–19."

87. FFR, 130.

88. On the bombing, *see* Richard H. Frost, *The Mooney Case* 80–102 (1968). On Mooney's trial, *see id.* at 173–93.

89. "Report on the Mooney Dynamiting Cases in San Francisco," 1/28/1918, Official Bulletin, at 15 in FFLC, Box 194, Folder "1918." *See* Frost, *The Mooney Case*, 164–72, 493–95.

90. TR to FF, 12/19/1917, at 1, FFLC, Box 98, Folder "Roosevelt, Theodore 1917–18 & undated."

91. *Id.* at 3–4.

92. FF to ERB, 11/28/1917 tel., FFLC, Box 31, Folder "Buckner, Emory R. 1917–18."

93. FF to TR, 1/7/1918, at 1–5, FFLC, Box 98, Folder "Roosevelt, Theodore 1917–18 & undated."

94. TNR, 1/18/1922, at 212–14; *id.* at 215–21; *id.* at 221–22; TNR, 10/19/1921, at 218–19; TNR, 10/12/1921, at 189–90.

95. Mooney v. Holohan, 294 U.S. 103, 110 (1935); Frost, *The Mooney Case*, 483–85.

96. FF to WL, 11/22/1917, at 1–2.

97. WL to WW, 6/15/1917, 42 WWP at 525; WW to WL, 6/16/1917, *id.* at 528.

98. NDB to WW, 8/20/1917, 43 WWP at 532.

99. WL COH at 93–97.

100. *Id.* at 95; WL to Graham Wallas, 9/18/1917, at 1, WLP, Reel 32, Box 33, Folder 1245.

101. Waldron and Gregory to WW, 5/11/1917, 42 WWP at 321–22.

102. WL Diary, 10/10/1917, at 96, WLP, Reel 160, Box 236, Folder 1.

103. FF to MD, 8/19/1917, at 2, FFLC, Box 5, Folder "Denman, Marion A. 1917 #6." ("I have to rush to Boston for a day to see the real cabinet of the Wilson administration."). *See* Neu, *Colonel House*, ix, xi (describing the origins of House's title and his role as "high-level political intermediary" in the Wilson administration).

104. WL to EMH, 4/12/1917, PPWL at 65–66.

105. WL to EMH, 9/24/1917, *id.* at 72. *See* Lawrence E. Gelfand, *The Inquiry* (1963).

106. WL to FF, 10/3/1917, WLP, Reel 9, Box 10, Folder 420.

107. WL Diary, 10/6/1917, at 90, WLP, Reel 160, Box 236, Folder 1.

108. WL Diary, 10/6/1917 & 10/7/1917, at 90–91. *See* HC to Willard Straight, 9/27/1917, at 1–2, DWSEP, Reel 14.

109. WL Diary, 10/7/1917, at 91.

110. NYT, 10/11/1917, at 8.

111. WL Diary, 10/10/1917, at 95–96.

112. WL to FF, 10/12/1917, WLP, Reel 9, Box 10, Folder 420.

113. FF to EMH, 9/1/1917 tel., EMHP, Box 45, Folder 1443; FF to WL, 10/22/1917, at 2–3.

114. WL to FF, 10/3/1917.

115. FF to WL, 10/22/1917, at 2–3. *See* FF to LDB, 10/20/1917, at 9.

116. WL to FF, 10/30/1917, at 1, WLP, Reel 9, Box 10, Folder 420.

117. *Id.* at 2.

118. FF to WL, 11/22/1917, at 1; FF to WL, 12/3/1917, FFLC, Box 77, Folder "Lippmann, Walter 1914–19."

119. WW to EMH, 9/2/1917, 44 WWP at 121.

120. EMH to WW, 9/4/1917, *id.* at 149.

121. House Diary, 1/8/1913, 27 WWP at 23; House Diary, 1/17/1913, *id.* at 61; House Diary, 1/24/1913, *id.* at 71; House Diary, 2/13/1913, *id.* at 110; Neu, *Colonel House*, 78–79, 82.

122. House Diary, 1/28/1916, Series II, Vol. 4, at 37; Neu, *Colonel House*, 254–55.

123. EMH to WW, 9/20/1917, 44 WWP at 226.

124. *Id.*

125. PPL, 9/27/1917, at 1; PPL, 9/28/1917, at 1.

126. Christopher Lasch, *The New Radicalism in America, 1889–1963*, at 225, 227 n. 4, 234–35, 236 (1965). On the Colcord-House relationship, *see* EMHP, Box 29, Folders 904–8. On the Bullitt-House relationship, *see* EMHP, Box 21, Folders 676–86.

127. PPL, 10/24/1917, at 1.

128. EMH to WW, 10/3/1917, 44 WWP at 298.

129. WW to Herbert Brougham, 9/29/1917, 44 WWP at 279. *See* Brougham to WW, 9/28/1917, *id.* at 275–76; Lawrence to WW, 10/3/1917, *id.* at 299–300.

130. FF to WL, n.d., WLP, Reel 164, Box 1, Folder 29.

131. Catherine Drinker Bowen, *Family Portrait* 117–18 (1970). *See* EDB Memoir, 1939–40, 7/15/1939, Ernesta Drinker Barlow Papers, Box 5, Folder 5:1 (describing Kitty Bowen as always having "great charm, spirit, wit and talent, but no physical beauty").

132. Will Brownell and Richard N. Billings, *So Close to Greatness* 53 (1987) (citing Bullitt's Yale classmate Philip Platt). This is also evident in Frankfurter's letters to Lippmann.

133. Bowen, *Family Portrait*, at 90–91; EDB Memoir, 1939–40, 7/15/1939.

134. EDB Memoir, 1939–40, 7/15/1939.

135. Bowen, *Family Portrait*, 131.

136. EDB Memoir, 1939–40, 7/15/1939.

137. On his mother's Jewish roots, *see* Brownell and Billings, *So Close to Greatness*, 12–16. On most brilliant senior at Yale, *see id.* at 29–33. He graduated in 1913 because of illness. *Id.* Beatrice Farnsworth, *William C. Bullitt and the Soviet Union* 4–5 (1967).

138. Brownell and Billings, *So Close to Greatness*, 34–36.

139. EDB Memoir, 1939–40, August 1939, at 97–107.

140. Brownell and Billings, *So Close to Greatness*, 49–61.

141. WCB to WL, 3/23/1917, WLP, Reel 5, Box 5, Folder 206. *See* FF to MD, 4/22/1917, at 4, Box 5, Folder "Denman, Marion A. Apr.–June 1917 #5"; EDB Memoir, 1939–40.

142. FF, "Memorandum on Breach of 'Confidence,'" at 1, n.d., FFLC, Box 67, Folder "House, Edward M. 1918–33 & undated."

143. *Id.* at 2.

144. WCB to Ernesta Drinker Bullitt, circa 1917, WCBP, Box 12, Folder 248.

145. WL to General G. O. Squier, 12/15/1917, WLP, Reel 5, Box 5, Folder 206. For WL-WCB correspondence, *see id.*

146. Colcord to EMH, 6/16/1917, at 1, EMHP, Box 29, Folder 904. Eustace Percy was also there that morning.

147. WL to FF, 12/28/1917, at 1–2, WLP, Reel 9, Box 10, Folder 420.

148. WL to EMH, n.d. 1917, EMHP, Box 70, Folder "1917 Jan–Sep. Walter Lippmann."

149. FF, "Memorandum on Breach of 'Confidence,'" at 3.

150. WCB to EMH, 7/5/1917, at 1, EMHP, Box 21, Folder 676 & WCBP, Reel 1.

151. WCB to EMH, 10/25/1917, at 1–2, EMHP, Box 21, Folder 676.

152. "A Memorandum by Sidney Edward Mezes, David Hunter Miller, and Walter Lippmann," circa 12/1917, 45 WWP at 459–74.

153. House Diary, 1/4/1918, *id.* at 458–59 & n. 1. For Wilson's draft of the Fourteen Points, *see id.* at 476–95.

154. "An Address to a Joint Session of Congress," 1/8/1918, *id.* at 534–39.

155. WL to EMH, Memorandum, 12/1917, PPWL at 84–86 & n. 1.

156. FF to WL, 11/5/1917, WLP, Reel 9, Box 10, Folder 420.

157. FF to NDB, Memorandum, 12/25/1917, 45 WWP at 356.

158. FF to WL, 12/28/1917 #21, at 3, WLP, Reel 9, Box 10, Folder 420.

CHAPTER 11

1. CHP, 6/6/1891, Georgia, Confederate Pension Applications, 1879–1960, GCP-203, at 1029.

2. CHP to PPL, 1/14/1916, at 1. The document had been missing from Box 16, Folder 2 of the Stone Mountain Memorial Collection at Emory, but a copy is on file thanks to David Freeman. See David B. Freeman, *Carved in Stone* 57 & n. 3 (1997). For Plane's earlier recollection on the origins of the project, *see* AC, 9/26/1915, at C6.

3. Letter from William H. Terrell, AC, 5/26/1914, at 8; Augusta Chronicle 5/28/1914, at 6.

4. Scholars have attributed Graves's article to the June 14, 1914, *Atlanta Georgian.* *See* Lucian Lamar Knight, *Georgia's Landmarks, Memorials, and Legends* 250 (1916). That article, however, cannot be found. It may have been in Graves's *New York American* column later that summer. *See* John Temple Graves, "World's Grandest Monument Waiting in Sight for the Confederate Dead," 7/19/1914, New York American, in American Memory, Library of Congress, Printed Ephemera Collection, Portfolio 14, Folder 39.

5. Sam Venable to CHP, 8/8/1914 & Venable to CHP, 11/9/1914, SMC, Box 16, Folder 1.

6. BaltSun, 8/6/1915, at 6.

7. CHP to John Temple Graves, 1/18/1915, SMC, Box 16, Folder 1; AC, 8/17/1915, at 4.

8. GB to Captain Manly, 7/12/1915, GBP, Box 114, Folder "Stone Mountain 1915."

9. GB to Seeley, 7/11/1915, *id.*

10. GB to CHP, 8/9/1915 tel., SMC, Box 16, Folder 1.

11. NYT, 2/17/1924, at XX10; Gerald W. Johnson, *The Undefeated* 6 (1927).

12. Robert J. Casey and Mary Borglum, *Give the Man Room* 174 (1952).

13. *Id.* at 175; Johnson, *The Undefeated*, 7–9; WP, 1/2/1916, at MT1, MT5.

14. GB to CHP, 8/17/1915, at 1–2, CHPP, Box 16, Folder 1.

15. AC, 9/26/1915, at C6.

16. TNR, 1/15/1916, at 275–77. On Bourne, *see* Bruce Clayton, *Forgotten Prophet* 117–40 (1998); Stansell, *American Moderns*, 210–22; Lasch, *The New Radicalism in America*, 69–103.

17. Gutzon Borglum, "Art That Is Real and American," The World's Work, 6/1914, at 200.

18. Gutzon Borglum, "The Betrayal of the People by a False Democracy," The Craftsman, 4/1912, at 7.

19. Robert Lincoln to GB, 2/6/1908, at 1, GBP, Box 26, Folder "Lincoln, Robt. T. and letter re A. Lincoln 1907–08" (describing Borglum's bust as "the most extraordinarily good portrait of my father I have ever seen"); CHP to PPL, 1/14/1916, at 1–2 (she "knew a great deal of Gutzon Borglum's creations").

20. "Carving a Mountain into a Memorial," Stone, 11/01/1915, at 588. *See* GB to CHP, 8/20/1915, HPP, Box 16, Folder 1.

21. CHP to GB, 12/17/1915 Extract, SMC, Box 16, Folder 2 (emphasis in original). After meeting with William J. Simmons, the Klan Imperial Wizard, nearly two years later, she repeated the suggestion of Klan representation on the memorial and Klan involvement in fundraising. CHP to GB, 12/4/1917, at 4–5, GBP, Box 114, Folder "Stone Mountain 1917."

22. AC, 11/28/1915, at A1; Wyn Craig Wade, *The Fiery Cross* 144–45 (1987).

23. GB to CHP, 1/27/1916, at 1, SMC, Box 16, Folder 3.

24. NYT, 1/2/1916, at SM1; WP, 1/2/1916, at MT1; HarCour, 1/30/1916, at X10; SPD, 1/16/1916, at B16; NYSun, 1/2/1916, §5, at 1.

25. WP, 1/2/1916, at MT1; NYT Magazine, 1/2/1916, at SM1-2; AC, 5/22/1916, at 7.

26. AC, 5/21/1916, at 5.

27. Johnson, *The Undefeated*, 17–19.

28. Gutzon Borglum, "The Confederate Memorial," The World's Work, 8/1917, at 438, 446.

29. GB to MB, 1/22/1917, at 3, GBP, Box 114, Folder "Works SM 1917."

30. "One Man War," GBP, Box 138, Folder "Biographic Material."

31. FFR, 55. For biographical information on Borglum, *see* Taliaferro, *Great White Fathers*, 65–86; Robin Borglum Carter, *Gutzon Borglum* 12–25 (1998); Shaff and Shaff, *Six Wars at a Time*; Rex Alan Smith, *The Carving of Mount Rushmore* 46–59 (1985); Casey and Borglum, *Give the Man Room*, 30–54.

32. Richard L. Jensen, *The Mormon Years of the Borglum Family* 12 (1979).

33. *Id.* at 14.

34. *Id.* at 15–16.

35. 1870 Census, Nebraska, Roll M593_839, Page 502B, Image 284, Line 31 & A. Mervyn Davies, *Solon H. Borglum* 18 (1974). *See* August Borglum to MB, 10/17/1947, at 3, GBP, Box 46, Folder "W" & GBJT, Box 2, Folder II.D (recalling it as a "mutual separation of a second wife who did not really belong in the family"); MB to Dorothy, n.d., GBJT, Box 2, at 1–2 (claiming that the "first wife was so violently jealous of the second wife that she made life miserable for her").

36. "Chapter I: In the Beginning," at 6, GBP, Box 138, Folder "Biographical Papers: Give the Man Room #2"; Casey and Borglum, *Give the Man Room*, 28.

37. Joseph Wilson, Compiled Military Service Records of Volunteer Union Soldiers in 54th Mass. Regiment, at 17, NARA, M 1898, Roll 18 (listing his complexion as "light"); 1880 Census, Muncie, Indiana, Roll 274, FHFilm 1254274, Page 406B, E.D. 184, Image 0454, lines 7–10 (listing Joseph as "black" and two children as "mulatto"); 1876–77 Muncie City Directory, at 78 (listing Joseph Wilson as a blacksmith and "(c)" for "colored"); Joseph Wilson, Beech Grove Cemetery Listing, 6/1/1880 (listing him as black but erroneously listing him as a member of the Eighteenth Regiment of the U.S.C.T.). This is the first account to reveal that Christine Wilson's husband was a black man. *Cf.* Shaff and Shaff, *Six Wars at a Time*, 18–19 (claiming she had married a man named Harry Wilson from Chicago); Taliaferro, *Great White Fathers*, 70 (indicating she remarried, moved to California, and died of tuberculosis); Smith, *The Carving of Mount Rushmore*, 48 (indicating Christina "withdrew from the marriage" in Omaha, joined her parents there, and later remarried).

38. Joseph Wilson, Compiled Military Service Records of Volunteer Union Soldiers in 54th Mass. Regiment, at 17 (listing N. P. Hallowell as mustering him into the 54th Mass. Regiment on May 12, 1863).

39. Deposition of Christine Wilson, 9/7/1887, at 1, Widow of Joseph Wilson, Civil War Pension Application, 54th Mass. Infantry, Certificate #240886, Application #35771, NARA, Washington, DC.

40. Joseph Wilson and Christena Mickleson, 10/8/1872, "Indiana Marriages, 1811–1959," Henry County, FHL Microfilm, 001887510.

41. "Chapter II: Alone," at 1–2, GBP, Box 138, Folder "Biographical Papers: Give the Man Room #2."

42. *Id.* at 3–4. Casey and Borglum, *Give the Man Room*, at 31–33.

43. Shaff and Shaff, *Six Wars at a Time*, 18–19.

44. Davies, *Solon H. Borglum*, 77.

45. Muncie Daily News, 6/2/1880, at 1. All the barbershops were closed in his honor. *Id. See* Joseph Wilson, Beech Grove Cemetery Listing, 6/1/1880.

46. Deposition of Christine Wilson, 9/7/1887, at 1–2.

47. Dagmar Wilson Death Certificate, 4/13/1895, Los Angeles, California; Harry Wilson Death Certificate, 4/7/1896, Solon H. Borglum and Borglum Family Papers, Box 1, Folder 2.

48. 1900 Census, E.D. 54, Sheet 2A, Household 31, Line 39; Los Angeles City Directory 1900–1901, at 796.

49. LAT, 2/4/1901, at 12; Notes from LA County Vital Records, Vol. 4, 1898–1901 (on file with author).

50. Casey and Borglum, *Give the Man Room*, 37–39.

51. LAT, 9/15/1889, at 12.

52. Jessie Fremont to GB, 4/15/1896, GBP, Box 17, Folder "Fremont, Jessie B."; *The Letters of Jessie Benton Fremont* 540–46 (Pamela Herr and Mary Lee Spence, eds., 1993); Jean Stern and Gerald J. Miller, "John Gutzon Borglum and the Los Angeles Art Community, 1884–1901," in *Out of Rushmore's Shadow* 21–23 (Rosa Portell, ed., 1999); Casey and Borglum, *Give the Man Room*, 42–43.

53. NYT, 3/1/1922, at 97.

54. Casey and Borglum, *Give the Man Room*, 45–46.

55. NYT, 10/25/1912, at 12. *See* Casey and Borglum, *Give the Man Room*, 47–49.

56. Shaff and Shaff, *Six Wars at a Time*, 44–45.

57. Davies, *Solon H. Borglum*, 10–12, 38–39; Phil Kovinick, "South Dakota's Other Borglum," *South Dakota History* 1, no. 3 (Summer 1971): 207–30; NYSun, 10/27/1912, at SM11.

58. GB to Mr. Drake, 3/12/1904, GBP, Box 13, Folder "D" (acknowledging the confusion in the press).

59. WES, 4/5/1902, at 19.

60. Davies, *Solon H. Borglum*, 7.

61. *Id*. at 7 & 245 n. 16.

62. CHP to PPL, 1/14/1916, at 2 (mentioning Solon's "Gordon equestrian statue" but describing Solon as Gutzon's "younger brother and pupil").

63. AC, 5/21/1916, at B5.

64. Shaff and Shaff, *Six Wars at a Time*, 80–81.

65. Robin Borglum Kennedy, *Mary's Story* (2014); Casey and Borglum, *Give the Man Room*, 104–5.

66. NYT, 12/7/1901, at BR17.

67. NYT, 5/20/1909, at 1; Casey and Borglum, *Give the Man Room*, 104–5.

68. Gutzon Borglum Account with Meyer, 10/15/1910, GBP, Box 32, Folder "Meyer"; Mary Borglum note, 1946, *id.*, Folder "Eugene Meyer, Jr." (recalling the interest was 5 percent). It was not just Meyer. Paul Warburg owned a mortgage on Borglum's New York studio and often took his commissions as collateral. The two men had a falling-out over the sculptor's indebtedness. *See* Mary Borglum Note, "Correspondence with Paul Warburg," GBP, Box 46, Folder "W."

69. NYT, 6/16/1909, at 8.

70. *See* GB to WW, 6/24/1914, 1/29/1915, & 1/3/1916, WWP, Reel 377, Series 4, No. 5043. On the White House meeting, *see* GB to JT, 5/7/1915, *id.*; WES, 5/12/1915, at 2.

71. GB to JT, 11/14/1917, WWP, Reel 377, Series 4, No. 5043.

72. WW to JT, 11/16/1917, *id.*; JT to GB, 11/16/1917, GBP, Box 48, Folder "Wilson, Woodrow Aug. 1905, Jan. 1916, Nov. 1917 to April 1918."

73. GB to JT, 11/22/1917, WWP, Reel 240, Series 4, No. 206A.

74. WW to JT, n.d., *id.*

75. NDB to JT, 11/28/1917, 45 WWP at 156 & Reel 240, Series 4, No. 206A.

76. GB to E. F. McDonald Jr., 2/6/1941, at 1–3, GBP, Box 46, Folder "W"; "Chapter X: Aircraft Investigations in World War I," at 7–8, GBP, Box 55, Folder "Aircraft Investigation 1918"; NYT, 9/11/1910, at 1 (mentioning shed idea).

77. NYT, 9/18/1908, at 1.

78. GB to Orville Wright, 9/20/1908, at 1–2, WBP, Box 13, Folder 23.

79. GB to E. F. McDonald Jr., 2/6/1941, at 2–3; "Chapter X: Aircraft Investigations in World War I," at 8; NYT, 12/22/1908, at 3; NYT, 6/11/1909, at 2.

80. "Chapter X: Aircraft Investigations in World War I," at 9–10.

81. WW to GB, 12/5/1917, 45 WWP at 214; "Memorandum for the President," 12/3/1917, WWP, Reel 240, Series 4, No. 206A.

82. GB to WW, 12/25/1917, 45 WWP at 356–58. *See* GB to WW, 12/12/1917, WWP, Reel 240, Series 4, No. 206A.

83. WW to JT, 12/30/1917, 45 WWP at 397 & Reel 240, Series 4, No. 206A.

84. NDB to WW, 1/2/1918, 45 WWP at 426–27 & Reel 240, Series 4, No. 206A.

85. WW to GB, 1/2/1918, 45 WWP at 427 & Reel 240, Series 4, No. 206A.

86. "Order of Events," GBP, Box 54, Folder "Aircraft Investigation I"; "Daily Record," 1/7/1917, *id.*

87. Borglum, "Chapter I: Aircraft Investigation in World War I," at 41–42, GBP, Box 55, Folder "Aircraft Investigation (1918)." *See* "Order of Events."

88. Daily Record, 1/12/1916.

89. Claude Moore Fuess, *Stanley King of Amherst* 36 (1955); SK to NDB, 7/2/1918, NDBP, Reel 4, Page 602.

90. Walter Lippmann, introduction, Gertrude Besse King, *Alliances for the Mind* viii–ix (1934).

91. OWH to FF, 2/7/1912, H-FF Corr., at 3.

92. *Id.* at 4 n. 1. *See* Gertrude King to FF, 2/14/12, JPC, Box 1, Folder 6.

93. Fuess, *Stanley King of Amherst*, 81.

94. *Id.* at 89–90.

95. *Id.* at 90, 96.

96. Borglum, "Chapter I: Aircraft Investigation in World War I," at 25; Daily Record, 1/17/1916, at 1–5; Undated Typescript Re: King, at 1–3, GBP, Box 54, Folder "Aircraft Investigation I."

97. WW to GB, 1/23/1918, 46 WWP at 82.

98. NDB to WW, 1/21/1918, 46 WWP at 57–58.

99. GB to WW, 1/26/1918, 46 WWP at 106 & Reel 377, Series 4, No. 5043.

100. WW to GB, 1/29/1918, GBP, Box 48, Folder "Woodrow Wilson" & WWP, Reel 377, Series 4, No. 5043.

101. GB to WW, 1/24/1918, 46 WWP at 94 & Reel 240, Series 4, No. 206A. The report is dated three days earlier.

102. Borglum, "Preliminary Report on Aeronautic Conditions," 1/21/1918, at 1, GBP, Box 53, Folder "Aircraft Woodrow Wilson 1918."

103. GB to WW, 1/24/1918, 46 WWP at 95.

104. Borglum, "Chapter I: Aircraft Investigation in World War I," at 12–13; Borglum Memorandum at 1, GBP, Box 57, Folder "Aircraft Investigation, 1918."

105. Borglum, "Preliminary Report on Aeronautic Conditions," 1/21/1918, at 3.

106. *Id.*

107. GB to Deeds, 3/5/1913, GBP, Box 13, Folder "D"; GB to A. M. Kittredge, 4/16/1914, GBP, Box 130, Folder "Wright Bros. Memorial 1912–14"; GB to Deeds, 12/12/1915, *id.*; Contract, *id.*

108. GB to Deeds, 5/22/1917, GBP, Box 13, Folder "D"; GB to Deeds, 7/30/1917 (with notation by MB 1951), *id.*

109. Borglum, "Preliminary Report on Aeronautic Conditions," 1/21/1918, at 8.

110. WW to EMH, 2/25/1918, 46 WWP at 445 (enclosing GB to WW, 2/24/1918).

111. WW to NDB, 2/1/1918, 46 WWP at 206.

112. NDB to WW, 2/1/1918, 46 WWP at 208–9.

113. FF to EM, 1/11/1957, at 1, FFLC, Box 84, Folder "Meyer, Eugene 1938–57."

114. LDB to FF, 1/24/1913, HBHS, at 21.

115. On Walter Meyer, *see* FF to EM, 1/11/1957, at 1–2 & EM to FF, 1/12/1957, FFLC, Box 84, Folder "Meyer, Eugene 1938–57." On Eugene Meyer, *see* Merlo J. Pusey, *Eugene Meyer* (1974).

116. Agnes socialized with Brandeis, Frankfurter, Laski, and Holmes. *See* Agnes Meyer Diary at 7, 43, 52, 106, 122, 132 (Brandeis); *id.* at 106 ("Took Felix Frankfurter home [from Brandeis's] and told him I could marry him but nobody else I knew. Also that he would not marry as he could not hold down all he expected in the lady–"); *id.* at 108 (met Frankfurter and Harold Laski for dinner); & *id.* at 109-10 (lunch with Frankfurter, met Holmes, and described Holmes as "a marvel"), Agnes Meyer Papers, Box 1, Folder "1917."

117. Eugene Meyer COH, Vol. I, Pt. 3, at 372.

118. *Id.*

119. FF to Mrs. Ezra Thayer, 1/7/1916, "Third Year Men," at 1, Frankfurter SMC, HLS. *See* FF to EM, 1/24/1935, FFLC, Box 84, Folder "Meyer, Eugene M. 1935–37" (describing Henderson as having "the best lawyer's head of them all" among New York lawyers Frankfurter knew, including Joe Cotton, Dwight Morrow, and Charles P. Howland).

120. EM to FF, 1/22/1935, *id.* See Katharine Graham, *Personal History* 252 (1997) (describing Henderson as one of "three main people on whom my father had bestowed his love and affection and respect").

121. Pusey, *Eugene Meyer*, 13–14.

122. NDB to WW, 2/1/1918, 46 WWP at 208.

123. NDB to WW, 2/3/1918, 46 WWP at 230.

124. Pusey, *Eugene Meyer*, 152; WSJ, 8/9/1916, at 6.

125. Agnes Meyer Diary, 2/1/1918, at 36–37. *See id.* at 37 ("This work and his work in the air-craft service makes him feel nearer to the powers that be and the change in him is very interesting.").

126. NDB to WW, 2/3/1918.

127. GB to EM, 3/11/1918, GBP, Box 52, Folder "Aircraft M, 1917–21, 1926, 1935, 1941."

128. *Id.*

129. GB to EM, 11/16/1930 & EM to GB, 11/29/1930, EMP, Box 12, Folder "Borglum, Gutzon 1920–39."

130. GM to EM, 3/11/1918.

131. WW to GB, 3/15/1918, 47 WWP at 41.

132. NYT, 3/17/1918, at 5.

133. Herbert Bayard Swope to JT, 3/17/1918, 47 WWP at 51; NYW, 3/18/1918, at 6.

134. NYT, 3/19/1918, at 3.

135. GB to WW, 4/3/1918, 47 WWP at 234–35.

136. GB to WW, 4/8/1918, *id.* at 297.

137. NYW, 4/13/1918, at 6.

138. GB to WW, 4/13/1918, 47 WWP at 335.

139. WW to GB, 4/15/1918, *id.* at 344.

140. NYT, 4/28/1918, at 4.

141. NYT, 4/30/1918, at 12.

142. NYT, 5/1/1918, at 12.

143. NYT, 5/3/1918, at 1.

144. WashTimes, 5/10/1918, at 1–2. Senator Thomas aired the charges on the Senate floor and reprinted all of Borglum's government correspondence in the Congressional Record. Cong. Rec. (Senate) 6326–30 (5/10/1918).

145. BG, 5/11/1918, at 2.

146. GB to WW, 5/10/1918, 47 WWP at 511 (emphasis in original).

147. JT to WW, 5/10/1918, *id.* at 587.

148. WW to JT, 5/10/1918, *id.* at 588.

149. NYT, 5/17/1918, at 4.

150. *Id.*

151. Pusey, 1 *Charles Evans Hughes*, 132–80.

152. Borglum, Memorandum, 5/26/1922, at 7, GBP, Box 54, Folder "Aircraft Investigation"; Borglum Memorandum, n.d., at 15, GBP, Box 57, Folder "Aircraft Investigation 1918." *See* GB to WW, 5/15/1918 tel., WWP, Reel 240, Series 4, No. 206A (praising Wilson's choice of Hughes).

153. WW to CEH, 5/17/1918, CEHP, Reel 3.

154. GB to Smallberg, 11/16/1940, at 1, GBP, Box 52, Folder "Aircraft Hughes 1918."

155. Hughes Report at 2, Reel 115, CEHP. *See* Pusey, 1 *Charles Evans Hughes*, 376–77 ("Because of the quiet nature of the investigation, many defects in the

makeshift aircraft procurement system were corrected without publicity as Hughes brought them to official attention.").

156. Borglum, Memorandum, 5/26/1922, at 7. *Cf.* GB to CEH, 8/21/1918, GBP, Box 57, Folder "Aircraft Investigation 1918" (praising his investigation).

157. Pusey, 1 *Charles Evans Hughes*, 377–82.

158. Hughes Report at 181.

159. Aircraft Report Supp. at 7 in Pusey, 1 *Charles Evans Hughes*, at 382.

160. Air Service Journal, 1/25/1919, at 2.

161. NYT, 2/18/1920, at 10. For Baker's defense of Deeds, *see* NYT, 2/20/1919, at 14; NYT, 2/4/1919, at 1.

162. NYW, 12/4/1918, in GBP, Box 59.

163. The majority report in the House validated Borglum's claims. Speech of Hon. James A. Frear, Cong. Rec. 4467–81 (3/10/1920) in GBP, Box 51, Folder "F 1913, 1918–21, 1938-39"; NYT, 2/17/1920, at 17; NYT, 2/18/1920, at 10; NYT, 3/7/1920, at 1; NYTrib, 10/21/1920, at 6.

164. Seward W. Livermore, *Politics Is Adjourned* 126–30, 133 (1966); Cooper, *Woodrow Wilson*, 434.

165. For a nuanced portrait, *see* Taliaferro, *Great White Fathers*, 163–73.

166. Borglum Memorandum, n.d., at 18–19.

167. Borglum Application, United States Public Service Reserve, 7/3/1918, at 4, GBP, Box 55, Folder "Aircraft Investigation 1918" (emphasis in original).

168. Albert Douglas to Frederic Bancroft, 2/7/1919, GBP, Box 52, Folder "Metropolitan Club 1919."

CHAPTER 12

1. FF to LDB, 12/14/1917, at 4–6, FFLC, Box 29, Folder "Louis D. Brandeis from Frankfurter Undated #88" & LDB-Louisville, Reel 596. *See* FF to LDB, 12/12/1917, *id.*

2. *See* FF to LDB, 12/12/1917, *id.*

3. FF, Memorandum, 1/7/1918, at 3, FFLC, Box 189, Folder "War Department 1918 #3" & NDBP, Reel 4, Box 5, Folder "F 1918."

4. *Id.* at 4.

5. *Id.* at 5.

6. *Id.* at 6–7.

7. FF to NDB, 1/4/1918, NBP, Reel 5, Folder "F 1918."

8. *Id.*

9. House Diary, 1/9/1918, Series II, Vol. 6, at 11.

10. *Id.*

11. LDB to EMH, 1/9/1918, at 1, FFLC, Box 26, Folder "Brandeis, Louis D. 1918."

12. *Id.*

13. *Id.* at 1–2.

14. *Id.* at 2.

15. House Diary, 1/17/1918, Series II, Vol. 6, at 24.

16. *Id.*

17. House Diary, 1/9/1918, Series II, Vol. 6, at 11.

18. House Diary, 2/23/1918, Series II, Vol. 6, at 69.

19. *See* chapter 10 nn. 90–94.

20. NDB to FF, 1/27/1918, FFLC, Box 189, Folder "War Department 1918."

21. House Diary, 1/30/1918, Series II, Vol. 6, at 42; HL to OWH, 1/31/1918, 1 HLL at 132–33.

22. Walter Hines Page to Arthur W. Page, 2/24/1918, at 13–14, Walter Hines Page Papers, Box 989, #128. *See* Walter Hines Page to Arthur W. Page, 2/1/18, at 2, *id.*, #124.

23. FF to MD, 1/30/1918 & 1/31/1918, FFLC, Box 5, Folder "Marion A. Denman 1918 #7."

24. FF to MD, 2/29/1918, at 2, *id.*; Journal entries, FFLC, Box 189, Folder "War Department 1918."

25. FF to MD, 2/29/1918, at 3.

26. FF to KL, 3/14/1918, at 1, FFLC, Box 80, Folder "Ludington, Katharine 1918–50."

27. *Id.* at 2–3.

28. FF to EMH, 2/24/1918, at 12–13, FFLC, Box 189, Folder "War Department 1918."

29. *Id.* at 16.

30. House Diaries, 3/27/1918, Series II, Vol. 6, at 91.

31. MD Passport Application, 5/3/1918, at 2, U.S. Passport Applications, 1/2/1906–3/31/1925, NARA, ARC ID 583830, MLR # A1 534, NARA Series M1490, Roll 511.

32. MD to Fosdick, 4/19/1918, NARA, Records of War Department and General and Special Staffs, RG 165, General Corr. 1917–21, NM 84, Entry 393, Box 51, at 25337.

33. MD French I.D. Card, 3/23/18, FFLC, Box 18, Folder "Misc. Documents concerning Family 1894–1957 & Undated"; MD Passport Application, 5/3/1918, at 2.

34. Liva Baker, *Felix Frankfurter*, 75–76 (1969).

35. MD to FF, 5/7/1918, at 2, FFLC, Box 5, Folder "Marion A. Denman 1918 #8."

36. NYT, 5/10/1918, at 10.

37. NYT, 6/2/1918, at 16.

38. FF to MD, 6/9/1918, at 2, FFLC, Box 5, Folder "Marion A. Denman 1918 #9."

39. http://www.maritimequest.com/liners/kronprinz_wilhelm_1901/kronprinz_wilhelm_data.htm.

40. Baker, *Felix Frankfurter*, 76 (based on interview with Helen Denman).

41. FF to KL, 8/9/1918, at 3–4, FFLC, Box 80, Folder "Ludington, Katharine 1918–50."

42. "Report of Roentgen Findings in the Case of Miss Marion Denman," 7/25/1918, FFLC, Box 5, Folder "Marion A. Denman 1918 #10."

43. FF to MD, 8/13/1918, at 1, *id.*

44. Fosdick Memorandum, 11/9/1918, NARA, Records of War Department and General and Special Staffs, RG 165, General Corr. 1917–21, NM 84, Entry 393,

Box 115, at 42194 (ordering that Denman's report be given "wide publicity"); Fosdick to Frederick Keppel, 12/2/1918, *id.*, Box 130, at 45351.

45. Memorandum to Major Foote, 7/12/1919, *id.* Box 153, at 50545; *see id.*, Box 160, at 52181.

46. "Statement of Newton D. Baker," 1/28/1918, Investigation of the War Department, Committee on Military Affairs, US Senate, 65th Cong., 2d Sess., Pt. 4, at 1925–86; NYT, 1/29/1918, at 1. *See* Kennedy, *Over Here*, 124–26; Beaver, *Newton D. Baker and the American War Effort*, 97–109.

47. NYT, 2/28/1918, at 10; NYT, 3/1/1918, at 1.

48. Robert Woolley and Matthew Hale to WW, 4/19/1918, 47 WWP at 376–79.

49. Woolley to Wilson, 4/25/1918, *id.* at 425–26.

50. Wilson to Woolley, 4/27/1918, *id.* at 449.

51. FF and SK to NDB, 4/30/1918, NDBP, Reel 5, Folder "1918 F."

52. NYTrib, 5/12/1918, at 8.

53. NYT, 5/26/1918, at SM2.

54. NYTrib, 5/15/1918, at 4.

55. ERB to FF, 5/16/1918, at 1, FFLC, Box 31, Folder "Buckner Emory R. 1917–18."

56. TNR, 5/18/1918, at 71.

57. FF to HC, 5/9/1918, at 1–2, FFLC, Box 50, Folder "Croly, Herbert 1918."

58. Hammer v. Dagenhart, Brief for Appellees, 18 *Landmark Briefs and Legal Arguments of the Supreme Court of the United States: Constitutional Law* 921 (Philip B. Kurland and Gerhard Casper, eds., 1975).

59. "The Sequel to the Dagenhart Case," The American Child, 1/1924, at 3. *See* Logan E. Sawyer III, "Creating *Hammer v. Dagenhart*," 21 Wm. & Mary Bill Rights. J. Rights 67 (2012).

60. Hammer v. Dagenhart, 247 U.S. 251, 273–74 (1918).

61. *Id.* at 271–72.

62. OWH to HL, 5/25/1918, 1 HLL at 157.

63. Hammer, 247 U.S. at 277–79 (Holmes J., dissenting).

64. *Id.* at 281 (Holmes, J., dissenting).

65. HL to OWH, 5/12/1918, 1 HLL, at 155; FF to OWH, H-FF Corr., 5/18/1918, at 72.

66. TNR, 6/15/1918, at 195.

67. Meeting Minutes, War Labor Policies Board, 7/12/1918, at 2 & Memorandum of Contract Clause Committee, at 4, FFLC, Box 191, Folder "War Labor Policies Board Minutes 1918 #29."

68. FF to HL, 7/25/1918, at 1, FFLC, Box 74, Folder "Laski, Harold 1915–19."

69. Max Freedman, *Roosevelt and Frankfurter* 10 (1967).

70. *See* chapter 4 nn. 39–41.

71. *See* War Labor Policies Board Minutes, FFLC, Box 191.

72. Herbert Ehrmann in *Felix Frankfurter: A Tribute* 101 (Wallace Mendelson, ed., 1964).

73. Freedman, *Roosevelt and Frankfurter*, 12.

74. Eleanor Roosevelt to Sara Delano Roosevelt, 10/1918, at 3, FDRL, Roosevelt Family Papers Donated by the Children, Eleanor Roosevelt 1903–1945 and Undated, Folder "Eleanor Roosevelt to Sara Delano Roosevelt, October–December & Undated 1918." This letter is often incorrectly cited as 5/12/1918. *See From the Diaries of Felix Frankfurter* 93 n. 56 (Joseph P. Lash, ed., 1975); Joseph P. Lash, *Eleanor and Franklin* 214 & 731 n. 13 (1981); Blanche Wiesen Cook, *Eleanor Roosevelt*, vol. 2, *The Defining Years, 1933–1938*, at 317 (1992).

75. Joseph E. Persico, *Franklin & Lucy* 215 (2008) ("There was never a complete break between Franklin and Lucy. … the signal might become faint at times, but never ceased entirely."). On Eleanor's discovery of the letters, *see id.* at 11; Lash, *Eleanor and Franklin*, at 225–27.

76. Barnard, *The Forging of an American Jew*, 210–11. Columbia law dean Harlan Fiske Stone and the judge advocate general also served on the board. *See* Jeremy K. Kessler, "The Administrative Origins of Modern Civil Liberties Law," 114 Columbia L. Rev. 1083, 1111–43 (2014).

77. FF to General Crowder, 9/30/1918, NARA, WLPB Records, RG 1, Corr. of Chairman and Exec. Sec., May 1918–Feb. 1919, Entry 2, Box 30, Folder "War Department Mar.–May 1918."

78. OWH to HL, 3/15/1918, 1 HLL at 142.

79. OWH to HL, 5/8/1918, *id.* at 153.

80. FFR 110–11; Édouard Jean Réquin, *America's Race to Victory* 132–38 (1919).

81. Clara E. Laughlin, *Foch the Man* 15–16, 74–75 (1918).

82. TNR, 6/8/1918, at 176–77.

83. OWH to FF, 6/15/1918, H–FF Corr., at 72.

84. FF to MD, 8/15/1918, at 2, FFLC, Box 5, Folder Marion A. Denman 1918 #10." Hale lived near the House at 1833 S Street. 1917 DC City Directory at 550.

85. FF to BB, 8/22/1918, NARA, WLPB Records, RG 1, Corr. of the Chairman and the Exec. Sec., May 1918–Feb. 1919, Entry 2, Box 3, "B-Bills," Folder "Baruch, Bernard."

86. FF to EP, 6/3/1918, at 2, FFLC, Box 89, Folder "Percy, Eustace 1917–1918."

87. "Report of President's Mediation Commission to the President of the United States," 1/9/1918, at 21, FFLC, Box 191, Folder "War Labor Policies Board Miscellaneous #35."

88. "Report to War Labor Policies Board: Eight-Hour Law," 6/22/1918, at 1, FFLC, Box 190, Folder "Committee on Eight-Hour Statutes."

89. *Id.* at 3.

90. *Id.* at 3–5.

91. Meeting Minutes, War Labor Policies Board, 6/28/1918, at 1 (agreeing to recommendations to extend "the eight-hour principle where feasible and advisable") (attaching "Report of Committee on Eight-Hour Laws"), FFLC, Box 191, Folder "War Labor Policies Board Minutes 1918 #28."

92. Executive Minutes, 5/11/1918, at 30, NARA, National War Labor Board Records, RG 2, Box 1.

93. *Id.* at 31–45.

94. *Id.* at 45.

95. WHT to WBW, 10/15/1918, at 1, FFLC, Box 190, Folder "War Labor Policies Board: Eight Hour Day–Olander & War Labor Board Correspondence"; Walsh to FF, 9/16/1918, *id.*; FF to WHT, 10/16/1918, FFLC, Box 191, Folder "War Labor Policies Board Miscellaneous #35."

96. FF to MD, 10/15/1918, at 5, FFLC, Box 5, Folder "Marion A. Denman 1918 #12."

97. FF to MD, 9/8/1918, FFLC, Box 5, Folder "Marion A. Denman 1918 #11"; "Memorandum of Action of War Labor Policies Board with Respect to the Eight Hour Day," NARA, National War Labor Board Records, RG 2, Box 50, Folder "War Policies"; FF to Olander, 9/9/1918, at 1, FFLC, Box 190, Folder "War Labor Policies Board: Eight Hour Day–Olander & War Labor Board Correspondence."

98. Walsh to FF, 9/2/1918, FFLC, Box 190, Folder "War Labor Policies Board: Eight Hour Day–Olander & War Labor Board Correspondence."

99. FF to H. F. Perkins, 7/1/1918, NARA, WLPB Records, RG 1, Corr. of Chairman and Exec. Sec., May 1918–Feb. 1919, Entry 2, Box 12, Folder "Eight Hour Day"; FF to Gary, 7/9/1918, FFLC, Box 190, Folder "War Labor Policies Board Gary Correspondence."

100. Gary to FF, 7/19/1918, NARA, Records, Corr. Chairman and Exec. Sec., May 1918–Feb. 1919, Entry 2, RG 1, Box 12, Folder "Eight Hour Day."

101. FF to Gary, 7/19/1918, at 2, FFLC, Box 190, Folder "War Labor Policies Board Gary Correspondence."

102. FF to Gary, 7/25/1918, *id.*

103. FF to Gary, 9/17/1918 tel., *id.*

104. FF to Gary, 9/19/1918, *id.*; FFR, 140.

105. FFR, 140–41.

106. Gary Meeting Minutes, 9/20/1918, at 2, FFLC, Box 190, Folder "War Labor Policies Board Gary Correspondence."

107. *Id.* at 2–5, 6.

108. NYTrib, 9/25/1918, at 10.

109. Gary Meeting Minutes, 9/20/1918, at 7.

110. FFR, 141. *See* Melvin I. Urofsky, *Big Steel and the Wilson Administration* 269–78 (1969).

111. FF to BB, 9/25/1918 & FF to WBW, 9/25/1918 tel., NARA, WLPB Records, RG 1, Corr. of Chairman and Exec. Sec., May 1918–Feb. 1919, Entry 2, Box 12, Folder "Eight Hour Day"; FF to Gary, 9/20/1918, FFLC, Box 190, Folder "War Labor Policies Board: Gary Correspondence."

112. NYTrib, 9/25/1918, at 10.

113. FF to WBW, 9/25/18 tel., at 1 (handwritten note to MD), FFLC, Box 5, Folder "Marion A. Denman 1918 #11." *See* FF to BB, 9/25/1918.

114. *Cf.* Urofsky, *Big Steel and the Wilson Administration*, 278 (describing Frankfurter as "rather naïve" for thinking that U.S. Steel would move to an actual eight-hour day during a wartime labor shortage).

115. FF, "The Conservation of New Federal Standards," The Survey, 12/7/1918, at 291, FFLC, Box 194, Folder "1918."

116. WTD to SFV, 8/1/18, at 1–2, RGVP, Carton 15, Folder 63.

117. FF to Manley Hudson, 6/19/1918, NARA, WLPB Records, RG 1, Corr. of the Chairman and Exec. Sec., May 1918–Feb. 1919, Entry 2, Box 24, Folder "Reconstruction Jan.–Sept. 1918."

118. Report re: "Regulations Governing Night Work for Women," 9/16/1918, FFLC, Box 190, Folder "War Labor Policies Board: Eight Hour Day–Olander & War Labor Board Correspondence."

119. Meeting Minutes, War Labor Policies Board, 11/15/1918, FFLC, Box 191, Folder "War Labor Policies Board Minutes #34."

120. FF, "The Conservation of New Federal Standards," at 292.

CHAPTER 13

1. WL to FF, 11/5/1918, FFLC, Box 77, Folder "Lippmann, Walter 1914–19."

2. Sidney Mezes, David Miller, and Walter Lippmann, "The Present Situation: The War Aims and Peace Terms It Suggests," before 12/22/1927, 45 WWP at 459–74.

3. Bowman Diary, "Peace Conference," 10/5/1939, at 4, Bowman Papers, Series 13, Box 2 & in Steel, *Walter Lippmann and the American Century*, 134.

4. Blankenhorn COH at 99. *See* Steel, *Walter Lippmann and the American Century*, 141–54.

5. House Diaries, 10/17/1917, Series II, Vol. 5, at 314.

6. WL to EMH, 10/17/1917, at 1–2, WLP, Reel 14, Box 14, Folder 564.

7. House Diaries, 10/17/1917.

8. Blankenhorn COH at 99.

9. WL to EMH, 6/16/1918, WLP, Reel 14, Box 14, Folder 564 & PPWL at 92–93.

10. House Diaries, 7/5/1918, Series II, Vol. 6, at 174.

11. WL to Isaiah Bowman, 7/24/1918, PPWL at 93; Steel, *Walter Lippmann and the American Century*, 139–40; Bowman Diary, 10/5/1939.

12. WL Passport Application 7/5/1918, at 1; WL to FL, 7/15/1918, WLP, Reel 165, Box 2, Folder 55.

13. Blankenhorn COH at 100, 105.

14. *Id.* at 110.

15. Blankenhorn COH at 105–6.

16. WL to EMH, 8/15/1918, WWP, Series II, Reel 98.

17. WL to EMH, 8/9/1918, at 2, *id.* & PPWL at 94.

18. Id. at 1–2; WL to EMH, 8/15/1918, at 1–2.

19. WL to EMH, 8/15/1918, at 1.

20. Heber Blankenhorn, *Adventures in Propaganda* 34 (1919).

21. *A Journalist's Diplomatic Mission: Ray Stannard Baker's World War I Diary* 82 (John Maxwell Hamilton and Robert Mann, eds., 2012).

22. *Id.* at 138. *See id.* at 129, 131–32.

23. WW to EMH, 8/31/1918, 49 WWP at 402.

24. *Id.*

25. WW to Lansing, 9/3/1918, *id.* at 423.

26. EMH to WW, 9/3/1918, *id.* at 429. *See* Lansing to WW, 9/4/1918, *id.* at 433–34.

27. WW to Lansing, 9/5/1918, *id.* at 447.

28. Benedict Crowell to WW, 9/8/1918, *id.* at 487–88.

29. WL to Mezes, 9/5/1918, PPWL at 95.

30. WL to EMH, 10/26/1918, *id.* at 96.

31. NYT, 11/1/1918, at 4. *See* CT, 11/6/1918, at 17; NYSun, 11/1/1918, at 3.

32. EMH to WW, 10/29/1918 tel., 51 WWP at 495.

33. House Diaries, 10/29/1918, at 12, Series II, Vol. 6a, at 12.

34. WL to EMH, 11/7/1918, WLP, Reel 14, Box 14, Folder 564 & PPWL at 107–8.

35. WL to NDB, 11/12/1918, PPWL at 108.

36. WL to EMH, circa 11/1918, *id.* at 105.

37. *Id.* at 106–7.

38. NYTrib, 11/27/1918, at 3.

39. WL to FL, 11/15/1918 & 11/17/1918, WLP, Reel 165, Box 2, Folder 58.

40. WL to FL, 11/20/1918, at 1, *id.*

41. WL to FL, 11/9/1918, at 2, *id.*; WL to FL, 11/14/1918, at 1–2, *id.*

42. WL to FL, 11/20/1918, at 2, *id.*

43. House Diaries, 11/30/1918, Series II, Vol. 6a, at 46.

44. WL to FL, 11/26/1918, at 1, WLP, Reel 165, Box 2, Folder 58.

45. WL to FL, 11/28/1918, *id.*

46. TNR, 12/7/1918, at 163.

47. WL to FL, 12/1/1918, WLP, Reel 165, Box 2, Folder 59; WL to DS, 12/1/1918, PPWL at 108–9.

48. WL to DS, 12/1/1918.

49. Charles Seymour to his family, 12/10/1918, 53 WWP at 357. Seymour edited a history of the Paris Peace Conference with Colonel House as well as House's papers. The conservative president of Yale from 1937 to 1950, Seymour perpetuated quotas against Jews and was described by his successor as "'descended from a long line of bronze statues.'" Geoffrey Kabaservice, *The Guardians* 154 (2004). *See id.* at 48–49 (on Jewish quotas).

50. WL to FL, 12/15/1918, at 1, WLP, Reel 165, Box 2, Folder 59.

51. WL to FL, 12/28/1918, at 1, *id.*

52. WL to FL, 12/15/1918, at 2–3, *id.*

53. WL to FL, 12/21/1918, at 2, *id.*

54. Ernest Sutherland Bates, "Walter Lippmann: The Career of 'Comrade Fool,'" *Modern Monthly*, June 1933, at 270. This rumor was perpetuated by Lippmann's nemesis on the Inquiry, Isaiah Bowman. See Bowman, "Peace Conference," 10/5/1939, at 3–4 (contending twenty years later that Lippmann was sent home not by Colonel House but by "the President himself").

55. Steel, *Walter Lippmann and the American Century*, 611.

56. RH to NDB, ca. 12/18/1918, at 5–7, NDBP, Box 6, Folder "H 1918."

57. RH to NDB, 12/22/1918, at 2, *id*.

58. RH to NDB, 12/26/1918, at 1, *id*.

59. WL to FL, 12/28/1918, at 1–2.

60. TNR, 1/11/1919, at 291.

61. On Quentin Roosevelt, *see* Eric Burns, *The Golden Lad* (2016).

62. FF to WL, 1/13/1919, at 1, WLP, Reel 9, Box 10, Folder 420a.

63. *Id.* at 2.

64. FF to WL, circa 2/1919 #26, at 1–2, *id*.

65. HL to WL, 1/29/1919, WLP, Reel 16, Box 17, Folder 688.

66. HL to OWH, 2/23/1919, 1 HLL at 186. *See* HL to OWH, 2/8/1919, *id*. at 184.

67. WL to FL, 11/24/1918, at 3, WLP, Reel 165, Box 2, Folder 58.

CHAPTER 14

1. FF to MD, 1/11/1919, at 1–2, FFLC, Box 6, "Folder Marion A. Denman Jan. 1919 #15."

2. *Id.* at 1–3.

3. FF to WBW, 2/8/1919, FFLC, Box 191, Folder "War Labor Policies Board Miscellany #36."

4. FF to HL, 1/24/1919, FFLC, Box 74, Folder "Laski, Harold 1915–19."

5. FF to RP, 2/22/1919, at 2, FFLC, Box 6, Folder "Marion A. Denman Feb. 1919 #19."

6. Balfour to Baron de Rothschild, 11/2/1917, 7 CWP at iv.

7. CW to LDB, 3/5/1918, 8 CWP at 96.

8. CW to LDB, 11/26/1918, 9 CWP at 38; CW to LDB, 12/3/1918, *id*. at 52; CW to AA, 12/23/1918, *id*. at 80.

9. *See* Jewish Advocate, 12/9/1910, at 1.

10. Jacob de Haas, *Louis D. Brandeis: A Biographical Sketch* 52 (1929).

11. *Id.* at 51–53. *See id.* at 151–54; Jewish Advocate, 12/9/1910, at 1, 8.

12. Louis Lipsky, *A Gallery of Zionist Profiles* 172 (1956).

13. LDB to JWM, 3/19/1915, 3 LLDB at 487; Barnard, *The Forging of an American Jew*, 172–98.

14. Brandeis, "The Rebirth of the Jewish Nation," in de Haas, *Louis D. Brandeis*, 163; Jewish Advocate, 10/2/1914, at 6; LDB to Jacob de Haas, 11/14/1914, 3 LLDB at 355 n. 1.

15. LDB to Louis Kirstein, 9/10/1915, 3 LLDB at 587.

16. New State Ice Co. v. Liebmann, 285 U.S. 262, 311 (1932) (Brandeis, J., dissenting).

17. FF to MD, 2/9/1919, at 1, Box 6, Folder "Marion A. Denman Feb. 1919 #17."

18. *Id.* at 1–2.

19. *Id.* at 3.

20. MD to FF, circa 2/15/1919, at 1, *id.*

21. FF to MD, 2/11/1919, *id.*

22. FF to MD, 2/26/1919, at 1, 3, FFLC, Box 6, Folder "Marion A. Denman Feb. 1919 #19."

23. FF to RP, 2/22/1919, at 1–2.

24. FF to MD, 2/26/1919, at 1–2.

25. FF to MD, 2/28/1919, at 2–3, *id.*

26. *Id.* at 3. On Weitzmann, *see* Isaiah Berlin, "Chaim Weitzmann," FFLC, Box 162, Folder "Palestine–Chaim Weizmann, 1948–64" & Isaiah Berlin, *Chaim Weizmann* (1959).

27. FF to MD, 2/28/1919, at 3.

28. *Id.*

29. Aaron Aaronsohn, "Agricultural and Botanical Explorations in Palestine," 8/4/1910, Bulletin No. 180, Bureau of Plant Industry, US Dept. of Agriculture (Washington, DC: GPO, 1910).

30. Louis Marshall to Adolph Lewisohn, 11/20/1909, 2 *Louis Marshall: Champion of Liberty* at 705 (1957); Marshall to Jacob Schiff, 3/22/1910, *id.* at 706.

31. LDB to Alfred Brandeis, 1/7/1912, 2 LLDB at 537.

32. *Jewish Advocate*, 5/23/1913, at 1.

33. LDB to NH, 6/16/1913, 3 LLDB at 117.

34. Aaron Aaronsohn Journal, 3/15/1913, at 1–2, WCBP, Box 174.

35. *Id.* at 3.

36. LDB to Julius Rosenwald, 2/4/1915 tel., 3 LLDB at 421 & n. 2.

37. LDB to WW, 3/5/1915, *id.* at 465.

38. LDB to Arthur Ruppin, 3/8/1915, *id.* at 473.

39. Alexander Aaronsohn, *With the Turks in Palestine* (1916); Alexander Aaronsohn, "Our Swords Are Red, O Sultan," Pt. 1, Atlantic Monthly (7/1916): 1–12 & Pt. 2 (8/1916): 188–96.

40. Aaronsohn, *With the Turks in Palestine*, 1–3.

41. *Id.* at 7–17, 23–26.

42. *Id.* at 26–27.

43. *Id.* at 29–31.

44. *Id.* at 31–34.

45. *Id.* at 37–44.

46. *Id.* at 70–85.

47. LDB to JWM, 10/19/1915, 3 LLDB at 613.

48. OWH to FF, 10/11/1915, H-FF Corr., at 34.

49. Aaronsohn, *With the Turks in Palestine*, 49–52; AA to JWM (AA's Confession), 10/9/1916, at 1–2, NILI Archives, 21_1_56.

50. AA to JWM (AA's Confession), 10/9/1916, at 5.

51. *Id.* at 1–4.
52. *Id.* at 9–10.
53. *Id.* at 12.
54. *Id.* at 8–9, 12.
55. Addenda, 10/9/1916, at 1, *id.*
56. *Id.*
57. *Id.* at 1–2.
58. Alex Aaronsohn, "The 'NILI' or 'A' Organization," in *Agents of Empire* 309 (Anthony Verrier, ed., 1995).
59. *See* AA Diary, *Agents of Empire*, 224–93; *id.* at 325–26 nn. 23 & 26.
60. AA to JWM (AA's Confession), 10/9/1916, at 9.
61. AA Diary, 11/16/1917, *Agents of Empire*, 294; CW to AA, 11/16/1917, 8 CWP at 6.
62. AA Diary, 12/1/1917, *Agents of Empire*, 295.
63. Aaronsohn, "The 'NILI' or 'A' Organization," at 312–13 (carrier pigeon); Shmuel Katz, *The Aaronsohn Saga* 241–62 (2007) (villagers); Patricia Goldstone, *Aaronsohn's Maps* 201–13 (2003) (British government).
64. Aaronsohn, "The 'NILI' or 'A' Organization," at 313.
65. AA Diary, 12/1/1917, NILI Archives, 46_3_10 Sept till Dec. 1917 I (translated from French). *Cf. Agents of Empire*, at 295.
66. FF to MD, 1/4/1918 (or 1/11/1918), at 3–4, FFLC, Box 5, Folder "Marion A. Denman #7."
67. AA to Oubi, 2/4/1918, at 2, WCBP, Box 173.
68. Percy, *Some Memories*, 59.
69. EP to AA, 12/19/1917, NILI Archives, 23_9_4.
70. WL to JWM, 12/1/1917, WLP, Reel 18, Box 19, Folder 765.
71. Aaron to Alex, 8/18/1918, at 3, WCBP, Box 173.
72. AA Diary, 11/29/1918, *Agents of Empire*, 300.
73. AA Diary, 7/25/1917, *id.* at 285.
74. AA Diary, 3/18/1918, NILI Archives, 48_3_3 March 1918 A (translated from French).
75. CW to LDB, 3/5/1918, 8 CWP at 96.
76. SSW to LDB, 1/11/1918, at 1–2, LDB-Louisville, Reel 82; LDB to CW, 1/13/1918, *id.*
77. AA to LDB, 2/24/1918, NILI Archives, 34_1_60.
78. AA to FF, 4/19/1918, NILI Archives, 34_1_62.
79. AA to Alex, 11/26/1918, at 1–2, WCBP, Box 173.
80. *Id.* at 2.
81. AA to Alex, 12/6/1918, WCBP, Box 173.
82. FF to MD, 3/10/1919, at 1, FFLC, Box 6, Folder "Marion A. Denman Mar. 1919 #21." *See* FF to LDB, 3/3/1919, at 9, *id.*, Folder "Marion A. Denman Mar. 1919 #20."
83. Ella Winter, *And Not to Yield* 50 (1963). Through Frankfurter, Winter met her future husband in Paris, journalist Lincoln Steffens. *Id.* at 52–54, 57–66.

84. CW to Balfour, 7/17/1918, 8 CWP at 228–30; CW to AA, 10/4/1918, *id.* at 276; CW to AA, 12/12/1918, 9 CWP at 62–63.

85. 9 CWP at 86–87.

86. FF to LDB, 3/3/1919, at 2–3.

87. FF, Memorandum, n.d., at 1, FFLC, Box 162, Folder "Prince Feisal Correspondence 1919–65." On Lawrence's connection to Frankfurter and Aaron Aaronsohn, *see* Ronald Florence, *Lawrence and Aaronsohn* (2007); Goldstone, *Aaronsohn's Maps*; Katz, *The Aaronsohn Saga.*

88. FF to LDB, 3/3/1919, at 3 (handwritten to Marion).

89. *Id.*

90. FF, Memorandum, n.d., at 2.

91. NYT, 3/5/1919, at 7.

92. Prince Feisal to FF, 3/1/1919, at 1, FFLC, Box 162, Folder "Palestine–Prince Feisal Correspondence 1919–65."

93. FF to T. E. Lawrence, 3/23/1919, *id.*, Folder "Palestine–Correspondence Zionist Commission Mar.–May 1919."

94. FF to Feisal, 3/23/1919, *id.*, Folder "Palestine–Prince Feisal Correspondence 1919–65."

95. FF to MD, 3/27/1919, at 1–2, FFLC, Box 6, Folder "Marion A. Denman 1919 3/19–4/19 #23."

96. AA Diary, 2/18/1919, *Agents of Empire*, 302; FF to LDB, 3/3/1919, at 9.

97. FF to LDB, 3/23/1919, at 3, FFLC, Box 162, Folder "Palestine–Correspondence Zionist Commission Mar.–May 1919."

98. Gen. Edmund Allenby to Alex Aaronsohn, 5/27/1919, NILI Archives, 1_2_12; Gen. A. W. Money to Eder, 7/11/1919, *id.*, 10_1.b._41; Capt. W. Ormsby-Gore, *Zionist Review*, 7/1919, at 35, *id.*, 10_1.a._5.

99. FF to LDB, 3/23/1919, at 3.

100. FF to LDB, 3/3/1919, at 9 (emphasis in original).

101. EDB to WCB, circa 1917, at 1–2, WCBP, Box 12, Folder 248.

102. CW to AA, 1/19/1919, 9 CWP at 96.

103. AA Diary, 1/16/1919, *Agents of Empire*, 301–2.

104. *Id.*; AA Diary, 2/18/1919, *id.* at 302.

105. FF to LDB, 3/3/1919, at 9 (handwritten in margin).

106. *Id. See* WCB to WL, 4/1/1919, WLP, Reel 5, Folder 206; FF to MD, 4/17/1919, at 4, FFLC, Box 7, Folder "Marion A. Denman Apr. 1919 #24."

107. FF to LDB, 3/3/1919, at 9–10.

108. FF to MD, 3/18/1919, at 4, FFLC, Box 6, Folder "Marion A. Denman Mar. 1919 #22."

109. House Diaries, 12/31/1918, Series II, Vol. 6a, at 85. Balfour later tried to claim to Brandeis that Lenin was a Jew. Frankfurter, Memorandum re: Brandeis Interview with Balfour, 6/24/1919, *Documents on British Foreign Policy 1919–1939*, First Series, Vol. IV, 1919, at 1276 (1952).

110. FF to MD, 3/18/1919, at 3.

111. *Id.* at 5.

112. NYT, 3/5/1919, at 7.

113. Alex Aaronsohn to AA and FF, 5/8/1919, NILI Archives, 29_4_24.

114. FF to LDB, 3/28/1919 tel., FFLC, Box 162, Folder "Palestine–Correspondence Zionist Commission Mar.–May 1919"; FF to EMH, 4/14/1919, FFLC, Box 162, Folder "Palestine: FF-WWilson Correspondence 1919."

115. David P. Billington, *Lothian* 24–25 (2006). *See* WL COH at 98 (mistakenly remembering Kerr as House resident).

116. FF to MD, 4/11/1919, FFLC, Box 7, Folder "Marion A. Denman Apr. 1919 #24" ("acetic intellectual …"); FF to MD, 4/13/1919, at 2, *id.* ("because in a way I belong …"). On Kerr, *see* FF to MD, 3/20/1919, at 1–2, FFLC, Box 6, Folder "Marion A. Denman 3/19–4/19 #23."

117. FF to MD, 4/13/1919, at 1–2. *See* Winter, *And Not to Yield*, 51.

118. Percy, *Some Memories*, 60, 73–74.

119. FF to MD, 5/22/1919, at 1–2, FFLC, Box 7, Folder "Marion A. Denman May 1919 #31"; FF to MD, 4/25/1919, *id.*, Folder "Marion A. Denman April 1919 #26."

120. FF to WW, 5/8/1919, at 1, FFLC, Box 162, Folder "Palestine–FF-WWilson Correspondence 1919" & WWP, Series 5B, Reel 405.

121. WW to FF, 5/13/1919, *id.*

122. FF to WW, 5/14/1919, at 1–2, *id.*

123. WW to FF, 5/14/1919, *id.*

124. Henry Alsberg to FF, 5/12/1919, at 1–3, FFLC, Box 162, Folder "Palestine–Correspondence Zionist Commission Mar.–May 1919."

125. *Id.* at 3–4.

126. FF to EMH, 5/18/1919, *id.*

127. FF to MD, 5/29/1919, FFLC, Box 7, Folder "Marion A. Denman May 1919 #32."

128. FF to MD, 4/17/1919, at 4, *id.*, Folder "Marion A. Denman Apr. 1919 #24."

129. FF to MD, 5/24/1919, at 1, 5, *id.*, Folder "Marion A. Denman May 1919 #31."

130. FF to LDB, 3/3/1919, at 9; FF to LDB, 3/23/1919, at 3.

131. FF to MD, 5/17/1919, at 4, FFLC, Box 7, "Folder Marion A. Denman May 1919 #30."

132. Alex Aaronsohn to AA and FF, 5/8/1919.

133. FF to Walter Gribbon, 5/13/1937, at 2, FFLC, Box 57, Folder "Gri."

134. FF to MD, 4/4/1919, at 1, FFLC, Box 6, Folder "Marion A. Denman 3/19–4/19 #23."

135. CW to Julius Simon, Victor Jacobson, and Shmarya Levin, 5/17/1919, 9 CWP at 142.

136. Goldstone, *Aaronsohn's Maps*, 252–56, 259; Katz, *The Aaronsohn Saga*, 340–41.

137. ToL, 5/23/1919, at 14.

138. Goldstone, *Aaronsohn's Maps*, 256; Katz, *The Aaronsohn Saga*, 340.

139. Goldstone, *Aaronsohn's Maps*, 251–59; Katz, *The Aaronsohn Saga*, 340–41; H. V. F. Winstone, *The Illicit Adventure* 355 (1962).

140. FF to David Fairchild, 5/16/1919, FFLC, Box 162, Folder "Palestine–Correspondence Zionist Commission Mar–May 1919 #1."

141. FF to MD, 5/27/1919, at 2; FF to MD, n.d., FFLC Box 7, Folder "Marion A. Denman May 1919 #32"; FF to MD, 5/26/1919, at 5, *id.* & FF to MD, 5/21/1919, *id.*, Folder "#31"; LDB to FF, 5/20/1919, FFLC, Box 162, Folder "Palestine–Correspondence Zionist Commission Mar–May 1919 #1"; FF to Friedenwald, 5/21/1919, *id.*

142. FF and CW to EF, 5/19/1919 tel., FFLC, Box 162, Folder "Palestine–Correspondence Zionist Commission Mar–May 1919 #1"; FF to Friedenwald, 5/19/1919 tel., *id.*

143. FF to MD, 5/17/1919, at 1.

144. MD to FF, 5/19/1919, at 1, FFLC, Box 7, Folder "Marion A. Denman May 1919 #30."

145. FF to MD, 6/10/1919, at 1, 3, *id.*, Box 8, Folder "Marion A. Denman June 1919 #34." The writer was Bill Ryall. *Id.*; Manchester Guardian, 5/20/1919, at 6.

146. Barnard, *The Forging of an American Jew*, 110. *See id.* at 107–10.

147. LDB to FF, 5/20/1919 tel., FFLC, Box 162, Folder "Palestine–Correspondence Zionist Commission Mar–May 1919 #1."

148. FF to MD, 6/10/1919, at 2.

149. WCB to Alex, 4/9/1920, NILI Archives, 9_5_5.

150. *Id.* Three boxes of Aaronsohn's diaries and letters ended up in Bullitt's personal papers. WCBP, Boxes 173–75.

151. FF to MD, 4/17/1919, at 4.

152. Steffens to Peter, 1/3/1920, 1 *The Letters of Lincoln Steffens* 522 (Ella Winter and Granville Hicks, eds., 1938); Steffens, *The Autobiography of Lincoln Steffens*, 790–802.

153. FF to MD, 5/26/1919, at 4.

154. *Id.* at 3–4.

155. WCB to WL, 4/1/1919, WLP, Reel 5, Box 5, Folder 206.

156. The Bookman, 5/1919, Vol. 49, at 6.

157. HC to WL, 2/27/1919, at 2, WLP, Reel 7, Box 7, Folder 303; HC to WL, 3/6/1919, at 1–2, *id.*

158. HC to WL, 3/6/1919, at 1.

159. Walter Lippmann, *The Political Scene* xii–xiii (1919).

160. *Id.* at 70, 70–73, 77–79, 81.

161. HL to WL, 3/24/1919, at 1, WLP, Reel 16, Box 17, Folder 688.

162. HL to OWH, 3/28/1919, 1 HLL at 193.

163. HL to OWH, 3/18/1919, *id.* at 192; OWH to HL, 4/20/1919, *id.* at 198.

164. LH to WL, 3/29/1919, at 1–3, WLP, Reel 12, Box 12, Folder 490.

165. FF to MD, 5/7/1919, at 3, FFLC, Box 7, Folder "Marion A. Denman May 1919 #28."

166. FF to WL, 7/11/1919, at 1, WLP, Reel 9, Box 10, Folder 420a.

167. *Id.* at 1–3.

168. WL to FF, 7/28/1919, at 1–2, *id.*

169. Walter Lippmann, "The Peace Conference," *Yale Review* (July 1919): 719–21.

170. LDB to FF, 5/16/1919, HBHS, at 28–29 & FFLC, Box 26, Folder "Brandeis, Louis D. 1919"; FF to LDB, 5/21/1919 tel., FFLC, Box 162, Folder "Palestine–Correspondence Zionist Commission Mar–May 1919 #1"; FF to LDB, 5/27/1919 tel., id.; FF to LDB, 5/30/1919, id.; FF to MD, 5/30/1919, at 1, FFLC, Box 7, Folder "Marion A. Denman May 1919 #32."

171. FF to LDB, 5/21/1919 tel. See LDB to FF, 6/5/1919, HBHS, at 31; FF to MD, 6/6/1919, at 1, FFLC, Box 8, Folder "Marion A. Denman June 1919 #33."

172. FF to MD, 6/6/1919, at 1–2 (emphasis in original).

173. Id. at 2–3. See HBHS, at 32 n. 1.

174. WP, 6/10/1919, at 4; NYT, 6/15/1919, at 12. LDB to FF, 6/9/1919, HBHS, at 31–32 & 4 LDB at 397 & FFLC, Box 8, Folder "Marion A. Denman June 1919 #34."

175. FF to MD, 6/20/1919, at 3, FFLC, Box 8, Folder "Marion A. Denman June 1919 #36."

176. LDB to AGB, 6/22/1919, 4 LLDB at 404.

177. FF to MD, 6/21/1919, at 3, FFLC, Box 8, Folder "Marion A. Denman June 1919 #37."

178. LDB to AGB, 6/22/1919, 4 LLDB at 403. See FF to MD, 6/21/1919, at 1–2.

179. FF, "Memorandum re: Brandeis Interview with Balfour," 6/24/1919, at 1276–77.

180. Id. at 1277–78.

181. FF to MD, 6/25/1919, at 2, FFLC, Box 8, Folder "Marion A. Denman June 1919 #37."

182. Id. at 1–3.

183. LDB to AGB, 6/24/1919, 4 LLDB at 406. See LDB to AGB, 6/25/1919, id. at 406–7.

184. FF to MD, 6/13/1919, at 3–5, FFLC, Box 8, Folder "Marion A. Denman June 1919 #35."

185. FF to MD, 6/19/1919, at 2, FFLC, Box 8, Folder "Marion A. Denman June 1919 #36"; FF to MD, 6/25/1919, at 5.

186. FF to MD, 6/25/1919, at 5.

187. Id. at 1, 4–5.

188. FF to MD, 6/13/1919, at 1.

189. FF to MD, 6/30/1919, at 2, FFLC, Box 8, Folder "Marion A. Denman June 1919 #38"; FF to Hugh Gibson, 6/28/1919, id.

190. WL to FF, 7/28/1919, at 1; WL to EMH, 7/19/1919, at 1, EMHP, Group #466, Series I, Box 70, Folder 2327.

191. Philip Kerr to Sir Percy Wyndham, 7/16/1919, FFLC, Box 8, Folder "Marion A. Denman July 1919 #41."

192. WL to FF, 7/28/1919, at 1.

193. FF to MD, 7/27/1919, at 3–4, FFLC, Box 8, Folder "Marion A. Denman July 1919 #43"; FF to MD, 7/31/1919, at 4–5, id.; FF to MD, 8/2/1919, at 1–2, id., Box 9, Folder "Marion A. Denman Aug. 1919 #44."

194. FF to WL, 7/30/1919, at 1–2, WLP, Reel 9, Box 10, Folder 420a.

195. LDB to AGB, 7/10/1919, 4 LLDB at 417–18.

196. LDB to AGB, 8/1/1919, *id.* at 419–20.
197. *Id.* at 420.
198. *Id. See* FF to MD, 8/2/1919, at 2–3; Allenby to Churchill, 8/6/1919, *Documents on British Foreign Policy, 1919–39*, First Series, Vol. IV, 1919, at 328.
199. LDB to AGB, 8/20/1919, 4 LLDB at 423.
200. LDB to AGB, 8/8/1919, *id.* at 421.
201. FF to MD, 8/4/1919, at 2, FFLC, Box 9, Folder "Marion A. Denman Aug. 1919 #44."
202. Steffens to Laura & Allen, 8/2/1919, 1 *The Letters of Lincoln Steffens*, at 478.
203. FF to MD, 8/4/1919, at 2.
204. *Id.*
205. FF to MD, 8/10/1919, at 1–2, FFLC, Box 9, Folder "Marion A. Denman Aug. 1919 #44."
206. FF to MD, 8/16/1919, at 1–2, *id.*, Folder "Marion A. Denman Aug. 1919 #45."
207. CW to FF, 8/27/1919, 9 CWP at 205.
208. FF to MD, 8/29/1919, FFLC, Box 9, Folder "Marion A. Denman Aug. 1919 #46"; FF to MD, n.d., *id.* Folder "Marion A. Denman Sept. 1919 #47."
209. FF to MD, 8/14/1919, at 4–5, *id.*, Folder "Marion A. Denman Aug. 1919 #45."

CHAPTER 15

1. SFV to FF, circa 2/4/1919, at 1, FFLC, Box 108, Folder "Valentine, Sophia 1912–31."
2. *Id.* at 1–2, 4–5.
3. *Id.* at 6–7.
4. MD to FF, 2/4/1919, at 1–2, FFLC, Box 6, Folder "Marion A. Denman Feb. 1919 #17."
5. MD to FF, 4/14/1919, at 4, FFLC, Box 7, Folder "Marion A. Denman Apr. 1919 #24."
6. *Id.* at 4–5. For more on Marion's views of Sophie and Charlotte, *see* FFLC, Box 11, Folder "Marion A. (Frankfurter) Denman 1924 #78."
   Marion was a good judge of character. Charlotte received an undergraduate degree from Radcliffe in 1938 and another degree from Harvard Extension School in 1969. She married in October 1936 and had three children. Charlotte Valentine Taylor died on October 12, 1998, at age eighty-eight. *See* BG, 12/27/1998, at C24.
7. FF to MD, 3/10/1919, at 3, FFLC, Box 6, Folder "Marion A. Denman Mar. 1919 #21."
8. MD to FF, 4/14/1919, at 5. King had been the last House of Truth resident, living there in 1919 after Frankfurter left for Paris.
9. *Id.*

10. The law firm was Denison & Curtis. James F. Curtis, Class of 1899, Harvard Alumni Bulletin, Vol. 22 at 45.

11. WTD to SFV, 2/7/1919, at 3, RGVP, Carton 15, Folder 64 (misfiled in 61).

12. *Id.* at 2. In 1925, Sophia Valentine sold the House of Truth along with her real estate on R Street. *See* RGVP, Carton 15, Folder 95.

CHAPTER 16

1. FF to LH, 1/8/1919, at 1, LHP, Box 104A, Folder 104-7.

2. Besides Frankfurter, the list included Loring Christie, Francis Hackett, Learned Hand, Arthur D. Hill, Harold Laski, Julian W. Mack, John G. Palfrey, and Samuel J. Rosensohn. Hand agreed to contribute his $40 share. *Id.*; LH to FF, 1/10/1919, *id. See* "Relief Portrait of Justice Holmes," Newsclipping, n.d., John G. Palfrey Collection of OWHP, Box 64, Folder 4.

3. *See* Thomas Healy, *The Great Dissent* 29–38 (2013); Geoffrey R. Stone, *Perilous Times* 198–203, 208 (2004); Richard Polenberg, *Fighting Faiths* 218–28 (1987); White, *Law and the Inner Self*, 421–30; David M. Rabban, *Free Speech in Its Forgotten Years* 342, 350–55 (1997); G. Edward White, "Justice Holmes and the Modernization of Free Speech Jurisprudence," 80 Cal. L. Rev. 391, 419–33 (1992).

4. White, "Justice Holmes and the Modernization of Free Speech Jurisprudence," at 462.

5. For the few exceptions, *see* Healy, *The Great Dissent*, 128–31; Rabban, *Free Speech in Its Forgotten Years*, 352.

6. FF to NDB, 9/18/1917, "Treatment of Conscientious Objectors," FFLC, Box 132, Folder "Conscientious Objectors 1917–32 & Undated." *Cf.* Kessler, "The Administrative Origins of Modern Civil Liberties Law," 1111–32 (offering a statist view of protecting conscientious objectors) *with* Laura M. Weinrib, *The Taming of Free Speech: America's Civil Liberties Compromise* (2016) & Laura M. Weinrib, "Freedom of Conscience in War Time: World War I and the Civil Liberties Path Not Taken," 65 Emory L. Rev. 1051 (2016) (countering with antistatist view).

7. *See* chapter 13 n. 6 (citing WL to EMH, 10/17/1917).

8. Schenck v. United States, 249 U.S. 47, 49–51 (1919).

9. *Id.* at 52.

10. Frohwerk v. United States, 249 U.S. 204, 205–7 (1919).

11. Debs v. United States, 249 U.S. 211, 212–15 (1919).

12. *Id.* at 212; Frohwerk, 249 U.S. at 206.

13. Patterson v. Colorado, 205 U.S. 454, 464–65 (1907).

14. Fox v. Washington, 236 U.S. 273, 278 (1915).

15. Masses Publishing Co. v. Patten, 244 F. 535, 540 (S.D.N.Y. 1917), rev'd., 246 F. 24 (2d. Cir. 1917).

16. LH to OWH, 6/22/1918, OWHP, Reel 61, Pages 559–61, Box 80, Folder 10. On Hand's influence on Holmes and free speech, *see* Gerald Gunther, *Learned Hand* 161–67 (1994).

17. OWH to LH, 6/24/1918, at 1, OWHP, Reel 61, Page 565, Box 80, Folder 10.

18. Baltzer v. United States, October Term 1918, at 2, OWHP, Reel 70, Page 1130. *Cf.* Novick, *Honorable Justice* 473–74 n. 87 (using the unpublished dissent as evidence that Holmes's views on free speech did not change) *with* White, *Law and the Inner Self* 414 & Rabban, *Free Speech in Its Forgotten Years*, 294 (disagreeing with Novick's thesis).

19. OWH to HL, 3/16/1919, 1 HLL at 190. *See* OWH to Charlotte Moncheur, 4/4/1919 & OWH to Wigmore, 6/7/1919, MDHP, Box 20, Folder 8.

20. OWH to FP, 4/5/1919, 2 H-P Letters at 7.

21. OWH to HL, 3/16/1919, 1 HLL at 190.

22. HL to OWH, 3/18/1919, *id.* at 191.

23. TNR, 4/19/1919, at 362.

24. OWH to HL, 4/20/1919, 1 HLL at 197. On Debs, *see* Ernest Freeberg, *Democracy's Prisoner* (2008); Nick Salvatore, *Eugene V. Debs* (1982).

25. LH to OWH, late 3/1919, at 1–2, OWHP, Box 80, Folder 10, Reel 61, Pages 571–72.

26. OWH to LH, 4/3/1919, OWHP, Box 36, Folder 4, Reel 26, Page 519.

27. TNR, 5/3/1919, at 14.

28. *Id.*

29. OWH to HL, 5/13/1919, 1 HLL at 202 & *id.* at 203–4 (containing unsent letter from OWH to HC, 5/12/1919).

30. OWH to FP, 4/5/1919, 2 H-P Letters at 7; OWH to LE, 4/5/1919, H-E Letters at 184.

31. NYT, 5/1/1919, at 3; AC, 5/1/1919, at 6.

32. OWH to HL, 5/1/1919, 1 HLL, at 199. *See* OWH to LE, 5/22/1919, H-E Letters at 186; OWH to Kaneko, 6/21/1919, at 1–2, OWHP, Box 36, Folder 4, Reel 26, Pages 527–28.

33. Healy, *The Great Dissent*, 28–38; Rabban, *Free Speech in Its Forgotten Years*, 353–54; Polenberg, *Fighting Faiths*, 225–26; Kramnick and Sheerman, *Harold Laski*, 125–27.

34. Zechariah Chafee Jr., "Harold Laski and the Harvard Law Review," 63 Harv. L. Rev. 1398, 1399–400 (1950).

35. RP to FF, 6/3/1918, at 1–2, FFLC, Box 90, Folder "Roscoe Pound 1918." On Laski as a future law school faculty member, *see* chapter 7 n. 140.

36. *Harvard Alumni Bulletin*, Vol. 22, at 67.

37. OWH to HL, 3/7/1919, 1 HLL at 189 & n. 1, OWH to HL, 4/8/1919, *id.* at 194.

38. OWH to HL, 4/8/1919, *id.*

39. See Donald Smith, *Zechariah Chafee Jr.* 30–32 (1986); White, *Law and the Inner Self*, 427–30; Rabban, *Free Speech in Its Forgotten Years*, 353–54; Polenberg, *Fighting Faiths*, 223–24; Stone, *Perilous Times*, 202–3; David S. Bogen, "The Free Speech Metamorphosis of Mr. Justice Holmes," 11 Hofstra L. Rev. 97 (1982); Fred D. Ragan, "Justice Oliver Wendell Holmes Jr., Zechariah Chafee Jr., and the Clear and Present Danger Test for Free Speech: The First Year, 1919," *Journal of American History* 5 (1971): 24–45.

40. In June 1919, the Harvard Corporation initially declined to promote Chafee from assistant professor, though it increased his salary. Pound, however, intervened. *See* F. W. Hunnewell to RP, 6/5/1919, RP to ALL, 6/7/1919 & RP to Hunnewell, 6/7/1919, Lowell Official Papers, Box 113, Folder 834. On Chafee's Rhode Island roots, *see* Smith, *Zechariah Chafee Jr.*, 58–76. On finishing second in the class, *see id.* at 74.

41. On Chafee's free speech scholarship, *see* Smith, *Zechariah Chafee Jr.*, 17–35; Rabban, *Free Speech in Its Forgotten Years*, 316–35; Mark A. Graber, *Transforming Free Speech* 122–64 (1991); Jerold S. Auerbach, "The Patrician as Libertarian: Zechariah Chafee Jr. and Freedom of Speech," *New England Quarterly* 42, no. 4 (1969): 511–31; Charles L. Barzun, "Politics or Principle?," 2007 B.Y.U. L. Rev. 259.

42. Zechariah Chafee Jr., "Freedom of Speech in War Time," 32 Harv. L. Rev. 932, 943–44 (1919).

43. *Id.* at 968 & 969 (quoting Holmes, "Natural Law," 40).

44. HL to ZC, 7/23/1919, Chafee Papers, Box 14, Folder 10, Reel 12, Page 489. On Holmes's summertime visits to Laski in Rockport, *see* OWH to HL, 7/12/1919, HL-Syracuse, Box 1; OWH to HL, 1/18/1927, 2 HLL at 914.

45. ZC to Charles Amidon, 9/30/1919, at 2–3, Chafee Papers, Box 4, Folder 1, Reel 3, Pages 11–12.

46. OWH to FP, 6/21/1920, 2 H-P Letters at 45 ("Chafee is a professor at the Harvard Law School and is said to be a very good man. In the few minutes talk I had with him a year ago he seemed unusually pleasant and intelligent. ...").

47. HL to OWH, 2/8/1919, 1 HLL at 185.

48. John A. Dolan, *Hale and Dorr: Background and Styles* 43–44 (1993); Richard Walden Hale, *Some Table Talk of Mr. Justice Holmes and The Mrs.* 5–7 (1935). Hale was instrumental in arranging the publication of the Holmes-Pollock Letters and assisted Catherine Drinker Bowen with her bestselling book about the Justice. Bowen, *Yankee from Olympus* ix (1944); Hale to Charles Warren, 1/11/1941, at 2–4, CDBP, Box 60.

49. FFR, 175; Henry Aaron Yeomans, *Abbott Lawrence Lowell, 1856–1943*, at 86 (1948).

50. FF to LH, 5/20/1920, at 5–6, LHP, Box 104A, Folder 104-9. *See* FFR, 174.

51. FFR, 175.

52. OWH to HL, 4/4/1919, 1 HLL at 193. *See* OWH to FP, 4/5/1919, 2 H-P Letters at 8.

53. HL to OWH, 4/20/1919, 1 HLL at 196.

54. OWH to HL, 5/1/1919, *id.* at 200.

55. TR to FF, 12/19/1917, at 1, FFLC, Box 98, Folder "Roosevelt, Theodore 1917–18 & undated."

56. Martin Mayer, *Emory Buckner* 36–40 (1968).

57. HL to OWH, 5/11/1919, 1 HLL at 201.

58. RP to JWM, 3/1/1919, RPP, Reel 78, Page 554.

59. FF to MD, 5/15/1919, at 1, FFLC, Box 7, Folder "Marion A. Denman May 1919 #30."

60. FF to TNP, 6/13/1918, TNP to FF, 7/1/1918, TNP to FF, 7/3/1918, RPP, Reel 7, Pages 28–30.

61. TNP to FF, 2/12/1919 & FF to TNP, 4/14/1919, FFLC, Box 89, Folder "Perkins, Thomas Nelson 1918–19."

62. RP to FF, 4/28/1919, at 1, FFHLS, Pt. III, Reel 17, Page 890, Box 187, Folder 3 & FFLC, Box 90, Folder "Pound, Roscoe 1919–23 #3."

63. FF to MD, 5/15/1919, at 3–4.

64. RP to FF, 5/17/1919, at 1–2, FFHLS, Pt. III, Box 187, Folder 3, Reel 17, Page 892 & FFLC, Box 90, Folder "Pound, Roscoe 1919–23 #3."

65. RP to LDB, 5/24/1919, at 1–2, LDB-Louisville, Reel 48.

66. FF to RP, 6/3/1919, at 1, RPP, Reel 7, Page 46.

67. FF to LDB, 6/6/1919 tel., LDB-Louisville, Reel 48.

68. FF to MD, 6/21/1919, at 4–5, FFLC, Box 8, Folder "Marion A. Denman June 1919 #37." On meeting at City Club, see LDB to RP, 6/10/1911, RPP, Reel 3, Page 83.

69. FF to MD, 6/21/1919, at 6–7.

70. Id. at 6.

71. Id. at 7.

72. FF to MD, 6/24/1919, at 7, FFLC, Box 8, Folder "Marion A. Denman June 1919 #37."

73. Id. at 6–7.

74. LDB to AGB, 6/14/1919, 4 LLDB at 400.

75. OWH to Charlotte Moncheur, 4/9/1918, at 2, OWHP, Box 36, Folder 3, Reel 26, Page 476; OWH to HL, 4/9/1918, 1 HLL at 148; OWH to HL, 12/3/1918, id. at 176.

76. OWH to HL, 5/18/1919, 1 HLL at 204–5. See OWH to FP, 5/26/1919, 1 H-P Letters, at 13; OWH to LE, 5/22/1919, H-E Letters at 187; OWH to NG, 9/2/1919, at 1, OWHP, Box 32, Folder 11, Reel 23, Page 648.

77. FF to MD, 6/21/1919, at 7. See chapter 17 n. 96.

78. OWH to HL, 5/18/1919.

79. RP to OWH, 5/29/1919, OWHP, Box 48, Folder 20–23, Reel 36, Page 736.

80. OWH to HL, 6/1/1919, 1 HLL at 210–11.

81. OWH to ALL, 6/2/1919, 1 HLL at 211 n. 2. For the original of Holmes's letter, see Lowell Official Papers, Box 102, Folder 250.

82. ALL to OWH, 6/10/1919, Lowell Official Papers, Box 102, Folder 250. Lowell's response was thought to have been lost. See 1 HLL at 211 n. 2; Healy, The Great Dissent, 276.

83. FF to MD, 6/21/1919, at 8, FFLC, Box 8, Folder "Marion A. Denman June 1919 #37."

84. OWH to FP, 6/17/1919, 2 H-P Letters at 15.

85. WashHerald, 6/3/1919, at 1.

86. CT, 6/3/1919, at 1.

87. Id.; NYT, 6/3/1919, at 1; WashHerald, 6/3/1919, at 2.

88. WashHerald, 6/3/1919, at 2.

89. NYT, 6/3/1919, at 1.

90. WP, 6/4/1919, at 1. The bombings had only just begun. On September 16, 1920, a bomb exploded on Wall Street. *See* Beverly Gage, *The Day Wall Street Exploded* (2009).

91. NYTrib, 6/13/1919, at 6.

92. Kenneth D. Ackerman, *Young J. Edgar* 6–7 (2007).

93. Cameron McWhirter, *Red Summer* (2011); Carl Sandburg, *The Chicago Race Riots* 1 (1919).

94. Eric M. Freedman, *Habeas Corpus* 69 & tbl. 2 (2001). On the riots in Elaine, Arkansas, *see* Robert Whitaker, *On the Laps of Gods* (2008); Grif Stockley, *Blood in Their Eyes* (2001); Richard C. Cortner, *A Mob Intent on Death* (1988).

95. Chicago Daily News, 10/18/1919, at 1; Walter F. White, "'Massacring Whites' in Arkansas," The Nation, 12/6/1919, at 715–16. *See* Walter Francis White, *A Man Called White* 49–51 (1948) & CDEF, 4/22/1922, at 2 (recounting White's escape from Arkansas before the townspeople planned to harm him for passing as white).

96. "An Open Letter to the Governor," The Nation, 6/15/1921, at 847–48.

97. "A Poor Way with Dissenters," Outlook, 9/7/1921, at 129–30.

98. BG, 9/10/1919, at 1.

99. *Id.*

100. HCrim, 10/10/1919; HCrim, 10/11/1919.

101. BG, 10/16/1919, at 5. *See* BP, 10/16/1919, at 24; BET, 10/16/1919, at 14.

102. BH, 10/9/1919, at 2.

103. BH, 10/12/1919, at D6. *See* "The Boston Police Strike," *Harvard Alumni Bulletin*, 10/23/1919, Vol. 22, No. 5, at 106.

104. Hall to Lowell, 11/20/1919, at 1–2 & Hall to Paul Tuckerman, 11/13/1919, at 1, Lowell Official Papers, Box 141, Folder 46(a).

105. HCrim, 10/22/1919; HCrim, 10/17/1919; Isaac Kramnick, "The Professor and the Police," *Harvard Alumni Magazine*, Sept.–Oct. 1989, 44.

106. HL to JWM, 10/15/1919, RPP, Reel 36, Page 901.

107. HL to OWH, 10/28/1919, 1 HLL at 218.

108. NYT, 11/9/1919, at 1.

109. *Id.* at 3; BaltSun, 11/9/1919, at 16; NYT, 11/22/1919, at 1; WP, 12/22/1919, at 1.

110. Zechariah Chafee Jr., "A Contemporary State Trial–The United States *versus* Jacob Abrams *et al.*," 33 Harv. L. Rev. 747, 750 (1920).

111. Abrams v. U.S., 250 U.S. 616, 624 (1919).

112. *Id.* at 627–28 (Holmes, J., dissenting).

113. *Id.* at 627.

114. *Id.* at 629–30.

115. *Id.* at 630.

116. OWH to RP, 11/13/1919, OWHP, Reel 26, Page 547, Box 36, Folder 5.

117. WL to OWH, 11/18/1919, OWHP, Reel 35, Page 348, Box 46, Folder 27.

118. WL to OWH, 11/13/1919, *id.*, Page 347. *See* TNR, 11/26/1919, at 377–83.

119. TNR, 11/26/1919, at 360.
120. *Id.* at 361.
121. Walter Lippmann, *Liberty and the News* 11 (1920).
122. AA Diary, 11/29/1918, in *Agents of Empire*, 300.
123. Meeting Minutes, 2/22/1919, *Papers Relating to the Foreign Relations of the United States: The Paris Peace Conference,* Vol. XI, at 70–71 (1945).
124. WL to Ellery Sedgwick, 4/7/1919, at 1, PPWL at 112 & Sedgwick Papers, Carton 7, Folder "Lippmann, Walter (nd–1928)."
125. *The Bullitt Mission to Russia* (1919).
126. WCB to WL, 1/21/1920, at 1–2, WLP, Reel 5, Box 5, Folder 206.
127. Lippmann, *Liberty and the News*, 13.
128. OWH to HL, 2/10/1920, 1 HLL at 240.
129. HL to OWH, 2/15/1920, *id.* at 242.
130. TNR, 12/24/1919, at 103–9. See OWH to FF, 1/28/1920, H-FF Corr., at 81; Keynes to FF, 9/12/1919 & 9/19/1919 tel. & 9/20/1919 & 9/23/1919, WLP, Reel 9, Box 10, Folder 420a.
131. HL to OWH, 1/4/1920, 1 HLL at 231.
132. WL to FF, 6/24/1921, at 1–2, FFLC, Box 77, Folder "Lippmann, Walter, 1920–23 #2."
133. FF to WL, 6/28/1921, at 1–2, WLP, Reel 9, Box 10, Folder 422.
134. HC to FF, August 1921, at 5–6, FFLC, Box 50, Folder "Croly, Herbert 1921–23."
135. TNR, 3/1/1922, at 10–14; TNR, 3/8/1922, at 44–48; TNR, 5/3/1922, at 286–88 (Dewey review).
136. HL to OWH, 11/12/1919, 1 HLL at 220.
137. RP to LDB, 10/31/1919, LDB-Louisville, Reel 48.
138. HL to Upton Sinclair, 8/16/1922, at 1; Upton Sinclair Papers-IU, Box 4; Upton Sinclair, *The Goose-Step* 83 (1923). *See* HL to Wigglesworth, 12/20/1919, Lowell Official Papers, Box 141, Folder 46a.
139. *Harvard Alumni Bulletin*, 1/22/1920, Vol. 22, No. 17, at 399.
140. *Boston Globe* editor Lawrence F. Winship, n.d., Memorandum, at 2, FFLC, Box 151, Folder "Laski, Harold 1893–1950 & undated #1."
141. *Harvard Lampoon*, 1/16/1920, Vol. 78, at 413.
142. NH to LDB, 2/19/1920, at 4, LDB-Louisville, Reel 48, Folder SC-1.
143. OWH to FF, 2/11/1920, H-FF Corr., at 82.
144. FF to ALL, 2/13/1920, Lowell Official Papers, Box 141, Folder 46a. *See* ALL to FF, 2/14/1920, *id.* ("The attack of the Lampoon was vulgar and altogether deplorable; but the only wise thing is treat it with silence and contempt.").
145. OWH to HL, 2/10/1920, 1 HLL at 239. *See* HL to OWH, 2/15/1920, *id.* at 240 ("That was a grand letter and it gave me a real lift in the world. The *Lampoon* is off my mind now, though it makes me sigh for clearer skies.").
146. HL to OWH, 1/4/1920, *id.* at 230–31.
147. Sedgwick to FF, 1/29/1920, FFLC, Box 102, Folder "Sedgwick, Ellery 1918–59." See FF to Sedgwick, 1/15/1920, FFHLS, Pt. 3, Reel 33, Page 729.

148. OWH to FF, 2/20/1922, 1 H-FF Corr., at 137.

149. HL to Upton Sinclair, 8/16/1922, at 1, Upton Sinclair Papers-IU, Box 4 ("academic freedom could not have been more loyally defended than it was by President Lowell in my case. He threatened his resignation if I were dismissed. He never called me to account either for my opinions or for the expression I gave to them."); HL to ALL, 1/28/1920 & 4/19/1921, Lowell Official Papers, Box 141, Folder 46a; HL to FF, 3/20/1921, at 2–3, *id.*; Yeomans, *Abbott Lawrence Lowell*, at 317 (Lowell told Mark DeWolfe Howe Sr.: "If the Overseers ask for Laski's resignation they will get mine!"); Harold J. Laski, *The American Democracy* 357 (1948).

150. Winship, Memorandum, n.d., at 2.

151. Upton Sinclair to HL, 9/1/1922, HL-Syracuse, Box 1. Laski blamed Harvard's alumni. HL to Upton Sinclair, 8/16/1922, at 1–2.

152. Sinclair, *The Goose-Step*, at 83. *But see* ALL to ZC, 10/4/1922, ZCP, Reel 12, Page 551 (describing Sinclair's comments as "a purely slanderous attack upon me" that "shows a complete disregard of the truth …"). Others questioned Lowell's motives. Samuel Eliot Morison, *Three Centuries of Harvard* 466 (1936) (remarking that "Laski was not *persona grata* to Lowell"); Winship, Memorandum, n.d., at 1–2 (questioning whether it was a "victory of academic freedom").

153. FF to OWH, 11/12/1919, H-FF Corr., at 75.

154. Howe, *Justice Oliver Wendell Holmes: The Shaping Years*, 200–201 & n. i.

155. Garson Kanin, "Trips to Felix," in *Felix Frankfurter: A Tribute*, 39–40.

156. FF to MD, 11/3/1919, FFLC, Box 9, Folder "Marion A. Denman Nov. 1919 #55."

157. FF to MD, 11/4/1919, at 2, *id.*

158. FF to MD, 11/6/1919, at 3, *id.*

159. NYH, 11/6/1919, at 1.

160. *Id.*

161. Belknap Diary, 3/30/1916 & 4/6/1916.

162. Belknap COH, 5/6/1975, at 21–22, 27–28. Belknap never left Denison & Curtis, which eventually became the New York law firm of Patterson, Belknap—with Belknap as its most senior partner.

163. OWH to NG 11/6/1919 at 2, OWHP, Reel 23, Page 684, Box 32, Folder 12.

164. MD to FF, 11/8/1919, at 2, FFLC, Box 9, Folder "Marion A. Denman November 1919 #55."

165. WTD to SFV, 5/9/1918, at 1–2, RGVP, Carton 15, Folder 63.

166. WTD to SFV, 12/10/1918, at 3, *id.*

167. *Id.* at 2–3.

168. WTD to SFV, 5/20/1919, at 2–3, *id.*, Folder 64.

169. *Id.* at 6–7.

170. Dr. Isaac Adler to FF, 3/18/1916, at 2, FFLC, Box 19, Folder "'A' misc. Ad."

171. FF to Ellery Sedgwick, 12/8/1915 & 4/28/1916, Sedgwick Papers, Carton 4, Folder "Frankfurter, Felix n.d.–1927."

172. WL to FL, Thursday night, n.d., circa Summer 1917, WLP, Reel 165, Box 2, Folder 54.
173. WTD to SFV, 9/24/1917, at 3, RGVP, Carton 15, Folder 62.
174. WTD to SFV, 5/20/1919, at 7–8.
175. Wedding list, 10/14/1919, FFLC, Box 9, Folder "Marion A. Denman October 1919 #52."
176. FF to MD, 11/8/1919, at 2–3, FFLC, Box 9, Folder "Marion A. Denman November 1919 #55."
177. FF to MD, 11/7/1919, at 1–2, id. See FF to MD, 11/9/1919, at 2, id.
178. FF to OWH, 11/12/1919.
179. OWH to HL, 11/3/1919, 1 HLL at 218.
180. HL to OWH, 11/5/1919, id. at 219. See HL to OWH, 11/14/1919, id. at 221.
181. ERB to FF, 11/14/1919, FFLC, Box 31, Folder "Buckner, Emory R. 1919–21 #15."
182. FF to ERB, 12/1919, id.; LH to FF, 12/3/1919 at 1, FFLC, Box 63, Folder "Hand, Learned 1914–19."
183. HL to OWH, 1/14/1920, 1 HLL at 233.
184. RP to LDB, 10/31/1919.
185. BG, 11/12/1919, at 6.
186. Russian Meeting, 11/11/1919, FFLC, Box 89, Folder "Perkins, Thomas Nelson 1918–19."
187. FF to TNP, 11/25/1919, at 1, id. See Ellery Sedgwick to FF, 11/20/1919, FFLC, Box 102, Folder "Sedgwick, Ellery 1918–59." See FFR, 174–75.
188. OWH to FF, 12/4/1919, H–FF Corr., at 78; P.S., 12/5/1919, id.
189. Bruce A. Kimball, "The Disastrous First Fund-Raising Campaign in Legal Education," *Journal of the Gilded Age and the Progressive Era* 12, no. 4 (October 2013): 574–75 (indicating that the activities of Frankfurter, Pound, and Laski "did not cost many contributions," and Lowell believed that his stand for academic freedom generated "greater contributions than any that were lost").
190. FF to ERB, 12/17/1919, FFLC, Box 31, Folder "Buckner, Emory R. 1919–21 #15" (emphasis in original). On Henderson, see chapter 11 nn. 118–20; Ernst, *Tocqueville's Nightmare*, 20–22.
191. JWM to RP, 4/20/1920, RPP, Reel 36, Page 898; JWM to RP, 4/26/1920, id., Pages 895–96; JWM to RP, 6/12/1920, id., Page 897.
192. RP to LDB, 4/24/1920, at 1–2, LDB-Louisville, Reel 48.
193. OWH to RP, 4/27/1920, RPP, Reel 77, Page 535.
194. FF to OWH, 5/15/1920, H–FF Corr., at 89–90.
195. RP to LDB, 5/15/1920, LDB-Louisville, Reel 48. *See Harvard Alumni Bulletin*, 10/12/1920, Vol. 23, No. 2, at 37.
196. FF to Roger Baldwin, 2/18/1920, American Civil Liberties Union Papers, Reel 16, Vol. 120, Page 30. *See* Baldwin to FF, 2/13/1920, FFLC, Box 125, Folder "American Civil Liberties Union 1920–34 Baldwin, Roger." On Frankfurter's ACLU involvement, *see* FFLC, Box 125. On the founding of the

ACLU, *see* Weinrib, *The Taming of Free Speech*; Robert C. Cottrell, *Roger Nash Baldwin and the American Civil Liberties Union* (2001); Samuel Walker, *In Defense of American Liberties* (1990).

197. Colyer v. Skeffington, 265 F. 17, 20–21 (D. Mass. 1920). *See* FFR, 170–71.

198. Colyer, 265 F. at 21–22.

199. *Id.* at 30–49.

200. *Id.* at 69–71, 79–80.

201. *See* Skeffington v. Katzeff, 277 F. 129 (1st Cir. 1922); BH, 12/29/1920 in FFLC, Box 159, Folder "National Popular Government League 1919–22 #2."

202. National Popular Government League, *To the American People* 3 (1920). On the National Popular Government League, *see* FFR, 173–74; David Williams, "The Bureau of Investigation and Its Critics, 1919–1921," *Journal of American History* 68, no. 3 (December 1981): 560–79; William Anthony Gengarelly, "Resistance Spokesmen: Opponents of the Red Scare, 1919–1921" (PhD diss., 1972).

203. *To the American People*, at 3.

204. *Id.* at 4.

205. "Correspondence between Attorney General Palmer and Professors Frankfurter and Chafee Regarding Aliens Held for Deportation," at 1, FFLC, Box 159, Folder "National Popular Government League 1919–22 #2."

206. AMP to FF, 6/4/1920 tel., *id.*, Folder "National Popular Government League 1919–22 #1."

207. FF and ZC to AMP, 6/4/1920 tel., *id. See* NYT, 6/5/1920, at 27.

208. BaltSun, 3/6/1921, at ED17.

209. Memorandum from George Kelleher to Frank Burke, "Attention of J. E. Hoover, Esq.," 5/26/1920, at 1 (quoting 5/20/1920 tel.), Investigative Case Files of the Bureau of Investigation, 1908–1922, Old German File #120964, NARA, M1085, Roll 504.

210. *See* Investigative Case Files of the Bureau of Investigation, 1908–1922, NARA, M1085, Rolls 504 & 831, Old German File #379228, Old German File #120964. On Frankfurter's foreign travel, *see* Hoover to W. L. Hurley, 6/10/1920, Roll 504, OG 120964, at 76; Hurley to Hoover, 6/11/1920, *id.* at 87.

211. "Memorandum to Mr. Hoover In re Felix Frankfurter, Zachariah [*sic*] Chafee, Lawrence G. Brooks et al.," 6/15/1920, at 12, OG 379228, at 105.

212. *Diaries of Drew Pearson, 1949–1959*, at 284 (Tyler Abell, ed., 1974). Whether Hoover actually said this is unclear. In a 1921 letter, Hoover wrote that Frankfurter and thirty-one others were "all known to be actors in this [Bolshevik] movement." Sam Crockett, *Frankfurter's Red Record* 1 (1961) (quoting letter from Hoover to Hurley, 2/23/1921, NARA, State Department File, 1910–29, 861.00/8795). *See* Rep. Louis T. McFadden, 3/13/1934, Cong. Rec.-House at 4449 ("I recall that Theodore Roosevelt, the year that he passed on, made a statement to the effect that Felix Frankfurter is the most dangerous man in the United States to our form of government.").

213. FFR, 169–70.

214. RP to OWH, 11/26/1919, OWHP, Reel 36, Page 798, Box 48, Folder 20–23.

215. OWH to RP, 11/28/1919, RPP, Reel 77, Page 534 & OWHP, Reel 26, Page 549, Box 36, Folder 5.

216. RP to OWH, 6/26/1920, OWHP, Reel 36, Page 799, Box 48, Folder 20–23.

217. Chafee, "A Contemporary State Trial," at 774.

218. *Id.* at 771.

219. RP to Henry Bates, 5/25/1921, at 1, Henry Moore Bates Papers, Box 1, Folder "Bates, Henry Moore Correspondence 1920–1921" (indicating the case against the other professors "collapsed in about five minutes" because of fabricated evidence).

220. Smith, *Zechariah Chafee Jr.*, 36–57; Peter H. Irons, "'Fighting Fair,'" 94 Harv. L. Rev. 1205 (1981); Auerbach, "The Patrician as Libertarian," 524–27.

221. FF to WL, 5/24/1921, at 1, WLP, Reel 9, Box 10, Folder 422. *See* FFR, 175–77; Handwritten notes of "trial" and prosecution's briefs, FFLC, Box 142, Folder "Harvard Law School Miscellany."

222. ZC to OWH 5/29/1921, at 6–7, OWHP, Reel 31, Page 58, Box 41, Folder 12; Yeomans, *Abbott Lawrence Lowell*, 317–27.

223. Yeomans, *Abbott Lawrence Lowell*, 323. The majority found that Chafee was not negligent in his article, but the minority thought that Chafee should correct the article's factual errors. Francis J. Swayze, "Report of the Committee to Visit the Law School," circa 6/23/1921, Lowell Official Papers, Box 170, Folder 970.

224. The Nation, 8/17/1921, at 163.

225. 35 Harv. L. Rev. 9, 10–14 (1921). *See* ZC to ALL, 9/30/1921, Lowell Official Papers, Box 170, Folder 970; ALL to ZC, 10/1/1921, *id.*; ALL to ZC, 6/27/1921, *id.*

226. Zechariah Chafee Jr., *Free Speech in the United States* v (1941).

227. ZC to OWH, 5/29/1921, at 6.

228. *Id.* at 1–2, 7.

229. Dean Acheson to Alexander Bickel, 6/2/1960, Acheson Papers, Reel 2, Box 3, Folder 34. In his memoirs, Acheson did not mention Day by name, and said that Mrs. Holmes had agreed that her husband should not dissent. This is according to Holmes's secretary Stanley Morrison, who told Acheson, then Brandeis's secretary. *Id.*; Acheson, *Morning and Noon*, 119 (1965). Acheson's letter to Bickel is even more revealing than the memoir. Acheson recalled that the meeting had occurred after the justices' conference vote but probably before the circulation of Holmes's dissent. The three justices (and Mrs. Holmes) believed that Holmes had adopted "a somewhat quixotic view in the present case and had been influenced toward it by Justice Brandeis's arguments. They believed that, in light of Justice Holmes's great reputation, enhanced by his military record, etc., a dissent by him in an espionage act case would do harm of which he was not aware." Acheson to Bickel, 6/2/1960.

230. John H. Wigmore, "Abrams *v.* U.S.: Freedom of Speech and Freedom of Thuggery in War-time and Peace-time," 14 Ill. L. Rev. 539, 539, 550 (1920). *See* Andrew Porwancher, "The Justice and the Dean," *Journal of Supreme Court History* 37, no. 3 (2012): 266–82.

231. OWH to FF, 4/25/1920, H-FF Corr., at 88; FF to OWH, 4/19/1920, *id.* at 86.

232. "Justice Holmes's Dissent," *The Review*, 12/6/1919, at 636.

233. OWH to FF, 11/30/1919, H-FF Corr., at 77.

234. OWH to NG, 12/10/1919, OWHP, Box 36, Folder 5, Reel 26, Page 557 & OWH to Mrs. Curtis, 12/7/1919, at 1, *id.* at Page 554.

CHAPTER 17

1. HL to OWH, 6/8/1920, 1 HLL at 267.

2. Holmes, *Collected Legal Papers*, v.

3. OWH to FP, 12/18/1910, 1 H-P Letters at 172 ("It soon will be time for me to resolve whether I will leave when I have done my ten years (Dec. 8, 1912) but not quite yet.").

4. OWH to Sheehan, 12/15/1912, H-S Corr. at 56. *See* Howe, *The Proving Years*, 49.

5. Howe, *The Shaping Years*, at 75–76. On his Harvard years, *see id.* at 35–79.

6. OWH to Wu, 6/21/1928, H-Wu Corr. at 48; OWH to Hays, 4/20/1928, OWHP, Reel 27, Page 240, Box 36, Folder 23; Howe, *The Shaping Years*, 65–68.

7. Howe, *The Shaping Years*, 76.

8. Richard F. Miller, *Harvard's Civil War* 104 (2005). *See id.* at 102–4.

9. Plan of the Battle at Ball's Bluff, Holmes Civil War Scrapbook at 198, Harvard Law School Library, Holmes Digital Suite.

10. OWH to Mother, 10/23/1861, *Touched with Fire: Civil War Letters and Diary of Oliver Wendell Holmes Jr.* 18 (Mark DeWolfe Howe, ed., 1946).

11. *Id.* at 13, 23–25.

12. Miller, *Harvard's Civil War*, 80–83 (revealing that the Twentieth Massachusetts had 88 officers and men wounded at Ball's Bluff and 113 captured).

13. Holmes Civil War Scrapbook, at 5; Howe, *The Shaping Years*, 100.

14. OWH to FP, 6/28/1930, 2 H-P Letters at 270.

15. Howe, *The Shaping Years*, 125–28; White, *Law and the Inner Self*, 57–59; Miller, *Harvard's Civil War*, 170–76.

16. OWH to FP, 6/28/1930. *See* OWH to FP, 7/27–30/1930, 2 H-P Letters at 273.

17. Norwood P. Hallowell, "Reminisces," 12/25/1897, *Selected Letters and Papers of N. P. Hallowell* 17–18 (1963).

18. *Id.* at 17.

19. He saved the note for his scrapbook and noted: "I wrote the above when I was lying in a little house on the field of Antietam which was for a while within the enemy's lines, as I thought I might faint & so be unable to tell who I was." Holmes Civil War Scrapbook, at 61.

20. OWH to Lady Ellen Askwith, 9/17/1919, at 1, OWHP, Box 13, Folder 1, quoted in Howe, *The Shaping Years*, 128. N. P. Hallowell does not recall this story, but visiting the Nicodemus House in 1868, he "startled the old lady by asking after a little clock which had stood in a certain place on that day." Hallowell, "Reminiscences," 21

21. Hallowell, "Reminiscences," 18–19.

22. "The Man Who Rescued 'The Captain,'" *Atlantic*, 8/1947, at 80; Oliver Wendell Holmes Sr., "My Hunt after 'The Captain,'" *Atlantic Monthly*, 12/1862, at 738.

23. Holmes, "My Hunt After 'the Captain,'" at 747–48; Anna Kennedy Findlay, "Where 'The Captain' Was Found," *Maryland Historical Magazine*, Vol. 33, 6/1938, at 118; Belknap Diary, 3/8/1916.

24. Findlay, "Where 'The Captain' Was Found," 118, 123.

25. Belknap Diary, 3/8/1916.

26. OWH to parents, 9/22/1862, *Touched with Fire*, 67–68.

27. "My Hunt after 'The Captain,'" at 738–61.

28. *Id.* at 740–42, 747–48, 751–53.

29. *Id.* at 759–60.

30. *Id.* at 760.

31. Belknap, "Justice Holmes at Work and Play," at 7 (based on transcriptions of Belknap's Diary, 3/8/1916).

32. Henry Abbott to George, 12/21/1862, *Fallen Leaves* at 154 (Robert Garth Scott, ed., 1991).

33. OWH to Mother, 5/3/1863, *Touched with Fire* at 92.

34. *Id.*; OWH to Father, 5/4/1863, *id.* at 93.

35. Henry Abbott to his father, 9/18/1863, *Fallen Leaves* at 215.

36. *Id.*

37. Henry Abbott to his father, 8/17/1863, *id.* at 201.

38. Henry Abbott to OWH, 8/18/1863, *id.* at 226.

39. Norwood P. Hallowell, "The Negro as Soldier," *Selected Letters and Papers of N. P. Hallowell*, at 35–47.

40. Alexander Woollcott, "'Get Down, You Fool!,'" Atlantic Monthly, Feb. 1938, 169–70.

41. OWH to HL 3/27/1921, 1 HLL at 339 ("my private show—Fort Stevens where I saw Lincoln when the big guns were firing and our skirmishes going up the opposite slope and the enemy got their nearest to Washington.") & OWH to HL, 3/26/1922, *id.* at 414 ("Did I ever take you to my little private show of Fort Stevens—the point where the enemy made his nearest approach to Washington in '64—and where I saw Lincoln *et al* and a brisk little fight?"); OWH to LE, 3/27/1912, H-E Letters at 67 ("to Fort Stevens where in '64 I saw my General walking and down the earthworks and President Lincoln standing within it and the big guns going and the skirmish line over on the opposite slope going up to the closest approach to the city that was made. ..."). *See* Howe, *The Shaping Years*, 167–69; White, *Law and the Inner Self*, 64–65, 506.

42. The two main sources of the quotation are Harold Laski and Felix Frankfurter. Laski, who had initially told the story to Alexander Woollcott, later wrote:

> He often liked to speak of one of his memories of the war. Lincoln visited the regiment when it was engaged in the defence of Washington against the rebels. He asked Holmes to show him where the rebels stood. Holmes pointed across to the Virginia Hills [*sic*], and the President, raising his tall, gaunt figure to see better, became at once a target for snipers. "I lost my nerve," Holmes used to say, "and yelled at the President, 'Get down, you fool!' The President turned to me quietly, and said with a twinkle

in his eye, 'Colonel Holmes, I am glad to see you know how to talk to a civilian.'"

Harold Laski, "Memories of a Great American," The Listener, 3/13/1941, at 359. Mark DeWolfe Howe pointed out some erroneous facts in Laski's version of the story and concluded that it "casts new doubt on the accuracy of Woollcott's story." Howe to Cramer, 5/21/1946, Mark DeWolfe Howe Papers, Box 28, Folder 18.

Felix Frankfurter perpetuated a more restrained version of the story in which Holmes did not know that he was yelling at President Lincoln. "But I believe it to be essentially accurate for I did hear it from the Justice's own mouth," Frankfurter recalled. "He did say to a stranger who for the moment he did not recognize as President Lincoln, more in anxiety than in irritation, some such as words as 'Get down, you damn fool, before you get shot.'" FF to James Cramer, 5/19/1943, FFLC, Box 50, Folder "Cramer, John H. 1943–48"; FF to Frederick Bernays Wiener, 3/21/1949, FFLC, Box 111, Folder "Wiener, Frederick Bernays 1948–55" (claiming that Holmes told him the story and to Henry Stimson as well); John Henry Cramer, Lincoln under Enemy Fire 116 (1946). Frankfurter's account was confirmed by Holmes's niece Esther Owen, who also heard the Lincoln story with the quotation from Holmes. Cramer, Lincoln under Enemy Fire, 118–19.

Two days after the alleged Fort Stevens incident, Holmes met John Hay and Robert Todd Lincoln when they visited the Sixth Corps in Virginia. Id. at 66; Benjamin Franklin Cooling III, The Day Lincoln Was Almost Shot 202 (2013). Holmes did not appear to mention the incident. In an 1870 letter, General Wright first recalled telling Lincoln to get down at Fort Stevens. George Thomas Stevens, Three Years in the Sixth Corps 382 n. (2d ed. 1870); Cramer, Lincoln under Enemy Fire, 30–31; WashTimes, 6/15/1900, at 3.

Holmes later told the story of seeing Lincoln at Fort Stevens to his admirers and secretaries, but without the words "Get down, you damn fool." Cramer, Lincoln under Enemy Fire, 114–15 (recounting Mark DeWolfe Howe's experiences hearing the story from Holmes without the quotation); Arthur Sutherland, "Recollections of Justice Holmes," at 12, Sutherland Papers, Box 24, Folder 24-7 (describing a trip to Fort Stevens during the 1927 Term: "The Justice showed me where the federal skirmish-line was, and spoke of seeing the President in the works; but until I read of it in a magazine, years after his death, I never heard of the Justice saying 'Get Down, you damn fool' to Abraham Lincoln."); Mark DeWolfe Howe Diary, 10/30/1933, at 5, Howe Papers, Box 29, Folder 29–1 & Monagan Papers, Box 1, Folder 1-12 ("And in the center of the fort he saw Mr. Lincoln standing."). Other secretaries doubted the "get down, you fool" version. See Chauncey Belknap to Catherine Drinker Bowen, 5/31/1944, at 3–4, CDBP, Box 61, Folder "Yankee from Olympus Fan Mail 1943–44'"; Irvin Olds to Catherine Drinker Bowen, 7/31/1944, at 3–4, id, Box 60, Folder "Yankee from Olympus Correspondence July 1943–Feb. 1957 & undated."

The scholarly consensus is that Holmes may have been there, but that the quotation is apocryphal. See Cooling, The Day Lincoln Was Almost Shot,

179 (concluding "that shocking utterance may have been emitted by almost anyone"); White, *Law and the Inner Self*, 64–65, 506 n. 63 (speculating that Mark DeWolfe Howe wrote about the story in "elliptical fashion" so as not to annoy Frankfurter); Frederick C. Hicks, "Lincoln, Wright, and Holmes at Fort Stevens," *Journal of the Illinois State Historical Society* 39 (September 1946): 323–32 (casting doubt on Woollcott's story); Howe to Catherine Drinker Bowen, 1/ 12/1957, at 1, CDBP, Box 2, Folder "H" Miscellany ("It would be easy to say OF COURSE Holmes yelled at Lincoln—FF says so. If despite the credentials of the witness I have lingering doubts about the tale should I not so indicate?").

43. OWH Diary, 5/29/1864, *Touched with Fire*, 134.

44. Howe, *The Shaping Years*, 169–75.

45. OWH to Mother, 6/7/1864, *Touched with Fire*, 143 & n. 2; OWH to Mother, 7/ 8/1864, *id.*, 152.

46. OWH to Parents, 5/16/1864, *id.* at 122.

47. Howe, *The Shaping Years*, 165 (quoting Holmes, "Memorial Day Address," in *The Mind and Faith of Justice Holmes*, 15 (Max Lerner, ed., 1943)).

48. Holmes, "The Soldier's Faith," 5/30/1895, *Speeches*, 56–66 & *The Mind and Faith of Justice Holmes*, 23–24.

49. Holmes, "Memorial Day Address," 5/30/1884, *The Mind and Faith of Justice Holmes*, 16.

50. White, *Law and the Inner Self*, 84 (citing Holmes, "Parts of the Unimaginable Whole," 6/28/1911, *The Mind and Faith of Justice Holmes*, 25–27).

51. Marion Denman Frankfurter, 8/10/1932, at 5, Mark DeWolfe Howe Research Materials, Box 22, Folder 26. A coxcomb is "a vain and conceited man; a dandy."

52. Louis Menand, *The Metaphysical Club* 201–32 (2001). On the impact of Holmes's Civil War experiences on his worldview, *see id.* at 3–69; Catharine Pierce Wells, "Oliver Wendell Holmes Jr. and the American Civil War," *Journal of Supreme Court History* 40 (2015): 282–313.

53. William James to G. W. James, 3/21/1866, James Family Papers, Harvard University Archives, quoted in Baker, *Justice from Beacon Hill*, 173, 698.

54. William James to Henry P. Bowditch, 8/12/1869, 1 *Letters of William James* 154–55 (Henry James, ed., 1920); James to Bowditch, 5/22/1869, *The Selected Letters of William James* 83 (Elizabeth Hardwick, ed., 1980).

55. OWH to Mrs. Howard Kennedy, 3/11/1872, in "Where the Captain Was Found," 121.

56. Catherine Drinker Bowen to Francis Biddle, 7/10/1944, at 2, Biddle Papers, Georgetown University, Box 9, Folder 67 ("Mrs. Arthur Hill, Mrs. Palfrey, Richard Hale, all either indicated or said outright that he made Fanny desperately unhappy, especially during those pre-Washington years.").

57. William James to Henry James, 2/13/1873, 1 *Letters of William James*, 168. *See* William James to Thomas W. Ward, 5/24/1868, *The Selected Letters of William James*, 76.

58. Howe, *The Proving Years*, 5–7.

59. *Id.* at 9 & 8 n. 18 (quoting Holmes to Mrs. Charles S. Hamlin, 10/12/1930, OWHP, Reel 33, Page 59, Box 43, Folder 28).

60. Oliver Wendell Holmes, *The Common Law* 1 (1891).

61. Holmes, "Memorial Day Address," 5/30/1884, *Speeches*, 11–12 & *The Mind and Faith of Justice Holmes*, 16; Holmes, "The Soldier's Faith," 5/30/1895, *Speeches*, 56–66 & *The Mind and Faith of Justice Holmes*, 18–25.

62. Holmes, "The Path of Law," 10 Harv. L. Rev. 457 (1897) & *The Mind and Faith of Justice Holmes*, 82.

63. Howe, *The Shaping Years*, 1–25; White, *Law and the Inner Self*, 9–14.

64. OWH to LE, 3/24/1923, H-E Letters at 212 & n. 37.

65. OWH to FF, 6/26/1928, H-FF Corr., at 231; Donald Hiss in *The Making of the New Deal*, 39 & Donald Hiss Interview with Louchheim, 11/4/1981, at 38, Louchheim Papers, Box 72, Folder 9.

66. On Holmes's quest for recognition, *see* White, *Law and the Inner Self*, 354–77; Brad Snyder, "The House That Built Holmes," 30 Law & History Rev. 661, 667–70 (2012).

67. WP, 1/31/1904, at B3.

68. OWH to Sheehan, 9/6/1904, H-S Corr., at 14–15; OWH to HL, 3/4/1920, 1 HLL at 248. *See* Northern Securities Co. v. United States, 193 U.S. 197, 364 (1904) (Holmes, J., dissenting).

69. Lochner v. New York, 198 U.S. 45, 75 (1905) (Holmes, J., dissenting).

70. NYT, 4/18/1905, at 1; CT, 4/18/1905, at 1; WP, 4/18/1905, at 11.

71. Roscoe Pound, "Liberty of Contract," 18 Yale L.J. 454, 480 (1909). *See* Edward S. Corwin, "The Supreme Court and the Fourteenth Amendment," 7 Mich. L. Rev. 643, 669–70 (1909) (criticizing Holmes's dissent); Frank M. Cobb, "Reasonableness of Maximum Rates as a Constitutional Limitation upon Rate Regulation," 21 Harv. L. Rev. 175, 179 (1908) (same); Ernst Freund, "Limitations of Hours of Labor," 17 Green Bag 411 (1905) (ignoring it).

72. WP, 3/9/1911, at 2.

73. AC, 3/9/1911, at 9; HarCour, 3/9/1911, at 13.

74. *See, e.g.*, BG, 10/15/1911, at 4; BG, 9/20/1911, at 4; BG, 8/20/1911, at 5.

75. OWH to Clara Stevens, 3/6/1909, OWHP, Reel 38, Page 34, Box 50, Folders 9–11. *See* OWH to Sheehan, 9/3/1910, H-S Corr. at 36–37; G. Edward White, "Holmes's Life Plan," 65 N.Y.U. L. Rev. 1409, 1462 (1990).

76. OWH to NG, 12/25/1908, OWHP, Reel 23, Page 466, Box 32, Folder 3.

77. New York Evening Post, 8/12/1902, at 4, OWHP, Reel 53, Page 910, Box 69, Folder 6.

78. OWH to NG, 3/18/1911, at 2, OWHP, Reel 23, Page 531, Box 32, Folder 5.

79. OWH to JCG, 5/10/1914, at 1–2, OWHP, Reel 24, Page 525, Box 33, Folder 25.

80. JCG to WHT, 11/9/1912, WHTP, Reel 452, No. 2, Image 175. President Taft advised his son, Robert, to decline the offer to be Holmes's secretary for the coming year. *See* Robert Taft to WHT, circa 11/13/1912, at 2, *id.*, Image 174; WHT to JCG, 11/19/1912, *id.*, Image 176; WHT to Robert Taft, 11/19/1912, *id.*, Image 177; White, *Law and the Inner Self*, 312–13.

81. JCG to OWH, 6/15/1913, at 1, OWHP, Reel 24, Page 482, Box 33, Folder 23; OWH to JCG, 5/10/1914, at 1, *id.*, Page 525, Box 33, Folder 25.

82. OWH to LE, 4/17/1914, H-E Letters at 90.

83. FF to OWH, 11/22/1920, H-FF Corr., at 97.

84. HC to OWH, 11/30/1920, at 1, OWHP, Reel 30, Page 366, Box 40, Folder 21.

85. OWH to Charlotte Moncheur, 4/4/1919, OWHP, Reel 36, Page 520, Box 36, Folder 4; HL to OWH, 7/18/1920, 1 HLL at 270; OWH to HL, 11/17/1920, *id.* at 291.

86. HC to OWH, 11/30/1920, at 2.

87. TNR, 2/2/1921, at 294.

88. *Id.* at 295. For Cohen-Holmes correspondence, *see Portrait of a Philosopher*, 313–60.

89. OWH to MC, 1/30/1921, at 1, OWHP, Reel 30, Page 37, Box 40, Folder 10.

90. TNR, 2/23/1921, at 380.

91. OWH to My Dear, 2/20/1921, at 1, OWHP, Reel 26, Page 646, Box 36, Folder 7.

92. James Bryce, Book Review, 4 J. Comp. Legis. & Int'l L. 119 (1922); Hampton L. Carson, Book Review, 69 U. Pa. L. Rev. 291 (1921); Walter Wheeler Cook, Book Review, 30 Yale L.J. 775 (1921); Robert Eugene Cushman, Book Review, 8 *Mississippi Valley Historical Review* 208 (1921); Julius Goebel Jr., Book Review, 7 Va. L. Rev. 494 (1921); Charles Noble Gregory, Book Review, 15 Am. J. Int. L. 490 (1921); Learned Hand, Book Review, 36 *Political Science Quarterly* 528 (1921); Charles Merrill Hough, Book Review, 21 Colum. L. Rev. 296 (1921); Austin Kocourek, Book Review, 16 Ill. L. Rev. 156, 156 (1921); Edwin W. Patterson, Book Review, 6 Iowa L. Bull. 250 (1921); Francis S. Philbrick, "A Genial Sceptic," The Freeman, 6/29/1921, at 378–79; C.W.P., Book Review, 6 Cornell L.Q. 353 (1921); Thomas Reed Powell, "Mr. Justice Holmes," The Nation, 2/9/1921, at 238; James H. Tufts, "The Legal and Social Philosophy of Mr. Justice Holmes," 7 A.B.A. J. 359 (1921).

93. Hand, Book Review, at 528.

94. OWH to FF, 8/30/1921, H-FF Corr., at 122.

95. FF to OWH, 9/1/1921, *id.* at 123.

96. LH to Arthur Train, 5/29/1941, at 1, LHP, Box 81, Folder 81-7. *See* LH to Charles P. Curtis Jr., 1/14/1954, at 1, *id.*, Box 86, Folder 86-21.

97. OWH to NG, 3/5/1921, at 2–3, OWHP, Reel 23, Pages 774–75, Box 32, Folder 15.

98. U.S. Ex Rel. Milwaukee Social Democratic Pub. Co. v. Burleson, 255 U.S. 407, 438 (1921) (Holmes, J., dissenting).

99. FF to OWH, 3/16/1921, H-FF Corr., at 106.

100. TNR, 3/30/1921, at 124.

101. Biddle, *Mr. Justice Holmes*, 167.

102. OWH to Mrs. Curtis, 3/17/1921, at 1, OWHP, Reel 21, Page 666, Box 36, Folder 7.

103. Biddle, *Mr. Justice Holmes*, 168. I quote Biddle's dialogue with caution, knowing that the attorney general invented both scenes and dialogue. FF to FB, 6/

25/1942, at 1, Biddle Papers, Georgetown University, Box 9, Folder 69. Biddle, however, attended the birthday celebration and witnessed Holmes's reaction firsthand. FB to Mrs. Holmes, 3/1/1921, OWHP, Reel 42, Box 55, Folder 12.

104. OWH to Mrs. Curtis, 3/17/1921, at 1. *See* OWH to HL, 3/10/1921, 1 HLL at 318.

105. Biddle, *Mr. Justice Holmes*, 168.

106. Roscoe Pound, "Judge Holmes's Contributions to the Science of Law," 34 Harv. L. Rev. 449, 453 (1921).

107. TNR, 3/9/1921, at 34.

108. OWH to Lady Scott, 3/15/1921, OWHP, Reel 26, Page 664, Box 36, Folder 7. *See* OWH to Charlotte Moncheur, 5/2/1921, at 1, *id.*, Page 677, Box 36, Folder 8 ("For one to whom intellectual ambition is the strongest the only reward that counts for much is when those whom he deems competent say that he has touched the superlative. And I have had more than I ever dared to hope.").

109. NYT, 4/3/1921, at 41. *See* WP, 7/17/1921, at 47.

110. OWH to HL, 11/17/1920, 1 HLL at 291.

111. OWH to unknown, 11/30/1921, OWHP, Reel 26, Page 720, Box 36, Folder 9; OWH to NG, 11/30/1921, at 1, MDHP, Box 4, Folder 3.

CHAPTER 18

1. GB to WGH, 12/7/1921, GBP, Box 22, Folder "Warren G. Harding 1921–23." For his earlier attempts with Wilson, *see* GB to J. W. Staggers, 7/17/1919 & Staggers to WW, 7/24/1919, WWP, Reel 377, Series 4, No. 5043.

2. GB to Mr. Lemke, 8/28/20, GBP, Box 82, Folder "Politics 1920"; GB to WGH, 12/6/20, at 1, GBP, Box 22, Folder "Warren G. Harding."

3. GB to WGH, 6/12/1920, GBP, Box 82, Folder "Politics 1920."

4. GB to WGH, 1/3/1920, *id.*

5. WGH to GB, 12/15/1920, GBP, Box 22, Folder "Warren G. Harding."

6. WGH to GB, 1/12/1920, *id.*; GB to WGH, 1/28/1922, at 1, *id.*, Folder "Warren G. Harding 1921–23."

7. GB to CHP, 8/1/1918, SMC, Box 16, Folder 4.

8. Report of CHP, 4/23/1919, Fourth Annual Meeting of Stone Mountain Memorial Association, GBP, Box 115, Folder "Works: Stone Mountain 1923."

9. Mary Borglum, Note, circa 1946, GBP, Box 32, Folder "Eugene Meyer Jr."; GB to BB, 9/11/1920, at 1, GBP, Box 115, Folder "Works: Stone Mountain 1918–1920."

10. NY Trib, 6/4/1920, at 7.

11. GB to WGH, 12/7/1921, at 1.

12. BaltSun, 7/20/1919, at 6.

13. AC, 4/3/1921, at G7.

14. *Id.*

15. NYT, 7/2/1922, at 40.
16. CHP to GB, 2/1/1919 & GB to CHP, 2/6/1919 & GB to CHP, 4/2/1919, GBP, Box 115, Folder "Works: Stone Mountain 1918–1920."
17. AC, 4/24/1919, at 5; AC, 4/22/1919, at 6.
18. AJ, 1/16/1919, in GBP, Box 115, Folder "Works: Stone Mountain 1918–1920."
19. Walter Chambliss to GB, 10/15/1919, id.
20. GB to Chambliss, 10/18/1919, id.
21. Bernard Baruch, *Baruch: My Own Story*, Vol. 1, at 5–12, 47 (1957).
22. In 1925, Baruch endowed the United Daughters of the Confederacy Mrs. Simon Baruch United Award in honor of his mother to fund works of southern history. *History of the United Daughters of the Confederacy*, Vol. 1, at 269 (2005).
23. GB to BB, 9/11/1920, at 1–2, GBP, Box 115, Folder "Works: Stone Mountain 1918–1920."
24. GB to BB, 8/16/1920, id.
25. Gutzon Borglum, "Dr. Isidore Singer as I Know Him," American Hebrew and Jewish Messenger, 11/7/1919, at 628.
26. GB to Frazier Curtis, 3/19/1920, GBP, Box 12, Folder "Curtis, Frazier C." (emphasis in original).
27. JGT to GB, 7/10/1920, GBP, Box 115, Folder "Works: Stone Mountain 1918–1920."
28. JGT to GB, 1/16/1921, id., Folder "Works: Stone Mountain 1921."
29. AC, 1/7/1921, at 4.
30. AC, 1/9/1921, at 2.
31. AC, 1/12/1921, at 8.
32. AC, 1/14/1921, at 10.
33. Davies, *Solon H. Borglum*, 232 (emphasis in original).
34. Shaff and Shaff, *Six Wars at a Time*, 192–93 (quoting interview with Monica Davies).
35. *Id.* at 193 (claiming, perhaps based on their Davies interview, that Gutzon was so overcome with grief he could not come to the funeral). Gutzon, however, did come to the memorial service, where the priest even insulted him out of earshot. *See* Mary Borglum to Dr. Guthrie, n.d., GBP, Box 18, Folder "G"; GB to Dr. Guthrie, 2/14/1922, id.; Dr. Guthrie to GB, 2/18/1922, id.; GB to Dr. Guthrie, 2/27/1922, id.
36. NYT, 3/5/1922, at 97.
37. GB to Guthrie, 2/27/1922; GB to Robert Garrison, 3/9/22, at 2, GBP, Box 8, Folder "G."
38. GB to Robert Garrison, 3/9/1922, at 2.
39. *Id.*
40. CHP to GB, 12/17/15, Excerpt, SMC, Box 16.
41. GB to BB, 9/11/1920, at 1; GB to BB, 4/30/1923, GBP, Box 115, Folder "Works: Stone Mountain 1922."
42. JGT to GB, 1/6/1922, GBP, Box 115, Folder "Works: Stone Mountain 1922."
43. NYT, 9/12/1921, at 12.

44. AC, 5/4/1922, at 14; GB to E.Y. Clark[e], 6/7/1922, at 1, GBP, Box 115, Folder "Works: Stone Mountain 1922."

45. GB to E. Y. Clark[e], 6/7/1922, at 1.

46. GB to Frazier Curtis, 5/26/1922, GBP, Box 12, Folder "Curtis, Frazier C."

47. GB to E. Y. Clark[e], 6/7/1922, at 2.

48. AC, 4/26/1922, at 6.

49. GB to JGT, 6/28/1922 & JGT to GB, 7/14/1922 & Budget 7/14/1922, GBP, Box 115, Folder "Works: Stone Mountain 1922."

50. AC, 8/2/1922, at 1.

51. AC, 8/4/1922, at 6.

52. SLPD, 5/19/1922, at 41; SLPD, 6/18/1922, at A49B; CT, 11/22/1922, at 5.

53. Bausch & Lomb to Charles D'Emery, 7/12/1922, GBP, Box 115, Folder "Works: Stone Mountain 1922"; Borglum, "Moulding a Mountain," The Forum, 10/1923, at 5.

54. Borglum, "Moulding a Mountain," at 5.

55. Memorandum re: Projector, n.d., at 1, GBP, Box 115, Folder "Works: Stone Mountain 1923."

56. Casey and Borglum, *Give the Man Room*, 185. *Cf.* Johnson, *The Undefeated*, 37 ("Oh, Daddy, Daddy! Look at the soldiers, coming through the woods!").

57. Stone Mountain Confederate Memorial Association, Meeting Minutes, 1/17/1923, at 1–3, GBP, Box 115, Folder "Works: Stone Mountain 1923."

58. GB to Clark Howell, editor, Atlanta Constitution, 9/2/1922, at 1, Box 115, Folder "Works: Stone Mountain 1922."

59. GB to WGH, 12/14/1922 tel., WGHP, Reel 215, File 1230, Folder 1, Page 1094. This may have been some sort of Klan code. To Indiana Klansman David C. Stephenson, Borglum referred to Dr. Evans as the "Old Man in West." GB to Stephenson, 8/28/1923 tel., GBP, Box 43, Folder "David C. Stephenson."

60. George Christian to GB, 12/14/1922 tel., WGHP, Reel 215, File 1230, Folder 1, Page 1095. *See* Christian to GB, 12/16/1922, two tels., WGHP, Reel 215, File 1230, Folder 1, Pages 1096–97.

61. *See* Christian to Will W. Alexander, 5/5/1922, WGHP, Reel 218, Folder 1500, Page 992; Christian to Charleston A. Klenman, 4/18/1922, *id.* at Page 976; NYT, 4/25/1922, at 2. Historians have never substantiated whether Harding was a member of the Klan. *See* Phillip G. Payne, *Dead Last* 118–19, 243–44 n. 60 (2009) (reciting the evidence). For a balanced view of Harding on race, *see* John W. Dean, *Warren G. Harding* 123–26 (2004).

62. CT, 12/19/1922, at 16.

63. Christian to GB & GB to Christian, 12/16/1922, tels.; AC, 12/20/1922, at 1. *See* Evans to GB, n.d. tel., GBP, Box 83, Folder "Politics 1923" ("Will arrive in Washington at New Willard Hotel next Monday Morning for stay several days stop. Make appointment as per your suggestion H. W. Evans"); GB to WGH, n.d., handwritten tel., *id.*

64. AC, 12/20/1922, at 1.

65. Venable to GB, 12/21/1922 tel., GBP, Box 115, Folder "Works: Stone Mountain 1922."

66. Stone Mountain Confederate Memorial Association, Meeting Minutes, 1/17/1923, at 1, 4.

67. *Id.* at 4–5.

68. GB to Forrest Adair, 1/31/1923, at 1–3, GBP, Box 115, Folder "Works: Stone Mountain 1923."

69. Adair to GB, 2/3/1923, *id.*

70. GB to E. Y. Clarke, 2/21/1923, GBP, Box 116, Folder "Works: Stone Mountain 1923."

71. NYT, 2/24/1923, at 4.

72. GB to Clarke, 3/8/1923, GBP, Box 116, Folder "Works SM: 1923."

73. Handwritten Inscription on Photograph, 4/12/1925, *id.*, "Works SM: 1924."

74. GB to Frederick L. Savage, 3/5/1923, at 1, WGHP, Reel 233, Pages 208–9.

75. GB to WGH, 3/6/1923, at 1, *id.*, Page 210. *See* GB to D. C. Stephenson, 3/9/1923, GBP, Box 43, Folder "David C. Stephenson."

76. NYT, 2/25/1923, at E1; NYTrib, 2/25/1923, at A3.

77. Memorandum re: Projector, at 2.

78. *Id.*; AC, 3/2/1923, at 1, 14; Casey and Borglum, *Give the Man Room*, 185–86.

79. Austin C. Lescarboura, managing editor, Scientific American, to GB, 11/16/1922 & GB to Lescarboura, 3/20/1923, GBP, Box 115, Folder "Works: Stone Mountain 1922"; GB to Arthur Young, 3/20/1923, *id.*; *Popular Mechanics*, 4/1923, 492, 494. *Cf.* Borglum, "Moulding a Mountain," at 5 (one to three years); Casey and Borglum, *Give the Man Room*, 186 (two to three years).

80. AC, 3/2/1923, at 2.

81. *Id.*

82. GB to JGT, 3/20/1923 tel., GBP, Box 116, Folder "Works: Stone Mountain 1923." *See* JGT to GB, 3/20/1923 tel. & JGT to GB 3/19/1923 tel., *id.*

83. BaltSun, 4/22/1923, at 2.

84. NYTrib, 4/22/1923, at 1.

85. BaltSun, 4/22/1923, at 2.

86. NYTrib, 4/22/1923, at 1.

87. BaltSun, 4/22/1923, at 2.

88. Leona St. George Rodgers Schuyler to GB, 5/25/1923, GBP, Box 115, Folder "Works: Stone Mountain 1923" (regarding New York *World* telegram, 4/22/1923).

89. GB to Schuyler, 6/1/1923, at 1–2, *id.*

90. Randolph to GB, 4/4/1923, at 2, *id.*

91. BaltSun, 4/13/1923, at 1.

92. AC, 4/14/1923, at 4; GB to WGH, 4/10/1923 tel., WGHP, Reel 230, Folder 1, Page 1118; Christian to GB, 4/12/1923 tel., *id.*, Page 1117; GB to Christian, 4/19/1923 tel., *id.*, Page 1121; Christian to GB, *id.*, Page 1122.

93. AC, 4/21/1923, at 6.

94. AC, 4/23/1923, at 1, 5.

95. AC, 6/1/1923, at 1. *See* GB to AC, 5/31/1923 tel., GBP, Box 116, Folder "Works: Stone Mountain 1924"; WP, 6/1/1923, at 2.

96. Memphis Commercial Appeal, 8/30/1923, at 1; BaltSun, 8/30/1923, at 1.

97. Mary Borglum to GB, 9/3/1923, GBP, Box 115, Folder "Works SM: 1923."

98. Gutzon Borglum entry, 13 *Who's Who in America* 460 (1924–25).

99. Charlotte Pierce died on April 24, 1947, in Los Angeles. She was seventy years old. LAT, 4/26/1947, at 8.

100. W. E. B. Du Bois, *The Souls of Black Folk* vii (1903). *See* Daniel J. Sharfstein, *The Invisible Line* (2011).

101. GB to Stephenson, 6/2/1923, at 1, GBP, Box 43, Folder "David C. Stephenson."

102. GB to Stephenson, 9/5/1923, *id.* (enclosing "Suggestions for Immigration").

103. GB to Stephenson, 6/2/1923, at 4.

104. *Pictorial Edition Stone Mountain* 17 (1923).

105. *Id.* at 2.

106. *Id.* at 2, 4, 6, 9.

107. *Id.* at 1, 2, 4, 9, 16.

108. AC, 6/3/1923, at 1, 12; AC, 6/9/1923, at 5.

109. AC, 6/9/1923, at 5.

110. JGT to GB, 7/2/1923 tel. & GB to JGT, 7/3/1923 tel., GBP, Box 116, Folder "Works: Stone Mountain 1923"; GB to Harvey, 7/31/1923, *id.*, Folder "Works SM: 1924."

111. JGT to GB, 7/3/1923, GBP, Box 116, Folder "Works: Stone Mountain 1923."

112. AJ Magazine, 5/6/1923, at 13. *See Margaret Mitchell: Reporter* (Patrick Allen, ed., 2010).

113. GB to Rivers, 7/1/1923, GBP, Box 116, Folder "Works: Stone Mountain 1923."

114. JGT to GB, 7/3/1923.

115. AC, 9/11/1923, at 7.

116. JGT to GB, 8/20/1923, GBP, Box 116, Folder "Works: Stone Mountain 1923."

117. GB to Eugene Black, 8/26/1923, GBP, Box 115, Folder "Works: Stone Mountain 1922."

118. David Webb to GB, 8/20/1923, GBP, Box 115, "Folder Works: Stone Mountain 1923."

119. JGT to GB, 8/20/1923, GBP, Box 116, Folder "Works: Stone Mountain 1923."

120. AC, 9/13/1923, at 7.

121. GB to JGT, 9/25/1923, GBP, Box 116, Folder "Works: Stone Mountain 1923" & GB to JGT, 9/14/1923 tel., *id.*

122. JGT to GB, 10/15/1923 tel., *id.*

123. JGT to GB, 10/1/1923, *id.* Box 115, Folder "Works: Stone Mountain 1923."

124. JGT to GB, 10/23/1923 tel. & 10/27/1923 tel., *id.*, Box 116, Folder "Works: Stone Mountain 1923."

125. JGT to GB, 10/23/1923 tel.; AC, 12/2/1923, at 14.

126. JGT to GB, 10/29/1923, at 1, GBP, Box 116, Folder "Works: Stone Mountain 1923."

127. GB to JGT, 9/30/1923 tel., *id.*; AC, 12/2/1923, at 14.

128. Borglum, "Moulding a Mountain," at 6.

129. AC, 12/16/1923, at A2.

130. Photograph, GBP, Box 116, Folder "Works: Stone Mountain 1924"; GB to Edward Rumely, 1/24/1924, at 1, GBP, Box 117, Folder "Works: Stone Mountain 1924"; NYT, 1/27/1924, at RP4–RP5.

131. AC, 1/13/1924, at 9.

132. *Id.*

133. AC, 1/20/1924, at 9–10; AJ, 1/20/1923, at 7.

134. AJ, 1/19/1924, at 2.

135. *Id.* at 1; AC, 1/20/1924, at 9.

136. AJ, 1/19/1924, at 1; AC, 1/20/1923, at 9.

137. GB to Edward Rumely, 1/24/1924, at 1.

138. AJ, 1/19/1924, at 1; AC, 1/20/1924, at 9.

139. AC, 1/20/1924, at 9.

140. GB to Edward Rumely, 1/24/1924, at 1.

CHAPTER 19

1. Walter Lippmann, *Public Opinion* 19 (1922).

2. OWH, "John Marshall," 2/4/1901, in *The Mind and Faith of Justice Holmes*, 385.

3. OWH to HL, 4/22/1922, 1 HLL at 417.

4. OWH to FP, 5/21/1922, 2 H-P Letters at 96.

5. Block v. Hirsh, 256 U.S. 135, 158 (1921).

6. FF to OWH, 4/18/1921, H-FF Corr., at 108.

7. OWH to FP, 5/21/1922. *See* OWH to My dear friend, 6/2/1922, OWHP, Reel 26, Page 761, Box 36, Folder 10; Brandeis-Frankfurter Conversations at 15, FFLC, Box 224.

8. *See* chapter 12 nn. 92–96.

9. WHT to Elihu Root, 12/21/1922, at 1, Elihu Root Papers, Box 166, Folder 12.

10. TNR, 1/18/1922, at 191 (quoting TNR, 7/27/1921, at 231).

11. Truax v. Corrigan, 257 U.S. 312, 328 (1921).

12. *Id.* at 339–40.

13. TNR, 1/18/1922, at 193–94.

14. Truax, 257 U.S. at 342 (Holmes, J., dissenting) (quoted in TNR, 1/18/1922, at 193) & *id.* at 344.

15. United Mine Workers v. Coronado Coal Co., 259 U.S. 344, 391, 413 (1922).

16. TNR, 8/16/1922, at 328–30. *See* LDB to FF, 8/31/1922, HBHS, at 104 (arguing Frankfurter went too easy on Taft). Taft may have changed his vote in the case because of Brandeis and brought the rest of the Court with him. *See* Alexander M. Bickel, *The Unpublished Opinions of Mr. Justice Brandeis* 77–97 (1957).

17. Bailey v. Drexel Furniture Co., 259 U.S. 20, 43–44 (1922).

18. TNR, 7/26/1922, at 248. *See* LDB to FF, 5/16/1922, HBHS, at 100–101.

19. TNR, 1/25/1922, at 238.

20. Brandeis-Frankfurter Conversations, July 9 [1922], at 4 ("LDB thinks if [there would have been] no XIV [Amendment] there would have been extension of application of contract clause").

21. TNR, 1/25/1922, at 238 (quoting Truax v. Corrigan, 257 U.S. 312, 344 (1921) (Holmes, J., dissenting)).

22. Robert La Follette, 6/14/1922, at 2, La Follette Family Papers, Box I:B226, Folder "Supreme Court Ruler of Nation."

23. Id. at 15.

24. OWH to HL, 6/14/1922, 1 HLL at 431.

25. Id.; BG, 7/2/1922, at 50.

26. OWH to FP, 6/23/1922, 2 H-P Letters at 99; OWH to NG, 6/27/1922, OWHP, Reel 26, Page 765, Box 36, Folder 10.

27. OWH to HL, 7/7/1922, 1 HLL at 434.

28. FF to WL, 7/21/1922, at 1, WLP, Reel 10, Box 10, Folder 423. See FF to RP, 7/24/1922, at 1–2, RPP, Reel 74, Pages 294–95.

29. OWH to HL, 8/19/1922, 1 HLL at 439.

30. NYW, 6/30/1922, at 11.

31. OWH to Ellen A. Curtis, 8/11/1922, OWHP, Reel 26, Page 772, Box 36, Folder 10 & John G. Palfrey Collection, Box 15, Folder 8, Seq. 5.

32. OWH to Ellen A. Curtis, 8/12/1922, id., & id. at Seq. 13.

33. OWH to John Hessin Clarke, 9/6/1922, MDHP, Box 20, Folder 14, Seq. 27.

34. John Hessin Clarke to WW, 9/9/1922, 68 WWP at 130. See Hoyt Landon Warner, The Life of Mr. Justice Clarke 112–15 (1959); Carl Wittke, "Mr. Justice Clarke in Retirement," 1 Western Res. L. Rev. 28, 33–35 (1949).

35. See Walter F. Murphy, "In His Own Image: Mr. Chief Justice Taft and Supreme Court Appointments," 1961 Sup. Ct. Rev., 159, 162–63.

36. OWH to HL, 9/22/1922, 1 HLL at 447.

37. OWH to HL, 9/28/1922, id. at 453. See OWH to FP, 10/15/1922, 2 H-P Letters at 103.

38. OWH to FP, 11/19/1922, 2 H-P Letters at 104. See LDB to FF, 10/19/1922, HBHS, at 122.

39. Pennsylvania Coal Co. v. Mahon, 260 U.S. 393, 413–16 (1922).

40. Id. at 416 (Brandeis, J., dissenting).

41. LDB to FF, 1/3/1923, HBHS, at 132. See FF to WL, 1/4/1924, WLP, Reel 10, Box 10, Folder 425 (blaming Benjamin); Brandeis-Frankfurter Conversations at 21 (Brandeis: "I account for [Mahon] by what one would think Holmes is [the] last man to yield to–class bias. He came back to views not of his manhood but childhood.").

42. OWH to HL, 1/13/1923, 1 HLL at 473. See OWH to FF, 2/14/1923, H-FF Corr., at 150.

43. TNR, 1/3/1923, 136–37. See OWH to HL, 1/13/1923, 1 HLL at 473 (identifying Acheson as the author and indicating that he "was not greatly impressed").

44. TNR, 12/20/1922, at 84.

45. Id. at 85.

46. OWH to FF, 12/22/1922, H-FF Corr., at 149–50.

47. WHT to LH, 3/3/1923, at 1–2, WHTP, Reel 251. See LDB to FF, 12/28/1922, HBHS, at 130; LDB to FF, 1/3/1923, id. at 132.

48. TNR, 12/6/1922, at 27–28; TNR, 12/13/1922, at 53–54 & 65–66; TNR, 12/20/1922, at 81–82; The Nation, 12/6/1922, at 593; The Nation, 12/13/1922, at 653 & 660–61. On Butler's nomination, *see* David J. Danelski, *A Supreme Court Justice Is Appointed* (1964); David Schneider, "More Than a Fraction" (PhD diss., 2009); John Paul Frank, "The Confirmation of Pierce Butler" (MA thesis, 1940).

49. TNR, 12/13/1922, at 66; The Nation, 12/13/1922, at 660.

50. Pierce Butler to FF, 1/18/1919, FFLC, Box 38, Folder "Butler, Pierce 1918–23"; FF to Pierce Butler Jr., 12/9/1922, *id.*; Pierce Butler Jr., to FF, 1/28/1923, *id.*; FF to Senator Knute Nelson, undated, *id.* (refusing to testify).

51. Adkins v. Children's Hospital, 261 U.S. 525, 542–43 (1923).

52. FF to Jesse Adkins, 10/21/1920, Adkins Papers, Box 6, Folder "JCA MWG, 1920–21" (remarking that it had been ten years since they had worked together).

53. Jesse Adkins to Winfred Denison, 9/11/14, Adkins Papers, Box 6, Folder "JCA 6-22, Correspondence–Resignation fr. Justice Department," 1914–16.

54. Adkins to FF, 6/6/1921, Adkins Papers, Box 6, Folder 6–36 MWG, 1920–21.

55. 52 App. D.C. 109, 284 F. Supp. 623–26 (Smyth, C.J., dissenting).

56. FF to Adkins, 9/14/1921, Adkins Papers, Box 6, Folder 6–35 Minimum Wage Board 1921–.

57. Lochner v. New York, 198 U.S. 45 (1905).

58. Muller v. Oregon, 208 U.S. 412 (1908). *See* chapter 2 nn. 55–57.

59. Bunting v. Oregon, 243 U.S. 426 (1917); Stettler v. O'Hara, 243 U.S. 629 (Apr. 9, 1917) (per curiam). *See* chapter 7 nn. 77, 82, chapter 9 nn. 15-22, 31-37.

60. Block v. Hirsh, 256 U.S. 135 (1921).

61. Acheson to FF, 2/1/1923 & 2/2/1923, FFLC, Box 153, Folder "Minimum Wage Decision D.C. 1923."

62. LDB to FF, 1/29/1923, HBHS, at 134 ("Very glad you and Marion consent to the expense fund."); FF to Adkins, 9/14/1921, at 1 (describing conversation with justice and saying he would disqualify himself because of his daughter).

63. FF to MDF, 3/12/1923, at 1–2, FFLC, Box 11, Folder "Marion A. Frankfurter 1923 #72."

64. *Id.* at 3–4.

65. Ernest Knaebel, court reporter, to FF, 4/21/1923, FFLC, Box 154, Folder "Minimum Wage Decision D.C. 1923."

66. Adkins v. Children's Hospital, 261 U.S. 525, 546 (1923).

67. *Id.* at 562, 564 (Taft, C.J., dissenting).

68. WHT to Robert Taft, 4/16/1923, at 3–4, WHTP, Reel 252, Series 3.

69. Adkins v. Children's Hospital, 261 U.S. 525, 570–71 (1923) (Holmes, J., dissenting).

70. OWH to HL, 4/14/1923, 1 HLL at 495. Holmes was referring to the free speech case of Socialist Benjamin Gitlow, which was argued for the first of two times on April 12, 1923. *See* chapter 21 nn. 8–12; Gitlow v. New York, 268 U.S. 652 (1925). On Taft's views, *see* WHT to OWH, 4/4/1923, at 1, OWHP, Reel 71, Page 728 (describing Holmes's opinion as "very strong" but "I feel as if I ought to say something on the subject.").

71. LDB to OWH, Holmes Supreme Court Reports O.T. 1922, OWHP, Reel 71, Page 727.
72. HL to OWH, 4/26/1923, 1 HLL at 496–97.
73. OWH to FF, 4/13/1923, H-FF Corr., 152.
74. FFR, 103.
75. FF to LH, 4/11/1923, at 1, LHP, Box 104-A, Folder 104-10.
76. Meyer v. Nebraska, 262 U.S. 390, 402–3 (1923). *See* OWH to FF, 6/6/1923, H-FF Corr., at 153 ("Many thanks for your encouragement in all my solitude. As to teaching the young, you will find that I said little and that cautiously and was willing to agree with the Court as to the fool law against German alone.").
77. Bartels v. Iowa, 262 U.S. 404, 412 (1923) (Holmes, J., dissenting). Holmes, however, agreed that an Ohio law that singled out German violated due process. *Id.* at 413 (citing Bohning v. Ohio).
78. FF to LH, 6/5/1923, LHP, Box 104A, Folder 104-10 & FFLC, Box 63, Folder "Hand, Learned 1923–24." Some have argued that Frankfurter "seems to agree with" Brandeis, who joined the majority opinion in *Meyer v. Nebraska*. Hirsch, *The Enigma of Felix Frankfurter*, 135. Though Brandeis and Frankfurter discussed the "application of due process as to freedom of speech and foreign language cases" and "agreed" as to a "right of education," it is unclear from the notes how much of the discussion constitutes Brandeis's views or Frankfurter's. *See* Brandeis-Frankfurter Conversations, 7/19/1921(?) [*sic*], at 20. This conversation almost certainly occurred in the summer of 1923 after *Meyer v. Nebraska*. Less than a month later, they also "agreed" that the Fourteenth Amendment should be repealed. *Id.*, 8/10/(1923?), at 24.
79. Moore v. Dempsey, 261 U.S. 86, 89–90 (1923).
80. *Id.* at 91. Brandeis attributed the change in outcome from the *Frank* case to the Court's change in personnel, namely, the departures of Chief Justice Edward White and Justices Mahlon Pitney and William Day. Brandeis-Frankfurter Conversations, 7/3/1923, at 17.

   Scholars have debated whether *Moore v. Dempsey* was a departure from *Frank v. Mangum* or, unlike *Frank*, a clearer example of a mob-dominated criminal trial that violated due process. *Cf.* Paul M. Bator, "Finality in Criminal Law and Federal Habeas Corpus for State Prisoners," 76 Harv. L. Rev. 441, 488–93 (1963) (arguing *Moore* did not discredit *Frank v. Mangum*) *with* Gary Peller, "In Defense of Federal Habeas Corpus Relitigation," 16 Harv. C.R.-C.L. L. Rev. 579, 643–49 (1982) (arguing *Moore* "overturned" *Frank* because due process no longer depended on the state's appellate procedure but on the "violation of ... federal rights"). Peller's reading is the better one—it was consistent with Holmes's, Brandeis's, and McReynolds's readings at the time. *See* Michael J. Klarman, "The Racial Origins of Modern Criminal Procedure," 99 Mich. L. Rev. 48, 58–61 (2000) (describing *Frank* and *Moore* as "technically consistent" but *Moore* was "more solicitous of the defendants' rights" and arguing that *Moore* was not attributable to the Court's changing membership but to the "external context" about lynching); Freedman, *Habeas Corpus*, 49–91.

81. Moore, 261 U.S. at 93 (McReynolds, J., dissenting).

82. *Id.* at 102.

83. Scipio Jones to Walter White, 1/13/1925 tel., NAACP Records, Pt. I, Box D-44, Folder "Cases Supported: Arkansas Riots."

84. The Nation, 3/7/1923, at 256.

85. Outlook, 1/30/1924, at 173.

86. TNR, 3/21/1923, at 84. *See* TNR, 3/14/1923, at 55–57.

87. FF to Florence Kelley, 6/12/1922, at 1, National Consumers' League Records, Reel 83, Page 300 (against child labor amendment).

88. FF to Florence Kelley, 10/19/1923, *id.* at Page 385. *See* FF to Florence Kelley, 10/25/1923, *id.* at Page 374; FF to Florence Kelley, 7/29/1924, *id.* at Page 430 (rejecting 7–2 proposal because: "My own conviction that the remedy lies otherwise–in a repeal of the Due Process Clause (or other restriction to procedural matters) a persistent process of education from Bar and Bench."). *See* TNR, 3/14/1923, at 59–60 (discussing Borah's bill).

89. Stenographer's Report of Minimum Wage Conference Called by National Consumers' League, 4/20/1923, at 4–5, National Consumers' League Records, Reel 82, Pages 691–92.

90. *Id.* at 12, Page 695.

91. *Id.* at 7, Page 693 (referring to Lippmann, *Public Opinion*, 12). The quote is not directly from the book (though the transcript refers to "Lippmann's new book"), and a word is missing from the transcript.

92. RP to Florence Kelley, 7/3/1924, at 1, National Consumers' League Records, Reel 83, Page 449.

93. FF to ERB, 5/19/1923, at 2, FFLC, Box 31, Folder "Buckner Emory R. 1923."

94. Felix Frankfurter, "Twenty Years of Mr. Justice Holmes' Constitutional Opinions," 36 Harv. L. Rev. 909 (1923). For Holmes's reaction, *see* OWH to FF, 7/3/1923, H-FF Corr., at 154.

95. Frankfurter, "Twenty Years of Mr. Justice Holmes' Constitutional Opinions," 915–16, 918.

96. *Id.* at 914.

97. *Id.* at 915.

98. *Id.* at 918.

99. *Id.* at 919.

100. *Id.* at 920.

101. Id. at 932.

102. *Archibald MacLeish: Reflections* 19 (Bernard A. Drabeck and Helen E. Ellis, eds., 1986).

103. "Honor to Justice Holmes," Time, 7/16/1923.

104. TNR, 9/12/1923, at 62.

105. FF to WL, 7/10/1922, at 2, WLP, Reel 10, Box 10, Folder 423.

106. *Id.* See LDB to FF, 5/14/1923, HBHS, at 140 (mentioning he would bring Supreme Court Reports); Brandeis-Frankfurter Conversations, FFLC, Box 224 & Melvin I. Urofsky, "The Brandeis-Frankfurter Conversations," 1985 Sup. Ct. Rev. 299.

107. HCrim, 6/6/1922.

108. NYTrib, 6/23/1922, at 1.

109. ALL to JWM, 3/14/1922, FFLC, Box 81, Folder "Mack, Julian W. 1922."

110. James Beck, "A Reply to Mr. Frankfurter," TNR, 1/18/1922, at 212; Felix Frankfurter, "In Answer to Mr. Beck," TNR, 1/18/1922, at 14; Felix Frankfurter, Letter to the Editor, TNR, 10/19/1921, at 215; James Beck, Letter to the Editor, 10/12/1921, TNR, at 189. See ALL to JWM, 3/20/1922, FFLC, Box 81, Folder "Mack, Julian W. 1922."

111. ALL to JWM, 3/20/1922.

112. ALL to JWM, 6/14/1922, id.

113. Barnard, The Forging of an American Jew, 291–300.

114. FF to ALL, 6/19/1922, FFLC, Box 126, Folder "Anti-Semitism Lowell, Abbot Lawrence 1922."

115. ALL to FF, 6/20/1922, FF to ALL, 6/21/1922, ALL to FF, 6/24/1922, FF to ALL, 6/29/1922, id. On the safe Jews comment, see FF to WL, 6/8/1922, at 1, WLP, Reel 10, Box 10, Folder 423; FF to LH, 6/4/1922, LHP, Box 104A, Folder 104-10; FF to LH, 6/7/1922, id.

116. FF to WL, 5/25/1922, circa 6/22, & 6/8/1922, WLP, Reel 10, Box 10, Folder 423.

117. FF to WL, 5/25/1922, at 2–3, id.

118. WL to FF, 4/21/1922, FFLC, Box 77, Folder "Lippmann, Walter 1920–23."

119. WL to Lawrence J. Henderson, 10/27/1922, PPWL at 150.

120. American Hebrew and Jewish Messenger, 4/14/1922, at 575.

121. WL to Arthur N. Holcolmbe, 6/14/1922, PPWL at 148.

122. WL to Lawrence J. Henderson, 10/27/1922, id. at 149.

123. Committee Report, 4/9/1923, at 2, FFLC, Box 128, Folder "Anti-Semitism."

124. School and Society, 9/30/1922, at 380; The Nation, 10/4/1922, at 322.

125. Committee Report, 4/9/1923 at 3; Memorandum from Wallace Donham to Lowell projecting Jewish student admissions for 1922–23 under the "new plan," 4/9/1923, Lowell Official Papers, UAI.5.1.160.6, Box 1.

126. FF to WL, 1/29/1923, WLP, Reel 10, Box 10, Folder 424.

127. NYT, 4/10/1923, at 1; Heywood Broun, "It Seems to Me," NYW, n.d., Julian Mack Papers, American Jewish Archives, Box 2, Folder "Clippings 2/3."

128. TNR, 7/4/1923, at 147.

129. BH, 6/21/1923, at 2, FFLC, Box 126, Folder "Amherst Controversy 1923–24 & undated."

130. Id.

131. Id.

132. FF to WL, 6/21/1923, FFLC, Box 126, Folder "Amherst Controversy Meiklejohn, Alexander 1923 & undated."

133. FF to LH, 8/24/1923, at 3, LHP, Box 104A, Folder 104-11.

134. NYW, 6/24/1923, Editorial Section, at 1.

135. FF to WL, 6/30/1923, at 1–2, WLP, Reel 10, Box 10, Folder 424. See Dr. Alfred Cohn to FF, 7/9/1923, at 4, FFLC, Box 126, Folder "Amherst Controversy Meiklejohn, Alexander 1923 & undated."

136. TNR, 7/4/1923, at 146–48.
137. FF to My dear New Republicans, 7/6/1923, at 1, FFLC, Box 126, Folder "Amherst Controversy Meiklejohn, Alexander 1923–24 & undated."
138. FF to WL, 7/27/1923, at 1, WLP, Reel 10, Box 10, Folder 424.
139. Alvin Johnson to FF, 7/17/1923, FFLC, Box 126, Folder "Amherst Controversy Meiklejohn, Alexander 1923–24 & undated."
140. TNR, 7/25/1923, at 221.
141. TNR, 9/5/1923, at 49.
142. FF to WL, 7/8/1923 & 7/22/1923 & 7/27/1923 & 8/6/1923, WLP, Reel 10, Box 10, Folder 424.
143. WL to FF, 7/10/1923, WL to FF, n.d. "Friday," FF to WL, 7/10/1923, WL to FF, 8/3/1923, FFLC, Box 78, Folder "Lippmann, Walter undated."
144. FF to WL, 8/6/1923, *id.*
145. *Id.*
146. WL to FF, 11/8/1923, *id.* & WLP, Reel 10, Box 10, Folder 424. *See* WL to FF, 11/23/1923, FFLC, Box 126, Folder "Amherst Controversy 1923–24 & Misc." ("The Meiklejohn business I am not going to take up with you because we shall talk about that someday soon.").
147. TNR, 6/20/1923, at 86.
148. FF to Dartmouth College president Ernest Hopkins, 11/2/1923, at 6–7, FFLC, Box 126, Folder "Amherst Controversy, Hopkins, Ernest 1923."

CHAPTER 20

1. FF to WL, 8/6/1923, WLP, Reel 10, Box 10, Folder 424.
2. OWH to HL, 2/13/1924, 1 HLL at 591.
3. HL to OWH, 2/24/1924, *id.* at 594.
4. LDB to FF, 10/24/1923, HBHS, at 145.
5. CT, 6/3/1924, at 16.
6. NYTrib, 6/3/1924, at 8.
7. *Id.*
8. LDB to FF, 6/3/1924, HBHS, at 170.
9. NYTrib, 6/3/1924, at 8.
10. OWH to LE, 6/4/1924, H-E Letters at 226. *See* OWH to Clara Stevens, 3/29/1926, at 3, OWHP, Reel 27, Page 48, Box 36, Folder 17.
11. NYW, 6/4/1924, at 10.
12. FF to OWH, 6/7/1924, H-FF Corr., at 174.
13. TNR, 4/30/1924, at 247–48.
14. William H. Harbaugh, *Lawyer's Lawyer: The Life of John W. Davis* 191–92 & 572 n. 32 (1973).
15. CCB to FF, 10/23/1924, at 1, FFLC, Box 163, "Presidential Election of 1924 Oct.–Nov."
16. LDB to FF, 4/6/1924, HBHS, at 163.
17. TNR, 4/16/1924, at 193–94.

18. LDB to FF, 4/16/1924, HBHS, at 165.

19. WL to FF, 1/3/1924, WLP, Reel 10, Box 10, Folder 425; FF to WL, 3/24/1924, *id.*; WL to FF, 3/24/1924, *id.*

20. NYW, 4/2/1924, at 10 & in FFLC, Box 163, Folder "Election of 1924 #2."

21. FF to WL, 4/2/1924, WLP, Reel 10, Box 10, Folder 425.

22. LDB to FF, 4/6/1924, HBHS, at 164.

23. FF to WL, 6/19/1924, WLP, Reel 10, Box 10, Folder 425.

24. FF to WL, 6/20/1924, at 1–2, *id.*

25. *Id.* at 1.

26. Robert M. La Follette, Introduction, vi, in Roe, *Our Judicial Oligarchy.*

27. OWH to HL, 7/10/1924, 1 HLL at 631. On Brandeis as running mate, *see* NYT, 7/3/1924, at 1; CSM, 7/9/1924, at 1.

28. Belle Case La Follette & Fola La Follette, 2 *Robert M. La Follette* 1115-16 (1953).

29. LDB to Alfred Brandeis, 7/19/1924, 5 LLDB at 134.

30. WL to FF, 7/17/1924, WLP, Reel 10, Box 10, Folder 425a.

31. FF to WL, 7/18/1924, at 1–2, WLP, Reel 10, Box 10, Reel 425a & FFLC, Box 163, Folder "Election of 1924 July–Sept. #2." *See* FFR at 199 ("The specific program of La Follette meant nothing to me, but the general direction in which he was going meant everything to me.").

32. FF to WL, 7/11/1924, at 1, WLP, Reel 10, Box 10, Folder 425a.

33. NYW, 7/22/1924, at 6.

34. FF to Editor of the World, 7/22/1924, at 4, FFLC, Box 163, Folder "Presidential Election of 1924 #4."

35. FF to WL, 7/25/1924 tel., WLP, Reel 10, Box 10, Folder 425a.

36. FF to WL, 7/28/1924, *id.* & FFLC, Box 163, Folder "Presidential Election of 1924 #4."

37. WL to FF, 7/28/1924, *id.*

38. FF to WL, 7/30/1924, *id.*

39. "Editor's Note, John W. Davis," NYW, 8/3/1924, at 2E.

40. FF to WL, 8/3/1924, FFLC, Box 163, Folder "Presidential Election of 1924 #4" & WLP, Reel 10, Box 10, Folder 425a; FF to Editor of the World, 8/3/1924, FFLC, Box 163, Folder "Election of 1924 July–Sept. #2."

41. WL to FF, 8/5/1924, FFLC, Box 163, Folder "Election of 1924 July–Sept. #2" & WLP, Reel 10, Box 10, Folder 425a.

42. FF to WL, 8/8/1924, at 2–3, *id.*

43. WL to FF, 8/11/1924, *id.*

44. FF to WL, 8/13/1924, *id.*

45. TNR, 7/23/1924, at 225–26 & *in* FFLC, Box 194, Scrapbook "Writings 1913–1924," at 272. *See* HC to DS, ca. 7/1927, at 3–4, DWSEP, Reel 15 (expressing unease about Frankfurter's lead editorial about Davis and that Croly had "toned it down").

46. TNR, 8/6/1924, at 285–87.

47. Gutzon Borglum, "Mountain Sculpture," DuPont Magazine, Summer 1932, at 8–10.

48. Borglum and Casey, *Give the Man Room*, 188.

49. AC, 3/9/1924, at C2.

50. AC, 5/4/1924, at 9.

51. NYHT, 6/30/1924, at 2.

52. NYT, 6/29/1924, at 1; NYT, 6/30/1924, at 1; NYHT, 4/29/1924, at 2.

53. NYT, 7/10/1924, at 1; NYHT, 6/21/1924, at 2.

54. GB to Lester Barlow, 7/3/1924, at 1, GBP, Box 83, Folder "Politics 1924."

55. GB to Robert La Follette, 7/4/1924, *id.*

56. GB to Barlow, 7/3/1924, at 2.

57. GB to James Watson, 7/19/1924, *id.*

58. GB to Burton Wheeler, n.d., at 1, *id.*

59. LAT, 9/13/1924, at A4; Max Bentley, "The Ku Klux Klan in Indiana," McClure's, May 1924, at 22.

60. NYT, 5/14/1924, at 2.

61. GB to D. C. Stephenson, 6/11/1924, at 1–2, GBP, Box 43, Folder "David C. Stephenson."

62. Basil Manley to GB, 7/14/1924 tel. & 7/15/1924, at 1, GBP, Box 83, Folder "Politics 1924"; WDN, 8/15/1924, at 1, in *id.*; NYT, 8/24/1924, at RPA7.

63. GB to Arthur Garfield Hays, 9/21/1924, GBP, Box 83, Folder "Politics 1924."

64. NYHT, 7/22/1924, at 3.

65. GB to Stephenson, 10/6/1923, GBP, Box 43, Folder "David C. Stephenson." *See* GB to Hon. Roy O. Woodruff, 10/8/1924, GBP, Box 83, Folder "Politics 1924"; GB to Oswald Garrison Villard, 9/16/1924 tel., at 1, *id.*

66. GB to Villard, 9/16/1924 tel., at 2, *id. See* Villard to GB, 9/16/1924 tel., *id.*

67. GB to La Follette, 9/29/1924, *id.*

68. GB to Bascomb Slemp, secretary to President Coolidge, 9/21/1924 tel., *id.*

69. GB to CC, 10/6/1924, *id. See* GB to Slemp, 10/9/1924, *id.*

70. GB to Daisy Harriman of Democratic National Committee, 10/8/1924, at 3, *id.*

71. AC, 11/9/1924, at 13.

72. *Id.*

73. GB to Stephenson, 8/27/1924, at 1, GBP, Box 43, Folder "David C. Stephenson."

74. *Id.*

75. TNR, 10/1/1924, at 110.

76. *Id.* at 111.

77. *Id.*

78. *Id.* at 112–13.

79. *Id.* at 113.

80. *Id.*

81. FF to Editor of the Boston Herald, 10/8/1924, FFLC, Box 163, Folder "Presidential Election of 1924 Oct.–Nov. #1"; FF to Editor of the Independent, 10/14/1924, *id.*; FF to Editor of the Boston Herald, 10/21/1924, *id.*; FF to Editor of the Boston Herald, 11/3/1924, *id.*; FF to the Boston Herald, 11/4/1924, *id.*; Frankfurter Statement for Boston Traveler, n.d., *id.* Folder "Presidential

Election of 1924 Miscellany #4"; Frankfurter Statement for Boston American, 10/22/1924, *id. See* Boston Traveler, 11/1/1924, at 6, BH, 10/4/1924; HCrim, 10/14/1924, at 1, 6 in *id.*, Folder "Presidential Election of 1924 Newspaper Clippings #5."

82. *See* Raymond Fosdick to FF, 10/1/1924, FFLC, Box 163, Folder "Presidential Election of 1924 Oct.–Nov. #1"; FF to LH, 10/3/1924, *id.*; FF to George Roberts, 10/3/1924, *id.*; CCB to FF, 10/20/1924, *id.*; Stephen Wise to FF, 9/28/1924, *id.*, Folder "Presidential Election of 1924–Sept"; LDB to FF, 11/7/1924, HBHS, at 180 (re: Mack).

83. TNR, 10/22/1924, at 200–201.

84. TNR, 10/29/1924, at 218.

85. *Id.* at 219.

86. WL to FF, 11/26/1924, at 1, WLP, Reel 10, Box 10, Folder 425a.

87. FF to WL, 10/21/1925, at 2, WLP, *id.*, Folder 426.

88. LDB to FF, 10/20/1925, HBHS, at 217.

89. TNR, 12/2/1925, at 54.

CHAPTER 21

1. HL to OWH, 11/3/1924, 1 HLL at 670.

2. OWH to HL, 11/13/1924, *id.* at 671.

3. HL to OWH, 11/26/1924, *id.* at 678.

4. OWH to HL, 1/11/1925, *id.* at 701; OWH to Ellen A. Curtis, 1/10/1925, OWHP, Reel 26, Page 950, Box 36, Folder 15; BET, 1/7/1925, at 1, 3.

5. OWH to FP, 5/17/1925, 2 H-P Letters at 161. *See* OWH to FF, 1/10/1925, H-FF Corr., at 180; OWH to HL, 5/21/1925, 1 HLL at 742.

6. LDB to FF, 10/6/1924, HBHS, at 175; LDB to FF, 3/17/1925, *id.* at 200; LDB to FF, 6/2/1925, *id.* at 204.

7. FF to OWH, 1/7/1925, H-FF Corr., at 179.

8. Gitlow v. New York, 268 U.S. 652, 658 (1925).

9. TNR, 7/1/1925, at 141.

10. Gilbert v. Minnesota, 254 U.S. 325, 343 (1920) (Brandeis, J., dissenting).

11. Gitlow, 268 U.S. at 666, 669.

12. *Id.* at 672–73 (Holmes, J., dissenting).

13. OWH to FF, 6/14/1925, H-FF Corr., at 184. *See* OWH to HL, 6/14/1925, 1 HLL at 752; OWH to LE, 7/11/1925, H-E Letters at 244; OWH to FP, 6/18/1925, 2 H-P Letters at 163.

14. OWH to FF, 7/2/1925, H-FF Corr., at 186.

15. FF to OWH, 6/30/1925, *id.* at 185.

16. NYW, 6/10/1925, at 10. The Powell-Lippmann relationship did not last long; Lippmann ended the arrangement. WL to Thomas Reed Powell, 10/14/1926 & Thomas Reed Powell to WL, 10/15/1926, TRPP, Box A, Folder "A1b Correspondence to 1929: F–L."

17. TNR, 7/1/1925, at 142.
18. *Id.*; NYT, 12/12/1925, at 1.
19. TNR, 7/1/1925, at 142.
20. Felix Frankfurter and James M. Landis, "The Compact Clause of the Constitution–A Study of Interstate Adjustments," 34 Yale L.J. 685 (1925).
21. Felix Frankfurter and James M. Landis, "The Business of the Supreme Court of the United States–A Study in the Federal Judicial System," 38 Harv. L. Rev. 1005 (1925).
22. TNR, 6/17/1925, at 85.
23. Pierce v. Society of Sisters, 268 U.S. 510, 534–35 (1925).
24. TNR, 6/17/1925, at 86.
25. *Id.*
26. *Id.* at 87.
27. *Id.*
28. Harold J. Laski, *A Grammar of Politics* (1925).
29. OWH to FF, 7/30/1925, H-FF Corr., at 188.
30. HL to OWH, 7/28/1925, 1 HLL at 770.
31. OWH to HL, 8/7/1925, *id.* at 772.
32. OWH to HL, 12/17/1925, 1 HLL at 807.
33. OWH to FF, 12/17/1925, H-FF Corr., at 196.
34. OWH to NG 12/19/1925 at 2, OWHP, Reel 24, Page 88, Box 33, Folder 7. *See* OWH to Elizabeth Shepley Sergeant, 1/12/1926, ESSP, Yale, Box 3, Folder 80 (discussing Robert Frost).
35. FF to ESS, 6/7/1926, at 1, ESSP, Yale, Box 2, Folder 52.
36. Thomas G. Corcoran, *Rendezvous with Democracy*, Holmes D/2-1–Holmes D/2-40, TGCP, Box 586; Corcoran Interview, 8/18/1979, Monagan Papers, Box 1, Folder 1–3; Corcoran Interview in Louchheim, *The Making of the New Deal*, 21–25.
37. OWH to FF, 1/27/1926, H-FF Corr., at 198.
38. TNR, 3/17/1926, at 88.
39. NYW, 3/8/1926, at 10. *See* FF to WL, 3/8/1926, WLP, Reel 10, Box 10, Folder 427; WL to OWH, 3/10/1926, Edward J. Holmes Collection of OWHP, Box 1, Folder 6.
40. LH to FF, 3/9/1926, LHP, Box 104B, Folder 104-12. *See* FF to LH, 3/8/1926 & 3/10/1926, *id.*; LH to FF, 3/17/1926, *id.*, Folder 104-13.
41. TNR, 12/8/1926, at 63. *See* LH to ESS, 9/30/1926, ESSP, Yale, Box 3, Folder 76.
42. NYW, 3/8/1926, at 10.
43. NYT, 3/7/1926, at SM1.
44. NYT, 3/7/1926, at E8.
45. Time, 3/15/1926.
46. *See* American Newspaper Annual and Directory 1927, at 834 (N. W. Ayer & Son) (listing circulation for 1926 at 103,391); Alan Brinkley, *The Publisher* 110, 122–23 (2010); Robert T. Elson, 1 *Time Inc.* 105 (1968).

47. Time, 3/15/1926.
48. Weaver v. Palmer Bros. Co., 270 U.S. 402, 416 (1926) (Holmes, J., dissenting).
49. Time, 3/15/1926.
50. *Id.*

CHAPTER 22

1. Shaff and Shaff, *Six Wars at a Time*, 215.
2. Borglum Diary, 2/25/1925, GBP, Box 163, Folder "Diary 1925"; Casey and Borglum, *Give the Man Room*, 212.
3. AC, 2/26/1925, at 2; AJ, 2/26/1925, at 1.
4. Borglum Diary, 2/25/1925; Casey and Borglum, *Give the Man Room*, 212.
5. Casey and Borglum, *Give the Man Room*, 212; Johnson, *The Undefeated*, 76–77; MB to Lester Barlow 3/3/1925 tel., GBP, Box 8, Folder "Lester Barlow."
6. AJ, 4/26/1925, at 16.
7. *Id.* at 1; Shaff and Shaff, *Six Wars at a Time*, 215.
8. Borglum Diary, 2/25/1925.
9. AC, 2/22/1925, at 1.
10. MB note, 1946, GBP, Box 32, Folder "Eugene Meyer Jr."
11. HarCour, 3/7/1925, at 2; GB to Gerald Johnson, 7/7/1925, at 11, GBP, Box 119, "Works SM 1925."
12. HarCour, 10/29/1925, at 11.
13. AC, 2/22/1925, at 6.
14. *Id.*
15. *Id.*
16. AC, 2/23/1925, at 2; AC, 2/24/1925, at 2.
17. NYT, 3/2/1925, at 2 (claiming he had backed Randolph's re-election as association president in April 1924 so as not to "hurt the McAdoo cause"); AC, 3/8/1925, at 7 (same).
18. NYHT, 2/27/1925, at 6; AC, 2/28/1925, at 12. *See* NYT, 2/23/1925, at 3.
19. NYT, 3/4/1924, at 8.
20. NYAN, 3/11/1925, at 16.
21. GB to NYW editor, 4/30/1925, GPB, Box 118, Folder "Works SM 1925"; NYW, 4/20/1925, at 14, *id.*
22. NYT, 3/4/1925, at 8.
23. GB to CC, 1/21/1925, at 2, GBP, Box 118, Folder "Works SM 1925."
24. E. T. Clark, president's acting personal secretary, to GB, 1/25/1925, *id. See* C. B. Slemp to GB, 1/26/1925, *id.*
25. GB to CC, 2/5/1925, at 1, *id.*
26. GB to Andrew Mellon, 3/4/1925, *id.*
27. Mellon to GB, 3/6/1925, *id.*
28. RNO, 2/28/1925, at 1; NYT, 2/28/1925, at 15; NYT, 3/5/1925, at 8.
29. AC, 3/1/1925, at 1.

30. AC, 3/2/1925, at 1.
31. Court Order, 3/7/1925, Guilford County Superior Court, GBP, Box 118, Folder "Works SM 1925"; AC, 3/8/1925, at 1.
32. GB to Gerald Johnson, 7/7/1925, at 13. *See* GB to Anna Barlow, 5/13/1925, at 1, GBP, Box 119, Folder "Works SM 1925."
33. NYT, 3/18/1925, at 27.
34. GB to Anna Barlow, 5/13/1925, at 1. *See* GB to Frank Borglum, 5/13/1925, at 1, GBP, Box 119, Folder "Works SM 1925."
35. "Borglum, as Seen by Fellow Artists," Literary Digest, 3/21/1925, at 26–28; NYT, 3/19/1925, at 6; AC, 3/17/1925, at 12; AC, 3/13/1925, at 1.
36. AC, 3/11/1925 at 20.
37. AC, 4/23/1925, at 1.
38. AC, 4/25/1925, at 4, 5.
39. *Id.* at 4.
40. GB to W. W. Fuller, n.d. tel., GBP, Box 119, Folder "Works SM 1925."
41. AC, 3/19/1925, at 1.
42. RNO, 7/19/1925, editorial section, at 1; AC, 7/19/1925, at 1; NYT, 7/20/1925, at 17; NYT, 7/21/1925, at 12.
43. GB to MB, 6/3/1925 tel., GBP, Box 119, Folder "Works SM 1925."
44. Doane Robinson, "Inception and Development of the Rushmore Idea," Black Hills Engineer, 11/1930, at 335.
45. DR letter to the editor, n.d. circa 1924, GBP, Box 160, Folder "Doane Robinson Papers (Photostat) 1925."
46. DR to Loredo Taft, 12/28/1923, *id.*
47. DR to Taft, 1/26/1924, *id.*
48. DR to GB, 8/29/1924, Doane Robinson Papers, Mt. Rushmore Correspondence 1923–25, Folder #149.
49. DR, "Inception and Development of the Rushmore Idea," at 335.
50. Olean (SD) Evening Times, 9/2/1924, at 1.
51. DR, "Inception and Development of the Rushmore Idea," at 336.
52. DR to PN, 9/28/1924, GBP, Box 160, Folder "Doane Robinson Papers (Photostat) 1925."
53. *Id.*
54. DR, "Inception and Development of the Rushmore Idea," at 337–38.
55. *Id.* at 336.
56. DR to PN, 9/28/1924.
57. GB to DR, 11/21/1924 tel. & DR to GB, 11/22/1924, GBP, Box 160, Folder "Doane Robinson Papers (Photostat) 1925"; GB to DR, 1/26/1925, at 2, *id.* (thought Norbeck suggested TR).
58. DR to PN, 11/26/1924, *id.* & GBP, Box 159, Folder "Peter Norbeck Papers (photostat) 1924 thru 1926."
59. PN to DR, 1/20/1925, at 1, *id.*, Box 160, Folder "Doane Robinson Papers (Photostat) 1925."

60. *Id.* at 2.
61. AC, 3/15/1925, at 6.
62. DR to GB, 5/5/1925 & GB to DR, 5/11/1925 & GB to DR, 5/27/1925, GBP, Box 160, Folder "Doane Robinson Papers (Photostat) 1925."
63. PN to DR, 3/2/1925, GBP, Box 159, Folder "Peter Norbeck Papers (photostat) 1924 thru 1926"; DR to PN, 3/6/1925, *id.*
64. Greensboro Daily News, 3/8/1925, at 1, 12; NYT, 3/8/1925, at 21; NYT, 3/9/1925, at 3; NYT, 3/15/1925, at XX13.
65. GB to DR, 5/11/1925, at 2, GBP, Box 160, Folder "Doane Robinson Papers (Photostat) 1925."
66. GB to DR, 10/22/1924, *id.*; GB to DR, 12/2/1924, *id.*
67. Borglum Diary, 8/12–14/1925, GBP, Box 163, Folder "Diary 1925."
68. Borglum Diary, 8/13–14/1925, *id.*
69. GB to PN, 8/28/1925, at 2, GBP, Box 159, Folder "Peter Norbeck Papers (photostat) 1924 thru 1926." *See* PN to DR, 8/31/1925, at 2, *id.*
70. Charles Rushmore to DR, 12/14/1925, available at http://www.nps.gov/moru/learn/historyculture/charles-rushmore-letter-to-doane-robinson.htm.
71. Borglum Diary, 8/13–14/1925.
72. DR to GB, 9/12/1925 tel., GBP, Box 150, Folder "Borglum-Robinson Corr. 1925–27."
73. GB to DR, 9/8/1925 tel., GBP, Box 160, Folder "Doane Robinson Papers (Photostat) 1925."
74. GB to DR, 9/14/1925 tel. & 9/15/1925 tel., GBP, Box 150, Folder "Borglum-Robinson Corr. 1925–27"; Evening Republican (Mitchell, SD), 9/15/1925, at 1.
75. RCJ, 10/1/1925, at 1; DR, "Inception and Development of the Rushmore Idea," at 338, 340–41; CSM, 10/27/1925, at 9.
76. RCJ, 10/2/1925, at 1.
77. NYT, 3/15/1925, at XX13.
78. OWH to FP, 4/30/1926, 2 H-P Letters at 181.
79. GB to DR, 10/25/1924, at 2, GBP, Box 160, Folder "Doane Robinson Papers (Photostat) 1925" ("I can truthfully say that were it not for Stone Mountain, and overcoming the almost insurmountable engineering difficulties there, a project such as I have outlined for you could not be launched.").

CHAPTER 23

1. Elizabeth Glendower Evans, "Mr. Justice Brandeis," The Survey, 11/1/1931, at 138.
2. EGE to OWH, 1/28/1932, FFLC, Box 225, Folder "Holmes, Oliver Wendell Correspondence with Mrs. Glendower Evans"; OWH to EGE, 2/2/1932, *id.*
3. FFR, 210.
4. "A Fight for the Underdog, Elizabeth Glendower Evans," Springfield Sunday Union and Republican, 5/1/1932 & 5/8/1932, in FFHLS, Pt. III, Reel 33, Pages 354–57.
5. "Personalia," The Chautauquan, 2/28/1914, at 26.

6. 1914 photo, Library of Congress, available at http://hdl.loc.gov/loc.mss/mnwp.150006.
7. 1 SV Trial Tr. at 75, 77.
8. 2 SV Trial Tr. at 1726, 1731–32 (Vanzetti); *id.* at 1846, 1866, 1912 (Sacco).
9. Felix Frankfurter, *The Case of Sacco and Vanzetti* 5–6 (1927); TNR, 6/9/1926, at 76.
10. G. Louis Joughin and Edmund M. Morgan, *The Legacy of Sacco and Vanzetti* 48–49 (1948).
11. "A Fight for the Underdog, Elizabeth Glendower Evans," Springfield Sunday Union and Republican, 5/8/1932; Vanzetti to EGE, 7/22/1921, in Nicola Sacco and Bartolomeo Vanzetti, *The Letters of Sacco and Vanzetti* 81 (Marion Denman Frankfurter and Gardner Jackson, eds., 1928).
12. FFR, 210.
13. *Id.* Some have questioned Frankfurter's assertion that he had not paid attention to the initial trial. *See* Moshik Temkin, *The Sacco-Vanzetti Affair* 234–35 n. 50 (2009); Robert Montgomery, "Felix Frankfurter and President Lowell in the Sacco-Vanzetti Case," at 11–17, Sacco-Vanzetti/Montgomery Papers, Box 8, Folder M7(15) (observing that Frankfurter was in the country at the time of the murders, the New England Civil Liberties Committee had used his name to raise money for the legal defense fund as early as 1921, and Frankfurter had misdated the Proctor motion as 1925 when it was filed in 1923). Frankfurter may have made some minor factual errors in his 1960 reminiscences, but at the time he insisted that he had not paid attention to the trial and did not become interested in the case until the Proctor motion in 1923. *See* FF to Shattuck, 4/27/1927, WLP, Reel 10, Box 10, Folder 428b.
14. *See* Elizabeth Gurley Flynn, *Rebel Girl* 330 (rev. ed. 1973) (recalling that Frankfurter had recommended Thompson to be the pair's lawyer on appeal).
15. 1 SV Trial Tr. at 896.
16. FFR, 212–13.
17. 4 SV Trial Tr. at 4269; Commonwealth v. Sacco, 255 Mass. 369 (May 12, 1927).
18. FF to HL, 9/23/1926, at 1, FFLC, Box 74, Folder "H Laski 1925–26."
19. FF to LH, 12/16/1925, LHP, Box 104B, Folder 104-12 (introducing Gates to Hand and explaining that Gates came to Harvard Law School thanks to early constitutional historian Max Farrand's control of the Commonwealth Fund).
20. Sylvester Gates to W. G. Gates, 1/5/1927, Gates Family Papers (on file with author) (declining Holmes's advice on advice of father); Sylvester Gates to W. G. Gates, 12/25/1926, at 2-3, *id.* (weighing offer with father); Corcoran to FF, n.d., at 2, JGPC/OWHP, Box 58, Folder 27 ("Has Gates lost his nerve over the difficulties of the job again? If he has I'd like to talk to or write him. The old fellow would like Gates–and I do so want him to get someone he'll like.").
21. *See* Sylvester Gates to W. G. Gates, 5/30/1926, at 3, Gates Family Papers (on file with author) (indicating he had just finished and sent off the article); FF to WL, 6/11/1926, WLP, Reel 10, Box 10, Folder 427a (confiding his and Gates's authorship).

22. FF to WL, 6/8/1926, WLP, Reel 10, Box 10, Folder 427a.

23. TNR, 6/9/1926, at 75–76.

24. *Id.* at 76.

25. *Id.* at 76–77.

26. FF to WL, 6/13/1926, WLP, Reel 10, Box 10, Folder 427a.

27. WL to FF, 6/14/1926, *id.*

28. 5 SV Trial Tr. at insert before 4360.

29. *Id.* at 4632.

30. *Id.* at 4641.

31. Ehrmann, in *Felix Frankfurter: A Tribute*, 101.

32. *Id.* at 100.

33. *Id.* at 106–7.

34. Herbert B. Ehrmann, *The Untried Case* (1933).

35. NYW, 9/20/1926, at 6.

36. FF to WL, 9/20/1926, WLP, Reel 10, Box 10, Folder 427a.

37. 5 SV Trial Tr., Defendant's Amended Bill of Exceptions for a Motion for a New Trial, 10/28/1926, at 4362.

38. FF to WL, 9/22/1926, WLP, Reel 10, Box 10, Folder 427a.

39. WL to FF, 9/23/1926, *id.*

40. FF to WL, 10/25/1926 tel., *id.*, Folder 427b.

41. WL to FF, 10/25/1926 tel., *id.*

42. BH, 10/26/1926, reprinted in NYW, 5/3/1927, at 14.

43. LDB to FF, 10/29/1926, HBHS, at 258.

44. FF to MD, 11/18/1926, at 1, FFLC, Box 14, Folder "Marion A. Denman 1926 #114."

45. FF to MD, 11/17/1926, at 2, *id.*

46. FFR, 214.

47. Memorandum, 10/25/1924 & Bankruptcy Petition, 10/1924, DWSEP, Reel 16.

48. Levy, *Herbert Croly of* The New Republic, 272, 288. *But see* Newspaper Annual and Directory, 1920, at 677 (N. W. Ayer & Son) (listing circulation at 37,000 for previous year); Forcey, *The Crossroads of Liberalism*, 190–91 (claiming the magazine had reached a high of 43,000 in 1920).

49. Bliven COH at 28.

50. Bruce Bliven, *Five Million Words Later* 176–77 (1970). *See* Robert Morss Lovett, *All Our Years* 192 (1948) ("Croly withdrew more and more into the religion of liberalism."); Eric F. Goldman, *Rendezvous with Destiny* 288 (1952) (describing Croly during the 1920s as declaring progressivism finished, focusing on "the redemption of the individual," and bringing a guru to *New Republic* meetings who believed that "what the world needed was the self-discipline of Yoga"); Levy, *Herbert Croly of* The New Republic, 263–300 (describing cost to magazine of breaking with Wilson over the Treaty of Versailles, Croly's religious mysticism, and the editor's "years of despair").

51. HC to R. G. Kincaid, 12/51924, DWSEP, Reel 16; HC to Dorothy Whitney Straight, 11/18/1924, *id.*, Reel 15.

52. FFR, 214.

53. *Id. See* FF to ES, n.d., ESP, Carton 4, Folder "Frankfurter, Felix nd–1927" ("You may or may not remember Mrs. King from House of Truth days. . . ."); FF to ES, 12/8/1915 (handwritten postscript), *id.* ("Win is getting on—I think decidedly. He's gained 13 pounds!"). Denison was class of 1896 at Harvard College; Sedgwick was class of 1894.

54. FFR, 214. *See* Ellery Sedgwick, *The Happy Profession* 156 (1946) (on buying the *Atlantic Monthly* for $50,000 and taking on its $5,000 deficit).

55. ES to McReynolds, 3/23/1927, at 1, ESP, Carton 4, Folder "Frankfurter, Felix nd–1927."

56. FFR, 214.

57. American Newspaper Annual and Directory (N. W. Ayer & Son), 1928, at 466 (132,348 for *Atlantic Monthly*) & 766 (25,000 for *New Republic*).

58. Bliven, *Five Million Words Later,* 183 ("When I came to *The New Republic* in 1923, I had already been writing about the case for three years and I—and many others—went on doing everything we could think of to help these two men, until the end."). Bliven had been a contributor to the liberal *New York Globe.* Bliven COH at 24; Lovett, *All Our Years,* 184 (indicating that he had followed the case through Frankfurter); Levy, *Herbert Croly of* The New Republic, 285–87 (discussing the magazine's extensive coverage of the case).

59. Edmund Wilson to Arthur Schlesinger Jr., 1964, in Edmund Wilson, *Letters on Literature and Politics 1912–1972,* at 197 (1977) ("We had been handling this without Herbert's supervision, and—though goodness knows we had hardly been incendiary—he thought that we had gone much too far."); HC to FF, 8/24/1927, at 1, FFHLS, Pt. III, Reel 24, Page 768 (describing his return from Honolulu, writing a leader that was "not very good," but that nonetheless replaced Lovett's proposed leader, which "would have aroused the feelings of a great many of our readers, but it was out of key with the way in which we have treated the matter throughout the whole controversy.").

60. FFR, 215.

61. *See* Robert H. Montgomery, *Sacco-Vanzetti: The Murder and the Myth* 335 (1960) (describing "significant differences" between the article and the book, including two critical pieces of evidence left out of the article).

62. ES to FF, 1/18/1927 (FF's handwritten postscript), FFHLS, Pt. III, Reel 24, Page 558; FF to ES, 8/15/1927, *id.*, at Page 602.

63. FF to Shattuck, 4/27/1927, at 2.

64. *See* chapter 9 nn. 23-27 (on allegations of racism and anti-Semitism); chapter 19 n. 34 (on his clashes with John Hessin Clarke).

65. Brandeis-Frankfurter Conversations, July 3, 1923, at 18, FFLC, Box 224, Folder "Conversations between L.D.B. and F.F." *See id.* at 9 ("McR is the Court's

problem. ... Holmes now explains him as a 'savage' with all the irrational impulses of a savage. The Chief complained that McR is everyday becoming more
'meticulous' as to others though his own opinions are simply dreadful–he is
lazy, stays away from the Court when he doesn't feel like coming (more re-
arguments were ordered because McR was absent and didn't listen to arguments and called for a re-argument)."); OWH to HL, 10/19/1923, 1 HLL at
554–55 ("McReynolds has improved wonderfully and I think is a useful and
quite suggestive man. He has some special knowledge and experience and his
doubts and difficulties are always worth considering. He controls his impulses
much more than at first and now that Clarke has gone, with whom he couldn't
get along (queer, for they both are kindly men). ....").

66. *See* chapter 9 nn. 28–30.
67. McReynolds to ES, circa 3/23/1927, at 1, ESP, Carton 4, Folder "Frankfurter, Felix nd–1927."
68. Sedgwick to McReynolds, 3/23/1927, at 2, *id.*
69. McReynolds to ES, 3/26/1927, at 1–2, ESP, Carton 7, Folder "McReynolds, James Clark."
70. Felix Frankfurter, "Prefatory Note," *The Case of Sacco Vanzetti.*
71. NYW, 3/5/1927, at 10.
72. FF to WL, 3/17/1927, WLP, Reel 10, Box 10, Folder 428a; WL to FF, 3/18/1927, *id.*
73. "Radicals: Committee," Time, 6/13/1927, at 11.
74. WGT to FF, 2/10/1927, at 1–2, FFHLS, Pt. III, Reel 24, at 564–65. *See* WGT to FF, 12/21/1927, at 1, *id.*, Reel 25, at 854.
75. FF, Memorandum, 2/12/1927, at 1–2, FFHLS, Pt. III, Reel 24, Pages 566–67. *See* WGT to FF, 12/21/*and* 1927, at 1.
76. 5 SV Trial Tr. at 4880; Commonwealth v. Sacco, 259 Mass. 128, 139–41 (Apr. 5, 1927).
77. NYW, 4/10/1927, at 1–2; BH, 4/10/1927, at 1; BET, 4/9/1927, at 1, 15.
78. 5 SV Trial Tr. at 4896.
79. *Id.* at 4896–903.
80. *Id.* at 4904.
81. *Id.* at 4904–5.
82. *Id.* at 4905.
83. BH, 4/10/1927, at 1.
84. NYW, 4/10/1927, at 2.
85. LDB to FF, 4/6/1927, HBHS, at 281. *See* LDB to FF, 4/9/1927, *id.* at 283.
86. Charles Merz (Lippmann's deputy editorial page editor) to FF, 4/6/1927 tel., WLP, Reel 10, Box 10, Folder 428a; FF editorial, 4/10/1927 tel., unpublished, *id.*
87. WGT to Stoughton Bell, 4/11/1927, RPP, Reel 74, Page 492; FF to Bell, 4/9/1927, *id.*, Page 491; Bell to FF, 4/8/1927, *id.*, Page 490.
88. FF to RP, 4/6/1927, RPP, Pt. I, Series II, Reel 74, Page 487.
89. Jack Maguire to RP, 6/11/1927, *id.*, Page 499. *See* FF to Maguire, 6/12/1927, at 1, *id.*, Page 500 ("It has just as much, and no more, relation to truth as would have a charge that Moorfield Storey killed Charles Summer.").

90. BET, 4/27/1927, at 2. *See* LDB to FF, 5/2/1927, HBHS, at 289 ("It was natural that the Transcript should resurrect the Roosevelt letter. I had been thinking of the Mooney case & wondering whether your S.V. action might not lead some able, courageous man who cares, to write up the terrible Mooney story."); FF to Frank Buxton, 8/4/1929 (handwritten reply), FFLC, Box 38, Folder "Buxton, Frank 1926–29" ("That T.R. reprint in the Herald [in 1919] has been the source of more ill-feeling against me than anything else that's ever been done in regard to me.").

91. BET, 4/29/1927, at 13. *See* LDB to FF, 5/6/1927, HBHS, at 290 ("If the Transcript's public can still 'sit & read' your answer to the Colonel should add to their education."); chapter 10 n. 93.

92. FF to LDB, 4/22/[1927], at 1, FFLC, Box 29, Folder "Brandeis, Louis Und. #98."

93. FF to RP, 8/25/1927, at 1–2, RPP, Reel 74, Pages 509–10.

94. Ehrmann, in *Felix Frankfurter: A Tribute*, 99 (recalling "a warm friendship between them which lasted until Felix's famous review of the Sacco-Vanzetti case was published in the *Atlantic Monthly*"). *See* FF to LH, 4/24/1925, LHP, at 1–2, Box 104B, Folder 104-12 ("Let me let you in on a dread secret–and don't you dare breathe it to a soul! The trouble with that gent is not that he is 'seeking the Empyrean.' It's a very different trouble: he has one of the most enslaving 'inferiority complexes' of anyone I know intimately. I know you'd never suspect it–but *that's* the explanation of many of the characteristics in him which you have noticed. And now–mum's the word.").

95. RP to Richard Child, 1/3/1927, RPP, Reel 35, Page 397; RP to WL, 1/26/1927, at 1–2, *id.*, Pages 398–99 (refusing to allow Lippmann to print Pound's letter to Child in the New York *World*); RP to Spencer Montgomery, 5/12/1927, FFHLS, Pt. III, Reel 24, Page 663; Hull, *Roscoe Pound and Karl Llewellyn*, 158–59.

96. Wigmore, "Abrams *v.* United States," 539; chapter 16 n. 230.

97. Jeremy K. Kessler, "The Administrative Origins of Modern Civil Liberties Law," 114 Colum. Law Review 1083, 1108–11, 1126–27 (2014).

98. Francis S. Philbrick to FF, 5/3/1927, FFHLS, Pt. III, Reel 25, Page 661 ("Somebody–probably Costigan–once quoted to me Wigmore's characterization of you as 'the most dangerous person in the U.S.' A very great compliment, since you always stand for liberalism and decency.").

99. "Memorandum as to Genesis of Wigmore Article on Sacco-Vanzetti Case," n.d., FFHLS, Pt. III, Reel 24, Page 645. *See* Judge Thayer to Wigmore, n.d. & Judge Thayer to Wigmore, 12/8/1927, JHWP, Box 47, Folder 26 (thanking Wigmore).

100. NYT, 4/11/1927, at 8.

101. Wigmore to Chief, Bureau of Investigation, 3/31/1927, JHWP, Box 47, Folder 26.

102. Grinnell to Wigmore, 4/16/1927 tel., *id. See* "Memorandum as to Genesis of Wigmore Article on Sacco-Vanzetti Case," n.d.

103. Boston Evening Transcript editor Henry Claus to Wigmore, 4/20/1927 tel., JHWP, Box 47, Folder 26.
104. BET, 4/25/1927, at 1, 12.
105. *Id.* at 1; FFR, 215–16.
106. FFR, at 216. Frankfurter heard this from William G. Thompson. Sedgwick, however, defended the *Atlantic Monthly* in print. BET, 4/26/1927, Pt. 2, at 3.
107. FF to JWM, 10/6/1927, at 1, FFHLS, Pt. III, Reel 34, Page 927.
108. BH, 4/26/1927, at 1.
109. BET, 5/10/1927, at 15.
110. BET, 5/11/1927, Pt. 2, at 3
111. BET, 5/23/1927, in FFLC, Box 246, Folder "S-V Clippings Vol. III, May 1927."
112. ERB to FF, 5/16/1927, FFLC, Box 31, Folder "Buckner, Emory R. 1927."
113. H. L. Mencken to FF, 6/21/1927, FFHLS, Pt. III, Reel 33, Page 629.
114. NYW, 5/1/1927, at 1E; NYW, 5/19/1927, at 13.
115. NH, 5/3/1927, Norman Hapgood's Weekly Letter, at 2, in FFLC, Box 246, Folder "S-V Clippings Vol. III, May 1927."
116. Hutchins to FF, 4/29/1927, FFHLS, Pt. III, Reel 25, Page 430.
117. Corcoran to FF, 4/28/1927, *id.*, Reel 24, Page 837.
118. The Nation, 5/11/1927 in FFLC, Box 246, Folder "S-V Clippings Vol. III, May 1927."
119. FF to Crowder, 12/19/1927, at 2, FFLC, Box 50, Folder "Crowder, Enoch H. 1920–27 & undated." *See* Earl Dean Howard to FF, 5/6/1927, FFHLS, Pt. III, Reel 25, Page 415 ("He does not seem to be able to recover from his war experiences. He has made a rather spectacal [*sic*] of himself several times in his attitude toward questions involving what he conceives to be loyalty to the flag."). For a pro-Wigmore view, *see* Montgomery, *Sacco-Vanzetti*, 337–41.
120. This Holmes quotation was compiled by Tom Corcoran, his secretary during the 1926 Term. TGCP, Box 144. *See* n. 117.
121. FFR, 217. *See* Michael Parrish notes on Frankfurter's 1927 Diary, 11/22/1927 (noting lunch with Hapgood in which Hapgood discussed "in detail" his two-and-a-half-hour interview with Lowell and that "Hapgood took notes of this interview which I shall try to incorporate in this diary") (on file with author). The 1927 diary has been stolen. *See* ALL to WHT, 11/1/1927, WHTP, Series 3, Reel 296 ("We certainly started with no prejudice against Sacco and Vanzetti. Indeed, all I had read was Frankfurter's article in the Atlantic, which, though a partisan argument, I supposed stated the facts correctly; and that naturally left the impression that something was wrong with the trial; but on reading all the facts, none of us had the least question about the men's guilt. The proof seemed to be conclusive. On the other hand, there was gross misstatement in the propaganda in their favor, and, as you say, the judge by his folly gave them an opportunity to attack him; and Wigmore's ridiculous article looked as if there was nothing serious to be said on the side of the courts."), reprinted in Yeomans, *Abbott Lawrence Lowell*, at 494–95.

122. Thompson and Ehrmann to Governor Fuller, 5/4/1927, 5 SV Trial Tr. at 4907.
123. Vanzetti to Governor Fuller, 5/3/1927, *id.* at 4910–23.
124. *Id.* at 4924, 4926, 4928. *See* Judge Charles Wyzanski's handwritten notes inside *Commonwealth vs. Sacco and Vanzetti* (Robert P. Weeks, ed., 1958), Georgetown University Law Center Library (describing Thayer as not "a discreet or unprejudiced judge"); Wyzanski to Francis Russell, 3/31/1986, Francis Russell Papers, Folder "1986 March 1–31" (Wyzanski's father "found Thayer the most indiscreet judge he had ever known well").
125. 5 SV Trial Tr. at 5065, 5418–19; NYW, 5/8/1927, at 2.
126. NYW, 4/18/1927, at 10.
127. Ralph Pulitzer to Bruce Bliven, 4/29/1927, FFHLS, Pt. III, Reel 34, Page 158 (declining Bliven's request to write Governor Fuller and explaining: "I fear that should I write personally I would not be able to contain myself and to use the tone of moderation and understatement which has been possible in our editorials, and yet I feel strongly that such a tone of moderation is the only one that will have the slightest chance of winning over a man who is in doubt but I fear leans definitely towards the opposite side.").
128. WL to FF, 4/18/1927, WLP, Reel 10, Box 10, Folder 428b ("I am just back and all fit again. What is the real situation about Sacco and Vanzetti now? What do you understand to be the Governor's state of mind and what do you think is the effect on his mind and on public opinion in Massachusetts of the radical demonstrations?").
129. NYW, 4/19/1927, at 15.
130. WL to FF, 5/3/1927, WLP, Reel 10, Box 10, Folder 428b.
131. FF to WL, 5/1/1927, *id.*
132. NYW, 5/6/1927, at 14.
133. NYW, 5/12/1927, at 12.
134. *Id.*; NYT, 5/10/1927, at 9; Hull, *Roscoe Pound and Karl Llewellyn*, 159–60.
135. NYW, 5/14/1927, at 12; Hull, *Roscoe Pound and Karl Llewellyn*, 160–61 (observing that Pound submitted his own petition).
136. FF to WL, 5/9/1927, at 1, WLP, Reel 10, Box 10, Folder 428b.
137. WL to FF, 5/10/1927, *id.*
138. NYHT, 5/6/1927, in FFLC, Box 246, Folder "S-V Clippings Vol. III, May 1927." *See* NYHT, 5/12/1927, at 24 (referring to Frankfurter's "fantastic charge" and "silly vituperation" about Thayer's memorandum and Wigmore's "demolition" of Frankfurter).
139. FF to Markel, 6/9/1927, WLP, Reel 10, Box 10, Folder 428b. *See* Markel to FF, 6/8/1927, *id.*; Memorandum by Frankfurter, n.d., *id.* For Wells's take, *see* NYT, 10/16/1927, at SM3.
140. NYW, 5/6/1927, at 14, in FFLC, Box 246, Folder "S-V Clippings Vol. III, May 1927."
141. NYW, 5/16/1927, at 12, in *id.*
142. FF to WL, 7/12/1927, at 5, WLP, Reel 10, Box 10, Folder 428b. *See* FF to ES, 7/12/1927, ESP, Carton 4, Folder "Frankfurter, Felix n.d.–1927."

143. FF to WL, 7/12/1927, at 4–5.

144. BET, 6/2/1927, in FFLC, Box 246, Folder "S-V Clippings Vol. IV, June–July 1927."

145. FF to WL, 7/12/1927, at 5, WLP, Reel 10, Box 10, Folder 428b.

146. *Id.* at 6.

147. NYW, 7/20/1927, in FFLC, Box 246, Folder "S-V Clippings Vol. IV, June–July 1927."

148. NYW, 7/22/1927, at 12 & in *id.*

149. WL to FF, 7/21/1927, WLP, Reel 10, Box 10, Folder 428b. Less than a month later, anarchists bombed a juror's home. NYT, 8/17/1927, at 1. Five years later, they bombed and destroyed Judge Thayer's Worcester home, and falling debris injured his wife and housekeeper. NYT, 9/28/1932, at 1.

150. FF to WL, 7/25/1927, at 2, *id.*

151. *Id.* at 1 (emphasis in original).

152. FF to WL, 7/26/1927, at 1, *id.*

153. WL to FF, 7/27/1927, *id.*

154. BH, 8/3/1927, at 24, in FFLC, Box 247, Folder "Clippings V S-V Aug. 1–5, 1927."

155. BH, 8/4/1927 & BET, 8/4/1927, in *id.*

156. FF to WL, 8/4/1927 tel., 8 a.m., WLP, Reel 10, Box 10, Folder 428b.

157. WL to FF, 8/3/1927 [*sic*] tel. typewritten copy, *id.*; WL to FF, 8/4/1927, handwritten, FFHLS, Pt. III, Reel 25, Pages 492–93.

158. NYW, 8/5/1927, in FFLC, Box 247, Folder "Clippings V S-V Aug. 1–5, 1927."

159. NYW, 8/6/1927, at 10.

160. NYW, 8/5/1927, in FFLC, Box 247, Folder "Clippings V S-V Aug. 1–5, 1927."

161. NYW, 8/6/1927, at 11.

162. NYW, 8/8/1927, at 10.

163. NYW, 8/12/1927, at 13.

164. NYW, 8/17/1927, at 11.

165. *Id.*

166. WL to Franklin Adams, 8/16/1927, at 2, WLP, Box 1, Folder 9, Reel 1. *See* Adams to WL, 8/18/1927, at 1, *id.* (indicating that he was "greatly depressed by the Broun tragedy").

167. WL to Adams, 8/19/1927, at 1, *id. See* Steel, *Walter Lippmann and the American Century*, 229–34.

168. FF to Mears, FF Wiretap Transcript, 8/16/1927, at 8, FFHLS, Pt. III, Reel 38, Box 215, Folder 6.

169. FF to GJ, 8/20/1927, FFHLS, Pt. III, Reel 24, Page 603.

170. *See* Attorney General Arthur K. Reading to Commissioner of Public Safety Gen. Alfred F. Foote, 8/1/1927, FF Wiretap Transcripts, FFHLS, Pt. III, Reel 38, Page 392, Box 215, Folder 5. Reading also authorized wiretapping room 301 at the Hotel Bellevue in Boston, the headquarters of the Sacco-Vanzetti Defense Committee. Reading to Foote, 8/8/1927, *id.* at Page 393. Only the Frankfurter transcripts survive. State officials released them after fifty years. NYT, 9/13/1977, at 16; NYT, 9/15/1977, at 46.

171. MDF to Mrs. Moors, FF Wiretap Transcript, 8/20/1927, at 3–4, FFHLS, Pt. III, Reel 38, Pages 505–6, Box 215, Folder 6.

172. FF to Mears, FF Wiretap Transcript, 8/16/1927, at 4–5, *id.*, Pages 467–68; FF to WGT, 8/20/1927, at 3–6, FFHLS, Pt. III, Reel 25, Page 794.

173. Gardner Jackson COH at 182–86. Jackson's professor, historian Arthur M. Schlesinger Sr., encouraged him to go: "You're going to be fully participating in an event that will be the making of history, while all I do is just try to teach history." *Id.* at 184. On Jackson, *see* Richard Polenberg, Introduction, *The Letters of Sacco and Vanzetti* xix–xxi (2007).

174. FF to JWM, FF Wiretap Transcript, 8/11/1927, at 1, FFHLS, Pt. III, Reel 38, Page 405, Box 215, Folder 5 ("The whole burden of making the truth known rests on Jackson. He can't carry it.").

175. FF to Mears, *id.*, 8/16/1927, at 11a, FFHLS, Pt. III, Reel 38, Page 478, Box 215, Folder 6.

176. NYW, 9/12/1927, at 6, in FFLC, Box 249, Folder "Sept.–Dec. 1927."

177. *Id.*

178. EGE to FF, 7/12/1927, at 1, 3, FFHLS, Pt. III, Reel 33, Pages 346, 348.

179. FF to Ehrmann, 7/14/1927, at 1–2, FFHLS, Pt. III, Reel 24, Pages 871–72.

180. BG, 8/10/1927, at 9. *See* TNR, 2/1/1928, at 294–96, in FFLC, Box 294, Folder "Newspaper Clippings 1928" (reprinting Vanzetti's last statement to Thompson on 8/22/1927).

181. William A. Truslow, *Arthur D. Hill* 6–9, 14–15 (1996).

182. FF to OWH, 3/28/1916, H-FF Corr., at 50.

183. Truslow, *Arthur D. Hill*, at 7.

184. ADH to OWH, 3/7/1919, at 1–2, OWHP, Box 18, Folder 12.

185. OWH to RP, 3/29/1916, at 1–2, RPP, Reel 7, Pages 939–40.

186. HLS Report to President, 1916–17, at 140; HLS Report to President, 1918–19, at 128; Springfield Republican, 8/5/1927; BH, 8/5/1927, at 1, 3, in FFLC, Box 247, Folder "S-V Clippings Aug. 1–5, 1927"; BG, 8/5/1927, at 6; BG, 6/7/1919, at 9; Truslow, *Arthur D. Hill*, at 15–16.

187. Herbert Ehrmann in *Felix Frankfurter: A Tribute*, 93.

188. "Arthur Dehon Hill, 1869–1947," at 4, in FFLC, Box 67, Folder "Hill, Arthur Dehon undated miscellany."

189. BG, 3/17/1923, at 1.

190. FF to ADH, 8/8/1927, FFLC, Box 67, Folder "Hill, Arthur Dehon 1918–27."

191. ADH to FF, 10/20/1927, *id.*, ADH to FF, 10/8/1927, at 1–2, *id.*; ADH to FF, 10/6/1927, *id.*; ADH to FF, 10/6/1927, *id.* (re associates Evarts and Field); FF to JWM, FF Wiretap Transcript, 8/21/1927, at 11, FFHLS, Pt. III, Reel 38, Page 541, Box 215, Folder 7 ("whatever was reasonable").

192. ADH to FF, 10/20/1927.

193. BG, 12/2/1947, at 14.

194. 5 SV Trial Tr. at 5428–30.

195. BG, 8/9/1927, at 1.

196. 5 SV Trial Tr. at 5433–61; BET, 8/6/1927, in FFLC, Box 247, Folder "S-V VI Clippings Aug. 6–9, 1927."
197. BET, 8/10/1927, at 1, in FFLC, Box 247, Folder "S-V VII Clippings August 10–16, 1927."
198. BP, 8/11/1927, at 12.

CHAPTER 24

1. Photo of Beverly Farms, 9/20/1928, Holmes Digital Suite, olvwork392157.
2. OWH to LE, H-E Letters, 5/19/1927, at 268 ("Frankfurter potently abetting, over the trial of Sacco & Vanzetti some years ago, I feel as if I was going to a perturbed teapot when I turn North in June.").
3. BG, 8/6/1927, at 3.
4. OWH to FF, 3/18/1927, at 211.
5. FFLC, Box 259, Folder "Related Material Removed from the Book *The Case of Sacco and Vanzetti*."
6. OWH to HL, 4/25/1927, 2 HLL at 938.
7. OWH to HL, 8/18/1927, *id*. at 971.
8. FF to ADH, 8/6/1927, at 1–2, FFLC, Box 67, Folder "Hill, Arthur Denon 1918–27" (emphasis in original).
9. MDF to WGT, 10:15 a.m., FF Wiretap Transcript, 8/10/1927, at 1, FFHLS, Pt. III, Reel 28, Page 399, Box 215, Folder 5.
10. Frank v. Mangum, 237 U.S. 309, 345 (1915) (Holmes. J., dissenting). On the *Frank* case and the aftermath (including Frank's letter to Holmes and lynching), *see* chapter 6 nn. 122–30.
11. Moore v. Dempsey, 261 U.S. 86, 89–90 (1923). On the Elaine Riots and Holmes's decision in *Moore v. Dempsey, see* chapter 16 nn. 94–97, chapter 19 nn. 79–86.
12. BP, 8/11/1927, at 12.
13. *Id*. at 1.
14. 5 SV Trial Tr. at 5533.
15. MDF to Thelma Irving, FF Wiretap Transcript, 8/10/1927, at 3–4, FFHLS, Pt. III, Reel 38, Pages 401–2, Box 215, Folder 5.
16. FF to Michael Musmanno, *id*. at 5–6, Pages 403–4.
17. *Id*. at 6, Page 404.
18. BP, 8/11/1927, at 1.
19. *Id*. at 1, 12; BG, 8/11/1927, at 10.
20. 5 SV Trial Tr. at 5532.
21. OWH to HL, 8/18/1927, 2 HLL at 971. *But see* MDH, Memorandum of talk with FF, 8/10/1964, at 1, MDHP, Box 22, Folder 26 (recalling that "OWH said to Thompson that of course [the] men couldn't have a fair trial in a community as infected by bias as the community seemed to be in Thompson's description of it.").
22. BG, 8/6/1927, at 3.

23. NYT, 8/7/1927, at 4.

24. OWH to HL, 8/18/1927, 2 HLL at 971; OWH to LE, 8/14/1927, H-E Letters at 272; BP, 8/11/1927, at 12.

25. OWH to HL, 8/18/1927, 2 HLL at 971.

26. *Id.*

27. OWH to LE, 8/14/1927, H-E Letters at 272.

28. FF to MDF, FF Wiretap Transcript, 8/18/1927, at 4, FFHLS, Pt. III, Reel 38, Page 494, Box 215, Folder 6; FF to MDF, 8/19/1927, at 2, *id.*, Page 499, FF to Paul Kellogg, 8/20/1927, at 7–8, *id.*, Pages 509–10.

29. FF to JWM, FF Wiretap Transcript, 8/11/1927, at 2, FFHLS, Pt. III, Reel 38, Page 406, Box 215, Folder 5.

30. *Id.* at 1, *id.*, Page 405. On Lippmann, Broun, and the *World, see* chapter 23 nn. 160–67.

31. FF to GJ, FF Wiretap Transcript, 8/14/1927, at 5, FFHLS, Pt. III, Reel 38, Page 439, Box 215, Folder 5. *See id.* (discussing the visit with Frankfurter by reporter Chamberlain of the *World* for "a good many hours. He knows a great deal now, and I was perfectly delighted when he himself made the suggestion that 'I think I will go to New York and talk with Mr. Lithman [*sic*].'").

32. *Id.* at 6, *id.*, Page 440. *See* Gardner Jackson COH at 226; FF to GJ, FF Wiretap Transcript, 8/14/1927, at 6, FFHLS, Pt. III, Reel 38, Page 440, Box 215, Folder 5 (confirming discussion between Frankfurter and Jackson about publishing an editorial in the *World* and reprinting part of it as an advertisement in the *Times*); FF to Paul Kellogg, 8/16/1927, at 14, *id.*, Page 482, Folder 6 ("I am going to New York. W.L. says he will give me all the time in the world to get the details together."); MDF to Paul Kellogg, *id.*, 8/18/1927, at 2, *id.*, Page 492, Folder 6 ("The World is going to do a lot of things he persuaded them to do. [Frankfurter] had a hard time with the Heward-Bruin [*sic*] situation. . . . He said he had real hopes.").

33. LDB to FF, 4/26/1927, HBHS, at 287. *See* FF to LDB, 4/22/[1927], FFLC, Box 29, Folder "Brandeis, Louis Und. #98" ("C. C. Burlingham is doing effective work for S.V."); CCB to FF, 4/22/1927, FFHLS, Reel 33, Page 206; CCB to FF, 4/24/1927, *id.*, Page 207; CCB to FF, 6/18/1927, *id.*, Page 208; CCB to FF, 9/13/1927, *id.*, Pages 209–10; George Martin, *CCB* 268–74 (2005).

34. GJ to MDF & FF to MDF, 8/18/1927, FFHLS, Pt. III, Reel 38, Pages 493–94, Box 215, Folder 6 ("really did a job with Walter"); Gardner Jackson COH at 230 (recalling Frankfurter spent "many hours" with Lippmann).

35. NYW, 8/19/1927, at 12–13. *See* FF to MDF, FF Wiretap Transcript, 8/18/1927, at 4–5, FFHLS, Pt. III, Reel 38, Pages 494–95, Box 215, Folder 6 ("They thought Lowell was Lowell, but when doubts appeared they began to go the other way.").

36. Gardner Jackson COH at 280.

37. FF to Mears, FF Wiretap Transcript, 8/16/1927, at 5, FFHLS, Pt. III, Reel 38, Page 468, Box 215, Folder 6.

38. FF to JWM, FF Wiretap Transcript, 8/20/1927, at 23, *id.*, Page 525; FF to Paul Kellogg, 8/20/1927, at 7–8, *id.*, Pages 509–10.

39. NYT, 8/19/1927, at 11.

40. FF to MDF, 8/19/1927, at 1A, 1B, 2, FFHLS, Pt. III, Reel 38, Pages 497–99, Box 215, Folder 6; Martin, *CCB*, 271–72 & n. 98.

41. NYT, 8/20/1927, at 14.

42. *Id.* at 4.

43. FF to GJ, FF Wiretap Transcript, 8/21/1927, at 14, FFHLS, Pt. III, Reel 38, Page 544, Box 215, Folder 7. *See* FF to JWM, FF Wiretap Transcript, 8/21/1927, at 11, *id.*, Page 541.

44. 5 SV Trial Tr. at 5499–503.

45. *Id.* at 5527–31.

46. *Id.* at 5534–35.

47. FF to GJ, FF Wiretap Transcript, 8/21/1927, at 14.

48. See *Buck v. Bell* Record at 53, NARA (characterizing Emma Buck as "feeble-minded" and having "the mentality of a child of twelve"); Paul A. Lombardo, *Three Generations, No Imbeciles* 106 (2008) (describing Emma Buck as having scars on her arms from possible drug use and mentioning "her record noted that she had been arrested for prostitution and given birth to illegitimate children"); Adam Cohen, *Im·be·ciles* 19–20, 22–23 (2016) (describing Emma Buck's sad history and questionable IQ test labeling her a "Moron").

49. *Buck v. Bell* Record at 67, NARA.

50. Lombardo, *Three Generations, No Imbeciles*, 74–75, 154–55; Cohen, *Im·be·ciles*, 179–211.

51. WHT to OWH, 4/23/1923, at 1, OWHP, JGPC, Box 22, Folder 25. *See* Buck v. Bell, 274 U.S. 200, 207 (1927).

52. Buck, 274 U.S. at 207–8.

53. OWH to HL, 4/25/1927, 2 HLL at 938–39; OWH to FF, 5/14/1927, H-FF Corr., at 212 ("I think my cases this term have been rather a high average of interest e.g., the Virginia Sterilization Act."); OWH to LE, 5/19/1927, H-E Letters at 267 ("One decision that I wrote gave me pleasure, establishing the constitutionality of a law permitting the sterilization of imbeciles."); OWH to Charlotte Moncheur, 6/18/1927, OWHP, Reel 27, Page 168, Box 36, Folder 21 ("I have had very interesting cases to write, ... a Virginia law for the sterilization of imbeciles was constitutional. ... which I wrote with some gusto of approval. ...").

54. OWH to LH, 6/24/1918, OWHP, Reel 26, Page 486, Box 36, Folder 3. *See* Thomas C. Leonard, *Illiberal Reformers* (2016).

55. Lombardo, *Three Generations, No Imbeciles*, 105, 139–41; Cohen, *Im·be·ciles*, 19, 21, 24–25.

56. Lombardo, *Three Generations, No Imbeciles*, 190–91 (photograph); Cohen, *Im·be·ciles*, 292.

57. OWH to FF, 5/14/1927, H-FF Corr., at 212.

58. FF to OWH, 6/5/1927, *id.* at 213.

59. Felix Frankfurter, "Mr. Justice Holmes and the Constitution: A Review of His 25 Years on the Supreme Court," 41 Harv. L. Rev. 121, 153 (1927).

60. OWH to LE, 5/19/1927, H-E Letters 267.

61. "I am amused (between ourselves) at some of the rhetorical changes suggested, when I purposely used short and rather brutal words for an antithesis, polysyllables that made them mad." Holmes, who had tempered his language in prior opinions, kept his sharp rhetoric in *Buck.* "This time, though I had said, Never again, I did the same thing in a milder form, and now as then have to accept criticism that I think pretty well justified." OWH to HL, 4/29/1927, 2 HLL at 939. Laski mentioned *Buck* in passing but did not praise the decision. HL to OWH, 5/7/1927, *id.* at 940.

62. *The Memoirs of Frida Laski,* at 19 (on file with author); Kramnick and Sheerman, *Harold Laski,* 30–34.

63. *The Memoirs of Frida Laski,* at 21–22; Kramnick and Sheerman, *Harold Laski,* 37, 58–59.

64. CDEF, 6/30/1927, at A1.

65. Louis Marshall to James Weldon Johnson, 1/13/1927, Johnson to James Cobb, 1/12/1927, Johnson to Marshall, 1/12/1927, Arthur Spingarn to Johnson, 1/11/1927, NAACP Records, Pt. 1, Box D64, Folder 1 "Nixon v. Herndon Jan.–Feb. 1927." *See* Will Guzmán, *Civil Rights in the Texas Borderlands* (2015); Charles L. Zelden, *The Battle for the Black Ballot* (2004).

66. NYW, 3/8/1927, at 1; WES, 3/8/1927, in NAACP Records, *id.,* Folder 5, "Nixon v. Herndon News Clippings."

67. Nixon v. Herndon, 273 U.S. 536, 541 (1927). Notice Holmes's use of "the blacks" as he later used the phrase in his second Sacco-Vanzetti opinion, a term the *Chicago Defender* criticized. *See infra* text accompanying notes 112–13. On Holmes's curious decision to rely on the Fourteenth rather than the Fifteenth Amendment, *see* WHT to OWH, n.d., OWHP, Reel 72, Page 572 ("I concur though I suspect that some of the brethren who are sensitive as to the non-application of the 15th Amendment under our decision to a primary may ask for a little more elaborate statement of what our decision here is confined to. Perhaps not–Certainly I don't ask it. It suits me–WHT.").

68. Holmes draft *Buchanan* dissent, at 1, OWHP, Reel 61, Page 651, Box 80, Folder 12. *See* Alexander M. Bickel and Benno C. Schmidt Jr., *History of the Supreme Court of the United States: The Judiciary and Responsible Government, 1910–1921,* vol. 9, insert after 592, 804–10 (1984); David E. Bernstein, "Philip Sober Controlling Philip Drunk: *Buchanan v. Warley* in Historical Perspective," 51 Vand. L. Rev. 797, 855–56 (1998).

69. Giles v. Harris, 189 U.S. 475, 488 (1903). *See* chapter 6 n. 131.

70. Berea College v. Kentucky, 211 U.S. 45 (1908) (Holmes, J., concurring in the judgment).

71. Bailey v. Alabama, 219 U.S. 219, 245 (1911) (Holmes, J., dissenting). *See* Bickel and Schmidt, *The Judiciary and Responsible Government,* at 866–71; chapter 6 nn. 132–33.

72. McCabe v. Atchison, Topeka & Santa Fe Ry., 235 U.S. 151, 164 (1914) (Holmes, J., concurring in the judgment).

73. Hughes to OWH, 11/29/1914, in Bickel and Schmidt, *The Judiciary and Responsible Government*, insert after 592, 780. *See* White, *Law and the Inner Self*, 333 ("But Holmes cannot easily be identified as a supporter of civil rights, for blacks or anyone else, in the years between 1903 and 1916. In fact, the Court's civil rights decisions during those years suggest that on more than one occasion Holmes's posture was sufficiently hostile to the claim of a petitioner to cause him to depart from his typical stance of deference toward the legislature in constitutional cases."); *id.* at 333–43 (discussing these cases and explaining why Holmes's early abolitionism did not translate into the protection of the right of blacks from 1903 to 1916); Yosal Rogat, "Justice Holmes: A Dissenting Opinion," 15 Stan. L. Rev. 254 (1963) (detailing Holmes's failure to enforce the Civil War amendments).

74. Abrams v. U.S., 250 U.S. 616, 629 (1919) (Holmes, J., dissenting).

75. Nixon v. Herndon, 273 U.S. 536, 541 (1927).

76. OWH to Wu, 6/21/1928, H-Wu Corr., at 48 (describing Laski's "passion for Equality, with which I have no sympathy at all. Yet in my youth I was an abolitionist and shuddered at a Negro Minstrel Show, as belittling a suffering race and I am glad I was and did.").

77. LDB to FF, 3/9/1927, HBHS, at 278.

78. NYAN, 3/16/1927, at 14.

79. Walter White to Holmes, 3/10/1927, NAACP Records, Pt. 1, Box D64, Folder 2, "Nixon v. Herndon Mar. 11–28, 1927."

80. Corcoran to FF, 3/17/1927, at 2, OWHP, JGPC, Box 58, Folder 27.

81. OWH to HL, 8/24/1927, 2 HLL at 974.

82. Bard v. Chilton Record at 253 & Bard v. Chilton Brief at 46, NARA, U.S. Supreme Court Appellate Case Files, File Nos. 33017–18, RG 267, Box 8356.

83. George C. Wright, *Racial Violence in Kentucky, 1865–1940*, at 262–66 (1990).

84. Bard v. Chilton Record at 383–87 (containing article from Madisonville Messenger, 4/11/1926); Louisville News, 5/1/1926, at 1, NAACP Records, Pt. I, Box G-76, Folder 8 "Louisville, KY Jan.–Oct. 1926."

85. Bard v. Chiton Record at 250, 262–63; William Warley to James Weldon Johnson, 10/25/1926, at 2, NAACP Records, Pt. I, Box G-76, Folder 8 Louisville, KY Jan.–Oct. 1926; Louisville News, 4/24/1926, at 1, *id.*, Folder 10.

86. Bard v. Chilton Record, at 412; CDEF, 5/8/1926, at 2.

87. Bard v. Chilton Record at 246–47.

88. Bard v. Chilton Record at 236; CDEF, 5/8/1926, at 2.

89. Bard v. Chilton Brief at 58; Louisville Leader, 4/30/1927, at 1, 8.

90. G. P. Hughes to Walter White, 7/15/1927 tel., NAACP Records, Pt. I, Box G-76, Folder 11 "Louisville, KY July–Dec. 1927" ("JUSTICE HOLMES GRANT STAY WILL HEAR CASE NEXT TERM SUPREME COURT"); Hughes to White, 7/16/1927 tel., *id.* ("ANSWERING TELEGRAM ATTORNEY WHO ARGUED BEFORE JUSTICE HOLMES HAS NOT RETURNED WILL FORWARD DETAILS WHEN HE COMES.").

91. Handwritten order, 7/14/1927, Bard v. Chilton, NARA, U.S. Supreme Court Appellate Case Files, File Nos. 33017–18, RG 267, Box 8356.
92. CDEF, 8/13/1927, at 4; NYAM, 8/10/1927, at 4; NJ&G, 8/6/1927, at 1; Philadelphia Tribune, 7/28/1927, at 5.
93. NYHT, 8/21/1927, at 6.
94. BP, 8/21/1927, at 10.
95. Holmes Handwritten Denial, 8/20/1927, at 1–3, OWHP, Box 69, Folder 10.
96. 5 S-V Trial Tr. at 5516.
97. *Id.* at 5517.
98. *Id.* at 5516.
99. CDEF, 8/27/1927, at A2.
100. OWH to FF, 7/25/1927, H-FF Corr., at 215 ("I am taking life pretty leisurely although there are always letters to be answered and although I have gone over 30 odd *certioraris* for next term and have granted one and denied another application for a stay when men are to be executed forthwith."). The grant is Bard and Fleming. The denial I have not been able to pinpoint. It was probably the Louisiana capital murder case of Joe Genna and Molton Brasseaux, who were convicted of murdering a New Orleans man. Genna and Brasseux filed their cert petitions on July 3. The Court officially denied cert on October 10. Nos. 347 & 351, 275 U.S. 522 (Oct. 10, 1927).
101. GJ to FF, FF Wiretap Transcript, 8/20/1927, at 15–16, FFHLS, Pt. III, Reel 38, Pages 517–18, Box 215, Folder 6.
102. ADH to FF, FF Wiretap Transcript, 8/20/1927, *id.* at 17, Page 519.
103. GJ to FF, FF Wiretap Transcript, 8/21/1927, at 2–3, FFHLS, Pt. III, Box 215, Folder 7, Reel 38, Pages 529–30.
104. FF to GJ, FF Wiretap Transcript, 8/21/1927, at 3, *id.*, Page 530.
105. BH, 8/22/1927, at 1.
106. FF to ADH, FF Wiretap Transcript, 8/21/1927, at 4–5, FFHLS, Pt. III, Box 215, Folder 7, Reel 38, Pages 531–32.
107. Norman Hapgood, "Justice Brandeis: Apostle of Freedom," The Nation, 10/5/1927, at 331.
108. *See* Gilbert v. Minnesota, 254 U.S. 325, 334 (1920) (Brandeis, J., dissenting); Schaefer v. United States, 251 U.S. 466, 482 (1920) (Brandeis, J., dissenting). Holmes only joined the first of the two dissents; he concurred in the judgment in *Gilbert*. Brandeis had regretted joining Holmes's opinions in *Schenck* and *Debs*: "I had not then thought the issues of freedom of speech out–I thought at the subject, not through it. Not until I came to write the Pierce and Schaefer cases did I understand it." Brandeis-Frankfurter Conversations, at 23, FFLC, Box 224, Folder "Conversation between L.D.B. and F.F."
109. Time, 10/19/1925, at 8.
110. TNR, 11/10/1926, at 311; NYW, 11/13/1926, at 12.
111. NYW, 11/13/1926, at 12. *See* FF to LH, 11/21/1926, LHP, Box 104-B, Folder 104-13 (praising what Hand had written about Brandeis); Learned Hand

COH at 102 ("Well, I think [Brandeis] had an overbearing will. I didn't like him.").

112. WHT to HLS, 5/18/1928, at 2, HLSP, Reel 75, Page 867 (discussing Holmes's and Brandeis's dissents from Taft's presidential removal power opinion in Myers v. United States, 272 U.S. 62 (1926); *id.* at 240 Brandeis, J., dissenting; *id.* at 295 Holmes, J., dissenting).

113. NYW, 11/13/1926, at 12.

114. Whitney v. California, 274 U.S. 357, 372 (1927) (Brandeis, J., concurring). Brandeis nearly published his *Whitney* concurrence as a dissent in *Ruthenberg v. Michigan*, which was mooted when the petitioner died. LDBP, Harvard Law School, Box 44, Folder 11, Reel 34; Ronald K. L. Collins and David M. Skover, "Curious Concurrence: Justice Brandeis' Vote in *Whitney v. California*," 2005 Supreme Ct. Rev. 333.

115. "Radicals: The Case of Miss Whitney," Time, 11/2/1925, at 7.

116. Whitney, 274 U.S. at 373–74 (Brandeis, J., concurring). *See* Graber, *Transforming Free Speech*, 101–3.

117. Whitney, 274 U.S. at 376 (Brandeis, J., concurring).

118. *Id.* at 377, 379.

119. Time, 5/23/1927, at 9.

120. Clement C. Young, *The Pardon of Charlotte Anita Whitney*, June 30, 1927, at 8–9, 13–14 (California State Printing Office, 1927). *See* NYT, 5/18/1927, at 24 (praising Brandeis's opinion).

121. *See* chapter 7 nn. 88–91.

122. LDB to May Nerney, 9/18/1914, 3 LLDB at 298 ("I have great doubt, however, whether it would be worth your while to come to Boston for that purpose alone, as it does not seem to me possible that I should be able to give you any advice of value in regard to the Jim Crow car situation, and the work which I have on hand would prevent my entering upon an investigation of the matter."). *See* LDB to Chapin Brinsmade, 9/29/1914, *id.* at 305 ("I should greatly doubt whether the Interstate Commerce Commission would, upon the filing of a formal petition, enter upon a general investigation of conditions of service to colored people on interstate trains.").

123. TNR, 11/27/1915, at 88–89. *See* chapter 6 n. 141.

124. On Brandeis on race, *see* Urofsky, *Louis D. Brandeis*, 639–40; Larry M. Roth, "The Many Lives of Louis Brandeis," 34 Southern U. L. Rev. 123 (2007); Christopher A. Bracey, "Louis Brandeis and the Race Question," 52 Ala. L. Rev. 859 (2001). *See also* Richard A. Posner, "The Rise and Fall of Judicial Self-Restraint," 100 Cal. L. Rev. 519, 528 (2012) (describing Brandeis as "a Jeffersonian with a Southerner's hostility to strong central government").

125. Corrigan v. Buckley, 271 U.S. 323 (1926). *See* South Covington & C St. Ry. Co. v. Kentucky, 259 U.S. 399 (1920) (upholding Kentucky law segregating streetcars that traveled in interstate commerce).

126. Richard Kluger, *Simple Justice* 125 (1976). *See* Genna Rae McNeil, *Groundwork: Charles Hamilton Houston and the Struggle for Civil Rights* 72 (1983).

127. OWH to HL, 1/18/1927, 2 HLL at 913. "Bery black" was stereotypical black dialect common in nineteenth-century fiction.
128. Olmstead v. U.S., 277 U.S. 438, 472 (1928) (Brandeis, J., dissenting); David E. Bernstein, *Rehabilitating Lochner* 98 (2011).
129. National Register of Historic Places, Inventory-Nomination Form at 2 (on file with author).
130. 1 LLDB at 110 n. 2; Strum, *Louis D. Brandeis*, at 42; Mason, *Brandeis*, 78. The original source of this quotation cannot be found.
131. BH, 8/22/1927, at 1.
132. Louis Bernheimer to FF, FF Wiretap Transcript, 8/21/1927, noon, at 8, FFHLS, Pt. III, Reel 38, Page 538, Box 215, Folder 7. *See* Sherman to FF, 8/21/1927, noon, at 5, *id.*, Page 532; JWM to FF, 8/21/1927, 3:30 p.m., at 9, *id.*, Page 539; BH, 8/22/1927, at 1.
133. BH, 8/22/1927, at 1.
134. BP, 8/22/1927, at 4; CT, 8/12/1921, at 3.
135. FF to MDF, 6/12/1927, at 2–3, FFLC, Box 14, Folder "Marion A. Frankfurter 1927 #116."
136. Mrs. Brandeis's donation was leaked to the *Boston American*. *See* EGE to Fred Moore, 8/21/1921, at 1, SVDCBPL, Box 13, Folder 10; EGE to Moore, 9/4/1921, *id.*, "Mrs. Brandeis Aids Sacco Defense Fund," Boston American, n.d., 1921, *id.*, Moore to EGE, 9/6/1921, *id.* (explaining he had given *Boston American* the defense fund's donor list, and the newspaper had chosen to publish Mrs. Brandeis's name). *See* NYW, 8/22/1927, at 1 (noting that "both Mrs. Brandeis and Miss Susan Brandeis had discussed the case with friends who were sympathetic toward Sacco and Vanzetti.").
137. LDB to FF, 10/29/1926, HBHS, at 258.
138. LDB to FF, 6/2/1927, HBHS, at 296 ("I have realized that S.V., inter alia, must have made heavy demands for incidental expense, as well as time, & meant to ask you when we meet whether an additional sum might not be appropriate this year. Let me know."). For critics of Brandeis's legal ethics, *see* Murphy, *The Brandeis/Frankfurter Connection*, 78–82 (citing Sacco-Vanzetti); Clyde Spillenger, "Elusive Advocate," 105 Yale. L.J. 1145 (1996); David W. Levy and Bruce Allen Murphy, "Preserving the Progressive Spirit in a Conservative Time," 78 Mich. L. Rev. 1252, 1302 (1980) (citing Sacco-Vanzetti). *But see* Robert Cover, "The Framing of Justice Brandeis," TNR, 5/5/1982, at 17–21 (defending Brandeis). For more neutral views of the financial relationship, *see* Nelson L. Dawson, *Louis D. Brandeis, Felix Frankfurter, and the New Deal* 4–5 (1980); Urofsky and Levy, HBHS, at 6–9.
139. LDB to FF, 8/5/1927, HBHS, at 306.
140. BH, 8/22/1927, at 1.
141. Alpheus Thomas Mason, *Harlan Fiske Stone: Pillar of Law* 125–41 (1956).
142. FF to WL, 4/7/1924, at 1, WLP, Box 10, Folder 425, Reel 10, Page 40. *See* Mason, *Harlan Fiske Stone*, 148.
143. HFS to FF, 4/15/1924, WLP, Box 10, Folder 425, Reel 10, Page 40. *See* Mason, *Harlan Fiske Stone*, 148.

144. FF to HFS, 5/15/1924, LHP, Box 104-B, Folder 104-13 & FFLC, Box 104, Folder "Stone, Harlan Fiske 1924 #1."

145. FF to WL, 4/17/1924, WLP, Box 10, Folder 425, Reel 10, Page 44; FF to WL, 4/3/1924, *id.*, Page 35; Mason, *Harlan Fiske Stone*, 141.

146. HFS to FF, 1/19/1925, at 2, FFLC, Box 104, Folder "Stone, Harlan Fiske 1925–1928 #2."

147. FF to HFS, 1/22/1925, at 3–4, *id.*

148. FF to LH, 11/10/1924, at 2, 4, LHP, Box 104A, Folder 104-11.

149. HFS to OWH, n.d., OWHP, Reel 72, Page 250 (joining Beech-Nut Packing Co. v. P. Lorillard Co., 273 U.S. 629 (1927)).

150. FF to MDF, 6/12/1927, at 2 (Brandeis told Frankfurter: "He is really fierce about Harlan Stone–and says Van Devanter has 'unmeasured contempt for him.'").

151. FF to LH, 3/10/1926, at 2, LHP, Box 104-B, Folder 104-12. Frankfurter based his assessment on Stone's "writings, on his performances and on correspondence with him when he was Attorney General. But it is wholly confirmed by what T. R. Powell tells me of his attitudes as Dean of Columbia." *Id.*

152. BP, 8/22/1927, at 4.

153. FF to Sherman, FF Wiretap Transcript, 8/22/1927, noon, at 6, FFHLS, Pt. III, Reel 38, Pages 533, Box 215, Folder 7.

154. BP, 8/22/1927, at 4.

155. BH, 8/22/1927, at 1.

156. 5 S-V Trial Tr. at 5517; BG, 8/23/1927, at 9.

157. BP, 8/23/1927, at 12.

158. Truslow, *Arthur D. Hill*, 17 (reprinting Hill diary entry, 8/22/1927).

159. BH, 8/22/1927, at 6; BP, 8/22/1927, at 4; BP, 8/21/1927, at 10; BET, 8/20/1927, at 1. The lawyer who had failed to bring a copy of the record was Michael Musmanno.

160. WHT to Henry Taft, 8/22/1927, at 2–3, WHTP, Series 3, Reel 294; WHT to Musmanno, 8/22/1927, *id.*; three telegrams, two from Musmanno to Taft, 8/21/1927 & undated telegram, WHTP, Series 3, Reel 293; Michael A. Musmanno, *After Twelve Years* 351–54 (1939).

161. Musmanno, *After Twelve Years*, 347–51.

162. OWH to LE, 9/11/1927, H-E Letters at 273; BH, 8/23/1927, at 7; BP, 8/23/1927, at 12.

163. FF to GJ, FF Wiretap Transcript, 8/21/1927, at 15, FFHLS, Pt. III, Reel 38, Page 545, Box 215, Folder 7.

164. Josephson, "Profiles: Jurist-II," at 46.

165. Gardner Jackson, COH at 295–97; Polenberg, Introduction, *The Letters of Sacco and Vanzetti*, xxi–xxv (2007).

166. LDB to FF, 8/24/1927, HBHS, at 306.

167. TNR, 9/28/1927, at 137. Email from David W. Levy to author, 5/7/2015 ("it sounded very much like HC" & "I would now bet money on HC.").

168. TNR, 9/28/1927, at 138.

169. Julius Rosenwald to President and Fellows of Harvard College, 12/24/1927, Julius Rosenwald Papers, Box 17, Folder 19. Lowell initially balked at such a large publication fund in Frankfurter's hands. *See* ALL to Rosenwald, 12/2/1927, *id.*, Box 36, Folder 7; JWM to ALL, 12/4/1927, *id.*

170. FF to JWM, 10/15/1927, at 1–3, FFHLS, Pt. III, Reel 34, Pages 946–48; FF to Oswald Garrison Villard, 8/23/1927, FFHLS, Pt. III, Reel 26, Page 25.

171. "Memorandum of SV Discussion at Overseers' Meeting Sept. 27," FFHLS, Pt. III, Reel 34, Pages 896–97; JWM to RP, 9/3/1927, at 1–2, *id.*, Pages 855–56.

172. FF to RP, 8/23/1927, at 1, Page 825.

173. *Id.* at 2, Page 826; FF to RP, 8/31/1927, at 1–3, RPP, Reel 74, Pages 513–15.

174. RP to JWM, 9/16/1927, at 1-2, FFHLS, Pt. III, Reel 34, Pages 875–76. *See* Hull, *Roscoe Pound and Karl Llewellyn*, 157–65.

175. FF to ALL, 8/16/1927, at 1–11, FFHLS, Pt. III, Reel 34, Pages 689–99.

176. FFR, 202.

177. FF to RP, 8/23/1927, at 2. This story has been often repeated without proper context or attribution. *See* Josephson, "Profiles: Jurist-II," at 46; DFF at 124.

178. Memorandum of SV Discussion at Overseers' Meeting Sept. 27 at 1–2; JWM to RP, 9/28/1927.

179. FF to RP, 9/24/1928 or 27, RPP, Reel 26, Page 490.

180. On Margold, *see* JWM to RP, 3/3/1928, at 1–3, RPP, Reel 78, Pages 572–74; RP to JWM, 3/5/1928, *id.* at 575; Thomas Reed Powell to Harry Bigelow, 2/4/1938, at 1–2, TRPP, Box A, Folder "A3b Correspondence 1929–40: B–Bo"; Powell, "The Harvard Law School," n.d., at 6–7, *id.*, Folder "A9 Harvard Law School"; Kalman, *Legal Realism at Yale, 1927–1960*, at 58–61. On Landis, *see* Incident at Harvard I, Diary Entries 6/14–28/1928, DFF, at 124–31.

181. FF to RP, 1/2/1928, at 6, FFHLS, Pt. III, Reel 18, Page 76.

182. Matthew Josephson, "Profiles: Jurist-III," New Yorker, 12/14/1940, at 32.

183. NYW, 8/24/1927, at 12.

184. "It Seems to Heywood Broun," The Nation, 9/14/1927, at 243.

185. Michael Parrish Notes on Frankfurter 1927 Diary, 10/4/1927 (on file with author); HC to FF, 8/24/1927, at 1–2, FFHLS, Pt. III, Reel 24, Pages 768–69; FF to HC, FF Wiretap Transcript, 9/1/1927, at 3, FFHLS, Pt. III, Box 215, Folder 7, Reel 38, Page 564 (referring to "a long letter about the kind of a dinner I think you should have").

186. Michael Parrish Notes on Frankfurter 1927 Diary, 10/4/1927 (quoting Frankfurter's speech).

187. GJ to FF, 10/7/1927, at 1–3, FFHLS, Pt. III, Reel 33, Pages 493–95. *See* CCB to FF, 10/5/1927, *id.*, Page 214 ("What you said last night went to the heart of the business. ... I admire Hill, but I couldn't help feeling last night that he was assuming a sort of protective pose and I was to have you upset it."); CCB to JWM, 10/6/1927, *id.*, Reel 34, Page 929 ("That was an interesting dinner the other night, was it not–Thompson a bit too long. Hill's professional prose

rather amused me, but he's a fine brave chap. I approved every word that Felix uttered.").

188. Gardner Jackson COH at 282.

189. LH to WL, 9/7/1927, at 3, WLP, Reel 12, Box 12, Folder 499. Hand was more outraged about the foreign press's sensationalistic coverage of the case and "was delighted at the way you treated that miserable son-of-a-bitch, Broun, whom I always disliked for a complacent piece of emptiness." *Id.* at 4–5. On Hand's relationship with Frankfurter and Hand's psychology about the Sacco-Vanzetti case and liberal causes, *see* Learned Hand COH at 101; Gunther, *Learned Hand,* 388–96. Gunther does not discuss Lippmann's equally important response.

190. WL to LH, 9/11/1927, LHP, Box 106, Folder 106-17, in *Reason and Imagination: The Selected Correspondence of Learned Hand, 1897–1961,* at 146–47 (Constance Jordan, ed., 2013).

191. Steel, *Walter Lippmann and the American Century,* 233. *See id.* at 232–34.

192. FF to HC, FF Wiretap Transcript, 9/1/1927, at 3, FFHLS, Pt. III, Box 215, Folder 7, Reel 38, Page 564 (Croly: "Bruce [Bliven] wishes me to tell you that there has been no finer piece of work done in the United States in the past six months than what you have done."). "*The Nation's* Honor Roll for 1927" included Frankfurter, Thompson, and Elizabeth Glendower Evans. The Nation, 1/4/1928, at 4, in FFLC, Box 249, Folder "Newspaper Clippings 1928." *See* Oswald Garrison Villard to FF, 8/26/1927, Villard Papers, #1196 ("I have been feeling a great deal for you in these last few days.").

193. Rosenwald to Bernard Flexner, 11/23/1927, Rosenwald Papers, Box 36, Folder 7 ($5000 from Rosenwald and Rockefeller); Flexner to Rosenwald, 1/28/1929, *id.* (receiving another $5000 from Rosenwald to pay deficit); CCB to Elihu Root, 3/27/1928, FFHLS, Pt. III, Reel 33, Page 217. *Cf.* Ehrmann, in *Felix Frankfurter: A Tribute,* 110 (arguing Frankfurter "raised part of the money himself") *with* Martin, *CCB,* 273 & n. 605 (crediting Burlingham and arguing that the sponsors asked Frankfurter to stay out of the project). Martin's account misses Frankfurter's behind-the-scenes leadership. Frankfurter used fellow Zionist Flexner, Burlingham, Buckner, and Fosdick to make the project happen while keeping his own name out of it by design. This is consistent with Frankfurter's philosophy after the publication of the book. The state of Massachusetts's wiretaps capture Frankfurter's leadership role in publishing the record. *See* FF to GJ, FF Wiretap Transcript, 9/20/1927, at 2–3, FFHLS, Pt. III, Box 215, Folder 8, Reel 38, Page 617 ("I am more desirous every day to get our record out, also the stenographic minutes of the Lowell committee.").

194. FF, Letter to the Editors of the *Illinois Law Review,* 22 Ill. L. Rev. 465–68 (1927).

195. Historians have continued to debate Sacco's and Vanzetti's innocence, a subject beyond the scope of this book. The scholarly consensus is that Sacco was guilty, but Vanzetti probably not. *Cf.* William Young and David E. Kaiser, *Postmortem* (1985) (concluding they were innocent) *with* Francis Russell, *Tragedy in Dedham* (1962) & Francis Russell, *Sacco and Vanzetti* (1986)

(concluding Sacco was guilty); http://www.nybooks.com/articles/archives/1986/may/29/sacco-and-vanzetti-an-exchange/; Charles Wyzanski to Francis Russell, 3/31/1986, at 3, Francis Russell Papers, Folder "1986 March 1–31" ("*I myself am persuaded by your writings that Sacco was guilty.* It *seems* to me that Vanzetti was *not proven* guilty either of murder or being accessory *before* the fact. If he were an accessory *after* the fact he ought not to have been convicted of a capital crime and electrocuted. Even if he were guilty of some crime, the evidence was not such as to prove guilt beyond a reasonable doubt of any crime whatsoever.") (emphasis in original).

 Upton Sinclair believed that Sacco and Vanzetti were guilty and nearly abandoned his historical novel about the case. Upton Sinclair, *Boston* (1928). In a 1929 letter discovered in 2005, Sinclair revealed that the pair's trial lawyer, Fred Moore, had confessed that "the men were guilty" and that Moore "had framed a set of alibis for them." Moore, however, was a cocaine addict who had resigned as defense counsel after a bitter clash with the defense committee. Sinclair went ahead with his book that portrayed Sacco and Vanzetti as victims of an unfair trial but not as innocent of the crime. Sinclair to John Beardsley, 8/29/1929, at 1–2 (on file with author).

196. FF to EGE, FF Wiretap Transcript, 9/21/1927, FFHLS, Pt. III, Box 215, Folder 8, Reel 38, Page 623.

197. Corcoran to FF, 9/10/1927, at 1, OWHP/JGPC, Box 58, Folder 27 (informing Frankfurter that the night guard was leaving and "I'm really very sorry that I hurt you as I know I did by telling you about the guards and feeling of danger at all."). Mrs. Holmes requested the guards. Corcoran, *Rendezvous with Democracy*, Holmes D/2 at 23–24.

198. NYT, 8/22/1927, at 16.

199. OWH to HL, 9/1/1927, 2 HLL at 975.

200. OWH to FF, 9/9/1927, H-FF Corr., at 216–17.

201. FF to JWM, FF Wiretap Transcript, 9/6/1927, at 5, FFHLS, Pt. III, Box 215, Folder 7, Reel 38, Page 581.

202. Daily Worker, 8/23/1927, at 4.

203. OWH to HL, 9/1/1927, 2 HLL at 976.

204. Felix Frankfurter, "Mr. Justice Holmes and the Constitution," 41 Harv. L. Rev. 121, 127–28 (1927).

205. Felix Frankfurter and James M. Landis, *The Business of the Supreme Court* iii (1928).

206. TNR, 9/14/1927, at 83. *See* FF to JWM, FF Wiretap Transcript, 9/6/1927, at 5; Murphy, *The Brandeis/Frankfurter Connection*, 81.

207. WL to LDB, 8/24/1927, American Jewish Archives, Harry Barnard Papers, Folder "Brandeis, Louis D. 1921–29."

208. Marshall to Johnson, 7/14/1927, at 2, Records of the National Association for the Advancement of Colored People Branch Files, Pt. I, Box G-76, Folder 11, "Louisville, KY July–Dec. 1927."

209. *Id.* at 2–3.

210. *Id.* at 4.

211. Walter White to Marshall, 7/19/1927, *id.*; White to G. P. Hughes, 7/19/1927, *id.*; Louisville Chapter to Johnson, 7/27/1927, *id.*

212. Docket Book, 1927 Term, Justice Harlan Fiske Stone, Bard v. Chilton & Fleming v. Chilton. Nos. 565 & 566 (Cert. Denied, 11/21/1927), Office of the Curator, Supreme Court of the United States. Justice Sutherland was absent that day and did not vote.

213. CDEF, 12/3/1927, at 1.

214. NYW, 11/26/1927, NAACP Records, Pt. I, Box G-76, Folder 11, "Louisville, KY July–Dec. 1927."

215. PC, 11/5/1927, at 1; PC, 12/3/1927, at 1; CDEF, 12/3/1927, at 1.

216. "The Times and the N.A.A.C.P.," Louisville Leader, n.d., NAACP Records, Pt. I, Box G-76, Folder 11, "Louisville, KY July–Dec. 1927" (commenting on "Somewhat Similar," Louisville Times, 11/22/1927, *id.*).

217. Gong Lum v. Rice, 275 U.S. 78, 80 (1927). *See* Jeannie Rhee, "In Black and White: Chinese in the Mississippi Delta," 19 J. Sup. Ct. Hist. 117, 122 (Dec. 1994) (suggesting the Rosedale school district's accreditation may have prompted state officials to act).

218. Rice v. Gong Lum, 104 So. 105, 108 (1925).

219. Gong Lum, 275 U.S. at 87.

220. Arthur Sutherland, "Recollections of Mr. Justice Holmes," circa 1935, at 19, Sutherland Papers, Box 24, Folder 24-7.

221. Houston to FF, 12/29/1925, FFLC, Box 67, Folder "Houston, Charles H. 1925–50."

CHAPTER 25

1. Gardner Jackson COH at 247. There is some dispute whether Jackson met with Frankfurter in person (as he remembered in his Columbia Oral History) or phoned him (as he seemed to indicate in his 5/28/1928 letter to Borglum, *see infra* n. 3).

2. GB to GJ, 5/25/1928 tel., Borglum Historical Center, Keystone, South Dakota. *See* Jackson COH at 247–48 (recalling Borglum's response arriving "five hours later" and Borglum saying, "Of course, you're right.").

3. GJ to GB, 5/28/1928, at 1–2, Shaff Collection, Box 4, Folder 2 & Borglum Historical Center.

4. GB to GJ, 6/12/1928, GBP, in Shaff and Shaff, *Six Wars at a Time*, 252 & Shaff Notes n.d., Shaff Collection, Box 5, Folder 2.

5. GJ to MB, 5/15/1946, at 1, GBP, Box 41, Folder "S Misc."; Jackson COH at 248.

6. Shaff and Shaff, *Six Wars at a Time*, 252 (quoting conversations with Mrs. Gardner Jackson, who was known by her friends as Dodi).

7. SAL, 4/5/1931, pt. 2, at 6.

8. *Id.*; Jackson COH at 248.

9. GB to CC, 9/23/1926, CC-Forbes Collection, Reel 11, Folder "PPF Borglum Memorial (Mount Rushmore)"; CC to GB, 9/27/1926, *id.*

10. GB to CC, 4/1/1927, at 1, GBP, Box 165, Folder "Coolidge, Calvin 1926–29."

11. "President Coolidge in the Black Hills," Black Hills Engineer, 11/1927, at 230–31.

12. DR to GB, 7/13/1927, GBP, Box 102, Folder "Rushmore 1918–27" ("I hope we may get the president over to Rushmore for the opening but he is pretty 'techy' about things and an extraordinary demand is being made upon him for appearances.").

13. GB to CC, 7/22/1927, at 1, CC-Forbes Collection, Reel 11, Folder "PPF Borglum Memorial (Mount Rushmore)."

14. SFAL, 8/10/1927, at 2.

15. RCJ, 8/11/1927, at 2.

16. Edmund W. Starling, *Starling of the White House* 257–58 (1946); NYT, 8/11/1927, at 1; NYHT, 8/11/1927, at 1; LAT, 8/11/1927, at 1.

17. RCJ, 8/10/1927, at 1; Hill City (SD) News, 8/12/1927, at 1; NYT, 8/11/1927, at 1.

18. CT, 8/11/1927, at 1; BHW, 8/12/1927, at 1, 8.

19. NYHT, 8/11/1927, at 6.

20. *Id.*

21. RCJ, 8/11/1927, at 1.

22. DR to PN, 8/16/1927, GBP, Box 159, Folder "Peter Norbeck Papers 1927–." Robinson wrote: "Wasn't that a fine bit of Yankeeness?" *Id.*

23. RCJ, 8/19/1927, at 1.

24. GB to DR, 8/31/1927, GBP, Box 159, Folder "Peter Norbeck Papers 1927–."

25. GB to PN, 9/11/1927, at 1–2, *id.*; GB to DR, 8/31/1927, *id.*; GB to JGT, 8/31/1927, at 2, *id.*

26. GB to JGT, 8/31/1927, at 2.

27. DR to C. A. Cairns, 1/25/1928, DRP, Folder #151, Mount Rushmore Corr. 1928–46.

28. GB to JGT, 8/31/1927, at 2.

29. PN to DR, 2/24/1927, GBP, Box 159, Folder "Peter Norbeck Papers 1927–."

30. PN to DR, 1/15/1927, *id.*; PN to DR, 1/24/1927, *id.*

31. GB, 1/17/1927, Message left with Secretary Mellon, *id.*, Folder "Peter Norbeck Papers 1927"; GB to PN, 2/15/1927, *id.* PN to DR, 2/17/1927, *id.*

32. PN to Boland, 4/9/1928, GBP, Box 159, Folder "Peter Norbeck Papers 1928."

33. PN to DR, 5/22/1928, *id.*

34. William Allen White, *A Puritan in Babylon: The Story of Calvin Coolidge* 360 (1938).

35. Calvin Coolidge, *The Autobiography of Calvin Coolidge* 190 (1929).

36. PN to GB, 5/31/1928 tel., GBP, Box 102, Folder "Rushmore 1928–1929"; PN to GB, 5/28/1931, *id.*

37. SAL, 3/25/1928, at 2.

38. Shaff Notes, GB to GJ, 6/12/1928, Shaff Collection, Box 5, Folder 2.
39. Gardner Jackson, "The Way of Boston," The Nation, 9/26/1928, at 292–93.
40. NYW, 8/24/1928, at 6; BP, 8/23/1928, at 7; BH, 8/23/1928, at 17; BET, 8/23/
    1928, at 11.
41. GJ to GB, 8/27/1928, GBP, Box 23, Folder "Gardner Jackson."
42. TNR, 9/5/1928, at 70–71.
43. *Id.* at 57.
44. NYW, 8/24/1928, at 1; BET, 8/24/1928, at 3.
45. NYW, 8/24/1928, at 6.
46. *Id.* at 1, 6. *See* NYT, 8/24/1928, at 5.
47. NYW, 8/24/1928, at 6.
48. GJ to GB, 8/27/1928, GBP, Box 23, Folder "Gardner Jackson."
49. GJ to GB, 8/23/1928 tel., Borglum Museum.
50. NYW, 8/24/1928, at 1; BET, 8/24/1928, at 3.
51. BG, 11/23/2014; NYT, 10/4/1947, at 30; NYT, 8/23/1937, at 7. A bronze version
    of the plaster draft also hangs in the Borglum Historical Center in Keystone,
    South Dakota, and aluminum castings in the Gardner Jackson Reading Room
    at Brandeis University and the Community Church in Boston. Adrienne M.
    Naylor, "Memorializing Sacco and Vanzetti in Boston," *Inquires Journal/Student
    Pulse* 2, no. 1 (2010), in http://www.studentpulse.com/articles/117/memori-
    alizing-sacco-and-vanzetti-in-boston. According to Borglum's granddaughter
    Robin Borglum Kennedy, the final bronze version of the memorial is thought
    to have been stolen shortly after Borglum's death in 1941.
    Borglum's widow, Mary, publicly opposed Gardner Jackson's 1947 efforts
    to display the memorial on Boston Common because she considered one of
    the many illustrious people supporting the effort to be a Communist–labor
    leader Philip Murray (even though Murray and Jackson had broken with the
    Communist-backed CIO). *See* MB to GJ, 9/15/1947, GBP, Box 41, Folder "S
    Misc."; MB to Gov. Robert Bradford, 10/9/1947, *id.* She wrote: "Gutzon used
    to be very friendly with Gardner Jackson and Felix Frankfurter but I found
    a note in his memorandum book not to mention Felix. I know he thought
    Gardner was harmless and liked him personally but he didn't think he had any
    constructive ideas. There are no recent letters to or from him, I mean during
    the last twenty years." MB to Rupert Hughes?, 9/8/1947, at 2, *id.* A year ear-
    lier, Mary Borglum had contacted Frankfurter about buying the bas-relief, and
    he referred her to Jackson yet recalled his Bull Moose days with Borglum
    with fondness. *See* FF to MB, 5/4/46, GBP, Box 16, Folder "F" ("Your letter
    flooded me with happy exciting memories. Strange some things fade out of
    one's consciousness and others have a vividness unimpaired by the passage of
    thirty or forty years. All my happy days with Gutzon have that vividness."); FF
    to Max Lowenthal, 4/8/1963, FFLC, Box 79, Folder "Lowenthal, Max 1961-
    64 & undated" (describing Borglum as among "intrinsically great" men during
    the House of Truth period).

CHAPTER 26

1. NYW, 7/21/1920, at 10.
2. NYW, 6/30/1928, at 10.
3. FF to WL, 6/16/1928, at 2, WLP, Reel 10, Box 10, Folder 429a.
4. Herbert Hoover, *American Individualism* 8 (1922).
5. FF to WL, 6/16/1928, at 2.
6. WL to FF, 7/3/1928, at 2, WLP, Reel 10, Box 10, Folder 429b. Lippmann was not alone in predicting economic disaster. *See* LDB to FF, 6/15/1928, HBHS, at 333 ("Al Smith should be able to beat Hoover, depressed by a stock market smash."). For Lippmann's expertise on the American economy, *see* Craufurd D. Goodwin, *Walter Lippmann: Public Economist* (2014).
7. Allan J. Lichtman, *Prejudice and the Old Politics* (1979).
8. NYW, 6/29/1928, at 12.
9. NYHT, 6/28/1924, at 6.
10. FDR Speech, 6/26/1924, at 9, FDR Library, in https://fdrlibrary.files.wordpress.com/2012/09/19241.pdf; NYT, 6/27/1924, at 4. The "Happy Warrior" line from Wordsworth was apparently insisted upon by a Smith aide, New York Judge Joseph M. Proskauer. *See* Robert A. Slayton, *Empire Statesman* 434–35 n. 23 (2001).
11. NYHT, 6/28/1928, at 2; Time, 3/5/1928, at 15.
12. FDR to WL, 8/6/1928, WLP, Reel 27, Box 29, Folder 1061.
13. NYT, 6/28/1928, at 3.
14. *See* WL to Belle Moskowitz, 6/25/1928, WLP, Reel 20, Box 21, Folder 845 ("I have given a lot of thought to the telegram which the Governor proposes to send when he is notified of his nomination. The part dealing with prohibition seems to me fine and ought not to be changed. ..."). *See* RH to John Hessin Clarke, 6/28/1928, at 1, NDBP, Box 115, Folder "Ralph Hayes 1928" ("Lippmann urged strongly that the Governor should not delay reiterating his position on the Volstead Act.").
15. FDR to WL, 8/6/1928, WLP, Reel 27, Box 29, Folder 1061.
16. FDR to James Bonbright, 3/11/1930, in *F.D.R.: His Personal Letters, 1928–45*, Vol. 3, at 109–10 (Elliott Roosevelt, ed., 1950).
17. FF to WL, 7/26/1927, at 1, WLP, Reel 10, Box 10, Folder 429b.
18. WAW to Helen Mahin, 12/18/1928, WAW Papers, Box C-138, Folder "Mahin, Helen O."
19. NYW, 8/1/1928, at 10.
20. FF to WAW, 8/1/1928, WAWP, Box C-137, Folder "Frankfurter, Felix" & FFLC, Box 163, Folder "Election of 1928 May–Sept."
21. WL to FF, 8/2/1928, WLP, Reel 10, Box 10, Folder 429b.
22. FF to WL, 8/4/1928, *id.* On Sacco-Vanzetti, *see* WAW to FF, 5/9/1927, WAW Papers, Box C-120, Folder "Frankfurter, Felix"; FF to WAW, 5/19/1927, *id.*; WAW to FF, 6/1/1927, *id.*; WAW to Gov. Alvan Fuller, 6/1/1927, *id.*, Folder "Fuller, Alvan."

23. FF to WL, 9/12/1928, WLP, Reel 10, Box 10, Folder 429b.

24. NYW, 9/24/1928, at 12.

25. NYW, 9/26/1928, at 12.

26. FF to Samuel Williston, 10/18/1928, at 2, FFLC, Box 163, Folder "Election of 1928 Oct. #2."

27. FF to Belle Moskowitz, 8/11/1928, at 1, *id.*, Folder "Election of 1928 May–Sept. #1."

28. FF to WL, 8/24/1928, at 1, WLP, Reel 10, Box 10, Folder 429b.

29. Walter Lippmann, "Hoover and Smith," Vanity Fair, 9/1928, at 39.

30. *Id.* at 40.

31. FF to WL, 10/9/1928, WLP, Reel 10, Box 10, Folder 429b.

32. FF to Joseph Proskauer, 8/15/1928, FFLC, Box 163, Folder "Election of 1928 May–Sept. #1"; FF to WL, 8/15/1928, WLP, Reel 10, Box 10, Folder 429b. *See* Thomas Reed Powell, Memorandum, n.d., at 2–6, TRPP, Box A, Folder "A2b Correspondence to 1929 R-Z" (discussing dinner for Smith for forty Harvard faculty members and chaired by Frankfurter); LDB to FF, 8/24/1928, HBHS, at 338 ("Your Hoover power material will doubtless be made good use of. Smith should, in connection with power, bring out clearly its significance to the farmers with his expanding use of electricity."). Frankfurter had worked on electric power in the Wilson administration, and he and Landis had written about it in their Compact Clause article. Frankfurter and Landis, "The Compact Clause of the Constitution," 685.

33. FF to WL, 10/9/1928, WLP, Reel 10, Box 10, Folder 429b; FF to WL, 10/10/1928, WLP, Reel 10, Box 10, Folder 429b; TNR, 10/17/1928, at 240–43.

34. FF to WL, 10/2/1928, WLP, Reel 10, Box 10, Folder 429b; FF to Henry Moskowitz, 10/17/1928, FFLC, Box 163, Folder "Election of 1928 Oct. #2"; WL to Magruder, 10/9/1928, PPWL at 233–34.

35. LDB to HL, 11/29/1929, Laski-Brandeis Papers, Yale Law School, Box 733.

36. HC to FF, 10/18/1928, FFLC, Box 163, Folder "Election of 1928 Oct. #2."

37. FF, "Why I Am for Smith," TNR, 10/31/1928, at 293–95.

38. FF to WL, 11/2/1928, WLP, Reel 10, Box 10, Folder 429b.

39. Opening Remarks of FF at Symphony Hall, 11/4/1928, at 1, FFLC, Box 163, Folder "Election of 1928 Misc. #6."

40. WL to ES, 11/20/1928, WLP, Reel 28, Box 30, Folder 1104. Lippmann was not just second-guessing. *See* WL to FF, 9/13/1928, WLP, Reel 10, Box 10, Folder 429b ("I am very much afraid that Smith has wholly miscalculated the strategy in starting the campaign at this date. But for over a year he's been stubbornly convinced that his political judgment is infallible. The only way he should have dealt with the whispering campaign which everybody foresaw was to have identified himself a year ago with issues of such importance that people would have had something else to think about. He wouldn't do it because he couldn't get it out of his head that he'd always turned the trick in New York in the

last three weeks of campaigning. A real case of provincial-mindedness."). On Roosevelt's criticism of Lippmann's Prohibition advice, *see supra* notes 14–16.

41. WL to ES, 12/4/1928, WLP, Reel 28, Box 30, Folder 1104.
42. FF to Belle Moskowitz, 11/8/1928, at 1, FFLC, Box 163, Folder "Election of 1928 Nov. #3." Frankfurter's mother had died on January 10, 1928.
43. FF to Joseph Proskauer, 11/21/1928, at 3–4, *id.* ("Surely the history of the Democratic Party, if it is to be the liberal party, has warrant in its tradition for demanding a better reasoned and a more consistent program. ... From the point of view of liberal politics it is essential that it be the purposes of the new group and of its leader to be right rather than to be President.").
44. FF to WL, 11/8/1928, at 1–2, WLP, Reel 10, Box 10, Folder 429b.

CHAPTER 27

1. FF to WL, 5/31/1928, at 1, WLP, Reel 10, Box 10, Folder 429a.
2. WHT to HLS, 5/18/1928, at 2, HLSP, Reel 75, Page 867.
3. Quaker City Cab Co. v. Commonwealth, 277 U.S. 389 (1928).
4. *Id.* at 403 (Holmes, J., dissenting).
5. *Id.* at 403–12 (Brandeis, J., dissenting).
6. Black & White Taxicab & T. Co. v. Brown & Yellow Taxicab & T. Co., 276 U.S. 518 (1928). *See* OWH to FP, 5/17/1928, 2 H-P Letters at 219.
7. South Pacific Co. v. Jensen, 244 U.S. 205, 222 (1917) (Holmes, J., dissenting).
8. FF to OWH, 4/14/1928, H-FF Corr., at 225.
9. OWH to FF, 4/21/1928, *id.* at 226.
10. Olmstead v. United States, 277 U.S. 438, 478 (1928) (Brandeis, J., dissenting). *See* Samuel D. Warren and Louis D. Brandeis, "The Right to Privacy," 4 Harv. L. Rev. 193 (1890). On the drafting of Brandeis's *Olmstead* dissent, *see* Brad Snyder, "The Judicial Genealogy (and Mythology) of John Roberts: Clerkships from Gray to Brandeis to Friendly to Roberts," 71 Ohio St. L. J. 1149, 1181–82 (2010).
11. Olmstead, 277 U.S. at 469–70 (Holmes, J., dissenting). *See* OWH to FP, 6/20/1928, 2 H-P Letters at 222 ("Brandeis wrote much more elaborately, but I didn't agree with all that he said. I should have not printed what I wrote, however, if he had not asked me to.").
12. Arthur Sutherland [Holmes's secretary during the 1927 Term], "Recollections of Justice Holmes," circa 1935, at 34, Sutherland Papers, Box 24, Folder 24-7 ("I sat in the courtroom and heard the old man read his dissent. His words and voice and manner were disdainful. It seemed as though he were obliged to hold something unpleasant in his hands. I can still hear his careful voice speaking of 'this dirty business.'").
13. Olmstead, 277 U.S. 470 (Holmes, J., dissenting).
14. WHT to Horace Taft, 6/12/1928, at 1, typescript in MDHP, Group II, Box 17, Folder 44.

15. Casey v. United States, 276 U.S. 413 (1928).

16. *Id.* at 421–24 (Brandeis, J., dissenting). *See* OWH to WHT, 2/1/1928, typescript in MDH Papers, Group II, Box 17, Folder 44 (of Brandeis's dissent, Holmes wrote: "I sympathize with him but can't quite see my way to agreeing.").

17. OWH to FP, 2/17/1928, 2 H-P Letters at 215.

18. BET, 5/23/1928, §3, at 1. See FF to OWH, 6/13/1928, H-FF Corr., at 228; OWH to FF, 6/26/1928, *id.* at 230.

19. FF to WL, 6/6/1928, at 1, WLP, Box 10, Folder 10, Reel 429a.

20. NYW, 6/6/1928, at 12.

21. NYW, 6/7/1928, at 12.

22. FF to OWH, 6/13/1928, H-FF Corr., at 228–29.

23. BNC to FF, 6/3/1928, at 1–2, OWHP, Reel 28, Pages 1038–39, Box 38, Folder 27 & H-FF Corr., at 229 n. 1. On Cardozo as Smith's choice for the Supreme Court, *see* NYHT, 8/13/1928, at 4 (according to Norman Hapgood).

24. WHT to Charles Taft, 3/10/1928, MDHP, Box 17, Folder 44.

25. NYHT, 7/11/1928, at 16. *See* CT, 7/11/1928, at 10; FF to OWH, 7/11/1928, H-FF Corr., at 231.

26. OWH to NG, 7/29/1928, at 1, OWHP, Reel 24, Page 241, Box 33, Folder 13.

27. G. Edward White, *The Eastern Establishment and the Western Experience* 67–73, 184–202 (1968). Like many members of the aristocracy, Wister was an anti-Semite. His memoir of Theodore Roosevelt included a reference to Frankfurter's role in the Bisbee deportation case: "Wilson sent an Oriental to investigate the rights of the matter, and report." Wister, *Roosevelt*, 221. Reviewers noted Wister's veiled shot at Frankfurter. NYHT, 6/14/1930, at 9. Wister also attributed Holmes's and Brandeis's different views in *Pennsylvania Coal v. Mahon* to Brandeis's "sublime genius of its Oriental race." Wister, *Roosevelt*, 137. *See id.* at 134–35.

28. OWH to Wister, 7/16/1928, at 1, Francis Biddle Papers, Georgetown University Special Collections, Box 10, Folder 4 & OWHP, Box 51, Folders 35–39, Reel 39. *See* OWH to FP, 7/12/1928, 2 H-P Letters at 226 (indicating that he had received the book from Wister). Ted White has attributed Holmes's canonization to the justice's self-identification as an "epistemological modernist." G. Edward White, "The Canonization of Holmes and Brandeis," 70 N.Y.U. L. Rev. 576, 580 (1995). Holmes's interest in *The Sun Also Rises* supports White's thesis.

29. OWH to Wister, 7/16/1928. *See* Wister, *Roosevelt*, 134.

30. OWH to NG, 7/29/1928, at 2, OWHP, Reel 24, Page 242, Box 33, Folder 13; OWH to LE, 7/28/1928, H-E Letters at 287.

31. OWH to FP, 4/4/1928, 2 H-P Letters at 218.

32. OWH to NG, 10/4/1928, OWHP, Reel 24, Page 248, Box 33, Folder 13. *See* OWH to FF, 9/10/1928, H-FF Corr., at 234 ("It looks now as if I might outlive Taney which would be accomplished on or about October 21.").

33. NYW, 10/5/1928, at 12.

34. FF to WL, n.d. Friday 1928, WLP, Reel 10, Box 10, Folder 429b.

35. OWH to LE, 7/12/1927, H-E Letters at 271; LDB to HL, 3/30/1924, Laski-Brandeis Papers, Box 733.

36. OWH to LE, 6/17/1928, H-E Letters at 284.

37. OWH to NG, 11/30/1928, at 2, OWHP, Reel 24, Page 253, Box 33, Folder 13.

38. OWH to NG, 3/4/1929, at 2, *id.*, Page 269, Box 33, Folder 14. That fall, Hoover sent Holmes flowers. *See* OWH to Hoover, 10/3/1929, OWHP, Reel 27, Page 330, Box 36, Folder 26. Later that term, Holmes "persuaded" Mrs. Hoover to lunch with him and "let fall that I realized the President was a great man after reading what had been written by my friend Einstein. ..." OWH to LE, 1/16/1930, H-E Letters at 303.

39. OWH to Lady Leslie Scott, n.d., MDHP, Box 20, Folder 29.

40. LDB to FF, 4/21/1929, HBHS, at 370–71. *See* Memorandum, 5/2/1929, at 1, LHP, Box 104B, Folder 104-16; OWH to LE, 2/28/1929, H-E Letters at 294 ("My wife had a tumble which left her very uncomfortable just after recovering from a long and trying pull down that I suppose was the grippe.").

41. LDB to Susan Brandeis, 5/3/1929, FLLDB at 481.

42. OWH to NG, 5/15/1929, at 2, OWHP, Reel 24, Page 296, Box 33, Folder 15.

43. Memorandum, 5/2/1929, at 2. *See* FF to WL, 5/4/1929, at 1, WLP, Reel 10, Box 10a, Folder 430. Taft told this to Frankfurter at Fanny's funeral.

44. OWH to LE, 6/1929, H-E Letters at 297.

45. OWH to FP, 5/24/1929, 2 H-P Letters at 243. *See* OWH to Lady Leslie Scott, 5/23/1929, MDHP, Box 20, Folder 29.

46. WHT to Charles Taft, 5/12/1929, typescript in MDHP, Box 17, Folder 44.

47. LDB to FF, 4/21/1929, HBHS, at 371. *See* Lockwood to FF, 5/24/1929, at 2, FFLC, Box 145, Folder "Oliver Wendell Holmes 1929–30" (revealing his intention to take a month off before joining Holmes at Beverly Farms).

48. Lockwood to FF, 5/7/1929, FFLC, Box 145, Folder "Oliver Wendell Holmes 1929–30."

49. LDB to FF, 5/11/1929, HBHS, at 372.

50. WHT to Charles Taft, 5/12/1929; LDB to FF, 5/11/1929, HBHS, at 372.

51. Beth S. Wenger, "Radical Politics in a Reactionary Age: The Unmaking of Rosika Schwimmer, 1914–1930," *Journal of Women's History* 2 (Fall 1990): 66–99.

52. United States v. Schwimmer, 279 U.S. 644, 651–52 (1929).

53. *Id.* at 653–55 (Holmes, J., dissent). Justice Edward Sanford dissented separately that he agreed with the court of appeals.

54. TNR, 6/12/1929, at 92.

55. Lockwood to FF, 5/31/1929, FFLC, Box 145, Folder "Oliver Wendell Holmes 1929–30."

56. FF to OWH, 5/29/1929, H-FF Corr., at 240. *See* OWH to FF, 5/31/1929, *id.* at 240–41.

57. NYT, 5/29/1929, at 28.

58. E. B. White, Comment, New Yorker, 6/22/1929, at 11.

59. Rosika Schwimmer to OWH, 1/28/1930, at 1–2, JGPC/OWHP, Box 21, Folder 38. For Schwimmer's letters, *see id.*, Box 21, Folder 38. For Holmes's responses, *see* OWH to Schwimmer, 1/30/1930 & 2/5/1930, MDHP, Box 17, Folder 27.
60. FF to WL, 5/31/1929, WLP, Reel 10, Box 10a, Folder 430.
61. WL to FF, 6/4/1929, *id.*
62. FF to WL, 6/5/1929, at 1, 3, *id.* Those six justices included Harlan Fiske Stone, whose liberal credentials Frankfurter doubted even before Stone was named to the Court. *See* chapter 24 nn. 148–51.
63. WL to FF, 6/11/1929, WLP, Reel 10, Box 10a, Folder 430. *See* WL to LH, 6/6/1929, LHP, Box 106, Folder 106-18 (enclosing Frankfurter's letter and asking if it is "a bit trying"); LH to WL, 6/7/1929, *id.* ("I think it is more than 'a bit trying,' I think it is intolerable. Nobody has a right to address anybody, even an old friend, in that tone. … It is a great limitation that one can never dissent from Holmes, Brandeis and Cardozo without being guilty of sinning against the Holy Ghost. I think his estimate of the ability of these three men is entirely justified, but it is preposterous to suppose that even the best men can never be wrong. It is almost a clansmen's spirit.").
64. FF to WL, 6/12/1929, at 1, 3, WLP, Reel 10, Box 10a, Folder 430.
65. WL to FF, 6/13/1929, *id.*

CHAPTER 28

1. "Address by Hon. Peter Norbeck of South Dakota," 2/22/1929, in Black Hills Engineer, 11/1930, at 346.
2. GB to PN, 2/25/1929, at 1, GBP, Box 102, Folder "Rushmore 1928–29."
3. Everett Sanders (Coolidge's private secretary) to GB, 2/26/1929 tel. & letter, GBP, Box 165, Folder "Calvin Coolidge 1926–30."
4. PN to DR, 3/13/1929 tel., GBP, Box 102, Folder "Rushmore 1928–29" (describing Borglum's idea as "splendid"); DR to PN, 3/13/1929, GBP, Box 159, Folder "Peter Norbeck Papers 1929" ("the publicity will probably be worth what it costs" but doubting Borglum could pull it off).
5. PN to GB, 5/3/1929, GBP, Box 102, Folder "Rushmore 1928–29."
6. MB to PN, 5/6/1929, at 1, *id.*
7. GB to PN, 2/1/1929, at 7, GBP, Box 159, Folder "Peter Norbeck Papers 1929."
8. NYT, 2/14/1929, at 13.
9. GB to PN, 2/1/1929, at 7.
10. PN to John Boland, 5/17/1929, GBP, Box 159, Folder "Peter Norbeck Papers 1929." *See* Memorandum PN to Boland, 5/17/1929, at 2, *id.* (on Hoover's refusal to meet with Borglum).
11. NYHT, 6/30/1929, at SM15.
12. Mount Rushmore National Memorial, June 1930, at 22, GBP, Box 172, Folder "Brochures 1930, 1941."
13. GB to Associated Press, 8/19/1929 tel., at 1–2, GBP, Box 102, Folder "Rushmore 1928–29."

14. JGT to John Boland, 11/29/1929 & Boland to Joseph Cullinan, 12/4/1929 & Boland to Cullinan, 12/19/1929, GBP, Box 174, Folder "Tucker, J.G. 1929." Borglum believed that Tucker had "completely lost his head in the Black Hills" and had stopped following the sculptor's instructions. GB to PN, 2/1/1929, at 5.

15. GB to Associated Press, 8/19/1929 tel., at 1.

16. GB to PN, 9/22/1929, at 1–2, GBP, Box 102, Folder "Rushmore 1928–29."

17. GB to Associated Press, 8/19/1929 tel., at 2.

18. CT, 11/21/1929, at 20.

19. Annual Report of the Mount Rushmore National Memorial Commission, 12/19/1929, Mount Rushmore National Memorial, June 1930, at 29, GBP, Box 172, Folder "Brochures, 1930, 1941."

20. NYT, 4/21/1929, at 52.

21. GB to CC, 12/2/1929 tel., GBP, Box 165, Folder "Calvin Coolidge 1926–30"; GB to CC, 3/19/1930, id.

22. GB to CC, 3/19/1930, id.; SAL, 2/16/1930, at 10.

23. CC to GB, 4/1/1930, GBP, Box 165, Folder "Calvin Coolidge 1926–30."

24. CC to GB, 4/14/1930, id.

25. GB to CC, 4/22/1930, id.

26. CC to GB, 4/26/1930, id.

27. NYT, 5/13/1930, at 28. See CT, 5/13/1930, at 1; LAT, 5/13/1930, at 1; NYHT, 5/13/1930, at 13.

28. GB to Coleman du Pont, 5/17/1930, at 1, GBP, Box 84, Folder "Politics 1930."

29. NYT, 7/24/1930, at 27.

30. Williamson to Cullinan, 8/2/1930 (containing Coolidge's reply), GBP, Box 165, Folder "Coolidge Inscription 1930."

31. NYT, 11/20/1930, at 2. See "Gutzon's Progress," Time, 12/1/1930, at 42, in GBP, Box 102, Folder "Rushmore 1930–31."

32. NYT, 3/29/1930, at 22.

33. George Akerson, secretary to the president, to GB, 6/20/1930 (declining for President Hoover) & GB to HH, 6/21/1930 tel. (asking for Coolidge), GBP, Box 172, Folder "Mt. Rushmore Unveiling 1930."

34. Cullinan & GB to CC, 6/24/1930 tel., GBP, Box 165, Folder "Calvin Coolidge 1926–30." & id. at 2, Box 172, Folder 1930 "Mt. Rushmore Unveiling."

35. Smith, *The Carving of Mount Rushmore*, 283.

36. NYT, 7/5/1929, at 1. See GB to Coolidge, 3/10/1930, at 1, GBP, Box 165, Folder "Calvin Coolidge 1926–30" (suggesting letterhead bearing title "America's Shrine for Political Democracy").

37. "Ceremonies at the Unveiling of the Head of George Washington," 7/4/1930, The Program, at 7, Mount Rushmore National Memorial, No. 2, The Jefferson Number, 1931, GBP, Box 172, Folder "Brochures 1930, 1941"; NYT, 7/5/1930, at 1.

38. "Personality in Stone: Mr. Borglum's Informal Remarks," Mount Rushmore National Memorial, No. 2, The Jefferson Number, 1931, at 11, GBP, Box 172 Folder "Brochures 1930, 1941."

39. NYT, 7/6/1930, at 15.

40. AC, 8/24/1930, at 12A

41. AC, 7/27/1930, at 6K.

42. AC, 8/28/1930, at 1.

43. AC, 9/1/1930, at 1.

44. RCJ, 7/5/1930, at 7.

45. *Id.*

CHAPTER 29

1. Felix Frankfurter, *The Public and Its Government* 161, 163 (1930).

2. *Id.* at 76–77, 80.

3. Alger Hiss to FF, 2/10/1930, at 2–3, FFLC, Box 145, Folder "Holmes, Oliver Wendell 1929–30."

4. LDB to FF, 1/9/1930, FFLC, Box 27, Folder "Brandeis, Louis D. 1930 #46" & HBHS, at 405.

5. LDB to FF, 1/11/1930, FFLC, Box 27, Folder "Brandeis, Louis D. 1930 #46" & HBHS, at 406.

6. FF to WL, 1/10/1930, WLP, Reel 10, Box 10a, Folder 431.

7. NYHT, 2/4/1930, at 1; NYT, 2/4/1930, at 1; WP, 2/4/1930, at 1.

8. FF to WL, 4/2/1930, *id.*

9. Historians have debated the importance of Cotton's meeting with Hoover. A few days after the meeting, Cotton told Frankfurter about it. Cotton said that Hoover had phoned Hughes to see if the former justice was interested (and under the expectation that Hughes would decline the job). Hughes biographer Merlo Pusey discounted the importance of the Cotton meeting; Frankfurter viewed Cotton as one of Hoover's most important legal advisers. For the Pusey-Frankfurter debate, *see* FFLC, Box 147, Folder "Charles Evans Hughes 1952–58"; Pusey, 2 *Charles Evans Hughes*, 650–53. In 1937, Hoover denied discussing the Supreme Court vacancy with Cotton or that Stone had been Hoover's first choice. HH to CEH, 2/19/1937 & 2/25/1937, CEHP, Reel 5, Box 8, Folder "General Correspondence 1937, Jan.–Apr."

10. FF to WL, 2/5/1930, at 1, WLP, Reel 10, Box 10a, Folder 131.

11. *Id.*; NYW, 2/5/1930, at 10.

12. FF to WL, 2/5/1930, at 1.

13. FF to LH, 2/4/1930, at 2, LHP, Box 104B, Folder 104-17.

14. FF to WL, 2/5/1930, at 1.

15. NYW, 2/14/1930, at 10.

16. FF to WL, 2/19/1930, WLP, Reel 10, Box 10a, Folder 131.

17. Cong. Rec.–Senate at 3372–73 (2/10/1930) (Senator Norris); Cong. Rec.–Senate at 3448–53 (2/11/1930) (Sen. Borah & Sen. Wheeler); Pusey, 2 *Charles Evans Hughes*, 654–62.

18. Cong. Rec.–Senate at 3491 (2/13/1930).

19. Pusey, 2 *Charles Evans Hughes*, 659.
20. Cong. Rec.–Senate at 5007–10 (3/8/1930).
21. LDB to FF, 1/28/1930, HBHS, at 408.
22. FF to WL, 4/2/1930, at 1, WLP, Reel 10, Box 10a, Folder 431 (quoting memorandum).
23. NYT, 3/22/1930, at 1.
24. LDB to FF, 3/17/1930, HBHS, at 417 ("I hear that considerable pressure is being brought to secure Parker's nomination for U.S.S.C. & that he is being seriously considered. Would it not be well for you to get to some of insurgents via Max [Lowenthal] or otherwise, the objections to him?"). *See* Peter G. Fish, "Spite Nominations to the United States Supreme Court," 77 Ky. L. J. 545, 555–60 (1988–89) (on the liberal opposition to Parker).
25. TNR, 4/2/1930, at 178.
26. FF to WL, 3/27/1930 tel., WLP, Reel 10, Box 10a, Folder 431. Chafee shared a memorandum and digest of Parker's opinions with Frankfurter. *See* Chafee, 3/1930, "Memorandum about Judge John J. Parker," FFLC, Box 184, Folder "Supreme Court Miscellany #10."
27. NYW, 4/1/1930, at 12.
28. FF to WL, 4/1/1930, WLP, Reel 10, Box 10a, Folder 431.
29. FF to LH, 3/22/1930, LHP, Box 104B, Folder 104-18. Chauncey Belknap Diary Transcript at 8, MDHP, Box 22, Folder 26 (recalling Holmes's categorization of lawyers and judges); Wyzanski to FF, 3/18/1958, at 1–2, FFLC, Box 113, "Folder Wyzanski, Charles E. 1957–58" (recalling that Holmes had told his secretary Alger Hiss who told Wyzanski that Parker was "in the 'kitchen knife' category of judges." Wyzanski continued: "As of 1930 this was a fair judgment. But perhaps because of his chastening by the Senate, it seems to me that Parker ended up with a record high in the second quarter of the federal judiciary and well above a majority of the men appointed to the Supreme Court after his own failure."). *Id.* at 1–2. In 1955, however, Parker wrote an unsigned opinion limiting *Brown v. Board of Education* to ending state-sponsored racial segregation rather than compelling integration. *See* Briggs v. Elliott, 132 F. Supp. 776 (E.D.S.C. 1955) (per curiam).
30. FF to WL, 4/1/1930, at 2.
31. WL to FF, 4/2/1930, WLP, Reel 10, Box 10a, Folder 431. *See* NYW, 4/3/1930, at 14.
32. UMW v. Red Jacket Consol. Coal & Coke Co., 18 F.2d 839 (4th Cir. 1927). *See* Peter G. Fish, "*Red Jacket* Revisited," *Law and History Review* 5 (1987): 51.
33. Parker Confirmation Hearings at 28, 33. *See id.* at 27 ("The power of reaction will be strengthened, and the broad minded, humane, progressive influence so courageously and patriotically exercised by minority members of the highest judicial tribunal in the land correspondingly weakened.").
34. Parker Confirmation Hearings at 74 (quoting Greensboro Daily News, 4/19/1920).

35. *Id.* at 75.
36. White, *A Man Called White*, 106.
37. White to Hoover, 4/12/1930, NAACP Papers, Box C-397, Folder "Judge Parker April 14, 1930"; White to Hoover, 4/24/1930, *id.*, Folder "Judge Parker April 25, 1930"; White to Hoover, 5/5/1930 tel., NAACP Papers, Box C-398, Folder "Judge Parker May 4–May 6, 1930"; White to Curtis, 5/7/1930 tel., *id.*, Folder "Judge Parker May 7–May 8, 1930"; White, *A Man Called White*, 104–15; Kenneth W. Goings, *The NAACP Comes of Age* 19–53 (1990).
38. FF to Walter White, 11/6/1929, FFLC, Box 111, Folder "White, Walter F. 1929–32"; Arthur Spingarn to FF, 11/12/1929, *id.*; White to FF, 11/12/1929, *id.* Frankfurter, however, turned down White's invitation to serve on the NAACP's executive board because it would have required too many absences from Cambridge to attend NAACP board meetings.
39. White Testimony, 4/5/1930, FFLC, Box 111, Folder "White, Walter F. 1929–32"; White to FF, 4/23/1930 tel., *id.*
40. FF to White, 4/24/1930, *id.*
41. White to FF, 4/25/1930, *id.*
42. LDB to FF, 4/21/1930, HBHS, at 422 ("W.L.'s absence seems very fortunate.").
43. NYW, 4/17/1930, at 12.
44. NYW, 4/15/1930, at 14. *See* NYW, 4/13/1930, at 2E.
45. FF to WL, 5/3/1930, at 1–2, WLP, Reel 10, Box 10a, Folder 431.
46. NYW, 5/6/1930, at 12.
47. FF to WL, 5/8/1930, WLP, Reel 10, Box 10a, Folder 431.
48. LDB to FF, 5/8/1930, HBHS, at 424–25.
49. FF to LDB, 5/10/1930, at 1, FFLC, Box 29, Folder "Brandeis, Louis D. 1930–34 #90." *See* FF to LH, 5/26/1930, LHP, Box 104B, Folder 104-18 (describing Roberts as "a real gain").
50. LDB to FF, 5/21/1930, HBHS, at 428. *See* FF to Owen Roberts, 5/10/1930, Owen J. Roberts Papers, Box 1, Vol. 1 ("Who says Senate Rows do not good!"); LDB to Roberts, 5/21/1930, *id.*
51. *See* David Riesman, 5/18/1935, "Owen J. Roberts," FFLC, Box 184, Folder "Supreme Court Miscellany #10" (trying to make sense of Roberts's constitutional jurisprudence); Fish, "Spite Nominations," 560–75 (analyzing divide between Roberts's economic views and liberal hopes for him on the Court).
52. Felix Frankfurter, "The United States Supreme Court Molding the Constitution," Current History, 5/1930, 239–40. During the spring of 1930, Frankfurter's strategy was to educate the public about the Court's conservative economic rulings. *See* FF to Max Lowenthal, 2/19/1930, FFLC, Box 183, Folder "Supreme Court 1870–1935."
53. Frankfurter, "The United States Supreme Court Molding the Constitution," 239. *See* New State Ice Co. v. Liebmann, 285 U.S. 262, 311 (1932) (Brandeis, J., dissenting).
54. Frankfurter, *The Public and Its Government*, 76 (quoting Missouri, Kansas & Texas Ry. Co. v. May 194 U.S. 267, 270 (1904)).

55. *Id.* at 77, 80.

56. Cong. Rec.–Senate at 5008–10 (3/8/1930).

57. Harold Laski, "Mr. Justice Holmes: For His Eighty-Ninth Birthday," Harper's, 3/1930, at 415–17.

58. OWH to FP, 6/9/1930, 2 H-P Letters at 268.

59. NYW, 3/21/1930, at 14.

60. LH to FF, 2/6/1930, at 2, LHP, Box 104B, Folder 104-17.

61. Alger Hiss to FF, 2/27/1930, at 2–3, FFLC, Box 145, Folder "Holmes, Oliver Wendell 1929–30."

62. Alger Hiss to FF, 10/14/1929, at 2–3, *id.*

63. Alger Hiss to FF, 12/13/1929, at 4–5, *id.*; Hiss Interview in Louchheim, *The Making of the New Deal*, 25–26. On Hiss's deceptive way of persuading the Justice to allow Hiss to read to him, *see* G. Edward White, *Alger Hiss's Looking-Glass Wars* 17–20 (2004).

64. OWH to LE, 5/7/1930, H-E Letters at 308.

65. Alger Hiss to FF, 12/13/1929, FFLC, Box 145, Folder "Holmes, Oliver Wendell 1929–30." On Hiss's decision to marry during his year with Holmes, the way he informed the Justice at the last minute, and Holmes's irritation, *see* White, *Alger Hiss's Looking-Glass Wars*, 20–24.

66. Alger Hiss to FF, 3/20/1930, at 4, FFLC, Box 145, Folder "Holmes, Oliver Wendell 1929–30."

67. OWH to FF, 3/25/1930, H-FF Corr., at 253.

68. Alger Hiss to FF, 4/8/1930, at 2–4, FFLC, Box 145, Folder "Holmes, Oliver Wendell 1929–30."

69. Baldwin v. Missouri, 281 U.S. 586, 595 (1930) (Holmes, J., dissenting). *See* Farmers' Loan & Trust Co. v. Minnesota, 280 U.S. 204, 216 (1929) (Holmes, J., dissenting); Safe Deposit & Trust Co. v. Virginia, 280 U.S. 83, 96 (1929) (Holmes, J., dissenting).

70. LDB to FF, 5/26/1930, HBHS, at 429. *See* OWH to HL, 5/28/1930, 2 HLL at 1253–54 ("I was amused by McReynolds's remark that all 'with unclouded minds' could see &c. But to my regret I believe that the phrase does not appear in print. He readily lapses into a certain arrogance of tone—yet I believe him to be a man of feeling with a disguised tender side."); OWH to HL, 6/8/1930, *id.* at 1259 ("I suspect that McReynolds may regard me as a bird that befouls its own nest, although nothing could be farther from my wishes or intent. We are on excellent terms together, but our notions are different.").

71. LDB to FF, 5/26/1930, HBHS, at 429.

72. FF to WL, 5/29/1930, WLP, Reel 10, Box 10a, Folder 431a.

73. NYW, 6/3/1930, at 10.

74. H. L. Mencken, "Mr. Justice Holmes," American Mercury, 5/1930, 122–24 (reviewing *The Dissenting Opinions of Mr. Justice Holmes* (Alfred Lief, ed. 1930)). *See* H. L. Mencken, "The Great Holmes Mystery," American Mercury, 5/1932, 123–26.

75. Memorandum, 5/30/1930, FFLC, Box 27, Folder "Brandeis, Louis D. 1930 #46."

76. OWH to FP, 6/9/1930, 2 H-P Letters at 268; OWH to FF, 5/29/1930, H-FF Corr., at 256.

77. FF to LH, 6/6/1930, LHP, Box 104B, Folder 104-19.

78. FF to WL, 6/16/1930, WLP, Reel 10, Box 10a, Folder 431a.

79. OWH to HL, 6/21/1930, 2 HLL at 1260. Of tiring after an hour and a half, *see* OWH to HL, 6/26/1930, *id*. at 1263. Alger Hiss was there for the visit with Frankfurter, Hand, and Lippmann. Alger Hiss Interview in Louchheim, *The Making of the New Deal*, 29–30.

80. OWH to HL, 8/9/1930, 2 HLL at 1272. *See* OWH to DF, 8/7/1930, OWHP, Reel 27, Page 419, Box 36, Folder 28 ("He is a beautiful spirit, unless I greatly err, and I was enchanted to have a long talk with him."). Alger Hiss was at the Cardozo visit. Alger Hiss Interview by Monagan, pt. 2, 1/18/1980, at 40, Monagan Papers, Box 1, Folder 1–8.

81. OWH to FP, 6/28/1930, 2 H-P Letters at 270. *See* OWH to FP, 7/27 & 30/1930, *id*. at 273.

82. Miller, *Harvard's Civil War*, 170–76.

83. On legal realism, *see* Hull, *Roscoe Pound and Karl Llewellyn*; John Henry Schlegel, *American Legal Realism and Empirical Social Science* (1995); Morton J. Horwitz, *The Transformation of American Law, 1870–1960* (1992); Kalman, *Legal Realism at Yale, 1927–1960*; Edward A. Purcell Jr., *The Crisis of Democratic Theory* (1973).

84. OWH to FF, 10/17/1930, H-FF Corr., at 258–59. On Llewellyn, *see* OWH to HL, 11/10/1930, 2 HLL at 1296 ("I was particularly struck by the tone of a N.Y. professor. . . . They utter harmless things that I should not think could provoke antagonism, and that do not seem to me dazzlingly new, as if they were voices crying in the wilderness—or heroes challenging the world.").

85. OWH to FF, 1/27/1931, H-FF Corr., at 260.

86. FF to OWH, 2/6/1931, *id*. at 261.

87. Felix Frankfurter, ed., *Mr. Justice Holmes* (1931).

88. George W. Wickersham, Review of *Mr. Justice Holmes*, *American Bar Association Journal*, 9/1931, 613.

89. FF, Letter to the Editor, 9/8/1931, *American Bar Association Journal*, 11/1931, 776.

90. FF to Arthur Schlesinger Sr., 3/20/1931, FFLC, Box 101, Folder "Schlesinger, Arthur Sr. 1928–63."

91. FF to MDF, 3/7/1931, FFLC, Box 14, Folder "Marion A. Denman 1931."

92. HL to OWH, 3/2/1931, 2 HLL at 1308.

93. Harold J. Laski, "The Political Philosophy of Mr. Justice Holmes," 40 Yale L.J. 683 (1931); Frederick Pollock, "Ad Multos Annos," 31 Colum. L. Rev. 349 (1931); Morris R. Cohen, "Justice Holmes and the Nature of Law," *id*. at 352; Tributes, 44 Harv. L. Rev. 677 (1931).

94. HH to OWH, 3/7/1931, JGPC/OWHP, Box 18, Folder 12. *See* OWH to HH, 3/7/1931, OWHP, Reel 27, Page 465, Box 36, Folder 29 (thanking him for letter).

95. "A Living Judge," The Nation, 3/11/1931, at 262.

96. TNR, 3/11/1931, at 87.

97. After showing the galleys to Frankfurter, Croly declined to publish his final book, *The Breach in Civilization*, and repaid his advance to the publisher. *See* FF to Louise Croly, 3/15/1945, at 1, FFLC, Box 50, "Folder Mrs. Herbert Croly 1940–45 & und."; FFLC, Box 215, Folder "The Breach of Civilization 1920 #2" (containing Frankfurter's comments on the draft); Levy, *Herbert Croly of The New Republic*, 292–99.

98. *See* chapter 23 n. 59.

99. WL to Lynn Weldon, 3/23/1931, PPWL at 271–72.

100. NYHT, 2/27/1931, at 1. *See* "The End of the *World*," The Nation, 3/11/1931, at 261.

101. NYHT, 3/26/1931, at 19.

102. *Id.*

103. FF to Hayes, 9/9/1931, Ralph Hayes Papers, Container 9, Folder 177 & in Steel, *Walter Lippmann and the American Century*, 280.

104. HL to OWH, 3/23/1931, 2 HLL at 1311.

105. GB to OWH, 3/8/1931, JGPC/OWHP, Box 59, Folder 11.

106. BB to GB, 5/13/1931, GBP, Box 102, Folder "Rushmore 1930–1931" (declining to contribute).

107. GB to HH, 10/2/1931, at 1, GBP, Box 167, Folder "Herbert Hoover 1931–32"; GBP to HH, 12/18/1931, *id.*

108. GB to HH, 10/2/1931, at 2–3.

109. BG, 3/9/1931, at 12. *See* HCrim, 3/7/1931.

110. Alger Hiss Interview by Monagan, pt. 2, 1/18/1980, at 41–42.

111. NYT, 3/9/1931, at 18.

112. Charles Clark to OWH, 3/3/1931, OWHP, Reel 29, Page 644, Box 39, Folder 21.

113. NYT, 3/9/1931, at 1.

114. *Id. See* "A Little Finishing Canter," Time, 3/16/1930, at 18; NYHT, 3/9/1931, at 1; CSM, 3/10/1931, at 16; BaltSun, 3/9/1931, at 8; LAT, 3/10/1931, at A4.

115. CT, 3/10/1931, at 3.

116. OWH to Clark, 3/12/1931, OWHP, Reel 27, Page 468, Box 36, Folder 29.

117. Clark to OWH, 3/14/1931, JGPC/OWH, Box 15, Folder 13 & OWHP, Reel 29, Page 645, Box 39, Folder 21.

118. OWH to FP, 7/27/1931, at 2 H-P Letters at 292.

119. BG, 3/16/1931, at 13.

120. OWH to HL, 6/20/1931, 2 HLL at 1319.

121. OWH to HL, 10/9/1931, *id.* at 1334; Chapman Rose Interview with Monagan, 9/17/1980, at 3, Monagan Papers, Box 1, Folder 1-14.

122. OWH to J. Weston Allen, 9/10/1931, in 17 A.B.A. Journal 1717 (1931).

123. OWH to FF, 10/23/1931, H-FF Corr., at 266.

124. LDB to FF, 9/28/1931, HBHS, at 466.

125. LDB to FF, 10/5/1931, *id.* at 468.

126. Chapman Rose Interview with Monagan 9/17/1980, at 5.

127. LDB to FF, 10/25/1931, HBHS, at 469.

128. Chapman Rose Interview with Monagan, 9/17/1980, at 11.

129. LDB to FF, 12/27/1931, HBHS, at 472.

130. Hughes, Autobiographical Notes Folder, "Chief Justice–1930–41," at 11, CEHP, Box 182, Reel 140. *See The Autographical Notes of Charles Evans Hughes* 299 (David J. Danelski and Joseph S. Tulchin, eds., 1973) (describing it as a "disagreeable duty").

131. Pusey, 2 *Charles Evans Hughes* at 681 (based on interview with Hughes about the meeting).

132. Chapman Rose Interview with Monagan, 9/17/1980, at 12.

133. LDB to FF, 1/10/1932, HBHS, at 472.

134. Rose to FF, 1/12/1932 tel., FFLC, Box 145, Folder "Rose, H. Chapman 1931–32."

135. NYHT, 1/14/1932, at 21.

136. NYHT, 1/21/1932, at 19.

137. TNR, 1/27/1932, at 279.

138. Andrew L. Kaufman, *Cardozo* 455–71 (1998); Andrew L. Kaufman, "Cardozo's Appointment to the Supreme Court," 1 Cardozo L. Rev. 23 (1979); Ira H. Carmen, "The President, Politics and the Power of Appointment," 55 Va. L. Rev. 616 (1969). Kaufman's 1979 *Cardozo Law Review* article is the most complete account and accords with my views.

139. Wise to FF, 1/19/1932, Andrew Kaufman Papers, Box 15, Folder 43.

140. HFS to George Hellman, 11/30/1939, at 1, HFSP, Box 16.

141. Mason, *Harlan Fiske Stone,* 336.

142. LDB to FF, 2/25/1932, HBHS, at 478 ("I doubt whether Cardozo would be helped by having him now set wise about McR. As I wrote you, it is not only McR, but Butler and Van who protested in advance to the A.G. Whether they represented Sutherland also, Harlan did not know.").

143. Van Devanter to Mrs. John W. Lacey, 1/11/1932, at 2–3, Van Devanter Papers, Box 16, Book 45.

144. Van Devanter to Hon. Frank B. Kellogg, 1/14/1932, at 1–2, *id.*

145. LDB to FF, 1/26/1932, HBHS, at 474.

146. HFS to FF, 2/9/1932, FFLC, Box 105, Folder "Stone, Harlan F. 1932 #5."

147. FF to HFS, 2/5/1932, *id.*

148. FF to HLS, 2/9/1932, FFLC, Box 103, Folder "Stimson, Henry L. 1932." *See* LDB to FF, 2/13/1932, HBHS, at 475 ("Glad you wrote Stimson about R. R. would be the supreme calamity.").

149. Diary Entry of 1/16/1932, HLSD, Vol. 20, Reel 4, Page 58; FF to HLS, 2/10/1932, at 1, FFLC, Box 103, Folder "Stimson, Henry L. 1932"; FF to LH, 1/22/1932, at 2, LHP, Box 104B, Folder 104-21.

150. FF to HLS, 2/10/1932, at 1–2.

151. Diary Entry of 1/24/1932, HLSD, Vol. 20, Reel 4, Page 88 (noting that he had discussed vacancy with Hoover a few days earlier).

152. Diary Entry of 1/19/1932, at 3, *id.* at Page 72; Diary Entry of 1/22/1932, at 3, *id.* at Page 86.

153. HLS to FF, 2/12/1932, FFLC, Box 103, "Folder Stimson, Henry L. 1932."

154. LDB to FF, 2/16/1932, HBHS, at 476.

155. Diary Entry of 2/14/1932, at 3, HLSD, Vol. 20, Reel 4, Page 171.

156. Telephone Memorandum, 2/15/1932, Hoover Presidential Library, Post-presidential Subject File, Cardozo appointment, 1938; Kaufman, *Cardozo*, 467.

157. Herbert Hoover, 2 *The Memoirs of Herbert Hoover* 268–69 (1952).

158. Van Devanter to Mrs. John W. Lacey, 2/29/1932, at 4, Van Devanter Papers, Box 16, Book 45. *See* Van Devanter to Hon. Frank B. Kellogg, 3/10/1932, at 2, *id.* ("I understand that some of the senators told the President they would oppose the nomination of any one whose views were not in keeping with those of the retiring Justice, and I think that even Mitchell advised the selection of such a man.").

159. FF to HLS, 2/17/1932, FFLC, Box 103, Folder "Stimson, Henry L. 1932."

160. FF to HFS, 2/15/1932, FFLC, Box 105, Folder "Stone, Harlan Fiske 1932 #6."

161. LDB to FF, 2/16/1932, HBHS, at 476 (describing Cardozo's nomination as an "unexpected boon"); LDB to FF, 3/17/1932, *id.* at 480 ("Yes, Borah did a good job on B.N.C. & I think S.S.W. is entitled to much of credit.")

162. Hoover and his private secretary insisted that Borah had nothing to do with the final decision. HH to Irving Dilliard, 7/22/1938, Hoover Presidential Library, Post-presidential Subject File, Cardozo Appointment, 1938; Walter Newton, Secretary to Hoover, Letter to the Editor, NYT, 11/22/1938, at 22, in *id.*

163. FF to HH, 2/16/1932, FFLC, Box 67, Folder "Hoover, Herbert 1919–32."

164. TNR, 2/24/1932, at 28.

CHAPTER 30

1. FF, "Pledges of Hoover Not Fulfilled," 10/23/1932, FFLC, Box 164, Folder "1932 Election Miscellaneous #5" (see typewritten comments).

2. Freedman, *Roosevelt and Frankfurter*, 52 (surmising that "Roosevelt assigned Walter Lippmann a high place among his 'deliberate editorial cads.'").

3. *Id.* at 45 ("During all this period Frankfurter often presented Roosevelt's case to Lippmann, arguing with a freedom which the Governor hesitated to exercise.").

4. NYHT, 1/8/1932, at 19.

5. FF to SK, 4/1/1932, at 2, FFLC, Box 164, Folder "Presidential Election of 1932 Mar.–Sept. #2." Frankfurter was referring to Newton Baker's devoted aide, Ralph Hayes.

6. James C. Bonbright (Columbia Business School) to FF, 2/3/1932, FFLC Box 164, Folder "Presidential Election of 1932 February #1." On Bonbright, *see* FF to LH, 10/22/1929, LHP, Box 104B, Folder 104-17.

7. FDR to Morris Llewellyn Cooke, 1/18/1932, *F.D.R.: His Personal Letters, 1928–1945*, Vol. 3, at 254.

8. FF to SSW, 2/6/1932, at 1, FFLC, Box 164, Folder "Presidential Election of 1932 February #1."

9. FF to ES, 2/10/1932, at 1, *id.*

10. FF, "Extract from a Letter to a Friend," 1/9/1932, at 1, FFLC, Box 164, Folder "Presidential Election of 1932 #5."

11. *Id.* at 1–2.

12. *Id.* at 2.

13. FF to ES, 2/10/1932, at 2.

14. FF to Proskauer tel., 2/22/1932, FFLC, Box 164, Folder "Presidential Election of 1932 February #1."

15. Proskauer to FF, 2/23/1932, *id.*

16. FF to Proskauer, 2/27/1932, at 1–2, *id.*

17. FF to ES, 2/10/1932, at 3.

18. NYHT, 2/12/1932, at 13.

19. FF to Belle Moskowitz, 3/17/1932, at 1, FFLC, Box 164, Folder "Presidential Election of 1932 March to September #2." *See* FF to Proskauer, 3/5/1932, *id.*

20. NYHT, 4/20/1932, at 19.

21. NYHT, 4/28/1932, at 7.

22. NYHT, 4/28/1932, at 17.

23. NYHT, 5/6/1932, at 19.

24. WL to NDB, 5/9/1932, NDBP, Box 149, Folder "Walter Lippmann 1932."

25. NYHT, 6/29/1932, at 19.

26. Craig, *Progressives at War*, 318–22.

27. NYT, 7/3/1932, at 8.

28. WL to NDB, 7/18/1932, at 1, NDBP, Box 149, Folder "Walter Lippmann 1932." *See* WL to NDB, 7/29/1932, at 2, *id.*

29. "Memorandum of Telephone Conversation between Felix Frankfurter and Governor Roosevelt," 7/2/1932, *Roosevelt and Frankfurter*, 74.

30. NYT, 6/23/1932, at 23.

31. LDB to FF, 6/26/1932, HBHS, at 492 (counseling him to turn it down); LDB to FF, 7/7/1932, *id.* at 494–95 (revealing Thompson's and Ehrmann's disappointment).

32. Chapman Rose to FF, 6/30/1932, at 2–4, FFLC, Box 98, Folder "H. Chapman Rose 1931–58" (including Frankfurter note dated 7/7/1932); Rose to FF, 7/8/1932, *id.*; FF, "Memorandum of Conversation with Chapman Rose, secretary to Justice Holmes," 7/8/1932, *id.*

33. FF to Ely, 6/29/1932, FFLC, Box 53, Folder "Ely, Joseph B. 1932–49" (indicating letter was backdated by one day).

34. FF to FDR, 7/22/1932, *Roosevelt and Frankfurter*, 78.

35. FF to Rosenman, 7/11/1932, FFLC, Box 164, Folder "Presidential Election of 1932 March–Aug. #2"; FF to Molly Dewson, 7/18/1932, *id.*; FF to Frances Perkins, 7/18/1932, *id.*

36. FF to Dewson, 7/18/1932, *id.*

37. NYHT, 7/31/1932, at 15.

38. FF to FDR, 8/5/1932, *Roosevelt and Frankfurter*, at 80–81.

39. FF to FDR, 9/2/1932, *id.* at 85.

40. NYT, 9/7/1932, at 18.

41. Paul Dickson and Thomas B. Allen, *The Bonus Army* 6 (2004).

42. NYHT, 9/11/1932, at SM8.

43. NYHT, 10/7/1932, at 21.

44. NYHT, 9/22/1932, at 19; NYHT, 10/21/1932, at 19.

45. FF to WL, 10/13/1932, *Roosevelt and Frankfurter*, 89.

46. NYHT, 9/27/1932, at 19.

47. GB, "Why I Am a Republican," Typescript, at 1–2, 6–7, GBP, Box 84, Folder "Politics 1931" (emphasis in original).

48. GB to HH, 10/2/1931, GBP, Box 84, Folder "Politics 1931"; GB to Mrs. Harry K. Daugherty, 5/9/1932, *id.*

49. GB to Mrs. Ellis A. Yost, 6/23/1932, GBP, Box 84, Folder "Politics 1932."

50. Chas. F. Scott to GB, 7/6/1932, *id.*

51. GB to Frank Hitchcock, 9/2/1932, at 1, *id.*; CT, 9/5/1932, at 2.

52. NYT, 9/5/1932, at 3.

53. "Gutzon Borglum's Remarks in Part," 9/7/1932, at 1–3, GBP, Box 84, Folder "Politics 1932." See NYHT, 9/7/1932, at 2.

54. GB to Mrs. William B. Meloney, NYHT editorial department, 9/19/1932, at 3, GBP, Box 84, Folder "Politics 1932."

55. NYT, 6/27/1932, at 8; NYT, 6/10/1932, at 4.

56. GB to Mrs. William B. Meloney, 9/19/1932, at 3.

57. GB to PN, 8/12/1932, GBP, Box 159, Folder "Peter Norbeck Papers 1930 to 1934."

58. PN to GB, 4/12/1934, at 1, *id.*

59. *See* chapter 11 n. 136.

60. GB to WAW, 10/4/1932, GBP, Box 84, Folder "Politics 1932."

61. NYHT, 9/26/1932, at 1; NYT, 9/26/1932, at 1.

62. GB to Sen. George Norris, 9/25/1932, at 1, GBP, Box 84, Folder "Politics 1932."

63. GB to GJ, 11/7/1932, at 2, 4, GBP, Box 12, Folder "J."

64. EGE, "Felix Frankfurter: Citizen, Teacher, Friend," Typescript, at 6–7 & Springfield Republican, 1/15/1933, EGE Papers, Reel 9, Folder 157.

65. Hans Zinsser to FF, 11/1932, at 3, FFLC, Box 164, Folder "Presidential Election of 1932 Sept.–Nov. #3"; Zinsser to FF, 11/2/1932, *id.*

66. SSW to FF, 9/8/1932, at 1, *id.*, Folder "Presidential Election of 1932 Mar.–Sept. #2."

67. FF to SSW, 9/14/1932, at 1, 3, *id.*

68. FF to Swope, 10/6/1932, *id.*; FF to Belle Moskowitz, 10/14/1932, *id.*
69. FF to Al Smith, 10/24/1932, *id.*
70. FF to Swope, 10/26/1932 tel., *id.*
71. FF to Swope, 11/2/1932, *id.*
72. FF to WL, 10/28/1932, *Roosevelt and Frankfurter*, 92.
73. HCrim, 10/15/1932, in FFLC, Box 197, Folder "Writings of Felix Frankfurter, 1932–1938."
74. NYT, 10/16/1932, at 30.
75. FF, "Pledges of Hoover Not Fulfilled," 10/23/1932.
76. Freedman, *Roosevelt and Frankfurter*, 93.
77. FF, "Campaign Speech over W.B.J.," 11/5/1932, at 3, 5, FFLC, Box 197, Folder "Writings of Felix Frankfurter, 1932–1938."
78. NYHT, 11/10/1932, at 19.
79. FF to FDR, 11/7/1932 tel., *Roosevelt and Frankfurter*, 93.
80. FF to FDR, 11/10/1932, *id.*

CHAPTER 31

1. OWH to HL, 11/7/1932, 2 HLL at 1415.
2. Eleanor Roosevelt, *This I Remember* 53–54 (1949) ("Franklin had known him quite well when he, Franklin, was Assistant Secretary of the Navy, and he often joined the Sunday-afternoon meetings that Justice Holmes held with some of the young men in Washington at that time."); Harvey Bundy COH at 64 (recalling that Roosevelt "would turn up at tea-time").
3. OWH to HL, 11/23/1932, 2 HLL at 1420.
4. The original source of the quotation was James MacGregor Burns, *Roosevelt: The Lion and the Fox* 157 (1956). Burns claimed that Holmes had made the comment after meeting President Roosevelt on March 8, 1933. *Id.* Burns listed his source for the quote as "confidential." *Id.* at 507. Burns interviewed both Frankfurter and Tom Corcoran for the book. *See id.* at 492. Corcoran, notorious for telling tall tales, was the most likely source. He was not at the Holmes-Roosevelt meeting, though he recalled seeing the justice "a couple of days later." Corcoran, *Rendezvous with Democracy*, Chapter 4-10, TGCP, Box 586. Corcoran's unpublished memoir repeats the "second-class intellect, but a first-class temperament" line several times. *See id.* at Chapter 4-12 & Holmes D/2-38 (crossed out).

    Many scholars believe that the quote refers to Theodore, not Franklin. In his letters, Holmes frequently referred to Theodore's intellect as "ordinary." *See* OWH to FP, 2/9/1921, 2 H-P Letters at 64 ("He was very likeable, a big figure, a rather ordinary intellect, with extraordinary gifts, a shrewd and I think pretty unscrupulous politician. He played all his cards–if not more. *R.i.p.*"); OWH to LE, 1/17/1928, H-E Letters at 277 ("You surprise me by your great interest in [Theodore] Roosevelt; not that he is not an interesting and striking figure but because I think he was entirely right in regarding his intellect as ordinary. I don't doubt that it had some extraordinary qualities, especially memory, but his reactions on what he knew seemed to me to be commonplace. ..."). *See* Richard A. Posner, Introduction, *The Essential Holmes* xiv–xv (1992) (describing the "first-class temperament" quote as "apocryphal" and as referring to Theodore, "though it is not clear that [Holmes] ever stated it so pithily").

5. FF and MDF Memorandum, 8/10/1932, at 1, 3, MDHP, Box 22, Folder 26, "Anecdotes, 1895–1964." On Holmes's later years, *see* Monagan, *The Great Panjandrum*.

6. HL to OWH, 10/9/1932, 2 HLL at 1409 ("You, I hear from Felix, are immersed (oh wise judge!) in detective stories, with an emphasis on the need for action on every page.").

7. OWH to LE, 3/16/1932, H-E Letters at 338.

8. Oliver Wendell Holmes, Introduction, *Mr. Justice Brandeis* ix (Felix Frankfurter, ed., 1932).

9. FF and MDF Memorandum, 8/10/1932, at 1–3.

10. *Id.* at 4 (emphasis in original).

11. *Id.*

12. Arthur Hill to Francis Biddle, 2/19/1932, Biddle Papers, Georgetown University, Box 9, Folder 71. In the spring of 1933, Mrs. Ralph (Elizabeth) Ellis asked Holmes: "How do you pass your time! Do you take vivid interest in the work of the Supreme Court?" Holmes replied: "No I do not. What I want is that my days should pass as a rock in a bed of a river, with the water flowing over it." N.d., MDHP, Box 22, Folder 26, Anecdotes, 1895–1964.

13. Powell v. Alabama, 141 So. 201, 214 (1932) (Anderson, C.J., dissenting). After the U.S. Supreme Court's 1932 decision, the defendants were retried three times and were found guilty three times even though one of the women had recanted her rape allegations. *See* James Goodman, *Stories of Scottsboro* (1994); Dan T. Carter, *Scottsboro* (revised ed., 1979).

14. Powell v. Alabama, 287 U.S. 45, 71 (1932). Justice Butler, joined by Justice McReynolds in dissent, rejected the claim that the defendants had been denied the right to counsel. *Id.* at 73–74 (Butler, J., dissenting). They also objected to the majority opinion's invocation of the Due Process Clause to interfere with state criminal trials as an "extension of federal authority into a field hitherto occupied exclusively by the several States." *Id.* at 76.

15. NYT, 11/13/1932, at E1.

16. NYHT, 2/16/1933, at 1; NYT, 2/17/1933, at 1. A woman initially claimed to have grabbed the gunman. Some doubt the woman's story based on another eyewitness who claimed that he had grabbed the gunman's arm. *See* Blaise Picchi, *The Five Weeks of Giuseppe Zangara* 17–18, 28–32 (1998).

17. Picchi, *The Five Weeks of Giuseppe Zangara*, 28.

18. CT, 2/16/1933, at 1.

19. FF to FDR, 2/23/1933, *Roosevelt and Frankfurter*, 108.

20. Samuel I. Rosenman, *Working with Roosevelt* 89–91 (1952) (describing the last-minute insertion of the "fear itself" paragraph into Roosevelt's inaugural address).

21. FFR, 241–42 (recalling he had arranged it two days before Christmas Day when he and Marion had stayed overnight at Hyde Park).

22. Donald Hiss Interview by John Monagan, 10/13/1979 & 6/3/1980, Monagan Papers, at 6, 25, 43–45, Box 1, Folder 9 & Monagan, *The Grand Panjandrum*, 1; Donald Hiss Interview by Katie Louchheim, 11/14/1981, Tape I, Side I, Pages 7–10, in Louchheim Papers, Box 79, Folder 79, Folder 6 & "Recollection of Donald Hiss," in *The Making of the New Deal*, 37. *See* FFR, 242 (recalling the champagne had been produced by the wife of the justice's nephew Edward Holmes and that she said it was from the French embassy).

23. "Memorandum by Frankfurter of a Visit with Roosevelt on March 8, 1933, When the President Asked Frankfurter to Become Solicitor General," 3/15/1933, *Roosevelt and Frankfurter*, 110. For less contemporaneous recollections, *see* FFR, 242; Donald Hiss Interview in Monagan, *Grand Panjandrum*, 1–3; Donald Hiss Interview in *The Making of the New Deal*, 36–38.

24. FF, Memorandum, 3/15/1933, *Roosevelt and Frankfurter*, at 110 (recalling Holmes had three or four glasses); Hiss Interview in Monagan, *The Grand Panjandrum*, 1 (quoting Holmes).

25. FF, Memorandum, 3/15/1933, *Roosevelt and Frankfurter*, at 110.

26. FDR: Day by Day, 3/8/1933, FDR Library http://www.fdrlibrary.marist.edu/daybyday/daylog/march-8th-1933/ (noting the time as 5:40 p.m.); Eleanor Roosevelt to Lorena Hickok, 3/8/1933, at 3, Lorena Hickok Papers, Franklin Delano Roosevelt Library, Box 1 "Mar.–Nov. 1933" ("At 5:30 pm, Franklin, James, and I went to Justice Holmes'."); FF, Memorandum, 3/15/1933, *Roosevelt and Frankfurter*, 113 ("So I turned up at Holmes' at 5:30 when President and Mrs. Roosevelt and James came to call.")

27. Donald Hiss Interview by Monagan, 10/13/1979, Pt. 2, at 45; Monagan, *The Grand Panjandrum*, 1–2.

28. Donald Hiss Interview in *The Making of the New Deal*, 37.

29. BG, 3/9/1933, at 9.

30. An AP photograph shows Roosevelt with a cane (hidden behind his son James's back). AP photo, 3/8/1933, 330308064 (on file with author). *Cf.* FFR, 247 (recalling that "it took the President about half an hour to negotiate the stairs of that old brownstone house. There was no ramp. … After an hour FDR stumped out on those stairs. It was hard for him to manage.") *with* Donald Hiss Interview by Monagan, 10/13/1979, Pt. 2, at 47 & Donald Hiss Interview in *The Making of the New Deal*, 37 (recalling that the Secret Service had installed a ramp and that Roosevelt had used a wheelchair) & Corcoran, *Rendezvous with Democracy*, Chapter 4-10–4-11 (recalling that Holmes's housekeeper, Mary Donnellan, had told him a few days later "how the President's wheelchair had been muscled in the elevator to the second floor"). *See* James

Tobin, *The Man He Became* 285–86 (2013) (arguing that as governor Roosevelt only used "his wheelchair without self-consciousness" among intimate friends, and his "fear of falling between chairs" was the main reason he did not use a wheelchair in public) & *id.* at 1–4 (describing his use of braces during his 1933 inauguration as president); Hugh Gregory Gallagher, *FDR's Splendid Deception* 97 (1985) ("The president moved quite literally in a ramped world. Wherever he went, the Secret Service went first. They built ramps for his use at every point."); Michael F. Reilly, *Reilly of the White House* 160 (1947) ("Because the Boss couldn't use normal steps, it was necessary to build ramps wherever his plane was to land. ..."); Rosenman, *Working with Roosevelt*, 22 (recalling the "strenuous physical ordeal for him to get in and out of automobiles. ... He could not climb stairs and often we had to carry him up some back stairs of a hall and down again."). The brownstone had one step, a landing, seven steps, another landing, and one more step. "Residence of Justice Oliver Wendell Holmes, 1720 I Street," 1935, Library of Congress, Prints and Photographs, Lot 10304 (G).

31. NYHT, 3/9/1933, at 3.
32. Donald Hiss Interview in *The Making of the New Deal*, 37–38.
33. *Id.*; Donald Hiss Interview by Monagan, 10/13/1979, Pt. 2, at 45–46; Monagan, *The Grand Panjandrum*, 1–2.
34. James Roosevelt and Sidney Shalett, *Affectionately, F.D.R.* 92 (1959).
35. FFR, 247.
36. Eleanor Roosevelt to Lorena Hickok, 3/8/1933, at 3.
37. Donald Hiss Interview in Monagan, *The Grand Panjandrum*, 2–3. *See* Donald Hiss Interview in *The Making of the New Deal*, 38.
38. White, *Law and the Inner Self*, 470 & 587 n. 107. As White points out, the quote comes from Alger Hiss, who was not there and most likely paraphrased his brother's recollections. *See* Alger Hiss, *Recollections of a Life* 33 (1988).
39. Donald Hiss Interview with Louchheim, Tape 1, Side 1, Page 11, in *The Making of the New Deal*, 38.
40. *Id.*; Monagan, *The Grand Panjandrum*, 2.
41. Donald Hiss Interview in Monagan, *The Grand Panjandrum*, 2; FFR, 247.
42. Frankfurter, Memorandum, 3/15/1933, *Roosevelt and Frankfurter*, 113.
43. NYT, 3/9/1933, at 17; Time, 3/20/1933, at 9.
44. BG, 3/9/1933, at 9; Eleanor Roosevelt to Lorena Hickok, 3/8/1933, at 1.
45. BG, 3/9/1933, at 9.

EPILOGUE

1. Frankfurter, Memorandum, 3/15/1933, *Roosevelt and Frankfurter*, 111–12; NYT, 3/9/1933, at 9. Roosevelt's initial choice for attorney general, Senator Thomas Walsh of Montana, had opposed Frankfurter for solicitor general. Walsh, however, died two days before the inauguration, and Roosevelt's second choice

for attorney general, Homer Cummings, consented to Frankfurter as solicitor general.

2. Frankfurter, Memorandum, 3/15/1933, *Roosevelt and Frankfurter*, 114 ("Brandeis said for me to take the Solicitor Generalship would be 'absurd.'").

3. *Id.* at 111–12.

4. *Id.* at 112–13.

5. FF to MDF, 4/8/1933, at 2, 4, FFLC, Box 14, Folder "Marion A. (Frankfurter) Denman 1933 #123."

6. MDF to EGE, 2/13/1934, EGEP, Reel 4, Folder 59.

7. DFF, 5/8/1933, at 138–40; Ben Cohen Interview by Joseph Alsop, 8/5/1938, at 1–4, JSAP, Box 93, Folder 3; Raymond Moley, *After Seven Years* 179–84 (1939); Kenneth Crawford Interview in *The Making of the New Deal*, 114–16; Parrish, *Felix Frankfurter and His Times*, 232–37; Jordan A. Schwarz, *The New Dealers* 145–47 (1993).

8. Moley, *After Seven Years*, 284–86 (recalling Cohen's and Corcoran's work on the 1934 Securities Act); Corcoran, *Rendezvous with Democracy*, Folio for Chapter 4-4-4-16, TGCP, Box 586; Parrish, *Felix Frankfurter and His Times*, 249–50 (on the Public Utility Holding Company Act); Schwarz, *The New Dealers*, 149–51 (on the Public Utility Holding Company Act).

9. BG, 5/15/1933, at 18.

10. General Hugh S. Johnson, "Think Fast, Captain!," Saturday Evening Post, 10/26/1935, at 7. *See* "Felix Frankfurter," Fortune, 1/1936, at 63 & *Roosevelt and Frankfurter*, 303 (quoting Johnson's criticisms and the *New York American*'s description of him as the "Iago" of the Roosevelt administration); Parrish, *Felix Frankfurter and His Times*, 228–30; Schwarz, *The New Dealers*, 126–28; Sujit Raman, "Felix Frankfurter and His Protégés," *Journal of Supreme Court History* 39, no. 1 (Spring 2014): 79–106; G. Edward White, "Felix Frankfurter, the Old Boy Network, and the New Deal," 39 Ark. L. Rev. 631 (1986); WP, 3/11/1934, at B1; NYHT, 10/27/1935, at A1.

11. Of the "overabundance" of Jewish lawyers during the New Deal, *see* 1/ Auerbach, *Unequal Justice*, 187–88; Peter H. Irons, *The New Deal Lawyers* 126–28 (1982); Schwarz, *The New Dealers*, 128–30; Moley, *After Seven Years*, 130 (mentioning Nathan Margold as solicitor in the Interior Department, Charles Wyzanski Jr. in the Labor Department, and Jerome Frank in the Agricultural Adjustment Administration). Others included Herbert Feis in the State Department, Paul Freund in the Justice Department, and David Lilienthal in the Tennessee Valley Authority.

12. David Nasaw, *The Patriarch* 574 (2012) (quoting Kennedy's "Diary Notes on the 1944 Political Campaign").

13. Johnson, "Think Fast, Captain!," 85. *See* FF to Alfred Cohn, 10/30/1935, in *Roosevelt and Frankfurter*, 288–91 (indicating that Frankfurter spurned Johnson's offer to become general counsel of the National Recovery Administration and Frankfurter's subsequent relations with Johnson); Moley, *After Seven Years*,

307 (recalling that "Hugh stamped around Washington hurling imprecations against Felix" because of Frankfurter's opposition to the Johnson-administered National Industrial Recovery Act).

14. Frank Watson Interview, Tape 1, Side 1, Page 1, Louchheim Papers, Box 79, Folder 1 "The Making of the New Deal" & in *The Making of the New Deal*, 105–6.

15. Katie Louchheim, "The Little Red House," *Virginia Quarterly Review* 1/1980.

16. FDR to FF, 1/15/1937, *Roosevelt and Frankfurter*, at 377 ("Very confidentially, I may give you an awful shock in about two weeks. Even if you do not agree, suspend final judgment and I will tell you the story."); FF to FDR, 2/7/1937, *id.* at 380–81 ("Yes, you 'shocked' me. ... But beyond that–well, the momentum of a long series of decisions not defensible in the realm of reason nor justified by settled principles of Constitutional interpretation had convinced me, as they had convinced you, that means had to be found to save the Constitution from the Court, and the Court from itself.").

17. Though Congress rejected the plan, the Court became more deferential to state and federal laws after Roosevelt's initial announcement. Some scholars have vigorously disputed whether the court-packing plan caused a "switch in time that saved nine." *See* Barry Cushman, *Rethinking the New Deal Court* (1998) (arguing the Court had already switched in 1934 with *Nebbia v. New York*). As Cushman points out, the justices had voted to overrule *Adkins v. Children's Hospital* and to uphold a state minimum wage law in *West Coast Hotel v. Parrish* prior to Roosevelt's announcement.

18. Freedman, *Roosevelt and Frankfurter*, 372 & FF to FDR, 2/18/1937, *id.* at 383–87; Joseph Lash, "A Brahmin of the Law," in DFF, 60–63; Jeff Shesol, *Supreme Power* 333–34 (2010); Edward A. Purcell Jr., *Brandeis and the Progressive Constitution*, 206–7 (2000).

19. Brad Snyder, "Frankfurter and Popular Constitutionalism," 47 U.C. Davis. L. Rev. 343, 411–13 (2013).

20. FFR, 284.

21. ToL, 4/14/1958, at 16.

22. Freedman, *Roosevelt and Frankfurter*, 744.

23. Corcoran, *Rendezvous with Democracy*, at Chapter 4-11, TGCP, Box 586.

24. FF to WL, 3/11/1933, *Roosevelt and Frankfurter*, 117.

25. NYHT, 3/7/1933, at 15.

26. Freedman, *Roosevelt and Frankfurter*, 115. Freedman was Frankfurter's authorized biographer.

27. Walter Lippmann, *An Inquiry into the Principles of the Good Society* 45–155 (1937) (comparing the "gradual collectivism" of the New Deal with the rise of collectivist and totalitarian regimes in Russia, Italy, and Germany).

28. LDB to FF, 4/29/1933, HBHS, at 520 ("I guess the Jews of Germany had better make up their minds to move on, all of them. Of course, the nation is crazy now, but life there will never be safe, and it has been distinctly degrading to the present generation of Jews. ... Hitlerism shows that the Allies were right in

1914, in opposing with all available force German aggression. If only they had not been wrong in 1919."); Felix Frankfurter, "Persecution of Jews in Germany," *The World Today*, 4/1934, at 36–38, *in* FFLC, Box 197, Scrapbook "Writings 1932–1938," at 162–64.

29. NYHT, 5/19/1933, at 19. *See* NYHT, 5/12/1933, at 13.

30. FF to WL, 11/28/1936, FFLC, Box 77, Folder "Lippmann, Walter 1933 #21)" (quoting NYHT, 5/19/1933, at 19). *See* Gunther, *Learned Hand*, 490–93.

31. The Nation, 7/5/1933, at 7, 10.

32. The Nation, 7/12/1933, at 36, 37.

33. The Nation, 7/19/1933, 70.

34. The Nation, 8/2/1933, at 126.

35. FF to Amos Pinchot, 7/7/1933, Amos Pinchot Papers, Box 67, Folder "Walter Lippmann."

36. HL to Gruening, 7/14/1933, *id. See* HL to FF and MDF, 4/30/1933, FFLC, Box 74, Folder "Harold Laski 1933 #8" (after a meeting with Lippmann, describing him as "pompous?" and "eagerly isolationist, childishly of the belief that we have only to make Germany prosperous to ruin Hitler …").

37. Amos R. Pinchot, "Roosevelt-Laski Scheme," *Scribner's Commentator*, at 62, Amos Pinchot Papers, Box 95, Folder "Laski 1941."

38. See ALL to FDR, 2/20/1936; FDR to FF, 2/24/1936; FF to FDR, 2/29/1936; FDR to FF, 2/29/1936; FF to FDR, 3/4/1936; FDR to Lowell, 3/6/1936; ALL to FDR, 4/14/1936; FDR to FF, 4/16/1936; FDR to FF, 4/29/1936; FDR to ALL, 4/29/1936, Lowell Personal Papers, Box 83, Folder 6 & FFLC, Box 257, Folder "Roosevelt, Franklin D., Harvard Tercentenary 1936" & *Roosevelt and Frankfurter*, 322–31.

39. Steel, *Walter Lippmann and the American Century*, 320–21.

40. *Id.*; LH to Lessing Rosenthal, 6/5/1936, *Roosevelt and Frankfurter*, 331. *See* LDB to FF, 6/3/1936, HBHS, at 581 ("Yes, W.L. is clearly aiming at you. I suppose he thinks he is disinterested.").

41. LH to Bernard Berenson, 8/3/1938, *Reason and Imagination*, 210; LH to Berenson, 4/27/1940, *id.* at 217; Gunther, *Learned Hand*, 496–502; Steel, *Walter Lippmann and the American Century*, 361; *see id.* at 342–63.

42. Walter Lippmann COH at 166–67.

43. FF to LH, 4/27/1943, LHP, Box 105A, Folder 105-10, *Reason and Imagination*, 242–43.

44. FF to LH, 12/29/1950, at 1, FFHLS, Pt. III, Reel 27.

45. Isaiah Berlin to Marie Berlin, 12/21/1955, in Isaiah Berlin, *Enlightening: Letters 1946–1960*, at 517 (Henry Hardy and Jennifer Holmes, eds., 2009).

46. Steel, *Walter Lippmann and the American Century*, 318 (against Roosevelt in 1936), 386–87 (on Willkie).

47. *Id.* at 445 (coining the phrase for a series of articles in 1947), *id.* at 557–72 (on his relationship with LBJ and Vietnam), *id.* at 573–84 (breaking with Johnson and criticizing the war effort). *See* Matthew A. Wasniewski, "Walter Lippmann,

Strategic Internationalism, the Cold War, and Vietnam, 1943–1967" (PhD diss., 2004).

48. PN to Gov. L. B. Hanna, 6/20/1934, GBP, Box 159, Folder "Peter Norbeck Papers 1930 to 1934."

49. Dawson, *Louis Brandeis, Felix Frankfurter, and the New Deal* 57–58 (quoting Memorandum by Milo Perkins, 6/5/1935, in Rex Tugwell Papers). *See* Oliphant Interview with Joe Alsop, JSAP, Box 93, Folder 3; Purcell, *Brandeis and the Progressive Constitution*, 87; Schlegel, *American Legal Realism and Empirical Social Science*, 15–20, 195, 221–24.

50. GB to FDR, 11/7/1935, at 1, GBP, Box 173, Folder "Roosevelt, F.D. & Pres. Secretaries 1933–34."

51. GB Speech, 8/30/1936, at 2–3, Box 173, Folder "Roosevelt's Visit to Rushmore 1936."

52. GB to Oliphant, 8/7/1935, GBP, Box 169, Folder "Herman Oliphant 1934–35."

53. FF to GB, 12/28/1939 & GB to FF, 1/24/1940, GBP, Box 16, Folder "F."

54. GB to FF, 1/24/1940, *id.* After Augustus Lukeman and others failed to finish Lukeman's design, a new sculptor was hired in 1962, started from scratch, and carved Jackson, Lee, and Davis into the mountain. *See* Freeman, *Carved in Stone*, 157–82.

On Frankfurter's "vivid" memories of Borglum a few years after the sculptor's death, *see* chapter 25 n. 51.

55. FDR to GB, 7/2/1936, GBP, Box 173, Folder "Roosevelt's Visit to Rushmore."

56. GB, 8/30/1936, GBP, Box 173, Folder "Roosevelt's Visit to Rushmore."

57. Informal Extemporaneous Remarks by the President, Mount Rushmore National Memorial, 8/30/1936, at 1, Franklin D. Roosevelt, Day by Day, FDRL, in http://www.fdrlibrary.marist.edu/daybyday/resource/august-1936-3/.

58. Nebbia v. New York, 291 U.S. 502 (1934). Holmes's former secretary, Arthur E. Sutherland Jr., had argued the case for Nebbia before the Supreme Court.

59. Mark DeWolfe Howe Diary, 3/6/1934, at 29, MDHP, Box 29, Folder 29-1 & Monagan Papers, Box 1, Folder 1-7.

60. FDR to OWH, 3/8/1934, OWHP, Reel 40, Page 2, Box 52, Folder 20.

61. James Rowe to FF, 2/23/1935, FFLC, Box 145, Folder "Rowe, James Jan.–Feb. 1935."

62. FF to Francis Biddle, 3/14/1935, Biddle Papers, Georgetown, Box 9, Folder 69; James Rowe to FF, 3/22/1935, at 1, FFLC, Box 145, Folder "Rowe, James Mar.–June 1935."

63. WES, 3/6/1936, at A-1, A-5.

64. NYT, 3/7/1935, 1.

65. EGE to AGB, 4/4/1935, at 3, EGEP, Reel 2, Folder 35.

66. Mark DeWolfe Howe Diary, 10/30/1933, at 5, MDHP ("In the morning Gutzon Borglum called–a very active man of whom Holmes is fond."); *see id.*, 11/5/1933, at 7 ("Suddenly he announced that he thought artists were more fun to talk to than anyone else–or words to that effect."); BET, 3/7/1935 (mentioning Borglum and the death mask).

67. WES, 3/8/1935, at A-4.
68. Mark DeWolfe Howe to MB, 12/4/1953, GBP, Box 20, Folder "H"; MB to Griswold, n.d., *id.*; Griswold to MB, 12/11/1953, GBP, Box 18, Folder "G."
69. NYT, 3/9/1935, at 16. "At the grave in Arlington there was a brief pause until the White House car arrived. Supported by an aide the President walked slowly to the open grave." John Knox, "Some Correspondence with Holmes and Pollock," 21 *Chicago Bar Record* 209, 224 (Mar. 1940), in John Knox Papers, Box 1, Folder 53. For accounts of Holmes's final days, *see* White, *Law and the Inner Self*, 471–75, 488; Monagan, *The Grand Panjandrum*, 144–47.
70. Photograph of OWH funeral, HLS Holmes Digital Suite.
71. FF to FDR, 3/7/1935, *Roosevelt and Frankfurter*, 257 (emphasis in original).
72. NYHT, 3/9/1935, at 10. *See* NYT, 3/9/1935, at 16 (same); LDB to FF, 3/12/1935, HBHS, at 563 ("It was good to see something of Marion as well as much of you.").
73. WP, 3/1/1935, at 1. *See* NYT, 3/6/1935, at 1; NYHT, 3/6/1935, at 1A & 16; NYT, 3/7/1935, at 16; WP, 3/9/1935, at 1; NYT, 3/7/1935, at 17 (future justice Robert H. Jackson described Holmes as "the champion of liberalism in the days when liberalism was not popular."). *But see* Oswald Garrison Villard, "Issues and Men: The Great Judge," The Nation, 3/20/1935, at 323 ("It is odd, indeed, that [Holmes] became known as a great liberal, for that, in most respects, he precisely was not. Like his father, he had no use for reformers and liberals per se.").

APPENDIX

* RGVP, Carton 9, Folder 55 (identifying Mrs. Gordon as the author on typewritten version); LHP, 104B, Folder 104-12 (containing handwritten version).

Selected Bibliography

ABBREVIATIONS

AA	Aaron Aaronsohn
AAP	Aaron Aaronsohn Papers
AC	Atlanta Constitution
ADH	Arthur D. Hill
AGB	Alice G. Brandeis
AJ	Atlanta Journal
ALL	A. Lawrence Lowell
AMP	A. Mitchell Palmer
BAA	Baltimore Afro-American
BaltSun	Baltimore Sun
BB	Bernard Baruch
BET	Boston Evening Transcript
BG	Boston Globe
BH	Boston Herald
BHP	Benjamin Huebsch Papers
BHW	Black Hills Weekly
BNC	Benjamin N. Cardozo
BP	Boston Post
CC	Calvin Coolidge
CC–Forbes	Calvin Coolidge-Forbes Library Collection
CCB	C. C. Burlingham
CCBP	C. C. Burlingham Papers
CDBP	Catherine Drinker Bowen Papers
CDEF	Chicago Defender
CEH	Charles Evans Hughes
CEHP	Charles Evans Hughes Papers
CEW	Charles E. Wyzanski Jr.
CHP	C. Helen Plane

CHPP	C. Helen Plane Papers
COH	Columbia Oral History
CPD	Cleveland Plain Dealer
CSM	Christian Science Monitor
CT	Chicago Tribune
CW	Chaim Weizmann
CWP	Chaim Weizmann Papers
DFF	Diaries of Felix Frankfurter
DR	Doane Robinson
DS	Dorothy Whitney Straight
DWSEP	Dorothy Whitney Straight Elmhirst Papers
ECS	Elizabeth Caldwell Stevens
EDB	Ernesta Drinker Bullitt
EDBP	Ernesta Drinker Barlow Papers
EG	Elbert Gary
EGE	Elizabeth Glendower Evans
EGEP	Elizabeth Glendower Evans Papers
EM	Eugene Meyer Jr.
EMH	Colonel Edward M. House
EMHP	Colonel Edward M. House Papers
EMP	Eugene Meyer Papers
EP	Eustace Percy
ERB	Emory R. Buckner
ES	Ellery Sedgwick
ESP	Ellery Sedgwick Papers
ESS	Elizabeth Shepley Sergeant
ESSP	Elizabeth Shepley Sergeant Papers
FA	Faye Albertson
FB	Francis Biddle
FBP	Francis Biddle Papers
FDRL	Franklin Delano Roosevelt Library
FF	Felix Frankfurter
FFHLS	Felix Frankfurter Papers, Harvard Law School
FFLC	Felix Frankfurter Papers, Library of Congress
FFR	Felix Frankfurter Reminisces
FFSyr	Felix Frankfurter Papers, Syracuse University
FH	Fanny Holmes

FL	Faye Lippmann
FLLDB	Family Letters of Louis D. Brandeis
FP	Frederick Pollock
GB	Gutzon Borglum
GBJT	Gutzon Borglum–John Taliaferro Collection
GBP	Gutzon Borglum Papers
GJ	Gardner Jackson
HarCour	Hartford Courant
HBHS	Half Brother, Half Son (LDB–FF Correspondence)
HC	Herbert Croly
HCL	Henry Cabot Lodge
HCrim	Harvard Crimson
HEP	Herbert Ehrmann Papers
H–E Letters	Holmes-Einstein Letters
H–FF Corr.	Holmes Frankfurter Correspondence
H–P Letters	Holmes-Pollock Letters
H–S Corr.	Holmes-Sheehan Correspondence
H–Wu Corr.	Holmes-Doctor Wu Correspondence
HFS	Harlan Fiske Stone
HFSDB	Harlan Fiske Stone Docket Books
HFSP	Harlan Fiske Stone Papers
HH	Herbert Hoover
HL	Harold Laski
HL–Syracuse	Harold Laski Papers-Syracuse University
HLL	Holmes-Laski Letters
HLP–Hull	Harold Laski Papers, Hull History Centre
HLP–LSE	Harold Laski Papers, London School of Economics
HLS	Henry L. Stimson
HLSD	Henry L. Stimson Diaries
HLSP	Henry L. Stimson Papers
JCG	John Chipman Gray
JGPC/OWHP	John G. Palfrey Collection, Holmes Digital Suite
JGT	J. G. Tucker
JHWP	John Henry Wigmore Papers
JSAP	Joseph and Stewart Alsop Papers
JT	Joseph Tumulty
JWM	Julian W. Mack

KL	Katharine Ludington
LAT	Los Angeles Times
LCC	Loring C. Christie
LCCP	Loring C. Christie Papers
LDB	Louis D. Brandeis
LDB-Louisville	Louis D. Brandeis Papers, University of Louisville
LDBHLS	Louis D. Brandeis Papers, Harvard Law School
LE	Lewis Einstein
LH	Learned Hand
LHP	Learned Hand Papers
LLDB	Letters of Louis D. Brandeis
MB	Mary Borglum
MD	Marion Denman
MDF	Marion Denman Frankfurter
MDH	Mark DeWolfe Howe
MDHP	Mark DeWolfe Howe, Holmes Research Papers, Holmes Digital Suite
NAACPP	NAACP Papers
NARA	National Archives and Records Administration
NDB	Newton D. Baker
NDBP	Newton D. Baker Papers
NG	Nina Gray
NH	Norman Hapgood
NHP	Norman Hapgood Papers
NJ&G	Norfolk Journal & Guide
NYAN	New York Amsterdam News
NYH	New York Herald
NYHT	New York Herald–Tribune
NYSun	New York Sun
NYT	New York Times
NYTrib	New York Tribune
NYW	New York World
OWH	Oliver Wendell Holmes Jr.
OWHP	Oliver Wendell Holmes Jr. Papers
PC	Pittsburgh Courier
PN	Peter Norbeck
PPL	Philadelphia Public Ledger

PPWL	Public Philosopher, Selected Letters of Walter Lippmann
RBP	Robert Borden Papers
RCJ	Rapid City Journal
RGV	Robert Grosvenor Valentine
RGVP	Robert Grosvenor Valentine Family Papers
RH	Ralph Hayes
RHP	Ralph Hayes Papers
RNO	Raleigh News & Observer
RP	Roscoe Pound
RPB	Robert P. Bass
RPP	Roscoe Pound Papers
RSBP	Ray Stannard Baker Papers
SAL	San Antonio Light
SFAL	Sioux Falls Argus–Leader
SFV	Sophie French Valentine
SK	Stanley King
SKP	Stanley King Papers
SMC	Stone Mountain Collection
SPD	St. Louis Post-Dispatch
SSW	Rabbi Stephen S. Wise
SVBA	Sacco-Vanzetti Collection, Boston Athenaeum
SV Trial Tr.	Sacco-Vanzetti Trial Transcripts
SVDCBPL	Sacco-Vanzetti Defense Committee Records, Boston Public Library
TGCP	Thomas G. Corcoran Papers
TNP	Thomas Nelson Perkins
TNR	The New Republic
ToL	Times of London
TR	Theodore Roosevelt
TR-HCL	Theodore Roosevelt–Henry Cabot Lodge Letters
TRP	Theodore Roosevelt Papers
TRPP	Thomas Reed Powell Papers
WashBee	Washington Bee
WashHerald	Washington Herald
WashTimes	Washington Times
WAW	William Allen White
WAWP	William Allen White Papers
WBP	Wright Brothers Papers

WBW   William B. Wilson
WCB   William C. Bullitt
WCBP   William C. Bullitt Papers
WDN   Washington Daily News
WES   Washington Evening Star
WGH   Warren G. Harding
WGHP   Warren G. Harding Papers
WGT   William G. Thompson
WHT   William Howard Taft
WHTP   William Howard Taft Papers
WL   Walter Lippmann
WLB   War Labor Board
WLP   Walter Lippmann Papers
WLPB   War Labor Policies Board
WP   Washington Post
WS   Willard Straight
WSP   Willard Straight Papers
WTD   Winfred T. Denison
WTDP   Winfred T. Denison Papers
WW   Woodrow Wilson
WWP   Woodrow Wilson Papers
ZC   Zechariah Chafee
ZCP   Zechariah Chafee Papers

MANUSCRIPTS

Aaron Aaronsohn Papers, NILI Museum-Beit Aaronsohn, Tel Aviv, Israel
Aaron and Alexander Aaronsohn Papers, American Jewish Archives, Cincinnati, OH
Dean Gooderham Acheson Papers, Yale University Library, New Haven, CT
Jesse Corcoran Adkins Papers, Georgetown University Law Library, Washington, DC
Martin Agronsky Papers, Library of Congress, Washington, DC
Joseph and Stewart Alsop Papers, Library of Congress, Washington, DC
American Civil Liberties Union Papers, Seeley G. Mudd Manuscript Library, Princeton, NJ
American Commission to Negotiate Peace Records, Library of Congress, Washington, DC
Gordon Auchincloss Papers, Yale University Library, New Haven, CT
Newton Baker Papers, Library of Congress, Washington, DC
Ray Stannard Baker Papers, Library of Congress, Washington, DC

Ernesta Drinker Barlow Papers, Georgetown University, Washington, DC

Harry Barnard Papers, American Jewish Archives, Cincinnati, OH

Henry Moore Bates Papers, University of Michigan, Bentley Historical Library, Ann Arbor, MI

Francis B. Biddle Papers, Franklin D. Roosevelt Presidential Library, Hyde Park, NY

Francis B. Biddle Papers, Georgetown University Library, Washington, DC

Edwin Montefiore Borchard Papers, Yale University Library, New Haven, CT

Sir Robert Laird Borden Papers, National Archives of Canada, Ottawa, Canada

Gutzon Borglum–John Taliaferro Collection, National Park Service, Mount Rushmore, SD

Gutzon Borglum Historical Center, Keystone, SD

Gutzon Borglum Papers, Calvin Coolidge Collection, Library of Congress, Washington, DC

Gutzon Borglum Papers, Library of Congress, Washington, DC

Solon H. Borglum and Borglum Family Papers, Smithsonian Institution, Washington, DC

Randolph Silliman Bourne Papers, Columbia University Library, New York, NY

Catherine Drinker Bowen Papers, Library of Congress, Washington, DC

Isaiah Bowman Papers, Johns Hopkins University, Baltimore, MD

Louis D. Brandeis Papers, Harvard Law School Library, Cambridge, MA

Louis D. Brandeis Papers, University of Louisville Library, Louisville, KY

William C. Bullitt Papers, Yale University Library, New Haven, CT

Charles Culp Burlingham Papers, Harvard Law School Library, Cambridge, MA

Calvin Coolidge-Forbes Library Collection, Northampton, MA

Zechariah Chafee Jr. Papers, Harvard Law School Library, Cambridge, MA

Loring Cheney Christie Papers, Public Archives of Canada, Ottawa, Canada

Benjamin V. Cohen Papers, American Jewish Archives, Cincinnati, OH

Benjamin V. Cohen Papers, Library of Congress, Washington, DC

Thomas G. Corcoran Papers, Library of Congress, Washington, DC

Edward S. Corwin Papers, Seeley G. Mudd Manuscript Library, Princeton, NJ

Winfred T. Denison Papers, Maine Historical Society, Portland, ME

Mark DeWolfe Howe Papers, Harvard University Library, Cambridge, MA

Irving Dilliard Papers, University of Missouri–St. Louis, St. Louis, MO

Herbert B. Ehrmann Papers, Harvard University Library, Cambridge, MA

Dorothy Whitney Straight Elmhirst Papers, Cornell University Library, Ithaca, NY

Elizabeth Glendower Evans Papers, Radcliffe Institute, Schlesinger Library, Cambridge, MA

Walter L. Fisher Papers, Library of Congress, Washington, DC

Felix Frankfurter Letters, Syracuse University Library, Syracuse, NY

Felix Frankfurter Papers, Harvard Law School Library, Cambridge, MA

Felix Frankfurter Papers, Library of Congress, Washington, DC

Arthur Gleason Papers, Library of Congress, Washington, DC

Ruth Gordon and Garson Kanin Papers, Library of Congress, Washington, DC

Thomas Montgomery Gregory Papers, Howard University Library, Washington, DC

Hermann Hagedorn Papers, Syracuse University Library, Syracuse, NY

Robert Lee Hale Papers, Columbia University Library, New York, NY

Learned Hand Papers, Harvard Law School Library, Cambridge, MA

Norman Hapgood Papers, Library of Congress, Washington, DC

Warren G. Harding Papers, Ohio History Connection, Columbus, OH

Harvard Law School Faculty Minutes, Harvard Law School Library, Cambridge, MA

Ralph Hayes Papers, Western Reserve Historical Society, Cleveland, OH

Oliver Wendell Holmes Collection, Library of Congress, Washington, DC

Oliver Wendell Holmes Papers, Harvard Law School Library, Cambridge, MA

Herbert Hoover Papers, Hoover Presidential Library, West Branch, IA

J. Edgar Hoover Official and Confidential File, FBI Files, National Archives and Records Administration, College Park, MD

Colonel Edward House Papers, Yale University Law School, New Haven, CT

Charles H. Houston Papers, Howard University, Washington, DC

Benjamin W. Huebsch Papers, Library of Congress, Washington, DC

Charles Evans Hughes Papers, Library of Congress, Washington, DC

Gus J. Karger Papers, American Jewish Archives, Cincinnati, OH

Andrew Kaufman Papers, Harvard Law School Library, Cambridge, MA

Stanley King Papers, Amherst College Archives, Amherst, MA

John Knox Papers, Georgetown University, Washington, DC

La Follette Family Papers, Library of Congress, Washington, DC

James McCauley Landis Papers, Harvard Law School Library, Cambridge, MA

Laski-Brandeis Papers, Yale Law School Library, New Haven, CT

Harold Laski Papers, Hull History Centre, Yorkshire, United Kingdom

Harold Laski Papers, International Institute of Social History, Amsterdam, Netherlands

Harold Laski Papers, London School of Economics Library, London

Harold Laski Collection, Syracuse University Library, Syracuse, NY

Walter Lippmann Papers, Yale University Library, New Haven, CT

Katie Louchheim Papers, Library of Congress, Washington, DC

A. Lawrence Lowell Official Papers, Harvard University Library, Cambridge, MA

A. Lawrence Lowell Personal Papers, Harvard University Library, Cambridge, MA

Max Lowenthal Papers, University of Minnesota, Minneapolis, MN

Julian William Mack Papers, American Jewish Archives, Cincinnati, OH

Martin Mayer Papers, Columbia University, New York, NY

James Clark McReynolds Papers, University of Virginia Law Library, Charlottesville, VA

Agnes Meyer Papers, Library of Congress, Washington, DC

Eugene Meyer Papers, Library of Congress, Washington, DC

John S. Monagan Papers, Harvard Law School Library, Cambridge, MA

Henry Morgenthau Sr. Papers, Library of Congress, Washington, DC

National Association for the Advancement of Colored People Collection, Library of Congress, Washington, DC

National Consumers' League Records, Library of Congress, Washington, DC

National War Labor Board Records, National Archives and Records Administration, College Park, MD

Walter Hines Page Papers, Houghton Library, Harvard University, Cambridge, MA

Amos Pinchot Papers, Library of Congress, Washington, DC

Gifford Pinchot Papers, Library of Congress, Washington, DC

Roscoe Pound Papers, Harvard Law School Library, Cambridge, MA

Owen J. Roberts Papers, Library of Congress, Washington, DC

Doane Robinson Collection, South Dakota State Archives, Pierre, SD

Theodore Roosevelt Papers, Library of Congress, Washington, DC

Julius Rosenwald Papers, University of Chicago, Chicago, IL

Elihu Root Papers, Library of Congress, Washington, DC

Sacco-Vanzetti Defense Committee Records, Boston Public Library, Boston, MA

Sacco-Vanzetti Papers, Harvard Law School Library, Cambridge, MA

Sacco-Vanzetti/Robert Montgomery Papers, Boston Public Library, Boston MA

Jacob H. Schiff Papers, American Jewish Archives, Cincinnati, OH

Austin Wakeman Scott Papers, Harvard Law School Library, Cambridge, MA

Ellery Sedgwick Papers, Massachusetts Historical Society, Boston, MA

Howard and Audrey Karl Shaff Collection, Augustana College Library, Sioux Falls, SD

Upton Beall Sinclair Papers, Indiana University Library, Bloomington, IN

Henry Lewis Stimson Papers, Yale University Library, New Haven, CT

Stone Mountain Collection, Emory University Library, Atlanta, GA

Harlan Fiske Stone Papers, Library of Congress, Washington, DC

Willard Straight Papers, Cornell University Library, Ithaca, NY

Supreme Court of the United States, Clerk's Office Files, National Archives and Record Administration, Washington, DC

George Sutherland Papers, Library of Congress, Washington, DC

William H. Taft Papers, Library of Congress, Washington, DC

Thomas Thacher Papers, Columbia University Library, New York, NY

James Bradley Thayer Papers, Harvard Law School Library, Cambridge, MA

Robert G. Valentine Family Papers, Massachusetts Historical Society, Boston, MA

Willis Van Devanter Papers, Library of Congress, Washington, DC

Oswald Garrison Villard Papers, Houghton Library, Harvard College, Cambridge, MA

War Department General and Special Staffs Records, National Archives and Records Administration, College Park, MD

War Labor Policies Board Records, National Archives and Records Administration, College Park, MD

Felix M. Warburg Papers, American Jewish Archives, Cincinnati, OH

William Allen White Papers, Library of Congress, Washington, DC

John Henry Wigmore Papers, Northwestern University Library, Evanston, IL

Arthur Willert Papers, Yale University Library, New Haven, CT
Woodrow Wilson Papers, Library of Congress, Washington, DC
William Wiseman Papers, Yale University Library, New Haven, CT
Wilbur and Orville Wright Papers, Library of Congress, Washington, DC
Alfred Zimmern Papers, University of Oxford, Bodleian Library, Oxford, United
    Kingdom

ORAL HISTORIES

Columbia Center for Oral History
Heber Blankenhorn
Bruce Bliven
Harvey Bundy
Learned Hand
Gardner Jackson
Walter Lippmann
Eugene Meyer
John Lord O'Brian
George Rublee
Ordway Tead
On File with Author
Chauncey Belknap Diary 1914–15
Gates Family Papers
Frida Laski Oral History
Dorothy Koval Collection (additional papers relating to Robert G. Valentine)
Michael Parrish Notes on Felix Frankfurter Diaries

NEWSPAPERS AND MAGAZINES

Atlanta Constitution
Atlanta Journal
Black Hills Weekly
Boston Evening Transcript
Boston Globe
Boston Herald
Chicago Daily News
Chicago Defender
Chicago Tribune
Christian Science Monitor
Daily Worker (NY)
Harper's Weekly
Hartford Courant
Harvard Crimson

The Independent
Los Angeles Times
Memphis Commercial Appeal
Mitchell (SD) Evening Republican
The Nation
New Republic
New York Amsterdam News
New York Herald
New York Herald-Tribune
New York Sun
New York Times
New York Tribune
New York World
Outlook
Philadelphia Public Ledger
Philadelphia Tribune
Pittsburgh Courier
Portland Oregonian
Rapid City Journal
Sioux Falls Argus-Leader
Sioux Falls Press
Springfield Republican
The Survey
Time
Washington Daily News
Washington Evening Star
Washington Herald
Washington Post
Washington Times

BOOKS

Acheson, Dean. *Morning and Noon.* Boston: Houghton Mifflin, 1965.

Ackerman, Kenneth D. *Young J. Edgar: Hoover, the Red Scare, and the Assault on Civil Liberties.* New York: Carroll and Graf, 2007.

Alschuler, Albert W. *Law without Values: The Life, Work, and Legacy of Justice Holmes.* Chicago: University of Chicago Press, 2000.

Alsop, Joseph, and Robert Kintner. *Men around the President.* New York: Doubleday, 1939.

Auerbach, Jerold S. *Rabbis and Lawyers: The Journey from Torah to Constitution.* Bloomington: Indiana University Press, 1990.

——. *Unequal Justice: Lawyers and Social Change in Modern America.* New York: Oxford University Press, 1976.

Baker, Leonard. *Brandeis and Frankfurter: A Dual Biography.* New York: Harper and Row, 1984.

Baker, Liva. *Felix Frankfurter*. New York: Coward-McCann, 1969.

——. *The Justice from Beacon Hill: The Life and Times of Oliver Wendell Holmes*. New York: HarperCollins, 1991.

Barnard, Harry. *The Forging of an American Jew: The Life and Times of Judge Julian W. Mack*. New York: Herzl Press, 1974.

Beaver, Daniel R. *Newton D. Baker and the American War Effort, 1917–1919*. Lincoln: University of Nebraska Press, 1966.

Bent, Silas. *Justice Oliver Wendell Holmes: A Biography*. New York: Vanguard Press, 1932.

Berg, A. Scott. *Wilson*. New York: Putnam, 2013.

Bernstein, David E. *Rehabilitating Lochner: Defending Individual Rights against Progressive Reform*. Chicago: University of Chicago Press, 2011.

Berlin, Isaiah. *Enlightening: Letters 1946–1960*, edited by Henry Hardy and Jennifer Holmes. London: Chatto and Windus, 2009.

Best, Gary Dean. *Harold Laski and American Liberalism*. New Brunswick, NJ: Transaction, 2006.

Bickel, Alexander M., and Benno C. Schmidt Jr. *History of the Supreme Court of the United States: The Judiciary and Responsible Government, 1910–21*. Vol. 9. New York: Macmillan, 1984.

Bickel, Alexander M. *The Unpublished Opinions of Mr. Justice Brandeis: The Supreme Court at Work*. Cambridge, MA: Belknap Press of Harvard University Press, 1957.

Biddle, Francis. *A Casual Past*. New York: Doubleday, 1961.

——. *Mr. Justice Holmes*. New York: Scribner, 1943.

Billington, David P. *Lothian: Philip Kerr and the Quest for World Order*. Westport, CT: Praeger, 2006.

Blankenhorn, Heber. *Adventures in Propaganda: Letters from an Intelligence Officer in France*. New York: Houghton, 1919.

Bliven, Bruce. *Five Million Words Later: An Autobiography*. New York: J. Day, 1970.

Blum, John Morton. *Joe Tumulty and the Wilson Era*. Boston: Houghton Mifflin, 1951.

——, ed. *Public Philosopher: Selected Letters of Walter Lippmann*. New York: Ticknor and Fields, 1985.

Bothwell, Robert. *Loring Christie: The Failure of Bureaucratic Imperialism*. New York: Garland, 1988.

Bowen, Catherine Drinker. *Family Portrait: With Illustrations*. Boston: Little, Brown, 1970.

——. *Yankee from Olympus*. Boston: Little, Brown, 1944.

Brandeis, Louis D. *The Curse of Bigness*. New York: Viking, 1934.

——. *Other People's Money and How the Bankers Use It*. New York: Frederick A. Stokes, 1914.

Brownell, Will, and Richard N. Billings. *So Close to Greatness: A Biography of William C. Bullitt*. New York: Macmillan, 1987.

The Bullitt Mission to Russia: Testimony before the Committee on Foreign Relations of the United States Senate of William C. Bullitt. New York: B. W. Huebsch, 1919.

Burns, James MacGregor. *Roosevelt: The Lion and the Fox.* New York: Harcourt, Brace, 1956.

Burton, David, ed. *Holmes-Sheehan Correspondence: The Letters of Justice Oliver Wendell Holmes and Canon Patrick Augustine Sheehan.* Port Washington, NY: Kennikat Press, 1976.

———, ed. *Progressive Masks: Letters of Oliver Wendell Holmes Jr. and Franklin Ford.* Newark: University of Delaware Press, 1982.

Carter, Dan T. *Scottsboro: A Tragedy of the American South.* Rev. ed. Baton Rouge: Louisiana State University Press, 1979.

Carter, Robin Borglum. *Gutzon Borglum: His Life and Work.* Austin, TX: Eakin Press, 1998.

Casey, Robert J., and Mary Borglum. *Give the Man Room: The Story of Gutzon Borglum.* Indianapolis: Bobbs-Merrill, 1952.

Chafee, Zechariah, Jr. *Free Speech in the United States.* Cambridge, MA: Harvard University Press, 1941.

Clayton, Bruce. *Forgotten Prophet: The Life of Randolph Bourne.* Columbia: University of Missouri Press, 1998.

Cohen, Adam. *Im·be·ciles: The Supreme Court, American Eugenics, and the Sterilization of Carrie Buck.* New York: Penguin Press, 2016.

Collins, Ronald K. L., ed. *The Fundamental Holmes: A Free Speech Chronicle and Reader: Selections from the Opinions, Books, Articles, Speeches, Letters, and Other Writings by and about Oliver Wendell Holmes Jr.* Cambridge: Cambridge University Press, 2010.

Cooling, Benjamin Franklin, III. *The Day Lincoln Was Almost Shot: The Fort Stevens Story.* Lanham, MD: Scarecrow Press, 2013.

Cooper, John Milton, Jr. *The Warrior and the Priest: Woodrow Wilson and Theodore Roosevelt.* Cambridge, MA: Belknap Press, 1985.

———. *Woodrow Wilson: A Biography.* New York: Knopf, 2009.

Coquillette, Daniel R., and Bruce A. Kimball. *On the Battlefield of Merit: Harvard Law School, the First Century.* Cambridge, MA: Harvard University Press, 2015.

Craig, Douglas B. *Progressives at War: William G. McAdoo and Newton D. Baker, 1863–1941.* Baltimore: Johns Hopkins University Press, 2013.

Cramer, John Henry. *Lincoln under Enemy Fire: The Complete Account of His Experiences during Early's Attack on Washington.* Baton Rouge: Louisiana State University Press, 1948.

Croly, Herbert. *Progressive Democracy.* New York: Macmillan, 1914.

———. *The Promise of American Life.* New York: Macmillan, 1909.

Daniels, Josephus. *The Wilson Era: Years of Peace, 1910–1917.* Chapel Hill: University of North Carolina Press, 1944.

Davies, Alfred Mervyn. *Solon H. Borglum, "A Man Who Stands Alone": A Biography.* Chester, CT: Pequot Press, 1974.

Dawson, Nelson L. *Louis D. Brandeis, Felix Frankfurter, and the New Deal.* Hamden, CT: Archon, 1980.

Dean, Robert J. *Living Granite: The Story of Borglum and the Mount Rushmore Memorial*. New York: Viking, 1949.

de Haas, Jacob. *Louis D. Brandeis: A Biographical Sketch*. New York: Bloch, 1929.

Diner, Steven J. *A Very Different Age: Americans of the Progressive Era*. New York: Hill and Wang, 1998.

Dolan, John A. *Hale and Dorr, Backgrounds and Styles*. Boston: 1993.

Duxbury. Neil. *Frederick Pollock and the English Juristic Tradition*. New York: Oxford University Press, 2004.

Ehrmann, Herbert B. *The Case That Will Not Die: Commonwealth vs. Sacco and Vanzetti*. Boston: Little, Brown, 1969.

——. *The Untried Case: The Sacco-Vanzetti Case and the Morelli Gang*. New York: Vanguard Press, 1933.

Ernst, Daniel R. *Lawyers against Labor: From Individual Rights to Corporate Liberalism*. Urbana: University of Illinois Press, 1995.

——. *Tocqueville's Nightmare: The Administrative State Emerges in America, 1900–1940*. New York: Oxford University Press, 2014.

Farnsworth, Beatrice. *William C. Bullitt and the Soviet Union*. Bloomington: Indiana University Press, 1967.

Fiss, Owen M. *History of the Supreme Court of the United States: Troubled Beginnings of the Modern State, 1888–1910*. Vol. 8. New York: Macmillan, 1993.

Fite, Gilbert. *Mount Rushmore*. Norman: University of Oklahoma Press, 1952.

Florence, Ronald. *Lawrence and Aaronsohn: T. E. Lawrence, Aaron Aaronsohn, and the Seeds of the Arab-Israeli Conflict*. New York: Viking, 2007.

Forbath, William E. *Law and the Shaping of the American Labor Movement*. Cambridge, MA: Harvard University Press, 1991.

Forcey, Charles. *The Crossroads of Liberalism: Croly, Weyl, Lippmann, and the Progressive Era, 1900–1925*. New York: Oxford University Press, 1961.

Frankfurter, Felix. *The Case of Sacco and Vanzetti: A Critical Analysis for Lawyers and Laymen*. Boston: Little, Brown, 1927.

——, ed. *Mr. Justice Holmes*. New York: Coward-McCann, 1931.

——. *Law and Politics: Occasional Papers of Felix Frankfurter, 1913–1938*, edited by Archibald MacLeish, and E. F. Prichard Jr. New York: Harcourt, Brace, 1939.

——. *Mr. Justice Holmes and the Constitution: A Review of His Twenty-Five Years on the Supreme Court*. Cambridge, MA: Dunster House Bookshop, 1927.

——. *The Public and Its Government*. New Haven, CT: Yale University Press, 1930.

——. *Of Law and Men*, edited by Philip Elman. New York: Harcourt, Brace, 1956.

Frankfurter, Felix, and Nathan Greene. *The Labor Injunction*. New York: Macmillan, 1930.

Frankfurter, Felix, and James M. Landis. *The Business of the Supreme Court: A Study in the Federal Judicial System*. New York: Macmillan, 1928.

Freeberg, Ernest. *Democracy's Prisoner: Eugene V. Debs, the Great War, and the Right to Dissent*. Cambridge, MA: Harvard University Press, 2008.

Freedman, Eric. *Habeas Corpus: Rethinking the Great Writ of Liberty*. New York: New York University Press, 2001.

Freedman, Max, ed. *Roosevelt and Frankfurter: Their Correspondence, 1928–1945*. Boston: Little, Brown, 1967.

Freeman, David B. *Carved in Stone: The History of Stone Mountain*. Macon, GA: Mercer University Press, 1997.

Frost, Richard H. *The Mooney Case*. Palo Alto, CA: Stanford University Press, 1968.

Fuess, Claude Moore. *Stanley King of Amherst*. New York: Columbia University Press, 1955.

Gage, Beverly. *The Day Wall Street Exploded: A Story of America in Its First Age of Terror*. New York: Oxford University Press, 2009.

Gallagher, Hugh Gregory. *FDR's Splendid Deception*. New York: Dodd, Mead, 1985.

Goldman, Eric F. *Rendezvous with Destiny: A History of Modern American Reform*. New York: Knopf, 1952.

Goldstone, Patricia. *Aaronsohn's Maps: The Untold Story of the Man Who Might Have Created Peace in the Middle East*. Orlando, FL: Harcourt, 2007.

Goodman, James. *Stories of Scottsboro*. New York: Pantheon, 1994.

Goodwin, Doris Kearns. *The Bully Pulpit: Theodore Roosevelt, William Howard Taft, and the Golden Age of Journalism*. New York: Simon and Schuster, 2013.

Gordon, Robert W., ed. *The Legacy of Oliver Wendell Holmes Jr*. Stanford, CA: Stanford University Press, 1992.

Gould, Lewis L. *Chief Executive to Chief Justice: Taft betwixt the White House and Supreme Court*. Lawrence: University Press of Kansas, 2014.

——. *Four Hats in the Ring: The 1912 Election and the Birth of Modern American Politics*. Lawrence: University Press of Kansas, 2008.

——. *The William Howard Taft Presidency*. Lawrence: University Press of Kansas, 2009.

Graber, Mark A. *Transforming Free Speech: The Ambiguous Legacy of Civil Libertarianism*. Berkeley: University of California Press, 1991.

Gray, Roland, ed. *John Chipman Gray*. Boston: Merrymount Press, 1917.

Gunther, Gerald. *Learned Hand: The Man and the Judge*. New York: Knopf, 1994.

Hagedorn, Hermann, ed. *The Works of Theodore Roosevelt: Social Justice and Popular Rule*. Vol. 17. National ed. New York: Charles Scribner's Sons, 1926.

Hale, Richard Walden. *Some Table Talk of Mr. Justice Holmes and "the Mrs.," Etc.* Boston: A. C. Getchell, 1935.

Hallowell, Norwood P. *Reminiscences Written for My Children by Request of Their Mother*. West Medford, MA, 1897.

——. *Selected Letters and Papers of N. P. Hallowell*. Peterborough, NH: R. R. Smith, 1963.

Hamilton, John Maxwell, and Robert Mann, eds. *A Journalist's Diplomatic Mission: Ray Stannard Baker's World War I Diary*. Baton Rouge: Louisiana State University Press, 2012.

Hapgood, Hutchins. *A Victorian in the Modern World*. New York: Harcourt, Brace, 1939.

Harbaugh, William H. *Lawyer's Lawyer: The Life of John W. Davis*. New York: Oxford University Press, 1973.

——. *The Centennial History of the Harvard Law School, 1817–1917*. Cambridge, MA: Harvard Law School Association, 1918.

Hardwick, Elizabeth, ed. *The Selected Letters of William James*. Boston: Godine, 1980.

Harvard College, Class of 1896 Secretary's Reports. Second, Third, Fourth, and Fifth Reports.

Healy, Thomas. *The Great Dissent: How Oliver Wendell Holmes Changed His Mind—and Changed the History of Free Speech in America*. New York: Henry Holt, 2013.

Hemingway, Ernest. *A Moveable Feast*. New York: Simon and Schuster, 1996.

Hicks, Frederick C. *William Howard Taft: Yale Professor of Law & New Haven Citizen*. New Haven, CT: Yale University Press, 1945.

Hirsch, H. N. *The Enigma of Felix Frankfurter*. New York: Basic Books, 1981.

Hofstadter, Richard. *The Age of Reform: From Bryan to FDR*. New York: Knopf, 1955.

Holmes, Oliver Wendell. *Collected Legal Papers*. New York: Harcourt, Brace, 1921.

——. *The Common Law*. Cambridge, MA: Belknap Press of Harvard University Press, 1881, rev. ed. 2009.

——. *Speeches*. Boston: Little, Brown, 1891 and rev. ed., 1913.

Hoover, Herbert. *The Memoirs of Herbert Hoover: The Great Depression, 1929–1941*. New York: Macmillan, 1952.

Horwitz, Morton J. *The Transformation of American Law, 1870–1960: The Crisis of Legal Orthodoxy*. New York: Oxford University Press, 1992.

Howe, Mark DeWolfe, ed. *Holmes-Laski Letters: The Correspondence of Mr. Justice Holmes and Harold J. Laski, 1916–1935*. Cambridge, MA: Harvard University Press, 1953.

——, ed. *Holmes-Pollock Letters: The Correspondence of Mr. Justice Holmes and Sir Frederick Pollock, 1874–1932*. 2 vols. Cambridge, MA: Harvard University Press, 1941.

——. *Justice Oliver Wendell Holmes: The Shaping Years, 1841–1870*. Cambridge, MA: Belknap Press of Harvard University Press, 1957.

——. *Justice Oliver Wendell Holmes: The Proving Years 1870–1882*. Cambridge, MA: Harvard University Press, 1963.

——, ed., *Touched with Fire: Civil War Letters and Diary of Oliver Wendell Holmes, Jr., 1861–1864*. Cambridge, MA: Harvard University Press, 1946.

Hull, N. E. H. *Roscoe Pound and Karl Llewellyn: Searching for an American Jurisprudence*. Chicago: University of Chicago Press, 1997.

Irons, Peter H. *The New Deal Lawyers*. Princeton, NJ: Princeton University Press, 1993.

Jensen, Richard L. *The Mormon Years of the Borglum Family*. Salt Lake City, UT: Historical Department, the Church of Jesus Christ of Latter-day Saints, 1979.

Johnson, Alvin. *Pioneer's Progress: An Autobiography*. New York: Viking, 1952.

Johnson, Gerald W. *The Undefeated*. New York: Minton, Balch, 1927.

Jordan, Constance, ed. *Reason and Imagination: The Selected Correspondence of Learned Hand, 1897–1961*. New York: Oxford University Press, 2013.

Justice Holmes to Doctor Wu: An Intimate Correspondence, 1921–32. New York: Central Book Co., 1947.

Kabaservice, Geoffrey. *The Guardians: Kingman Brewster, His Circle, and the Rise of the Liberal Establishment*. New York: Henry Holt, 2004.

Kalman, Laura. *Legal Realism at Yale, 1927–1960*. Chapel Hill: University of North Carolina Press, 1986.

——. *The Strange Career of Legal Liberalism*. New Haven, CT: Yale University Press, 1998.

Katz, Shmuel. *The Aaronsohn Saga*. Jerusalem: Geen, 2007.

Kaufman, Andrew L. *Cardozo*. Cambridge, MA: Harvard University Press, 1998.

Kennedy, David M. *Freedom from Fear: The American People in Depression and War, 1929–1945*. New York: Oxford University Press, 1999.

——. *Over Here: The First World War and American Society*. New York: Oxford University Press, 1980.

——, ed. *Progressivism: The Critical Issues*. Boston: Little, Brown, 1971.

Kennedy, Robin Borglum. *Mary's Story: Mary Borglum's Story from the Mountains of Anatolia to the Mountains of South Dakota*. North Charleston, SC: CreateSpace, 2013.

Kens, Paul. *Judicial Power and Reform Politics: The Anatomy of Lochner v. New York*. Lawrence: University Press of Kansas, 1990.

Kloppenberg, James T. *Uncertain Victory: Social Democracy and Progressivism in European and American Thought, 1870–1920*. New York: Oxford University Press, 1986.

——. *The Virtues of Liberalism*. New York: Oxford University Press, 1998.

Kluger, Richard. *Simple Justice: The History of Brown v. Board of Education and Black America's Struggle for Equality*. New York: Knopf, 1976.

Knox, John. *The Forgotten Memoir of John Knox: A Year in the Life of a Supreme Court Clerk in FDR's Washington*, edited by Dennis J. Hutchinson and David J. Garrow. Chicago: University of Chicago Press, 2002.

Kramnick, Isaac, and Barry Sheerman. *Harold Laski: A Life on the Left*. New York: Allen Lane/Penguin Press, 1993.

Kurland, Philip B., ed. *Felix Frankfurter on the Supreme Court: Extrajudicial Essays on the Court and the Constitution*. Cambridge, MA: Belknap Press of Harvard University Press, 1970.

——, ed. *Mr. Justice Frankfurter and the Constitution*. Chicago: University of Chicago Press, 1971.

——, ed. *Of Law and Life and Other Things That Matter: Papers and Addresses of Felix Frankfurter, 1956–1963*. Cambridge, MA: Belknap Press of Harvard University Press, 1965.

La Follette, Belle Case, & Fola La Follette. *Robert M. La Follette: June 14, 1855–June 18, 1925*. 2 vols. New York: Macmillan, 1953.

Larson, Erik. *Dead Wake: The Last Crossing of the Lusitania*. New York: Crown, 2015.

Lasch, Christopher. *The New Radicalism in America, 1889–1963: The Intellectual as a Social Type*. New York: Knopf, 1965.

Lash, Joseph P. *Eleanor and Franklin: The Story of Their Relationship Based on Eleanor Roosevelt's Private Papers*. New York: Norton, 1971.

——, ed. *From the Diaries of Felix Frankfurter: With a Biographical Essay and Notes.* New York: Norton, 1975.

Laski, Harold J. *The American Democracy.* New York: Viking, 1948.

——. *Authority in the Modern State.* New Haven, CT: Yale University Press, 1919.

——. *A Grammar of Politics.* New Haven, CT: Yale University Press, 1925.

Lerner, Max, ed. *The Mind and Faith of Justice Holmes: His Speeches, Essays, Letters, and Judicial Opinions.* Boston: Little, Brown, 1943.

Levy, David W. *Herbert Croly of* The New Republic*: The Life and Thought of an American Progressive.* Princeton, NJ: Princeton University Press, 1985.

Link, Arthur S. *Wilson: Campaigns for Progressivism and Peace, 1916–1917.* Vol. 5. Princeton, NJ: Princeton University Press, 1965.

——. *Wilson: Confusions and Crises, 1915–16.* Vol. 4. Princeton, NJ: Princeton University Press, 1964.

——. *Wilson: The New Freedom.* Vol. 2. Princeton, NJ: Princeton University Press, 1956.

——. *Wilson: The Road to the White House.* Vol. 1. Princeton, NJ: Princeton University Press, 1947.

——. *Wilson: The Struggle for Neutrality, 1914–1915.* Vol. 3. Princeton, NJ: Princeton University Press, 1960.

——. *Woodrow Wilson and the Progressive Era, 1910–1917.* New York: Harper, 1954.

Lippmann, Walter. *American Inquisitors: A Commentary on Dayton and Chicago.* New York: Macmillan, 1928.

——. *Drift and Mastery: An Attempt to Diagnose the Current Unrest.* New York: M. Kennerley, 1914.

——. *Early Writings,* edited by Arthur Schlesinger Jr. New York: Liveright, 1970.

——. *An Inquiry into the Principles of the Good Society.* Boston: Little, Brown, 1937.

——. *Interpretations, 1931–1932.* New York: Macmillan, 1932.

——. *Men of Destiny.* New York: Macmillan, 1927.

——. *The Phantom Public.* New York: Harcourt, Brace, 1925

——. *The Political Scene: An Essay on the Victory of 1918.* New York: H. Holt, 1919.

——. *A Preface to Morals.* Boston: Beacon Press, 1929.

——. *A Preface to Politics.* London: T. F. Unwin, 1913.

——. *Public Persons,* edited by Gilbert A. Harrison. New York: Liveright, 1976.

——. *Public Philosopher: Selected Letters of Walter Lippmann.* John Morton Blum, ed. New York: Ticknor and Fields, 1985.

——. *Public Opinion.* New York: Harcourt, Brace, 1922.

——. *The Stakes of Diplomacy.* New York: H. Holt, 1915.

——, and Charles Merz. *Liberty and the News.* New York: Harcourt, Brace and Howe, 1920.

Livermore, Seward W. *Politics Is Adjourned: Woodrow Wilson and the War Congress, 1916–1918.* Middleton, CT: Wesleyan University Press, 1966.

Lombardo, Paul A. *Three Generations, No Imbeciles: Eugenics, the Supreme Court, and Buck v. Bell.* Baltimore: Johns Hopkins University Press, 2008.

Louchheim, Katie, ed. *The Making of the New Deal: The Insiders Speak.* Cambridge, MA: Harvard University Press, 1983.

Lovett, Robert Morss. *All Our Years: The Autobiography of Robert Morss Lovett.* New York: Viking, 1948.

Luhan, Mabel Dodge. *Movers and Shakers.* New York: Harcourt, Brace, 1936.

Lurie, Jonathan. *William Howard Taft: The Travails of a Progressive Conservative.* New York: Cambridge University Press, 2012.

Martin, George Whitney. *CCB: The Life and Century of Charles C. Burlingham, New York's First Citizen, 1858–1959.* New York: Hill and Wang, 2005.

Martin, Kingsley. *Harold Laski, 1893–1950, a Biographical Memoir.* New York: Viking, 1953.

Mason, Alpheus Thomas. *Brandeis: A Free Man's Life.* New York: Viking, 1946.

——. *Harlan Fiske Stone: Pillar of the Law.* New York: Viking, 1956.

——. *William Howard Taft: Chief Justice.* New York: Simon and Schuster, 1965.

Mayer, Martin. *Emory Buckner.* New York: Harper and Row, 1968.

McCraw, Thomas. *Prophets of Regulation: Charles Francis Adams, Louis D. Brandeis, James M. Landis, Alfred E. Kahn.* Cambridge, MA: Harvard University Press, 2009.

McGerr, Michael. *A Fierce Discontent: The Rise and Fall of the Progressive Movement in America, 1870–1920.* New York: Free Press, 2003.

McLellan, David S., and David C. Acheson, eds. *Among Friends: Personal Letters of Dean Acheson, 1893–1971.* New York: Dodd, Mead, 1980.

McNeil, Genna Rae. *Groundwork: Charles Hamilton Houston and the Struggle for Civil Rights.* Philadelphia: University of Pennsylvania Press, 1983.

McPherson, James. *Battle Cry of Freedom: The Civil War Era.* New York: Ballantine Books, 1989.

McWhirter, Cameron. *Red Summer: The Summer of 1919 and the Awakening of Black America.* New York: Henry Holt, 2011.

Menand, Louis. *The Metaphysical Club.* New York: Farrar, Straus and Giroux, 2001.

Mendelson, Wallace, ed. *Felix Frankfurter: The Judge.* New York: Reynal, 1964.

——, ed. *Felix Frankfurter: A Tribute.* New York: Reynal, 1964.

——. *Justices Black and Frankfurter: Conflict in the Court.* Chicago: University of Chicago Press, 1961.

Mennel, Robert M., and Christine L. Compston, eds. *Holmes and Frankfurter: Their Correspondence, 1912–1934.* Hanover: University Press of New England for University of New Hampshire, 1996.

Milkis, Sidney M. *The President and the Parties: The Transformation of the American Party System since the New Deal.* New York: Oxford University Press, 1993.

——. *Theodore Roosevelt, the Progressive Party, and the Transformation of American Democracy.* Lawrence: University Press of Kansas, 2009.

Miller, Richard F. *Harvard's Civil War: A History of the Twentieth Massachusetts Volunteer Infantry.* Hanover, NH: University Press of New England, 2005.

Moley, Raymond. *After Seven Years.* New York: Harper, 1939.

Monagan, John S. *The Grand Panjandrum: Mellow Years of Justice Holmes.* Lanham, MD: University Press of America, 1988.

Montgomery, David. *The Fall of the House of Labor: The Workplace, the State, and American Labor Activism, 1865–1925.* New York: Cambridge University Press, 1987.

Montgomery, Robert H. *Sacco-Vanzetti: The Murder and the Myth.* New York: Devin-Adair, 1960.

Moody, John. *The Truth about the Trusts: A Description and Analysis of the American Trust Movement.* New York: Moody, 1904.

Moran, Gerald Paul. *John Chipman Gray: The Harvard Brahmin of Property Law.* Durham, NC: Carolina Academic Press, 2010.

Morris, James McGrath. *Pulitzer: A Life in Politics, Print and Power.* New York: Harper, 2010.

Morison, Elting E., ed. *The Letters of Theodore Roosevelt, The Square Deal: 1901–1903.* Cambridge, MA: Harvard University Press, 1951.

——. *Turmoil and Tradition: A Study of the Life and Times of Henry L. Stimson.* Boston: Houghton Mifflin, 1960.

Mowry, George E. *Theodore Roosevelt and the Progressive Movement.* Madison: University of Wisconsin Press, 1946.

Murphy, Bruce Allen. *The Brandeis/Frankfurter Connection: The Secret Political Activities of Two Supreme Court Justices.* New York: Oxford University Press, 1982.

Musmanno, Michael A. *After Twelve Years.* New York: Knopf, 1939.

Nasaw, David. *The Patriarch: The Remarkable Life and Turbulent Times of Joseph P. Kennedy.* New York: Penguin Press, 2012.

National Popular Government League. *To the American People.* Washington, DC: National Popular Government League, 1920.

Neu, Charles E. *Colonel House: A Biography of Woodrow Wilson's Silent Partner.* New York: Oxford University Press, 2015.

Newby, Richard. *Kill Now, Talk Forever: Debating Sacco and Vanzetti.* Bloomington, IN: 1st Books, 2001.

Nourse, Victoria F. *In Reckless Hands*: Skinner v. Oklahoma *and the Near Triumph of American Eugenics.* New York: Norton, 2008.

Novick, Sheldon M. *Honorable Justice: The Life of Oliver Wendell Holmes.* Boston: Little, Brown, 1989.

Oney, Steve. *And the Dead Shall Rise: The Murder of Mary Phagan and the Lynching of Leo Frank.* New York: Pantheon, 2003.

Painter, Nell Irvin. *Standing at Armageddon: The United States, 1877–1919.* New York: Norton, 1987.

Palmer, Frederick. *Newton Baker: America at War.* 2 vols. New York: Dodd, Mead, 1931.

Paper, Lewis J. *Brandeis.* Englewood Cliffs, NJ: Prentice Hall, 1983.

Parrish, Michael E. *Felix Frankfurter and His Times.* New York: Free Press, 1982.

Peabody, James Bishop, ed. *The Holmes-Einstein Letters: Correspondence of Mr. Justice Holmes and Lewis Einstein, 1903–1935.* New York: Macmillan, 1964.

Peppers, Todd C., and Artemus Ward, eds. *In Chambers: Stories of Supreme Court Law Clerks and Their Justices.* Charlottesville: University of Virginia Press, 2012.

Percy, Eustace. *Some Memories*. London: Eyre and Spottiswoode, 1958.

Perry, Elisabeth Israels. *Belle Moskowitz: Feminine Politics and the Exercise of Power in the Age of Alfred E. Smith*. Boston: Northeastern University Press, 1992.

Persico, Joseph E. *Franklin and Lucy: President Roosevelt, Mrs. Rutherfurd, and the Other Remarkable Women in His Life*. New York: Random House, 2008.

Phillips, Harlan B., ed. *Felix Frankfurter Reminisces*. New York: Reynal, 1960.

Polenberg, Richard. *Fighting Faiths: The Abrams Case, the Supreme Court, and Free Speech*. New York: Viking, 1987.

Portell, Rosa, ed. *Out of Rushmore's Shadow: The Artistic Development of Gutzon Borglum (1867–1941)*. Stamford, CT: Stamford Museum and Nature Center, 1999.

Posner, Richard, ed. *The Essential Holmes: Selections from the Letters, Speeches, Judicial Opinions, and Other Writings of Oliver Wendell Holmes Jr.* Chicago: University of Chicago Press, 1992.

Price, Willadene. *Gutzon Borglum: Artist and Patriot*. Chicago: Rand McNally, 1961.

Pringle, Henry F. *The Life and Times of William Howard Taft: A Biography*. 2 vols. New York: Farrar and Rinehart, 1939.

Purcell, Edward A., Jr. *Brandeis and the Progressive Constitution*. New Haven, CT: Yale University Press, 2000.

——. *The Crisis of Democratic Theory: Scientific Naturalism and the Problem of Value*. Lexington: University Press of Kentucky, 1973.

Pusey, Merlo J. *Charles Evans Hughes*. 2 vols. New York: Macmillan, 1951.

——. *Eugene Meyer*. New York: Knopf, 1974.

Rabban, David M. *Free Speech in Its Forgotten Years*. Cambridge: Cambridge University Press, 1997.

Redmond, Charles, and Henry Cabot Lodge, eds. *Selections from the Correspondence of Theodore Roosevelt and Henry Cabot Lodge*. Vol. 1. New York: Charles Scribner's Sons, 1925.

Reilly, Michael F. *Reilly of the White House*. New York: Simon and Schuster, 1947.

Renstrom, Peter G. *The Taft Court: Justices, Rulings, and Legacy*. Santa Barbara, CA: ABC-CLIO, 2003.

Rodgers, Daniel T. *Atlantic Crossings: Social Politics in a Progressive Age*. Cambridge, MA: Belknap Press of Harvard University Press, 1998.

——. *Contested Truths: Keywords in American Politics since Independence*. New York: Basic Books, 1987.

Roe, Gilbert E. *Our Judicial Oligarchy*. New York: B. W. Huebsch, 1912.

Roosevelt, Eleanor. *This I Remember*. Westport, CT: Greenwood Press, 1949.

Roosevelt, James, and Sidney Shalett. *Affectionately, F.D.R.: A Son's Story of a Lonely Man*. New York: Harcourt, Brace, 1959.

Ropes, John Codman, and Worthington Chauncey Ford, eds. *War Letters, 1862–1865, of John Chipman Gray and John Codman Ropes*. Boston: Houghton Mifflin, 1927.

Rosen, Jeffrey. *Louis D. Brandeis: American Prophet*. New Haven, CT: Yale University Press, 2016.

Rosenfield, Leonora Cohen, ed. *Portrait of a Philosopher: Morris R. Cohen in Life and Letters.* New York: Harcourt, Brace and World, 1962.

Rosenman, Samuel I. *Working with Roosevelt.* New York: Harper, 1952.

Russell, David R. *Writing in the Academic Disciplines, 1870–1990: A Curricular History.* 2d ed. Carbondale: Southern Illinois University Press, 2002.

Russell, Francis. *Sacco and Vanzetti: The Case Resolved.* New York: Harper and Row, 1986.

———. *Tragedy in Dedham: The Story of the Sacco-Vanzetti Case.* New York: McGraw-Hill, 1962.

Ryan, Alan. *The Making of Modern Liberalism.* Princeton, NJ: Princeton University Press, 2012.

Sandburg, Carl. *The Chicago Race Riots, July, 1919.* New York: Harcourt, Brace, 1919.

Sacco, Nicola, and Bartolomeo Vanzetti. *The Letters of Sacco and Vanzetti,* edited by Marion Denman Frankfurter and Gardner Jackson. New York: Viking, 1928.

Schlegel, John Henry. *American Legal Realism and Empirical Social Science.* Chapel Hill: University of North Carolina Press, 1995.

Schlesinger, Arthur, Jr. *The Crisis of the Old Order, 1919–1933.* Boston: Houghton Mifflin, 1957.

Schwarz, Jordan A. *The New Dealers: Power Politics in the Age of Roosevelt.* New York: Knopf, 1993.

Scott, Robert Garth, ed. *Fallen Leaves: The Civil War Letters of Major Henry Livermore Abbott.* Ohio: Kent State University Press, 1991.

Sedgwick, Ellery. *The Happy Profession.* Boston: Little, Brown, 1946.

Seideman, David. *The New Republic: A Voice of Modern Liberalism.* New York: Praeger, 1986.

Shaff, Howard, and Audrey Karl Shaff. *Six Wars at a Time: The Life and Times of Gutzon Borglum, Sculptor of Mount Rushmore.* Sioux Falls, SD: Center for Western Studies, 1985.

Shesol, Jeff. *Supreme Power: Franklin Roosevelt v. the Supreme Court.* New York: Norton, 2010.

Sinclair, Upton. *The Goose-Step: A Study of American Education.* Pasadena, CA: 1923.

Sklar, Kathryn Kish, and Beverly Wilson Palmer, eds. *The Selected Letters of Florence Kelley, 1869–1931.* Champaign: University of Illinois Press, 2009.

Sklar, Martin J. *The Corporate Reconstruction of American Capitalism, 1890–1916: The Market, the Law, and Politics.* New York: Cambridge University Press, 1988.

Smith, Donald L. *Zechariah Chafee Jr., Defender of Liberty and Law.* Cambridge, MA: Harvard University Press, 1986.

Smith, Rex Alan. *The Carving of Mount Rushmore.* New York: Abbeville Press, 1985.

Social Register, Washington, D.C. 1911, 1913, 1916, 1918, 1919. New York: Social Register Association.

Southern, David W. *The Progressive Era and Race: Reaction and Reform, 1900–1917.* New York: Wiley, 2005.

Srodes, James. *On Dupont Circle: Franklin and Eleanor Roosevelt and the Progressives Who Shaped Our World.* San Francisco: Counterpoint, 2012.

Stansell, Christine. *American Moderns: Bohemian New York and the Creation of a New Century.* New York: Metropolitan Books, 2000.

Staples, Harry Lee, and Alpheus Thomas Mason. *The Fall of a Railroad Empire: Brandeis and the New Haven Merger Battle.* Syracuse, NY: Syracuse University Press, 1947.

Steel, Ronald. *Walter Lippmann and the American Century.* Boston: Little, Brown, 1980.

Steffens, Lincoln. *The Autobiography of Lincoln Steffens.* New York: Harcourt, Brace, 1931.

———. *The Letters of Lincoln Steffens.* 2 vols. New York: Harcourt, Brace, 1938.

Stimson, Henry L., and McGeorge Bundy. *On Active Service in Peace and War.* New York: Harper, 1948.

Stone, Geoffrey R. *Perilous Times: Free Speech in Wartime from the Sedition Act of 1798 to the War on Terrorism.* New York: Norton, 2004.

Strum, Philippa. *Louis D. Brandeis: Justice for the People.* Cambridge, MA: Harvard University Press, 1984.

Sullivan, Patricia. *Lift Every Voice: The NAACP and the Making of the Civil Rights Movement.* New York: New Press, 2009.

Sutherland, Arthur E. *The Law at Harvard: A History of Ideas and Men, 1817–1967.* Cambridge, MA: Belknap Press, 1967.

Taft and Roosevelt: The Intimate Letters of Archie Butt, Military Aide. 2 vols. New York: Doubleday, Doran, 1930.

Taliaferro, John. *Great White Fathers: The Story of the Obsessive Quest to Create Mount Rushmore.* New York: Public Affairs, 2002.

Temkin, Moshik. *The Sacco-Vanzetti Affair: America on Trial.* New Haven, CT: Yale University Press, 2009.

Tobin, James. *The Man He Became: How FDR Defied Polio to Win the Presidency.* New York: Simon and Schuster, 2013.

Todd, A.L. *Justice on Trial.* New York: McGraw-Hill, 1964.

Truslow, William A. *Arthur D. Hill.* Boston: Hill and Barlow, 1996.

Tuchman, Barbara W. *The Zimmerman Telegram.* New York: Viking, 1958.

Urofsky, Melvin I. *Big Steel and the Wilson Administration: A Study in Business-Government Relations.* Columbus: Ohio State University Press, 1969.

———. *Felix Frankfurter: Judicial Restraint and Individual Liberties.* Boston: Twayne, 1991.

———. *Louis D. Brandeis: A Life.* New York: Pantheon, 2009.

Urofsky, Melvin I., and David W. Levy, eds. *The Family Letters of Louis D. Brandeis.* Norman: University of Oklahoma Press, 2002.

———, eds. *"Half Brother, Half Son": The Letters of Louis D. Brandeis to Felix Frankfurter.* Norman: University of Oklahoma Press, 1991.

———, eds. *Letters of Louis D. Brandeis.* 5 vols. Albany: State University of New York Press, 1971–78.

Verrier, Anthony, ed. *Agents of Empire: Anglo-Zionist Intelligence Operations, 1915–1919: Brigadier Walter Gribbon, Aaron Aaronsohn, and the NILI Ring.* London: Brassey's, 1995.

Von Drehle, David. *Triangle: The Fire That Changed America.* New York: Atlantic Monthly Press, 2003.

Wade, Wyn Craig. *The Fiery Cross: The Ku Klux Klan in America.* New York: Oxford University Press, 1987.

Walker, Samuel. *In Defense of American Liberties: A History of the ACLU.* New York: Oxford University Press, 1990.

Warner, Hoyt Landon. *The Life of Mr. Justice Clarke: A Testament to the Power of Liberal Dissent in America.* Cleveland, OH: Western Reserve University Press, 1959.

Weinrib, Laura. *The Taming of Free Speech: America's Civil Liberties Compromise.* Cambridge, MA: Harvard University Press, 2016.

Whitaker, Robert. *On the Laps of Gods: The Red Summer of 1919 and the Struggle for Justice That Remade a Nation.* New York: Crown, 2008.

White, G. Edward. *Alger Hiss's Looking-Glass Wars: The Covert Life of a Soviet Spy.* New York: Oxford University Press, 2004.

——. *The Eastern Establishment and the Western Experience: The West of Frederic Remington, Theodore Roosevelt, and Owen Wister.* New Haven, CT: Yale University Press, 1968.

——. *Justice Oliver Wendell Holmes: Law and the Inner Self.* New York: Oxford University Press, 1993.

White, Walter Francis. *A Man Called White: The Autobiography of Walter White.* New York: Viking, 1948.

Wiebe, Robert H. *The Search for Order, 1877–1920.* New York: Hill and Wang, 1967.

Wigdor, David. *Roscoe Pound: Philosopher of Law.* Westport, CT: Greenwood Press, 1974.

Willert, Sir Arthur. *Washington and Other Memories.* Boston: Houghton Mifflin, 1972.

Wilson, Edmund. *Patriotic Gore: Studies in the Literature of the American Civil War.* New York: Oxford University Press, 1962.

Winstone, H. V. F. *The Illicit Adventure: The Story of Political and Military Intelligence in the Middle East from 1898 to 1926.* London: J. Cape, 1982.

Winter, Ella. *And Not to Yield: An Autobiography.* New York: Harcourt, 1963.

Wister, Owen. *Roosevelt: The Story of a Friendship, 1880–1919.* New York: Macmillan, 1930.

Wright, George C. *Racial Violence in Kentucky, 1865–1940.* Baton Rouge: Louisiana State University Press, 1990.

Yellin, Eric S. *Racism in the Nation's Service: Government Workers and the Color Line in Woodrow Wilson's America.* Chapel Hill: University of North Carolina Press, 2013.

Yeomans, Henry Aaron. *Abbott Lawrence Lowell, 1856–1943.* Cambridge, MA: Harvard University Press, 1948.

Young, William, and David E. Kaiser. *Postmortem: New Evidence in the Case of Sacco and Vanzetti.* Amherst: University of Massachusetts Press, 1985.

Zelden, Charles L. *The Battle for the Black Ballot:* Smith v. Allwright *and the Defeat of the All-White Primary.* Lawrence: University Press of Kansas, 2004.

ARTICLES

Athey, Louis L. "Florence Kelley and the Quest for Negro Equality." *Journal of Negro History* 56, no. 4 (October 1971): 249–61.

Auerbach, Jerold S. "The Patrician as Libertarian: Zechariah Chafee Jr. and Freedom of Speech." *New England Quarterly* 42, no. 4 (December 1969): 511–31.

Barsh, Russel Lawrence. "Progressive-Era Bureaucrats and the Unity of Twentieth-Century Indian Policy." *American Indian Quarterly* 15, no. 1 (January 1991): 1–17.

Bernstein, David. "Philip Sober Controlling Philip Drunk: *Buchanan v. Warley* in Historical Perspective." *Vanderbilt Law Review* 51, no. 4 (1998): 797–879.

Blumenthal, Henry. "Woodrow Wilson and the Race Question." *Journal of Negro History* 48, no. 1 (January 1963): 1–21.

Bogen, David S. "The Free Speech Metamorphosis of Mr. Justice Holmes." *Hofstra Law Review* 11, no. 1 (1982): 97–190.

Borglum, Gutzon. "Aesthetic Activities in America: An Answer to His Critics." *Craftsman* 15, no. 2 (December 1908): 301–7.

——. "Art That Is Real and American." *The World's Work* (June 1914): 200–17.

——. "The Betrayal of the People by a False Democracy." *Craftsman* 22, no. 1 (April 1912): 3–9.

——. "The Confederate Memorial," *The World's Work* (August 1917): 437–46.

——. "Engineering Problems to Be Met in Mountain Sculpture." *Black Hills Engineer* 18, no. 4 (November 1930): 308–34.

——. "Individuality, Sincerity and Reverence in American Art." *Craftsman* 15, no. 1 (October 1908): 3–6.

——. "The Political Importance and the Art Character of the National Memorial at Mount Rushmore." *Black Hills Engineer* 18, no. 4 (November 1930): 285–99.

Bracey, Christopher A. "Louis Brandeis and the Race Question." *Alabama Law Review* 52, no. 3 (2001): 859–910.

Brauneis, Robert. "'The Foundation of Our "Regulatory Takings" Jurisprudence': The Myth and Meaning of Justice Holmes's Opinion in *Pennsylvania Coal Co. v. Mahon.*" *Yale Law Journal* 106, no. 3 (December 1996): 613–702.

Callard, K. "The Heart and Mind of Harold Laski." *Canadian Journal of Economics and Political Science / Revue Canadienne d'Economique et de Science Politique* 20, no. 2 (May 1954): 243–51.

Carmen, Ira H. "The President, Politics and the Power of Appointment: Hoover's Nomination of Mr. Justice Cardozo." *Virginia Law Review* 55, no. 4 (1969): 616–59.

Chafee, Zechariah, Jr. "A Contemporary State Trial: The United States versus Jacob Abrams et al." *Harvard Law Review* 33, no. 6 (1920): 747–74.

——. "Harold Laski and the Harvard Law Review." *Harvard Law Review* 63, no. 8 (June 1950): 1398–1400.

Clifford, John G. "Grenville Clark and the Origins of Selective Service." *Review of Politics* 35, no. 1 (January 1973): 17–40.

Cohen, Morris R. "The Place of Logic in the Law." *Harvard Law Review* 29, no. 6 (1916): 622–39.

Collins, Ronald K. L., and David M. Skover. "Curious Concurrence: Justice Brandeis's Vote in *Whitney v. California.*" *Supreme Court Review* (2005): 333–97.

Derby, Augustin. "Recollections of Mr. Justice Holmes." *New York University Law Quarterly Review* 12 (March 1935): 345–51.

Du Bois, W. E. Burghardt. "My Impressions of Woodrow Wilson." *Journal of Negro History* 58, no. 4 (October 1973): 453–59.

Ernst, Daniel R. "Ernst Freund, Felix Frankfurter, and the American Rechtsstaat: A Transatlantic Shipwreck, 1894–1932." *Studies in American Political Development* 23 (October 2009): 171–88.

——. "Review of *Law and Inner Self* by Oliver Wendell Holmes." *Virginia Quarterly Review* 70, no. 4 (Autumn 1994): 740–51.

Filene, Peter G. "An Obituary for 'The Progressive Movement.'" *American Quarterly* 22, no. 1 (April 1970): 20–34.

Fish, Peter G. "*Red Jacket* Revisited: The Case That Unraveled John J. Parker's Supreme Court Appointment." *Law and History Review* 5 (1987): 51–104.

——. "Spite Nominations to the United States Supreme Court: Herbert C. Hoover, Owen J. Roberts, and the Politics of Presidential Vengeance in Retrospect." *Kentucky Law Journal* 77 (1988–89): 545–76.

Foer, Franklin. "Foreword." In Herbert Croly, *The Promise of American Life.* Princeton, NJ: Princeton University Press, 2014.

Frankfurter, Felix. "The Case of Sacco and Vanzetti." *Atlantic Monthly*, March 1927: 409–32.

——. "The Constitutional Opinions of Justice Holmes." *Harvard Law Review* 29, no. 6 (November 1916): 683–702.

——. "The Early Writings of O. W. Holmes Jr." *Harvard Law Review* 44, no. 5 (March 1931): 717–827.

——. "Hours of Labor and Realism in Constitutional Law." *Harvard Law Review* 29, no. 4 (February 1916): 353–73.

——. "The Law and the Law Schools." *Reports of the American Bar Association* 1, no. 4 (October 1915): 532–40.

——. "Mr. Justice Brandeis." *Harvard Law Review* 55, no. 2 (December 1941): 181–83.

——. "Mr. Justice Brandeis and the Constitution." *Harvard Law Review* 45, no. 1 (November 1931): 33–111.

——. "Mr. Justice Holmes and the Constitution: A Review of His Twenty-Five Years on the Supreme Court." *Harvard Law Review* 41, no. 2 (December 1927): 121–73.

——. "Mr. Justice Holmes. 8 March 1841–6 March 1935." *Harvard Law Review* 48, no. 8 (June 1935): 1279–80.

——. "Twenty Years of Mr. Justice Holmes' Constitutional Opinions." *Harvard Law Review* 36, no. 8 (June 1923): 909–39.

——. "Valentine, Robert Grosvenor." *Dictionary of American Biography* 19. Edited by Dumas Malone (New York: Charles Scribner's Sons, 1936): 142–43.

Frankfurter, Felix, and James M. Landis. "The Compact Clause of the Constitution: A Study in Interstate Adjustments." *Yale Law Journal* 34, no. 7 (1925): 685–758.

Franklin, John Hope. "*Birth of a Nation*–Propaganda as History." In *Race and History: Selected Essays, 1938–1988.* 10–24. Baton Rouge: Louisiana State University Press, 1989.

Freund, Ernst. "Constitutional Limitations and Labor Legislation." *Illinois Law Review* 4 (April 1910): 609–23.

——. "Limitation of Hours of Labor and the Federal Supreme Court." *Green Bag* 17 (1905): 411–17.

——. "Limitation of Hours of Labor and the Supreme Court." *Journal of Political Economy* 13, no. 4 (1905): 597–99.

Garraty, John A. "Holmes's Appointment to the U.S. Supreme Court." *New England Quarterly* 22, no. 3 (September 1949): 291–303.

German, James C., Jr. "The Taft Administration and the Sherman Antitrust Act." In *The Monopoly Issue and Antitrust, 1900–1917*, edited by Robert F. Himmelberg. 172–86. New York: Garland, 1994.

Greeley, Louis M. "Changing Attitude of the Courts toward Social Legislation." *Illinois Law Review* 5 (1910): 222–32.

Greene, Jamal. "The Anticanon." *Harvard Law Review* 125, no. 2 (2011): 380–475.

Grey, Thomas C. "Holmes, Pragmatism, and Democracy." *Oregon Law Review* 71, no. 3 (1992): 521–42.

——. "Holmes and Legal Pragmatism." *Stanford Law Review* 41, no. 4 (1989): 787–870.

——. "Holmes's Language of Judging–Some Philistine Remarks." *St. John's Law Review* 70, no. 1 (1996): 5–12.

——. "Judicial Review and Legal Pragmatism." *Wake Forest Law Review* 38, no. 2 (2003): 473–512.

Gunther, Gerald. "In Search of Judicial Quality on a Changing Court: The Case of Justice Powell." *Stanford Law Review* 24, no. 6 (June 1972): 1001–35.

Hand, Learned. "Due Process of Law and the Eight-Hour Day." *Harvard Law Review* 21, no. 7 (May 1908): 495–509.

——. "Mr. Justice Holmes." *Harvard Law Review* 43, no. 6 (1930): 857–62.

——. "Review of Collected Legal Papers, by Oliver Wendell Holmes." *Political Science Quarterly* 36, no. 3 (1921): 528–30.

Hollinger, David. "The 'Tough-Minded' Justice Holmes, Jewish Intellectuals, and the Making of an American Icon." In *The Legacy of Oliver Wendell Holmes Jr.*, edited by Robert W. Gordon. 216–28. Stanford, CA: Stanford University Press, 1992.

Holmes, Oliver Wendell. "Ideals and Doubts." *Illinois Law Review* 10 (May 1915): 1–4.

——. "Natural Law." *Harvard Law Review* 32, no. 1 (November 1918): 40–44.

"Holmes, Peirce and Legal Pragmatism." *Yale Law Journal* 84, no. 5 (April 1975): 1123–40.

Howe, Mark De Wolfe. "The Positivism of Mr. Justice Holmes." *Harvard Law Review* 64, no. 4 (1951): 529–46.

Irons, Peter. "'Fighting Fair': Zechariah Chafee Jr., the Department of Justice, and the 'Trial at the Harvard Club.'" *Harvard Law Review* 94, no. 6 (1981): 1205–36.

Jantzen, Franz. "From the Urban Legend Department: McReynolds, Brandeis, and the Myth of the 1924 Group Photograph." *Journal of Supreme Court History* 40, no. 3 (2015): 325–33.

Josephson, Matthew. "Jurist-I." *New Yorker*. November 23, 1940: 24–32.

——. "Jurist-II." *New Yorker*. December 7, 1940: 36– 46.

——. "Jurist-III." *New Yorker*. December 14, 1940: 32–42.

Kaufman, Andrew L. "Cardozo's Appointment to the Supreme Court." *Cardozo Law Review* 1, no. 1 (1979): 23–54.

Kennedy, David M. "Overview: The Progressive Era." *Historian* 37, no. 3 (May 1975): 453–68.

Kessler, Jeremy K. "The Administrative Origins of Modern Civil Liberties Law." *Columbia Law Review* 114, no. 5 (2014): 1083–166.

Kimball, Bruce A. "The Disastrous First Fund-Raising Campaign in Legal Education." *Journal of the Gilded Age and the Progressive Era* 12, no. 4 (October 2013): 535–78.

Kloppenberg, James T. "Liberalism." In *The Princeton Encyclopedia of American Political History*. Vol. 1, 475–84. Princeton, NJ: Princeton University Press, 2010.

Kolasky, William. "George Rublee and the Origins of the Federal Trade Commission." *Antitrust* 26, no. 1 (Fall 2011): 106–12.

Kramnick, Isaac. "The Professor and the Police." *Harvard Alumni Magazine*, September–October 1989, 42–45.

Kurland, Philip B. "Review of Harlan Fiske Stone: Pillar of the Law by Alpheus Thomas Mason." *Harvard Law Review* 70, no. 7 (May 1957): 1318–25.

Landis, James M. "Mr. Justice Brandeis and the Harvard Law School." *Harvard Law Review* 55, no. 2 (1941): 184–90.

Lash, Joseph P. "A Brahmin of the Law." In *From the Diaries of Felix Frankfurter: With a Biographical Essay and Notes*, edited by Joseph P. Lash, 3–98. New York: W. W. Norton, 1974.

Lennig, Arthur. "Myth and Fact: The Reception of 'The Birth of a Nation.'" *Film History* 16, no. 2 (January 2004): 117–41.

Levinson, Sanford. "The Democratic Faith of Felix Frankfurter." *Stanford Law Review* 25 (1973): 430–48.

Levy, David W., and Bruce Allen Murphy. "Preserving the Progressive Spirit in a Conservative Time: The Joint Reform Efforts of Justice Brandeis and Professor Frankfurter, 1916–1933." *Michigan Law Review* 78, no. 8 (1980): 1252–304.

Lippmann, Walter. "The World Conflict in Its Relations to American Democracy." *Annals of the American Academy of Political and Social Science* 72 (July 1917): 1–10.

Louchheim, Katie. "The Little Red House." *Virginia Quarterly Review* 56, no. 1 (Winter 1980).

Lower, A. R. M. "Loring Christie and the Genesis of the Washington Conference of 1921–22." *Canadian Historical Review* 47, no. 1 (March 1966): 38–48.

Lunardini, Christine A. "Standing Firm: William Monroe Trotter's Meetings with Woodrow Wilson, 1913–1914." *Journal of Negro History* 64, no. 3 (July 1979): 244–64.

MacLeish, Archibald. "Mr. Justice Frankfurter." *Life*, February 12, 1940: 34–36, 80–84.

McDonnell, Janet A. "Land Policy on the Omaha Reservation: Competency Commissions and Forced Fee Patents." *Nebraska History* 63 (Fall 1982): 399–411.

Luban, David. "Justice Holmes and the Metaphysics of Judicial Restraint." *Duke Law Journal* 44, no. 3 (1994): 449–523.

Messinger, I. Scott. "The Judge as Mentor: Oliver Wendell Holmes Jr. and His Law Clerks." *Yale Journal of Law and the Humanities* 11, no. 1 (1999): 119–52.

——. "Legitimating Liberalism: The New Deal Image-makers and Oliver Wendell Holmes Jr." *Journal of Supreme Court History* 20, no. 1 (1995): 57–72.

Monagan, John S. "The Love Letters of Justice Holmes." *Boston Globe Magazine*, March 24, 1985, 15.

Morison, Elting E. "Theodore Roosevelt Appoints a Judge." *Proceedings of the Massachusetts Historical Society*, 3d ser., 72 (October 1957): 309–22.

Murphy, Walter F. "In His Own Image: Mr. Chief Justice Taft and Supreme Court Appointments." *Supreme Court Review* (1961): 159–93.

Nourse, Victoria F. "A Tale of Two Lochners: The Untold History of Substantive Due Process and the Idea of Fundamental Rights." *California Law Review* 97, no. 3 (2009): 751–99.

O'Connell, Jeffrey, and Nancy Dart. "The House of Truth: Home of the Young Frankfurter and Lippmann." *Catholic University Law Review* 35, no. 1 (1985): 79–96.

——, and Thomas E. O'Connell. "Review: The Rise and Fall (and Rise Again?) of Harold Laski." *Maryland Law Review* 55, no. 4 (1996): 1384–420.

O'Reilly, Kenneth. "The Jim Crow Policies of Woodrow Wilson." *Journal of Blacks in Higher Education*, no. 17 (October 1997): 117–21.

Polenberg, Richard. "Introduction." In *The Letters of Sacco and Vanzetti*. Marion Denman Frankfurter & Gardner Jackson, eds. New York: Penguin Books, 2007.

Pollock, Frederick. "Abrams v. United States." *Law Quarterly Review* 36, no. 4 (1920): 334–38.

Porwancher, Andrew. "The Justice and the Dean." *Journal of Supreme Court History* 37, no. 3 (2012): 266–82.

Pound, Roscoe. "Judge Holmes's Contributions to the Science of Law." *Harvard Law Review* 34, no. 5 (March 1921): 449–53.

——. "Liberty of Contract." *Yale Law Journal* 18, no. 7 (May 1909): 454–87.

Powell, Thomas Reed. "Review of *The Case for the Shorter Work Day* by Felix Frankfurter." *Political Science Quarterly* 31, no. 3 (1916): 469–71.

Putney, Diane T. "Robert Grosvenor Valentine, 1909–12." In *The Commissioners of Indian Affairs*, edited by Robert N. Kvasnicka and Herman J. Viola. 233–42. Lincoln: University of Nebraska Press, 1979.

Ragan, Fred D. "Justice Oliver Wendell Holmes Jr., Zechariah Chafee Jr., and the Clear and Present Danger Test for Free Speech: The First Year, 1919." *Journal of American History* 58, no. 1 (June 1971): 24–45.

Raman, Sujit. "Felix Frankfurter and His Protégés: Re-examining the 'Happy Hot Dogs.'" *Journal of Supreme Court History* 39, no. 1 (Spring 2014): 79–106.

Risen, Clay. "The House of Truth." *Morning News*, July 19, 2006.

Robinson, Doane. "Inception and Development of the Rushmore Idea." *Black Hills Engineer* 18, no. 4 (November 1930): 334–43.

Rogat, Yosal. "Mr. Justice Holmes: A Dissenting Opinion." *Stanford Law Review* 15, no. 1 (December 1962): 3–44.

——. "Mr. Justice Holmes: A Dissenting Opinion." *Stanford Law Review* 15, no. 2 (March 1963): 254–308.

Roth, Larry. "The Many Lives of Louis Brandeis: Progressive-Reformer. Supreme Court Justice. Avowed Zionist. And a Racist?" *Southern University Law Review* 34, no. 2 (Summer 2007): 123–68.

Sawyer, Logan E., III. "Creating *Hammer v. Dagenhart.*" *William and Mary Bill of Rights Journal* 21, no. 1 (2012): 67–123.

Scheiber, Harry N. "What Wilson Said to Cobb in 1917: Another View of Plausibility." *Wisconsin Magazine of History* 52, no. 4 (July 1969): 344–47.

Siegel, Stephen. "John Chipman Gray, Legal Formalism, and the Transformation of Perpetuities Law." *University of Miami Law Review* 36, no. 3 (1982): 439–64.

——. "John Chipman Gray and the Moral Basis of Classical Legal Thought." *Iowa Law Review* 88, no. 5 (2001): 1513–600.

Snyder, Brad. "Frankfurter and Popular Constitutionalism." *UC Davis Law Review* 47, no. 1 (November 2013): 343–417.

——. "The House That Built Holmes." *Law and History Review* 30, no. 3 (August 2012): 661–720.

——. "The Judicial Genealogy (and Mythology) of John Roberts: Clerkships from Gray to Brandeis to Friendly to Roberts," *Ohio State Law Journal* 71, no. 6 (2010): 1149–1244.

Spillenger, Clyde. "Elusive Advocate: Reconsidering Brandeis as People's Lawyer." *Yale Law Journal* 105, no. 6 (1996): 1145–535.

"To Justice Oliver Wendell Holmes: An Anniversary Oblation." *Illinois Law Review* 10, no. 9 (1916): 617–32.

Tushnet, Mark. "The Logic of Experience: Oliver Wendell Holmes on the Supreme Judicial Court." *Virginia Law Review* 63, no. 6 (October 1977): 975–1052.

Urofsky, Melvin I. "Attorney for the People: The 'Outrageous' Brandeis Nomination," *Yearbook: 1979 Supreme Court Historical Society*: 8–19.

———. "State Courts and Protective Legislation during the Progressive Era: A Reevaluation." *Journal of American History* 72, no. 1 (June 1985): 63–91.

———. "Wilson, Brandeis, and the Supreme Court Nomination," *Journal of Supreme Court History* 28, no. 2 (July 2003): 145–56.

Valentine, Robert G. "The Human Element in Production." *American Journal of Sociology* 22, no. 4 (January 1917): 477–88.

———. "Introduction in English at the Institute." *Technology Review* 1, no. 4 (1899): 441–56.

———. "On Criticism of Themes by Students." *Technology Review* 4, no. 4 (1902): 459–78.

———. "Work and Pay: A Suggestion for Representative Government in Industry." *Quarterly Journal of Economics* 31, no. 2 (February 1917): 241–58.

Vose, Clement E. "The National Consumers' League and the Brandeis Brief." *Midwest Journal of Political Science* 1, nos. 3/4 (November 1957): 267–90.

Wagner, Richard H. "A Falling Out: The Relationship between Oliver Wendell Holmes and Theodore Roosevelt." *Journal of Supreme Court History* 27, no. 2 (December 2002): 114–37.

Weiss, Nancy J. "The Negro and the New Freedom: Fighting Wilsonian Segregation." *Political Science Quarterly* 84, no. 1 (March 1969): 61–79.

Wells, Catharine Pierce. "Oliver Wendell Holmes Jr. and the American Civil War." *Journal of Supreme Court History* 40, no. 3 (2015): 282–313.

White, G. Edward. "The Canonization of Holmes and Brandeis: Epistemology and Judicial Reputations." *New York University Law Review* 70, no. 3 (1995): 576–621.

———. "Felix Frankfurter, the Old Boy Network, and the New Deal: The Placement of Elite Lawyers in Public Service in the 1930s." *Arkansas Law Review* 39, no. 4 (1986): 631–68.

———. "Holmes as Correspondent." *Vanderbilt Law Review* 43, no. 6 (1990): 1707–62.

———. "Holmes's Life Plan: Confronting Ambition, Passion, and Powerlessness." *New York University Law Review* 65, no. 6 (1990): 1409–80.

———. "Justice Holmes and the Modernization of Free Speech Jurisprudence: The Human Dimension." *California Law Review* 80, no. 2 (1992): 391–468.

———. "Looking at Holmes in the Mirror." *Law and History Review* 4, no. 2 (October 1986): 439–65.

———. "The Rise and Fall of Justice Holmes." *University of Chicago Law Review* 39, no. 1 (1971): 51–77.

Wigmore, John H. "Abrams *v.* U.S.: Freedom of Speech and Freedom of Thuggery in War-Time and Peace-Time." *Illinois Law Review* 14, no. 8 (1920): 539–61.

———. "Justice Holmes and the Law of Torts." *Harvard Law Review* 29, no. 6 (1916): 601–16.

Williams, David. "The Bureau of Investigation and Its Critics, 1919–1921." *Journal of American History* 68, no. 3 (December 1981): 560–79.

Winerman, Marc. "The Origins of the FTC: Concentration, Cooperation, Control, and Competition." *Antitrust Law Journal* 71, no. 1 (2003): 1–97.

Wittke, Carl. "Mr. Justice Clarke in Retirement." *Western Reserve Law Review* 1, no. 1 (June 1949): 28–48.

Wolgemuth, Kathleen L. "Woodrow Wilson and Federal Segregation." *Journal of Negro History* 44, no. 2 (April 1959): 158–73.

Wyzanski, Charles E., Jr. "The Democracy of Justice Oliver Wendell Holmes." *Vanderbilt Law Review* 7, no. 3 (1954): 311–24.

Yale, William. "Ambassador Henry Morgenthau's Special Mission of 1917." *World Politics* 1, no. 3 (April 1949): 308–20.

DISSERTATIONS

Gengarelly, William Anthony. "Resistance Spokesmen: Opponents of the Red Scare, 1919–1921." PhD diss., Boston University, 1972.

Putney, Diane T. "Fighting the Scourge: American Indian Morbidity and Federal Policy, 1897–1928." PhD diss., Marquette University, 1980.

Scheuer, Michael Frank. "Loring Christie and the North Atlantic Community, 1913–41." PhD diss., University of Manitoba, 1986.

Wasniewski, Matthew A. "Walter Lippmann, Strategic Internationalism, the Cold War, and Vietnam, 1943–1967." PhD diss., University of Maryland, 2004.

Weinrib, Laura. "The Liberal Compromise: Civil Liberties, Labor, and the Limits of State Power, 1917–1940." PhD diss., Princeton University, 2011.

Acknowledgments

Oliver Wendell Holmes Jr. remarked "that if a man was to do anything he must do it before 40." By his standard, I have failed miserably. During the summer of 2008, I conceived of a book about the relationship between Holmes and his young friends at the House of Truth. At the time, I was living only a few blocks from 1727 Nineteenth Street in Dupont Circle. I was thirty-six, about to be married, and figured that the book would take me no more than three or four years to complete. More than eight years have passed and so has my forty-fourth birthday. But, as most writers can attest, better late than never. It has been a long and worthwhile journey.

Numerous people have made it possible for me to finish this book, starting with the lifeblood of every historian—librarians and archivists.

My big break came thanks to the kindness and generosity of a Vermont archivist, Dorothy Koval. Koval had preserved the papers of the owner and leader of the House of Truth, Taft's commissioner of Indian affairs, Robert G. Valentine. From 1991 to 1998, she had worked with Valentine's daughter, Charlotte Valentine Taylor, in organizing the collection of letters and documents. The papers were stored in "files, closets, chests, and barns" in the Taylor family home in Manchester-by-the-Sea, Massachusetts. After Charlotte's death in 1998, her daughter Anne cleared out the house and barn and gave the papers to Koval. Koval donated them to the Massachusetts Historical Society (MHS), and they remained there unprocessed. Thanks to grant funding obtained by MHS, the Valentine Papers are now open to researchers. They reveal the hidden history of the House of Truth and the depth of Valentine's friendships with Felix Frankfurter and Winfred T. Denison. The correspondence with Valentine's wife documents how he and his friends turned 1727 Nineteenth Street into one of the city's foremost political salons. Koval alerted me to this research goldmine, sent me additional materials in her possession, and answered countless queries. To say that I am in her debt is a massive understatement.

At my home institution, the University of Wisconsin Law Library has gone above and beyond the call of duty—from purchasing a new microfilm machine to requesting and retrieving every conceivable book, database, and primary source. The word "no" is not in their vocabulary. I thank Steve Barkan, Vicky Coulter, Lilly Li, Mary Jo Koranda, Cheryl O'Connor, Bonnie Shucha, Eric Taylor, Jay Tucker, Peter Wehrle, and Jenny Zook. Jennifer Hanrahan also assisted me at Wisconsin. During my time as a visiting professor at Georgetown University Law Center, the library staff including Craig Lelansky, Jeremy McCabe, Yelena Rodriguez, Erie

Taniuchi, and Michelle Wu treated me like a member of their permanent faculty. T.C. Anthony, George E. Belton, Betsy Kuhn, and Jennifer Lane also assisted me at Georgetown.

My home away from home during this project is every historian's dream—the Manuscript Division of the Library of Congress. For the last three years, I have lived three blocks from the library, and I can see the manuscript division from my house. By the end of the project, my goal was to stay out of the manuscript room so that I could finish writing. The librarians and archivists are knowledgeable, professional, and friendly beyond measure. I thank my many friends there past and present including Fred Augustyn, Jennifer Brathovde, Jeff Flannery, Dave Kelly, Lia Kerwin, Patrick Kerwin, Bruce Kirby, Joe Jackson, Ryan Reft, Lewis Wyman, and Daun van Ee.

I also could not have finished this book without the assistance of Jane Kelly, Ed Moloy, Margaret Peachy, and the indefatigable Lesley Schoenfeld at the Harvard Law School Special Collections Library. They have been helping me with this project for many years, answered questions big and small, and helped me explore every research angle. The Oliver Wendell Holmes Digital Suite, with more than 100,000 documents and 1,000 photos, is one of the world's best digitization projects and represents the future of primary source research and preservation.

The Massachusetts Historical Society allowed me to see the Robert Valentine Papers when they were unprocessed and worked quickly to get them processed. They gave me grant funding, took me to lunch, and helped me all along the way. I thank Anna Clutterbuck-Cook, Daniel Hinchen, Elaine Grublin, Brenda Lawson, Laura Lowell, Tracey Potter, Kate Viens, and Conrad Wright.

Many other archivists have helped me in ways large and small: Robert Ellis, Paul Harrison, Christina Jones, Richard McCulley, and Richard Peuser at the National Archives; Zane Martin at the National Park Service, Mount Rushmore; Robert Clark, William Baehr, Kirsten Carter, and Matthew Hanson at the FDR Library; Clare Cushman and Jennifer Lowe at the Supreme Court Historical Society; Matthew Hofstedt and Franz Jantzen at the Supreme Court of the United States Curator's Office; Nina Gershuni and Illanit Levy at the Aaronsohn Museum; Kimberly Reynolds at the Boston Public Library; Lisa Marine at the Wisconsin Historical Society; David A. Olson at Columbia University; Rossy Mendez and Rachel Van Unen at Princeton University's Mudd Manuscript Library; Jim Stimpert at Johns Hopkins University; Dana Herman at the American Jewish Archives; Ann Sindelar at Western Reserve Historical Society; Scott Taylor at Georgetown University Special Collections; Brandon Pieczko at the Ball State University Library; Scott Campbell at the University of Louisville Law Library; Ken Stewart at the South Dakota State Archives; Jamie Kingman Rice at the Maine Historical Society; Timothy Driscoll at the Harvard University Archives; Nicolette A. Dobrowolski at the Syracuse University Archives; Cate Kellett, Ryan Greenwood, Fred Shapiro, and Michael Widener at the Yale Law School Library; Judy Burg and Simon Wilson at Hull History Centre; Ella

Molenaar, Teun de Reijke, and M. van der Pal at the International Institute of Social History; Jo-Ellen El-Bashir at the Moorland–Spingarn Research Center at Howard University; Elizabeth Thrond and Harry Thompson at Augustana College; Christina Senezak (formerly) at Patterson Belknap; David K. Frasier at Indiana University's Lilly Library; Karen Jania at University of Michigan Bentley Historical Library; Janet Olson at Northwestern University Library; Anne Engelhart and Sarah Hutcheon at Harvard University's Schlesinger Library; Kathleen E. Shoemaker at Emory University's Rose Library; Judith Wright at University of Chicago Law School Library; Donna F. Slaton at the Historical Society of Hopkins County. Special thanks to Louis F. Bacharach and Lauren Post for permission to publish a photograph and political cartoon by their talented relatives.

Several research assistants have worked with me on this project, none more talented and more important than Debbie Sharnak. A history graduate student at the University of Wisconsin, Debbie worked with me for three years on this project, visited archives in Austin, Minneapolis, New Haven, and New York, and spent countless hours at microfilm machines. I could not have finished the research without her assistance and good cheer. I look forward to reading her books one day. Special thanks to all the students who have gathered material and proofread for this project including Mihal Ancik, David Blinka, Amy Butner, Steven Curry, Cory Dodds, Antonia Ferguson, Cat Foley, Timothy Garrett, Alison Kahn, Eryn Killian, Jake Lieberman, Patrick Proctor-Brown, Irina Rodina, and Annie Ziesing.

Numerous scholars and their families lent their time, expertise, and research including Robin Borglum Kennedy, Robert Bothwell, Dan Coquillette, Sam Erman, Bruce Kimball, Isaac Kramnick, Charles and Rosemary Monagan, I. Scott Messinger, Michael Parrish, Audrey Shaff, Daniel Sharfstein, Ronald Steel, John Taliaferro, William Truslow, and G. Edward White. Special thanks to David Tanenhaus for the editing and peer review of my *Law and History Review* article.

I benefited greatly from comments and suggestions at faculty and student workshops at the Boston College Legal History Roundtable, Brooklyn Law School, University of Chicago Public Law and Legal Theory Workshop, Georgetown University Law Center, New Legal Realism Tenth Anniversary Conference at University of California–Irvine Law School, New York University Legal History Colloquia, Randy Barnett's "Recent Books on the Constitution" seminar at Georgetown University Law Center, Tulane Law School, University of Virginia Law School Legal History Workshop, and the University of Wisconsin Conlaw Schmooze.

A few generous people in academia read the entire manuscript and gave me valuable feedback, including John Milton Cooper, Daniel R. Ernst, Laura Kalman, David W. Levy, and Victoria Nourse. Several scholars read parts of the manuscript and supplied me with written comments, including Randy Barnett, John Q. Barrett, R.B. Bernstein, Ben Kerschberg, Bill Nelson, Frank Stewart, Mel Urofsky, Bruce Watson, and Larry Zacharias. I hope to return the favor one day (just not all at once!). All the aforementioned people helped me improve the book. All errors are my own.

I am indebted to the work of scholars of Frankfurter (Liva Baker, Max Freedman, H. N. Hirsch, Joseph P. Lash, Michael Parrish, Harlan B. Phillips, Melvin Urofsky); Holmes (Liva Baker, Francis Biddle, Catherine Drinker Bowen, Thomas Healy, Mark DeWolfe Howe, Louis Menand, John S. Monagan, Sheldon Novick, Catharine P. Wells, G. Edward White); Lippmann (John M. Blum, Ronald Steel, Matthew A. Wasniewski); and Borglum (Howard and Audrey Karl Shaff, Rex Allen Smith, John Taliaferro).

During more than eight years in academia, I have learned so much from my friends and colleagues at the University of Wisconsin Law School. Wisconsin took a chance on me, and I hope that I have made Willard Hurst's institution proud. I could not have done it without the law school and graduate school's summer funding and research support. I also greatly enjoyed visiting and learning from my friends and colleagues at Brooklyn Law School and Georgetown University Law Center.

My agent, Philippa "Flip" Brophy of Sterling Lord Literistic, believed in this book when no one else did, and every publisher either turned it down or wanted to turn it into something else. She fought for me as if I were her most important client, and this book were her largest advance. The memory of Richard Ben Cramer binds us, but we have forged our own enduring friendship. Flip and her amazing assistant Holly Hilliard helped me at every phase of this project, and Flip is always in my corner.

The editors and production staff at Oxford University Press are equally first rate. My editor Tim Bent line-edited the entire manuscript, edited the introduction and conclusion multiple times, and taught me a lot about writing and storytelling. His editorial assistant Alyssa O'Connell is a wizard with photographs, permissions, and everything else in between. And their colleague David McBride has his finger on the pulse of legal history and guided me into Tim's steady hands. Thanks to Deepti Agarwal for supervising the book's production and to Susan Ecklund for her excellent copyediting.

The two people most responsible for who am I today are my parents, Harry and Linda Snyder. My mother is a gifted writer and amateur photographer who took several photographs for this book. My father remains my biggest fan and publicist. They have been supportive of everything I have ever tried to do. My brother Ivan, his wife, Tamara, and my amazing nieces Elana and Maya have encouraged me throughout this project (yes, Ivan, the book is finally done).

This book is dedicated to the three most important people in my life—my wife, Shelby, and my children, Lily and Max. They have put up with me during the book's many ups and downs and have enriched my life more than they possibly know. Holmes, who missed out on the joys and unconditional love of children, was wrong about not being able to accomplish anything after age forty. Being a husband and father has made me feel like the luckiest person in the world. Shelby, Lily, and Max are my house of truth.

Index

Aaronsohn, Aaron, *238*
  Brandeis and, 245, 248–49
  Brandeis on, 242
  Bullitt, W., and, 258–59
  death of, 257–58
  Frankfurter and, 241–42,
    245–48, 256–57
  at House of Truth, 246–47
  Lippmann and, 247–48
  Mack and, 245
  NILI spy network and, 245–46
  Percy and, 247
  Roosevelt, T., and, 243
  Zionist cause and, 241–49, 252
Abbott, Henry, 312–13, *314*
abolitionism, 392
  Holmes, Jr., on, 306–7, 312, 313, 704n73
Abrams, Jacob, 302, 352
  Frankfurter on, 426
Abrams v. United States
  Brandeis and, 304, 459
  Chafee and, 303
  Frankfurter on, 295
  Holmes, Jr., on, 289–95, 303–4, 318,
    665n229
  Laski on, 293
  Lippmann on, 291–92
  Red Scare and, 289–90
Acheson, Dean, 348, 350,
    665n229, 678n43
  in Treasury Department, 567
ACLU. *See* American Civil
    Liberties Union
Adair, Forrest, 330–31
Adamson Act, 143
  Supreme Court and, 163–64
Addams, Jane, 449
Adkins, Jesse, 349, 679n62
Adkins v. Children's Hospital, 349–51, 355
  Holmes, Jr., on, 351

AFL. *See* American Federation of Labor
aircraft industry corruption
  Baker on, 197–98
  Borglum and, 196–208
  Dayton-Wright and, 200–201
  Deeds and, 200–201, 206–7
  Hughes and investigation on, 206–7
  Marshall Committee, 203–4
  Meyer, E., and, 202–3
  Wilson on, 196–98
Albertson, Faye
  Holmes, Jr., and, 173
  at House of Truth, 172–73
  Lippmann and marriage to, 172–73
Allenby, Edmund, 266
Alsberg, Henry, 255
American Civil Liberties Union
    (ACLU), 299
American Federation of Labor (AFL), 93
  on Parker, J., 520–22
American Individualism (Hoover,
    H.), 489–90
American isolationism, 137, 571
  World War I and, 164, 166
American liberalism, 363
  in American party system, 3
  Broun on, 469–70
  fair criminal trials and, 413–14
  Frankfurter on, 391, 507
  Holmes, Jr., as face of, 342–43, 364
  House of Truth and, 3, 577–78
  Lippmann on, 3, 382–83, 507, 570
  Meiklejohn affair and, 364
  network of, 577–78
  1924 election and basic issues
    of, 365–83
  political power and, 577
  Sacco-Vanzetti case and,
    413–14, 467–68
American Sugar Refining Company, 9

American Tobacco Company, 20–21
    antitrust actions against, 13
American Zionist movement, 239
Ames, James Barr, 73
anarchism
    bombings and, 378–79, 698n149
    Espionage Act and, 276
    Galleani, 278–79
    Immigration Act of 1918 and, 279
    Mooney case and, 179
    Red Summer of 1919 and, 287
    Sacco-Vanzetti case and, 410–11, 415
    Zangara and, 560
Anderson, George W., 445
Antietam, Civil War, 188, 308, 528
anti-immigrant views, 377, 486
    Palmer Raids and, 300–301
antilynching legislation, 329, 354
anti-Semitism, 718n27
    Borglum and, 325
    Brandeis and, 124–25, 133,
        619n67, 619n70
    Harvard College Jewish quota and,
        357, 359
    House and, 183, 211, 253
    Kennedy, J., and, 567
    Lippmann on, 360
    Lowell and, 357
    McReynolds and, 626n22
    Taft and, 619n67
    Zionist cause and, 253
antitrust laws, 4
    American Tobacco Company and, 13
    Clayton Antitrust Act, 143
    Frankfurter on, 14–15
    Holmes, Jr., on, 50
    Sherman Antitrust Act, 13–18, 20–21
    Standard Oil Company, 13
    Stimson on, 14–15
    sugar trust, 8–9
    Supreme Court and enforcement
        of, 13–14
    Taft on, 15
    United Mine Workers and, 345
Arab-Jewish alliance, 249–51
"the Arab Question," 249–50
Armed Neutrality Bill, 166
Armstrong, Hamilton Fish, 571
Armstrong, Marie, 105

Astor, Nancy, 254
Atlanta Constitution, 328
Atlanta Journal, 324
Atlantic Monthly
    Holmes, Sr., writings in, 306, 311, 315
    Lippmann and writing in, 291–92
    "My Hunt after 'The Captain,'" 311
    Sedgwick and, 696n106
    "The Portentous Case of Sacco
        and Vanzetti: A Comprehensive
        Analysis of a Trial of Grave
        Importance," 420–23
    on Turkish atrocities, 243–44
Authority in the Modern State (Laski), 279

Baker, Newton D., 167, 425–26, 472
    on aircraft industry corruption, 197–98
    on civil liberties, 544
    Frankfurter and, 167–68, 209–10,
        473, 543–44
    League of Nations supported by, 543
    Lippmann and, 171–72, 231, 543–44
    1932 presidential election and, 543–44
    on wartime government
        reorganization, 210–11
Baldwin, Elbert F., 30
Baldwin v. Missouri, 526–27
Balfour, Arthur, 169, 253
    Brandeis and, 263–64, 267, 651n109
    Balfour Declaration, 238
    Frankfurter and, 154–55
Ballinger-Pinchot Affair, 21–22, 125, 132
Ball's Bluff, Civil War, 307
Bard, Nathan, 455–56
    execution of, 474, 475
Bard-Fleming case
    Cobb and, 474
    habeas corpus for, 455
    Holmes, Jr., on, 455–56, 456, 705n100
    NAACP and, 473–75
    Sacco-Vanzetti case and, 474–75
    Supreme Court and, 473–74
Barlow, Lester, 397, 399
Bartels v. Iowa, 680n77
Baruch, Bernard, 216
    Borglum and, 324–25
    United Daughters of the Confederacy
        and, 324, 673n22
Bass, Robert P., 152

Denison and, 59
  Valentine, R., and, 54–56
Beard, Charles, 449
Beck, James, 179, 358
Belknap, Chauncey, *103*, 533–34,
  662n162
  Christie and, 106
  Denison and, 295–96
  Frankfurter and, 102
  as Holmes, Jr., secretary, 102–5
  at House of Truth, 104
Berlin, Isaiah, 572
Bickel, Alexander, 665n229
Biddle, Francis, 54, 100, 533–34, 671n103
  Holmes, Jr., and, 49
  at House of Truth, 48–49
  on National Labor Relations
    Board, 567
Bill of Rights, 527
birth control movement, 452
The Birth of a Nation (film), 190–91, 326
  Ku Klux Klan and, 120–21
  New Republic on, 121
Bissell, Louis G., 82, 320
  at House of Truth, 101–2
Black and White Taxicab case, 499–500
Black Hills, South Dakota
  Coolidge in, 480–81
  tourism, 511–12
Blankenhorn, Herber, 227–28
Bliven, Bruce, 449, 693n58
  Pulitzer and, 697n127
Board of Inquiry, 220
Bolshevism, 289
  Bullitt, W., on, 252, 259
bombings
  anarchist, 378–79, 698n149
  Galleani, 378–79
  of Hardwick residence, 379
  of Palmer residence, 286–87
  Preparedness Day Parade, 178–79
Bonbright, James, 543
Bonus Army, 548, 550
Borah, William E., 537, 539, 729n162
Borgland, 196
Borglum, Gutzon, 1, *47*, 82, *189*, *330*.
  See also Mount Rushmore, South
  Dakota; Stone Mountain memorial,
  Georgia

on aircraft industry corruption,
    196–208
  anti-immigrant views of, 377, 486
  anti-Semitism, 325
  arrest of, 400
  Baruch and, 324–25
  Borgland, 196
  Brandeis and, 198
  brother Solon and, 195, 326–27, 673n35
  Confederate war hero monument, 1, *2*,
    188–92, 321–22, *323*, 583n2
  Coolidge and, 377–78, 399,
    482–83, 512–13
  death of, 574
  Deeds and, 201
  dynamite used by, 374–75
  financial difficulties, 196, 322–23,
    398, 637n68
  Frankfurter and, 46, 477–79,
    573, 714n51
  Harding and, 322, 333–34
  Holmes, Jr., and, 408, 531–32
  Holmes, Jr., plaster death mask by,
    575, *578*
  Hoover, H., and, 508–10, 532, 550–51
  House of Truth and, 3
  interest in airplanes, 197–98
  Jackson, G., and, 552, 714n51
  King, S., and, 199–200
  Ku Klux Klan and, 327–35,
    375–76, 399
  La Follette and, 376–77
  La Follette-Wheeler campaign medal-
    lion, *372*, 377
  Lincoln statue, 46–47, 190, 635n19
  The Mares of Diomedes, 196
  Mellon and, 484
  Meyer, E., and, 196, 202–3, 323,
    398, 637n68
  Montgomery and, 196
  mother leaving family and marrying
    black Union army veteran, 193–94
  1924 presidential election and, 374–78
  on 1932 presidential election, 550–51
  Norbeck and, 403–4, 509–10
  Oliphant and, 572–73
  personal attacks on, 205
  personal history of, 192–96
  Plane and, 188–89, *336*, 401

Borglum, Gutzon (*Cont.*)
  politics of, 550
  postwar work, 323–24
  Putnam and, 194
  Randolph and, 397–400
  Return of the Boer, 196
  Robinson, D., and, 402–3, 484
  Rodin and, 194
  Roosevelt, F., and, 551–52
  Roosevelt, T., supported by, 46–48,
    139, 194
  Sacco-Vanzetti bas-relief by, 477–79,
    478, 486
  Stephenson and, 376, 398
  Stone Mountain half dollar, 398–400
  Stone Mountain memorial and firing
    of, 396–98
  Stone Mountain Memorial Association
    and, 397–99
  Stone Mountain memorial model and,
    396, *397*
  on Taft, 47
  Treasury Department and, 484, 572
  Tucker and, 484, 511
  United Daughters of the Confederacy
    and, 190
  Valentine, R., and, 48
  Wars of America monument, 324
  wartime efforts of, 192
  Wilson and, 196–98, 204
Boston, Charles, 533
Boston Evening Transcript, "J. H. Wigmore
  Answers Frankfurter Attack on
  Sacco-Vanzetti Verdict," 426–27
Boston Herald, 418–19, 427
Boston & Maine Railroad, 21
Bourne, Randolph, 190
Bowman, Isaiah, 233–34
Brandeis, Louis D., 4, *23*, *466*
  on Aaronsohn, 242
  Aaronsohn and, 245, 248–49
  on *Abrams* dissent, 459, 665n229
  in American Zionist movement, 239
  anti-Semitism and, 124–25, 133,
    619n67, 619n70
  Balfour and, 263–64, 267, 651n109
  Ballinger-Pinchot Affair and, 21–22,
    125, 132
  on *Black and White Taxicab*, 499–500

Borglum and, 198
confirmation of, 127
on conservatism, 347–48
Croly and, 125, 616n17
enemies, 124
Evans, E., and, 409
Frankfurter and, 19–20, 22, 58, 356–57,
    464, 473, 500
Frankfurter and confirmation of,
    126–27, 129
Frankfurter and nomination of, 134
on free speech, 459–60, 680n78,
    705n108
Gitlow v. New York dissent, 387–89
Hand on, 459–60, 705–6n111
Harvard Law School and, 21,
    130–31, 588n54
Hill and, 458–59, 462
Holmes, Jr., and, 128, 284–85, 459–60,
    498–501, *499*, 534
Holmes, Jr., on, 556–57
on Holmes, Jr., 517
House and, 183
at House of Truth, 69, 125–26
as Jew, 617n33
on Jewish state, 240, 263–64
on labor laws, 21
La Follette and, 50–51, 371
law career of, 21–22
on Lippmann, 368–69
Lippmann and, 127–29, 134, 473
Lochner v. New York, 21
on maximum hour laws, 114
McReynolds and, 725n70
on minimum wage laws, 114–15
Muller v. Oregon, 21
New Republic and, 125–26, 129–30,
    131, 133
nomination to Supreme Court, 134–35
opponents to nomination of, 129–32
*Other People's Money and How Bankers
  Use It*, 125
Palestine trip, 262–67, *267*
on Parker, J., 723n24
on *The Phantom Public*, 383
philosophy of, 128
Pound and, 283–84
on privacy, 501
on race, 461, 706n122

on racial segregation, 461
on Roosevelt, T., 50–51
on Sacco-Vanzetti case, 461–62,
    707n136
Sacco-Vanzetti case and, 473
on Sacco-Vanzetti sentencing, 424
on *Schaefer v. United States*, 705n108
on Sherman Act, 20–21
on Supreme Court, 459–60
Supreme Court nomination,
    122–36, *123*
Taft on nomination of, 125,
    132–33, 619n67
Valentine, R., and, 149–50, 154
on wartime government reorganiza-
    tion during, 211
Weizmann and, 268
on *Whitney v. California*, 706n114
Wilson and, 52, 58
Wilson and nomination to Supreme
    Court of, 122, *123*
on wiretapping, 500
Zionist cause and, 239, 264–65
Brasseaux, Molton, 705n100
The Breach in Civilization (Croly), 727n97
Brooks, Van Wyck, 91
Brough, Charles H., 287–88
Broun, Heywood, 428, 430, 710n189
    on American liberalism, 469–70
    Lippmann and, 436, 470
    Pulitzer and, 435–36
    on Sacco-Vanzetti case, 435–36
    World and resignation of, 436–37
Brown v. Board of Education, 568
Bruce, Roscoe Conkling, Jr., 361
Bruère, Robert W., 147
Bryce, James, 25, 66
Buchanan v. Warley, 453
Buck, Carrie, 450–51
Buck, Emma, 702n48
Buckner, Emory R., 428, 472
    Frankfurter and, 25, 39, 45, 65, 82
    Sacco-Vanzetti case record publication
        and, 710n193
    Valentine, R., and, 74
Buck v. Bell, 461, 702n48
    eugenics and, 451–52
    Holmes, Jr., on, 450–51, 703n61
Bullard, F. Lauriston, 418

Bullitt, Ernesta Drinker, 183–85, *184*
Bullitt, William Marshall, 68
Bullitt, William "Billy"
    Aaronsohn and, 258–59
    on Bolshevism, 252, 259
    Frankfurter and, 183–85
    House and, 186–87
    on League of Nations, 291
    Zionist cause and, 252
Bundy, Harvey, 610nn17–18
    as Holmes, Jr., secretary, 101–2, 533–34
    at House of Truth, 101–2
Bureau of Indian Affairs, 26–27, 30–31
Burlingham, Charles C., 82, 380,
    447–48, 472
    Lippmann and, 448
    Sacco-Vanzetti case record publication
        and, 710n193
Burns, James MacGregor, 732
The Business of the Supreme Court
    (Frankfurter), 473
Butler, Pierce, 348–49, *390*, 679n50
    on *Buck v. Bell*, 451
    on *Powell v. Alabama*, 733n14
Butt, Archie, 604n133

Cabot, Richard C., 529
capitalism, 489
Cardozo, Benjamin, 464, 517–18,
    535–37, *540*
    Frankfurter and, 537–39
    on *Gitlow v. New York*, 388
    Holmes, Jr., and, 528, 726n80
    on Holmes, Jr., 501–2
    Hoover, H., and, 539, 729n162
    on Schwimmer case, 506–7
    Supreme Court nomination, 539
*The Case of Sacco and Vanzetti: A Critical
    Analysis for Lawyers and Laymen*
    (Frankfurter), 421
    backlash against, 424–25
    Holmes, Jr., on, 442–43
    Wigmore on, 425–28
Catholicism, 491
    Tammany Hall issue and, 493
CBS. *See* Columbia Broadcasting System
censorship, 275
    Lippmann on, 231
    under Wilson, 227–28

Cermak, Anton, 560
Chafee, Zechariah, Jr., *303*, 357–58
  on *Abrams* dissent, 304
  charges filed against, 302–3
  Free Speech in the United States, 303
  on *Gitlow v. New York*, 386–89
  at Harvard Law School,
    658n40, 658n46
  Holmes, Jr., and, 279–80
  Hoover, J. E., and investigation of, 301
  Laski and, 280
  Lowell and, 302
  Palmer Raid immigrants and, 300–301
  on Parker, J., 519–20
Child, Richard Washburn, 147
child labor, 69
  Hammer v. Dagenhart, 218–19
  Keating-Owen Child Labor Act,
    143, 217–18
  laws, 143, 345
  minimum wage laws for, 349–50
  Supreme Court on, 464
Christie, Loring, *35*, 44, 66, 569
  Belknap and, 106
  Frankfurter and, 34
  Holmes, Jr., and, 105
  at House of Truth, *62*, 72
  on *Lusitania* sinking, 108
civil liberties, 275–76
  ACLU, 299
  Baker on, 544
  Frankfurter and, 299
  majority rule and, 451
  wartime suppression of, 275, 577
civil rights
  Lippmann on, 506
  Supreme Court on, 704n73
Civil War
  abolitionism views and, 306–7,
    312–13
  Antietam, 188, 308, 528
  Ball's Bluff, 307
  Holmes, Jr., and experiences
    in, 105, 307–13, *310*, 528, 558,
    666nn19–20, 667n41
  Lincoln at, 312–13, 667nn41–42
  Nicodemus House, 308
Clark, Charles, 533
Clarke, E. Y., 327, 329, 331

Clarke, John Hessin, 143, 158, 164, 350,
  421, 694n65
  resignation of, 347
Clarke, Stanley, 72, 100–101
Clayton Antitrust Act, 143
Cleveland Crime Survey, 414–15
Cobb, James, 474
Cohen, Morris R., 318, 487
  in Public Works Administration, 567
Colcord, Lincoln, 183
Collected Legal Papers (Holmes, Jr.), 305
  reviews of, 318–19
collective bargaining, 109
collectivism, 737n27
Columbia Broadcasting System
  (CBS), 532–33
The Common Law (Holmes, Jr.), 315, 500
Communism
  Espionage Act and, 276
  Gitlow v. New York and, 387–88
  labor policy and, 282
  in postwar Europe, 489
  red-baiting of Frankfurter and Pound,
    274–75, 280–86
  Schwimmer and, 504
Compact Clause, 389, 716n32
Congress, Supreme Court and, 346
conscientious objectors, 275–76,
  426, 544
  Board of Inquiry on, 220
conservatism
  Brandeis on, 347–48
  Holmes, Jr., and, 348
  Lippmann and, 471, 543
  in Supreme Court, 343, 347, 349, 516
Constitution. *See also* Fourteenth
  Amendment
  Compact Clause, 389, 716n32
  Due Process Clause of, 343, 345–46
  Fifth Amendment, 500
  Fourth Amendment, 500, 568
  Holmes, Jr., on, 394, 524
  minimum wage laws and, 350
  Supreme Court and, 523–24
Cook, Waldo, 449
Coolidge, Calvin, 288, 365
  in Black Hills, 480–81
  Borglum and, 377–78, 399,
    482–83, 512–13

death of son of, 485
Frankfurter on, 367
Hand promoted by, 385
Holmes, Jr., and, 366–67, 384
judicial appointments, 385
Laski on, 384
Mount Rushmore and, 407, 480–83,
    483, 511–14
Mount Rushmore inscription
    and, 512–13
1924 presidential election and, 367,
    377–78, 382
Roosevelt Medal ceremony and, 385
Supreme Court and, 378–80
Coppage v. Kansas, 113–14
copper mining strikes, Arizona, 178
Corcoran, Thomas Gardiner,
    533–34, 732n4
Holmes, Jr., and, 392–93
"The Little Red House," 567–68
in Reconstruction Finance
    Corporation, 567
Securities Act of 1933 and, 566
on Wigmore, 428
corruption
in aircraft industry, 196–208
in Harding administration, 367
Tammany Hall, 491–93, 541, 543,
    547–49, 570
Cotton, Joseph P., 51, 152
Hoover, H., and, 722n9
Council of Five, 241
Coupal, James F., 482
Craig, John, 119
Creel, George E., 228
criminal justice system, racial prejudice
    and, 454–55
criminal trials, fair
American liberalism and, 413–14
Due Process Clause and right to,
    352–53, 444
Frank v. Mangum, 116–18
habeas corpus and, 568
mob-dominated, 118, 446,
    455–56, 680n80
Moore v. Dempsey and, 353–54,
    475, 680n80
Olmstead v. United States,
    500–501, 717n10

Powell v. Alabama, 560
race and, 446, 474
rape, 474
Red Scare in America and, 352–53
Sacco-Vanzetti case, 415
Scottsboro Boys and, 558–60
Supreme Court and, 4, 116–18, 500
criminal trials, state
habeas corpus and, 568
Supreme Court and, 444, 457, 559
Croly, Herbert, 66, 82, 84, 92, 692n50
Brandeis and, 125, 616n17
The Breach in Civilization, 727n97
Frankfurter and, 88, 217,
    495–96, 606n30
Hand and, 606n30
health problems, 495
Holmes, Jr., and, 98–100
on Holmes, Jr., 530–31
La Follette supported by, 380–81
Lippmann and, 87–90, 174,
    259–60, 292
New Republic founding and, 89–92
New Republic postwar and, 419
Progressive Democracy, 95, 99, 608n89
The Promise of American Life, 87–88
Roosevelt, T., and, 93
on Treaty of Versailles, 419, 530
Valentine and, 88
Wilson and, 145, 164–65
Cullinan, Joseph, 514
cultural nationalism, 190
Curtis, Edwin U., 288

Darrow, Clarence, 487
Davis, Cliff, 374, 406
Davis, Jefferson, 1, 2. See also Stone
    Mountain memorialGeorgia
Davis, John W., 369, 472
Frankfurter on, 367–68, 371–74
Lippmann on, 368, 372–73, 381
Morgan and, 368, 373
1924 presidential election and, 368
Supreme Court and, 379–80
Dawson, Charles I., 455
Day, William R., 348
Dayton-Wright, aircraft industry corrup-
    tion and, 200–201
Debs, Eugene V., 277–79

Deeds, Edward A.
  aircraft industry corruption and,
    200–201, 206–7
  Borglum and, 201
de Haas, Jacob, 239, 265
  Frankfurter and, 241
democracy
  Fourteenth Amendment and, 345
  House of Truth and, 578–79
  industrial, 149
  Lippmann on, 341, 572
Democratic National Convention for
    1924 presidential election, 369–70
Democratic Party
  Frankfurter on, 717n43
  1928 presidential elections and, 494
Democratic Party primary elections,
    blacks banned from participating
    in, 452–53
Democrats, Wilson, 3
Denison, Winfred T., 7, 11, 18–19,
    20, 80
  as assistant attorney general, 44
  Bass and, 59
  Belknap and, 295–96
  Board of Appraisers investigation, 67
  departure from Philippines, 154–55
  Frankfurter and, 4, 18, 69, 77, 296–97
  health problems, 155
  at House of Truth, 33–34, 273
  House of Truth and departure
    of, 77–78
  Lippmann and, 173
  McReynolds and, 68–69
  mental illness, 296
  1912 presidential election and, 59
  political career of, 18
  post-Philippines, 272–73
  Roosevelt, T., and, 44, 111–12
  as secretary of the interior for the
    Philippines, 77–80, 111–12
  Stimson and, 15–16
  suicide of, 295–97
  in Taft Administration, 59
  Taft and, 613n95
  Valentine, R., and, 77, 78, 154–56
  Valentine, S., and, 296
  "White Hope Speech," 111–12
  Wickersham and, 44, 59, 79

Denman Frankfurter, Marion, 71, 76,
    174–75, 214
  Frankfurter and, 213–15, 240
  at Holmes, Jr., funeral, 575, 576
  on Holmes, Jr., 557–58
  marriage to Frankfurter, 297–98
  on Sacco-Vanzetti case, 412
  Valentine, S., and, 272
  in War Department Commission on
    Training Camp Activities, 270–72
  wartime social work, 214–15
deportations, 410, 455
  Hoover, J. E., and, 289
Dewey, John, 383, 449
Dewson, Molly, 547
Dodge, Mabel, 172
Doheny, Edward, 370
Donnellan, Mary, 561, 734n30
Dos Passos, John, 445
Dred Scott decision, 40
Drift and Mastery (Lippmann), 95
  Holmes, Jr., on, 99
Du Bois, W. E. B., 119
  Wilson and, 143–44
Due Process Clause
  Buck v. Bell, 451
  Frankfurter on, 343, 352, 355–56,
    388, 681n88
  free speech and, 352–53
  Gitlow v. New York and, 388
  Holmes, Jr., on, 526
  judicial power and, 352
  labor laws and, 388
  Moore v. Dempsey and, 353–54,
    680n80
  Powell v. Alabama and, 733n14
  right to fair criminal trial and,
    352–53, 444
  socioeconomic legislation and, 388
  Supreme Court and, 498
  Truax v. Corrigan, 344 Early, Jubal, 312

E. C. Knight decision, 40–41
economic liberty, 351
education
  Brown v. Board of Education, 568
  compulsory public education law
    and, 390
Egypt, 174–76

Ehrmann, Herbert "Brute," 438
    Frankfurter and, 417, 695n94
eight-hour-workday, 221–24
Elaine Riots, 287–88
    Moore v. Dempsey, 353
Eliot, Charles W., 130–32
Ellis, Franklin, 102
Emerson, Guy, 82
Equal Protection Clause, Supreme Court
    and, 498
Espionage Act
    free speech and, 276
    Holmes, Jr., on, 276–78
    Socialism and, 276–77
eugenics, 451–52
Europe
    Frankfurter in wartime, 212–13
    labor disputes in wartime, 212–13
    Lippmann in wartime, 227–36
    postwar, 489
    Socialism in postwar, 489
    World War I in, start of, 94–97
Evans, Elizabeth Glendower, *413*
    Brandeis and, 409
    political and social causes, 409–10
    Roosevelt, F., and, 553
    Sacco-Vanzetti bas-relief unveiling
        and, 487
    Sacco-Vanzetti case and, 411, 438
    at Sacco-Vanzetti sentencing, 423–24
    Socialism and, 409
Evans, H. W., 378
exculpatory evidence, in Sacco-Vanzetti
    case, 412–13

A Farewell to Arms (Hemingway), 525
Farley, Thomas, 548
fascism, 530
Federal Power Act, 544
Federal Reserve Act, 143
Federal Trade Commission, 567
Federal Trade Commission Act, 143
Feis, Herbert, 736n11
Fess, Simeon D., 482
Fifth Amendment, 500
Finerty, John, 467
Fisher, Walter L., 27
    Valentine, R., and, 55–56
Fiske, Fanny Howe, 53

Fleming, Bunyan, 455–56. *See also*
    Bard-Fleming case
    execution of, 474, *475*
Flexner, Bernard, 241, 472
    Sacco-Vanzetti case record publication
        and, 710n193
foreign language
    Bartels v. Iowa, 680n77
    free speech and, 680n78
    Meyer v. Nebraska, 680n76, 680n78
foreign policy
    La Follette on, 382
    Lippmann on, 571–72
    Wilson on, 96
Forrest, Nathan Bedford, 327, 329
Fosdick, Raymond, 380, 472
    Sacco-Vanzetti case record publication
        and, 710n193
Fourteen Points, Wilson's, 226
Fourteenth Amendment, 379. *See also*
    Due Process Clause
    democracy and, 345
    Dred Scott decision, 40
    Frankfurter on, 345–46
    Holmes, Jr., on, 113–14, 453–54
    Moore v. Dempsey and, 354
    Nixon v. Herndon and, 453, 703n67
    race and, 560
    subterranean mining rights
        and, 347–48
Fourth Amendment, 568
    wiretapping and, 500
Fox, Austen G., 302
Frank, Jerome, 736n11
    Law and the Modern Mind, 529
Frank, Leo, 116–18, *117*
    Holmes, Jr., on, 444
    lynching of, 118
Frankfurter, Felix, 1, 6–12, *7, 14, 168,*
    210, 268
    Aaronsohn and, 241–42,
        245–48, 256–57
    on Abrams, 426
    on *Abrams* dissent, 295
    Adkins v. Children's Hospital,
        349–51, 355
    on American liberalism, 391, 507
    on antitrust policy, 14–15
    on "the Arab Question" in, 249–50

Frankfurter, Felix (*Cont.*)
  as assistant US attorney, 9
  Baker and, 167–68, 209–10,
    473, 543–44
  Balfour Declaration and, 254–55
  Belknap and, 102
  Borglum and, 46, 477–79, 573, 714n51
  Brandeis and, 19–20, 22, 58, 356–57,
    464, 473, 500
  Brandeis confirmation and,
    126–27, 129
  Brandeis nomination and, 134–35
  on *Brown v. Board of Education*, 568
  Buckner and, 25, 39, 45, 65, 82
  on *Buck v. Bell*, 452
  Bullitt, W., and, 183–84
  in Bureau of Insular Affairs, 12–13
  The Business of the Supreme Court, 473
  Cardozo and, 537–39
  *The Case of Sacco and
    Vanzetti: A Critical Analysis
    for Lawyers and Laymen*, 421,
    424–28, 441–48
  Christie and, 34
  civil liberties and, 299
  Cleveland Crime Survey, 414–15
  on Coolidge, 367
  Croly and, 88, 217, 495–96, 606n30
  on Davis, J. W., 367–68, 371–74
  death of, 569
  death of father, 134
  de Haas and, 241
  on Democratic Party, 717n43
  Denison and, 4, 18, 69, 77, 296–97
  Denman and, 174–75, 213–15, 240
  on Due Process Clause, 343, 352, 355–
    56, 388, 681n88
  Eastman Fellowship at Oxford, 565–66
  education, 6–8
  Ehrmann and, 417, 695n94
  eight-hour-workday and, 221–24
  European wartime trip of, 212–13
  on Fourteenth Amendment, 345–46
  on free speech, 680n78
  Gary and, 222–23
  on *Gitlow v. New York*, 389
  on government service, 516
  Hand and, 710n189
  Hapgood and, 613n104

  "Happy Hot Dogs," 567
  on Harvard Jewish quota, 359
  at Harvard Law School, 7–8
  as Harvard Law School professor,
    72–76, 112, 281–82, 284, 298–99,
    425, 468
  Holmes, Jr., and, 22–24, 69–70, 75, 348,
    355, 473, 500
  at Holmes, Jr., funeral, 575, 576, 577
  on Holmes, Jr., 356, 523–24, 667n42
  Hoover, H., and, 170, 488–89, 495, 539
  Hoover, J. E., and investigation of, 301
  on Hoover, H., 518, 555
  House and, 182–83
  at House of Truth, 1–3, 33–34, 62,
    159, 271
  House of Truth managed by, 169–70
  on Hughes, 518
  the Inquiry and, 182–83
  Jackson, E., and, 701n32, 712n1
  Jackson, G., and, 479
  as Jew, 8, 359–60, 585n10, 617n33
  "J. H. Wigmore Answers Frankfurter
    Attack on Sacco-Vanzetti
    Verdict," 426–27
  on judicial power, 352
  labor laws defended by, 134, 349–50
  on labor-management
    relations, 156–57
  on labor strikes, 177–80
  on La Follette, 370–71, 684n31
  La Follette supported by, 380–81
  Landis and, 389
  Laski and, 141
  on League of Nations, 253
  liberalism and, 364, 471–72
  on Lippmann, 543
  Lippmann and, 170–71, 236, 365, 370,
    382, 416, 447–48
  Lippmann and disagreements with,
    357, 361–63, 372–74, 380–81,
    506–7, 570–72
  Lowell and, 357–58, 468–69
  Lowell on, 428–29
  Mack and, 468–69
  marriage to Denman, 297–98
  on maximum hour law, 160–61
  McReynolds and, 162–63, 421–22
  on Meiklejohn affair, 361–64

minimum wage conference called by, 354–55
minimum wage laws and, 160–61, 354–55
Mooney case and, 281–82, 425, 695n90
Morgenthau, Sr., and, 265
Morgenthau Mission, 174–76, 237
on Morrow, 363
NAACP and, 522
National War Labor Board and, 221–22
"Necessary Reorganization of the Functions Exercised by the Secretary of War" memorandum, 210–11
on New Deal, 566–67
New Republic founding and, 91–92
1912 presidential election and, 42, 57–59
at 1924 Democratic National Convention, 369–70
on 1924 presidential election, 365, 370, 378–79
on 1928 presidential elections, 490–91, 493–95
1932 presidential election and, 541–45
nomination to Massachusetts Supreme Court, 547
on Palestine, 240
Palmer and, 301
Palmer Raid immigrants and, 300–301
on Paris peace conference, 249, 261
on Parker, J., 519–20, 522–23
Perkins and, 281, 298–99
on *The Phantom Public*, 383
on *Pierce v. Society of Sisters* majority opinion, 389–91
Poland trip, 265–66
on *The Political Scene*, 261–62
"The Portentous Case of Sacco and Vanzetti: A Comprehensive Analysis of a Trial of Grave Importance," 420–23
Pound and, 299, 425
Prince Feisal and, 250–51
on progressivism, 56
protégés, 567, 736n10
The Public and Its Government, 540
on *Public Opinion*, 342

red-baiting of, 274–75, 280–86
on religious intolerance, 493
reputation as radical, 179
resignation from War Labor Policies Board, 237
on Robinson, J. T., 538
Roosevelt, F., and, 219–20, 541–42, 547–48, 552–53, 560–61, 565–66
Roosevelt, F., and influence of, 566–67
Roosevelt, T., on, 179
on Roosevelt, T., 41–42, 56–57
on Sacco-Vanzetti case, 411–15, 434–35
Sacco-Vanzetti case and, 447, 691n13
Sacco-Vanzetti case record publication and, 471–72, 710n193
Sacco-Vanzetti trial summation by, 419–20
"The Same Mr. Taft" editorial, 344–45
Schlesinger and, 529–30
on Schwimmer dissent, 505
on Scottsboro Boys, 559–60
Securities Act of 1933 and, 566
Sedgwick and, 420, 544
on Sherman Antitrust Act, 15–16
"The Sherman Law and Our Industrial Problem" speech, 14–18
Smith, A., and, *489*, 490–93, 545, 553–54
socioeconomic legislation and, 566–67
Solicitor General post offered to, 565–66, 735n1
Stimson and, 6, 8, 42, 68, 74–75, 343, 538–39
Stimson gubernatorial campaign and, 9–12
Stone and, 463–65
on Supreme Court, 568–69
Supreme Court and, 69–70, 158–61, 343–44, 352, 355–56, 378–80, 389–90
Supreme Court criticized by, 356–57, 500, 516, 523–24
Supreme Court nomination of, 568
on Taft, 13, 17–18, 41
in Taft administration, 42, 57–59
Taft and, 221–22, 343, 677n16
ten-hour law argument before Supreme Court, 161–63
"A Tentative Social Program," 61–63
on Thayer, 443–44

Frankfurter, Felix (*Cont.*)
　Valentine, R., and, 11, 25, 57–58, 61–66,
　　75–76, 151–54, 624n39
　in War Department, 68,
　　167–69, 174–80
　on War Labor Policies Board, 237, 541
　as War Labor Policies
　　chairman, 216–17
　on wartime government reorganiza-
　　tion during, 210–11
　wartime labor relations and, 180
　wartime service, 237
　in Washington D. C., 13, 167–69
　Weizmann and, 268, 359
　White, E., and, 159–60
　White, W., and, 522
　"Why I Am for Smith," 496
　"Why I Am Voting for
　　Roosevelt," 554–55
　Wigmore and, 426–28
　on Wilson, 145–46
　in Wilson administration, 68, 74, 212
　on wiretapping, 501
　wiretapping of phone, 437, 698n170
　Wister on, 718n27
　Yale lectures, 516
　"The Zeitgeist and the
　　Judiciary," 69–70
　Zionist cause and, 237–69
Frank v. Mangum, 680n80
　Holmes, Jr., on, 116–18, 353, 444
free press
　abridged, 386
　Gitlow v. New York and, 388
free speech
　abridged, 386
　Brandeis on, 459–60, 680n78, 705n108
　Due Process Clause and, 352–53
　Espionage Act and, 276
　foreign language and, 680n78
　Frankfurter on, 680n78
　Gitlow v. New York and, 388
　Hand on, 277
　Holmes, Jr., on, 274–77, 280–81,
　　289–90, 304, 351, 504–5, 679n70
　Red Scare in America and, 352–53
　Schwimmer and, 504–5
　Supreme Court and, 4
　Whitney and, 460–61

Free Speech in the United States
　(Chafee), 303
Freedman, Max, 220
French, Daniel Chester, 190
Freund, Ernst, 278, 449
Freund, Paul, 736n11
Freund, Sanford, 45
Frohwerk, Jacob, 276–77
Fuller, Alvan T., 429, 445–46
　Hill and, 440–41
　on Sacco-Vanzetti case retrial, 433–35
　Sacco-Vanzetti Defense Committee
　　appeal to, 449
　Sacco-Vanzetti petition to, 430
　stay of execution for Sacco-Vanzetti
　　case, 446
Furman, Bess, 564

Galleani, Luigi, 278–79
Garner, John Nance, 546
Garrison, Lindley M., 68, 74
Gary, Elbert, 222–23
Gates, Sylvester, 691n20
　"The Portentous Case of Sacco and
　　Vanzetti: A Comprehensive Analysis
　　of a Trial of Grave Importance,"
　　419, 421
　"The Sacco and Vanzetti Case," 414–15
Genna, Joe, 705n100
Gilbert v. Minnesota, 705n108
Giles v. Harris, 453
Gitlow, Benjamin, 386, *387*, 679n70
Gitlow v. New York, 386–88
　dissent, 387–89
Glavis, Louis, 21
Goldmark, Josephine, 159–60
Gompers, Samuel, 93
Gong Lum v. Rice, 475–76
Goodwin, Elliot, 54, 66
Gordon, Pauline, 581–82
Gordon, Thurlow M., 54, 113, 740
Gould, Roy, 416
government
　big, 8
　liberalism and role of, 114
　limits of, 577
　Lippmann on, 235
　progressivism and, 8
　wartime reorganization of, 211

A Grammar of Politics (Laski), 391
Grant, Robert, 431
Gray, John Chipman, 22, 73,
  98–99, 588n62
  Holmes, Jr., and, 317
Gray, Nina, 296, 319, 503
Great Depression, 515, 567
  New Deal, 87, 546–47, 566–67, 736n11
  stock market crash of 1929, 511, 715n6
Green, William, 520–22
Greenway, John C., 179
Greenwich House, 29
Gregg, Richard, 150, 152
Griffith, D. W., *The Birth of a Nation*,
  120–21, 190–91, 326
Gunderson, Carl, 407

habeas corpus
  for Bard-Fleming case, 455
  criminal trials and, fair, 568
  for Sacco-Vanzetti case, 442–47, 450
Hackett, Francis, 82, 84, 121
Haines, Lynn, 328
Hale, Richard W., 281, 486
Hale, Shelton, 221, 618n59
Hall, Edwin, 288–89
Hallowell, Norwood Penrose, *309*,
  317, 666n20
  Holmes, Jr., and, 193, 307–9
Hallowell, Robert, 84
Hamilton, Alexander, 87
Hamilton, Alice, 449
Hammer v. Dagenhart, 218–19
Hand, Learned, 66, 75, 82, 380
  on Brandeis, 459–60, 705–06n111
  on *Collected Legal Papers*, 319
  Coolidge promotion of, 385
  Croly and, 606n30
  Frankfurter and, 710n189
  on free speech, 277
  Holmes, Jr., and, 277–78, 393–94
  at Holmes, Jr., Harvard Law School
    portrait unveiling, 524–25
  on Holmes, Jr., 525
  the Inquiry and, 181
  Lippmann and, 470–71, 571
  on minimum wage, 109–10
  on *The Political Scene*, 261
  on Sacco-Vanzetti case, 710n189

Wilson and, 142–43
Hapgood, Norman, 113, 135, 449
  Frankfurter and, 613n104
  Laski and, 140–41
  Lowell and, 696n121
  on Wigmore, 428
Harding, Warren
  Borglum and, 322, 333–34
  corruption in administration of, 367
  death of, 365
  Ku Klux Klan and, 329–31, 674n61
  Stone Mountain memorial
    and, 333–34
  Supreme Court nominees, 348–49
  Taft and, *344*
Hardwick, Thomas, 279, 335
Harney Memorial Association, 404
Harper's, 524
Harrison, George, 101, 610n13
Hart, Edward H., 104, 320
  at House of Truth, 101–2
Harvard College, black students at, 361
Harvard Crimson, 554–55
Harvard Lampoon, 275, 293–94,
  661nn144–45
Harvard Law School
  backlash against Frankfurter and, 425
  Brandeis and, 21, 130–31, 588n54
  Chafee at, 658n40, 658n46
  Frankfurter at, 7–8
  Frankfurter on faculty at, 72–76, 112,
    281–82, 284, 298–99, 468
  Holmes, Jr., portrait at, 524–25
  Jewish student quota, 357, 359–61,
    682n125
  Laski at, 294
  Pound and, 301
  Red Scare in America at,
    274–75, 280–86
  Valentine, R., at, 28–29
Hayes, Ralph, 234–35, 546, 729n5
  on Lippmann, 531
Haynes, John, 470
Hays, Arthur Garfield, 377
Heike, Charles R., 9, 11
Hemingway, Ernest
  A Farewell to Arms, 525
  The Sun Also Rises, 502
Henderson, Gerard C. "Gerry," 202

Herzl, Theodore, 239
Hill, Arthur Dehon
    Brandeis and, 458–59, 462
    Fuller and, 440–41
    Holmes, Jr., and, 439, 456–57
    Sacco-Vanzetti case and,
        439–41, 449–50
    Stone and, 465–66
    Thayer and, 440
    writ of habeas corpus and, 442–47
Hiss, Alger, 525–26, 526, 528, 532,
    723n29, 725n65
Hiss, Donald, 561–62
Hitler, Adolf, 570, 737n28
Hitz, William, 115
Holcombe, Arthur, 360
Holmes, Fanny, 1, 71, 314, 602n67
    death of, 503
    funeral for, 503–4
    Holmes, Jr., seventy-fifth birthday
        party and, 104–5
Holmes, Oliver Wendell, Jr., 26, 306, 466,
    526, 559, 563
    abolitionism and, 306–7, 312,
        313, 704n73
    Abrams dissent, 289–95, 303–4, 318,
        665n229
    as acting chief justice, 516–17, 525
    Adkins v. Children's Hospital, 351
    Albertson and, 173
    American liberalism and, 342–43, 364
    on antitrust policy, 50
    attempted bombings of, 279
    on Baldwin v. Missouri, 527
    on Bard-Fleming case, 455–56, 456,
        705n100
    Belknap as secretary to, 102–5
    Biddle and, 49
    on Black and White Taxicab, 499–500
    Borglum and, 408, 531–32
    Borglum plaster death mask of,
        575, 578
    on Brandeis, 556–57
    Brandeis and, 128, 284–85, 459–60,
        498–501, 499, 534
    Brandeis on, 517
    on Buck v. Bell, 450–51, 703n61
    Bundy as secretary for, 101–2, 533–34
    Cardozo and, 528, 726n80

    Cardozo on, 501–2
    on The Case of Sacco and
        Vanzetti: A Critical Analysis for
        Lawyers and Laymen, 442–43
    Chafee and, 279–80
    Christie and, 105
    Civil War experiences, 105,
        307–13, 310, 528, 558,
        666nn19–20, 667n41
    Collected Legal Papers, 305, 318–19
    The Common Law, 315, 500
    conservatism and, 348
    on Constitution, 394, 524
    conversational skill of, 24
    Coolidge and, 366–67, 384
    Corcoran and, 392–93
    criticism of, 527
    Croly and, 98–100
    Croly on, 530–31
    death of, 574
    death of wife and, 503–4
    Debs opinion, 277–79
    Denman on, 557–58
    on Drift and Mastery, 99
    on Due Process Clause, 526
    eightieth birthday, 320
    eighty-fifth birthday
        celebration, 393–94
    on Espionage Act, 276–78
    on Fourteenth Amendment,
        113–14, 453–54
    Frankfurter and, 22–24, 69–70, 75, 348,
        355, 473, 500
    Frankfurter on, 356, 523–24, 667n42
    on Frank v. Mangum, 116–18, 353, 444
    on free speech, 274–77, 280–81,
        289–90, 304, 351, 504–5, 679n70
    funeral, 575, 576, 577, 740n69
    Gitlow v. New York dissent, 386–89
    Gray and, 317
    Hallowell, N., and, 193, 307–9
    on Hammer v. Dagenhart, 218
    Hand and, 277–78, 393–94, 524–25
    Hand on, 525
    Harper's essay on, 524
    Harvard Law School portrait
        of, 524–25
    health problems, 346–47, 525–26,
        534, 556

Hill and, 439, 456–57
Hiss, A., and, 525–26, *526*
Holmes, Sr., and, 305–6, 308, 311–12,
    314–16, 320–21
Hoover, H., and, 556, 719n38
on Hoover, H., 503
house, 22, 24, *101*, 442, *443*
at House of Truth, 3, 66, 70–71, 220–21,
    317–18, 530, 576
Hughes and, *517*, 535
on ideology, 558
influence on Supreme Court, 498, 558
"jobbist" philosophy of, 313–14
King, G., and, 199
Laski and, 141, 277–79, 305, 365–66,
    392, 530
Laski on, 524
law career of, 24
liberalism and, 113, 274, 391–92,
    527–28, 575–76, 740n73
on "liberty of contract," 351
Lincoln and, 312–13, 667–69nn41–42
Lippmann and, 98–100, 393
Lippmann on, 531
Lochner decision, 574
Lochner dissent, 316
Lowell and, 285–86
on maximum hour laws, 70
McReynolds and, 526–27, 693n65
as Mephistopheles, 589n68
in Metaphysical Club, 314
Milwaukee Leader case, 319–20
on minority rights, 450–51
Moore v. Dempsey and, 353, 444
on moral causes, 313
New Republic and, 98, *99*,
    113–14, 530–31
newspaper profiles of, 394–95
ninetieth birthday, 529–33
ninetieth birthday radio
    broadcast, 532–33
ninety-second birthday, 561–64
ninety-third birthday, 574
on 1932 presidential election, 556
on *Nixon v. Herndon*, 453, 703n67
Northern Securities decision and, 50
as oldest sitting justice, 502–3
Percy and, 106
philosophy of, 128, 313–14

on *The Political Scene*, 261
on privacy, 501
on *Progressive Democracy*, 99
on *Public Opinion*, 341–42
on race, 118–19, 453–55,
    614n131, 703n67
recognition craved by, 315–19,
    502–3
recognition of, 356, 366–67, 394, 502,
    524–25, 533
on rent control law, 348
resignation of, 535
in retirement, 556–58, 733n12
retirement considered by, 385–86
Roosevelt, E., and, 562–64, 732n2
Roosevelt, F., and visit with, 561–64,
    732nn2–3, 734n30
Roosevelt, T., and, 49–50, 316,
    596n82, 732–33n4
on Roosevelt, F., 556
Roosevelt Medal received by,
    366–67, *385*
on Sacco-Vanzetti case, 446–47, 450,
    457, 472–73
on Sacco-Vanzetti writ of habeas
    corpus, 442–47
on Schwimmer, 505
secretaries, 100, 392–93,
    533–34, 610n26
seventy-fifth birthday party, 104–5
on Sherman Act, 24
skepticism, 307, 393–94
on Socialism, 391
"The Soldier's Faith" address,
    105, 313
on state taxes, 526–27
on sterilization laws, 702n53
Stone and, 464–65
study, *101*
summer home, 442, *443*
on Supreme Court, 316, 348–49, *390*
symbolism and, 348
on Taft, 49
Taft and, 502–4, 670n80
ten-hour law argument and, 162–63
Valentine, R., and, 45
Wigmore and, 425, 428
on wiretapping, 500–501
World editorials on, 393–94

Holmes, Oliver Wendell, Sr.
  Holmes, Jr., and, 305–6, 308, 311–12,
    314–16, 320–21
  "My Hunt after 'The Captain,'" 311
  writings in *Atlantic Monthly*, 306,
    311, 315
Hoover, Herbert, 264, 481, *549*
  American Individualism, 489–90
  Borglum and, 508–10, 532, 550–51
  Cardozo nomination and, 539,
    728n162
  Cotton and, 722n9
  Frankfurter and, 170, 488–89, 495, 539
  Frankfurter on, 518, 555
  Holmes, Jr., on, 503, 556, 719n38
  at House of Truth, 170, 488–89
  Hughes nominated by, *536*
  judicial nominations of, 518–20,
    535–38, *536*
  liberalism of, 488
  Lippmann on, 170, 488–89
  Mount Rushmore and, 508–10,
    513–14, 551
  1928 presidential elections and, 496
  1932 presidential election and,
    545, 548–49
  Parker, J., nominated by, *536*
  public opinion of, 548
  religious intolerance and, 493
  Smith, A., and, 495
  Supreme Court and, 498, 517–18
  war veteran protest and, 548
  World on, 488
Hoover, J. Edgar, 287
  defense lawyers investigated by, 301,
    664n212
  deportations by, 289
  Palmer Raids and, 289
House, Edward M., 171, *232*
  anti-Semitism, 183, 211, 253
  Brandeis and, 183
  Bullitt, W., and, 186–87
  Frankfurter and, 182–83
  Lippmann and, 180–81, 228, 230–31
  on wartime government reorganiza-
    tion during, 211
House of Truth, 1–2, *33*, 67, 581–82
  Aaronsohn at, 246–47
  Albertson as first female in, 172–73
  American liberalism and, 3, 577–78

Belknap at, 104
Biddle at, 48–49
Bissell at, 101–2
Borglum and, 3
Brandeis at, 69, 125–26
Bundy at, 101–2
Christie at, *62*, 72
dark sides of, 579
democracy and, 578–79
Denison and departure from, 77–78
Denison at, 33–34, 273
dinners at, 169–70
Ellis at, 102
end of, as political salon, 270–72
formation of, 33–37
Frankfurter at, 1–3, 33–34, *62*, *159*, *271*
Frankfurter management of, 169–70
Hart at, 101–2
Holmes, Jr., and, 3, 66, 70–71, 220–21,
  317–18, 530, 576
Hoover, H., at, 170, 488–89
influence of, 2–3
legacy of, 579
Lippmann at, 3, 172–73
"The Little Red House" and, 567–68
Mack at, 221
Mount Rushmore and, 578–79
naming of, 36–37
network, 578–79
New Republic and, 85, 92–93
Percy and departure from, 80–82
Percy at, *159*, *271*
professional network built by, 3
on racial justice, 119
residents of, 4–5, 33–34, *62*
Roosevelt, T., support and, 2–4,
  37, 45–46
Valentine, R., and absence
  from, 65–66
Valentine, R., at, 31–34, 148
wartime, 164, 220–21
Wilson support in, 124, 136–46
Houston, Charles Hamilton, 476
Howe, Mark DeWolfe, 574–75
Howland, Charles P., 472
Hughes, Charles Evans, 17, 533
  aircraft industry investigation, 206–7
  Frankfurter on, 518
  Holmes, Jr., and, *517*, 535
  Hoover, H., and nomination of, *536*

Lippmann on, 518–19
in 1916 presidential race, 138–40
on Supreme Court, 518–19
human rights, 391
Hutchins, Robert Maynard, 428

Immigration Act of 1918, 279
individualism, 489–90
industrial democracy, 149
industrialization
labor and effects on, 489
scientific management and, 109
industrialization effects on workers. *See
also* child labor; maximum hour
laws; minimum wage laws; workers'
compensation laws
strikes and, 61–62
Valentine, R., and, 63–64
industrial relations regulation, 15
Industrial Workers of the World (IWW),
61–62, 93
the Inquiry, 181–87, 226–36
infighting in, 233–34
leak regarding, 183, 185–86
IWW. *See* Industrial Workers of
the World

Jackson, Edwin L., 376
Frankfurter and, 701n32, 712n1
Sacco-Vanzetti memorial and, 487
Jackson, Gardner "Pat"
Borglum and, 552, 714n51
Frankfurter and, *479*
Sacco-Vanzetti memorial and, 448,
458, 477–78
Jackson, Robert H., 740n73
Jackson, Stonewall, 1, 2. *See also* Stone
Mountain memorialGeorgia
James, Henry, 314
James, William, 314–15
Jewish state
Brandeis on, 240, 263–64
in Palestine, 240, 253–54
Jews. *See also* anti-Semitism
Arab-Jewish alliance, 249–51
Brandeis as, 617n33
Frankfurter as, 8, 359–60,
585n10, 617n33
Harvard Law School quota for, 360–61,
682n125

Lippmann as, 360
in Poland, 265–66
"J. H. Wigmore Answers
Frankfurter Attack on
Sacco-Vanzetti Verdict"
(Wigmore), 426–27
Jim Crow policy, 361
Johnson, Alvin, 362–63
Johnson, Hiram, 55
Johnson, Hugh S., 567
Johnson, Lyndon B., 572
Jones, "Dakota Clyde," 482
Jones, Eliot, 152
judicial power, curbing, 346
Due Process Clause and, 352
judiciary, 4. *See also* Supreme Court;
specific judges
influencing, 579
La Follette on, 370–71
Roosevelt, T., on, 41
"The Zeitgeist and the
Judiciary," 69–70

Kallen, Horace M., 486–87
Katzmann, Frederick G., 415
Keating-Owen Child Labor Act,
143, 217–18
Kelley, Florence, 544, 681n88
Kellogg, Paul, 449
Kendall, Henry P., 109, 152
Kennedy, David, 608n91
Kennedy, Joseph, 567
Kerr, Philip, 254
King, Gertrude, 199
King, Stanley, 152, 169, 543
Borglum and, 199–200
Kirby, Rollin, 431, *432*, 493, *494*
Ku Klux Klan, 1
The Birth of a Nation and, 120–21
Borglum and, 327–35, 375–76, 399
compulsory public education law
and, 390
Democratic National Convention
and, 369–70
Harding and, 329–31, 674n61
McAdoo and, 369–70, 375
religious intolerance and, 493
Stephenson and, 335, 376, 674n59
Stone Mountain memorial and, 191,
327–29, 331–34, 635n21

labor. *See also* child labor
    auditing, 147–48
    organized, 92–94, 109, 149
    Roosevelt, T., on, 93–94
labor disputes
    in Europe, 212–13
    in lumber industry, 209
    New York City transit system, 147
labor issues, 579. *See also specific issues*
    industrialization and, 489
    Roosevelt, T., on, 93–94
labor laws
    Brandeis on, 21
    child, 143, 345
    Due Process Clause and, 388
    Frankfurter and defense of,
        134, 349–50
    social scientific evidence defense
        of, 21
    Supreme Court and, 158
labor-management relations
    Frankfurter on, 156–57
    protocol (management and labor
        agreement), 149–50
labor policy
    Communism and, 282
    War Industries Board and, 218–19
    World War I and, 209–10
labor relations
    National Labor Relations Board, 567
    National War Labor Board, 221–22
    wartime, 180
labor strikes, 61–62
    copper mining, in Arizona, 178
    Frankfurter and investigation
        of, 177–80
    Truax v. Corrigan, 344
    United Mine Workers, 93
La Follette, Robert, 39, 44, 346,
    366, 593n7
    Borglum and, 376–77
    Borglum and La Follette-Wheeler
        campaign medallion, *372*, 377
    Brandeis and, 50–51, 371
    Croly and support of, 380–81
    Frankfurter and support of, 380–81
    Frankfurter on, 370–71, 684n31
    on judiciary, 370–71
    Lippmann on, 371, 381–82

1924 presidential election and,
    370–71, 376–77
    politics of, 381–82
    Supreme Court and, 380
    Wheeler and, 376–77
Lamar, Joseph R., 17, 116
Landis, James M., 389, 495
    in Federal Trade Commission, 567
    in SEC, 567
    Securities Act of 1933 and, 566
Lane, Franklin K., 66
Langdell, Christopher Columbus, 73
Lansing, Robert, 176, 229, 241, 256, 259
Lardner, Ring, 533
Laski, Harold, 140–42, *142*, 152, 667n42
    on *Abrams* dissent, 293
    Authority in the Modern State, 279
    Bolshevism charged at, 289
    on Boston police strike, 288–89
    on *Buck v. Bell*, 452
    Chafee and, 280
    on Coolidge, 384
    Frankfurter and, 141
    A Grammar of Politics, 391
    Hapgood and, 140–41
    Harvard Lampoon and, *275*, 293–94,
        661nn144–45
    at Harvard Law School, 294
    Holmes, Jr., and, 141, 277–79, 305,
        365–66, 392, 530
    on Holmes, Jr., 524
    on Lippmann, 531, 571
    Lippmann and, 236, 738n36
    Lowell and, 294, 662n149
    on *The Political Scene*, 261
    Pound and, 279
    Sinclair on, 294
    on Supreme Court, 161
    Valentine, R., and, 153
Lathrop, Julia, 53–54, 64
Law and the Modern Mind (Frank,
    J.), 529
Lawrence, T. E., 250
League of Nations, 234
    Baker and support of, 543
    Bullitt, W., and testimony on, 291
    Frankfurter on, 253
Leary, John J., 417–18
LeDuc, William G., 309–10

Lee, Robert E., 1, *2, 323*. *See also* Stone
    Mountain memorialGeorgia
    Stone Mountain memorial head carv-
        ing of, 338–39
legal liberalism, 584n9
legal realism, 529
Lehmann, Frederick W., 13, 143
Leupp, Francis E., 30–31
Lewis, William Henry, 68
liberalism. *See also* American liberalism
    definitions of, 3, 584n7
    Frankfurter and, 364, 471–72
    Holmes, Jr., and, 113, 274, 391–92, 527–
        28, 575–76, 740n73
    of Hoover, H., 488
    legal, 584n9
    Lippmann and, 471, 531
    privacy and, 501–2
    progressivism and, 608n91
    on role of government, 114
    of Stone, 463–64
    Wilson and, 227–28
Liberty and the News (Lippmann), 291–92
"liberty of contract," 21, 343
    Holmes, Jr., on, 351
    maximum hour law and, 350–51
    Sutherland, G., on, 351–52
Lilienthal, David, 736n11
Lincoln, Abraham, 40. *See also* Mount
    Rushmore, South Dakota
    Borglum statue of, 46–47, 190, 635n19
    at Civil War, 312–13, 667nn41–42
    Holmes, Jr., and, 312–13, 667nn41–42
    Smith, A., and, 492
Lippmann, Walter, 84–86, *85, 542*
    Aaronsohn and, 247–48
    on *Abrams* dissent, 291–92
    on American liberalism, 382–83,
        507, 570
    on anti-Semitism, 360
    in *Atlantic Monthly*, 291–92
    Baker and, 171–72, 231, 543–44
    on *Baldwin v. Missouri*, 527
    Bowman and, 233–34
    Brandeis and, 127–29, 134–35, 473
    Brandeis on, 368–69
    Broun and, 436, 470
    Burlingham and, 448
    on censorship, 231

on civil rights, 506
Cold War and, 572
conservatism of, 471, 543
criticism of, 570
Croly and, 87–90, 174, 259–60, 292
on Davis, J. W., 368, 372–73, 381
on democracy, 341, 572
Denison and, 173
Drift and Mastery, 95, 99
on foreign policy, 571–72
Frankfurter and, 170–71, 236, 365, 370,
    382, 416, 447–48
Frankfurter and disagreements
    with, 357, 361–63, 372–74, 380–81,
    506–7, 570–72
Frankfurter on, 543
on government, 235
Hand and, 470–71, 571
Hayes on, 531
on Hitler, 570
Holmes, Jr., and, 98–100, 393
on Holmes, Jr., 531
Hoover, H., and, 170, 488–89
House and, 180–81, 228, 230–31
at House of Truth, 3, 172–73
on Hughes, 518–19
on industrial democracy, 149
the Inquiry and, 181–87, 226–36
as Jew, 360
journalism focus of, 291–93
on La Follette, 371, 381–82
Laski and, 236, 738n36
Laski on, 531, 571
liberalism of, 471, 531
Liberty and the News, 291–92
marriage to Albertson, 172–73
Meiklejohn and, 362–63
on minimum wage, 109–10
on New Deal, 570
New Republic and, 292
New Republic and return of, 259–60
New Republic founding and, 89–92
at *New York Herald-Tribune*, 531, 542
1924 presidential election and, 365, 370
on 1928 presidential elections,
    490–91, 493–95
1932 presidential election and, 541–45
at 1924 Democratic National
    Convention, 369–70

Lippmann, Walter (*Cont.*)
  on organized labor, 94
  on Paris Peace Conference, 262
  on Parker, J., 519–20
  Percy and, 229
  The Phantom Public, 382–83
  Pinchot, A., on, 570
  political advising by, 572
  political intelligence gathering
    by, 230–31
  The Political Scene, 260–61
  Powell and, 686n16
  A Preface to Politics, 86–87
  on Prohibition, 491
  on public opinion, 291, 572
  Public Opinion, 341–42
  public *versus* private politics of, 544
  on religious intolerance, 493
  Roosevelt, F., and, *227*, 492, 541–43,
    569–70, 729n3
  Roosevelt, T., and, 93–94, 138
  on Roosevelt, F., 545–46, 548–50, 571
  on Sacco-Vanzetti advisory
    committee, 435
  on Sacco-Vanzetti case, 416, 418, 422,
    434–36, 447–48, 470–71
  Sacco-Vanzetti case supported
    by, 429–30
  Schwimmer case and, 506–7
  Smith, A., and, 490–91, 493–96
  on Socialism, 570
  The Stakes of Diplomacy, 108, 165
  "stereotypes," 341
  Straight, W., and, 232–33
  on Tammany Hall issue, 570
  "The Opposition to Justice
    Parker," 520
  on "The Portentous Case of Sacco
    and Vanzetti: A Comprehensive
    Analysis of a Trial of Grave
    Importance," 422
  "The Prejudices of Judge
    Thayer," 430–31
  on Valentine, R., 151–52
  in War Department, 180–87, 226
  wartime ambitions of, 171
  in wartime Europe, 227–36
  wartime propaganda and, 227–30
  on Wilson, 261–62

  Wilson and, 144, 164–65
  Wilson on, 229–30
  Wilson support from, 139–40
  at *World*, 293, *342*
  on World War I, 108, 260
Littell, Philip, 84, 91, 105, 318, 419, 529
"The Little Red House," 567–68
Lloyd George, David, 153, 254
Lochner v. New York, 21, 40–41, 70
  Holmes, Jr., dissent on, 316
  Holmes, Jr., on, 574
  Mayer and, 599n155
Lockwood, John, 504–05
Lodge, Henry Cabot, 139
Louisville Leader, 474
Louisville Times, 474
Lovett, Robert Morss, 486
Lowell, A. Lawrence, *358*
  anti-Semitism of, 357
  on Boston police strike, 288
  Chafee and, 302
  on Frankfurter, 428–29
  Frankfurter and, 357–58, 468–69
  Hapgood and, 696n121
  Holmes, Jr., and, 285–86
  Jewish student quota and, 360–61,
    682n125
  Jim Crow policy, 361
  Laski and, 294, 662n149
  in *New Republic*, 357
  Pound and, 285–86
  on Sacco-Vanzetti advisory
    committee, 431–32
  Sacco-Vanzetti case and, 448–49
Lowenthal, Max, 176, 219, 220, 349
Ludington, Arthur, 45–46, 66
"Ludlow Massacre," 93
Lukeman, Augustus, 400,
    485–86, 739n54
Lum, Martha, 475–76
lumber industry, labor disputes in, 209
Lunn, George, 86
Lurton, Horace H., 16–17, 70
Lusitania, sinking of, 107–8
lynching, 455, 680n80
  antilynching legislation, 329, 354
  of Frank, L., 118
  legalized, 117
  Wilson, W., and, 144, 180

MacArthur, Douglas, 548
Mack, Julian W., 25, 35, 53–54, 380, 537
    Aaronsohn and, 245
    on Board of Inquiry, 220
    Frankfurter and, 468–69
    on garment industry, 147
    at House of Truth, 221
    Valentine, R., and, 149, 152
MacLeish, Archibald, 356
Magruder, Calvert, 495
majority rule, 451
Manifest Destiny, 579
The Mares of Diomedes (Borglum), 196
Margold, Nathan, 469, 709n180, 736n11
Marshall, John, 50, 341, 524
Marshall, Louis, 242, 245, 452–53, 522
    Bard-Fleming case and, 474
Marshall Committee, 203–4
Marston, George, 119
Massachusetts Minimum Wage
        Commission, 110
maximum hour laws, 4, 40, 69, 158–61
    Adamson Act, 143, 163–64
    Brandeis on, 114
    eight-hour-workday, 221–24
    Holmes, Jr., on, 70
    "liberty of contract" and, 350–51
    Supreme Court on, 161–62
    ten-hour law, 160–63
Mayer, Julius M., 599n155
McAdoo, William Gibbs, 136, 369–70, 375
McClennen, Edward F., 127
McCoy, Frank R., 46
McLean, Angus W., 400
McReynolds, James C., 66, 124,
        390, 626n22
    anti-Semitism of, 626n22
    Brandeis and, 725n70
    Denison and, 68–69
    Frankfurter and, 162–63, 421–22
    Holmes, Jr., and, 526–27, 693n65
    Moore v. Dempsey and, 353–54
    Pierce v. Society of Sisters majority
        opinion, 389–91
    on "The Portentous Case of Sacco and
        Vanzetti: A Comprehensive Analysis
        of a Trial of Grave Importance," 421
    on *Powell v. Alabama*, 733n14
    Sedgwick and, 421–22

Medeiros, Celestino F., 416–17
Meiklejohn, Alexander, 361–64
    Lippmann and, 362–63
    Sacco-Vanzetti bas-relief unveiling
        and, 486
Mellon, Andrew, 368–69, 399–400
    Borglum and, 484
Mencken, H. L., 428, 527
Merz, Charles, 229, 292, 419, 501, 522
Metaphysical Club, 314
Meyer, Eugene, Jr., 201–2, 567
    Borglum and, 196, 202–3, 323,
        398, 637n68
Meyer v. Nebraska, 680n76, 680n78
Mezes, Sidney, 226
Miller, David Hunter, 226
Miller, Kelly, 454
Milwaukee Leader case, 319–20
minimum wage conference, 354–55
minimum wage laws, 4, 69, 158–61
    Brandeis on, 114–15
    for children, 349–50
    constitutionality of, 350
    Frankfurter and, 160–61, 354–55
    Hand on, 109–10
    Lippmann on, 109–10
    Massachusetts Minimum Wage
        Commission, 110
    Supreme Court on, 115–16, 163, 391
    Valentine, R., on, 110
    for women, 349–50
mining
    copper, strikes, 178
    rights, subterranean, 347–48
minority rights, 450–51
Missouri Staats Zeitung, 276
Mitchell, Margaret, 337
Mitchell, William D., 518, 537
Mitchell-Innes, Alfred, 54, 66, 72, 80
mob-dominated criminal trials, 446,
        455–56, 680n80
    Frank, L., lynching and, 118
Montgomery (Borglum), Mary, 195–96
Mooney, Tom, 178–80, 281–82, 425
    Preparedness Day Parade bombing
        and, 178–79
Mooney case
    anarchism and, 179
    Frankfurter and, 281–82, 425, 695n90

Moore, Fred H., 429, 710n195
Moore v. Dempsey
    Due Process Clause and,
        353–54, 680n80
    Elaine Riots and, 353
    fair criminal trials and, 353–54,
        475, 680n80
    Fourteenth Amendment and, 354
    Holmes, Jr., and, 353, 444
    McReynolds and, 353–54
    NAACP and, 353
    Powell v. Alabama and, 558–59
    race and, 475
    racial justice and, 353–54
    Scottsboro Boys and, 558–59
Moors, John, 469
Morawetz, Victor, 472
Morelli gang, 417
Morgan, J. P., 21
    Davis, J. W., and, 368, 373
Morgenthau, Henry, Jr., 572
Morgenthau, Henry, Sr., 174–76
    Frankfurter and, 265
Morgenthau Mission, 174–76, 237
Morison, Samuel Eliot, 416, 532–33
Morrow, Dwight, 362–63
Morton, James M., Jr., 449–50
Moskowitz, Belle, 553–54
Mount Rushmore, South Dakota, 1, 5,
        583n2
    ceremonial carving of Washington
        head at, 482–84
    Coolidge and, 407, 480–83,
        483, 511–14
    dark sides of, 579
    dedication, 407
    federal funding of, 508, 552
    funding of, 403–5, 480, 484, 532
    hall of records, 574
    Hoover, H., and, 508–10, 513–14, 551
    House of Truth and, 578–79
    initial survey of, 405–6
    inscription, 512–13
    Jefferson head dedication, 573
    Lincoln head, 573
    model for, *512*
    Native Americans and, 407, 481, 579
    Norbeck and, 508–9
    public opinion of, 515

Randolph and, 404–5
Robinson, D., and, 401–2, 508–9
Roosevelt, F., and, 572–73
Roosevelt, F., at dedication of, *566*
Roosevelt, T., head and, 573–74
sketch, *406*
Stone Mountain memorial
    and, 514–15
Stone Mountain Memorial Association
    and, 404–5
Tucker and, 406, 482–84
Washington carving, 482–84, *509*, 511
Washington head, 482–84, 513–14
Mount Rushmore National Memorial
    Commission, 485
    inscription and, 513
    Rosenwald and, 510
Muller v. Oregon, 21
Musmanno, Michael, 466–67, 708n159
Myers v. United States, 706n112
"My Hunt after 'The Captain'" (Holmes,
    Sr.), 311

NAACP. *See* National Association for the
    Advancement of Colored People
Nagel, Charles, 16, 472
National Association for the
    Advancement of Colored People
    (NAACP), 119, 121
    Bard-Fleming case and, 473–75
    Frankfurter and, 522
    Moore v. Dempsey, 353
    Nixon v. Herndon, 452–53
    Parker, J., and, 521–22
    Scottsboro Boys and, 558
National Consumers' League, 21, 349
National Industrial Recovery Act
    (NIRA), 736n13
nationalism
    cultural, 190, 328
    New Nationalism, 87
National Labor Relations Board, 567
National Progressive League, 552–53
National War Labor Board, 221–22
"A Nation's Prayer" (Valentine,
    R.), 48, 64
Native Americans, 30
    Mount Rushmore and, 407, 481, 579
    religious garb order, 26–27, 43, 55–56

self-governance for, 43
Valentine, R., and, 27, 31
The Nature of the Judicial Process (Cardozo,
B.), 355
Nevins, Allen, 548
New Deal, 546–47
Frankfurter on, 566–67
lawyers, 736n11
Lippmann on, 570
New Nationalism, 87
New Republic (newspaper), 84–85
on *The Birth of a Nation*, 121
Brandeis and, 125–26, 129–30, *131*, 133
Croly and founding of, 89–92
Croly and postwar, 419
founding of, 2, 89–92
Frankfurter and founding of, 91–92
Frankfurter-Lippmann debate in, 373–74
funding of, 90–91
Holmes, Jr., and, 98, *99*, 113–14, 530–31
House of Truth and, 85, 92–93
Lippmann and founding of, 89–92
Lippmann and return to, 259–60
Lowell in, 357
on *Lusitania* sinking, 107
1928 presidential elections in, 495–96
"Open letter to Dwight
Morrow," 362–63
on Parker, J., 519–20
The Political Scene published in, 260–61
post WWI political shift in,
260–61, 419
on racial justice, 119, 144
on Roosevelt, T., 96–97
on Sacco-Vanzetti case, 467–68
Sacco-Vanzetti case dinner hosted
by, 470
"The Same Mr. Taft" editorial, 344–45
Schwimmer dissent in, 505
"The Sacco and Vanzetti Case," 414–15
"Why I Am for Smith," 496
Wilson support in, 136–37, 145, 164–65
World War I and neutrality in, 107
New York, New Haven & Hartford
Railroad, 21, 130, 133
New York City transit system labor
dispute, 147
New York Herald-Tribune
Lippmann at, 531, 542

on Roosevelt, F., 542–43, 550
New York Times, 513
Nicodemus House, 308
NILI spy network, 245–46
NIRA. *See* National Industrial
Recovery Act
Nixon, Lawrence Aaron, 452
Nixon v. Herndon, 452–53
Fourteenth Amendment and,
453, 703n67
Holmes, Jr., on, 453, 703n67
voting rights and, 475
White, W., on, 454
Norbeck, Peter, 407, 480
Borglum and, 403–4, 509–10
Mount Rushmore and, 508–9
Mount Rushmore National Memorial
Commission, 485
Northern Securities decision, 50
Noyes (Hart), Frances, 104, 320

Oliphant, Herman, 572–73
Olmstead, Roy, 500–501
Olmstead v. United States, 500–501, 717n10
"Open letter to Dwight Morrow"
(Johnson, A.), 362–63
"The Opposition to Justice Parker"
(Lippmann), 520
organized labor, 92–93
Lippmann on, 94
Roosevelt, T., on, 94
scientific management and, 109
Valentine, R., on, 109, 149
*Other People's Money and How Bankers Use
It* (Brandeis), 125

pacifism, 166, 505
Palestine, 237
Arab-Jewish alliance and, 249–51
"the Arab Question" in, 249–50
Balfour Declaration, 154–55, 238
Brandeis trip to, 262–67, *267*
British Empire in, 254
British Mandate for, 253–54
Frankfurter on, 240
Jewish state in, 240, 253–54
Turkey and, 243–44
Zichron Ya'akov community
in, 243–44

Palfrey, John, 152, 503
Palmer, A. Mitchell
    bombing and, 286–87
    Frankfurter and, 301
Palmer Raids, 358
    deportations and, 410, 445
    Frankfurter and, 300–301
    Gitlow and, 386
    Hoover, J. E., and, 289
    immigrants rounded up during,
        300–301
    Sacco-Vanzetti case and, 412
Panama Canal, 16, 68
Paris Peace Conference
    Frankfurter on, 249, 261
    Lippmann on, 262
    Wilson at, 256, 262
Parker, Dorothy, 445, 470
Parker, John J., 521
    Brandeis on, 723n24
    Chafee on, 519–20
    Frankfurter on, 519–20, 522–23
    Hoover, H., and nomination
        of, 536
    NAACP and, 521–22
    opposition to, 520–22
    on Supreme Court, 723n29
    "The Opposition to Justice
        Parker," 520
    World on, 522–23
Percy, Eustace, 34–35, 36, 46, 66, 569
    Aaronsohn and, 247
    "blue memorandum," 81
    at British embassy, 169
    Holmes, Jr., and, 106
    at House of Truth, 159, 271
    House of Truth and departure
        of, 80–82
    Lippmann and, 229
    on Lusitania sinking, 108
    on war effort, 106
    Zionist cause and, 254
Perkins, Thomas Nelson, 281, 298–99
Pershing, John J., 79, 481
The Phantom Public (Lippmann),
    382–83
Phillips, Orie L., 537–38
Phillips, Wendell, 307
Pierce v. Society of Sisters, 389–91
Pinchot, Amos, 570–71

Pinchot, Gifford, 26
    Ballinger-Pinchot Affair, 21–22,
        125, 132
Pitney, Mahlon, 17, 115, 348, 385
Plane, C. Helen, 322–23, 339
    Borglum and, 188–89, 336, 401
    Griffith and, 190–91
    Stone Mountain memorial and,
        188–91, 400–401
    United Daughters of the Confederacy
        and, 188
the Players Club, 88, 89
Plessy v. Ferguson, 475–76
Polakoff, Sol, 154
Poland
    Frankfurter trip to, 265–66
    Jews in, 265–66
police strike, Boston, 288–89
The Political Scene (Lippmann), 260–61
Pollak, Walter H., 472
"The Portentous Case of Sacco and
    Vanzetti: A Comprehensive Analysis
    of a Trial of Grave Importance"
    (Frankfurter), 420–23
Pound, Roscoe, 73–74, 130–32, 283
    Brandeis and, 283–84
    Frankfurter and, 299, 425
    as Harvard Law School dean, 301
    Laski and, 279
    Lowell and, 285–86
    red-baiting of, 274–75, 280–86
    Sacco-Vanzetti case and, 425
Powell, Thomas Reed, 388, 563
    Lippmann and, 686n16
Powell v. Alabama, 733n13
    Frankfurter on, 559–60
    McReynolds and, 733n14
    Moore v. Dempsey and, 558–59
    Sutherland, A., on, 559
Powys, John Cowper, 487
A Preface to Politics (Lippmann), 86–87
"The Prejudices of Judge Thayer"
    (Lippmann), 430–31
Preparedness Day Parade bombing, San
    Francisco, 178–79
presidential election (1912), 38–60
    cartoon, 53
    Denison and, 59
    Frankfurter and, 42, 57–59
    outcome of, 60

Valentine, R., and, 56–57
presidential election (1916)
  Hughes in, 138–40
  Wilson in, 136–46
presidential election (1924), 365–83
  Borglum and, 374–78
  Borglum and La Follette-Wheeler
    campaign medallion, 372, 377
  Coolidge and, 367, 377–78, 382
  Davis, J. W., candidacy, 368
  Democratic National
    Convention, 369–70
  Frankfurter-Lippmann debate on,
    372–74, 380–81
  Frankfurter on, 365, 370, 378–79
  La Follette and, 370–71, 376–77
  Lippmann and, 365, 370
  McAdoo and, 369–70, 375
  outcome of, 382
  Smith, A., and, 370
  Supreme Court and, 365
presidential election (1928)
  Democratic Party and, 494
  Frankfurter on, 490–91, 493–95
  Hoover, H., and, 496
  Lippmann on, 490–91, 493–95
  in New Republic, 495–96
  outcome of, 496–97
  religious intolerance and, 494
  Republican Party and, 494
  Smith, A., and, 487, 496
presidential election (1932), 541–55
  Baker and, 543–44
  Borglum on, 550–51
  Frankfurter and, 541–45, 553–54
  Holmes, Jr., on, 556
  Hoover, H., and, 545, 548–49
  Lippmann and, 541–45
  Roosevelt, F., and, 541–46
  Roosevelt, F., victory in, 555
  Smith, A., and, 544–46, 553–54
Prince Feisal, 249–50
  Frankfurter and, 250–51, 258
privacy
  Brandeis on, 501
  Holmes, Jr., on, 501
  liberalism and, 501–2
  right to, 500
  Supreme Court on, 500–502
Proctor, William, 412

Progressive Democracy (Croly), 95, 608n89
  Holmes, Jr., on, 99
progressivism, 95
  big government and, 8
  definitions of, 3
  Frankfurter on, 56
  liberalism and, 608n91
  National Progressive League, 552–53
  on Supreme Court, 13–14
Prohibition, 369
  Lippmann on, 491
  Smith, A., and, 491–92
The Promise of American Life
  (Croly), 87–88
Proskauer, Joseph, 545
the protocol (management and labor
  agreement), 149–50
The Public and Its Government
  (Frankfurter), 540
public education law, compulsory, 389–91
public opinion, 416
  of Hoover, H., 548
  Lippmann on, 291, 572
  of Mount Rushmore, 515
  of Sacco-Vanzetti case, 422, 447
Public Opinion (Lippmann)
  Frankfurter on, 342
  Holmes, Jr., on, 341–42
  symbolism in, 341–42
Public Utility Holding Company Act of
  1935, 566
Public Works Administration, 567
Pulitzer, Ralph, 430
  Bliven and, 697n127
  Broun and, 435–36
Putnam, Elizabeth "Lisa" Jaynes, 194

race, 579
  black soldiers in armed forces, 180
  Brandeis on, 461, 706n122
  Dred Scott decision and, 40
  fair criminal trials and, 474
  Fourteenth Amendment, 560
  Holmes, Jr., on, 118–19, 453–55,
    614n131, 703n67
  Moore v. Dempsey and, 475
  Parker, J., on, 521–22
  Plessy v. Ferguson, 475–76
  Scottsboro Boys, 558–60, 733n13
  Supreme Court and, 558

racial justice
  black students at Harvard College, 361
  House of Truth on, 119
  Moore v. Dempsey and, 353–54
  New Republic on, 119, 144
racial prejudice
  criminal justice system and, 454–55
  Democratic Party primary elections
    and, 452–53
  Gong Lum v. Rice, 475–76
  Jim Crow policy, 361
  Nixon v. Herndon, 452–53
  of Wilson, 120, 143–44
racial segregation
  Brandeis on, 461
  Gong Lum v. Rice, 476
  Plessy v. Ferguson, 475–76
  Supreme Court and, 568
  in Washington D. C., 120
  Wilson administration and, 120
racial violence
  The Birth of a Nation and, 121
  postwar, 287–88
racism
  The Birth of a Nation, 120–21,
    190–91
  Stone Mountain memorial
    and, 190–91
Randolph, Hollins, 375–76
  Borglum and, 397–400
  Lukeman hired by, 400
  Mount Rushmore and, 404–5
rape
  fair criminal trials and, 474
  Frank and, 116–18
  Scottsboro Boys and, 558–60
Rapid City Journal, 515
reasonable doubt, 473
Reconstruction Finance
    Corporation, 567
Red Scare in America
  Abrams dissent and, 289–90
  criminal trials and, right to
    fair, 352–53
  free speech and, 352–53
  at Harvard Law School,
    274–75, 280–86
  Palmer Raids, 289
Red Summer of 1919, 287
Reed, John, 84

religious intolerance, 493. *See also*
    anti-Semitism
rent control law, 343, 350
  Supreme Court on, 348–49
Republican Party, 1928 presidential elec-
    tions and, 494
Réquin, Édouard, 220–21
Return of the Boer (Borglum), 196
The Revolutionary Age (Socialist
    manifesto), 386
Ripley, Walter, 415
Roberts, George, 380
Roberts, Owen J., 523
Robinson, Doane, 401–2, 508–9
  Borglum and, 402–3, 484
Robinson, Joseph T., 538
Robinson, William James, 399
Rockefeller, John D., Jr.
  "Ludlow Massacre" and, 93
  Sacco-Vanzetti case record publication
    and, 472
Rodin, Auguste, 194
Roe, Gilbert, 370
Rolland, Romain, 487
Roosevelt, Eleanor, 220, 557
  Holmes, Jr., and, 562–64, 732n2
  at Holmes, Jr., funeral, 575, *576*
Roosevelt, Franklin Delano, 3, 286,
    554, 557
  assassination attempt, 560
  Borglum and, 551–52
  "court-packing plan," 568, 737n17
  criticisms of, 541, 571
  Evans, E., and, 553
  Frankfurter and, 219–20, 541–43,
    552–53, 560–61, 565–66
  Frankfurter and influence on, 566–67
  Frankfurter as legal advisor to, 547–48
  as governor of New York, 541
  Holmes, Jr., and visit with, 561–64,
    732nn2–3, 734n30
  Holmes, Jr., on, 556
  at Holmes, Jr., funeral, 740n69
  inauguration of, 561
  Lippmann and, *227*, 492, 541–43,
    569–70, 729n3
  Lippmann on, 545–46, 548–50, 571
  Mount Rushmore and, 572–73
  at Mount Rushmore dedication, *566*
  New Deal, 546–47

New York Herald-Tribune on, 542–43, 550
1932 presidential election and, 541–46
1932 presidential election victory of, 555
opposition to, 544
presidential nomination of, 546, 549
Smith, A., and, 491–92, 545–46, 553–54
Supreme Court and, 568
Tammany Hall issue and, 541, 543, 547–49
Valentine, R., and, 66–67
Walker hearings and, 548–49
water power policy, 542
wheelchair, 734n30
"Why I Am Voting for Roosevelt," 554–55
Wise on, 553
Roosevelt, James, 557, 562
Roosevelt, Theodore, *39. See also* Mount Rushmore, South Dakota
Aaronsohn and, 243
"Armageddon Speech," 51
assassination attempt, 60
Borglum and support of, 46–48, 139, 194
Brandeis on, 50–51
"Charter of Democracy" speech, 40
"Confession of Faith" speech, 55
Croly and, 93
death of, 235
Denison and, 44, 111–12
Frankfurter criticized by, 179
Frankfurter on, 41–42, 56–57
Holmes, Jr., and, 49–50, 316, 596n82, 732n4
House of Truth and support for, 2–4, 37, 45–46
on judiciary, 41
labor platform, 93–94
Lippmann and, 93–94, 138
New Republic on, 96–97
Northern Securities decision and, 50
Ohio Constitutional Convention speech, 39–40
on recalling state judges, 40
Smith, H., and, 54
Square Deal, 546
Stimson and, 8, 10–11
Stimson on, 42
Supreme Court and, 40–41, 380

Taft and, 38–39
third-party presidential bid, 4
third term presidential campaign, 38–39, 44–46, 51
on trusts, 40
Valentine, R., and, 30, 42–43, 51–52, 152
Weyl and, 93
on Wilson, 138
Roosevelt Medal, 366–67, *385*
Root, Elihu, 343
Roosevelt Medal received by, *385*
Sacco-Vanzetti case record publication and, 472
Rose, Chapman, 534–35
Rosenman, Sam, 547
Rosensohn, Sam, 45, 66, 82, 151, 182, 219, 220
Rosenwald, Julius, 76, 150, 199, 202, 242–3, 245, 468
Mount Rushmore and, 510, 551
Sacco-Vanzetti case record publication and, 472, 710n193
Rowe, James, 574
Rublee, George, 51, 66, 113, 135
Rugg, Arthur P., 385
"rule of reason," 14
Rushmore, Charles, 405
Russell, Richard B., Jr., 551
Sacco, Nicola, *410*, 410–11
appeal, 412–13
The Case of Sacco and Vanzetti: A Critical Analysis for Lawyers and Laymen, 421
execution of, 467
innocence of, 710n195
"The Portentous Case of Sacco and Vanzetti: A Comprehensive Analysis of a Trial of Grave Importance," 420–21
at sentencing, 423–24
"The Sacco and Vanzetti Case," 414–15

"The Sacco and Vanzetti Case" (Frankfurter and Gates), 414–15
Sacco-Vanzetti advisory committee, 431–33
Lippmann on, 435
Lowell on, 431–32

Sacco-Vanzetti bas-relief, 477–79, *478*
  unveiling of, 486–87
Sacco-Vanzetti case
  American liberalism and,
    413–14, 467–68
  anarchism and, 410–11, 415
  ballistics testimony and, 412–13,
    416, 429
  Bard-Fleming case and, 474–75
  Brandeis and, 424, 473
  Brandeis on, 461–62, 707n136
  Broun on, 435–36
  Evans, E., and, 411, 438
  exculpatory evidence in, 412–13
  eyewitnesses, 415
  fair criminal trial for, 415
  Frankfurter and, 471–72, 691n13
  Frankfurter and nomination to
    Massachusetts Supreme Court
    and, 547
  Frankfurter on, 411–15, 434–35
  Frankfurter summation of, 419–20
  Fuller and, 430, 433–35, 446, 449
  habeas corpus and, 442–47, 450
  Hand on, 710n189
  Hill and, 439–41, 449–50
  Holmes, Jr., on, 442–47, 450,
    457, 472–73
  Lippmann on, 429–30, 434–36,
    447–48, 470–71
  Lowell and, 448–49
  Medeiros confession and, 416–17
  Medeiros motion, 418
  new evidence and, 423
  New Republic on, 467–68
  in newspapers, 429–33, 447–48,
    457, 472–73
  new trial motion denied in, 423
  Palmer Raids and, 412
  pardon petition, 429
  Pound and, 425
  public appeals for, 449
  public opinion of, 422, 447
  record publication of, 472, 710n193
  retrial, 414, 418
  "The Sacco and Vanzetti Case," 414–15
  sentencing, 423–24, 438
  stay of execution for, 442, 447–67
  Stone on, 465–66
  Supreme Court and, 450, 473

Thompson and, 414
World on, 417–18, 429–31, *432*, 433,
  435–36, 448, 469
Sacco-Vanzetti Defense Committee,
  421, 424
  appeal to Fuller, 449
Sacco-Vanzetti memorial, 477–79, 487
Salsedo, Andrea, 411
"The Same Mr. Taft"
  (Frankfurter), 344–45
Sanderson, George, 440
Sanford, Edward Terry, 348–49, 386, *390*
  Adkins v. Children's Hospital, 351
  death of, 519
Schaefer v. United States, 705n108
Schenck, Charles, 276, 705n108
Schlesinger, Arthur, Sr., 529–30
Schwab, Charles M., 221
Schwimmer, Rosika, 504–7, *506*
  free speech and, 504–5
scientific management, organized labor
  and, 109
Scott, Emmett J., 180
Scottsboro Boys, 733n13. *See also Powell
  v. Alabama*
  Frankfurter on, 559–60
  Moore v. Dempsey and, 558–59
  NAACP and, 558
  Sutherland, G., on, 559
Seabury, Samuel, 547–48
Seager, Henry, 449
SEC. *See* Securities and Exchange
  Commission
Securities Act of 1933, 566
Securities and Exchange Commission
  (SEC), 567
Securities Exchange Act of 1934, 566
Sedgwick, Ellery, 294, 599n3, 693n53
  Atlantic Monthly and, 696n106
  Frankfurter and, 420, 544
  on "J. H. Wigmore Answers
    Frankfurter Attack on Sacco -
    Vanzetti Verdict," 427
  McReynolds and, 421–22
Sedition Act, 276
separate but equal doctrine. *See also* racial
  segregation
  Gong Lum v. Rice and, 476
  Plessy v. Ferguson and, 475–76
Sergeant, Elizabeth Shepley, 392

Seymour, Charles, 647n49
Sheridan, Philip, 46, 324
Sherman Antitrust Act
  amending, 15–16
  Brandeis on, 20–21
  Frankfurter on, 15–16
  Holmes, Jr., on, 24
  "The Sherman Law and Our
    Industrial Problem" speech, 14–18
  Socialism and, 15
  Stimson on, 15–16
  Supreme Court and enforcement
    of, 13–14
  Taft on, 16
Sinclair, Upton, 487, 662n152
  on Laski, 294
  Sacco-Vanzetti case record publication
    and, 710n195
Sioux, Mount Rushmore and, 407, 481
slavery, Dred Scott decision and, 40. See
  also abolitionism
Smith, Al, 370
  Catholicism and, 491
  Frankfurter and, 489, 490–96,
    545, 553–54
  Hoover, H., and, 495
  Lincoln and, 492
  Lippmann on, 490–91, 493–96
  as 1928 Democratic presidential nomi-
    nee, 487, 496
  1932 presidential election and,
    544–46, 553–54
  opposition to, 545
  Prohibition and, 491–92
  Roosevelt, F., and, 491–92,
    545–46, 553–54
  Tammany Hall issue and, 491–93, 494
  voting record of, 492
  White, W. A., and, 492
  "Why I Am for Smith," 496
Smith, Herbert Knox, 46, 55
  in Roosevelt, T., campaign, 54
Smoot, Reed, 79
Socialism, 93, 279
  Espionage Act and, 276–77
  Evans and, 409
  Gitlow v. New York and, 386–88
  Holmes, Jr., on, 391
  La Follette on, 382
  Lippmann on, 570

in postwar Europe, 489
The Revolutionary Age manifesto, 386
  Sherman Act and, 15
"social legislation," 70
social scientific evidence, labor laws de-
  fended with, 21
socioeconomic legislation
  Due Process Clause and, 388
  Frankfurter and, 566–67
  New Deal, 566–67
"The Soldier's Faith" address (Holmes,
  Jr.), 105, 313
South Braintree robbery and murders,
  410–11. See also Sacco-Vanzetti
  case
  eyewitness to, 416
  Medeiros confession to, 416–17
sovereignty, 279
Spingarn, Arthur, 452
Square Deal, 546
The Stakes of Diplomacy (Lippmann),
  108, 165
Standard Oil Company, 13
Starling, Edmund, 480
Steffens, Lincoln, 86, 650n83
Stephens, Alexander H., 485
Stephenson, David C., 335, 674n59
  Borglum and, 376, 398
sterilization laws, 450–51
  eugenics and, 451–52
  Holmes, Jr., on, 702n53
Stillman, James, 29
Stimson, Henry, 7, 17
  on antitrust policy, 14–15
  Denison and, 15–16
  Frankfurter and, 6, 8, 42, 68, 74–75,
    343, 538–39
  Frankfurter in Taft administration
    and, 57–58
  gubernatorial campaign, 9–12, 11
  Roosevelt, T., and, 8, 10–11
  on Roosevelt, T., 42
  as secretary of war, 12
  on Sherman Antitrust Act, 15–16
  "The Sherman Law and Our
    Industrial Problem" speech, 14–18
  sugar trust prosecuted by, 8–9
  Taft supported by, 42
  as US attorney, 8
stock market crash of 1929, 511, 715n6

Stone, Harlan Fiske, 385, *390, 466*, 537–38
  Frankfurter and, 463–65
  Hill and, 465–66
  Holmes, Jr., and, 464–65
  liberalism of, 463–64
  on Sacco-Vanzetti case, 465–66
  on Supreme Court, 463–64, 518
Stone Mountain half dollar, 398–400
Stone Mountain memorial, Georgia, 1, *2*,
    188–92, *323*, 551–52, 583n2, 739n54
  Borglum fired from, 396–98
  carving process, 335–37
  dedication, 191
  dynamite used on, 374–75
  funding for, 190–91, 322–29, 337,
    378, 398
  Harding and, 333–34
  Ku Klux Klan and, 191, 327–29,
    331–34, 635n21
  Lee head carving, 338–39
  Lukeman and, 400, 485–86
  master model, 375
  model, 338
  model for, 396, *397*
  Mount Rushmore and, 514–15
  Plane and, 188–91, 400–401
  plans for, 191
  racism and, 190–91
  technological difficulties of,
    328–29, 331–32
Stone Mountain Memorial
    Association, 375
  Borglum and, 397–99
  Mount Rushmore and, 404–5
  Stone Mountain half dollar and,
    399–400
Storey, Moorfield, 424–25, 452
  Bard-Fleming case and, 474
Straight, Dorothy, 90, 323
Straight, Willard, 84, 138
  Lippmann and, 232–33
  New Republic funding from, 90–91
  on Wilson, 145
Stratton, Harold, 487
Stratton, Samuel Wesley, 431
Strauss, Lewis, 264
St. Vincent Millay, Edna, 487
sugar trust
  E. C. Knight decision, 40–41

Stimson and prosecution of, 8–9
Sullivan, Mark, 537
The Sun Also Rises (Hemingway), 502
Supreme Court, *390*
  Abrams v. United States, 289–95, 303–4,
    318, 459
  Adamson Act upheld by, 163–64
  Adkins v. Children's Hospital,
    349–51, 355
  antilabor decisions, 345–46
  antitrust laws and, enforcement
    of, 13–14
  Baldwin v. Missouri, 526–27
  Bard-Fleming case and, 473–74
  Bartels v. Iowa, 680n77
  Black and White Taxicab case, 499–500
  Brandeis nomination to, 122–36,
    123, 134–35
  Brandeis on, 459–60
  Brown v. Board of Education, 568
  Buchanan v. Warley, 453
  Buck v. Bell, 450–51, 461,
    702n48, 703n61
  The Business of the Supreme Court, 473
  Cardozo nominated to, 539
  on child labor, 464
  on civil rights, 704n73
  Congress and, 346
  conservatism in, 343, 347, 349, 516
  Constitution and, 523–24
  Coolidge and, 378–80
  Coppage v. Kansas, 113–14
  criminal trials, fair and, 4, 116–18, 500
  criminal trials, state and, 444, 457, 559
  Davis, J. W., and, 379–80
  democratic political process and, 4
  Due Process Clause and, 343, 498
  E. C. Knight decision, 40–41
  Equal Protection Clause and, 498
  Frankfurter and, 69–70, 158–61, 343–
    44, 352, 355–56, 378–80, 389–90
  Frankfurter and criticism of, 356–57,
    500, 516, 523–24
  Frankfurter nomination to, 568
  Frankfurter on, 568–69
  Frank v. Mangum, 116–18, 353,
    444, 680n80
  on free speech, 4
  Frohwerk v. United States, 276–77

Gilbert v. Minnesota, 705n108
Giles v. Harris, 453
Gitlow v. New York, 386–89
Gong Lum v. Rice, 475–76
Hammer v. Dagenhart, 218–19
Harding and nominees for, 348–49
Holmes, Jr., as acting chief justice
   of, 516–17
Holmes, Jr., influence on, 498, 558
Holmes, Jr., on, 316, 348–49, *390*
Holmes, Jr., resignation from, 535
Hoover, H., and, 498, 517–18
Hoover, H., nominations to,
   518–20, 535–38
Hughes on, 518–19
judicial power and, 346
labor laws and, 158
La Follette and, 380
Laski on, 161
on maximum hour law, 161–62
Meyer v. Nebraska, 680n76, 680n78
Milwaukee Leader case, 319–20
on minimum wage laws, 115–16,
   163, 391
Moore v. Dempsey and, 353–54, 680n80
Muller v. Oregon, 21
Myers v. United States, 706n112
1924 presidential election and, 365
Nixon v. Herndon, 452–54, 475, 703n67
Olmstead v. United States,
   500–501, 717n10
Parker, J., on, 723n29
Pierce v. Society of Sisters, 389–91
Plessy v. Ferguson, 475–76
pre-WWI, 4
on privacy, 500–502
progressives on, 13–14
race and, 558
racial segregation and, 568
on rent control law, 348–49
role of, 126, 516, 568–69
Roosevelt, F., and, 568
Roosevelt, F., "court-packing plan" for,
   568, 737n17
Roosevelt, T., and, 40–41, 380
Sacco-Vanzetti case and, 473
Sacco-Vanzetti writ of habeas corpus
   and, 450
Schaefer v. United States, 705n108

on Schwimmer case, 505–7
on Scottsboro Boys, 558–60
on state taxes, 526–27
Stone on, 463–64, 518
on subterranean mining rights, 347–48
Sutherland, G., on, 347, *390*
Taft and, 16–17
Taft on, 343–45, 516
ten-hour law argument, 161–63
Whitney v. California, 460–61, 706n114
Sussex crisis, 137
Sutherland, Arthur, Jr., 472–73, 476,
   717n12, 739n58
Sutherland, George
   on *Adkins v. Children's Hospital*, 355
   on "liberty of contract," 351–52
   Moore v. Dempsey and, 353–54
   on Scottsboro Boys, 559
   on Supreme Court, 347, *390*
Swope, Herbert Bayard, 553–54
symbolism
   Holmes, Jr., and, 348
   in *Public Opinion*, 341–42
Szold, Robert, 113, 243

Taft, William Howard, 13
   Adkins v. Children's Hospital, 351
   anti-Semitism, 619n67
   antitrust policy and, 15
   Ballinger-Pinchot Affair and, 21–22
   Borglum on, 47
   on Brandeis nomination, 125,
      132–33, 619n67
   cartoon, *19*
   death of, 519
   Denison and, 59, 613n95
   Frankfurter and, 221–22, 343, 677n16
   Frankfurter on, 13, 17–18, 41
   Harding and, *344*
   health problems, 516
   Holmes, Jr., and, 49, 502–4, 670n80
   on National War Labor Board, 221–22
   renomination campaign of, 51–52
   Roosevelt, T., and, 38–39
   "The Same Mr. Taft" editorial, 344–45
   on Sherman Antitrust Act, 16
   on "The Sherman Law and Our
      Industrial Problem" speech, 18
   son, 100

Taft, William Howard (*Cont.*)
    Stimson support of, 42
    on Supreme Court, 343–45, *390*, 516
    Supreme Court and, 16–17
    on *Truax v. Corrigan*, 344
    Valentine, R., and, 26–27, 56–57
    on wiretaps, 501
Tammany Hall issue, 491–92, *494*
    Catholicism and, 493
    Lippmann on, 570
    Roosevelt, F., and, 541, 543, 547–49
    Walker hearings and, 548–49
Taney, Roger B., 502
    Dred Scott decision, 40
taxation
    Baldwin v. Missouri, 526–27
    corporate, 498–99
    Supreme Court on state, 526–27
Taylor, Frederick W., 63, 109
Tead, Ordway, 150, 152
Teapot Dome scandal, 367
ten-hour law, Oregon, 160–63
    Holmes, Jr., on, 162–63
"A Tentative Social Program"
    (Frankfurter, Valentine, R.), 61–63
Thayer, James Bradley, 73, 126
Thayer, Webster, 415, 418
    bias and prejudice of, 429–30, 444
    Frankfurter on, 443–44
    Hill and, 440
    Sacco-Vanzetti case and, 429
    Sacco-Vanzetti case new trial motion
        denied by, 423
    "The Prejudices of Judge
        Thayer," 430–31
    Wigmore and, 426–27
Thompson, William G., 412
    Medeiros motion, 418
    Sacco-Vanzetti case and, 438
    Sacco-Vanzetti case retrial and, 414
    on "The Portentous Case of Sacco
        and Vanzetti: A Comprehensive
        Analysis of a Trial of Grave
        Importance," 422–23
    writ of habeas corpus, 444–45
Time magazine, 394–95
totalitarianism, 737n27
trade, "rule of reason" and restraint of, 14
Treasury Department, 567

Borglum and, 484, 572
    Mellon and, 368–69, 484
Treaty of Versailles, 543, 577
    Croly on, 419, 530
Trinkle, Lee, 335
Trotter, William Monroe, 120–21
Truax v. Corrigan, 344
trusts, Roosevelt, T. on, 40
Tucker, Jesse George
    Borglum and, 484, 511
    ceremonial carving of Washington
        head at Mount Rushmore, 482–84
    dynamite used by, 374
    Mount Rushmore survey and, 406
    Stone Mountain Memorial and, 191,
        325, 328, 337, 396–98
Tumulty, Joseph, 197
Turkey, 174–76
    Palestine and, 243–44
Tweed, Boss, 536

Ullman, Isaac, 132–33, 619n67
UMW. *See* United Mine Workers
unfair competition, regulating, 69
Union Pacific Railway, 29
United Daughters of the
    Confederacy, 333
    Baruch and, 324, 673n22
    Borglum and, 190
    Plane and, 188
United Mine Workers (UMW),
    345, 520–21
United Shoe Machinery Company,
    129, 133
U.S. Steel, 222–23

Valentine, Robert G., 4, 25–28, *28, 64,
    89, 148*
    Bass and, 54–56
    Borglum and, 48
    Brandeis and, 149–50, 154
    Buckner and, 74
    in Bureau of Indian affairs, 30–31
    celebration of life of, 153–54
    as commissioner of Indian affairs,
        26–27, 31
    Croly and, 88
    death of, 151–53
    Denison and, 77, *78*, 154–56

financial difficulties, 56
Fisher and, 55–56
Frankfurter and, 11, 25–26, 57–58,
   61–66, 75–76, 151–54, 624n39
at Harvard, 28–29
health issues, 29, 32–33, 590n91,
   591n118
Holmes, Jr., and, 45
at House of Truth, 31–34, 62, 148
as industrial counselor, 63–64,
   82, 108–9
on industrial democracy, 149
as labor auditor, 147–48
Laski and, 153
Leupp and, 30–31
Lippmann on, 151–52
Mack and, 149, 152
on minimum wage, 110
"A Nation's Prayer," 48, 64
New York City transit system labor
   dispute and, 147
on 1912 presidential election, 56–57
on organized labor, 109, 149
religious garb order, 27, 43, 55–56
resignation from Taft
   administration, 56–57
Roosevelt, F., and, 66–67
Roosevelt, T., and, 30, 42–43,
   51–52, 152
on scientific management, 109
Taft and, 26–27
"A Tentative Social Program," 61–63
on Wall Street, 29
wife and daughter of, 31–33, 32, 56
on Wilson, 146
on World War I, 110–11
Valentine, Sophia "Charlotte," 31–33, 32,
   56, 273, 655n6
Valentine, Sophie, 31–33, 32, 56, 270
   Denison and, 296
   Denman and, 272
Van Devanter, Willis, 17, 390
Vanophem, Jean, 374
Vanzetti, Bartolomeo, 410, 410–11. See also
   Sacco-Vanzetti case
   appeal, 412–13
   The Case of Sacco and
      Vanzetti: A Critical Analysis for
      Lawyers and Laymen, 421

execution of, 467
innocence of, 710n195
"The Portentous Case of Sacco
   and Vanzetti: A Comprehensive
   Analysis of a Trial of Grave
   Importance," 420–21
at sentencing, 423–24
"The Sacco and Vanzetti
   Case," 414–15
Venable, Sam, 188–90, 326, 398
Villa, Hugo, 406
Villard, Oswald Garrison, 121, 487
voting rights, 452–53
   Nixon v. Herndon, 475

Walker, Jimmy, 548–49, 553
Walsh, Frank P., 216
Walsh, Thomas, 735n1
Wamblee-Tokaha, 481
Warburg, Paul, 637n68
War Industries Board, 216
War Labor Policies Board
   eight-hour-workday, 221–24
   Frankfurter on, 216–17, 541
   Frankfurter resignation from, 237
   Hammer v. Dagenhart and, 218–19
   labor policy and, 218–19
Warren, Charles, 115, 355
Warren, Edward "Bull," 73, 130
Wars of America monument, 324
war veteran protest, 548
Washington, Booker T., 119
Washington, George. See Mount
   Rushmore, South Dakota
Watson, James E., 376
Wehle, Louis Brandeis, 119
Weizmann, Chaim, 175, 237, 241, 249
   Brandeis and, 268
   Frankfurter and, 268, 359
   Zionist cause and, 238–39
Weyl, Walter, 419
   New Republic founding and, 91
   Roosevelt, T., and, 93
Wheeler, Burton, 376–77
   Borglum and La Follette-Wheeler
      campaign medallion, 372
White, E. B., 505–6
White, Edward Douglass, 17, 115
   Frankfurter and, 160

White, Walter, 287–88, 660n95
    Frankfurter and, 522
    on *Nixon v. Herndon*, 454
    on Parker, J., 521–22
White, William Allen, 487, 552
    on Smith, A., 492
"White Hope Speech" (Denison), 111–12
Whitney, Charlotte "Anita," 460–61
Whitney v. California, 460–61, 706n114
"Why I Am for Smith"
    (Frankfurter), 496
"Why I Am Voting for Roosevelt"
    (Frankfurter), 554–55
Wickersham, George W., 12, 21, 132
    Denison and, 44, 59, 79
Wickersham Commission, 544
Wigmore, John Henry, 304
    on *The Case of Sacco and
        Vanzetti: A Critical Analysis
        for Lawyers and Laymen*
        (Frankfurter), 425–28
    criticism of, 428
    Frankfurter and, 426–28
    Holmes, Jr., and, 425, 428
    "J. H. Wigmore Answers Frankfurter
        Attack on Sacco-Vanzetti
        Verdict," 426–27
    Thayer and, 426–27
Willert, Arthur, 72, 80, 82, 169
Willkie, Wendell L., 572
Wilson, Joseph, 192–93
Wilson, Woodrow, 42
    on aircraft industry corruption, 196–98
    on American isolationism, 137
    The Birth of a Nation screening
        by, 120–21
    Borglum and, 196–98, 204
    Brandeis and, 52, 58, 122, *123*
    censorship under, 227–28
    Croly and, 145, 164–65
    declaration of war requested by, 166
    Du Bois and, 143–44
    Espionage Act, 276
    Fourteen Points, 226
    Frankfurter and, 68, 74, 212
    Frankfurter on, 145–46
    Hand and, 142–43
    House of Truth support of,
        124, 136–46

    international policy of, 137–38
    liberalism and, 227–28
    on Lippmann, 229–30
    Lippmann and, 144, 164–65
    Lippmann and support of, 139–40
    Lippmann on, 261–62
    Lusitania sinking and, 107
    lynching and, 144, 180
    Mexico policy, 96
    New Republic support of, 136–37,
        145, 164–65
    at Paris Peace Conference,
        256, 262
    racial prejudice, 120, 143–44
    reelection of, 136–46
    Roosevelt, T., on, 138
    Straight, Willard, on, 145
    support for, 52
    Trotter and, 120
    Valentine, R., on, 146
    war policies of, 136–37
    wartime government changes
        under, 216
Wilson Democrats, 3
Winship, Blanton, 482
wiretapping, 500–501
    of Frankfurter, 437, 698n170
Wise, Stephen, 380, 537
    on Roosevelt, F., 553
Wister, Owen, 502, 718n27
women
    minimum wage laws for, 349–50
    sterilization laws, 450–51
    suffrage, 410
Wood, Leonard, 46, 139
workers' compensation laws, 4, 69
World (newspaper)
    Broun resignation from, 436–37
    "Calmness and Fairness
        Needed," 429–30
    Frankfurter-Lippmann debate on 1924
        election and, 372–74
    on Holmes, Jr., 393–94
    on Hoover, H., 488
    Lippmann at, 293, *342*
    on Parker, J., 522–23
    on Sacco-Vanzetti case, 417–18, 429–31,
        432, 433, 435–36, 448, 469
    sale of, 531

"The Breaking Wave" cartoon, *432*
"The Opposition to Justice
    Parker," 520
"The Prejudices of Judge
    Thayer," 430
wiretapping editorials, 501
World War I
    aircraft industry corruption during,
        196–208
    American declaration of war, 166
    American isolationism and, 164, 166
    Borglum and efforts during, 192
    civil liberties in, 275, 577
    end of, 224
    government reorganization
        during, 211
    House of Truth and, 164, 220–21
    the Inquiry, 181–87
    labor policy and, 209–10
    Lippmann on, 108, 260
    on *Lusitania* sinking, 107
    National War Labor Board, 221–22
    New Republic neutrality and, 107
    New Republic post-, 260–61, 419
    propaganda, 228–30
    racial violence post-, 287–88
    start of, in Europe, 94–97
    support for, 166

Valentine, R., on, 110–11
    Zimmermann telegram and, 166
Wright, Horatio, 312–13
Wyman, Bruce, 76
Wyzanski, Charles, 736n11

Young, Owen, 545

Zangara, Giuseppe, 560
"The Zeitgeist and the Judiciary"
    (Frankfurter), 69–70
Zimmermann telegram, 166
Zionist cause
    Aaronsohn and, 241–49, 252
    in America, 239
    anti-Semitism and, 253
    Arab-Jewish alliance and, 249–51
    on "the Arab Question" and,
        249–50
    Balfour Declaration and, 154–55, 238
    Brandeis and, 239, 264–65
    Bullitt, W., and, 252
    Frankfurter and, 237–69
    Jewish state in Palestine and,
        240, 253–54
    Percy and, 254
    Polish Jews and, 255
    Weizmann and, 238–39